Med▾

Pocket
English
Dictionary

Edited by

Peter Collin

MEDWAY

First Published in Great Britain 2003

By Medway Publishing Ltd

152a Park Street Lane, Park Street

St Albans AL2 2AU

ISBN: 1-902712-01-3

Printed in India by Replika Press

About This Dictionary

This entirely revised dictionary lists the words most commonly used in English, giving definitions and in many cases examples of use. Grammar notes are given in many entries - irregular plurals for nouns, comparatives and superlatives for adjectives, past forms for verbs. Where a word is commonly used with a preposition, that preposition is given in bold letters.

To make the dictionary as compact as possible, many derived words are listed under the main headwords and do not appear separately: so package is to be found under pack, secrecy under secret, etc.

Abbreviations used in the Dictionary

adj.	adjective	*inf.*	informal
adv.	adverb	*inter.*	interjection
Am.	American	*n.*	noun
approx.	approximately	*pl.*	plural
def.	definite	*prep.*	preposition
e.g.	for example	*sl.*	slang
esp.	especially	*sth.*	something
indef.	indefinite	*v.*	verb

Pronunciation

The following signs are used to show the pronunciation of words in the dictionary.

Where there are several pronunciations which are current only the most common are indicated, -r is never pronounced at the end of words, but when a word ending in -r is followed by a vowel the -r can be pronounced.

Words are also marked with a sign (') to show where the strong beat should be placed, but this is only a guide; the pronunciation of a word can change depending on the position of the word in a sentence.

æ	back	ə	afraid	ð	then	r	round
ɑː	farm	əʊ	boat	dʒ	just	s	some
ɒ	top	əʊə	lower	f	fog	ʃ	short
aɪ	pipe	ɛː	word	g	go	t	too
aʊ	how	iː	heap	h	hand	tʃ	chop
aɪə	fire	ɪ	hit	j	yes	θ	thing
aʊə	flower	ɪə	hear	k	catch	v	voice
ɔː	bought	χː	school	l	last	w	was
ɔɪ	toy	ʊ	book	m	mix	z	zoo
e	fed	ʌ	but	n	nut	ʒ	treasure
eə	hair	b	back	ŋ	sing		
əɪ	take	d	dog	p	penny		

Alphabet

These are the letters of the English alphabet, showing their pronunciation.

Aa	eɪ	Hh	eɪtʃ	Oo	əʊ	Vv	viː
Bb	biː	Ii	aɪ	Pp	piː	Ww	'dʌbljuː
Cc	siː	Jj	dʒe	Qq	kjuː	Xx	eks
Dd	diː	Kk	keɪ	Rr	ɑː	Yy	waɪ
Ee	iː	Ll	el	Ss	es	Zz	zed
Ff	ef	Mm	em	Tt	tiː		
Gg	dʒiː	Nn	en	Uu	juː		

Aa

a, an [stressed eɪ, æn: unstressed ə, ən] (a before words beginning with a consonant, and before words beginning with u pronounced juː; an before a, e, i, o, or u and before h where h is not pronounced) indefinite article (a) one; give me a stamp and an envelope. (b) not a particular one; he has a big nose. (c) for each one/in each one; thirty kilometres an hour. (d) a certain: I know a Dr Smith.

A1 [eɪ'wʌn] in very good condition.

aardvark [ɑːdvɑːk] n. ant-eating animal of South Africa.

AB ['eɪbiː] n. ordinary seaman.

aback [ə'bæk] adv. taken aback = surprised, usu. unpleasantly.

abacus [ə'bækəs] n. (pl.-ses) device for counting, made of small beads which slide along rods in a frame.

abaft [ə'bɑːft] adv. (of ships) behind the other.

abalone [æbə'ləʊnɪ] n. type of Pacific shellfish.

abandon [ə'bændon] v. (a) to leave. (b) to give up. **abandonment** n. giving up.

abase [ə'beɪs] v. (a) (formal) to make s.o. low; to a. oneself = to grovel/to apologise. (b) to humiliate.

abashed [ə'bæʃt] adj. ashamed.

abate [ə'bɪt] v. to become less strong. **abatement** n. reduction (in tax).

abattoir ['æbətwɑː] n. slaughterhouse/ place where animals are killed for meat.

abbess ['æbes] n. (pl.-es) woman in charge of nuns in a convent.

abbey ['æbɪ] n. Christian religious establishment with living quarters, etc., grouped round a church.

abbot ['æbət] n. man in change of monks in an abbey.

abbreviate [ə'briːvieɪt] v. to shorten (words, names). **abbreviation** [əbriːvɪ'eɪʃn] n. group of letters representing a larger word.

ABC [eɪbiːsiː] n. the letters of the alphabet.

abdicate ['æbdɪkeɪt] v. to give up the throne. **abdication** ['æbdɪ'kerʃn] n. giving up (of a throne).

abdomen ['æbdəmen] n. lower part of the body, containing the stomach, bowels, etc. **abdominal** [æb'dɒmɪnl] adj. referring to the abdomen.

abduct [æb'dʌkt] v. to remove (s.o.) by force. **abduction** n. removal (of s.o.) by force. **abductor** n. person who abducts s.o.

abeam [ə'biːm] adv. (of ships) side by side

aberration [æbə'reɪʃn] n. (a) change from what is usual. (b) sudden attack of forgetfulness: mental a. = slight confusion. **aberrant** [a'berənt] adj. abnormal/not usual.

abet [ə'bet] v. (abetted) to aid and a. s.o. = to be s.o.'s accomplice in a crime. **abettor** n. person who abets s.o.

abeyance [ə'beɪəns] n. suspension (of a law, etc.); in a = not being applied.

abhor [əb'hɔː] v. to feel hatred/horror for (sth). **abhorrent** [əv'hɒrənt] adj. disgusting/which makes you shudder. **abhorrence** n. horror/great dislike.

abide [ə'baɪd] v. (a) to stick to/to follow: to a. by a promise = to stand by what you have promised. (b) (only with negative) to like; I can't a. the smell of garlic. **abiding** adj. which stays/ remains.

ability [ə'bɪlɪtɪ] n. power to do sth: capability; to the best of my a. = as best I can.

ab initio [æbɪ'nɪʃɪəʊ] adj. (course) which starts from the beginning.

abject ['æbdʒekt] adj. (a) very miserable. (b) cowardly/extremely humble. **abjectly** adv. in a miserable/ humble way.

abjure [æb'dʒuə] v. to swear not do sth.

ablation [æ'blerʃn] n. operation to remove an organ.

ablaze [ə'bleɪz] adv. in flames.

able ['eɪbl] adj. having the ability (to do sth): a. seaman = first class seaman in the Royal Navy. **ably** ['eɪblɪ] adv. very efficiently.

ablutions [æ'bluʃənz] n. pl. washing (face/hands, etc.)

abnormal [æb'nɔːml] adj. not normal **abnormally** adv. not normally/

unusually. **abnormality** [æbnɔː'mælɪtɪ] *n.* (*pl.*abnormalities) being abnormal; unusualness/peculiarity.

ABO [eɪbiː'əʊ] *n.* system of classifying blood by the letters A, B and O.

aboard [ə'bɔːd] *adv. & prep.* on/in (a ship/aircraft/train/bus).

abode [ə'bəʊd] *n.* (formal) home; of no fixed a. = with no permanent address; right of a. = the right to live in a country.

abolish [ə'bɒlɪʃ] *v.* to cancel/to remove. **abolition** [æbə'lɪʃn] *n.* act of abolishing. **abolitionist** *n.* person who is in favour of abolition (esp. of slavery/ capital punishment).

abominable [ə'bɒmɪnəbl] *adj.* horrible/disgusting; the a. snowman = yeti. **abominably** *adv.* in a horrible way. **abominate** [ə'bɒmɪneɪt] *v.* to dislike intensely. **abomination** [əbɒmɪ'neɪʃn] *n.* unpleasant/nasty thing.

aborigine [æbə'rɪdʒɪnɪ] *n.* member of a race which was living in a country before the country was colonised; original inhabitant. **aboriginal.1** *adj.* referring to aborigines.. **2** *n.* aborigine.

abortion [ə'bɔːʃn] *n.* (deliberate) miscarriage of an unborn child. **abort** *v.* (a) to cause an abortion to (s.o.). (b) to stop (a project) taking place. **abortionist** *n.* person who carries out an illegal abortion. **abortive** *adj.* (plan) which fails.

abound [ə'baʊnd] *v.* (in) to be full of.

about [ə'baʊt] *adv. & prep.* (a) in various places; cups lying a. on the floor; there's a lot of flu a. (b) concerning; tell me a your book; what do you want to speak to me a.? how a. a cup of tea? = would you like a cup of tea? (c) (in the army) round; a. turn = facing the opposite direction. (d) approximately; a. three metres square; at a four o' clock. (e) on the point (of doing sth); just a. to go out. (f) in the process of doing sth; while you're a. it can you post this letter?

above [ə'bʌv] *adv. & prep.* (a) higher than; a the clouds; the temperature was a. 40°.(b) louder than; I can't hear you a. the noise. (c) they're living a. their means = more extravagantly than they can afford. (d) earlier on (in a book); higher up (on a page). **aboveboard** *adj.* open/honest; not corrupt.

abracadabra [æbrəkə'dæbrə] *n.* traditional magic spell.

abrade [æ'breɪd] *v.* to scrape off (a surface). **abrasion** [ə'breʒn] *n.* scraping off (of the skin). **abrasive 1** [ə'breɪzɪv] *adj.* (a) grinding (substance). (b) sharp/rude (manner, comment). **2** *n.* rough substance for smoothing a surface.

abreast [ə'brest] *adv.* in a row; level (with sth); cycling three a. = three bicycles side by side; to keep a. of/with sth = to keep up with the latest newss.

abridged [ə'brɪdʒd] *adj.* shortened. **abridgement** *n.* shortened version (of a long book).

abroad [ə'brɔd] *adv.* in or to another country.

abrogate ['æbrəgeɪt] *v.* (formal) to end (a law, a treaty). **abrogation** [æbrə'geɪʃn] *n.* ending (of a treaty).

abrupt [ə'brʌpt] *adj.* sudden (departure); brusque (way of speaking). **abruptly** *adv.* suddenly; brusquely. **abruptness** *n.* suddenness; brusqueness.

abscess ['æbses] *n.* (*pl.*-es) collection of pus in the body.

abscond [əb'skɒnd] *v.* to run away.

abseil ['æbseɪl] *v.* to come down a cliff or wall by means of a fixed rope coiled around one's body.

absence ['æbsəns] *n.* (a) not being there; she was sentenced in her a. (b) lack; in the a. of a map we had to ask our way. **absent 1** ['æbsənt] *adj.* not present. **absent.2** [əb'sent] *v.* to a. oneself = to stay away (from class/a meeting) deliberately. **absentee** [æbsən'tiː] *n.* person who s absent; a. landlord = landowner who does not live near his land and takes no interest in it. **absenteeism** *n.* deliberately staying away from work. **absent-minded** *adj.* forgetful. **absent-mindedly** *adv.* forgetfully. **absent-mindedness** *n.* being often forgetful.

absolute ['æbsəluːt] *adj.* complete; the president assumed a. power = become a dictator; the government has an a. majority of ten = has a majority of ten over all the other parties in Parliament. **absolutely** *adv.* totally. **absolutism** *n.* political theory that governments should have absolute power.

absolution [æbsəlu"ʃn] n. blessing by a priest to forgive sin.

absolve [əb'zɒlv] v. to remove blame for a sin from (s.o.); to release (s.o.) from a promise.

absorb [əb'zɔːb] v. (a) to soak up (liquid); to deaden (a shock); to accept (a stranger/outside body) into a group. (b) absorbed in = completely busy with; it's an absorbing story = it holds your attention. **absorbent** adj. which absorbs; a. cotton = cotton wool. **absorber** n. shock a. = part of a car which softens the shock of a bump to the passengers. **absorption** [əb'zɔːpʃn] n. act of absorbing.

abstain [əb'stem] v. (from) not to do sth deliberately; Mr Smith abstained = refused to vote. **abstainer** n. person who does not drink alcohol.

abstemious [əb'stiːmɪəs] adj. not drinking (or eating) too much. **abstemiousness** n. not drinking (or eating) too much.

abstention [əb'sti'mɪəs] n. refusal to do sth; several abstentions = several people did not vote.

abstinence ['æbstməns] n. not drinking/eating to excess; total a. = not drinking any alcohol.

abstract 1 ['æbstrækt] adj. not concrete; (painting) which does not reproduce sth recognisable. **abstract 2** ['æbstraækt] n. (a) quality of not being concrete; in the a. = without mentioning specific cases. (b) abstract picture. (c) summary. **abstract 3** [əb'strækt] v. (a) to remove; to steal. (b) to summarise. **abstracted** adj. vague/dreamy; thoughtful. **abstraction** n. (a) removing; stealing. (b) vague idea.

abstruse [əb'struːs] adj. very difficult to understand.

absurd [əb'sɜːd] adj. very odd; ridiculous. **absurdity** n. fact of being absurd. **absurdly** adv. ridiculously.

abundant [ə'bʌndənt] adj. in large quantities. **abundance** n. large quantity. **abundantly** adv. copiously; very much.

abuse 1 [ə'bjuːs] n. (a) wrong use/bad use. (b) evil. (c) rude words/insults; term of a. = rude/insulting word. (d) very bad treatment (often sexual) of a person such as a child. **abuse 2** [ə'bkuːz] v. (a) to

put to wrong use; he abused my confidence = he took advantage of my confidence. (b) to insult. (c) to ill-treat; to make bad use of. **abusive** [ə'bjuːsɪv] adj. insulting.

abut [ə'bʌt] v. (abutted) (formal) to a. on a property = to be next to a property.

abysmal [ə'bʌt] adj. extremely large; the weather was a. = very bad. **abysmally** adv. extremely badly.

abyss [ə'bɪs] n. (pl.-es) very deep hole; very deep part of the sea.

Ac symbol for actinium.

AC abbrev. for alternating current.

A/C = account.

acacia [ə'kerʃə] n. common tropical tree which produces gum.

academic 1 [æk'demɪk] adj. (a) abstract (idea. question). (b) relating to study, esp. at a university; a staff = teaching staff at university. **academic 2** n. university teacher. **academically** adv. referring to academic matters/to teaching at university. **academician** [ækædəmɪʃn] n. member of an academy.

academy [ə'kædəmɪʃn] n. (a) specialised teaching establishment; (in Scotland) selective secondary school; military a. = training school for army officers; a. music = school for musicians. (b) society for the promotion of art/ science.

ACAS ['eɪkæs] n. the Advisory Conciliation and Arbitration Service.

accede [ək'siːd] v. (a) to a. the throne = to become king or queen. (b) (formal) to agree (to).

accelerate [æk'seləreɪt] v. (to cause to) go faster. **acceleration** [ækselə'reɪʃn] n. going faster. **accelerator** [æk'seləretə] n. pedal (in a car) which allows more petrol into the engine. and increases speed.

accent ['æksənt] n. (a) way of pronouncing; an Irish a. (b) small sign over a letter to show that it is pronounced differently. (c) stress.

accentor n. small brown singing bird.

accentuate [ək'sentjuert] v. to stress/ to make more obvious. **accentuation** [əksentju'erʃn] n. stressing.

accept v. (a) to take (thing which is offered). (b) to agree (to do sth). (c) accepted custom = sth which is usually done. **acceptability** n. being acceptable. **acceptable** *adj.* which you can easily accept. **acceptance** *n.* (a) receiving (of thing offered). (b) agreement (to do sth).

access 1 ['ækses] *n.* way of getting to person/place; a road leading off a main road to buildings; to have easy a. to = to be able to get sth easily. **access 2** *v.* to call up information which is stored in a computer. **accessible** [ək'sesɪbl] *adj.* able to be reached easily. **accessibility** [əksesɪ'bɪltɪ] *n.* being accessible.

accession [ək'seʃn] *n.* a. (to the throne) = becoming king or queen; the treaty of A. = the treaty by which the UK become a member of the EC. **accessions** *n. pl.* new books added to a library. **accessory 1** [ək'sesərɪ] *n.* (a) piece of minor equipment which is added to main items; a bag = bag for carrying extra items to attach to a camera. (b) non-essential items of clothing (handbag, gloves, hat, etc.) (c) charged with being an a. to the crime = with helping to commit the crime. **accessory 2** *adj.* non-essential.

accident ['æksɪdənt] *n.* thing which happens by chance, often with unfortunate results; I discovered the documents by a.; fatal a. = accident where s.o. is killed. **accidental 1** [æksɪ'dentl] *adj.* by accident; not on purpose. **accidental 2** *n.* (in music) additional sharp, flat or natural. **accidentally** *adv.* by accident; not on purpose. **accident-prone** *adj.* (person) who is likely to have a lot of accidents.

acclaim 1 [ə'kleɪm] *n.* great shout of praise. **acclaim 2** *v.* to greet with a shout of praise. **acclamation** [æklə'meɪʃn] *n.* act of acclaiming.

acclimatize, *Am.* **acclimate** [ə'klaɪmətaɪz, ə'klaɪmət] *v.* to make (sth/s.o.) used to a new climate or a new way of living. **acclimatization,** *Am.* **acclimation** [əklaɪmətaɪ'zerʃn, əklaɪ'merʃn] *n.* becoming acclimatised.

accolade ['ækɒleɪd] *n.* sign of praise; giving of a knighthood to s.o.

accommodate [ə'kɒmədeɪt] *v.* (a) to adapt; to supply (s.o.) with sth. (b) to provide lodging for (s.o.).

accommodating *adj.* helpful; giving satisfaction; always ready to help.

accommodation [əkɒmə'deɪʃn] *n.* (a) place to live/to sleep; all the a. in the town has been booked. (b) agreement/compromise. (c) adjustment.

accompany [ə'kʌmpnɪ] *v.* (a) to go with; sauce to a. the fish = to be served with the fish. (b) to play (usu. the piano) while s.o. sings or plays another instrument. **accompaniment** *n.* (a) thing which accompanies. (b) music played to accompany a soloist. **accompanist** *n.* person who accompanies a soloist.

accomplice [ə'kʌmplɪs] *n.* person who helps another person commit a crime.

accomplish [ə'kʌmplɪʃ] *v.* to finish/to carry out (a plan, etc). **accomplished** *adj.* gifted/talented; skilled. **accomplishment** *n.* (a) finishing (of a task). (b) accomplishments = talents.

accord [ə'kɔːd] *n.* (a) agreement; with one a. = all together/in agreement. (b) of your own a. = spontaneously/with no prompting. **accordance** *n.* agreement; in a. with your instructions = following your instructions. **accordingly** *adv.* in consequence. **according to** *adv.* (a) as s.o. says or writes; as stated by s.o. (b) by/in relation to; separate the children into groups a. to their ages.

accordion [ə'kɔːdɪən] *n.* (piano) a. = musical instrument with a bellows and a keyboard. **accordionist** *n.* person who plays an accordion.

accost [ə'kaʊnt] *v.* to go/to come up to (s.o.) and speak to them.

account 1 *n.* (a) story/description; by all accounts = according to what everyone said. (b) statement of money; bank a. = money deposited in a bank; current a. = account from which you can draw money without giving notice; savings a. = account where you put money regularly; deposit a. = account where you leave money for some time and on which interest is paid; to pay money on a. = to pay part of the total bill in advance; expense a. = money which a businessman is allowed to spend on entertainment and personal expenses which are paid for by his firm. (c) accounts (of a firm) = statement showing the financial position of a firm; accounts department = department in a company dealing with money. (d) he turned the accident to a. = he was able to profit from the accident. (e) he was called to a. = he was asked to explain; she gave a good a. of herself = she came out of the game/examination, etc. very well. (f) to take sth into a. = to make allowances for sth. (g) on a. of = because of; I was worried on her a. = I was afraid sth might happen to her; on no a. = not under any circumstances. **account 2** v. to a. for sth = to explain.

accountability. [əkaʊntə'bɪlɪtɪ] n. being accountable (for sth).

accountable adj. responsible.

accountancy n. theory/profession of being an accountant. **accountant** n. person who deals with the accounts (of a company); chartered a. = person who has passed high level examinations in accountancy. **accounting** n. accountancy.

accoutrements [ə'ku:trəmənts] n. pl. (usu. bulky or complicated) equipment which is carried.

accredit [ə'kredɪt] v. to authorise.

accretion [ə'kri:ʃn] n. increase in size by gradual additions.

accrue [ə'kru:] v. to increase by addition. **accrual** n. increase made by addition.

acct. abbrev. for account.

accumulate [ə'kju:mjulɪt] v. to pile up. **accumulation** [əkju:mju'leɪʃn] n. act of accumulating; pile/heap.

accumulator [ə'kju:mleɪtə] n. electric battery which can be recharged.

accurate ['ækjurət] adj. completely correct. **accuracy** n. being accurate; complete correctness. **accurately** adv. completely correctly.

accuse [ə'ku:z] v. to say that s.o. has done sth wrong; the police accused him of stealing the car. **accusation** [ækju'zeɪʃn] n. saying that s.o. has done sth wrong. **accusative** [ə'kju:zətɪv] adj. & n. (in grammar) (case) which shows the object of a verb. **accused** n. person who has been accused of a crime.

accuser n. person who accuses s.o.

accusing adj. in an a. tone = as if accusing. **accusingly** adv. as if accusing.

accustom [ə'kʌstəm] v. to make (s.o.) used (to sth).

ace [eɪs] n. (a) playing card which shows only one spot; the a. of diamonds. (b) person who is very brilliant at doing sth; an a. pilot. (c) (in tennis) shot which your opponent cannot return.

acerbate ['æsəbeɪt] v. to make worse.

acerbity [ə'sɜbɪt] n. (formal) sharpness (of flavour/character).

acetate ['æsɪteɪt] n. type of man-made fibre.

acetic [ə'si:tɪk] adj. referring to vinegar.

acetone ['æsɪtəʊn] n. colourless liquid, used to dissolve solids.

acetylene [ə'setɪli'n] n. gas which burns with a very bright light.

ache 1 [eɪk] n. pain; (see toothache, headache, etc.). **ache 2** v. to hurt.

aching adj. which hurts.

achieve [ə'tʃi:v] v. to succeed in doing (sth); to reach (a goal). **achievement** n. what you achieve; successful under taking/exploit.

Achilles' heel [ə'kɪli:z'hi:l] n. weak spot. **Achilles' tendon** n. tendon at the back of the ankle.

achromatic [ækrəʊ'mætɪk] adj. without colour.

acid 1 ['æsɪd] n. usually liquid chemical substance which contains hydrogen, corrodes some metals, and turns litmus paper red; a drops = boiled sweets with a sharp taste; the a. test = test which will show the true value of sth. **acid 2** adj. bitter/unpleasant.

acidify [ə'sɪdɪtɪ] v. to make substances acid. **acidity** [ə'sɪdɪtɪ] n. (a) acid contents. (b) bitterness. **acid rain** n. rain with a high level of acidity, caused by pollution.

acknowledge [ək'nɒlɪdʒ] v. (a) to admit (that sth is true). (b) to replay to say you have received (a letter).

acknowledgement n. admission (that sth is true); reply stating that you have received sth; my letter has not had any a. = no one has replied to it; (in a book) acknowledgements = the list of people the author thanks for help.

acme ['ækmɪ] n. highest point.

acne ['æknɪ] n. skin disease, with spots on the face/neck, etc.

acolyte ['ækəlaɪt] n. person who helps a priest during religious ceremonies.

aconite ['ækənaɪt] n. small spring flower which is poisonous.

acorn ['eɪkɔːn] *n.* fruit of an oak tree.
acoustic 1 [ə'kuːstɪk] *adj.* referring to
sound; a coupler = device for linking a
computer to a telephone handset,
allowing data to be transmitted; a. guitar
= ordinary guitar, (as opposed to an
electric guitar). **acoustic 2** *n.*
acoustics = (i) study of sound; (ii) ability
to carry sound without distortion.
acquaint [ə'kweɪnt] *v.* (a) to inform.
(b) to be acquainted with = to know.
acquaintance *n.* (a) knowing; to
make the a. of = to get to know. (b)
person you know (slightly).
acquiesce [ækwɪ'es] *v.* (formal) to
agree. **acquiescence** *n.* agreement.
acquiescent *adj.* in agreement.
acquire [ə'kwaɪə] *v.* to get into your
possession; acquired immunodeficiency
syndrome (AIDS) = condition, caused by
a virus, where the body's immune
system breaks down, making the patient
susceptible to any infection.
acquisition [ækwɪ'zɪʃn] *n.* (a) act of
acquiring. (b) thing you have acquired.
acquisitive [ə'kwɪzɪtɪv] *adj.* always
ready to acquire things.
acquisitiveness *n.* love of acquiring
things.
acquit [ə'kwɪt] *v.* (acquitted) (a) to
decide that someone is innocent. (b) he
acquitted himself well = he did well.
acquittal *n.* decision that a person is
innocent.
acre ['eɪkə] *n.* unit for measuring the
area of land (4840) square yards or 0.45
hectares). **acreage** ['eɪkrɪdʒ] *n.* area in
acres.
acrid ['ækrɪd] *adj.* bitter/pungent
(smell).
acrimonious [ækrɪ'məʊnɪəs] *adj.*
bitter (argument). **acrimony**
['ækrɪmənɪ] *n.* bitterness (of argument).
acrobat ['ækrəbæt] *n.* person who does
spectacular physical exercises.
acrobatic [ækrə'bætɪk] *adj.* referring
to spectacular exercises. **acrobatics** *n.*
pl. spectacular physical exercises.
acronym ['ækrənɪm] *n.* word (like
NATO) formed from the initials of other
words.
acropolis [ə'krɒpəlɪs] *n.* castle,
protecting a town in ancient Greece.
across [ə'krɒs] *adv. & prep.* (a) from
one side to the other; it is 500 metres a.

(b) on the other side; a. the street. (c) I
came/ran a. this = I found it. **across
the- board** *adj.* which applies to every
thing or everyone.
acrostic [ə'krɒstɪk] *n.* poem/puzzle in
which the first letters of each line form a
word.
acrylic [ə'krɪlɪk] *adj. & n.* (material/
paint) made from acid.
act 1 [ækt] *n.* (a) thing which is done;
we caught him in the a. = as he was
doing it; a. of God = natural disaster
which cannot be prevented. (b) A. (of
Parliament) (c) large section of a play.
act 2 *v.* (a) to play (a part in a play). (b)
to do sth; to a on behalf of = represent; to
a. as = do the work of (c) to behave (d)
to take effect/to work. **acting. 1** *adj.* a.
chairman = person who is taking the
place of the chairman. **acting. 2** *n.*
profession of an actor. **action** ['ækʃn] *n.*
(a) doing; out of a = not working. (b)
thing done. (c) the a. of the play = what
happens in it. (d) mechanism (of a
watch). (e) lawsuit; an a. for libel. (f)
warfare; killed in a. = on the battlefield.
actionable *adj.* (sth) for which s.o.
could bring a lawsuit against you.
activate ['æktɪveɪt] *v.* to put into
action. **active** ['æktɪv] *adj.* vigorous/
agile; (volcano) which still erupts; on a.
service = on the battlefront. **actively**
adv. in an active way. **activist** *n.*
person who actively supports a political
policy. **activity** [æk'tɪvɪtɪ] *n.* (a)
movement/being active. (b) occupation.
actor, actress ['æktə, 'æktrəs] *n.* (*pl.*-
es) person who acts in the theatre/films/
on television.
actinium [æk'tɪnɪəm] *n.* (element: Ac)
radioactive metal.
actual ['æktjʊəl] *adj.* real; in a fact =
really. **actuality** [æktjʊ'ælɪtɪ] *n.* reality.
actually *adv.* really.
actuary ['æktjʊərɪ] *n.* person who
calculates insurance rates. **actuarial**
[æktjʊ'eərɪəl] *adj.* referring to insurance
rates.
actuate ['æktjʊeɪt] *v.* to set in motion/
to start off.
acuity [ə'kjuːɪtɪ] *n.* sharpness (of sight).
acumen ['ækjuːmən] *n.* ability to make
shrewd decisions.
acupuncture ['ækjʊpʌŋktʃə] *n.* way
of healing and curing by placing the tips

of needles in the skin. **acupuncturist** *n.* doctor who practises acupuncture.

acute [ə'kju:t] *adj.* (a) very sharp (angle). (b) sudden serious (illness/pain). (c) perceptive. **acutely** *adv.* very sharply (aware). **acuteness** *n.* sharpness (of pain); seriousness (of illness); clearness (of hearing).

ad [æd] *n. inf.* advertisement; small ads = small advertisement for staff/articles for sale, etc.

AD ['eɪ'di:] abbreviation for Anno Domini (Latin for in the year of our Lord) (used to show dates after the birth of Christ) 923 AD.

adage ['ædɪdʒ] *n.* old wise saying.

adagio [ə'dɑ:dʒɪəʊ] *n.* slow piece of music.

Adam ['ædəm] *n. inf.* I don't know him from A. = I have no idea who he is; A.'s apple = lump in the front of a man's neck.

adamant ['ædəmənt] *adj.* fixed in your opinion/intentions.

adapt [ə'dæpt] *v.* to change (sth) so that it fits; to make (sth) more suitable. **adaptability** [ədæptə'bɪlɪtɪ] *n.* case of adapting yourself to new circumstances. **adaptable** *adj.* able to (be) adapt(ed) easily. **adaptation** [ædæp'teɪʃn] *n.* written work which is adapted from another. **adapter, adaptor** *n.* electric plug which allows several plugs to be fitted to the same socket; small disc which allows a record with a large central hole to be fitted on a turntable.

add [æd] *v.* (a) to join (sth to sth else). (b) to say/to write sth more. (c) to make a total. **addendum** [ə'dendəm] *n.* (*pl.*addenda) piece added, as at the end of a book. **add up** *v.* to make a total of (figures); these figures don't add up = the total given is incorrect.

adder ['ædə] *n.* viper.

addict ['ædɪkt] *n.* person who cannot stop himself from doing sth (usu. which is harmful to himself); drug a. = person who cannot stop taking a drug; TV a. = person who is always watching television. **addicted** [ə'dɪktɪd] *adj.* (to) (person) who cannot stop (taking a drug). **addiction** [ə'dɪkʃn] *n.* drug a. = inability to stop taking a drug. **addictive** *adj.* which causes addiction. **addition** [ə'dɪʃn] *n.* (a) act of adding;

in a. = added to this; also. (b) thing added. **additional** *adj.* further.

additive ['ædɪtɪv] *n.* substance, *usu.* chemical, which is added.

addled ['ædld] *adj.* rotten (egg).

address 1 [ə'dres] *n.* (*pl.*-es) number of house. name of street, town country, etc., where a person lives/where an office is situated; a book = book containing a list of addresses. (b) formal speech.

address 2 *v.* (a) to write the name and address of the person/the firm to whom sth is being sent. (b) to speak to (s.o.). (c) (in golf) to aim at the ball.

addressee [ædre'si:] *n.* person to whom a letter is addressed.

adduce [ə'dju:s] *v.* (formal) to bring added proof (of sth).

adenoids [ædənɔɪdz] *n. pl.*small growths in the back of the throat. **adenoidal** [ædɪ'nɔɪdl] *adj.* referring to the adenoids.

adept ['ædept] *adj. & n.* (person who is) clever (at doing sth).

adequate ['ædɪkwət] *adj.* (large) enough. **adequately** *adv.* enough.

adhere [əd'hɪə] *v.* to stick (to). **adherence** *n.* sticking/attachment. **adherent** *n.* person who belongs to (a society, etc). **adhesion** [əd'hi:ʒn] *n.* attachment/sticking; ability to stick. **adhesive 1** [əd'hi:zɪv] *adj.* which sticks; a. tape = plastic tape which sticks; a plaster = material used to stick bandages over wounds. **adhesive 2** *n.* glue.

ad hoc [æd'hɒk] *adj.* which applies to a particular case.

adieu [ə'dju:] *n.* (poetic) goodbye.

ad infinitum [ædɪnfɪ'naɪtəm] *adv.* for ever.

adipose ['ædɪpəʊs] *adj.* fatty (tissue).

adjacent [ə'dʒeɪsənt] *adj.* (to) next to/ touching/side by side.

adjective ['ædʒəktɪv] *n.* word used to describe a noun. **adjectival** [ædʒek'taɪvl] *adj.* used like an adjective. **adjectivally** *adv.* like an adjective.

adjoin [ə'dʒɔɪn] *v.* to be next to sth/to touch sth.

adjourn [ə'dʒɜːn] *v.* to put off (a meaning) to a later date; let's a. to the bar = let's stop talking here and continue in the bar. **adjournment** *n.* putting off (a meeting) to a later date.

adjudicate [ə'dʒuːdɪkeɪt] v. to give a decision (in a dispute); to be the judge (in a competition). **adjudication** [ədʒuːdɪ'keɪʃn] n. decision (in a dispute); judging (of a competition). **adjudicator** [ə'dʒuːdɪkeɪtə] n. judge.

adjunct ['ædʒʌŋkt] n. thing additional (to sth).

adjust [ə'dʒʌst] v. to put right by making a slight change. **adjustable** adj. which can be changed slightly. **adjuster, adjustor** n. person who calculates the extent of losses in an insurance claim. **adjustment** n. slight change made (to a mechanism).

adjutant ['ædʒətənt] n. army officer who assists in administration.

ad-lib ['æd'lɪb] v. (ad-libbed) inf. to speak without a script.

administer [əd'mɪnɪstə] v. to govern/to rule (a country/an office); to run (a company/an estate); to a. an oath to s.o. = to make s.o. swear an oath. **admin** n. informal administrative work.

administrate v. to see that justice is done. **administration** [ədmɪnɪ'streɪʃn] n. ruling (of a country); the government. **administrative** adj. which administers; referring to administration. **administrator** n. person who rules/governs.

admirable ['ædmərəbl] adj. see admire.

admiral ['ædmərəl] n. highest-ranking officer in the navy; red a. = type of red and black butterfly. **the Admiralty** n. British government department dealing with the navy.

admire [əd'maɪə] v. to look at (sth) with, pleasure. **admirable** ['ædmərəbl] adj. remarkable; excellent. **admirably** adv. remarkably; excellently. **admiration** [ædmə'reɪʃn] n. feeling of pride/pleasure. **admirer** [əd'maɪərə] n. person who admires. **admiring** adj. (look) showing admiration. **admiringly** adv. in an admiring way.

admission [əd'mɪʃn] n. (a) being allowed to enter; no a. = no one can enter. (b) saying that sth is true.

admissible [əd'mɪsɪbl] adj. (evidence) that can be admitted.

admit [əd'mɪt] v. (admitted) (a) to allow to enter. (b) to say that sth is true. (c) to accept (evidence/idea.

etc). **admittance** n. entrance. **admittedly.** adv. according to general opinion.

admixture [æd'mɪkstʃə] n. thing which is added to make a mixture.

admonish [əd'mɒnɪʃ] v. to scold s.o./ to tell s.o. off. **admonition** [ædmə'nɪʃn] n. scolding.

ad nauseam [æd'nɔːzɪəm] adv. until one is sick of it.

ado [ə'duː] n. without any more a. = without any more fuss.

adobe [ə'dəʊbɪ] n. bricks made from clay dried in the sun.

adolescence [ædə'lesns] n. period between childhood and being an adult. **adolescent** adj. &n. (referring to) a young person between child and adult.

adopt [ə'dɒpt] v. (a) to take (s.o.) legally as your son or daughter. (b) to follow/to take up (a line of argument); to put on (an air), (c) to prescribe (a book) for use in class. **adoption** [ə'dɒpʃn] n. (a) legal taking of a child as your own. (b) prescribing (of a book) for use in class. **adoptive** adj. who has (been) adopted.

adore [ə'dɔː] v. to love very strongly. **adorable** adj. pretty/lovely. **adoration** [ædə'reɪʃn] n. strong love/ worship. **adorer** n. person who adores.

adorn [ə'dɔːn] v. to cover with ornaments/to decorate. **adornment** n. adorning; ornament.

adrenal [ə'driːnəl] adj. referring to the kidneys. **adrenalin(e)** [ə'drenəlɪn] n. secretion which is produced by a gland when s.o. is excited/afraid.

adrift [ə'drɪft] adv. to cast a boat a. = to let a boat float without control; to cut yourself a. = to separate yourself.

adroit [ə'drɔɪt] adj. skilful/clever (with your hands). **adroitly** adv. smartly.

adsorb [æd'zɔːb] v. to form a thin film on the surface of sth.

adulation [ædjʊ'leɪʃn] n. wild praise/ excessive flattery.

adult ['ædʌlt, ə'dʌlt] adj. & n. grown-up (person); fully grown (animal)

adulterate [ə'dʌltəreɪt] v. to water down; to add sth of inferior quality to (a substance). **adulterer, adulteress** [ə'dʌltərə, ə'dʌltərəs] n. person who commits adultery. **adulterous** adj. referring to adultery. **adultery** n. (of married person) having sexual intercourse with s.o. to whom he/she is not married.

ad valorem [ædvə'lɔːrəm] *adj.* (tax) calculated on the value of the thing being taxed.

advance 1 [əd'vɑːns] *n.* (a) forward movement; a guard = troops sent ahead of the main force. (b) in a. = early; beforehand. (c) to make advances to = to try to attract. (d) payment made early.

advance 2 *v.* (a) to go forward. (b) to put forward; he advanced me £10 = he gave me £10 as an early payment.

advanced *adj.* (a) (subject) which is studied after several years initial study; a. student = student who has studied for several years. (b) the season is well a. = the season is coming to an end; in an a. state of decay = very decayed.

advancement *n.* progress (of science, etc.).

advantage [əd'vɑːntɪdʒ] *n.* useful thing which will help you to be successful; to take a. of = to profit from; to take a. of s.o. = to cheat for your own benefit; her dress shows off her figure to a. = makes her figure look perfect.

advantageous [ædvən'teɪdʒəs] *adj.* profitable/useful.

advent ['ædvent] *n.* (a) coming; arrival. (b) Advent = church season before Christmas.

adventitious [ædven'tɪʃəs] *adj.* (root) which develops from a plant's stem and not from another root.

adventure [əd'ventʃə] *n.* new, exciting and dangerous experience. **adventurer** *n.* person who aims to make a fortune by taking risks. **adventurous** *adj.* bold (person); exciting (life). **adventurously** *adv.* boldly. **adventurousness** *n.* being adventurous.

adverb ['ædvɜːb] *n.* word used to describe a verb/an adjective/another adverb. **adverbial** [əd'vɜːbɪəl] *adj.* used as an adverb. **adverbially** *adv.* like an adverb

adversary ['ædvəsrɪ] *n.* person your are fighting against. **adverse** ['ædvɜːs] *adj.* (a) contrary (winds). (b) bad; unfavourable (conditions). **adversely** *adv.* badly. **adversity** [əd'vɜːsɪtɪ] *n.* difficulty.

advert 1 ['ædvɜːt] *n. inf.* advertisement. **advert 2** [æd'vɜːt] *v.* (formal) to refer to. **advertise** ['ædvətaɪz] *v.* to show that sth is for sale/to publicise sth; he advertised for a new secretary = put an advertisement in the paper asking people to apply for the job; there's no need to a. the fact = there's no need to tell everyone the secret. **advertisement** [əd'vɜːtɪsmənt] *n.* announcement that sth is for sale/is wanted. **advertiser** *n.* person who advertises. **advertising** *n.* action of announcing the sale of sth; business of describing goods for sale; a agency = firm which designs and places advertisements.

advice [əd'vaɪs] *n.* (a) suggestion as to what should be done; a piece of a. (b) a. note = paper which tells you that goods have been shipped. **advise** [əd'vaɪz] *v.* to suggest what should be done.

advisability *n.* being recommended. **advisable** *adj.* which you would recommend. **advisedly** *adv.* after a lot of thought. **adviser, advisor** *n.* person who gives advice, **advisory** *adj.* in an a. capacity = as an adviser.

advocacy [ædvɒkəsɪ] *n.* pleading for; support for. **advocate 1** ['ædvɒkət] *n.* (a) person who pleads for a cause. (b) (In Scotland) lawyer who pleads in court. **advocate 2** ['ædvɒkeɪt] *v.* to recommend/to plead.

adze [ædz] *n.* axe with the blade at right angles to the handle.

aegis ['iːdʒɪs] *n.* (formal) under the a. of = supported/patronised by.

aeolian [iː'əʊlɪən] *adj.* caused by the wind.

aeon ['iːɒn] *n.* very long time.

aerate [eə'reɪt] *v.* to fill sth with air or gas.

aerial 1 ['eərɪəl] *adj.* referring to the air. **aerial 2** *n.* device for sending or receiving radio or TV signals.

aerie ['ɪːrɪ] *n. Am.* see eyrie.

aerobatics [eərə'bætɪks] *n. pl.* trick flying (as a display).

aerobic [eə'rəʊbɪk] *adj.* needing oxygen to take place or to exist. **aerobics,** *n. pl.* exercises to improve the body's use of oxygen.

aerodrome ['eərədrəʊm] *n.* small airfield.

aerodynamics [eərədaɪ'næmɪks *n.* science of movement of flying bodies in the air.

aerofoil ['eərəfɔɪl] *n.* wings surface of a plane.

aeronautical [eərə'nɔːtɪkl] *adj.* referring to aircraft flying. **aeronautics** *n.* science of flying aircraft.

aerophagia [eərəʊ'feɪdʒɪə] *n.* habit of swallowing air.

aeroplane ['eərəpleɪn] *n.* machine that flies.

aerosol ['eərəsɒl] *n.* canister filled under pressure, which sends out a spray when the button is pushed.

aerospace ['eərəʊspeɪs] *n.* the space around the earth, including the atmosphere.

aesthete ['iːsθiːt] *n.* person who appreciates beauty in art. **aesthetic** [iːs'θetɪk] *adj.* pleasing from an artistic point of view. **aesthetically** *adv.* from an artistic point of view.

afar [ə'fɑː] *adv.* from a. = from a long way away.

affable ['æfəbl] *adj.* pleasant/ courteous. **affability** [æfə'bɪlɪtɪ] *n.* pleasantness/courtesy. **affably** *adv.* in a pleasant/friendly way.

affair [ə'feə] *n.* (a) business; that's my a. = it's my business and not your; his affairs = his business. (b) he's having an a. with her = he's her lover. (c) the present state of affairs = how things are at present.

affect [ə'fekt] *v.* (a) to pretend/to put on (b) to touch/to change sth. **affectation** [æfek'teɪʃn] *n.* pretence. **affected** *adj.* pretended/put on. **affecting** *adj.* touching/which makes you feel emotion.

affection [ə'fekʃn] *n.* liking/love. **affectionate** *adj.* showing love or fondness for s.o. **affectionately** *adv.* in a loving way.

affidavit [æfɪ'deɪvɪt] *n.* written sworn statement.

affiliate [ə'fɪlɪeɪt] *v.* to link (a small group to a larger one). **affiliation** [əfɪlɪ'eɪʃn] *n.* political a. = political link.

affinity [ə'fɪnɪtɪ] *n.* (*pl.*affinities) closeness/similarity of character; strong attraction.

affirm [ə'fɜːm] *v.* (a) to state. (b) to make a statement (in court, instead of taking the oath). **affirmation**

[æfə'meɪʃn] *n.* statement. **affirmative 1** [ə'fɜːmətɪv] *adj.* agreeing. **affirmative 2** *n.* the answer is in the a. = the answer is yes. **affirmatively** *adv.* he answered a. = he answered yes.

affix [ə'fɪks] *v.* (formal) to attach.

afflict [ə'flɪkt] *v.* to torture/to torment. **affliction** [ə'flɪkʃn] *n.* torment; cause of distress.

affluence ['æflʊəns] *n.* wealth. **affluent** *adj.* rich; a. society = society where most people have enough money.

afford [ə'fɔːd] *v.* to have enough money to pay for (sth).

afforestation [æfɒrɪ'steɪʃn] *n.* planting tress to make a forest.

affray [ə'freɪ] *n.* (formal) fight between several people in public.

affront 1 [ə'frʌnt] *n.* offence. **affront 2** *v.* to insult.

afield [ə'fiːld] *adv.* to go far a. = to go a long way.

afire [ə'faɪə] *adj.* on fire.

aflame [ə'fleɪm] *adj.* (formal) on fire.

aflatoxin [æflə'tɒksɪn] *n.* poisonous substance which forms on seeds and nuts.

afloat [ə'fləʊt] *adv.* floating.

afoot [ə'fʊt] *adv.* there's a plan a. = a plan is being prepared: there's sth a. = sth is being plotted.

aforesaid [ə'fɔːsed] *adj.* (formal) which has been mentioned before.

aforethought [ə'fɔːθɔːt] *adj.* (formal) with malice a. = having planned the crime beforehand.

afraid [ə'freɪd] *adj.* (a) frightened (by) she's a. of the dark. (b) sorry to have to say; I'm a. she's ill.

afresh [ə'freʃ] *adv.* (all over) again.

African ['æfrɪkən] *adj. & n.* (person) from Africa; A. violet = small house plant with blue or pink flowers.

Afro- ['æfrəʊ] prefix meaning African/ between Africa and another country.

Afro ['æfrəʊ] *adj. & n.* A. (hairstyle) = type of bouffant hairstyle.

aft [ɑːft] *adv.* at/towards the back of a ship.

after 1 ['ɑːftə] *adv.* next/later. **after 2** *prep.* next to/following: the police are a. you = the police are looking for you: what's he a.? = what does he want? a. you = please go first. **after 3** *conj.* following the time when. **afterbirth.**

placenta which comes out of the womb after the birth of young. **aftercare** n. care for people after an operation, etc. **aftereffects** n. pl.effects that follow on sth. **afterglow** n. glow in the sky after the sun has set. **afterhours** adj. (trading) after a stock exchange has closed. **aftermath** n. what takes place after a catastrophe. **afternoon** n. part of the day between 12 noon and evening. **afters** n. pl.(in a meal) inf. sweet pudding/dessert. **aftersales service** n. maintenance (of a car/a machine, etc.) by the manufacturer/the agent after it has been sold. **aftershave** n. a. (lotion) = lotion for soothing the face after shaving. **aftershock** n. lighter earth tremor felt after a major earthquake. **afterthought** n. thing which you think of later.

afterwards adv. after that; next/later.

Ag symbol for silver.

again [ə'geɪn, ə'gen] adv. once more; once a. = another time; a. and a. = several times; now and a. = sometimes; inf. come a. ? = could you repeat that?

against [ə'genst] prep. (a) touching. (b) contrary to (rules, etc). he's a. lending her any more money = he's opposed to lending her money.

agaric [ə'gærɪk] n. type of fungus.

agate ['ægət] n. semi-precious stone, usu. with bands of different colours.

age 1 [eɪdʒ] n. (a) number of years you have lived; under a. = below the legal age (to do sth). (b) period; the Stone A. (c) for ages = a very long time. **age 2** v. to become old. **aged 1** [eɪdʒd] adj. a. 74 = 74 years old. **aged 2** ['eɪdʒɪd] adj. & n. (a) very old. (b) the a. = old people. **ageless**. adj. which does not grow old or look old.

agency ['eɪdʒənsɪ] n. (a) office which represents a larger firm/which works on behalf of another firm; we have the a. for Ford cars = we are the distributors for Ford cars. (b) means.

agenda [ə'dʒendə] n. list of things to be discussed at a meeting.

agent ['eɪdʒənt] n. (a) person who represents s.o. else; secret a. = spy. (b) substance which has an effect on another; a. provocateur = person who provokes people to commit crimes, esp. crimes against the state.

agglomeration [əglɒmə'reɪʃn] n.

large urban area.

aggrandizement [ə'grændɪzmənt] n. making larger/more powerful.

aggravate ['ægrəveɪt] v. to make worse. **aggravating** adj. inf. annoying. **aggravation** [ægrə'veɪʃn] n. worsening (of a quarrel); inf. annoyance.

aggregate ['ægrɪgət] n. (a) total; in the a. = as a total. (b) mixture of sand, gravel, etc., with cement.

aggression [ə'greʃn] n. hostility; attacking; act of a. = attack. **aggressive** [ə'gresɪv] adj. hostile; attacking. **aggressively** adv. violently. **aggressiveness** n. being aggressive. **aggressor** n. attacker.

aggrieved [ə'griːvd] adj. upset; hurt.

aggro ['ægrəʊ] n. (no pl.) SI. violent quarrelling/disagreement.

aghast [ə'gɑːst] adj. horrified.

agile ['ædʒaɪl] adj. light-footed; (animal/person) who can climbs/swing/run, etc. very easily. **agility** [ə'dʒɪlɪtɪ] n. being agile.

agio ['ædʒɪəʊ] n. charge made for converting money to another currency.

agitate ['ædʒɪteɪt] v. to stir up public opinion (for/against sth). **agitation** [ædʒɪ'teɪʃn] n. (a) worry. (b) political a. = political unrest. **agitator** ['ædʒɪteɪtə] n. person who stirs up political unrest.

AGM [eɪdʒiːem] Annual General Meeting.

agnostic [æg'nɒstɪk] adj. & n. (person) who believes that nothing can be known about God. **agnosticism** n. belief that nothing can be known about God.

ago [ə'gəʊ] adv. in the past; three years a.

agog [ə'gɒg] adj. all a. = very eager.

agonize ['ægənaɪz] v. to worry (over a decision). **agonized** adj. as if in pain/in agony. **agonizing** adj. (a) very sharp (pain). (b) upsetting. painful (decision).

agony ['ægənɪ] n. extreme pain/extreme discomfort; a. column = letters and advice about personal problems in a newspaper.

agoraphobia [ægərə'fəʊbɪə] n. irrational fear of public places or open spaces.

agrarian [ə'greərɪən] adj. dealing with the land.

agree [ə'griː] v. (a) (with) to say that you think the same ways as (s.o.). (b) (to) to say yes to (a suggestion). (c) eggs don't a. with me = make me feel ill. **agreeable** adj. (a) pleasant. (b) in agreement; are you a. to this? = do you agree? **agreeably** adv. pleasantly, **agreement** n. act of saying yes; to be in a. with = to agree with.

agriculture ['ægrɪkʌltʃə] n. use of the land for growing crops/raising animals, etc. **agricultural** [ægrɪ'kʌltʃərəl] adj. referring to agriculture. **agribusiness** n. farming and making products for farmers, seen as a business.

agronomy [ə'grɒnəmɪ] n. study of agriculture.

aground [ə'graʊnd] adv. no longer afloat; the ship went a.

ahead [ə'hed] adv. in front; in advance (of a time); full speed a. = go forward as fast as possible.

ahoy [ə'hɔɪ] inter. used by sailors to call a ship.

AI = artificial insemination.

aid 1 [eɪd] n. (a) help; first a. = help to injured/sick people; first-a. kit = box with bandages/medicines, etc.; in a. of the Red Cross = to help the Red Cross. (b) instrument to help; a hearing a. **aid 2** v. to help.

AID = artificial insemination by donor.

aide [eɪd] n, assistant (of a president, etc). **aide-de-camp** [eɪddə'kɒŋ] n. (pl.aides-) officer who assists a senior officer.

AIDS = acquired immunodeficiency syndrome.

ail [eɪl] v. (old) to be ill. **ailing** ['eɪlɪŋ] adj. sick.

ailment ['eɪlmənt] n. minor illness.

aileron ['eɪlərɒn] n. flap on the edge of an aircraft's wing.

aim 1 [eɪm] n. target; what you are trying to do; he took a. = he pointed his gun at the target. **aim 2** v. (a) to plan/to intend to do. (b) to point (at). **aimless, (adj.) aimlessly** adv. with no particular plan.

air 1 ['eə] n. (a) mixture of gases which we breathe, and which surrounds the earth; travel by a. = in an aircraft; in the a. = not yet decided; on the a = a speaking live on TV/on radio. (b) little tune. (c) appearance/feeling. **air 2** v. to

freshen (a room. clothes, etc.). (b) giving more air. **airbase** n. military airfield.

airbed n. inflatable plastic/rubber mattress. **airborne** adj. carried in the air. **airbrake** n. (a) movable part on an aircraft to slow it down. (b) brake (on trucks) which works by compressed air. **air-conditioned** adj. cooled by an air-conditioner. **air-conditioner** n. machine which keeps a room at the right temperature. **air conditioning** n. cooling of the air by an air-conditioner. **aircooled** adj. (engine) cooled by air, not by water. **aircraft** n. (pl.aircraft) machine which files. **aircraft carrier** n. large warship which carries aircraft and has a long deck for landing and taking off. **aircraftman, aircraftwoman** n. (pl.-men-women) lowest rank in the Royal air Force. **aircrew** n. the crew of an aircraft. **airfield** n. small private or military aerodrome. **air force** n. military air defence organisation. **airfreight, 1** n. shipping goods by air. **airfreight, 2** v. to ship goods by air. **airgun** n. gun which shoots pellets using compressed air. **air hostess** n. woman who woks on a passenger aircraft, serving meals and looking after the passengers. **airily** adv. in an airy way. **airless** adj. with no air or wind; stuffy. **air letter** n. very light piece of writing paper which, when folded and stuck down, becomes its own envelope. **airlift, 1** n. transport of emergency supplies/people by air. **airlift 2** v. to transport emergency supplies/people by air. **airline** n. company which runs passenger or cargo air services. **airlock** n. blockage in the flow of a liquid in a pipe (caused by air). **airmail** n. & adv. (mail) sent by air. **airman** n. (pl.men) man serving in an air force. **airmattress** n. mattress which can be inflated. **airplane** n. Am. aeroplane. **air pocket** n. sudden turbulence in air. **airport** n. commercial installation where passenger and cargo planes land and take off. **air raid** n. attack by military aircraft. **airship** n. large inflated balloon driven by an engine. **airsick** adj. sick because of travelling by air. **airsickness** n. feeling of being airsick. **airspeed** n. speed of an aircraft in the air. **airstrip**

n. small runway where planes can land and take off. **air terminal** *n.* station in a town where air passengers can take buses to an airport. **airtight** *adj.* not letting in any air. **air traffic control** *n.* control of the movement of aircraft by people on the ground. **airway** *n.* passage (such as the throat) through which air passes in the body. **airworthiness** *n.* safety of an aircraft for use. **airy** *adj.* (-ier, -iest) (a) full of air. (b) vague (promise). **airyfairy** *adj.* impractical (plan).

aisle [aɪl] *n.* gangway; side part in a church parallel to the nave.

ajar [ə'dʒɑː] *adj.* (of door/window) slightly open.

aka [eɪkeɪ'eɪ] = also known as.

akimbo [ə'kɪmbəʊ] *adv.* with her arms a. = with her hands on her hips.

akin [ə'kɪn] *adj.* similar (to).

Al symbol for aluminium.

alabaster ['æləbɑːstə] *n.* smooth white stone.

a la carte [ælæ'kɑːt] *adv. & adj.* (meal) made of several dishes ordered separately from a menu.

alacrity [ə'lækrɪtɪ] *n.* speed.

à la mode [ælæ'mɒd] *adv. Am.* served with ice cream.

alarm 1 [ə'lɑːm] *n.* thing which gives a loud warning; false a. = warning signal which is false; fire a. = bell which rings when a fire breaks out; a. (clock) = clock which rings at a certain time. **alarm 2** *v.* to warn (s.o.); to frighten (s.o.). **alarmist** *adj. & n.* (person) who is unnecessarily worried by sth.

alas [ə'læs] *inter.* showing sadness.

albatross ['ælbətrɒs] *n.* (*pl.*-es) very large white sea bird.

albedo [æl'biːdəʊ] *n.* ability to reflect light.

albeit [ɔːl'biːɪt] *conj.* (formal) although.

albino [æl'biːnəʊ] *n.* animal or person born with pale skin, white hair, and pink eyes.

album ['ælbəm] *n.* (a) large book for sticking things in. (b) long-playing record.

albumenalbumin ['ælbjʊmən] *n.* white part of an egg.

alchemy ['ælkəmɪ] *n.* medieval chemistry, aimed at converting metals to gold. **alchemist** *n.* person who studied

alchemy.

alcohol ['ælkəhɒl] *n.* intoxicating liquid distilled from a fermented mixture. **alcoholic 1** [ælkə'hɒlɪk] *adj.* referring to alcohol. **alcoholic 2** *n.* person who is addicted to drinking alcohol. **alcoholism** *n.* addiction to drinking alcohol.

alcove ['ælkəʊv] *n.* small recess in a wall.

alder ['ɔːldə] *n.* tree which often grows near water.

ale [eɪl] *n.* type of beer.

alert 1 [ə'lɜːt] *adj.* watchful; lively. **alert 2** *n.* to be on the a. = to be watchful/to watch out for sth: he gave the a. = he gave a warning signal. **alert 3** *v.* to a. s.o. to = to warn s.o. of. **alertness** *n.* watchfulness; promptness (in doing sth).

alfalfa [æl'fælfə] *n.* lucerne.

alfresco [æl'freskəʊ] *adj. & adv.* in the open air; an a. meal.

algae ['ældʒiː] *n. pl.* tiny water plant with no stems or leaves.

algebra ['ældʒɪbrə] *n.* branch of mathematics where numbers are replaced by letters. **algebraic** [ældʒɪ'breɪk] *adj.* referring to algebra.

algorithm ['ælgərɪðm] *n.* plan for working out a complicated calculation.

alias 1 ['eɪlɪəs] *adv.* otherwise known as. **alias 2** ['eɪlɪaɪ] *n.* (*pl.*-es) assumed name.

alibi *n.* proof that you were some where else when a crime was committed.

alien 1 ['eɪlɪən] *adj.* foreign (to). **alien 2** *n.* foreigner. **alienate** ['eɪlɪəneɪt] *v.* to turn away/to repeal. **alienation** [eɪlɪə'neɪʃn] *v.* turning away/repelling.

alight 1 [ə'laɪt] *v.* (formal) to a. from = to get off (a train/bus, etc). **alight 2** *adj.* on fire.

align [ə'laɪn] *v.* to put (yourself/sth) in line; to put (yourself) on the same side as. **alignment** *n.* row (of objects); putting (countries) on the same side.

alike [ə'laɪk] *adv.* almost the same.

alimentary [ælɪ'mentərɪ] *adj.* which feeds; a canal = tube by which food goes into the stomach, and passes through the body.

alimony ['ælɪmənɪ] *n.* money paid regularly by a husband to his divorced wife.

alive [ə'laɪv] adj. (a) living/not dead.
(b) a. to = aware of. (c) lively.

alkali ['ælkəlaɪ] n. substance which will
neutralize an acid, and which turns
litmus paper blue. **alkaline** adj. not
acid.

all 1 [ɔːl] adj. & pron. (a) everything
everyone; a the children; a of us prefer
beer. (b) (in tennis) fifteen a. = fifteen
points each. (c) once (and) for a. = for
the last time; not at a. = certainly not; a.
but = nearly. **all 2** adv. completely;
dressed a. in blue; a at once/a. of a
sudden = suddenly; inf. not a. there =
mad. **all in** adj. (a) inf. worn out. (b) a.
in = including everything; a.-in price.

all-night adj. which goes on for the
whole night. **all-out** adj. complete
(strike) we must make an a.-out effort =
we must do everything. **all right**
[ɔːl'raɪt] adj. (a) fine; well, (b) yes, I
will. **all-round** adj. general; a.-round
athlete = person who is good at all sorts
of sports. **all-rounder** n. person who
can do anything, esp. cricketer who can
play in any position. **all-star** adj. with
many stars appearing. **all-time** adj.
(greatest level, etc.) ever.

Allah ['ælæ] n. Muslim name for God.

allay [ə'leɪ] v. to calm (fear/anger).

allegation [ælɪ'geɪʃn] n. suggestion as
if it were fact. **allege** [ə'ledʒ] v. to
suggest (as a fact that). **alleged** adj.
suggested. **allegedly** [ə'ledʒɪdlɪ] adv.
as is alleged.

allegiance [ə'liːdʒəns] n. faithfulness;
they swore a. to the President = they
swore to obey him.

allegory ['ælɪgərɪ] n. piece of writing
where the characters represent abstract
qualities or defects. **allegorical**
[ælɪ'gɒrɪkl] adj. referring to allegory.

allegro [ə'legrəʊ] adv. & adj. (in
music) played quite fast.

allergy ['ælədʒɪ] n. illness caused by a
reaction to irritant substances. **allergen**
n. substance (such as pollen) which
produces an allergic reaction. **allergic**
[ə'lədʒɪk] adj. reacting badly against; I
am a. to grass pollen; she is a; to jazz =
dislikes it intensely.

alleviate [ə'liːvɪeɪt] v. to lessen/to
soften. **alleviation** [əliːvɪ'eɪʃn] n.
lessening.

alley ['ælɪ] n. (a) very narrow street. (b)

skittle a./bowing a. = long narrow area
for playing skittles.

alliance [ə'laɪəns] e. link between two
groups or countries

allied ['ælaɪd] adj. (a) linked by an
alliance; the a powers = western
countries linked against communist
states. (b) linked.

alligator ['ælɪgeɪtə] n. large flesh-
eating reptile living in tropical rivers.

alliteration [əlɪtə'reɪʃn] n. use of
repeated consonants at the beginning of
words in poetry.

allocate ['æləkeɪt] v. to give (sth) as a
share (for a particular purpose.

allocation [ælə'keɪʃn] n. division/
giving as a share; amount allocated.

allot [ə'lɒt] v. (allotted) to share out
between several people. **allotment** n.
(a) sharing out. (b) small plot of land
leased by a town to a citizen (esp. for
growing vegetables.

allow [ə'laʊ] v. (a) to a. s. o. to do sth =
to let (s. o. do sth). (b) to give; we will a.
you six weeks to pay. **allowable** adj.
which is permitted; a expenses =
expenses which are allowed against tax.

allowance n. (a) money paid
regularly; family a. = money paid each
week by the State to families with
children. (b) to make allowances for =
take into account.

alloy 1 ['ælɔɪ] n. mixture of two or
more metals. **alloy 2** v. to mix (metals).

allspice ['ɔːlspaɪs] n. small round
tropical seed used as a spice.

allude [ə'luːd] v. to a. to sth = to refer to
sth indirectly or briefly.

allure [ə'ljʊə] v. to attract. **alluring**
adj. attractive.

allusion [ə'luːʒn] n. slight reference.
allusive adj. which makes reference to
sth.

alluvial [ə'luːvɪəl] adj. (soil/land)
which has been deposited by rivers.

alluvium n. soil which has been
deposited by a river.

ally 1 ['ælaɪ] n. person/country who is
on the same side as you in a quarrel or
war. **ally 2** [ə'laɪ] v. to a. oneself to = to
join forces with/to support.

alma mater [ælmə'meɪtə] n. school or
college which s.o. has attended.

almanac ['ɔːlmənæk] n. calendar which
also contains advice or information.

almighty 1 [ɔːl'maɪtɪ] *adj. inf.* very powerful; an a. row = a very loud noise. **almighty 2** *n.* the A. = God.

almond ['ɑːmənd] *n.* nut from a tree of the peach family.

almoner ['ɑːmənə] *n.* (old) person in a hospital who sees that the patients are happy and well fed.

almost ['ɔːlməʊst] *adv.* nearly; not quite.

alms [ɑːmz] *n. pl.*(old) gift to old/sick/ poor people. **almshouses** *n. pl.*houses formerly built as homes for the poor.

aloe ['æləʊ] *n.* desert plant with thick leaves and bitter juice.

aloft [ə'lɒft] *adv.* (formal) high up (in the air).

alone [ə'ləʊn] *adj. & adv.* with no one else.

along 1 [ə'lɒŋ] *prep.* a. the road = from one end of the road to the other; for some distance down the road. **along 2** *adv.* come a. with me = come with me; all a. = from the beginning; they don't get a. very well together = they do not agree.

alongside *adv. & prep.* beside.

aloof [ə'luːf] *adv. & adj.* coldly/ unfriendly; they kept a. = they did not mix with others. **aloofness** *n.* cold superciliousness.

alopecia [æləʊ'piːsɪə] *n.* baldness.

aloud [ə'laʊd] *adv.* loud enough to be heard; in a loud voice.

alp [ælp] *n.* mountain or mountain meadow in Switzerland.

alpaca [æl'pækə] *n.* wool from a llama.

alpha ['ælfə] *n.* first letter of the Greek alphabet.

alphabet ['ælfəbet] *n.* letters used to write words laid out in a set order (A, B, C, etc.). **alphabetical** [ælfə'betɪkl] *adj.* in a. order = in order based on the first letter of each word. **alphabetically** *adv.* in alphabetical order.

alpine ['ælpaɪn] *adj. & n.* referring to high mountains; (plant) which grows on high mountains. **alpinist** *n.* person who climbs mountains.

already [ɔːl'redɪ] *adv.* by now.

alright [ɔːl'raɪt] *adj. & inter. inf.* = all right.

alsatian [æl'seɪʃn] *n.* large dog (of German origin) often used as a guard dog.

also ['ɔːlsəʊ] *adv.* as well/at the same time.

altar ['ɒltə] *n.* table in church/temple for religious ceremonies.

alter ['ɒltə] *v.* to change. **alteration** [ɒltə'reɪʃn] *n.* change.

altercation [ɔːltə'keɪʃn] *n. (formal)* argument.

alternate 1 [ɔːl'tɜːnət] *adj.* every other/ missing one each time. **alternate 2** ['ɔːltəneɪt] *v.* to put (sth) in place of sth else, and then switch them round

alternately [ɔːl'tɜːnətlɪ] *adv.* in turns; one first and then the other **alternating** *adj.* (electric current) which flows one way and then the other. **alternative** [ɔːl'tɜːnətɪv] *n. & adj.* thing in place of sth else. **alternatively** *adv.* on the other hand. **alternator** ['ɔːltəneɪtə] *n.* device which produces alternating current.

although [ɔːl'ðəʊ] *conj.* in spite of the fact that.

altimeter ['æltɪmiːtə] *n.* instrument for measuring altitude. **altitude** ['æltɪtjuːd] *n.* height (measured above the level of the sea).

alto ['æltəʊ] *n.* (*pl.*-os) (man with a) high-pitched voice, (woman with a) low-pitched voice.

altogether [ɔːltə'geðə] *adv.* considering everything together.

altruism ['æltrʊɪzəm] *n.* being unselfish. **altruistic** *adj.* unselfish.

alum ['æləm] *n.* natural mineral salt.

aluminium *Am.* **aluminum** [ælju'mɪnjəm], [ə'luːmɪnəm] *n.* (element Al) light white metal.

alumnus [ə'lʌmnəs] *n.* (*pl.*alumni[ə'lʌmnaɪ] *Am.* graduate (of a college/university).

always ['ɔːlweɪz] *adv.* every time/all the time.

alyssum ['ælɪsəm] *n.* low garden plant with small white flowers.

Alzheimer's disease ['æwltseɪməz dɪ'ziːz] *n.* condition where a patient becomes prematurely senile.

am [æm] *v.* see be.

a.m. ['eɪ'em] *adv.* in the morning.

amalgam [ə'mælgəm] *n.* (formal) mixture of substances. **amalgamate** [ə'mælgəmeɪt] *v.* to mix together/to link up. **amalgamation** [əmælgə'meɪʃn] *n.* amalgamating; things amalgamated.

amanuensis [æmænju:ensɪs] *n,* person who writes for s.o., else.

amaryllis [æmə'rɪlɪs] *n.* lily.

amass [ə'mæs] *v.* to pile up (a fortune).

amateur ['æmətɜ:] *n. & adj.* (person) who is not paid to do sth; (person) who does sth because he likes doing it. **amateurish** *adj.* not very well done.

amatory ['æmətərɪ] *adj.* referring to love.

amaze [ə'meɪz] *v.* to surprise. **amazed** *adj.* surprised. **amazement** *n.* surprise. **amazing** *adj.* very surprising.

ambassador, ambassadress [æm'bæsədə, -dres] *n.* person who represents a country in another country.

amber ['æmbə] *n.* (a) yellow or orange translucent stone made of fossilized resin. (b) orange traffic light between green and red.

ambergris ['æmbəgrɪ] *n.* substance from sperm whales, used in making perfume.

ambidextrous [æmbɪ'dekstrəs] *adj.* (person) who can use either right or left hand equally well.

ambience ['æmbɪəns] *n.* surroundings.

ambient *adj.* which surrounds; a temperature = temperature of the air around sth.

ambiguous [æm'bɪgjʊəs] *adj.* which has two possible meanings. **ambiguity** [æmbɪ'gju:ɪtɪ] *n.* state of having two possible meanings; vagueness.

ambit ['æmbɪt] *n.* general area covered by sth.

ambition [æm'bɪʃn] *n.* desire to improve your status in the world. **ambitious** *adj.* wanting to get on in the world; (project) which aims very high.

ambivalent [æm'bɪvələnt] *adj.* undecided/with two points of view.

amble ['æmbl] *v.* he was ambling along = walking slowly along.

ambrosia [æm'brəʊzɪə] *n.* delectable food.

ambulance ['æmbjʊləns] *n.* van for taking sick people to hospital. **ambulanceman** *n.* man who drives, or helps in, an ambulance.

ambush 1 ['æmbʊʃ] *n.* (*pl.*-es) surprise attack. **ambush 2** *v.* to attack by surprise.

ameliorate [ə'mi:lɪjəreɪt] *v.* (formal) to make better. **amelioration** [əmi:lɪjə'reɪʃn] *n.* becoming better.

amen [ɑ:'men, eɪ'men] *inter.* word (meaning let this be so) which is used at the end of Christian prayers; I say a. to that = I agree entirely.

amenable [ə'mi:nəbl] *adj.* docile/easygoing; a to new ideas = willing to accept new ideas.

amend [ə'mend] *v.* to change (for the better). **amendment** *n.* change esp. suggested change to a proposal.

amends *n.* to make a. for something = to compensate for an injury, etc.

amenity [ə'mi:nɪtɪ] *n.* (a) pleasantness (of a place); a. bed = bed in a separate room in a public hospital. (b) sport and entertainment facility; a. centre = building housing (for example) a cinema, auditorium, gymnasium, swimming pool.

American 1 [ə'merɪkən] *adj.* referring to America; A. plan = full board (in a hotel). **American 2** *n.* person from the United States.

amethyst ['æməθɪst] *n.* purple precious stone.

amiable ['eɪmɪəbl] *adj.* pleasant. **amiability** [eɪmɪə'bɪlɪtɪ] *n.* being amiable. **amiably** *adv.* pleasantly.

amicable ['æmɪkəbl] *adj.* friendly. **amicably** *adv.* in a friendly way.

amid(st) [ə'mɪd(st)] *prep.* in the middle of.

amidships *adv. & prep.* in the middle of a ship.

amino acid [ə'mi:nəʊ 'æsɪd] *n.* acid found in protein, necessary for growth.

amiss [ə'mɪs] *adv. & adj.* don't take it a = don't be annoyed; something is a. = has gone wrong.

amity ['æmɪtɪ] *n.* friendship

ammeter ['æmɪtə] *n.* device for measuring electricity in amperes.

ammonia [ə'məʊnɪə] *n.* gas made of hydrogen and nitrogen, which has a strong smell.

ammonite ['æmənaɪt] *n.* fossil shell like that of a large snail.

ammunition [æmjʊ'nɪʃn] *n.* (no *pl.*) bullets/shells, etc., for using in warfare/hunting, etc.

amnesia [æm'ni:zɪə] *n.* medical state when you forget everything.

amnesty 1 ['æmnəstɪ] *n.* pardon (to criminals). **amnesty 2** *v.* to offer (criminals) a pardon.

amniotic fluid ['æmnɪɒtɪk 'fluːd] *n.* liquid surrounding a baby in the womb.

amœba [ə'miːbə], [ə'miːbɪ] *n.* (*pl.*amoebas, amoebae) tiny organism consisting of a single cell.

amok [ə'mɒk] *adv.* to run a. = to run wild killing people.

among(st) [ə'mʌŋ(st) *prep.* (a) in the middle of. (b) out of.

amoral [eɪ'mɒrəl] *adj.* with no sense of values/of morality.

amorous ['æmərəs] *adj.* tending to fall in love; showing (sexual) love.

amorphous [ə'mɔːfəs] *adj.* having no particular shape.

amortize ['æmɔːtaɪz] *v.* to write off (a debt).

amount 1 [ə'maʊnt] *n.* (a) quantity. (b) sum (of money). **amount 2** *v.* to add up (to); it amounts to the same thing = it means the same.

amour propre [æmuːə 'prɒpr] *n.* respect for oneself.

amp, ampere [æmp, 'æmpɛə] *n.* quantity of electricity flowing in a current.

ampersand ['æmpəsænd] *n.* printing sign (&) meaning 'and'

amphetamine [æm'fetəmiːn] *n.* drug which stimulates.

amphibian [æm'fɪbɪən] *n.* (a) animal which lives both in water and on land. (b) (military) vehicle that moves in water and on land. **amphibious** *adj.* which lives/travels in water and on land.

amphitheatre ['æmfɪθɪətə] *n.* (a) Greek or Roman circular theatre. (b) lecture hall with rows of seats rising in tiers.

amphora ['æmfərə] *n.* Greek or Roman wine jar.

ample ['æmpl] *adj.* (a) large. (b) enough/sufficient. **amply** *adv.* in large enough quantity. **amplify** ['æmplɪfaɪ] *v.* (a) to make (a sound, etc). louder. (b) to develop (sth) in more detail. **amplification** [æmplɪfɪ'keɪʃn] *n.* development; making louder. **amplifier** *n.* machine which amplifies a sound.

ampoule ['æmpuːl] *n.* small container containing liquid for injections.

amputate ['æmpjʊteɪt] *v.* to cut off (a limb). **amputation** [æmpjʊ'teɪʃn] *n.* cutting off.

amuck amok.

amulet ['æmjulet] *n.* lucky charm.

amuse [ə'mjuːz] *v.* to give (s.o.) pleasure; to a. yourself = to spend time happily. **amusement** *n.* pleasure; a arcade = hall with slot machines for playing games, etc. **amusing** *adj.* which makes you laugh.

an [æn, ən] see a.

anabolic steroids ['ænə'bɒlɪk'sterɔɪdz] *n.* chemical substances which make the body create more tissue.

anachronism [ə'nækrɒnɪzəm] *n.* thing which is out of keeping with the period. **anachronistic** [ənækrɒ nɪstɪk] *adj.* which is not in keeping with the period.

anaconda [ænə'kɒndə] *n.* very large snake.

anaemia, Am. anemia [ə'niːmɪə] *n.* illness caused by lack of red cells in the blood.

anaemic [ə'niːmɪk] *adj.* looking pale; suffering from anaemia

anaerobic [ænɛə'rəʊbɪk] *adj.* not needing oxygen to take place.

anaesthetic, Am. anesthetic [ænəs'θetɪk] *n.* substance which makes you lose consciousness; local a. = substance which numbs part of the body. **anaesthesia** [ænɪs'θiːzɪə] *n.* loss of consciousness from being given an anaesthetic. **anaesthetist** [ə'niːsθətɪst] *n.* doctor who gives anaesthetics. **anaesthetize** [ə'niːsθətaɪz] *v.* to give (s.o.) an anaesthetic.

anaglypta [ænə'glɪptə] *n.* wallpaper with an embossed pattern.

anagram ['ænəgræm] *n.* word or phrase containing the letters of another word or phrase jumbled up (e.g. Cathy and yacht).

anal ['eɪnl] *adj.* referring to the anus.

analgesic [ænəl'dʒiːzɪk] *adj. & n.* (drug) which relieves pain. **analgesia** *n.* absence of pain.

analogous [ə'næləgəs] *adj.* similar/parallel.

analog ['ænəlɒg] *adj.* (computer) working on a more or less continuous signal.

analogy [ə'nælədʒɪ] *n.* similarity/parallel.

analyse [ˈænəlaɪz] v. to examine (sth) closely to see how it is formed. **analysis** [əˈnælɪsɪs] n. (pl.analyses [əˈnælɪsiːz]) close examination. **analyst** [ˈænəlɪst] n. (a) person who carries out analyse. (b) psychoanalyst. **analytical** [ænəˈlɪtɪkl] adj. which examines closely in detail.

anarchy [ˈænəkɪ] n. total lack of order or government. **anarchic** [əˈnɑːkɪk] adj. lacking in order. **anarchist** n. person who believes in anarchy.

anathema [əˈnæθəmə] n. curse; it's a. to him = he dislikes it intensely.

anatomy [əˈnætəmɪ] n. structure (esp. of a body). **anatomical** [ænəˈtɒmɪkl] adj. relating to the structure of the body.

ancestor [ˈænsestə] n. member of your family many generations ago. **ancestral** [ænˈsestrəl] adj. a. home = home of a family for many generations. **ancestry** [ˈænsestrɪ] n. origin (of a family).

anchor 1 [ˈæŋkə] n. (a) heavy metal hook dropped to the bottom of the sea to hold a ship in one place; they dropped a. in the bay; the ship was at a. (b) thing which holds secure/which gives security. **anchor 2** v. to drop anchor; hold (a ship) with an anchor. **anchorage** n. place where ships can anchor safely. **anchorman** n. main presenter on a TV news show.

anchovy [ˈæntʃəvɪ, ænˈtʃəʊvɪ] n. small fish with a strong taste.

ancient [ˈeɪnʃənt] adj. very old.

ancillary [ænˈsɪlərɪ] adj. secondary; a. workers = cleaners/porters, etc., in hospitals.

and [ænd, ənd] conj. showing connection between two things; try a. sing = try to sing.

andante [ænˈdæntɪ] adv. & adj. (in music) played quite slowly.

andiron [ˈændaɪən] n. metal stand to hold logs in a hearth.

android [ˈændrɔɪd] adj. shaped like a man.

anecdote [ˈænɪkdəʊt] n. short humorous story told by s.o.

anemia [əˈniːmɪə] n. Am. see anaemia.

anemometer [ænɪˈmɒmɪtə] n. instrument for measuring wind.

anemograph n. instrument which records wind force on paper.

anemone [əˈnemənɪ] n. small flower; sea a. = animal living in the sea which looks likes a flower.

aneroid [ˈænərɔɪd] adj. a. barometer = barometer which measures atmospheric pressure by the movement of a vacuum box.

anesthetic [ænɪsˈθetɪk] n. Am. see anaesthetic.

aneurism [ˈænjʊrɪzəm] n. swelling of an artery.

anew [əˈnjuː] adv. (formal) again.

angel [ˈeɪndʒl] n. heavenly being with wings; inf. kind person. **angelic** [ænˈdʒelɪk] adj. looking innocent/like an angel. **angelica** [ænˈdʒelɪkə] n. sweet-smelling plant of which the green stalks are preserved in sugar and used in desserts. **angelus** [ˈændʒeləs] n. service said in Roman Catholic churches, esp. at sunset.

anger 1 [ˈæŋgə] n. great annoyance. **anger 2** v. to make (s.o.) annoyed.

angina [ænˈdʒaɪnə] n. pains in the chest.

angle 1 [ˈæŋgl] n. (a) corner; right a. = angle of 90°; acute a. = angle of less than 90° obtuse a. = angle of more than 90°. (b) point of view. **angle 2** v. (a) to kick a ball/to shoot at an angle and not straight. (b) to a. for a rise = to try to get an increase in salary by dropping hints.

angler n. person who fishes with a rod. **angling** n. fishing with a rod.

Anglican [ˈæŋglɪkən] adj. &n. (person) belonging to the Church of England. **anglicism** [ˈæŋglɪsɪzəm] n. way of saying sth which is English or influenced by English.

Anglo [ˈæŋgləʊ] prefix meaning English/between England and another country. **anglophile** n. person who likes England. **anglophobe** n. person who hates England.

angora [æŋˈgɔːrə] n. & adj. (animal) with thick very soft wool; a. cat; a. rabbit; a jumper.

angostura [æŋgəˈstuːrə] n. bitter substance used to flavour drinks.

angry [ˈæŋgrɪ] adj. (-ier, -iset) very annoyed. **angrily** adv. in an angry way.

angstrom [ˈæŋstrɒm] n. unit of measurement of wavelengths.

anguish [ˈæŋgwɪʃ] n. great suffering. **anguished** adj. showing great suffering.

angular ['æŋgjʊlə] *adj.* (of rock) sharp/with sharp angles; (of person) with prominent bones.

aniline ['ænɪliːn] *n.* liquid produced from coal, used to make paint and plastics.

animal ['ænɪml] *n.* living creature which is not a plant. **animate** ['ænɪmeɪt] *v.* (a) to make lively. (b) to draw on a film a series of cartoon figures, each with slightly different poses, so that when the figures are projected the figures appear to move; animated cartoon. **animation** [ænɪ'meɪʃn] *n.* (a) liveliness/vivacity. (b) of making an animated cartoon. **animosity, animus** [ænɪ'mɒsɪtɪ, 'ænɪməs] *n.* unfriendly attitude/hostility (towards).

anion [æ'naɪən] *n.* negative ion.

aniseed ['ænɪsiːd] *n.* plant whose seeds are used to flavour sweets and drinks.

ankle ['æŋkl] *n.* part of your body joining the foot to the leg; a. socks = short socks which stop just above the ankles; a.-deep = up to one's ankles.

annals ['ænlz] *n. pl.* written yearly account of events/discoveries, etc. which have taken place.

anneal [ə'niːl] *v.* to strengthen (sth) by heating and cooling.

annex [ə'neks] *v.* to join (one country to another). **annexation** [ænek'seɪʃn] *n.* joining a of one county to another.

annexe ['æneks] *n.* (a) building attached to another building. (b) document attached to another document.

annihilate [ə'naɪəleɪt] *v.* to destroy completely. **annihilation** [ənaɪ'leɪʃn] *n.* complete destruction.

anniversary [ænɪ'vɜːsərɪ] *n.* day which falls on the same date as an important event in the past.

annotate ['ænəteɪt] *v.* to make notes on (sth); to add notes to (a book). **annotation** *n.* adding of notes; note added.

announce [ə'naʊns] *v.* to tell publicly. **announcement** *n.* public statement. **announcer** *n.* person on radio or TV who announces programmes, reads the news, etc.

annoy [ə'nɔɪ] *v.* to make (s.o.) angry. **annoyance** *n.* state of being annoyed. **annoyed** *adj.* angry; irritated.

annual 1 ['ænjʊəl] *adj.* which happens once a year. **annual 2** *n.* plant which comes out in a new edition each year.

annualized *adj.* shown on an annual basis. **annually** *adv.* every year.

annuity [ə'njʊɪtɪ] *n.* sum of money which is paid annually. **annual** [ə'nʌl] *v.* (annulled) to end/to cancel.

annulment *n.* cancellation.

annular ['ænjʊlə] *adj.* shaped like a ring.

anode ['ænəʊd] *n.* positive electric terminal. **anodize** *v.* to cover (metal) with a film by using it in electrolysis.

anodyne ['ænədaɪn] *adj. & n.* (medicine) which makes pain less strong; (thing) which stops you worrying.

anoint [ə'nɔɪnt] *v.* to put oil on (a person) as part of a religious ceremony.

anomaly [ə'nɒmɒlɪ] *n.* thing which is unusual/which does not fit into the normal pattern. **anomalous** *adj.* abnormal/strange.

anon 1 [ə'nɒn] *adv.* soon. **anon 2** anonymous.

anonymous [ɔ'nɒnɪməs] *adj.* (person) who does not give his name; a letter = a letter with no signature. **anonymity** [ænɔ'nɪtɪmɪtɪ] *n.* hiding of your name. **anonymously** *adv.* without giving your name.

anopheles [æ'nɒfcliːz] *n.* mosquito which transmits malaria.

anorak ['ænəræk] *n.* waterproof jacket with a hood.

anorexia nervosa [ænə'reksɪə nɜː'vəʊsə] *n.* condition where you refuse to eat because of worry that you may become fat.

another [ə'nʌðə] *adj. & pron.* (a) (one) more. (b) a different one. (c) one a. = each other.

answer 1 ['ɑːnsə] *n.* replay. **answer 2** *v.* to replay; to a back = replay rudely.

answerable *adj.* responsible (for something to person). **answering** *adj.* in answer; a service = recorded message on the telephone which answers automatically for s.o. who is out.

ant [ænt] *n.* small insect living in large communities. **anteater** *n.* animal which eats ants. **anthill** *n.* mound of earth containing an ants' nest.

antagonize [æn'tægənaɪz] *v.* to arouse s.o. hostility. **antagonism** *n.* hostility/

opposition. **antagonist** *n.* opponent.
antagonistic [æntægə'nıstık] *adj.*
hostile.
antarctic [æn'tɑːktık] *adj. & n.*
(referring to) the area around the South
Pole. **Antarctica** *n.* region around the
South Pole.
ante ['æntı] *n.* money gambled by a
player at the beginning of a game of
poker.
ante- ['æntı] prefix meaning before.
antecedent [æntı'siːdənt] *n.* earlier
form of sth; thing which comes before.
antedate ['æntıdeıt] *n.* v. to put an
earlier date on (a cheque); to happen
earlier.
antediluvian [æntıdı'luːvıən] *adj.* very
ancient.
antelope ['æntıləʊp] *n.* type of deer
found in Africa.
antenatal [æntı'neıtl] *adj.* before birth;
a. clinic = clinic for pregnant women.
antenna [æn'tenə] *n.* (a) (*pl.*-
ae[æn'teniː]) feeler/sensitive apparatus
for sensing. (b) (*pl.*-as) *Am.* aerial.
anterior [æn'tıərıə] *adj.* which comes
earlier.
anteroom ['æntıruːm] *n.* small room
leading to a larger room.
anthelmintic [ænθel'mıntık] *adj. & n.*
(substance) to remove worms.
anthem ['ænθəm] *n.* choral music (for
a special occasion); national a. = official
music of a country, played to honour the
state.
anther ['ænθə] *n.* tip of a stamen which
carries pollen.
anthology [æn'θɒlədʒı] *n.* collection
of poems/stories, etc., by various people
in one book. **anthologize** *v.* to put (a
poem) into an anthology.
anthracite ['ænθrəsaıt] *n.* hard coal
which gives off a lot of heat but not
much smoke or flame.
anthrax ['ænθræks] *n.* serious disease
of cattle, which can be caught by people.
anthropoid ['ænθrəpɔıd] *adj. & n.*
(ape) which is like a man.
anthropology [ænθrə'pɒlədʒı] *n.*
study of man. **anthropological**
[ænθrəpə'lɒdʒıkl] *adj.* referring to the
study of man. **anthropologist**
[ænθrə'pɒlədʒıst] *n.* scientist who
studies man. **anthropomorphic**
[ænθəpə'mɔːfık] *adj.* (religion, etc.)

which gives gods, animals, etc., the form
of human beings.
anti ['æntı] prefix meaning against;
antitank gun; anti-malaria tablet; anti-
inflationary measures. **anti-semitic**
adj. against Jews.
antibiotic [æntıbaı'ɒtık] *adj. &n.*
(drug) which kills bacteria.
antibody ['æntıbɒdı] *n.* chemical
substance built up in the body to fight a
particular disease.
anticipate [æn'tısıpeıt] *v.* (a) to act
because you see sth is about to happen.
(b) expect sth to happen. **anticipation**
[æntısı'peıʃn] *n.* expectation that sth
will happen. **anticipatory** *adj.* which
anticipates.
anticlimax [æntı'klaımæks] *n.* (*pl.*-es)
feeling of being let down when sth
exciting does not happen.
anticlockwise [æntı'klɒkwaız] *adj. &
adv.* in the opposite direction to the
hands of a clock.
antics ['æntıks] *n. pl.*playing around;
fooling.
anticyclone [æntı'saıkləʊn] *n.* area of
high atmospheric pressure.
antidote ['æntıdəʊt] *n.* (to) things
which counteracts the effects of a poison.
antifreeze ['æntıfriːz] *n.* liquid put in
the radiator of a car to prevent it freezing
in cold weather.
antigen ['æntıdʒən] *n.* substance which
produces antibodies.
antihistamine [æntı'hıstəmiːn] *n.*
medicine which prevents allergies.
antimony ['æntımənı] *n.* (element; Sb)
white metal used to make alloys.
antipathy [æn'tıpəθı] *n.* (to) feeling of
not liking s.o./sth.
antiperspirant [æntı'pɜːspırənt] *n.*
spray which stops you perspiring.
antiphon ['æntıfɒn] *n.* (religious) chat
for two sets of singers, each singing in
turn. **antiphonal** *adj.* (sung) like an
antiphon.
antipodes [æn'tıpədiːz] *n. pl.*opposite
side of the earth, esp. Australia and New
Zealand. **antipodean** [æntıpə'diːən]
adj. from the antipodes.
antipyretic [æntıparə'retık] *adj. & n.*
(substance) which reduces fever.
antiquary [æn'tıkwərı] *n.* person who
collects, studies, or sells antiques.
antiquarian [æbtı'kweərıən] *adj.* a.

bookseller = bookseller who sells old books. **antiquated** ['æntɪkweɪtɪd] *adj.* old (and decrepit). **antique 1** [æn'tiːk] *adj.* very old (and valuable). **antique 2** *n.* old and valuable object; a. shop = shop which sells old objects. **antiquity** [æn'tɪkwɪtɪ] *n.* ancient times.

antirrhinum [æntɪ'raɪnəm] *n.* summer flower, the snapdragon.

antiseptic [æbtɪ'septɪk] *adj. & n.* (substance) which prevents a wound becoming septic.

antisocial [æntɪ'səʊʃl] *adj.* disliking society bad for society; a. hours = hours of work outside the normal period.

antistatic [æntɪ'stætɪk] *adj.* which stops the effect of static electricity.

antithesis [æn'tɪθəsɪs] *n.* (*pl.*-theses[-θəsiːz]) opposite.

antitoxin [æntɪ'tɒsɪn] *n.* substance which counteracts the effects of a toxin. **antitoxic** *adj.* which counteracts a toxin.

antivenene [æntɪ'veniːn] *n.* substance which counteracts snake bites.

antivivisectionist [æntɪvɪvɪ'sekʃənɪst] *n.* person who is opposed to using live animals for experiments.

antler ['æntlə] *n.* horn. (on deer).

antonym ['æntənɪm] *n.* word which means the opposite of another word.

anus ['eɪnəs] *n.* (*pl.*-es) hole through which animals produce waste matter from the bowels.

anvil ['ænvɪl] *n.* (a) block on which a blacksmith beats hot metal. (b) one of the ossicles in the ear.

anxiety [æŋ'zaɪətɪ] *n.* (a) great worry (about). (b) eagerness (to). **anxious** *adj.* (a) very worried. (b) eager (to). **anxiously** *adv.* worriedly.

any 1 ['enɪ] *adj. & pron.* (a) it does not matter which. (b) some; have you a. sugar? I haven't got a; he hasn't a. money. **any 2** *adv.* I can't go a further = I can go no further.

anybody ['enɪbɒdɪ] *pron.* (a) it does not matter who. (b) some person; hardly a. = very few.

anyhow 1 ['enɪhaʊ] *adv.* carelessly. **anyhow 2** *conj.* = anyway.

anyone ['enɪwʌn] *pron.* = anybody.

anything ['enɪθɪŋ] *pron.* (a) it does not matter what; hardly a. = almost nothing. (c) like a. = very strongly; raining like a.

= pouring down.

anyway ['enɪweɪ] *adv. & conj.* in any case.

anywhere ['enɪweə] *prep.* (a) it does not matter where. (b) some where; can you see it a.?

AOB [eɪəʊ'biː] = any other business.

aorta [eɪ'ɔːtə] *n.* main artery taking blood from the heart.

apace [e'peɪs] *adv.* (formal) fast.

apart [ə'pɑːt] *adv.* (a) separated. (b) separate; the watch came a. = fell to pieces; can you tell them a.? = can you say which is which? (c) a. from = except.

apartheid [ə'pɑːtaɪt] *n.* policy in South Africa of segregating the black people from the white.

apartment [ə'pɑːtmənt] *n.* (a) set of rooms in a large building, as a separated living unit. (b) *Am.* flat; a; block = block of flats.

apathy ['æpəθɪ] *n.* lack of interest. **apathetic** [æpə'θetɪk] *adj.* uninterested.

ape 1 [eɪp] *n.* large man-like monkey with no tail. **ape 2** *v.* to imitate (s.o.).

aperient [ə'pɪərɪənt] *adj. & n.* substance which makes the bowels work.

aperitif [ə'perɪtiːf] *n.* drink taken before a meal to give you an appetite.

aperture ['æpətʃə] *n.* hole; opening.

apex ['eɪpeks] *n.* (*pl.*-es) top (of a triangle).

aphasia [ə'feɪzjə] *n.* being unable to speak, caused by brain damage.

aphid, aphis ['eɪfɪd, 'eɪfɪs, 'æfɪs] *n.* (*pl.*aphides) small insect which sucks the sap from plants.

aphorism ['æfərɪzəm] *n.* short wise saying.

aphrodisiac [æfrə'dɪzɪæk] *n. & adj.* (substance) which increases sexual desire.

apiary ['eɪpɪərɪ] *n.* place where bees are kept. **apiarist** *n.* (formal) beekeeper.

apiculture ['æpɪkʌltʃə] *n.* keeping of bees (for honey).

apiece [ə'piːs] *adv.* each.

aplomb [ə'plɒm] *n.* calmness/self-confidence.

apocalyptic [əppə'lɪptɪk] *adj.* which prophesies doom. **Apocalypse** *n.* last book of the New Testament, prophesying doom. **apocryphal** [ə'pɒkrɪfl] *adj.* probably untrue. **Apocrypha** *pl.*

collection of texts of the Old Testament which are not accepted as genuine.

apogee ['æpədʒiː] n. highest point (in the orbit of a planet/in the career of a statesman, etc.).

apologetic [əpɒlə'dʒetɪk] adj. making excuses; saying you are sorry.

apologetically adv. in an apologetic way. **apologist** n. person who writes or speaks on behalf of a cause.

apologize v. to say you are sorry.

apology n. saying you are sorry; my apologies for being late = I' m sorry I' m late.

apoplexy ['æpəpleksɪ] n. sudden inability to move caused by a stroke.

apoplectic [æpə'plektɪk] adj. (a) referring to apoplexy. (b) red-faced.

apostasy [æ'pɒstəsɪ] n. abandoning a religious belief. **apostle** [ə'pɒsl] n. one of the twelve men who were the original disciples of Jesus; a spoon = small spoon with the figure of an apostle on the end of the handle. **apostate** [ə'pɒsteit] n. person who has given up his beliefs. **apostolic** [æpəs'tɒlɪk] adj. of the apostles.

a posteriori [eɪpɒsteri'ɔːrɪ] adj. based on observed facts.

apostrophe [ə'pɒstrəfɪ] n. printing sing (') which shows either that a letter has been left out (weren't) or with s to show possession (a boy's coat, the girls' team).

apotheosis [æpɒθɪ'əʊsɪs] n. making s.o. into a god.

appal [ə'pɔːl] v. to frighten/to make horrified. **appalling** adj. horrible/frightening. **appallingly** adv. frighteningly.

apparatus [æpə'reɪtəs] n. (no pl.) equipment (for doing scientific tests, etc.

apparel [ə'pærəl] n. (formal) clothes.

apparent [ə'pærənt] adj. which seems.

apparition [æpə'rɪʃn] n. ghost; thing which seems strange.

appeal 1 [ə'piːl] n. (a) asking for (help, etc). (b) request to the law courts to reconsider a verdict. (c) attraction; sex a. = asking for. (b) to a. to = (i) to ask (s.o.) to judge; (ii) to attract. **appealing** adj. attractive; as if asking for help.

appelant n. person who appeals.

appear [ə'prə] v. (a) to come into sight.

(b) to be present (at). (c) to act (in a play). (d) to seem. **appearance** n. (a) how a thing or person looks. (b) being present; to put in an a. = to be present.

appease [ə'piːz] v. to try to avoid/to soothe. **appeasement** n. policy of avoiding conflict.

appellation [æpə'leɪʃn] n. (formal) name.

append [ə'pend] v. to attach/to join. **appendage** n. thing attached. **appendix** [ə'pendɪks] n. (a) (pl.appendixes) small tube attached to main intestine. (b) (pl.appendices[ə'pendɪsiːz]) section at the back of a book giving information which is additional to the text. **appendectomy** [æpen'dektəmɪ] n. operation to remove an appendix. **appendicitis** [əpendɪ'saɪtɪs] n. illness caused by inflammation of the appendix.

appertain [æpə'teɪn] v. (formal) to be relevant.

appetite ['æpɪtaɪt] n. desire to eat, etc. **appetizer** n. snack taken with drinks before the main meal. **appetizing** adj. which makes you want to eat.

applaud [ə'plɔːd] v. to clap or cheer to show you appreciate sth. **applause** n. clapping and cheering.

apple ['æpl] n. common hard fruit growing on a tree which bears this fruit.

appliance [ə'plaɪəns] n. (a) machine/device. (b) fire engine.

appliqué [ə'pliːkeɪ] n. decoration made by sewing shaped pieces of cloth on to a larger piece.

apply [ə'plaɪ] v. (a) to put (sth) on sth. (b) to be relevant. (c) to ask s.o. for sth (esp. a job). (d) to a. yourself = to work hard. **applicable** [ə'plɪkəbl] adj. which refers to. **applicant** ['æplɪkənt] n. person who applies for a job; candidate. **application** [æplɪ'keɪʃn] n. (a) action of putting something; for external a. only = to be used on the skin. (b) asking for (a job, etc.); a form = from to be filled in when applying. **applied** adj. (science) which is put to practical use.

appoint [ə'pɔɪnt] v. to give (s.o.) a job (as). **appointed** adj. (a) arranged/stated. (b) equipped/furnished. **appointment** n. (a) being given a job. (b) meeting time which has been agreed. (c) appointments = furniture and equipment.

apportion [ə'pɔːʃn] v. (formal) to divide up/to share out.

apposite ['æpəzɪt] adj. fitting/ appropriate (remark). **apposition** n. putting a word next to another; noun in a. = noun used as an adjective to describe another noun.

appraise [ə'preɪz] v. to judge the value of (sth). **appraisal** n. evaluation.

appreciate [ə'priːʃɪeɪt] v. (a) to feel the value of (sth). (b) to increase in value. **appreciable** adj. which can be felt. **appreciably** adv. in a way which could be felt. **appreciation** [əpriːʃɪ'eɪʃn] n. (a) estimation (of the value of sth). (b) increase in value. **appreciative** [ə'priːʃjətɪv] adj. praising.

apprehend [æprɪ'hend] v. to arrest (a criminal) **apprehension** [æprɪ'henʃn] n. fear. **apprehensive** adj. afraid/ nervous. **apprehensively** adv. nervously.

apprentice [ə'prentɪs] n. youth who works with a skilled man to learn from him. **apprenticeship** n. time you spend as an apprentice.

apprise [ə'praɪz] v. (formal) to inform (s.o. of sth).

appro ['æprəʊ] n. inf. on a. = on approval.

approach 1 [ə'prəʊtʃ] n. (pl.-es) (a) way of dealing (with a problem). (b) he made approaches to her to join his firm = he contacted her to ask her to join his firm = he contacted her to ask her to join his firm. (c) way into; a road = road leading to a main road. **approach 2** v. (a) to go near. (b) to deal with (a question). **approachable** adj. easy to talk to. **approaching** adj. which is coming closer.

approbation [æprə'beɪʃn] n. (formal) approval.

appropriate 1 [ə'prəʊprɪət] adj. suitable/which fits. **appropriate 2** [ə'prəʊprɪeɪt] v. to seize (sth which belongs to s.o. else). **appropriation** [əprəʊprɪ'eɪʃn] n. (a) seizure. (b) money voted to a budget.

approve [ə'pruːv] v. to express agreement (with sth); to allow; to a of sth = to be in agreement with sth. **approval** n. allowing (sth); on a. = on trial.

approving adj. which shows

agreement. **approvingly** adv. showing agreement.

approximate 1 [ə'prɒksɪmət] adj. rough (calculation). **approximate 2** [ə'prɒksɪmeɪt] v. to be nearly correct. **approximately** adv. roughly. **approximation** [əprɒksɪ'meɪʃn] n. rough estimate.

appurtenance [ə'pɜːtənəns] n. (formal) thing which is connected to or belongs to sth else.

APR = Annual (ized) Percentage Rate.

aprés-ski [æpreɪ'skiː] n. (parties) which take place in the evening after a day's skiing.

apricot ['eɪprɪkɒt] n. yellow fruit with large stone grown in warm countries tree which bears apricots.

April ['eɪprəl] n. 4th month of the year. **April Fool** n. person who is tricked on April 1st. **April Fool's Day** n. April 1st/day when people are tricked.

a priori [eɪpraɪ'ɔːrɪ] adj. based on theory or assumptions.

apron ['eɪprən] n. (a) piece of cloth worn over clothes to protect them when working. (b) area in an airport where aircraft are parked.

apropos [æprə'pəʊ] adv. referring to.

apse [æps] n. rounded end of a church.

apt [æpt] adj. (a) expression which fits well. (b) likely (to). **aptitude** n. ability; test = test to see if you are fitted for a job. **aptly** adv. fittingly. **aptness** n. fitness (of an expression).

aqualung ['ækwəlʌŋ] n. skindiver's portable oxygen apparatus.

aquamarine 1 [ækəmə'riːn] adj. dark blue-green. **aquamarine 2** n. semi-precious blue stone.

aquaplane ['ækwəpleɪn] v. (of car) to slide along the wet surface of a road.

aquarium [ə'kweərɪəm] n. (a) tank for keeping fish. (b) exhibition where fish are displayed.

Aquarius [ə'kweərɪəs] n. one of the signs of the Zodiac, shaped like a man carrying water.

aquatic [æ'kwætɪk] adj. which lives in water; a plants.

aquatint ['ækwətɪnt] n. print which has been shaded to like a drawing.

aqueduct ['ækwɪdʌkt] n. channel which takes water over land.

aqueous ['ækwɪəs] adj. containing water.

aquifer ['ækwɪfə] n. layer of porous rock in which water gathers.

aquiline ['ækwɪlaɪn] adj. hooked (nose).

Ar symbol for argon.

Arab 1 ['ærəb] adj. referring to Arabia. **Arab 2** n. Muslim person living in Arabia or some other Near Eastern countries. **Arabian** [ə'reɪbɪən] adj. referring to Arabia. **Arabic 1** ['ærəbɪk] n. language spoken by Arabs. **Arabic 2** adj. arabic numerals = signs for numbers written 1, 2, 3, 4, etc.

arabis n. small garden plant, with little white flowers.

arabesque [ærə'besk] n. complicated design of leaves/flowers

arable ['ærəbl] adj. & n. (land) which is good for growing crops.

arachnid [ə'ræknɪd] n. type of animal with eight legs, such as a spider.

arbitrage ['ɑːbɪtreɪdʒ] n. buying shares in a company which is likely to be taken over, so as to sell them later at a profit. **arbitrageur** n. person whose business is arbitrage. **arbitrate** ['ɑːbɪtreɪt] v. to judge between two parties in a quarrel. **arbiter** n. person who decides (usu. on questions of fashion). **arbitrarily** adv. at random. **arbitrary** adj. (decision) taken at random. **arbitration** [ɑːbɪ'treɪʃn] n. judgement in a dispute. **arbitrator** ['ɑːbɪtreɪtə] n. person who judges a dispute.

arboreal [ɑː'bɔːrɪəl] adj. living in trees. **arboretum** [ɑːbə'riːtəm] n. collection of trees grown for study.

arbour [c'ɑːbə] n. shady place where trees are trained to form a shelter.

arc [ɑːk] n. (a) part of circle. (b) electric spark jumping between two points. **arclamp, arc-light** n. very bright light. **arc-welding** n. welding by an electric arc.

arcade [ɑː'keɪd] n. covered area with an arched roof; shopping a. = row of shops covered by a roof.

arcane [ɑː'keɪn] adj. mysterious/secret.

arch 1 [ɑːtʃ] n. (pl.-es) (a) vault/ rounded structure forming a roof, or top of a door. (b) triumphal a. = large construction with a rounded vault over a carriageway, usu. built to celebrate a victory. (c) rounded part under the foot. **arch 2** v. to make (sth) round.

arch 3 adj. wicked and playful.

arched adj. made with an arch.

archway n. passage/entrance with an arch.

arch- [ɑːtʃ] prefix meaning greatest; arch-enemy.

archaeology [ɑːkɪ'blədʒɪ] n. study of ancient civilization; industrial a. = study of old machinery/factories/mines, etc. **archaeological** [ɑːkɪə'lɒdʒɪkl] adj. referring to archaeology. **archaeologist** [ɑːkɪ'ɒlədʒɪst] n. person who studies archaeology.

archaic [ɑː'keɪk] adj. very ancient.

archangel ['ɑːkeɪndʒl] n. highest rank of angel.

archbishop [ɑːtʃ'bɪʃəp] n. very important bishop/leader of bishops.

archer ['ɑːtʃə] n. person who shoots with a bow and arrow. **archery** n. sport of shooting arrows at a target.

archetype ['ɑːkɪtaɪp] n. original version from which other versions can be copied. **archetypal** adj. original; perfect (example).

archipelago [ɑːkɪ'peləgəʊ] n. (pl.-os) group of islands.

architect ['ɑːkɪtekt] n. person who designs buildings. **architecture** n. design of buildings. **architectural** adj. referring to architecture.

architrave ['ɑːkɪtreɪv] n. moulding around a door or window.

archives ['ɑːkaɪvz] n. pl.collection of documents, esp. public or historical records. **archivist** ['ɑːkɪvɪst] n. librarian who looks after archives.

arctic ['ɑːktɪk] adj. &n. (referring to) the area around the North Pole; extremely cold (weather).

ardent ['ɑːdənt] adj. very strenuous; keen. **ardently** adv. strenuously/ fiercely.

ardour, Am. **ardor** ['ɑːdə] n. violence (of emotions).

arduous ['ɑːdjʊəs] adj. very difficult/ hard (task). **arduously** adv. with great difficulty.

are [ɑː] v. see be.

area ['eərɪə] n. (a) space; measure of the surface of sth. (b) region; the sterling a. = the countries where the £ sterling is the main exchange currency. (c) general subject.

areca [ə'riːkə] n. type of tropical nut.

arena [ə'riːnə] *n.* space where sports and fights take place.

Argentine, Argentinian 1 ['ɑːdʒəntaɪn, ɑːdʒən'tɪnjən] *adj.* referring to Argentina. **Argentinian 2** *n.* person from Argentina.

argon ['ɑːgɒn] *n.* (element; Ar) inert gas.

argue ['ɑːgjuː] *v.* to discuss without agreeing; to quarrel. **arguable** *adj.* which is open to discussion. **argument** *n.* (a) quarrel/discussion without agreement. (b) reasoning.

argumentative [ɑːgjʊ'mentətɪv] *adj.* (person) who likes to quarrel.

aria ['ɑːrɪə] *n.* long solo song in opera.

arid ['ærɪd] *adj.* very dry. **aridity** [ə'rɪdɪtɪ] *n.* extreme dryness.

Aries ['eəriːz] *n.* one of the signs of the Zodiac, shaped like a ram.

arise [ə'raɪz] *v.* (arose; arisen) (a) to appear; to start. (b) to result; from.

aristocrat ['ærɪstəkræt] *n.* person who is born into the aristocracy. **aristocracy** [ærɪ'stɒkrəsɪ] *n.* top rank (by birth) of society. **aristocratic** [ærɪstə'krætɪk] *adj.* referring to the aristocracy; superior (attitude).

arithmetic [ə'rɪθmetɪk] *n.* calculations with figures. **arithmetical** [ærɪθ'metɪkl] *adj.* referring to arithmetic.

arm1 [ɑːm] *n.* (a) part of the body between hand and shoulder; a. in a. = with their arms linked. (b) thing shaped like an arm; piece at the side of a chair to rest your arms on. (c) narrow stretch of sea running inland. (d) arms = weapons; up in arms about = very angry/furious. **arm 2** *v.* to equip with weapons.

armaments *n. pl.* heavy weapons/war equipment. **armband** *n.* piece of cloth worn round your arm. **armchair** *n.* chair with arms. **armed** *adj.* equipped with weapons the a. forces = the army, navy and air force. **armful** *n.* load carried in your arms. **armhole** *n.* hole in a piece of clothing through which you put your arms. **armour**, *Am.* **Armor** *n.* (a) metal protective clothes for medieval covering ships or tanks. **armoured** *adj.* protected by metal; a car = military car made of thick metal which carries a small gun. **armour-plated** *adj.* protected by thick metal plates.

armoury *n.* place where weapons are kept; all arms (belonging to a country).

armpit *n.* part of your body under where your arm joins the shoulder.

armrest *n.* thing which you rest your arm on.

army *n.* all the soldiers of a country.

armada [ɑː'mɑːdə] *n.* fleet of warships.

armadillo [ɑːmə'dɪləʊ] *n.* small South American animal covered with a flexible shell.

armageddon [ɑːmə'gedən] *n.* great final battle.

armature ['ɑːmətjə] *n.* moving part of an electric motor; coil in a dynamo.

armistice ['ɑːmɪstɪs] *n.* decision to stop fighting temporarily.

aroma [ə'rəʊmə] *n.* (pleasant) smell (of coffee/wine, etc).

aromatic [ærə'mætɪk] *adj.* (herb) with a strong pleasant smell.

arose [ə'rəʊz] *v.* see arise.

around 1 [ə'raʊnd] *adv.* (a) surrounding a place. (b) in an indefinite place. **around 2** *prep.* (a) surrounding. (b) approximately.

arouse [ə'raʊz] *v.* (a) to wake. (b) to excite (emotion).

arpeggio [ɑː'pedʒɪəʊ] *n.* (*pl.*-os) chord with the notes played one after the other and not all together.

arrange [ə'reɪndʒ] *v.* (a) to put in order. (b) to adapt (a piece of music). (c) to organize. **arrangement** *n.* (a) way in which something is laid out. (b) organizing. (c) agreement.

arrant ['ærənt] *adj.* (old) complete.

array 1 [ə'reɪ] *n.* display. **array 2** *v.* (a) to set out in order. (b) (formal) to dress (in fine costume).

arrears [ə'rɪəz] *n.* to be in a. = to be late (in doing sth).

arrest 1 [ə'rest] *n.* being held (by the police) on a charge; he's under a; cardiac a. = stoppage of the heart. **arrest 2** *v.* hold (s.o.) for breaking the law. **arresting** *adj.* which attracts the attention.

arris ['ærɪs] *n.* a. rail = horizontal triangular plank which holds the upright planks of fence.

arrive [ə'raɪv] *v.* to reach a place; (of baby) to be born. **arrival** *n.* (a) reaching a place. (b) person who has arrived.

arrogant ['ærəgənt] *adj.* very proud.
  arrogance *n.* being very proud;
  thinking that you are superior.
  arrogantly *adv.* proudly.
arrow ['ærəʊ] *n.* (a) long stick with a
  sharp point which is shot by a bow, (b)
  sign showing the way to a place.
arrowroot *n.* flour made from the root
  of an American plant.
arse [ɑːs] *n.* (vulgar) buttocks.
arsenal ['ɑːsənl] *n.* store of weapons.
arsenic ['ɑːsnɪk] *n.* (element; As)
  powerful poison.
arson ['ɑːsn] *n.* criminal act of setting
  fire to a property. **arsonist** *n.* person
  who sets fire to property.
art [ɑːt] *n.* painting, drawing, sculpture
  and music; a. gallery = museum of
  paintings, sculptures, etc., arts subjects =
  subjects (such as languages, history, etc)
  which are not sciences. **artful** *adj.*
  clever; up to the latest tricks. **artfully**
  adv. cleverly. **artless** *adj.* natural/not
  forced; native.
artefact ['ɑːtɪfækt] *n.* object (usu. a
  tool) made by man.
arteriosclerosis [ɑːtɪərɪəʊsklə'rəʊsɪs]
  n. hardening of the arteries (esp. in old
  age).
artery ['ɑːtərɪ] *n.* (a) tube that blood
  flows through from the heart to other
  parts of the body. (b) important road.
arterial [ɑː'tɪərɪəl] *adj.* referring to an
  artery.
artesian [ɑː'tiːʒn] *adj.* a. well = well
  drilled in the ground which does not
  require a pump to make the water rise.
arthritis [ɑː'θraɪtɪs] *n.* illness where
  joints become swollen and stiff.
  arthritic [ɑː'θrɪtɪk] *adj.* stiff from
  arthritis. **arthrodesis** [ɑːθrəʊ'diːsɪs] *n.*
  operation to fix a hip joint so that it does
  not move. **arthroplasty** ['ɑːθrəʊplæstɪ]
  n. operation to replace a hip joint with
  an artificial one.
arthropod. *n.* animal with a body
  formed of joined sections, such as a
  spider.
artichoke ['ɑːtɪtʃəʊk] *n.* (a) (globe) a.
  = green vegetable like the flower of a
  thistle. (b) (Jerusalem) a. = root
  vegetable like a bumpy potato.
article ['ɑːtɪkl] *n.* (a) clause (in
  agreement). (b) piece of writing in a
  news paper, etc. (c) thing/object. (d) part

of speech; the is a definite a.; 'a' is an
  indefinite a.
articulate 1 [ɑː'tɪkjʊleɪt] *v.* (a) to speak
  (a word). (b) to join; articulated lorry =
  lorry with a trailer. **articulate 2**
  [ɑː'tɪkjʊlət] *adj.* clear-speaking.
articulation [ɑːtɪkjʊ'leɪʃn] *n.* joint.
artifice ['ɑːtɪfɪs] *n.* trick. **artificer** *n.*
  skilled craftsman (esp. on a ship).
artificial [ɑːtɪ'fɪʃl] *adj.* which is an
  imitation/not the real thin; a respiration
  = reviving s.o. who is nearly dead.
  artificiality *n.* falseness/not being
  sincere. **artificially** *adv.* unnaturally.
artillery [ɑː'tɪlərɪ] *n.* section of the army
  concerned with guns; the a. = the guns.
  artilleryman *n.* (*pl.*-men) soldier
  working on guns.
artisan [ɑːtɪ'zæn] *n.* skilled workman/
  craftsman.
artist ['ɑːtɪst] *n.* person who draws,
  paints, or plays music. **artistic** [ɑː'tɪstɪk]
  adj. (person) who has a felling or skill for
  art; (thing) which looks good because it is
  made by an artistic person. **artistically**
  adv. with art. **artistry** ['ɑːtɪstrɪ] *n.* skill
  in art. **artiste** [ɑː'tiːst] *n.* performer in a
  theatre (esp. dancer/acrobat).
arty ['ɑːtɪ] *adj. inf.* pretending to be
  artistic.
arum ['eərəm] *n.* lily with a tall white
  flower.
as [æz, əz] *conj.* (a) like, (b) because. (c)
  at the same time that. (d) doing the job
  of; acting the part of. (e) in a certain
  way. (f) as for = referring to/concerning. (g) as
  from = starting from. (h) as if/as though
  = like/seeming. (i) as long as = on
  condition that. (j) as soon as =
  immediately. (k) as to = referring to. (l)
  as well as = in addition to.
As symbol for arsenic.
asap [eɪeseɪ'piː] = as soon as possible.
asbestos [æs'bestəs] *n.* mineral
  substance which is fireproof.
asbestosis [æsbes'təʊsɪs] *n.* lung
  disease caused by breathing in particles
  of asbestos.
ascend [ə'send] *v.* (formal) to go up.
  ascendancy *n.* influence.
  ascendant *n.* rising; in the a. =
  becoming powerful/popular. **ascension**
  ascent [ə'senʃn, ə'sent] *n.* going up.
ascertain [æsə'teɪn] *v.* (formal) to
  check/to find out (the facts).

ascertainable *adj.* which can be checked.

ascetic 1 [ə'setɪk] *adj.* (way of life) where you do not allow yourself any comfort or pleasure. **ascetic 2** *n.* religious person who does not allow himself any pleasures. **asceticism** *n.* belief in an ascetic way of life.

ASCII ['æski] American Standard Code for Information Interchange.

ascorbic [æ'skɔːbɪk] *adj.* a. acid = vitamin C occurring in oranges, vegetables, etc.

ascot ['æskət] *n. Am.* cravat.

ascribe [æ'skraɪb] *v.* (formal) to attribute (sth to s.o.). **ascribable** *adj.* which can be ascribed.

aseptic [ə'septɪk] *adj.* sterilized/with no infection.

asexual ['eɪseksjuəl] *adj.* not involving sex.

ash [æʃ] *n.* (*pl.*ashes) (a) common tree in northern countries; wood of this tree (b) dust left after something has burnt (c) ashes = remains of a person's body after cremation. (d) the Ashes = cricket trophy, played for by teams from England and Australia. **ashcan** *n. Am.* container for putting rubbish in. **ashen** ['æʃən] *adj.* very pale. **ashpan** *n.* (in a stove) box for collecting ash. **ashtray** *n.* small bowl for putting ash from cigarettes, etc.

ashamed [ə'ʃeɪmd] *adj.* sorry because of sth wrong.

ashlar ['æʃlə] *n.* (no *pl.*) building stones cut square.

ashore [ə'ʃɔː] *adv.* on land.

Asian ['eɪʒn] *adj. & n.* (person) from Asia. **Asiatic** [eɪsɪ'ætɪk] *adj.* referring to Asia.

aside 1 [ə'saɪd] *adv.* to one side; *Am.* a from = apart from. **aside 2** *n.* words spoken in a play which the other characters are not supposed to hear.

asinine ['æsɪnaɪn] *adj.* stupid.

ask [ɑːsk] *v.* (a) to put a question (about); to a. after s.o. = to inquire about s.o.'s health. (b) to a. for = to request/to want (sth) to be given to you. (c) to invite (s.o. to a party, etc.). **asking** *n.* it's yours for the a. = you only have to ask for it and you will get it.

askance [ə'skɑːns] *adv.* to look at sth/s.o. a. = to be suspicious of.

askew [ə'skjuː] *adv.* not straight.

aslant [ə'slɑːnt] *adv.* sloping.

asleep [ə'sliːp] *adj.* sleeping.

asp [æsp] *n.* small poisonous snake.

asparagus [ə'spærəgəs] *n.* cultivated plant of which you eat the new shoots as a vegetable.

aspect ['æspekt] *n.* (a) direction which a house faces. (b) side; way of looking at sth.

aspen ['æspən] *n.* small tree with leaves which tremble in the wind.

asperity [æ'sperɪtɪ] *n.* sharpness.

aspersions [ə'spɜːʃnz] *n. pl.* *pl.*bad comments (on s. o).

asphalt 1 ['æsfælt] *n.* mixture of tar and sand which is used for surfacing roads. **asphalt 2** *v.* to cover with asphalt.

asphyxiate [əs'fɪksɪeɪt] *v.* to stifle/to kill (s.o.) by preventing them from breathing. **asphyxia, asphyxiation** [əsfɪksɪ'eɪʃn] *n.* being unable to breathe.

aspic ['æspɪk] *n.* meat jelly.

aspidistra [æspɪ'dɪstrə] *n.* type of indoor plant.

aspirate ['æspɪrət] *adj. & n.* (sound) which has to be breathed (a s' h' in 'horse').

aspire [ə'spaɪə] *v.* (to) to have the ambition to do sth. **aspirant** ['æspərənt] *n.* person who aspires to do sth. **aspiration** [æspɪ'reɪʃn] *n.* ambition. **aspiring** *adj.* ambitious/hopeful.

aspirin ['æsprɪn] *n.* (tablet of) common drug taken to stop headaches/colds, etc.

ass [æs] *n.* (*pl.*-es) (a) donkey. (b) stupid person. (c) *Am. Sl.* buttocks.

assailant [ə'seɪlənt] *n.* person who attacks (s.o.).

assassinate [ə'sæsɪneɪt] *v.* to kill (s.o.) for political reasons. **assassin** *n.* person who kills for political reasons. **assassination** [əsæsɪ'neɪʃn] *n.* political murder.

assault 1 [ə'sɔːlt] *n.* attack; a course = ground where soldiers practise attacks. **assault 2** *v.* to attack.

assay 1 [ə'seɪ] *n.* test to see how pure metal is. **assay 2** *v.* to test (metal) to see how pure it is.

assegai ['æsəgaɪ] *n.* native spear from Southern Africa.

assemble [ə'sembl] *v.* to get together; to put together. **assembly** *n.* (a) meeting. (b) putting together; a. line = continuous moving line in a factory. where machines, etc., are put together.

assent 1 [ə'sent] *n.* agreement; Royal A. = formality by which a Bill approved by Parliament becomes an Act. **assent 2** *v.* to agree (to).

assert [ə'sɜːt] *v.* to state firmly; to a. yourself = take a firm position. **assertion** [ə'sɜːʃn] *n.* statement (of rights). **assertive** *adj.* forceful.

assess [ə'ses] *v.* (a) to calculate the amount of damages/of tax which should be paid. (b) to value. (c) to estimate. **assessment** *n.* (a) calculation of damages/of tax. (b) calculation of value. (c) estimate. **assessor** *n.* person who assesses.

asset [ˈæset] *n.* (a) valuable thing which belongs to you. (b) *pl.* assets = anything owned which can be sold to pay debts. **asset-stripper** *n.* person who buys a company and sells its assets.

assiduous [ə'sɪdjʊəs] *adj.* regular and very careful. **assiduity** [æsɪ'djuːɪtɪ] *n.* regularity of work. **assiduously** *adv.* regularly and very carefully; without fail.

assign [ə'saɪn] *v.* (a) to appoint (s.o. to do sth). (b) to transfer sth to s.o. **assignation** [æsɪg'neɪʃn] *n.* (a) transfer (of property). (b) lovers meeting. **assignment** *n.* (a) delegation (of a task to s.o.). (b) work which you have been told to do.

assimilate [ə'sɪmɪleɪt] *v.* to digest (food); to learn and understand (facts). **assimilation** [ə'sɪmɪ'leɪʃn] *n.* act of assimilating food or information.

assist [ə'sɪst] *v.* to help (s.o.). **assistance** *n.* help. **assistant 1** *n.* person who helps. **assistant 2** *adj.* deputy.

assizes [ə'saɪzɪz] *n. pl.* (old) local courts held in various parts of England and Wales at regular intervals (now the Crown Courts).

associate 1 [ə'səʊsɪeɪt] *v.* (with) to link (with s.o.) /to be linked (to s.o./sth). **associate 2** *n.* person who is linked to s.o. **association** [əsəʊsɪ'eɪʃn] *n.* group/society; a. football = soccer.

assonance [ˈæsənəns] *n.* rhyme using vowels only.

assorted [ə'sɔːtɪd] *adj.* (a) matched.

(b) mixed. **assortment** *n.* collection/mixture.

assuage [ə'sweɪdʒ] *v.* (formal) to calm/to soothe.

assume [ə'sjuːm] *v.* (a) to take (power responsibility) upon yourself. (b) to suppose. **assumed** *adj.* false. **assumption** [ə'sʌmpʃn] *n.* (a) taking up (of office). (b) belief that sth is true. even if it has not been proved.

assure [ə'ʃʊə] *v.* (a) to make safe/certain. (b) to state/to affirm. **assurance** *n.* (a) promise. (b) life a. insurance against death. (c) calm; feeling of certainty. **assured** *adj.* certain. **assuredly** [ə'ʃʊərədlɪ] *adv.* certainly.

aster [ˈæstə] *n.* garden plant with star shaped flowers.

asterisk [ˈæstərɪsk] *n.* sign (*) to indicate some special mention.

astern [ə'stɜːn] *adv.* behind a ship; (of ship) to go a. = to go backwards.

asteroid [ˈæstərɔɪd] *n.* very small planet.

asthma [ˈæsmə] *n.* wheezing, *usu.* caused by allergy. **asthmatic** [æs'mætɪk] *adj. & n.* (person) who suffers from asthma.

astigmatism [ə'stɪgmətɪzəm] *n.* condition of the eyes where the image focuses correctly at one angle but not at another. **astigmatic** [æstɪg'mætɪk] *adj.* referring to astigmatism.

astonish [ə'stɒnɪʃ] *v.* to surprise. **astonishing** *adj.* surprising. **astonishingly** *adv.* surprisingly. **astonishment** *n.* surprise.

astound [ə'staʊnd] *v.* to surprise completely. **astounding** *adj.* very surprising.

astrakhan [æstrə'kæn] *n.* dark fur from the skin of black lambs.

astral [ˈæstrəl] *adj.* referring to stars.

astray [ə'streɪ] *adv.* lost; to go a. = get lost; to lead a. = to lead into bad habits.

astride [ə'straɪd] *adv. & prep.* with your legs on either side (of).

astringent 1 [ə'strɪndʒənt] *adj.* harsh/severe (comments, etc.). **astringent 2** *n.* medicine/cosmetic for closing pores, etc. **astringency** *n.* being astringent.

astrology [ə'strɒlədʒɪ] *n.* art of foretelling events from the stars and planets. **astrologer** *n.* person who gives advice based on reading the

position of the stars. **astrological**
[æstrə'lɒdʒɪkl] *adj.* referring to
astrology.

astronaut ['æstrənɔ:t] *n.* person who
travels in a spacecraft.

astronomy [ə'strɒnəmɪ] *n.* science of
studying the stars, the sun and the
universe. **astronomer** *n.* person who
studies astronomy. **astronomical**
[æstrə'nɒmɪkl] *adj.* (a) referring to
astronomy. (b) *inf.* very large.
astronomically *adv.* (a) using
astronomy. (b) *inf.* enormously.

astrophysics [æstrəʊ'fɪzɪks] *n.* study
of the physics of the universe.

astute [ə'stju:t] *adj.* clever/wise.
astutely *adv.* cleverly. **astuteness** *n.*
being astute.

asunder [ə'sʌndə] *adv.* (old) apart.

asylum [ə'saɪləm] *n.* (a) place of
refuge; political a. = permission to stay
in a country when one is politically
undesirable in one's own. (b) (old)
mental hospital.

asymmetry cə'sɪmətrɪ] *n.* lack of
symmetry. **asymmetrical**
[æwsɪ'metrɪkl] *adj.* not symmetrical.

at [æt, ət] *prep.* (a) (showing time or
place) at the office; at night. (b)
(showing speed or rate) at 100 miles an
hour; at 20p a pound. (c) (showing
cause) she laughed at my old coat. (d)
busy; at work. (e) at first = at the
beginning: at once = immediately.

ataraxia [ætə'ræksɪə] *n.* excessive
calmness.

atavistic [ætə'vɪnstɪk] *adj.* reverting to
the characteristics of one's ancestors.

ataxia [æ'tæksɪə] *n.* being unable to
coordinate the use of muscles.

ate [et] *v.* see eat.

atheism ['eɪθɪɪzəm] *n.* believing there
is no god. **atheist** *n.* person who
believes there is no god. **atheistic**
[eɪθɪ'ɪstɪk] *adj.* referring to atheism.

athlete ['æθli:t] *n.* person who takes
part in sport, in particular, running,
jumping, throwing; athlete's foot = skin
infection on the feet, **athletic** [æθ'letɪk]
adj. referring to sport, **athletics** *n.*
organized sports where you run, jump or
throw.

Atlantic [ət'læntɪk] *n.* the A. (Ocean) =
ocean separating Europe and Africa from
North and South America.

atlas ['ætləs] *n.* (*pl.*-es) book of maps.

atmosphere ['ætməsfɪə] *n.* (a) air
which surrounds the earth. (b) general
feeling (at a party, etc.) **atmospheric**
[ætməs'ferɪk] *adj.* referring to the
atmosphere. **atmospherics** *n. pl.*
electric disturbances which interfere
with radio or TV signals.

atoll ['ætɒl] *n.* tropical coral island.

atom ['ætəm] *n.* (a) basic particle of
matter. (b) very small thing. **atomic**
[ə'tɒmɪk] *adj.* referring to physical
atoms; a. bomb = bomb which uses
nuclear energy; a. number = number of
protons in one atom of a chemical
element; a. weight = ratio of the mass of
an atom of an element to the mass of
carbon 12 **atomize** ['æəmaɪz] *v.* to
reduce to very fine particles. **atomizer**
n. device for atomizing, esp. a spray for
scent.

atonal [eɪ'təʊnəl] *adj.* without any
tones.

atone [ə'təʊn] *v.* to make amends (for).
atonement *n.* making amends (for a sin).

atrium ['ætrɪəm] *n.* (a) central court of
a large building, *usu.* with a glass roof.
(b) one of the chambers of the heart.

atrocious [ə'trəʊʃəs] *adj.* (a) very
wicked. (b) very bad. **atrociously** *adv.*
very badly. **atrocity** [ə'trɒsɪtɪ] *n.* very
wicked deed.

atrophy 1 ['ætrəfɪ] *n.* wasting away (of
a limb). **atrophy 2** *v.* to waste away.

attach [ə'tætʃ] *v.* to fasten.

attaché [ə'tæʃeɪ] *n.* specialized
member of the staff on an embassy; a
commercial a. **attaché case** *n.* small
case for carrying papers.

attachment *n.* (a) device which is
attached to something else (b) affection.

attack 1 [ə'tæk] *n.* (a) starting to fight.
(b) sudden start of a disease. **attack 2**
v. to start fighting (s.o.). **attacker** *n.*
person who attacks.

attain [ə'teɪn] *v.* to reach (an age, an
ambition). **attainable** *adj.* which can
be reached. **attainment** *n.* (a)
reaching. (b) attainments = talents/
intellectual capacities.

attainder [æ'teɪndə] *n.* former method
of punishing a state criminal, by passing
an Act of Parliament.

attempt 1 [ə'tempt] *n.* try. **attempt 2**
v. to try.

attend [ə'tend] v. (a) to a. to s.o. = to look after s.o. (b) to be present at. **attendance** n. being present. **attendant** n. person (in a museum) who guards the exhibits; person who is on duty (in a public lavatory, etc.). **attention** [ə'tenʃn] n. (a) careful thought about sth. (b) (of soldiers) to stand to a. = to stand straight with heels together. **attentive** [ə'tentɪv] adj. (a) paying attention; careful. (b) taking care of (s.o.). **attentively** adv. with attention.

attenuate [ə'tenjʊeɪt] v. (formal) to make thinner/weaker; attenuating circumstances = circumstances which reduce the blame attached to a crime. **attenuation** n. becoming weaker.

attest [ə'test] v. (formal) (to) to say that sth is true.

attic ['ætɪk] n. room under the roof of a house.

attire [ə'taɪə] n. (no pl.) (formal) clothing. **attired** adj. (in) wearing.

attitude ['ætɪtjuːd] n. (a) way of standing/sitting, etc. (b) way of thinking.

attorney [ə'tɜːnɪ] n. (as) esp. Am. lawyer. (b) power of a. = power to act on behalf of s.o., else.

attract [ə'trækt] v. to make (sth come towards you. **attraction** [ə'trækʃn] n. (a) pull. (b) ability to attract (s.o.) /to make (s.o.) interested. (c) thing which attracts people. **attractive** adj. pleasant-looking. **attractively** adv. in an attractive way.

attribute 1 ['ætrɪbjuːt] n. (a) quality. (b) symbol. **attribute 2** [ə'trɪbjuːt] v. to a. sth to s.o. = to say that sth belongs to s.o. **attributable** [ə'trɪbjʊtəbl] adj. which can be attributed to s.o.

attrition [ə'trɪʃn] n. wearing down; war of a. = war to be won by wearing down your enemy's forces.

attuned to [ə'tjuːnd tʊ] adj. aware of (latest fashions, etc.).

Au symbol for gold.

aubergine ['əʊbəʒiːn] n. eggplant.

aubrietia [ɔː'briːʃə] n. low growing plant with bright purple flowers.

auburn ['ɔːbən] adj. reddish chestnut coloured (hair).

auction 1 ['ɔːkʃn] n. sale where the item is sold to the highest bidder. **auction 2** v. to sell (sth) to the highest

bidder. **auctioneer** n. person who is in charge of an auction. **auction off** v. to sell (sth) by auction to get rid of it. **auction rooms** n. pl. place where auctions are carried out.

audacious [ɔː'deɪʃəs] adj. very daring. **audaciously** adv. daringly. **audacity** [ɔː'dæsɪtɪ] n. daring.

audible ['ɔːdɪbl] adj. which can be heard. **audibility** [ɔːdɪ'bɪlɪtɪ] n. capacity for being heard. **audibly** ['ɔːdɪblɪ] adv. in an audible way.

audience ['ɔːdɪəns] n. (a) people listening to a concert/watching a film or play, etc. (b) (formal) hearing.

audio-typist [ɔːdɪəʊ'taɪpɪst] n. typist who types from a recorded tape.

audio-visual [ɔːdɪəʊ'vɪzjʊəl] adj. referring to a method of teaching using tapes, records, films, etc.

audit 1 ['ɔːdɪt] n. official checking of accounts. **audit 2** v. to check (the accounts of a company). **auditor** n. expert accountant who checks the accounts of a company, etc. **audition 1** [ɔː'dɪʃn] n. testing of the suitability of actors/dancers, etc., for a job. **audition 2** v. (a) to test the suitability of (an actor/dancer, etc., for a job). (b) (of actor) to a. for a part = to go to a test for a part. **auditorium** [ɔːdɪ'tɔːrɪəm] n. huge hall for meetings/concerts, etc.

au fait [əʊ'feɪ] adj. familiar (with).

auf Wiedersehen [aʊf'viːdəzeɪn] (German) goodbye.

auger ['ɔːgə] n. tool for boring holes.

augment [ɔːg'ment] v. to increase. **augmentation** [ɔːgmen'teɪʃn] n. increase.

augur ['ɔːgə] v. to be a sign for the future.

august [ɔː'gʌst] adj. solemn and dignified.

August ['ɔːgəst] n. 8th month of the year.

auk [ɔːk] n. large black and white sea bird.

aunt [ɑːnt] n. sister of your mother or father; wife of an uncle. **auntie, aunty** n. familiar name for an aunt.

au pair [əʊ'peə] adj. & n. (pl. au pairs) she is going to France as an au pair (girl) = she is going to live with a French family to do light housework (and learn French).

aura ['ɔːrə] *n.* general feeling surrounding a person/a place.

aural ['ɔːrəl] *adj.* using the ear. **aurally** *adv.* by listening.

au revoir [əʊrə'vwɑːr] (French) goodbye.

auricle ['ɒrɪkl] *n.* (a) outside part of the ear. (b) space in the heart which fills with blood and then pumps it into the ventricles.

aurora [ə'rɔːrə] *n.* a. borealis = the Northern lights/bright lights seen in the sky in the far North.

auscultation [ɔːskəl'teɪʃn] *n.* listening to the chest of a patient, using a stethoscope.

auspices ['ɔːspɪsɪz] *n. pl.* (a) forecast/ signs of the future. (b) patronage; under the a. of = subsidized/organized by.

auspicious [ɔː'spɪʃəs] *adj.* favourable/ lucky. **auspiciously** *adv.* favourably.

Aussie ['ɒzɪ] *n. & adj. inf.* Australian.

austere [ɔː'stɪə] *adj.* cold/severe; without luxury. **austerity** [ɔː'sterɪtɪ] *n.* absence of luxury.

Australian 1 [ɒs'treɪlɪən] *adj.* referring to Australia. **Australian 2** *n.* person from Australia.

Australasian *adj.* referring to Australasia (the part of the Southern Hemisphere including Australia, New Zealand, and the Pacific Islands).

Austrian 1 ['ɒstrɪən] *adj.* referring to Austria. **Austrian 2** *n.* person from Austria.

autarchy ['ɔːtɑːkɪ] *n.* self rule, situation where a state rules itself.

autarky ['ɔːtɑːkɪ] *n.* self-sufficiency.

authentic [ɔː'θentɪk] *adj.* real; genuine. **authenticate** [ɔː'θentɪkeɪt] *v.* to swear that sth is true. **authenticity** [ɔːθen'tɪsɪtɪ] *n.* being authentic.

author ['ɔːθə] *n.* person who writes books, etc. **authorship** *n.* identity of the author.

authority [ɔː'θɒrɪtɪ] *n.* (a) power. (b) permission. (c) source. (d) ruling committee or group. (e) expert.

authoritarian [ɔːθɒrɪ'teərɪən] *adj.* exercising strict control. **authoritative** [ɔː'θɒrɪtətɪv] *adj.* (a) commanding. (b) which sounds as if it is correct.

authoritatively *adv.* in an authoritative way. **authorize** ['ɔːθəraɪz] *v.* to give (s.o.) permission.

authorization [ɔːθəraɪ'zeɪʃn] *n.* permission.

autistic [ɔː'tɪstɪk] *adj.* suffering from autism. **autism** *n.* mental illness which makes you withdrawn and unable to communicate.

auto- ['ɔːtəʊ] Prefix meaning self; automatic; automobile.

autobiography [ɔːtəbaɪ'ɒgrəfɪ] *n.* life story of a person written by himself. **autobiographical** [ɔːtəbaɪə'græfɪkl] *adj.* referring to the life of the writer.

autocracy [ɔː'tɒkrəsɪ] *n.* system of government by one man. **autocrat** ['ɔːtəkræt] *n.* dictator/person who does not allow anyone else to rule him. **autocratic** [ɔːtə'krætɪk] *adj.* ruled by one man. **autocratically** *adv.* like a dictator.

autocue ['ɔːtəʊkjuː] *n.* trademark for a screen with the text printed on it to help television announcers to speak while looking into the camera.

autogamy [ɔː'tɒgəmɪ] *n.* self fertilization.

autograph 1 ['ɔːtəgrɑːf] *n.* signature (of a famous person). **autograph 2** *v.* to a. a book for s.o. = to write your signature in it.

automat ['ɔːtəmæt] *n.* automatic vending machine. **automatic** *adj.* controlled by automation. **automatic** [ɔːtə'mætɪk] *adj. & n.* (device) which works by itself. **automatically** *adv.* working by itself. **automation** [ɔːtə'meɪʃn] *n.* installation of machinery to make a process more automatic.

automaton [ɔː'tɒmətən] *n.* (*pl.*-ta) doll which moves with a motor inside it; person who acts like a robot.

automobile ['ɔːtəməbiːl] *n.* esp. *Am.* car.

automotive. [ɔːtə'məʊtɪv] *adj.* referring to cars.

autonomy [ɔː'tɒnəmɪ] *n.* self-government. **autonomous** *adj.* (region) which governs itself.

autopsy ['ɔːtɒpsɪ] *n.* cutting up of a dead body to discover the cause of death.

autosuggestion [ɔːtəsə'dʒestʃən] *n.* state where a person makes himself believe sth about himself.

autumn ['ɔːtəm] *n.* season of the year when the leaves fall of the trees. **autumnal** [ɔː'tʌmnl] *adj.* referring to autumn.

auxiliary 1 [ɔːgˈzɪlɪərɪ] n. (a) helper. (b) verb which is used to form part of another verb. **auxiliary 2** adj. (person/machine) which helps.

avail 1 [əˈveɪl] v. to a. oneself of = to use. **avail 2** n. of no a. = no use.

availability [əveɪləˈbɪlɪtɪ] n. being available. **available** adj. ready to be used; which can be obtained.

avalanche [ˈævəlɑːnʃ] n. fall of snow down a mountainside.

avant-garde [ævɒŋˈgɑːd] adj. experimental (music/drama).

avarice [ˈævərɪs] n. state of not wanting to spend money. **avaricious** [ævəˈrɪʃəs] adj. wanting to hoard money and not spend it.

avenge [əˈvendʒ] v. to pay s.o. back for (a crime). **avenger** n. person who pays back a crime.

avenue [ˈævənjuː] n. (a) wide, treelined, road in a city. (b) two parallel rows of trees. (c) way of approaching a problem.

aver [əˈvɜː] v. (formal) to state.

average 1 [ˈævərɪdʒ] n. (a) figure arrived at when a total is divided by the number of figures added. (b) on a. = as a general rule. (c) sharing of costs of an insurance. a. adjuster = person who calculates how much insurance should be paid. **average 2** adj. general; ordinary. **average 3** v. to work out as an average.

averse [əˈvɜːs] adj. he is a. to hard work = he dislikes it. **aversion** [əˈvɜːʃn] n. (a) (to) dislike. (b) my pet a. = thing I dislike most.

avert [əˈvɜːt] v. (a) to turn away (one's eyes). (b) to prevent (a disaster).

aviary [ˈeɪvɪərɪ] n. building for keeping birds in.

aviation [eɪvɪˈeɪʃn] n. art/technology of flying (aircraft). **aviator** [ˈeɪvɪeɪtə] n. aeroplane pilot.

avid [ˈævɪd] adj. eager/enthusiastic. **avidly** adv. eagerly.

avocado (pear) [ævəˈkɑːdəʊ (ˈpeəl)] n. (pl.-os) green tropical fruit with a large stone in the middle, eaten as a vegetable.

avocet [ˈævəset] n. white wader with a long bill which is curved upwards.

avoid [əˈvɔɪd] v. (a) to try not to do (sth). (b) to keep away from. **avoidable**

adj. which you could have avoided. **avoidance** n. act of avoiding.

avoirdupois [ævədəˈpɔɪz] n. system of weights based on ounces, pounds, etc.

avowal [əˈvaʊəl] n. (formal) admission. **avowed** [əˈvaʊd] adj. stated; admitted.

avuncular [əˈvʌŋkjʊlə] adj. like an uncle.

await [əˈweɪt] v. to wait for.

awake 1 [əˈweɪk] v. (awoke; awoken) (a) to wake (s.o.) up. (b) to become aware of. **awake 2** adj. not sleeping. **awaken** [əˈweɪkn] v. to wake wake/to arouse. **awakening** n. a rude a. = a sharp shock.

award 1 [əˈwɔːd] n. (a) prize. (b) decision which settles a dispute. **award 2** v. to give (a prize, etc.)

aware [əˈweə] adj. knowing.

awareness n. state of being aware.

awash [əˈwɒʃ] adj. covered with a liquid.

away [əˈweɪ] adv. (a) not here/far; a. match = at another team's ground. (b) the birds were singing a. = they were going on singing; right a. = immediately.

awe [ɔː] n. fear/terror. **awe-inspiring, awesome** adj. frightening. **awestruck** adj. frightened/full of terror.

awful adj. (a) (old) very frightening. (b) very bad/very strong; unpleasant. **awfully** adv. infl. very.

awhile [əˈwaɪl] adv. for a short time.

awkward [ˈɔːkwəd] adj. (a) difficult. (b) embarrassing. (c) clumsy. **awkwardly** adv. with difficulty; inconveniently. **awkwardness** n. (a) embarrassment. (b) difficulty.

awl [ɔːl] n. tool used for making small holes.

awning [ˈɔːnɪŋ] n. canvas roof stretched out to protect from the sun or rain.

awoke, awoken [əˈwəʊk, əˈwəʊkn] v. see awake.

AWOL [ˈeɪwɒl] = absent without leave.

awry [əˈraɪ] adv. not straight.

axe, Am. **ax 1** [æks] n. instrument with a sharp metal head for chopping wood; to have an a. to grind = a particular point of view to put across. **axe 2** v. to reduce (expenditure); to sack (staff).

axil [ˈæksɪl] n. place where a leaf joins a stem.

axiom ['æksɪəm] *n.* well-known saying/ obviously true statement. **axiomatic** [æksɪə'mætɪk] *adj.* obvious; wellknown.

axis ['æksɪs] *n.* (*pl.*axes['æksi:z]) imaginary line through centre of a sphere.

axle ['æksl] *n.* rod going through the middle of a wheel.

ayatollah [aɪə'tɒlə] *n.* Muslim leader.

aye [aɪ] *n.* yes; the ayes have it = more people have voted yes than no.

azalea [ə'zeɪlɪə] *n.* small shrub with showy scented flowers.

azo ['eɪzəʊ] *n.* a. dyes = dyes added to food to give it a better colour.

azure ['eɪʒə] *adj.* blue like the sky.

Bb

Ba Symbol for barium.

BA [bi:'eɪ] Bachelor of Arts.

babble 1 [bæbl] *n.* trickling sound (of water). (b) to chatter. **babble 2** *v.* (a) to make a trickling sound; (formal) baby.

babe [beɪb] *n.* (formal) baby.

babel ['beɪbl] *n.* loud noise of talking.

baboon [bə'bu:n] *n.* large African monkey.

baby ['beɪbɪ] *n.* very young child; to have a b. = to give birth to a baby; the b. of the family = the youngest of the children; he was left holding the b. = he had to sort out all the problems left to him by others. (b) small animal. (c) small object; b. grand (piano). **baby carriage** *n. Am.* prAm. **baby carrier** *n.* canvas cot with handles for carrying a baby. **babyish** *adj.* like a baby.

babysit *v.* (baby-sat) to look after children while their parents are out.

baby-sitter *n.* person who baby-sits.

bachelor ['bætʃələ] *n.* unmarried man; b. pad = small flat for a single person; b. girl = unmarried woman. (b) holder of a first degree from a university.

bacillus [bə'sɪləs] *n.* (*pl.*bacilli[bæ'sɪlaɪ]) type of bacterium.

back 1 [bæk] *n.* (a) part of body down the spine between neck and buttocks; he did it behind my b. = without my knowing; I was glad to see the b. of him = I was glad to see him go; to put s.o.'s b. up = to annoy s.o.; we've broken the b. of the work = we have done most of the work. (b) opposite part/side to the front; he knows London like the b. of the his hand = very well indeed; I have an idea at the b. of my mind = I have the beginnings of an ideal, in the b. of beyond = away out of a town/in an inaccessible place; b. to front = the wrong way round. (c) sportsman who plays in a defensive position in football/ hockey, etc. **back 2** *adj.* (a) referring to the rear; he's had to take a b. seat = he's had to take a less prominent position. b. seat driver = passenger in a car who offers the driver unwanted advice. (b) in arrears; b. pay = pay which is owed to s.o. **back 3** *adv.* (a) to the rear; stand b. = move backwards; please sit b., I can't see = please lean backwards in your chair. (b) in return; I'll call you b. = I'll phone you again; as soon as I return to the office. (c) ago; a few years b. **back 4** *v.* (a) to (make sth) go backwards; can you b. the car into the garage? he backed away from the madman. (b) to support (with money). (c) to gamble on (a horse). (d) (of wind) to blow in another direction. **backache** *n.* pain in the back. **back bencher** *n.* ordinary member of parliament. **backbiting** *n.* sharp criticism. **backbone** *n.* spine/ column of bones forming the main support of the back. **backbreaking** *adj.* very hard (work). **backchat** *n.* replaying rudely. **backcloth** *n.* (in theatre) painted sheet at the back of the stage. **backdate** *v.* to put an earlier date than true on (a cheque). **back down** *v.* retreat from your former position. **backdrop** *n.* (in theatre) painted sheet at the back of the stage. **backer** *n.* person who supports sth with money; person who gambles money on horse racing. **backfire** *v.* (of a car) to make a small bang, due to misfiring of the ignition; (of a plan) to go wrong with unfortunate consequences for the planner. **backgammon** *n.* game like draughts paled on a special board. **background** *n.* the back part of a painting against which the foreground stands out; he comes from a working class b. = his family is working class; b. music = music played quietly in a film or in a restaurant. **backhand** *adj. & n.* (tennis/table tennis shot) played with the back of the racket/bat. **backhanded** *adj.* (compliment) that could be taken also as an insult. **backhander** *n.* (a) blow/shot with the back of the hand. (b) *Sl.* bribe. **backing** *b.* (a) material used on the back of sth to strengthen it. (b) musical accompaniment to a singer or instrument. (c) (financial) support. (d) reversing (of a car). **backlash** *n.* reverse effect (of apolitical or social move); white b. = reaction among white people. **backless** *adj.* (dress, etc) with no back. **backlog** *n.* work not done/ bills not paid. **back number** *n.* old copy of a magazine or newspaper. **back out** *v.* (a) to reverse out. (b) to decide not to continue (with a project). **backpack** *n.* bag carried on a walker's back. **backpacker** *n.* person who goes backpacking. **backpacking** *n.* going for a long walk, carrying your clothes, food, tent, etc., in a backpack. **backpedal** *v.* (-pedalled) (a) to pedal backwards. (b) to reverse your opinions. **backside** *n. inf.* buttocks. **backsliding** *n.* going back to a bad habit after having reformed. **backspace** *n.* moving a cursor back one space on a computer monitor. **backstage** *adv. & adj.* in the parts of a theatre where the audience can't go; behind the scenes/ hidden from view. **backstairs** *n.* stairs (for servants) in the back part of a large house. **backstroke** *n.* style of swimming on your back. **backtrack** *v.* (a) to change your opinion. **back up** *v.* (a) to support (s.o.). (b) to make a copy of a computer file, for security reasons. (c) *Am.* to reverse a car. **backup (copy)** *n.* copy of a computer file or disk. **backward** *adj.* (a) slow/retarded (child); (country) which is not industrially advanced. (b) b. in paying bills = slow in paying. **backwardness** *n.* being backward. **backwards** *adv.* in reverse/towards the rear; he knows the song b. = extremely well. **backwater** *n.* (a) small slow-moving branch of a river. (b) quiet/old-fashioned place. **backwoods** *n. pl.*forest; they live in the b. = they live far from other houses.

backwoodsman *n.* (*pl.*-men) person who lives in the forest; *inf.* old reactionary peer. **backyard** *n.* small paved area behind a house.
bacon ['beɪkn] *n.* pork which has been salted or smoked; *inf.* it saved his b. = it got him out of the difficult situation.
bacterium [bæk'tɪərɪəm] *n.* (*pl.*bacteria) microscopic organism which produces germs or decay. **bacterial, bacteriological** [bæktɪərɪə'lɒdʒɪkl] *adj.* referring to bacteria; b. warfare = method of conducting war by using bacteria to kill the enemy. **bacteriologist** [bæktɪərɪ'ɒlədʒɪst] *n.* scientist who specializes in bacteriology.
bacteriology *n.* study of bacteria.
bad 1 [bæd] *adj.* (worse, worst) (a) not good; b. meat; b. driver. (b) wicked. (c) unpleasant; b. news; she's in a b. temper. (d) serious; b. accident. (e) diseased; injured; b. leg. **bad 2** *n.* (a) there's a lot of b. in these potatoes = a lot of rotten bits. (b) I'm £10 to the b. = I have lost/ wasted £10. **baddy** *n. inf.* villain.
badlands *n. Am.* land which cannot be cultivated. **badly** *adv.* (worse, worst) (a) not well done. (b) seriously (wounded). (c) very much; he b. needs a shave.
bade [bæd] *v.* see bid.
badge [bædʒ] *n.* small sign worn to show that you belong to a group, or simply as a decoration.
badger 1 [bædʒə] *n.* wild animal with striped black and white head which lives underground and comes out at night.
badger 2 *v.* to bother (s.o.); he badgered me into giving him £5.
badinage [bædɪ'nɑːʒ] *n.* light teasing talk.
badminton ['bædmɪntən] *n.* game for two or four people, played with rackets and a shuttlecock.
baffle 1 ['bæfl] *n.* shield (to cut out noise). **baffle 2** *v.* (a) to puzzle. (b) to frustrate. **bafflement** *n.* being baffled.
bag 1 [bæg] *n.* (a) thing made of paper/ cloth/plastic which you can carry things in; carrier b. = bag made of stiff paper with two handles for shopping. shopping b. = large bag for carrying shopping; *inf.* bags of money = lots of money. (b) bags under the eyes = puffy layer of skin

beneath the eyes showing that you are ill or tired. (c) *inf.* it's in the b. = the deal is agreed. (d) animals killed while hunting. (e) *inf.* old b. = dirty old woman. **bag 2** *v.* (bagged) to catch (an animal when hunting); *inf.* bags I go first = I claim the right to go first. **baggy** *adj.* (-ier, -iest) (of clothes) too big/hanging in folds.

bagasse [bæ'gæs] *n.* residue left after crushing sugar cane.

bagatelle [bægə'tel] *n.* (a) game where small metal balls are sent round a board. (b) unimportant thing.

baggage ['bægɪdʒ] *n.* (no *pl.*) luggage.

bagpipe ['bægpaɪps] *n. pl.* musical instrument made of an air sack attached to pipes.

bail [beɪl] *n.* (a) small piece of wood resting on the top of stumps in cricket. (b) money pad to a court as surety for a prisoner's temporary release; he was released on b. of £500. **bailer** *n.* scoop for removing water from a boat. **bailout** *v.* to scoop water out of (a boat); to help (s.o.) who is in financial difficulties. (b) to bale out. (c) to pay money to let a prisoner out temporarily between hearings.

Bailey bridge ['beɪlɪ'brɪdʒ] *n.* prefabricated bridge which is supported by boats.

bailiff ['beɪlɪf] *n.* court official who can seize property in payment of debts. (b) landowner's agent on an estate.

bairn ['beən] *n.* (in Scotland) child.

bait 1 [beɪt] *n.* fly. worm, etc., used to attract fish or animals. **bait 2** *v.* to attach bait to (a hook or trap).

baize [beɪz] *n.* green cloth made of wool.

bake [beɪk] *v.* to cook (in an oven). **bakehouse** *n.* building with ovens for baking. **baker** *n.* person who makes bread and cakes. **baker's** *n.* shop selling bread and cakes. **bakery** *n.* shop and workshop of a baker. **baking 1** *n.* cooking (in an oven); b. dish = fireproof dish which can be put in the oven; b. tray = flat sheet of metal for baking biscuits, etc., on. **baking 2** *adv.* b. hot = extremely hot. **backing power** *n.* powder which when added to a cake mix helps it to rise.

balaclava [bælə'klɑːvə] *n.* b. (helmet) = knitted woollen helmet covering the whole head and neck, with a round opening for the face.

balalaika [bælə'kækə] *n.* Russian stringed instrument like a small guitar.

balance 1 ['bæləns] *n.* (a) machine which weighs; the result hangs in the b. = you cannot tell which way the result will turn out. (b) staying steady; to keep/ to lose one's b.; the b. of power = the division of power between countries. (c) what remains after all payments have been made; we have a b. of £25 in the bank; b. of payments = difference between money obtained from exports and money paid for imports by a country; b. sheet = statement drawn up at the end of a year showing the financial situation of a company. **balance 2** *v.* (a) to remain in one position without falling. (b) to make (sth stand without falling). (c) to counteract the effect of (sth). (d) to make the accounts b. = to make the total of income and expenditure cancel each other out. **balanced** *adj.* level; sensible.

balcony ['bælkənɪ] *n.* (a) small terrace jutting out from an upper floor. (b) upper terrace of seats in a theatre/cinema.

bald [bɔːld] *adj.* (a) with no hair. (b) not elaborate; a b. statement of fact. **balding** *adj.* becoming bald. **baldly** *adv.* drily. **baldness** *n.* lack of hair.

balderdash ['bɔːldədæʃ] *n.* nonsense.

bale 1 [beɪl] *n.* large bundle. **bale 2** *v.* to b. out = to jump out of a crashing aircraft with the help of a parachute.

baleful ['beɪlfʊl] *adj.* threatening/ unpleasant; a b. look. **balefully** *adv.* in a baleful way.

balk [bɔːk] *v.* (a) to prevent s.o. from doing sth. (b) to b. sth = to refuse to do sth.

ball [bɔːl] *n.* round object for playing games; keep the b. rolling = keep everything moving. I'll start the b. rolling = I'll start things off; he's on the b. = he knows his job very well/he is up to date; they won't play b. = they won't cooperate with us. (b) thing with a round shape; a b. of wool. (c) formal dance. (d) *Am.* baseball; b. park = area set aside for playing baseball. **ball-and-socket** *adj.* (joint) where a ball at the end of one rod/ bone fits a socket at the end of another. **ball bearing** *n.* bearing using a ring of

little steel balls; one of these steel balls.
ballboy, ballgirl *n.* boy or girl who picks up the balls during a tennis match.
ballcock *n.* mechanism with a value operated by a floating ball (for filling cisterns). **ballpoint** *adj.* b. pen = pen with a tiny ball which is automatically coated with ink from a tube. **ballroom** *n.* large room for formal dances; b. dancing = formal dancing.
ballad ['bæləd] *n.* romantic popular song or poem telling story.
ballade *n.* form of poetry, with a repeated refrain.
ballast ['bæləst] *n.* (a) material carried in ship/balloon to give extra weight. (b) stones used to bed down railway sleepers.
ballet ['bæleɪ] *n.* (a) dancing as a spectacle for public performance; b. dancer. (b) piece danced for performance; the ballet "Swan Lake'. (c) company which performs ballets.
ballerina ['bælə'riːnə] *n.* woman ballet dancer.
ballistics [bə'lɪstɪks] *n.* science of shooting bullets or shells.
balloon [lə'luːn] *n.* large round object which is inflated; hot-air b. = large passenger-carrying balloon inflated with hot air. **ballooning** *n.* sport of racing large passenger-carrying balloons.
ballot 1 ['bælət] *n.* voting by pieces of paper; a secret b. = election where the votes of individual voters are not disclosed; postal b. = election where voters can send their votes by post; b. paper = paper with names of candidates against which the voter makes a cross; b. box = sealed box for putting ballot papers in. **ballot 2** *n.* to vote by pieces of paper. **ballot-rigging** *n.* illegal arrangement of votes in a ballot, so that one side wins.
ballyhoo [bælɪ'huː] *n.* Am. energetic publicizing (during an election campaign, etc.).
balmy ['baːmɪ] *adj.* fragrant/soft (air/ breeze).
balsa ['bɔːlsə] *n.* very light wood (used for making models).
balsam ['bɔːlsəm] *n.* fragrant flowering plant.
balustrade [bælə'streɪd] *n.* stone fence made of small carved pillars along the

edge of a terrace/balcony, etc.
baluster ['bæləstə] *n.* small pillar.
bamboo [bæm'buː] *n.* tropical plant which provides tall strong, jointed canes; b. shoot = young shoots of bamboo which can be eaten.
bamboozle [bæm'buːzl] *v.* to trick/to puzzle (s.o.).
ban 1 [bæn] *n.* law/instruction which forbids sth; a b. on smoking in cinemas.
ban 2 *v.* (banned) to forbid (sth).
banal [bə'nɑːl] *adj.* ordinary/trivial.
banality [bə'nwlntɪ] *n.* ordinariness.
banana [bə'bɑːnə] *n.* long yellow tropical fruit; b. republic = corrupt central American state.
band 1 [bænd] *n.* (a) thin loop of material for tying things together. (b) bands = strips of white cloth worn round the neck by lawyers/clergymen. (c) group of frequencies in radio transmission. (d) group of people. (e) group of musicians, esp. playing brass and percussion instruments. **band 2** *v.* to form a group.
bandmaster *n.* leader of a brass band.
bandsman *n.* (*pl.*bandsmen) musician playing in a band. **bandstand** *n.* small state (in public gardens) for outdoor concerts. **bandwagon** *n.* to jump on the b. = to join a popular movement/to start to do sth which is already proving popular.
bandage 1 ['bændɪdʒ] *n.* piece of cloth to tie round a wound/round a twisted ankle, etc. **bandage 2** *v.* to tie a cloth round a wound.
bandanna [bæn'dænə] *n.* large silk handkerchief.
bandeau ['bændeʊ] *n.* ribbon to tie back the hair.
bandit ['bændɪt] *n.* robber/brigand.
bandy 1 ['bændɪ] *adj.* he had b. legs = when he stands with feet together his knees do not touch.
bandy 2 *v.* (bandied) to b. about = to shout/write (words to several people).
bane [beɪn] *n.* it's the b. of my life = it's what annoys me most.
bang 1 [bæŋ] *n.* (a) loud noise. supersonic b. = loud noise made when an aircraft goes faster than the speed of sound. (b) sharp blow. (c) hair cut straight across the forehead. **bang 2** *v.* to make a bang (by hitting sth). **bang 3** inter showing noise of an explosion; the

gun suddenly went b.; b. in the middle = right in the middle. **banger** n. (a) firework that goes bang. (b) Sl. old car. (c) inf. sausage. **banging** n. noise of repeated bangs.

bangle ['bæŋgl] n. bracelet made of metal or rigid material.

banish ['bænɪʃ] v. to send (s.o.) away/ to exile (s.o.); to get rid of (sth).

banisters ['bænɪstəz] n. pl.set of vertical rods with a handrail along the side of stairs.

banjo ['bændʒəʊ] n. stringed instrument with a round body.

bank 1 [bæŋk] n. (a) long mound of earth/sand/snow, etc. (b) edge of a river or canal. (c) row (of lights). (d) institution for keeping or lending money; merchant b. = bank which deals with lending large sums of money to business clearing banks = banks which issue cheques; b. charges = charges made by a bank for its services; b. holiday = public holiday when the banks are closed. **bank 2** v. (a) to pile up in a long mound; they banked up the side of the canal = they reinforced the canal banks; the snow banked up along the road = the wind blew the snow into banks. (b) (of plane) to roll to one side. (c) to put money into a bank; to use a bank; where do you b.? = which bank do you use? (d) I'm banking on taking two weeks off next month = I'm counting on/relying on taking two weeks off. **banker** n. person who directs a bank. **banking** n. the profession of being a banker. **banknote** n. paper money issued by a bank. bankroll, v. inf. to pay for (a project).

bankrupt adj. & n. (person) whose debts exceeds his assets and who has been declared incapable of meeting his debts; he has been declared b.

bankruptcy n. state of being bankrupt.

banksia ['bæŋksɪə] n. Australian shrub with yellow flowers.

banner ['bænə] n. (a) long flag b. headlines = very large headlines in a newspaper. (b) large piece of material with a slogan written on it, carried in a procession or protest march.

banns [bænz] n. pl. official statement in church of intention to marry.

banquet ['bæŋkwɪt] n. large formal

dinner. **banqueting hall** n. large rooms where banquets are held.

bantam ['bæntəm] n. breed of very small chickens. **bantamweight** n. light weight in boxing between flyweight and featherweight.

banter ['bæntə] n. sarcastic teasing comments. **bantering** adj. (tone of voice) used when making light sarcastic comments.

banyan ['bænjæn] n. tropical tree with roots which come down from the branches.

baobab ['bæəʊbæb] n. very large tropical tree, found in Africa.

bap [bæp] n. soft flat white bread roll.

baptize [bæp'taɪz] v. to admit s.o. to the church and give them a Christian name.

baptism ['bæptɪzm] n. church ceremony where s.o. is given a Christian name. **baptismal** [bæp'tɪzml] adj. referring to baptism.

bar 1 [bɑː] n. (a) long piece (of metal/ chocolate, etc.). (b) obstacle; harbour b. = ridge of sand at the entrance to a harbour; colour b. = objection to persons because of the colour of their skin. (c) place where drinks are served; saloon b. = room in a pub with carpets and comfortable chairs; public b. = room in pub which is less comfortable than the saloon bar; milk b./snack b./sandwich b. = counter/shop where milk/snacks/ sandwiches are served. (d) place where a prisoner stands in court; b. of the house = place where people who are not MPs are asked to appear before the House of Commons. (e) officially recognized lawyers; he was called to the b. = he became a barrister. (f) division (in music). (g) unit of atmospheric pressure. **bar 2** v. (a) (barred) to block (a road); to stop (s.o. from doing sth). **bar 3** prep. b. none = with no exceptions. **bar code** n. system of lines printed on a product which can be read by a computer.

barring prep. excepting.

barb [bɑːb] n. small tooth (on a fishhook or arrow). **barbed** adj. with sharp points; b. comment = sharp critical comment; b. wire = wire (for fences) with sharp spikes.

barbarian [bɑː'beərɪən] n. wild/ uncivilized person. **barbaric** [bɑː'bærɪk] adj. cruel/uncivilized.

barbarity [bɑːˈbærɪtɪ] *n.* cruelty.
barbarous [ˈbɑːbərəs] *adj.* cruel/uncivilized.
barbecue 1 [ˈbɑːbɪkjuː] *n.* (a) charcoal fire/grill for cooking food outdoors. (b) meal cooked on a barbecue. **barbecue 2** *v.* to cook on a barbecue.
barber [ˈbɑːbə] *n.* man who cuts men's hair.
barbiturate [bɑːˈbɪtjʊrət] *n.* drug which sends you to sleep.
bard [bɑːd] *n.* (formal) poet.
bare 1 [ˈbeə] *adj.* (a) naked/not covered with clothes or leaves. (b) just enough; a b. living = just enough to live on; b. necessities = absolutely essential items for existence; elected with a b. majority = with a very small majority. **bare 2** *v.* to strip naked; he bared his soul = he told all his innermost thoughts.
bareback *adj. & adv.* riding a horse with no saddle. **barefaced** *adj.* crude/cynical (lie). **barefoot** *adv.* with no shoes on. **barefooted** *adv.* with no shoes on. **bareheaded** *adv. & adj.* with no hat on. **barely** *adv.* hardly/scarcely; I b. had enough money to pay the bill. **bareness** *n.* nakedness.
bargain 1 [ˈbɑːgɪn] *n.* (a) thing bought; sale agreed; to strike a b. = to agree on a sale; he drives a hard b. = he is a tough negotiator. (b) thing bought more cheaply than it usually is; into the b. = as well as everything else; b. basement = part of a shop where cheap items are sold. b. offer = special offer of goods at low prices. **bargain 2** *v.* (a) to negotiate a sale; I got more then I bargained for = more than I expected. (b) to haggle. **bargaining** *n.* discussion about prices/wages, etc.; collective b. = discussion between management and unions to fix new salaries for union members.
barge 1 [ˈbɑːdʒ] *n.* large flat-bottomed cargo boat on inland waters. **barge 2** *v.* to bump heavily (into). **bargee** [bɑːˈdʒiː] *n.* man in charge of a barge. **barge pole** *n.* long pole for moving a barge along; *inf.* I wouldn't touch it with a b. p. = I don't recommend getting involved with it in any way.
baritone [ˈbærɪtəʊn] *adj. & n.* (singer with a) voice between tenor and bass.
barium [ˈbeərɪəm] *n.* (element: Ba)

white soft metal, b. meal = liquid which you drink before having your stomach X-rayed which will show up clearly on the X-ray.
bark 1 [bɑːk] *n.* (a) outer part of a tree. (b) loud noise made by dog; his b. is worse than his bite = he is not as terrifying as he sounds **bark 2** *v.* (a) he barked his shin on the rock = he scraped the skin off his shin. (b) to make a loud call like a dog; to b. up the wrong tree = to get the wrong idea. **barker** *n.* person who calls out to advertise sth in the street. **barking** *n.* continuous calls of dogs.
barley [ˈbɑːlɪ] *n.* cereal crop; pearl b. = grains of barley used in cooking b. sugar = sweet make of boiled sugar; b. wine = very strong beer.
barmaid [ˈbɑːmeɪd] *n.* woman who serves drinks in a bar. **barman** [ˈbɑːmən] *n.* (*pl.*-men) man who serves drinks in a bar.
barmy [ˈbɑːmɪ] *adj.* (-ier, -iest) *inf.* mad.
barn [bɑːn] *n.* large farm building for storing grain or hay. **barnyard** *n.* yard in a farm.
barnacle [ˈbɑːnək] *n.* (a) small shellfish which clings to the bottoms of ships/to submerged wooden posts, etc. (b) b. goose = common northern goose.
barney [ˈbɑːnɪ] *n.* *Sl.* argument.
barometer [bəˈrɒmɪtə] *n.* instrument for measuring atmospheric pressure and therefore for forecasting the weather. **barometric** [bærəˈmetrɪk] *adj.* referring to a barometer. b. pressure.
baron [ˈbærən] *n.* lowest rank of hereditary peers, now also title of life peers. **baroness** *n.* wife of a baron; title of a life peeress. **baronet** *n.* hereditary knight. **baronial** [bəˈrəʊnɪəl] *adj.* large/sumptuous (castle).
baroque [bəˈrɒk] *adj.* in the ornate style of architecture of the late 17th and 18th centuries.
barrack 1 [ˈbærək] *n.* barracks = buildings where soldiers, sailors, or airmen are housed; b. room = dormitory for soldiers, etc.; b. room lawyer = person who organizes protests against authority without knowing the true facts. **barrack 2** *v.* to shout to show displeasure; they barracked our football team.

barracuda [bærə'kju:də] n. large tropical fish.

barrage ['bærɑ:ʒ] n. (a) dam across a river, etc. (b) rapid fire (of guns/questions).

barrel ['bærəl] n. (a) large wooden container (for wine/oil/fish/oysters, etc.) he's got me over a b. = in a very awkward situation. (b) firing tube (on a gun). (c) b. organ = machine for making music when a handle is turned.

barren ['bærən] adj. unproductive (land); (woman/animal) who cannot have young; (tree) which does not produce fruit. **barrenness** n. being barren.

barricade 1 [bærɪ'keɪd] n. makeshift heap of cars/rubbish, etc., made to blocks a street. **barricade 2** v. to block (a street/a door).

barrier ['bærɪə] n. thing which stops you moving forward.

barrister ['bærɪstə] n. lawyer who is allowed to speak in court.

barrow ['bærəʊ] n. (a) small wheeled truck which is pushed by hand. (b) mound of earth piled over a prehistoric tomb. **barrow boy** n. man who sells things from a barrow in the street.

bartender ['bɑ:tendə] n. barman.

barter 1 ['bɑ:tə] n. exchange (of one product for another). **barter 2** v. to exchange (one product for another).

basalt ['bæsɔ:lt] n. black volcanic rock.

base 1 [beɪs] n. (a) bottom part. (b) military camp; air force b. (c) substance which is the main part of a mixture. (d) chemical compound which reacts with an acid to form a salt. **base 2** v. to b. sth on = to use sth as a base. **base 3** adj. low/cheap; b. metal = not a precious metal. **baseball** ['beɪsbɔ:l] n. American team game played with a bat and ball. **baseboard** n. Am. decorative board running along the bottom edge of a wall in a room. **baseless** adj. (accusation) without any basis in fact.

basement n. floor beneath the ground floor.

bash 1 [bæʃ] n. (pl.-es) (a) your car has had a b. = something has bumped into your car. (b) inf. go on, have a b. = go on, try to do it. **bash 2** v. to hit (sth) hard. **bashful** ['bæʃfʊl] adj. shy/modest. **bashfully** adv. shyly. **bashfulness** n. being bashful.

basic ['beɪsɪk] adj. elementary b. vocabulary = most commonly used words. **basically** adv. at bottom.

basics n. pl. simple and important facts; to get back to b. = to consider the basic points again.

BASIC ['beɪsɪk] Beginners All-purpose Symbolic Instruction Code.

basil ['bæzl] n. type of scented herb.

basilica [bə'zɪlɪkə] n. (a) large rectangular church. (b) large catholic church.

basin ['beɪsɪn] n. large bow; wash b. = bowl in a bathroom with taps giving running water for washing the hands.

basis ['beɪsɪs] n. (pl.bases) (scientific) reason.

bask [bɑ:sk] v. to lie (in the sun/in glory).

basket ['bɑ:skɪt] n. container made of woven straw/cane, etc.; b. chair = chair made of woven cane. **basketball** ['bɑ:skɪtbɔ:l] n. team game where you try to throw a ball into a small net high up. **basketwork** n. making of baskets; objects made of woven straw/cane, etc.

bas-relief ['bæsrɪli:f] n. type of carving in stone where the figures stand out against (but are joined to) the background.

bass 1 [bæs] n. type of edible freshwater fish. **bass 2** [beɪs] adj. & n. (pl.-es) low/deep voice or music; double b. = instrument like a very large cello; b. guitar/trombone = large guitar/trombone tuned to play low notes; b. clef = sign in music showing that the notes are lower.

basset ['bæsɪt] n. b. (hound) = breed of dog with short legs and long ears.

bassoon [bə'su:n] n. low-pitched wind instrument. **bassoonist** n. person who plays a bassoon.

bastard ['bɑ:stəd] adj. & n. (person) not born of married parents; (things) which is not pure; inf. nasty person/thing.

baste [beɪst] v. (a) to sew (material) loosely. (b) to spread juices over (meat which is cooking).

bastion ['bæstɪən] n. fortified part/stronghold.

bat 1 [bæt] n. (a) small mammal which flies by night and hangs upside down to rest. (b) instrument for hitting a ball (in some games); he did it of his own b. =

he did it on his own initiative. **bat 2** v. (batted) (a) to be one of the two batsmen (in cricket); (of a cricket team) to have the turn to strike. (b) she never batted an eyelid = she did not show any suprise. **batsman** n. (pl.-men) cricketer who is at the wicket.

batch [bætʃ] n. (pl.-es) quantity of bread/cakes baked at one time; group of letters/goods taken together.

bated ['beɪtɪd] adj. with b. breath = holding your breath.

bath 1 [bɑːθ] n. (a) large container for washing all the body. (b) container for a liquid; container full of a liquid;. (c) act of washing all the body; to have a b. (d) bath full of water; will you run my b. for me? = will you fill the bath with water for me? (e) public baths = large (public) building with a swimming pool. **bath 2** v. to wash (s.o./yourself) all over; he is bathing the baby. **bathmat** n. small mat to step on as you get out of the bath. **bath oil** n. scented oil to put in a bath. **bathrobe** n. (a) loose coat of towelling worn before or after a bath. (b) Am. man's dressing gown. **bathroom** n. room with a bath, wash basin and sometimes a toilet. **bathsalts** n. pl. scented crystals to put in a bath. **bathtowel** n. very large towel for drying yourself after a bath. **bathtub** n. esp. Am. bath/container for washing all the body. **bathe 1** [beɪð] n. swim. **bathe 2** v. (a) to swim. (b) to wash (a wound) carefully. (c) Am. to have a bath. **bather** n. person who is swimming. **bathing** n. swimming (in the sea, river or a pool); b. costume = piece of clothing worn when swimming.

bathos ['beɪθɒs] n. sudden drop from a serious subject to a trivial one.

bathysphere ['bæθɪsfɪə] n. round pressurized cabin for exploring deep pressurized cabin for exploring deep parts of the sea. **bathyscaph** n. type of small submarine, used for underwater research.

batik [bæ'tiːk] n. type of cloth, coloured in patterns by dyeing it with wax designs on it.

batman ['bætmən] n. (pl.-men) officer's servant.

baton ['bætn] n. stick (of orchestra conductor or policeman).

batrachian [bə'treɪkɪən] n. amphibian, such as a toad.

battalion [bə'tælɪən] n. part of the army often commanded by a lieutenant colonel.

batten 1 ['bætn] n. thin strip of wood. **batten 2** v. (on ship) to bb. down the hatches = to close down the hatch covers before a storm.

batter 1 ['bætə] n. thin liquid mixture of flour/eggs/milk, for making pancakes, etc. **batter 2** v. to hit hard and continuously. **battered** adj. which has been hit hard; b. babies/wives = babies/wives who have been constantly illtreated. **battering ram** n. long beam used to break down castle gates. **battery** ['bætərɪ] n. (a) group of artillery guns. (b) container with a cell or several cells charged with electricity. (c) hut with cages for raising large numbers of chickens. (d) assault and b. = criminal charge of attacking s.o. with violence. **battery-powered** adj. worked by an electric battery.

battle 1 ['bætl] n. important fight between large enemy forces; the B. of Trafalgar; a b. royal = a great struggle. **battle 2** v. to fight (against). **battleaxe** n. inf. large fierce woman. **battlefield** n. site of a battle. **battlefront** n. line along which fighting is taking place. **battlements** n. pl. top part of a castle wall, with a walk for soldiers. **battleship** n. very large warship.

batty ['bætɪ] adj. inf. mad.

bauble ['bɔːbl] n. (formal) cheap piece of jewellery.

baud rate ['bɔːdreɪt] n. number of signal changes transmitted per second.

baulk [bɔːlk] v. see balk.

bauxite ['bɔːksaɪt] n. mineral from which aluminium is produced.

bawdy ['bɔːdɪ] adj. rude/coarse.

bawl [bɔːl] v. to shout loudly. **bawl out** v. Am. to criticize (s.o.).

bay 1 [beɪ] n. (a) fragrant shrub whose leaves are used in cooking. (b) large rounded inlet in a coast; the B. of Biscay. (c) arch of a bridge; section of church between pillars; b. windows = window which projects from an outside wall. (d) special section set back from the road; parking b. = place marked for parking;

loading b. = place where lorries can be parked with a high platform for loading. (e) light brown horse. (f) to keep attackers at b. = to keep them away. **bay 2** v. (of hunting dog) to bark.

bayonet ['beɪənət] n. sharp blade attached to the end of a rifle.

bazaar [bə'zɑː] n. (a) oriental market. (b) market selling goods for charity.

bazooka [bə'zuːkə] n. small anti-tank gun.

b. & b. = bed and breakfast.

BBC [biːbiː'siː] British Broadcasting Corporation.

BC ['biː'siː] abbrev. for before Christ; Julius Caesar died in 44 BC.

be 1 [biː] v. (I am, you are, he is, we/they are; I/he was, we/you/they were; he has been) (a) describing a person or thing; the house is big. (b) to add up to; two and three are five. (c) to exist/to live; where are we? there he is; how are you today? tomorrow is Friday. (d) to feel; I am cold; they are hungry. (e) to go; have you ever been to New York? the police had been into every room. (f) (showing time) it is four o'clock. (g) (showing future) he is to see the doctor tomorrow. **be 2** (used to make part of verbs) I am coming; he has been waiting for hours; (passive use) he was killed by a train.

being 1 adj. for the time b. = temporarily/for now. **being 2** n. (a) existence; the association came into b. in 1946. (b) human b. = person.

beach 1 [biːtʃ] n. (pl.-es) stretch of sand/pebbles by the side of the sea. **beach 2** v. to bring (a boat) on to the beach. **beachcomber** n. person who collects things thrown up on the beach by the sea. **beachhead** n. small area occupied by troops at the beginning of an invasion from the sea. **beachwear** n. (no pl.) clothes to wear on the beach.

beacon ['biːkən] n. light (used as a signal); radio b. = radio transmitter which guides aircraft into an airport. Belisha b. = orange globe light which marks a zebra crossing.

bead [biːd] n. (a) small ornament with a hole so that it can be threaded. (b) small drop of liquid. **beading** n. thin strip of wood (usu. carved in a pattern/used to

decorate. **beady** adj. b. eyed = with eyes small and bright like beads.

beagle ['biːgl] n. breed of dog used for hunting.

beak [biːk] n. hard covering of a bird's mouth.

beaker ['biːkə] n. metal/plastic cup, usu. with no handle; glass container used in scientific experiments.

beam 1 [biːm] n. (a) large block of wood used in building. (b) ray (of light/sound); radio b. = wavelength for radio transmission. (c) width of a ship inf. he's broad in the b. = rather fat. **beam 2** v. to send out rays. (b) to smile. **beaming** adj. radiant (sunshine/smile/face).

beam in on v. to take (sth) as a target.

bean [biːn] n. (a) vegetable with edible seeds (and pods); inf. full of beans = full of vigour. (b) coffee beans = fruit of the coffee plant which, when roasted and ground, are used to make coffee.

bear 1 ['beə] n. (a) large furry wild animal; polar b. = large white bear living in Arctic regions; teddy b. = toy bear. (b) person who believes the stock market prices will fall. **bear 2** v. (bore; has borne) (a) to carry; this tree has borne fruit every year; the deposit bears interest at 5%. (b) to stand/to put up with; I can't b. noise. (c) to support; will this branch b. my weight? (d) to turn; b. right at the crossroads. (e) to aim; the enemy brought their guns to b. on our ship. **bearable** adj. which you can put up with. **bear down on** v. to advance heavily towards (s.o.). **bearer** n. person who carries sth. **beargarden** n. don't turn the place into a b. = don't make a row and mess everywhere. **bearing** n. (a) ball bearings = set of small balls around an axle to spread the weight evenly and make the wheel turn smoothly. (b) to get your bearing = to find out where you are; to lose your bearings = to lose all idea of where you are. (c) stately b. = stately way of standing/walking. **bear out** v. to confirm. **bearskin** n. tall fur hat worn by a soldier. **bear up** v. to survive cheerfully. **bear with** v. to endure patiently.

beard [bɪəd] n. hair on the lower part of a man's face; whiskers on a mussel/oyster, etc. **bearded** adj. with a beard. **beardless** adj. with no beard.

beast [biːst] *n.* (a) wild animal; b. of burden = donkey/horse, etc., trained to carry load. (d) nasty person. **beastliness** *n.* nastiness (of person). **beastly** *adj.* nasty.

beat 1 [biːt] *n.* (a) regular sound; heart b. (b) regular measure in music. (c) area regularly patrolled by a policeman. **beat 2** *v.* (beat; has beaten) (a) to hit hard several times. (b) to chase (birds); we b. a hasty retreat = we went way very quickly; don't b. about the bush = get to the point quickly; *Sl.* b. it! = go away!. (c) to defeat. (d) to do better than (a record). (e) to stir (eggs, etc.) vigorously. **beat back** *v.* to push back. **beat down** *v.* (a) to flatten (corn). (b) I beat down his price = I reduced the price he was asking by haggling; he beat me down = he made me reduce my price. (c) (of the sun) to strike hard on. **beaten** *adj.* off the b. track = away from other houses from other houses. **beater** *n.* (a) person who drives birds towards the people who will shoot them. (b) machine for beating eggs. **beating** *n.* act of hitting. **beat up** *v.* (a) to whip (cream). (b) to attack (s.o.).

beatify [biːˈætɪfaɪ] *v.* to declare (s.o.) blessed (as the first step to declaring s.o. a saint). **beatification** [biːætɪfɪˈkeɪʃn] *n.* declaring s.o. blessed.

Beaufort scale [ˈbəʊfətˈskeɪl] *n.* scale for measuring wind strengths.

beautiful [ˈbjuːtɪfəl] *adj.* very pleasing to look at. **beaut** *n. inf.* (esp. Australian) a beautiful thing/person. **beautician** *n.* person who makes people beautiful (by applying makeup. etc.). **beautifully** *adv.* in a very pleasing way. **beautify** *v.* to make sth beautiful. **beauty** *n.* state of being beautiful; b. salon = clinic specializing in women's appearance; b. spot = (i) famous beautiful place; (ii) dark spot, *usu.* on the face.

beaver 1 [ˈbiːvə] *n.* small American mammal which lives in water and makes dams with trees which it gnaws down. **beaver 2** *v.* to b. away at sth = to work hard at sth.

becalmed [biːˈkɑːmd] *adj.* (of a sailing ship) not able to move because there is no wind.

became [bɪˈkeɪm] *v.* see become.

because [bɪˈkɒz] *conj.* for the reason that; owing to the fact that. **because of** *prep.* on account of.

beck [bek] *n.* (a) (in North of England) mountain streaM. (b) he is always at her b. and call = he always does exactly what she wants him to do.

beckon [ˈbekən] *v.* to make a sign (to s.o.) to come.

become [bɪˈkʌm] *v.* (became; has become) to change into sth different; what became of him? = what happened to him? **becoming** *adj.* her dress is very b. = her dress suits her very well.

becquerel [ˈbekərel] *n. Sl.* unit of radiation.

bed 1 [bed] *n.* (a) piece of furniture for sleeping on; double b. = bed for two people; single b. = bed for one person; to go to b. = to lie down in bed to sleep for the night; he took to his b. = he was ill and had to stay in bed; to make the b. = to straighten the bedclothes after getting out of bed. (b) bottom (of a river/lake); oyster b. = collection of oysters at the bottom of the sea; watercress b. = mass of watercress growing in a river. (c) area of garden kept for plants. **bed 2** *v.* (bedded) (a) to b. down = to give (horses) fresh straw; to b. down railway sleepers = to lay them on ballast. (b) to b. out plants = to put out plants in a flower bed. **bedclothes** *n. pl.* sheets/blankets, etc. on a bed. **bedcover** *n.* cloth which covers a bed during the daytime. **bedding** *n.* (a) bedclothes (mattress/pillows, etc,); straw (for horses). (b) bedding out = putting out (of plants) into flower beds; bedding plants = plants suitable for putting into flower beds. **bedfellow** *n.* person who sleeps in the same bed; person who is associated with s.o. **bedjacket** *n.* warm jacket worn in bed. **bedpan** *n.* bowl for passing waste water into when lying in bed. **bedridden** *adj.* forced to stay in bed because of illness. **bedrock** *n.* bottom rock beneath various mineral seams. **bedroom** *n.* room for sleeping in. **bedside** *n.* side of a bed; b. manner = attitude of a doctor to his sick patient. **bed-sitting room, bed-sitter, bedsit** [bedˈsɪtɪŋ ruːm] *n. inf.* bedroom and living room combined. **bedsore** *n.* sore which is caused by lying in bed for long periods. **bedspread** *n.* decorative cloth to put over a bed. **bedstead** *n.* solid frame of a bed. **bedtime** *n.* time to go to bed; it's past your b. = it's later than the time you usually go to bed.

bedevilled [bɪ'devld] *adj.* surrounded (with difficulties).

bedlam ['bedləm] *n.* loud noise; chaos.

bedraggled [bɪ'drægld] *adj.* wet and dirty.

bee [biː] *n.* small insect which makes honey. **bee-eater** *n.* small tropical bird, which eats insects such as bees.

beehive *n.* box in which a colony of bees lives. **beekeeper** *n.* person who keeps bees. **beekeeping** *n.* keeping of bees (for honey). **beeline** *n.* straight line; he made a b. for the drinks = he went straight to the drinks. **beeswax** *n.* wax produced by bees, used as a polish.

beech [biːtʃ] *n.* (*pl.*-es) large northern tree; wood of this tree.

beef 1 [biːf] *n.* (a) meat from a bull of cow; corned b. = beef which has been salted. (b) *inf.* grumble **beef 2** *v. inf.* to grumble (about). **beefburger** ['biːfbɜːgə] *n.* round flat cake of minced beef. **beefy** *adj.* (-ier, -iest) muscular.

beep 1 [biːp] *n.* short high sound made by an electronic device, such as a computer. **beep 2** *v.* to make a short high-pitched sound.

beer ['bɪə] *n.* alcoholic drink made from malt, flavoured with hops; a glass of this drink. **beery** *adj.* referring to beer.

beet [biːt] *n.* (a) sugar b. root vegetable grown for processing into sugar. (b) beetroot. **beetroot** *n.* dark red root vegetable.

beetle ['biːtl] *n.* small winged insect with a hard cover over its wings.

beetling ['biːtlɪŋ] *adj.* (cliff) which is high and looks threatening.

befall [bɪ'fɔːl] *v.* (befell; has befallen) (formal) to happen (to).

befit [bɪ'fɪt] *v.* (formal) (befitted) to suit.

before [bɪ'fɔː] *adv., prep & con.j.* (a) in front (of). (b) earlier (than).

beforehand *adv.* in advance.

befriend [bɪ'frend] *v.* to be friendly to and help (s.o.).

beg [beg] *v.* (begged) (a) to ask for money. (b) to ask; to b. a favour of s.o. = to ask s.o. a favour; I. b. your pardon = excuse me. **beggar** *n.* person who asks

for money; *inf.* lucky beggar! = what a lucky person! **beggarly** *adj.* small/ poor (wage). **begging** *n.* asking for money; it's going b. = no one wants it.

beget [bɪ'get] *v.* (beget; begot; has begotten) (old) to give birth to; to produce.

begin [bɪ'gɪn] *v.* (began; has begun) to start; b. again = start from the beginning. **beginner** *n.* person who is starting to do sth. **beginning** *n.* first part/start; at the b. = to start with.

begonia [bɪ'gəʊnɪə] *n.* pot plant with large bright flowers.

begrudge [bɪ'grʌdʒ] *v.* to feel resentment because of sth s.o. has or does; I don't b. him his money.

beguile [bɪ'gaɪl] *v.* to make (time) pass quickly and pleasantly.

behalf [bɪ'hɑːf] *n.* I am speaking on b. of the association = I am speaking to get support for the association. (b) acting on my b. = acting for me. (c) don't worry on my b. = do not worry about me.

behave [bɪ'heɪv] *v.* to act; to b. yourself = be good. **behaved** *adj.* well-behaved child = polite/quite child; badly behaved child = child who is rude/dirty/nosy.

behaviour, *Am.* **behavior** *n.* conduct/ way of acting. **behavioural** *adj.* concerning the behaviour of human beings.

behead [bɪ'hed] *v.* to cut off a head.

behind 1 [bɪ'haɪnd] *adv.* (a) after; he stayed b. = he stayed at the place everyone started from. (b) late; I am b. with my work. **behind 2** *prep.* (a) at the back of; what is really b. it all? = what is the real cause of it all? I'm b. you completely = I'm in full support. (b) late/ retarded (by comparison with s.o. else); less advanced than (s.o.). **behind 3** *n. inf.* buttocks. **behindhand** *adv.* late.

behold [bɪ'həʊld] *v.* (beheld) (formal) to see. **beholder** *n.* person who sees. **beholden** [bɪ'həʊlden] *adj.* (formal) grateful to s.o. for sth).

behove [bɪ'həʊv] *v.* to be fitting.

beige [beɪʒ] *adj.* pale fawn colour.

belated [bɪ'leɪtɪd] *adj.* late. **belatedly** *adv.* late.

belay [bɪ'leɪ] *v.* to attach a rope.

belch 1 [beltʃ] *n.* (*pl.*-es) noise made when bringing up gas from the stomach. **belch 2** *v.* (a) to make a noise by bringing up gas from the stomach through the mouth. (b) to pour out (smoke, flames). **beleaguered** [bɪ'liːgəg] *adj.* in a difficult position; surrounded by enemies.

belfry ['belfrɪ] *n.* tower for bells.

Belgian 1 ['beldʒən] *adj.* referring to Belgium. **Belgian 2** *n.* person from Belgium.

belie [bɪ'laɪ] *v.* (formal) to hide/to show (sth) wrongly.

believe [bɪ'liːv] *v.* to feel sure of (sth), without any proof; I b. so = I think that is correct; to b. in sth = to believe that sth exists. **belief** *n.* feeling sure of sth. **believable** *adj.* which one can believe. **believer** *n.* person who believes in sth, esp. God.

belittle [bɪ'lɪtl] *v.* to make (sth) seem small or unimportant.

bell [bel] *n.* metal cup-shaped object which makes a ringing sound when hit; mechanism to make a ringing sound; that rings a b. = that reminds me of something. **bellboy, Am.bellhop** *n.* messenger boy employed in a hotel. **bellpush** *n.* button which rings a bell when pushed. **bell tower** *n.* tower for bells.

belladonna ['belədɒnə] *n.* deadly nightshade, a poisonous plant.

belle [bel] *n.* beautiful women.

bellicose ['belɪkəʊs] *adj.* (formal) warlike.

belligerent 1 [bə'lɪdʒərənt] *adj.* warlike. **belligerent 2** *n.* country fighting a war. **belligerency** *n.* being belligerent.

bellow 1 ['beləʊ] *n.* loud cry (of bull/angry person). **bellow 2** *v.* to make a loud cry.

bellows ['beləʊz] *n. pl.* apparatus for blowing air into a fire to make it burn brightly.

belly ['belɪ] *n.* (*pl.*-ies) *inf.* abdomen. **bellyache 1** *n.* pain in the stomach. **bellyache 2** *v. inf.* to complain bitterly (about sth). **bellyflop** *n. inf.* to do a b. = to fall flat on to the water instead of diving into it. **bellyful** *n. inf.* I've had a b. of his complaints = I've had as many of his complaints as I can stand.

belong [bɪ'lɒŋ] *v.* to b. to s.o. = to be s.o.'s property. (b) to be to a club = to be

a member (of a club). **belongings** *n. pl.*personal property.

beloved 1 [bɪ'lʌvɪd] *adj.* whom s.o. loves. **beloved 2** *n.* person who is loved by s.o.

below 1 [bɪ'ləʊ] *adv.* lower down. **below 2** *prep.* lower than; the temperature never goes b. 25°.

belt 1 [belt] *n.* (a) strap which goes round your waist; seat b. = belt in a car or aircraft which holds you safely in place. (b) zone; green b. = area round a town where building is not permitted. **belt 2** *v.* (a) *Sl.* to b. along = to go very fast. (b) *Sl.* b. up! = keep quiet!. (c) *inf.* they were belting out a song very loudly.

bemoan [bɪ'məʊn] *v.* (formal) to complain about (sth).

bemused [bɪ'mjuːzd] *adj.* bewildered/puzzled.

bench [bentʃ] *n.* (*pl.*-es) (a) long hard seat (for several people). (b) the b. = group of magistrates who try cases in court. (c) table (for working).

benchmark *n.* standard against which something can be tested.

bend 1 [bend] *n.* (a) curve; S-bend = double curve in a pipe; *inf.* round the b. = quite mad. (b) the bends = illness in divers caused by coming up from a deep dive too quickly. **bend 2** *v.* (bent) to make (a straight object) curved; to curve. **bend down** *v.* to stoop.

beneath 1 [bɪ'niːθ] *adv.* underneath/below. **beneath 2** *v. prep.* under; he thinks it is b. him = he thinks it is too unimportant for him to deal with.

benediction [benɪ'dɪkʃn] *n.* blessing (in church).

benefactor, benefactress ['benɪfæktə, 'benɪfæktrəs] *n.* person who gives s.o./a society money.

beneficent [bɪ'nefɪsənt] *adj.* which does good. **beneficial** [benɪ'fɪʃl] *adj.* which does good; useful. **beneficiary** [benɪ'fɪʃərɪ] *n.* (*pl.*-es) person who inherits sth from a person who has died.

benefit 1 ['benfɪt] *n.* (a) profit/advantage. (b) payment; unemployment b. = payment (by the state) to unemployed people; maternity b. = payment to a woman who has had a baby. **benefit 2** *v.* to be profit.

benevolence [bə'nevələns] *n.* goodness/charity. **benevolent** *adj.*

good/charitable; b. dictatorship = dictatorship which provides for the wellbeing of the people. **benevolently** adv. in a benevolent way.

benighted [bɪ'naɪtɪd] adj. uneducated.

benign [bɪ'naɪn] adj. (a) pleasant (person). (b) non-malignant (growth).

bent 1 [bent] adj. (a) curved. (b) he is b. on becoming a sailor = he s very keen to become a sailor. (c) Sl. dishonest.

bent 2 n. she has a natural b. to be a nurse = she has an instinct to become a nurse. **bent 3** v. see also bend.

benzene ['benziːn] n. liquid obtained from coal, which is used as a fuel and causes cancer.

benzine ['benziːn] n. liquid mixture obtained from petroleum, and used for cleaning.

bequeath [bɪ'kwiːð] v. to leave (property/money) to s.o. when you die. **bequest** [bɪ'kwest] n. property left to s.o.

berberis ['bɜːbərɪs] n. plant with small red berries, grown for decoration.

bereaved [bɪ'riːvd] n. the b. = (i) widow/widower; (ii) family of a person who has died. **bereavement** n. loss of member of the family through death.

beret ['bereɪ] n. round cloth or felt cap with no peak.

beriberi [berɪ'berɪ] n. tropical disease of the nervous system.

berry ['berɪ] n. (pl.-ies) fruit of a shrub.

berserk [bə'zɜːk] adj. to go b. = to go wild/mad.

berth 1 [bɜːθ] n. (a) place where a ship ties up to a quay; to give sth a wide b. = to avoid sth at all costs. (b) bed in a ship/ train). **berth 2** v. to tie up (a ship).

beryl ['berɪl] n. type of precious stone.

beseech [bɪ'siːtʃ] v. (beseeched/ besought[bɪ'sɔːt]) (formal) to ask (s.o. to do sth).

beset [bɪ'set] v. (beset) to surrounded, causing problems. **besetting sin** n. defect which is always present.

beside [bɪ'saɪd] prep. at the side of b. the point = nothing to do with the subject.

besides 1 [bɪ'saɪdz] prep. other than.

besides 2 adv. also/in any case.

besiege [bɪ'siːdʒ] v. (of troops/ newspaper reporters) to surround.

besought [bɪ'sɔːt] v. see beseech.

bespoke [bɪ'spəʊk] adj. b. tailor = tailor who makes clothes to measure.

best 1 [best] adj. & n. (superlative for good and well) very good; better than anyone/anything else; b. man = friend of the bridegroom who helps him at a wedding; the b. of it is that = the most interesting/funniest part of the story is that; do you b. = do as well as you can; for the b. part of an hour = for almost a whole hour; to the b. of my knowledge = as far as I know. **best 2** adv. in a way which is better than anyone else; bestdressed = wearing the most fashionable clothes. **bestseller** n. book/article that sells in very large number.

bestial ['bestjəl] adj. like a beast. **bestiality** [bestɪ'ælɪtn] n. being bestial.

bestir [bɪ'stɜː] v. (formal) to b. yourself = to get the energy to do sth.

bestow [bɪ'stəʊ] v. (formal) to give.

bet 1 [bet] n. money put down as a pledge when you try to forecast the result of a race, etc., and which you lose if you guess wrongly. **bet 2** v. (bet) to offer to pay money if what you think will happen does not happen; he b. me £10 the Prime Minister would lose the election; I b. you he's going to be late = I am quite sure. **better** n. person who bets.

betting n. placing of bets; b. shop = office where you can bet money on horse races.

beta ['biːtə] n. second letter of the Greek alphabet. **beta blocker** n. drug which reduces the heart's activity.

betake [bɪ'teɪk] v. (betook) (formal) to take.

betel [biːtl] v. type of tropical nut.

béta noire [bet'nwɑː] n. thing which you dislike particularly.

betide [bɪ'taɪd] v. (formal) to happen to (s.o.).

betray [bɪ'treɪ] v. to reveal a secret about s.o. to his enemies. **betrayal** n. giving s.o. up to his enemies.

betroth [bɪ'trəʊð] v. (formal) to engage s.o. to marry. **betrothal** n. act of betrothing s.o.

better 1 ['betə] adj. (comp. of good and well) superior; of higher quality; less ill; finer (weather). **better 2** adv. I'm feeling b = I'm feeling less ill; he thought b. of it = he decided not to do what he had planned; you'd b. be going = it's time you went; he's b. off where he is = he's in a better position where he is. **better 3** v. to b. oneself/one's position = to improve one's position.

between [bɪ'twiːn] prep. with things on both sides; b. you and me = privately; in b. = in the middle of.

betwixt [bɪ'twɪkst] prep. (old) between.

bevel 1 ['bevl] n. angled edge of a flat surface. **bevel 2** v. (bevelled) to give a flat surface an angle edge.

beverage ['bevərɪdʒ] n. drink.

bevy ['bevɪ] n. (pl.-ies) group (esp. of girls).

bewail [bɪ'weɪl] v. (formal) to complain about (sth).

beware [bɪ'weə] v. to b. of = to watch out for.

bewilder [bɪ'wɪldə] v. to puzzle. **bewilderment** n. puzzle/surprise.

bewitch [bɪ'wɪtʃ] v. to charm/to cast a spell on. **bewitching** adj. charming (girl).

beyond [bɪ'jɒnd] adv. further than; on the other side of; it's b. a joke = it's no longer funny.

biannual [baɪ'ænjʊəl] adj. which happens twice a year. **biannually** adv. twice a year.

bias ['baɪəs] n. (a) to cut material on the b. = slantwise/diagonally; be binding = narrow strip of material cut on the bias, used for hemming. (b) slant/strong opinion in one direction. (c) tendency to turn in one direction (of a bowl in a game of bowls). **biased** adj. showing strong opinion in one direction/ prejudiced.

bib [bɪb] n. (small cloth tied under a baby's chin.

bible ['baɪbl] n. (a) book of Christian or Jewish scriptures. (b) important book of reference. **biblical** ['bɪblɪkl] adj. referring to the bible.

bibliography [bɪblɪ'ɒɡrəfɪ] n. list of books/articles referring to a special subject. **bibliographer** n. person who writes a bibliography. **bibliographical** ['bɪblɪlɪə'ɡræfɪk] adj. (details) referring to a particular subject. **bibliophile** ['bɪblɪəʊfaɪ] n. person who loves books.

bibulous ['bɪbjuːləs] adj. fond of drinking.

bicameralism [baɪ'kæmərəlɪzm] n. system of government where there are two parts of parliament, such as a national assembly and a senate.

bicarbonate [baɪ'kɑːbənət] n. b. of soda = chemical used as a medicine for stomach pains or as an ingredient in cooking.

bicentenary [baɪsen'tiːnərɪ] n. anniversary of 200 years. **bicentennial** [baɪsen'tenɪəl] adj. referring to a bicentenary.

biceps ['baɪseps] n. large muscle in the top part of the arm.

bicker ['bɪkə] v. to quarrel.

bicycle 1 ['baɪsɪkl] n. two-wheeled vehicle driven by pedals. **bicycle 2** v. to ride on a bicycle.

bid 1 [bɪd] n. offer/attempt; he made a b. for power = he tried to seize power; takeover b. = attempt to take over a company. **bid 2** v. (a) (bid/bade[bæd]; has bidden) to wish; he bade me farewell. (b) (bid; has bid) to make an offer at an auction. **bidder** n. person who makes an offer at an auction.

bidding n. (a) command; I did it at his b. = did it because he told me to do it. (b) offers made at an auction.

bide [baɪd] v. to b. your time = to wait for the right moment.

bidet ['biːdeɪ] n. low washbasin for washing the genitals.

biennial [baɪ'enjəl] adj. & v. (plant) which flowers in its second year; (event) which occurs every two years. **biennially** adv. every two years.

bier ['bɪə] n. table/hearse for carrying a coffin.

biff 1 [bɪf] n. inf. hit. **biff 2** v. inf. to hit.

bifocal [baɪ'fəʊkl] adj. & n. spectacles/bifocals = spectacles with two types of lens in each frame, one for reading and one for long distance.

bifurcate ['baɪfəkɔɪt] v. to split. **bifurcation** [baɪfə'keɪʃn] n. splitting (of a road).

big 1 [bɪɡ] adj. (bigger, biggest) large, b. game = large animals (lions, etc.), which are hunted for sport. **big 2** adv. to talk b. = to pretend to be important. **bighead** n. inf. person who is proud of himself and shows off. **bigwig** n. important person in an official position.

bigamy ['bɪgəmɪ] *n.* action of illegally marrying a second wife/husband, when the first is still alive and has not been divorced. **bigamist** *n.* person who is illegally married to two people at the same time. **bigamous** *adj.* b. marriage = illegal marriage when you are already married to s.o. else.

bight [baɪt] *n.* (a) loop of a rope. (b) wide curved bay.

bigot ['bɪgət] *n.* person with a narrow minded attitude to religion/politics; fanatic. **bigoted** *adj.* with very unbending ideas about religion/politics, etc. **bigotry** *n.* narrow minded attitude to religion/politics etc.

bike [baɪk] *n. inf.* bicycle.

bikini [bɪ'ki:nɪ] *n.* brief two-piece bathing costume for women.

bilateral [baɪ"lætərəl] *adj.* one two sides; b. agreement = agreement between two sides.

bilberry ['bɪlbərɪ] *n.* small edible blue berry growing in northern mountains; paint which bears these berries.

bile [baɪl] *n.* bitter fluid produced by the liver to digest fat.

bilge [bɪldʒ] *n.* dirty water (in a ship's hull); *inf.* nonsense.

bilingual [baɪ'lɪŋwəl] *adj.* using two languages; (person) who can speak two languages equally fluently.

bilious ['bɪlɪəs] *adj.* sick; he had a b. attack = he was sick. **billousness** *n.* feeling sick.

bilk [bɪlk] *v.* to cheat (s.o.) of sth.

bill [bɪl] *n.* hard covering of a bird's mouth. (b) note showing the amount of money you have to pay. (c) proposed act of parliament. (d) *Am.* banknote. (e) poster (showing what is on at a theatre); to top the b. = to be mentioned at the top of a list as the most important item; will fill the b. = will be very suitable. (f) b. of fare = menu. billboard, n. *Am.* large wooden panel for posters. **billfold.** *n. Am.* wallet for banknotes. **billhook** *n.* large hooked knife, used for cutting small branches.

billabong ['bɪləbɒŋ] *n.* (in Australia) loop in a river where there is no current.

billet 1 ['bɪlɪt] *n.* lodgings (for soldiers). **billet 2** *v.* to lodge (soldiers) on s.o.

billiards ['bɪljədz] *n.* game involving hitting balls with a long rod on a smooth

green-covered table. **billiard ball, billiard table** *n.* ball/table used in the game of billiards.

billion ['bɪljən] *n.* one million millions. *Am.* one thousand millions; billions of letter = a great many letters.

billow 1 ['bɪləʊ] *n.* large wave. **billow 2** *v.* to move in large waves.

billy can ['bɪlɪkæn] *n.* small can used (esp. by hikers) for cooking.

billy goat ['bɪlɪgəʊt] *n.* male goat. biltog, n. dried beef, eaten in Southern Africa.

bimbo ['bɪmbəʊ] *n. Sl.* attractive young girl.

bimonthly 1 [baɪ'mʌnθlɪ] *adj.* every to months; twice a month. **bimonthly 2** *n.* magazine appearing every fortnight.

bin [bɪn] *n.* storage box; pedal b. = rubbish container which opens with a pedal; bread b. = box for keeping bread fresh.

binary ['baɪnərɪ] *adj.* in twos; b. system = where numbers are shown by the figures 1 and 0 only.

bind 1 [baɪnd] *n. Sl.* nuisance. **bind 2** *v.* (bound[baʊnd]) (a) to tie. (b) to cover (a book). (c) to oblige (s.o.) to do sth.; b. (s.o.) over = to make s.o. promise to obey the law for a period of time.

binder *n.* (a) bookbinder. (b) stiff cover for holding and protecting loose sheets of paper/magazines. **bindery** *n.* factory which binds books. **binding 1** *adj.* this contract is b. on both parties = both have to do what is says. **binding 2** *n.* outside cover of the book. **bindweed** *n.* type of climbing weed.

binge [bɪndʒ] *n. inf.* wild drunken party.

bingo ['bɪŋgəʊ] *n.* game (played in public) where the aim is to cover up all the numbers on a card as they are called out.

binnacle ['bɪnəkl] *n.* box containing the compass on a ship.

binocular 1 [bɪ'nɒkjʊlə] *adj.* b. vision = ability to see the same object with two eyes, and therefore to judge distance. **binocular 2** *n. pl.*binoculars = double glasses for seeing long distances.

binomial [baɪ'nəʊmɪəl] *adj.* (theory) based on two figures; b. classification = way of classifying plants and animals, using two Latin names.

biochemistry [baɪəʊˈkemɪstrɪ] *n.* science of the chemical constituents of animals or plants. **biochemical** *adj.* referring to biochemistry. **biochemist** *n.* person who studies the chemical composition of animals or plants.

biodegradable [baɪəʊdɪˈgreɪdəbl] *adj.* which decomposes naturally to form harmless material.

biography [baɪˈɒgrəf] *n.* story of the life of s.o. **biographer** *n.* person who writes a biography. **biographical** [baɪəˈgræfɪkl] *adj.* referring to a biography.

biology [baɪˈɒlədʒɪ] *n.* study of living things. **biological** [baɪəˈlɒdʒɪkl] *adj.* referring to living things. b. warfare = war in which germs are used. **biologist** *n.* person who studies biology.

biomass [ˈbaɪəʊmæs] *n.* all living organisms in a certain place.

bionic [baɪˈɒnɪk] *adj.* with powers reinforced by electronic devices.

biophysics [baɪəʊˈfɪzɪks] *n.* science of the physics of living things.

biopsy [ˈbaɪɒpsɪ] *n.* operation to remove a growth/a piece of tissue.

biorhythms [ˈbaɪəʊrɪðmz] *n. pl.* cycles of activity which are said to recur regularly in each person's life.

bipartite [baɪpɑːˈtaɪt] *adj.* with two sides taking part.

biped [ˈbaɪped] *n.* animal with two legs.

biplane [ˈbaɪpleɪn] *n.* aircraft with two sets of wings, one above the other.

birch 1 [bɜːtʃ] *n.* (*pl.*-es) silver b. = common northern tree with white bark. **birch 2** *v.* to beat with a bundle of twigs.

bird [bɜːd] *n.* (a) animal with wings and feather. (b) *inf.* person. (c) *inf.* girl. **bird's-eye view** *n.* view from high up looking down. **bird watcher** *n.* person who studies birds. **bird watching** *n.* study of birds.

biretta [bɪˈretə] *n.* small cap worn by a Catholic priest.

biro [ˈbaɪrəʊ] *n.* (*pl.*-os) trademark for a ballpoint pen.

birth [bɜːθ] *n.* being born; he is French by b. = he has French nationality because his parents are French; b. certificate = official document showing date and place of s.o.'s birth; b. control = method of preventing pregnancy; b. rate

= average number of children born per thousand population; to give b. to = to have (a child) /to produce (young).

birthday *n.* date on which you were born; in his b. suit = naked/with no clothes on. **birthmark** *n.* mark on the skin which is there from birth.

birthplace *n.* place where s.o. was born/sth was invented. **birthright** *n.* right which you inherit at birth.

biscuit [ˈbɪskɪt] *n.* small hard cake, *usu.* sweet; cheese and biscuits = cheese with dry unsweetened biscuits; water biscuits = biscuits made of flour and water.

bisect [baɪˈsekt] *v.* to cut into two equal parts.

bisexual [baɪˈseksjʊəl] *adj.* who is attracted to both sexes.

bishop [ˈbɪʃəp] *n.* (a) church leader in charge of a diocese. (b) piece in chess shaped like a bishop's hat. **bishopric** *n.* post of bishop.

bismuth [ˈbɪzməθ] *n.* (element: Bi) white metal used in medicine.

bison [ˈbaɪsn] *n.* (*pl.*bison) large wild ox or cow.

bistro [ˈbiːstrəʊ] *n.* (*pl.*-os) small restaurant serving continental food.

bit [bɪt] *n.* (a) small piece; a b. longer = a little while longer; the chair has come to bits = has fallen apart; she's thrilled to bits = very pleased; he is a b. of a nuisance = he is rather a nuisance; b. by b. = in stages; not a b. of use = of no use at all; he's every b. as ugly as you said = just as ugly; b. part = small part (in a play). (b) piece of metal for making holes which is placed in a drill. (c) piece of metal going through a horse's mouth to which the reins are attached. (d) small piece of information (in a computer) (e) *v.* see also. **bitty** *adj. inf.* disconnected; made of many little bits.

bitch 1 [bɪtʃ] *n.* (*pl.*-es) (a) female dog. (b) *inf.* unpleasant women. **bitch 2** *v. inf.* to complain

bite 1 [baɪt] *v.* (bit; has bitten) (a) to cut with teeth; he bit my head off = he spoke angrily to me. (b) to work/to have effect. **bite 2** *n.* (a) mouthful. (b) place where you have been bitten. **biting** *adj.* sharp (wind); piercing (cold); sharp (remark). **bitten** [ˈbɪtn] *v.* see bite.

bitter 1 [ˈbɪtə] *adj.* (a) not sweet; sour. (b) resentful/cruel; to the b. end = right

to the very end. (c) very cold. **bitter 2**
n. light-coloured beer which is not
sweet. **bitterly** *adv.* sharply/resentfully.
bitterness *n.* resentment.

bittern ['bɪtən] *n.,.* marsh bird which
makes a booming call.

bitumen ['bɪtjʊmən] *n.* black
substance, like tar. **bituminous**
[bɪ'tjuːmɪnəs] *adj.* referring to bitumen.

bivalve ['baɪvælv] *n.* shellfish with two
shells hinged together.

bivouac ['bɪvʊæk] *v.* (bivouacked) to
camp out in the open without a tent.

bizarre [bɪ'zɑː] *adj.* very strange.

blab [blæb] *v. inf.* to talk too much/to
gossip.

black 1 [blæk] *adj.* (-er, -est) (a) of a
very dark colour, the opposite of white;
b. coffee = coffee without milk or cream;
b. economy = section of the economy
where earnings are not declared for tax;
b. ice = dangerous layer of thin ice on a
road; I'm in his b. books = he's angry
with me; b. box = device which stores
information about an aircraft's flight; b.
market = selling illegally, at high prices,
products which are not normally
available. (b) bad; b. spot = place which
traffic accidents often happen. **black 2**
n. (a) very dark colour, opposite to
white; to be in the b. = to have money in
a bank account. (b) person whose skin is
very dark coloured. **black 3** *v.* to refuse
to handle (goods) in support of a strike.
blackball *v.* to vote against (s.o.)
joining a club. **blackberry** *n.* common
wild fruit, growing on long prickly
stems. **blackbird** *n.* common northern
bird, the male of which has black
feathers and yellow beak. **blackboard**
n. board on the wall which can be
written on. **blackcurrant** *n.* common
black soft fruit grown in the garden.
blacken *v.* to make black.
blackfellow *n.* (in Australia)
aborigine. **blackfly** *n.* small black
aphis. **blackguard** ['blægɑːd] *n.*
scoundrel/wicked person. **blackhead**
n. blocked pore which shows up as a
black dot on the skin. **blackish** *adj.*
rather black. **blackleg** *n.* person who
goes to work in spite of order to go on
strike. **blacklist 1** *n.* list of undesirable
things or people. **blacklist 2** *v.* to put
(s.o.'s name) on a list of undesirable

people. **blackmail 1** *v.* to make s.o.
pay money by threatening to reveal some
unpleasant or shameful detail about
them. **blackmail 2** *n.* act of
blackmailing. **blackmailer** *n.* person
who blackmails. **Black Maria** *n. Sl.*
police van used to transport prisoners.
blackness *n.* total darkness. **black
out** *v.* (a) to wipe off/to cover up (a
name). (b) to faint/to lose consciousness.
(c) to cut off the electricity. **blackout** *n.*
(a) loss of consciousness. (b) sudden
stoppage of electricity supply.
blacksmith *n.* man who makes
horseshoes, gates etc., out of metal.
blackthorn *n.* wild prickly bush, with
white flowers.

bladder ['blædə] *n.* (a) bag in the body
where urine is stored. (b) bag inside a
ball which is inflated.

blade [bleɪd] *n.* cutting part of knife,
etc. (b) thin leaf of grass. (c) one arm of
a propeller. (d) flat part at the end of an
oar.

blame 1 [bleɪm] *n.* criticism of s.o. for
having done sth; to get the b. for = to be
said to be responsible for. **blame 2** *v.*
to b. s.o. for sth = to say that sth was
caused by s.o.; he is to b. for the accident
= he is responsible for the accident; I
don't b. you = I think you were quite
right. **blameless** *adj.* pure/innocent.
blameworthy *adj.* (person) who can
rightly be blamed.

blanch [blɑːntʃ] *v.* (a) to put quickly
into boiling water. (b) turn white.

blancmange [blə'mɒnʒ] *n.* dessert
like a cream jelly flavoured with
chocolate/strawberry. etc.

bland [blænd] *adj.* smooth/not striking;
(food) without much flavour. **blandly**
adv. in a smooth casual way.
blandness *n.* smoothness; lack of any
striking features.

blandishments ['blændɪʃmənts *n. pl.*
attractive flattery.

blank 1 [blæŋk] *adj.* (-er, -est) (a)
(paper, etc.) with nothing on it; b.
cheque = cheque where the figures are
not written in; b. verse = poetry which
does not rhyme; he looked b. = he looked
lost/surprised. (b) b. cartridge = with no
bullet in it. **blank 2** *n.* (a) white space
(with nothing printed on it); my mind is
a b. = I cannot remember anything; he

drew a b. = he failed to make any progress. (b) cartridge with no bullet in it. **blankly** *adv.* with vacant expression.

blanket 1 ['blæŋkɪt] *n.* woollen bed covering; electric b. = electrically heated pad to warm a bed; b. order = order which covers many items. **blanket 2** *v.* to cover (with fog, etc.).

blare 1 ['bleə] *n.* loud noise. **blare 2** *v.* to make a loud noise.

blarney ['blɑːnɪ] *n.* talk which it in tended to trick.

blasé ['blɑːzeɪ] *adj.* with a couldn't-care-less attitude.

blaspheme [blæs'fiːm] *v.* to swear; to talk without respect for God. **blasphemer** *n.* person who swears. **blasphemous** ['blæsfəməs] *adj.* showing no respect for religion; anti-religious (talk). **blasphemy** *n.* disrespect for religion; swearing.

blast 1 [blɑːst] *n.* (a) sharp blowing of wind. (b) short whistle. c) going full b. = working at full power. (d) explosion; shock wave from an explosion. **blast 2** *v.* (a) to blow up. (b) to run. **blast furnace** *n.* furnace used to make steel. **blast off** *v.* (of rocket) to take off. **blast-off** *n.* departure of a rocket.

blatant ['bleɪtənt] *adj.* obvious/unmistakable. **blatantly** *adv.* obviously/unmistakably.

blaze 1 [bleɪz] *n.* (a) fierce fire; she worked like blazes = she worked extremely hard. (b) white mark made by cutting away the bark of a tree; white mark on the forehead of an animal. **blaze 2** *v.* (a) to burn fiercely. (b) to b. a trail = to mark a path by cutting the bark on trees/to be the first to do something. **blazing** *adj.* fiery; a b. row = a violent quarrel. **blazer** ['bleɪzə] *n.* jacket worn with a badge to show membership of a club/school.

blazon ['bleɪzn] *n.* coat of arms. **blazon 2** *v.* to proclaim (sth).

bleach 1 [bliːtʃ] *n.* substance which takes the colour out of something. **bleach 2** *v.* to take the colour out of sth. **bleachers** *n. pl.*Am. raised tiers of seats at a sports stadium.

bleak [bliːk] *adj.* (-es, -est) cold/inhospitable. **bleakly** *adv.* in a cold/inhospitable way.

bleary ['blɪərɪ] *adj.* water/dim (eyes). **bleary-eyed** *adj.* with watery eyes.

bleat 1 [bliːt] *n.* noise made by a sheep or goat. **bleat 2** *v.* to make a noise like a goat/sheep; what is he bleating about? = what does he keep on complaining about?

bleed 1 [bliːd] *n.* a nose b. = loss of blood from the nose. **bleed 2** *v.* (bled) to lose blood; my heart bleeds for you = I am very sorry for your.

bleep 1 [bliːp] *n.* small noise made by a radio/a radar screen. **bleep 2** *v.* (of a radio) to make a small noise. **bleeper** *n.* machine which makes a bleep.

blemish 1 ['blemɪʃ] *n.* (*pl.*-es) imperfection/mark. **blemish 2** *v.* to spoil.

blench [blenʃ] *v.* to tremble with fear.

blend 1 [blend] *n.* mixture (of coffee/tea/tobacco. **blend 2** *v.* to mix **blender** *n.* machine for mixing food.

bless [bles] *v.* to make sacred; to bring happiness/wealth to (s.o.); well I'm blessed! = I am surprised; *inf.* b. you! = phrase said when someone sneezes. **blessed** ['blesɪd] *adj.* (a) protected by God. (b) *inf.* cursed/annoying. **blessing** *n.* (a) thing which is useful/which brings happiness; it's a b. in disguise = it doesn't look like it, but it is very useful. (b) short prayer, esp. before or after a meal.

blether ['bleðə] *n.* silly talk.

blew [bluː] *v.* see blow.

blight 1 [blaɪt] *n.* fungiod disease (attacking vegetables/leaves etc). **blight 2** *v.* to spoil/to ruin. **blighter** *n. inf.* fellow/man.

blimp [blɪmp] *n.* small airship.

blind 1 [blaɪnd] *n.* (a) covering (over a window). Venetian b. = blind made of many horizontal flat strips of wood or plastic. (b) the b. = people who connot see. **blind 2** *adj.* not able to see; to turn a b. eye to sth = pretend not to notice; b. alley = (i) alley with no way out; (ii) position with no prospect of progress; b. spot = (i) part of the road which a motorist cannot see; (ii) thing which s.o. is incapable of understanding. **blind 3** *v.* to prevent s.o. from seeing; to make s.o. blind. **blind 4** *adv.* flying b. = flying an aircraft, using the instruments only. **blindfold 1** *n.* bandage put over

s.o.'s eyes to prevent him from seeing.
blindfold 2 *v.* to put a bandage over
s.o.'s eyes. **blindly** *adv.* without being
able to see. **blindness** *n.* not being
able to see.
blink 1 [blɪŋk] *n.* *inf.* on the b. = not
working properly. **blink 2** *v.* to close
your eyelids very quickly. **blinkers** *n.*
shades put on a horse's eyes to prevent it
from looking sideways.
blip [blɪp] *n.* small dot of light on a
radar screen.
bliss [blɪs] *n.* great happiness. **blissful**
adj. extremely happy. **blissfully** *adv.*
happily.
blister 1 ['blɪstə] *n.* bump on the skin
(with water underneath) made by
rubbing; b. pack = type of container,
where the product is covered by a stiff
plastic bubble. **blister 2** *v.* to make
bumps on the surface (of sth).
blithely ['blaɪðlɪ] *adv.* in a happy
carefree way.
blithering ['blɪðərɪʃ] *adj.* *inf.* awful.
blitz 1 [blɪts] *n.* (*pl.*-es) (a) bombing (of
a town). (b) *inf.* b. on sth = sudden
campaign to clear sth up. **blitz 2** *v.* to
bomb.
blizzard ['blɪzəd] *n.* heavy snowstorm
with strong winds.
bloated ['bləʊtɪd] *adj.* full; too fat.
bloater ['bləʊtə] *n.* dried salt herring.
blob [blɒb] *n.* large spot.
bloc [blɒk] *n.* (political) group.
block 1 [blɒk] *n.* (a) piece/lump of
stone or wood. (b) large building. *Am.*
he lives two blocks away = there are two
crossroads between here and his house.
(c) group; b. vote = vote by a group
voting together. (d) b. capitals/letters =
capital letters. (e) b. and tackle =
arrangement of pulleys and ropes for
lifting heavy objects. **block 2** *v.* to
prevent sth going past; the lorry blocked
the road for hours. **blockade 1**
[blɒ'keɪd] *n.* preventing supplies being
brought into a place. **blockage 2** *v.* to
prevent supplies being brought into a
place. **blockage** *n.* blocking. **block
up** *v.* to stop (a hole) to fill (a pipe).
bloke [bləʊk] *n.* *inf.* man.
blond, blonde [blɒnd] *adj. & n.* (man/
woman) with fair hair.
blood [blʌd] *n.* red liquid in the body;
b. group = type of blood a person has; b.

donor = person who gives blood to be
used in operations; b. pressure =
pressure at which the heart pumps blood;
b. transfusion = giving blood to a sick
person; it makes my b. boil = it makes
me very angry; his b. ran cold = he was
scared. **blood bank** *n.* place where
blood is stored until it is needed for
transfusions. **bloodbath** *n.* massacre.
bloodcurdling *adj.* very frightening.
bloodhound *n.* dog trained to follows
tracks. **bloodless** *adj.* with no blood;
b. revolution = revolution where no one
was killed. **bloodshed** *n.* killing.
bloodshot *adj.* red (eyes). **blood
sports** *n.* *pl.*sports which involve
killing animals. **bloodstain** *n.* stain
caused by blood. **bloodstained** *adj.*
stained with blood. **bloodstock** *n.*
race horses. **bloodstream** *n.* flow of
blood round the body. **bloodsucker** *n.*
animal which sucks your blood.
bloodtest *n.* test to show the
condition of the blood. **bloodthirsty**
adj. cruel/liking gory details. **blood
vessel** *n.* vein/artery which carries
blood **bloody** *adj.* (-ier, -iest) (a)
covered with blood; where much blood
has been shed;. (b) *Sl.* awful. **bloody-
mined** *adj.* *inf.* awkward/
uncooperative.
bloom 1 [bluːm] *n.* flower; the apple
trees are in full b. = all the apple flowers
are out. (b) velvety skin (of a peach);
dust (on skin of a grape). (c) b. of youth
= healthy glow of a young person. (d)
layer of algae on the surface of the water.
bloom 2 *v.* to flower/to flourish.
bloomer *n.* *inf.* mistake. (b) *inf.*
bloomers = wide knickers.
blossom 1 ['blɒsəm] *n.* flower (on
trees). **blossom 2** *v.* to flower.
blot 1 [blɒt] *n.* dirty spot; drop (of ink
on paper). **blot 2** *v.* (blotted) to drop a
spot (of ink) on sth; to dry the ink on a
letter.
blotter *n.* pad of blotting paper.
blotting paper *n.* thick absorbent
paper for drying ink.
blotto ['blɒtəʊ] *adj.* *inf.* drunk.
blotch [blɒtʃ] *n.* large patch of colour.
blotchy *adj.* (face) with patch of red.
blouse [blaʊz] *n.* (woman's) shirt.
blow 1 [bləʊ] *n.* knock/punch. **blow 2**
v. (blew[bləʊ]; has blown) to make air

move; (of air) to move; it's blowing hard = there is a strong wind; he blew his nose = he cleared his nose by blowing down t into a handkerchief; to b. a fuse = to burn out a fuse by overloading it. **blow away** v. to move (sth) away by blowing. **blow down** v. to fall down/to make (sth) fall down by blowing. **blow dry** v. (blow drying) to dry (s.o.'s hair) with a blower. **blow-dry** n. act of drying hair with a blower. **blower** b. (a) device which blows. (b) Sl. telephone. **blowfly** n. large blue-green fly that is attracted by meat. **blowlamp** n. lamp with strong gas jet for stripping old paint. **blow off** v. to go off/to make (sth) go off by blowing. **blow out** v. to go out/to make (sth) go out by blowing. **blowout** n. (a) inf. huge meal. (b) bursting (of a tyre). **blowover** v. (of storm) to end; to knock (sth) down by blowing. **blowpipe** n. pipe through which poison arrows can be blown. **blowtorch** n. blow lamp. **blow up** v. (a) to explode. (b) to destroy by explosives. (c) to fill (sth) with air. (d) to enlarge (a photograph). **blowy** adj. windy.

blowsy ['blaʊzɪ] adj. common, redfaced (woman).

blubber 1 ['blʌbə] n. fat (of a whale/seal). **blubber 2** v. to cry noisily.

bludgeon 1 ['blʌdʒən] n. large stick for hitting people. **bludgeon 2** v. to beat (s.o.) with a stick.

blue 1 [bluː] adj. (-er, -est) (a) coloured like the sky; b. baby = baby with blue skin caused by heart disease; once in a b. moon = very seldom. (b) pornographic b. movies. (c) sad. **blue 2** n. (a) colour like that of the sky; out of the b. = as a complete surprise. (b) blues = Black American folk music, the basis of jazz. **bluebell** n. common blue wild flower/wild hyacinth. **blueberry** n. Am. small blue berry; plant which bears this berry. **bluebottle** n. large blue-green fly that is attracted to meat. **blue chip (share)** n. share in a safe company. **blue collar worker** n. manual worker. **blue-eyed** adj. with blue eyes; blue eyed boy = favourite. **Blue laws** n. Am. laws which regulate what can be done on a Sunday. **blue-pencil** v. (-pencilled) to censure. **blueprint** n. detailed plan.

bluish adj. rather blue.

bluff 1 [blʌf] n. (a) steep rocky hill. (b) trick; to call s.o.'s b. = to claim (successfully) that s.o. is tricking/is lying. **bluff 2** adj. down-to-earth/straightforward (person). **bluff 3** v. to trick/to pretend. **bluffly** adv. in a straightforward way. **bluffness** n. being blunt/straightforward.

blunder 1 ['blʌndə] n. mistake. **blunder 2** v. (a) to make a mistake. (b) to b. into = to bump into. **blundering** adv. clumsy.

blunt 1 [blʌnt] adj. (a) not sharp. (b) straightforward/almost rude. **blunt 2** v. to make blunt. **bluntly** adv. frankly/almost rudely. **bluntness** n. being blunt.

blur 1 [blɜː] n. indistinct picture **blur 2** v. (blurred) to make indistinct.

blurb [nlɜːb] n. piece of publicity describing a book.

blurt [blɜːt] v. to let out (a secret).

blush 1 [blʌʃ] n. (pl.-es) red shade (on skin). **blush 2** v. to go red (with embarrassment).

bluster 1 ['blʌstə] n. swaggering talk; air to defiance. **bluster 2** v. to swagger/to show off. **blustery** adj. strong (wind/gale).

BMA [biːem'eɪ] British Medical Association.

boa ['bəʊə] n. b. constrictor = large tropical sake which kills animals by wrapping itself round them and squeezing them; feather b. = type of scarf make of feathery material.

boar [bɔː] n. male pig. usu. wild.

board 1 [bɔːd] n. (a) large flat piece of wood, etc.; ironing b. = narrow table for ironing. (b) food; b. and lodging = food and housing; full b. = bed and all meals (in a hotel). (c) group of people in charge of a business. (d) to go on b. = to go on to a ship/into an aircraft. **board 2** v. (a) to go on to a ship/bus), into (an aircraft). **boarder** n. child who lives at school. **boarding** adj. (a) b. card = card which allows you to go into an aircraft. (b) b. house = house where you pay to lodge; b. school = school where the children live during term.

boardroom n. room where a board of directors meets. **board up** v. to cover (windows/doors) with boards to prevent

burglars getting into an empty house.
boast 1 [bəʊst] n. act of boasting.
boast 2 v. (a) (of/about) to talk about how clever/strong/handsome, etc., you are. (b) to possess (sth), and be proud. **boaster** n. person who is always boasting. **boastful** adj. very proud; always boasting.
boat [bəʊt] n. ship; b. train = train which connects with a boat; we're all in the same b. = we're all in equal circumstances. **boater** n. flat straw hat. **boathouse** n. shed for rowing boats. **boating** n. rowing (for pleasure). **boatman** n. (pl.= men) man in charge of boats. **boatswain** ['bəʊsn] n. (at sea) man in charge of the boats and sails.
bob 1 [bɒb] n. (a) little curtsy. (b) hair tied in a knot. **bob 2** v. (bobbed) (to move quickly up and down).
bobbin ['bɒbɪn] n. small reel for holding thread (for a sewing machine/a spinning machine).
bobble [bɒbl] n. little fluffy ball; b. hat = woolly hat with a fluffy ball.
bobby ['bɒbɪ] n. inf. policeman. **bobby-pin** n. Am. flat hairpin. **bobby-socks** n. pl.Am. girls' ankle socks.
bobsleigh ['bɒbsleɪ] n. sledge with two runners, used for racing.
bode [bəʊd] v. it bodes ill = it promises to bring ruin.
bodgie ['bɒdʒɪ] n. (in Australia) hooligan.
bodice ['bɒdɪs] n. top part (of a dress)
bodkin ['bɒdkɪn] n. large thick needle used for threading tape or elastic.
body ['bɒdɪ] n. (pl.-ies) (a) main structure of an animal or person; main part of an animal or person not including the head and limbs; dead b. = corpse. (b) group of people. (c) main part (of a building/a car, etc.). (d) strength (of wine). **bodily 1** adj. of the body; to cause s.o. grievous b. harm = to attack s.o. and beat him up. **bodily 2** adv. they carried him out b. = they lifted him up and carried him. **bodyguard** n. person or ground of people who guards s.o. **bodywork** n. outer covering of a car.
boffin ['bɒfɪn] n. inf. scientist/inventor.
bog 1 [bɒg] n. (a) area of marshland. (b) Sl. toilet. **bog 2** v. (bogged) to get bogged down = to get stuck (in mud);

the discussion got bogged down in details = they got stuck in details.
boggy adj. marshy.
bogey ['bəʊgɪ] n. (a) (also bogeyman) thing which frightens children. (b) (in golf) normal number of strokes which a player should take to play a hole.
boggle ['bɒgl] v. to be reluctant (at = to do sth); the mind boggles = it is impossible to imagine.
bogie ['bəʊgɪ] n. pivoted set of wheels on a railway carriage.
bogus ['bəʊgəs] adj. false.
bohemian [bəʊ'hi:mɪən] adj. & n. (person) living a wild/unconventional life.
boil 1 [bɔɪl] n. (a) swelling in the body full of infected matter. (b) the kettle is one the b. = the water is boiling; bring the water to the b. = make the water boil.
boil 2 v. (a) to heat (a liquid) until it bubbles. (b) to cook in boiling water; hard-boiled egg = egg which has been cooked until it is solid (usu. eaten cold).
boil away v. to evaporate (through boiling). **boil down** v. (a) to evaporate (through boiling); to reduce (a piece of writing). (b) to be reduced to; it all boils down to whether he will resign willingly or not = the main question is, will he resign willingly or not. **boiler** n. large metal receptacle for boiling water; main heater for central heating. b. suit = blue overalls. **boiling 1** n. action of heating a liquid until it bubbles; 100°C is the b. point of water. **boiling 2** adj. which is boiling or very hot; it is b. in this room = it is very hot. **boiling 3** adv. b. hot = very bot. **boil over** v. to rise in a pan when boiling, and run over the sides.
boisterous ['bɔɪstrəs] adj. noisy/violent (crowd/wind/sea, etc.). **boisterously** adv. in a boisterous way. **boisterousness** n. noise/violence.
bold [bəʊld] adj. (-er, -est) (a) strongly marked (colour/outline). (b) daring/brave. **boldly** adv. bravely/defiantly. **boldness** n. daring/bravery.
bole [bəʊl] n. tree trunk.
bolero [bə'leərəʊ] n. (a) type of Spanish dance. (b) ['bɒlərəʊ] short sleeveless jacket worn by women.
boll [bɒl] n. seed head of the cotton plant.
bollard ['bɒlɑːd] n. low post on a quay

for a ship's rope, or in the road to indicate where traffics should go.
bolshie ['bɒlʃɪ] *adj. inf.* difficult/ uncooperative (person).
bolster 1 ['bəʊlstə] *n.* long pillow going right across a bed. **bolster 2** *v.* (also to bolster up) to support (s.o. who is falling).
bolt 1 [bəʊlt] *n.* (a) flash of lightning with thunder; it came as a b. from the blue = it came as a complete surprise. (b) metal rod which slides into a hole to secure a door. (c) metal rod with a screw which fastens with a nut. (d) to make a b. for = to rush towards. **bolt 2** *v.* (a) to run fast/to escape; the horse bolted = the horse got out of control. (b) to eat quickly and with big mouthfuls. (c) to fasten (a door) with a bolt. (d) to fasten with a bolt and nut. **bolt 3** *adv.* sitting b. upright = sitting straight upright.
bomb 1 [bɒm] *n.* (a) large explosive weapon, often dropped from an aircraft; b. disposal = removing the fuse from an unexploded bomb. it went like a b. = it went very well indeed. (b) (in Australia) old car. (c) *inf.* lot of money. **bomb 2** *v.* to drop bombs on. **bombard** [bɒm'bɑːd] *v.* to attack (repeatedly). **bombardment** *n.* attack (with bombs/ shells/questions). **bomber** *n.* special aircraft for dropping bombs. **bombshell** *n.* great (unpleasant) surprise.
bombastic [bɒm'bæstɪk] *adj.* flowery/ boasting (way of speaking).
bona fide 1 ['bəʊnə'faɪdɪ] *adj.* made in good faith; a bona fide offer. **bona fide 2** *n.* the police are checking on his bona fides = they are checking that he is speaking the truth.
bonanza [bə'nænzə] *n.* great wealth (discovered suddenly).
bond 1 [bɒnd] *n.* (a) link; joining together. (b) paper showing that money has been lent to the government; premium bonds = bonds which are eligible to win in a lottery. (c) contract. (d) in b. = in a customs warehouse. **bond 2** *v.* to link/to join (with glue). **bondage** *n.* slavery. **bonded warehouse** *n.* warehouse containing goods in bond.
bone 1 [bəʊn] *n.* one of the solid white pieces which make up the framework of the body; b. dry = completely dry; b. idle = completely lazy; I've got a b. to pick

with you = I want to complain about sth which you've done. **bone 2** *v.* to take the bones out of (meat fish). **boneless** *adj.* with no bone **bony** *adj.* with big bones; with many bones.
bonfire ['bɒnfaɪə] *n.* outdoor fire for burning rubbish or as a celebration.
bongo ['bɒngəʊ] *n.* small drum, tapped with the hand.
bonkers ['bɒŋkez] *adj. Sl.* mad.
bonnet ['bɒnɪt] *n.* (a) child's/woman's hat; with a brim framing the face. (b) hinged cover for the front part of a car.
bonny ['bɒnɪ] *adj.* (-ier, -iest) good-looking and healthy.
bonsai ['bɒnsaɪ] *n.* (art of growing) trees in small pots, pruned so that they remain small.
bonus ['bəʊnəs] *n.* (*pl.*-es) extra money; cost-of living b. = extra pay to compensate for the increased cost of living; (on motor insurance) no claim b. = reduced payment if you have never made a claim.
boo 1 [buː] *in.ter.* call to show disapproval or to surprise. **boo 2** *v.* to show disapproval by saying 'boo'.
boob [buːb] *n. Sl.* (a) mistake. (b) breast.
booby ['buːbɪ] *n.* silly person. **booby prize** *n.* (silly) prize given to the last person in a competition. **boobytrap 1** *n.* trap to catch s.o. unaware.
boobytrap 2 *v.* (boobytrapped) to set a trap (in a place).
book 1 [bʊk] *n.* (a) printed pages attached together with a cover. (b) exercise b. = book of blank pages with lines for writing on; cheque b. = book of blank cheques; I'm in his bad books = he disapproves of me. (c) script (of musical). (d) b. of tickets = several tickets fastened together and sold as a unit; b. of matches = cardboard matches fastened together in a card holder. **book 2** *v.* (a) to reserve (a place/seat/table) on plane/in theatre/in restaurant. (b) he was booked for speeding = the police have made a charge against him for speeding.
bookable *adj.* which can be reserved in advance. **bookbinder** *n.* person who puts covers on printed sheets to make a book. **bookbinding** *n.* art of binding books. **bookcase** *n.* cabinet/ set of shelves for keeping books. **bookie**

n. inf. person who collects bets before a race. **book in** *v.* to register (at a hotel). **booking** *n.* (a) reservation (of seat/place); b. office = office (at theatre) where you can book seats in advance. (b) arrangement (for actor, etc.) to appear at a theatre. **bookish** *adj.* learned/studious. **book-keeper** *n.* person who works in the accounts department (in a firm). **book-keeping** *n.* keeping of accounts. **booklet** *n.* small book with only a few pages. **booklover** *n.* person who loves (and collects) books. **bookmaker** *n.* person who collects bets before a race. **bookmark(er)** *n.* long, narrow, piece of card/cloth/leather used to keep your place in a book. **bookmobile** ['bʊkməbiːl] *n.* travelling library. **bookseller** *n.* person who sells books. **bookshelf** *n.* shelf for keeping books. **bookshop** *n.* shop selling books. **bookstall, bookstand** *n.* kiosk (in railway station, etc.) selling books and magazines. **bookstore** *n. Am.* bookshop. **book trade** *n.* the book producing and selling industry. **book up** *v.* to reserve. **bookworm** *n.* person who reads many books.

boom 1 [buːm] *n.* (a) floating barrier across a harbour. (b) long rod attached to the lower edge of a sail; long rod (for holding a microphone over speakers' heads). (c) low muffled sound. (d) sudden increase (in value/sales/general prosperity). **boom 2** *v.* (a) to make a low muffled sound. (b) to increase suddenly/to become more prosperous.

boomerang ['buːməræŋ] *n.* curved piece of wood which, when thrown comes back to the thrower. **boomerang 2** *v.* to backfire/to rebound.

boon 1 [buːn] *n.* advantage/blessing. **boon 2** *adj.* b. companion = great friend.

boor [bɔː, 'bʊə] *n.* rough/uncouth man. **boorish** *adj.* rude/uncouth.

boost 1 *n.* help/publicity. **boost 2** *v.* to help/to promote. (b) to increase (voltage in electricity cable).

booster *n.* (a) apparatus for increasing voltage. (b) b. rocket = rocket which helps keep up the speed of the main rocket. b. shot = injection which keeps up the protection given by a former injection.

boot 1 [buːt] *n.* (a) footwear which goes above the ankle; the b. is on the other foot = the situation is just the opposite. (b) back part of a car (where the luggage can be put). **boot 2** *v.* (a) to kick. (b) (computers) to carry out a set of instructions automatically. **bootee** *n.* small knitted boot for babies. **bootlaces** *n. pl.* very long laces for boots **bootleg** *adj.* illegal (whisky, etc). **bootlegger** *n.* person who makes/transports illegal spirits.

booth [buːð] *n.* (a) (covered) stall at a market/fair. (b) small enclosed space for one person.

booty ['buːtɪ] *n.* treasure captured in a war.

booze 1 [buːz] *n. inf.* alcoholic drink. **booze 2** *inf.* to drink (alcohol). **boozer** *n. inf.* (a) person who drinks a lot. (b) bar/public house.

boracic [bə'ræsɪk] *adj.* chemical substance used in ointments.

borax ['bɔːræks] *n.* white powder used in making glass and as an antiseptic.

Bordeaux mixture ['bɔːdəʊ'mɪkstʃə] *n.* sulphur spray, used on plants.

border 1 ['bɔːdə] *n.* frontier/edge; flower b. = edging of flowers along a flower bed. **border 2** *v.* France borders on Germany = France touches Germany; it is a film which borders on the indecent = which is almost indecent. **bordering** *adj.* close to **borderline** *n.* line between two surfaces; b. case = case which is on the dividing line (between two types).

bore 1 [bɔː] *n.* (a) width of a tube. (b) person/thing which makes you fed up; what a b. = what a nuisance. (c) wave in a river caused by the tide. **bore 2** *v.* (a) to make (a hole). (b) to make (s.o.) fed up (with you); I'm bored stiff = very bored. (c) see also **bear**. **boredom** *n.* being bored. **borehole** *n.* exploratory hole made to see if there are any mineral/oil deposits in the ground. **boring** *adj.* which makes you lose interest completely.

born [bɔːn] *adj.* he was b. in 1962 = his birth took place in 1962; she's a b. actress = she has always had a gift for acting; I wasn't b. yesterday = I'm not as stupid as you think.

borne [bɔːn] *v.* see **bear**.

boron ['bɔːrɒn] n. (element: B) brown powder which resists high temperatures and is used to make borax.

borough ['bʌrə] n. large town (with a governing council).

borrow ['bɒrəʊ] v. to take (sth) for a short time with the owner's permission; to take (money) from a bank, etc. for a time, usu. paying interest on it. **borrower** n. person who borrows (money, etc.). **borrowing** n. (a) act of borrowing money. (b) money borrowed.

borzoi ['bɔːˈzɔɪ] n. breed of long-haired hound.

bosom ['bʊzəm] n. breast; b. companion = close friend.

boss 1 [bɒs] n. (pl.-es) inf. (a) person who is in charge. (b) round knob. **boss 2** v. inf. to command/to give order; she bosses him around = she is always telling him what to do. **boss-eyed** adj. Sl. squinting. **bossiness** n. being bossy. **bossy** adj. (-ier, -iest) (person) always giving order.

bosun ['bəʊsn] n. (at sea) man in charge of the boats and sails.

botany ['bɒtənɪ] n. study of plants. **botanical** [bə'tænɪkl] adj. relating to plants; b. gardens = gardens scientifically arranged to show different species of plants. **botanist** ['bɒtənɪst] n. person who studies plants.

botch [bɒtʃ] v. to ruin/to make a mess of (a job).

both 1 [bəʊθ] adj. & pron. two persons/objects together. **both 2** adv. at the same time.

bother 1 ['bɒðə] n. worry/annoyance. **bother 2** v. (a) to annoy (s.o.). (b) to take trouble (to do sth). **bothered** adj. worried/embarrassed.

bottle 1 ['bɒtl] n. (a) tall glass/plastic container for liquids; hot water b. = container for hot water which is used for warming beds. (b) (slang) courage. **bottle 2** v. to put into a bottle; bottled fruit = fruit preserved in sealed jars. **bottle bank** n. public container for old bottles. **bottle-feeding** n. feeding of babies by a bottle, not at the breast. **bottleneck** n. (a) narrow part of a bottle. (b) narrow road (where traffic often gets jammed). **bottle up** v. (a) to hold back (one's feelings). (b) to jam (traffic). **bottling** n. putting into

bottles, esp. preserving fruit in sealed jars.

bottom 1 ['bɒtəm] n. (a) lowest part; base; prices have touched rock b. = they are at their lowest; he came b. of the class = he had the worst marks. (b) buttocks. **bottom 2** adj. lowest. **bottomless** adj. with no bottom. **bottomry** n. mortgage of a ship.

botulism ['bɒtjʊlɪzəm] n. illness caused by bacteria in food.

bouclé ['buːkleɪ] n. wool with many loops in it.

boudoir ['buːdwɑː] n. small private room for a woman.

bouffant ['buːfɒn] adj. fluffy (hairstyle).

bougainvillea [buːgən'vɪlɪə] n. tropical climbing plant with purple of pink flowers.

bough [baʊ] n. large branch.

bought [bɔːt] v. see buy.

boulder ['bəʊldə] n. large rock.

boulevard ['buːləvɑːd] n. wide road.

bounce 1 [baʊns] n. (a) springiness; the bed has a lot of b. in t. (b) he's got a lot of b. = he is full of energy. **bounce 2** v. (a) to spring up and down; to make (sth) spring up and down; the ball bounced down the stairs. (b) inf. his cheque bounced = there was not enough money in the account to pay the sum on the cheque. **bouncer** n. (a) (in cricket) ball which bounces very high. (b) person who throws undesirable customers out of a restaurant/club, etc. **bouncing** adj. (ball) which bounces; b. baby = healthy-looking baby. **bouncy** adj. (a) which bounces well. (b) (person) who is full of energy.

bound 1 [baʊnd] n. leap. **bound 2** adj. (a) b. for South America = leaving for/on the way to South America; homeward b. = on the way home. (b) tied up. (c) obliged. (d) very likely; they are b. to be late. (e) see also bind. **bound 3** v. to leap. **bounden** adj. b. duty = obligation. **boundless** adj. without any limits. **bounds** n. limits/edges; out of b. = (place) where people are not allowed to go. **boundary** ['baʊndrɪ] n. frontier/outer limit of sth; (in cricket) to his a b. = to hit the ball beyond the edge of the field.

bounty ['baʊntɪ] n. (a) giving (of

money). (b) money given as a reward or in excess of usual wages. **bountiful** *adj.* generous.

bouquet [bʊˈkeɪ] *n.* artistically arranged bunch of flowers.

bourbon [ˈbɔːbən] *n. Am.* corn whisky.

bourgeois [ˈbʊəʒwɑː] *adj. & n.* middleclass (person).

bourgeoisie [bʊəʒwɑːˈziː] *n.* the middle class.

bout [baʊt] *n.* (a) sports contest. (b) attack (of illness).

boutique [buːˈtiːk] *n.* small shops selling fashionable clothes/perfume, etc.; small clothing department in a large store.

bovine [ˈbəʊvaɪn] *adj.* referring to cows and bulls; b. spongiform encephalopaty = disease of cattle, which affects the brain, and is possibly connected to scrapie.

bow [ˈbəʊ] *n.* (a) long piece of wood with taut string joining both ends, used for shooting arrows. (b) wooden rod with hair stretched taut between its ends, used for playing a violin or other stringed instrument. (c) ribbon/tie knotted to look like a butterfly. **bow-legged** *adj.* with legs which curve apart at the knee. **bow tie** *n.* short necktie tied in bow. **bow window** *n.* window projecting out from the wall in a curve. **bow2 1** [ˈbəʊ] *n.* (a) salute made by bending the body forward. (b) (*usu.* bows) front part of a ship. (c) rower who sits nearest the bow of a rowing boat. **bow2 2** *v.* to bend forward. **bowsprit** *n.* horizontal mast going forward from the bows of a ship.

bowdlerize [ˈbaʊdləraɪz] *v.* to cut indecent part from (a book).

bowels (sometimes bowel) [ˈbaʊəlz] *n.* intestines; in the b. of the earth = deep underground.

bower [ˈbaʊə] *n.* shelter covered by trees or plants.

bowl 1 [ˈbəʊl] *n.* (a) wide container (of china/plastic, etc.). (b) wooden ball for playing game of bowls. (c) bowls - game where wooden balls are rolled to try to get nearest to small target ball. **bowl 2** *v.* (a) throw a ball, esp. in cricket. (b) to roll a bowl. (in a game of bowls).

bowler *n.* (a) person who plays bowls. (b) (in cricket) person who throws the ball to the opposing batsman. (c) b. (hat) = black round-topped man's hat.

bowling *n.* (a) game of bowls; b. green = grass pitch for playing bowls. (b) game of knocking down skittles with a large ball; b. alley = hall for bowling. **bowl over** *v.* to knock down/to surprise.

box 1 [bɒks] *n.* (*pl.*-es) (a) container with a lid; letter b.,/pillar b. = box in the street for posting letters; letter b. = slit in a door for delivering letters or newspapers; b. number = number of a box in the post office/newspaper office where letters will be kept for you and delivered in bulk. (b) evergreen tree, with very small leaves; hard wood from this tree. (c) small balcony room in a theatre; cubicle for a horse; place where a witness gives evidence in court. (d) smack (on the ear). **box 2** *v.* (a) to b. s.o.'s ears = to smack s.o. on the ears. (b) to fight an opponent in the boxing ring.

boxer *n.* (a) man who practises the sport of boxing. (b) breed of large dog with short hair. **boxing** *n.* sport of fighting with gloves in a ring; B. Day = day after Christmas Day, 26th December. **box office** *n.* office in a theatre where you buy tickets. **boxroom** *n.* small room for keeping boxes, cases, unused objects. **box spanner** *n.* spanner with a ring-shaped end which fits over nuts.

boy [bɔɪ] *n.* male child; old b. = old friend/old man/former pupil of a school. **boyfriend** *n.* young male friend. **boyhood** *n.* youth/time of life when you are a boy. **boyish** *adj.* like a boy, **Boy Scouts** *n.* social/educational organization for boys.

boycott 1 [ˈbɔɪkɒt] *n.* act of boycotting. **boycott 2** *v.* to refuse to have anything to do with s.o./sth.

BP [biːˈpiː] British Pharmacopœia; British Petroleum.

BR [biːˈɑː] British Rail.

bra [brɑː] *n. inf.* brassiere/woman's undergarment for supporting the breasts.

brace 1 [breɪs] *n.* (a) support; (on teeth) metal clamp to make teeth grow straight. (b) braces = elastics straps over the shoulders to hold up trousers. (c) pair; a b. of grouse = two grouse. (d) tool for holding a bit to drill holes. **brace 2** *v.* to support/to strengthen; he braced himself for the ordeal = he stiffened his muscles to prepare himself for the

ordeal. **bracing** *adj.* invigorating/
healthy (climate).

bracelet ['breislət] *n.* ornamental
chain/band worn round the wrist.

bracken ['brækən] *n.* wild fern
growing often in open country.

bracket 1 ['brækɪt] *n.* (a) support (for
shelf, etc. against a wall). (b) printing
symbol showing that sth is separated
from the rest of the text. (c)
(administrative) group; the middle-
income b. **bracket 2** *v.* (a) to put
(words) into brackets. (b) to link; his
name was bracketed with that of the
major.

brackish ['brækɪʃ] *adj.* salty/
undrinkable water.

bract [brækt] *n.* part of a plant which is
shaped like a leaf but can be coloured
like a flower.

brad [bræd] *n.* small nail with a flat
head.

bradawl ['brædɔːl] *n.* boring tool for
making holes (esp. in leather).

brag [bræg] *v.* (bragged) to boast.

Brahmin ['brɑːmɪn] *n.* highest-ranking
Hindu; *Am.* very important person (esp.
in the civil service).

braid 1 [breɪd] *n.* plaited decoration.
braid 2 *v.* to plait (hair) with ribbon.

braille [breɪl] *n.* system of raised dots
on paper for the blind to read by touch.

brain 1 [breɪn] *n.* nervous centre of the
head which thinks and directs they body;
use your b. = think hard; she's got brains
= she's intelligent; *inf.* b. drain =
departure of highly intelligent people to
other countries in order to work for
higher salaries. **brain 2** *v.* to knock s.o.
out by hitting him on the head.

brainchild *n.* original idea/plan
thought up by s.o. **braininess** *n.*
intelligence. **brainless** *adj.* idiotic/
stupid. **brainpower** *n.* intelligence/
ability to think or reason. **brainstorm**
n. sudden mad idea. **brainwash** *v.* to
indoctrinate (s.o.) to make s.o. think in a
totally different manner than before.

brainwave *n.* brilliant idea **brainy**
adj. (-ier, -iest) *inf.* intelligent.

braise [breɪz] *v.* to cook (meat/
vegetables) in a covered pot with very
little liquid.

brake 1 [breɪk] *n.* mechanism for
stopping a car/bicycle, etc.; hand b. =

brake operated by a hand lever. **brake 2**
v. to stop/to slow down by applying the
brakes. **braking** *n.* putting on the
brakes; b. distance = distance a car
travels after the brakes are applied before
it comes to a halt.

bramble ['bræmbl] *n.* wild blackberry.

bran [bræn] *n.* skins of wheat seeds
which are separated from the flour.

branch 1 [brɑːntʃ] *n.* (*pl.*-es) (a) limb
of a tree. (b) offshoot; b. of a river; b.
line = minor railway line. (c) office (of a
bank, etc.); store (of a chain of stores).

branch 2 *v.* to b. out = to spread out/to
diversify.

brand 1 [brænd] *n.* (a) identification
mark made (on cattle) by a hot iron. (b)
named product made by one
manufacturer. **brand 2** *v.* (a) to mark
(cattle) with a hot iron. (b) he was
branded as a thief = he was called a
thief. **branded** *adj.* (a) marked (cattle,
etc.). (b) (goods) with a brand name.

brand name *n.* name applied to one
product. **brand-new** *adj.* completely
new.

brandish ['brændɪʃ] *v.* to wave (sth)
about.

brandy ['brændɪ] *n.* strong alcohol
distilled from wine; glass of this alcohol;
b. snap = thin rolled biscuit flavoured
with ginger.

brash [bræʃ] *adj.* vulgar, pushing.

brass [brɑːs] *n.* (a) yellow metal made
from copper and zinc; to b. = directors/
high ranking officers; to get down to b.
tacks = to discuss the basic problem. (b)
musical instruments made of brass; a. b.
band. (c) *inf.* money (d) (in church)
memorial plate made of brass. **brass
rubbing** *n.* reproduction of a brass
plate by covering it with paper and
rubbing with wax. **brassy** *adj.* (a)
(noise) like that of brass instruments. (b)
rude, loud-mouthed (person).

brassicas ['bræsɪkəz] *n. pl.* plants of
the cabbage family.

brassiere ['bræzɪə] *n.* woman's
undergarment for supporting the breasts.

brat [bræt] *n.* rude child.

bravado [beə'cɑːdəʊ] *n.* reckless
bravery.

brave 1 [breɪv] *adj.* (-er, -est) not
afraid; courageous. **brave 2** *v.* to defy.
brave 3 *n.* male American Indian

fighter. **bravely** *adv.* with courage.
bravery *n.* courage. **bravo** [brɑːˈvəʊ]
inter showing approval.
brawl 1 [beɔːl] *n.* wild fight. **brawl 2**
v. to fight wildly. **brawler** *n.* person
who is fighting wildly.
brawn [brɔːn] *n.* (a) chopped meat
mixed with jelly to form a loaf. (b)
muscle power. **brawny** *adj.* muscular/
strong.
bray [breɪ] *v.* to make a loud call like a
donkey.
brazen 1 [ˈbreɪzn] *adj.* (a) like brass/
made of brass. (b) shameless. **brazen 2**
v. he brazened it out = he impudently
got through the awkward situation.
brazier [ˈbreɪzɪə] *n.* metal basket for
burning coal.
Brazilian 1 [brəˈzɪlɪən] *adj.* referring to
Brazil. **Brazilian 2** *n.* person from
Brazil.
breach 1 [briːtʃ] *n.* (*pl.*-es) (a) crack (in
a defence/dam). (d) breaking (of a law/
promise); b. of the peace = rowdy action;
b. of faith = going back on what has been
promised; b. of promise = refusing to
marry s.o. after having promised to do
so. **breach 2** *v.* to split; to make a
crack in (a wall).
bread [bred] *n.* (no. *pl.*) food made
from flour, water and yeast backed in an
oven; wholemeal b. = bread made from
flour which contains the whole grain;
bread-and-butter letter = letter written to
say thank you for hospitality; b. bin =
metal/plastic container for keeping bread
fresh. **breadcrumbs** *n. pl.* bread
broken up into very small pieces.
breadline *n.* he's on the b. = he has
hardly enough money to live on.
breadwinner *n.* person who earns
money to feed the family.
breadth [bredθ] *n.* (a) measurement of
how broad or wide sth is. (b) wideness
(of views).
break 1 [breɪk] *n.* (a) split/crack (where
two parts have broken). (b) quarrel. (c) b.
in the weather = change in the weather.
(d) rest period; coffee b. = period where
you stop work for a cup of coffee;
morning b. = short period of play during
the morning at school. (e) he had a lucky
b. = his bad luck changed. (f) at b. of day
= at dawn. (g) series of shorts in snooker.
break 2 *v.* (broke; has broken) (a) to

fall to pieces/to smash (sth) into pieces;
we'll b. our journey at Edinburgh = we'll
stop for a while at Edinburgh; my watch is
broken = my watch has stopped working;
it broke her heart = she was extremely
upset; he broke the record for the high
jump = did better then anyone had ever
done before. (b) we are breaking even =
we are not making a loss or a profit. (c)
not to keep (a promise/a rule). (d) the
storm broke = storm suddenly started;
the day was braking = daylight was
coming. (e) (of boy's voice) to become
deeper as the boy grows older. (f) to
cushion (a fall). (g) (of wave) to grow tall
and crash down. **breakable** *adj.* which
can easily be broken. **breakables** *n.*
*pl.*fragile objects (glasses/cups, etc.).
breakages *n. pl.*braking (of glass,
etc.); things which have been broken.
break away *v.* to escape/to be
detached (from). **breakaway** *adj.*
which has become detached; the b.
nationalist party = the nationalist party
which has split off from a larger party.
break down *v.* (a) to smash (sth). (b)
to collapse / to go wrong. (c) to list
(items). **breakdown** *n.* (a) collapse;
nervous b. = state where you become
severely depressed. (b) list under various
headings. (c) we had a b. on the
motorway = our car stopped working; b.
truck = truck which tows away cars
which do not work. **breaker** *n.* (a) big
wave which is breaking. (b) person who
buys old cars, etc., to take them to bits
and sell the parts. **breakfast 1**
[ˈbrekfəst] *n.* first meal of the day; b.
cup = large cup; wedding b. = meal
(often lunch) after a wedding;
continental b. = breakfast of bread and
coffee. English b. = breakfast with
cereals, bacon and eggs, toast and coffee
or tea. **breakfast 2** *v.* to eat the first
meal of the day. **break in** *v.* (a) to
smash in. (b) to interrupt. (c) to train (a
horse). **break-in** *n.* burglary.
breaking *n.* (a) action of smashing/
falling to pieces. (b) b. and entering =
crime of breaking into s.o.'s property.
break into *v.* to smash in order to
enter. **break loose** *v.* to escape.
breakneck *adj.* at b. speed =
extremely fast. **break off** *v.* (a) to split
away/to crack; to remove (sth) by

breaking. (b) to stop; they have broken of negotiations. **break open** v. to smash (in order to open). **break out** v. (a) to start; war has broken out. (b) to escape; three prisoners broke out from prison. **breakout** n. escape. **break through** v. to smash in order to go through. **breakthrough** n. sudden success (in science). **break up** v. (a) to smash to pieces; break it up! = stop fighting; they had a quarrel and broke up = did not work/live together any more. (b) to go on holiday; school breaks up on Tuesday. (c) (of weather) to get worse. **breakup** n. coming to pieces/falling apart.

breakwater n. wall/fence going into the sea to prevent waves from battering the coast.

bream [bri:m] n. (pl.bream) type on fat edible fish.

breast [brest] n. (a) one of two milk giving organs in a woman's body; b. feeding = feeding a child with milk from the breast. (b) chest/front part of the top of the body; b. pocket = pocket on the front of a jacket; b. stroke = swimming stroke where both arms stretch out together and are brought back to the chest.

breath [breθ] n. air which goes into and out of the body; out of b./gasping for b. = having difficulty in breathing; don't waste your b. on them = don't waste time talking to them; it took my b. away = I was completely astonished; he muttered under his b. = quietly; a b. of wind = a slight breeze. **breathalyse** ['breθəvaɪz] v. to test (a driver) to see if he is drunk. **breathalyser** n. instrument for testing if a driver has drunk to much alcohol. **breathless** adj. out of breath/panting. **breathlessly** adv. in a rush/without taking time to breath. **breathtaking** adj. so exciting/beautiful that it takes your breath away.

breathe [bri:ð] v. to suck air in or out through the nose or mouth; b. deeply = take in lots of air; don't b. a word about it! = don't say anything about it.

breather n. rest period; I'm going out for a b. = I'm going out to get fresh air.

breathing n. act of taking air in an out of the body; b. apparatus = mask, etc., which allows your to breathe when in gas/smoke, etc.; b. space = rest period.

bred [bred] v. see breed.

breech [bri:tʃ] n. (pl.-es) (a) back part of a gun where the ammunition is loaded. (b) b. birth = birth in which the baby's buttocks appear first. (c) breeches = trousers which come down to below the knees; breeches buoy = device, like a canvas seat. used to rescue people at sea.

breed 1 [bri:d] n. particular race of animal **breed 2** v. to produce young animals/plants; I was born and bread in the country = I was born and grew up in the country; well-bred person = s.o. who is polite/who has been well educated.

breeder n. (a) person who breeds (animals). (b) (fast) b. reactor = nuclear machine which makes a surplus of nuclear material. **breeding** n. (a) production of animals. (b) training in good manners.

breeze 1 [bri:z] n. slight wind; a stiff breeze = quite a strong wind. **breeze 2** v. he breezed into the restaurant = he rushed in looking very pleased with himself. **breeze-block** n. light building block used for building inside walls. **breezily** adv. in a happy-go-lucky way. **breezy** adj. (a) windy. (b) happy-go-lucky.

brethren ['breðrən] n. pl.(religious) brothers.

breve [bri:v] n. long note in music.

breviary ['bri:vjərɪ] n. book of Roman Catholic prayers.

brevity ['brevɪtɪ] n. conciseness/shortness.

brew 1 [bru:] n. liquid which has been brewed. **brew 2** v. (a) to make (beer/tea). (b) there's trouble brewing = there is trouble coming. **brewer** n. person who makes beer; brewer's yeast = yeast used in brewing beer, and taken in tablet form as a source of vitamin B. **brewery** n. place where beer is made.

briar ['braɪə] n. prickly wild bush (esp. rose) **briar pipe** n. pipe made from briar wood.

bribe 1 [braɪb] n. money given illegally to s.o. to get sth done. **bribe 2** v. to give (s.o.) money illegally to get sth done. **bribery** n. act of bribing.

bric-à-brac ['brɪkəbræk] n. (no. pl.) ornaments or furniture of little value.

brick [brɪk] n. block of baked clay, used for building; he dropped a. b. = he made

an unfortunate remark by mistake.
brick-built *adj.* built of bricks.
bricklayer *n.* person who builds with bricks. **brick up** *v.* to fill in (window/doorway) with bricks. **brickwork** *n.* bricks built up a wall. **brickworks** *n.* factory where bricks are made.
bride [braɪd] *n.* woman who is about to get married or who has just got married. **bridal** *adj.* referring to a wedding. **bridegroom** *n.* man who is about to get married or who has just got married. **bridesmaid** *n.* unmarried woman who is the bride's attendant at a wedding.
bridge 1 [brɪdʒ] *n.* (a) construction to take a road/railway across a river/road/railway line. (b) top part of a ship where a captain stands. (c) top of the nose. (d) (in a violin) support for the strings. (e) type of card game for four people.
bridge 2 *v.* to build a bridge across (a river, etc.). **bridgehead** *n.* preliminary position held by attackers who have attacked across water. **bridge roll** *n.* small long soft roll of white bread. **bridging loan** *n.* short-term loan, esp. one to help s.o. buy a house before he has sold his old one.
bridle 1 [braɪdl] *n.* headstraps (for a horse). **bridle 2** *v.* (a) to hold back (a horse). (b) to take offence. **bridlepath**, **bridleway** *n.* path for horseriders.
brief 1 [briːf] *adj.* short. **brief 2** *n.* (a) paper concerning a legal case. (b) instruction. (c) briefs = short knickers/underpants. **brief 3** *v.* to give a case to (a lawyer); to give (s.o.) information/instructions. **briefcase** *n.* small case for carrying papers. **briefing** *n.* conference where information is given. **briefly** *adv.* short/speaking for a short time
brigade [brɪˈgeɪd] *n.* (a) army group smaller than a division. (b) fire b. = group of people whose job is to fight fires. **brigadier** [brɪgəˈdɪə] *n.* army officer in charge of a brigade, rank in the army above colonel.
brigand [ˈbrɪgənd] *n.* robber.
bright [braɪt] *adj.* (-er, -est) (a) shining very strongly/having a very vivid colour; to look on the b. side of things = to be optimistic. (b) intelligent. **brighten** *v.* (a) to make bright. (b) she brightened up when she saw him = she became more

cheerful. the weather is brightening up = it is getting finer. **brightly**, *adv.* (a) with a storng light. (b) in an intelligent/cheerful tone of voice. **brightness** *n.* strength (of light); intelligence (of person).
brill [brɪl] *n.* (*pl.*brill) type of flat white edible sea fish.
brilliant 1 [ˈbrɪljənt] *adj.* (a) very shiny. (b) very clever. **brilliant 2** *n.* diamond. **brilliance** *n.* brightness; intelligence.
brim 1 [brɪm] *n.* edge. **brim 2** *v.* (brimmed) the glass was brimming over with wine. = the glass was overflowing. **brimful** *adj.* very full/full to overflowing.
brindled [ˈbrɪndld] *adj.* (of animals) brown with streaks of another colour.
brine [braɪn] *n.* salt water.
bring [brɪŋ] *v.* (brought[ˈbrɔːt]; has brought) to take (sth/s.o.) to this place. **bring about** *v.* to cause/to make (sth) happen. **bring along** *v.* to bring with you. **bring-and-buy** *n.* type of market where people bring or buy homemade or secondhand goods. **bring back** *v.* to return (here); that picture brings it all back to me = makes me remember it all. **bring down** *v.* to make (sth/s.o.) fall down; to lower (sth). **bring forward** *v.* to bring forward the date of the meeting = to arrange an earlier date for it. **bring in** *v.* to make (sth/s.o.) come in. **bring off** *v.* to succeed in; he brought it off - he did it successfully. **bring on** *v.* to produce/to make grow; you've brought it on yourself = it's your own fault. **bring out** *v.* to make (sth/s.o.) come out; to b. out a new book = to publish a new book; to b. out the colour = to make the colour more noticeable/more effective. **bring round** *v.* (a) to carry (sth) to s.o.'s house. (b) to revive (s.o.) who is unconscious. **bring up** *v.* (a) to raise (a subject). (b) to vomit. (c) to educate in manners.
brink [brɪŋk] *n.* edge (of cliff); on the b. of a nervous breakdown = very close to having a nervous breakdown.
briny [ˈbraɪnɪ] *adj.* salty; *inf.* the b. = the sea.
brisk [brɪsk] *adj.* (-er, -est) rapid. **briskly** *adv.* rapidly.
brisket [ˈbrɪskɪt] *n.* beet from the breast of an animal.

brisling ['brɪzlɪŋ] n. small sea fish, like a sardine.

bristle 1 ['brɪsl] n. short stiff hair (on animal/brush). **bristle 2** v. (a) to take offence. (b) to b. with = to be full of/ covered with.

bristly adj. covered with short stiff hair.

British ['brɪtɪʃ] adj. & n. referring to Great Britain; the B. = the people of Great Britain; the B. Isles = group of islands off the north coast of Europe, including England, Wales, Scotland, Ireland and many smaller islands. **Brit** n. Sl. a Briton **Briton** ['brɪtn] n. person from Great Britain.

brittle ['brɪtl] adj. which breaks easily. **brittleness** n. fragility.

broach [brəʊtʃ] v. (a) to open (a cask of wine, etc.). (b) to start talking about (a problem).

broad [brɔːd] adj. (-er, -est) very wide; in b. daylight = in full daylight; a b. Scottish accent = a strong accent; b. beans = type of bran with large flat seeds. **broadcast 1** n. radio/television programme; outside b. = radio/television programme recorded in the open air, not in a studio. **broadcast 2** v. (broadcast) (a) to sow (by throwing seed by hand). (b) to send out by radio/television; they b. an appeal to the people. (c) to tell everyone (the news); don't b. the fact = keep it a secret. **broadcast 3** adv. (sowing) by throwing the seed by hand **broadcast 4** adj. sent by radio/ television. **broadcaster** n. person who speaks on the radio/television. **broaden** v. to make wider; travel broadens the mind = travel makes your knowledge/ interest more extensive. **broadloom** adj. (carpet) woven in a very wide strip. **broadly** adv. b. speaking = in a general way. **broadminded** adj. tolerant; not easily taking offence. **broad-shouldered** adj. with wide shoulders. **broadside** n. (a) firing of all the guns of one side of a ship. (b) sharp written or spoken criticism. (c) b. on = with the side moving forwards.

brocade [brə'keɪd] n. thick cloth with a raised pattern.

broccoli ['brɒkəlɪ] n. (pl.broccoli) cabbage-like vegetable of which the flower-heads are eaten.

brochure ['brəʊʃə] n. small book; small publicity pamphlet.

brogue [brəʊg] n. (a) heavy shoe with patterned leather top. (b) accent (usu. Irish).

broil [brɔɪl] v. to grill. **broiler** n. chicken specially bred for roasting.

broke [brəʊk] adj. inf. to be flat b. = b. = to have no money; see also break.

broken ['brəʊkən] adj. (a) in pieces; a b. home = home where the parents have separated. (b) spoken with a foreign accent and with many mistakes. (c) see also break. **broken-down** adj. not working. **broken-hearted** adj. very upset/sad. **broker** ['brəʊkə] n. person who deals in shares/insurance; honest b. = person who tries to mediate.

brokerage n. fee charged by a broker for his work.

brolly ['brɒlɪ] n. inf. umbrella

bromide ['brəʊmaɪd] n. (a) chemical used to make a calming medicine. (b) photographic paper.

bronchial ['brɒŋkɪəl] adj. referring to the respiratory tubes; b. asthma = asthma in the lungs. **bronchi** n. pl.air passages leading into the lungs. **bronchitis** [brɒŋ'kaɪtɪs] n. decease of the respiratory tubes.

bronze [brɒnz] n. metal made from copper and tin. B. Age = prehistoric period when men used weapons of bronze. **bronzed** adj. tanned/sunburnt.

brooch [brəʊtʃ] n. ornament to pin on to clothing.

brood 1 [bruːd] n. group of chicks/ small children. **brood 2** v. to have gloomy thoughts; she's brooding over a plan = she is pondering a plan. **broody** adj. (a) (hen) preparing to sit on a clutch of eggs. (woman) who wants to have a baby. (b) (person) who has gloomy thoughts.

brook 1 [brʊk] n. small streAm. **brook 2** v. to allow/to accept.

broom [bruːm] n. (a) shrub with yellow flowers. (b) brush with long handle for sweeping the floor. **broomstick** n. long handle of a broom.

bros [brɒs] = brothers.

broth [brɒθ] n. light soup; Scotch b. = thick soup with barley, vegetables and lamb.

brothel [brɒθl] n. house of prostitutes.

brother ['brʌðə] n. (a) male child of the same parents as another child. (b) man belonging to a monastic order.
brotherhood n. fraternity; companionship (between men).
brother-in-law n. (pl.brothers-in-law) brother of your husband or wife; husband of your sister; husband of the sister of your husband or wife.
brotherly adj. as of brothers.
brought [brɔːt] v. see bring.
brow [braʊ] n. (a) forehead/top part of the face above the eyes. (b) line of hair above each eye. (c) rounded top of a hill.
browbeat v. (browbeat; has browbeaten) to intimidate (s.o.).
brown 1 [braʊn] adj. (-er, -est) coloured like the colour of wood or soil.
brown 2 n. colour of wood or soil.
brown 3 v. to go brown; to make brown. **browned off** adj. inf. fed up.
brownie n. (a) girl in the younger section of the Girl Guides. (b) Am. small chocolate cake. **brownish** adj. rather brown.
browse [braʊz] v. (a) (of animal) to wander about eating grass. (b) (of person) to wander round a shop looking at goods for sale. **browser** n. person who is browsing in a shop.
brucellosis [brəsel'əʊsɪs] n. disease caught from drinking infected milk.
bruise 1 bruːz] n. mark made on the skin by a blow. **bruise 2** v. to get/to make marks on the skin from a blow.
bruiser n. fighter.
brunch [brʌntʃ] n. large meal (as a combination of breakfast and lunch) taken in the middle of the morning.
brunette [bruːˈnet] adj. & n. (woman) with brown hair.
brunt [brʌnt] n. to bear b. of = to suffer most from.
brush 1 [brʌʃ] n. (pl.-es) (a) instrument with a handle and hair/wire/nylon bristles for painting or cleaning. (b) scrub land. (c) cleaning with a brush. (d) short argument/fight with an opponent. (e) piece of carbon which makes an electric contact. (f) tail. (of a fox).
brush 2 v. (a) to clean with a brush. (b) to go past sth touching it gently.
brush aside v. to reject. **brush away** v. to clear away with a brush. **brush down** v. to brush (sth) off vigorously.

brush off, v. to clean (sth) off with a brush. **brush-off** n. to give s.o. the b. off = to send s.o. away without agreeing to what they want. **brush up** v. (a) to make (yourself) smart. (b) to improve (your knowledge of). **brushwood** n. low undergrowth.
brusque [bruːsk] adj. abrupt/impolite. **brusquely** adv. rudely.
Brussels sprouts ['brʌslz'spraʊts] n. pll. vegetable like tiny cabbages.
brute [bruːt] n. (a) animal. (b) rude/violent person; to use b. force = to use rough methods. **brutal** adj. violent.
brutality [bruːˈtælɪtɪ] n. violent action. **brutalize** v. to heat (s.o.). **brutally** adv. in a brutal way. **brutish** adj. rude/violent
bryony ['braɪənɪ] n. type of climbing plant with poisonous berries.
BSc [biːesˈsiː] Bachelor of Science.
BSE [biːesˈiː] bovine spongiform encephalopathy.
bubble 1 [bʌbl] n. small amount of air trapped in liquid. **bubble 2** v. to make bubbles. **bubbly 1** adj. with bubbles. **bubbly 2** n. inf. champagne
bubonic plague [bjuːˈbɒnɪk] 'pleɪg] n. fatal disease transmitted by rats.
buck 1 [bʌk] n. (a) male deer/rabbit. (b) Am. inf. dollar. (c) inf. to pass the b. = to hand responsibility on to s.o. else. **buck 2** v. (of horse) to jump in the air (with rounded back). **bucked** adj. inf. very pleased and encouraged. **buckteeth** n. pl.teeth which stick out in front. **buck up** v. inf. to make (s.o.) feel more lively. (b) inf. buck up! = hurry up!/cheer up!
bucket 1 ['bʌkɪt] n. round container with an open top and a handle. **bucket 2** v. inf. (of rain) to b. down = to pour down. **bucketful** n. quantity contained in a bucket. **bucket seat** n. rounded seat (in a car). **bucket shop** n. cheap travel agent.
buckle 1 ['bʌkl] n. metal fastener for attaching a belt/strap/shoe. **buckle 2** v. (a) to attach (sth) with a metal clasp. (b) to bend/to collapse.
buckram ['bʌkrəm] n. thick cloth for covering books.
buckshee [bʌkˈʃiː] adv. inf. free.
buckwheat ['bʌkwiːt] n. dark grain, giving brown flour.

bucolic [bju:'kɒlɪk] *adj.* referring to the countryside.

bud 1 [bʌd] *n.* (a) point on a plant where a new shoot is appearing; flower not yet opened; the roses are in b. = the flowers are ready to open. (b) *Am.* inf. friend. **bud 2** *v.* (budded) (a) to make buds. (b) to graft a bud. **budding** *adj.* (flower) not yet open; b. concert pianist = person who hopes to be a concert pianist.

Buddhism ['bʊdɪzəm] *n.* religion following the teaching of Buddha. **Buddhist** *adj. & n.* (person) who follows the teaching of Buddha.

buddleia ['bʌdlɪə] *n.* garden shrub with long purple flowers.

buddy ['bhdɪ] *n. Am.* inf. friend.

budge [bʌdʒ] *v.* to move.

budgerigar ['bʌdʒərɪgɑ:] *n.* blue to green tropical bird like a small parrot.

budget 1 ['bʌdʒɪt] *n.* list of proposed expenditure; the B. = the government's declaration of proposals for tax and expenditure. **budget 2** *v.* to b. for = to plan how to spend money on sth.

budgie ['bʌdʒɪ] *n. inf.* budgerigar

buff 1 [bʌf] *adj. & n.* (of a) pale yellow-brown colour. (b) *n. inf.* enthusiast. **buff 2** *v.* to polish/to shine.

buffalo *n.* (pl.-oes) large wild ox or cow (in American and tropical countries).

buffer ['bʌfə] *n.* (a) shock-absorbing pad, esp. at end of railway line; b. state = small country between two larger states, which may be antagonistic to each other; b. zone = area between to areas of fighting. (b) *Sl.* old b. = old man.

buffet1 ['bʊfeɪ] *n.* (a) self-service snack bar (in railway station, etc.); b. car = railway coach containing a buffet. (b) self-service meal. (c) sideboard. **buffet2** ['bʌfɪt] *v.* to bank/to jolt.

buffoon [bə'fu:n] *n.* fool/clown. **buffoonery** *n.* foolish action.

bug 1 [bʌg] *n.* (a) small insect which sucks. (b) *Am.* any small insect. (c) *inf.* germ. (d) hidden microphone. (e) defect in a computer progrAm. **bug 2** *v.* (bugged) (a) to install a hidden microphone in (a room). (b) *inf.* what's bugging you? = what's bothering you?

bugbear *n.* thing which you hate.

bugle ['bju:gl] *n.* military trumpet.

bugler *n.* person who blows bugle.

build 1 [bɪld] *n.* size/shape (of person).

build 2 *v.* (built[bɪlt]; has built) to construct; to make by putting pieces together. **builder** *n.* person who constructs houses, etc. **building** *n.* (a) constructing; b. land = land for construction of houses. (b) construction; house/office block; b. society = society which lends money to people to buy houses. **build up** *v.* to construct/to create/to increase. **built-in** *adj.* (cupboards, etc.) which are constructed as part of a building. **built-up** *adj.* built-up area = area of a town where there are many buildings.

bulb [bʌlb] *n.* (a) fleshy underground stem of a plant, which produces leaves and flowers in spring. (b) glass globe full of gas which produces light when an electric current passes through it. **bulbous** *adj.* fat and rounded.

bulge 1 [bʌldʒ] *n.* swelling. **bulge 2** *v.* to swell out (with).

bulimia [bʊ'lɪmɪə] *n.* disease where you have a craving to eat and force yourself to vomit.

bulk 1 [bʌlk] *n.* large quantity; size in b. = in large quantities; b. purchase = purchase in large quantities; the b. of our sales = most of our sales. **bulk 2** *v.* to b. large = to be important; to take up a lot of room. **bulkhead** *n.* dividing wall in a ship or aircraft. **bulkiness** *n.* being bulky. **bulky** *adj.* (-ier, -iest) very large/taking up an inconvenient amount of room).

bull [bʊl] *n.* (a) male ox. (b) male of certain species. (c) person who believes the stock market prices will rise. (d) official pronouncement by the pope. (e) *Sl.* rubbish/nonsense. **bulldog** *n.* breed of squat, flatfaced dogs. **bulldoze** *v.* (a) to knock down/to clear using a bulldozer. (b) to force; he bulldozed his proposal though the committee = forced them to agree to it. **bulldozer** *n.* large tractor with a shovel in front for moving earth. **bullfight** *n.* entertainment in Spain, where a man fights a bull. **bullfighter** *n.* man who fights bulls. **bullfinch** *n.* small finch with red breast **bullfrog** *n.* large frog. **bullock** *n.* castrated bull. **bullring** *n.* arena where bullfights take place **bull's-eye**

n. centre point of a target.
bullet ['bʊlɪt] *n.* piece of metal fired from a revolver or small gun. **bullet-proof** *adj.* (waistcoat/window) specially made so that bullets cannot pierce it.
bulletin ['bʊlɪtɪn] *n.* piece of information; report on a situation.
bullion ['bʊljən] *n.* gold or silver bars.
bully 1 ['bʊlɪ] *n.* person who frightens people who are weaker than he is; b. boys = thugs. **bully 2** *v.* to intimidate (s.o.) **bully beef** *n. inf.* corned beef. **bully off** *v.* (in hockey) to start the game.
bulrush ['bʊlrʌʃ] *n.* (*pl.*-es) tall reed with a brown furry head.
bulwark ['bʊlwək] *n.* side or a ship which rises higher than the deck.
bum 1 [bʌm] *n. inf.* (a) buttocks. (b) *Am.* tramp; person who loafs about doing nothing. **bum 2** *v.* (bummed) *inf.* to b. off s.o. = to live at s.o.'s expense.
bumble ['bʌmbl] *v.* move/do things in a clumsy way. **bumblebee** *n.* large furry bee.
bumf [bʌmf] *n. Sl.* paper (usu. useless documents); toilet paper.
bump 1 [bʌmp] *n.* (a) slight shock from hitting sth lightly. (b) small bulge on the body (from being hit). **bump 2** *v.* to hit sth (lightly); I bumped into him at the station = I met him by chance. **bump off** *v. inf.* to murder. **bumpy** *adj.* (-ier, -iest) uneven (path/flight) **bumper** [bʌmpə] *n.* (a) something very large; a b. crop. (b) metal or rubber strip at front and rear of a car to protect it when it is hit.
bumptious ['bʌmpʃəs] *adj.* (person) full of his own importance.
bun [bʌn] *n.* (a) small cake. (b) hair wound round in a knot at the back of the head.
bunch 1 [bʌntʃ] *n.* (*pl.*-es) (a) cluster (of things) tied together; the pick of the b. = the best out of the group. (b) group (of racing cyclists). **bunch 2** *v.* (in sport) to form a group.
bundle 1 ['bʌndl] *n.* parcel (of papers, etc.). **bundle 2** *v.* to tie (several things) together.
bung 1 [bʌŋ] *n.* stopper; thing which stops up a hole (in a cask). **bung 2** *v.* to block/to stop up a hole. (b) *inf.* b. it in

the wastepaper basked = throw it in the wastepaper basket.
bungalow ['bʌŋɡələʊ] *n.* house with only a ground floor.
bungle ['bʌŋgl] *v.* to do (sth) badly. **bungler** *n.* person who has done a job badly.
bunion ['bʌnjən] *n.* painful swelling at the base of the big toe.
bunk [bʌŋk] *n.* (a) bed attached to a wall; b. beds = two beds, one on top of the other. (b) *inf.* to do a b. = to run away. (c) *inf.* nonsense. **bunker** ['bʌŋkə] *n.* (a) coalhole. (b) sandy pit on a golf course. (c) fortified gun emplacement.
bunny ['bʌnɪ] *n.* pet name for a rabbit.
bunting ['bʌntɪŋ] *n.* (a) type of small singing bird. (b) (no *pl.*) strings of small flags.
buoy 1 [bɔɪ] *n.* floating marker showing a channel (in a river/at the entrance to a harbour). **buoy 2** *v.* to b. s.o. up = to cheer s.o. up **buoyancy** *n.* ability to float; b. aid = type of life jacket made of blocks of light substance, worn by yachtsmen. **buoyant** *adj.* (a) which can flat easily. (b) full of vigour.
burble 1 ['bɜːbl] *n.* low murmur. **burble 2** *v.* to murmur softly.
burden 1 [bɜːdn] *n.* (a) heavy load; sth which is hard to do/to bear; beast of b. = animal (like a donkey) used to carry loads; to make s.o.'s life a b. = to make things difficult for s.o. (b) theme music of a song. **burden 2** *v.* to load.
bureau ['bjʊərəʊ] *n.* (*pl.*bureaux ['bjʊərəʊz]) (a) office; information b. = office which collects and hands out information. (b) (antique) desk; *Am.* chest of drawers.
bureaucracy [bjʊə'rɒkrəsɪ] *n.* rule by civil servants. **bureaucrat** *n.* civil servant. **bureaucratic** [bjʊərə'krætɪk] *adj.* referring to the civil service.
burgeon ['bɜːdʒən] *v.* to begin to grow.
burgh ['bʌrə] *n.* (Scotland) borough.
burglar ['bɜːglə] *n.* person who enters a house to steal; b. alarm = electric alarm which rings if a burglar attempts to enter the house. **burglary** *n.* robbery committed by a burglar. **burgle** *v.* to steal form (a house).
burgundy ['bɜːgəndɪ] *n.* type of French red wine.

burial ['berɪə] n. act of burying (a dead body); b. ground = cemetery.

burlap ['bɜːlæp] n. thick canvas.

burlesque [bɜːˈlesk] adj. & n. light satirical (play)

burly ['bɜːlɪ] adj. (-ier, -iest) strong/solid (man).

Burmese 1 [bɜːˈmiːz] adj. coming from Burma. **Burmese 2** n. (a) person from Burma. (b) language spoken in Burma.

burn 1 [bɜːn n. (a) place (on the body) which has been burnt. (b) (in Scotland) streAm. **burn 2** v. (burnt/burned; has burnt/burned) (a) destroy by fire; he burnt his fingers = he suffered a loss/he did not do at all as well as he expected; he's burnt his boats/his bridges = he can't go back now. (b) to use as a fuel.

burn down v. to destroy by fire.

burner n. apparatus for burning. **burn out** v. the fire has gone out because there was nothing left to burn. **burnt** adj. which has gone black with fire.

burnish ['bɜːnɪʃ] v. to make (sth) shine by rubbing.

burp 1 [bɜːp] n. noise made when bringing up gas from the stomach through the mouth. **burp 2** v. to make a burp.

burr [bɜː] n. (a) prickly part of a plant, containing seeds, which clings to clothes, etc. (b) country accent with a strongly pronounced 'r'. (c) rough edge to a piece of cut metal.

burrow 1 ['bʌrəʊ] n. hole in the ground where rabbits live. **burrow 2** v. to make a long hole underground.

bursar ['bɜːsə] n. person in charge of the finances of a school/college.

bursary n. scholarship/money given to a student to help him pay for his studies.

burst 1 [bɜːst] n. (a) sudden explosion; b. of gunfire; b. of laughter. (b) sudden attack; b. of speed. **burst 2** v. (burst; has burst) to explode/to break open; she b. into the room = she rushed into the room; the boy b. into tears = he started to cry; he was bursting to tell everyone the secret = he was eagerly waiting to tell the secret. **burst open** v. to (make sth) come open with a bang. **burst out** v. to shout out; he burst out laughing.

bury ['berɪ] v. to put (sth) into a hole in the ground.

bus 1 [bʌs] n. (pl.-es) motor vehicle for carrying passengers; school b. = bus which takes children to school. **bus 2** v. (bussed) to take (children) to school in a different part of the town in order to mix racial groups. **busman** n. (pl.-men) person who works on a bus; a busman's holiday = spending your spare time doing sth similar to your normal job.

bussing n. action of sending children to school in a different art of the town in order to mix racial groups. **bus stop** n. place where a bus stops regularly to let people on or off.

busby ['bʌzbɪ] n. tall fur hat worn by some soldiers.

bush [bʊʃ] n. (pl.-es) (a) plant which is smaller than a tree. (b) the b. = wild uncultivated land (in Africa/Australia); b. fire = fire in wild uncultivated land; pilot = pilot of a plane flying in the bush.

bushed adj. tired out. **bushman** n. (pl.-men) native of the African bush.

bushy adj. growing thickly.

bushel ['bʊʃl] n. measure for grain (= 8 gallons).

business ['bɪznəs] n. (pl.-es) (a) affair; it's none of your b. = it has nothing to do with you. (b) commercial work; to do b. with s.o. = to trade with s.o.; do you think he means b.? = do you think he is serious?. (c) commercial firm.

businesslike adj. practical/serious. **businessman, businesswoman** n. (pl.-men/-women) person who works in a commercial company.

busker ['bʌskə] n. person who signs/plays a musical instrument, to entertain people in the street.

bust 1 [bʌst] n. (a) sculpture of head and shoulders. (b) measurement round a woman's breasts. **bust 2** adj. inf. broken **bust 3** v. (busted/bust) inf. to break.

bustard ['bʌstəd] n. large brown bird which, runs fast.

bustle 1 ['bʌsl] n. (a) pad at the back of address (in Victorian time). (b) rushing around. **bustle 2** v. to rush around.

busy ['bɪzɪ] adj. (-ier, -iest) occupied with doing sth; he is b. mending the car; b. street = street with lots of pedestrians and traffic. **busily** adj.v. in a busy way.

busybody n. person who interferes in other people's affairs.

but [bʌt] *con.j. adv. & prep.* (suggesting the opposite/a reservation) he is tall b. his sister is short; nothing b. = only; b. for his letter, we would not have known he was here = if it had not been for his letter.

butane [ˈbjuːteɪn] *n.* gas (often used for cooking or heating).

butch [bʊtʃ] *adj. Sl.* (of woman) very masculine.

butcher 1 [ˈbʊtʃə] *n.* (a) person who prepares and sells meat. (b) *Sl.* butcher's = look; let's have a butcher's at it.

butcher 2 *v.* (a) to kill in cold blood. (b) to chop (sth) about. **butcher's** *n.* shop which sells meat. **butchery** *n.* massacre/brutal killing.

butler [ˈbʌtlə] *n.* main male servant in a large house.

butt 1 [bʌt] *n.* (a) large barrel for keeping water. (b) end of a cigarette. (c) shoulder end of a rifle. (d) place where you practise shooting (e) person who is often teased. (f) push (with the head). (g) *Am.* inf. buttocks. **butt 2** *v.* (a) to push (s.o.) with your head. (b) to b. in = to interrupt a conversation.

butter 1 [ˈbʌtə] *n.* solid yellow fat made from creAm. **butter 2** *v.* to spread butter on (sth); to b. s.o. up = to flatter s.o. **buttercup** *n.* common bright yellow wild flower.

butterfingers *n.* person who can't catch/who drops things. **butterfly** *n.* insect with brightly coloured wings.

buttermilk *n.* thin milk left after butter has been churned. **butterscotch** *n.* sweet made from butter and sugar.

buttock(s) [ˈbʌtək(s)] *n.* fleshy part of the body which you sit on.

button 1 [ˈbʌtn] *n.* small object stitched to clothes for attaching one part of clothing to another; small round object which you press to make a machine work; b. mushroom = small round mushroom which is not fully grown. **button 2** *v.* to attach with buttons **buttonhole 1** *n.* (a) hole for putting a button through. (b) flower stuck in the hole in a lapel. **buttonhole 2** *v.* to b. s.o. = to traps s.o. and talk to him at length.

buttress 1 [ˈbʌtrəs] *n.* (*pl.*-es) supporting pillar (reinforcing a wall). **buttress 2** *v.* to support.

butty [ˈbʌti] *n. Sl.* sandwich.

buxom [ˈbʌksəm] *adj.* plumb and attractive (women).

buy 1 [baɪ] *v.* (bought[bɔːt] has bought) to get by paying money. **buy 2** *n.* thing which you have bought/which you might buy; a good b. = a bargain. **buyer** *n.* person who buys, esp. person who buys stock for a large store. **buy out** *v.* to buy a partner's share in a business.

buzz 1 [bʌz] *n.* (a) (*pl.*-es) noise like a bee. (b) *inf.* telephone call; give me a b. tomorrow. **buzz 2** *v.* (a) to make a noise like a bee. (b) (of aircraft) to fly close to (another aircraft) to force it to go away. **buzzer** *n.* device which makes a buzzing noise. **buzz off** *v. inf.* to go away. **buzz word** *n.* word which is frequently used.

buzzard [ˈbʌzəd] *n.* kind of bird of prey.

by 1 [baɪ] *prep.* (a) near. (b) before; by ten o'clock. (c) using; by airmail; by car. (d) painting by Rembrandt = which Rembrandt painted; play by Shakespeare = which Shakespeare wrote. (e) by yourself = alone. (f) by the dozen = a dozen at a time. **by 2** *adv.* (a) near; put some money by for a rainy day = put money to one side/save money. (b) past; he drove by without stopping. **by-election** *n.* election to fill a place left vacant by the death/resignation of a representative. **bygone 1** *adj.* past/former. **bygone 2** *n.* thing which comes from the past; let bygones be bygones = forget past insults. **by-law** *n.* law which is passed by a municipal council. **bypass 1** *n.* (a) road which goes round a town. (b) heart b. = operation to insert a tube to go round a diseased part of an artery. **bypass 2** *v.* to go round (a town), avoiding the centre; to avoid (sth) by going round it. **by-product** *n.* secondary product made as a result of manufacturing something else. **by road** *n.* small local road. **bystander** *n.* person standing near the scene of action. **byway** *n.* small path/road. **byword** *n.* (for) famous example.

bye [baɪ] *n.* (in cricket) run scored without the batsman having hit the ball; to have a b. = to pass to the next round of a sporting tournament without having to play. **bye(-bye)** [baɪ(baɪ)] *in.ter.* used when leaving someone.

byre ['baɪə] *n.* cowshed.

byte [baɪ] *n.* series of bits processed by a computer as one piece.

Cc

C Symbol for carbon.

Ca symbol for calcium.

cab [kæb] *n.* taxi. **cab-driver** *n.* person who drivers a taxi.

cabal [kæ'bɑːl] *n.* small group of politician who plot in secret.

cabaret ['kæbəret] *n.* entertainment given in a restaurant or club.

cabbage ['kæbɪdʒ] *n.* green leafy vegetable; c. white = common type of white butterfly.

caber ['keɪbə] *n.* long of wood thrown in Scottish games.

cabin ['kæbɪn] *n.* (a) small room on a ship. (b) small hut. (c) interior of an aircraft; c. crew = air hostesses and stewards.

cabinet ['kæbɪnət] *n.* (a) piece of furniture with shelves. (b) central committee of ministers in a government; shadow c. = committee formed by the main opposition party to parallel the actual cabinet. **cabinetmaker** *n.* woodworker who makes furniture.

cable 1 ['keɪbl] *n.* (a) thick rope/wire; pulled up a steep hill by a cable. (b) telegraph wire for sending messages under the sea. (c) message sent by telegraph. (d) c. TV = television sent by cable. **cable 2** *v.* to send a message to (s.o.) by telegraph. **cablecar** *n.* cabin on a cable railway. **cablegram** *n.* telegram sent by cable.

caboodle [kə'buːdl] *n.* *inf.* the whole c. = everything.

cacao [kə'kɑːəʊ] *n.* tropical tree, of which the seeds provide cocoa and chocolate.

cache [kæʃ] *n.* hidden store.

cachet ['kæʃeɪ] *n.* special mark.

cackle 1 ['kækl] *n.* noise made by hens; *Sl.* cut the c. = stop chattering.

cackle 2 *v.* to chatter.

cacophony [kə'kɒfənɪ] *n.* loud unpleasant mixture of sounds. **cacophonous** *adj.* unpleasantly noisy.

cactus ['kæktəs] *n.* (*pl.*cacti[kæktaɪ] prickly plant which grows in the desert.

cad [kæd] *n.* (old) unpleasant/dishonest person. **caddish** *adj.* like a cad.

cadaver [kə'dɑːvə] *n.* corpse. **cadaverous** *adj.* looking like a corpse.

CAD/CAM = computer-assisted design/computer-assisted manufacture.

caddie 1 ['kædɪ] *n.* person who carries the clubs for a golfer. **caddie 2** *v.* to act as a caddie (for s.o.).

caddis fly ['kædɪsflaɪ] *n.* insect living near water.

caddy ['kædɪ] *n.* (*pl.*caddies) box for keeping tea in.

cadence ['keɪdəns] *n.* rhythm (of music/poetry).

cadenza [kə'denzə] *n.* flowery piece for a solo instrument in the middle of concerto/symphony etc.

cadet [kə'det] *n.* young person training for the armed services.

cadge [kædʒ] *v.* to scrounge/to try to get (sth) without having to pay for it. **cadger** *n.* person who cadges.

cadmium ['kædmɪəm] *n.* (element: Cd) grey metal which can be poisonous to human beings.

cadre ['kɑːdə] *n.* (a) small group of expert people in a political party of the army. (b) active specialist working in a political party.

caecum ['siːkəm] *n.* wide part of the large intestine.

caesarean [sɪ'zeərɪən] *n.* c. (section) - operation on a pregnant woman to deliver her baby through the wall of the womb.

café ['kæfeɪ] *n.* small restaurant selling snacks or light meals, but not alcoholic drinks. **cafeteria** [kæfɪ'tɪərɪə] *n.* self-service restaurant.

caffeine ['kæfiːn] *n.* stimulating substance in coffee and tea.

cage 1 [keɪdʒ] *n.* enclosure of wire of with metal bars for keeping birds or animals. **cage 2** *v.* to put in a cage.

cagey ['keɪdʒɪ] *adj.* (cagier, cagiest) secretive/unwilling to reveal sth. **cagily**

adv. in a cagey way. **caginess** *n.* being cagey.

cahoots [kə'hu:ts] *n. inf.* to be in c. with s.o. to work with s.o., against another person.

cairn [keən] *n.* heap of stones to mark an important spot.

cairngorm *n.* type of semi-precious stone found in Scotland.

caisson [kə'su:n] *n.* watertight enclosure, as in dry dock.

cajole [kə'dʒəʊl] *v.* to persuade by flattering. **cajolery** *n.* act of flattering.

cake 1 [keɪk] *n.* (a) cooked food made of eggs, flour and sugar, *usu.* eaten cold; *Sl.* it's a piece of c. = it is very easy; you can't have your c. and eat it = you cant benefit from two quite opposite things. (b) block of soap. **cake 2** to form a dry crust.

calamine ['kæləmaɪn] *n.* c. lotion = pink liquid put on skin to soothe and stop itching.

calamity [kə'læmɪtɪ] *n.* disaster. **calamitous** *adj.* very unfortunate/ disastrous.

calcareous [kæl'keərɪəs] *adj.* (soil) containing chalk.

calceolaria [kælsɪəʊ'leərɪə] *n.* house plant, with coloured boat-shaped flowers.

calcinate ['kælsɪneɪt] *v.* to burn to ashes.

calcium ['kælsɪəm] *n.* (a) (element: Ca) grey metal which forms bones. (b) white substance found in water lime, etc.

calcify *v.* to turn (sth) into calcium.

calculate ['kælkjʊleɪt] *v.* to work out (a sum); to estimate (quite accurately); calculated insult = deliberate insult. **calculable** *adj.* which can be calculated. **calculating** *adj.* (person) who plans clever schemes. **calculation** [kælkjʊ'leɪʃn] *n.* act of calculating; sum which has been calculated. **calculator** *n.* electronic machine for doing sums. **calculus** *n.* (a) mathematical way of calculating. (b) stone formed inside the body.

caldron ['kɔːldrən] *n. Am.* see cauldron.

calendar ['kæləndə] *n.* sheet showing the days and months of a year; c. month, c. year = month/year as shown on a calendar.

calendula [kə'lendju:lə] *n.* yellow flower, the marigold.

calf [kɑːf] *n.* (*pl.* calves [kɑːvz]) (a) young cow/bull; young (of elephant, etc.) (b) leather (from cow's skin). (c) fleshy back part of the leg between the ankle and the knee.

calibre, *Am.* **caliber** ['kælɪbə] *n.* (a) interior diameter of a gun. (b) standing/ intellectual ability. **calibrate** *v.* to mark/to correct degrees on (a thermometer) /to mark units on (a scale). **calibration** *n.* marking of degrees; degree marked.

calico ['kælɪkəʊ] *n.* thick cotton cloth.

calipers ['kælɪpəz] see callipers.

call 1 [kɔːl] *n.* shout/cry; song of a bird; I want a c. at 7 o'clock = I want to be woken at 7 o'clock; on c. = available for duty. (b) conversation on the telephone. (c) visit. (d) need; there's no c. for alarm. **call 2** *v.* (a) to shout; c. me at 7 'o clock. (b) to telephone. (c) to give (s.o.) a name. (d) to visit. **call back** *v.* (a) to telephone in replay; to telephone again. (b) to come back to visit again. **callbox** *n.* street telephone box. **callboy** *n.* (a) young man in a theatre who tells performers when it is time for them to go on stage. (b) young man in a hotel who runs messages. **caller** *n.* (a) person who comes to visit. (b) person who telephone. **call for** *v.* (a) he called for help = he shouted to ask for help. (b) to c. for s.o. = to go to s.o.'s house to collect them. (c) to need/to require. **call-girl** *n.* prostitute who can be called by telephone. **call in** *v.* to call to (s.o.) to make them come in. **calling** *n.* vocation; job. **call off** *v.* to cancel. **call on** *v.* (a) to visit. (b) to appeal to (s.o.). **call out** *v.* (a) to shout. (b) to ask (police/soldiers) to come to help. **call sign** *n.* letters/worlds which identify a radio station. **call up** *v.* (a) to telephone. (b) to order (s.o.) to join the army. **call-up** *n.* order to join the army.

calligraphy [kə'lɪgrəfɪ] *n.* art of fine handwriting. **calligraphic** [kælɪ'græfɪk] *adj.* referring to calligraphy.

callipers, calipers ['kælɪpəz] *n. pl.* (a) instrument for measuring the diameter of sth round (like a pipe). (b) metal frame to support the leg of a disabled person.

callisthenics [kælɪs'θenɪks] *n.* exercises which are supposed to make the body strong and beautiful.

callous ['kæləs] *adj.* hard/unfeeling. **callously** *adv.* cruelly. **callousness** *n.* cruelty.

callow ['kæləʊ] *adj.* young and inexperienced.

callus ['kæləs] *n.* (*pl.*-es) hard patch on the skin.

calm 1 [kɑːm] *adj.* (-er, -est) quiet/not rough. **calm 2** *n.* period of quiet. **calm 3** *v.* to become to make quiet. **calmly** *adv.* quietly. **calmness** *n.* period of quiet.

calorie ['kælərɪ] *n.* measure of heat/of energy-giving value of food. **calorific** [kælə'rɪfɪk] *adj.* referring to heat.

calumny ['kæləmnɪ] *n.* lie/false statement. **calumniate** [kə'lʌmnɪeɪt] *v.* to tell lies about (s.o.).

calve 1 [kɑːv] *v.* to give birth to a calf. **calve 2** *n. pl.*see calf.

calypso [kə'lɪpsəʊ] *n.* type of topical song sung in the West Indies.

calyx ['kælɪks] *n.* (*pl.*-es) outer covering of a flower bud.

cam [kæm] *n.* ring on a camshaft, which makes pistons move up and down.

camaraderie [kæmə'rædərɪ] *n.* friendship among comrades, esp. in the armed forces.

camber ['kæmbə] *n.* bend/curve (in a surface); way in which the road slopes. **cambered** *adj.* sloping/rounded (surface).

cambric ['kæmbrɪk] *n.* thin cotton cloth.

camcorder ['kæmkɔːdə] *n.* portable cinecamera which records pictures for video.

came [keɪm] *v.* see come.

camel ['kæml] *n.* desert animal with one or two humps, used for riding. **camel hair** *n.* thick pale brown wool, used for making coats, etc.

camellia [kə'miːlɪə] *n.* evergreen bush with pink or white flowers.

cameo ['kæmɪəʊ] *n.* (a) small stone with a design of a head which stands out against a darker background. (b) small but sharply defined part in a play/film.

camera ['kæmərə] *n.* (a) machine for taking photographs. (b) in c. = in closed session/in secret. **cameraman** *n.* (*pl.*- men) man who operates a cine-camera.

camomile ['kæməmaɪl] *n.* fragrant plant, of which the dried leaves are used for making hot drinks.

camouflage 1 ['kæməflɑːʒ] *n.* hiding (sth) by means of colouring, so that it is difficult to see it against the background. **camouflage 2** *v.* to hide (sth) so that it is difficult to see it against the background.

camp 1 [kæmp] *n.* place where people live in tents or cabins in the open; c. bed = folding bed; c. fire = fire round which campers sit at night; holiday c. = place where people spend holidays in cabins and enjoy organized entertainment. **camp 2** *v.* (a) to live (on holiday) in a tent. (b) to c. it up = to put on an affected style. **camp 3** *adj.* in an affected (often humorously homosexual) style. **camper** *n.* (a) person who lives in a tent or caravan. (b) *Am.* small van equipped with beds, tables, cooking facilities, etc. **camping** *n.* going on holiday with a tent or caravan. **campsite** *n.* area specially laid out for tents and caravans.

campaign 1 [kæm'peɪn] *n.* (a) organized military movements. (b) organized method of working; a sales c. **campaign 2** *v.* (a) to take part in a war. (b) (for) to work in an organized fashion to achieve an end. **campaigner** *n.* person who campaigns.

campanology [kæmpə'nɒlədʒɪ] *n.* study of ringing church bells.

campanula [kæm'pænjuːlə] *n.* the bell flower, with blue bell-shaped flowers.

camphor ['kæmfə] *n.* strong-smelling substance which comes from certain trees; c. balls = small white balls impregnated with camphor which prevent moths from attacking clothes. **camphorated** *adj.* impregnated with camphor.

campion ['kæmpjən] *n.* wild plant with small pink flowers.

campus ['kæmpəs] *n.* (*pl.*-es) land on which a university/polytechnic is built.

camshaft ['kæmʃɑːft] *n.* shaft with projecting rings which open and close pistons in turn.

can 1 [kæn] *n.* (a) metal box for liquids, esp. for preserving food or drink. (b) watering c. = bucket with a long spout for watering plants. **can 2** *v.* (a) (I/he can; neg. cannot; short form can't; past. I/he could; neg. could not; short form couldn't) able to do sth/knowing how to do sth. (b) (canned) to put (fruit/ vegetables etc.) into cans to preserve them. **canned** *adj.* in a metal box; c. music = recorded music. **cannery** *n.* canning factory.

Canada goose [kænədə'gu:s] *n.* large wild goose, with black neck and white chin, originally native of N. America.

Canadian 1 [kb'neɪdjən] *adj.* referring to Canada. **Canadian 2** *n.* person from Canada.

canal [kə'næl] *n.* (a) artificial waterway. (b) passage in the body.

canapé ['kænəpeɪ] *n.* small cocktail snack.

canary [kə'neərɪ] *n.* small yellow singing bird.

cancan ['kænkæn] *n.* French cabaret dance, where the dancers kick their legs in the air.

cancel ['kænsl] *v.* (cancelled) (a) to stop (sth which had been planned). (b) to mark a postage stamp with a rubber stamp. **cancellation** [kænsə'leɪʃn] *n.* act of cancelling; seat/ticket which is on sale because a purchaser cannot use it.

cancel out *v.* to balance (sth) and so remove its force.

cancer ['kænsə] *n.* (a) disease of the blood or tissue. (b) Cancer = one of the signs of the Zodiac, shaped like a crab; Tropic of C. = imaginary line 23° 28' north of the equator. **cancerous** *adj.* referring to cancer.

candelabra [kændi'lɑ:brə] *n.* *pl.*branched candlesticks; chandeliers.

candid ['kændɪd] *adj.* frank/open. **candidly** *adv.* in a candid way.

candidate ['kændɪdət] *n.* person standing for election; person who has entered for a competition/an examination. **candidacy, candidature** *n.* act of standing as a candidate.

candied ['kændɪd] *adj.* dried and sugared; c. peel = dried orange/lemon peel.

candle ['kændl] *n.* stick of wax with a wick in the centre; to burn the c. at both ends = to work hard during the day and enjoy yourself late into the night.

candlelight *n.* light from a candle. **candlelit** *adj.* lit by candles.

candlestick *n.* holder for a candle. **candlewick** *n.* cotton maternal for bedcovers, with patterns of tuffs.

candour, *Am.* **candor** ['kændə] *n.* frankness/openness.

candy ['kændɪ] *n.* *Am.* sweet. **candyfloss** *n.* molten sugar spun to make a fluffy mass. **candy-striped** *adj.* with stripes of colour on a white background like certain sweets.

candytuft *n.* plant with pink or blue flowers.

cane 1 [keɪn] *n.* (a) stem (esp. of jointed plants like bamboo). (b) walking stick (cut from such plants). **cane 2** *v.* to hit with a cane. **caning** *n.* beating with a cane.

canine 1 ['keɪnaɪ] *adj.* referring to dogs.

canine 2 *n.* c. (tooth) = round pointed tooth.

canister ['kænɪstə] *n.* round metal box.

canker ['kæŋkə] *n.* disease/sore which eats into flesh/into wood of trees.

canna ['kænæ] *n.* tropical plant, with large leaves and red or orange flowers.

cannabis ['kænəbɪs] *n.* plants, parts of which can be smoked to give a pleasant feeling of relaxation.

canneloni [kæne'ləʊnɪ] *n.* type of pasta, like small pancakes with a meat or spinach filling.

cannibal ['kænɪbl] *n.* person who eats people. **cannibalism** *n.* custom of eating people. **cannibalize** *v.* to take pieces of old machinery to repair another machine.

cannon 1 ['kænən] *n.* (a) large gun; gun in an aircraft. (b) (in billiards) hitting of one ball off the other two.

cannon 2 *v.* to bounce off (another ball/the cushion); to bump (into sth).

cannonball *n.* large metal ball fired by a cannon.

cannot ['kænət] *v.* see can.

canny ['kænɪ] *adj.* (-ier, -iest) wise/ clever. **cannily** *adv.* cleverly.

canoe 1 [kə'nu:] *n.* boat propelled by one or more people with paddles. **canoe 2** *v.* (canoed) to travel in a canoe.

canoeing *n.* sport of going in a canoe. **canoeist** *n.* person who paddles a canoe.

canon ['kænən] *n.* (a) religious rule or instructions; c. law = the church's laws.

(b) clergyman attached to a cathedral.
canonical *adj.* referring to a canon.
canonization *n.* declaring s.o. a saint.
canonize *v.* to declare (s.o.) a saint.
canopy ['kænəpɪ] *n.* small roof over a platform/balcony, etc.
cant [kænt] *n.* (a) hypocrisy/insincere language. (b) jargon/language of a certain group of people.
can't [kɑːnt] *v.* see can.
cantaloupe ['kæntəluːp] *n.* type of melon with pink flesh.
cantankerous [kæn'tæŋkrəs] *adj.* bad tempered. **cantankerousness** *n.* continual bad temper.
cantata [kæn'tɑːtə] *n.* musical piece for several voices and orchestra (usu. on a religious theme).
canteen [kæn'tiːn] *n.* (a) private self-service restaurant. (b) box containing knives, forks and spoons. (c) portable flask for water.
canter 1 ['kæntə] *n.* gentle gallop.
canter 2 *v.* to go at a canter; he cantered home = he won easily.
canticle ['kæntɪkl] *n.* religious song.
cantilever ['kæntɪliːvə] *n.* projecting support which holds up a balcony/a bridge. **cantilevered** *adj.* held up by a cantilever.
canto ['kæntəʊ] *n.* (*pl.*-os) long section of an epic poem.
canton ['kæntɒn] *n.* administrative division of Switzerland.
canvas ['kænvəs] *n.* (*pl.*-es) thick cloth (for making tents/sails, or for painting on); a painting on canvas; holiday under c. = camping holiday.
canvass ['kænvəs] *v.* to try to persuade people to vote for s.o./to buy sth. **canvasser** *n.* person who canvasses. **canvassing** *n.* going from door to door to persuade people to vote.
canyon ['kænjən] *n.* (in America) large valley with perpendicular sides.
cap 1 [kæp] *n.* (a) hat with a peak; c. and gown = hat and robes worn by graduates of a university. (b) top/cover (of a bottle, pen, etc.). (c) small piece of paper with gunpowder. **cap 2** *v.* (capped) (a) to top with a cap; to fix a cover on (a pipe) to stop it leaking. (b) to name (s.o.) to a national side (in football/rugby/cricket). (c) to surpass/to do better than.

CAP Common Agricultural Policy.
capable ['keɪpəbl] *adj.* competent/able.
capability [keɪpə'bɪlɪtɪ] *n.* ability.
capably ['keɪpəblɪ] *adv.* competently/efficiently.
capacity [kə'pæsɪtɪ] *n.* (a) amount which a container can hold; seating c. = number of seats (in a bus/cinema, etc.). (b) engine c. = power of an engine. (c) ability to do something. (d) position; in his c. as manager. **capacitor** *n.* device for storing an electric charge.
capacious *n.* very large/which contains a lot.
cape [keɪp] *n.* (a) long cloak. (b) headland jutting into the sea.
caper 1 ['keɪpə] *n.* (a) jumping/leaping. (b) small bitter seed used in cooking. (c) *inf.* trick. **caper 2** *v.* to c. about = to jump/to leap.
capillary [kə'pɪlərɪ] *adj. & n.* very thin (tube); very thin blood vessel; c. attraction = physical phenomenon where water is drawn up in a thin tube.
capital 1 ['kæpɪtl] *n.* (a) decorated stone on the top of a column. (b) large letter. (c) main city of a country/a state, etc. (d) money which is invested. (e) c. punishment = execution/legal killing of a criminal. **capital 2** *adj.* (a) very important. (b) *inf.* very good. **capitalism** *n.* economic system based on ownership of resources by individuals or companies and not by the state. **capitalist** *adj. & n.* (person) who supports the theory of capitalism; businessman.
capitalization [kæpɪtəlaɪ'zeɪʃn] *n.* amount of capital invested in a company.
captalize ['kæpɪtəlaɪz] *v.* (a) to invest capital in a company. (b) to c. on = to take advantage of (sth). **capitation** [kæpɪteɪʃn] *n.* amount of money allowed to a school for spending on books and equipment for each pupil.
Capitol ['kæpɪtəl] *n.* building where the US Congress meets; on C. Hill = in the US Congress.
capitulate [kə'pɪtjʊleɪt] *v.* to give in/to surrender. **capitulation** [kəpɪtjʊ'leɪʃn] *n.* surrendering.
capon ['keɪpɒn] *n.* fat castrated chicken.
cappucino [kæpuː'tʃiːnəʊ] *n.* frothy Italian coffee, with milk and chocolate.
caprice [kə'priːs] *n.* whim/sudden

fancy. **capricious** [kə'prɪʃəs] adj. whimsical/prone to change your mind. **capriciousness** n. tendency to change your mind suddenly.

Capricorn ['kæprɪkɔːm] n. one of the signs of the zodiac, shaped like a goat; Tropic of C. = imaginary line 23° 28' south of the equator.

capsicum ['kæpsɪkəm] n. green pepper (plant).

capsize [kæp'saɪz] v. (of bats) to turn over.

capstan ['kæpstən] n. machine which turns to haul in a rope or anchor.

capsule ['kæpsjuːl] n. enclosed case; small case for a dose of medicine which melts when swallowed; space c. = living compartment in a space rocket.

captain 1 ['kæptɪn] n. (a) officer in charge of a ship or aircraft. (b) rank in the army above lieutenant; rank in the navy above commander. (c) leader of sports teAm. **captian 2** v. to lead (an expedition/a team). **captaincy** n. (a) rank of caption (in army/navy). (b) post of leader of a sports team.

caption ['kæpʃn] n. phrase printed beneath picture.

captious ['kæpʃəs] adj. continually finding fault.

captivate ['kæptɪveɪt] v. to charm/to seduce. **captive 1** ['kæptɪv] n. prisoner. **captive 2** adj. held c. = held as a prisoner. **captivity** [kæp'tɪvɪti] n. imprisonment. **captor** n. person who captures s.o. **capture 1** ['kæptʃə] n. taking of s.o./sth captive. **capture 2** v. (a) to take (s.o.) captive. (b) they have captured 10% of the market = they have captured 10% of the possible sales.

capybara [kæpɪ'bɑːrə] n. very large rodent, native of S. America.

car [kɑː] n. (a) private motor vehicle; c. park = special parking place for cars. (b) railway wagon. **car pool** n. group of people who each take turns in driving all their children to school, etc. **carport** n. shelter for a car. **carsick** adj. feeling ill when travelling by motor vehicle. **car wash** n. place where cars are washed automatically.

carafe [kə'ræf] n. glass jug for serving wine.

caramel ['kærəmel] n. (a) sweet made with sugar and butter. (b) burnt sugar; c.

custard = pudding of egg custard topped with browned sugar. **caramelize** v. to heat sugar until it becomes brown.

carapace ['kærəpeɪs] n. outside shell (of an animal).

carat ['kærət] n. (a) measure of purify of gold; 18-c. gold. (b) weight of a diamond.

caravan ['kærəvæn] n. (a) van with beds, table, washing facilities, etc., which can be towed by a car. (b) group of vehicles/animals travelling together. (esp. across a desert). **caravanning** n. going on holiday in a caravan.

caraway ['kærəweɪ] n. spicy seed used to flavour cakes and biscuits.

carbamate ['kɑːbəmeɪt] n. type of pesticide.

carbine ['kɑːbaɪn] n. type of light riffle.

carbohydrate [kɑːbəʊ'haɪdreɪt] n. chemical substance containing carbon, hydrogen and oxygen, and derived from sugar. she eats too many carbohydrates = too much fattening food.

carbolic [kɑː'bɒlɪk] adj. referring to an acid used to disinfect. c. soap.

carbon ['kɑːbən] n. (element: C) substance found in charcoal, soot, diamonds; c. dioxide = colourless gas (CO2) forming a small part of the atmosphere; c. monoxide = colourless poisonous gas (CO) present in car exhaust fumes; c. paper = paper with black substance on one side, used to make copies in typing; c. copy = identical copy. **carbonate** n. salt of carbonic acid. **carbonic** [kɑː'bɒnɪk] adj. referring to carbon; c. acid = acid formed when carbon dioxide is dissolved in water. **carboniferous** [kɑːbə'nɪfərəs] adj. coal-bearing. **carbonize** ['kɑːbənaɪz] v. to make into carbon by burning.

carboxyhaemoglobin n. compound of carbon monoxide and haemoglobin formed when a person inhales car exhaust fumes.

carborundum [kɑːbə'rʌndəm] n. hard substance used for polishing or sharpening.

carboy ['kɑːbɔɪ] n. very large glass bottle for containing liquids.

carbuncle ['kɑːbʌŋkl] n. (a) red precious stone. (b) large inflamed spot on the skin.

carburettor [kɑːbə'retə] n. device in a car for changing liquid petrol into vapour.

carcase/carcass ['kɑːkəs] n. (a) body of a dead animal ready for the butcher; bones left after you have eaten a cooked bird. (b) body (of a person).

carcinogen [kɑː'sɪgədʒən] n. substance which causes cancer.

carcinoma [kɑːsɪ'nəʊmə] n. cancer

card 1 [kɑːd] n. (a) small rectangle of stiff paper for writing on. (b) rectangle of stiff paper with a design on it, used for playing games; playing cards = ordinary cards, marked in four designs (diamonds, hearts, clubs, spades); c. games = games using packs of special cards; they were playing cards = they were playing games of cards (for money). (c) (visiting) c. = small piece of stiff paper with your name and address printed on it; banker's c./cheque c. = plastic card given by a bank which guarantees payment of a cheque. credit c. = plastic card which allows you to buy goods without paying for them immediately; smart c. = plastic car with a built-in microprocessor; (d) cards = official record of an employee; he got his cards = he was told to leave. **card 2** v. to comb (raw wool). **cardboard** n. thick card, used for packing. **card-index 1** n. series of small cards classified into alphabetical or numerical order. **card-index 2** v. to classify (sth) on to small filing cards. **card-sharper** n. person who cheats at cards to win money.

cardiac ['kɑːdɪæk] adj. referring to the heart; c. arrest = heart attack.

cardigan ['kɑːdɪgən] n. woollen jacket which buttons at the front.

cardinal 1 ['kɑːdɪnl] adj. very important (rule, etc.). (b) c. numbers = numbers which show quantity (1, 2, 3, etc). **cardinal 2** n. (a) high dignitary of the Catholic church. (b) bright red North America bird.

cardiogram ['kɑːdɪəgræm] n. chart showing heart beats. **cardiograph** n. machine for recording heart beats in the form of cardiogrAm. **cardiology** [kɑːdɪ'ɒlədʒɪ] n. study of the heart and its diseases. **cardiologist** n. doctor specializing in cardiology.

cardiovascular adj. referring to the heart and the blood circulation system.

care 1 ['keə] n. (a) worry. (b) looking after s.o./sth; to take c. = to watch out/to be careful; in the c. of = being looked after by; (on a letter) Mr. White, c. of Mrs. Green = Mr. White, at Mrs. Green's house. **care 2** v. (a) to worry; I don't c. if I never see you again. (b) to like; would you c. for a cake? (c) to c. for = to look after. **carefree** adj. without any worries. **careful** adj. cautious/taking care. **carefully** adv. with care. **careless** adj. not paying attention/not taking care. **carelessly** adv. in a careless way. **carelessness** n. being careless. **carer** n. person who looks after another person. **caretaker** n. person who looks after a building; (government) which runs a country temporarily (until a permanent one is elected). **careworn** adj. tired because of worries.

careen [kə'riːn] v. (a) to tilt (a boat) over, so as to clean the bottom. (b) inf. to go along very fast.

career 1 [kə'rɪə] n. (a) life of professional work. (b) forward rush. **career 2** v. to rush forward out of control. **careerist** adj. & n. (person) only aiming at advancing his career.

caress 1 [kə'res] n. (pl.-oes) gentle touch. **caress 2** v. to stroke gently.

caret ['kærɪt] n. c. (sign) = sign used to show that sth is missing.

cargo ['kɑːgəʊ] n. (pl.-oes) goods carried (esp. on a ship). c. boat = ship which carries only goods and no passengers.

caribou ['kærɪbuː] n. (pl.caribou) reindeer of North America.

caricature 1 ['kærɪkətjʊə] n. amusing drawing which satirizes by emphasizing s.o.'s particular features. **caricature 2** v. to satirize by emphasizing s.o.'s bad features.

caries ['keəriːz] n. (pl.caries) decayed place in a tooth.

carillon ['kærɪlɒn] n. set of bells, usu. in a tower, on which tunes can be played.

carminative ['kɑːmɪnətɪv] n. medicine which relieves indigestion. **carmine** ['kɑːmɪn] adj. & n. bright red (colour).

carnage ['kɑːnɪdʒ] n. bloodshed/ massacre/killing.

carnal ['kɑːnl] *adj.* referring to the body; sensual.

carnation [kɑː'neɪʃn] *n.* strongly scented flower often worn as a buttonhole.

carnet ['kɑːnet] *n.* permit to take goods from one country to another.

carnival ['kɑːnɪvl] *n.* festival often with dancing and eating in the open air.

carnivore ['kɑːnɪvɔː] *n.* animal which eats flesh. **carnivorous** [kɑː'nɪvərəs] *adj.* flesh-eating.

carol 1 ['kærəl] *n.* special song sung at a particular time of the year; Christmas c. **carol 2** *v.* (carolled) to sing Christmas carols. **carol-singer** *n.* person singing Christmas carols (to collect money for charity).

carotid [kæ'rɒtɪd] *n.* artery in the neck.

carouse [kə'raʊz] *v.* to drink alcohol and enjoy yourself. **carousal** *n.* (formal) drunken party. **carousel** [kæru:'sel] *n.* (a) circular conveyor belt which distributes luggage. (b) *Am.* merry-go-round.

carp 1 [kɑːp] *n.* (*pl.*carp) fat edible fish often bred in captivity for eating. **carp 2** *v.* to keep on finding fault with things.

carpel ['kɑːpəl] *n.* female part of a flower.

carpenter ['kɑːpəntə] *n.* person who works with wood, esp. in building. **carpentry** *n.* art of working with wood.

carpet 1 ['kɑːpɪt] *n.* woven or knotted covering for the floor; *inf.* to have s.o. on the c. = to criticize s.o. **carpet 2** *v.* (a) to cover (as) with a carpet. (b) *inf.* to criticize (s.o.). **carpetbagger** *n.* politician who tries to make his fortune in a part of the country which is not his home. **carpeting** *n.* covering with a carpet, wide piece of carpet. **carpet sweeper** *n.* device which cleans carpets by means of rotating brushes.

carriage ['kærɪdʒ] *n.* (a) action of carrying goods; c. paid = the price includes payment of transport. (b) open vehicle pulled by a horse; railway c. = passenger wagon on a train. (c) way of walking. (d) movable part on a typewriter which goes from side to side. **carriageway** *n.* surface of the road on which traffic moves.

carrier ['kærɪə] *n.* (a) thing/person who carries; company which transports goods; luggage c. = grid on the back of a bicycle for carrying parcels; c. pigeon = pigeon specially trained for carrying messages; c. bag = large paper or plastic bag with handles. (b) person who carries the germ of a disease without suffering and can infect others with it. (c) aircraft c. = ship which carries air-craft.

carrion ['kærɪən] *n.* (no *pl.*) rotting meat. **carrion crow** *n.* type of large black crow.

carrot ['kærət] *n.* bright orange root vegetable.

carry ['kærɪ] *v.* (a) to lift (sth) up and move it from one place to another. (b) to win (a vote). (c) (of sound) to be heard at a distance. (d) to keep (in a shop). **carry along** *v.* to carry (sth) which cannot prevent it. **carry away** *v.* (a) to take away/to demolish. (b) to get carried away = to get overcome with emotion/excitement. **carrycot** *n.* rectangular box with handles for carrying a baby.

carry foward *v.* (in book-keeping) to take (a sum) on to the next page or column. **carry off** *v.* (a) to win/to take away. (b) he carried it off very well = he got through a potentially embarrassing situation very well. **carry on** *v.* (a) to continue/to go on. (b) *inf.* to be very angry. **carry out** *v.* to do (sth) successfully. **carry through** *v.* to bring (sth) to a finish.

cart 1 [kɑːt] *n.* vehicle pulled by a horse; to put the c. before the horse = not to put first things first. **cart 2** *v.* to carry (sth heavy). **carter** *n.* person who drives a cart; company which transports goods by road. **carthorse** *n.* large strong horse. **cartload** *n.* quantity carried in a cart. **cartwheel** *n.* (a) wheel of a cart. (b) to turn cartwheels = to turn over and over sideways on your outstretched hands and feet.

carte blanche [kɑːt'blɒnʃ] *n.* to have c. b. to do sth = to be able to do whatever you want.

cartel [kɑː'tel] *n.* group of companies which try to fix the price of sth.

cartilage ['kɑːtɪlɪdʒ] *n.* strong flexible material which acts as a cushion in joints in the body. **cartilaginous** [kɑːtɪ'lædʒɪnəs] *adj.* made of cartilage.

cartographer [kɑː'tɒgrəfə] *n.* person

who draws maps. **cartographic** *adj.* referring to maps. **cartography** *n.* science of drawing maps.

carton ['kɑːtən] *n.* cardboard box.

cartoon [kɑːˈtuːn] *n.* (a) funny (often political) drawing. (b) film made of moving drawings. (c) sketch for a painting. **cartoonist** *n.* person who draws (political) cartoons.

cartridge ['kɑːtrɪdʒ] *n.* (a) tube packed with gunpowder and a bullet for firing from a gun. (b) film/recording tape enclosed in a plastic case which fits directly into the camera/tape recorder; tube of ink which fits into a pen. (c) part of a record player which holds the stylus. (d) c. paper = kind of thick rough paper.

carve [kɑːv] *v.* (a) to cut (meat) up at table. (b) to cut (stone/wood) to make a shape. **carver** *n.* (a) person who carves. (b) carving knife. (c) dining chair with arms. **carving** *n.* (a) cutting up cooked meat; c. knife = large sharp knife for cutting meat. (b) art of cutting stone/wood into shapes. (c) an object which has been made by carving.

caryatid [kær'jætɪd] *n.* statue of female figure, which acts as a column holding up a roof.

cascade 1 [kæs'keɪd] *n.* (artificial) waterfall. **cascade 2** *v.* to fall in large quantities.

case 1 [keɪs] *n.* (a) box (of goods). (b) protective box or covering. (c) suitcase. (d) way in which sth happens; example; in any c. = anyway; in c. of fire = if fire breaks out; just in c. = to guard against a possible emergency. (e) sick person c. history = details of a patient's past history, progress, etc. (f) legal affair. **case 2** *v.* to put (sth) in a case.

casein ['keɪsɪɪn] *n.* protein found in milk.

casement ['keɪsmənt] *n.* window that opens on hinges; frame around such a window.

cash 1 [kæʃ] *n.* money (in coins and notes); c. crop = crop grown for sale; c. desk = place in a shop where you pay; c. register = machine which shows the amount to be paid and has a drawer for keeping money. **cash 2** *v.* to change (a cheque) into cash; to c. in on = to make a lot of money by profiting from sth. **cash and carry** *n.* discount warehouse,

selling items to the general public. **cash flow** *n.* rate at which money comes into and is paid out of a business.

cashew [kə'ʃuː] *n.* small sweetish nut, often eaten salted.

cashier 1 [kə'ʃiə] *n.* person who deals with money. **cashier 2** *v.* to expel (an officer) from the armed forces.

cashmere ['kæʃmɪə] *adj. & n.* (made of) fine soft goat's wool.

casing ['keɪsɪŋ] *n.* hard covering which protects something.

casino [kə'siːnəʊ] *n.* (pl.-os) building where you can gamble.

cask [kɑːsk] *n.* large barrel.

casket ['kɑːskɪt] *n.* (a) ornamental box (for jewels) (b) Am. coffin.

cassata [kə'sɑːtə] *n.* Italian ice cream with dried fruit in it.

casserole ['kæsərəʊl] *n.* (a) oven-proof covered dish. (b) food cooked in a covered dish in the oven.

cassette [kə'set] *n.* (a) magnetic tape in a plastic case which can fit directly into a playing or recording machine; c. player = machine for playing cassettes; c. recorder = machine for recording and playing back cassettes. (b) film in a plastic case which fits directly into a camera.

cassock ['kæsək] *n.* long, *usu.* black gown worn by priests, choirboys, etc.

cast 1 [kɑːst] *n.* (a) throwing (of a fishing line). (b) plaster shape made from a mould. (c) worm c. = small pile of earth thrown up by a worm. (d) list of actors in a play/film; all the actors in a play/film. (e) c. of mind = way of thinking. (f) squint (in an eye). **cast 2** *v.* (cast) (a) to throw. (b) to mould metal/plaster. (c) to choose actors for a play/film. **cast 3** *adj.* which has been cast in a mould; a cast-iron excuse = a perfect excuse. **cast about for** *v.* to look for. **cast adrift** *v.* to abandon (a boat/a family). **cast aside** *v.* to throw away. **cast away** *v.* to throw away; cast away on a desert island = shipwrecked on a desert island. **castaway** *n.* person who has been shipwrecked. **cast down** *v.* to throw down; they were cast down = they were miserable. **casting 1** *n.* (a) moulding of a shape/thing which has been moulded. (b) choosing of actors. **casting 2** *adj.* c. vote = vote which

decides when the other votes are equal.
cast off v. (a) to calculate roughly the number of pages in (a book), before it is printed. (b) to untie the ropes holding a boat. (c) (in knitting) to finish stitches.
cast-off clothing, cast-offs n. pl. clothes which have been thrown away.
cast on v. to put (stitches) on to the needles when knitting.
castanets [kæstə'nets] n. pl.hollow clappers made of wood which are held in the hand and clicked in time to music by Spanish dancers.
caste [kɑːst] n. hereditary class (in Indian society).
castigate ['kæstɪgeɪt] v. (formal) to punish/to beat s.o. as a punishment; to criticize s.o. sharply.
castle ['kɑːsl] n. (a) large fortified building. (b) piece in chess which looks like a castle.
castor/caster ['kɑːstə] n. (a) sugar c. = pot with holes in the lid for sprinkling sugar; c. sugar = fine sugar. (b) wheel screwed on to the leg of a chair. **castor oil** n. oil from a palm which is used as laxative.
castrate [kæ'streɪt] v. to remove the testicles from (a male animal).
castration [kæ'streɪʃn] n. act of castrating.
casual ['kæʒjʊəl] adj. (a) not formal; c. labour = workers taken on for very short periods. (b) not serious. **casually** adv. by chance; in a informal way.
casualness n. being casual.
casualty ['kæʒjʊəltɪ] n. person injured or killed in a battle/an accident; person or thing destroyed or damaged; c. department = section of a hospital for accident victims. casuistry['kæzjuːɪstrɪ] n. debating principles in very fine detail.
cat [kæt] n. (a) furry domestic pet, which purrs and has a long tail; wild animal of the same family as the domestic cat; inf. be let the c. out of the bag = he revealed the secret; c. burglar = burglar who climbs wall or drainpipes to enter a house. (b) inf. woman who makes spiteful remarks. **catcall** n. whistle/ hoot (to show displeasure). **catfish** n. (pl.catfish) large ugly freshwater fish with whiskers. **catgut** n. gut used as thread. **catmint** n. plant much liked by cats. **catnap** n. shot nap. **cat's eyes**

n. small glass reflectors showing the centre or sides of a road. **catwalk** n. open metal gangway running along the outside of a ship/building.
catabolism [kæ'tæbɒlɪzm] n. breaking down of complex substances into simple chemicals.
cataclysm ['kætəklɪzəm] n. disaster. **cataclysmic** [kætə'klɪzmɪk] adj. disastrous.
catacombs ['kætəkuːmz] n. pl. underground rooms (used in ancient times for burying the dead).
catalepsy ['kætəlepsɪ] n. state where s.o. becomes unconscious and stiff. **cataleptic** adj. referring to catalepsy.
catalogue, Am. **catalog 1** ['kætəlɒg] n. list of things for sale/in a library/in a museum. **catalogue 2** v. to make a list of books in a library/of treasures in a museum/of things for sale. **cataloguer** n. person who specializes in the making of catalogues.
catalysis [kə'twlɪsɪs] n. chemical reaction which is helped by a substance which does not itself change. **catalyst** ['kætəlɪst] n. chemical substance which helps to produce a chemical reaction; anything which helps sth to take place. **catalytic** adj. referring to catalysis; c. converter = device attached to the exhaust pipe of a car to reduce carbon monoxide.
catamaran [kætəmə'ræn] n. boat with two parallel hulls.
catapult 1 ['kætəpʌlt] n. strong elastic band on a forked stick, used for throwing stones; c. launching gear = mechanism on an aircraft carrier for sending an aircraft into the air. **catapult 2** v. to send (an aircraft, etc.) into the air; to put (s.o.) into a new job quickly.
cataract ['kætərækt] n. (a) waterfall on a river. (b) film which grows over the eye and eventually prevents you from seeing.
catarrh [kə'tɑː] n. type of cold caused by inflammation of the nose and bronchial tubes. **catarrhal** [kə'tɑːrəl] adj. referring to catarrh.
catastrophe [kə'tæstrəfɪ] n. disaster. **catastrophic** [kætə'strɒfɪk] adj. disastrous.
catatonic [kætə'tɒnɪk] adj. (condition) where a patient either violent or stays without moving at all.

catch 1 [kætʃ] *n.* (*pl.*-es) (a) things which have been caught; we had a good c. = we caught a lot of fish; he's a good c. = he is a good prospective husband/worker. (b) action of catching. (a ball, etc.). (c) awkwardness/hitch; there must be a c. in it = there must be something wrong with it/there must be a trap: c. 22 = vicious circle which cannot be escaped from. **catch 2** *v.* (caught) (a) to grab hold of (sth) which is moving; I didn't c. what you said = I was not able to hear. (b) to get (a disease). (c) to find (s.o.) by surprise. **catching** *adj.* (disease) which can be caught/which is infectious.

catchment area *n.* (a) land from which a river gets its water. (b) area round a school from which all pupils must come. **catch on** *v.* (a) to understand. (b) to become fashionable.

catch out *v.* to find that (s.o.) has made a mistake; to ask (s.o.) a question to which he does not know the answer.

catch phrase *n.* popular phrase, *usu.* associated with an entertainer or advertisement. **catch up** *v.* to move faster than s.o. so as to draw level with him. **catchword** *n.* popular phrase. **catchy** *adj.* (tune) which is easy to remember.

catechize ['kætɪkaɪz] *v.* to ask questions. **catechism** ['kætɪkɪzəm] *n.* book of religious instruction; religious classes.

category ['kætɪgərɪ] *n.* classification of things/people. **categoric(al)** [kætɪ'gɒrɪk(l)] *adj.* straightforward/definite. **categorically** *adv.* definitely.

cater ['keɪtə] *v.* to supply food and drink (at a party, etc.). **caterer** *n.* person who supplies food. **cater for** *v.* to provide for. **catering** *n.* supplying of food.

caterpillar ['kætəpɪlə] *n.* insect larva which tuns into a moth or butterfly; c. track = endless metal belt running round a pair of wheels (on a tank, etc.); c. tractor = tractor which runs on caterpillar tracks.

caterwaul ['kætəwɔːl] *v.* to howl (like cats at night).

cathedral [kə'θiːdrəl] *n.* large church which is the seat of a bishop.

catherine wheel ['kæθrɪnwiːl] *n.* firework which spins round and round.

catheter ['kæθɪtə] *n.* very thin tube which can be inserted into the body to remove fluid.

cathode ['kæθəʊd] *n.* negative electric pole; c. ray tube = tube (as in a television set) where a stream of electrons hits a screen.

catholic 1 ['kæθlɪk] *adj.* (a) wide/general (taste). (b) referring to the Roman Catholic Church. **catholic 2** *n.* Catholic = member of the Roman Catholic Church. **catholicism** [kə'θɒlɪsɪzəm] *n.* beliefs of the Roman Catholic church.

catkin ['kætkɪn] *n.* flower of a willow or hazel tree.

catsup ['kætsəp] *n. Am.* ketchup.

cattle ['kætl] *n. pl.* animals of the cow family (such as bulls, calves, oxen, etc.).

cattlegrid *n.* rails forming a bridge, which prevent farm animals from getting out on to the road.

catty ['kætɪ] *adj.* (-er, -est) nasty/sharp tongued (woman).

caucus ['kɔːkəs] *n.* (*pl.*-es) group of party members who plan electoral strategy and choose candidates.

caught [kɔːt] *v.* see catch.

cauldron, *Am.* caldron ['kɔːldrəən] *n.* large deep pan for cooking.

cauliflower ['kɒlɪflaʊə] *n.* cabbage-like vegetable with a large white flower head which is eaten; c. ear = permanently swollen ear, found in boxers.

caulk ['kɔːk] *v.* to fill the cracks in a boat's hull to make it watertight.

cause 1 [kɔːz] *n.* (a) thing which makes sth happen; he died from natural causes = he died naturally, and was not killed in an accident or murdered. (b) reason for doing sth. (c) noble aim/charity to which it is good to give money. **cause 2** *v.* to make (sth) happen. **cause célèbre** *n.* famous court case.

causal *adj.* referring to a cause.

causeway ['kɔːzweɪ] *n.* road/path built up on a bank above marshy ground or water.

caustic ['kɔːstɪk] *adj.* (a) burning; c. soda = chemical used for cleaning. (b) sharp (wit).

caustically *adv.* in a sharp/witty way.

cauterize ['kɔːtəraɪz] *v.* to burn (a wound) to stop infection. **cauterization**

[kɔːtəraɪˈzeɪʃn] n. cauterizing.
caution 1 [ˈkɔːʃn] n. care/precaution.
caution 2 v. to warn. **cautionary**
adj. which warns. **cautious** adj.
careful/prudent. **cautiously** adv. in a
cautious way. **cautiousness** n. being
cautious.
cavalcade [ˈkævəlkeɪd] n. procession
(usu. of horseriders).
cavelier [kævəˈlɪə] adj. high-handed/
with no respect for other people or
customs.
cavalry [ˈkævəlrɪ] n. soldiers on
horseback.
cave 1 [keɪv] n. large underground hole
in rock or earth; c. bears = prehistoric
bears which lived in caves; c. paintings
= paintings on walls of caves done by
cavemen. **cave 2** v. to c. in = to
collapse. **caveman** n. (pl.-men)
primitive man who lived in caves.
caveat [ˈkævɪæt] n. warning (esp.
against doing sth); c. emptor = let the
buyer beware.
cavern [ˈkævən] n. very large cave.
cavernous adj. like a cavern.
caviar(e) [ˈkævɪɑː] n. very expensive
delicacy consisting of the eggs of a
sturgeon.
cavil [ˈkævɪl] n. (cavilled) to c. at sth =
to object to sth.
cavity [ˈkævɪtɪ] n. hole; c. wall = wall
made of two rows of bricks with a gap in
between.
cavort [kəˈvɔːt] v. to rush about in
excitement.
caw [kɔː] v. to make a croaking sound
like a crow.
cayenne [ˈkeɪen] n. type of hot red
pepper.
cayman [ˈkeɪmən] n. alligator.
CB [ˈsiːˈbiː] abbrev. for citizens' band.
cc [ˈsiːsiː] abbrev. for cubic centimetre.
Cd   symbol for cadmium.
CD   abbrev. for compact disk. CD-ROM
= CD-read only memory
cease [siːs] v. to stop. **ceasefire** n.
agreement to stop shooting (in a war).
ceaseless adj. without stopping.
ceaselessly adv. without stopping.
cedar [ˈsiːdə] n. large evergreen tree
with sweet-smelling wood; wood from
this tree. **cedarwood** n. wood from a
cedar.
cede [siːd] v. to pass (property/land) to

s.o. else.
cedilla [sɪˈdɪlə] n. accent placed under
the letter 'c'. showing that it is
pronounced 's'.
ceilidh [ˈkeɪlɪ] n. (in Scotland, Ireland)
party with performances of songs and
dances.
ceiling [ˈsiːlɪŋ] n. (a) inside roof over a
room. (b) upper limit.
celandine [ˈseləndaɪn] n. small wild
plant with yellow flowers.
celebrate [ˈselɪbreɪt] v. (a) to
remember a special day with parties and
feasts. (b) to perform (a mass).
celebrant n. priest who celebrates
mass. **celebrated** adj. very famous.
celebration [selɪˈbreɪʃn] n. festivity.
celebrity [səˈlebrɪtɪ] n. (a) famous
person. (b) being famous.
celeriac [sɪˈlerɪæk] n. vegetable with a
thick root tasting like celery.
celerity [səˈlerɪtɪ] n. speed.
celery [ˈselərɪ] n. white- or green-
stemmed plant, eaten as a vegetable, esp.
raw as a salad.
celestial [səˈlestjəl] adj. (formal)
heavenly/referring to the sky.
celibate [ˈselɪbət] adj. not married,
esp. because to religious vows.
celibacy n. state of being celibate.
cell [sel] n. (a) room in a prison/in a
monastery; condemned c. = cell for a
person who has been condemned to
death. (b) basic unit of an organism. (c)
basic political group. (d) part of an
electric battery. **cellular** adj. made up
of many small cells; (cloth) with open
holes in it. **cellulitis** n. inflammation
of tissue under the skin. **cellar** [ˈselə] n.
underground room or rooms beneath a
house.
cello [ˈtʃeləʊ] n. large stringed musical
instrument, smaller than a double bass.
cellist n. person who plays the cello.
cellophane [ˈseləfeɪn] n. trademark for
transparent flexible sheet for wrapping
or covering.
cellulose [ˈseljʊləʊs] n. chemical
substance found in plants, used for
making paper and paint.
Celsius [ˈselsɪəs] adj. & n. (scale for)
measuring temperature, where the
boiling point of water is 100°, and the
freezing point 0°.
Celt [kelt] n. descendant of a European

people now found in Scotland, Ireland, Wales, Brittany. etc. **Celtic** *adj.* referring to ancient or modern Celts.

cement 1 [sɪ'ment] *n.* (a) power made from limestone heated with clay, which when mixed with water dries hard. (b) mortar. (c) strong glue. **cement 2** *v.* (a) to stick together with cement. (b) strengthen/to make close. **cement mixer** *n.* machine for mixing cement.

cemetery ['semətrɪ] *n.* burial ground.

cenotaph ['senətɑːf] *n.* war memorial; empty tombs.

censer ['sensə] *n.* (in church) metal receptacle on a chain for burning incense.

censor 1 ['sensə] *n.* official who inspects letters/newspaper articles/plays/books, etc., to see if they can be sent or published. **censor 2** *v.* to forbid the publication of (sth) because it may be obscene or may reveal secrets. **censorious** [sen'sɔːrɪəs] *adj.* critical/which criticizes. **censorship** *n.* office of censor; act of censoring.

censure 1 ['senʃə] *n.* condemnation/criticism. **censure 2** *v.* to condemn/to criticize (s.o.).

census ['sensəs] *n.* (pl.-es) official counting of the population of a country.

cent [sent] *n.* small coin/one-hundredth part of a dollar.

centaur ['sentɔː] *n.* mythical animal; half man, half horse.

centenary [sen'tiːnərɪ] *n.* hundredth anniversary. **centanerian** [sentɪ'neərɪən] *n.* person who is 100 years old or more. **centennial** [sen'tenjəl] *adj.* referring to a centenary. **centigrade** ['sentɪgreɪd] *adj. & n.* (scale for) measuring temperature where the boiling point of water is 100° and the freezing point 0°. **centilitre,** *Am.* **centiliter** ['sentɪliːtə] *n.* liquid measure, on hundredth part of a litre. **centimetre** *Am.* **centimeter** ['sentɪmiːtə] *n.* measure of length, one hundredth part of a meter. **centipede** ['sentɪpiːd] *n.* creeping animal with a large number of legs.

centre, *Am.* **center 1** ['sentə] *n.* (a) middle; c. party = political party in the centre, neither right nor left. (b) large building containing several different units. (c) player who plays in the middle

of the field. **centre** *Am.* **Center 2** *v.* (a) to place in the centre. (b) to put the main emphasis (on). **central** *adj.* in the middle; c. heating = heating for a whole building which comes from one heating apparatus. **centralization** [sentrəlaɪ'zeɪʃn] *n.* act of centralizing. **centralize** *v.* to put under the control of a central system. **centrally** *adv.* in the middle. **centre forward** *n.* (in football) player in the centre of the forward line.

centrifugal [sentrɪ'fjuːgl] *adj.* which tends to go away from the centre.

centripetal [sentrɪ'piːtl] *adj.* which tends to go towards the centre.

century ['sentʃərɪ] *n.* (a) hundred years. (b) (in games) score of one hundred.

ceramic [sə'ræmɪk] *adj.* made of pottery. **ceramics** *n.* art of working in pottery.

cereal ['sɪərɪəl] *n.* (a) grain crop such as wheat, barley, maize, etc. (b) (breakfast) c. = grain foods eaten with sugar and milk for breakfast.

cerebellum [serɪ'beləm] *n.* Back part of the brain, which governs balance.

cerebral ['serɪbrəl] *adj.* (a) referring to the brain. (b) intellectual (rather than emotional). c. palsy = disorder of the brain which affects spastics. **cerebrum** *n.* main part of the brain.

ceremony ['serɪmənɪ] *n.* official occasion; solemn behaviour on an official occasion; don't stand on c. = be informal. **ceremonial 1** [serɪ'məʊnɪəl] *n.* way of conducting a ceremony. **ceremonial 2** *adj.* referring to a ceremony. **ceremonially** *adv.* with ceremony. **ceremonious** *adj.* with a lot of ceremony. **ceremoniously** *adv.* with a lot of ceremony.

cerise [sə'riːz] *n.* bright cherry pink colour.

cert [sɜːt] *n. inf.* (a) certainty; it's a dead c. = it is bound to happen. (b) certificate.

certain ['sɜːt] *adj.* (a) sure. (b) particular. **certainly** *adv.* of course. **certainty** *n.* (a) being certain. (b) sure/certain thing.

certificate [sə'tɪfɪkət] *n.* official document which proves/shows sth. **certifiable** [sɜːtɪ'faɪəbl] *adj.* (person) who should be declared insane; (thing)

which should be certified. **certification**
[sɜ:tɪfɪ'keɪʃn] n. act of certifying.
certify ['sɜ:tɪfaɪ] v. to write a certificate;
to put in writing an official declaration to
declare (s.o.) insane.
certitude ['sɜ:tɪtju:d] n. certainty.
cervix ['sɜ:vɪks] n. (pl.-es) neck, esp.
the neck of the womb. **cervical** adj.
referring to the cervix.
cessation [se'seɪʃn] n. stopping.
cession ['seʃn] n. ceding.
cesspit, cesspool ['sespɪt, 'sespu:l]
n. underground tank for collecting
sewage.
cf abbrev. for confer, meaning to
compare.
CFC abbrev. for chlorofluorcarbon.
cg abbrev. centigram
chafe [tʃeɪf] v. (a) to rub/to wear out by
rubbing. (b) to become irritated/annoyed.
chafing dish n. dish which keeps
food hot.
chaff [tʃɑ:f] n. (a) dried corn stalks left
after the grain is extracted. (b) good
humoured teasing.
chaffinch ['tʃæfɪntʃ] n. common pink
breasted finch.
chagrin ['ʃægrɪn] n. annoyance/
sadness.
chain 1 [tʃeɪn] n. (a) series of rings joined
together; c. reaction = events/chemical
reactions which build up rapidly.(b) row (of
mountains).(c) c. store = group of shops
belonging to the same company. **chain 2** v.
to attach with a chain. **chainsaw** n. saw
where the teeth are set in a continuous chain
driven by a motor. **chain-smoke** v. to
smoke (cigarettes) one after the other.
chain-smoker n. person who chain
smokes.
chair 1 ['tʃeə] n. (a) piece of furniture
for one person to sit on. (b) position of
chairman at a meeting; position of
professor at a university; in the c. = in
charge of a meeting. **chair 2** v. to be in
charge of (a meeting). **chairlift** n.
chairs on a cable which take skiers up a
mountain. **chairman** n. (pl.-men)
person who is in charge of a meeting;
head of a company. **chairmanship** n.
position of chairman; art of being a
chairman. **chairperson** n. person who
is in charge of a meeting. **chairwoman**
n. (pl.women) woman who is charge of
a meeting.

chaise longue n. chair with a long
seat.
chalcedony [ʃeɪz'lɒŋg] n. whitish
stone, a variety of quartz.
chalet ['ʃæleɪ] n. small (holiday)
house, usu. made of wood.
chalice ['tʃælɪs] n. metal cup in which
wine is offered at a communion service.
chalk 1 [tʃɔ:k] n. (a) soft white rock. (b)
stick of white or coloured material for
writing on a blackboard. **chalk 2** v. to
mark of write with chalk. **chalk up** v.
to mark (a score/a victory). **chalky** adj.
white like chalk; gritty like chalk.
challenge 1 ['tʃæləndʒ] n. invitation
to fight/struggle; to take up the c. =
accept the invitation of fight. **challenge
2** v. to ask (s.o.) to fight; to ask (s.o.) to
prove that they are right. **challenger** n.
person who challenges. **challenging**
adj. provocative.
chamber ['tʃeɪmbə] n. (a) room/hall;
council c. = room where a town council
meets; c. of commerce = official group of
businessmen in a town; lawyer's
chambers = offices of a lawyer. (b) space
in a piece of machinery, esp. one of the
spaces for cartridges in a revolver. (c)
space in an organ, such as the heart. (d)
c. music = music for a few instruments,
originally played in a small room.
chambermaid n. woman who cleans
room in a hotel. **chamberpot** n. pot in
which you can urinate, and which is usu.
kept in the bedroom.
chameleon [kə'mi:lɪən] n. lizard
which changes its colour according to its
natural surroundings.
chamfer ['ʃæmfə] v. to bevel the edge
of (sth).
chammy leather ['ʃæmɪleðə] n. very
soft leather used for washing windows,
etc.
chamois ['ʃæmwɑ:] n. (a) mountain
goat. (b) ['ʃæmɪ] very soft leather.
champ 1 [tʃæmp] n. inf. champion.
champ 2 v. to chew hard and noisily;
c. at the bit = to be impatient to go.
champagne [ʃæm'peɪn] n. sparkling
French white wine. **champers** n. inf.
champagne.
champion 1 ['tʃæmpɪən] n. best
person/animal in a particular
competition. **champion 2** v. to support
(a cause) strenuously. **championship**

n. (a) support of a cause. (b) contest to determine who is the champion.

chance 1 [tʃɑːns] *n.* (a) luck; games of c. = games where you gamble on the possibility of winning; to take chances = to take risks. (b) possibility/opportunity.

chance 2 *v.* (a) to happen unexpectedly. (b) to risk. **chancy** *adj. inf.* risky.

chancel [ˈtʃɑːnsl] *n.* part of a church near the altar where a choir sits.

chancellery [ˈtʃɑːnsəlrɪ] *n.* office of a chancellor; office attached to an embassy. **chancellor** [ˈtʃɑːnsələ] *n.* (a) government minister; (in Germany/Austria) = Prime Minister; C. of the Exchequer = British finance minister. (b) titular head of a university. **Chancery** [ˈtʃɑːnsərɪ] *n.* one of the divisions of the British High Court.

chandelier [ʃændəˈlɪə] *n.* light-fitting hanging from the ceiling with several branches for holding lights.

chandler [ˈtʃɑːndlə] *n.* person who supplies stores for ships.

change 1 [tʃeɪndʒ] *n.* (a) difference from what was before; c. of clothes = new set of clothes to wear; to ring the changes = (i) to ring peals of bells; (ii) to try several alternatives to see which works best. (b) money given back when you pay a larger amount than the price asked; (small) c. = money in coins.

change 2 *v.* (a) to make (sth) different; to become different. (b) to put on different clothes; changing room = room where you can change into sports clothes. (c) (for) to give sth in place of sth else; to c. (trains) = to get off one train to catch another. **changeability** [tʃeɪndʒəˈbɪlɪtɪ] *n.* being changeable. **changeable** *adj.* which changes often/is likely to change. **changeless** *adj.* which never changes. **changeling** *n.* baby supposed to have been substituted for another by fairies.

channel 1 [ˈtʃænl] *n.* (a) piece of water connecting two seas. (b) bed (of a stream); ditch/gutter along which liquid can flow. (c) means/ways; channels of communication = ways of communicating. (d) frequency band for radio or TV. **channel 2** *v.* (channelled) to direct/to persuade to take a certain direction.

chant 1 [tʃɑːnt] *n.* regular singing of a repeated phrase; monotonous song.

chant 2 *v.* to sing to a regular beat.

chaos [ˈkeɪɒs] *n.* confusion. **chaotic** [keɪˈɒtɪk] *adj.* confused/disorderly.

chap 1 [tʃæp] *n.* (a) *inf.* man. (b) cooked cheek (of a pig). **chap 2** *v.* to crack (skin). **chaps** *n. pl.* wide leggings worn by cowboys.

chapel [ˈtʃæpl] *n.* (a) small church; part of a large church with a separate altar; place of worship for nonconformists. (b) branch of a trades union (in the printing and publishing industry)

chaperon(e) 1 [ˈʃæpərəʊn] *n.* older woman who goes around with a young girl on social visits. **chaperon(e) 2** *v.* to protect (a young girl) who is going to a social occasion.

chaplain [ˈtʃæplɪn] *n.* priest (attached to a private individual or in the armed services). **chaplaincy** *n.* position of chaplain.

chapped [tʃæpt] *adj.* (of skin) cracked (with cold).

chapter [ˈtʃæptə] *n.* (a) division of a book; a c. of accidents = a series of accidents. (b) group of priests who administer a cathedral.

char 1 [tʃɑː] *n.* (a) small freshwater fish. (b) *inf.* charwoman. (c) *inf.* tea.

char 2 *v.* (charred) (a) *inf.* to do housework for s.o., (b) to burn black.

character [ˈkærəktə] *n.* (a) central being of a person which makes him an individual who is different from all others. (b) person in a play/novel. (c) odd person. (d) letter/symbol used in writing or printing. **characteristic 1** [kærəktəˈrɪstɪk] *adj.* special/typical. **characteristic 2** *n.* special/typical feature. **characteristically** *adv.* typically **characterization** [kærəktəraɪˈzeɪʃn] *n.* indication of character. **characterize** [ˈkærəktəraɪz] *v.* to be a typical feature of (sth). **characterless** *adj.* ordinary/with no special features.

charade [ʃəˈrɑːd] *n.* (a) game where spectators have to guess a word from a scene acted by others. (b) action which has no meaning/which is simply a pretence.

charcoal [ˈtʃɑːkəʊl] *n.* black material formed by partly burnt wood; c. grey = dark, dull grey colour.

chard [tʃɑːd] *n.* (*pl.*chard) green vegetable like spinach.

charge 1 [tʃɑːdʒ] *n.* (a) care (of s.o./ sth). (c) accusation (of an offence). (d) attack (by soldiers running forward). (e) amount of gunpowder in a cartridge/ bomb. (f) amount of electric current.

charge 2 *v.* (a) to make (s.o.) pay for sth. (b) (with) to accuse (of an offence). (c) to put a cartridge in (a gun); to put electricity into (a battery). (d) to attack (by running forward). **chargeable** *adj.* which can be charged. **chargehand** *n.* leader of a group of workers under a foreman. **chargepayer** *n.* person who pay the community charge. **charger** *n.* (a) battle horse. (b) device for putting electricity into a car battery (c) large dish for serving meat.

chargé d'affaires [ʃɑːʒeɪdæˈfeə] *n.* deputy of an ambassador, and official who takes the place of an ambassador.

chariot [tʃærɪət] *n.* two-wheeled vehicle pulled by horses. **charioteer** [tʃærɪəˈtɪə] *n.* person who drives a chariot.

charisma [kəˈrɪzmə] *n.* personal appeal. **charismatic** [kærɪzˈmætɪk] *adj.* which appeals to the people.

charity [ˈtʃærɪtɪ] *n.* (a) organisation which collects money to help the poor or support some cause; giving of money to the poor. (b) kindness (to the poor/the oppressed). **charitable** *adj.* (a) which refers to a charity. (b) kind/not critical. **charitably** *adv.* in a charitable way.

charlady [ˈtʃɑːleɪdɪ] *n.* charwoman.

charlatan [ˈʃɑːlətən] *n.* person who says he is an expert,. but really is not.

charlie, charley [ˈtʃɑːlɪ] *n. Sl.* a proper c. = a complete fool.

charlotte [ˈʃɑːlɒt] *n.* pudding with fruit and waters on the outside.

charm 1 [tʃɑːm] *n.* (a) supposed magic object; c. bracelet = bracelet hung with little ornaments. (b) attractiveness.

charm 2 *v.* (a) to bewitch/to put under a spell; he has a charmed life = he is very lucky. (b) to attract (s.o.) /to make (s.o.) pleased. **charmer** *n.* person who charms. **charming** *adj.* attractive.

chart 1 [tʃɑːt] *n.* (a) map of the sea, a river or lake. (b) diagram showing statistics; the charts = the list of most popular records. **chart 2** *v.* (a) to make

a map of (the sea, a river or lake). (b) to make a diagram of; to show (information) in a diagrAm. **charter 1** [ˈtʃɑːtə] *n.* (a) aircraft hired for a particular flight. (b) legal document giving rights or privileges to a town/a university). **charter 2** *v.* to hire (an aircraft or boat). **chartered** *adj.* (accountant, etc.) who has passed his examinations.

charwoman [ˈtʃɑːwʊmən] *n.* (*pl.*women) woman who does housework for s.o.

chary [ˈtʃeərɪ] *adj.* reluctant to do sth; cautious.

chase 1 [tʃeɪs] *n.* hunt; wild goose c. = useless search. **chase 2** *v.* to run after (s.o.) to try to catch them. **chaser** *n.* alcoholic drink such as beer, drunk after another, stronger, alcoholic drink.

chasm [ˈkæzəm] *n.* huge crack in the ground.

chassis [ˈʃæsɪ] *n.* (*pl.*chassis[ˈʃæsɪz]) metal framework of a car; undercarriage of an aircraft.

chaste [tʃeɪst] *adj.* (sexually) pure. **chastity** [ˈtʃæstɪtɪ] *n.* being chaste.

chasten [ˈtʃeɪsn] *v.* to reprimand; to make (s.o.) less proud. **chastened** *adj.* to make/less proud.

chastise [tʃæˈstaɪz] *v.* (formal) to punish. **chastisement** *n.* punishing.

chasuble [ˈtʃæzʊbl] *n.* long sleeveless coat worn by priests at ceremonies.

chat 1 [tʃæt] *n.* casual friendly talk.

chat 2 *v.* (chatted) to talk in a casual and friendly way; *inf.* to c. s.o. up = to get into conversation/to flirt with. **chat show** *n.* TV show where famous people talk to the host. **chatty** *adj.* (person) who likes to chat; (letter) full of unimportant news.

chattel [ˈtʃætl] *n.* object which you possess.

chatter 1 [ˈtʃætə] *n.* quick talking. **chatter 2** *v.* to talk quickly and not seriously; his teeth were chattering = were rattling because of cold. **chatterbox** *n.* person who cannot stop talking.

chauffeur [ˈʃəʊfə] *n.* person who is paid to drive a car for s.o. else.

chauvinism [ˈʃɒvɪnɪzəm] *n.* excessive pride in your native country. **chauvinist** *n.* person who is excessively proud of his native country; male c. = man who feels that men are superior to women. **chauvinistic** [ʃəʊvˈnɪstɪk] *adj.* nationalistic.

cheap [tʃiːp] *adj.* (-er, -est) (a) not costing a lot of money; on the c. = in the cheapest possible way. (b) low/sly (joke, etc.) **cheapen** *v.* to reduce the value of (sth). **cheaply** *adv.* not expensively/for a low price. **cheapness** *n.* low cost.

cheat 1 [tʃiːt] *n.* person who tricks s.o. so that he loses. **cheat 2** *v.* (a) to trick (s.o.) so that he loses. (b) to try to win by trickery.

check 1 [tʃek] *n.* (a) making sure; examination/test. (b) sudden halt (c) (in chess) state where your opponent has to move to protect his king. (d) pattern of squares in different colours. (e) ticket. (f) *Am.* bill (in a restaurant) (g) *Am.* = cheque. **check 2** *v.* (a) to make sure; to examine. (b) to bring (s.o.) to a halt. (c) (in chess) to put the opponent's king in danger. (d) to hold back. (e) *Am.* to tick/to mark with a sign to show that sth is correct. **checked** *adj.* with a squared pattern. **checkers** *n. Am.* = draughts. **check in** *v.* (a) to register when you arrive at a hotel/at an airport/at work. (b) to hand in (luggage) for safe keeping. **checklist** *n.* list which is used for checking. **checkmate 1** *n.* (in chess) position where the king cannot move. **checkmate 2** *v.* to put your opponent's king in a position from which he cannot escape. **check out** *v.* (a) to leave a hotel; to take (luggage) out of safe keeping. (b) *Am.* to verify/to see if sth is correct. **checkout** *n.* cash desk in a supermarket. **check over** *v.* to look over sth to make sure it is all there/all in working order. **checkroom** *n. Am.* cloakroom. **check up on** *v.* to verity/to see if sth is correct. **checkup** *n.* complete medical examination; general examination (of a car).

cheek 1 [tʃiːk] *n.* (a) fat side of the face on either side of the nose and below the eye. (b) *inf.* rudeness. (c) *Sl.* buttock. **cheek 2** *v. inf.* to be rude to (s.o.). **cheekily** *adv.* in a cheeky way. **cheekiness** *n.* being cheeky. **cheeky** *adj.* (-ier, -iest) rude.

cheep 1 [tʃiːp] *n.* little cry. like that made by a baby bird. **cheep 2** *v.* to make a little cry.

cheer 1 ['tʃɪə] *n.* (a) shout praise or encouragement. cheers! = (i) (when drinking) here's to you; (ii) (when receiving sth) thank you. **cheer 2** *v.* (a) to shout encouragement. (b) to comfort; to make happier. (c) to c. up = to make happier. (c) to c. up = to make or become happier; c. up! = don't be miserable. **cheerful** *adj.* happy. **cheerfully** *adv.* in a cheerful way. **cheerfulness** *n.* being cheerful. **cheerily** *adv.* in a cheery way **cheering** *n.* cheers of encouragement. **cheerio** *in.ter. inf.* goodbye. **cheerleader** *n.* person who directs the cheering of a crowd.

cheerless *adj.* gloomy/sad, **cheery** *adj.* happy.

cheese [tʃiːz] *n.* solid food made from milk; a c. = a whole round cheese. **cheeseburger** *n.* hamburger with melted cheese on top. **cheese cake** *n.* tart of sweet pastry and cream cheese with fruit. **cheesecloth** *n.* thin cotton cloth such as cheeses are wrapped in (often used for light shirts). **cheesed (off)** *adj. inf.* fed up. **cheeseparing 1** *adj.* mean. **cheeseparing 2** *n.* meanness. **cheesy** *adj. inf* smelling of cheese.

cheetah ['tʃiːtə] *n.* large animal like a leopard, which can run very fast.

chef [ʃef] *n.* (chief) cook (in a restaurant). **chef d'œuvre** *n.* masterpiece.

chemical 1 ['kemɪkl] *adj.* referring to chemistry. **chemical 2** *n.* substance (either natural or man-made) which is formed by reactions between elements. **chemically** *adj.* by a chemical process. **chemist** *n.* (a) person who specializes in chemistry. (b) person who makes or sells medicines. **chemistry** *n.* science of chemical substances, elements, compounds, and their reactions. **chemotherapy** ['kiːməʊˈθerəpɪ] *n.* using chemical drugs to fight disease.

chenille [ʃəˈniːl] *n.* soft cotton cloth, with a tufted surface.

cheque, *Am.* **check** [tʃek] *n.* note to a bank asking them to pay money from one account to another; c. book = book of blank cheques; c. (guarantee) card = card which guarantees that the bank will pay a cheque; blank c. = cheque which has no details filled; crossed c. = cheque which has two lines drawn across it and can only be paid into a bank.

chequers ['tʃekəz] *n. pl.* squares in a pattern. **chequered** *adj.* (a) laid out in a pattern of squares; c. flag = flag used to show the end of a motor race. (b) varied/with good and bad parts.

cherish ['tʃerɪʃ] *v.* to love/to treat kindly; to nourish (a hope).

cheroot [ʃə'ru:t] *n.* long think cigar with both ends open.

cherry ['tʃerɪ] *n.* small summer fruit, growing on a long stalk; c. (tree) = tree which bears cherries.

cherub ['tʃerəb] *n.* small fat child-like angel; child who looks like an angle. **cherubic** [tʃə'ri:bɪk] *adj.* round and innocent (face).

chervil ['tʃɜ:vɪl] *n.* herb used to flavour soups.

chess [tʃes] *n.* (no *pl.*) game for two people played on a board with sixteen pieces on each side. **chessboard** *n.* black and white squared board you play chess on. **chessmen** *n. pl.* pieces used in chess.

chest [tʃest] *n.* (a) piece of furniture, like a large box; c. of drawers = piece of furniture with several drawers for keeping clothes in; c. freezer = freezer of which the top is a lid. (b) top front part of the body, where the heart and lungs are; to get sth off your c. = to speak frankly about sth which is worrying you.

chesterfield ['tʃestəfi:ld] *n.* sofa with soft back and arms.

chestnut ['tʃesnʌt] *n.* (a) bright red-brown nut; large tree which grows these nuts; wood of this tree; sweet c. = edible chestnut. (b) red-brown colour. (c) red-brown horse. (d) *inf.* old joke; cliché.

chevron ['ʃevrən] *n.* sign shaped like a V.

chew [tʃu:] *v.* to make (sth) soft with your teeth. **chewing gum** *n.* sweet gum which you chew but do not swallow. **chewy** *adj.* which can be chewed for along time.

chianti [ki'æntɪ] *n.* Italian red wine.

chic [ʃi:k] *adj.* elegant; radical c. = fashionable left-wing opinions or people who hold them.

chicane [ʃɪ'keɪn] *n.* twisting piece of track on a racecourse for motor cars.

chicanery *n.* trickery.

chick [tʃɪk] *n.* baby bird. esp. hen.

chickpea *n.* type of yellow pea.

chickweed *n.* common weed with small yellow flowers. **chicken 1** ['tʃɪkɪn] *n.* young farmyard bird, esp. young hen; meat from a (young) hen.

chicken 2 *v. inf.* to c. out = to back out of a fight/argument because you out afraid. **chickenfeed** *n.* not much money/profit. **chicken-livered** *adj.* scared/frightened. **chickenpox** *n.* disease (usu. of children) which gives red itchy spots.

chicory ['tʃɪkərɪ] *n.* vegetable of which the leaves are used for salads, and the roots are dried and ground to mix with coffee to make it bitter.

chide [tʃaɪd] *v.* (chided/chid; was chided) (formal) to criticize.

chief 1 [tʃi:f] *adj.* most important; commander-in-chief = commander above all other officers. **chief 2** *n.* leader. **chiefly** *adv.* mainly. **chieftain** ['tʃi:ftən] *n.* leader of a tribe.

chiffchaff ['tʃɪftʃæf] *n.* European warbler.

chiffon ['ʃɪfɒn] *n.* type of very thin material.

chignon ['ʃɪ:njɒn] *n.* hair tied together in a knot at the back of the head.

chihuahua [tʃɪ'wɑ:wɑ:] *n.* breed of very small dog.

chilblain ['tʃɪlbleɪn] *n.* painful swelling on hands, feet, etc., caused by the cold.

child [tʃaɪld] *n.* (*pl.*children['tʃɪldrən]) young boy or girl; it's child's play = it is very easy. **childbirth** *n.* act of giving birth to a child. **childhood** *n.* state of being a child; time when you are a child. **childish** *adj.* like a child; silly/foolish. **childishly** *adv.* in a childish way. **childishness** *n.* being childish. **childless** *adj.* with no children. **childlike** *adj.* innocent like a child.

Chilean 1 ['tʃɪlɪən] *adj.* referring to Chile. **Chilean 2** *n.* person from Chile.

chill 1 [tʃɪl] *n.* (a) coldness in the air. (b) illness caused by cold. **chill 2** *v.* to cool. **chilliness** *n.* coldness. **chilly** *adj.* cold; not very welcoming.

chilli, Am. chili ['tʃɪlɪ] *n.* dried speed pod of the pepper plant, used to make very hot sauces.

chime 1 [tʃaɪm] *n.* ringing of bells.
chime 2 *v.* (of bells) to ring. **chime in**
v. inf. to enter a conversation.

chimney ['tʃɪmnɪ] *n.* tall tube or brick
column for taking smoke away from a
fire. **chimney pot** *n.* round top to a
chimney on a house. **chimney stack**
n. tall chimney rising above the roof of a
factory; group of chimneys on the roof of
a house. **chimney sweep** *n.* person
who cleans chimneys.

chimpanzee, chimp
[tʃɪmpæn'ziːtʃɪmp] *n. inf.* type of
intelligent ape from Africa.

chin [tʃɪn] *n.* front part of the bottom
jaw.

china ['tʃaɪnə] *n.* (no *pl.*) porcelain;
cups, plates, etc., made of fine white
clay. c. clay = fine white clay, used for
making china.

chinchilla [tʃɪn'tʃɪlə] *n.* grey fur from
a small American animal.

chine [tʃaɪn] *v.* to cut the rib bones from
the backbone of a joint of meat).

Chinese 1 [tʃaɪ'niːz] *adj.* referring to
China. C. lantern = garden plant, whose
seed pods form bright red balls.

Chinese 2 *n.* (a) (pl Chinese) person
from China. (b) language spoken in
China.

chink 1 [tʃɪŋk] *n.* (a) little crack. (b)
noise of chinking. **chink 2** *v.* to make a
noise by knocking glasses/metal objects
together.

chintz [tʃɪnts] *n.* think cotton cloth with
bright flower patterns, used for
upholstery.

chip 1 [tʃɪp] *n.* (a) little piece of wood/
stone, etc., to have a c. on your shoulder
= to be permanently indignant about sth
where you feel you have been treated
unfairly. (b) long piece of potato fried in
oil. (c) *Am.* potato crisp. (d) silicon c. =
small piece of silicon, able to store data,
used in computers. **chip 2** *v.* (chipped)
to break off a small piece of. **chipboard**
n. thick board made of small chips of
wood glued together, and used in
building. **chip in** *v.* (a) to contribute.
(b) to interrupt. **chip off** *v.* to break off.
chipped *adj.* c. potatoes = long pieces
of potato fired in oil. **chippings** *n. pl.*
small bits of stone used to make roads.
chipmunk ['tʃɪpmʌŋk] *n.* small North
American animal, like a striped squirrel.

chipolata [tʃɪpə'lɑːtə] *n.* long thin
sausage.

chiropodist [kɪ'rɒpədɪst] *n.* person
who specializes in chiropody.
chiropody *n.* treatment of feet.

chiropractor ['kaɪrəpræktə] *n.* person
who heals by message and manipulation
of joints.

chirp 1 [tʃɜːp] *n.* sharp short call of
birds/grasshoppers. **chirp 2** *v.* (of
birds/grasshoppers) to call. **chirpy** *adj.*
inf. bright and cheerful.

chisel 1 ['tʃɪzl] *n.* metal tool for cutting
small pieces of wood/stone, when hit
with a hammer. **chisel 2** *v.* (chiselled)
(a) to cut wood/stone with a chisel. (b)
Sl. to swindle.

chit [tʃɪt] *n.* (a) note/small invoice. (b)
young girl. **chitchat** ['tʃɪttʃæt] *n.*
gossip/talk.

chitterlings ['tʃɪtəlɪŋz] *n. pl.* fried
pig's intestines.

chivalrous ['ʃɪvəlrəs] *adj.* courteous/
very polite. **chivalry** *n.* politeness/
courtesy.

chives [tʃaɪvz] *n. pl.* onion-like plant
with small green leaves.

chivvy ['tʃɪvɪ] *v. inf.* to c. s.o. up/along
= to make s.o. hurry.

chlorine ['klɔːriːn] *n.* (element Cl)
greenish gas used to disinfect swimming
pools, etc. **chloride** ['klɔːraɪd] *n.*
compound of chlorine with another
substance **chlorinate** ['klɔːrɪneɪt] *v.* to
disinfect with chlorine. **chlorination**
[klɔrɪ'neɪʃn] *n.* disinfecting with
chlorine.

chlorofluorocarbon
[klɒrəʊfluˈɔːrəʊˈkɑːbən] *n.* compound of
chlorine and fluorine, used in aerosols,
which remains in the upper atmosphere
and contributes to the greenhouse effect.
chloroform 1 ['klɒrəfɔːm] *n.* chemical,
whose vapour when breathed makes you
unconscious. **chloroform 2** *v.* to make
unconscious with chloroform.

chlorophyll ['klɒrəfɪl] *n.* substance
which makes plants green.

choc [tʃɒk] *n. inf.* chocolate. **choc-ice**
n. hard black of ice-cream covered with
chocolate.

chock [tʃɒk] *n.* small block of wood
which prevents wheels turning. **chock-
a-block, chock-full** *adj.* completely
full.

chocolate ['tʃɒklət] n. (a) food made from cacao tree seeds; plain c. = bitter chocolate; milk c. = sweet chocolate made with milk; hot c. = hot drink made of powdered chocolate. (b) small sweet made from chocolate. (c) dark brown colour.

choice [tʃɔɪs] n. thing which you choose; I haven't any c. = I have to do it; c. peaches = peaches which have been specially selected.

choir ['kwaɪə] n. (a) group of people singing together. (b) part of the church where the choir sits. **choirboy** n. boy who sings in a church choir.

choirmaster n. person who conducts and rehearses a choir.

choke 1 [tʃəʊk] n. (a) blockage in the throat. (b) (in a car engine) valve which increases the flow of air to the engine; knob on the dashboard which activates this valve. (c) central inedible part of a globe artichoke. **choke 2** v. (a) to block (a pipe, etc.). (b) to stop breathing because you have swallowed sth. **choke back** v. to hold back (tears). **choker** n. piece of ribbon, etc., worn tightly round the neck. **choking** adj. stifling.

cholera ['kɒlərə] n. serious infectious disease causing severe diarrhoea.

cholesterol [kɒ'lestərɒl] n. substance in fats and eggs, also produced by the liver, which deposits fat in the arteries.

chomp [tʃɒmp] v. chew noisily.

chook, chookie [tʃʊk(ɪ)] n. inf. (in Australia) chicken.

choose [tʃuːz] v. (chose; chosen) to decide to take (sth) /to do one particular thing. **choosing** n. act of making a choice. **choosy** adj. difficult to please.

chop 1 [tʃɒp] n. (a) piece of meat with a rib bone. (b) inf. dismissal. (c) jaw esp. in animal. **chop 2** v. (chopped) (a) to cut into small pieces with an axe/a knife. (b) to c. and change = to do first one thing, then another. **chop down** v. to cut down (a tree) with an axe. **chop off** v. to cut off. **chopper** n. (a) axe for cutting meat. (b) inf. helicopter. **choppy** adj. quite rough (sea). **chop suey** n. Chinese dish of fried meat and bean sprouts. **chop up** v. to cut up into little bits. **chopsticks** ['tʃɒpstɪks] n. pl. long sticks used by oriental people for eating food.

choral ['kɔːrəl] adj. referring to a choir.

chord [kɔːd] n. (a) several notes played together in harmony. (b) line which joins two points on the circumference of a circle.

chore [tʃɔː] n. piece of routine work, esp. house work. **choreography** [kɒrɪ'ɒgrəfɪ] n. art of working out the steps for a ballet. **choreographer** n. person who works out the steps for a ballet.

chorister ['kɒrɪstə] n. person who sings in a choir.

chortle v. to chuckle loudly.

chorus 1 [kɔːrəs] n. (a) group of people who sing or dance together. (b) part of a song which is repeated by every one together. **chorus 2** v. to say sth all together. **chorus-girl** n. girl who appears as a member of a chorus in a variety show.

chose, chosen [tʃəʊz], ['tʃəʊzən] v. see choose.

chough [tʃʌf] n. large black bird with a red bill.

chow [tʃaʊ] n. (a) type of Chinese dog with thick fur. (b) inf. food.

chowder ['tʃaʊdə] n. Am. fish soup.

christen ['krɪsn] v. (a) to give name to (a baby) in church; to give a name to (a ship/a bell, etc.) at a ceremony. (b) to use (sth) for the first time. **christening** n. ceremony in church where a baby is given a name.

Christian 1 ['krɪstʃən] n. person who believes in Christianity **Christian 2** adj. referring to Christianity; C. name = first name given at a ceremony in church. **Christianity** [krɪstɪ'ænɪtɪ] n. religion based on the doctrine preached by Jesus Christ and followed by Christian ever since. **Christmas** ['krɪsməs] n. Christians festival on December 25th; C. Day = December 25th; Father C. = man dressed in red robes with a long white beard who is believed to bring gifts to children on Christmas Day. **Christmassy** adj. like Christmas.

chromatic [krə'mætɪk] adj. referring to colours or to a musical scale.

chrome [krəʊm] n. chromium; c. yellow = bright yellow. **chromium** ['krəʊmɪəm] n. (element: Cr) hard shiny metal which does not rust.

chromosome ['krəuməsəum] *n.* one of several elements which form a biological cell, and which carries the genes.

chronic ['krɒnɪk] *adj.* continual/ repeating (illness, etc); *inf.* very bad. **chronically** *adv.* very badly.

chronicle 1 ['krɒnɪk] *n.* record of things which take place; news story **chronicle 2** *v.* to write the history of (events) in the order in which they took place. **chronicler** *n.* person who writes a chronicle.

chronology [krɒ'nɒlədʒɪ] *n.* statement of the order in which things happened. **chronological** [krɒnə'lɒdʒɪkl] *adj.* in order of when the events happened. **chronologically** *adv.* in chronological order. **chronometer** [krə'nɒmɪtə] *n.* very accurate watch (as used for timing races).

chrysalis ['krɪsəlɪs] *n.* (*pl.*-es) hardcased stage through which a caterpillar passes before turning into a butterfly or moth.

chrysanthemum [krɪ'sænθəməm] *n.* bright-coloured autumn flower.

chub [tʃʌb] *n.* (*pl.*chub) fat river fish.

chubby ['tʃʌbɪ] *adj..* (-ier, -est) quite plump.

chuck 1 [tʃʌk] *n.* (a) part of a drill which hold the bit. (b) type of beef steak. **chuck 2** *v. inf.* to throw. **chucker-out** *n. inf.* person whose job is to throw undesirable people out of night-clubs.

chuckle 1 ['tʃʌkl] *n.* quiet laugh. **chuckle 2** *v.* to give a quiet laugh.

chuffed [tʃʌfd] *adj. Sl.* (a) happy/ pleased. (b) unhappy/annoyed.

chug [tʃʌg] *v.* (chugged) to make a regular puffing noise like a steam engine.

chukka ['tʃʌkə] *n.* period of play in a polo match.

chum [tʃʌm] *n. inf.* friend. **chummy** *adj.* friendly.

chump [tʃʌmp] *n.* (a) silly fool. (b) c. chop = large lamb chop.

chunk [tʃʌŋk] *n.* large thick piece. **chunky** *adj.* made of large pieces.

church [tʃɜːtʃ] *n.* (*pl.*-es) (a) large building for Christian religious ceremonies. (b) group of Christians together. **churchgoer** *n.* person who goes to church (regularly).

churchwarden *n.* senior member of a parish. **churchyard** *n.* cemetery round a church.

churlish ['tʃɜːlɪʃ] *adj.* rude. **churlishly** *adv.* rudely. **churlishness** *n.* rudeness.

churn 1 [tʃɜːn] *n.* large metal container for milk; container in which cream is churned. **churn 2** *v.* to turn cream to make butter. **churn out** *v. inf.* to produce in a series. **churn up** *v.* to mix/stir up.

chute [ʃuːt] *n.* (a) slide into water (in a swimming pool). (b) slide for sending things to a lower level.

chutney ['tʃʌtnɪ] *n.* highly-flavoured sauce *usu.* made with tomatoes, onions, vinegar and spices.

CIA [siːaɪ'eɪ] abbreviation for Central Intelligence Agency.

CID [siːaɪ'diː] abbreviation for Criminal Investigation Department.

cider ['saɪdə] *n.* alcoholic drink made from fermented apple juice.

c.i.f. [siːaɪ'ef] abbrev. for cost, insurance, freight.

cigar [sɪ'gɑ] *n.* tight roll of tobacco leaves which you can light and smoke.

cigarette [sɪgə'ret] *n.* chopped tobacco rolled in very thin paper which you can light and smoke. **cigarette case** *n.* special case for holding cigarettes. **cigarette end** *n.* end of the cigarette which has been smoked. **cigarette holder** *n.* holder for putting cigarettes in to smoke.

cinch [sɪntʃ] *n. inf.* (a) things which is very easy to do. (b) sth. which is certain to work.

cinders ['sɪndəz] *n. pl.* lumps of coarse ash left after coal has been burnt. **cinder track** *n.* race track covered with cinders.

cine- [sɪnɪ] *prefix* referring to moving pictures; cine-film. **cine-camera** ['sɪnɪkæmərə] *n.* camera for taking moving pictures.

cinema ['sɪnɪəmə] *n.* (a) theatre for showing films. (b) art of making moving pictures. **cinematographic** [sɪnəmætə'græfɪk] *adj.* referring to the cinema.

cineraria [sɪnə'reərɪə] *n.* houseplant with blue, pink or purple flowers.

cinnamon ['sɪnəmən] *n.* spice made from the bark of a tropical tree.

cipher ['saɪfə] *n.* (a) code/secret message. (b) monogram/initials of a name linked together artistically. (c) zero; person of no importance.

circa ['sɜːkə] *prep.* (used of dated) about.

circle 1 ['sɜːkl] *n.* (a) line forming a round shape. (b) row of seats above the stalls in a theatre. (c) group of people/ society. **circle 2** *v.* (a) to go round in a ring. (b) to draw a circle round (sth).

circuit ['sɜːɪt] *n.* (a) trip around sth. (b) area visited by a judge who travels from court to court. (c) path of electricity; printed c. board = flat card with metal tracks printed on it to form an electric circuit; short c. = fault (caused by crossed wires, etc.) when electricity follows a shorter path than usual; closed c. television = private television operating over a short area by cable. **circuitous** [sə'kjuːɪtəs] *adj.* roundabout (way).

circular ['sɜːkjʊə] *adj. & n.* (sth) round in shape; publicity leaflet given out to many people. **circularize** *v.* to send circulars to (people). **circulate** ['sɜːkjʊleɪt] *v.* (a) to distribute to pass round. (b) to move round. **circulation** [sɜːkjʊ'leɪʃn] *n.* (a) act of circulating; banknotes in c. = notes which are in use. (b) movement of blood round the body. (c) number of copies of a newspaper, etc., which are sold. **circulatory** *adj.* referring to circulation of the blood.

circumcise ['sɜːkəmsaɪz] *v.* to remove the foreskin of (a male person). **circumcision** [sɜːkəm'sɪʒn] *n.* act of removing the foreskin.

circumference [sə'kʌmfərəns] *n.* (distance round) the edge f a circle.

circumlocution [sɜːkəmlə'kjuːʃn] *n.* roundabout way of saying sth.

circumnavigate [sɜːkəm'nævɪgeɪt] *v.* (formal) to sail round (the world). **circumnavigation** [sɜːkəmnævɪgeɪʃn] *n.* sailing round the world.

circumscribe [sɜːkəm'skraɪb] *v.* (formal) to draw a line round sth; to set limits to sth. **circumscription** [sɜːkəm'skrɪpʃən] *n.* limiting; a limited area.

circumspect ['sɜːkəmspekt] *adj.* very careful.

circumstances ['sɜːkəmstənsɪz] *n. pl.* (a) way in which something took place; in the c. = as things have turned out like this/as it happens. (b) state of one's finances. **circumstantial** [sɜːkəm'stænʃl] *adj.* giving details; c. evidence = evidence which suggests sth but does not offer firm proof. **circumstantiate** *v.* to give details to prove (sth).

circumvent [sɜːkəm'vent] *v.* to avoid. **circumvention** *n.* avoidance.

circus ['sɜːkəs] *n.* (pl.-es) (a) travelling show, often given under a large tent, which animals, clowns, etc. (b) busy roundabout in the centre of a large town.

cirrhosis [sɪ'rəʊsɪs] *n.* disease of the liver caused, esp. by alcohol.

cirrus ['sɪrəs] *n.* small very high fleecy cloud.

cissy ['sɪsɪ] *n. inf.* man/boy who acts like a girl.

cistern ['sɪstən] *n.* water tank.

citadel ['sɪtədəl] *n.* fort guarding a town.

cite [saɪt] *v.* (a) to quote (a reference, a person) as proof. (b) to call (s.o.) to appear in court. **citation** [saɪ'teɪʃn] *n.* (a) official document recognzing an act of bravery. (b) quotation of sth as a reference or proof. (c) summons to appear in court.

citizen ['sɪtɪzn] *n.* (a) inhabitant of a town. (b) person with full rights as an inhabitant of a country; citizen's arrest = arrest of a suspected criminal by an ordinary citizen; citizens' band = private radio, mainly used by drivers of road vehicles. **citizenship** *n.* state of being a citizen.

citric ['sɪtrɪk] *adj.* c. acid = acid found in citrus fruit.

citrus ['sɪtrəs] *n.* c. fruit = fruit such as oranges, lemons or grapefruit.

city ['sɪtɪ] *n.* (a) very large town. (b) town created by charter, often with a cathedral; the C. = the old centre of London, now the main financial district.

civet ['sɪvɪt] *n.* wild cat, which provides a substance used in making perfume.

civic ['sɪvɪk] *adj.* referring to a city; c. centre = social/sports centre run by a city, c. authorities = leaders of a city.

civics *n.* study of municipal affairs.
civil ['sɪvl] *adj.* (a) belonging to the
general public, not to the army; c. service
= the government bureaucracy; c. servant
= person who works in a government
department. (b) referring to the ordinary
citizen; c. rights = the rights of a citizen;
c. rights movement = campaign to
ensure that all citizens have equal rights;
c. war = war between groups in the same
country; c. defence = defence by
ordinary citizens, not the army; c. law =
law referring to the citizen, not to
criminals; c. action = court action
brought by one citizen against another; c.
engineer = person who designs road,
bridges, etc. (c) polite. **civilian**
[sɪ'vɪljən] *adj. & n.* (person) not
belonging to the armed forces; private
citizen. **civility** *n.* politeness. **civilly**
adv. politely. **civilize** ['sɪvɪlaɪz] *v.* (a)
to educate (primitive people) to a higher
level of society. (b) to make (s.o.) less
rude/uncouth. **civilization** [sɪvɪlaɪzeɪʃn]
n. regular civilized way of conducting
society, making s.o. civislized. **civvy**
['sɪvɪ] *adj. inf.* civilian. **civvies** *n. pl.*
inf. civilian clothes.
Cl symbol for chlorine.
clad [klæd] *adj.* covered. **cladding** *n.*
material used for the outside covering of
walls.
claim 1 [kleɪm] *n.* (a) demand. (b)
statement/assertion. **claim 2** *v.* (a) to
demand as one's right. (b) to state/to
assert (without any proof) (c) to say you
own (sth) which has been left/lost.
claimant *n.* person who claims a right.
clairvoyant [kleə'vɔɪnt] *n.* person who
can see in his mind things which are
happening elsewhere/who can foretell
the future. **clairvoyance** *n.* act of
communicating with sprits/of foretelling
the future.
clam [klæm] *n.* large shellfish with a
hinged shell.
clamber ['klæmbə] *v.* to climb with
difficulty.
clammy ['klæmɪ] *adj.* (-ier, -iest) damp
and cold; humid (weather).
clamminess *n.* being clammy.
clamour *Am.* **clamor 1** ['klæmə] *n.*
shouting. **clamour 2** *v.* to shout/to
demand loudly. **clamorous** *adj.* noisy/
shouting.

clamp 1 [klæmp] *n.* (a) metal pieces
which are screwed tightly to hold sth
together. (b) pile of vegetables covered
with earth for storage. **clamp 2** *v.* (a) to
hold tight with a clamp. (b) to c. down
on = to stop (petty crime, etc.).
clampdown *n.* (on) severe action to
stop sth.
clan [klæn] *n.* Scottish family tribe.
clannish *adj.* loyal to the clan;
supporting your own group.
clannishness *n.,* being clannish.
clansman *n.* (*pl.*-men) member of a
clan.
clandestine [klæn'destɪn] *adj.* secret/
undercover.
clang 1 [klæn] *n.* loud noise of metal
ringing. **clang 2** *v.* to make a loud
ringing noise. **clanger** *n. inf.* very bad
mistake.
clank 1 [klæn] *n.* noise of metal hitting
metal. **clank 2** *v.* to make a noise of
metal hitting other metal.
clap 1 [klæp] *n.* (a) beating of hands
against each other to show pleasure. (b)
friendly tap (with the hand). (c) loud
noise (of thunder). (d) *Sl.* gonorrhoea.
clap 2 *v.* (clapped) (a) to beat your
hands together to show you are pleased.
(b) to give (s.o.) a friendly tap with the
hand. (c) to put (s.o. in jail) suddenly.
clapped out *adj. Sl.* worn out/broken
down (car, etc). **clapper** *n.* swinging
metal piece inside a bell which strikes
the bell; *inf.* like the clappers = very fast.
clapperboard *n.* black board with a
striped hinged section at the top, used in
film-making to indicate the start of a
scene. **clapping** *n.* applause. **claptrap**
['klæptræp] *n. inf.* rubbish.
claret ['klærət] *n.* red Bordeaux wine.
clarify ['klærɪfaɪ] *v.* (a) to make clear.
(b) to heat (butter, etc) until it becomes
transparent. **clarification**
[klærɪfɪ'keɪʃn] *n.* making clear/
explanation.
clarinet [klærɪ'net] *n.* wind instrument
in the woodwind group. **clarinettist** *n.*
person who plays a clarinet.
clarion ['klærɪən] *n.* trumpet; c. call =
loud clear call.
clarity ['klærɪtɪ] *n.* clearness.
clash 1 [klæʃ] *n.* (*pl.*-es) (a) loud noise
of things hitting each other. (b) battle/
conflict; shock of two colours seen side

by side. **clash 2** v. (a) to bang together making a loud noise. (b) not to agree/to be in conflict. (c) to fight.

clasp 1 [klɑːsp] n. (a) device for holding sth shut. (b) brooch. (c) act of holding in your hand. **clasp 2** v. to hold (sth) tight. **claspknife** n. (pl.-knive) pocket knife which folds.

class 1 [klɑːs] n. (pl.-es) (a) group of people with the same position in society; middle c. = class of professional people/ buorgeoisie; working c. = class of people who do mainly manual labour; upper c. = the rich/the aristocracy. (b) group of people (usu. children) who study together. (c) category/group into which things are classified. first c. = very good; to travel first c. = in the most expensive seats; tourists c./economy c. = less expensive seats on aircraft and ships. **class 2** v. to put (sth) in a category. **classifiable 1** adj. which can be classified. **classifiable 2** v. to put (sth) in a category. **classification** [klæsɪfɪ'keɪʃn] n. way of ordering things into categories. **classify** ['klæs] v. to arrange things into groups; classified information = information which is officially secret. **classless** adj. with no division into social classes. **class room** n. room in which a class taught. **classy** adj. (-ier, -iest) int. chic/ expensive looking.

classic 1 ['klæsɪk] n. (a) great book/ play piece of music/writer/composer, etc. (b) the classics = Ancient Greek and Roman literature, culture, etc. **classic 2** adj. (a) (style) which is elegant and based on that of Greek of Roman architecture/literature, etc. (b) typical. **classical** adj. (a) referring to the classics. (b) serious (music). **classicist** n. person who studies the classics.

clatter 1 ['klætə] n. noise of things hitting together. **clatter 2** v. to make a noise.

clause [klɔːz] n. (a) paragraph in a treaty or legal document. (b) part of a sentence; main c. = the central part of a sentence; subordinate clauses = clauses which depend on the main clause.

claustrophobia [klɒstrə'fəʊbɪə] n. terror of being shut inside a closed place.

claustrophobic adj. referring to claustrophobia.

clavichord ['klævɪkɔːd] n. old musical instrument like a small piano, with a very quiet sound.

clavicle ['klævɪkl] n. collarbone.

claw 1 [klɔː] n. (a) nail (of animal/bird). (b) pincer/part of a crab or lobster which pinches. **claw 2** v. to scratch with a claw. **claw back** v. to take back money which has been allocated. **claw hammer** n. hammer with the back of the head curved and split for removing nails.

clay [kleɪ] n. stiff soil found in river valleys; stiff earth used for making bricks or china. **clayey** adj. containing clay.

claymore n. sword used in Scotland.

clean 1 [kliːn] adj. (-es, -est) not dirty; c. break = complete break; to come c. = confess (to a crime etc.). **clean 2** adv. completely. **clean 3** v. to remove dirt. **cleaner** n. person/thing which removes dirt; vacuum c. = machine for sucking up dirt; (dry) cleaner's = shop where clothes can be taken to be cleaned; oven c. = strong substance for cleaning dirty ovens. **cleaning** n. removing dirt **cleanliness, cleanness** ['klenlɪnəs, kliːnnəs] n. state of being clean. **cleanly** adv. in a clean way. **cleanshaven** adj. with no beard or moustache. **cleanse** [klenz] v. to make very clean; cleansing cream = cream for cleansing the skin. **cleanser** n. material which removes dirt.

clear 1 ['klɪə] adj. (-er, -est) (a) pure; transparent. (b) with nothing in the way. (c) easily understood. (d) complete. (e) free. (of). **clear 2** adv. in a clear way. **clear 3** v. (a) to remove (obstacles); to c. the table = to remove dirty china and cutlery; to c. one's throat = to cough slightly to get ready for speaking (b) to make clear/pure; to become clear/pure. (c) to show that s.o. is innocent. (d) not to hit. **clearance** n. (a) act of removing obstacles; act of removing plants from land; c. sale = sale where all the goods are reduced in price to clear them from the shelves. (b) space for sth to pass through. **clearaway** v. to remove (sth) which is in the way; to remove (dirty dishes) from a table. **clear-cut** adj. definite/distinct. **clear-headed** adj. clever/with a sharp understanding. **clearing** n. (a) act of removing obstacles. (b) area in a wood where the trees have been cut down. (c) c. bank = bank which issues cheques. **clearly** adv. (a) in a way which is easily understood or heard. (b) obviously. **clearness** n. being clear. **clearoff** v. (a) to pay off (one's debts). (b) to run away. **clear out** v. (a) to throw out rubbish from (a room). (b) to go away. **clear up** v. (a) to make clear/pure. (b) to become brighter. **clearway** n. road where no parking is allowed.

cleat [kli:t] n. wooden/metal device for attaching ropes on ships.

cleave [kli:v] v. (clove/cleft; has. cloven/cleft) (old) (a) to split. (b) to cling (to). **cleavage** ['kli:vɪdʒ] n. space between the breasts. **cleaver** ['kli:və] n. large axe used by butchers.

clef [klef] n. sign at the beginning of a piece of music which shows whether it is bass or treble.

cleft [kleft] adj. & n. split; c. palate = split roof of the mouth; in a c. stick = in an awkward situation.

clematis [klə'mənt] n. climbing garden plant with large purple or pink flowers.

clement ['klemənti:n] adj. (formal) king/soft (weather). **clemency** n. mercy (to a criminal).

clementine ['klemənti:n] n. small sweet orange with a skin which is easily removed.

clench [klenʃ] v. to close tightly.

clerestory ['klɪəstɔ:rɪ] n. high row of windows in a medieval church.

clergy ['klɜ:dʒɪ] n. priests. **clergyman** n. (pl.-men) priest or minister, esp. of Anglican Church.

cleric ['klerɪk] n. (formal) priest/clergyman. **clerical** ['klerɪkl] adj. (a) referring to a clerk. (b) referring to clergy; c. dress = back suit and stiff white collar fastening at the back.

clerihew ['klerɪ'hju:] n. short four-lined humorous poem.

clerk [klɑ:k. am. klɜ:k] n. (a) person who works in an office; town c. = person who administers a town. (b) Am. salesman in a shop.

clever ['klevə] adj. intelligent/able to learn quickly; c. with one's hands = good at making things. **cleverly** adv. in a clever way. **cleverness** n. being clever.

cliché ['kli:ʃeɪ] n. saying/phrase which is frequently used.

click 1 [klɪk] n. short sharp sound.

click 2 v. (a) to make a short sharp sound; to c. one's heels = to bring the heels of one's boots together to make a noise. (b) to be surprisingly successful; it suddenly clicked = it was suddenly understood.

client ['klaɪənt] n. person with whom you do business/to whom you give a service. **clientele** [kli:ɒn'tel] n. all the customers (of a shop).

cliff n. high rock face, usu. by the sea.

cliffhanger n. suspense story, situation where one does not know what will happen.

climacteric [klaɪ'mæktərɪk] n. critical point in life, when changes take place in your body.

climate ['klaɪmət] n. general weather conditions. **climatic** [klaɪ'mætɪk] adj. refereeing to climate. **climatology** [klaɪmə'tɒlədʒɪ] n. study of climate.

climax ['klaɪmæks] n. (pl.-es) peak/greatest amount/highest point **climactic** [klaɪ'mætɪk] adj. referring to a climax.

climb 1 [klaɪm] n. act of going up, place where you go up. **climb 2** v. to go up. **climb down** v. (a) to come down a mountain/a ladder. (b) to give in/not to do what you had previously insisted on doing. **climber** n. person who climbs; plant which climbs.

climbing n. sports of climbing mountains.

clime [klaɪm] n. (formal) country.

clinch 1 [klɪntʃ] n. (pl.-es) (a) (in boxing) a position where both boxers hold on to each other. (b) inf. close embrace. **clinch 2** v. (a) (in boxing) to hold tight to the other boxer. (b) to settle (a deal).

cling [klɪŋ] v. (clung) to hold tight to (sth).

clinic ['klɪnɪk] n. specialized medical office or hospital. **clinical** adj. medical; c. thermometer = thermometer for taking a person's temperature; to take a c. view of something = to look at is coolly. **clinically** adv. in a clinical way.

clinician n. doctor who treats patients in hospital, but not a surgeon.

clink 1 [klɪŋk] n. (a) noise of glasses/metal objects hitting each other (b) Sl. prison. **clink 2** v. (of glasses/metal objects) to make a noise (when hitting together). **clinker** ['klɪŋkə] n. (a) hard waste material after coal has been burnt. (b) (of boat) made with planks which overlap.

clip 1 [klɪp] n. (a) piece of bent wire for attaching papers, etc., together (b) inf. smack. (c) inf. at good c. = quite fast.

clip 2 v. (clipped) (a) to attach (papers) together (b) to cut with scissors or shears. to punch holes in (tickets) to show they have been used. **clipper** n. (old) fast sailing vessel, used mainly for carrying tea. **clippers** n. pl.small scissors; instrument with a movable blade for cutting hair. **clipping** n. small piece cut out of a newspaper; cut off a hedge, etc.

clique [kliːk] n. small select group of people. **cliquey, cliquish** adj. like a clique.

clitoris ['klɪtərɪs] n. small erectile part (in female genitals).

cloak 1 [kləʊk] n. long outer coat with no sleeves. **cloak 2** v. to cover/to hide as if with a cloak. **cloakroom** n. (a) place where you leave your coat in a restaurant/theatre, etc. (b) toilet.

clobber 1 ['klɒbə] n. (no pl.) inf. belongings **clobber 2** v. inf. to ask for money/to tax.

cloche [klɒʃ] n. small glass or polythene tent used gardening for covering young plants.

clock 1 [klɒk] n. machine for telling the time; alarm c. = clock which rings a bell to wake you up; to work right round the c. = to work all day long. **clock 2** v. to c. in/out, on/off = to record your time of arrival or departure at work. **clock golf** n. game like golf where you hit the ball into a central hole from point round a circle. **clockwise** adv. in the same direction as the hands of a clock. **clockwork** n. (no. pl.) machine which works on a spring which is wound up with a key; like c. = smoothly.

clod [klɒd] n. large lump of earth.

clog 1 [klɒg] n. wooden shoe **clog 2** v. (clogged) to block.

cloisonné ['klwæzɒneɪ] n. type of enamel decoration where the sections of enamel are separated by little ridges of metal.

cloister ['klɔɪstə] n. (in a monastery)

covered walk round a courtyard. **cloistered** adj. shut up (as in a monastery).

clone [kləʊs] n. plant/animal which is grown from a piece of another plant/animal, and not from a seed.

close1 1 [kləʊs] adj. (-es, -iest) (a) very near (to); to keep a c. watch on someone = to watch someone attentively; c. election = election where the winner is separated from the loser by only a small number of votes. (b) shut; c. season = season when hunting is forbidden. (c) stuffy. (d) very friendly. **close1 2** adv. near; she is c. on forty. **close1 3** n. gardens and houses round a cathedral; small road with houses. **close-fisted** adj. miserly. **close-fitting** adj. tight (dress). **closely** adv. (a) attentively. (b) tightly. **closeness** n. (a) nearness. (b) stuffiness. **close-up** n. photograph taken at very close range.

close 2 1 [kləʊz] n. end. **close 2 2** v. (a) to shut. (b) to end (an argument/a debate). (c) to fight (with s.o.). **closed** adj. shut; c. shop = system whereby a firm can only employ members of a certain trade union. **close down** v. to shut a shop, etc., (permanently); to stop transmitting radio/TV programmes. **close in** v. (a) the days are becoming shorter. (b) to close in one s.o. = to run s.o. to earth/to come close to s.o.; one is chasing. **closing 1** adj. final; c. bid = last bid at an auction. **closing 2** n. shutting (of a shop, etc.); early c. day = day when a shop is shut in the afternoon; c. time = time when a pub, etc., closes. **closure** ['kləʊʒə] n. shutting.

closet 1 ['klɒzɪt] n. (a) small room/private office. (b) Am. cupboard. **closet 2** v. to shut oneself up with s.o.

clot 1 [klɒt] n. (a) lump of solidified blood, etc. (b) inf. fool. **clot 2** v. (clotted) to form lumps; clotted cream = cream which has been heated until it solidifies.

cloth [klɒθ] n. (a) piece of woven material. (b) woven material. **clothe** [kləʊð] v. to dress. **clothes** [kləʊðz] n. pl.things you wear; c. brush = brush for cleaning clothes; c. line = long rope for hanging wet clothes to dry; c. horse = wooden or metal frame for hanging went clothes to dry; c. peg. *Am.* & in Scotland c. pin = small plastic or wooden clip for attaching wet clothes to a clothes line; c. rail = rail where several dresses/coats can be hung. **clothing** [kləʊðɪŋ] *n.* (no. pl) clothes.

cloud 1 [klaʊd] *n.* mass of vapour/smoke (in the air); under a c. = (a) gloomy; (b) unpopular with the authorities. **cloud 2** *v.* to hide with a cloud. **cloudburst** *n.* sudden downpour of rain. **cloudcapped** *adj.* (mountain) topped with clouds. **cloudiness** *n.* being cloudy. **cloudless** *adj.* (sky) which no clouds. **cloudy** *adj.* (-ier, -iest) covered with clouds; not clear/not transparent.

clout 1 [klaʊt] *n.* (a) blow (with the fist). (b) *inf.* power/influence. **clout 2** *v.* to give (s.o.) a blow with the fist.

clove [kləʊv] *n.* (a) spice formed by small dried flower buds of a tropical tree. (b) piece of garlic. **clove hitch** *n.* type of knot. **cloven** [kləʊvn] *adj.* split.

clover [kləʊvə] *n.* common weed, used as fodder for cattle; to be in c. = to live very comfortably; c. leaf intersection = crossroads formed by two motorways and their linking road, which when seen form above looks like the leaf of clover.

clown 1 [klaʊn] *n.* (a) man who makes people laugh in circus. (b) stupid fool. **clown 2** *v.* (about, around) to play the fool.

cloy [klɔɪ] *v.* to be sickly sweet.

club 1 [klʌb] *n.* (a) large stick; golf c. = long stick with which you hit the ball when playing golf. (b) one of the four suits in a pack of cards. (c) group of people who allow others to join them (usu. on payment of a fee); golf c.; drama c. **club 2** *v.* (clubbed) (a) to hit with a club. (b) to put all your money together. **clubfoot** *n.* deformed foot. **clubhouse** *n.* house where members of a club meet.

cluck [klʌk] *v.* (of hen) to make a low noise in the throat.

clue [kluː] *n.* information which helps you solve a mystery/puzzle; I haven't a c. = I do not know at all. **clued up** *adj.* *inf.* expert/knowing a great deal. **clueless** *adj.* *inf.* stupid.

clump 1 [klʌmp] *n.* group of shrubs, trees, etc. **clump 2** *v.* to move making a dull noise.

clumsy [klʌmzɪ] *adj.* (-ier, -iest) not graceful; frequently breaking things. **clumsily** *adv.* in a clumsy way. **clumsiness** *n.* being clumsy.

clung [klʌŋ] *v.* see sling.

clunk [klʌŋk] *n.* noise of heavy metal objects hitting each other.

cluster 1 [klʌstə] *n.* group of small objects together. **cluster 2** *v.* to group (together).

clutch 1 [klʌtʃ] *n.* (*pl.*-es) (a) several eggs laid together in a nest. (b) clasp; into his clutches = into his hands. (c) mechanism for changing the gears in a car; c. pedal = pedal which works the clutch; to let in the c. = to make the gears connect; to let out the c. = to disengage the engine from the gears. **clutch 2** *v.* to grab.

clutter 1 [klʌtə] *n.* mass of things left lying about. **clutter 2** *v.* to fill (a room) with a mass of things.

cm abbrev. for centimetre.

co- [kəʊ] prefix meaning together.

co. [kəʊ, kʌmpɪnɪ] abbrev. for company.

Co. [kəʊ, kʌmpənɪ] symbol for cobalt.

CO [siːˈəʊ] commanding officer.

c/o abbrev. for care of.

coach 1 [kəʊtʃ] *n.* (*pl.*-es) (a) large bus for long distance travelling. (b) passenger wagon (on a train). (c) person who trains sportsmen, etc. **coach 2** *v.* (a) to train (sportsmen). (b) to give private lessons to.

coagulate [kəʊˈægjʊleɪt] *v.* to form into lumps/to cake. **coagulation** [kəʊægjʊˈleɪʃn] *n.* forming into lumps/caking.

coal [kəʊl] *n.* black mineral used as fuel; coal-fired boiler = boiler which is heated by coal. **coalfield** *n.* area of coal undergound. **coalhole** *n.* space in a cellar for storing coal; hole in the ground, through which coal can be delivered into a cellar. **coalmine** *n.* mine where coal is dug. **coalminer** *n.* person who mines coal. **coal scuttle** *n.* box for keeping coal near a fireplace.

coalesce [kəʊəˈles] *v.* to join together. **coalescence** *n.* joining together.

coalition [kəʊəˈlɪʃn] *n.* joining together; combination of political parties forming a government.

coarse [kɔːs] adj. (-er, -est) (a) not fine/ rough (laugh/etc.). (b) rude. (c) c. fishing = fishing in a river or lake. **coarsely** adv. in a coarse way. **coarsen** v. to make coarse. **coarseness** n. being coarse.

coast 1 [kəʊst] n. land by the sea; from c. to c. = across an area of land from one sea to another. **coast 2** v. (a) to ride a vehicle without using the engine or the pedals. (b) to sail along the coast. **coastal** adj. referring to the coast. **coaster** n. (a) ship which sails from port to port along the coast. (b) flat dish or small mat for standing a bottle/glass on. **coastguard** n. person who guards a piece of coast (watching out for wrecks/smugglers, etc.). **coastline** n. line of the coast.

coat 1 [kəʊt] n. (a) long piece of outdoor clothing which covers the top part of the body. (b) fur of an animal. (c) layer (of paint, etc.). (d) c. of arms = symbolic design on the shield of a family/town. **coat 2** v. to cover (sth) with a layer. **coat-hanger** n. piece of wood/wire/plastic on which you hang clothes. **coathook** n. hook (on a wall/door) for hanging a coat. **coating** n. covering (of paint, etc.).

coatrack n. rail where several coats can be hung.

coax [kəʊks] v. to persuade (s.o.) to do sth.

coaxial [kəʊˈæksɪəl] adj. c. cable = electric cable where several wires are laid parallel to each other.

cob [kɒb] n. (a) seed head (of corn/ maize, etc.); c. nut = hazel nut. (b) male swan. (c) short horse. (d) round loaf.

cobalt [ˈkəʊbɔːlt] n. (element: Co) white metal; blue colour obtained from the metal.

cobber [ˈkɒbə] n. (in Australia) inf. friend.

cobble [ˈkɒbl] v. to put things together roughly. **cobbled** adj. covered with cobblestones. **cobble (stone)** n. rounded stone formerly used for paving streets.

cobbler [ˈkɒblə] n. person who mends shoes.

cobra [ˈkɒbrə] n. large poisonous tropical snake.

cobweb [ˈkɒbweb] n. net of fine thread made by a spider.

cocaine [kəˈkeɪn] n. painkilling drug, also used as a stimulant.

coccus [ˈkɒkəs] n. (pl.cocci) ball-shaped bacterium.

coccyx [ˈkɒksɪks] n. (pl.-es) small bone at the end of the spine.

cochineal [kɒtʃɪˈniːl] n. red colouring used in cooking.

cochlea [ˈkɒtʃlɪə] n. spiral tube in the inner ear.

cock 1 [kɒk] n. (a) male bird (esp. a domestic chicken). (b) tap. (c) hammer on a gun which fires the cartridge. **cock 2** v. (a) to prick up (your ears). (b) to put (your) head to one side. (c) to set (a gun) ready for firing. **cock-a-doodle doo!** inter. showing the noise made by a cock. **cock-a-hoop** adj. triumphant at. **cock-crow** n. early morning. **cockade** [kɒˈkeɪd] n. rosette of ribbons worn on a hat. **cockatoo** [kɒkəˈtuː] n. type of large parrot. **cockchafer** [ˈkɒktʃeɪfə] n. large beetle. **cocker** [ˈkɒkə] n. type of spaniel. **cockerel** [ˈkɒkrəl] n. young cock. **cock-eyed** [ˈkɒkaɪd] adj. inf. stupid/odd (idea).

cockle 1 [ˈkɒkl] n. small edible shellfish with a double shell. **cockle 2** v. (of paper) to curl up/wrinkle.

cockney [ˈkɒknɪ] adj. & n. (person) who comes from the east part of London; way of speaking of a person from the east part of London.

cockpit [ˈkɒkpɪt] n. place where the pilot sits in an aircraft or boat.

cockroach [ˈkɒkrəʊtʃ] n. (pl.-es) large brown or black beetle.

cocksure [kɒkˈʃʊə] adj. very sure/self confident.

cocktail [ˈkɒkteɪl] n. mixed alcoholic drink; c. lounge = smart lounge bar in a hotel; c. snacks = snacks which are eaten with drinks; fruit c./prawn c. = mixture of fruit/prawns in salad; Molotov c. = grenade made of a bottle of petrol and a fuse which you light before throwing.

cock-up [ˈkɒkʌp] n. Sl. mistake/badly carried out work.

cocky [ˈkɒkɪ] adj. unpleasantly proud and conceited.

cocoa [ˈkəʊkəʊ] n. (no pl.) brown power ground from the seed of the cacao tree, used for a drink; drink made in this way.

coconut ['kəʊkənʌt] *n.* large nut from a palm tree; c. shy = stall at a fair where you try to hit coconuts with a ball; c. matting = rough matting made from the outer fibres of a coconut.

cocoon 1 [kə'ku:n] *n.* protective case of thread made by a larva before it turns into a moth or butterfly. **cocoon 2** *v.* to wrap (sth) p for protection (in).

cod [kɒd] *n.* (*pl.*cod) large sea fish; c. liver oil = oil from the livers of cod.

c.o.d. abbrv. for cash on delivery.

coda ['kəʊdə] *n.* last part of a piece of music.

coddle ['kɒdl] *v.* (a) to spoil/to pamper (s.o.). (b) to cook (eggs) in warm, but not boiling. water.

code 1 [kəʊd] *n.* (a) set of laws/of rules of behaviour; the Highway C. = rules for drivers; c. of practice = rules drawn up by a group, which all members of the group must follow. (b) secret signs agreed in advance for sending messages; the Morse c. = series of dots and dashes used for sending telegraphic messages; c. word = secret agreed word. **code 2** *v.* to write (a message) in code.

codeine ['kəʊdi:n] *n.* drug used to relieve pain and produce sleep.

codex ['kəʊdeks] *n.* very ancient manuscript of the Bible.

codger ['kɒdʒe] *n. inf.* man.

codicil ['kəʊdɪsɪl] *n.* additional clause to a will.

codify ['kəʊdɪfaɪ] *v.* to write (rules of conduct/laws) as a code. **codification** [kəʊdɪfɪ'keɪʃn] *n.* act of codifying.

co-director [kəʊdaɪ'rektə] *n.* one of two or more directors.

codling ['kɒdlɪŋ] *n.* small apple used for cooking; c. moth, moth whose larvae feed on apples.

co-educational [kəʊedjʊ'keɪʃənl] *adj.* (school) where boys and girls are taught together. **co-ed 1** *adj.* co-educational **co-ed 2** *n.* girl who goes to a co-education school.

coefficient [kəʊɪ'fɪʃənt] *n.* factor in mathematics.

coelacanth ['si:ləkænθ] *n.* prehistoric type of fish which is not extinct.

coeliac ['si:lɪæk] *adj.* referring to the abdomen.

coerce [kəʊ'ɜ:s] *v.* to force. **coercion** [kəʊ'ɜ:ʃn] *n.* force. **coercive** *adj.*

using force.

coeval [kəʊ'i:vəl] *adj.* belonging to the same generation.

coexist [kəʊɪg'zɪst] *v.* to exist/to live together **coexistence** *n.* living together; peaceful c. = where countries with different types of government exist side by side in peace. **coexistent** *adj.* living at the same time (as sth else).

coffee ['kɒfɪ] *n.* (a) seeds of a tropical plant, roasted and ground to make a drink. (b) made from these beans; instant c. = powdered extract of coffee which makes a drink when hot water is poured on it; c. table = low table for putting cups/glasses, etc., on; c. table book = large colourful art book. **coffee shop** *n.* small restaurant (often in a hotel) serving snacks.

coffers ['kɒfəz] *n. pl.* money chests. **coffer dam** *n.* watertight wall which allows work to be done on the bed of a river or the sea.

coffin ['kɒfɪn] *n.* long wooden box in which dead person is burned or cremated.

cog [kɒg] *n.* tooth (on a toothed wheel). **cog-wheel** *n.* wheel with teeth round the edge which fit into the teeth on another wheel and make it turn.

cogent ['kəʊdʒənt] *adj.* valid (argument); powerful (reason). **cogency** *n.* being cogent.

cogitate ['kɒdʒɪteɪt] *v.* to ponder/to think deeply. **cogitation** [kɒdʒɪ'teɪʃn] *n.* deep thought.

cognac ['kɒnæk] *n.* French brandy.

cognate ['kɒgneɪt] *adj.* (formal) with the same origin.

cognizance ['kɒgnɪzəns] *n.* knowledge (of a fact). **cognizant** *adj.* (of) knowing/being aware.

cognoscenti [kɒnjə'ʃentɪ] *n. pl.*specialists in the arts.

cohabit [kəʊ'hæbɪt] *v.* to live together as man and wife, esp. when not married.

cohere [kəʊ'hɪə] *v.* to hold together; to form a whole. **coherence** *n.* being coherent. **coherent** *adj.* clear/logical (ideas). **coherently** *adv.* clearly/ logically. **cohesion** [kəʊ'hi:ʒn] *n.* sticking together. **cohesive** [kəʊ'hi:sɪv] *adj.* which stick together.

cohort ['kəʊhɔ:t] *n.* division of a Roman army; large group of people.

coiffure [kwɑːˈfjʊə] *n.* hairstyle.
coiffeur [kwɑːˈfɜː] *n.* hairdresser.
coil 1 [kɔɪl] *n.* (a) roll (of rope); one loop (in sth coiled). (b) electric c. = wire wrapped round a shaft which conducts electricity. (c) contraceptive device. **coil 2** *v.* to roll up; to make loops.
coin 1 [kɔɪn] *n.* piece of metal money.
coin 2 *v.* (a) to strike/to produce (metal money). *inf.* to coin it = to make a lot.
coinage *n.* (a) system of money (of a country). (b) new word.
coincide [kəʊɪnˈsaɪd] *v.* to happen (by chance) at the same time as sth else.
coincidence [kəʊˈɪnsɪdəns] *n.* two things which happen together/by chance.
coincidental [kəʊɪnsɪˈdentl] *adj.* happening by coincidence.
coir [ˈkɔɪə] *n.* coconut fibre.
coition, coitus [kəʊˈɪʃn, ˈkəʊɪtəs] *n.* (formal) act of sexual intercourse.
coke [kəʊk] *n.* (a) (no *pl.*) fuel processed from coal, which gives a very fierce heat. (b) *inf.* Coca-Cola/trademark for a type of soft drink. (c) *inf.* cocaine.
col [kɒl] *n.* high pass between mountains.
colander [ˈkɒləndə] *n.* bowl with holes in it for draining water from vegetables.
cold 1 [kəʊld] *adj.* (-er, -est) (a) not hot; he got c. feet = he was not brave enough to continue; c. chisel = hard steel chisel; c. war = fight for power between countries without actually using weapons. (b) unfriendly (reception, manner). **cold 2** *n.* (a) state of being cold; left out in the c. = left on one side. (b) infectious illness when you sneeze and cough; to catch a c. **cold-blooded** *adj.* (a) (animal such as fish) with blood whose temperature varies with its surroundings. (b) with no feelings.
coldly *adv.* (a) in an unfriendly way.
coldness *n.* state of being cold. **cold-shoulder** *v.* to be deliberately unfriendly to (s.o.).
coleslaw [ˈkəʊlslɔː] *n.* cabbage salad.
coley [ˈkəʊlɪ] *n.* type of sea fish.
colic [ˈkɒlɪk] *n.* severe pain in the abdomen. **colitis** [kəˈlaɪtɪs] *n.* inflammation of the colon.
collaborate [kəˈlæbəreɪt] *v.* to work together. **collaboration** [kəlæbəˈreɪʃn] *n.* collaborating. **collaborator** *n.* person who collaborates.

collage [kɒˈlɑːʒ] *n.* picture made from piece of paper, etc., which are stuck on to a backing.
collagen [ˈkɒlədʒən] *n.* fibres which form tissue.
collapse 1 [kəˈlæps] *n.* falling down/ruin. **collapse 2** *v.* to fall down suddenly. **collapsible** *adj.* which can be folded up.
collar 1 [ˈkɒlə] *n.* part of clothing which goes round the neck. **collar 2** *v.* *inf.* to grab/to catch (s.o.). **collarbone** *n.* bone from the top of the ribs to the shoulder blade.
collate [kəˈleɪt] *v.* to compare texts, etc.
collation [kəˈleɪʃn] *n.* (formal) (a) light cold lunch. (b) comparison of texts.
collator *n.* someone who compares texts.
collateral [kəˈlætərəl] *adj. & n.* parallel; (security) which used as an additional guarantee.
colleague [ˈkɒliːg] *n.* person who works with you.
collect 1 [ˈkɒlɪkt] *n.* short prayer used on a particular day. **collect 2** [kəˈlekt] *v.* (a) to fetch and bring together. (b) to gather money for charity. (c) *Am.* to call c. = to ask the person you are phoning to pay for the call. **collected** *adj.* calm/not flustered. **collection** *n.* (a) group of objects brought together. (b) gathering of money; money which has been gathered; to take a c. for sth. **collective** *adj.* brought together; c. farm = farm where everything belongs to and is run by the workers on behalf of the state; c. bargaining = negotiations for new salaries carried out between union and management. **collectively** *adv.* all together. **collector** *n.* person who collects; tickets c. = person who takes used tickets from railway passengers.
colleen [kɒˈliːn] *n.* (in Ireland) girl.
college [ˈkɒlɪdʒ] *n.* teaching establishment (for adults and adolescents); c. of further education = college for study after secondary school; c. of education = college for training teachers. **collegiate** [kəˈliːdʒɪət] *adj.* belonging to/referring to a college.
collide [kəˈlaɪd] *v.* to c. with = to bump into.
collie [ˈkɒlɪ] *n.* type of sheepdog.
collier [ˈkɒlɪə] *n.* (a) coal miner. (b)

ship which carries coal. **colliery**
['kɒljərɪ] *n.* coalmine.
collision [kə'lɪʒən] *n.* bumping into
sth.
collocation [kɒlə'keɪʃn] *n.* (formal)
group.
colloid ['kɒlɔɪd] *n.* viscous liquid.
colloquial [kə'ləʊkwɪəl] *adj.* as is
commonly spoken; conversational.
colloquialism *n.* colloquial
expression. **colloquially** *adv.* as in
conversational speech.
collusion [kə'luːʒn] *n.* a secret illegal
agreement.
colon ['kəʊlən] *n.* (a) large part of the
intestines. (b) punctuation sign(:) to
show a break in a sentence.
colonel ['kɜːnl] *n.* officer in charge of a
regiment; army rank above lieutenant
colonel.
colonnade [kɒlə'neɪd] *n.* row of
columns.
colony ['kɒlənɪ] *n.* (a) territory ruled by
another country. (b) group of animals/
humans living together. **colonial**
[kə'ləʊnɪə] *adj.* referring to a colony/the
colonies. **colonialism** *n.* exploitation
of colonies. **colonialist** *n.* person who
advocates colonialism. **colonist**
['kɒlənɪst] *n.* person set form the home
country to settle in a colony.
colonization [kɒlənaɪ'zeɪʒn] *n.* act of
making a colony out of a territory.
colonize *v.* to occupy (land) and make
it a colony.
colophon ['kɒlɒfən] *n.* printed device
which identifies a publisher or printer.
color ['kʌlə] *n. & v. Am.* see colour.
coloration *n.* colouring.
Colorado beetle [kɒlərɑːdəʊ'biːtl] *n.*
striped beetle which attacks potato
plants.
colossal [kə'lɒs] *adj.* (a) very large/
huge. (b) splendid. **colossally** *adv.*
greatly/enormously. **colossus** *n.* (*pl.*-
es) huge statue; huge man.
colostomy [kɒ'lɒstəmɪ] *n.* operation to
attach a colon to an artificial hole in the
belly.
colour, *Am.* **color 1** ['kʌlə] *n.* (a)
shade/tint which an object has in light; c.
film/TV = not black and white; c.
scheme = arrangement of colours (as in
the furnishing of a room); off c. = feeling
unwell. (b) shade (of a person's skin); c.

bar = bar to s.o. because of the colour of
his skin. (c) paint; water colours = paints
which have to be mixed with water. (d)
colour(s) = flag; with flying colours =
with great success; in his true colours =
(i) coloured sports shirt; (ii) badge to
show that you belong to the first teAm.
colour 2 *v.* to paint with colour; to
make (sth) coloured. **colorant** *n.*
colouring material. **colour-blind** *adj.*
unable to distinguish some colours (usu.
red and green). **colour-blindness** *n.*
being colour-blind. **coloured** *adj.* (a)
(illustration) in colour. (b) adj. & n
(person) whose skin is not white.
colourful *adj.* brightly coloured;
picturesque/full of local colour.
colouring *n.* way in which sth is
coloured; substance which gives colour
to sth (such as food). **colourless** *adj.*
pale/uninteresting.
colt [kəʊlt] *n.* (a) young male horse. (b)
the colts = junior sports teAm.
coltsfoot *n.* wild plant with small
yellow flowers.
columbine ['kɒləmbaɪn] *n.* garden
plant with delicate pink or blue flowers.
column ['kɒləm] *n.* (a) tall pillar. (b)
thing which is round and long; spinal c.
= backbone; control c./steering c. = shaft
with a wheel on top for steering an
aircraft/a car. (c) line of soldiers; fifth c.
= subversive elements working behind
the enemy lines to weaken the morale of
the population. (d) long thin block of
printing on a page; regular article in a
newspaper. **columnist** ['kɒləmɪst] *n.*
journalist who writes regularly for a
paper.
coma ['kəʊmə] *n.* state of
unconsciousness. **comatose**
['kəʊmətəʊs] *adj.* (a) in a coma. (b)
sleepy/half awake.
comb 1 [kəʊm] *n.* (a) long-toothed
instrument for disentangling hair. (b) red
crest on the head of a bird (such as a
cock). (c) honeycomb. **comb 2** *v.* (a) to
disentangle (hair). (b) to search (an
area).
combat 1 ['kɒmbæt] *n.* fighting.
combat 2 *v.* to fight. **combatant**
['kɒmbətənt] *adj. & n.* (person) who
takes part in a fight. **combative** *adj.*
quarrelsome/argumentative.
combine 1 ['kɒmbaɪn] *n.* (a) financial

commercial group. (b) c. (harvester) = large machine for cutting and threshing grain. **combine 2** [kəm'baɪn] v. to join together. **combination** [kɒmbɪ'neɪʃn] n. (a) several things joined together. (b) series of numbers which open a lock; a c. lock. (c) motor-cycle c. = motorcycle with sidecar. (d) combinations = long one-piece winter underwear.

combs [kɒmz] n. pl. inf. combinations.

combustion [kəm'bʌstʃən] n. burning. **combustible** [kəm'bʌstɪb] adj. & n. (substance) which can easily catch fire and burn.

come [kʌm] v. (came; has come) (a) to arrive here; c. and see us; c. up to my room. (b) to happen; how does the door c. to be open? inf. how c.? = why/how did it happen? (c) to add up to; it comes to £5; c. to that = by the way/while we are talking of that. (d) to c. = in the future. **come across** v. to find. **come after** v. to follow. **come along** v. to arrive. **come back** v. to return.

comeback n. (a) repercussions. (b) return of a singer/sportsman) after retirement. **come by** v. to obtain.

come down v. to descend.

comedown n. humiliation. **come into** v. (a) to enter. (b) to inherit (money). **come off** v. (a) to fall off. (b) to result; he came off badly = the result was bad for him. **come on** v. (a) to hurry. (b) to arrive. **come out** v. (a) to move outside. (b) (of photograph, etc.) to result/to show. (c) to c. out (on strike).

come over v. (a) to cross. (b) to start to feel; what has c. over him? = what is the matter with him? **comer** n. person who comes; late comers; all comers.

come round v. (a) to visit. (b) to recover from unconsciousness. (c) to change one's way of thinking; to agree with s.o. else. **come to** v. to recover (from unconsciousness).

comeuppance n. inf. he got his c. = he was punished. **coming 1** adj. approaching. **coming 2** n. arrival; comings and goings.

comedy ['kɒmədɪ] n. play or film which makes you laugh; funny aspect (of an event). **comedian** [kəmi:dɪ'en] n. man who tells jokes to make people laugh. **comedienne** [kəmi:dɪ'en] n. woman who tells jokes to make people laugh.

comely ['kʌmlɪ] adj. attractive (woman).

comestibles [kʌ'mestɪbəlz] n. pl.(formal) food.

comet ['kɒmɪt] n. body which moves visibly through space with a bright tail.

comfort 1 ['kʌmfət] n. (a) thing which helps to relive suffering. (b) ease of living; Am. c. station = public toilet.

comfort 2 v. to relieve the suffering of (s.o. who is miserable, etc.).

comfortable adj. soft/relaxing, giving ease. **comfortably** adv. in a soft/ relaxing way; c. off = having plenty of money. **comforter** n. (a) person who comforts. (b) long woolly scarf. (c) Am. eiderdown. (d) baby's dummy.

comforting adj. consoling.

comfortless adj. harsh/hard. **comfy** adj. (-ier, iest) inf. comfortable.

comfrey ['kʌmfrɪ] n. herb, used both medicinally and also to make compost.

comic 1 ['kɒmɪk] adj. funny, amusing.

comic 2 n. (a) person who tells jokes to make people laugh. (b) children's paper with cartoon stories. **comical** adj. funny. **comically** adv. in a funny way.

comma ['kɒmə] n. (a) punctuation mark (,) showing a break in a sentence around a clause; inverted commas (" ") = printing signs showing speech. (b) small brown butterfly with ragged wings.

command 1 [kə'mɑːnd] n. (a) order; c. performance = play/film put on at the command of the king/queen; second-in-c. = officer/person directly under the main commander/director; in c. of = in charge of. (b) knowledge (of a language).

command 2 v. (a) to order. (b) to be in charge of. (c) to demand (a price).

commandant [kɒmən'dænt] n. officer in charge of a military base, etc.

commandeer [kɒmen'dɪə] v. to order that (sth) should be given over to the armed forces. **commander** [kə'mɑːndə] n. officer in charge (of a corps/ship); rank in the navy below captain.

commanding adj. in command.

commandment n. rule; the Ten Commandments = rules given by God to Moses. **commando** n. (pl -os); group of specially trained shock troops; member of such a group.

commemorate [kə'meməreɪt] v. to celebrate (the memory of something/a special occasion, etc.). **commemoration** [kəmemə'reɪʃn] n. commemorating. **commemorative** [kə'memərətɪv] adj. which commemorates.

commence [kə'mens] v. (formal) to begin. **commencement** n. (a) beginning (b) Am. day when degrees are awarded at a university.

commend [kə'mend] v. (formal) to praise. **commendable** adj. praiseworthy. **commendably** adv. in a praiseworthy way. **commendation** [kɒmen'deɪʃn] n. official praise. **commendatory** [kə'mendətrɪ] adj. which praises.

commensurate [kə'mensjʊrət] adj. c. with = in proportion to.

comment 1 ['kɒment] n. remark/what you feel about something; no c. = I refuse to discuss the matter. **comment 2** v. to make remarks (on).

commentary n. (a) remarks about a book, etc. (b) spoken report on a football match/horse race, etc. **commentator** n. person who reports on events on the radio r television.

commerce ['kɒmɜːs] n. business transactions; chamber of c. = association of businessmen. **commercial 1** [kə'mɜːʃl] adj. dealing with business; c vehicle = vehicle used for business purposes. **commercial 2** n. piece of publicity of television. **commercialization** [kəmɜːʃəlaɪ'zeɪʃn] n. making sth into a business proposition. **commercialize** v. to make into a business proposition. **commercially** adv. in a commercial way.

commiserate [kə'mɪzəreɪt] v. to sympathize (with s.o.). **commiseration** [kəmɪzə'reɪʃn] n. sympathizing.

commissar [kɒmɪ'sɑː] n. political leader (in a communist state). **commissariat** [kɒmɪ'seərɪət] n. department (esp. in the army) dealing with the supply of food.

commission 1 [kə'mɪʃn] n. (a) group of people which investigates problems of national importance. (b) document naming someone an officer. (c) order for sth to be made/to be used; out of c. = not

in working order. (d) percentage of sales value given to the salesman.

commission 2 v. (a) to authorize (s.o.) to be an officer/to authorize (an artist/architect, etc.) to do a piece of work; to put (a ship) into commission. (b) to authorize (a piece of work) to be done. **commissionaire** [kəmɪʃə'neə] n. doorkeeper (in a hotel/office block). **commissioner** [kə'mɪʃnə] n. (a) representative of authority; c. of police = highest ranking police officer; High C. = ambassador of a Commonwealth country. (b) c. for oaths = solicitor who can take sworn statements. (c) member of a commission.

commit [kə'mɪt] v. (committed) (a) to carry out (a crime). (b) to c. s.o. for trail = to send s.o. to the courts for trail. (c) to c. oneself = to promise to do sth. **committed** adj. firmly believing in (sth). **commitment** n. (a) promise. (b) agreement to do sth. (c) promise to pay money. **committal** n. sending of prisoner to the courts for trial.

committee [kə'mɪtɪ] n. official group of people who organize or discuss on behalf of a large body; to be one a c. = to be a member of it.

commode [kə'məʊd] n. (a) chest of drawers. (b) chair with a chamberport in the seat.

commodious [kə'məʊdɪəs] adj. spacious/large (room/house, etc).

commodity [kə'mɒdɪtɪ] n. merchandise; thing sold; basic commodities = basic foodstuffs and raw materials.

commodore ['kɒmədɔː] n. rank in the Navy above captain. (b) person who directs a yacht club.

common 1 ['kɒmən] adj. (-er, -est) (a) belonging to everyone/to the public in general; it is c. knowledge = everyone knows it. (b) belonging to two or more people; we have to two things in c.; C. Market = organization linking several European countries for purposes of trade. (c) ordinary/which happens frequently. (d) vulgar/of the lower class. **common 2** n. land which belongs to a community. **commoner** n. ordinary citizen/not a noble. **common law** n. law which is derived from decisions of courts, rather than from statutes; c.-1.

wife = woman who lives with a man as his wife, with out being married to him.
commonly *adv.* frequently.
common-or-garden *adj.* ordinary.
commonplace *adj. & n.* (thing) which happens frequently. **commons** *n.* (a) on short commons = not having enough food. (b) the (House of) C. = the lower (elected) house of the British parliament. **commonsense** *n.* ordinary good sense. **commonwealth** *n.* republic; group of states the (British) C. = association of countries which were formerly colonies of Britain but which are now independent.
commotion [kə'məʊʃən] *n.* confusion/trouble.
commune 1 ['kɒmjuːn] *n.* group of people who work together sharing everything. **commune 2** [kə'mjuːn] *v.* to be in touch (with s.o./sth) in spirit.
communal [kə'mjuːnəl] *adj.* (property) held in common/belonging to several people. **communally** *adv.* done by several people together.
communicate [kə'mjuːnɪkeɪt] *v.* (a) (with) to pass information to s.o./to be in touch with s.o. (b) communicating rooms = rooms with a connecting door; communicating door = door which links two rooms. **communicable** *adj.* which can be passed on to s.o.
communicant *n.* person who takes Holy Communion. **communication** [kəmjuːnɪ'keɪʃn] *n.* act of communicating/passing of information; c. cord = alarm signal on a train.
communicative [kə'mjuːnɪkətɪv] *adj.* talkative; (person) who is willing to give information. **communion** *n.* (a) fellowship with s.o.; (b) Holy C. = central Christian religious ceremony, celebrating the Last Supper.
communiqué [kə'mjuːnɪkeɪ] *n.* official news item given to the press.
communism ['kɒmjʊnɪzəm] *n.* political doctrine whereby the state owns all industry and land. **communist 1** *adj.* referring to communism.
communist 2 *n.* (a) person who believes in communism. (b) member of the Communist Party.
community [kə'mjuːnɪtɪ] *n.* (a) group of people living in one place; an urban c. = a town and its inhabitants; c. centre =

sports/arts centre belonging to a town; c. charge = tax levied on all adult which funds local government expenditure; the European C. = the Common Market; religious c. = group of monks or nuns. (b) the population as a whole.(c) group of organisms living in an area.
commute [kə'mjuːt] *v.* (a) to reduce (a legal penalty). (b) to travel to work in town every day. (c) to pay money instead of doing a piece of work. **commutable** *adj.* which can be commuted.
commutation [kɒmjʊ'teɪʃn] *n.* act of commuting a sentence. **commuter** *n.* person who travels to work in town every day; c. train = train for commuters; c. belt = area round a town where commuters live.
compact 1 ['kɒmpækt] *n.* (a) agreement. (b) small box for carrying face powder. (c) *Am.* small car.
compact 2 [kəm'pækt] *adj.* small; tight/close together. **compact 3** *v.* to make (sth) compact. **compact disk** *n.* metal recording disk, which can hold a larger amount of music than a plastic record, and which is read by a laser in a special player. **compactly** *adv.* tightly/close together.
companion [kəm'pænjən] *n.* (a) person who travels or lives with s.o. (b) handbook. **companionable** *adj.* friendly. **companionship** *n.* friendship. **companionway** *n.* stairway on a ship.
company ['kʌmpənɪ] *n.* (a) being together with other people; he is good c. = he is an entertaining companion; to part c. = to split up; to get into bad c. = to get in with bad c. = to get into bad companions. (b) group of soldiers within a battalion; crew of a ship. (c) theatrical c. = group of actors who play together. (d) (usu. written Co. in names) commercial firm.
compare [kəm'peə] *v.* to put two things side by side to see how they differ; he compared our bread to a lump of concrete = he said it was like a lump of concrete; his work doesn't c. very well with his brother's = is not as good as his brother's. **comparability** [kɒmpərə'bɪlɪtɪ] *n.* being comparable.
comparable ['kɒmprəbl] *adj.* which can be compared. **comparative 1**

[kəm'pærətɪv] *adj.* relative.
comparative 2 *n.* form of an
adjective/adverb showing an increase in
level; 'better' and 'more stupidly' are the
comparatives of 'good' and 'stupidly'.
comparatively *adv.* more or less;
relatively. **comparison** *n.* act of
comparing; there is no c. = you cannot
compare them, one is so much better
than the other.
compartment [kəm'pɑːtmənt] *n.*
division inside a box; separate section in
a railway carriage/in a ship.
compass ['kʌmpəs] *n.* (*pl.*-es) (a)
device which indicates the north by
means of a needle. (b) a pair of
compasses = instrument for drawing a
circle. (c) scope/range.
compassion [kəm'pæʃn] *n.* pity; to
have c. on s.o. = to take pity on s.o.
compassionate *adj.* merciful/
pitying; c. leave = extra holiday given to
s.o. to visit a sick relative, etc.
compatible [kəm'pætəbl] *adj.* able
to fit with sth. **compatibility**
[kəmpætə'bɪlɪtɪ] *n.* ability to fit
together.
compatriot [kəm'pætrɪət] *n.* person
who comes from the same country.
compel [kəm'pel] *v.* (compelled) to
force. **compelling** *adj.* which forces;
very exciting (story/film).
compendium [kəm'pendɪəm] *n.*
collection (of paper/notes/games)
compensate ['kɒmpenseɪt] *v.* to pay
(s.o.) for damage done; to pay for a loss.
compensation [kɒmpen'seɪʃn] *n.*
payment for damage **compensatory**
adj. which compensates.
compère 1 ['kɒmpeə] *n.* host/person
who introduces a show. **compère 2** *v.*
to act as host in a show/to introduce
different acts.
compete [kəm'piːt] *v.* to try to beat
others in a race/a game/a business.
competent ['kɒmpɪtənt] *adj.* able (to
do sth) /capable (of doing sth); efficient.
competence *n.* (a) capability/
efficiency. (b) professional
responsibilities; the case is outside the c.
of this court. **competently** *adv.* in a
capable/efficient way.
competition [kɒmpə'tɪʃn] *n.* (a) game
where several teams or people try to win.
(b) commercial rivalry/trying to sell

more than another firm. **competitive**
[kəm'petɪtɪv] *adj.* (person) who likes
entering competitions; (sport) which is
based on competitions; (prices) which
aim to compete with those of rival firms.
competitor *n.* person who goes in for
a competition; rival firm.
compile [kəm'paɪl] *v.* to draw up (a
list); to make a collection (of poetry); to
write (a dictionary). **compilation**
[kɒmpɪ'leɪʃn] *n.* act of compiling; work
which has been complied. **compiler**
[kəm'paɪlə] *n.* (a) person who complies.
(b) computer program which
converts
coded data to a machine readable
program.
complacent [kəm'pleɪsnt] *adj.* self-
satisfied. **complacency** *n.* being
complacent. **complacently** *adv.* in a
complacent way.
complain [kəm'pleɪn] *v.* to grumble
because sth is wrong. **complaint** *n.* (a)
grumble/statement that sth is wrong. (b)
illness.
complaisant [kəm'pleɪznt] *adj.* eager
to please.
complement 1 ['kɒmplɪmənt] *n.* (a)
number of people needed to fill sth. (b)
thing which adds to or fits in with sth
else. **complement 2** [kɒmplɪ'ment] *v.*
to complete/to fit in (with sth).
complementary [kɒmplɪ'mentərɪ] *adj.*
which fills/completes sth.
complete 1 [kəm'pliːt] *adj.* (a) full/
whole. (b) finished. **complete 2** *v.* (a)
to finish. (b) to fill in (a form).
completely *adv.* wholly.
completeness *n.* fullness (of success).
completion *n.* finishing; finish; c. of a
contract = signing of a contract.
complex 1 ['kɒmpleks] *adj.*
complicated. **complex 2** *n.* (*pl.*-es) (a)
series of building. (b) repressed
emotions/obsessions; inferiority c. =
feeling that you are inferior; (Œdipus c.
= feeling of hatred for one's father and
love and one's mother. **complexity**
[kəm'pleksɪtɪ] *n.* complicated nature.
complexion [kəm'plekʃn] *n.* colour of the
skin on your face; general way things are.
complicate ['kɒmplɪkeɪt] *v.* to make
things complicated. **complicated** *adj.*
with many small details/difficult to
understand. **complication**
[kɒmplɪ'keɪʃn] *n.* being complicated;

second illness which makes the first illness worse.

complicity [kəm'plɪsɪtɪ] *n.* being an accomplice to a crime.

compliment 1 ['kɒmplɪmənt] *n.* praise; send him my compliments = send him my good wishes. **compliment 2** ['kɒmplɪment] *v.* to praise.

complimentary [kɒmplɪ'mentərɪ] *adj.* which praises; c. ticket = free ticket.

compline ['kɒmplɪn] *n.* last service of the day.

comply [kəm'plaɪ] *v.* (with) to observe (a rule); to obey (an order). **compliance** *n.* agreement to do sth. **compliant** *adj.* (person) who agrees to do sth/who obeys the rules.

component [kəm'pəʊnənt] *adj. & n.* (piece) which forms part of sth.

compose [kəm'pəʊz] *v.* (a) to make up (music); to write (a letter/a poem). (b) c. yourself = be clAm. **composed** *adj.* calm/unflustered. **composer** *n.* person who writes music. **composite** ['kɒmpəzɪt] *adj.* made of several different parts. **composition** [kɒmpə'zɪʃn] *n.* (a) way in which sth is formed. (b) piece of music/poem/long essay. (c) artificial substance.

compositor [kəm'pɒzɪtə] *n.* person who sets type for printing.

composure [kəm'pəʊʒə] *n.* calmness.

compos mentis ['kɒmpɒs'mentɪs] *adj.* sane.

compost ['kɒmpɒst] *n.* rotted vegetable matter used as a fertilizer.

compound 1 ['kɒmpaʊnd] *adj.* made up of several parts; c. fracture = fracture where the broken bone pierces the skin; c. interest = interest calculated each year on the total sum including the previous year's interest. **compound 2** ['kɒmpaʊnd] *n.* (a) chemical made up of two or more elements. (b) yard enclosed by a fence. **compound 3** [kəm'paʊnd] *v.* (a) to come to an agreement with people to whom you owe money. (b) to keep information about (a crime) hidden. (c) to increase/to aggravate (a crime/a feeling).

comprehend [kɒmprɪ'hend] *v.* (a) to understand. (b) to include.

comprehensible *adj.* which can be understood/understandable.

comprehension *n.* understanding.

comprehensive *adj.* which includes everything; c. (school) = for children of different abilities; c. education = system of education where all children go to the same type of school without any selection. **comprehensiveness** *n.* wide range (of knowledge, etc.).

compress 1 ['kɒmpres] *n.* pad of material put on a bruise/sore **compress 2** [kəm'pres] *v.* to squeeze into a small space; compressed air = air under pressure. **compressor** *n.* machine which compresses air/gas, etc.

comprise [kəm'praɪz] *v.* to be formed of.

compromise 1 ['kɒmpraɪz] *n.* agreement of two opposing points of view, where each side give way to some extent. **compromise 2** *v.* (a) to come to an agreement by giving way. (b) to embarrass/to put in a difficult positions. **compromising** *adj.* embarrassing.

comptroller [kən'trəʊlə] *n.* (old) person who controls the finances in an establishment.

compulsion [kəm'pʌlʃn] *n.* force/ urge. **compulsive** *adj.* (person) who cannot stop himself doing sth; a c. smoker. **compulsory** *adj.* which you are forced to do.

compunction [kəm'pʌŋkʃn] *n.* remorse/regret.

compute [kəm'pjuːt] *v.* to calculate. **computation** [kɒmpjʊ'teɪʃn] *n.* calculation. **computer** *n.* electronic machine which calculates and keeps information automatically; c. bureau = office which does work on its computers for other companies; c. fraud = fraud committed by using a computer. **computer-assisted** *adj.* helped by using a computer; c. -a design. **computerization** *n.* act of computerizing. **computerize** *v.* (a) to process by computer. (b) to equip (a) business, etc.) with a computer.

comrade ['kɒmreɪd] *n.* friend/ companion; fellow member of a socialist or communist party. **comradeship** *n.* fellowship/friendliness.

con 1 [kɒn] *n.* (a) *inf.* deception; c. man = trickster. (b) argument against. **con 2** *v.* (conned) *inf.* to deceive/to trick (s.o.).

concatenation [kɒnkætɪ'neɪʃn] *n.* chain of events.

concave [kɒn'keɪv] *adj.* (surface) which is hollowed in the middle like a spoon.

conceal [kən'si:l] *v.* to hide. **concealed** *adj.* hidden; c. entrance = entrance which is difficult to see. **concealment** *n.* hiding.

concede [kən'si:d] *v.* (a) to admit (that you are wrong). (b) to admit that you have lost.

conceit [kən'si:t] *n.* high opinion of oneself. **conceited** *adj.* (person) who thinks too much of himself.

conceive [kən'si:v] *v.* (a) to become pregnant. (b) to think up (an idea). **conceivable** *adj.* which can be imagined. **conceivably** *adv.* in a conceivable way.

concentrate 1 ['kɒnsəntreɪt] *n.* concentrated substance. **concentrate 2** *v.* (a) (on) to pay great attention to (sth). (b) to put (all one's resources) together in one place. **concentrated** *adj.* very strong (juice after water has been extracted). **concentration** [kɒnsən'treɪʃn] *n.* (a) attentiveness. (b) putting all your resources into one area. (c) c. camp = camp where many political prisoners are held in captivity.

concentric [kən'sentrɪk] *adj.* (circles) inside each other, each with the same central point.

concept ['kɒnsept] *n.* idea/ philosophical notion. **conception** [kən'sepʃn] *n.* (a) becoming pregnant. (b) idea. **conceptual** *adj.* referring to concepts. **conceptualize** *v.* to form a concept of (sth).

concern 1 [kən'sɜːn] *n.* (a) worry. (b) interest; it is no c. of yours = it is none of your business. (c) firm/business; a big industrial c. **concern 2** *v.* (a) to deal with this concerns you = is about you; that does not c. him = it has nothing to do with him as far as money is concerned = with reference to money. (b) to be concerned (about) = to worry (about). **concerning** *prep.* about/ referring to.

concert ['kɒnsət] *n.* programme of music played in public. **concerted** [kən'sɜːtɪd] *adj.* done or planned jointly. **concert hall** *n.* large hall for giving concerts.

concertina 1 [kɒnsə'ti:nə] *n.* portable musical instrument with bellows and a set of keys at either end.

concertina 2 *v.* to become crushed/ crumpled.

concerto [kən'tʃeətəʊ] *n.* (*pl.*-os) piece to music for a solo instrument and orchestra, or for a small group of instruments.

concession [kən'seʃn] *n.* act of conceding/of admitting sth; to make c. = to change what you planned to fit in which s.o. else's wishes.

conch [kɒntʃ] *n.* (*pl.*-es) type of sea shell, like a large snail shell.

conchology [kɒŋ'kɒlədʒɪ] *n.* study of shells.

conciliate [kən'sɪlɪeɪt] *v.* to win over (s.o.) who was previously unfriendly; to reconcile. **conciliation** [kənsɪlɪ'eɪʃn] *n.* act of conciliating; c board = committee set up to arbitrate in industrial disputes. **conciliator** [kən'sɪlɪeɪtə] *n.* person who tries to reconcile people of opposing views. **conciliatory** [kən'sɪlɪətrɪ] *adj.* which is aimed at conciliating.

concise [kən'saɪs] *adj.* short; meaning a lot, but using few words. **concisely** *adv.* in a concise way. **conciseness, concision** [kən'sɪʒn] *n.* briefness.

conclave ['kɒŋkleɪv] *n.* religious assembly, esp. meeting of cardinals to elect a pope.

conclude [kən'klu:d] *v.* (a) to come to end. (b) to deduce/to come to an opinion. (c) to arrange (a treaty). **concluding** *adj.* final. **conclusion** [kən'klʊʒn] *n.* (a) end. (b) opinion reached by reasoning. **conclusive** *adj.* decisive/ which offers firm proof. **conclusively** *adv.* in a decisive way.

concoct [kən'kɒkt] *v.* (a) to make (a dish of food). (b) to make up/to invent (a story). **concoction** *n.* curious mixture of food or drink.

concomitant [kən'kɒmɪtənt] *adj.* (formal) which accompanies/goes with.

concord ['kɒŋkɔːd] *n.* harmony/peace. **concordance** [kən'kɔːdəns] *n.* alphabetical list of words used in a book. **concordat** [kɒn'kɔːdæt] *n.* agreement (between church and state).

concourse ['kɒŋkɔːs] *n.* (a) crowd/ mass of people. (b) large open space inside a railway station/concert hall, etc.

concrete 1 ['kɒnkri:t] *adj.* real/firm.

concrete 2 *adj. & n.* like substance made by mixing sand, gravel, cement and water. **concrete mixer** *n.* machine for mixing concrete.

concretion [kən'kri:ʃn] *n.* mass of things which have solidified together.

concubine ['kɒŋkjʊbaɪn] *n.* woman who lives with a man as his second wife, but who is not married to him.

concur [kən'kɜ:] *v.* to agree. **concurrence** [kən'kʌrəns] *n.* agreement. **concurrent** [kən'kʌrənt] *adj.* which happen at the same time. **concurrently** *adv.* happening at the same time.

concussion [kən'kʌʃn] *n.* shock to the brain caused by being hit on the head. **concussed** *adj.* in a state of concussion.

condemn [kən'dem] *v.* to blame; to sentence (a criminal); to declare (houses) to be unfit to live in. **condemnation** [kɒndem'neɪʃn] *n.* blame.

condense [kən'dens] *v.* (a) reduce the size of (sth); condensed milk = milk which has been concentrated and sweetened. (b) (of steam) to form drops of water. **condensation** [kɒnden'seɪʃn] *n.* act of condensing; steam which has formed into a film on a cold surface. **condenser** *n.* part of a machine which turns gas into liquid.

condescend [kɒndɪ'send] *v.* to speak/ to act as if you are superior to s.o. else. **condescending** *adj.* unpleasantly superior (voice/smile, etc.). **condescens** *n.* acting with a feeling of superiority.

condiment ['kɒndɪmənt] *n.* seasoning for food, such as salt, pepper, mustard.

condition 1 [kən'dɪʃn] *n.* (a) state. (b) term (of a bargain); on c. that = provided that. (c) bad state; a heart c. = a weak heart. **condition 2** *v.* (a) to put into good condition. (b) to make (s.o.) used to sth.; conditioned reflex = reaction to a stimulus which has been repeated many times. **conditional** *adj. & n.* provided that certain things happen; part of a verb which shows this; I would come' is a conditional form of 'to come'. **conditionally** *adv.* under certain conditions. **conditioner** *n.* lotion which puts sth (esp. hair) into good condition.

condole [kən'dəʊl] *v.* to c. with s.o. = to express your regrets for some tragedy which has happened. **condolences** *n. pl.* expressions of regret (at the death of s.o.).

condom ['kɒndəm] *n.* rubber contraceptive sheath.

condominium [kɒndə'mɪnɪəm] *n.* (a) joint ownership. (b) *Am.* building held in joint ownership.

condone [kən'dəʊn] *v.* to excuse/ forgive (a crime, etc.).

condor ['kɒndɔ:] *n.* large South American vulture.

conducive [kən'dju:sɪv] *adj.* favourable (to).

conduct 1 ['kɒndʌkt] *n.* way of behaving. **conduct 2** [kən'dʌkt] *v.* (a) to lead/to guide/to control (a business, an orchestra); conducted tour = tour led by a guide. (b) to allow (electricity/heat) to pass through. (c) to c. yourself = to behave. **conduction** [kən'dʌkʃn] *n.* passing of heat/electricity. **conductivity** [kɒndʌk'tɪvɪtɪ] *n.* ability to conduct electricity or heat. **conductor** *n.* (a) substance (such as metal) which conducts heat/electricity; c. rail = rail which carries electricity for electric trains. (b) person who directs an orchestra. (c) bus c. = person who collects money from the passengers on a bus. (d) *Am.* railway guard.

conductress *n.* (*pl.*-es) woman who collects money from passengers on a bus.

conduit ['kɒndɪt] *n.* tube along which liquids can be passed.

cone [kəʊn] *n.* geometrical figure, round at the base, rising to a point; Ice cream c. = cornet; fir c. = fruit of a fir tree; nose c. = pointed end of a rocket. **coneshaped** *adj.* shaped like a cone.

confab ['kɒnfæb] *n. inf.* chat/ discussion.

confection [kən'fekʃən] *n.* food made of a mixture of sweet things. **confectionery** [kən'fekʃənrɪ] *n.* sweets and cakes. **confectioner's** *n.* shop selling sweets and cakes.

confederate [kən'fedərət] *n.* person who has joined with others (usu. to do a crime). **confederacy** *n.* joining together. **confederation** [kənfedə'reɪʃn] *n.* group (of states/trade unions, etc.).

confer [kən'fɜː] v. (conferred) (a) to discuss. (b) to c. an honour on s.o. = to award s.o. an honour. **conference** ['kɒnfərəns] n. discussion; meeting of a group/society.

confess [kən'fes] v. to admit that you have done sth wrong. **confession** [kən'feʃn] n. admission of fault; to make your c. = to admit your sins to a priest. **confessional** n. small private box in a church where a priest hears confessions. **confessor** n. priest who hears confessions.

confetti [kən'fetɪ] n. small pieces of coloured paper thrown over the bride and bridegroom after a wedding.

confidant, confidante [kɒnfɪ'dænt] n. man/woman you tell secrets to.

confide [kən'faɪd] v. to c. in s.o. = to tell s.o. secret. **confidence** ['kɒnfɪdəns] n. (a) feeling sure. (b) secrecy; in c. = as a secret. (c) c. trick = trick whereby trickster gains s.o.'s confidence to steal money from him. **confident** adj. sure (of yourself). **confidently** adv. in a sure way. **confidential** [kɒnfɪ'deɪʃɪ] adj. secret/private; (secretary) entrusted with confidential matters. **confidentiality** n. being secret/private. **confidentially** adv. in a confidential way.

configuration [kənfɪgə'reɪʃn] n. (a) (formal) shape. (b) way in which computer hardware or software are planned.

confine [kən'faɪn] v. to restrict/to shut up; confined to bed = forced to stay in bed. **confinement** n. (a) imprisonment. (b) period when a woman gives birth to a baby.

confirm [kən'fɜːm] v. (a) to make definite/to make sure. (b) to be confirmed = to be made a full member of a church. **confirmation** [kɒnfə'meɪʃn] n. (a) making sure. (b) ceremony in which s.o. is made a full member of the church. **confirmatory** adj. which confirms. **confirmed** adj. permanent; he is a c. bachelor = he will never get married.

confiscate ['kɒnfɪskeɪt] v. to take away s.o.'s possessions as a punishment. **confiscation** [kɒnfɪs'keɪʃn] n. act of confiscating.

conflagration [kɒnflə'greɪʃn] n. (formal) big fire.

conflate [kən'fleɪt] v. to put together.

conflict 1 ['kɒnflɪkt] n. battle/fight. **conflict 2** [kən'flɪkt] v. to clash/to contradict.

confluence ['kɒnfluəns] n. (formal) place where two rivers joint together.

conform [kən'fɔːm] v. to fit in (to a pattern); to act in the same way as other people. **conformist** n. person who conforms **conformity** n. conforming.

confound [kən'faʊnd] v. to confuse/to bother.

confront [kən'frʌnt] v. to face up to (a danger); to c. s.o. with = to bring s.o. face to face with. **confrontation** [kɒnfrʌn'teɪʃn] n. bringing face to face; meeting between opposing sides.

confuse [kən'fjuːz] v. to mix/to muddle. **confused** adj. mixed-up/muddled. **confusedly** [kən'fjuːzɪdlɪ] adv. in a muddled way. **confusing** adj. mudding. **confusion** [kən'fjuːʒn] n. muddle/disorder.

confute [kən'fjuːt] v. (formal) to prove (sth) wrong. **confutation** [kɒnfjuː'teɪʃn] n. proving wrong.

congeal [kən'dʒiːl] v. to set solid; to become solid (as of dried blood).

congenial [kən'dʒiːnɪəl] adj. sympathetic/friendly.

congenital [kən'dʒenɪtl] adj. (illness/defect) present in a person since birth. **congenitally** adv. from birth.

conger eel ['kɒŋgəiːl] n. very large type of eel.

congested [kən'dʒestɪd] adj. blocked/crowded. **congestion** [kən'dʒestʃn] n. blocking (of streets); filling (of the lungs) with liquid.

conglomeration [kənglɒmə'reɪʃn] n. mass of things heaped together. **conglomerate** [kən'glɒmərət] n. (a) rock made of small piece fused together. (b) many subsidiary companies linked together.

Congolese [kɒŋgə'liːz] adj. & n. (person) from the Congo.

congratulate [kən'grætjʊleɪt] v. to give (s.o.) good wishes on a special occasion; to praise (s.o.) for some achievement. **congratulations** [kəngrætjʊ'leɪʃnz] n. good wishes. **congratulatory** [kən'grætjʊlətrɪ] adj. which give good wishes.

congregate ['kɒŋgrɪgeɪt] v. to gather together. **congregation** [kɒŋgrɪ'geɪʃn] n. people gathered together; people meeting together in a church.

congress ['kɒŋgres] n. meeting of a group people; Congress = the elected legislative body of the United states. **congressional** adj. referring to the US Congress. **congressman** n. (pl.-men) member of the Congress of the United States.

congruent ['kɒŋgrʊənt] adj. which fit together.

conical ['kɒnɪkl] adj. shaped like a cone.

conifer ['kɒnɪkl] n. tree which bears cones. **coniferous** [kə'nɪfərəs] adj. referring to conifers.

conjecture 1 [kən'dʒektʃə] n. guess. **conjecture 2** v. to guess. **conjectural** adj. possible/which has been guessed at.

conjugal ['kɒndʒʊgl] adj. referring to marriage.

conjugate ['kɒndʒʊgeɪt] v. to show the different parts of (a verb). **conjugation** [kɒndʒʊ'geɪʃn] n. way in which a verb changes according to tense and person.

conjunction [kən'dʒʌŋkʃn] n. word which links different parts of a sentence; in c. with = together with.

conjunctivitis [kəndʒʌŋktɪvaɪtɪs] n. inflammation of the eyes.

conjuncture [kən'dʒʌŋktʃə] n. circumstances.

conjure ['kʌndʒə] v. (a) to do ticks with cards/rabbits, etc. (b) to call up (a spirit/a picture). **conjurer, conjuror** n. person who does tricks. **conjuring** n. magic tricks.

conk [kɒŋk] n. Sl. head. **conk out** v. inf. to stop working. **conker** ['kɒŋkə] n. horse chestnut.

connect [kə'nekt] v. to join/to link; this train connects with the 13.56 = this train arrives in time for your to get off it and catch the 13.56; they are connected to the Williams family = they are related to them. **connected** adj. joined/linked; well c. = with influential friends and relations. **connection, connexion** n. join/link; in c. with your visit = with reference to/concerning your visit; there is a connection to London = there is a train which connects with this one for

London; he has connections in the theatre = he has friends/relations in the theatre.

conning tower ['kɒnɪŋtaʊə] n. highest part of a submarine.

connive [kə'naɪv] v. to c. at sth = to allow it to take place. **connivance** n. conniving (at sth).

connoisseur [kɒnə'sɜː] n. expert/ person who knows a lot (about sth).

connote [kə'nəʊt] v. to imply sth in addition. **connotation** n. additional meaning.

connubial [kə'njuːbɪəl] adj. (formal) referring to marriage.

conquer ['kɒŋkə] v. to defeat by force. **conquering** adj. triumphant/ victorious. **conqueror** n. person who leads the invasion of a country; state which captures another country. **conquest** ['kɒŋkwest] n. (a) capturing. (b) thing/country which has been captured.

consanguinity [kɒnsæŋ'gwɪnɪti] n. (formal) connection by blood.

conscience ['kɒnʃɪ'ens] n. feeling which tells you if you have done right or wrong. **conscience-stricken** adj. ashamed.

conscientious [kɒnʃɪ'enʃəs] adj. who works carefully and well; c. object = person who refuses to join the services because he feels war is wrong. **conscientiously** adv. in a conscientious way.

conscious ['kɒnʃəs] adj. aware of things around you; a c. decision = a deliberate decision. **consciously** adv. in a conscious way. **consciousness** n. being conscious; to lose c. = to become unconscious.

conscript 1 ['kɒnskrɪpt] n. person who has been ordered to join the services. **conscript 2** [kən'skrɪpt] v. to order (people) to join the services. **conscription** [kən'skrɪpʃn] n. legal obligation to join in the services.

consecrate ['kɒnsɪkreɪt] v. to bless (a new church/a king); to devote (one's life to sth). **consecration** [kɒnsɪ'kreɪʃn] n. blessing; devoting (of your life).

consecutive [kən'sekjʊtɪv] adj. following one after the other. **consecutively** adv. in order.

consensus [kən'sensəs] *n.* generally agreed opinion.
consent 1 [kən'sent] *n.* agreement. **consent 2** *v.* to agree (to sth).
consequence ['kɒnsɪkwəns] *n.* (a) result. (b) importance; it is of no c. = it does not matter. **consequent** *adj.* c. on = resulting from. **consequential** [kɒnsɪ'kwenʃl] *adj.* resulting. **consequently** *adv.* because of this/for this reason.
conserve [kən'sɜːv] *v.* to save. **conservancy** *n.* body which controls a river, etc. **conservation** [kɒnsə'veɪʃn] *n.* preservation/saving (of energy, natural resources, old buildings; etc.). **conservationist** *n.* person who is interested in conservative.
conservatism *n.* (a) being conservative. (b) (in politics) policies of the Conservative party. **conservative** [kən'sɜːvətɪv] *adj.* (a) not wanting to change; C. party = political party which does not want to change to existing system of government, and which does not favour state control of industry; a C. = member of the Conservative Party. (b) at a c. estimate = at the lowest/most moderate estimate. **conservatively** *adv.* moderately.
conservatory *n.* (a) room with large windows, where you keep tropical flowers and plants. (b) also.
conservatoire [kən'sɜːvətwɑːr] academy of music.
consider [kən'sɪdə] *v.* to think deeply about (sth). **considerable** *adj.* quite large. **considerably** *adv.* to a great extent. **considerate** *adj.* full of feeling/understanding towards s.o. **considerately** *adv.* thoughtfully. **consideration** [kənsɪdə'reɪʃn] *n.* (a) being though about. (b) small sum of money. **considering** *prep.* when you think of/taking into account.
consign [kən'saɪn] *v.* to give (goods) into s.o.'s care. **consignee** *n.* (formal) person who receives goods from s.o. **consignment** *n.* (a) sending of goods. (b) goods which have been sent. **consignor** *n.* person who consigns goods to s.o.
consist [kən'sɪst] *v.* (a) (in) to have as a basis. (b) (of) to be made up of. **consistency.** *n.* (a) being the same

throughout. (b) thickness (of a paste, etc.). **consistent** *adj.* which does not contradict; always the same/unchanging. **consistently** *adv.* always/permanently.
consistory [kən'sɪstərɪ] *n.* meeting of the Pope and cardinals at which a decision is taken.
console 1 ['kɒnsəʊl] *n.* (a) flat table with the keyboard (of a organ/telex machine, (etc.). (b) cabinet for a TV set.
console 2 [kən'səʊl] *v.* to comfort (s.o.) after a loss. **consolation** [kɒnsə'leɪʃn] *n.* comfort; c. prize = prize given to s.o. who did not win, but who tried hard.
consolidate [kən'sɒlɪdeɪt] *v.* to make firm/solid. **consolidation** [kənsɒlɪ'deɪʃn] *n.* (a) making firm. (b) grouping together of small packets from different sources into one large shipment. **consolidator** *n.* shipping company which groups shipments together.
consommé [kən'sɒmeɪ] *n.* thin clear soup.
consonant 1 ['kɒnsənənt] *n.* (letter representing) a sound which is not a vowel. **consonant 2** *adj.* which agrees with.
consort 1 ['kɒnsɔːt] *n.* husband or wife (of a queen or king). **consort 2** [kən'sɔːt] *v.* to go around with s.o.
consortium [kən'sɔːtɪəm] *n.* (*pl.*-tia) group of companies who work together.
conspicuous [kən'spɪkjʊəs] *adj.* very obvious; he was c. by his absence = everyone noticed that he was not there. **conspicuously** *adv.* very obviously.
conspire [kən'spaɪə] *v.* to plot (to do sth). **conspiracy** [kən'spɪrəsɪ] *n.* plot. **conspirator** *n.* plotter. **conspiratorial** [kənspɪrə'tɔːrɪəl] *adj.* like s.o. who is plotting.
constable ['kʌnstəbl] *n.* policeman. **constabulary** [kən'stæbjʊlərɪ] *n.* police force of a district.
constant ['kɒnstənt] *adj.* (a) not changing or stopping (b) faithful. **constancy** *n.* faithfulness. **constantly** *adv.* all the time.
constellation [kɒnstə'leɪʃn] *n.* group of stars forming a pattern in the sky.
consternation [kɒnstə'neɪʃn] *n.* shock/surprise.

constipated ['kɒnstɪpeɪtɪd] *adj.*
unable to empty the bowels regularly.
constipation [kɒnstɪ'peɪʃn] *n.* slow
working of the bowels.
constituent 1 [kən'stɪtjʊənt] *adj.*
(part) which makes up a whole
constituent 2 *n.* (a) part which goes
to make up a whole. (b) person who may
vote in an electoral area. **constituency**
n. area which elects a member of
Parliament.
constitute ['kɒnstɪtjuːt] *v.* to make up;
to establish. **constitution**
[kɒnstɪ'tjuːʃn] *n.* (a) bodily health. (b)
laws and principles which form the basis
of a country's organization.
constitutional 1 *adj.* referring to the
legal basis of a state. (monarchy) where
the power is held by an elected
government. **constitutional 2** *n.* short
walk which is supposed to be good for
the health. **constitutionally** *adv.*
according to the constitution.
constrain [kən'streɪn] *v.* to force.
constraint *n.* force.
constrict [kən'strɪkt] *v.* to squeeze/to
strangle. **constriction** [kən'strkʃn] *n.*
constricting.
construct [kən'strʌkt] *v.* to build.
construction [kən'strʌkʃn] *n.* (a) act
of building; way in which sth is made
up. (b) thing which has been built.
constructive *adj.* which aims at
improving. **constructively** *adv.* in a
constructive way. **constructor** *n.*
builder/person who constructs.
construe [kən'struː] *v.* to take to mean.
consul ['kɒnsəl] *n.* country's
representative abroad, particularly
looking after the personal affairs of his
fellowcountrymen. **consular**
['kɒnsjʊlə] *adj.* referring to a consul; c.
department (of an embassy) =
department which looks after passports
and visas. **consulate** *n.* house/offices
of a consul.
consult [kən'sʌlt] *v.* to ask for advice.
consultant *n.* specialist who gives advice,
esp. medical specialist attached to a hospital.
consultation [kɒnsʌl'teɪʃn] *n.* act of
consulting. **consultative** [kən'sʌltətɪv]
adj. which gives advice; c. assembly =
assembly to advise the government.
consulting *n.* asking for advice; c. room
= doctor's office.

consume [kən'sjuːm] *v.* (a) to eat or
drink. (a) to use up. **consumables** *n.*
(a) consumer goods. (b) (computers)
paper, ribbons, etc., which are used in
peripherals. **consumer** *n.* person who
uses goods or eats food; c. goods =
goods which are bought by ordinary
members of the public (and not by
industry). **consumerism** *n.* fighting
for the rights of the consumer.
consummate 1 [kən'sʌmɪt] *adj.*
perfect (artist, etc.). **consummate 2**
['kɒnsəmeɪt] *v.* to complete; to c. a
marriage = to have sexual intercourse for
the first time after marriage.
consummation [kɒnsə'meɪʃn] *n.*
completion; end.
consumption [kən'sʌmpʃn] *n.* (a) act
of consuming; quantity consumed. (b)
(old) tuberculosis. **consumptive** *adj.*
looking as though one is suffering from
tuberculosis.
cont. abbrev. for continued.
contact 1 ['kɒntækt] *n.* (a) touch; c.
lenses = tiny lenses worn on the eyeballs,
replacing glasses. (b) person whom you
know/whom you have contacted.
contact 2 *v.* to get into
communication with (s.o.)
contagion [kən'teɪdʒn] *n.* passing on
of a disease by touching. **contagious**
[kən'teɪdʒəs] *adj.* (disease) which is
transmitted by touching.
contain [kən'teɪn] *v.* (a) to hold/to have
inside. (b) to hold back/to restrain (an
attack, anger). **container** *n.* (a) box/
bottle, etc., which holds sth else. (b)
large case for easy loading on a ship,
lorry, etc. **containerization** *n.* using
containers for shipping goods.
containment *n.* holding back (an
enemy).
contaminate [kɒn'tæmɪneɪt] *v.* to
make bad/dirty. **contaminant** *n.*
substance which contaminates.
contamination [kɒntæmɪ'neɪʃn] *n.* act
of contaminating.
contemplate ['kɒntempleɪt] *v.* (a) to
look at (sth) intently. (b) to plan to do
sth. **contemplation** [kɒntem'pleɪʃn] *n.*
meditation/deep thought.
contemplative [kən'templətɪv] *adj.*
which meditates.
contemporary [kən'temprərɪ] *adj.* &
n. (a) (with) (person) who lives at the

same time or is (about) the same age as another; (thing) which dates back to the same period as another thing. (b) modern/up-to-date. **contemporaneous** [kəntempə'reɪnɪəs] *adj.* of the same date/period.

contempt [kən'tempt] *n.* feeling of hatred/disrespect for s.o.; c. of court = conduct which a judge rules is offensive to a court. **contemptible** *adj.* which deserves contempt. **contemptuous** *adj.* scornful (of).

contend [kən'tend] *v.* (a) (with) to fight. (b) to state/to believe. **contender** *n.* person who challenges s.o. to a fight; person who fights.

content 1 [kən'tent] *adj.* (with) satisfied/happy. **content 2** [kən'tent] *n.* (a) satisfaction; to your heart's c. = as much as you like. (b) ['kɒntent] thing which is contained/which is in a container; table of contents = list of chapters/sections in a book; the contents of the letter = what was written in it; mineral c. of water = percentage of minerals in water. **content 3** [kən'tent] *v.* to satisfy. **contented** *adj.* satisfied/happy. **contentedly** *adv.* in a contented way. **contentedness, contentment** *n.* being contented.

contention [kən'tenʃn] *n.* (a) dispute; bone of c. = source of argument. (b) statement/belief. **contentious** [kən'tenʃəs] *adj.* (person) who likes arguments; (problem) which is a frequent source of dispute.

conterminous [kən'tɜːmɪnəs] *adj.* which has the same limits as sth, else.

contest 1 ['kɒntest] *n.* fight; competition. **contest 2** [kən'test] *v.* (a) to fight (an election). (b) to query; argue that (a will) is invalid. **contestant** *n.* competitor/person who enters a contest.

context ['kɒntekst] *n.* phrase in which a word occurs, which helps show its meaning; out of c. = with out the surrounding text. **contextual** [kən'tekstjʊəl] *adj.* referring to a context.

contiguous [kən'tɪgjʊəs] *adj.* (formal) next to/touching. **contiguity** [kɒntɪ'gjuːɪtɪ] *n.* being contiguous.

continent 1 ['kɒntɪnənt] *n.* large mass of land; on the C. = in Europe.

continent 2 *adj.* able to control the

passing of urine or excreta. **continental** [kɒntɪ'nentl] *adj.* (a) referring to a continent. (b) referring to Europe (excluding the British Isles); a Continental = a European (but not an inhabitant of the British Isles); c. breakfast = coffee and rolls or bread; c. climate = climate with hot dry summers and very cold winters, found in the central parts of continents; c. quilt = a duvet, a bag stuffed with feathers, used as the only covering for a bed.

contingent 1 [kən'tɪdfənt] *adj.* which depends on sth. **contingent 2** *n.* group of soldiers, etc. **contingency** *n.* emergency.

continue [kən'tɪnjuː] *v.* to go on doing sth. **continual** *adj.* which goes on all the time without stopping. **continually** *adv.* very frequently; all the time **continuation** [kəntɪnjʊ'eɪʃn] *n.* (a) (also continuance) going on without stopping. (b) extension/thing which has been continued. **continuity** [kɒntɪ'njʊɪtɪ] *n.* state of continuing without a break; c. girl = girl who ensures that each scene in a film follows on smoothly. **continuous** [kən'tɪnjʊəs] *adj.* with no break; c. stationery = computer paper, in one long strip, folded in concertina fashion. **continuously** *adv.* one after the other with no break in between.

continuum *n.* thing which continues.

contort [kən'tɔːt] *v.* to twist unnaturally. **contortion** [kən'tɔːʃn] *n.* twisting unnaturally. **contortionist** *n.* person in a show who twists his body into odd shapes.

contour ['kɒntʊə] *n.* shape of the outline of sth; c. (line) = line on a map drawn through points at the same height above sea level.

contra 1 ['kɒntræ] *prep.* against.

contra 2 *n.* c. entry = one entry made on one side of an account to balance an entry on the opposite side. **contra 3** *v.* to make a contra entry.

contraband ['kɒntrəbænd] *n.* (no *pl.*) goods on which customs duty has not been paid

contraception [kɒntrə'sepʃn] *n.* prevention of pregnancy.

contraceptive *adj. & n.* (thing) which prevents pregnancy.

contract 1 ['kɒntrækt] n. (a) legal agreement. (b) (in north of England) bus or train season ticket. **contract 2** [kən'trækt] v. (a) to get smaller; to make smaller; to tighten. (b) to sign an agreement to do some work. (c) to catch (a decease). **contraction** [kən'rækʃn] n. shortening; shrinking. **contractor** n. person who does work according to a signed agreement. **contractual** adj. according to a contract.

contradict [kɒntrə'dıkt] v. to deny what s.o. else says. **contradiction** [kɒntrə'dıkʃn] n. saying the opposite. **contradictory** adj. which says the opposite.

contralto [kə'træltəʊ] n. (pl.-os) (woman with a) low-pitched singing voice.

contraption [kən'træpʃn] n. machine/device.

contrapuntal [kɒntrə'pʌntl] adj. using counterpoint.

contrary 1 ['kɒntrərı] adj. (a) opposite; c. winds = winds blowing in the opposite direction to the one you want. (b) [kən'treərı] rude; always doing the opposite of what you want. **contrary 2** n. the c. = the opposite; one the c. = quite the opposite; to the c. = stating sth different/opposite. **contrary 3** adv. in an opposite way (to). **contrarily** adv. in a contrary way. **contrariness** [kən'treərınəs] n. always doing the opposite of what people doing the opposite of what people want/awkwardness (of a child).

contrast 1 ['kɒntrɑːst] n. sharp difference. **contrast 2** [kən'trɑːst] v. to show up the difference between.

contravene [kɒntrə'viːn] v. to break the law/the regulations. **contravention** [lɒmtrə'venʃn] n. breaking of a law.

contribute [kən'trıbjuːt] v. (a) to help towards; to c. to = write articles for (a newspaper. etc.). (b) to give money (to a charity). **contribution** [kɒntrı'bjuːʃn] n. (a) article submitted to a newspaper. (b) money, etc. given to help sth. **contributor** [kən'trıbjʊtə] n. a person who contributes. **contributory** adj. which helps; c. factors = factors which have helped produce the situation.

contrite ['kɒntraıt] adj. (person) who is sorry. **contrition** [kən'trıʃn] n. regret.

contrive [kən'traıv] v. to manage; to plan. **contrivance** n. machine/device. **contrived** adj. artificial/not natural.

control 1 [kən'trəʊl] n. (a) authority/power; keeping in order; under c. = in order; birth c. = limiting of the number of babies born. (b) the controls = the gears/levers, etc., for directing a machine. (c) standard with which the results of an experiment can be compared. **control 2** v. (controlled) (a) to direct. (b) to limit/to regulate. **controllable** adj. which can be controlled. **controller** n. person who controls. **control tower** n. high building at an airport, which houses the radio operators who direct planes on landing or take off.

controversy [kən'trɒvəsı] n. violent discussion. **controversial** [kɒntrə'vɜːʃl] adj. (subject) which provokes violent discussions. **controvert** v. (formal) to deny. **controvertible** adj. which can be denied.

contumacious [kɒntjʊ'meıʃəs] adj. (formal) persistently disobedient. **contumely** ['kɒntjʊmlı] n. (formal) rudeness/insults.

contusion [kən'tjuːʒn] n. (formal) bruise.

conundrum [kə'nʌndrəm] n. riddle.

conurbation [kɒnə'beıʃn] n. very large spread of a built-up area.

convalesce [kɒnvə'les] v. to recover after an illness/an operation. **convalescence** n. period when you are convalescing. **convalescent** adj. & n. (person) who is convalescing; c. home = rest home for people who are convalescing.

convection [kən'vekʃn] n. upward movement of heat in air/liquid. **convector** n. heater which warms the air moving through it.

convene [kən'viːn] v. to call together (a meeting). **convenor** n. person who convenes.

convenience [kən'viːnıəns] n. (a) suitableness; at your earliest c. = as soon as it suits you. (b) public toilet. (c) all modern conveniences = all modern comforts (in a house). (d) c. foods = dishes which are easy/quick to prepare. **convenient** adj. suitable; practical.

conveniently *adv.* handily.

convent [ˈkɒnvənt] *n.* religious house for women.

convention [kənˈvenʃn] *n.* (a) custom/ usual way of doing things. (b) contract (c) congress/general meeting of an association/political party. **conventional** *adj.* ordinary/usual; c. weapons = ordinary (not nuclear) weapons. **conventionally** *adv.* in a conventional/ordinary/usual way.

converge [kənˈvɜːdʒ] *v.* to come together at a certain place. **convergence** *n.* meeting. **convergent** *adj.* meeting at a certain point.

conversant [kənˈvɜːsənt] *adj.* familiar (with a subject). **converse 1** [ˈkɒnvɜːs] *n.* the opposite. **converse 2** [kənˈvɜːs] *v.* to talk. **conversation** [kɒnvəˈseɪʃn] *n.* talk. **conversational** *adj.* in conversation. **conversationalist** *n.* person who converses well.

conversely *adv.* in the opposite way

conversion [kənˈvɜːʒn] *n.* (a) changing (of one thing into another). (b) turning of a person to another religion. (c) (in Rugby) converting a goal.

convert 1 [ˈkɒnvɜːt] *n.* person who has changed religion. **convert 2** [kənˈvɜːt] *v.* (a) to turn (s.o.) from one religion to another (b) to change; (in Rugby) to c. a goal = to kick the ball over the crossbar between the goal posts after a try has been scored. **converter** *n.* machine which converts. **convertibility** [kənvɜːtɪˈbɪlɪtɪ] *n.* easiness of change of one currency to another. **convertible 1** [kənˈvɜːtəbl] *adj.* which can easily be changed (esp. of a currency). **convertible 2** *n.* car with a roof which folds back.

convex [ˈkɒnveks] *adj.* (surface) which is rounded outwards like the back of a spoon.

convey [kənˈveɪ] *v.* to transport/to carry; to give (greetings, etc.). **conveyance** *n.* (a) transporting. (b) means of transport. (c) transfer of property from one owner to another. **conveyancing** *n.* transferring of property. **conveyor** *n.* person who transports/thing which transports; c. belt = long moving surface used in a factory to move products through the production processes.

convict 1 [ˈkɒnvɪkt] *n.* criminal who has been sentenced to prison. **convict 2** [kənˈvɪkt] *v.* to find (s.o.) guilty; to sentence (a criminal) to prison. **conviction** [kənˈvɪkʃn] *n.* (a) being found guilty. (b) firm belief.

convince [kənˈvɪns] *v.* to c. s.o. of sth = to persuade/to make (s.o.) believe sth. **convincing** *adj.* (argument) which convinces. **convincingly** *adv.* in a convincing way.

convivial [kənˈvɪvɪəl] *adj.* lively/jolly. **conviviality** [kənvɪvɪˈælɪtɪ] *n.* liveliness.

convoke [kənˈvəʊk] *v.* to call (a meeting). **convocation** [kɒnvəˈkeɪʃn] *n.* (a) calling of a meeting. (b) meeting of a church assembly/university.

convoluted [ˈkɒnvəluːtɪd] *adj.* (a) twisted. (b) very complicated (story, etc.). **convolution** [kɒnvəˈluːʃn] *n.* twisting; complication.

convolvulus [kənˈvɒlvjʊləs] *n.* common climbing weed.

convoy 1 [ˈkɒnvɔɪ] *n.* group of ships/ lorries travelling together in line under protection. **convoy 2** *v.* to escort/to protect (esp. a line of merchant ships).

convulse [kənˈvʌls] *v.* to make (sth/ s.o.) shake. **convulsions** *n. pl.* violent shaking of the body; violent spasms which make the body twitch. **convulsive** *adj.* which causes violent shaking.

coo [kuː] *v.* to make soft noises (like a pigeon). **cooing** *n.* noise made by a pigeon.

cook 1 [kʊk] *n.* person who prepares food by heating it. **cook 2** *v.* (a) to prepare (food) by heating. (b) (of food) to be prepared; dinner is cooking. (c) *inf.* to c. the books/the accounts = to falsify the entries in account books. **cookbook** *n.* book of recipes. **cooker** *n.* (a) stove for cooking. (b) cooking apple. **cookery** *n.* (no *pl.*) art of cooking. c. book = cookbook. **cookie** *n. Am.* biscuit. **cooking** *n.* action of preparing food, *usu.* by heating; c. apple = sour green apple for cooking.

cool 1 [kuːl] *adj.* (-er, -est) (a) quite cold. (b) calm. (c) unfriendly (reception). **cool 2** *n.* (a) state of being cool; place where it is cool; in the c. of the evening. (b) *Sl.* calmness; she lost her c. = she lost her temper. **cool 3** v. to make cool; to become cool. **coolant** n. substance (usu. water) used to keep engines cool.

cool down v. (a) to become cool. (b) to become clAm. **cooler** n. (a) thing/machine which cools. (b) Sl. prison.

cooling 1 adj. refreshing (drink, etc.).

cooling 2 n. action of becoming cool.

coolly adv. in a cool, calm way.

coolness n. (a) being cool. (b) calmness. (c) unfriendliness (of a reception, etc.). **cool off** v. become cooler.

coolie ['ku:lɪ] n. workman/porter (in the Far East).

coop 1 [ku:p] n. cage for chickens.

coop 2 v. to be cooped up = to be shut up inside.

co-op ['kəʊɒp] n. inf. cooperative stores.

cooper [kəʊ:pə] n. person who makes barrels.

cooperate [kəʊ'ɒpəreɪt] v. to work with s.o. **cooperation** [kəʊɒpə'reɪʃn] n. working together. **cooperative 1** [kəʊ'ɒprətɪv] adj. & n. (shop, etc.) which works on a profit-sharing basis. **cooperative 2** adj. willing to works with s.o.

co-opt [kəʊ'ɒpt] v. to ask (s.o.) to join a committee without being formally elected to it. **co-option** n. act of co-opting.

co-ordinate 1 [kəʊ'ɔ:dɪnət] n. (a) set of figures which fix a point on a map graph. (b) co-ordinates = matching outer clothes for women. **co-ordinate 2** v. to make things work together; fit in with each other. **co-ordination** [kəʊɔ:dɪ'neɪʃn] n. co-ordinating. **co-ordinator** n. person who co-ordinates.

coot [ku:t] n. black water bird with a white forehead.

co-ownership [kəʊ'əʊnəʃɪp] n. ownership by several people or groups.

cop [kɒp] n. inf. policeman

cope 1 [ləʊp] n. long coloured cloak worn by a priest. **cope 2** v. to deal with.

copilot ['kəʊplaɪət] n. pilot who is second in command to the caption of an aircraft.

coping ['kəʊpɪŋ] n. c. stone = to stone on a wall, which protects the wall from the weather.

copious ['kəʊpɪəs] adj. plentiful/in good supply. **copiously** adv. in large quantities.

copper ['kɒpə] n. (a) (element: Cu) reddish metal which turns green when exposed to air. (b) large pan for boiling water and washing clothes. (c) inf. policeman. (d) small coin made of copper or other brown metal.

copperplate n. old-fashioned neat round handwriting.

coppice, copse 1 ['kɒpɪs, kɒps] n. wood of young trees. **coppice, copse 2** v. to coppice = to cut trees down to the ground regularly, so as to produce strong straight shoots.

copra ['kɒprə] n. dried coconut kernel used to make oil.

copulate ['kɒpjʊleɪt] v. to have sexual intercourse. **copulation** [kɒpjʊ'leɪʃn] n. sexual to intercourse.

copy 1 ['kɒpɪ] n. (a) an imitation/reproduction. (b) book; newspaper. (c) material to be used in a newspaper article/in an advertisement, etc. **copy 2** v. to imitate/to make a reproduction of (sth). **copier** n. machine which makes copies.

copying n. imitation. **copyright** n. right to publish a book/put on a play, etc., and not to have it copied without permission; in c. = protected by the laws of copyright. **copywriter** n. person who writes copy for advertisements.

coquette [kɒ'ket] n. women who flirts. **coquettish** adj. flirtatious. **coquetry** ['kɒketrɪ] n. being coquettish.

coracle ['kɒrəkl] n. light round boat made of skin.

coral ['kɒrəl] n. rock-like substance formed of the skeletons of tiny animals in the sea.

cor anglais ['kɔ:'ɒŋgleɪ] n. bass oboe.

corbel ['kɔ:bl] n. piece of stone or wood which juts out from a wall and supports sth (usu. a roof beam).

cord [kɔ:d] n. (a) string/thin rope. (b) string-like part of the body; spinal c. (c) inf. cords = corduroy trousers.

cordial 1 ['kɔ:dɪəl] adj. friendly. **cordial 2** n. concentrated juice of a fruit to which water is added. **cordiality** [kɔ:dɪ'ælɪtɪ] n. friendliness. **cordially** adv. in a cordial way.

cordite [ˈkɔːdaɪt] n. type of explosive.

cordon 1 [ˈkɔːdən] n. (a) barrier to prevent s.o. escaping; line of police/soldiers surrounding a point. (b) fruit tree grown as a single stem, with side shoots cut back. **cordon 2** v. to c. of a street = to put up a cordon across a street. **cordon bleu** [kɔːdɒŋˈblɜː] adj. top quality (cooking).

corduroy [ˈkɔːdjʊrɔɪ] n. velvet-like cloth with ribs.

core 1 [kɔː] n. central part; rotten to the c. = rotten right through; to take a c. sample = to cut a long round sample of rock with a drill. **core 2** v. to scoop out the core of (an apple, etc).

co-respondent [kəʊrɪˈspɒndənt] n. person cited in a divorce case.

corgi [ˈkɔːgɪ] n. breed of small dogs, with short hair and pointed faces.

coriander [kɒrɪˈændə] n. small plant whose seeds and leaves are used for flavouring.

cork 1 [kɔːk] n. (a) (material made from) very light bark of a type of oak tree; c. oak = tree with very light bark. (b) stopper which closes wine bottles. **cork 2** v. to put a cork into (a bottle).

corkage n. charge made by a restaurant for uncorking a customer's own wine bottle. **corked** adj. (wine) which has an unpleasant taste because of a rotting cork. **corkscrew** n. special screwing device for taking corks out of bottles.

corm [kɔːm] n. fat root which can be planted like a bulb.

cormorant [ˈkɔːmərənt] n. large dark seabird which eats fish.

corn [kɔːn] n. (a) cereal crops. (b) maize. sweet c. = maize grown for human consumption; c. cob = head of maize with many seeds. (c) painful hard growth (on a foot). **corncrake** n. small bird which lives in corn fields. **cornfield** n. field in which corn is grown. **cornflakes** n. pl.breakfast cereal of crisp pieces of toasted maize. **cornflour** n. maize powder, used in cooking. **cornflower** n. blue flower growing in corn fields. **cornstarch** n. Am. cornflour. **corny** adj. (-ier, -iest) inf. old/out-of-date (joke).

cornea [ˈkɔːnɪə] n. transparent covering of the eyeball. **corneal** adj. referring to the cornea.

corned [kɔːnd] adj. salted/preserved (beef).

corner 1 [ˈkɔːnə] n. (a) angle made by two flat surfaces joining; she has turned the c. = she is beginning to recover from an illness. (b) (in football) free kick taken from the corner of the pitch. **corner 2** v. (a) to turn a corner. (b) to monopolize (a market). (c) to drive (s.o.) into a corner. **cornerstone** n. (a) stone at the bottom of a corner of a building. (b) strong foundation/basis.

cornet [ˈkɔːnɪt] n. (a) cone-shaped biscuit for holding ice creAm. (b) trumpet-like brass musical instrument.

cornice [ˈkɔːnɪs] n. decorated moulding round a ceiling/round the eaves (of a building).

cornucopia [kɔːmjʊˈkəʊpɪə] n. (formal) horn overflowing with fruit and flowers, the symbol of rich harvest.

corolla [kəˈrɒlə] n. petals near the centre of a flower. **corollary** [kəˈrɒlərɪ] n. natural result/thing which follows naturally.

corona [kəˈrəʊnə] n. ring of light; ring of light visible when the sun is totally eclipsed.

coronary [ˈkɒrənrɪ] adj. referring to the arteries to the heart; c. thrombosis, inf. a c. = heart attack caused by blocking of an artery.

coronation [kɒrəˈneɪʃn] n. crowning (of a king/queen/emperor).

coroner [ˈkɒrənə] n. person who directs a court to investigate sudden or accidental deaths.

coronet [ˈkɒrənət] n. small crown.

corporal 1 [ˈkɔːprəl] adj. referring to the body. c. punishment = beating/whipping/caning. **corporal 2** n. non-commissioned rank in the army below sergeant. **corporate** [ˈkɔːpərət] adj. forming a body; c. plan = overall plan for a whole company. **corporation** [kɔːpəˈreɪʃn] n. (a) town council. (b) large firm. (c) inf. large stomach.

corps [kɔː] n. (pl.corps) military or organized group.

corpse [kɔːps] n. dead body.

corpulent adj. fat. **corpulence** n. fatness.

corpus [ˈkɔːpəs] n. all the works (of an author).

corpuscle ['kɔːpʌsl] *n.* red or white cell in blood.

corral *Am.* **1** [kɒ'rɑːl] *n.* fence to enclose cattle. **corral** *Am.* **2** *v.* to enclose (cattle).

correct 1 [kə'rekt] *adj.* accurate/right/ true. **correct 2** *v.* to show the mistakes in (sth); to remove the mistakes from (sth). **correction** [kə'rekʃn] *n.* making correct. **corrective** *adj.* & *n.* (thing) which corrects. **correctly** *adv.* accurately. **correctness** *n.* accuracy (of answer, etc.); rightness (of clothes).

correlate ['kɒrəleɪt] *v.* to correspond to/to be linked to. **correlation** [kɒrə'leɪʃn] *n.* correspondence/link.

correspond [kɒrɪ's'pɒnd] *v.* (a) (to) to fit in with; to match. (b) to write letter; to exchange letter (with s.o.).

correspondence *n.* (a) matching. (b) exchange of letters; letters which have come; c. course = course of study taken at home with lessons sent by post.

correspondent *n.* person who writes letters; journalists who writes articles for newspapers on particular subjects.

corresponding *adj.* which fits/ matches. **correspondingly** *adv.* in a similar way.

corridor ['kɒrɪdɔː] *n.* long narrow passage.

corrigenda [kɒrɪ'dʒendə] *pl. n.* corrections (in a text).

corroborate [kə'rɒbəreɪt] *v.* to confirm (a statement). **corroboration** [kərɒbə'reɪʃn] *n.* confirmation of a statement. **corroboratory** *adj.* which corroborates.

corrode [kə'rəʊd] *v.* to rot (metal) to rust. **corrosion** [kɔ:'rəʊʒn] *n.* rusting/ eating away (of metal). **corrosive** [kə'rəʊsɪv] *adj.* & *n.* (substance) which eats away metal.

corrugated ['kɒrəgeɪtɪd] *adj.* bent into waves; c. iron; c. paper.

corrupt 1 [kə'rʌpt] *adj.* not honest (judge, etc.) who take bribes. **corrupt 2** *v.* to make dishonest/to bribe.

corruptibility [kərʌptə'bɪlɪtɪ] *n.* being corruptible. **corruptible** *adj.* (person) who can be bribed. **corruption** [kə'rʌpʃn] *n.* dishonesty/bribery.

corsage [kɔː'sɑːʒ] *n.* flowers worn on the front of a dress.

corset ['kɔːsɪt] *n.* tight underwear worn by women to support their bodies.

cortege [kɔː'teks] *n.* (formal) procession at a funeral.

cortex ['kɔːteks] *n.* outer covering of part of the body, esp. the brain.

cortisone ['kɔːtɪzəʊn] *n.* hormone medicine used against skin allergies/ arthritis, etc.

corvette [kɔː'vet] *n.* small naval gunboat.

cos [kɒz] *n.* short for cosine. **cos lettuce** ['kɒs'letɪs] *n.* type of tall lettuce.

cosh 1 [kɒʃ] *n.* (*pl.*-es) *inf.* short stick for hitting. **cosh 2** *v. inf.* to hit s.o. on the head.

cosine ['kəʊsaɪn] *n.* (in mathematics) ratio between the length of a side forming an acute angle to that of the hypotenuse in a right-angled triangle.

cosmetic [kɒz'metɪk] *adj.* & *n.* (substance) used in beautifying in face/in improving the look of sth.; c. surgery = surgery to improve someone's appearance.

cosmic ['kɒzmɪk] *adj.* referring to the universe.

cosmonaut *n.* soviet astronaut.

cosmos *n.* (formal) the universe.

cosmopolitan [kɒzmə'pɒlɪtən] *adj.* (a) made up of people from different parts of the world. (b) at ease in different cities/with people of different nationalities.

cosset ['kɒsɪt] *v.* to spoil (s.o.) with comfort.

cost 1 [kɒst] *n.* amount which you have to pay for sth; at all costs = at no matter what price; c. of living = money paid for food, clothing, housing, etc., shown as a monthly index figure. **cost 2** *v.* (a) (cost) to have a price of. (b) **costing** *n.* calculation of a selling price.

coastlines *n.* expensiveness.

costly *adj.* (-ier, -iest) expensive.

co-star 1 ['kəʊstɑː] *n.* famous actor/ actress starring in a film/play with other famous actors/actresses. **co-star 2** *v.* (co-starred) to act in a play/film as a co-star.

costermonger ['kɒstəmʌŋgə] *n.* person who sells things from a barrow in the street.

costume ['kɒstjuːm] *n.* (a) set of clothes; bathing/swimming c. = woman's swimsuit; c. jewellery = cheap imitation jewellery. (b) set of clothes for the theatre.

cosy 1 [kəʊzɪ] adj. (-ier, -iest) warm and comfortable. **cosy 2** n. woollen cover (for a teapot, etc.). **cosily** adv. comfortably/warmly. **cosiness** n. being cosy.

cot [kɒt] n. child's bed with sides; c. death = sudden unexplained death of a sleeping baby. possibly caused by overheating.

cottage [ˈkɒtɪdʒ] n. little house in the country; c. cheese = soft white cheese made from curds; c pie = minced meat cooked with mashed potatoes on top; c. industry = handicrafts made in people's houses. **cottager** n. person who lives in a cottage.

cotter pin [ˈkɒtəpɪn] n. pin with a split end, used to hold parts of a machine together.

cotton 1 [ˈkɒtn] n. (a) fibre from the downy seed heads of a tropical plant. (b) cloth made of this fibre. (c) thread (for sewing). **cotton 2** v. inf. to c. on = to understand. **cotton candy** n. Am. candy; floss. **cotton wool** n. fluffy cotton stuff, used for wiping wounds, applying ointment, etc.

cotyledon [kɒtɪˈliːdən] n. first leaf on a seedling.

couch [kaʊtʃ] n. (pl.-es) sofa/low bed.

couch grass [kuːtʃ] n. weedlike grass which spreads from underground roots.

couchette [kuːˈʃet] n. folding bed in a train.

cougar [ˈkuːgə] n. Am. large brown American wild cat.

cough 1 [kɒf] n. sending air out of the lungs suddenly because of an irritation in the throat; c. pastille = medicated sweet sucked to relieve irritation in the throat.

cough 2 v. send air out of the lungs suddenly because of irritation. Sl. to c. up = to pay. **coughing** n. series of coughs.

could, couldn't [kʊd, ˈkʊdnt] v. see can.

coulomb [ˈkuːlɒm] n. unit of the quantity of electricity passed in one second over a given point by a current of one ampere.

coulter [ˈkuːltə] n. blade of a plough.

council [ˈkaʊnsl] n. elected committee; esp. town c. = elected committee which runs the affairs of a town; c. house = house rented out by a town council; c. estate = group of council houses or flats; c. chamber = room in which a town council meets. **councillor** n. elected member of a town council.

counsel [ˈkaʊnsl] n. (a) advice (b) lawyer/barrister. **counselling** n. giving advice. **counsellor** n. adviser.

count 1 [kaʊnt] n. action of counting/adding figures; to lose c. = to have no longer any idea of what the total is. (b) accusation. (c) lower ranks of noble.

count 2 v. (a) to add up a total. (b) to say numbers in order. (c) to rely (on). (d) to be important. **count down** v. to count backwards (9, 8, 7, 6. etc.).

countdown n. counting backwards.

counting n. action adding up a total.

countless adj. which cannot be counted/numerous.

countenance 1 [ˈkaʊntnəns] n. (formal) face. **countenance 2** v. (format) to approve of (s.o.'s action).

counter 1 [ˈkaʊntə] n. (a) machine which counts. (b) small round disc used in games. (c) long flat surface in a shop for displaying goods, or in a bank for placing money. **counter 2** adj., adv. & prefix. opposite (to). **counter 3** v. (a) to stop/to block. (b) to reply with an opposing response.

counteract v. to neutralize/to stop the effects of (sth).

counterattack 1 n. attack in return/attack against s.o., who has just attacked you. **counterattack 2** v. to attack in return.

counterattracton n. attraction aimed at luring customers away from a rival.

counterbalance v. to compensate for a force in one direction by going in the opposite direction.

counterblast n. strong written or spoken reply to an attack.

countercharge n. accusation against s.o., who has just accused you.

counterclaim n. claim made in response to another claim.

counterclockwise adj. & adv. Am. anticlockwise.

counter-demonstration n. rival/opposed demonstration in reply to a demonstration.

counterespionage n. secret service working against spies.

counterfeit 1 ['kaʊntəfɪt] adj. false/forted (money). **counterfeit 2** v. to forge/to make false money.

counterfoil n. slip of paper which you retain after giving s.o., a cheque/an invoice, etc.

countermand v. to say that (an order) should not be carried out.

countermeasure n. way of stopping the effects of sth.

counterpane n. bedcover.

counterpart n. person who has a similar job/is in a similar situation; parallel thing.

counterpoint n. combination of melodies in a piece of music.

counterpoise n. heavy weight which counterbalances.

counter-productive adj. which produces a contrary effect to the one intended.

Counter Reformation n. movement in the Catholic church in the 16th century, a response to the Protestant Reformation.

counter-revolution n. revolt against a revolution. **counter-revolutionary** adj. & n. (person who is) in revolt against a revolution.

countersign v. to sign (a document) which s.o., else has signed, in order to authorize it.

countersink v. (countersank; countersunk) to make a hole for the head of (a nail or screw) to fit into so that it is level with the surface.

country ['kʌntrɪ] n. (a) political or geographical unit of land. (b) region. (c) not town; in the c. **countrified** adj. like the country. **countryman** n. (pl.-men) person who comes from the same country as you. **countryside.** n. the country/the land (excluding towns and cities).

county ['kaʊntɪ] n. (a) small administrative district; c. court = court in England and Wales which hears minor civil cases; c. town = main town of a county. (b) inf. upper-class landowners.

coup [kuː] n. (pl.coups) (a) coup d'etat. (b) successful move. **coup d'état** [kuːdeɪ'tɑː] n. armed overthrow of a government.

coupé ['kuːpeɪ] n. car with two doors and a fixed roof.

couple 1 ['kʌpl] n. pair/two things/two people together; two people together, esp. a man and woman; a husband and wife; a c. of = (i) two (ii) a few. **couple 2** v. to link together.

couplet n. two lines of poetry which rhyme.

coupling n. metal links for joining two pieces of machinery/two wagons together.

coupon ['kuːpɒn] n. piece of paper which acts in place of money/in place of a ticket; football c. = form on which you fill up your forecast for the football pools.

courage ['kʌrɪdʒ] n. (no pl.) bravery. **courageous** [kə'reɪdʒəs] adj. brave. **courageously** adv. bravely.

courgette [kʊə'ʒet] n. very small marrow.

courier ['kʊrɪə] n. person who carries messages; a guide with a package tour.

course 1 [kɔːs] n. (a) passing of time; in the c. of = during; in due c. = eventually. (b) road; direction. (c) of c. = naturally; as a matter of c. = in the usual way. (d) series of lessons; book/series of books for studying. (e) series of treatments for an illness. (f) dish of food for a meal. (g) track (for racing). (h) golf c. = area of land specially designed for playing golf. (i) line of bricks (in a wall). **course 2** v. to flow fast.

court 1 [kɔːt] n. (a) tribunal where a judge (and jury) try criminals. (b) group of people living round a king or queen. (c) area where a game of tennis/squash, etc., is played. **court 2** v. (a) to try to persuade (a woman) to marry you. (b) to look for; to try to win (praise, etc.); to risk (disaster). **courteous** ['kɜːtjəs] adj. very polite. **courteously** adv. politely. **courtesy** ['kɜːtəsɪ] n. politeness; by c. of = with the kind permission of; c. car = free car waiting for hotel guests at an airport. **courtier** ['kɔːtjə] n. member of a royal court. **court-martial 1** [kɔːt'mɑːʃl] n. trial of a soldier by other soldiers. **court-martial 2** v. (court-martialled) to try (a soldier). **courtroom** n. room where a trial is held. **courtship** n. courting a woman. **courtyard** n. square yard surrounded by buildings.

cousin ['kʌzn] *n.* son or daughter of an uncle or aunt.

couturier [ku:'tjʊrɪeɪ] *n.* dress-designer.

cove [kəʊv] *n.* (a) small bay. (b) *inf.* man.

coven ['kʌvn] *n.* group of witches.

covenant 1 ['kʌvənənt] *n.* contract/agreement; deep of c. = official signed agreement (to pay s.o., a sum each year). **covenant 2** *v.* to agree by contract.

Coventry ['kɒvəntrɪ] *n.* to send s.o. to C. = to refuse to speak to s.o.

cover 1 ['kʌvə] *n.* (a) thing which is put over sth to protect it; under c. of night = under the protection of the dark. (b) lid. (c) (cardboard) binding of a book; outer pages of a magazine. (d) shelter; to take c. (e) protection (guaranteed by insurance). **cover 2** *v.* (a) to put sth over (sth) to protect it. (b) to travel (a certain distance). (c) to point a gun at. (d) to be enough to pay for. (e) to deal with. (f) to protect with insurance. (g) to be a reporter at (an event). **coverage** *n.* amount of space/time devoted to an event in a newspaper/on TV. **covering 1** *n.* thing which covers. **covering 2** *adj.* c. letter = explanatory letter sent with a form/with another letter, etc. **cover up** *v.* to hide completely. **cover-up** *n.* hiding (of a scandal).

coverlet ['kʌvələt] *n.* cover for a bed.

covert ['kʌvət] *adj.* (formal) hidden/secret.

covet ['kʌvɪt] *v.* to want (sth which belongs to s.o., else). **covetous** *adj.* wanting sth which belongs to s.o., else.

covey ['kʌvɪ] *n.* group (of partridges).

cow 1 [kaʊ] *n.* (a) female animal of bull family kept to give milk. (b) female of certain animals, e.g. the elephant. (c) (in Australia) *Sl.* unpleasant thing/person.

cow 2 *v.* to frighten. **cowboy** *n.* (a) man who drives herds of cattle in America. (b) *inf.* bad workman who charges too much. **cowhand, cowherd, cowman** *n.* man who looks after cattle. **cow parsley** *n.* common wild plant with tall white flowers.

cowpat *n.* round flat cake of cow dung. **cowshed** *n.* shed for cows.

cowslip *n.* common yellow wild flower.

coward ['kaʊəd] *n.* person who is not brave. **cowardice** *n.* lack of bravery. **cowardly** *adj.* not brave.

cower ['kaʊə] *v.* to crouch down because of fear.

cowl [kaʊl] *n.* hood (for a monk's habit); cover for a chimney. **cowling** *n.* cover for an engine.

cowrie ['kaʊrɪ] *n.* colourful seashell.

cox 1 [kɒks] *n.* (*pl.*-es) person who steers a rowing boat. **cox 2** *v.* to steer a rowing boat. **coxed** *adj.* (boat) without a cox. coxless, adj. (boat) without a cox. **coxswain** ['kɒksn] *n.* (a) officer in charge of a boat. (b) person who steers a rowing boat. **coxwainless** *adj.* coxless.

coy [kɔɪ] *adj.* timid; shy. **coyly** *adv.* in a coy way. **coyness** *n.* being coy.

coyote [kɔɪ'əʊtɪ] *n.* small American wolf.

coypu ['kɔɪpu:] *n.* small animal like a beaver.

CPU [si:pi:'ju:] central processing unit.

crab [kræb] *n.* edible ten-footed crustacean with large pincers, which walks sideways; to catch a c. = to miss a stroke when rowing; c. apple = bitter wild apple. **crabbed** *adj.* (a) bad-tempered. (b) (handwriting) which is difficult to read. **crabby** *adj. inf.* bad-tempered.

crack 1 [kræk] *n.* (a) sharp dry sound. (b) sharp blow. (c) thin break; split; at c. of dawn = at daybreak. (d) *inf.* to have a c. at sth = to try to do sth. (e) *Sl.* strong form of cocaine. **crack 2** *adj. inf.* first-class. **crack 3** *v.* (a) to make a sharp sound. (b) to make a thing split in (sth). (c) to c. jokes = to tell jokes. (d) *inf.* get cracking! = start (working, etc.); cracking pace = very fast pace. (e) to decipher (a code). **crack down on** *v. inf.* to campaign against. **cracker** *n.* (a) small firework which makes a bang. (b) paper tube which makes a little explosion when it is pulled. (c) dry unsweetened biscuit. **crackers** *adj. inf.* mad. **crackpot** *adj. & n. inf.* mad (person). **crack up** *v. inf.* (a) to praise (sth) extravagantly. (b) to collapse.

crackle 1 ['krækl] *n.* small explosive sounds. **crackle 2** *v.* to make little explosive sounds. **crackling** *n.* hard cooked pork skin.

cradle 1 ['kreɪdl] n. (a) baby's bed which can be rocked. (b) support (for a piece of machinery). (c) starting point (for civilization, etc.). **cradle 2** v. to rock (in your arms).

craft [krɑːft] n. (a) artistry; skill; crafts = types of work done by hand. (b) ship. (c) cunning; slyness. **craftily** adv. cunningly. **craftiness** n. cunning; slyness. **craftsman** n. (pl.-men) artist person who is expert in using his hands. **craftsmanship** n. skill of a craftsman. **crafty** adj. (-er, -iest) sly.

crag [kræg] n. steep rock cliff. **craggy** adj. rough (rock or person's face).

cram [kræm] v. (crammed) (a) to squeeze (into). (b) to learn facts hurriedly before an examination. **cramfull** adj. very full; overflowing.

cramp 1 [kræmp] n. sudden pain where the muscles tighten up and cannot be relaxed. **cramp 2** v. to hinder; to squeeze tight.

crampon n. metal hook/spike attached to boots for climbing in ice and snow.

cranberry ['krænbəri] n. wile red edible berry.

crane 1 [kreɪn] n. (a) tall metal construction for lifting heavy weights. (b) long-legged tropical bird. **crane 2** v. to stretch (one's neck). **cranefly** n. common insect with long legs.

cranium ['kreɪnɪəm] n. bones covering the top part of the skull. **cranial** adj. referring to the cranium; c. nerves = the nerves which link the brain with the head and neck.

crank 1 [kræŋk] n. (a) shaft with a right angled bend, used for communicating motion. (b) very odd person. **crank 2** v. to turn or lift with a crank. **crankshaft** n. rod which is turned by a crank **cranky** adj. odd/bizarre (person).

cranny ['kræni] n. small crack/small gap.

crap [kræp] n. Sl. shit/rubbish.

craps [kræps] n. Am. game played with two dice.

crash 1 [kræʃ] n. (pl.-es) (a) loud noise. (b) accident, c. helmet = helmet worn by motorcyclists to protect them in case of a crash; c. barrier = strong fence by the side of a road to prevent cars from running off the road. (c) financial collapse. (d) complete breakdown of a computer. **crash 2** v. (a) to explode; to make a great noise. (b) to damaged/destroyed in an accident; to c. into = to hit in an accident (c) to collapse financially. (d) (of a computer) to break down completely. **crash 3** adj. urgent; a c. course = very rapid course. **crash-land** v. to land heavily, without using the undercarriage, so that the aircraft is damaged. **crash-landing** n. act of landing heavily.

crass [kræs] adj. (a) rude/coarse. (b) complete.

crate 1 [kreɪt] n. large rough wooden box. **crate 2** v. to put into a crate.

crater ['kreɪtə] n. hole at the top of a volcano; hole made by a bomb.

cravat [krə'væt] n. type of scarf worn by men knotted round the neck in place of a tie.

crave [kreɪv] v. to want (sth) very much. **craving** n. strong desire (for).

craven ['kreɪvn] adj. cowardly.

crawl 1 [krɔːl] n. (a) creeping on hands and knees. (b) fast swimming stroke with arms going overarm. (c) very slow progress. **crawl 2** v. (a) to move around on hands and knees. (b) to creep along slowly. (c) to be covered (with creeping things).

crayfish ['kreɪfɪʃ] n. (pl.crayfish) kind of fresh-water crustacean like a small lobster.

crayon ['kreɪɒn] n. stick of coloured material for drawing.

craze [kreɪz] n. mania (for sth). **crazily** adv. madly. **craziness** n. madness. **crazy** adj. (-ier, -iest) mad; c. paving = different-shaped paving stones fitted together.

creak 1 [kriːk] n. squeaky cracking noise. **creak 2** v. to make a squeaky cracking noise. **creaky** adj. which makes a creaking noise.

cream 1 [kriːm] n. (a) rich fatty part of milk; single c. = runny cream; double c. = thick cream; c. cheese = rich soft cheese; the c. of the undergraduates = the top few. (b) smooth paste; face c. **cream 2** adj. coloured like cream; very pale fawn. **cream 3** v. (a) (off) to take away the best. (b) to whip into a smooth paste. **creamery** n. dairy. **creamy** adj. (-er, -est) smooth; full of cream.

crease 1 [kriːs] n. fold made by

ironing; fold made accidentally. **crease 2** v. (a) to iron a fold into (sth). (b) to make folds accidentally in (sth).

create [kri'et] v. (a) to make; to invent. (b) inf. to make a disturbance/a fuss. **creation** [kri'eɪʃn] n. thing which has been made. **creative** adj. full of ideas; always making sth. **creativity** [kriɜ'tɪvtɪ] n. aptitude for creating. **creator** n. person who makes/ invents sth.

creature ['kri:tʃə] n. animal person.

crèche [kreʃ] n. nursery where babies can be left while their parents are at work, etc.

credence ['kri:dəns] n. belief (that sth is correct/true). **credentials** [kri'denʃəlz] n. pl.papers which prove your identify or rank so that people can trust you. **credible** [kredɪbl] adj. which can be believed. **credibility** [kredɪ'bɪlɪtɪ] n. ability to be believed; he suffers from a c. gap = people do not believe him. **credibly** adv. reliably.

credit 1 ['kredɪt] n. (a) merit; recognition of quality; it does you c. = you are to be praised for it; he's a c. to the school = he has made the school proud of him. (b) belief; faith. (c) time given to pay; c. card = car which allows you to buy goods without having to pay immediately; on c. = without paying immediately. (d) side of an account showing money in hand or which is owed to you; c. note = not showing that money is owed you. (e) credits = list of actors'/directors' names which appear at the beginning or end of a film/TV programme. **credit 2** v. (credited) (a) to c. s.o. with = to attribute a quality, etc., to s.o. (b) to believe (c) to promise to pay (s.o.); to pay money into (an account). **creditable** adj. honourable (deed). **creditably** adj. honourably. **creditor** n. person who is owed money.

credulous ['kredjʊləs] adj. (person) who believes anything easily. **credulity, credulousness** [kri'dju:lɪtɪ] n. belief/ trust. **credulously** adv. in a credulous way.

creed [kri:d] n. statement of what you believe; the Apostles' C. = the statement of Christian faith.

creek [kri:k] n. little inlet of the sea; Am. small river.

creel [kri:l] n. basket to put fish in.

creep 1 [kri:p] n. (a) inf. sly; unpleasant person. (b) he gives me the creeps = he makes me shudder. **creep 2** v. (crept[krept]) (a) to move around stealthily. (b) creeping plant = plant which spreads close to the ground/which climbs up a wall. (c) it made my flesh c. = it made me shudder. **creeper** n. plant which climbs over walls. **creepy** adj. (-ier, -iest) inf. which makes you shudder. **creepy-crawly** n. inf. insect.

cremate [kri'meɪt] v. to burn (a dead body). **cremation** n. burning of a dead body. **crematorium** [kremə'tɔ:rɪəm] n. (pl.-ia) place where bodies are burnt.

crenellated ['krɛnəleɪtɪd] adj. (castle wall) with openings to shoot through.

creole ['kri:əʊl] adj. & n. (person) of mixed West Indian and European descent.

creosote 1 ['krɪəsəʊt] n. dark brown liquid, used for protecting wood from rotting. **creosote 2** v. to paint which creosote.

crepe [kreɪp] n. (a) c. paper = slightly crinkly coloured paper; c. bandage = bandage made of wrinkled elastic cloth. (b) c. soles = thick wrinkled rubber soles for shoes.

crept [krept] v. see creep.

crescendo [kri'ʃendəʊ] n. (pl.-os) increasing noise (esp. in music).

crescent ['kresnt] n. (a) curved shape, like a new moon. (b) street which forms a semicircle.

cress [kres] n. (no pl.) small green salad plant, usu. eaten with seedlings of mustard.

crest [krest] n. (a) top (of hills/waves). (b) plumes/fleshy growth on the head of a bird. (c) coat of arms. **crestfallen** adj. discouraged/depressed.

cretin [kretɪn] n. person who is mentally weak; inf. very stupid person. **cretinous** adj. very stupid.

crevasse [kri'væs] n. deep crack in a glacier.

crevice [krevɪs] n. small crack in a rock/wall.

crew [kru:] n. (a) people who work on a boat/aircraft/bus, etc. (b) gang. **crewcut** n. very short haircut.

crib 1 [krɪb] n. (a) manger/box for food

for horses or cows. (b) baby's bed (c) model of the scene of the first Christmas displayed in a church at Christmas time. (d) word-for-word translation/list of answers to help a bad student with homework. **crib 2** v. (cribbed) to copy.

cribbage ['krɪbɪdʒ] n. card game where the points are marked by pegs on a special board.

crick 1 [krɪk] n. c. in the neck = sprain/pulled muscle in the neck. **crick 2** v. to pull a muscle in (one's neck).

cricket ['krɪkɪt] n. (a) small jumping insect, like a grasshopper. (b) game played between two teams of eleven players using bats, hard balls and wickets as targets; inf. it isn't c. = it is not fair. **cricketer** n. person who plays cricket.

crime [kraɪm] n. illegal act. **criminal 1** ['krɪmɪnl] adj. referring to an illegal act. **criminal 2** n. person who commits a crime. **criminally** adv. so bad as to be against the law. **criminology** [krɪmɪ'nɒlədʒɪ] n. study of crime.

crimp [krɪmp] v. to press into waves or folds.

crimson ['krɪmzn] adj. & n. deep red colour.

cringe [krɪndʒ] v. (a) bend to avoid a blow. (b) to be excessively humble.

crinkle ['krɪŋkl] v. to fold making many small creases. **crinkly** adj. (-ier, -iest) with many creases/curls.

crinoline ['krɪbɪliːn] n. (old) very wide skirt.

cripple 1 ['krɪpl] n. person who is disabled or lame. **cripple 2** v. (a) to make (s.o.) disabled. (b) to prevent (a machine/a factory) from working.

crisis ['kraɪsɪs] n. (pl. crises['kraɪsiːz]) critical moment; turning point.

crisp 1 [krɪsp] adj. (-er, -est) dry and brittle; sharp/cold (air), crunchy (lettuce). **crisp 2** n. (potato) crisps = thin slices of potato fried until they are crisp. **crispness** n. being crisp. **crispy** adj. very crisp.

criss-cross 1 ['krɪskrɒs] adj. with lines crossing in two directions. **criss-cross 2** v. to go backwards and forwards in different directions.

criterion [kraɪ'tɪərɪən] n. (pl. criteria) standard by which things are judged.

critic ['krɪtɪk] n. (a) person who

examines sth and comments on it, esp. person who writes comments on new plays and films for a newspaper. (b) person who comments unfavourably on sth/who finds fault with sth. **critical** adj. (a) dangerous (situation); extremely urgent/important (decision); very serious (medical condition). (b) unfavourable (comment). **critically** adv. in a critical way. **criticism** ['krɪtɪsɪ] n. (a) comment; literary c. = comment on a work of literature. (b) unfavourable comment. **criticize** v. to comment unfavourably on (sth). **critique** [krɪ'tiːk] n. piece of careful literary criticism.

croak 1 [krəʊk] n. hoarse noise (like that made by frogs). **croak 2** v. to make a hoarse sound. **croaky** adj. (-ier, -iest) hoarse (voice).

crochet 1 ['krəʊʃeɪ] n. type of knitting using one needle with a hook at the end. **crochet 2** v. (crocheted['keəʊʃetd]; crocheting['krəʊʃeɪŋ]) to make (sth) using a hooked needle. **crochet-hook** n. hooked needle for crocheting.

crock [krɒk] n. (a) rough earthenware pot. (b) inf. broken-down car or person. **crockery** n. (no pl.) rough pottery tableware.

crocodile ['krɒkədaɪl] n. (a) large meateating reptile living in rivers in Africa; she went c. tears = she pretended to cry when she was not in any way sad. (b) long line of schoolchildren walking in pairs.

crocus ['krəʊkəs] n. (pl.-es) purple, yellow or white spring flower.

croft [krɒft] n. (in Scotland) small farm held by a tenant. **crofter** n. farmer who holds a croft.

croissant ['krwæsɒŋ] n. rolled pastry, made in the shape of a crescent.

crone [krən] n. ugly old witch. **crony** ['krəʊnɪ] n. old friend.

crook 1 [krʊk] n. (a) bend. (b) long stick with a bend top. (c) inf. criminal. **crook 2** adj. (in Australia) Sl. ill. **crooked** ['krʊkɪd] adj. (a) bent. (b) dishonest. **crookedly** adv. in a bent way; not straight.

croon [kruːn] v. to sing in a low voice. **crooner** n. person who croons.

crop 1 [krɒp] n. (a) vegetables/grain, etc. grown for food. (b) part of a bird's throat shaped like a bag. (c) small whip used by a rider. (d) short haircut. **crop 2** v. (cropped) (a) to cut (a hedge/s.o.'s hair) short. (b) (of sheep) to eat (grass) so that it is very short. **cropper** n. inf. became a c. = (i) he fell badly; (ii) his plans did not succeed. **crop up** v. to occur.

croquet ['krəʊkeɪ] n. lawn game played with hoops, balls and mallets.

croquette [krə'ket] n. small ball of mashed potato, covered with breadcrumbs and fried.

crosier ['krəʊzɪə] n. staff (like a crook) carried by a bishop.

cross 1 [krɒs] n. (a) shape with two lines cutting across each other at right angles. (b) shape of a vertical line, with another cutting across it at right angles, forming the symbol of the Christian church; wooden construction of this shape; the Red C. = international rescue and medical organisation. (c) thing which is hard to bear. (d) mixture of two breeds; mixture of two different things. **cross 2** v. (a) to c. oneself = to make a sign of the cross on oneself. (b) to put two lines across (a cheque) so that it can only be paid into a bank account. (c) to go across; to place across; crossed line = telephone connection where you can hear other people talking. (d) to breed (two animals/plants) together. **cross 3** adj. (a) opposed/contrary; they are at c. purposes = they are in disagreement; to talk at c. purposes = to misunderstand what each other is saying. (b) bad-tempered/angry. **crossbar** n. beam which goes across a space. **crossbill** n. type of bird, with a bill of which the top part crosses over the bottom. **crossbreed** n. animal produced by crossing two animals of different breeds. **crosscheck** v. to check again to make sure. **cross-country** adj. & n. (race) across fields and along roads, not on a tack. **cross-examination** n. searching questioning by an opposing lawyer. **cross-examine** v. to ask (s.o.) searching questions. **crosseyed** adj. (person) whose eyes do not face forward; (person) with a squint. **crossfertilize** v. to fertilize (one plant) with another variety. **crossfire** n. gunfire from two directions, so that the fire crosses. **cross-grained** adj. bad-tempered.

crossing n. (a) act of going across. (b) place where you cross; pedestrian c. = place were pedestrians can cross a street; level c. = place where a road crosses a railway line. **crosslegged** adj. & adv. with one ankle over the other. **crossly** adv. in an angry way. **cross off, cross out** v. to draw a line through (sth written). **cross-question** v. to cross examine. **cross-questioning** n. cross examining. **cross-reference** n. line in a reference book telling you to look in another section for further information. **crossroads** n. pl.place where two roads cross. **cross-section** n. (a) diagram as if a cut had been made across sth. (b) sample. **crosswalk** n. Am. pedestrian crossing. **crosswind** n. wind blowing across a road, etc. **crosswise** adv. in the shape of a cross. **crossword** n. puzzle where small squares have to be filled with letters forming words to which clues are given.

crosse [krɒs] n. stick with a net, used in playing lacrosse.

crotch [krɒtʃ] n. (pl.-es) where the two legs fork.

crotchet ['krɒtʃɪt] n. note in music lasting two quavers or half as long as a minim. **crotchety** adj. (a) bad-tempered. (b) odd/slightly mad; capricious.

crouch [kraʊtʃ] v. to bend down low.

croup [kruːp] n. (a) infection in the throat, which makes children cough noisily. (b) rear part of a horse.

croupier ['kruːpɪə] n. person who is in charge of a gaming table.

crow 1 [krəʊ] n. large common black bird; as the c. flies = in a straight line.

crow 2 v. (a) (of a cockerel) to call. (b) to c. over s.o. = to exclaim happily because you have beaten s.o. **crowbar** n. large metal lever for opening boxes. **crow's-feet** n. little wrinkles at the outer corners of the eyes. **crow's nest** n. platform on top of a mast for a lookout.

crowd 1 [kraʊd] n. mass of people.

crowd 2 v. to group together.

crown 1 [kraʊn] n. (a) gold and jewelled headdress for a king/queen, etc. (b) symbol of monarchy; counsel for the c. = lawyer representing the state. (c) top (of the head, a tooth, etc.). (d) type of coin. **crown 2** v. (a) to make (s.o.) king/queen/emperor, etc., by placing a crown on his head. (b) to be a splendid end to (sth). (c) inf. to hit (s.o.) on the head. (d) to reward. (e) to put a false top on (a tooth). **crown cork** n. metal and cork cap on a bottle. **Crown Court** n. court in various places in England and Wales which tries major criminal cases. **Crown Prince** n. eldest son of a king, who will inherit the throne.

crucial ['kruːʃl] adj. extremely important/critical. **crucially** adv. vitally/critically.

crucible ['kruːsɪbl] n. small pot used for heating substances in chemical experiments.

crucifix ['kruːsɪfɪks] n. (pl.-es) statue representing Jesus Christ on the cross. **crucifixion** [kruːsɪ'fɪkʃn] n. killing by nailing to a cross. **crucify** v. to kill (s.o.) by nailing to a cross.

crude 1 [kruːd] adj. (-ier, -est) (a) unpurified; unrefined (oil). (b) rude/ illmannered. **crude 2** n. unrefined oil. **crudely** adv. in a crude way. **crudeness, crudity** n. being crude.

cruel ['kruːəl] adj. (crueller, cruellest) which causes pain/suffering. **cruelly** adv. savagely/unkindly. **cruelty** n. being cruel.

cruet ['kruːɪt] n. set of containers for salt, pepper, mustard, etc.

cruise 1 [kruːz] n. long pleasure voyage in a ship calling at different ports. **cruise 2** v. (a) to go about steadily (in a boat) visiting places. (b) to travel at an even speed. **cruiser** n. larger warship, smaller than a battleship; cabin c. = motor boat with a cabin for living in.

crumb [krʌm] n. small piece (of bread, etc.).

crumble 1 ['krʌmbl] n. dessert made of fruit covered with a mixture of flour, fat and sugar. **crumble 2** v. to break into small pieces **crumbly** adj. which easily falls to pieces.

crummy ['krʌmɪ] adj. (-ier, -iest) inf. rotten/no good.

crumpet ['krʌmpɪt] n. thick round butter cake, served toasted with butter.

crumple ['krʌmpl] v. to crush/to screw up into a ball.

crunch 1 [krʌntʃ] n. (pl.-es) (a) sound

of sth crisp being crushed. (b) inf. crisis point; when it comes to the c. **crunch 2** v. to crush (sth crisp); to chew (sth hard). **crunchy** adj. hard and crisp.

crupper ['krʌpə] n. piece of leather which fastens round a horse's tail to keep the saddle in place.

crusade 1 [kruː'seɪd] n. (a) medieval campaign by Christians against Muslims who occupied the Holy Land. (b) campaign. **crusade 2** v. to campaign/ to fight (against of for). **crusader** n. person who goes on a crusade.

crush 1 [krʌʃ] n. (a) drink made of fruit juice. (b) mass of people squeezed together. (c) girl's infatuation. **crush 2** v. to squash.

crust [krʌst] n. hard exterior (of bread/ cake/the earth, etc.). **crusty** adj. (-ier, - iest) (bread) with a hard crust.

crustacean [krʌ'steɪʃn] n. one of many types of animals with hard shells, mainly living in the sea, such as lobsters, crabs, etc.

crutch [krʌtʃ] n. (pl.-es) (a) lame person's long stick which goes under the armpit. (b) crotch.

crux [krʌks] n. central point of a problem; the c. of the matter.

cry 1 [kraɪ] n. (a) act of making tears. (b) shout; exclamation (esp. of pain). (c) call (of a bird/animal). **cry 2** v. (a) to make tears. (b) (also cry out) to shout; to exclaim (in pain). **crying** adj. scandalous/which needs putting right. **cry off** v. to decide not to do sth which you had promised to do.

cryogenics [kraɪəʊ'dʒenɪks] n. study of very low temperatures.

crypt [krɪpt] n. cellar under a church.

cryptic ['krɪptɪk] adj. secret; mysterious.

crypto- ['krɪptəʊ] prefix hidden.

cryptogam ['krɪptəgæm] n. plant (like moss) which has no flowers.

cryptogram ['krɪptəgæm] n. message written in a secret language; coded message. **cryptography** n. study of codes.

crystal ['krɪstl] n. (a) chemical formation of regular-shaped solids. (b) very clear bright glass. **crystalline** adj. shaped like a crystal; clear as a crystal. **crystallization** [krɪstəlaɪ'zeɪʃn] n. formation of crystals. **crystallize**

['krɪstəlaɪz] v. (a) to form crystals. (b) to preserve fruit in sugar. (c) to take shape. **crystallography** [krɪstə'lɒgrəfɪ] n. study of crystals.

Cu symbol for copper.

cub [kʌb] n. (a) young animal (esp. bear/fox). (b) C. Scout = boy in the younger section of the Boy Scouts.

Cuban 1 ['kjuːbn] adj. referring to Cuba. **Cuban 2** n. person from Cuba.

cubby-hole ['kʌbɪhəʊl] n. small dark cupboard/hiding place.

cube 1 [kjuːb] n. (a) geometric solid shape where all six sides are square and join each other at right angles. (b) the result where a number is multiplied by itself twice; c. root = number which when multiplied by itself twice produces a given number. **cube 2** v. (a) to multiply (a number) by itself twice. (b) cubed sugar = sugar in square lumps.

cubic adj. solid; c. capacity = capacity to hold something; c. centimetre = (i) cube where each side measures one centimetre; (ii) the volume of this size.

cubicle ['kjuːbɪkl] n. small room (in a dormitory); changing room (in a shop/at swimming baths).

cubism ['kjuːbɪzəm] n. art movement where geometric shapes predominate. **cubist** adj. & n. (painter) using geometric shapes.

cuckoo 1 ['kʊkuː] n. common summer bird, which lays its eggs in other bird's nests. **cuckoo 2** adj. inf. stupid. **cuckoo clock** n. clock where a small bird makes a noise like a cuckoo to call the time.

cucumber ['kjuːkʌmbə] n. long vegetable used in salads or for pickling.

cud [kʌd] n. food chewed a second time.

cuddle 1 ['kʌdl] n. a hug. **cuddle 2** v. to hug and kiss (s.o.). **cuddlesome, cuddly** adj. warm and soft.

cudgel 1 ['kʌdʒl] n. large stick for hitting people with; to take up the cudgels on s.o.'s behalf = to go to defend s.o. **cudgel 2** v. (cudgelled) to c. one's brains = to think hard.

cue [kjuː] n. (a) (in a play) the line which indicates that you speak or act next; to take your c. from s.o. = to follow s.o. closely/to do as s.o. does. (b) long stick for playing billiards/snooker.

cuff 1 [kʌf] n. (a) end of the sleeve round the wrist; speaking of the c./an off the c. speech = speech made without any notes; impromptu speech. (b) Am. folded part at the bottom of each leg of a pair of trousers. (c) smack (with an open hand). **cuff 2** v. to give (s.o.) a smack. **cuff-links** n. pl.fasteners, usually linked with a chain, for attaching shirt cuffs.

cuirass [kwiː'ræs] n. armour for the top part of the body.

cuisine [kwɪ'ziːn] n. style of cooking.

cul-de-sac ['kʌldəsæk] n. small street open at only one end.

culinary ['kʌlɪnərɪ] adj. referring to cooking.

cull [kʌl] v. to kill (some animals in a herd) when there are too many of them.

cullet ['kʌlɪt] n. broken glass for recycling.

culminate ['kʌlmɪneɪt] v. to reach a climax/to end (in). **culmination** [kʌlmɪ'neɪʃn] n. final point/grand ending.

culottes [kjʊ'lɒts] n. pl.woman's wide shorts, like a split skirts.

culpable ['kʌlpəbl] adj. guilty. **culpability** [kʌlpə'bɪlɪtɪ] n. guilty.

culprit ['kʌlprɪt] n. person who has done something wrong.

cult [kʌlt] n. religious or semi-religious worship; c. hero = person worshiped by a group of admirers.

cultivate ['kʌltɪveɪt] v. (a) to dig and water (the land) to grow plants; to grow (plants). (b) to do everything to win (s.o.'s friendship). **cultivated** adj. (person) who has been educated/who is civilized. **cultivation** [kʌltʊ'veɪʃn] n. (a) act of cultivating. (b) education. **cultivator** n. (a) farmer/person who cultivates. (b) small motor-powered plough.

culture ['kʌltʃə] n. (a) cultivation of plants/pearls. (b) growing (of germs in a laboratory). (c) civilization. **cultural** adj. referring to culture. **cultured** adj. (a) civilized; well educated (person). (b) (pearl) which has been artificially grown.

culvert ['kʌlvət] n. drain which goes under a road in a pipe.

cumbersome ['kʌmbəsəm] adj. large and heavy.

cumin ['kʌmɪn] n. herb whose seeds are used for flavouring.

cummerbund ['kʌməbʌnd] n. type of decorative belt worn by men.

cumulative ['kjuːmjʊlətɪv] adj. which accumulates, which grows by adding new parts.

cumulus ['kjuːmjʊləs] n. type of large white mass of clouds; rounded masses of clouds.

cuneiform ['kjuːnɪfɔːm] adj.& n. type of ancient writing done on wet clay with a stick.

cunning 1 ['kʌnɪŋ] n. (a) cleverness. (b) trickery. **cunning 2** adj. (a) clever. (b) tricky/sly.

cup 1 [kʌp] n. (a) bowl with a handle for drinking tea or coffee, etc. (b) silver goblet or vase given as a prize in sporting events/competions, etc.; c. final = match for a football championship; c. tie = preliminary match for a football championship. **cup 2** v. (cupped) to put (hands) in the shape of a cup. **cupful** n. quantity held by a cup. **cupboard** ['kʌbəd] n. large piece of furniture with shelves and doors; alcove in a wall with shelves and doors.

cupidity [kjuː'pɪdɪtɪ] n. greed; desire for sth.

cupola ['kjuːpələ] n. small dome.

cuppa ['kʌpə] n. inf. cup of tea

cur [kɜː] n. dirty dog.

curare [kjʊə'rɑːrɪ] n. S. American poison, now used to relax the muscles.

curate ['kjʊərət] n. minor priest who helps the parish priest. **curacy** n. post of curate. **curator** [kjʊ'reɪtə] n. person in charge of a museum.

curb 1 [kɜːb] n. (a) = kerb (b) brake/ thing which hold you back. **curb 2** v. to brake; to hold back.

curd [kɜːd] n. solid food made from sour milk. **curdle** ['kɜːdl] v. to (cause to) go sour.

cure 1 ['kjʊə] n. (a) making better. (b) remedy. **cure 2** v. (a) to make better. (b) to preserve (fish/pork, etc.) by salting/smoking, etc.; to preserve (skins) to make leather. **curable** adj. (disease) which can be cured. **curative** adj. which can cure.

curettage [kjʊre'tɑːʒ] n. scraping of the inside of part of the body. **curette** n. surgical instrument for scraping.

curfew ['kɜːfjuː] n. period when no one is allowed on the streets.

curie ['kjʊərɪ] n. unit of measurement of radioactivity.

curio ['kjʊərɪəʊ] n. (pl.-oes) old/rare object. **curiosity** [kjʊərɪ'ɒsɪtɪ] n. (a) desire for knowledge. (b) odd/rare object. **curious** ['kjʊərɪəs] adj. (a) wanting to know. (b) odd/peculiar. **curiously** adv. oddly.

curl 1 [kɜːl] n. lock of wavy twisted hair. **curl 2** v. (a) to make (hair) wave/ twist. (b) to grow in waves/twists naturally. **curler** n. small tube for wrapping hair round to make it curl. **curling** n. team game where heavy weights are slid across ice towards a target. **curl up** v. to roll up into a ball. **curly** adj. (-ier, -iest) with natural waves twists.

curlew ['kɜːljuː] n. brown wading bird with a long curved beak.

currant ['kʌrənt] n. (a) small black or red soft fruit; bush of this fruit. (b) small dried grape.

currency ['kʌrənsɪ] n. (a) (system of) money; hard c. = money which can be easily exchanged internationally. (b) being well known; to gain c. = to become more frequently heard. **current 1** ['kʌrənt] n. flow of water/air/ electricity. **current 2** adj. of the present time; frequent; c. affairs = things which are happening at the present moment; c. account = bank account from which you can draw money without giving notice. **currently** adv. at the present time.

curriculum [kə'rɪkjʊləm] n. list of subjects studied in a school, etc.; c. vitae['viːtaɪ] = summary of biographical details, esp. details of education and work experience.

curry 1 ['kʌrɪ] n. hot spice; dish made with hot spice; c. powder. **curry 2** v. (a) to cook with hot spices. (b) to brush down (a horse). (c) to c. favour with s.o. = to try to make s.o. favour you. **currycomb** n. stiff brush for brushing a horse.

curse 1 [kɜːs] n. (a) evil magic spell. (b) swear word. (c) calamity/evil. (d) inf. the c. = woman's menstrual periods. **curse 2** v. (a) to cast an evil spell on (s.o.). (b) to swear.

cursive ['kɜːsɪv] adj. (writing) with the letters joined together.

cursor ['kɜ:sə] n. spot of light which moves round a computer screen, showing where work is being done.

cursory ['kɜ:sərɪ] adj. rapid/superficial (inspection/glance). **cursorily** adv. rapidly.

curt [kɜ:t] adj. (-er, -est) abrupt. **curtly** adv. abruptly. **curtness** n. being curt.

curtail [kɜ:'teɪl] v. to shorten; to reduce. **curtailment** n. act of curtailing.

curtain 1 ['kɜ:tn] n. long piece of material hanging by hooks from a pole, covering a window or cutting off the stage in a theatre. **curtain 2** v. (also c. off) to hide/to cover with a curtain. **curtaincall** n. calling of an actor to take a bow after the end of a performance. **curtainrod** n. rod on which a curtain is hung.

curtsy 1 ['kɜ:tsɪ] n. respectful movement made by women/girls, by bending the knees and putting one foot forward. **curtsy 2** v. to c. to s.o. = to make a curtsy to s.o.

curve 1 [kɜ:v] n. rounded shape like a semi-circle. **curve 2** v. to make rounded shape. **curvaceous** [kɜ:'veɪʃəs] adj. (girl) with a rounded figure. **curvature** ['kɜ:vətʃə] n. bending of something into a curve; c. of the spine = abnormal bending of the spine. **curved** adj. rounded.

cushion 1 ['kʊʃn] n. bag filed with feathers, etc., for sitting/leaning on. **cushion 2** v. to soften (a blow).

cushy ['kʊʃɪ] adj. (-ier, -iest) inf. easy (job).

cusp [kʌsp] n. point where two curves meet.

cuspidor ['kʌspɪ'dɔ:] n. bowl into which one can spit.

cussed ['kʌsɪd] adj. inf. awkward and contrary. **cussedness** ['kʌsɪdnəs] n. inf. being cussed.

custard ['kʌstəd] n. cream made with eggs, milk and sugar; also with a special power and milk. **custard tart** n. pastry case filled with custard and baked.

custody ['kʌstədɪ] n. keeping. **custodial sentence** n. sentence which sends a convicted person to prison. **custodian** [kʌ'stəʊdɪən] n. person who keeps sth safe; guardian of an ancient monument, etc.

custom ['kʌstəm] n. (a) habit. (b) using of a shop; custom-built/custom-made = made to special order.

customarily adv. usually.

customary adj. habitual. **customer** n. client/person who buys in a shop.

customize v. to convert (car) to a customer's special and peculiar requirements. **customs** n. (a) tax on goods imported into a country. (b) Customs and Excise = the government department/office which inspects imports, imposes taxes on alcohol and deals with VAT.

cut 1 [kʌt] n. (a) reduction (in salary); breaking of (electricity supply). (b) opening made with a sharp blade; small wound. (c) short c. = way which is shorter than usual. (d) way in which a suit/jacket, etc., is made. (e) piece/slice of meat. (f) inf. share (of profits, etc.).

cut 2 (cut) (a) to make an opening (using a sharp blade); to wound (with a knife); to shorten; to reduce. (b) to divide (a pack of playing cards) in half. (c) not to look at (s.o.) whom you know. (d) to miss (a lecture). **cut 3** adj. which has been cut. **cut down** v. to chop down (a tree); to reduce (an amount). **cut in** v. to interrupt a conversation; to move in quickly in front of another car in traffic. **cut off** v. to disconnect (electricity supply); to remove; to stop (s.o.) reaching a place. **cut out** v. (a) to stop (eating sth, etc.). (b) to remove a small piece by cutting it from a large piece (of paper, etc.); he is not cut out for the army = he does not fit in with/is not suitable for the army. **cut price** adj. cheap.

cutter n. (a) person who cuts. (b) machine which cuts. (c) small, fast boat.

cut-throat adj. vicious/intense.

cutting 1 adj. which cuts; sharply critical (remark). **cutting 2** n. (a) small piece of paper cut out of a newspaper. (b) little piece of a plant which will take root if stuck in the ground. **cut up** v. to make into small pieces by cutting; inf. cut up = very upset.

cutaneous [kju:'teɪnɪəs] adj. referring to the skin.

cute [kju:t] adj. inf. nice. **cuteness** n. niceness.

cuticle ['kju:tɪkl] n. skin round a fingernail or toenail.

cutlass ['kʌtləs] *n.* short sword, used in the navy and in cavalry.

cutlery ['kʌtləri] *n.* (no *pl.*) knives, forks and spoons.

cutlet ['kʌtlət] *n.* (a) thin slice of meat (usu. with the rib bone attached). (b) fried patty made with meat, etc.

cuttlefish ['kʌtlfɪʃ] *n.* animal (like a squid) which lives in the sea and squirts ink when attacked.

cv [si:vi:] *n.* curriculum vitae.

cwt abbrev. for hundred weight.

cyanide ['saɪənaɪd] *n.* strong poison.

cybernetics [saɪbə'netɪks] *n.* science of the communication of information.

cyclamen ['sɪkləmən] *n.* common indoor plant with pink flowers which grow from a corm.

cycle 1 [saɪkl] *n.* (a) period during which sth returns. (b) series of songs or poems. (c) bicycle. **cycle 2** *v.* to go on a bicycle. **cyclic, cyclical** ['sɪklɪk(l)] *adj.* occurring in cycles.

cycling *n.* riding a bicycle as a sport.

cyclist *n.* person who rides a bicycle.

cyclone ['saɪkləʊn] *n.* tropical storm.

cyclostyled ['saɪkləʊstaɪld] *adj.* (copy) produced from a stencil.

cyclotron ['saɪkləʊtron] *n.* machine which accelerates the spiral movement of particles, used in nuclear processes.

cygnet ['sɪgnət] *n.* baby swan.

cylinder ['sɪlɪndə] *n.* shape like a tube; part of an engine, of this shape, in which a piston moves. **cylindrical** [sɪ'lɪndrɪkl] *adj.* tube-shaped.

cymbals ['sɪmbəlz] *n.* *pl.*pair of round metal plates which are banged together to make a loud noise in music.

cynic ['sɪnɪk] *n.* person who mocks/who doubts that anything is good. **cynical** *adj.* referring to a cynic. **cynically** *adv.* in a cynical, mocking way. **cynicism** ['sɪnɪsɪzəm] *n.* being cynical.

cynosure ['saɪnəsjʊə] *n.* centre of attraction.

cypress ['saɪprəs] *n.* (*pl.*-es) tall slim evergreen tree.

Cypriot 1 ['sɪprɪət] *adj.* referring to Cyprus. **Cypriot 2** *n.* person from Cyprus.

cyst [sɪst] *n.* small growth on or inside the body. **cystitis** [sɪs'taɪtɪs] *n.* inflammation of the bladder.

cystoscopy *n.* operation to examine the bladder by means of a very small telescope on the end of a tube.

cytology [saɪ'tɒlədʒɪ] *n.* study of cells.

Czech 1 [tʃek] *adj.* referring to Czech Republic. **Czech 2** *n.* (a) person from Czech Republic. (b) language spoken in Czech Republic.

Dd

dab 1 [dæb] *n.* (a) light tap. (b) *inf.* a d. hand at poker = very good at playing poker. (c) small flat fish. (d) small quantity. **dab 2** *v.* (dabbed) to give (sth) a light tap; to d. (sth) on = to apply (paint, etc.) by pressing lightly.

dabble [dæbl] *v.* to paddle (in water); he dabbles in politics = he does a little political work.

dabchick [dæbtʃrk] *n.* common small dark warterbird with a red forehead.

dace [ders] *n.* (*pl.*dace) small edible freshwater fish.

dachshund [dækshund] *n.* breed of long low dog (originally from Germany).

dactyl [dækrl] *n.* measure (one long and two short syllables) used in Latin poetry.

dad, daddy [dæd],[dædr] *n.* *inf.* father. **daddy-long-legs** *n.* insect with very long legs.

dado [derdəu] *n.* (*pl.*-os) lower part of a wall, which is panelled or painted differently from the upper part.

daffodil [dæfədr] *n.* spring flower in shades of yellow, with a trumpet shaped centre.

daft [da:ft] *adj.* *inf.* silly.

dagger [dægə] *n.* short knife; at daggers drawn = bitter enemies.

daguerreotype [də'gerɪəutarp] *n.* photographic process, where the image is captured on silver-coated plate.

dahlia ['deɪhə] *n.* autumn garden flower (produced from a bulbous root).

Dáil [dɔɪl] *n.* lower house of the Irish Parliament.

daily 1 ['deɪh] *adj.* every day. **daily2** *adv.* twice d. = two times a day. **daily3** *n.* (a) newspaper published every weekday. (b) woman who comes to a house everyday to do housework.

dainty [ˈdeɪntɪ] *adj.* (-ier, -iest) delicate; small. **daintily** *adv.* delicately.

dairy [ˈdeərɪ] *n.* place where milk, cream and butter are processed or sold; d. produce = milk, butter, cream and cheese; d. farm = farm which produces milk. **dairyman** *n.* (*pl.*-men) man who looks after dairy cows.

dais [ˈdeɪs] *n.* low platform (in large hall).

daisy [ˈdeɪzɪ] *n.* small pink and white summer flower; d. wheel printer = typewriter/computer printer, where the characters are on the ends of spokes of a wheel.

dale [deɪl] *n.* (in north of England) valley.

dally [ˈdælɪ] *v.* to idle; to spend time doing nothing. **dalliance** *n.* (old) idling.

dalmatian [dælˈmeɪʃn] *n.* large white dog with black spots.

dam1 [dæm] *n.* (a) wall (of earth or concrete) blocking a river, etc. (b) female mammal which is a mother. **dam2** *v.* (dammed) to block (a river) by building a wall across it.

damage 1 [ˈdæmrdʒ] *n.* (a) harm (done to things, not to people). (b) damages = payment ordered by a court to a victim. (c) *inf.* total of a bill. **damage2** *v.* to spoil or harm (sth).

damask [ˈdæməsk] *n.* kind of patterned material, used esp. for tablecloths, etc. **damascene** *adj.* (steel) decorated with patterns of silver or gold.

dame [deɪm] *n.* (a) (in a pantomime) old woman (usu. played by a man). (b) *Am. inf.* woman (c) title given to women (equivalent to Sir for men).

damn1 [dæm] *n.* curse. **damn2** *v.* to condemn; to curse; to criticize. **damn3** *inter. inf.* expressing annoyance. **damnable** *adj.* cursed. **damnation** [dæmˈneɪʃn] *n.* state of being eternally condemned. **damned** *adj. inf.* very annoying. **damning** *adj.* which shows that sth is wrong.

damp1 [dæmp] *n.* wetness; rising d. = humidity which creeps up walls of a house; d. course = strip of material inserted in a wall to prevent damp rising. **damp2** *adj.* (-er, -est) rather wet. **damp3** *v.* to wet; to reduce (enthusiasm). **dampen** *v.* to damp.

damper *n.* (a) gloom. (b) plate at the back of a fireplace which regulates the draught. (c) soft pad which touches a piano string to soften the tone. (d) (in Australia) flat bread made from flour and water, cooked on a fire. **dampness** *n.* state of being wet. **damp-proof** *adj.* resistant to wet.

damsel [ˈdæmzl] *n.* (old) girl.

damson [ˈdæmzən] *n.* small purple plum; tree which bears this fruit.

dance1 [dɑːns] *n.* (a) way of moving to music. (b) evening entertainment where people dance. **dance2** *v.* (a) to move (in time to music). (b) to jump up and down (with excitement). **dancer 1** *n.* person who dances; ballet d. = person who dances in ballet.

dandelion [ˈdændrlarən] *n.* wild plant with yellow flowers and bitter sap.

dandruff [ˈdændrʌf] *n.* small pieces of dry skin (in the hair).

dandy [ˈdændr] *n.* man who is too interested in clothes. **dandified** *adj.* like a dandy.

Dane [deɪn] *n.* person from Denmark; Great d. = breed of very large shorthaired dog.

danger [ˈdeɪndʒə] *n.* risk; possibility of harm or death; in d. = at risk; out of d. / off the d. list = no longer likely to die; d. money = extra payment to a worker in a dangerous job. **dangerous** *adj.* which can cause injury or death. **dangerously** *adv.* in a dangerous way.

dangle [ˈdæŋgl] *v.* to (cause to) hang limply.

Danish1 [ˈdeɪntʃ] *adj.* referring to Denmark; d. pastry = sweet pastry cake with jam or fruit folded in it. **Danish2** *n.* language spoken in Denmark.

dank [dæŋk] *adj.* cold and damp.

daphne [ˈdæfnɪ] *n.* small shrub with pink flowers which appear very early in the spring.

dapper [ˈdæpə] *adj.* smart/elegant.

dappled [ˈdæpld] *adj.* covered with patches of light and dark colour.

Darby and Joan [daːbrəndʒəun] *n.* happy old couple.

dare1 [ˈdeə] *n.* act of daring s.o. to do sth. **dare2** *v.* (a) to be brave enough (to do sth); I d. say = perhaps/probably. (b) to challenge (s.o.) to do sth by suggesting it is cowardly not to do it.

daredevil *adj.& n.* (person) full of reckless bravery. **daring 1** *adj.* brave but foolish. **daring 2** *n.* foolish bravery.

dark 1 [da:k] *adj.* (-er, -est) (a) with little or no light. (b) not a light colour; d. horse = person/thing which succeeds though not expected to do so; d. Ages = period between the end of the Roman civilization in Northern Europe and the Middle Ages. (c) keep it d. = keep it a secret. (d) gloomy. **dark2** *n.* (a) absence of light. (b) to keep s.o. in the d. = to keep sth a secret from s.o. **darken** *v.* to become dark. **darkly** *adv.* in a gloomy way. **darkness** *n.* absence of light. **darkroom** *n.* room with a special light, in which you can develop and print films.

darling ['da:lɪŋ] *n.& adj.* (person) loved; lovable.

darn1 [da:n] *v.* to mend (holes in clothes). **darn 2** *n.* place where clothes have been mended. **darning** *n.* action of mending; clothes which are waiting to be mended.

dart1 [da:t] *n.* (a) light arrow with a sharp point. (b) small heavy arrow with feathers (for playing a game with); darts = games where two teams throw small heavy arrows at a round target. (c) small tuck sewn into a garment to make it fit. (d) quick rush. **dart2** *v.* to run fast. **dartboard** *n.* round target at which darts are thrown.

dash1 [dæʃ] *n.* (*pl.*-es) (a) small amount. (b) little line. (c) sudden rush. **dash2** *v.* (a) to rush. (b) to smash (sth). **dashboard** *n.* instrument panel in a car. **dashing** *adj.* very smart and energetic (person).

dastardly [da:stədlt] *adj.* cowardly and unpleasant.

data ['deɪtə] *n.* statistical information; d. bank = store of information in a computer; d. protection = keeping information or computer records safely, so that they cannot be copied; see also datum. **database** *n.* data stored in a computer, which can be used to provide information of various kinds. **data processing** *n.* analysis of statistical information using a computer.

date1 [deɪt] *n.* (a) number of a day, month or year; up to d. = recent; he is bringing the book up to d. = he is revising the book to put in most recent information; out of d. = not modern; the book is three years out of d. (b) agreed meeting time. (c) fruit of a date palm.

date2 *v.* (a) to write the number of the day on (sth). (b) to give the date of (an antique, etc.). (c) *Am.* to agree to meet (s.o. of the opposite sex) at a particular time. (c) this house dates from 1600 = this house has existed since 1600. (d) to seem old-fashioned. **datable** *adj.* which can be dated. **dated** *adj.* old-fashioned. **dateless** *adj.* with no date. **dateline** *n.* heading (with date and place) of a report from a foreign correspondent. **date line** *n.* line of longitude (in the Pacific Ocean) which indicates the change in date from east to west. **date palm** *n.* palm tree which provides small, very sweet brown fruit.

dative ['deɪtɪv] *adj.& n.* (in grammar) (case) showing giving.

datum ['deɪtəm] *n.* (*pl.*data) piece of information.

daub1 [dɔ:b] *n.* (a) smear. (b) *inf.* bad painting. **daub2** *v.* to smear with paint/ with mud, etc.

daughter ['dɔ:tə] *n.* female child (of a parent). **daughter-in-law** *n.* (*pl.*daughters-in-law) son's wife.

daunt [dɔ:nt] *v.* to discourage; nothing daunted = not frightened. **dauntless** *adj.* fearless.

davenport ['dævənpɔ:t] *n.* (a) *Am,* sofa. (b) small writing desk.

davit ['dævɪt] *n.* (on a ship) small crane for lowering the lifeboats into the sea.

dawdle ['dɔ:dl] *v.* to walk slowly and aimlessly.

dawn1 [dɔ:n] *n.* (a) beginning of day, when the sun rises. (b) beginning of (of civilization). **dawn2** *v.* (a) (of day) to begin. (b) it dawned on him that = he began to realize that.

day [deɪ] *n.* (a) period of time lasting 24 hours. (b) period of time from morning to night. (c) light. (d) two apples a d. = every day. (e) one d. /some d. = sometime in the future. (f) period (in the past). **daybreak** *n.* early morning when the sun is about to rise. **day centre** *n.* place where elderly or disabled people can meet and be looked after during the day. **daydream1** *n.*

dream which you have during the day when you are not asleep. **daydream2** v. to think about other things; not to concentrate. **daylight** n. light of day; d. saving time = system of advancing the clocks in summer to take advantage of the longer daylight period. **day release** n. system where a worker is allowed time from work to attend a course of study. **daytime** n. in the d. = during the day.

daze1 [deɪz] n. state of not being mentally alert. **daze2** v. to stun(s.o.).

dazzle ['dæzl] v. to blind (temporarily). **dazzling** adj. very bright (light).

db, dB abbrev. for decibel.

D & C abbrev. for dilation and curettage.

DC abbrev. for direct current.

DDT [diːdiːtiː] n. common insecticide.

deacon ['diːkən] n. minor priest. **deaconess** n. woman who can direct services (in some Protestant churches).

dead 1 [ded] adj. (a) not alive; (telephone line, etc.) not working. (b) complete (silence, etc.). (c) no longer used. **dead 2** n. (a) the d. = dead people. (b) at d. of night = in the middle of the night. **dead 3** adv. (a) completely. (b) exactly. **dead beat** adj. inf. tired out. **deaden** v. to make (a sound) quieter; to make (a blow) soft. **dead end** n. (street/way) leading nowhere. **dead heat** n. race where two people come in equal first. **dead letter** n. (a) letter which cannot be delivered. (b) low which is no longer obeyed. **deadline** n. date by which sth has to be done. **deadliness** n. being deadly. **deadlock 1** n. state where two sides cannot agree. **deadlock 2** v. to (cause to) be unable to agree. **deadly** adj. (-ier, -iest) so strong as to kill; d. nightshade = very poisonous plant. **deadpan** adj. not showing any emotion.

deaf 1 [def] adj. (-er, -est) unable to hear; having difficulty in hearing. **deaf 2** n. the d. = people who cannot hear. **deafaid** n. small device which helps a deaf (by a loud noise). **deafening** adj. so loud as to make you deaf. **deafness** n. state of being deaf.

deal1 [diːl] n. (a) large quantity; a good d. better = much better. (b) handing out

(playing cards). (c) (business) affair. (d) wood from a pine tree. **deal2** v. (dealt[delt]) (a) to hand out. (b) to d. with = to organize to solve a problem. (c) to d. in = to buy and sell. **dealer** n. person who buys and sells. **dealership** n. business of a dealer. **dealings** n. pl.business/affairs.

dean [diːn] n. person in charge of lecturers or priests. **deanery** n. position or house of a dean (in a cathedral).

dear 1 [dɪə] adj. (-er, -est) (a) well liked; loved. (b) (addressing someone at the beginning of a letter) d. Mr Smith; d. Sir. (c) expensive. **dear 2** inter. oh d. ! = how annoying! **dearly** adv. tenderly; very much.

dearth [dɜːθ] n. scarcity.

death [deθ] n. act of dying. d. duty = tax paid on money left by dead person; d. mask = plaster mask made of s.o.'s face, after death; d. rate = number of people who die (as a percentage of the population). **deathbed** n. bed on which s.o. is dying. **deathtrap** n. dangerous place. **death watch beetle** n. beetle which bores holes in wood and makes a clicking sound.

deb [deb] n. inf.debutante.

débâcle [der'baːkl] n. (a) sudden defeat/collapse. (b) breakup of ice on a river in spring.

debar [dɪ'baː] v. (debarred) to d. s.o., from sth = to forbid s.o. to do sth.

debase [dɪ'beɪs] v. to degrade; to reduce the value of (sth, esp. the value of the metal in coinage). **debasement** n. act of debasing.

debate1 [dɪ'beɪt] n. formal discussion. **debate2** v. to discuss. **debatable** adj. not absolutely certain.

debauched [dɪ'bɔːtʃt] adj. (person) who spends his time in wild living and enjoys immoral pleasures. **debauchery** n. wild living.

debenture [dɪ'bentʃə] n. document showing that a company agrees to repay a debt, and to pay a fixed interest on it, the money being secured on the company's assets.

debilitate [dɪ'bɪlɪteɪt] v. to make weak. **debility** n. weakness.

debit 1 ['debɪt] n. (money) which is owed; on the d. side = against (a proposal). **debit 2** v. to deduct money from (an account).

debonair [debə'neə] adj. carefree/ relaxed (air).

debrief ['di:bri:f] v. to ask (s.o.) questions to obtain information about a mission which he has just completed. **debriefing** n. obtaining information about a mission by questioning the person who carried it out.

debris ['debri:] n. pieces (of a demolished building/crashed aircraft, etc.).

debt n. money owed to s.o.; he is in d. = he owes money. **debtor** n. person who owes money.

debug [di:'bʌg] v. (debugged) to remove bugs from (sth); to correct errors in a computer program.

debunk [dr'bʌŋk] v. inf. to disprove.

debut ['deɪbju:] n. first appearance (of an artist/actor, etc.). **debutante** n. girl who goes into adult society for the first time.

deca- ['dekə] prefix meaning ten.

decade ['dekeɪd] n. period of ten years.

decadence ['dekədəns] n. decline in moral values. **decadent** adj. declining in moral values.

decaffeinated [di:'kæfɪneɪtɪd] adj. (coffee) which has had the caffeine removed.

decal ['di:kæl] n. Am. sticker/piece of plastic or paper with a pattern or slogan which you can stick to a surface as a decoration.

decamp [di:'kæmp] v. inf. to go away.

decant [dr'kænt] v. to pour (liquid, esp. wine) from a bottle into another container. **decanter** n. glass bottle which wine is poured into before serving.

decapitate [dr'kæpɪteɪt] v. to cut off the head of (s.o.). **decapitation** [dɪkæpɪ'teɪʃn] n. act of cutting off a head.

decarbonize [de'ka:bənaɪz] v. to remove carbon deposits from (a petrol engine).

decathlon [dr'kæθlən] n. sporting competition where each athlete competes in ten different types of sport.

decay1 [dr'keɪ] n. falling into ruin; rotting. **decay2** v. to fall into ruin; to rot.

decease [dɪ'si:s] n. death. **deceased** n. dead person.

deceit [dr'si:t] n. trickery. **deceitful** adj. tricking. **deceitfully** adv. in a deceitful way.

deceive [dɪ'si:v] v. to trick; to make (s.o.) believe sth which is not true.

decelerate [di:selereɪt] v. to (make sth) go slower. **deceleration** [di:selə'rerʃn] n. going slower.

December [dr'sembə] n. 12th month of the year.

decent ['di:sənt] adj. (a) honest. (b) quite good. **decency** n. honour; good morals. **decently** adv. in a decent way.

decentralize [di:'sentrəlaɪz] v. to move (authority/offices) from the centre. **decentralization** [di:sentrəlaɪ'zeɪʃn] n. act of decentralizing.

deception [dr'sepʃn] n. fraud; making s.o. believe sth which is not true. **deceptive** adj. not as it looks. **deceptively** adv. in a way which deceives.

decibel ['desɪbel] n. unit of measurement of noise.

decide [dɪ'saɪd] v. to make up your mind (to do sth). **decided** adj. (a) firm (tone, manner). (b) certain/obvious (difference, etc.). **decidedly** adv. (a) in a firm manner. (b) certainly.

deciduous [dr'sɪdjʊəs] adj. (tree) which loses its leaves in winter.

decimal 1 ['desɪml] adj. (system of mathematics) based on the number 10; d. point = dot indicating the division between units and parts which are less than one unit (such as 2.05). **decimal2** n. figure expressed on the base of 10. **decimalize** v. to change to decimals. **decimate** v. to remove one out of ten of; to cut down/to remove/to kill in large numbers.

decipher [dɪ'saɪfə] v. to make out (sth badly written, or written in code). **decipherment** n. act of deciphering.

decision [dɪ'sɪʒn] n. making up your mind; ability to make up your mind. **decisive** [dɪ'saɪsɪv] adj. firm (voice); (contest, etc.) which brings about a result. **decisively** adv. in a decisive way; firmly.

deck [dek] n. (a) floor (of ship/bus). flight deck = (i) control cabin (of plane); (ii) flat surface on an aircraft carrier

where aircraft land and take off. (b) *Am.* pack (of playing cards). (c) apparatus for playing records, tapes, cassettes.
deckchair *n.* collapsible canvas chair (for sitting in the sun). **decked** *adj.* decorated/covered with.
deckle-edged [dekl'edʒd] *adj.* (paper) with a ragged edge.
declaim [dɪ'kleɪm] *v.* to recite in a loud voice. **declamatory** [dɪ'kæmətərɪ] *adj.* as if in a loud voice.
declare [dɪ'kleə] *v.* (a) to state (officially). (b) (at customs) to say what (dutiable goods) one has. (c) (at cricket) to stop your innings and ask the other team to bat. (d) (at cards) to say which suit is trumps. **declaration** [deklə'reɪʃn] *n.* (official) statement.
decline 1 [dɪ'klaɪn] *n.* downward trend. **decline 2** *v.* (a) to refuse (an invitation). (b) to become weaker. (c) (in grammar) to show the different cases of (a word). **declension** *n.* form of the different cases of a word.
declivity [dɪ'klɪvɪtɪ] *n.* slope downwards.
declutch [dɪ'klʌtʃ] *v.* to disengage the clutch in a car.
decode [diː'kəʊd] *v.* to translate (a message) out of code. **decoder** *n.* person who decodes.
decoke [diː'kəʊk] *v. inf.* to clean carbon from (an engine).
decollate ['dekəlenɪt] *v.* to separate copies. **decollator** *n.* machine which separates copies (of computer printouts).
decompose [diːkəm'pəʊz] *v.* to rot. **decomposition** [diːkɒmpə'zɪʃn] *n.* act of rotting.
decompression [diːkəm'preʃn] *n.* reducing the pressure in sth; d. chamber = room where divers stay to get used gradually to normal pressures after working in very deep water.
decongestant [diːkən'dʒestənt] *n.* medicine which unblocks, esp. a blocked nose.
decontaminate [diːkən'tæmɪneɪt] *v.* to remove infection/radioactivity from (sth). **decontamination** [diːkəntæmɪ'neɪʃn] *n.* act of decontaminating.
decontrol [diːkən'trəʊl] *v.* to remove controls from sth.
decor ['deɪkɔː] *n.* (a) scenery (for a

play). (b) interior decoration (of a room).
decorate ['dekəreɪt] *v.* (a) to paint (a building); to put new wallpaper in (a room); to put up flags/lights (to celebrate an occasion). (b) to award (s.o.) a medal.
decorations [dbkə'reɪʃnz] *n.* (a) flags/lights, etc. used to celebrate an occasion. (b) medals. **decorative** ['dekərətɪv] *adj.* pleasant to look at; serving as a decoration. **decoratively** *adv.* in a decorative way. **decorator** *n.* person who paints houses; interior d. = person who designs ways of decorating the inside of buildings.
decorum [dɪ'kɔːrʌm] *n.* being decorous. **decorous** ['dekərəs] *adj.* very well behaved.
decoy 1 ['diːkɔɪ] *n.* object to attract and trap sth. **decoy 2** ['diːkrɪːs] *v.* to attract and trap (sth/s.o.).
decrease 1 *n.* fall; lessening. **decrease 2** *v.* to fall; to become less.
decree 1 [dɪ'kriː] *n.* legal order which has not been voted by Parliament; d. nisi['naisai]/d. absolute = granting by a judge of a provisional/complete divorce. **decree 2** *v.* to state as a legal order.
decrepit [dɪ'krepɪt] *adj.* falling to pieces; old and feeble (person). **decrepitude** *n.* being decrepit.
decry [dɪ'kraɪ] *v.* to say that (sth) is bad.
dedicate ['dedɪkeɪt] *v.* to place (a church) under the patronage of a saint; to write a book for/to offer a book to (s.o.); to spend (all your life) on sth. **dedicated** *adj.* (computer/program) reserved for a particular task. **dedication** [dedɪ'keɪʃn] *n.* (a) devotion. (b) inscription at the beginning of a book showing to whom it is dedicated.
deduce [dɪ'djuːs] *v.* to conclude (from examining evidence). **deduct** [dɪ'dʌkt] *v.* to remove (from a sum of money). **deductible** *adj.* which can be deducted. **deduction** [dɪ'dʌkʃn] *n.* (a) thing which is deduced; conclusion. (b) thing which is deducted; sum of money which is taken away.
deed [diːd] *n.* (a) (noble) act. (b) legal document; the deeds of a house = papers showing who owns the house; d. poll = legal document, signed by one party only, such as when s.o. changes his name.

deem [di:m] v. (formal) to consider.
deep 1 [di:p] adj. (-er, -est) (a) which goes down a long way. (b) rich/dark (colour). (c) low-pitched/bass (voice). **deep 2** adv. a long way down. **deep 3** n. the d. = the sea. **deepen** v. to go further down; to become deeper; to make (sth) deeper. **deep-freeze** n. refrigerator for freezing food and keeping it frozen. **deep-fried** adj. cooked in deep oil. **deeply** adv. profoundly; very much. **deep-rooted** adj. which goes down a long way. **deep-seated** adj. solid/firm.

deer [dɪə] n. (pl.deer) wild animal which runs fast, and of which the male usually has horns. **deerhound** n. large fastrunning dog, bred for chasing deer. **deerstalker** n. round tweed hat, with small peaks at the front and back.

deface [dɪ'feɪs] v. to spoil the surface of (sth); to write on (a wall); to mutilate (a statue). **defacement** n. act of defacing.

de facto [di:fæktəʊ] adj. existing in fact/real.

defamation [defə'meɪʃn] n. d. of character = saying bad things about s.o. **defamatory** [de'fæmətrɪ] adj. which says bad things about s.o. **defame** [dɪ'feɪm] v. to say bad things about s.o.

default 1 [di:fɔ:lt] n. (a) failing to carry out the terms of a contract. (b) (computers) set way of working; d. drive = the drive which is set to be accessed first. **default 2** v. to fail to carry out the terms of a contract. **defaulter** n. person who defaults; (in the army) soldier who is being punished.

defeat 1 [dɪ'fi:t] n. loss of (fight/vote). **defeat 2** v. to beat (s.o. in a fight/vote). **defeatism** n. feeling sure that you will lose. **defeatist** adj. sure that you will lose.

defecate ['defəkeɪt] v. to pass waste matter from the bowels.

defect1 ['di:fekt] n. fault. **defect2** [dɪ'fekt] v. to leave the army/your country, to go over to the enemy side. **defection** n. going over to the side of the enemy. **defective** adj. faulty. **defector** n. person who defects.

defence, Am. defense [dɪfens] n. (a) protection. (b) the d. = lawyers who speak on behalf of an accused person.

defenceless adj. unprotected.
defensibility n. being defensible.
defensible adj. which can be defended. **defensive 1** adj. which protects. **defensive 2** n. on the d. = feeling one has to justify oneself. **defensively** adv. in a defensive way.

defend [dɪ'fend] v. (a) to protect (from attack). (b) to speak on behalf of (an accused person). **defendant** n. person who is accused of doing sth illegal/ person who is sued in a civil law suit. **defender** n. person who defends.

defer [dɪ'fɜ:] v. (deferred) (a) to put off/ to put back. (b) to d. to s.o./to s.o.'s opinion = to accept the advice of s.o. who knows better. **deference** ['defərəns] n. respect. **deferential** adj. respectful. **deferment** n. postponement.

defiance [dɪ'faɪəns] n. acting against (law/authority). **defiant** adj. very proud and antagonistic.

defibrillator [di:fɪbrɪleɪtə] n. machine which stimulates a weak heart by giving it electric shocks.

deficiency [dɪ'fɪʃənsɪ] n. lack. **deficient** adj. (in) lacking (sth) mentally deficient = below normal intelligence. **deficit** ['defɪsɪt] n. amount by which expenditure is larger than receipts (in a firm's/a country's accounts).

defile 1 ['di:faɪl] n. narrow pass between mountains. **defile 2** v. to dirty/to pollute. **defilement** n. act of polluting.

define [dɪ'faɪn] v. (a) to explain clearly/ to give the meaning of. (b) to state the boundary of. **definable** adj. which can be defined.

definite ['defɪnət] adj. very clear; d. article = 'the' (as opposed to the indefinite article, 'a' or 'an'). **definitely** adv. certainly. **definition** [defɪ'nɪʃn] n. (a) clear explanation (of a word). (b) clearness (of a picture). **definitive** [dɪ'fɪnɪtɪv] adj. final/which cannot be improved.

deflate [dɪ'fleɪt] v. (a) to let the air out of (a tyre). (b) to reduce inflation in (the economy).

deflation [dɪ'fleɪʃn] n. reducing inflation. **deflationary** adj. which leads to deflation.

deflect [dɪˈflekt] v. to turn aside (an arrow/a bullet, etc.). **deflection** n. act of deflecting.

defoliate [diːˈfəʊlɪeɪt] v. to remove the leaves of (a tree, etc.). **defoliation** n. act of defoliating. **defoliant** n. chemical used to defoliate.

deforestation [diːfɒresˈteɪʃn] n. removal of trees from an area of land.

deformed [dɪˈfɔːmd] adj. badly shaped. **deformation** [defɔːˈmeɪʃn] n. spoiling the shape of sth. **deformity** n. badly shaped part of the body.

defraud [dɪˈfrɔːd] v. to cheat.

defray [dɪˈfreɪ] v. to pay (costs).

defreeze [diːˈfriːz] v. to thaw (frozen food).

defrock [diːˈfrɒk] v. to remove (a priest) from holy orders.

defrost [diːˈfrɒst] v. to melt the ice on (the inside of a refrigerator).

deft [deft] adj. (-er, -est) very agile/clever (with your hands). **deftly** adv. in a deft way. **deftness** n. being deft.

defunct [dɪˈfʌŋkt] adj. dead (person); (law) which is no longer applied.

defuse [diːˈfjuːz] v. to take the fuse out of (a bomb) so that it cannot explode; to make (a situation) less tense.

defy [dɪˈfaɪ] v. (a) to refuse to obey (law). (b) to challenge (s.o. to sth).

degenerate 1 [dɪˈdʒenərət] adj. which has degenerated/become depraved. **degenerate 2** [dɪˈdʒenəreɪt] v. (a) to become depraved. (b) to get worse. **degeneracy** n. being degenerate. **degeneration** [dɪdʒenəˈreɪʃn] n. becoming degenerate; becoming worse.

degrade [dɪˈgreɪd] v. (a) to humiliate (s.o.); to make (s.o.) like an animal. (b) to make (a chemical compound) simpler. **degradable** adj. which can be degraded. **degradation** [degreˈdeɪʃn] n. becoming like an animal. **degrading** adj. lowering; which humiliates/which makes a person like an animal.

degree [dɪˈgriː] n. (a) division of an angle or scale. (b) level; amount; to a certain d. = to some extent. (c) diploma (of a university).

dehiscence [diːˈhɪsəns] n. bursting of a seed pod.

dehumidifier [diːhjuːˈmɪdɪfaɪə] n. device which removes humidity from the air.

dehydrate [diːhaɪˈdreɪt] v. to remove water from (sth). **dehydration** n. becoming dehydrated.

de-ice [diːˈaɪs] v. to remove the ice from (sth). **de-icer** n. thing which de-ices.

deify [ˈdeɪfaɪ] v. to make (sth/s.o.) into a god. **deification** [deɪɪfɪˈkeɪʃn] n. making into a god.

deign [deɪn] v. to condescend (to sth).

deity [ˈdeɪtɪ] n. god.

déjà vu [dɪˈʒæˈvuː] adv. feeling that you have already seen sth before.

dejected [dɪˈdʒektɪd] adj. depressed/unhappy. **dejectedly** adv. in a gloomy way. **dejection** [dɪˈdʒekʃn] n. gloom/depression.

de jure [diːˈdʒʊərɪ] adv. correct according to the law.

dekko [ˈdekəʊ] n. Sl. to have a d. = to have a quick look.

delay 1 [dɪˈleɪ] n. time during which one is late. **delay 2** v. (a) to make late. (b) to wait; to put (sth) off until later.

delectable [dɪˈlektəbl] adj. very pleasant; very attractive. **delectation** [dɪlekˈteɪʃn] n. pleasure/enjoyment.

delegate 1 [ˈdelɪgət] n. person who represents others at a meeting. **delegate 2** [ˈdelɪgeɪt] v. to pass (authority/responsibility) on to a subordinate. **delegation** [delɪˈgeɪʃn] n. (a) group of representatives. (b) passing of authority to a subordinate.

delete [dɪˈliːt] v. to cross out (a word/text). **deletion** [dɪˈliːʃn] n. word/phrase which has been crossed out.

deleterious [delɪˈtrɪərəs] adj. (formal) harmful.

deliberate 1 [dɪˈlɪbərət] adj. (a) done on purpose. (b) slow and thoughtful (speech/manner). **deliberate 2** [dɪˈlɪbəreɪt] v. to debate/to discuss. **deliberately** adv. (a) on purpose. (b) slowly and thoughtfully. **deliberation** [dɪlɪbəˈreɪʃn] n. (a) thought; consideration. (b) the deliberations of a meeting = the debate/discussion.

delicacy [ˈdelɪkəsɪ] n. (a) sensitivity. (b) state of being delicate. (c) rare thing to eat. **delicate** adj. (a) easily damaged; very thin. (b) liable to get illnesses. (c) very fine. **delicately** adv. with care. **delicatessen** [delɪkəˈtesn] n. shop selling cold meat and foreign food, etc.

delicious [dɪ'lɪʃəs] *adj.* which tastes very good. **deliciously** *adv.* in a delicious way.

delight 1 [dɪ'laɪt] *n.* pleasure. **delight 2** *v.* to take pleasure (in). **delighted** *adj.* very pleased. **delightful** *adj.* very pleasant.

delineate [dɪ'lɪnɪeɪt] *v.* (formal) to draw. **delineation** [dnlɪnɪ'eɪʃn] *n.* (formal) drawing.

delinquency [dɪ'lɪŋkwənsɪ] *n.* minor crime; juvenile d. = crimes committed by young people. **delinquent** *adj.& n.* criminal.

delirious [dɪ'lɪrɪəs] *adj.* mad with fever/with happiness. **delirium** *n.* madness caused by fever; great excitement.

deliver [dɪ'lɪvə] *v.* (a) to bring (sth) to s.o. (b) to make (a speech). (c) to help the mother give birth to (a baby). **deliverance** *n.* (formal) rescue. **delivery** *n.* (a) brining sth to s.o. (b) birth (of a child).

dell [del] *n.* small hollow filled with trees.

delphinium [del'fɪnɪəm] *n.* garden plant with tall blue flowers.

delta ['deltə] *n.* (a) land around the mouth of a river made of mud brought by the river. (b) fourth letter of the Greek alphabet; d. wing aircraft = with wings forming a triangle.

delude [dɪ'luːd] *v.* to make (s.o.) believe sth which is wrong. **delusion** [dɪ'luːʒn] *n.* wrong belief.

deluge 1 ['deljuːdʒ] *n.* flood. **deluge 2** *v.* to flood (with).

de luxe [dn'lʌks] *adj.* very expensive; of very high quality.

delve [delv] *v.* to dig (into the past archives, etc.).

demagogue ['deməgɒg] *n.* politician who appeals to the crowd for support. **demagoguery** *n.* appealing for support from the crowd as a means of obtaining political power.

demand 1 [dɪ'mɑːnd] *n.* asking for sth; it is in d. = many people want it. **demand 2** *v.* to ask insistently for sth. **demanding** *adj.* (job) which takes up much time and energy.

demarcation [diːmɑː'keɪʃn] *n.* showing of boundaries; d. dispute = dispute between workers over who

démarche ['deɪmɑːʃ] *n.* official often diplomatic, approach to another party.

demean [dɪ'miːn] *v.* to d. yourself = to make yourself appear undignified or contemptible.

demeanour [dɪ'miːnə] *n.* behaviour/ manner

demented [dɪ'mentɪd] *adj.* mad. **dementia** [dɪ'menʃə] *n.* (formal) madness.

demerara [demə'reərə] *n.* type of coarse brown sugar.

demerit [diː'merɪt] *n.* fault; unattractive point.

demi- ['demɪ] prefix meaning half.

demijohn ['demɪdʒɒn] *n.* large bottle for alcoholic drink.

demilitarized [diː'mɪlɪtəraɪzd] *adj.* (zone) which no longer has armed forces in it.

demise [dɪ'maɪz] *n.* (formal) death.

demist [diː'mɪst] *v.* to clear condensation from the windows of a car. **demister** *n.* blower (in a car) to prevent the windows misting up.

demo ['deməʊ] *n.* inf. demonstration.

demob 1 [diː'mɒb] *v.* (demobbed) *inf.* to demobilize. **demob 2** *n.* inf. demobilization. **demobilize** [diː'məʊbɪlaɪz] *v.* to release (s.o.) from the armed forces. **demobilization** [diːməʊbɪlaɪ'zeɪʃn] *n.* being demobilized.

democracy [dɪ'mɒkrəsɪ] *n.* system of government by freely elected representatives of the people. **democrat** ['deməkræt] *n.* (a) person who believes in democracy. (b) Democrat = member of one of the two main political parties in the USA. **democratic** [demə'krætɪk] *adj.* referring to democracy. **democratically** *adv.* in a democratic way.

demographic [demə'græfɪk] *adj.* referring to demography. **demography** [dɪ'mɒgrəfɪ] *n.* study of population figures.

demolish [dɪ'mɒlɪʃ] *v.* to knock down. **demolition** [demə'lɪʃn] *n.* knocking down.

demon ['diːmən] *n.* devil. **demoniacal, demonic** [diːmə'naɪəkl, diː'mɒnɪl] *adj.* like a devil.

demonstrate ['demənstreɪt] *v.* (a) to show. (b) to form a crowd to protest

(against sth). **demonstrable** *adj.*
which can be demonstrated.
demonstration [demən'streɪʃn] *n.* (a)
showing. (b) march to protest against
sth; crowd which is protesting against
sth. **demonstrator** *n.* person who
marches/who forms part of a crowd to
protest against sth; person who shows
how to do sth. **demonstrative**
[dɪ'mɒnstrətɪv] *adj.* (person) who shows
his feelings openly.
demoralize [dɪ'mɒrəlaɪz] *v.* to lower
the morale/confidence of (s.o.).
demoralization [dɪmɒrəlaɪ'zeɪʃn] *n.*
lowering of morale. **demoralized** *adj.*
doubtful that you can win.
demote [di:'məʊt] *v.* to give (s.o.) a less
important job. **demotion** *n.* act of
demoting.
demur [dɪ'mɜ:] *v.* (demurred) to d. at =
to object to sth.
demure [dɪ'mjʊə] *adj.* quiet and
serious (girl). **demurely** *adv.* in a
demure way.
demurrage [di:'mʌrɪdʒ] *n.* payment for
keeping a ship in dock when unloading.
den [den] *n.* (a) place to hide away in.
(b) *inf.* small room where you can hide
away to work.
denationalize [di:'næʃnəlaɪz] *v.* to put
(a nationalized industry) into private
ownership. **denationalization**
[dɪnæʃnlaɪ'zeɪʃn] *n.* act of
denationalizing.
dendrochronology
[dendrəʊkrɒ'nɒlədʒɪ] *n.* finding the age
of wood by the study of the tree rings.
dengue ['deŋgɪ] *n.* tropical fever.
denial [dɪ'naɪəl] *n.* statement that sth is
not true.
denigrate ['denɪgreɪt] *v.* to say that (an
action) is worse than it is.
denim ['denɪm] *n.* thick cotton cloth;
denims = clothes made of this cloth.
denizen ['denɪzən] *n.* (formal)
inhabitant of a particular place.
denomination [dɪnɒmɪ'neɪʃn] *n.* (a)
unit of money (on a banknote/coin). (b)
religious sect; church. **denominational**
adj. belonging to a particular sect.
denominator [dɪ'nɒmɪneɪtə] *n.* figure
beneath the line in a fraction.
denote [dɪ'nəʊt] *v.* to mean.
dénouement [deɪ'nu:mɒŋ] *n.* ending
(of a plot).

denounce [dɪ'naʊns] *v.* to blame/to
accuse (s.o./sth) openly.
dense [dens] *adj.* (-er, -est) (a) very
thick; crowded together. (b) stupid.
denseness *n.* being dense. **densely**
adv. thickly. **density** *n.* (a) physical
degree of mass per unit of volume. (b)
high d. of population = many people per
unit of area.
dent 1 [dent] *n.* slight hollow (as made
by a blow). **dent 2** *v.* to make a slight
hollow in (sth).
dentist ['dentɪst] *n.* person who looks
after teeth. **dental** *adj.* referring to
teeth; d. floss = thin thread for cleaning
between teeth; d. surgery = dentist's
office. **dentifrice** *n.* toothpaste.
dentistry *n.* work of a dentist.
dentition *n.* arrangement of a person's
teeth. **dentures** ['dentʃəz] *n. pl.*false
teeth.
denude [dɪ'nju:d] *v.* to make (sth) bare;
to remove all the covering from (sth).
denunciation [dɪnʌnsɪ'eɪʃn] *n.* public
accusation/blame.
deny [dɪ'naɪ] *v.* to state that (sth) is not
correct; to prevent (s.o.) having sth; to d.
oneself = not to eat/drink, etc. very
much.
deodorant [dɪ'əʊdərənt] *n.* preparation
which removes unpleasant smells.
deodorize *v.* to remove unpleasant
smells from (sth).
deoxyribonucleic acid
[di:ɒksɪraɪbəʊnju:'kleɪɪk'æsɪd] *n.* DNA,
the basic genetic material in a cell.
depart [dɪ'pɑ:t] *v.* to go away.
departed *n.* the d. = the dead.
departure [dɪ'pɑ:tʃə] *n.* leaving d.
lounge = large waiting room at an airport
for passengers about to leave.
department [dɪ'pɑ:tmənt] *n.* section of
a large organization; d. store = large shop
with many different sections.
département *n.* administrative
divisions of France. **departmental**
[dɪpɑ:t'mentl] *adj.* referring to a
department.
depend [dɪ'pend] *v.* (a) (on) to be
decided according to sth. (b) to rely (on
sth). **dependable** *adj.* that can be
relied on. **dependant** *n.* member of
family supported by another.
dependence *n.* being dependent.
dependency *n.* country which is ruled

by another. **dependent** *adj.* (a) supported by s.o. else; relying on s.o. else. (b) addicted to (a drug).

depict [dɪ'pɪkt] *v.* (formal) to show. **depiction** *n.* showing.

depilatory [dɪ'pɪlətrɪ] *adj. & n.* (substance) which removes hair from the body.

deplete [dɪ'pliːt] *v.* to run down/to use up (stores).

deplore [dɪ'plɔː] *v.* to be extremely sorry that sth has happened; to dislike (an action/an attitude). **deplorable** *adj.* very bad (behaviour).

deploy [dɪ'plɔɪ] *v.* to spread out (soldiers, etc.) for action. **deployment** *n.* act of deploying.

depopulate [diː'pɒpjʊleɪt] *v.* to reduce the number of people living in an area. **depopulation** [diːpɒpjʊ'leɪʃn] *n.* act of being depopulated.

deport [dɪ'pɔːt] *v.* to expel (s.o.) from a country. **deportation** [diː[ɔː'teɪʃn] *n.* expulsion (of a foreigner).

deportment *n.* way of walking/sitting.

depose [dɪ'pəʊz] *v.* (a) to force (s.o.) to leave his position; to force (a king, etc.) to give up his throne,. (b) to state (in court). **deposition** [depə'zɪʃn] *n.* (a) forcing s.o. to leave his position. (b) statement (by a witness).

deposit 1 [dɪ'pɒzɪt] *n.* (a) money placed in (a bank); money given to secure sth you want to buy; d. account = bank account where you leave money for some time to earn interest. (b) mineral layer (in the ground); sediment/chemical left at the bottom of a container.

deposit 2 *v.* to put (money) in a bank. **depository** *n.* person who receives something which is deposited for safe keeping. **depositor** *n.* person with money in a bank. **depository** *n.* place for storing furniture, etc.

depot ['depəʊ] *n.* central warehouse; central garage; central barracks for a regiment.

depraved [dɪ'preɪvd] *adj.* corrupted/ wicked. **depravity** [dɪ'[rævɪtɪ] *n.* state of living a wicked life.

deprecate ['deprəkeɪt] *v.* to disapprove of (sth).

depreciate [dɪ'priːʃɪeɪt] *v.* to lose value. **depreciation** [dɪprɪʃɪ'eɪʃn] *n.* regular loss in value. **depreciatory**

adj. which depreciates.

depredation [deprə'deɪʃn] *n.* attack/ ruining.

depress [dɪ'pres] *v.* (a) to make miserable. (b) to push down (a button). **depressed** *adj.* miserable. **depressing** *adj.* gloomy. **depression** [dɪ'preʃn] *n.* (a) miserable feeling. (b) low pressure area brining bad weather. (c) economic crisis. (d) hollow (in the ground). **depressive** *adj.* which makes s.o. depressed.

deprive [dɪ'praɪv] *v.* to d. s.o. of sth = to take sth away from s.o. **deprivation** [deprɪ'veɪʃn] *n.* being deprived of sth. **deprived** *adj.* (person) who has not enjoyed any of society's benefits.

dept. = department.

depth [depθ] *n.* (a) how deep sth is; distance downwards; he 's out of his d. = (i) the water is too deep for him; (ii) it is too difficult for him to understand. (b) very deep point. **depth charge** *n.* type of bomb dropped into the sea which explodes deep beneath the surface.

deputation [depjʊ'teɪʃn] *n.* group of people who speak on behalf of others. **depute 1** [depjuːt] *n.* (in Scotland) deputy. **depute 2** [dɪ'pjuːt] *v.* to give responsibility (to s.o.). **deputize** ['depjʊtaɪz] *v.* to stand in (for s.o.). **deputy** ['depjʊtɪ] *n.* person who can take the place of another person.

derail [dɪ'reɪl] *v.* to make (a train) leave the rails.

derailment *n.* leaving the rails.

derailleur [dɪ'reɪljə] *n.* bicycle gear system, where the chain goes round a movable sprocket.

deranged [dɪ'reɪnʒd] *adj.* mad.

derby ['dɑːbɪ] *n.* (a) sporting contest between local teams. (b) Am.['dɜːbɪ] bowler hat.

deregulate [dɪ'regjuleɪt] *v.* to remove government restrictions over an industry. **deregulation** *n.* removal of official restrictions.

derelict 1 ['derəlɪkt] *n.* tramp/dosser. **derelict 2** *adj.* ruined and abandoned. **dereliction** [derə'lɪkʃən] *n.* neglecting (to do your duty).

derestricted [diːrɪ'strɪktɪd] *adj.* (road) with no speed limit.

deride [dɪ'raɪd] *v.* to laugh at (s.o.). **derision** [dɪ'rɪʒn] *n.* mockery.

derisive [dɪ'raɪsɪv] *adj.* mocking (laughter). **derisory** [dɪ'raɪzərɪ] *adj.* laughably small (amount).

de rigueur [dərɪ'gɜːə] *adv.* obligatory.

derive [dɪ'raɪv] *v.* to come originally (from sth). **derivation** [derɪ'veɪʃn] *n.* origin (of a word). **derivative** [dɪ'rɪvətɪv] *n.* thing which is derived.

dermatitis [dɜːmə'taɪtɪs] *n.* disease of the skin. **dermatologist** [dɜːmə'tɒlədʒɪst] *n.* person who studies dermatology. **dermatology** *n.* study of skin disease.

derogatory [dɪ'rɒgətrɪ] *adj.* showing contempt.

derrick ['derɪk] *n.* large metal construction (like a crane); oil d. = metal frame which holds the drilling equipment for an oil well.

derris ['derɪs] *n.* powder used to kill insects.

derv [dɜːv] *n.* fuel used in diesel engines.

desalinate [diː'sælɪneɪt] *v.* to remove salt (from sea water).

descant ['deskænt] *n.* musical part which is played/sung much higher than the rest.

descend [dɪ'send] *v.* (a) to go down (a staircase, etc.). (b) to d. from s.o. = to have s.o. as an ancestor. (c) to d. upon = to attack; *inf.* to visit unexpectedly.

descendant *n.* person whose family goes back to a certain ancestor. **descent** *n.* (a) going down. (b) he is of Irish descent = his family was Irish.

describe [dɪ'skraɪb] *v.* to say what (sth/s.o.) is like. **description** [dɪ'skrɪpʃn] *n.* picture in words of what sth is like. **descriptive** *adj.* which says what sth is like.

desecrate ['desɪkreɪt] *v.* to use (a church/a grave) in a disrespectful way. **desecration** *n.* act of desecrating.

desegregate [dɪ'segrəgeɪt] *v.* to end the segregation of(a group of people or institution). **desegregation** *n.* action of desegregating.

deselect [dɪsə'lekt] *v.* to remove the approval of a local political party for a candidate or for an MP. **deselection** *n.* removal of approval for an MP or a candidate.

desert 1 ['dezət] *adj.& n.* very dry, *usu.* sandy (place). **desert 2** [dɪ'zɜːt] *v.* to

leave the armed forces without permission; to leave (s.o.) all by himself. **deserted** *adj.* abandoned; with no inhabitants. **deserter** *n.* person who leaves the armed forces without permission. **desertion** *n.* act of deserting. **deserts** *n.* *pl.*(formal) just d. = rightful reward.

deserve [dɪ'zɜːv] *v.* to merit (sth). **deservedly** *adv.* in a way which is right. **deserving** *adj.* which ought to be supported/rewarded.

desiccate ['desɪkeɪt] *v.* to dry.

design 1 [dɪ'zaɪn] *n.* plan; drawing of sth before it is constructed; to have designs on = to plan to attack/take (sth). **design 2** *v.* to plan (sth). **designer** *n.* artist who plans sth. **designing** *adj.* crafty (person).

designate 1 ['dezɪgneɪt] *v.* to appoint (s.o.) to a post. **designate 2** suffix. showing person who has been appointed but has not started work; the ambassador designate. **designation** *n.* act of designating.

desire 1 [dɪ'zarə] *n.* want. **desire 2** *v.* to want. **desirability** *n.* being desirable. **desirable** *adj.* which a lot of people want. **desirous** *adj.* (of) wanting.

desist [dɪ'zɪst] *v.* (formal) (from) to stop doing (sth).

desk [desk] *n.* table for writing. **desktop publishing** *n.* creating finished printed documents using a computer and a special program.

desolate ['desələt] *adj.* bleak inhospitable (place). **desolation** [desə'leɪʃn] *n.* bleakness; ruin (of a place).

despair 1 [dɪ's[eə] *n.* hopelessness. **despair 2** *v.* he despaired of being rescued = he had given up all hope of being rescued. **desperate** ['desprət] *adj.* (a) hopeless. (b) wild (through being in despair). **desperately** *adv.* urgently; wildly. **desperation** [despə'reɪʃn] *n.* hopelessness.

despicable [dɪ'spɪkəbl] *adj.* worthless/ which you can look down on. **despise** [dɪ'spaɪz] *v.* to look down on (s.o.) /to think (s.o.) is not worth much.

despite [dɪ'spaɪt] *prep.* in spite of.

despoil [dɪ'spɔɪl] *v.* to ruin; to plunder.

despondency [dɪ'spɒndənsɪ] *n.*

discouragement. **despondent** *adj.* discouraged.

despot ['despɒt] *n.* tyrant/dictator. **despotic** [dɪ'spɒtɪk] *adj.* like a dictator. **despotism** *n.* tyranny/ dictatorship.

dessert [sɪ'zɜ:t] *n.* sweet course (in a meal). **dessertspoon** *n.* spoon for eating dessert.

destination [destɪ'neɪʃn] *n.* place a person/vehicle is going to. **destine** ['destɪn] *v.* to aim. **destiny** *n.* what may happen in the future.

destitute ['destɪtju:t] *adj.* with no money or belongings. **destitution** [destɪ'tju:ʃn] *n.* being destitute.

destroy [dɪ'strɔɪ] *v.* to remove/to kill/to ruin completely. **destroyer** *n.* medium-sized naval ship. **destruction** [dɪ'strʌkʃn] *n.* complete ruining. **destructive** [dɪ'strʌktɪv] *adj.* which destroys. **destructiveness** *n.* tendency to destroy things.

desultory ['dezəltrɪ] *adj.* haphazard/ with no connecting links.

detach [dɪ'tætʃ] *v.* to separate; detached house = house which is not attached to another. **detachable** *adj.* which you can separate. **detachment** *n.* (a) indifference; lack of immediate interest. (b) small group of servicemen, etc.

detail 1 ['di:teɪl] *n.* small item. **detail 2** *v.* (a) to list all the small items. (b) to d, s.o. off to do sth = to give a task or duty to s.o.

detain [dɪ'teɪn] *v.* (a) to keep (s.o. in prison). (b) to hold (s.o.) back; to stop (s.o.) from leaving. **detainee** [di:teɪ'ni:] *n.* person held in prison.

detect [dɪ'tekt] *v.* to discover; to notice. **detection** [dɪ'tekʃn] *n.* discovery. **detective** *n.* policeman who investigates crimes. **detector** *n.* instrument which discovers sth.

détente [deɪ'tɑ:nt] *n.* friendly atmosphere between two formerly hostile countries.

detention [dɪ'tenʃn] *n.* imprisonment, keeping s.o. from leaving, d. centre = place where young criminals are imprisoned for a short time.

deter [dɪ'tɜ:] *v.* (deterred) to discourage (s.o. from doing sth).

detergent [dɪ'tɜ:dʒənt] *n.* chemical

used instead of soap for washing clothes or dishes.

deteriorate [dɪ'tɪərɪəreɪt] *v.* to go bad; to get worse. **deterioration** [dɪtɪərɪə'reɪʃn] *n.* worsening.

determine [dɪ'tɜ:mɪn] *v.* (a) to fix (a date, etc.). (b) to decide finally (to). **determinant** *n.* thing which determines. **determination** [dɪtɜ:mɪ'neɪʃn] *n.* firm intention. **determined** *adj.* resolved (to).

deterrent [dɪ'terənt] *n.* thing which discourages; nuclear d. = nuclear weapon which it is hoped will discourage the enemy from attacking.

detest [dɪ'test] *v.* to dislike intensely. **detestable** *adj.* very unpleasant. **detestation** [di:tes'teɪʃn] *n.* strong dislike.

detonate ['detəneɪt] *v.* to set off (an explosive). **detonation** [detə'neɪʃn] *n.* explosion. **detonator** *n.* small explosive charge which will set off a large explosion.

detour ['di:tʊə] *n.* roundabout road taken to avoid an obstacle/to see sth not on the direct route.

detract [dɪ'trækt] *v.* (from) to remove part of sth/to make sth less important. **detractor** *n.* person who criticizes sth.

detriment ['detrɪmənt] *n.* hurt; damage; to the d. of = damaging to. **detrimental** [detrɪ'mentl] *adj.* which damages.

detritus [di:'traɪtəs] *n.* rubbish which is formed by the weathering of rock; any waste matter.

deuce [dju:s] *n.* (a) score in tennis when both players are at 40 points. (b) score of two (in cards).

deuterium [dju:'trərɪəm] *n.* heavy form of hydrogen.

Deutschmark ['dɔɪtʃmɑ:k] *n.* old currency used in Germany.

devalue [di:'vælju:] *v.* to reduce value of (a currency) in relationship to that of other countries. **devaluation** [di:væljuə'eɪʃn] *n.* reducing the international value of currency.

devastate ['devəsteɪt] *v.* to wreck/to lay waste(countryside). **devastating** *adj.* overwhelming. **devastation** [devə'steɪʃn] *n.* widespread damage.

develop [dɪ'veləp] *v.* (a) to use to good purposes. (b) to expand. (c) to start (a disease, etc.). (d) to produce and fix (a photograph) from film. (e) to grow **developer** *n.* (a) liquid for developing photographs. (b) person who builds property. **developing** *adj.* growing; d. countries = countries which are becoming indusrialized. **development** *n.* (a) growth. (b) developments = what will happen.

deviate ['di:vıeıt] *v.* to swerve/to turn away (from a direct line). **deviation** [di:vı'eı∫n] *n.* moving away from a direct or normal line. **deviance** *n.* deviation from normal human behaviour. **deviant** *adj. & n.* (person) who deviates from normal human behaviour.

device [dı'vaıs] *n* (a) small (useful) machine. (b) left to his own devices = left to do whatever he wanted. (c) emblem (on a coat of arms).

devil ['devl] *n* (a) evil spirit; *inf.* what the devil? = what on earth? d. 's advocate = person who argues the opposite point of view, in order to oppose a widely held opinion. (b) *inf.* person; lucky d. ! **devilish** *adj.* referring to the devil. **devilled** *adj.* cooked in spicy sauce. **devilment, devilry** *n.* wicked behaviour.

devious ['di:vıəs] *adj.* not straight forward; roundabout. **deviously** *adv.* in a devious way. **deviousness** *n.* not being straight forward.

devise [dı'vaız] *v.* to think up; to invent.

devoid [dı'vɔıd] *adj.* empty (of).

devolution [di:və'lju:∫n] *n.* removing of power from the centre. **devolve** [dı'vɒlv] *v.* to pass on (responsibility) to a deputy.

devote [dı'vəʊt] *v.* to d. time to sth = to spend time on sth. **devoted** *adj.* (person) who spend all his time on sth. **devotee** [devə'ti:] *n.* (of) person who is very enthusiastic about sth. **devotion** [dı'vəʊ∫n] *n.* (religious) attachment; devotions = prayers. **devotional** *adj.* religious.

devour [dı'vaʊə] *v.* (formal) to eat (greedily).

devout [dı'vaʊt] *adj.* pious, deeply concerned with religion

dew [dju:] *n.* water which forms at night on objects in the open air. **dew drop** *n.* drop of dew; *inf.* drop on the end of s.o.'s

nose. **dew claw** *n.* small claw on the side of a dog's foot **dewlap** *n.* skin which hangs in folds on the throat. **dewy** *adj.* covered in dew. **dewyeyed** *adj.* innocent and sentimental.

dexterity [dek'steratı] *n.* skill (with hands). **dextrous** ['dekstrəs] *adj.* clever (with one's hand).

dextrose ['dekstrəʊz] *n.* sweet substance found naturally.

dhow [daʊ] *n.* Arab sailing boat.

diabetes [daıə'bi:ti:z] *n.* (no *pl.*) illness where the sugar content of the blood rises because of lack of insulin **diabetic 1** [daıə'betık] *adj.* referring to diabetes; d. food = food with a low sugar content which can be eaten by people suffering from diabetes. **diabetic 2** *n.* person suffering from diabetes.

diabolic(al) [daıə'bɒlik(l)] *adj.* referring to the devil; evil.

diacritic [daıə'krıtık] *n.* sign written above a character to show pronunciation.

diadem ['daıədem] *n.* crown.

diaeresis [daı'rərısıs] *n.* to dots (.) put over a vowel to show that it is pronounced separately from another.

diagnose [daıəg'nəʊz] *v.* to identify (an illness). **diagnosis** *n.* (*pl.*-ses) identification (of an illness).

diagnostic [daıəg'nɒstık] *adj.* referring to diagnosis. **diagnostics** *n. pl.* test to find faults in computer hardware/software.

diagonal [daı'ægənl] *adj & n.* (line) going from one corner to another slantwise. **diagonally** *adv.* slantwise.

diagram ['daıəgræm] *n.* sketch/plan. **diagrammatic** [daıəgrə'mætık] *adj.* in the form of a diagram.

dial 1 ['daıəl] *n.* round face (of a clock/ meter/telephone). **dial 2** *v.* (dialled) to make a telephone number; to call the police you must dial 999. **dialling** *n.* making a number on the telephone, d. tone = sound on the telephone which shows you that you can dial; d. code = number which you dial to call a particular town or country.

dialect ['daıəlekt] *n.* variety of language spoken in a particular area. **dialectal** *adj.* referring to a dialect. **dialectic** [daıə'lektık] *n.* reasoned investigation of philosophical truth.

dialogue ['daɪəlɒg] *n.* conversation between two people/two groups.

dialysis [daɪ'ælɪsɪs] *n.* cleaning of the blood by passing it through a filter.

diameter [daɪ'æmɪtə] *n.* distance across the centre of a circle. **diametrically** [daɪə'metrɪklɪ] *adv.* d. opposed to = completely against/ opposite.

diamond ['daɪəmənd] *n.* (a) very hard transparent precious stone; d. wedding = 60th wedding anniversary. (b) one of the four suit in a pack of cards.

dianthus [daɪ'ænθəs] *n.* Latin name for carnations or pinks.

diaper ['daɪəpə] *n Am.* nappy

diaphanous [daɪ'æfənəs] *adj.* (cloth) which is so thin that you can see through it.

diaphragm ['daɪəfræm] *n.* (a) thin sheet which vibrates with noise. (b) thin wall of muscle separating the chest and the abdomen.

diarrhoea, Am. diarrhea [daɪə'rɪə] *n.* illness of the intestines where your bowel movements are very fluid.

diary ['daɪərɪ] *n.* (a) description of what has happened in your life day by day; he has kept a d. for years. (b) small book in which you write notes/appointments for each day of the week. **diarist** *n.* person who writes a diary.

diastase [daɪə'steɪz] *n.* enzyme which breaks down starch and converts it to sugar.

diastole [daɪə'stəʊl] *n.* phase in the beating of the heart when the heart swells and fills with blood.

diatom [daɪ'ætəm] *n.* type of microscopic sea creature.

diatribe ['daɪətrɪb] *n.* violent spoken or written criticism.

dibber, dibble ['dɪbə, 'dɪbl] *n.* stick used to make holes in the ground for planting.

dice1 [daɪs] *n.* small cube with one to six dots on each face (for games). **dice2** *v* (a) to cut up (vegetables etc.) into very small cubes. (b) to gamble. **dicey** *adj. inf.* dangerous/difficult.

dichotomy [daɪ'kɒtəmɪ] *n.* splitting into two (usu. contradictory) parts.

dickens ['dɪkɪnz] *n. inf.* the d. of = a lot of; what the d. ? = what on earth?

dicker ['dɪkə] *v inf.* to d. about = to hesitate.

dicky1 ['dɪkɪ] *n inf.* (a) false shirt front. (b) folding back seat in a car. **dicky2** *adj. inf.* ill; not working properly.

dicotyledon [daɪkɒtɪ'liːdən] *n.* plants who seedlings have two fleshy leaves.

dictate [dɪk'teɪt] *v.* (a) to say (sth) to s.o. who writes down your words. (b) to tell s.o. what to do. **dictation** [dɪk'teɪʃn] *n.* act of dictating (sth to be written down) **dictator** *n.* person who rules a country alone. **dictatorial** [dɪktə'tɔːrɪəl] *adj.* like a dictator. **dictatorship** *n.* rule of a country by one person.

diction ['dɪkʃn] *n.* way of speaking.

dictionary ['dɪkʃənrɪ] *n.* (a) book which lists words in alphabetical order, giving their meanings or translations. (b) list of correctly spelled words in a spelling checking program.

dictum ['dɪktəm] *n.* saying (made by a notable person).

did [dɪd] *v.* see do.

didactic [daɪ'dæktɪk] *adj.* which teaches.

diddle ['dɪdl] *v. inf.* to trick/to cheat.

die 1 [daɪ] *n.* metal stamp for making coins **die 2** *v.* to stop living; *inf.* I'm dying to read his book = I am very eager to read his book; I'm dying for a cup of tea = I'd love a cup of tea; the sound died away = become fainter; the wind died down = became less strong; the old customs are dying out = not being continued. **diecast** *adj.* cast from metal in a mould. **diehard** *adj & n. inf.* very reactionary (person).

dieldrin [daɪ'eldrɪn] *n.* powerful insecticide.

diesel ['diːzl] *n.* d. engine = engine which runs on thicker fuel than petrol; d. oil = oil used in diesel engines.

diet 1 ['daɪət] *n.* (a) kind of food you eat; to be on d. = to eat only one sort of food/to eat less. (b) (in some countries) parliament. **diet 2** *v.* to eat less food/ only one sort of food. **dietary** *adj.* referring to a diet. **dieter** *n.* person who is on a diet. **dietetics** *n.* study of food and its nutritional value. **dietician** [daɪə'tɪʃn] *n.* person who specializes in the study of diets.

differ ['dɪfə] *v.* to d. from = not to be the same as; I beg to d. = I must disagree.

difference ['dɪfrəns] *n.* way in which two things are not the same; it doesn't make any d. = it doesn't alter the situation. **different** *adj.* not the same; that's quite a d. thing = it is not at all the same. **differential 1** [dɪfə'renʃl] *adj.* showing up the difference; d. equation **differential 2** *n.* (a) part of the axle of a car which allows wheels to turn at different speeds at corners. (b) difference in salary between different grades of jobs. **differentiate** *v.* to make/to tell the difference (between). **differentiation,** *n.* act of differentiating. **differently** *adv.* not in the same way. **difficult** ['dɪfɪkʌlt] *adj.* not easy. **difficultly** *n.* thing which is not easy; she got into difficulties when swimming = she was in danger of drowning; he is in financial difficulties = he has problems to do with money.

diffidence ['dɪfɪdəns] *n.* being diffident. **diffident** *adj.* shy; lacking confidence. **diffidently** *adv* shyly.

diffract [dɪ'frækt] *v.* to split light into its different colours. **diffraction** [dɪ'frækʃn] *n.* splitting up of light into its different colours.

diffuse1 [dɪ'fjuːs] *adj.* vague/unclear; d. lighting = soft lighting, not giving any sharp shadows. **diffuse2** [du'fjuːz] *v.* to spread out; to send out; diffused lighting = soft lighting, not giving any sharp shadows. **diffusion** *n.* act of diffusing.

dig1 [dɪg] *n.* (a) poke; he gave me a d. in the ribs = he nudged me with his elbows. (b) satirical attack. (c) archaeological excavation. **dig2** *v.* (dug; has dug) to make a hole in the ground; we dug up a Roman coin in the garden = we found the coin when digging. **digger** *n.* person/machine that digs. **digging** *n.* action of making a hole in the ground. **dig in** *v.* (a) to bury (manure) in the ground. (b) *inf.* to start eating. **digs** *n. inf.* furnished room(s) let to students, etc.

digest1 ['daɪdʒest] *n.* summary. **digest2** [daɪ'dʒest] *v.* (a) to turn (food) into energy in the stomach and intestine; I cannot d. my dinner = I am feeling unwell after my dinner. (b) to ponder over (a piece of information). **digestible** *adj.* which can be digested. **digestion** *n.* action of turning food into energy. **digestive** *adj.* which

helps you to digest; d. biscuit = sweet wholemeal biscuit.

digit ['dɪdʒɪt] *n.* (a) single figure (from 0 to 9). (b) finger or toe. **digital** *adj.* which involves figures; d. watch = watch where the time is shown by figures (such as 11:52); d. computer = computer which works on a varied signal. **digitize** *v.* to convert information to digital form.

digitalin, digitalis [dɪdʒɪ'teɪlɪn, -ɪs] *n.* drugs made from foxgloves.

dignified ['dɪgnɪfaɪd] *adj.* solemn/ important-looking. **dignify** *v.* to honour (s.o.) with a title; to give dignity to (s.o.).

dignitary *n.* important person; civic dignitaries = the mayor, councillors, etc., of a town. **dignity** *n.* (a) solemn/ serious way of behaving; it is beneath his d. to clean his own shoes = he is too proud to clean them. (b) tittle (given to s.o. as an honour).

digress [daɪ'gres] *v.* to wander away from the subject when speaking,

digression *n.* speech/writing which does not deal with the subject.

dihedral [daɪ'hiːdrəl] *n.* angle at which an aircraft's wing varies from the horizontal.

dike [daɪk] *n.* (a) a long wall of earth to keep out of water. (b) long ditch.

diktat ['dɪktæt] *n.* official command.

dilapidated [dɪ'læpɪdeɪtɪd] *adj.* falling into ruin. **dilapidation** *n.* being in ruins.

dilate [daɪ'leɪt] *v.* to make (eyes) grow larger; (of the eyes) to grow larger.

dilate upon *v.* to talk at length about. **dilatation, dilation** [dɪlə'teɪʃn, daɪ'leɪʃn] *n.* act of dilating. **dilator** *n* drug used to make a part of the body (such as the eyes) grow larger. **dilatory** ['dɪlətərɪ] *adj* slow (to act).

dilatoriness *n.* slowness.

dilemma [dɪ'lemə] *n.* serious problem, where a choice has to be made between several bad alternatives; in a d. = not knowing which course of action to follow.

dilettante [dɪlɪ'tæntɪ] *n.* person who is interested in a subject, but not very seriously.

diligence ['dɪlɪdʒəns] *n.* hard work/ taking care. **diligent** *daj.* hard-working.

dill [dɪl] *n.* herb used for flavouring fish and pickles.

dilly-dally ['dɪlɪ'dælɪ] *v.* to hang back; to loiter.

dilute 1 [daɪ'ljuːt] *v.* to add water to (another liquid) to make it weaker. **dilute 2** *adj.* with water added. **dilution** *n.* act of diluting.

dim 1 [dɪm] *adj.* (dimmer, dimmest) (a) weak (light); I have a d. recollection of it = I can remember it vaguely. (b) rather stupid. **dim 2** *v.* (dimmed) to turn down (a light); the house lights dimmed = the lights in the theatre were turned down (as the play started). **dimly** *adv.* vaguely; unclearly. **dimmer** *n.* light switch which dims a light. **dimness** *n.* weakness (of light); vagueness(of memory).

dime [daɪm] *n. Am.* ten cent coin.

dimension [dɪ'menʃn] *n.* measurement (in figures). **dimensional** *adj* two-dimensional = having two dimensions, flat; three-dimensional = having three dimensions/in the round.

diminish [dɪ'mɪnɪʃ] *v.* to make (sth) smaller; to become smaller.

diminution [dɪmɪ'njuːʃn] *n.* becoming smaller. **diminutive 1** [dɪ'mɪnjʊtɪv] *adj.* very small. **diminutive 2** *n.* word used to show that sth is small; 'Kate' is a d. of 'Catherine'.

diminuendo [dɪmɪnjʊ'endəʊ] *n.* (in music) decreasing noise.

dimple ['dɪmpl] *n.* small hollow (in cheeks/in babies' fat elbows) **dimpled** *adj.*

din 1 [dɪn] *n.* loud noise. **din 2** *v.* (dinned) to force (a piece of information into s.o.'s head) by frequently repeating it.

dine [daɪn] *v.* to have dinner; to d. out = to have dinner away from home. **diner** *n.* (a) person eating dinner. (b) dining car. (c) *Am.* small restaurant selling hot food. **dining car** *n.* restaurant car (on a train). **dining room** *n.* room where people usually eat.

ding-dong 1 ['dɪŋdɒŋ] *n.* sound made by a bell. **ding-dong 2** *adj & n. inf.* vigorous (argument).

dinghy ['dɪŋgɪ] *n.* small boat.

dingo ['dɪŋgəʊ] *n.* Australian wild dog.

dingy ['dɪndʒɪ] *adj.* (-ier, -iest) dirty. **dinginess** *n.* dirt.

dinkum ['dɪŋkəm] *adj.* (in Australia) *inf.* real.

dinner ['dɪnə] *n.* main meal (usu. the evening meal); school d. = meat served to children in school in the middle of the day; d. break = school break at the middle of the day; d. table = table (where people eat); d. party = dinner to which guests are invited; d. service = set of plates for eating a main meal; d. jacket = formal (usu. black) jacket worn for dinner with a black bow tie.

dinosaur ['daɪnəsɔː] *n.* large prehistoric reptile.

dint [dɪnt] *n.* by d. of = through; by means of.

diocese ['daɪəsɪs] *n.* area under the charge of a bishop. **diocesan** [daɪ'ɒsɪzn] *adj.* referring to the diocese.

dioxide [daɪ'ɒksaɪd] *n.* oxide with two parts of oxygen to one part of another substance.

dip 1 [dɪp] *n.* (a) quick covering with liquid. (b) sudden drop (of a rod/of land). (c) savoury paste, onto which biscuits, etc. can be dipped as cocktail snacks. (d) short bathe/swim. (e) sheep d. = place where sheep are dipped in pesticide to kill ticks. **dip 2** *v.* (dipped) (a) to put (sth) quickly into a liquid. (b) to dive. (c) to d. your headlights = lower the beam of your headlights when another car is approaching. (d) to d. into a book = to read a few lines here and there. **dipper** *n.* (a) big d. = fairground railway which goes up and down steep slopes. (b) small brown bird which dives into water.

dipstick *n.* rod (in the engine of a car) which shows the level of oil in the engine.

diphtheria [dɪfθɪərɪə] *n.* (no *pl.*) serious infectious disease of babies.

diphthong ['dɪfθɒŋ] *n.* two vowel sounds which are pronounced together.

diploma [dɪ'pləʊmə] *n.* certificate showing that you have passed an examination

diplomacy [dɪ'pləʊməsɪ] *n.* art of negotiating between different parties. esp. between different countries

diplomat ['dɪpləmæt] *n.* person (such as an ambassador) who represents his country abroad. **diplomatic** [dɪplə'mætɪk] *adj.* (a) representing one's country. (b) careful not to give offence.

diplomatically *adv.* in a diplomatic way **diplomatist** [dɪˈpləʊmətɪst] *n.* diplomat.

dipsomania [dɪpsəˈmeɪnɪə] *n.* habitual drinking of alcohol. **dipsomaniac** *n.* a person who wants to drink alcohol all the time.

dire [ˈdaɪə] *adj.* very serious; d. necessity = urgent necessity.

direct 1 [daɪˈrekt/dɪˈrekt] *v.* (a) to aim towards a point. (b) to tell (s.o.) to do sth; to manage/organize(a film etc.). **direct 2** *adj.* straight; d. taxation = taxes which you pay to the tax office; d. hit = hit on the target; there is a d. flight to London = the plane does not stop between here and London. **direct 3** *adv.* straight; without stopping.

direction [daɪˈrekʃn] *n.* (a) point to which you are going/at which you are aiming. (b) instruction. (c) guiding (of the making of a film) **directional** *adj.* going in one direction. **directive** *n.* official instruction. **directly 1** *adv.* immediately; straight. **directly 2** *conj.* I will write the letter d. I get home = As soon as I get home **directness** *n.* frankness (of a reply) **director** [daɪˈrektə] *n.* (a) a person who is appointed by the share holders to help run a firm; managing d. = person who is in charge of a firm;. (b) person in charge of making a film/a play. **directorate** *n.* group of directors **directorship** *n.* position of director. **directory** *n.* list of people/businesses showing their telephone numbers and addresses; book giving list of people/business with their addresses and telephone numbers; classified d. = telephone directory where firms are classified into various groups.

dirge [dɜːdʒ] *n.* funeral song.

dirigible [dɪˈrɪdʒɪbl] *n.* large airship which can be steered.

dirk [dɜːk] *n.* short dagger.

dirndl [ˈdɜːndl] *n.* wide skirt gathered tight at the waist.

dirt [dɜːt] *n.* mud; earth; filth; d. cheap = extremely cheap. **dirtiness** *n.* being dirty/not being clean. **dirt-track** *n.* cinder-covered track for racing. **dirty 1** *adj.* (-ier, -iest) (a) not clean; covered with dirt. (b) d. weather = grey/drizzly weather; d. trick = low/unpleasant trick. **dirty 2** *v.* to cover with dirt.

disability [dɪsəˈbɪlɪtɪ] *n.* physically handicapped. **disabled 1** [dɪsˈeɪbld] *adj.* physically handicapped. **disabled 2** *n.* the d. = physically handicapped people.

disabuse [dɪsəˈbjuːz] *v.* to make (s.o.) see that he was wrong.

disadvantage [dɪsədˈvɑːntɪdʒ] *n.* handicap; drawback; lack of advantage **disadvantaged** *adj.* handicapped. **disadvantageous** [dɪsædvɑːnˈteɪdʒəs] *adj.* which does not give an advantage; unfavourable.

disaffected [dɪsəˈfektɪd] *adj.* discontented/rebellious.

disagree [dɪsəˈɡriː] *v.* not to agree; cabbage disagrees with me = makes me feel ill. **disagreeable** *adj.* unpleasant. **disagreement** *n.* lack of agreement.

disallow [dɪsəˈlaʊ] *v.* to refuse to accept; the team's second goal was disallowed = was not counted

disappear [dɪsəˈpɪə] *v.* to vanish. **disappearance** *n.* vanishing.

disappoint [dɪsəˈpɔɪnt] *v.* to let (s.o.) down; not to turn out as expected. **disappointing** *adj.* unsatisfactory; not coming un to expectations. **disappointment** *n.* sadness because what was expected did not take place.

disapprove [dɪsəˈpruːv] *v.* not to approve (of sth). **disapproval, disapprobation** [dɪsæprəʊˈbeɪʃn] *n.* lack of approval. **disapprovingly** *adv.* in a way which shows you do not approve.

disarm [dɪsˈɑːm] *v.* to remove weapons from (s.o.). **disarmament** *n.* abolition of weapons by a country. **disarming** *adj.* charming (manner) which prevents people from criticizing

disarrange [dɪsəˈreɪndʒ] *v.* to put (sth) into disorder.

disarray [dɪsəˈreɪ] *n.* lack of order.

disaster [dɪˈzɑːstə] *n.* catastrophe; very bad accident; air d. = crash of an aircraft killing many people. **disastrous** *adj.* very bad/catastrophic. **disastrously** *adv.* very badly.

disband [dɪsˈbænd] *v.* to send (soldiers) back home; to split up (a group of soldiers/musicians etc.).

disbar [dɪsˈbɑː] *v.* (disbarred) (formal) to remove (a lawyer) from the bar.

disbelief [dɪsbɪ'liːf] *n.* lack of belief.
disbeliever *n.* person who does not believe.

disbud [dɪs'bʌd] *v.* (disbudded) to remove some of the buds from (a plant).

disburse [dɪs'bɜːs] *v.* to pay out (money).

disc [dɪsk] *n.* round flat object esp. a record for playing on a record-player; slipped d. = painful condition where one of the cushioning discus in the spine has become displaced; d. brakes = brakes in a car which are in the form of discs; d. harrow = type of harrow formed of a series of metal discs; d. jockey = person who plays records on the radio/in a club, etc.

discard 1 ['dɪskɑːd] *n.* thing which has been discarded. **discard 2** [dɪs'kɑːd] *v.* to put (sth) to on one side; to reject

discern [dɪ'sɜːn] *v.* to see/to make out. **discernible** *adj.* which can be seen. **discerning** *adj.* (person) who has good judgement. **discernment** *n.* ability to judge correctly.

discharge 1 ['dɪstʃɑːdʒ] *n.* (a) liquid (coming out of a pipe etc); pus (coming out of a wound). (b) payment (of a debt.). (c) release (of a prisoner). **discharge 2** *v.* (a) to unload (a cargo); to let off (a gun). (b) to send (s.o.) away; he was discharged from the hospital = he was allowed to go home because he was better.(c) to release (a prisoner).(d) to pay(a debt.); discharged bankrupt = person who has paid off his debts according to the requirements of the court.

disciple [dɪ'saɪpl] *n.* follower (of a religious leader).

discipline 1 ['dɪsɪplɪn] *n.* keeping people under control. **discipline 2** *v.* to control, to punish (s.o.).
disciplinarian [dɪsɪplɪə'neəriən] *n.* person who believes in strict discipline.
disciplinary [dɪsɪ'plɪnəri] *adj.* (action) which keeps s.o. under control.

disclaim [dɪs'kleɪm] *v.* not to admit/to deny; he disclaims all knowledge of the payment = he says he knows nothing about the payment. **disclaimer** *n.* statement in which you disclaim all knowledge of sth.

disclose [dɪs'kləʊz] *v.* to reveal (a secret). **disclosure** [dɪs'kləʊʒə] *n.* revealing (of a secret).

disco ['dɪskəʊ] *n.* (*pl.*-os) *inf.* discotheque; place where people dance to recorded music; dancing to pop/rock records.

discolour, *Am.* **discolor** [dɪs'kʌlə] *v.* to change the colour of (sth).
discolouration [dɪskʌlə'reɪʃn] *n.* change of colour.

discomfort [dɪs'kʌmfət] *n.* lack of comfort.

disconcert [dɪskən'sɜːt] *v.* to surprise/ to embarrass. **disconcerting** *adj.* worrying/surprising.

disconnect [dɪskə'nekt] *v.* to undo (two things which are connected); they disconnected the refrigerator = they unplugged the refrigerator.
disconnected *adj.* disjointed; with no links.

disconsolate [dɪs'kkns̩əlt] *adj.* very sad. **disconsolately** *adv.* very sadly.

discontent [dɪskən'tent] *n.* state of not being satisfied. **discontented** *adj.* not satisfied.

discontinue [dɪskən'tɪnjuː] *v.* not to continue to produce (sth).
discontinuity [dɪskɒntɪ'njɒɪtɪ] *n.* being discontinuous. **discontinuous** *adj.* which stops and starts; intermittent.

discord ['dɪskɔːd] *n.* lack of agreement.
discordant [dɪs'kɔːdənt] *adj.* (a) not in agreement. (b) out of harmony.

discotheque ['dɪskətek] *n.* place where people dance to recorded music.

discount 1 ['dɪskaʊnt] *n.* percentage less than the normal price; d. store = shop where goods are cheaper than else where. **discount 2** [dɪs'kaʊnt] *v.* (a) not to pay any attention to (sth). (b) to put a discount on (a price).

discourage [dɪs'kʌrɪdʒ] *v.* not to encourage; to d. s.o. from doing sth = to stop s.o. doing sth. **discouragement** *n.* being discouraged; thing which stops you doing sth. **discouraging** *adj.* not encouraging.

discourse1 ['dɪskɔːs] *n.* (formal) talk/ speech. **discourse2** [dɪs'kɔːs] *v.* (formal) to speak.

discourteous [dɪs'kɜːtɪəs] *adj.* rude.
discourteously *adv.* rudely.
discourtesy *n.* rudeness.

discover [dɪs'kʌvə] *v.* to find (sth new).
discoverer *n.* person who finds sth.
discovery *n.* act of finding sth new.

discredit 1 [dɪs'kredɪt] *n.* doubt/lack of belief (in s.o.). **discredit 2** *v.* to make people doubt (s.o./sth); he has been discredited = no one believes him any more. **discreditable** *adj.* not honourable (conduct). **discreditably** *adv.* dishonourably.

discreet [dɪs'kriːt] *adj.* quiet; not allowing anyone to notice. **discreetly** *adv.* quietly; without anyone noticing.

discrepancy [dɪs'krepənsɪ] *n.* lack of agreement (between figures/accounts).

discrete [dɪs'kriːt] *adj.* separate/not connected. **discretion** [dɪs'kreʃn] *n.* wisdom/good sense; I leave it to your d. = I leave it for you to decide.

discretionary *adj.* (powers) used at s.o.'s discretion.

discriminate [dɪs'krɪmɪneɪt] *v.* to distinguish; to d. between = to treat (two things) differently; to d. against = to prefer (one thing to another).

discriminating *adj.* able to distinguish/judge. **discrimination** [dɪskrɪmɪ'neɪʃn] *n.* (a) judgement; a man of d. = of good taste. (b) preference (for or against sth); racial d. = preference for or against a race.

discursive [dɪs'kɜːsɪv] *adj.* not succinct/not to the point.

discus ['dɪskəs] *n.* (*pl.*-es) flat round disc which is thrown as a sport.

discuss [dɪs'kʌs] *v.* to talk about (a problem). **discussion** [dɪs'kʌʃn] *n.* talking about (a problem); the question under d. = the problem we are talking about.

disdain1 [dɪs'deɪn] *n.* looking down; feeling that s.o./sth is inferior. **disdain2** *v.* to look down on (sth); to refuse to do (sth) because it is beneath you.

disdainful *adj.* superior (air).

disdainfully *adv.* with a superior air.

disease [dɪ'ziːz] *n.* serious illness (of animals, plants, etc.). **diseased** *adj.* sick.

disembark [dɪsɪm'bɑːk] *v.* to get off a ship. **disembarkation** [dɪsembɑː'keɪʃn] *n.* getting off a ship.

disembodied [dɪsɪm'bɒdɪd] *adj.* not connected to a body.

disembowel [dɪsɪm'baʊəl] *v.* to remove the intestines from (s.o.).

disenchanted [dɪsɪn'tʃɑːntɪd] *adj.* (with) feeling that sth has not turned out as expected. **disenchantment** *n.* feeling that sth has not turned out as well as expected.

disenfranchise [dɪsɪn'fræntʃaɪz] *v.* to take away the right to vote.

disengage [dɪsɪn'geɪdʒ] *v.* (a) to break off; the troops disengaged = the troops broke off the fighting. (b) to separate (the gears of a car).

disentangle [dɪsɪn'tæŋgl] *v.* to untie (knotted string, etc.).

disfavour, *Am.* **disfavor** [dɪs'feɪvə] *n.* shame; lack of favour; the minister fell into d. = he was disgraced; the minister incurred the king's d. = he fell into disgrace with the king.

disfigure [dɪs'fɪgə] *v.* to make ugly. **disfigurement** *n.* act of disfiguring.

disfranchise [dɪs'fræntʃaɪz] *v.* to remove the right to vote from (s.o.). **disfranchisement** *n.* removal of the right to vote.

disgorge [dɪs'gɔːdʒ] *v.* (a) to pour out. (b) to give up (things which have been stolen).

disgrace 1 [dɪs'greɪs] *n.* shame; being out of favour with s.o.; the minister fell into d. = he was out of favour. **disgrace 2** *v.* to bring shame on. **disgraceful** *adj.* which you should be ashamed of. **disgracefully** *adv.* in a disgraceful way.

disgruntled [dɪs'grʌntld] *adj.* annoyed/discontented.

disguise 1 [dɪs'gaɪz] *n.* costume, wig. etc., to make a person look like s.o. else; in d. = dressed to look like s.o. else.

disguise 2 *v.* to dress so as to look like s.o. else; to make (sth) look/sound different; there is no disguising the fact = you cannot hide the fact.

disgust 1 [dɪs'gʌst] *n.* (at) strong dislike; feeling sick/very discontented. **disgust 2** *v.* to make (s.o.) feel sick. **disgusting** *adj.* which make you feel sick.

dish 1 [dɪʃ] *n.* (*pl.*-es) (a) a large plate (for serving food). (b) part of a meal; (plate of) prepared food. **dish 2** *v.* he is dishing up the food = he is serving the meal; *inf.* they are dishing out tickets = they are handing out tickets. **dishcloth** *n.* cloth for washing dishes.

dishwasher, *n.* machine for washing dishes. **dishwater** *n.* water which has been used for washing dishes. **dishy** *adj. inf.* attractive (girl).

disharmony [dɪs'hɑːmənɪ] *n.* not being in agreement/in harmony.

dishearten [dɪs'hɑːtn] *v.* to discourage. **disheartening** *adj.* discouraging.

dishevelled [dɪ'ʃevəld] *adj.* uncombed (hair).

dishonest [dɪs'ɒnɪst] *adj.* not honest. **dishonestly,** *adv.* not honestly; illegally. **dishonesty** *n.* lack of honesty.

dishonour, *Am.* **dishonor 1** [dɪs'ɒnə] *n.* lack of honour. **dishonour,** *Am.* **dishonor 2** *v.* (a) to treat rudely. (b) not to honour; dishonoured cheque = cheque which the bank will not pay.

dishonourable *adj.* not honourable; shameful. **dishonourably** *adv.* in a dishonourable way.

disillusion [dɪsɪ'luːʒn] *n.* feeling of being let down/that sth has not turned out as you expected. **disillusioned** *adj.* feeling that sth has not turned out as expected. **disillusionment** *n.* feeling of being let down/that sth has not turned out as expected.

disincentive [dɪsɪn'sentɪv] *n.* thing which discourages; the low salary is a d. to work = the salary does not encourage people to work.

disinclined [dɪsɪn'klaɪnd] *adj.* not inclined; she is feeling d. to go to work today = she does not want to go to work today. **disinclination** [dɪsɪnklɪ'neɪʃn] *n.* not wanting to do sth.

disinfect [dɪsɪn'fekt] *v.* to remove/to prevent infection. **disinfectant** *n.* chemical liquid for fighting infection.

disinformation [dɪsɪnfə'meɪʃən] *n.* false information to confuse an enemy.

disingenuous [dɪsɪn'dʒenjʊəs] *adj.* false; lacking frankness; pretending to be naive.

disinherit [dɪsɪn'herɪt] *v.* to change your will so that s.o. will no longer inherit your money when you die.

disintegrate [dɪs'ɪntɪgreɪt] *v.* to fall to pieces. **disintegration** [dɪsɪntɪ'greɪʃn] *n.* falling to pieces.

disinter [dɪsɪn'tɜː] *v.* (disinterred) to dig up (sth) which has been buried.

disinterested [dɪs'ɪntrəstɪd] *adj.* not in favour of one side or the other; he is a totally d. observer = he is an impartial

observer. **disinterestedness** *n.* being disinterested.

disjointed [dɪs'dʒɔɪntɪd] *adj.* without any links; unconnected.

disk [dɪsk] *n.* any round flat object, especially a piece of magnetized plastic used in computers to record information; floppy d. = small disk which can be inserted and removed from a computer; hard d. = disk with large capacity, which is permanently fixed in a computer. **diskette** *n.* small floppy disk. **disk drive** *n.* device which spins a disk in a computer and controls the access of information.

dislike 1 [dɪs'laɪk] *n.* lack of liking; to take a d. to = to start to hate. **dislike 2** *v.* not to like; I don't d. honey = I rather like honey.

dislocate ['dɪsləkeɪt] *v.* (a) to put (an arm/leg, etc.) out of joint. (b) to disorganize. **dislocation** [dɪslə'keɪʃn] *n.* (a) disorganization. (b) putting an arm/leg, etc., out of joint.

dislodge [dɪs'lɒdʒ] *v.* to detach/to remove.

disloyal [dɪs'lɔɪəl] *adj.* not loyal. **disloyalty** *n.* being disloyal.

dismal ['dɪzməl] *adj.* miserable. **dismally** *adv.* miserably; (to fail a test) very badly.

dismantle [dɪs'mæntl] *v.* to take to pieces.

dismay 1 [dɪs'meɪ] *n.* horror/ consternation. **dismay 2** *v.* to strike (s.o.) with horror.

dismember [dɪs'membə] *v.* to cut up (a body) into parts; to take apart.

dismiss [dɪs'mɪs] *v.* (a) to send (s.o.) away. (b) to remove (s.o.) from a job. (c) to refuse (a request.). **dismissal** *n.* removal from a job.

dismount [dɪs'maʊnt] *v.* to get off a horse/bicycle, etc.

disobey [dɪsə'beɪ] *v.* not to obey. **disobedience** [dɪsə'biːdɪəns] *n.* lack of obedience. **disobedient** *adj.* not obedient.

disorder [dɪs'ɔːdə] *n.* (a) lack of order; untidiness. (b) riot; disturbance.(c) illness. **disorderly** *adj.* wild(crowd).

disorganize [dɪs'ɔːgənaɪz] *v.* to put (sth) out of its usual order.

disorientate [dɪs'ɔːrɪənteɪt] *v* to make (s.o.) lose their sense of direction; to confuse (s.o.). **disorientation** *ln* feeling lost.

disown [dɪs'əʊn] *v* to refuse to acknowledge (sth) is yours.

disparage [dɪs'pærɪdʒ] *v* to say that (sth) is bad. **disparagement** *n* act of disparaging. **disparaging** *adj.* critical; saying that sth is bad.

disparate ['dɪspərət] *adj.* varied/ different. **disparity** [dɪs'pærɪtɪ] *n.* difference.

dispassionate [dɪs'pæʃnət] *adj.* calm and without emotion. **dispassionately** *adv.* calmly.

dispatch 1 [dɪs'pætʃ] *n.* (*pl.*-es) (a) sending; d. note = saying that goods have been sent. (b) speed (of doing sth). (c) message; d. box = box containing government papers; d. rider = motorcyclist who carries messages. **dispatch 2** *v.* (a) to send. (b) to finish quickly.(c) to kill off.

dispel [dɪs'pel] *v.* (dispelled) to clear away.

dispense [dɪs'pens] *v.* (a) to distribute. (b) to prepare and sell (medicine). (c) to d. = to do without. **dispensable** *adj.* which can be dispensed with.

dispensary *n.* place where a chemist prepares medicines. **dispensation** [dɪspən'seɪʃn] *n.* permission not to follow a rule, etc. **dispenser** *n.* automatic machine/box with a hole to allow one object to come out at a time. **dispensing** *adj.* d. chemist = chemist who has the qualifications to prepare medicines.

disperse [dɪs'pɜːs] *v.* to clear away; to scatter in different directions. **dispersal** **dispersion**, *n.* act of dispersing.

dispirited [dɪ'spɪrɪtɪd] *adj.* sad/ discouraged; feeling disappointed.

displace [dɪs'pleɪs] *v.* to move (sth) from its usual place; displaced persons = refugees who have fled from their home lands. **displacement,** *n.* moving (of sth); amount of water removed by a ship, (hence) the volume of the ship.

display 1 [dɪs'pleɪ] *n.* show/exhibition; air d. = exhibition of flying by various aircraft; d. screen = screen on which data is displayed; d. unit = special stand for showing goods for sale. **display 2** *v.* to put (sth) on show.

displease [dɪs'pliːz] *v.* not to please.

displeasure [dɪs'pleʒə] *n.* annoyance.

disport [dɪs'pɔːt] *v.* (formal) to d. oneself = to amuse oneself.

dispose [dɪs'pəʊz] *v.* to d. of sth = to get rid of sth. **disposable** *adj.* which can be thrown away after use; d. income = amount of income left after the tax has been deducted. **disposal** *n.* (a) waste d. unit = machine attached to a sink which grinds up waste. (b) I am at your d. = you can ask me to do anything you wish. **disposed** *adj.* he is well d. towards us = he favours us. **disposition** [dɪspə'zɪʃn] *n.* (a) character. (b) act of passing property to another person.

dispossess [dɪspə'zes] *v.* to d. s.o. of = to remove possessions from s.o.

disproportion [dɪsprə'pɔːʃn] *n.* being out of proportion. **disproportionate** *adj.* unusual; out of proportion. **disproportionately** *adv.* in disproportionate way.

disprove [dɪs'pruːv] *v.* to prove (sth) is wrong.

dispute1 [dɪs'pjuːt] *n.* argument. **dispute 2** *v.* to argue that (sth) is incorrect. **disputable** *adj.* which can be disputed. **disputant** *n.* person who disputes. **disputation** *n.* (formal) argument.

disqualify [dɪs'kwɒlɪfaɪ] *v.* to rule that (s.o.) is incapable of doing sth/not qualified to do sth. **disqualification** [dɪskwɒlɪfɪ'keɪʃn] *n.* rule that s.o. is disqualified.

disquiet [dɪs'kwaɪət] *n.* worry. **disquieting** *adj.* which makes you worried.

disquisition [dɪskwɪ'zɪʃn] *n.* (formal) long speech.

disregard 1 [dɪsrɪ'gɑːd] *n.* (for) indifference (to sth); lack of worry (about sth). **disregard 2** *v.* to take no notice of.

disrepair [dɪsrɪ'peə] *n.* in d. = needing to be repaired.

disrepute [dɪsrɪ'pjuːt] *n.* bad reputation. **disreputable** [dɪs'repjʊtəbl] *adj.* with a bad reputation; he is d. character = a wicked person.

disrespect [dɪsrɪ'spekt] *n.* lack of respect. **disrespectful** *adj.* lacking respect; rude.

disrobe [dɪs'rəʊb] *v.* (formal) to undress.

disrupt [dɪs'rʌpt] v. to break up/to interrupt (a meeting). **disruption** [dɪs'rʌpʃn] n. breaking up; interruption (of a meeting). **disruptive** adj. which disrupts.

dissatisfaction [dɪssætɪs'fækʃn] n. lack of satisfaction. **dissatisfied** [dɪs'sætɪsfaɪd] adj. not satisfied.

dissect [dɪ'sekt] v. to cut up (a dead body/plant) in order to examine the inside. **dissection** n. cutting up (a body or plant).

dissemble [dɪ'sembl] v. (formal) to hide one's feelings.

disseminate [dɪs'semɪneɪt] v. to spread (news) around. **dissemination** n. act of spreading news around.

dissension [dɪ'senʃn] n. lack of agreement.

dissent 1 [dɪ'sent] n. lack of agreement. **dissent 2** v. to d. from = not to agree with. **dissenter** n. person who does not agree (esp. with the established church).

dissertation [dɪsə'teɪʃn] n. short (university) thesis.

disservice [dɪs'sɜːvɪs] n. unintentional harm; you do yourself a d. = you are harming your reputation.

dissident ['dɪsɪdənt] adj. & n. (person) who does not agree with the opinion of his political party/with the state. **dissidence** n. disagreement (with the state).

dissimilar [dɪ'smɪlə] adj. not the same; they are not d. = they are quite alike.

dissimulate [dɪ'sɪmjʊleɪt] v. (formal) to hide one's feelings.

dissimulation n. (formal) hiding one's feelings.

dissipate ['dɪsɪpeɪt] v. to clear away; to get rid of. **dissipation** [dɪsɪ'peɪʃn] n. throwing away (a fortune); wide living.

dissociate [dɪ'səʊsɪeɪt] v. to d. yourself from = to say that you have nothing to do with. **dissociation** n. act of dissociating oneself.

dissolute ['dɪsəljuːt] adj. depraved; undisciplined.

dissolve [dɪ'zɒlv] v. (a) to make (a solid substance) become part of a liquid; to become part of liquid. (b) to bring to an end. **dissolution** n. act of dissolving (Parliament, etc.).

dissolvent n. substance which can

dissolve other substances.

dissonant ['dɪsənənt] adj. out of harmony.

dissuade [dɪ'sweɪd] v. to d. s.o. from sth = to persuade s.o. not to do sth. **dissuasion** n. persuading s.o. not to sth.

distal ['dɪstəl] adj. away from the centre of the body.

distance1 ['dɪstəns] n. space from one point to another; in the d. = quite a long way away. **distance2** v. to d. yourself from = to put yourself at a distance from. **distant** adj. far away; he is a d. relative = he is related to me, but not of my close family. **distantly** adv. in a distant way.

distaste [dɪs'teɪst] n. dislike. **distasteful** adj. unpleasant.

distemper 1 [dɪs'tempə] n. (a) water colour paint for walls. (b) sickness of dogs. **distemper 2** v. to put distemper on (a wall).

distend [dɪs'tend] v. to swell. **distension** n. swelling.

distil [dɪ'stɪl] v. (distilled) to make pure water/alcohol by heating and collecting the vapour; distilled water = pure water. **distillation** n. act of distilling (water/alcohol). **distiller** n. person who distils alcohol. **distillery** n. factory for distilling alcohol.

distinct [dɪ'stɪŋkt] adj. (a) separate. (b) clear. **distinction** [dɪ'stɪŋkʃn] n. (a) difference. (b) special excellence. **distinctive** adj. very noticeable; particular to one thing; which makes one thing different from others. **distinctly** adv. clearly. **distinctness** n. being distinct.

distinguish [dɪ'stɪŋgwɪʃ] v. (a) to see clearly; to make out (detail). (b) to make a difference (between two things). (c) he distinguished himself = he made himself noticed. **distinguishable** adj. which can be distinguished. **distinguished** adj. important/well-known (writer, painter, etc.).

distort [dɪ'stɔːt] v. to twist; to give a false impression of. **distortion** [dɪ'stɔːʃn] n. twisting; giving a false impression of.

distract [dɪ'strækt] v. to attract attention from. **distracted** adj. wild (with worry/grief). **distraction** [dɪ'strækʃn] n. (a) amusement. (b) worry; he loved her to d. = he was wild about her.

distrain [dɪs'treɪn] v. to seize goods to pay for debts.

distraught [dɪs'trɔːt] adj. wild (with worry/grief, etc.).

distress 1 [dɪ'sstres] n. (a) great sorrow/pain. (b) difficulty; d. signal = signal sent out by ship/aircraft in difficulties. **distress 2** v. to make (s.o.) very sad.

distressing adj. very sad; worrying.

distribute [dɪ'strɪbjuːt] v. to give to several people; we d. Japanese cars = we are the agents for Japanese cars.

distribution [dɪstrɪ'bjuːʃn] n. giving to several people. **distributive** [dɪ'strɪbjʊtɪv] adj. which distributes.

distributor n. (a) company which sells goods for another (usu. overseas) company. (b) (in a car engine) mechanism which passes the electric spark to each sparking plug in turn.

district ['dɪstrɪkt] n. area/region; Am. d. attorney = government official, a lawyer who prosecutes cases in a certain region; d. council = section of local government which administers a district.

distrust 1 [dɪs'trʌst] n. lack of trust. **distrust 2** v. not to trust.

disturb [dɪ'stɜːb] v. to bother/to worry (s.o.); to interrupt (s.o.). **disturbance** n. (a) noise. (b) crackling noise (on radio). **disturbing** adj. worrying.

disunited [dɪsjuː'naɪtəd] adj. no longer united.

disuse [dɪs'juːs] n. to fall into d. = not to be used any more. **disused** ['dɪsjuːzd] adj. not used.

ditch 1 [dɪtʃ] n. long trench for taking away water. **ditch 2** v. (a) to make ditch. (b) (of aircraft) to come down in the sea. (c) inf. to abandon; he ditched his car and walked = he left his car by the side of the road.

dither 1 ['dɪðə] n. all of a d. = very agitated. **dither 2** v. not to be able to make up one's mind.

ditto ['dɪtəʊ] n. the same thing; printer's sign (") meaning that the same thing is to be repeated.

ditty ['dɪtɪ] n. little song.

diuretic [daɪʊ'retɪk] adj. & n. (substance) which makes you produce more urine.

diurnal [daɪ'ɜːnəl] adj. (poetic) daily.

divan [dɪ'væn] n. low couch; bed with a solid base and no back or ends.

dive 1 [daɪv] n. (a) plunge downwards head first. (b) inf. disreputable bar/club. **dive 2** v. (dived, Am. dove[dəʊv]) to plunge head first.

diver n. person who works underwater. **diving board** n. plank at swimming pool from which people dive. **diving suit** n. heavy suit for divers working at great depths.

diverge [daɪ'vɜːdʒ] v. to split; to go in different ways. **divergence** n. split/difference. **divergent** adj. which split/which are different. **diverging** adj. splitting; d. opinions = opinions which are quite different.

diverse [daɪ'vɜːs] adj. varied. **diversification** [daɪvɜːsɪfɪ'keɪʃn] n. act of diversifying. **diversify** v. to vary; to do other sorts of work. **diversity** n. great variety. **diversion** [daɪ'vɜːʃn] n. (a) sending traffic another way. (b) amusement. (c) to create a d. = to do sth to distract s.o.'s attention from another thing which you do not wart him to see. **divert** v. (a) to send traffic another way. (b) to amuse. (c) I am trying to d. his attention = to distract his attention.

divest [daɪ'vest] v. (formal) to d. s.o. of sth = to take sth away from s.o.

divide [dɪ'vaɪd] v. (a) to cut into parts. (b) to calculate how many of one number there are in another. (c) (in the House of Commons) to vote. **dividers** n. pl. pair of compasses for measuring.

dividend ['dɪvɪdend] n. part of profits shared out among shareholders.

divine 1 [dɪ'vaɪn] adj. referring to God. **divine 2** v. to predict the future; to search for hidden sources of water. **divine 3** n. (formal) learned priest. **divination** [dɪvɪ'neɪʃn] n. predicting what will happen in the future. **diviner** n. person who finds hidden sources of water. **divinity** [dɪ'vɪnɪtɪ] n. god; state of being a god.

division [dɪ'vɪʒn] n. (a) splitting up into parts; calculation of how many of one number there are in another; long d. = working out of a complicated division (such as 2894 divided by 19) on paper. (b) (in British Parliament) counting of

votes. (c) important part (of army/firm).
divisional *adj.* referring to a division.
divisible [dɪ'vɪzəbl] *adj.* which can be divided. **divisive** *adj.* which produces quarrels. **divisor** [dɪ'vaɪzə] *n.* number which divides another.
divorce 1 [dɪ'vɔːs] *n.* legal separation of husband and wife leaving each free or remarry. **divorce 2** *v.* (a) to separate (two ideas, etc.). (b) to break off a marriage legally. **divorcee** [dɪvɔː'siː] *n.* person who is divorced.
divot ['dɪvət] *n.* small piece of turf.
divulge [daɪ'vʌldʒ] *v.* to reveal (a secret).
DIY [diːaɪ'waɪ] *abbrev.* for do it yourself; a DIY shop = shop selling paints/tools, etc.
dizzy ['dɪzɪ] *adj.* (-ier, -iest) feeling that everything is spinning round; I feel d. = my head is turning; d. heights = such great heights that they makes your head turn. **dizzily** *adv.* in a dizzy way. **dizziness** *n.* feeling that everything is turning round you.
DJ ['diːdʒeɪ] *abbrev.* for disc jockey.
DNA [diːen'eɪ] *abbrev.* for deoxyribonucleic acid.
do 1 [duː] *n.* (*pl.*dos) party; social gathering. **do 2** *v.* (did; done) (a) to work at (sth); to make/to complete (sth); I 'm doing my hair = I am combing my hair; she was doing the washing; he hasn't done the dishes; can you do today's crossword? well done! = congratulations; you have worked/run, etc., well !. (b) the potatoes aren't done yet = aren't cooked yet; the meat is done to a turn = the meat is well cooked; *inf.* I feel done in = I am tired out. (c) to be satisfactory; will this colour do? we will have to make do with paper plates = we will have to accept paper plates because there is no alternative. (d) to go (at a certain speed). (e) (used in negatives, questions and answers) it doesn't matter; we didn't laugh; do you live in England? - yes, I do; but your parents don't live there, do they? - no they do not. (f) (takes the place of another verb) can you swim as fast as he does? he speaks French better than I do; she arrived before we did. (g) (telling someone not to do something) don't throw that paper away! (h) how do you do? = hello! (i) (to

emphasize) why don't you work? - I do work! why didn't she tell you? - she did tell me! **do away** *v.* to do away with sth = to abolish sth; to do away with s.o. = to murder s.o. **do down** *v. inf.* to trick (s.o.). **do for,** *v. inf.* (a) to kill/to destroy. (b) to do house work for (s.o.).
do-gooder *n.* (*pl.*do-gooders) *inf.* person who tries to help others, but in an ineffectual or officious way. **do in** *v. inf.* to kill. **doing** *n.* (a) it takes some d. = it is quite difficult to do. (b) *inf.* doings = things. **do-it-yourself** *n* repairing building/painting by yourself, without employing a professional. **do out** *v.* to clean out (a room/a cupboard). **do up** *v.* (a) to fasten. (b) to renovate; they bought an old cottage and did it up. **do with** *v.* (a) *inf.* to need; I could do with a drink. (b) to concern; it is nothing to do with me = it is not my business; it has to do with the new book = it concerns/it is about the new book; what have you done with my hat? = where have you put my hat?
do without *v.* to manage without.
docile ['dəʊsaɪl] *adj.* quiet/not aggressive. **docility** [dɒ'sɪlɪtɪ] *n.* being docile.
dock 1 [dɒk] *n.* (a) artificial harbour; the docks = the whole harbour; the ship is in d. = is tied up at the quay; my car is in d. = being repaired; dry d. = dock where the water is pumped out to allow repairs to be done to a ship. (b) box in a law court, where the prisoner sits. (c) wild plant with very large leaves. **dock 2** *v.* (a) to put a ship into harbour; (of ship) to arrive in harbour. (b) to link two spacecraft together in space. (c) to cut off/to remove. **docker** *n.* man who works in the docks. **dockyard** *n.* place where ships are built.
docket 1 ['dɒkɪt] *n.* paper showing the list of contents (of a packet which has been sent). **docket 2** *v.* to attach a docket to (sth).
doctor 1 *n.* (shortened in names to Dr) person who looks after people's health; learned person with a superior degree from a university. **doctor 2** *v.* (a) to look after (a patient/a sick animal). (b) to change figures in (accounts). (c) to castrate (an animal).
doctoral *adj.* referring to a doctorate. **doctorate** ['dɒktərət] *n.* higher degree from a university.

doctrine ['dɒktrɪn] n. statement of what a group of people believe.
doctrinaire [dɒktrɪ'neə] adj. very dogmatic. **doctrinal** [dɒk'traɪnl] adj. referring to a doctrine.
document ['dɒkjʊmənt] n. paper with writing on it. **documentary 1** [dɒkjʊ'mentərɪ] n. factual film about a real subject. **documentary 2** adj. referring to documents.
documentation n. all the documents which refer to sth.
dodder ['dɒdə] v. to walk uncertainly/to totter. **doddery** adj old and trembly. **doddle** ['dɒdl] n. inf. it's a d. = it's very easy.
dodge 1 [dɒdʒ] n. trick. **dodge 2** v. to avoid/to get out of the way. **dodgems** n. pl.amusement at a fairground, where small electric cars are driven round and bump into each other. **dodgy** adj. inf. unsafe/unsure.
dodo ['dəʊdəʊ] n. large extinct bird; as dead as a d. = totally dead/finished.
doe ['dəʊ] n. female (deer/rabbit).
doff [dɒf] v. to take off (one's hat).
dog 1 [dɒg] n. (a) carnivorous animal which barks, often kept as a pet; let sleeping dogs lie = not to disturb the existing state of affairs. (b) male fox. (c) the dogs = dog races; to go to the dogs = to go to ruin. (d) d. days = very hot period in late summer. **dog 2** v. (dogged) to d. s.o.'s footsteps = to follow s.o. **dog-collar** n. leather band to go round a dog's neck. (b) inf. white collar worn by clergyman. **dog-eared** adj. (book) with its pages bent or torn. **dog-fish** n. huss/small white sea fish.
dogged ['dɒgɪd] adj. not giving in easily. **doggedly** adv. in a dogged way. **doggo** adv. inf. to lie d. = to stay quiet. **doghouse** n. Am. kennel; inf. in the d. = in disgrace. **dogrose** n. wild pink rose. **dogsbody** n. person who always has all the worst jobs to do. **dog-tired** adj. worn out. **dogwatch** n. (in the navy) one of the two watches in the evening. **dogwood** n. shrub with bright red stems.
doggerel ['dɒgərəl] n. bad poetry.
dogma ['dɒgmə] n. official belief. **dogmatic** [dɒg'mætɪk] adj. insistent that what you say is right.
dogmatically adv. in a dogmatic way.

dogmatism n. insistence that you are right. **dogmatize** v. to insist that you are right.
dolly ['dɒlɪ] n. decorated paper/lace serviette to put under a cake on a plate.
doldrums ['dɒldrəmz] n. pl.in the d. = not making any progress.
dole 1 [dəʊl] n. money given by the government to people without work; on the d. = unemployed and receiving government payments. **dole 2** v. to d. out = to hand out (in a half-hearted way).
doleful ['dəʊlfʊl] adj. gloomy.
dolefully adv. gloomily.
doll [dɒl] n. toy which looks like a baby. **dolled up** adj. inf. very smartly dressed. **dolly** n. (a) inf. doll. (b) wheeled platform for a TV camera.
dollar ['dɒlə] n. money used in the USA and many other countries.
dollop ['dɒləp] n. inf. large lump (of sth soft).
dolmen ['dɒlmən] n. prehistoric tomb with a flat stone supported by uprights.
dolphin ['dɒlfɪn] n. mammal like a small whale living in the sea.
dolphinarium [dɒlfɪ'neərɪəm] n. large aquarium, where people pay to watch dolphins perform tricks.
dolt [dəʊlt] n. silly person.
domain [də'meɪn] n. (a) area controlled by s.o. (b) area of knowledge.
dome [dəʊm] n. semi-spherical roof. **domed** adj. with a dome.
Domesday Book ['du:mzdeɪ bʊk] n. record of land and population in England, made for William I in 1086.
domestic [də'mestɪk] adj. (a) referring to the home; d. science = study of cooking and running a home; d. animals = animals which man keeps for wool/milk/meat, etc. (b) d. flights = flights inside a country. **domesticated** [də'mestɪkeɪtɪd] adj. (animal) trained to live in the house. **domesticity** [dɒme'stɪsɪtɪ] n. life at home.
domicile ['dɒmɪsaɪl] n. (formal) place where s.o. lives. **domiciliary** adj. which takes place in the home.
domiciled adj (formal) living; resident.
dominant ['dɒmɪnənt] adj. most important; supreme; commanding. **dominance** n. being dominant. **dominate** ['dɒmɪneɪt] v. (a) to rule. (b)

to be very obvious. **dominating** *adj.* ruling; over-shadowing. **domination** [dɒmɪ'neɪʃn] *n.* act of dominating.

domineer [dɒmɪ'nɪə] *v.* to rule (s.o.); a domineering wife = a wife who rules her husband. **dominion** [də'mɪnjən] *n.* (a) self-governing state in the Commonwealth. (b) rule (over a territory)

domino ['dɒmɪnəʊ] *n.* (*pl.*-oes) one of a set of small flat blocks, each divided into two sections, with upto six dots in each section; d. theory = theory that if event occurs, others will inevitably follow.

don 1 [dɒn] *n.* university teacher. **don 2** *v.* (donned) to put on (a piece of clothing). **donnish** *adj.* like a don.

donate [dəʊ'neɪt] *v.* to give. **donation** [dəʊ'neɪʃn] *n.* gift.

done [dʌn] *v.* see do.

donkey ['dɒŋkɪ] *n.* farm animal like a small horse but with long ears; *inf.* I haven't seen him for donkey's years = I have not seen him for long time; d. jacket = thick woollen jacket with a wide leather strip across the shoulders, worn esp. by workmen; d. work = hard dull work.

donor ['dəʊnə] *n.* person who gives; blood d. = person who gives blood for blood transfusions.

doodle ['duːdl] *v.* to make meaningless drawings/patterns on paper.

doom 1 [duːm] *n.* (a) fate. (b) unhappy ending/ruin. **doom 2** *v.* to condemn (s.o./sth). **Doomsday** *n.* end of the world.

door [dɔː] *n.* barrier of wood/metal, etc., which closes an entrance; front d. = main door of a house; back d. = door at the back of a house; he lives two doors down the street = he lives two houses away. **doorkeeper** *n.* person who is on guard at a main door. **doorknob** *n.* round handle for opening/shutting a door. **doorman** *n.* (*pl.*-men) person who is in attendance at a door (of a restaurant/hotel, etc.). **doormat** *n.* rough carpet in front of a door. **doorstep** *n.* block of stone/wood, etc., forming the base of a doorway. **doorway** *n.* space filled by a door.

dope [dəʊp] *n.* (a) *inf.* drug. (b) strong glue/varnish for making models. (c) *inf.*

information. (d) *inf.* stupid fool. **dopey** *adj.* *inf.* stupid/silly.

dormant ['dɔːmənt] *adj.* sleeping; d. account = bank account which is not used; d. plant = plant which is not growing because it is winter; d. volcano = volcano which is not erupting, but which is not extinct.

dormer ['dɔːmə] *n.* d. (window) = window with a small gable roof jutting out from a sloping roof.

dormitory ['dɔːmɪtrɪ] *n.* long room full of beds.

dormouse ['dɔːmaʊs] *n.* (*pl.*dormice) small mouse-like animal.

dorsal ['dɔːsl] *adj.* (muscle/fin) on the back of an animal.

DOS [dɒs] disk operating system.

dose 1 [dəʊs] *n.* (a) quantity of medicine. (b) *inf.* attack of a disease. (c) *Sl.* attack of venereal disease. **dose 2** *v.* to give (s.o.) medicine. **dosage** *n.* amount of medicine to be given.

doss [dɒs] *v.* *inf.* to d. down = to sleep on a rough bed/on the ground, etc. **dosser** *n.* *inf.* tramp/vagrant. **dosshouse** *n.* *inf.* cheap lodging for vagrants.

dossier ['dɒsɪə] *n.* collection of relevant papers.

dot 1 [dɒt] *n.* small round spot; he arrived on the d. of three = exactly at three o'clock; *inf.* since the year d. = for ever. **dot 2** *v.* (dotted) to mark with small spots; dotted line = line made up of small spots; the hill side is dotted with houses = there are houses here and there on the hillside. **dot-matrix printer** *n.* computer printer which forms letters from many small dots. **dotty** *adj.* (-ier, -iest) *inf.* slightly mad.

dote [dəʊt] *v.* to d. on s.o. = to be very fond of s.o. **dotage,** *n.* feebleness of mind from old age.

dotterel ['dɒtərəl] *n.* type of field bird.

dottle ['dɒtl] *n.* mass of unburnt tobacco at the bottom of a pipe.

double 1 ['dʌbl] *adj.* (a) with two parts; d. bed = bed for two people; d. cream = thick cream which can be whipped easily; d. figures = numbers from 10 to 99; d. chin = chin with a second fold of flesh beneath. (b) twice as big a d. whisky = two measures of whisky; it takes d. the time = twice as long; it is d. the distance = twice as far. **double 2** *adv.* I am seeing d. = I can see two things when there is only one there. **double 3** *n.* (a) at the d. = at a run. (b) he is my d. = he and I look exactly alike. (c) men's/women's/mixed doubles = tennis matches for two men or two women or one man and one women on each side. **double 4** *v.* (a) to multiply by two. (b) he doubled back = he turned round and came back along the same way. (c) she was doubled up in pain = was bent forwards. **double-barrelled** *adj.* (a) (gun) with two barrels. (b) (surname) with two parts linked with a hyphen. **double bass** *n.* very large stringed musical instrument. **double breasted,** *adj.* (jacket) which overlaps in front. **double-cross** *v.* to trick (s.o.) when he thinks that you are working on his side. **double-crosser** *n.* trickster/cheat. **double dealing** *n.* trickery. **double-decker** *n.* (a) bus with an upper as well as lower deck. (b) *inf.* sandwich made with three slices of bread. **double Dutch** *n. inf.* nonsense. **double-edged** *adj* (a) with two sharp edges. (b) which has two quite different meanings. **double glazing** *n.* two panes of glass in windows, which insulate. **double-jointed** *adj.* with very flexible finger joints; very flexibly. **double-park** *v.* to park alongside a car which is already parked at the side of the street. **double-parking** *n.* parking alongside a car which is already parked at the side of the street. **double-quick** *adj. & adv.* extremely fast. **double take** *n.* second reaction which comes after a first. **double-talk** *n* words which mean sth quite different from what they seem. **doubly** *adv.* twice. **doublet** ['dʌblət] *n.* (a) tight fitting jacket. (b) word of the same origin as another word.

doubt 1 [daʊt] *n.* not being sure; to have doubts about = not to be sure; no d. = of course/certainly; in d. = uncertain. **doubt 2** *n.* not to be sure of. **doubtful** *adj.* uncertain. **doubtfully** *adv.* hesitatingly. **doubtless** *adv.* certainly. **douche** [duːʃ] *n.* spray of water to clean part of the body. **dough** [dəʊ] *n.* (a) uncooked mixture of water and flour for making bread, etc. (b)

Sl. money. **doughnut** *n.* small round or ring-shaped cake cooked by frying in oil. **doughy** *adj.* soft and wet(like uncooked dough). **doughty** ['daʊtɪ] *adj.* (poetic) brave. **dour** ['dʊə] *adj.* gloomy/silent. **dourly** *adv.* gloomily. **douse** [daʊs] *v.* to throw water on (sth). **dove** [dʌv] *n.* (a) white domesticated pigeon. (b) politician who is in favour of negotiating for peace.(c) [ ]dBLv] *v. Am.* see dive. **dovetail** *v.* (a) to join (wood) together with a V-shaped joint. (b) to fit in neatly. **dovecote** *n.* house for doves. **dowager** ['daʊədʒə] *n.* widow of a nobleman who has kept her title. **dowdy** ['daʊdɪ] *adj.* (-ier, -iest) badly dressed (person); dull/unfashionable (clothes). **dowdily** *adv.* in a dowdy way. **dowel** ['daʊəl] *n.* round wooden peg like a nail for attaching pieces of wood together. **dowelling** *n.* a piece of d. = a long round stick of wood from which dowels can be cut. **dower** ['daʊə] *n.* share of property which belongs to a widow. **down 1** [daʊn] *adv, adj. & prep.* (a) towards the bottom; he fell d. = fell to the ground; d. with examinations! = let's do away with examinations; he tried to go up the d. escalator = the one which was going downwards. (b) at the bottom; she is d. with influenza = she has gone to bed with influenza; *inf.* d. under = in Australia and New Zealand; inflation is d. again = inflation is lower again.(c) to pour d. = to rain hard. **down.2** *n.* (a) soft feathers (of a duck). (b) the downs = rounded chalk hills in the South of England. **down 3** *v.* (a) to swallow quickly. (b) to down tools = to stop work/go on strike. **down-and-out** *n.* tramp/person with no money who lives in the street. **down-at-heel** *adj.* worn/ shabby (clothes). **downcast** *adj.* gloomy/depressed. **downfall** *n.* collapse/ruin. **downgrade** *v.* to reduce the status of (s.o.). **downhearted** *adj.* depressed/gloomy. **downhill** *adv.* towards the bottom (of a hill). **download** *v.* to load data/program into a computer. **down-market** *adj.* aiming at the cheaper end of the market. **down**

payment *n.* part of a total cost paid in advance. **downpour** *n.* heavy fall of rain. **downright.1** *adj.* complete/distinct. **downright.2** *adv.* completely/distinctly. **downside** *n.* negative/pessimistic view. **downstage** *adv.* towards the front of a stage.

downstairs *adv. & n.* on/to a lower, esp, the ground floor. **downstream** *adj.& adv.* towards the mouth of a river. **down-to-earth** *adj.* straightforward/matter-of-fact (way of speaking, etc.).

downtown *adv. & n.* (in/to the) central business district of a town.

downtrodden *adj.* oppressed/badly treated. **downward** *adj.* (movement) towards the bottom. **downwards** *adv.* towards the bottom. **downy** *adj.* covered with down/with soft feathers.

Downing Street ['daʊnɪŋstriːt] *n.* residence of the British Prime Minister; *inf.* the British Government.

Down's syndrome ['daʊnz'sɪndrəʊm] *n.* congenital defect, where the patient has slanting eyes, a wide flat face, and has difficulty in speaking.

dowry ['daʊrɪ] *n.* money or goods which a bride brings to her husband.

dowse [daʊz] *v.* to look for water using a forked twig which moves above water. **dowser** *n.* person who dowses.

doyen ['dɔɪən] *n.* senior member of a group.

doyly ['dɔɪlɪ] *n.* doily.

doze 1 [daʊz] *n.* short sleep. **doze 2** *v.* to be half asleep; he dozed off = he went into a light sleep. **dozy** *adj.* sleepy.

dozen ['dʌzn] *n.* twelve; half a d. apples = six apples; dozens of people/times = many people/times.

Dr ['dɒktə] abbreviation for Doctor.

drab [dræb] *adj.* lacking bright colours; brown, grey.

drachm [dræm] *n.* small measure used in pharmacy. **drachma** ['drækmə] *n.* old unit of money used in Greece.

draconian [drəˈɒblɪnɪ] *adj.* very severe/harsh (law, etc.).

draft 1 [drɑːft] *n.* (a) rough plan of a document. (b) *Am.* obligatory military service.(c) order for money to be paid by a bank. **draft 2** *v.* (a) to draw up a rough plan of. (b) *Am.* to call (s.o.) for service; see also draught.

drag 1 [dræg] *n.* (a) long uphill climb;

Sl. what a d. ! = how boring !. (b) *Sl.* wearing of women's clothes by a man; he was in d. (c) *inf.* one puff on a cigarette. **drag 2** *v.* (dragged) (a) to pull sth heavy along. (b) to hang back/to stay behind; to go slowly.(c) to pull a net along the bottom of (a lake) to try to find sth. **dragnet** *n.* net used to drag a lake; full search for criminals. **drag on** *v.* to continue slowly. **drag out** *v.* to pull out; to make (a story) last a long time.

dragon ['drægən] *n.* mythological animal which breathes fire. **dragonfly** *n.* common insect with brilliant transparent wings.

dragoon 1 [drəˈguːn] *n.* (old) soldier on horse back. **dragoon 2** *v.* to force.

drain 1 [dreɪn] *n.* (a) pipe for carrying waste water; *inf.* it's like pouring money down the d. = it is a waste of money. (b) d. on resources = gradual loss of money; brain d. = emigration of professional people to work overseas for better pay.

drain 2 *v.* (a) to remove (a liquid). (b) to drink the contents of (a glass).

drainage *n.* system of pipes for taking away waste water. **draining** *n.* removal of excess liquid; d. board = sloping surface next to a sink for draining water off dishes. **drainpipe** *n.* pipe which takes away waste water.

drake [dreɪk] *n.* male duck.

dram [dræm] *n.* small drink (of spirits).

drama ['drɑːmə] *n.* (a) serious theatrical performance; d. department = department which deals with plays. (b) series of serious events. **dramatic** [drəˈmætɪk] *adj.* (a) referring to drama. (b) surprising; giving a shock.

dramatically *adv.* very surprisingly. **dramatics** *n. pl.* putting on plays. **dramatist** ['dræmətɪst] *n.* person who writes plays. **dramatization** [dræmətaɪˈzeɪʃn] *n.* adaptation (of a novel) for the stage/for the TV.

dramatize ['dræmətaɪz] *v.* (a) to adapt (a novel) for the stage/for the TV. (b) to make (sth) seem much more dramatic than it really is.

drank [dræŋk] *v.* see drink.

drape 1 [dreɪp] *n. Am.* drapes = curtains. **drape 2** *v.* to hang (clothes) around sth. **draper** ['dreɪpə] *n.* person who sells cloth. **drapery** *n.* (a) cloth goods. (b) thin cloth draped around s.o.

drastic ['dræstɪk] *adj.* severe/sudden.
drastically *adv.* suddenly.
draught, *Am*. draft [drɑːft] *n.* (a)
pulling; d. horse = horse trained to pull
heavy loads; beer on d. /d. beer = beer
which is pumped out of a barrel, by
hand. (b) mouthful/swallow. (c) amount
of a ship's bottom which is under water;
boat with a shallow draught = boat
which does not go very deep into water.
(d) breeze (in a room). (e) draughts =
game played with black and white
counters on a board with black and white
squares. **draughtsman** ['drɑːftsmən] *n.*
(*pl.*-men) person who draws plans.
draughtsmanship *n.* skill at
drawing. **draughty** *adj.* (-ier, -iest) full
of breezes.
draw 1 [drɔː] *n.* (a) lottery. (b)
attraction. (c) he is quick on the d. = he
pulls out his gun and shoots quickly.(d)
game where neither side wins. **draw 2**
v. (drew, drawn) (a) to make a picture
with a pen or pencil. (b) to pull; he drew
the curtains = he opened/closed the
curtains; to d. lots = take a piece of
paper/stick, etc., from a bundle, the
person taking the marked paper/stick
being the one selected; he drew a blank
= he was unsuccessful in his search (c)
to move (sth) closer, etc. (d) not to have
a winner in a game; the match was
drawn = neither side won. (e) to collect
liquid; to d. blood = to cut s.o. so that
they bleed. (f) to take (money) from an
account. **draw aside** *v.* to take(s.o.) /to
move to one side. **draw back** *v.* he
drew back the curtains = he opened the
curtains; she drew back = she moved
backwards. **drawback** *n.* inconvenient
thing; obstacle. **drawbridge** *n.* bridge
which can be raised or lowered to give
access across water. **drawer** *n.* sliding
compartment in a desk or cupboard
which you open by pulling on a handle;
chest of drawers = piece of bedroom
furniture made of several sliding
compartments. **draw in** *v.* the days are
drawing in = becoming shorter.
drawing *n.* picture done with pen or
pencil; d. pin = pin with a large flat head
for pinning paper; d. board = large board
used by designers, on which paper is laid
for drawing on; it was back to the d.
board = he had to start the project all

over again. **drawing room** *n.* sitting
room; room for sitting and talking in, but
not eating. **drawn** *adj.* looking tired.
draw out *v.* to pull (sth) out; to make
(sth) last a long time. **drawstring** *n.*
string which when pulled closes a bag.
draw up *v.* to make (a plan, etc.).
drawl 1 [drɔːl] *n.* slow way of speaking.
drawl 2 *v.* to speak slowly, dragging
the words.
drawn [drɔːn] *v.* see draw.
dray [dreɪ] *n.* low flat lorry or cart for
carrying barrels.
dread 1 [dred] *n.* great fear. **dread 2** *v.*
to fear greatly. **dreadful** *adj.* awful.
dreadfully *adv.* awfully/extremely.
dream 1 [driːm] *n.* (a) things which you
think you see happening when you are
asleep. (b) lovely thing. **dream 2** *v.* (he
dreamed/he dreamt[dremt]) to think
you see things happening while you are
asleep; I wouldn't d. of wearing pink
socks = I wouldn't ever think of wearing
pink socks. **dreamer** *n.* person who
thinks a lot/who is out of touch with
practical things. **dreamily** *adv.* as in a
dreAm. **dreamless** *adj.* without
dreams. **dream up** *v.* to invent.
dreamy *adj.* like a dream.
dreary ['drɪərɪ] *adj.* (-ier, -iest) sad/
gloomy; not interesting. **drearily** *adv.*
sadly/gloomily. **dreariness** *n.* being
dreary; dreary appearance.
dredge [dredʒ] *v.* (a) to scrape the
bottom of (a river or lake) to remove
sand or mud. (b) to sprinkle (a cake)
with sugar, etc. **dredger** *n.* (a) a
machine for removing sand or mud from
the bottom of a river or lake; boat with
such a machine in it. (b) container with
holes in the top for sprinkling (sugar,
etc.).
dregs [dregz] *n.* sediment at the bottom
of a bottle; rubbish.
drench. [drentʃ] *v.* to soak; drenched =
wet through.
dress 1 [dres] *n.* (a) a piece of
woman's/girl's clothing, covering more
or less all the body. (b) special clothes; d.
rehearsal = rehearsal where the actors
wear their costumes; d. circle = first
balcony of seats above the stalls in a
theatre; d. coat = man's formal black
coat. **dress 2** *v.* (a) to put on clothes.
(b) to clean (a wound) /to put a bandage

on (a wound). (c) to arrange a display in (a shop window). (d) to prepare (a chicken) for cooking. **dress down** v. to criticize. **dresser** n. (a) person in a theatre who helps the actors with their costumes; window d. = person who arranges displays in shop windows. (b) piece of kitchen furniture with open shelves above and cupboards below.

dressing, n. (a) putting on clothes; d. room = room for getting dressed, esp. room where an actor puts on his costume; d. gown = long robe worn over pyjamas or nightdress; d. table = bedroom table with mirrors. (b) sauce (for salad); French d. = sauce made of oil and vinegar (c) bandage (for a wound).

dressmaker n. person who makes women's clothes. **dressmaking** n. making of women's clothes by hand.

dress up v. to put on a costume.

dressy adj. very showily dressed; showy (clothes). **dressage** ['dresɑːʒ] n. training of a horse which shows how obedient it is.

drew [druː] v. see draw.

drey [dreɪ] n. squirrel's nest.

dribble ['drɪbl] v. (a) to let drops of liquid run out of your mouth. **driblets, dribs and drabs** ['drɪbləts, 'drɪbzən'dræbz] n.pl. little bits; in dribs and drabs = a little at a time.

drier ['draɪə] n. = dryer.

drift 1 [drɪft] n. (a) general direction; I got the general d. of his argument = I understood the general sense of his argument. (b) pile of snow blown by the wind. (c) North Atlantic d. = current which crosses the North Atlantic. **drift 2** v. (a) to let yourself move. (b) (of snow) to pile up. **drifter** n. person with no set plan in life/person who moves aimlessly from job to job. **driftwood,** n. (no pl.) wood which floats and blows on to the shore.

drill 1 [drɪl] n. (a) machine for making holes (in wood/metal, etc.); pneumatic d. = machine driven by compressed air for making holes in roads. (b) military practice in marching, etc.; inf. what's the d. ? = what do we do now ? fire d. = practice in reaching the life boats on a ship/practice in evacuating a building in case of fire. (c) small furrow in the ground in which you sow seeds. (d) thick cotton cloth. **drill 2** v. to make holes; he is drilling for oil = he is making holes in the ground in the hope of finding oil. (b) to do military practice.

drily ['draɪlɪ] adv. = dryly.

drink. 1 [drɪŋk] n. liquid which you swallow; alcohol; soft drinks = non alcoholic drinks; he has a d. problem = he suffers from alcoholism; he was much the worse for d. = he was drunk. **drink. 2** (drank; has drunk) to swallow (liquid); he was drinking at the bar = he was drinking alcohol at the bar; she doesn't d. = she never drinks alcohol; let's d. to the success of the expedition = let us raise our glasses and wish it success. **drinkable** adj. nice to drink. **drinker** n. person who drinks (too much alcohol). **drinking** n. action of swallowing liquid; consumption of alcohol; alcoholism; d. water = water which is safe to drink.

drip 1 [drɪp] n. (a) small drop of water. (b) (in hospital) device which allows liquid to drip regularly into the blood stream of patient. **drip.2** v. (dripped) to fall in drops; the tap is dripping = drops of water are coming out of the tap which has not been turned of tightly enough; drip-dry shirt = shirt which does not crease if hung to dry while wet.

dripping n. fat left in a pan after roasting meat.

drive 1 [draɪv] n. (a) ride in a motor vehicle. (b) way in which a car is propelled or guided; car with front wheel d. = car where the engine is connected directly to the front wheels; car with left-hand d. = car where the driver sits on the left-hand side. (c) device in a computer which spins a disk. (d) short private road leading to a house. (e) stroke (in golf or cricket) where the ball is hit hard and far. (f) energy. (g) campaign (to collect money for charity). **drive 2** v. (drove; has driven) (a) to make a motor vehicle travel in a certain direction; I will d. you to the airport = I will take you to the airport in my car. (b) to force/to push; he was driven to it = he was forced to do it; she drives a hard bargain = she is very tough business women; the pressure of work was driving her frantic = making her become frantic. (c) (in golf or cricket) to hit the ball hard and far. **drive**

along v. to ride along a road in motor vehicle. **drive at** v. what is he driving at ? = what is he trying to say ? **drive away** v. (a) to force (sth/s.o.) to go away. (b) to ride away in a motor vehicle. **driveback** v. (a) to force back. (b) to go/to come back in a motor vehicle. **drive in** v. (a) to force in. (b) to go in by car; drive-in cinema/restaurant = cinema/restaurant where you can drive-in in a car and watch a film or eat while still sitting in the car. **drive on** v. to continue one's journey. **driver** n. person who drives (a motor vehicle); Am. driver's licence = permit which allows you to drive. **driveway** n. short private road leading to a house. **driving 1** adj. (rain/snow) blown by the wind. **driving.2** n. action of driving a motor vehicle; d. test = test taken before you can have a driving licence; d. school = school where you learn to drive; d. licence = permit which allows you to drive; d. wheel = wheel which moves a part of the machinery (in a machine) /steering wheel (in a car/lorry, etc.). **drivel** ['drɪvl] n. rubbish. **driven** ['drɪvn] v. see drive. **drizzle 1** ['drɪzl] n. thin continuous rain. **drizzle 2** v. to rain in a thin mist. **drizzly** adj. (weather) where it is raining in thin mist.

drogue [drəʊg] n. (a) funnel-shaped object, made of cloth, used to be pulled behind an aircraft for target practice. (b) parachute used as a brake.

droll [drəʊl] n. funny in an odd way.

dromedary ['drɒmədəri] n. camel with only one hump.

drone 1 [drəʊn] n. (a) male bee. (b) lazy person. (c) buzz (of an inset/an engine); monotonous noise. **drone 2** v. to buzz; to talk slowly and in a monotonous voice.

drool [dru:l] v. (a) to slobber. (b) inf. to show excessive pleasure about something.

droop [dru:p] v. to hang down; his spirits drooped = he was feeling miserable.

drop.1 [drɒp] n. (a) tiny quantity of liquid which falls; the doctor has given me some drops for my eyes = liquid to be put in the eyes in small quantities. (b) small round jewel; small round sweet.

(c) fall. (d) jumping by a group of people with parachutes. **drop.2** v. (dropped) to fall; to let (sth) fall; the wind dropped = stopped blowing hard; she dropped a stitch = she let a stitch slip in her knitting; inf. d. me a line when you are in Paris = send me a short letter when you are in Paris; shall I d. you at your door ? = shall I drive you back and leave you at your door ?; he has dropped the idea of going to live in Greece = he has given up the idea; the whole project has been dropped = has been stopped; d. it = stop talking about it. **drop in** v. to call on s.o. **drop-kick** n. kick in football where you drop the ball to the ground and kick it as it is falling. **droplet** n. little drop. **drop off** v. to fall off; he dropped off = he fell asleep. **drop out** v. to stop competing; he has dropped out = he has given up his studies/has stopped living conventionally. **drop-out** n. person who has stopped studying/stopped living conventionally. **dropper** n. glass tube for putting drops in eyes, etc. **droppings** n. pl. solid waste matter from birds/animals.

dropsy ['drɒpsɪ] n. disease where liquid forms in parts of the body. **dropsical** adj. suffering from dropsy.

dross [drɒs] n. worthless rubbish.

drought [draʊt] n. long period when there is no rain/when the land is dry.

drove.1 [drəʊv] n. large number (of people/animals). **drove.2** v. see drive.

drown [draʊn] v. (a) to die by being unable to breathe in water. (b) to flood (a field). (c) to cover up (a noise).

drowse [draʊz] v. to be half asleep. **drowsily** adv. sleepily. **drowsiness** n. feeling of wanting to go to sleep. **drowsy** adj. sleepy,

drubbing ['drʌbɪŋ] n. beating.

drudge [drʌdʒ] n. person who does hard/boring work. **drudgery** n. hard/boring work.

drug 1 [drʌg] n. (a) medicine. (b) substance which affects the nerves, and which can be habit forming. **drug 2** v. (drugged) to give a drug to (s.o.); his coffee had been drugged = s.o. had put a drug in his coffee. **druggist** n. chemist. **drugstore** n. Am. chemist's shop and snack bar.

druid ['dru:ɪd] *n.* priest of the old Celtic religion.

drum 1 [drʌm] *n.* large round percussion instrument, covered with tightly stretched material and played with a stick; d. major = head of a military band. (b) large barrel; cylindrical container. **drum 2** *v.* (drummed) (a) to bang on a drum; to tap your fingers quickly on a surface. (b) to d. up support = to encourage people vigorously to give their support. (c) to d. sth into s.o. = to make s.o. learn sth by constantly repeating it. **drummer** *n.* person who plays the drums. **drumstick** *n.* (a) wooden stick for playing a drum. (b) lower part of a leg (of a cooked chicken/turkey, etc.).

drunk 1 [drʌŋk] *adj.* excited/incapable because of drinking alcohol. **drunk 2** *n.* person who is drunk. **drunkard** *n.* person who is often drunk. **drunken** *adj.* referring to an excess of alcohol. **drunkenly** *adv.* in a drunken way. **drunkenness** *n.* (habit of) being drunk. **drupe** [dru:p] *n.* fruit with a large stone (like a peach).

dry 1 [draɪ] *adj.* (drier, driest) (a) not wet; he only had d. bread to eat = bread with no butter or jam; d. land = solid land; at the end of the film there wasn't a d. eye in the house = the film made all the audience cry. (b) (of wine) not sweet. (c) (area) where alcohol is forbidden. (d) uninteresting/boring (book). (e) d. sense of humour = where you make jokes without seeming to know they are funny. **dry 2** *v.* to stop being wet; to wipe (sth) until it is dry. **dry-clean** *v.* to clean (clothes) with chemicals. **dry cleaner's** *n.* shop where clothes are dry-cleaned. **dryer** *n.* machine for drying; spin d. = machine which dries washing by spinning it round very fast. **dry-goods store** *n. Am.* draper's shop. **dry ice** *n.* solid carbon dioxide, used to produce very cold temperatures. **drying** *n.* action of making something dry; I'll do the d. = I'll dry the dishes. **dryly** *adv.* in a dry/harsh, sarcastic way. **dryness** *n.* state of being dry. **dry out** *v.* to make (sth) dry. **dry rot** *n.* disease in wood which makes the wood powdery. **dry run** *n.* practice. **dry up** *v.* to stop flowing; he dried up in the middle of his speech = he stopped talking and could not continue.

dryad ['draɪæd] *n.* mythological wood goddess.

DTP desk top publishing.

dual ['djʊəl] *adj.* double; in a pair; he has d. nationality = he is a citizen of two countries; d. carriageway = main road separated into two parts by a central grass bank or fence.

duality [djʊ'ælɪtɪ] *n.* being dual.

dub [dʌb] *v.* (dubbed) (a) to make (s.o.) a knight. (b) to add a dialogue to (a film) in another language from the original.

dubbin ['dʌbɪn] *n.* type of thick oil for making boots soft and waterproof.

dubious ['dju:bɪəs] *adj.* (a) doubtful/vague; suspicious. (b) hesitant. **dubiously** *adv.* doubtfully. **dubiousness** *n.* doubt.

duchess ['dʌtʃes] *n.* wife/widow of a duke. **duchy** *n.* land ruled by a duke.

duck 1 [dʌk] *n.* (a) common water bird; female of this bird; meat of this bird used as food; lame d. = firm/person in financial difficulties. (b) score of zero (in cricket). (c) strong cotton cloth. **duck 2** *v.* (a) to lower your head quickly (to avoid hitting sth). (b) to push (s.o.) under water. (c) to avoid (an unpleasant job). **duckboards** *n. pl.* boards placed as a path across wet ground. **ducking** *n.* he got a d. = he fell/was pushed into the water. **duckling,** *n.* baby duck. **duckweed** *n.* green weed which floats on the surface of ponds.

duct [dʌkt] *n.* tube for carrying air/liquid etc.

ductile ['dʌktaɪl] *adj.* (metal) which can be pulled out to form thin wires

dud [dʌd] *n. inf.* failure; false coin/bank note; (shell) which will not explode; d. cheque = worthless cheque.

dude [dju:d] *n. Am.* dandy; visitor to a ranch.

dudgeon ['dʌdʒən] *n.* in high d. = very indignant.

due 1 [dju:] *adj.* (a) expected; when is the baby d. = when is the baby expected to be born?. (b) (money which is) owed. (c) just/deserved; d. to = caused by. (e) in d. course = subsequently. **due 2** *adv.* the plane flew d. west = straight in a westerly direction. **due 3** *n.* what is owed/deserved; to give him his d. he works very hard = to be just to him; harbour dues = money owed to the harbour authorities for using the harbour.

duel ['djʊəl] *n.* fight between two people (with swords/guns). **duellist** *n.* person who fights a duel.

duenna [dju:'enə] *n.* elderly Spanish lady, who act as chaperone.

duet [dju:'et] *n.* piece of music played/ sung by two people.

duff 1 [dʌf] *adj. inf.* rotten/no good. **duff 2** *n.* boiled pudding. **duffer** *n. inf.* stupid person.

duffel, duffle ['dʌfl] *n.* d. coat = thick coat (often with a hood) fastened with toggles; d. bag = tubular bag which is closed by a string.

dug [dʌg] *v.* see dig. **dugout** *n.* hole in the ground, made as a shelter for soldiers; d. canoe = boat made from a tree trunk which has been hollowed out.

duke [dju:k] *n.* highest rank of a noble man.

dulcet ['dʌlsɪt] *adj.* (voice etc.) which sounds pleasant.

dulcimer ['dʌlsɪmə] *n.* musical instrument with strings hit with little hammers.

dull [dʌl] *adj.* (duller, dullest) (a) not exciting/not interesting. (b) gloomy (weather). (c) not sharp (sound). (d) not bright; gloomy (colour). (e) rather stupid. **dullard** *n.* stupid person. **dullness** *n.* (a) lack of excitement. (b) gloominess (of colour/weather). (c) boredom. (d) slowness, stupidity. **dully** *adv.* in a dull way.

duly ['dju:lɪ] *adv.* properly; as you should.

dumb [dʌm] *adj.* (a) unable to speak. (b) stupid. **dumbbell** ['dʌmbel] *n.* bar with weights on each end used by weightlifters. **dumbfound** [dʌm'faʊnd] *v.* to surprise/to flabbergast; I am dumbfounded at the news = I am astonished at the news. **dumbly** *adv.* silently/without saying anything.

dumdum ['dʌmdʌm] *n.* soft-nosed bullet which flattens out when it hits its target.

dummy ['dʌmɪ] *n.* (a) plastic teat sucked by babies. (b) false thing; d. run = practice. (c) tailors d. = model of a person used to show clothes (in a shop window). (d) stupid fool.

dump 1 [dʌmp] *n.* place to put rubbish; what a d. ! = what an awful place. **dump 2** *v.* (a) to put (sth) heavily on the ground. (b) to throw away; to get rid of. (c) to sell (surplus goods) at a very cheap price (usu. overseas).

dumpling ['dʌmplɪŋ] *n.* small ball of dough served in stew; apple dumplings = apples baked in dough.

dumps [dʌmps] *n. pl.inf.* down in the d. = miserable.

dumpy ['dʌmpɪ] *adj.* short and squat.

dun 1 [dʌn] *n.* debt collector. **dun 2** *adj.* dull brown colour. **dun 3** *v.* (dunned) to pester (a debtor) for money.

dunce [dʌns] *n.* stupid person.

dune [dju:n] *n.* sand dunes = grass-covered sandy ridges by the seashore.

dung [dʌŋ] *n.* solid waste matter (of animals).

dungarees [dʌŋgə'ri:z] *n.* overalls/ working clothes, usually of thick blue cloth, worn over ordinary clothes.

dungeon ['dʌndʒən] *n.* dark and unpleasant underground prison.

dunk [dʌŋk] *v.* to dip (biscuit, etc) into a liquid.

dunlin ['dʌnlɪn] *n.* a small shore bird.

dunno [də'nəʊ] *v. inf.* = (I) don't know.

dunnock ['dʌnək] *n.* the hedge sparrow.

duo ['dju:əʊ] *n.* two people (usu. two performers).

duodecimal [dju:əʊ'desɪml] *adj.* (system of calculating) based on the number 12.

duodenum [dju:əʊ'di:nəm] *n.* part of the intestine immediately below the stomach.

duodenal *adj.* referring to the duodenum.

dupe 1 [dju:p] *n.* person who has been tricked. **dupe 2** *v.* to trick (s.o.).

duplex ['dju:pleks] *n.* (*pl.*-es) *Am.* two family house; d. apartment = flat with rooms on two floors.

duplicate 1 ['dju:plɪkət] *n & adj.* copy/ double. **duplicate 2** ['dju:plɪkeɪt] *v.* to make a copy (of a letter, etc.); you are just duplicating his work = you are simply doing his work all over again. **duplicating** *n.* action of making a copy. **duplication** [dju:plɪ'keɪʃn] *n.* copying; repetition. **duplicator** *n.*

machine which makes copies of documents.

duplicity [djuːˈplɪsɪtɪ] *n.* dishonesty; tricking s.o.

durable [ˈdjʊərəbl] *adj.* which lasts/which does not wear away. **durability** [djʊərəˈbɪlɪtɪ] *n.* ability to last/not wear out **durably** *adv.* in a durable way.

duration [djʊˈreɪʃn] *n.* period of time for which sth lasts.

duress [djʊˈres] *n.* force/illegal threats used to make s.o. do sth.

during [ˈdjʊərɪŋ] *prep.* for the time sth lasts.

durum [ˈdjʊərəm] *n.* hard wheat used for making pasta.

dusk [dʌsk] *n.* twilight/period in the evening just before it gets dark. **dusky** *adj.* dark-skinned.

dust 1 [dʌst] *n.* thin layer of dry dirt. **dust 2** *v.* (a) to remove dust from (sth). (b) to sprinkle (sugar) on a cake.

dustbin *n.* large container for household rubbish. **dust bowl** *n.* area where the dry surface soil has been blown away. **dust cover** *n.* paper cover round a book. **duster** *n.* (a) cloth for removing dust; feather d. = brush made of feathers for removing dust. (b) *inf.* flag (on a ship) **dusting** *n.* (a) removing of dust. (b) sprinkling (of sugar, etc.). **dust jacket** *n.* paper cover round a book. **dust man** *n.* (*pl.*-men) person employed by a town to remove household rubbish. **dustpan** *n.* small wide shovel for scooping up dirt. **dust up** *n.* *inf.* quarrel. **dusty** *adj.* (-ier, -iest) covered with dust; d. answer = unsatisfactory reply.

Dutch 1 [dʌtʃ] *adj.* referring to Holland. d. courage = courage which comes from being drunk; d. treat = party where each person pays his share.

Dutch 2 *n.* (a) language spoken in Holland. (b) the Dutch = the people of Holland. (c) to go d. = to split the expenses. **Dutchman, Dutchwoman** *(pl.* -men, - women) *man/woman from Holland.* A native of Holland/the Netherlands

duty [ˈdjuːtɪ] *n.* (a) what one has to do; service; to be on d. all day; d. chemist = chemist's shop which is open on Sundays; d. officer = officer who is in charge at a particular time. (b) money

which has to be paid; d. free shop = shop at an airport/on a boat where goods can be bought free of local tax. **dutiable** *adj.* (goods) on which a customs duty must be paid. **dutiful** *adj.* (person) who does what they should do. **dutifully** *adv.* as one should.

duvet [ˈduːveɪ] *n.* bag stuffed with feathers, used as the only covering for a bed.

dwarf 1 [dwɔːf] *n.* person who is much smaller than normal; variety of plant or animal which is smaller than usual; d. beans = beans which form low bushes an do not climb. **dwarf 2** *v.* to make (sth) appear small.

dwell [dwel] *v.* (dwelled/dwelt) to live. **dweller** *n. & suffix.* person who lives (in a place). **dwelling** *n.* house. **dwell on** *v.* to refer at length to (a subject).

dwindle [ˈdwɪndl] *v.* to get less. **dwindling** *adj.* which is getting less.

dye 1 [daɪ] *n.* colour used to stain cloth; fast d. = colour which will not come out when washed. **dye 2** *v.* to stain with a colour. **dyeing** *n.* staining (of cloth).

dying [ˈdaɪɪŋ] *adj.* about to die.

dyke [daɪk] *n.* see dike.

dynamic [daɪˈnæmɪk] *adj.* energetic/forceful (person). **dynamics** *n. pl.* study of objects in movement.

dynamite 1 [ˈdaɪnəmaɪt] *n.* high explosive. **dynamite 2** *v.* to blow up with dynamite.

dynamo [ˈdaɪnəməʊ] *n.* (*pl.*-os) small electricity generator.

dynasty [ˈdɪnəstɪ] *n.* several generations of one family, esp. a family of rulers.

dysentery [ˈdɪsəntrɪ] *n.* disease of the intestines.

dysfunction [dɪsˈfʌŋʃən] *n.* abnormal functioning of an organ.

dyslexia [dɪsˈleksɪə] *n.* being dyslexic. **dyslexic** *adj.* (child) who has great difficulty in reading and writing.

dyspepsia [dɪsˈpepsɪə] *n.* inability to digest food properly. **dyspeptic** *adj.* unable to digest food properly.

dystrophy [ˈdɪstrəfɪ] *n.* muscular d. = disease causing gradual weakening of the muscles. **dystrophic** [dɪsˈtrɒfɪk] *adj.* (lake) with acid peaty water.

Ee

each 1 [iːtʃ] *adj.* every. **each 2** *pron.* every person; everything. **each 3** e. other = both of two people or things; we write to e. other.

eager ['iːgə] *adj.* very willing to do sth. **eagerly** *adv.* in an eager way. **eagerness** *n.* being eager.

eagle ['iːgl] *n.* large bird of prey. **eagle-eyed** *adj.* (person) who can see very clearly/who notices small details.

ear ['ɪə] *n.* (a) part of the head, used for hearing; middle e. = space inside the head beyond the eardrum; inner e. = space inside the head, beyond the middle ear, which controls balance and hearing. (b) sense of hearing; sense of correct tone. (c) e. of corn = head of corn seeds. **earache** ['ɪəreɪk] *n.* pain in an ear. **eardrum** *n.* tight skin inside the ear which resonates to sound waves and so allows you to hear. **earlobe** *n.* lobe on an ear. **earmark** *v.* to reserve (sth such as money) for a special purpose. **earphone** *n.* part of a pair of headphones which fits over one ear. **earring** *n.* ring attached to the earlobe as an ornament. **earshot** *n.* within e./ out of e. = near enough to be heard/too far away to be heard.

earl [ɜːl] *n.* high-ranking nobleman.

early 1 ['ɜːlɪ] *adv.* before the proper time; at the beginning of a period of time; the train left five minutes e.; e. in the afternoon. **early 2** *adj.* which happens at the beginning of a period of time; which happens before the usual time; at an e. date = soon; e. closing day = day on which shops close in the afternoon.

earn [ɜːn] *v.* to be paid money for working. **earnings** ['ɜːnɪŋz] *n. pl.* amount of money earned; salary/wages.

earnest 1 ['ɜːnɪst] *adj.* serious. **earnest 2** *n.* (a) money paid as a guarantee. (b) in e. = seriously/really. **earnestly** *adv.* seriously. **earnestness** *n.* being earnest.

earth 1 [ɜːθ] *n.* (a) planet on which we live; *inf.* It costs the e. = a great deal of money; why one e. did you say that? =

what ever made you say that?. (b) soil. (c) e. wire = electric wire which connects with the ground. (d) fox's hole; to run s.o. to e. = to find s.o. after a difficult search. **earth 2** *v.* to connect (electrical apparatus) to the ground. **earthen** ['ɜːθən] *adj.* made of clay. **earthenware** *n. & adj.* (pottery) made of clay. **earthly** *adj. inf.* he hasn't an e. (chance) = has no chance at all. **earthquake** *n.* shaking of the earth caused by a fault or underground volcanic activity. **earth-shattering** *adj. Inf.* momentous (news). **earth up** *v.* to pile earth around a growing plant. **earthworks** *n. pl.* walls of earth built as defences. **earthworm** *n.* worm/ small animal which looks like a very small snake and lives in earth. **earthy** *adj.* (-ier, -iest) coarse/rude (humour).

earwig ['ɪəwɪg] *n.* small insect with curved pincers on its tail.

ease 1 [iːz] *n.* absence of difficulty; ill at e. = nervous/uncomfortable. **ease 2** *v.* (a) to make less difficult. (b) to make easy. (c) to make less tight. **ease off** *v.* to become less. **ease up** *v.* to slow down.

easel ['iːzl] *n.* vertical frame on legs (to support a blackboard/painting etc.).

easement ['iːzmənt] *n.* right to use a path across someone else's property.

east 1 [iːst] *n.* one of the points of the compass, the direction of the rising sun; the eastern part of a country the Far E. = countries to the east of India; the Middle E. = countries to the east of Egypt and west of Pakistan; the Near E. = countries at the eastern end of the Mediterranean. **east 2** *adj.* of the east; E. Germany = German Democratic Republic; E. Anglia = eastern part of England to the north-east of London. **east 3** *adv.* towards the east. **eastbound** *adj.* going towards the east. **easterly** *adj.* (a) e. wind = wind from the east. (b) towards the east. **eastern** *adj.* of the east. **easternmost** *adj.* furthest east. **eastward** *adj.* towards the east. **eastwards** *adv.* towards the east.

Easter ['iːstə] *n.* Christian festival (in March or April); E. Day = Sunday celebrating Christ's rising from the dead; E. egg = chocolate or sugar egg eaten at Easter.

easy 1 [ˈiːzɪ] *adj.* (-ier, -iest) not difficult; the house is within e. reach of the station = is conveniently close to the station; my boss is very e. to get on with = not difficult to work for. **easy 2** *adv.* to take things e. = to rest/to do only light work; e. now! = be careful/don't get excited! Go e. on/with the jam! = don't take too much of it. **easily** *adv.* without difficulty. **easiness** *n.* state of being easy/of not being difficult. **easy chair** *n.* large comfortable armchair. **easy-going** *adj.* (person who is) easy to get on with/not very critical.

eat [iːt] *v.* (ate[ ]et]; has eaten) to chew and swallow (food); eating apple = sweet apple; I had him eating out of my hand = he did everything I told him to do; he had to e. his words = to take back what he had said. **eatable** *adj.* which can be eaten. **eatables** *n. pl.* things to eat. **eat away** *v.* (of acid) to corrode. **eater** *n.* person who eats. **eat into** *v.* to reduce gradually. **eat up** *v.* to finish eating *inf.* car that eats up petrol = car that uses a lot of petrol.

eau de Cologne [əʊdəkəˈləʊn] *n.* liquid with a light scent.

eaves [iːvz] *n. pl.* edge of a roof overhanging the wall. **eavesdrop** *v.* (eavesdropped) to listen to a conversation which you are not supposed to hear. **eavesdropper** *n.* person who eavesdrops.

ebb 1 [eb] *n.* (of tide) going down. **ebb 2** *v.* (of tide) to go down.

ebony [ˈebənɪ] *n.* black tropical wood.

ebullient [ɪˈbʌljənt] *adj.* very excited/full of life. **ebullience** *n.* high spirits.

EC [ˈiːsiː] *n.* European Community.

eccentric [ɪkˈsentrɪk] *adj.* odd (person). **eccentrically** *adv.* in an eccentric way. **eccentricity** [eksenˈtrɪsɪtɪ] *n.* being eccentric.

ecclesiastical [ɪkliːzɪæstɪkl] *adj.* belonging to the church.

ECG [ˈiːsiːˈdʒiː] electrocardiogram.

echelon [ˈeʃəlɒn] *n.* (a) arrangement of separate things in steps, and not in a straight line. (b) group of people at a certain level in an organization.

echo 1 [ˈekəʊ] *n.* (*pl.*echoes) repeated sound reverberating in a cave, etc., e. sounder = device which measures depth by using echoes from the bottom of the sea. **echo 2** *v.* (of sound) to repeat.

éclair [eɪˈkleə] *n.* long cake made of pastry, filled with cream and covered with chocolate.

eclectic [ɪˈklektɪk] *adj.* taking ideas, etc., from several different sources.

eclipse 1 [ɪˈklɪps] *n.* temporary disappearance of (part of) the sun or moon, because another body passes across them. **eclipse 2** *v.* (a) to hide (another planet) by passing in front of it. (b) to be more brilliant/successful than s.o.

ecology [ɪˈkɒlədʒɪ] *n.* study of the relationship between plants and animals and their environment. **ecological** [iːkəˈlɒdʒɪkl] *adj.* referring to ecology. **ecologist** *n.* person who studies ecology.

economy [ɪˈkɒnəmɪ] *n.* (a) saving (of money or resources); e. pack = cheaper packet of goods. (b) way in which a country makes money; financial state of a country. **economic** [iːkəˈnɒmɪk] *adj.* referring to economy. **economical** *adj.* which saves money or resources. **economically** *adv.* without waste. **economics** *n.* (a) study of the finance of industry/of a country. (b) financial structure. **economist** [ɪˈkɒnəmɪst] *n.* person who specializes in the study of finance. **economize** *v.* to e. (on) = to save/not to waste.

ecru [eɪˈkruː] *n.* pale fawn colour.

ecstasy [ˈekstəsɪ] *n.* great happiness. **ecstatic** [ɪkˈstætɪk] *adj.* very happy. **ecstatically** *adv.* extremely happy.

ECT [iːsiːˈtiː] electroconvulsive therapy.

ectoplasm [ˈektəʊplæzəm] *n.* substance said to come from the body of a person in a trance.

ECU [ˈekjuː] European Currency Unit.

ecumenical [iːkjuːˈmenɪkl] *adj.* referring to Christian unity/concerned with joining together all Christian groups.

eczema [ˈeksɪmə] *n.* skin disease which causes itchy red spots.

eddy 1 [ˈedɪ] *n.* small swirl of water (in a stream). **eddy 2** *v.* to swirl around.

edelweiss [ˈeɪdəlvaɪs] *n.* alpine plant with white flowers.

edge 1 [edʒ] *n.* (a) (sharp) side of flat object; the violin set my teeth on e. = made me shudder; on e. = nervous/

jumpy. (b) sharpened side of a knife/axe, etc. (c) point at the outside of sth; a house at the e. of the forest. **edge 2** v. (a) to creep sideways. (b) to put along the edge; a dress edged with silk.

edgeways, edgewise adv. sideways.

edging n. material used to edge with.

edgy adj. nervous/jumpy.

edible ['edɪbl] adj. which can be safely eaten.

edict [iːdɪkt] n. official order.

edifice ['edɪfɪs] n. large building.

edify ['edɪfaɪ] v. (formal) to instruct and improve (s.o.). **edification** [edɪfɪ'keɪʃn] n. instruction and improvement.

edit ['edɪt] v. to make notes on (a text); to change (a text) to make it more acceptable; to prepare (a text) for publication; to cut up (a film/tape) and stick it together in correct order to make it ready to be shown/played. **edition** [ɪ'dɪʃn] n. (a) number of books/papers printed at the same time; first e. = copy of the first printing of a book. (b) form in which a book is published. **editor** n. (a) person who makes notes on a text/ who prepares a text for publication. (b) director of a newspaper or part of a newspaper; the sports e. (c) computer program for editing text. **editorial 1** [edɪ'tɔːrɪəl] adj. referring to editors/to editing. **editorial 2** n. leading article written by the editor of a newspaper.

educate ['edjʊkeɪt] v. to teach/to instruct (s.o.); an educated person = person who is cultivated. **education** n. (system of) teaching/being taught; adult e. = teaching of adults; further e. = teaching people who have left school.

educational adj. referring to education/teaching/schools; e. publisher = publisher who produces school books.

educationist n. person who specializes in the study of teaching methods.

Edwardian [ed'wɔːdjən] adj. referring to the time of Edward VII (1901 - 1910).

EEC [iːiːˈsiː] n. European Economic Community.

eel [iːl] n. long thin fish like a snake.

eerie ['ɪərɪ] adj. (eerier, eeriest) frightening/weird. **eerily** adv. in an eerie way. **eeriness** n. being eerie.

efface [ɪ'feɪs] v. to rub out. **effacement** n. rubbing out.

effect 1 [ɪ'fekt] n. (a) result/influence; this rule takes e./comes into e. from November 1st = starts to be applied. (b) meaning; words to that e. = words with that meaning. (c) (in theatre/film/on radio) sound effects = artificial or reproduced sounds (such as thunder, horses, creaking doors).

effect 2 v. to produce/to carry out.

effective adj. (a) which produces a (good) result. (b) which takes effect; a rule e. from November 1st.

effectively adv. in a way which produces a good result.

effectual adj. (formal) which produces the intended effect. **effectually** adv. in an effectual way. **effectuate** v. to carry out (sth) effectively.

effeminate [ɪ'femɪnət] adj. (of man) behaving in a feminine way. **effeminacy** n. being effeminate.

effervesce [efə'ves] v. (of liquid) to make bubbles giving off gas.

effervescence n. bubbles in liquid; act of making bubbles. **effervescent** adj. which bubbles.

effete [e'fiːt] adj. weak/with no strength left.

efficacious [efɪ'keɪʃəs] adj. (medicine, etc.) which produces the correct result.

efficacy ['efɪkəsɪ] n. being effective; power to produce the correct result.

efficiency [ɪ'fɪʃənsɪ] n. ability to produce the required result; business e. = ability to work effectively in business.

efficient adj. able to work well/to produce the required result. **efficiently** adv. in an efficient way.

effigy ['efɪdʒɪ] n. statue/model of s.o.

effluent ['efluənt] n. sewage; liquid waste (from a factory). **effluvium** n. hidden liquid which has a strong unpleasant smell.

effort ['efət] n. use of physical energy. **effortless** adj. without apparently using any energy.

effrontery [ɪ'frʌntərɪ] n. rudeness.

effusive [ɪ'fjuːsɪv] adj. too enthusiastic (in thanks). **effusively** adv. very enthusiastically.

e.g. [iːdʒiː] abbreviation for exempli gratia, meaning for example.

egalitarian [ɪgælɪ'teərɪən] adj. & n. (person) who believes in equality for everyone.

egg 1 [eg] *n.* (a) ovum produced by a female animal. (b) hard-shelled cell, produced by a bird, esp. that of a hen.

egg 2 *v.* to e. s.o. on = to encourage s.o. to do sth. **eggcup** *n.* holder for a boiled egg. **egghead** *n. inf.* clever person. **eggplant** *n.* aubergine/purple fruit eaten as vegetable. **eggshell** *n.* shell around an egg; e. finish = slightly shiny matt finish to paintwork.

eggtimer *n.* device for timing how long an egg is boiled.

ego ['i:gəʊ] *n.* yourself; high opinion of yourself; e. trip = action which boosts your opinion of yourself. **egocentric** [egəʊ'sentrɪk] *adj.* thinking only about yourself. **egoism** ['egəʊɪzəm] *n.* thinking about oneself. **egoist** *n.* person who only thinks of himself.

egotism ['egəʊtɪzəm] *n.* talking only about oneself. **egotist** *n.* person who only talks about himself. **egotistic(al)** [egəʊ'tɪstɪk(l)] *adj.* conceited.

egregious [ɪ'gri:dʒəs] *adv.* very bad; shocking.

egret ['i:grət] *n.* type of heron with beautiful white tail feathers.

Egyptian 1 [ɪ'dʒɪpʃn] *adj.* referring to Egypt. **Egyptian 2** *n.* person from Egypt.

eh [eɪ] inter showing surprise/enquiry.

eider ['aɪdə] *n.* type of duck.

eiderdown ['aɪdədaʊn] *n.* bed covering made of a large bag full of feathers.

eight [eɪt] (a) number 8 he is e. (years old); come to see us at e. (o' clock). (b) eight people (the crew of a rowing boat). Eighteen, number 18; the e. hundreds = the years between 1800 and 1899.

eighteenth, 18th *adj. & n..* referring to eighteen; the e. century = period from 1700 to 1799. **eighth, 8th** *adj. & n.* referring to eight. **eightieth, 80th** *adj. & n.* referring to eighty. **eighty** number 80.

Eire ['eərə] *n.* Irish Republic.

eisteddfod [aɪ'stedfəd] *n.* Welsh literary and musical competition.

either 1 ['aɪðə. 'i:ðə] *adj. & pron.* (a) one or the other; there are trees on e. side of our house. **either 2** *conj. & adv.* (showing choice) e. you come here or I go to you; (emphatic) he isn't French and he isn't English e.

ejaculate [ɪ'dʒækjʊleɪt] *v.* (a) (formal) to exclaim/to say (sth) suddenly. (b) (of male) to produce sperm. **ejaculation** [ɪdʒækjʊ'leɪʃn] *n.* act of ejaculating sperm which has been ejaculated.

eject [ɪ'dʒekt] *v.* to throw out. **ejector seat** *n.* seat in an aircraft which throws the pilot out in an emergency.

eke [i:k] *v.* to e. out = to economize (savings) /to try not to use up (resources).

elaborate 1 [ɪ'læbərət] *adj.* very detailed; very complicated. **elaborate 2** *v.* to go into details. **elaboration** [ɪlæbə'reɪʃn] *n.* being elaborate; detailed explanation. **elaborately** *adv.* in a complicated/detailed way.

eland ['i:lənd] *n.* large S. African antelope.

elapse [ɪ'læps] *v.* (of time) to pass.

elastic 1 [ɪ'læstɪk] *adj.* which stretches and contracts; not rigid e. band = loop of rubber for holding papers, etc., to gather. **elastic 2** *n.* piece of rubber which can stretch.

elasticate *v.* to fit with elastic. **elasticity** [ɪlæ'stɪsɪtɪ] *n.* ability to stretch.

elated [ɪ'leɪtɪd] *adj.* very excited and pleased. **elation** [ɪ'leɪʃn] *n.* feeling of excitement and pleasure.

elbow ['elbəʊ] *n.* joint in the arm. **elbowroom** *n.* space to move about.

elder 1 ['eldə] *adj.* older (person) e. statesman = statesman who is older (and wiser) than others. **elder 2** *n.* (a) older person. (b) common tree with white flowers and bunches of small purple berries. **elderberry** *n.* (a) elder tree. (b) fruit of an elder. **elderly** *adj.* quite old. **eldest** *adj.* oldest (of a group).

El Dorado [eldə'rɑːdəʊ] *n.* legendary country of gold.

elect 1 [ɪ'lekt] *v.* (a) to choose by voting. (b) to e. to do sth = to choose to do sth. **elect 2** suffix showing person who has been elected to a post, but who has not taken it up officially; the mayor-elect. **election** [ɪ'lekʃn] *n.* process of choosing by voting; general e. = election for the national Parliament.

electioneering *n.* working for an election campaign. **elective** *adj.* which can be chosen. **elector** *n.* person who is qualified to vote in an election. **electoral** *adj.* referring to an election; e. college = group of people elected to elect s.o. (such as a president); e. roll/register = list of people who are qualified to vote in a certain area. **electorate** *n.* all the people in a country who are qualified to vote. **electric** [ɪ'lektrɪk] *adj.* (a) generating/worked by electricity. (b) the atmosphere, was e. = full of excitement. **electrical** *adj.* referring to electricity. **electrically** *adj.* by electricity. **electric chair** *n.* chair used to execute criminals by passing a strong electric current through their bodies. **electrician** [elek'trɪʃn] *n.* person who works on electrical maintenance. **electricity** [elek'trɪsɪtɪ] *n.* form of energy used for power. **electrification** [ɪlektrɪfɪ'keɪʃn] *n.* changing to an electric source of power. **electrify** [ɪ'lektrɪfaɪ] *v.* (a) to convert to an electric source of power. (b) to startle and excite. **electrocardiogram** *n.* chart made by an electrocardiograph. **electrocardiograph** *n.* device for recording the electric impulses made by a beating heart. **electroconvulsive therapy** *n.* treatment of mental disorders by giving the patient small electric shocks. **electrocute** *v.* to kill by electricity. **electrocution** [ɪlektrə'kjuːʃn] *n.* killing by electricity. **electrode** *n.* rod which leads the electric current into or out of a cell. **electroencephalogram** *n.* chart made by an electroencephalograph. **electroencephalograph** *n.* device for recording the electric impulses made by the brain. **electrolysis** [ɪlek'trɒlɪsɪs] *n.* (a) separation of the parts of a compound liquid by passing an electric current through it. (b) removal of unwanted hair by electric current. **electrolyte** [ɪ'lektrəlaɪt] *n.* chemical solution which can be broken into its parts by electrolysis. **electromagnet** *n.* magnet made of material wound with a coil of wire with an electric current passing through it. **electromagnetic** *adj.* made by an electromagnet. **electromotive** *adj.* (force) which produces an electric current.

electron *n.* basic particle in an atom. **electronic** *adj.* referring to electrons or electronics. **electronically** *adv.* in an electronic way. **electronics** *n.* science of conduction of electrons; industry which makes TV sets/radios/calculators, etc. **electroplate** *v.* to coat (a metal *usu.* copper), with a thin layer of silver by means of electrolysis. **eleemosynary** [eliːməʊ'saɪnəri] *adj.* referring to charity. **elegant** ['elɪgənt] *adj.* well dressed; very fashionable. **elegance** *n.* being elegant. **elegantly** *adv.* fashionably. **elegy** ['eladʒɪ] *n.* sad poem about s.o. who is dead. **elegiac** [elɪ'dʒaɪək] *adj.* sad and regretful. **element** ['elɪmənt] *n.* (a) basic chemical substance. (b) basic part (of sth). (c) natural environment; he's in his e. when he's talking about gardening. (d) the elements = bad weather (wind/rain, etc.). (e) wire which heats in an electric heater/cooker, etc. **elementary** [elɪ'mentrɪ] *adj.* basic/simple; e. mathematics. **elephant** ['elɪfənt] *n.* very large African or Indian animal, with a trunk and tusks; white e. = expensive but useless thing. **elephantiasis** [elɪfən'taɪəsɪs] *n.* tropical disease where parts of the body become huge. **elephantine** [elɪ'fæntaɪn] *adj.* very large, heavy and difficult to move. **elevate** ['elɪveɪt] *v.* to raise up. **elevation** [elɪ'veɪʃn] *n.* (a) raising.(b) (drawing of) one side of a building. (c) height (above sea-level) **elevator** *n.* (a) device for lifting goods (Am. or people) inside a building; grain e. = large building for hoisting and storing grain. (b) part of the tail of an aircraft. **eleven** [ɪ'levn] *adj. & n.* (a) number 11. be arrived at (0'clock); he is e. (years old). (b) eleven people (as in a sports team). the England e. **elevenses** *n.* *pl.*inf. snack eaten in the mid-morning. **eleventh, 11th** *adj. & n.* referring to eleven; at the e. hour = at the last minute. the e. century = period from 1000 to 1099. **elf** [elf] *n.* (*pl.*elves[ ]xxxx]) small, *usu.* male, supernatural being. **elfin** *adj.* referring to elves.

elicit [ɪ'lɪsɪt] v. to obtain (information) (from s.o.).

elide [ɪ'laɪd] v. to omit a sound when speaking. **elision** [ɪ'lɪʒn] n. omitting of a sound.

eligible ['elɪdʒɪbl] adj. able to be chosen (for the sth); e. bachelor = man who has all the qualifications (esp. money) to be married. **eligibility** [elɪdʒə'bɪlɪtɪ] n. being eligible.

eliminate [ɪ'lɪmɪneɪt] v. to remove (waste, etc.). (b) to exclude (s.o.) after a test. **elimination** [ɪlɪmɪ'neɪʃn] n. act of eliminating. **eliminator** n. game, etc. which decides who is eliminated.

élite [eɪ'liːt] n. group of privileged people/the best people. **elitism** n. rule by an elite.

elixir [ɪ'lɪksə] n. medicine which people imagine will cure everything.

Elizabethan [elɪzə'biːθən] adj. referring to the time of Elizabeth I.

elk [elk] n. (pl.elk) large European deer with flat antlers.

ellipse [ɪ'lɪps] n. oval shape. **ellipsis** n. absence of a word which is needed to complete the meaning of a phrase. **elliptic(al)** adj. (a) oval. (b) difficult to understand because of a missing word or phrase.

elm [elm] n. large deciduous tree; Dutch e. disease = disease which kills elms.

elocution [elə'kjuːʃn] n. clear and elegant way of speaking.

elongate ['iːlɒŋgeɪt] v. to stretch out to make longer. **elongation** [iːɪɒŋ'geɪʃn] n. act of elongating.

elope [ɪ'ləʊp] v. to run away from home to get married (with s.o.) **elopement** n. act of eloping.

eloquence ['eləkwəns] n. art of speaking well. **eloquent** adj. good and persuasive (speech). **eloquently** adv. in an eloquent way.

else [els] adv. (a) otherwise come in or e. stay out; you had better pay, or e. = or I will force you to pay. (b) when anyone e. = any other person; nobody e. = no other person; anything e. = any other thing; nowhere e. = no other place; somewhere e. Am. some place e. = in some other place. **elsewhere** adv. somewhere else; in other places.

elucidate [ɪ'luːsɪdeɪt] v. to make clear/ to make easy to understand.

elucidation [ɪluːsɪ'deɪʃn] n. making clear.

elude [ɪ'luːd] v. to escape/to avoid (capture). **elusion** n. act of eluding.

elusive [ɪ'luːsɪv] adj. difficult to find.

elver ['elvə] n. baby eel.

em [em] n. space in printing equal to the width of the letter 'm'.

emaciated [ɪ'meɪsɪeɪtɪd] adj. extremely thin. **emaciation** n. being emaciated.

email ['iːmeɪl] n. electronic mail, a system of sending messages from one computer to another, using telephone lines.

emanate ['eməneɪt] v. to come from. **emanation** n. thing which comes.

emancipate [ɪ'mænsɪpeɪt] v. to make (s.o.) free. **emancipation** [ɪmænsɪ'peɪʃn] n. setting free.

emasculate [ɪ'mæskjʊleɪt] v. to make feeble. **emasculation** [ɪmæskjʊ'leɪʃn] n. making feeble.

embalm [ɪm'bɑːm] v. to treat (a dead body) with chemicals to prevent it from decaying.

embankment [ɪm'bæŋkmənt] n. artificial bank (along a river); road along such a bank.

embargo 1 [ɪm'bɑːgəʊ] n. (pl.-oes) official prohibition(on goods/traffic/ information). **embargo 2** v. to prohibit (sth) officially.

embark [ɪm'bɑːk] v. 1. to go on board a ship; the passengers embarked at Southampton. 2. to e. on sth = to start doing sth. **embarkation** [embɑː'keɪʃn] n. act of going on board a ship or aircraft.

embarrass [ɪm'bærəs] v. to make (s.o.) feel uncomfortable (by rudeness/indecency, etc.) **embarrassment** n. act of making s.o. feel uncomfortable.

embassy ['embəsɪ] n. home or offices of an ambassador.

embattled [ɪm'bætld] adj. under attack; constantly criticized.

embed [ɪm'bed] v. (embedded) to fix (sth) into a mass of concrete/flesh, etc.

embellish [ɪm'belɪʃ] v. to decorate/to make beautiful. **embellishments** n. pl.decorations/beautiful improvements.

embers ['embəz] n. pl.pieces of wood/ coal which are red hot.

embezzle [ɪm'bezl] v. to steal (money which you are looking after for s.o.).
embezzlement n. act of embezzling.
embezzler n. person who embezzles.
embittered [ɪm'bɪtəd] adj. (of person) made angry and sad (by disappointment/ envy).
emblem ['embləm] n. design which is adopted as the characteristic of a country/team/town, etc. **emblematic** [emblə'mætɪk] adj. which acts as an emblem.
embody [ɪm'bɒdɪ] v. to show (an idea) in a physical form. **embodiment** n. physical expression of an idea.
embolism ['embəlɪzəm] n. blocking of a blood vessel by a blood clot or a bubble of air.
emboss [ɪm'bɒs] v. to raise (a design) above a flat surface; embossed letterhead = address pressed on writing paper so that it stands above the surface.
embrace [ɪm'breɪs] v. (a) to hold and kiss (s.o.) as a gesture of affection. (b) to become a convert to (a belief).
embrocation [embrə'keɪʃn] n. liquid which you rub into parts of the body which are stiff.
embroider [ɪm'brɔɪdə] v. to make artistic patterns by sewing with coloured threads. **embroidery** n. art of sewing flower designs/patterns.
embroil [em'brɔɪl] v. to involve (s.o.) in a quarrel.
embryo ['embrɪəʊ] n. (pl.-os) earliest state of living organism; rudimentary idea. **embryology** n. study of embryos. **embryonic** [embrɪ'ɒnɪk] adj. original/in a very early state.
emend [i:'mend] v. to change/to make correct. **emendation** [i:men'deɪʃn] n. change/correction.
emerald ['emrəld] adj. & n. green precious stone; colour of this stone.
emerge [ɪ'mɜːdʒ] v. to come out (from inside sth); to become apparent/known. **emergence** n. act of emerging. **emergent** adj. e. nations = countries which are slowly becoming economically independent.
emergency [ɪ'mɜːdʒənsɪ] n. dangerous state where decisions have to be taken quickly (such as fire/ accident/breakdown of law and order), state of e. = when normal administrative processes are taken over by the police or armed forces; e. exit = door used when a fire breaks out; e. operation = operation carried out at short notice because the patient is seriously ill; e. services = the police, fire and ambulance services.
emeritus [ɪ'merɪtəs] adj. (professor) who has retired but keeps his title.
emery ['emərɪ] n. fine crystals used for polishing. **emery board** n. thin stick of cardboard covered with fine crystals, used for filing fingernails. **emery paper** n. fine sandpaper.
emetic [ɪ'metɪk] n. substance which makes you vomit.
emigrate ['emɪgreɪt] v. to leave a country to live in another. **emigrant** n. person who emigrates. **emigration** [emɪ'greɪʃn] n. act of leaving a country to live in another. **emigré** ['emɪgreɪ] n. person who has emigrated for political reasons.
eminence ['emɪnəns] n. high place; high rank. **eminent** ['emɪnənt] adj. very highly respected because of position or work. **eminently** adv. remarkably, particularly.
emir ['emɪə] n. Muslim ruler. **emirate** n. country ruled by an emir.
emissary ['emɪsərɪ] n. person sent to negotiate on s.o.'s behalf.
emit [ɪ'mɪt] v. (emitted) to send out (a sound/smoke, etc.). **emission** n. act of emitting; thing emitted.
emollient [ɪ'mɒlɪənt] adj. & n. (substance) which softens.
emolument [ɪ'mɒljʊmənt] n. (formal) payment/salary.
emotion [ɪ'məʊʃn] n. (strong) feeling. **emotional** adj. showing emotion. **emotionally** adv. in an emotional way. **emotive** adj. which is likely to cause strong feeling.
empanel [ɪm'pænəl] v. to chose (a jury).
empathy ['empəθɪ] n. being able to share the feelings of another person, by imagining yourself as that person.
emperor ['emprə] n. ruler of an empire.
emphasize ['emfəsaɪz] v. to stress the importance of (sth). **emphasis** ['emfəsɪs] n. stress (usu. in speech). **emphatic** [ɪm'fætɪk] adj. using

emphasis. emphatically *adv.* in a forceful way.

empire ['empaɪə] *n.* large territories ruled by a central government.

empirical [em'pɪrɪkl] *adj.* based on practical experiment and not on theory.

emplacement [ɪm'pleɪsmənt] *n.* place where guns are set.

employ [ɪm'plɔɪ] *v.* (a) to give (s.o.) regular work. (b) to use. **employee** [emplɔɪ'i:] *n.* person who is employed. **employer** *n.* person who gives work to people and pays them. **employment** *n.* regular paid work.

emporium [ɪm'pɔ:rɪəm] *n.* large shop.

empower [ɪm'paʊə] *v.* to give (s.o.) the authority to do sth.

empress ['emprəs] *n.* woman ruler of an empire; wife/widow of an emperor.

empty 1 ['emtɪ] *adj.* with nothing inside. **empty 2** *n.* thing, *usu.* bottle, which has nothing in it. **empty 3** *v.* to make (sth) empty; to remove (the contents) from sth. **emptiness** *n.* being empty. **empty-handed** *adj.* with no results; having received nothing.

EMS [i:em'es] European Monetary System.

emu ['i:mju:] *n.* large Australian bird which cannot fly.

EMU [i:em'ju:] European Monetary Union.

emulate ['emjʊleɪt] *v.* to try to do as well as or better than (s.o.). **emulation** [emjʊ'leɪʃn] *n.* act of emulating.

emulsion [ɪ'mʌlʃn] *n.* mixture of two liquids which do not unite completely such as oil and water; e. paint = paint made of colour added to an emulsion of oil and water. **emulsifier** *n.* thing which emulsifies. **emulsify** *v.* to make into an emulsion.

en [en] *n.* space in printing equal to the width of the letter 'n'.

enable [ɪ'neɪbl] *v.* to make it possible for s.o. to do sth.

enact [ɪ'nækt] *v.* to make (a law). **enactment** *n.* making (of a law).

enamel 1 [ɪ'næml] *n.* (a) very hard covering of colour. (b) hard coloured coating fixed to metal by heating. (c) hard coating on the teeth. **enamel 2** *v.* (enamelled) to cover with very hard colour.

enamoured [ɪ'næməd] *adj.* I'm not e. of her hair style = I don't like it very much.

en bloc [ɒŋ'blɒk] *adv.* all together as a group.

encamped [ɪn'kæmpd] *adj.* in a camp. **encampment** *n.* large camp.

encapsulate [ɪn'kæpsjʊleɪt] *v.* to put in a capsule; to put in a capsule; to put in a shortened form.

encase [ɪn'keɪs] *v.* to surround as if in a case.

enchant [ɪn'tʃɑ:nt] *v.* to charm. **enchanting** *adj.* very beautiful/ magical. **enchantment** *n.* magic spell.

encircle [ɪn'sɜ:kl] *v.* to surround completely.

enclave ['enkleɪv] *n.* small group/small area completely surrounded by another quite different and larger group/mass.

enclose [ɪn'kləʊz] *v.* to put (an object) inside sth; I am enclosing a bill with my letter. **enclosure** [ɪn'kləʊʒə] *n.* (a) fenced area for keeping animals. (b) paper enclosed with a letter in an envelope.

encode [en'kəʊd] *v.* to put data/a message into code.

encomium [ɪn'kəʊmɪəm] *n.* (formal) praise.

encompass [ɪn'kʌmpəs] *v.* to surround.

encore 1 ['ɒŋkɔ:] *n.* (a) calling (by the audience) for a performer to repeat a song, a piece of music. (b) song/piece of music repeated at the request of the audience. **encore 2** *v.* to call for a song, etc., to be repeated.

encounter 1 [ɪn'kaʊntə] *n.* (a) meeting. (b) short conflict. **encounter 2** *v.* to meet.

encourage [ɪn'kʌrɪdʒ] *v.* to give (s.o.) the confidence to do sth. **encouragement** *n.* giving s.o. the confidence to do sth. **encouraging** *adj.* which encourages.

encroach [ɪn'krəʊtʃ] *v.* to e. on = to occupy space belonging to s.o. else. **encroachment** *n.* act of encroaching.

encrust [ɪn'krʌst] *v.* to cover with a hard covering.

encumber [ɪn'kʌmbə] *v.* (formal) to weigh down (s.o.) with sth. **encumbrance** *n.* thing which encumbers.

encyclical [ɪn'sɪklɪkl] *n.* solemn letter from the Pope.

encyclopaedia, encyclopedia
[ɪnsaɪklə'piːdɪə] *n.* reference book which gives facts about things/people/events, etc. **encyclopaedic, encyclopedic** *adj.* like an encyclopaedia.

end 1 [end] *n.* (a) final part; *inf.* no e. of = very many; to throw s.o. in at the deep e. = to give s.o. a difficult job to start with; to be at a loose e. = to have nothing to do; to make ends meet = to have enough money to live on; big e. = end of the rod in a car engine which connects the piston to the camshaft. (b) final part of a period of time. (c) aim; to this e. = in order to do this. **end 2** *v.* to finish. **endgame** *n.* way of playing the last moves in chess game. **ending** *n.* way a story, etc., finishes. **endless** *adj.* with no apparent end. **endlessly** *adv.* with no apparent end. **endpapers** *n.* pages (usually left blank) at the beginning and end of a book. **endways** *adv.* with the end first.

endanger [ɪn'deɪndʒə] *v.* to put in danger.

endear [ɪn'dɪə] *v.* to e. s.o. to s.o. = to make s.o. loved by s.o. **endearment** *n.* term of e. = word showing that you love.

endeavour, *Am.* **endeavor 1** [ɪn'devə] *n.* (formal) attempt.
endeavour 2 *v.* (formal) to try hard.

endemic [en'demɪk] *adj.* (disease) which is often found in a particular place.

endive ['endɪv] *n.* salad vegetable with curly leaves.

endocardium [endəʊ'kɑːdɪəm] *n.* membrane lining the heart.

endocrine ['endəkraɪn] *adj.* e. gland = gland which makes hormones and passes them directly into the blood stream without using ducts.

endorse [ɪn'dɔːs] *v.* (a) to show approval; to e. a cheque = to sign it on the back to show it is yours. (b) his driving licence was endorsed = had a note attached to show he had been found guilty of a traffic offence. **endorsement** *n.* (a) approval. (b) note which endorses a driving licence.

endow [ɪn'daʊ] *v.* (a) to give a regular income to (a school/hospital, etc.). (b) endowed with = having (naturally) certain qualities. **endowment** *n.* (a) giving of money (to a school, etc.) to

provide a regular income. (b) e. policy = type of insurance policy where a sum of money is paid to be insured person on a certain date, or to his heirs if he dies.

endure [ɪn'djʊə] *v.* (a) to suffer. (b) to stay/to last. **endurable** *adj.* which can be endured. **endurance** *n.* ability to suffer hardship; e. test = test of a machine/person to see if it/he works well under bad conditions.

enema ['enɪmə] *n.* liquid medicine put into the rectum with a syringe.

enemy ['enəmɪ] *n.* opponent (in war).

energy ['enədʒɪ] *n.* force/strength; atomic e. = power from atomic reactions. **energetic** [enə'dʒetɪk] *adj.* using force; lively. **energetically** *adv.* using much force. **energize** *v.* to make (sth) vigorous.

enervate ['enəveɪt] *v.* to make (s.o.) lazy/sluggish.

enfeeble [ɪn'fiːbl] *v.* to make (s.o.) feeble.

enfold [ɪn'fəʊld] *v.* to wrap (sth) up in sth.

enforce [ɪn'fɔːs] *v.* to make sure (a law) is obeyed. **enforceable** *adj.* which can be enforced. **enforcement** *n.* act of enforcing.

enfranchise [ɪn'fræntʃaɪz] *v.* to give (s.o.) the right to vote in elections.

engage [ɪn'geɪdʒ] *v.* (a) to attach together (legally) to employ (new staff). (b) to make parts of a machine fit into each other; e. first gear = put your car into first gear. (c) to be occupied (in doing sth). (d) to attack (the enemy). **engaged** *adj.* (a) having officially stated one's intention to marry. (b) busy; occupied. **engagement** *n.* (a) appointment. (b) statement of intention to marry. e. ring = ring given by man to woman when they agree to marry. (c) battle. **engaging** *adj.* charming.

engender [ɪn'dʒendə] *v.* (formal) to produce.

engine ['endʒɪn] *n.* (a) machine/large motor which produces power. (b) locomotive/vehicle for pulling trains. **engined** *adj.* with an engine. single engined aircraft. **engine-driver** *n.* person who drives a locomotive.

engineer 1 [endʒɪ'nɪə] *n.* (a) person who looks after technical equipment. esp. engines. (b) in army) soldier who specializes in construction of bridges/

defences, etc.; civil e. = person who specializes in construction of roads/bridges etc. (c) *Am.* person who drives a locomotive. **engineer 2** *v.* to arrange (sth) by plotting. **engineering** *n.* science/study of technical equipment; civil e. = science of construction (esp. of roads/bridges, etc.).

English 1 ['ɪŋglɪʃ] *adj.* referring to England; I think he is E. although he speaks with an American accent.

English 2 *n.* (a) the E. = the people of England. (b) language of England, the USA, Australia and many other countries can you speak E.? what is that in E.? what's the E. for 'pommes frites'? Englishman, Englishwoman, n (*pl.*-men, - women) person from England.

engrave [ɪn'greɪv] *v.* to cut (a pattern/a letter) on to a hard surface. **engraver** *n.* artist who engraves. **engraving** *n.* picture printed from an engraved plate.

engross [ɪn'grəʊs] *v.* to draw up a legal document in its final form. **engrossed** [ɪn'grəʊst] *adj.* e. in = very interested/busy in.

engulf [ɪn'gʌlf] *v.* to swallow up.

enhance [ɪn'hɑːns] *v.* to increase (beauty/value). **enhancement** *n.* increase in value etc.).

enigma [ɪ'nɪgmə] *n.* mystery/puzzle. **enigmatic** [enɪg'mætɪk] *adj.* difficult to explain/difficult to understand.

enjoin [ɪn'dʒɔɪn] *v.* (formal) to command.

enjoy [ɪn'dʒɔɪ] *v.* to take pleasure in (sth) to e. yourself = to have a good time. **enjoyable** *adj.* pleasing **enjoyment** *n.* pleasure

enlarge [ɪn'lɑːdʒ] *v.* (a) to make bigger. (b) to e. upon = to give more details about. **enlargement** *n.* bigger photograph (than the original negative). **enlarger** *n.* device for enlarging photographs.

enlighten [ɪn'laɪtn] *v.* to e. s.o. on/ about sth = to give s.o. a clear picture of sth. **enlightened** *adj.* free of prejudice; holding approved ideas. **enlightenment** *n.* knowledge/absence of ignorance, the Enlightenment period in the 18th century when many scientific discoveries were made.

enlist [ɪn'lɪst] *v.* (a) (of soldier) to join the armed forces. (b) to e. s.o.'s help = to

get help from s.o. **enlistment** *n.* joining the armed forces.

enliven [ɪn'laɪvn] *v.* to make more lively.

en masse [ɒn'mæs] *adv.* all together in a crowd.

enmity ['enmɪtɪ] *n.* hatred towards s.o.

ennoble [ɪ'nəʊbl] *v.* to make (s.o.) a peer.

enormous [ɪ'nɔːməs] *adj.* very large. **enormity** *n.* seriousness (of a crime). **enormously** *adv.* very much.

enough 1 [ɪ'nʌf] *adj.* sufficient, as much as is needed; have you got e. money? **enough 2** *n.* sufficient quantity; have you had e. to eat? **enough 3** *adv.* sufficiently; it is not light e. to take pictures.

enquire [ɪŋ'kwaɪə] *v.* 1. to ask questions (about) 2. to conduct an official investigation. **enquiry** *n.* (a) question; asking for information; enquiries (desk) = place (in a shop, etc.) for dealing with questions. (b) official investigation.

enrage [ɪn'reɪdʒ] *v.* to make (s.o.) very annoyed.

enrapture [ɪn'ræptʃə] *v.* to charm (s.o.).

enrich [ɪn'rɪtʃ] *v.* to make richer. **enrichment** *n.* making richer.

enrol, *Am.* **enroll** *v.* (enrolled) to admit (new members/new students); be enrolled for a cookery class. **enrolment** *n.* action of admitting new members/students; list of all new students.

en route [ɒn'ruːt] *adv.* on the way.

ensconced [ɪn'skɒnst] *adj.* firmly settled.

ensemble [ɒn'sɒmbl] *n.* (a) group (of musicians/singers). (b) set of women's clothes which match. (c) group of things which fit together.

enshrine [ɪn'ʃraɪn] *v.* to enclose as if in a shrine.

ensign ['ensaɪn] *n.* (a) national flag used by a ship. (b) *Am.* junior naval officer.

enslave [ɪn'sleɪv] *v.* to make a slave of (s.o.).

ensnare [ɪn'sneə] *v.* to catch in a trap.

ensue [ɪn'sjuː] *v.* to follow. **ensuing** *adj.* which follows.

en suite [ɒn'swiːt] *adv.* joined in a series.

ensure [ɪnˈʃʊə] v. to make sure of.
ENT [ˈiːenˈtiː] ear, nose and throat.
entail [ɪnˈteɪl] v. to involve/to include.
entangle [ɪnˈtæŋgl] v. to be caught up (in string/bushes/problems).
  entanglement n. state of being entangled; barbed wire e. = mass of coiled barbed wire to protect soldiers.
entente [ɒnˈtɒnt] n. peaceful agreement (between countries).
enter [ˈentə] v. (a) to go in/to come in. (b) to write down (a name, etc). (c) to type information on a keyboard, and put it into a computer system. **enter for** v. to put your name on a list as a competitor; to e. for the marathon. **enter into** v. to take part in (an agreement).
enteritis [entəˈraɪtɪs] n. infection of the intestines. **enteric** [enˈterɪk] adj. referring to the intestines.
enterprise [ˈentəpraɪz] n. (a) new plan/adventure. (b) ability to plan. (c) method of working in business; private e. = business firms which are not State-owned. **enterprising** adj. with initiative
entertain [entəˈteɪn] v. (a) to amuse. (b) to offer (s.o.) a meal. (c) to consider (a suggestion/an idea). **entertainer** n. person/performer who entertains.
  entertaining adj. amusing.
  entertainment n. (a) amusement. (b) hospitality; e. allowance = money allowed for entertaining guests to meals.
enthralling [ɪnˈθrɔːlɪŋ] adj. extremely interesting.
enthrone [ɪnˈθrəʊn] v. to put (s.o.) on a throne.
enthusiasm [ɪnˈθjuːzɪæzəm] n. great interest. **enthuse** [ɪnˈθjuːz] v. inf. to show great interest (over sth).
  enthusiast n. person who shows great interest in sth. **enthusiastic** adj. showing great interest; he was very e. about my book. **enthusiastically** adv. with enthusiasm.
entice [ɪnˈtaɪs] v. to attract/to tempt.
  enticement n. act of enticing; thing which entices.
entire [ɪnˈtaɪə] adj. whole. **entirely** adv. wholly; I e. agree with you.
  entirety n. being whole; he translated the book in its e. = completely.
entitle [ɪnˈtaɪtl] v. (a) to give the right to; he is entitled to ten days holiday a

year. (b) go give a title to; a book entitled 'War and Peace'. **entitlement** n. right to have.
entity [ˈentɪtɪ] n. thing which exists as a separate unit.
entomb [ɪnˈtuːm] v. to bury.
entomology [entəˈmɒlədʒɪ] n. study of insects. **entomological** [entəməˈlɒdʒɪkl] adj. referring to entomology. **entomologist** [entəˈmɒlədʒɪst] n. person who studies insects.
entourage [ɒntuːˈrɑːʒ] n. group of people (secretaries/assistants/advisers, etc.) surrounding an important person.
entrails [ˈentreɪlz] n. pl. intestines of an animal.
entrance 1 [ˈentrəns] n. (act of) going in; (door for) going in; main e. = main doorway. **entrance 2** [ɪnˈtrɑːns] v. to bewitch. **entrancing** adj. very attractive/beautiful. **entrant** [ˈentrənt] n. person who enters for a race/a competition.
entreat [ɪnˈtriːt] v. to plead. **entreating** adj. pleading. **entreatingly** adv. pleadingly. **entreaty** n. plea.
entrée [ˈɒntreɪ] n. (a) freedom to go in. (b) small dish served before the main dish (in a formal meal).
entrench [ɪnˈtrenʃ] v. to put in trenches/to dig in. **entrenched** adj. firmly e. = (i) firmly established; (ii) holding firm opinions.
entrepreneur [ɒntrəprəˈnɜː] n. (a) person who directs a company and speculates commercially. (b) contractor who acts as a middleman.
  entrepreneurial [ɒntrəprəˈnɜːrɪəl] adj. speculative.
entrust [ɪnˈtrʌst] v. to e. sth to s.o./to e. s.o. with sth = to give s.o. the responsibility for sth.
entry [ˈentrɪ] n. (a) going in. (b) written information in a reference book/accounts ledger/computer system.
entwine [ɪnˈtwaɪn] v. to twist around.
E number [ˈiːnʌmbə] n. classification number for food additives, used in the EC.
enumerate [ɪˈnjuːməreɪt] v. to mention one by one/to make a list of.
  enumeration n. list at of enumerating.
enunciate [ɪˈnʌnsɪeɪt] v to speak (words) clearly. **enunciation** [ɪnʌnsɪˈeɪʃn] n. clear pronunciation.

envelop [ɪn'veləp] v. to cover/to surround with a covering. **envelope** ['envələʊp] n. paper covering for sending letters.

environment [ɪn'vaɪərənmənt] n. surroundings (in which you live). **environmental** [ɪnvaɪərən'mentl] adj. which refers to the surroundings of sth. e. health officer = official who monitors pollution, insanitary conditions etc. in an area. **environs** [ɪn'vaɪərənz] n. pl. area surrounding a place.

envisage [ɪn'vɪzɪdʒ] v. to foresees to plan (sth) which may take place.

envoy ['envɔɪ] n. person sent officially (by a country) /high ranking diplomat.

envy 1 ['envɪ] n. feeling of wishing to have sth which s.o. else has/of wanting to be or do sth else. **envy 2** v. to e. s.o. sth = to wish to have sth belonging to s.o. to be unhappy because you want to be like s.o. else. **enviable** adj. which one can envy. **envious** adj. feeling envy.

enzyme ['enzaɪm] n. substance which can make other substances change (as in digestion).

epaulette, Am. **epaulet** ['epəlet] n. decorative strip on the shoulder of a uniform.

ephemeral [ɪ'fiːmərəl] adj. which disappears quickly/does not last long. **ephemera** n. pl. printed papers (like tickets) which are thrown away after use.

epic 1 ['epɪk] n. long story/poem/film, esp. about war. **epic 2** adj. long and difficult.

epicentre ['episentə] n. point on the surface of the earth which an earthquake reaches first.

epicure ['epɪljʊə] n. person who is fond of and knows a lot about food. **epicurean** [epɪkjʊ'riːən] adj. & n (referring to) an epicure.

epidemic [epɪ'demɪk] n. wave of disease which affects a lot of people.

epidermis [epɪ'dɜːmɪs] n outer layer of skin.

epidural [epɪ'djʊərəl] adj. (anaesthetic) given in the spine.

epiglottis [epɪ'glɒtɪs] n. cartilage at the back of the throat which prevents food from being taken into the windpipe.

epigram ['epɪgræm] n. short witty saying. **epigrammatic** [ep:grə'mætik]

adj. witty, like an epigram.

epigraph n. text used to illustrate sth, (as at the end of a book).

epilepsy [epɪlepsɪ] n. disease which usu. gives convulsive fits. **epileptic 1** [epɪ'leptik] adj. referring to epilepsy. **epileptic 2** n. person who suffers from epilepsy.

epilogue ['epɪlɒg] n. short text at the end of a longer work; short moral programme at the end of a day's TV or radio programmes.

Epiphany [ɪ'pɪfənt n. Christian festival on January 6th, celebrating the visit of the Kings to the Christ child.

episcopal [ɪ'pɪskəpl] adj. referring to bishops; (church) which has bishops. **episcopalian** [ɪpɪskə'peɪlɪən] adj. & n. (member) of an episcopal church.

episode ['epɪsəʊd] n. (a) short piece of action in longer story. (b) short period (in your life).

epistemology [epɪstə'mɒlədʒi] n. study of knowledge.

epistle [ɪ'pɪsl] n. (formal) long letter.

epitaph ['epɪtɑːf] n. writing on a gravestone.

epithet ['epɪθet] n. special name describing s.o. William I has the e. of 'the Conqueror'.

epitome [ɪ'pɪtəmɪ] n. person who shows a particular quality very strongly. **epitomize** v. to show (a quality) very strongly.

epoch ['iːpɒk] n. major period of time. **epoch-making** adj. very important historically.

equable ['ekwəbl] adj. calm/not easily upset.

equal 1 ['iːkwəl] v. (equalled) to be exactly the same as/to add up to; two plus two equals four. **equal 2** adj. (a) exactly the same as/level with something; all things being e. = having considered everything carefully. (b) he wasn't e. to the task = he wasn't strong enough/brave enough to do it. **equal 3** n. person who is on the same level as s.o. else. **equality** [ɪ'kwɒlɪtɪ] n. state of being equal, e. of opportunity = state where everyone has the same chance of getting a job/of doing well. **equalize** ['iːkwəlaɪz] v. to make equal; to score and make the points of both teams the same. **equalizer** n. goal etc., which makes the score equal. **equally** *adv.* in exactly the same way.

equanimity [ekwə'nɪmɪti] *n.* not getting flustered/calmness.

equate [ɪ'kweɪt] *v.* to see (two things) as equal. **equation** [ɪ'kweɪʒn] *n.* mathematical or chemical formula showing two parts are equal. **equator** [ɪ'kweɪtə] *n.* imaginary line around the circumference of the earth which is the same distance from the North and South Poles. **equatorial** [ekwə'tɔːrɪel] *adj.* referring to the equator.

equerry ['ekwərɪ] *n.* man who is in attendance on a king/queen.

equestrian [ɪ'kwestrɪən] *adj. & n.* (person) riding on a horse.

equidistant [iːkwɪ'dɪstənt] *adj. & n.* at an equal distance from sth.

equilateral [iːkwɪ'lætərəl] *adj.* (triangle) with all sides of the same length.

equilibrium [iːkwɪ'lɪbrɪəm] *n.* state of being perfectly balanced.

equine ['ekwaɪn] *adj.* referring to horses.

equinox ['iːkwɪnɒks] *n.* time of the year when the day and night are of equal length. **equinoctial** [iːkwɪ'nɒʃl] *adj.* referring to an equinox.

equip [ɪ'kwɪp] *v.* (equipped) to provide (sth/s.o.) with arms/machinery/furniture, well equipped = with all the arms/ machinery, etc., which are thought necessary. **equipment** *n.* things which are provided to equip sth.

equity ['ekwɪtɪ] *n.* (a) state of justice; in e. = to be fair. (b) equities = ordinary shares (in a company). **equitable.** *adj.* fair/just. **equitably** *adv.* in an equitable way.

equivalent [ɪ'kwɪvələnt] *adj. & n.* (thing) of the same value/same strength (as sth). what is the British e. of the Secretary of State? **equivalence** *n.* being equivalent.

equivocate [i'kwɪvəkeɪt] *v.* to mislead/ to give an ambiguous answer. **equivocal** *adj.* uncertain/ambiguous. **equivocally** *adv.* in an equivocal way. **equivocation** *n.* ambiguous reply.

era ['ɪərə] *n.* long period of history, the Victorian e.

eradicate [ɪ'rædɪkeɪt] *v.* to wipe out/to destroy completely. **eradication**

[ɪrædɪ'keɪʃn] *n.* wiping out.

erase [ɪ'reɪz] *v.* to rub out (writing) /to remove (recorded material) from a tape; to remove data on a disk. **eraser** *n. Am.* rubber for erasing; ink e. = hand eraser for rubbing out ink. **erasure** [ɪ'reɪʒə] *n.* place where a piece of writing has been erased.

ere [eə] *prep.* (poetic) before.

erect 1 [ɪ'rekt] *adj.* straight upright.

erect 2 *v* to put up a mast/a building. **erectile** *adj.* (tissue) which can become erect. **erection** *n.* (a) action of putting up thing which has been erected. (b) state where the penis becomes erect.

erg [ɜːg] *n.* unit of measurement of work.

ergonomics [ɜːgə'nɒmɪks] *n.* study of people at work and their working environment.

ergot ['ɜːgɒt] *n.* poisonous disease of rye.

erica ['erɪkə] *n.* heather.

ERM [iːɑː'em] Exchange Rate Mechanism.

ermine ['ɜːmɪn] *n.* white fur (from the winter coat of a stoat).

erode [ɪ'rəʊd] *v.* to wear away. **erosion** [ɪ'rəʊʒn] *n.* act of wearing away.

erogenous [ɪ'rɒdʒənəs] *adj.* very sensitive sexually. **erotic** [ɪ'rɒtɪk] *adj.* strongly sexual. **eroticism** *n.* erotic quality.

err [ɜː] *v.* to make a mistake/to be fault; he erred on the right side = his mistake was to his advantage.

errand ['erənd] *n.* being sent out (esp. to buy sth); to run errands for s.o.

errant [erənt] *adj.* (knight) wandering in search of adventure.

erratic [ɪ'rætɪk] *adj.* irregular/wild. **erratically** *adv.* in a wild manner.

erratum [ɪ'rɑːtəm] *n.* (*pl.*errata) mistake in a printed book.

error ['erə] *n.* mistake; in e. = by mistake. **erroneous** *adj.* wrong. **erroneously** *adv.* by mistake.

ersatz ['eəzæts] *adj.* artificial, imitated.

erstwhile [ɜːstwaɪl] *adj.* former.

eructation [erʌk'teɪʃn] *n.* (formal) belching.

erudite ['erjuːdant] *adj.* learned. **erudition** [erjuːdrʃn] *n.* learning/ knowledge.

erupt [ɪ'rʌpt] *v.* (of volcano) to throw

out lava, ash, etc. (of person) to become angry suddenly. **eruption** n. (a) (of volcano) throwing out of lava/ash. (b) appearance of spots on the skin.

erysipelas [erɪ'sɪpələs] n. red rash on the skin.

escalate ['eskəleɪt] v. to get worse/more violent; to increase steadily. **escalation** [eskə'leɪʃn] n. getting worse/bigger. **escalator** n. moving stairs.

escalope [eskæ'lɒp] n. thin slice of meat esp. veal.

escapade ['eskəpeɪd] n. wild act.

escape 1 [ɪ'skeɪp] n. (a) action of getting away from prison/from an awkward situation; we had a narrow e. = we were almost killed; e. clause = part of a contract which allows one party to avoid the obligations of the contract. (b) key/program which controls the actions of a computer. **escape 2** v. (a) to get away (from prison/from an awkward situation), he escaped through the window. (b) to avoid/to miss; his name escapes me = I cannot remember his name. **escapee** [eskeɪ'piː] n. person who has escaped from prison.

escapement n. device in a watch or clock which regulates the movement.

escapism n. retreat from reality.

escapist adj. & n (person) who retreats from reality. **escapologist** [eskə'pɒlədʒɪst] n. performer who escapes from chains/sealed box, etc., before an audience.

escarpment [ɪ'skɑːpmənt] n. steep slope.

eschew [es'tʃuː] v. (formal) to avoid.

escort 1 ['eskɔːt] n. person or group of people accompanying s.o. **escort 2** [es'kɔːt] v. to accompany (s.o.).

Eskimo ['eskiməʊ] n & adj. (pl.-o or -os) one of a people living in the north of Canada and Greenland.

esophagus [ə'sɒfəgəs] n. Am. oesophagus.

esoteric [ɪsəʊ'terɪk] adj. understood by very few people; difficult to understand.

espadrille [espə'drɪŋ.-drɪl] n. canvas rope-soled shoe.

espalier [ɪ'spælɪə] n. artificial shape of a fruit tree, with a central stem and branches which form the shape of a ladder.

esparto [es'pɑːtəʊ] n. type of grass.

especial [e'speʃl] adj. particular. **especially** adv. particularly very.

espionage ['espɪənɑːʒ] n. spying; industrial e. = spying on a rival firm to try to find out trade secrets.

esplanade ['espləneɪd] n. level place (along a seafront) where people can walk.

espouse [es'paʊz] v. (formal) to support (a cause).

espresso [ɪ'spresəʊ] n. coffee made by forcing boiling water through ground coffee.

esprit de corps [espriː'də'kɔː] n. feeling of loyalty to a group (usually a military unit).

espy [ɪ'spaɪ] v. (old) to see.

Esq. [es'kwaɪə] abbreviation for esquire (very polite form of address written after man's name on envelope) George Martin, Esq.

essay 1 ['eseɪ] n. piece of prose writing on a particular subject. **essay 2** [e'seɪ] v. (formal) to attempt. **essayist** n. person who writes essays.

essence ['esəns] n. pure extract taken from sth; central part (of an argument).

essential [ɪ'senʃl] adj. & n. (thing) which is very important/indispensable; the bare essentials = the things which are absolutely necessary. **essentially** adv. basically/for the most important part.

establish [ɪ'stæblɪʃ] v. (a) to set up/to create. (b) to show sth to be true. **establishment** n. (a) creation/setting up. (b) commercial firm. (c) the E. = (small) group of people in positions of authority or influence.

estate [ɪ'steɪt] n. (a) large area of land belonging to one person; e. agent = person who arranges the sale of houses and land; housing e. = area of houses or flats built at one time; e. car/wagon = long car with room at the back for carrying luggage/equipment, etc. (b) property owned by a person at the time of death.

esteem 1 [ɪ'stiːm] n respect; to hold s.o. in (high) e. = to respect s.o. (very much). **esteem 2** v. (formal) to consider; I esteem it an honour. **esteemed** adj. highly respected. **estimable** adj. which can be respected.

ester ['estə] *n.* compound of an acid and an alcohol.

estimate 1 ['estɪmət] *n.* calculation which shows the worth/cost/number of sth; price quoted by a supplier; rough e. = an approximate calculation. **estimate 2** ['estɪmeɪt] *v.* to calculate (approximately) the cost/the number, etc., of sth; to calculate a price (before supplying the item). **estimation** [estɪ'meɪʃn] *n.* calculation of how much sth is worth; judgement of how valuable a person is.

estrange [ɪ'streɪndʒ] *v.* to make unfriendly. **estrangement** *n.* becoming estranged.

estuary ['estjʊərɪ] *n.* wide part of a river where the sea comes in at high tide.

etc. [et'setərə] abbreviation for et cetera meaning and so on/and the others.

etceteras [et'setərəz] *n. pl.* other things.

etch [etʃ] *v.* to engrave on metal with acid. **etching** *n.* picture reproduced from a metal plate which has been engraved with acid.

eternity [ɪ'tɜːnɪtɪ] *n.* never-ending period of time; *inf.* it will take an e. = it will take a very long time. **eternal** *adj.* everlasting. **eternally** *adv.* for ever; *inf.* all the time.

ether ['iːθə] *n.* very volatile liquid which burns easily and is used as an anaesthetic. **ethereal** [ɪ'θiːərɪəl] *adj.* very light like a fairy.

ethics ['eθɪks] *n.* moral principles. **ethical** *adj.* morally right.

ethnic ['eθnɪk] *adj.* relating to a particular race; e. minority = minority of a different racial origin than that of the majority. **ethnography** *n.* writing about different races. **ethnological** [eθnə'lɒdʒɪkl] *adj.* referring to ethnology. **ethnologist** [eθ'nɒlədʒɪst] *n.* person who studies ethnology. **ethnology** [eθ'nɒlədʒɪ] *n.* study of the customs of different races.

ethos ['iːθɒs] *n.* beliefs or characteristics (esp. of a group of people).

ethyl ['eθɪl] *n.* liquid formed from ether and alcohol, used to add to petrol.

etiquette ['etɪket] *n.* correct way of behaving in society; professional e. = the rules of behaviour of a particular group of people.

etymology [etɪ'mɒlədʒɪ] *n.* way in which a word and its meaning have developed historically. **etymological** [etɪmə'lɒdʒɪkl] *adj.* referring to etymology.

eucalyptus [juːkə'lɪptəs] *n.* evergreen tree which gives a strong-smelling oil used to treat colds.

eucharist ['juːkərɪst] *n.* Christian ceremony of taking consecrated bread and wine. **eucharistic** [juːkə'rɪstɪk] *adj.* referring to the eucharist.

eugenics [juː'dʒenɪks] *n.* science of breeding strong human beings.

eulogy ['juːlədʒɪ] *n.* (formal) speech or writing praising s.o. **eulogize** *v.* to praise (s.o.) strongly. **eulogistic** [juːlə'dʒɪstɪk] *adj.* which eulogizes.

eunuch ['juːnək] *n.* castrated man, usu., a servant.

euphemism ['juːfəmɪzəm] *n.* word or phrase used in place of a more offensive or unpleasant word. **euphemistic** [juːfə'mɪstɪk] *adj.* referring to euphemism. **euphemistically** *adv.* as a euphemism.

euphonium [juː'fəʊnɪəm] *n.* large brass wind instrument.

euphony ['juːfənɪ] *n.* pleasant sound.

euphoria [juːfə'rɪə] *n.* extreme happiness. **euphoric** [juː'fɒrɪk] *adj.* very happy.

eureka [juː'riːkə] *interj.* meaning a discovery has been made.

Euro ['jʊərəʊ] Currency used in twelve European countries; (•) prefix referring to Europe; Eurocurrency, Eurovision.

European [jʊərə'piːən] *adj. & n* (person) from Europe; the E. Community = group of twelve European countries linked together by the Treaty or Rome; the E. Parliament = the parliament to which members (MEPs) are elected from each country of the European Community; the E. monetary system = system of controlled exchange rates between some member states of the EC.

Eustachian [juː'steɪʃn] *adj.* E. tube = tube which connects the middle ear to the throat.

euthanasia [juːθə'neɪzɪə] *n.* painless killing of very sick or old persons to put them out of their misery.

eutrophic [juː'trɒfɪk] *adj.* (lake) which is rich in nutrients.

evacuate [ɪ'vækjʊeɪt] v. (a) to make (people) leave a dangerous place; to remove (troops) from a place; to remove people from (a place). (b) to empty (the bowels). **evacuation** [ɪvækjʊ'eɪʃn] n. (a) leaving of a dangerous place. (b) emptying of the bowels. **evacuee** [ɪvækjʊ'iː] n. person who has been evacuated.

evade [ɪ'veɪd] v. to avoid.

evaluate [ɪ'væljʊeɪt] v. to calculate value. **evaluation** [ɪvæljʊ'erʃn] n. act of calculating.

evanescent [ɪvə'nesənt] adj. (formal) which fades quickly.

evangelical [iːvæn'dʒelɪkl] adj. referring to certain Protestant churches and their teaching of the Bible.

evangelist [ɪ'vændʒəlɪst] n. (a) one of the four men who wrote the Gospels. (b) preacher.

evaporate [ɪ'væpəreɪt] v. (a) to turn liquid into vapour. (b) to disappear. **evaporation** [ɪvæpə'reɪʃn] n. process of turning liquid into vapour.

evaporated adj. e. milk = milk which has been reduced in volume by evaporation.

evasion [ɪ'verʒn] n. avoiding (a direct answer). **evasive** [ɪ'veɪsɪv] adj. which tries to avoid. **evasively** adv. trying to avoid a direct answer. **evasiveness** n. trying to avoid a direct answer.

eve [iːv] n. night before short time before; on the e. of our departure = just before we were due to leave Christmas E. = 24th December/day before Christmas; New Year's E. = 31st December.

even 1 [ˈiːvn] adj. (a) flat/level. (b) regular; a man of very e. temper = who never gets very excited. (c) equal (in a competition); to get e. with s.o. = try to have revenge on s.o.; the company is just breaking e. = it is making no profit, but no loss either. (d) e. number = number which can be divided by 2. **even 2** v. (a) to flatten/to smooth (sth). (b) to make equal; to e. things up = to make things equal. **even 3** adv. not only, he doesn't e. like strawberries = most people like strawberries, but he doesn't e. worse = worse than before; e. so = however if you consider everything e. now = right at this minute. **evenly** adv. (a) in a level way.

(b) equally; they are e. matched = they are equals (in competition). **evenness** n. being even.

evening [ˈiːvnɪŋ] n. late part of the day, as night falls; this e. = today in the evening. **evening dress** n. clothes worn to special occasions in the evening (long dress for women, black clothes and black or white bow tie for men).

evensong [ˈiːvənsɒŋ] n. Anglican church service held in the evening.

event [ɪ'vent] n. (a) happening; happy e. = birth of a child; in the course of events = as things turned out in the e. of his refusing = if he should refuse. (b) result; in any e. = whatever happens; at all events = in any case. (c) sporting competition; field events = jumping and throwing competitions; track events = running hurdling. **eventful** adj. exciting/full of unexpected happenings.

eventide [iːvn'taɪd] n. (old) evening.

eventual [ɪ'ventjʊəl] adj. final.

eventuality [ɪventjʊ'ælɪtɪ] n. thing which might happen; in that e. = if that should happen. **eventually** adv. in the end.

ever [ˈevə] adv. (a) at any time; I hardly e. see her = almost never see her. louder than e. = louder than before. (b) always; e. since then = from that time onwards; they lived happily e. after = always. from then on; I will love you for e. and e. = always; Scotland for e. ! = excl. to show support for Scotland or a Scottish teAm. (c) inf. e. so = extremely. (d) (emphatic) what e. is the matter ? = what on earth is the matter? = what e. is it for? = what can it be used for? **evermore** adv. always.

evergreen 1 [ˈevəgriːn] adj. (plant) which keeps its leaves all winter.

evergreen 2 n. tree which keeps its leaves all winter. **everlasting** [evə'lɑːstɪŋ] adj. going on for ever.

every [ˈevrɪ] adj. each; all (taken separately); e. other day = each alternate day. **everybody** pron. all people.

everyday adj. ordinary/very common.

everyone pron. everybody.

everything pron. all things.

everywhere adv. in all places.

evict [ɪ'vɪkt] v. to put (s.o.) out of their home. **eviction** [ɪ'vɪkʃn] n. act of putting s.o. out of their home.

evidence ['evɪdəns] n. (a) traces (of crime). (b) written or spoken report (at a trial); the criminal turned State's/ Queen's e. = gave information to the court which proved that his accomplices were guilty. (c) in e. = visible. **evident** adj. obvious. **evidently** adv. obviously; presumably.

evil 1 ['iːvl] adj. very wicked. **evil 2** n. wickedness; injustice.

evince [ɪ'vɪns] v. (formal) to show (a certain quality/feeling).

evoke [ɪ'vəʊk] v. (a) to call up (an image). **evocation** [ɪvəʊ'keɪʃn] n. act of evoking. **evocative** [ɪ'vɒkətɪv] adj. which calls up a sensation in the mind of the onlooker or reader.

evolve [ɪ'vɒlv] v. (a) to work out gradually (a scientific theory/a way of working). (b) to develop (gradually). **evolution** [iːvə'luːʃn] n. gradual development; the theory of e. = theory that man and other living organisms developed gradually from primitive forms of life. **evolutionary** adj. referring to evolution.

ewe [juː] n. female sheep.

ewer ['juːə] n. large jug.

ex- [eks] prefix meaning (a) former; who used to be; my ex-girlfriend. (b) out of; ex-factory = (price) direct from the factory.

exacerbate [ɪg'zæsəbeɪt] v. (formal) to make worse/more painful. **exacerbation** [ɪgzæsə'beɪʃn] n. making worse.

exact 1 [ɪg'zækt] adj. precise. **exact 2** v. to force (sth) from s.o. **exacting** adj. (person) who demands a lot (of effort). **exaction** n. (formal) demand (for money). **exactitude** n. precision. **exactly** adv. precisely; e.! = quite right.

exaggerate [ɪg'zædʒəreɪt] v. to make things seem larger/worse/better than they really are. **exaggeration** [ɪgzædʒə'reɪʃn] n. (statement, etc) making things seem larger/worse/better; without e. = quite truthfully.

exalted [ɪg'zɔːltɪd] adj. in a high position in authority; very happy. **exaltation** [egzəl'teɪʃn] n. exalted feeling.

examine [ɪg'zæmɪn] v. to inspect (sth) to see if it is correct; to test (a student);

to ask (a witness) questions. **exam** [ɪg'zæm] n. inf. written or spoken test. **examination** [ɪgzæmɪ'neɪʃn] n. inspection; written or spoken test. **examinee** [ɪgzæmɪ'niː] n. person being tested. **examiner** [ɪg'zæmɪnə] n. person who inspects or tests.

example [ɪg'zɑːmpl] n. case selected to show; to set an e. = to act well, so that others may copy you; to make an e. of s.o. = to punish s.o. so that others will learn not to do what he did; for e. = to name one thing out of many.

exasperate [ɪg'zɑːspəreɪt] v. to make (s.o.) furious. **exasperation** [ɪgzɑːspə'reɪʃn] n. fury.

excavate ['ekskəveɪt] v. to dig (a hole in the ground); to carry out an archaeological investigation of (a place). **excavation** [ekskə'veɪʃn] n. large hole; archaeological investigation. **excavator** n. machine for making holes in the ground.

exceed [ɪk'siːd] v. to go beyond (a limit). **exceedingly** adv. very.

excel [ɪk'sel] v. (excelled) to be very good (at sth). **excellence** ['eksələns] n. very good quality. **Excellency** n. title given to ambassadors. **excellent** adj. very good.

except 1 [ɪk'sept] prep & conj. not including; other than; all went well e. that James was sick = apart from the fact that. **except 2** v. not to include (sth). **exception** [ɪk'sepʃn] n. thing not included; he took e. to what she said = he was annoyed at what she said. **exceptionable** adj. not to be approved of. **exceptional** adj. outstanding. **exceptionally** adv. particularly.

excerpt 1 ['eksɜːpt] n. small part (of a larger piece of music/writing). **excerpt 2** v. to make an excerpt.

excess [ɪk'ses] n. (a) too much (of sth); in e. of = more than; to e = too much; e. baggage = more baggage than one is allowed to carry. (b) excesses = bad actions which are worse than is normally acceptable. **excessive** adj. more than is normal. **excessively** adv. too much.

exchange 1 [ɪks'tʃeɪndʒ] n. giving of one thing for another; he took my old car in part e. = he took my old car as part of the payment for the new one I was buying; foreign e. = exchange of the money of one country for that of another; e. rate = rate at which one money is given for another; telephone e. = place where telephone calls are linked; stock e. = place where stocks and shares are bought and sold. **exchange 2** *v.* to swap/to give (sth) for sth else; they exchanged addresses = each of them gave the other his address.

exchangeable *adj.* which can be exchanged.

exchequer [eks'tʃekə] *n.* British government department dealing with public money; Chancellor of the E. = British minister of finance.

excise 1 ['eksaɪz] *n.* tax on certain goods. **excise 2** [ɪk'saɪz] *v.* to cut out.

excision [ɪk'sɪʒn] *n.* cutting out.

excite [ɪk'saɪt] *v.* to arouse (s.o./sth) to make (s.o.) very emotional; he was excited at/by the thought of going on holiday. **excitability** [ɪksaɪtə'bɪlɪti] *n.* ease with which you are made very excited. **excitable** [ɪk'saɪtəbl] *adj.* easily excited. **excitement** *n.* state of being excited. **exciting** *adj.* which makes s.o. excited.

exclaim [ɪk'skleɪm] *v.* to say (sth) loudly and suddenly. **exclamation** [eksklə'meɪʃn] *n.* shouting out; exclamation mark = written sign (!) to show exclamation.

exclude [ɪk'sklu:d] *v.* to shut out (sth from somewhere). **excluding** *prep.* without; other than; not including.

exclusion [ɪk'sklu:ʒn] *n.* act of shutting out. **exclusive. 1** *adj.* (a) very select; not open to everyone. (b) e. right = right to do sth which no one else is then allowed to do. **exclusive 2** *adv.* not including. **exclusively** *adv.* solely/ only.

excommunicate [ekskə'mju:nɪkeɪt] *v.* to refuse communion to (a member of a church). **excommunication** [ekskəmju:nɪ'keɪʃn] *n.* refusal of communion.

excrement ['ekskrəmənt] *n.* solid waste matter produced by the body.

excrescence [ɪk'skresns] *n.* ugly growth/lump.

excrete [ɪk'skri:t] *v.* to produce (waste matter). **excreta** *n. pl.*(formal) waste matter produced by the body.

excruciating [ɪk'skru:ʃieɪtɪŋ] *adj.* very painful.

exculpate ['ekskʌlpeɪt] *v.* (formal) to remove blame from (s.o.).

excursion [ɪk'skɜ:ʃn] *n.* short pleasure trip; e. ticket = special cheap ticket.

excuse 1 [ɪk'skju:s] *n.* reason; apology. **excuse 2** [ɪk'skju:z] *v.* to pardon (s.o.); to allow (s.o.) not to do sth; e me = I am sorry; please may I be excused? = please may I go to the lavatory? **excusable** *adj.* which can be pardoned.

excusably *adv.* in an excusable way.

ex-directory ['eksdaɪ'rektrɪ] *adj.* (telephone number) which is not listed in the telephone directory.

execrate ['eksɪkreɪt] *v.* (formal) to curse/to hate (s.o.). **execrable** *adj.* extremely bad. **execrably** *adv.* extremely badly.

execute ['eksɪkju:t] *v.* to carry out (an official order) esp. to kill s.o. who has been condemned to death. **executant** [eg'zekjʊtənt] *n.* performer (of a piece of music). **execution** [eksɪ'kju:'ʃn] *n.* carrying out (of plan); legal killing of person sentenced to death. **executioner** [eksɪ'kju:ʃənə] *n.* official who executes people.

executive 1 *adj.* which carries out plans; which puts things into practice; e. committee = committee which runs the business, etc. **executive 2** *n.* (a) person in business who makes decisions/plans, etc. (b) Chief E. = main administrator in an organization; main administrator in a town. (c) the E. = the part of a Government which carries out laws.

executor [ɪg'zekjʊtə] *n.* person who sees that a dead person's will is carried out. **executrix** [ɪg'zekjʊtrɪks] *n.* woman who sees that a dead person' will is carried out.

exegesis [eksɪ'dʒi:sɪs] *n.* commentary (on the Bible).

exemplary [ɪg'zemplərɪ] *adj.* which serves as an example. **exemplar** *n.* perfect example. **exemplify** *v.* to show as an example.

exempt 1 [ɪg'zempt] *adj.* not forced to obey (law, etc). **exempt 2** *v.* to free (s.o.) from having to obey a rule or law/ from doing sth. **exemption** [ɪg'zempʃn] *n.* (from) ruling that s.o. does not have to do sth.

exercise 1 ['eksəsaɪz] *n.* use of physical or mental powers; e. book = book for writing out work at school. **exercise 2** *v.* (a) to make (an animal) take exercise. (b) to use (power) he exercised his right of veto.

exert [ɪg'zɜːt] *v.* to use (force/pressure, etc). **exertion** [ɪg'zɜːʃn] *n.* effort.

ex gratia [eks'greɪʃə] *adj.* (payment) made as a present, with no obligation implied.

exhale [eks'heɪl] *v.* (formal) to breathe out.

exhaust 1 [ɪg'zɔːst] *n.* escape (of steam/gas); e. (pipe) = pipe in a car which carries away fumes from the engine. **exhaust 2** *v.* to wear out; to finish. **exhausted** *adj.* (a) tired out. (b) completely used up. **exhaustion** [ɪg'zɔːstʃn] *n.* state of being very tired. **exhaustive** *adj.* very thorough. **exhaustively** *adv.* thoroughly.

exhibit 1 [ɪg'zɪbɪt] *n.* object displayed (in court/at an exhibition). **exhibit 2** *v.* to display. **exhibition** [eksɪ'bɪʃn] *n.* display (of works of art, flowers, etc.). **exhibitionist** *n.* person who acts in a strange way so that people will look at him. **exhibitor** *n.* person who displays sth at an exhibition.

exhilarate [ɪg'zɪləreɪt] *v.* to make extremely happy. **exhilarating** *adj.* which makes you full of energy. **exhilaration** [ɪgzɪlə'reɪʃn] *n.* extreme happiness.

exhort [ɪg'zɔːt] *v.* (formal) to urge/to encourage (s.o. to do sth). **exhortation** [ɪgzɔː'teɪʃn] *n.* encouragement.

exhume [ɪg'zjuːm] *v.* to dig up (a dead person who has been buried). **exhumation** [eksjʊ'meɪʃn] *n.* act of digging up a dead body which has been buried.

exigent ['egzɪdʒənt] *adj.* (formal) very urgent. **exigency** [eg'zɪdʒɪnsɪ] *n.* (formal) urgent need.

exiguous ['egzaɪl] *adj.* very small.

exile 1 *n.* (a) banishment (from home country); he went into e. (b) person who is banished. **exile 2** *v.* to send (s.o.) away from his home country as a punishment.

exist [ɪg'zɪst] *v.* to live/to be. **existence** *n.* life/being. **existent,**

existing *adj.* actual/which is present at this moment.

exit 1 ['egzɪt, eksɪt] *n.* way out; going out; he made his e. by the window = he went out by the window; emergency e. = door used in emergency; fire e. = door used on case of fire. **exit 2** *v.* (in a play) goes out; e Mr Smith.

ex libris [eks'liːbrɪs] *n.* printed label stuck in a book to show who it belongs to.

exocrine ['eksəʊkriːn] *adj.* (gland) with ducts.

exodus ['eksədəs] *n.* departure/leaving (usu. of a crowd).

ex officio [eksɒ'frʃɪəʊ] *adv. & adj.* because of your position.

exonerate [ɪg'zɒnəreɪt] *v.* to state that no blame should be attached to (s.o.). **exoneration** [ɪgzɒnə'reɪʃn] *n.* statement that no blame is attached to s.o.

exorbitant [ɪg'zɔːbɪtənt] *adj.* very high (price).

exorcize ['egzɔːsaɪz] *v.* to drive (a devil/a ghost) from a place. **exorcism** ['egzɔːsɪzəm] *n.* driving away a devil/a ghost. **exorcist** *n.* person who exorcizes.

exotic [ɪg'zɒtɪk] *adj.* unusual referring to a tropical place; from a foreign place. **exotically** *adv.* in an exotic way.

expand [ɪk'spænd] *v.* to increase in size/to become larger. **expanse** [ɪk'spæns] *n.* wide extent. **expansion** [ɪk'spænʃn] *n.* increase in size. **expansive** *adj.* (person) who talks freely. **expansiveness** *n.* being expansive.

expatiate [ɪk'speɪʃɪeɪt] *v.* (formal) to talk at great length on sth.

expatriate 1 [ɪk'spætrɪət] *n.* person who is not living in his home country. **expatriate 2** *v.* to send (s.o.) away from his home country.

expect [ɪk'spekt] *v.* to think/to hope/to assume sth is going to happen; I e. she is tired; he expects me to do all the housework; is it going to rain?- I e. so; we're expecting visitors = we are waiting for visitors to arrive; she's expecting = she is pregnant.

expectancy *n.* hope. life e. = number of years a person will probably live. **expectant** *adj.* expecting e. mother

pregnant woman. **expectantly** *adv.*
hopefully. **expectation** *n.* hope.
expectorant [ɪk'spektərənt] *n.* cough
medicine which makes you cough up
phlegm. **expectorate** *v.* (formal) to
cough up phlegm.
expediency [ɪk'spiːdɪənsɪ] *n.* most
simple/straight forward way of doing sth.
expedient 1 *n.* simple way of doing
sth. **expedient 2** *adj.* simple/
straightforward.
expedite ['ekspɪdaɪt] *v.* to make sth
happen faster. **expedition** [ekspi'dɪʃn]
n. (a) rapidity. (b) journey of
exploration; to go on an e. to the North
Pole. **expeditionary** *adj.* (army)
which is on a journey. **expeditious**
adj. prompt/rapid. **expeditiously** *adv.*
rapidly.
expel [ɪk'spel] *v.* (expelled) to throw
(s.o.) out; to send (s.o.) away.
expendable [ɪk'spendəbl] *adj.* which
is not worth keeping after it has been
used; he is e. = he can be sacked/left
behind/killed. **expenditure**
[ɪk'spendɪtʃe] *n.* amount spent.
expense [ɪk'spens] *n.* amount of
money spent; e. account = money which
a businessman is allowed to spend on
entertainment and personal expenses
which are paid for by his firm; they had
a good laugh at his e. = they laughed at
him. **expensive** *adj.* which costs a lot
of money.
experience 1 [ɪk'spɪərɪəns] *n.* thing
lived through; wisdom gained by living
through various situations; I have no e.
of travelling in the desert. **experience**
2 *v.* to live through (sth). **experienced**
adj. wise from plenty of practice.
experiment 1 [ɪk'sperɪmənt] *n.*
scientific test. **experiment 2** *v.* to
carry out a scientific test. **experimental**
[ɪksperɪ'mentl] *adj.* used as part of a
test. **experimentally** *adv.* as an
experiment. **experimentally.** *adv.* as
an experiment. **experimentation** *n.*
carrying out of experiments.
expert 1 ['ekspɜːt] *adv.* referring to s.o.
who knows a great deal about a subject;
e. system = computer program which has
been devised for a particular purpose.
expert 2 *n.* person who knows a great
deal about a subject. **expertise**
[ekspə'tiːz] *n.* specialist knowledge.

expiate ['ekspɪeɪt] *v.* (formal) to make
amends for (a crime). **expiation**
[ekspɪ'eɪʃn] *n.* making amends.
expire [ɪk'spaɪə] *v.* (a) to come to an
end. (b) (formal) to die. **expiration,**
expiry *n.* coming to an end; the e. date
of a ticket.
explain [ɪk'spleɪn] *v.* to give reasons for
(sth); to make (sth) clear. **explanation**
[eksplə'neɪʃn] *n.* reason for sth.
explanatory [ɪk'splænətərɪ] *adv.*
which gives reasons; which makes clear.
expletive [ɪk'spliːtɪv] *n.* swear word.
explicable [ɪk'splɪkəbl] *adj.* which can
be explained. **explicit** [ek'splɪsɪt] *adj.*
straightforward clear. **explicitly** *adv.*
clearly.
explode [ɪk'spləʊd] *v.* (a) (of bombs
etc) to go off/to blow up. (b) to make
(bombs) go off; to destroy (a theory).
exploit 1 ['eksplɔɪt] *n.* great/daring
achievement. **exploit 2** [ɪk'splɔɪt] *v.* to
take commercial advantage of (sth) to e.
the mineral resources of the North Sea.
exploitation [eksplɔɪ'teɪʃn] *n.* taking
advantage.
explore [ɪk'splɔː] *v.* to investigate/to
travel and discover (esp. unknown
lands). **exploration** [eksplə'reɪʃn] *n.*
investigation of (unknown lands).
exploratory [ɪk'splɒrətərɪ] *adj.*
tentative preliminary. **explorer** *n.*
person who explores unknown lands.
explosion [ɪk'spləʊʒn] *n.* blowing up
(of bombs/oil tanks etc.); population e. =
rapid increase in population. **explosive**
1 [ɪk'spləʊsɪv] *adj.* liable to blow up.
explosive 2 *n.* material (like
gunpowder) which can blow up.
exponent [ɪk'spəʊnənt] *n.* person who
practises a certain belief/a certain art.
exponential [ekspə'nenʃəl] *adj.*
growing in proportion to the original
number (i.e. growing faster as numbers
increase).
export 1 ['ekspɔːt] *n.* goods sent to a
foreign country for sale; e. manager =
person in charge of sales to foreign
countries. **export 2** [ɪk'spɔːt] *v.* to send
(goods) to a foreign country for sale.
exporter *n.* person or company which
sells goods to foreign countries.
expose [ɪk'spəʊz] *v.* (a) to show. (b) to
let light go on to a film. (c) to reveal (a
scandal). **exposed** *adj.* (a) open; in a

very e. position = not sheltered from the wind. (b) e. film = where the pictures have been taken but not developed. **exposition** [ekspə'zɪʃn] *n.* detailed explanation. **exposure** [ɪk'spəʊʒə] *n.* (a) state of not being sheltered from cold danger, etc. (b) time and amount of light needed for a picture to be taken on film; e. meter = device for calculating the exposure for a photograph. (c) revealing (of corruption, etc). (d) direction in which (a house) faces.

exposé [ɪk'spəʊzeɪ] *n.* newspaper report revealing corruption/wrongdoing, etc.

expostulate [ɪk'spɒstjʊleɪt] *v.* (formal) to protest/to reason (with s.o.). **expostulation** ['ɪkspɒstjʊ'leɪʃn] *n.* protest.

expound [ɪk'spaʊnd] *v.* to explain in detail.

express 1 [ɪk'spres] *adj.* done on purpose; I did it with the e. intention of killing him. **express 2** *adj. & n.* rapid (train/postal service). **express 3** *v.* (a) to put into words; I expressed myself badly = I did not make clear what I wanted to say. (b) to put symbols; to e. a fraction in decimals. **expression** [ɪk'spreʃn] *n.* (a) way of showing feeling on the face. (b) phrase. **expressive** *adj.* showing feeling. **expressly** *adv.* on purpose. **expressway** *n. Am.* fast road with few junctions.

expropriate [ɪk'sprəʊprɪeɪt] *v.* (of the state/a local authority) to take away (property) from a private owner. **expropriation** [ɪksprəʊprɪ'eɪʃn] *n.* taking of property away from a private owner.

expulsion [ɪk'spʌlʃn] *n.* act of being thrown out/sent away.

expunge [ek'spʌndʒ] *v.* (formal) to wipe out/to cross out.

expurgate ['ekspɜːgeɪt] *v.* to remove rude/offensive expressions from (a book). **expurgation** [ekspɜː'geɪʃn] *n.* act of expurgating.

exquisite [ɪk'skwɪzɪt] *adj.* very finely made/very refined. **exquisitely** *adv.* finely.

exserviceman [eks'sɜːvɪsmən] *n.* (*pl.* -men) man who used to be a member of the armed forces.

extant [ɪk'stænt] *adj.* still in existence. **extempore** [ɪk'stempərɪ] *adv. & adj.* without notes; he spoke for ten minutes e; an e. speech. **extemporize** *v.* to speak without preparation/without notes.

extend [ɪk'stend] *v.* (a) to stretch out extended family = family group which includes distant relatives. (b) to make longer. **extendable, extensible** *adj.* which can be extended. **extension** *n.* (a) act of extending; thing added on. (b) subsidiary telephone in an office.

extensive *adj.* very widespread; very vast. **extensively** *adv.* very greatly/widely. **extensor** *n.* muscle which makes a joint become straight.

extent [ɪk'stent] *n.* degree; size; range area.

extenuating [ɪk'stenjʊeɪtɪŋ] *adj.* which lessens or explains a crime; e. circumstances. **extenuation** [ɪkstenjʊ'eɪʃn] *n.* lessening (of the seriousness of a crime).

exterior 1 [ɪk'stɪərɪə] *adj.* outside. **exterior 2** *n.* outside; the e. of house.

exterminate [ɪk'stɜːmɪneɪt] *v.* to kill (large number of living things). **extermination** [ɪkstɜːmɪ'neɪʃn] *n.* act of killing (large numbers).

external [ɪk'stɜːnl] *adj.* outside; medicine for e. use only = which must not be drunk or eaten. **externally** *adv.* outside.

extinct [ɪk'stɪŋkt] *adj.* (volcano) which no longer erupts; (species) which has died out. **extinction** [ɪk'stɪŋkʃn] *n.* putting out (of a fire); dying out (of a species).

extinguish [ɪk'stɪŋgwɪʃ] *v.* to put out (a fire). **extinguisher** *n.* fire e. = apparatus for putting out fires.

extirpate ['ekstɜːpeɪt] *v.* (formal) to destroy completely.

extol [ɪk'stəʊl] *v.* (extolled) (formal) to praise very highly.

extort [ɪk'stɔːt] *v.* to get (money) from s.o. by threats. **extortion** [ɪk'stɔːʃn] *n.* getting money from s.o. by threats. **extortionate** *adj.* excessive (demands); very high (price).

extra 1 ['ekstrə] *adj.* more than normal; additional. **extra 2** *adv.* (a) more than usual; e. strong string. (b) in addition; the service charge is e. **extra 3** *n.* (a) person (not a star) appearing in crowd scenes in a film. (b) sth more than usual. **extra 4** extra prefix meaning outside; extracurricular = outside marriage; extramural = (course) for students who are not full members of a university; extrasensory = (perception) by other means than the five senses; extraterritorial = outside the territory.

extract 1 ['ekstrækt] n. thing reduced from sth larger; meat e. = substance concentrated from meat. **extract 2** v. to pull (sth) out; to produce (sth).

extraction [ik'strækʃn] n. (a) pulling out (of a tooth); production (of coal, etc). (b) origin; he is of French e. = his family originally was French. **extractor** n. e. fan = fan which sucks air out.

extradite ['ekstrədait] v. to bring back (a criminal) to his home country for trial (by agreement with the country where he was arrested). **extraditable** adj. (crime) for which you can be extradited. **extradition** [ekstrə'dıʃn] n. return of a criminal to his home country.

extraneous [ik'streiniəs] adj. not directly connected with sth.

extraordinary [ik'strɔːdnri] adj. marvellous; quite different from everything else; strange/unusual. **extraordinarily** adv. in an extraordinary way.

extrapolate [ik'stræpəleit] v. to calculate (sth unknown) on the basis of available information. **extrapolation** [ikstræpə'leiʃn] n. calculating sth unknown on the basis of available information.

extravagance [ik'strævəgəns] n. excessive expense and luxury. **extravagant** adj. (a) (person) who spends a lot of money. (b) expensive and luxurious. **extravagantly** adv. in an extravagant way. **extravaganza** [ikstrævə'gænzə] n. expensive and luxurious party/show/film.

extreme 1 [ik'striːm] adj. very great excessive; at the e. end = right at the end. **extreme 2** n. to go to extremes = to do everything in an excessive way. **extremely** adv. very; excessively. **extremist** n. person who has extreme views (usu. about politics). **extremity** [ik'stremiti] n. end point; the extremities = the hands and feet.

extricate ['ekstrikeit] v. to get (s.o.) out of a difficult situation.

extrovert ['ekstrəvɜːt] n. person who is very outgoing and jolly. **extroverted** adj. referring to an extrovert.

extrude [ik'struːd] v. to squeeze out under pressure. **extrusion** [ik'struːʒn] n. squeezing (of metal) under pressure.

exuberance [ig'zjuːbərəns] n. wild enthusiasm. **exuberant** adj. wildly enthusiastic.

exude [ig'zjuːd] v. to sent out/to give off (a smell/a feeling) in all directions; he exudes self-confidence.

exult [ig'zʌlt] v. to rejoice/to be glad; he exulted over his victim = he showed great pleasure at having a victim. **exultant** adj. full of triumph. **exultation** n. great rejoicing.

eye 1 [ai] n. (a) part of the head, used for seeing; keep your eyes open! = watch out! to set/clap eyes on sth = to see sth (suddenly); it catches the e. = it is very noticeable; inf. I'm up to my eyes in work = I have masses of work to do; to keep an e. on = to guard; they don't see e. to e. = they do not agree. (b) inf. private e. = private detective. (c) small hole in a needle for passing the thread through; small loop for attaching a hook; bud on a potato through which sprouts grow. **eye 2** v. to look at (s.o./sth) carefully. **eyeball** n. ball of the eye. **eyebath** n. small cup for bathing the eye. **eyebrow** n. small arch of hair above the eye. **eyeful** n. inf. good look at sth. **eyelash** n. one of the hairs growing round the rim of the eye. **eyelet** n. small hole (as in a shoe, for passing the lace through). **eyelid** n. covering for the eye. **eyeliner** n. substance for drawing a line round the eye. **eye-opener** n. thing which surprises you. **eyepiece** n. lens at the end of a telescope through which you look. **eyeshade** n. shade worn on the forehead for keeping bright light out of the eyes. **eyeshadow** n. substance for colouring the skin round the eye. **eyesight** n. (no pl.) ability to see; his e. is failing = he can see less well. **eyesore** n. thing which is hideous/unpleasant to look at. **eyestrain** n. (no pl.) tiredness of the eyes. **eyetooth** n. (pl.-teeth) canine. **eyewash** n. (no pl.)

liquid for bathing the eyes; *inf.* it's all e.
= it is rubbish. **eyewitness** *n.* person
who has seen sth happen.
eyrie, Am, aerie ['ɪərɪ] *n.* nest of an
eagle; high and inaccessible house.

Ff

F symbol for fluorine.
fable ['feɪbl] *n.* moral story *usu.* about
animals, making them seem like human
beings.
fabric ['fæbrɪk] *n.* (a) material. (b)
basic structure (of society). **fabricate**
['fæbrɪkeɪt] *v.* to invent (an untrue
story); to forge (a paper). **fabrication**
[fæbrɪkeɪʃn] *n.* invention.
fabulous ['fæbjʊəs] *adj.* (a) imaginary;
as in a fable. (b) *inf.* marvellous/
wonderful. **fabulously** *adv. inf.*
wonderfully.
facade [fə'sɑːd] *n.* front of a large
building; outward appearance which is
intended to give a false impression.
face 1 [feɪs] *n.* (a) front part of the
head; f to f. = talking and looking at each
other; to make a f. = to make a rude
expression; to lose f. = to feel
humiliated. (b) front of an object. **face 2**
v. (a) to put a facing/an outward
covering on (sth). (b) to turn your head
towards; the house faces east = the house
looks towards the east; to f. up to = to
accept bravely. **facecloth, faceflannel**
n. small piece of towelling for washing
the face or body. **faceless** *adj.*
threateningly anonymous. **facelift** *n.*
operation to remove wrinkles from your
face. **face pack** *n.* cream which is left
on the face to improve the skin. **face
value** *n.* value written on a coin/
banknote/share certificate; to take sth at
face value = to assume that the first/
obvious meaning is the correct one.
facing. *n.* material covering the
surface of a building/the edges of a
garment.
facet ['fæsɪt] *n.* (a) one of the flat sides
on a cut gem. (b) aspect (of a problem,
etc.).

facetious [fə'siːʃəs] *adj.* funny/joking
(in an offensive way). **facetiously** *adv.*
not seriously/in a joking way.
facetiousness *n.* being facetious.
facial 1 ['feɪʃl] *adj.* referring to a face.
facial 2 *n.* beauty treatment to make
your face more beautiful.
facile ['fæsaɪl] *adj.* done too easily.
facility *n.* (a) ease/absence of
difficulty. (b) facilities = equipment
which can be used (for sth). (c) large
industrial/scientific building. **facilitate**
v. to make (sth) easy.
facsimile [fæk'sɪmɪlɪ] *n.* (a) perfect
reproduction; perfect copy. (b) fax.
fact ['fækt] *n.* thing that is true; in f./as
a matter off. = really/actually.
faction ['fækʃn] *n.* group of people
linked together in opposition to a leader/
a government. **factional** *adj.* referring
to factions.
factor [fæktə] *n.* (a) one of the numbers
which produce a given number when
multiplied. (b) thing which is influential/
important. (c) person who buys debts at
a discount and then tries to reclaim the
full amount from the debtor.
factory ['fæktrɪ] *n.* building where
things are made; f. ship = ship which
freezes or cans fish which are caught by
smaller fishing boats.
factotum [fæk'təʊtəm] *n.* person who
does all types of work.
factual ['fæktjʊəl] *adj.* containing facts.
factually *adv.* in a factual way.
faculty ['fækəltɪ] *n.* (a) special ability.
(b) division of a university. (c) *Am.*
teaching staff (of a school/university/
college, etc.).
fad [fæd] *n.* strange temporary mania.
faddist *n.* person who follows a fad.
faddy *adj. inf.* (person) who has odd
likes and dislikes about food.
fade [feɪd] *v.* to lose colour brightness
or strength; to make (sth) lose colour.
faeces, Am. feces ['fiːsiːz] *n. pl.*
(formal) solid waste matter from the
body. **faecal** *adj.* referring to faeces.
fag 1 [fæg] *n.* (a) tiring/boring work. (b)
Sl. cigarette. (c) Sl. male homosexual.
fag 2 *v.* to work hard; Sl. fagged out =
tired out. **faggot** ['fægət] *n.* (a) bundle
of sticks for lighting a fire. (b) spiced
meat ball. (c) *inf.* nasty old woman. (d)
Sl. male homosexual.

Fahrenheit [færənheɪt] *adj.* (scale for) measuring heat where the boiling point of water is 212 and the freezing point 32.
faience [faɪˈɑːns] *n.* thick glazed earthenware.
fail 1 [feɪl] *v.* (a) to be unsuccessful in doing sth. (b) to grow weaker. (c) not to pass (a candidate) in an examination. **fail 2** *n.* without f. = certainly. **failing 1** *n.* weakness/bad point. **failing 2** *prep.* f. that = if that does not work. **fail-safe** *adj.* (machine) made so that if anything goes wrong it will stop working and so not be dangerous. **failure** [ˈfeɪljə] *n.* (a) breakdown/stoppage; heart f. = dangerous condition when the heart has stopped beating; power f. = breakdown in electricity supplies. (b) thing which did not work out satisfactorily.
faint 1 [feɪnt] *adj.* (a) not clear; difficult to see or hear; weak. **faint 2** *v.* to lose consciousness for a short time. **fainthearted** *adj.* timid. **faintly** *adv.* weakly. **faintness** *n.* being faint.
fair 1 [ˈfeə] *n.* (a) group of sideshows/amusements/food stalls, etc., set up in one place for a short time. (b) market for selling and advertising goods. **fair 2** *adj.* (-er, -est) (a) light-coloured (skin, hair). (b) honest/correct. (c) not bad. (d) (of weather) dry and warm. **fairground** *n.* place in the open air where a fair is held. **fairly** [ˈfeəlɪ] *adv.* (a) quite/not completely. (b) justly/correctly. **fairness** *n.* (a) light colouring. (b) honesty/correctness. **fairway** *n.* (a) part of a golf course where the grass is kept cut (b) navigable channel.
airy *n.* (a) small supernatural creature who is able to work magic; f. story = story about fairies/princesses/giants, etc.; f. godmother = kind person who gives you sthg; f. lights = small coloured electric lights for decorating trees, etc.; f ring = dark ring on grass, caused by a fungus. (b) Sl. male homosexual.
fairyland *n.* land where fairies are supposed to live. **fairytale** *n.* fairy story; a f. castle = romantic castle like those in fairytales.
aith [feɪθ] *n.* belief/trust; f. healer = person who heals by prayer; in good f. = honourably, even though wrongly.
faithful *adj.* (a) trusting/loyal. (b) completely correct. **faithfulness** *n.*

being faithful. **faithfully** *adv.* (a) loyally. (b) yours f. = used as an ending for business letters, when addressed to no specific person. **faithless** *adj.* disloyal.
fake 1 [feɪk] *n.* imitation/forgery; not the real thing. **fake 2** *v.* to make an imitation of (sth).
fakir [ˈfeɪkɪə] *n.* Indian holy man.
falcon [ˈfɔːlkən] *n.* small bird of prey, sometimes trained to catch other birds in sport. **falconry** *n.* sport of hunting with falcons.
fall 1 [fɔːl] *n.* (a) drop/collapse. (b) esp. *Am.* the autumn. (c) falls = waterfall. (d) f. from power = loss of a powerful position. **fall 2** *v.* (fell; has fallen) to drop down. **fall back** *v.* to retreat/to go back. **fall back on** *v.* to use (sth) which was kept as a reserve. **fall down** *v.* to drop to the ground. **fallen. 1** *adj.* dropped. **fallen 2** *n.* the f. = people who have been killed in battle/in a war. **fall for** *v.* (a) to fall in love with (s.o.). (b) to be tricked by (sth). **fall in** *v.* (in the army) to stand in line. **fall in with** *v.* to join with (s.o.); to agree with (an idea). **fall off** *v.* to become less. **fall out** *v.* (a) to drop. (b) to have an argument. **fallout** *n.* radioactive dust from a nuclear explosion. **fall through** *v.* to fail. **fall to** *v.* to start to do sth (esp. eat or work).
fallacy [ˈfæləsɪ] *n.* false argument; error. **fallacious** [fəˈleɪʃəs] *adj.* wrong.
fallibility [fælɪˈbɪlɪtɪ] *n.* being fallible. **fallible** [ˈfælɪbl] *adj.* (person) who can make a mistake.
Fallopian [fəˈləʊpɪən] *adj.* F. tube = tube in a woman from an ovary to the womb.
fallow [ˈfæləʊ] *adj.* (land) which is purposely not used for crops so that it can regain its goodness. **fallow deer** *n.* small deer with white spots.
false [fɔːls] *adj.* (-er,-est) (a) not true. (b) not real; f. teeth = artificial teeth; f. alarm = signal for an emergency when there isn't one. **falsehood** *n.* lie. **falsely** *adv.* in a false way. **falseness** *n.* being false. **falsification** *n.* act of falsifying. **falsify** *v.* to change (sth) thus making it invalid.
falsetto [fɒlˈsetəʊ] *n.* unnaturally high voice (used by a man singing).

falter ['fɔːltə] v. to move or speak hesitantly.

fame [feɪm] n. being well known. **famed** adj. well known.

familiar [fə'mɪljə] adj. (a) heard or seen before; well known; I am f. with that type of machine = I know that type of machine. (b) very informal/(too) friendly.

familiarity [fəmɪlɪ'ærɪtɪ] n. (a) (with) good knowledge of s.o./sth. (b) excessively informal way of speaking to s.o. **familiarization** [fəmɪljəraɪ'zeɪʃn] n. act of familiarizing. **familiarize** [fə'mɪljəraɪz] v. to f. yourself with sth = to become informed about sth.

familiarly adv. in a familiar way.

family ['fæmɪlɪ] n. (a) group of people who are closely related, esp. mother, father and their children; f. planning = birth control; f. tree = table of the family going back over many generations. (b) group of animals/plants, etc., which are closely related.

famine ['fæmɪn] n. very serious lack/shortage of food.

famished adj. inf. very hungry.

famous adj. well known.

fan 1 [fæn] n. (a) object/machine for moving air, to make things cooler or warmer; f. belt = loop of rubber which turns a fan to cool the engine of a car. (b) passionate admirer; a Liverpool f. = a supporter of Liverpool football teAm.

fan 2 v. (fanned) to make the air move. **fan club** n. organized group of admirers (of a pop star). **fan mail** n. admiring letters received by a pop star, etc. **fan out** v. to spread out (like a fan).

fanatic [fə'nætɪk] adj. & n. (person) who is madly enthusiastic about sth, esp. religion. **fanatical** adj. too enthusiastic. **fanatically** adv. in a fanatical way. **fanaticism** n. being fanatical.

fancier ['fænsɪə] n. person who has an interest (in a certain type of animal); pigeon f. = person who breeds and races pigeons.

fancy 1 ['fænsɪ] n. (a) imagination. (b) desire; it took his f. = made him want it. **fancy 2** adj. pretty/decorated. **fancy 3** v. (a) to imagine/to believe. (b) to like/to want to have; inf. I think she fancies you = she is attracted to you. **fancy dress** n. unusual costume (worn to a party).

fanciful adj. imaginative.

fanfare ['fænfeə] n. piece of music played on trumpets to signal the entrance of an important person/the start of a show.

fang [fæŋ] n. animal's long tooth.

fanlight ['fænlaɪt] n. small window over a door or a large window.

fantasy ['fæntəsɪ] n. invented story/not a true story. **fantasize** v. to imagine/to dreAm. **fantastic** [fæn'tæstɪk] adj. (a) strange/like a dreAm. (b) inf. wonderful/amazing. **fantastically** adv. in a fantastic way.

far 1 [fɑː] adv. (farther/further; farthest/furthest) (a) a long way away/not near; so f. = up to now. (b) much; by f. the best. **far 2** adj. distant/not near. **faraway** adj. distant/remote. **far-fetched** adj. difficult to believe. **far-reaching** adj. which has important results. **far-sighted** adj. looking to the future.

farad ['færæd] n. unit of electrical capacity.

farce [fɑːs] n. comedy based on slapstick and ridiculous situation; absurd situation. **farcical** adj. absurd.

fare 1 [feə] n. (a) price to be paid for a journey; return f. = fare from one place to another and back again. (b) passenger in a bus/taxi. (c) food. **fare 2** v. to get on; to do (well/badly).

farewell [feə'wel] inter & n. (formal) goodbye.

farinaceous [færɪ'neɪʃəs] adj. made of flour.

farm 1 [fɑːm] n. land used for growing crops and keeping animals. **farm 2** v. to look after a farm; to grow crops/to keep animals for sale. **farmer** n. man who looks after a farm, **farmhouse** n. house where the farmer and his family live. **farming** n. job of looking after a farm/growing crops/keeping animals for sale. **farm out** v. to hand over (work/child, etc.) to another person.

farmstead n. small farm. **farmyard** n. space outside a farmhouse, usu. surrounded by farm buildings or a wall.

farrago [fə'rɑːgəʊ] n. tangled mass.

farrier ['færɪə] n. blacksmith who shoes horses. **farriery** n. business of a farrier.

farrow ['færəʊ] v. to have a litter of piglets.

fart 1 [fɑːt] *n.* (vulgar) noise made when passing gas from the intestines through the anus. **fart 2** *v.* (vulgar) to make a fart.

farther [fɑːðə] *adj. & adv.* to a greater distance; more distant. **farthest** [ˈfɑːðəst] *adj. & adv.* to the greatest distance; most distant.

farthing [ˈfɑːðɪŋ] *n.* (old) small coin, worth half a halfpenny.

fascia [ˈfeɪʃə] *n.* (a) long board over the windows of a shop with the name of the shop written on it. (b) dashboard (of a car).

fascicle [ˈfæsɪkl] *n.* section of a large book, which is published in sections.

fascinate [ˈfæsɪneɪt] *v.* to attract/to charm. **fascinating** *adj.* attractive/ very interesting. **fascination** [fæsɪˈneɪʃn] *n.* attraction/charm. **fascinator** *n.* person who fascinates.

fascism [ˈfæʃɪzəm] *n.* extreme rightwing political movement. **fascist** *adj. & n.* (person) supporting fascism.

fashion 1 [fæʃn] *n.* (a) manner/way; after a f. = not very well. (b) most admired style at a particular moment. **fashion 2** *v.* to make. **fashionable** *adj.* in fashion. **fashionably.** *adv.* (dressed) in a fashionable way.

fast 1 [fɑːst] *adj. & adv.* (-er, -est) (a) quick; my watch is five minutes f. = my watch shows a time five minutes later than really is; f. film = film which requires very short exposure time; f. food = food which is prepared and served quickly. (b) tightly fixed; f. colours = colours in clothing which do not run when washed; to make sth f. = to attach sth tightly. (c) f. asleep = soundly sleeping. **fast 2** *n.* period when you stop eating. **fast 3** *v.* to stop eating (for a time). **fasten** [ˈfɑːsn] *v.* to fix tightly. **fastener** *n.* device which fastens/ attaches; zip f. = sliding fastener for attaching clothes, bags, etc. **fastening** *n.* thing which fastens.

fastidious [fæˈstɪdɪəs] *adj.* hard to please; easily shocked. **fastidiously** *adv.* in a fastidious way. **fastidiousness** *n.* being fastidious.

fastness [ˈfɑːsnəs] *n.* (*pl.*-es) stronghold in mountains.

fat 1 [fæt] *adj.* (fatter, fattest) (a) big and round; overweight; *inf.* a f. lot of good = very little good. (b) thick. (c) full of grease. **fat 2** *n.* (a) grease/white layer on an animal's body under the skin (b) cooking f. = refined oil (either vegetable or animal) used in frying, etc. **fatness** *n.* being fat. **fatstock** *n.* cows/sheep, etc., fattened for food.

fate [feɪt] *n.* destiny; thing that is certain to happen as we think it has been decided by a power beyond human control.

fatal *adj.* deadly/causing death. **fatalism** *n.* accepting fate. **fatalist** *n.* person who accepts what happens, knowing that it is usually bad and can not be avoided. **fatalistic** [feɪtəˈlɪstɪk] *adj.* like a fatalist. **fatalities** [fəˈtælɪtɪz] *n. pl.*deaths. **fatally** *adv.* causing death.

fated *adj.* destined/condemned by fate. **fateful** *adj.* (decision, etc.) important for its serious consequences in the future.

father 1 [ˈfɑːðə] *n.* (a) male parent; f. figure = older man who is consulted for advice. (b) originator. (c) title given to a priest. **father 2** *v.* to be the father of. **father in -law** *n.* (*pl.*fathers- in-law) father of your wife or husband. **fatherland** *n.* native country. **fatherless** *adj.* with no father. **fatherly** *adj.* like a father.

fathom 1 [ˈfæðəm] *n.* measure of depth of water (6 feet or 1. 8 metres). **fathom 2** *v.* (also fathom out) to find the meaning of (a mystery).

fatigue 1 [fəˈtiːg] *n.* (a) tiredness; metal f. = wearing out of metal used in a construction, causing weak points. (b) fatigues = (i) cleaning duty in the army; (ii) overalls worn when doing this. **fatigue 2** *v.* to tire (s.o.) out.

fatten [ˈfætn] *v.* to make fat. **fattening** *adj.* (foods) which make you fat. **fatty** *adj.* (food/tissue) which has a lot of fat in it.

fatuous [ˈfætjʊəs] *adj.* stupid/silly. **fatuously** *adv.* in a fatuous way. **fatuousness, fatuity** [fəˈtjuːɪtɪ] *n.* being fatuous.

faucet [ˈfɔːsɪt] *n. Am.* tap.

fault 1 [fɔːlt] *n.* (a) mistake; she's at f. = has made a mistake. (b) imperfection/ thing which is not as it should be. (c) (in geology) break in a rock layer where a section of rock slips down and another section rises. (d) (in tennis) error in serving. **fault 2** v. to criticize/to find (sth) wrong. **faultiness** n. being faulty. **faultless** adj. perfect. **faultlessly** adv. perfectly. **faulty** adj. (-ier, -iest) with mistakes or imperfections.

faun [fɔːn] n. mythical creature, like a man with goat's legs and horns.

fauna ['fɔːnə] n. wild animals (of an area).

faux pas [fəʊ'pɑː] n. piece of embarrassing behaviour.

favour, Am. **favor 1** ['feɪvə] n. (a) friendly act/kindness. (b) support for one group/one person at the expense of others; out of f. = disliked; the score is 3-2 in his f. = he is leading 3-2. (c) preference/liking; to be in f. of = to prefer. (d) ribbon/badge (worn by a supporter). **favour 2** v. (a) to like/to prefer. (b) to make things easy for (s.o.). **favourable** ['feɪvrəbl] adj. helpful/kind; good (impression). **favourably** adv. in a favourable way. **favoured** adj. preferred/liked. **favourite. 1** adj. preferred/liked. **favourite 2** n. (a) most liked thing/person. (b) horse, team, etc., which most people think will win. **favouritism** n. prejudice/preference for one thing/person.

fawn 1 [fɔːn] n. young deer. **fawn 2** adj. brownish cream colour. **fawn 3** v. to f. on s.o. = to try to get s.o. 's favour by doing everything they ask.

fax 1 [fæks] n. (pl.faxes) copy of a text or image sent by telephone. **fax 2** v. to sent an image by telephone.

FBI [efbiː'aɪ] n. US Federal Bureau of Investigation.

Fe symbol for iron.

fear 1 ['fɪə] n. terror/worry/feeling of being afraid; inf. no f. ! = certainly not! **fear 2** v. to be afraid of (sth). **fearful** adj. terrible. **fearfully** adv. terribly/very. **fearless** adj. with no feeling of terror. **fearlessly** adv. not feeling afraid. **fearsome** adj. frightening.

feasible ['fiːzəbl] adj. (a) which can be done. (b) likely/probable. **feasibility** [fiːzə'bɪlɪtɪ] n. ability to be done; f; study = study to see if sth can be done. **feasibly** adv. possibly.

feast 1 [fiːst] n. (a) special religious day when we remember a saint or special

event. (b) very large meal. **feast 2** v. (a) to eat expensive food. (b) to eat a very large meal.

feat [fiːt] n. unusually difficult act.

feather 1 ['feðə] n. one of many growths which form the covering of a bird's body; light as a f. = very light. **feather 2** v. (a) to f. one's nest = to make a lot of money (usu. fraudulently). (b) to make the blade of an oar skim fast across the surface of the water. **feather-brained** adj. silly and forgetful. **feathered** adj. with feathers. **featherweight** n. weight in boxing between bantamweight and lightweight. **feathery** adj. light/delicate (like a feather).

feature 1 ['fiːtʃə] n. (a) special part of the face (such as nose/mouth, etc.); important aspect. (b) important item in a news programme or article; important article on a special subject. (c) f. film = main long film. **feature 2** v. to have as the main actor/as the main subject, esp. on film, TV or in a newspaper; to appear as the main actor/subject in a film or on TV. **featureless** adj. with no striking features.

February ['februərɪ] n. 2nd month of the year.

feces ['fiːsiːz] n. pl.Am. see faeces.

feckless ['fekləs] adj. (person) who has no aim in life/who is incompetent.

fecund ['fekənd] adj. fertile/fruiting. **fecundity** [fɪ'kʌndɪtɪ] n. being fecund.

fed [fed] v. see feed. **fed up** adj. inf. bored/tired (with).

federation [fedə'reɪʃn] n. group of states or societies which have joined together. **federal** ['fedərəl] adj. referring to a system where a group of semi-independent states exist under a central government. **federate** ['fedəreɪt] v. to join (states) together in a federation.

fee [fiː] n. money paid to doctors, schools and lawyers, etc.

feeble ['fiːbl] adj. (-er, -est) weak. **feeble-minded** adj. of low intelligence. **feebleness** n. weakness. **feebly** adv. weakly.

feed 1 [fiːd] n. (a) food given to animals. (b) meal, esp. given to babies (c) means of putting material into a machine; sheet f. = device on a printer for inserting single sheets of paper. **feed 2** v. (fed) (a) to give food to (s.o./sth). (b) to eat. (c) to put (in). **feedback** n. (a) return of a signal in an electronic circuit causing a high-pitched noise. (b) information/details about sth which has been done. **feeder** n. (a) feeding bottle; device for feeding material into a machine. (b) baby's bib. (c) f. school = junior school which provides children for a senior school. **feeding** adj. giving milk, etc., to a baby. **feedlot** n. fenced area of land where cattle are fattened.

feel 1 [fiːl] n. touch, esp. with the fingers. **feel 2** v. (felt) (a) to touch, esp.; with your fingers; the knife felt cold; to f. one's way = act cautiously until one has more experience. (b) to have a feeling/sensation; he feels it would be unwise = he thinks it would be unwise; do you f. like a cup of tea ? = would; you like a cup of tea ? to f. up to doings sth = to feel strong enough to do it. **feeler** n. antenna/long part on an insect's head with which it touches; to put out a f. = to explore sth/to see if sth is acceptable. **feeling** n. (a) sense of touch. (b) thing felt inside/emotion.

feet [fiːt] n. pl.see foot.

feign [feɪn] v. (formal) to pretend.

feint 1 [feɪnt] n. false attack; move to confuse your opponent. **feint 2** adj. (paper) with very pale lines drawn on it. **feint 3** v. to make a move to confuse your opponent.

feisty ['feɪstɪ] adj. Am. aggressive.

felicity [fə'lɪsɪtɪ] n. (formal) happiness. **felicitous** adj. well chosen (words).

feline 1 ['fiːlaɪn] adj. referring to a cat; like a cat. **feline 2** n. member of the cat family.

fell 1 [fel] n. high moorland in the North of England. **fell 2** adj. (old) cruel; at one f. swoop = swiftly. **fell 3** v. to cut down (a tree); to knock (s.o.) down; see also fall.

fellow ['feləʊ] n. (a) man. (b) person who is in the same group, f. workers. (c) member of a college (at Oxford and Cambridge). **fellowship** n. (a) friendly feeling. (b) group of people with similar interests. (c) position of fellow (at Oxford and Cambridge).

felon ['felən] n. criminal. **felony** n. serious crime.

felt 1 [felt] n. thick, matted material made of wool; f. tipped pen = pen of which the writing end is made of hard felt. **felt 2** v. to cover (sth) with felt; see also feel. **felt-tip** n. felt tipped pen.

female 1 ['fiːmeɪl] adj. (a) referring to women/girls. (b) referring to the sex which has young. **female 2** n. (a) inf. woman/girl. (b) animal/insect/bird which gives birth to young or lays eggs; flower which produces seeds. **feminine** ['femənɪn] adj. (a) belonging to a woman; like a woman. (b) (in grammar) referring to words which have a particular form to indicate the female gender. **femininity** [femɪ'nɪnətɪ] n. womanliness; female qualities.

feminism ['femɪnɪzəm] n. being a feminist. **feminist** n. person (usu. woman) who actively supports the right of women to equal status with men.

femoral ['fiːmərəl] adj. referring to the femur.

femur ['fiːmə] n. thigh bone.

fen [fen] n. large area of marsh.

fence 1 [fens] n. (a) barrier of wood or wire, used to keep people or animals in or out of a place; to sit on the f. = to avoid giving a definite answer to a question. (b) SI person who takes stolen goods to resell them. **fence 2** v. (a) to f. in/off = to surround with a fence. (b) to fight with swords as a sport. **fencer** n. person who fences. **fencing** n. (a) material making up a fence. (b) sport of fighting with swords.

fend [fend] v. (a) to f. off = to push away. (b) to f. for yourself = to look after yourself. **fender** n. (a) low guard around of fireplace to stop coal or wood falling out into the room. (b) rope mat/rubber tyre, etc., hung against the side of a boat to protect it from bumps. (c) Am. mudguard of a car.

fennel ['fenl] n. herb with a smell like aniseed.

feral ['fɪərəl] adj. (animal) which is wild (having once been domesticated).

ferment 1 ['fɜːmənt] n. upset/agitation. **ferment 2** [fə'ment] v. to change by fermentation. **fermentation** [fɜːmen'teɪʃn] n. chemical change brought about in liquids, usu. leading to the production of alcohol.

fern [fɜːn] *n.* green plant often with feathery leaves which does not have flowers or seeds.

ferocious [fəˈrəʊʃəs] *adj.* fierce/angry. **ferociously** *adv.* in a ferocious way. **ferocity** [fəˈrɒsɪtɪ] *n.* fierceness.

ferret 1 [ˈferɪt] *n.* small weasel-like animal half-tamed and used to drive rabbits or rats from holes. **ferret 2** *v.* to f. out = to find out by endless searching.

Ferris wheel [ˈferɪswiːl] *n.* large vertical wheel in a funfair, with seats.

ferroconcrete [ferəʊˈkɒŋkriːt] *n.* concrete reinforced with steel bars.

ferrous [ˈferəs] *adj.* containing iron.

ferrule [ˈferuːl] *n.* metal cap on the end of an umbrella or stick.

ferry 1 [ˈferɪ] *n.* (a) (also ferryboat) boat which carries goods or people to and fro across a stretch of water (b) place where a boat crosses a stretch of water. **ferry 2** *v.* to take (s.o.) across in a boat; the bus ferried people to and from the station = took them back and forth. **ferryman** *n.* (*pl.*-men) man in charge of ferry.

fertile [ˈfɜːtaɪl, [xx]ˈfɜːtl] *adj.* rich enough to produce crops; (of female) able to produce young; he has a f. imagination = he is very imaginative/he can imagine things very easily. **fertility** *n.* ability to produce crops or young. **fertilization** *n.* the act of fertilizing. **fertilize** *v.* (a) to join male and female cells together, so that a new animal/plant will be made. (b) to spread fertilizer on. **fertilizer** *n.* chemical or manure spread over the ground to make it richer and more able to produce crops.

fervour, Am. fervor [ˈfɜːvə] *n.* passion. **fervent, fervid** *adj.* passionate. **fervently** *adv.* in a fervent way.

fescue [ˈfeskjuː] *n.* grass grown in meadows.

fester [ˈfestə] *v.* (of wound) to become bad and produce pus.

festival [ˈfestɪvl] *n.* (a) religious celebration which comes at the same time each year. (b) artistic celebration/entertainment which is put on at regular intervals; arts f. = competitions in music, drama, painting and handicrafts, etc. **festive** *adj.* happy; fit for a celebration. **festivity** [feˈstɪvɪtɪ] *n.* celebration.

festoon 1 [feˈstuːn] *n.* long chain of hanging decorations. **festoon 2** *v.* to hang with decorations.

fetch [fetʃ] *v.* (a) to go and bring (s.o./sth) back. (b) to be sold at (a certain price). **fetch in** *v.* to collect. **fetching** *adj.* attractive/pretty. **fetch up** *v. inf.* to arrive/to end up (in a certain place).

féte 1 [feɪt] *n.* public celebration, *usu.* in the open air, with stalls, sideshows and competitions. **fete 2** *v.* to celebrate (the arrival of an important person, (etc).

fetid [ˈfɪtɪd] *adj.* bad-smelling (water/breath).

fetish [ˈfetɪʃ] *n.* (a) object worshipped by s.o. (b) obsession.

fetlock [ˈfetlɒk] *n.* back part of a horse's leg just above the hoof.

fetter [ˈfetə] *v.* to chain (a prisoner). **fetters** *n. pl.*chains.

fettle [ˈfetl] *n.* in fine f. = in very good condition.

fetus [ˈfiːtəs] *n. Am.* see foetus.

feud 1 [fjuːd] *n.* bitter quarrel. **feud 2** *v.* to quarrel bitterly all the time. **feudal** [ˈfjuːdl] *adj.* f. system = medieval system of holding land in return for services to an overlord or king. **feudalism** *n.* feudal system.

fever [ˈfiːvə] *n.* (a) state when the body's temperature is higher than normal. (b) f. (pitch) = great excitement. **feverish** *adj.* suffering from a fever. **feverishly** *adv.* excitedly; impatiently.

few [fjuː] *adj. & n.* (a) (-er, -est) not many. (b) a f. = some/several.

fey [feɪ] *adj.* otherworldly (person); not interested in practical things.

fez [fez] *n.* round hat worn in some Muslim countries.

fiancé, fiancée [fɪˈɒnseɪ] *n.* man/woman who is engaged to be married.

fiasco [fɪˈækəʊ] *n.* (*pl.*-os) total failure.

fib 1 [fɪb] *n.* lie. **fib 2** *v.* (fibbed) to tell lies. **fibber** *n.* person who tells lies.

fibre, Am. fiber [ˈfaɪbə] *n.* small thread of material. (b) moral f. = strength of moral feelings. **fibreglass** *n.* (a) glass fibre wool used as insulation (b) strong material made of woven threads of glass plastic containing threads of glass. **fibre optics** *n.* use of thin strands of material through which light can be passed; in order to convey messages or images over long distances.

fibroid *adj.* (growth, etc) made of fibres. **fibrositis** [faɪbrəʊ'saɪtɪs] *n.* pain in tissues, muscles, etc. **fibrous** *adj.* made of fibres.

fibula ['fɪbjʊlə] *n.* thin bone between the knee and the ankle behind the tibia.

fickle ['fɪkl] *adj.* changeable/not steady. **fickleness** *n.* being fickle.

fiction ['fɪkʃn] *n.* (a) story that is not true. (b) novels. **fictional** *adj.* (character) who exists in fiction. **fictitious** [fɪk'tɪʃəs] *adj.* untrue/not real.

fiddle 1 ['fɪdl] *n. inf.* (a) violin. (b) dishonest/illegal dealings; on the f. = trying to make money illegally. **fiddle 2** *v. inf.* (a) to play the fiddle. (b) to play idly with sth. (c) *inf.* to handle (money) in a dishonest way. **fiddler** *n. inf.* violin player. **fiddlesticks** *n. inf.* nonsense. **fiddly** *adj. inf.* small and awkward to use.

fidelity [fɪ'delɪtɪ] *n.* faithfulness/accuracy (of a reproduction).

fidget 1 ['fɪdʒɪt] *n.* person who can not stay still. **fidget 2** *v.* to move restlessly. **fidgety** *adj.* restless.

field 1 [fi:ld] *n.* (a) piece of cultivated land surrounded by fences or hedges. (b) large surface/area; f. day = busy and exciting time. (c) piece of ground for playing games; f. events = jumping and throwing competitions. (d) special area of study. (e) area of influence (of a magnet/of gravity/of a charged particle). **field 2** *v.* (in cricket) (a) to stop (a ball hit by a batsman). (b) to be part of the side which is not batting. **fielder** *n.* (in cricket) member of the side which is not batting. **field glasses** *n. pl.*binoculars. **field hockey** *n. Am.* hockey. **field marshal** *n.* highest rank in the army. **fieldmouse** *n.* (*pl.*-mice) small type of country mouse. **fieldsman** *n.* (pl, -men) (in cricket) member of the side which is not batting. **fieldwork** *n.* scientific research done outside and not in a laboratory. **fieldworker** *n.* person engaged in fieldwork.

fiend [fi:nd] *n.* devil; monster; *inf.* addict. **fiendish** *adj.* devilish; very cruel.

fierce ['frəs] *adj.* ferocious/angry; which will attack anything; (of fire) very hot. **fiercely** *adv.* strongly and angrily. **fierceness** *n.* violence (of a battle); heat (of a fire).

fiery ['faɪərɪ] *adj.* burning/full of fire angry.

fiesta [fɪ'estə] *n.* Spanish festival.

fife [faɪf] *n.* small metal flute played in military bands.

fifteen [fɪfti:n] *n.* (a) number 15. (b) group of fifteen people (as in a Rugby team). **fifteenth, 15th** *adj. & n.* referring to fifteen. **fifth, 5th** [fɪfθ] *adj. & n.* referring to five; f. column = enemy sympathizers inside a country under attack. **Fifth Amendment** *n.* the Amendment to the Constitution of the USA which allows citizens not to give evidence in court which might incriminate themselves. **fifty** ['fɪftɪ] number 50; f. f. = each paying half of the cost. **fiftieth, 50th** *adj.* referring to fifty.

fig [fɪg] *n.* juicy sweet fruit of the tree.

fight 1 [faɪt] *n.* struggle/battle; boxing. **fight 2** *v.* (fought) to hit out; to struggle with (s.o./sth). **fighter** *n.* (a) person who fights. (b) fast attacking aircraft. **fighting** *n.* action of struggling with s.o.

figment ['fɪgmənt] *n.* f. of the imagination = thing which has been imagined.

figure 1 ['fɪgə. [ɑm..] 'fɪgjə] *n.* written number (such as 28). (b) geometric shape such as a triangle or circle; drawing/diagram in a book. (c) shape of a person. (d) f. of speech = colourfull expression used to illustrate a meaning. (e) pattern of movement (in skating/dancing). **figure 2** *v.* (a) to f. out = to try to understand; *inf.* that figures = that makes sense. (b) to appear (in a novel, etc). **figurative** ['fɪgjʊrətɪv] *adj.* (usage of a word) which is not the literal meaning. **figuratively** *adv.* in a figurative way. **figurehead** *n.* (a) wooden figure carved on the front of ship. (b) person who seems important but who has no real power. **figurine** ['fɪgjʊri:n] *n.* small figure (in china/wood, etc).

filament ['fɪləmənt] *n.* thin wire (in an electric bulb).

filbert ['fɪlbət] *n.* type of hazel nut.

filch [fɪltʃ] *v.* to steal.

file 1 [faɪl] *n.* (a) metal tool used for smoothing rough surfaces. (b) holder for papers and documents (c) section of data on a computer. (d) line of people l in single f. = one be behind the other. **file 2** *v.* (a) to smooth (a surface) with a file. (b) to put (papers) away in a folder or case (c) to walk in a line. **filing cabinet** *n.* box with drawers for putting files in. **filings** *n. pl.*small pieces of metal which come away when metal is filed smooth.

filial [fɪlɪəl] *adj.* (formal) referring to a son or daughter.

filibuster 1 [ˈfɪlɪbʌstə] *n.* attempt to prevent a law being passed by speaking for a very long time in the debate. **filibuster 2** *v.* to delay the passing of a law by speaking for a very long time in the debate.

filigree [ˈfɪlɪgriː] *n.* very decorative ornamental work done in precious metals.

Filipino [fɪlɪˈpiːnəʊ] *adj. & n.* (*pl.*-os) (person) from the Philippines.

fill [fɪl] *v.* to put as much as possible into (sth) /to make (sth) full; to become full; to drill a hole in (a bad tooth) and fill it up with metal, etc; to finds s.o. to do (a job). **filler** *n.* material used to fill holes and cracks in walls/wood work, etc. **fill in** *v.* (a) to fill a hole. (b) to complete the blank spaces in (a form/document). (c) *inf.* to f. s.o. in on = to tell/to inform (s.o.). **filling** *n.* thing that fills up sth else. **filling station** *n.* place where you can buy petrol and oil. **fill out** *v.* (a) to write everything that is asked for on (a form). (b) to get fatter. **fill up.** *v.* to fill (sth) until it is completely full; to become completely full; to complete (a form). **fillet 1** [ˈfɪlɪt] *n.* good cut of meat or fish from which all the bones have been removed. **fillet 2** *v.* to remove the bones from (a fish).

fillip [ˈfɪlɪp] *n.* sharp boost.

filly [ˈfɪlɪ] *n.* young female horse.

film 1 [fɪlm] *n.* (a) moving pictures shown on a screen. (b) roll of coated plastic put in a camera and used for taking photographs or moving pictures. (c) thin covering (of dust, etc). **film 2** *v.* to take pictures of (sth) with a cine-camera. **film star** *n.* well-known film actor or actress. **filmstrip** *n.* strip of

film with several still pictures which are projected one after the other. **filmy** *adj.* very thin/almost transparent.

filter 1 [ˈfɪltə] *n.* (a) device/material for straining liquids or air, stopping any solids from passing through. (b) glass on a camera which allows only certain colours or intensities of light to pass through. **filter 2** *v.* (a) to pass through a filter. (b) to move gradually and quietly; f. lane/lights = traffic lane/lights only for cars turning. (c) to f. through/down = to go/come slowly through or down. **filter paper** *n.* paper used for filtering liquids. **filtertip cigarettes** *n. pl.*cigarettes with a filter at the mouth end.

filth [fɪlθ] *n.* dirt; obscene words/books, etc. **filthy** *adj.* (-ire, -best) (a) very dirty. (b) very unpleasant and angry (temper). (c) obscene. **filthily** *adv.* in a filthy way. **filthiness** *n.* being filthy; filthy things.

filtrate [ˈfɪltreɪt] *n.* liquid which has been filtered. **filtration** *n.* action of filtering.

FIMBRA [fɪmbræ] Financial Intermediaries; Managers and Brokers Regulatory Association the organization which regulates the working of investment advisers, insurance brokers, etc.

fin [fɪn] *n.* (a) thin limbo on the body of a fish which it moves to swim. (b) piece shaped in a similar way on a bomb rocket or aircraft.

finagle [fɪˈneɪgl] *v. Am. inf.* to work dishonestly'; to get (sth) dishonestly.

final 1 [ˈfaɪnl] *adj.* coming at the end; last; the decision is f. = cannot be changed. **final 2** *n.* (a) last competition in a tournament between several teams or competitors. (b) finals = last examinations at the end of a university course, after which you get your degree. **finalist** *n.* person taking part in the final competition. **finality** [faɪˈnælɪtɪ] *n.* state of being at the end. **finalization** [faɪnəlarˈzeɪʃn] *n.* act of finalizing. **finalize** [ˈfaɪnəlaɪz] *v.* to finish making plans for sth. **finally** *adv.* at last; in the last place. **finale** [fɪˈnɑːlɪ] *n.* last part of a piece of music/of a show.

finance 1 [ˈfaɪnæns] *n.* money, esp. belonging to the public or to a company. **finance 2** *v.* to provide money for. **financial** [fɪˈnænʃl] *adj.* concerning money; f. year = 12 month period for which accounts are calculated. **financially** *adv.* regarding finance. **financier** [fɪ'nænsɪə] *n.* person who deals with money on a large scale.

finch [fɪntʃ] *n.* (*pl.*es) small seed- eating bird.

find 1 [faɪnd] *n.* good thing which you have discovered. **find 2** *v.* (found) to discover (sth hidden or lost); to be found = to exist; to f. out = to discover to learn; to f. s.o. out = discover s.o. is dishonest or naughty; it has been found that = it is a known fact that. **finder** *n.* person who finds. **findings** *n. pl.*facts discovered/recommendations.

fine 1 [faɪn] *n.* money to be paid as a punishment for doing wrong. **fine 2** *adj.* (-er, -est) (a) pure. (b) lovely/good. (c) (of weather) good; with no rain (d) very thin; very small. **fine 3** *inter.* f. ! = all right/agreed. **fine 4** *v.* (a) to make (sth) fine. (b) to punish by making s.o. pay a fine. **fine art** = painting/ sculpture, etc. **finely** *adv.* delicately/ thinly/beautifully. **finery** *n.* fine clothes.

finesse [fɪ'nes] *n.* skill (in dealing with awkward situations).

finger 1 ['fɪŋgə] *n.* (a) one of the five parts at the end of a hand, *usu.* other than the thumb; to keep your fingers crossed = to hope that sth will happen as you want it; to put your f. on sth = to identify it; to have a f. in every pie = to be involved in every plan. (b) part of a glove into which a finger goes. (c) thing shaped like a finger. **finger 2** *v.* to touch with the fingers. **fingering** *n.* use of the fingers when playing a musical instrument. **fingernail** *n.* thin horny substance which grows at the end of the fingers. **fingerprint** *n.* mark left by the end of the fingers. **fingerstall** *n.* cover put over a finger which has been hurt. **fingertip** *n.* end of the finger; he has it at his fingertips = he knows all about it.

finial ['fɪnɪəl] *n.* decoration on a gable.

finical, finicking, finickity, finicky ['fɪnɪkl,'fɪnɪkɪŋ,fɪ'nɪkɪtɪ,'fɪnɪkɪ] *adj. inf.* (a) awkward and detailed (work). (b) fussy (person) who dislikes things, esp. certain types of food.

finish 1 ['fɪnɪʃ] *n.* (a) end. (b) way in which sth is completed; appearance of sth when it is finished. **finish 2** *v.* to end. **finish off** *v.* (a) to complete (b) to kill. **finish up** *v.* (a) to end up. (b) to finish completely. **finish with** *v.* to. f. with s.o. = to stop being friendly with s.o. to f. with sth = to need sth no longer.

finite ['faɪnaɪt] *adj.* with an end/with a limit; f. verb = verb which indicates a tense.

Finn [fɪn] *n.* person from Finland. **Finnish 1** ['fɪnɪʃ] *adj.* referring to Finland. **Finnish 2** *n.* language spoken in Finland.

fiord ['fjɔːd] *n.* long arm of the sea among mountains in Norway.

fir [fɜː] *n.* f. (tree) = evergreen tree with needle-shaped leaves. **fir cone** *n.* hard scaly fruit of the fir.

fire 1 ['faɪə] *n.* (a) thing that is burning to catch. f = to start burning because of sth else which is in flames; to set f. to sth = to make sth start burning (b) great enthusiasm or excitement. (c) shooting of guns. **fire 2** *v.* (a) to make (sth) burn. (b) to make (s.o.) excited. (c) to bake/to heat. (d) to shoot (a gun); f. away = ask your question. (e) to dismiss (s.o.) from a job. **fire alarm** *n.* bell/siren which gives warning that a fire has started. **firearm** *n.* any gun held in the hand. **firebrand** *n.* agitator. **firebreak** *n.* strip of land which has been cleared of trees, to prevent forest fires from spreading. **firebrigade** *n.* people whose job is to put out fires. **firedamp** *n.* explosive gas in a mine. **fire engine** *n.* vehicle used by the fire brigade to carry pumps/hoses/ladders, etc; to put out fires. **fire escape** *n.* stairs/ladder which can be used by people to get out of buildings on fire. **fire extinguisher** *n.* portable cylinder filled with chemicals or foam to put out a small fire. **firefly** *n.* type of insect which glows at night. **fireguard** *n.* metal screen put in front of a fireplace. **firelight** *n.* light from a fire. **firelighter** *n.* block of inflammable material used to start a fire. **fireman** *n.* (*pl.*-men) (a) man whose job it is to put out fires. (b) man who keeps the fire burning in a furnace/a steam train. **fireplace** *n.* place where a fire is lit indoors. **fireproof** *adj.* which will not burn. **fireside** *n.* area around a fireplace in a room. **fire station** *n.* centre where fire engines are based. **firewarden** *n.* person whose job it is to look out for forest fires. **firewood** *n.* (no *pl.*) wood for making fires. **firework** *n.* small container holding chemical which will sparkle or explode when lit. **firm 1** [fɜ:m] *n.* business/company. **firm 2** *adj.* solid/fixed/strong. **firm 3** *adv.* to stand f. = to refuse to change your mind. **firmly** *adv.* in a strong way. **firmament** ['fɜ:məmənt] *n.* (formal) sky.

first 1 [fɜ:st] *adj. & adv.* (as a number can be written 1st) (a) at the beginning/ coming before everything else; at f. = at the beginning. (b) for the first time (c) in a first class seat. **first 2** *n.* thing/person coming before everything else; in f. = in first gear; a f. in Physics = a first class degree. **first aid** *n.* help given to a person who is hurt before a doctor or ambulance arrives. **First Amendment** *n.* the Amendment to the Constitution of the USA which grants citizens freedom of speech. **first class. 1** *adj.* excellent; highest; most expensive. **first class 2** *adv.* (travel) with the most expensive seats. **first day cover** *n.* special stamped envelope cancelled on the first day of issue of the stamp on it. **first floor** *n,* storey above the ground floor in a building; *Am.* ground floor. **firsthand** *adj. & adv.* direct from the original source. **First Lady** *n.* wife of the President of the USA. **firstly** *adv.* to start with. **first mate** *n.* second-in command of a merchant ship. **first night** *n.* evening when a play is performed for the first time. **first-rate** *adj.* excellent.

firth [fɜ:θ] *n.* (n Scotland) long arm of the sea.

fiscal ['fɪskl] *adj.* (a) referring to tax/ government revenue (b) (in Scotland) procurator f. = public prosecutor.

fish 1 [fɪʃ] *n.* (*pl.*fish, occasionally fishes) cold-blooded animal with fins and scales, that lives in water; he's like a f. out of water = awkward. because he feels he is not in his usual surroundings. **fish 2** *v.* (a) to try to catch fish; *inf.* to f. out = to take out. (b) to try to get (information). **fishbone** *n.* bone in a fish. **fishcake** *n.* round cake of fish

and potato mixed together. **fisherman** *n.* (*pl.*-men) man who catches fish, either as his job or for sport. **fishery** *n.* business of catching fish. **fish finger,** *Am.* **fish stick** *n.* frozen finger-shaped piece of fish covered in breadcrumbs. **fish-hook** *n.* metal hook at the end of a line which catches in the mouth of the fish. **fishing** *n.* catching fish. **fishing boat** *n.* boat used for fishing. **fishing rod.** *n.* long piece of wood to which is attached the line and hook. **fishing tackle** *n.* all the equipment used by a fisherman. **fishmonger** *n.* man who sells raw fish in a shop. **fishmonger's** *n.* shop selling raw fish. **fishplate** *n.* metal clamp which holds rails together. **fish shop** *n.* shop selling (i) raw fish or (ii) (also fish-and-chip shop) cooked fish and chips. **fish slice** *n.* flat utensil used for turning food and removing it from a frying pan. **fishy** *adj.* (a) like a fish. (b) *inf.* suspicious/odd (story, etc).

fission ['fɪʃn] *n.* breaking up of sth into parts; nuclear f. = breaking up of an atom in an explosion.

fissure ['fɪʃə] *n.* crack/split, esp. in a rock or in the ground.

fist [fɪst] *n.* tightly closed hand. **fistful** *n.* amount you can hold in your fist. **fisticuffs** *n.* *pl.*(old) fighting.

fit 1 [fɪt] *n.* sudden sharp attack of illness, etc; by fits and starts = at odd moments/ with continual stoppages. **fit 2** *adj.* (fitter, fittest) (a) right/suitable. (b) capable. (c) healthy. **fit 3** *v.* (fitted) (a) to be the right place. (b) to make suitable for. **fitful** *adj.* irregular. **fitfully** *adv.* irregularly. **fit in.** *v.* (a) to be suitable/to match (with). (b) to find room/time for (s.o./sth). **fitment** *n.* piece of furniture which is fixed in a room. **fitness** *n.* being fit. **fit out, fit up** *v.* to provide all the equipment/clothing necessary for. **fitted** *adj.* suitable/right; which has been made to fit. **fitter** *n.* (a) skilled mechanic who adjusts machines and their parts, (b) person who makes sure clothes fit. **fitting. 1** *adj.* suitable/right. **fitting 2** *n.* (a) action of making sth fit/of trying on a new piece of clothing; f. room = small room in shop where you can try on clothes before you buy them. (b) size (of shoe, etc). (c) thing which is fixed in a building but which could be removed.

five [faɪv] n. number 5. **fiver** n. inf. five pound note; five dollar bill. **fives** n. game in which a ball is hit off the walls of a court with the hands or a bat.

fix 1 [fɪks] n. (pl.-es) (a) difficult position. (b) Sl. injection of a drug such as heroin. **fix 2** v. (a) to fasten/to attach. (b) to arrange. (c) Am. to make/to prepare (a drink/meal, etc). (d) to pass (a photographic plate) through a liquid to stop the image changing. (e) to mend. **fixated** adj. obsessed. **fixation** [fɪk'seɪʃn] n. obsession. **fixative** ['fɪksətɪv] n. substance which fixes the colours on a painting. **fixed** adj. (a) attached firmly. (b) (price. etc.) arranged or agreed upon. **fixedly** ['fɪksɪdlɪ] adv. with eyes fixed on s.o. **fixer** n. person who can arrange sth. **fixity** n. state of being fixed. **fixture** ['fɪkstʃə] n. (a) (date for a) sports match. (b) fixtures = objects permanently fixed in a house (like radiators). **fix up** v. to arrange.

fizz 1 [fɪz] n. sound like a lot of bubbles. **fizz 2** v. to bubble up. **fizzy** adj. bubbly. **fizzle out** ['fɪzl'aʊt] v. inf. to come to nothing/not to work.

fjord ['fjɔːd] n. fiord.

flabbergast ['flæbəgɑːst] v. to amaze.

flabby ['flæbɪ] adj. (-iesr, best) (person) who is soft and fat. **flab** n. inf. soft excess flesh. **flabbiness** n. being flabby.

flaccid ['flæksɪd] adj. hanging loosely.

flag 1 [flæg] n. (a) piece of material with the emblem of a country/club. etc. on it (b) small paper badges sold in aid of charities. (c) large paving stone. (d) iris/marsh plant with long fat leaves and purple flowers. (e) mark inserted in a computer text. **flag 2** v. (flagged) (a) to grow tired (b) to f. down = to wave to make (a taxi) stop. (c) to insert a mark in a computer file. **flag day** n. day on which small paper flags are sold in aid of a charity. **flagpole, flagstaff** n. tall pole on which large flags are flown.

flagship n. ship on which the admiral sails. and which therefore flies his special flag. **flagstone** n. large flat stone used for making pavements/floors.

flagellate ['flædʒəleɪt] v. (formal) to whip. **flagellation** [flædʒə'leɪʃn] n. (formal) whipping.

flagon ['flægən] n. large round container for liquids.

flagrant ['fleɪgrənt] adj. (crime) which is obvious. **flagrance** n. being flagrant. **flagrantly** adv. in a flagrant way.

flail 1 [fleɪl] n. implement for threshing corn. **flail 2** v. to wave (your arms) about.

flair ['fleə] n. natural ability (for sth).

flak [flæk] n. (no pl.) gun fire against aircraft; sharp criticism.

flake 1 [fleɪk] n. tiny. thin piece. **flake 2** v. to f. off/away = to fall off in little pieces; Sl; to f. out = to collapse with tiredness. **flaky** adj. in thin pieces.

flamboyant [flæm'bɔɪənt] adj. brightly coloured; too bright. **flamboyance** n. being flamboyant. **flamboyantly** adv. in a flamboyant way.

flame [fleɪm] n. bright tongue of fire. **flameproof, flame-resistant** adj. specially treated so that it will not catch fire or melt. **flaming** adj. (a) in flames. (b) in a f. temper = furious/in a very bad mood.

flamingo [flə'mɪŋgəʊ] n. (pl.-os) water bird with long legs and neck. often with pink feathers.

flammable ['flæməbl] adj. easily set on fire/inflammable.

flan [flæn] n. open tart.

flange [flændʒ] n. rim/edge which sticks out on a pipe or wheel; f. coupling = joint with a rim sticking out.

flank 1 [flæŋk] n. side (esp. of an animal. an army). **flank 2** v. to be at the side of (sth).

flannel ['flænl] n. (a) warm woollen material; flannels = flannel trousers. (b) small piece of towelling for washing the face or body. **flannelette** n. warm cotton material, which feels like flannel.

flap 1 [flæp] n. (a) hinged part (which hangs down). (b) inf. excitement and worry. (c) movement like that of a bird's wing. **flap 2** v. (flapped) to move up and down like a bird's wing. **flapjack** n. flat cake made of oats. honey. etc.

flare 1 ['fleə] n. (a) device which gives a sudden blaze of light (esp. as a signal). (b) widening bottom part (of a skirt/of trousers). **flare 2** v. (a) to burn brightly. (b) (of a skirt/trousers) to widen gradually. **flare up** v. (a) to blaze suddenly. (b) to get angry.

flash 1 [flæʃ] n. (pl, -es) (a) short sudden burst of light or emotion; in a f. = very quickly. (b) apparatus for taking photographs in the dark. (c) short item of news. (d) coloured marking on a uniform. **flash 2** v. (a) to light up quickly and suddenly. (b) to show (sth) quickly. (c) to f. by/past = to move/to pass by quickly. **flashback** n. scene in a film, showing what happened at an earlier date. **flashbulb** n. photographic light bulb which makes a short burst of light when you take a photograph. **flashcube** n. square block of four flash bulbs. **flasher** n. inf. man who exposes his private parts. **flashgun** n. photographic device for holding a flashbulb. **flashily** adv. in a flashy way. **flashiness** n. being flashy. **flashing** n. metal strip which covers a joint in a roof. **flashlight** n. hand torch/lamp. **flashpoint** n. temperature at which gas or petrol vapour will ignite/moment at which a revolution will break out. **flashy** adj. showy and bright but of poor quality.

flask [flɑːsk] n. (small) bottle for liquids; thermos f./vacuum f. = insulated bottle for keeping liquids hot or cold.

flat 1 [flæt] adj. & adv. (flatter. flattest) (a) level/smooth; punctured (tyre); f. rate = fixed charge which never changes. (b) (of drink) no longer sparkling. (c) (of battery) no longer producing electricity. (d) (of music) below the correct pitch. (e) definite (refusal). (f) to go f. out = as fast as you can go; f. broke = with no money at all. **flat 2** n. (a) place which is level; f. racing = horse racing on a level course, not over jumps. (b) Am. puncture/flat tyre. (c) accommodation made up of a set of rooms. usu. on one floor, in a building containing several such groups of rooms. (d) note in music which is a semitone lower. **flatfish** n. type of fish with a flattened body. **flatlet** n. small flat. **flatly** adv. definitely. **flatten** v. to make flat. **flatworm** n. worm with a flat body. **flatter** ['flætə] v. (a) to praise (s.o.) insincerely. (b) to make (s.o.) feel honoured. (c) to f. yourself = to deceive yourself/to persuade yourself that sth is true. when it is not. **flatterer** n. person who flatters. **flattery** n. insincere praise.

flatulence ['flætjʊləns] n. gas in the intestine. **flatulent** adj. suffering from flatulence.

flaunt [flɔːnt] v. to display (sth) in a vulgar way to attract attention.

flautist ['flɔːtɪst] n. person who plays the flute.

flavour, Am. **flavor 1** ['fleɪvə] n. taste. **flavour 2** v. to add spices and seasoning in cooking; to add a flavour to (sth). **flavouring** n. substance added to food to give a particular taste.

flaw 1 [flɔː] n. fault/mistake; defect. **flaw 2** v. to spoil. **flawless** adj. perfect

flax [flæks] n. (no pl.) plant used for making linen cloth. **flaxen-haired** adj. fairhaired.

flay [fleɪ] v. (a) to strip the skin off (an animal). (b) to beat (s.o.) harshly.

flea [fliː] n. tiny blood-sucking insect that jumps. **flea bite** n. (a) place where a flea has bitten. (b) inf. very slight bother. **flea market** n. market for secondhand goods.

fleck 1 [flek] n. small spot. **fleck 2** v. to mark (sth) with spots.

fled [fled] v. see flee.

fledgling ['fledʒlɪŋ] n. small bird ready to fly from the nest.

flee [fliː] v. (fled) to run away (from).

fleece 1 [fliːs] n. wool of a sheep. **fleece 2** v. SI. to cheat (s.o.) and take their money. **fleecy** adj. made of fleece; covered with fleece; looking like fleece.

fleet 1 [fliːt] n. (a) group of ships belonging together. (b) collection of vehicles. **fleet 2** adj. rapid (footsteps). **fleeting** ['fliːtɪŋ] adj. short and quick. **fleetingly** adv. rapidly.

flesh [fleʃ] n. (a) soft part of the body covering the bones; in the f. = in reality (not on TV or in photographs); a f. wound = one which is not too deep; his own f. and blood = his relations/his family. (b) soft part of a fruit. **fleshy** adj. fat/plump.

fleur-de-lys [flɜːdə'liːs] n. lily design formerly the emblem of France.

flew [fluː] v. see fly.

flex 1 [fleks] n. flexible insulated cable for carrying electricity. **flex 2** v. to bend. **flexibility** [fleksɪ'bɪlɪtɪ] n. ability to bend easily/to adapt to new circumstances. **flexible** *adj.* (a) easy to bend (b) adaptable. **flexibly** *adv.* in a flexible way. **flexitime** *n.* system where workers can start and stop their day's work at various times.

flibbertigibbet ['flɪbətɪdʒɪbɪt] *n.* silly empty-headed woman.

flick 1 [flɪk] *n.* little sharp blow/tap. **flick 2** *v.* to hit lightly. **flick knife** *n.* knife with a blade which can fit inside the handle and which shoots out when a spring is released. **flick through** *v.* to glance at (the pages of a book) very rapidly. **flicker 1** ['flɪkə] *n.* trembling/quivering. **flicker 2** *v.* tremble/to quiver; to burn unsteadily.

flier ['flaɪə] *n.* see fly.

flight [flaɪt] *n.* (a) journey through the air; flying. (b) group of birds/air craft flying together. (c) f. of stairs = group of stairs in one direction. (d) running away; to put to f. = to chase away; to take f. = to run away. **flight deck** *n.* (a) flat surface on an aircraft carrier on which aircraft land and take off. (b) section at the front of a large aircraft where the pilots sit. **flightless** *adj.* (bird) which cannot fly. **flight lieutenant** *n.* rank in the air force below squadron leader.

flight recorder *n.* box carried on a plane where details of the flight are recorded automatically. **flighty** ['flaɪtɪ] *adj.* silly and empty-headed.

flimsy ['flɪmzɪ] *adj.* (of material) light and thin; poorly made; poor (excuse). **flimsily** *adv.* in a flimsy way. **flimsiness** *n.* being flimsy.

flinch [flɪntʃ] *v.* to move back in pain/fear.

fling 1 [flɪŋ] *n.* (a) wild dance. (b) to have one's f. = to let off one's high spirits. **fling 2** *v.* (flung) to throw wildly.

flint [flɪnt] *n.* (a) very hard type of rock which makes sparks when struck. (b) small piece of metal which makes a spark to light a cigarette lighter. **flinty** *adj.* hard/severe (look).

flip [flɪp] *v.* (flipped) to hit lightly; to f. over = to turn over quickly. **flip flops.** *n. pl.* rubber sandal held on by a strap between the toes. **flip side** *n.* second side of a record. **flippant** ['flɪpənt] *adj.* joking about things which should be taken seriously. **flippantly** *adv.* in a

flippant way. **flipper** ['flɪpə] *n.* (a) limb of a sea animal used for swimming. (b) long flat piece of rubber which you can attach to your foot to help you swim faster.

flirt 1 [flɜːt] *n.* person, esp. woman who flirts. **flirt 2** *v.* to play at attracting people of the opposite sex for amusement. **flirtation** [flɜː'teɪʃn] *n.* brief love affair. **flirtatious** *adj.* (person) who flirts a lot.

flit 1 [flɪt] *n.* to do a moonlight f. = to escape quietly at night. **flit 2** *v.* (fitted) (a) to move quickly and quietly. (b) to go away quietly without anyone noticing.

Flitch [flɪtʃ] *n.* (*pl.*-es) side of bacon.

float 1 [fləʊt] *n.* (a) piece of cork, etc., attached to a fishing line which will float on the surface of the water. (b) decorated lorry in a procession; milk f. = low electric truck for delivering milk. (c) cash taken from a central supply and used for small expenses. **float 2** *v.* to (make sth) lie on the top of a liquid; to start up (a company by selling shares in it; to let (a currency, such as the pound sterling) find its own exchange rate internationally and not fix it at a certain amount. **floating** *adj.* resting on the surface of a liquid; f. voter = person who is uncertain which party to vote for in an election.

flock 1 [flɒk] *n.* (a) group of similar animals together, esp. sheep/goats/birds. (b) waste cotton. **flock 2** *v.* to move in a group; to f. together = to come together in a group.

floe [fləʊ] *n.* large sheet of ice floating on the sea.

flog [flɒg] *v.* (flogged (a) to beat hard, usu. with a whip. (b) St. to sell.

flood 1 [flʌd] *n.* large amount of water over land which is *usu.* dry. (b) large amount of (tears/letters, etc.) **flood 2** *v.* to cover with water; they flooded in = came in large numbers. **floodgate** *n.* part of lock/sluice/dam in a river, which can be opened or shut and which helps control the flow of the water. **floodlight 1** *n.* powerful light often used for lighting the outside of a building or a football pitch at night. **floodlight 2** *v.* (floodlit) to light with floodlights.

floor 1 [flɔː] *n.* (a) part of a room on which you walk. (b) storey/one level of rooms in a building. (c) part of an assembly room where people discuss; to take the f. = to start speaking in a discussion. **floor 2** *v.* (a) to knock to the ground. (b) to amaze and puzzle (s.o.). **floorboard** *n.* long flat piece of wood used for making wooden floors. **floorcloth** *n.* cloth for washing floors. **floorshow** *n.* cabaret entertainment.

flop 1 [flɒp] *n* (a) *inf.* failure. (b) movement of sth falling limply. **flop 2** *v.* (flopped) (a) to fall/to sit/to lie limply or heavily. (b) *inf.* to fail. **floppy** *adj.* which hangs limply; f. disk = disk used in a computer.

flora ['flɔːrə] *n.* wild plants (of an area). **floral** *adj.* referring to flowers.

floret ['flɒrɪt] *n.* little flower which is part of a flowerhead.

floribunda [flɒrɪ'bʌndə] *n.* type of rose with many small flowers.

florid ['flɒrɪd] *adj.* red (face).

florin ['flɒrɪn] *n.* (old) British coin worth two shillings.

florist ['flɒrɪst] *n.* person who sells flowers.

floss [flɒs] *n.* waste silk threads; dental f. = thin thread for pulling between the teeth to remove pieces of food; candy f. = molten sugar spun to make a fluffy mass.

flotation [fləʊ'teɪʃn] *n.* starting of a new company by selling shares in it.

flotilla [flə'tɪlə] *n.* small group of boats.

flotsam ['flɒtsəm] *n.* (no *pl.*) rubbish floating in the water.

flounce 1 [flaʊns] *n.* border of ruffled cloth (attached to a skirt, etc). **flounce 2** *v.* to f. out = to go out of a room showing your impatience and annoyance. **flounced** *adj.* with flounces.

flounder 1 ['flaʊndə] *n.* common edible flat fish. **flounder 2** *v.* (also flounder about, around) to move (in water) with difficulty; to be uncertain of an answer to a question.

flour ['flaʊə] *n.* grain crushed to powder, used for making bread/cakes, etc. **flourmill** *n.* place where grain is ground into flour. **floury** *adj.* like flour.

flourish 1 ['flʌrɪʃ] *n.* (*pl.*-es) (a) wide movement of the arm in the air(b) large curve in handwriting. (c) fanfare (of trumpets). **flourish 2** *v.* (a) to grow well. (b) to wave (sth) in the air.

flout [flaʊt] *v.* to scorn/to disregard (sth).

flow 1 [fləʊ] *n.* movement of liquid/air, etc. **flow 2** *v.* to move along smoothly. **flowchart** *n.* diagram showing the stages in a process.

flower 1 ['flaʊə] *n.* colourful part of a plant which produces the seed. **flower 2** *v.* to make flowers. **flowerbed** *n.* part of a garden where flowers are grown. **flowerpot** *n.* container to grow plants in. **flowery** *adj.* (a) (also flowered) decorated with a pattern of flowers. (b) ornate (style).

flown [fləʊn] *v.* see fly.

flu [fluː] *n.* influenza/common illness like a bad cold, often with a high temperature.

fluctuate ['flʌktjʊeɪt] *v.* to move back wards and forwards/up and down.

fluctuation [flʌktjʊ'eɪʃn] *n.* movement backwards and forwards/up and down.

flue [fluː] *n.* pipe leading to a chimney.

fluency ['fluːənsɪ] *n.* case of speaking.
fluent *adj.* able to speak easily.
fluently *adv.* easily.

fluff 1 [flʌf] *n.* soft pieces of wool or hair. **fluff 2** *v. inf.* to do (sth) badly. **fluffiness** *n.* being fluffy. **fluffy** *adj.* like fluff; covered with fluff.

fluid 1 ['fluːɪd] *n.* liquid. **fluid 2** *adj.* (situation) which is not settled. **fluidity** [fluː'ɪdɪtɪ] *n.* being fluid.

fluke [fluːk] *n.* (a) *inf.* chance/lucky event. (b) one of the two flat parts of a whale's tail/of an anchor. (c) type of flatworm.

flummox ['flʌməks] *v. inf.* to confuse (s.o.).

flung [flʌŋ] *v.* see fling.

flunk [flʌŋk] *v. Am. inf.* to fail (an examination/a candidate).

flunkey ['flʌŋkɪ] *n.* servant.

fluorescence [flʊə'resns] *n.* ability to send out a glow of light when an electric current is applied. **fluorescent** *adj.* giving off light when electric current is applied.

fluorine ['flʊəriːn] *n.* (element: F) pale yellow-green gas. **fluoridation** [flʊəraɪ'deɪʃn] *n.* adding fluoride to water (to prevent tooth decay). **fluoride** ['flʊəraɪd] *n.* compound of fluorine; f. toothpaste = toothpaste with small amount of fluoride added in order to prevent tooth decay.

flurry ['flʌrɪ] n. (a) hurried excitement. (b) sudden small amount of snow, rain or wind.

flush 1 [flʌʃ] n. (pl.-es) (a) redness of the face. (b) rush of water. (c) (at cards) hand with all the cards of the same suit. **flush 2** v. (a) to go red in the face. (b) to f. out = to drive out of hiding. (c) to f. a lavatory = to wash it out by moving a handle which makes water flush through. **flush 3** adj. (a) f. with = level with. (b) inf. having plenty of money to spend.

fluster 1 ['flʌstə] n. nervous worry. **fluster 2** v. to worry/to confuse (s.o.).

flute [fluːt] n. (a) wind instrument played by blowing across a small hole at the end of a pipe. (b) long rounded groove. **fluted** adj. decorated with grooves or scallops. **flutist** n. Am. person who plays the flute.

flutter 1 ['flʌtə] n. (a) light movement, esp. of wings. (b) inf. small gamble. **flutter 2** v. (a) to move (wings, etc) quickly and lightly. (b) to move softly and quickly.

fluvial ['fluːvɪəl] adj. referring to rivers.

flux [flʌks] n. (a) constant change. (b) substance used in soldering.

fly 1 [flaɪ] n. (pl.flies) (a) small insect with two wings. f. fishing = sport of fishing = sport of fishing with an imitation fly as bait. (b) (also flies) trouser front fastened by a zip or buttons. **fly 2** v. (flew; has flown) (a) to move through the air (b) to move fast. (c) to put up (a flag). **fly 3** adj. inf. clever/sly. **flyblown** adj. rotten (meat). **fly-by-night** n. inf. unreliable company. **flycatcher** n. bird which catches flies. **flier, flyer** n. (a) person who pilots an aircraft. (b) paper advertising sth. **flying club.** n. club for people interested in flying aircraft. **flying doctor** n. doctor who visits patients using an aircraft. **flying fish** n. fish which jumps out of the water as it moves. **flying saucer** n. unidentified flying object which people claim to see and which they think comes from another planet. **flying squad** n. group of policemen who arrive quickly at the scene of a crime. **flying start** n. good beginning to a race/a new job, etc. **flying visit** n. very short visit. **flyleaf** n. blank leaf of paper at the beginning and end of a book. **flyover** n. road

built to pass over another. **flypast** n. flight of aircraft over a certain spot to celebrate sth. **flysheet** n. extra roof for a tent. **flyweight** n. lightest category of boxer. **flywheel** n. large heavy wheel which turns, keeping an engine working at a steady pace.

foal [fəʊl] n. young horse.

foam 1 [fəʊm] n. mass of small bubbles; f. rubber = rubber in blocks with many little holes in it, used for chair cushions, etc. **foam 2** v. to make froth. **foamy** adj. covered with foam.

fob 1 [fɒb] n. little ornament attached to a watch-chain. **fob 2** v. (fobbed) to f s.o. off with sth = to deceive s.o. into accepting sth which they don't really want. **fob watch** n. watch carried in a pocket attached to the end of a chain.

fo 'c' sle ['fəʊksl] n. front part of a ship where the crew lives.

focus 1 ['fəʊkəs] n. (a) (pl.foci) point where rays of light from an object meet; in. f. = clearly visible; out of f. = blurred/not clear. (b) centre of attention. **focus 2** v. to adjust so as to be able to see clearly. **focal** adj. referring to a focus.

fodder ['fɒdə] n. food for cows/sheep, etc.

foe [fəʊ] n. (formal) enemy/opponent.

foetus, Am. **fetus** ['fiːtəs] n. unborn child/reptile/birth, etc., which is developing from an embryo. **foetal** adj. referring to a foetus.

fog [fɒg] n. thick mist through which it is difficult to see. **fogginess** n. being foggy. **foggy** adj. misty. **foghorn** n. hooter used in fog as a warning to ships. **foglamp** n. car lamp used in fog.

fogey ['fəʊgɪ] n. old f. = reactionary old man.

foible ['fɔɪbl] n. odd way of behaving or thinking.

foil 1 [fɔɪl] n. (a) thin metal sheet; tin f./cooking f. = foil used for wrapping food before cooking. (b) long thin sword with a button on the end used in the sport of fencing. (c) person who contrasts sharply with another and so makes the other's qualities stand out. **foil 2** v. to defeat; to prevent (a plot) being put into effect.

foist [fɔɪst] v. to f. sth on s.o. = to force s.o. to accept sth which they don't want.

fold 1 [fəʊld] n. (a) small enclosure for sheep. (b) crease (in paper/cloth, etc.)

fold 2 v. (a) to bend (sth) so that one part is on top of another. (b) to f. your arms = to bend your arms together in front of your chest. **folder** n. cardboard envelope for holding papers. **folding** adj. able to be folded. **fold up** v. (a) to bend (sth) over to make a smaller area than before. (b) inf. to finish/to end.

foliage ['fəʊliɪdʒ] n. leaves in a tree or plant. **foliar** adj. referring to leaves.

folio ['fəʊliəʊ] n. (a) very large size of book. (b) page number.

folk [fəʊk] n. pl.people; my f. =,my family. **folk dance** n. traditional dance. **folklore** n. traditional stories and beliefs. **folksong** n. traditional song. **folkweave** n. traditional peasant cloth.

follicle ['fɒlɪkl] n. small hole (in the skin) out of which a hair grows.

follow ['fɒləʊ] v. (a) to go after/to come after; to continue along (a road). (b) to act in accordance with (a rule). (c) understand. **follower** n. supporter. **following** adj. which follows; next. **follow up** v. to investigate/to research (sth) further.

folly ['fɒlɪ] n. silly behaviour.

foment [fə'ment] v. (formal) to stir up (trouble). **fomentation** [fəʊmen'teɪʃn] n. act of stirring up trouble.

fond [fɒnd] adj. loving; I am f. of music = I like music. **fondly** adv. in a found way. **fondness** n. liking/love. **fondle** ['fɒndl] v. to stroke lovingly.

fondue ['fɒndjuː] n. dish of melted cheese into which pieces of bread are dipped or of hot oil into which pieces of meat are dipped.

font [fɒnt] n. basin holding holy water for baptism in a church.

fontanelle [fɒntə'nel] n. soft membrane between the pieces of the skull of a baby.

food [fuːd] n. substances eaten by people and animals or taken in by plants; f. poisoning = illness caused by sth eaten. **foodstuff** n. thing that can be eaten.

fool 1 [fuːl] n. (a) idiot/stupid person. (b) type of creamed fruit dessert. **fool 2** v. (a) to f. about/around = to play around in a silly way. (b) to trick (s.o.).

foolhardy adj. brav, but taking unnecessary risks. **foolish** adj.. silly/

stupid. **foolishly** adv. stupidly.
foolishness n. silliness/stupidity.
foolproof adj. so simple that even an idiot could use it safely. **foolscap** ['fuːlskæp] n. large size of writing paper.

foot 1 [fʊt] n. (pl.feet) (a) part of the leg on which you stand; on f. = walking; under f. = on the ground inf. to put your f. in it = to say sth embarrassing; to put your f. down = to be firm/not to give in. (b) base/end of sth. (c) measure of length (= 30. 5 cm); three feet wide. **foot 2** v. (a) to f. it = to walk. (b) to f. the bill = to pay the bill. **foot and mouth disease** n. disease of cows. **footage** n. (no pl.) cine film which has been exposed.

football n. (a) game played between two teams with a ball which is kicked; Rugby f. = game played between two teams with an oval ball which can be kicked or passed by hand. (b) ball used in the game of football. **footballer** n. person who plays football. **footbrake** n. break (on a machine or car) operated by the foot. **footbridge** n. small bridge for people to walk across. **footfall** n. footstep. **foothills** n. pl.lower slopes. **foothold** n. (a) place where you can put your foot when climbing. (b) small position on which you can build.

footing n. (a) safe place for your feet. (b) to put things on a firm f. = to base things firmly. **footlights** n. pl.row of lights along the front of the stage in a theatre. **footloose** adj. free to go anywhere; with no ties. **footman** n. (pl.-men) male servant. **footnote** n. explanation at the bottom of a page, ferring to sth on the page. **footpath** n. path for walkers. **footplate** n. platform in a steam engine for the driver and his helper. **footprint** n. mark left by the foot on the ground. **footslogging** n. walking. **food soldier** n. soldier who travels on foot. **footsore** adj. (person) with feet which hurt. **footstep** n. sound of a foot touching the ground. **footstool** n. small stool which supports the feet. **footwear** n. (no pl.) boots and shoes. **footwork** n. (no pl) way of using your feet (esp. in sports). **footling** ['fuːtlɪŋ] adj. silly/ insignificant.

for 1 [fɔː] prep. (a) in exchange. (b) in support of. (c) used as. (d) because of.

(e) in the direction of; the train f. London. (f) towards; my love f. you. (g) over a distance of/over a length of time; f. miles; f. a fortnight. (h) as a present to; belonging to; a letter f. you. (i) in the place of; can you write this letter f. me? (j) with the purpose of; to go f. a walk; run f. the bus = to catch the bus. (k) f. all that = in spite of everything; as f. = regarding; f. sale = able to be bought f. example = to name one thing out of many; f. ever/f good = always; f. the most part = usually. **for 2** *conj.* because.

forage 1 ['fɒrɪdʒ] *n.* food for horses and cattle. **forage 2** *v.* (a) to search for food/supplies. (b) to rummage/to look for sth. **forage cap** *n.* soft cap shaped like an upturned boat.

foray ['fɒreɪ] *n.* sudden attack.

forbade [fə'bæd] *v.* see forbid.

forbearance [fɔː'bearəns] *n.* patience. **forbearing** *adj.* patient/long-suffering.

forbid [fə'bɪd] *v.* (forbade[xxxxx] forbidden) to tell (s.o.) no to do sth. **forbidding** *adj.* sinister/looking dangerous.

force 1 [fɔːs] *n.* (a) strength/power; in f. = (i) in large numbers; (ii) (law which is) operating/working. (b) organized group of people; the armed forces = navy, army and air force. **force 2** *v.* (a) to move by using strength. (b) to compel/ to make (s.o.) do sth. (c) to make (plants) grow faster/earlier than normal. **force back** *v.* to push sth back very hard. **forced** *adj.* (a) compelled; f. landing = quick landing of an aircraft because sth is wrong. (b) artificial/not real. **force-feed** *v.* (force fed) to feed (s.o. on hunger strike) by force. **forceful** *adj.* strong/powerful. **forcefully** *adv.* in a forceful way. **forcefulness** *n.* being forceful. **force majeure** *n.* thing which happens (such as a war) which cannot be controlled by parties to a contract. **forcemeat** *n.* minced meat used as stuffing (for turkeys, etc.).

forceps ['fɔːseps] *n.* (no pl) pincers used by doctors in surgery.

forcible ['fɔːsɪbl] *adj.* done by/with force. **forcibly** *adv.* using force.

ford 1 [fɔːd] *n.* shallow part of a river where you can cross by going through the water. **ford 2** *v.* to cross a river by

going through a shallow part. **fordable** *adj.* (river) which can be forded.

fore 1 [fɔː] *n.* front part of a ship; f. and aft = front and back of a ship,to come to the f. = to become prominent. **fore 2** *adj.* front/before (used as a prefix in words such as forearm, foresee).

forearm. 1 ['fɔːrɑːm] *n.* part of the arm between the hand and the elbow.

forearm 2 *v.* to get ready for a fight in good time. **forebears** *n.* *pl.*(old) ancestors. **foreboding** [fɔː'bəʊdɪŋ] *n.* feeling that sth evil will take place.

forecast 1 *n.* description of what will happen in the future. **forecast 2** *v.* (forecast) to say what will happen in the future. **forecaster** *n.* person who says what will happen in the future, esp. concerning the weather. **forecastle** ['fəʊksl] *n.* front part of a ship where the crew live. **foreclose** [fɔː'kləʊz] *v.* to take away property because the owner cannot pay back money which he has borrowed on its security. **foreclosure** *n.* act of foreclosing. **forecourt** *n.* courtyard in front of a building.

forefather *n.* ancestor. **forefinger** *n.* index finger/first finger next to the thumb. **forefoot** *n.* front foot (of an animal). **forefront** *n.* to be in the f. of a campaign = to be one of the leaders.

forego [fɔː'gəʊ] *v.* (forwent, has foregone) to do without. **foregoing** *adj.* which has gone before. **foregone** *adj.* decided in advance; it was a f. conclusion = everyone knew.

foreground *n.* part of a picture/scene nearest the viewer. **forehand** *adj.* (in tennis) stroke played with the palm of the hand facing forwards. **forehead** ['fɒrɪd, 'fɔːhed] *n.* part of the head between the eyes and the hair.

foreknowledge *n.* knowledge in advance. **foreland** *n.* headland. **foreleg** *n.* front leg of an animal. **foreman** *n.* (pl, -men) (a) (in a factory) workman in charge of several others. (b) f. of a jury = spokesman for the jury. **foremost** *adj. & adv.* first/chief; first and f. = first of all. **forenoon** *n.* morning. **forepaw** *n.* front paw. **forerunner** *n.* person/thing coming before another more important one. **foresee** [fɔː'siː] *v.* (foresaw; has foreseen) to feel in advance that sth will happen. **foreseeable** *adj.* which can be foreseen. **foreshadow** [fɔː'ʃædəʊ] *v.* to be a sign of (sth to come). **foreshore** *n.* part of a beach which is covered by the sea at each high tide. **foresight** *n.* ability to see what will probably happen in the future; ability to plan for emergencies. **foreskin** *n.* loose skin covering the end of the penis. **forestall** [fɔː'stɔːl] *v.* to anticipate/to stop (s.o. doing sth). **foretaste** *n.* small bit of sth that will be had later on. **foretell** [fɔː'tel] *v.* (foretold) to predict/to say what will happen in the future. **forethought** *n.* thinking ahead. **forewarned** *adj.* warned in advance. **foreword** *n.* short section at the beginning of a book introducing it to the reader.

foreign ['fɒrən] *adj.* (a) not belonging to your own country (b) strange; f. exchange = exchanging the money of one country for money of another; f. to his nature = very strange for him to do it. (c) f. body = thing from outside which lodges in your body. **foreigner** *n.* person who does not belong to your country.

forensic [fə'rensɪk] *adj.* referring to the solving and punishment of crime; f. medicine = medicine concerned with crimes.

forest [fɒrɪst] *n.* large area covered with trees. **forester, forest ranger** *n.* person whose job it is to look after a forest. **forestry** *n.* job of looking after a forest and its trees; science of growing and maintaining forests.

forever [fə'revə] *adv.* always.

forfeit 1 ['fɔːfɪt] *n.* thing taken/lost as a punishment. **forfeit 2** *v.* to lost (sth) esp. as a punishment. **forfeiture** ['fɔːfɪtʃə] *n.* act of forfeiting.

forgather [fɔː'gæðə] *v.* (formal) to gather together.

forgave [fə'geɪv] *v.* see forgive.

forge 1 [fɔːdʒ] *n.* blacksmith's workshop where he makes horeshoes and other iron objects. **forge 2** *v.* (a) to work (metal) in a forge. (b) to copy (sth) illegally. (c) to f. ahead = to go forward quickly. **forged** *adj.* copied illegally. **forger** *n.* person who copies sth illegally. **forgery** *n.* (a) making an illegal copy. (b) illegal copy.

forget [fə'grt] *v.* (forgot; has forgotten) not (to be able) to remember; to leave (sth) behind. **forgetful** *adj.* often unable to remember. **forgetfulness** *n.* being forgetful. **forget-me-not** *n.* small blue-flowered plant.

forgive [fə'gɪv] [fə'geɪv] *v.* (forgave; has forgiven) to pardon/to stop being angry with (s.o.). **forgivable** *adj.* able to be pardoned/understandable. **forgiveness** *n.* pardon (ing).

forgo [fɔː'gəʊ] *v.* (forwent;has forgone) to do without.

forgot [fə'gɒt] *v.* see forget.

fork 1 [fɔːk] *n.* (a) object with a handle at one end and sharp points at the other, used for picking things up. (b) place where a branch leaves a tree trunk. (c) place where two roads split. **fork 2** *v.* (a) to f. over the soil = to turn the soil over with a fork. (b) to turn off a road. (c) (of a road) to split into two parts. (d) *inf.* to f. out = to pay for sth, *usu.* unwillingly. **forked** *adj.* divided into two. **forklift truck** *n.* motor vehicle which can lift heavy loads on metal arms.

forlorn [fə'lɔːn] *adj.* left alone and feeling sad; f. hope = very slight hope. **forlornly** *adv.* sadly.

form 1 [fɔːm] *n.* (a) shape. (b) paper with blank spaces for you to fill in. (c) condition of an athlete/racing animal; he's in good f. = he' s in a good mood/ he's very amusing. (d) structure/style of a piece of writing/a piece of music (e) school class. (f) long wooden seat with no back. (g) custom/behaviour. (h) hare's nest. **form 2** *v.* (a) to shape; to take shape. (b) to be. (c) to organize; they formed a club.

formation [fɔː'meɪʃn] *n.* shaping/ forming of sth. **formative** ['fɔːmətɪv] *adj.* referring to the early years of life when a person's character is a being formed.

formal ['fɔːml] *adj.* (a) ceremonial/done according to certain rules. (b) regular; clearly written (agreement). **formality** [fɔː'mælɪtɪ] *n.* thing which has to be done to conform with the rules but which does not mean much. **formalization** *n.* making formal. **formalize** *v.* to make (an agreement) formal/regular. **formally** *adv.* according to rules/ceremonially.

formaldehyde [fɔːˈmældɪhaɪd] *n.* gas used in solution to make formalin.

formalin *n.* solution used as a disinfectant and preservative.

format 1 [ˈfɔːmæt] *n.* (a) shape/size (in which sth is made). (b) dimensions of a page/book. **format 2** *v.* (formatted) to arrange text on a computer, so that it is ready for final printing; to set a computer disk so that it is ready to receive data.

forme [fɔːm] *n.* frame in which type is fixed for printing.

former [ˈfɔːmə] *adj.* (a) earlier. (b) first thing mentioned (of two). **formerly** *adv.* at an earlier time.

formic [ˈfɔːmɪk] *adj.* f. acid = acid found in the sting of ants.

formica [fɔːmaɪkə] *n.* trade name for a hard plastic.

formidable [ˈfɔːmɪdəbl] *adj.* frighteningly difficult; very impressive (person).

formula [ˈfɔːmjʊlə] *n.* (*pl.*-ac) (a) statement, *usu.* of a scientific fact and often by means of symbols. (b) Formula I race = car race where the cars all have engines of the largest classification. (c) *Am.* milky food for babies. **formulate** *v.* (a) to express (sth) as a formula. (b) to express (an idea) clearly. **formulation** *n.* expressing clearly.

fornicate [ˈfɔːnɪkeɪt] *v.* to have sexual intercourse (when note married). **fornication** *n.* act of fornicating.

forsake [fɔːˈseɪk] *v.* (forsook; has forsaken) to leave behind. **forsaken** *adj.* abandoned/deserted.

forswear [fɔːˈsweə] *v.* (formal) to swear not to do (sth).

forsythia [fɔːsaɪθ ɪə] *n.* common garden shrub with yellow flowers.

fort [fɔːt] *n.* strong building which can be defended against enemy attacks; to hold the f. = to be in charge while s.o. is away.

forte 1 [ˈfɔːtɪ] *n.* (a) loud piece of music (b) particular ability. **forte 2** *adv.* played loudly.

forth [fɔːθ] *adv.* (formal) forward; back and f. = backwards and forwards; and so on. f. = and so on. **forthcoming** *adj.* (a) soon to appear. (b) *inf.* friendly/full of information. **forthright** *adj.* direct/blunt (way of speaking). **forthwith** *adv.* immediately.

fortify [ˈfɔːtɪfaɪ] *v.* to make strong; fortified wine = wine (like sherry/port) with extra alcohol added. **fortification** [fɔːtɪfɪˈkeɪʃn] *n.* (a) making strong. (b) fortifications = walls/towers built to defend a city.

fortissimo [fɔːˈtɪsɪməʊ] *adv.* very loudly (in music).

fortitude [ˈfɔːtɪtjuːd] *n.* strength of mind/bravery, esp. when in pain.

fortnight [ˈfɔːtnaɪt] *n.* two weeks. **fortnightly** *adj. adv.* once every two weeks.

fortress [ˈfɔːtrəs] *n.* (*pl.*-es) strong building/castle.

fortuitous [fɔːˈtjuːɪtəs] *adj.* accidental/happening by chance. **fortuitously** *adv.* by chance/accidentally.

fortune [ˈfɔːtjuːn] *n.* (a) luck/chance. (b) what will happen in the future. (c) large amount of money. **fortunate** [ˈfɔːtʃənət] *adj.* lucky. **fortunately** *adv.* by good luck. **fortune-teller** *n.* person who says what will happen in the future by looking at cards or lines on your hand.

forty [ˈfɔːtɪ] *n.* number 40; *inf.* f. winks = shorts sleep in the daytime. **fortieth, 40th** *adj. & n.* referring to 40.

forum [ˈfɔːrəm] *n.* (a) place where matters of general interest can be discussed. (b) public discussion.

forward 1 [ˈfɔːwəd] *adj.* (a) towards the front. (b) advanced/well ahead. (c) too confident. **forward 2** *adv.* (a) from that day f. = from then on. (b) to the front; to look f. to sth = to wait for sth with pleasure. **forward 3** *n.* (in football, etc) player in an attacking/front position. **forward 4** *v.* (a) to send on (a letter) to another address. (b) to help (sth) progress. **forward-looking** *adj.* thinking ahead/dealing with the future optimistically. **forwards** *adv.* to the front.

fossick [ˈfɒsɪk] *v.* (Australian) to look for sth/to search.

fossil [ˈfɒsl] *n.* remains of an animal/plant left in a rock; *inf.* elderly old-fashioned person. **fossilization** *n.* becoming fossilized. **fossilized** [ˈfɒsɪlaɪzd] *adj.* turned into a rock.

foster [ˈfɒstə] *v.* (a) to bring up (a child who is not your own). (b) to encourage (an idea, etc). **foster-child** *n.* (*pl.*-

children) child brought up by parents who are not his own. **foster home** n. family/home where a foster-child is brought up. **foster-mother** n. mother who fosters a child. **foster-parents** n. pl.parents who foster a child.

fought [fɔːt] v. see fight.

foul 1 [faʊl] adj. (-er, -est) (a) bad/dirty/ unpleasant (taste, language, air, etc.) (b) against the rules of a game. (c) f. play = murder. (d) to fall f. of = to get into trouble with. **foul 2** n. action against the rules of the game. **foul 3** v. (a) to make dirty. (b) to do sth against the rules of the game. (c) the boat fouled its anchor = its anchor got stuck in weeds, etc; inf. to f. sth up = to make a mess of sth/to create a problem. **foully** adv. in a foul way. **foulmouthed** adj. with foul language. **foulness** n, being foul.

found [faʊnd] v. (a) to establish/to begin (sth). (b) to base (a story, etc.) (c) to melt (metal); to make (sth) out of molten metal; see also find.

foundation [faʊn'deɪʃn] n. (a) establishing/beginning. (b) foundations = base below ground on which a building is laid; f stone = stone in a wall which records the start of building. (c) organization which provides money for certain projects. (d) f. (cream) = coloured cream put on the face under powder.

founder 1 n. person who establishes/ beings sth; f. member = one of the first to establish a club etc. **founder.2** v. (of a boat, scheme) to collapse/to sink.

foundling n. baby abandoned by its parents and found by s.o. else.

foundry n. works where things are made from molten metal, etc.

fount [fɒnt],[faʊnt] n. (a) set of type of one particular size and design. (b) (old) fountain. **fountain** ['faʊntɪn] n. jet of water in a street of garden; f. pen = pen which you can fill up with ink.

four [fɔː] n. (a) number 4; on all fours = on hands and knees. (b) four people (in a rowing boat). **fourfold** adv. & adj. four times as much. **fourpart** adj. (music) for four different voices. **fourposter (bed)** n. bed with a tall post at each corner and curtains. **foursome** n. (a) activity/game played by four people. (b) group of four people. **fourteen** n. number 14. **fourteenth, 14th** adj.

referring to fourteen. **fourth, 4th. 1** adj. referring to four. **fourth, 4th. 2** n. quarter.

fowl [faʊl] n. (pl.fowl) domestic birds kept for food or eggs (chickens, ducks, turkeys and geese); wild f. = game birds which are shot for sport. **fowling piece** n. gun for shooting wild fowl.

fox 1 [fɒks] n. wild animal with reddish fur and a bushy tail. **fox 2** v. to puzzle/ to trick. **fox cub** n. young fox. **foxglove** n. tall purple and white flower found in woods. **foxhound** n. dog used for hunting foxes. **foxhunting** n. chasing foxes to catch and kill them, usu. with dogs. **fox terrier** n. type of small dog. **foxtrot** n. type of ballroom dance. **foxy** adj. crafty/cunning.

foyer ['fɔɪeɪ] n. large entrance hall at the front of a hotel/theatre.

fracas ['fræka:] n. noisy disturbance.

fraction ['frækʃn] n. (a) very small piece/amount. (b) (in mathematics) less than a whole number. **fractional** adj. very small. **fractionally** adv. by a very small amount.

fractious ['frækʃəs] adj. bad-tempered/crying (child). **fractiousness** n. being fractious.

fracture 1 ['fræktʃə] n. break (esp. in bones); simple f. = clean break of a bone; compound f. = one where the broken bone has pierced the skin. **fracture 2** v. to break (a bone).

fragile ['frædʒaɪl] adj. easily broken/ delicate; inf. feeling weak and ill after drinking too much alcohol. **fragility** [frə'dʒɪlɪtɪ] n. being easily broken.

fragment 1 ['frægmənt] n. small piece. **fragment 2** [fræg'ment] v. to break into small pieces. **fragmentary** adj. in pieces/not complete. **fragmentation** n. breaking into small pieces.

fragrance ['freɪgrəns] n. pleasant smell. **fragrant** adj. sweet-smelling.

frail [freɪl] adj. weak. **frailty** n. weakness.

frame 1 [freɪm] n. (a) supporting structure of a building/ship/aircraft/ bicycle/glasses, etc; f. tent = tent supported on a framework of poles; Am. f. house = wooden house. (b) bone structure of a person/animal; f. of mind = temper/ mood. (c) border of wood/metal round a picture/mirror/window. (d) one picture in

a length of cine film. (e) glass box for protecting young plants in a garden.
frame 2 *v.* (a) to put into words. (b) to put a border around (sth). (c) *inf.* to make (an innocent person) appear guilty.
frame-up *n. inf.* arrangement whereby an innocent person is framed.
framework *n.* (a) structure supporting a building, etc. (b) basis of a plan.
franc [fræŋk] *n.* unit of money in Switzerland.
franchise 1 ['fræntʃaɪz] *n.* (a) right to vote. (b) permit to sell a company's products in a certain region/to trade using a well-known brand name.
franchise 2 *v.* to license a product to others who will use it for trade and pay a fee for its use. **franchisee** *n.* person who runs a business under franchise.
franchisor *n.* person who licenses s.o. to operate a franchise.
Franco ['fræŋkəʊ] prefix meaning between France and another country.
frank 1 [fræŋk] *adj.* plain-speaking (person) who says what he thinks. **frank 2** *v.* to stamp (a letter) on a special machine. **frankly** *adv.* speaking truthfully. **frankness** *n.* saying what you think.
frankfurter ['fræŋkfɜːtə] *n.* long spiced sausage, which is boiled and sometimes eaten with a roll.
frankincense ['fræŋkɪnsens] *n.* gum from a tree, burnt as incense.
frantic [fræntɪk] *adj.* worried and wildly excited. **frantically** *adj.* in an excited and worried way.
fraternal [frə'tɜːnl] *adj.* brotherly. **fraternally** *adv.* in a fraternal way. **fraternity** *n.* (a) society of men with similar interests; *Am.* student f. = student association for men. (b) brotherly feeling. **fraternization** [frætənaɪ'zeɪʃn] *n.* act of fraternizing. **fraternize** ['frætənaɪz] *v.* to become friendly (with s.o.). **fratricide** ['frætrɪsaɪd] *n.* murder of your brother.
fraud [frɔːd] *n.* (a) (piece of) dishonesty. (b) person pretending to be sth he is not; thing that is not what you expect. **fraudulence** *n.* dishonesty. **fraudulent** *adj.* dishonest.
fraught [frɔːt] *adj.* (a) (with) full of (problems, danger). (b) *inf.* full of anxiety; worrying (situation).

fray 1 [freɪ] *n.* fight; ready for the f. = ready to fight/ready to take part in the action. **fray 2** *v.* (of material) to become worn/to unravel so that threads are loose.
frazzle ['fræzl] *n.* state of exhaustion.
freak [friːk] *n.* (a) unusual type of person/animal/plant. (b) extraordinary change in the weather. (c) person who is fanatic about sth. **freakish** *adj.* unusual/extraordinary. **freak out** *v. inf.* to become very excited because of the effect of drugs.
freckle ['frekl] *n.* small brown mark on the skin often caused by the sun. **freckled** *adj.* covered in freckles.
free 1 [friː] *adj.* (freer, freest) (a) not imprisoned/not tied down. (b) not occupied. (c) not costing any money. (d) able to do what you want; to be f. with sth = to give sth away generously. (e) to be f. from/of sth = to be with out sth (usu. unpleasant). **free 2** *v.* (a) to get (a person) out of prison. (b) to release from a difficult situation. **freedom** *n.* state of being free; f. of speech = ability to say what you like. **free-for-all** *n.* general fight/general argument among several people. **freehand** *adj. & adv.* (drawing) drawn without the help of rulers/compasses, etc. **freehold** *n. & adj.* right to own a property for ever. **freeholder** *n.* person who owns a freehold property. **freehouse** *n.* pub which is not owned by one brewery company but can sell any brand of drink. **freelance 1** *adj. & n.* independent (worker); not employed by one particular company. **freelance 2** *adv.* (to work) independently. **freelance 3** *v.* to work independently. **freeloader** *n. inf.* person who lives on gifts which he cadges from other people. **freely** *adv.* in a frank manner/without being tied. **Freemason** *n.* member of a secret society. **freemasonry** *n.* brotherhood/ fraternity. **free-range** *adj.* (hens) kept in the open, not in boxes. **free style** *n.* (in sport) any style; (in swimming) any stroke, *usu.* crawl. **free trade** *n.* system of trade agreements between countries where goods are imported and exported free of tax. **freeway** *n. Am.* fast motorway with few junctions. **freewheel** [friː'wiːl] *v.* to go along on a

bicycle without pedalling. **free will** *n.* ability to decide for yourself.

freesia ['fri:ʒə] *n.* scented flower grown from a bulb.

freeze 1 [fri:z] *n.* (a) period of frost. (b) wage f./price f. = period of standstill in wages or prices. **freeze 2** *v.* (froze; has frozen) (a) to change from liquid to solid because of the cold. (b) to become very cold. (c) to stay very still (d) to store (food) at below freezing point. (e) to keep prices or wages at the present level. (f) to prevent the owner from using or selling (assets).

freezer *n.* deep-freeze/refrigerator for freezing food and keeping it frozen.

freezing point *n.* temperature at which a liquid becomes solid.

freight 1 [freit] *n.* (a) transport of goods by air, sea or land. (b) goods transported; f. train = train used for transporting goods; *Am.* f. car = goods wagon.

freight 2 *v.* to transport (goods).

freighter *n.* aircraft/ship which carries goods. **freightliner** *n.* train carrying goods in containers.

French 1 [frentʃ] *adj.* referring to France; F window = door made of glass *usu.* opening on to a garden; F beans = beans grown on low bushes and eaten when green in their pods; F dressing = salad dressing made of oil and vinegar; *Am.* F. fries/F. fried potatoes = chips; to take F. leave = to go away without permission; F leave = to go away without permission; F. horn = brass instrument with a coiled tube. **French 2** *n.* (a) language spoken in France and some other countries. (b) the F. = the people of France. **Frenchman, Frenchwoman** *n.* (*pl.*-men, -women) person from France. **French polish** *v.* to polish (wood) with a resin polish.

frenetic [frə'netik] *adj.* wildly excited.

frenzy ['frenzi] *n.* wild excitement. **frenzied** *adj.* wildly excited. **frenziedly** *adv.* in a frenzied way.

frequent 1 ['fri:kwənt] *adj.* happening often/often seen. **frequent 2** [fri'kwent] *v.* go (somewhere) very often.

frequency *n.* (a) rate at which sth happens. (b) number of vibrations per second made by a radio wave.

frequently *adv.* often.

fresco ['freskəʊ] *n.* (*pl.*-oes) painting done on wet plaster on a wall.

fresh [freʃ] *adj.* (-er, -est) (a) new/not used; f. air = open air. (b) recent (news); newly-made (cakes). (c) not tinned or frozen. (d) quite strong (wind). (e) healthy-looking. (f) cheeky/rather rude.

freshen *v.* to become/to make fresh.

fresher, freshman *n.* (*pl.*-men) new student in his/her first year at college.

freshly *adv.* newly; recently.

freshness *n.* being fresh. **fresh water** *n.* water in rivers or lakes.

freshwater *adj.* referring to river or lake water not salt water.

fret 1 [fret] *n.* raised metal strip crossing the neck of a guitar against which you press the strings. **fret 2** *v.* (fretted) to worry/be unhappy. **fretful** *adj.* crying and unhappy (child). **fretfully** *adv.* in a fretful way.

fretwork ['fretwɜ:k] *n.* patterns in wood cut with a very fine saw. **fretsaw** *n.* fine saw used for cutting patterns in wood.

Freudian ['frɔɪdɪən] *adj.* referring to Freud and his theories of psychoanalysis; a F. slip = a mistake in speaking which seems to show your real feelings, when you are trying to hide them.

friable ['fraɪəbl] *adj.* (earth) which can be crumbled easily.

friar ['fraɪə] *n.* member of a Christian religious order.

fricassée [frɪkæseɪ] *n.* dish of pieces of meat cooked in a rich sauce.

friction ['frɪkʃn] *n.* (a) rubbing one thing against another. (b) disagreement between two or more people.

Friday ['fraɪdeɪ] *n.* fifth day of the weekday between Thursday and Saturday; Good F. = the Friday before Easter Day; Man F. = general helper.

fridge [frɪdʒ] *n. inf.* refrigerator/ apparatus for keeping thighs cold.

fried [fraɪd] *v.* see fry.

friend [frend] *n.* person whom you know well and like; supporter (of a cause); the Society of Friends = religious society, also called the Quakers.

friendless *adj.* having no friends.

friendliness *n.* friendly feeling.

friendly 1 *adj.* like a friend/kind/ helpful. **friendly 2** *n. inf.* game which does not count in a tournament.

friendship *n.* state of being friends.

frieze [fri:z] *n.* decorative border round the top of walls, pillars, etc.

frigate ['frɪgət] *n.* small fast-moving naval ship.

fright [fraɪt] *n.* (a) fear (b) *inf.* awful looking person. **frightful** *adj. inf.* terrible/awful. **frightfully** *adv. inf.* extremely/terribly/very. **frightfulness** *n.* unpleasantness. **frighten** ['fraɪtn] *v.* to make (s.o.) afraid. **frightened** *adj.* afraid/scared (of). **frightening** *adj.* causing fear.

frigid ['frɪdʒɪd] *adj.* (a) very cold/icy. (b) unfriendly/not showing any warm feelings; (woman) not interested in sex. **frigidity** [frɪdʒɪdɪtɪ] *n.* (a) great cold. (b) coldness of feelings, esp. lack of interest in sex. **frigidly** *adv.* in a cold way.

frill [frɪl] *n.* (a) piece of material gathered together and sewn on to a dress, etc. (b) frills = unnecessary ornaments. **frilled** *adj.* with frills. **frilly**, with many frills.

fringe [frɪndʒ] *n.* (a) hair lying over the forehead. (b) edging of material consisting of loose threads hanging down (on a shawl/dress/carpet, etc/) (c) outer edge of an area; f. benefits = extra benefits on to of a salary (such as a free car, etc.) f. theatre = *usu.* experimental drama, often not using a traditional theatre building.

frippery ['frɪpərɪ] *n.* useless ornament.

frisk [frɪsk] *v.* (a) to jump (about) (b) to search (s.o.) by running your hands over him to see if he is carrying a weapon. **friskily** *adv.* in a frisky way. **friskiness** *n.* feeling full of life. **frisky** *adj.* lively.

fritillary [frɪ'tɪlərɪ] *n.* type of small butterfly.

fritter 1 ['frɪtə] *n.* piece of meat/fruit/vegetable dipped in a mixture of flour, egg and milk and fried. **fritter 2** *v.* f. away = to waste (time, money).

frivolous ['frɪvələs] *adj.* silly/not serious. **frivolously** *adv.* in a frivolous way. **frivolousness, frivolity** [frɪ'vɒlɪtɪ] *n.* silliness/lack of seriousness.

frizzle ['frɪzl] *v. inf.* (a) (of hair) to be very tightly curled. (b) to fry in hot fat. **frizzy** ['frɪzɪ] *adj. inf.* tightly curled (hair). **frizz** *v. inf.* to put (hair) into tight curls.

fro [frəʊ] *adv.* to and f. = backwards and forwards.

frock [frɒk] *n.* (a) dress/piece of female clothing covering more or less all the body. (b) long robe worn by monks or priests.

frog [frɒg] *n.* (a) small tailless reptile which lives on both land and water; to have a f. in your throat = to feel you have sth in you throat which stops you speaking clearly. (b) decorated fastening on a uniform. **frogman** *n.* (*pl.*-men) underwater diver. **frogmarch** *v.* to force (s.o., esp. a prisoner) to move by carrying him by his arms (and sometimes legs). **frogspawn** *n.* (no *pl.*) transparent jelly containing frog's eggs.

frolic 1 ['frɒlɪk] *n.* happy game/party. **frolic 2** *v.* (frolicked) to play happily.

from [frɒm] *prep.* (a) (showing movement away) the plane f. London. (b) (showing where something started) f. beginning to end; f. now on; f. time to time = sometimes. (c) (showing difference) I can't tell better f. margarine. (d) sent by; a letter f. Peter. (e) because of; he died f. pneumonia. (f) according to; f. what I heard.

frond [frɒnd] *n.* large leaf of a fern or palm tree.

front 1 [frʌnt] *n.* (a) part which faces forward; most prominent part; in f. of = before. (b) road which runs beside the sea in a seaside town. (c) line of an army nearest the enemy in battle. (d) (of weather) line separating cold and warm masses of air. (e) business used to hide illegal activity. **front 2** *adj.* foremost/first (seat, door, etc.) **front 3** *v.* to face (on to). **frontage** ['frʌntɪdʒ] *n.* (a) length of a property along a road. (b) land between a building and the road. **frontal** *adj.* of/in the front; belonging to the front. **frontier** ['frʌntɪə] *n.* (a) boundary line between two countries or states. (b) the frontiers of science = the furthest point in human knowledge. **frontispiece** ['frʌntɪspiːs] *n.* picture opposite the title page of a book.

frost [frɒst] *n.* (a) weather when the temperature is below the freezing point of water; ten degrees of f. = ten degrees below freezing. (b) white covering on the ground/trees, etc., when the temperature

is below freezing. **frostbite** n. damage
to a part of the body due to cold.
frostbitten adj. attacked by frostbite.
frosted adj. (a) covered in frost;
damaged by frost. (b) (glass) which has a
rough surface through which it is
difficult to see. (c) (cake) covered with
sugar. **frostily** adv. coldly/in an
unfriendly way. **frosting** n. icing on a
cake. **frosty** adj. (a) very cold; covered
with frost (b) cold/unfriendly (manner).
froth 1 [frɒθ] n. mass of bubbles on top
of a liquid. **froth 2** v. to have masses of
bubbles. **frothy** adj. having bubbles on
top.
frown 1 [fraʊn] n. pulling down the
eyebrows as a sign of anger/puzzlement,
etc. **frown 2** v. to pull down the
eyebrows; to f. on (sth) = to disapprove
of sth.
frowsty ['fraʊztɪ] adj. smelling dirty
and stale.
frowzy ['fraʊzɪ] adj. untidy and dirty.
froze [frəʊz] v. see freeze. **frozen**
['frəʊzn] adj. (a) very cold. (b) at a
temperature below freezing point; f. food
= food stored at a temperature below
freezing point; see also freeze.
frugal ['fruːgl] adj. spending/costing
very little money. **frugality** [fruːgælɪtɪ]
n. being frugal. **frugally** adv. in a
frugal way.
fruit 1 [fruːt] n. (a) (pl.usu. fruit) part of
a plant which contains the seeds and
which is often eaten; f. salad = pieces of
fresh fruit mixed and served cold. (b)
product (of hard work). **fruit 2** v. to
carry/to produce edible parts. **fruitcake**
n. cake with a lot of dried fruit in it.
fruiterer n. person who sells fruit.
fruitful adj. (work) which produces
good results. **fruitfully** adv. in a
fruitful way. **fruition** [fruː'ɪʃn] n. to
come to f. = to be accomplished with
good results. **fruitless** adj. producing
no results. **fruitlessly** adv. in a
fruitless way. **fruit machine** n.
gambling machine where pictures of
different fruits revolve when you pull a
handle. **fruity** adj. (a) tasting of fruit.
(b) inf. deep and tuneful (voice).
frump [frʌmp] n. person, usu. a woman,
who wears old-fashioned clothes.
frumpish adj. (wearing) out-of-date
clothes.

frustrate [frʌ'streɪt] v. to prevent (s.o.)
doing what he wants to do. **frustration**
[frʌ'streɪʃn] n. feeling of anger and
impatience when stopped from doing
what you want.
fry 1 [fraɪ] n. (pl.fry) baby fish; small f.
= unimportant people. **fry 2** v. to cook
in oil/fat. **frying pan** n. shallow, open
pan used for frying; to jump out of the
frying pan into the fire = to go from one
difficult situation to sth worse.
fuchsia ['fjuːʃə] n. garden plant with
colourful hanging flowers.
fuddle ['fʌdl] v. to make (s.o.) feel hazy
and confused.
fuddy-duddy ['fʌdɪdʌdɪ] n. inf. old-
fashioned person.
fudge 1 [fʌdʒ] n. soft sweet made from
butter, sugar and milk. **fudge 2** v. to f.
the issue = to avoid making a decision
on an issue.
fuel 1 ['fjʊəl] n. substance (coal/gas/oil/
wood, etc.) which can be burnt to give
heat/power; to add f. to the flames = to
make matters worse. **fuel 2** v. (fuelled)
to provide fuel for.
fug [fʌg] n. inf. stuffy/hot atmosphere.
fugginess n. being fuggy. **fuggy** adj.
stuffy/hot.
fugitive ['fjuːdʒɪtɪv] n. & adj. (person)
who is running away.
fugue [fjuːg] n. piece of music where a
tune is repeated in several patterns.
fulcrum ['fʊlkrəm] n. point on which a
level rests/on which a seesaw balances.
fulfil [fʊl'fɪl] v. (fulfilled) to complete
(sth) satisfactorily. **fulfilment** n.
satisfactory ending.
full 1 [fʊl] adj. (-er, -est) (a) containing
as much as possible; f. up = with no
more room; I'm f. (up) = I have eaten as
much as I can; f. skirt = wide skirt made
from lots of material. (b) as many (as
possible). (c) complete; f. stop = dot (.)
at the end of a sentence. (d) round and
plump (face); f. moon = moon when
completely round. **full 2** n. in f. =
completely/entirely; to the f. =
completely. **full back** n. (in games)
defensive player near the goal.
fullblooded adj. (a) vigorous
(argument) (b) (of horses) strongly
typical. **full-blown** adj. (a) (of a
flower) wide open (b) he is a full-blown
doctor = he has passed all his

examinations and is qualified. **full-grown** *adj.* adult. **full-length** *adj.* (a) from head to toe. (b) long (story/film). **fullness** *n.* (a) state of containing as much as possible. (b) state when all is completed; in the f. of time = eventually/in the end. **fullscale** *adj.* complete/total. **full time** *n.* end of a sports match. **full-time** *adj. & adv.* all the time. **fully** *adv.* completely/entirely. **fully-fledged** *adj.* experienced/qualified.

fulmar ['fʊlmɑː] *n.* grey and white northern seabird.

fulminate ['fʌlmɪneɪt] *v.* (formal) to protest angrily. **fulminations** [fʌlmɪ'neɪʃnz] *n. pl.* angry protests.

fulsome ['fʊlsəm] *adj.* excessive/too much.

fumarole ['fjuːmərəʊl] *n.* hole in the side of volcano through which smoke escapes.

fumble ['fʌmbl] *v.* (with to touch/to feel clumsily. **fumbling** *adj.* clumsy.

fume 1 [fjuːm] *n. pl.* fumes = smoke/gas. **fume 2** *v.* to be angry.

fumigate ['fjuːmɪgeɪt] *v.* to clean (a room) by smoking out germs and insects. **fumigation** [fjuːmi'geɪʃn] *n.* smoking out germs/insects.

fun [fʌn] *n.* amusement/pleasure; to make f. of/to poke f. at = to laugh nastily at/to mock; for f./in f. = not seriously/as a joke. **funfair** *n.* group of amusements, sideshows, etc., collected together.

function 1 ['fʌŋkʃn] *n.* (a) job/duty (b) gathering of people; party. **function 2** *v.* (a) to work. (b) to serve (as). **functional** *adj.* useful but not decorative. **functionally** *adv.* in a functional way. **functionary** *n.* official. **function key** *n.* key on a computer keyboard which activates a set of instructions.

fund 1 [fʌnd] *n.* (a) sum of money set aside for a special purpose. (b) collection. **fund 2** *v.* to provide money for (a special purpose).

fundamental [fʌndə'mentl] *adj.* basic/essential. **fundamentally** *adv.* basically.

funeral ['fjuːnərəl] *n.* ceremony where a dead person is buried/cremated. **funerary** *adj.* used in a funeral.

funereal [fjuː'nɪərɪəl] *adj.* sad and gloomy.

fungus ['fʌŋgəs] *n.* (*pl.* fungi[fʌŋgaɪ]) plant which has no green leaves or flowers and which frequently lives on other plants. **fungicide** ['fʌndʒɪsaɪd] *n.* chemical which kills fungus. **fungicidal** *adj.* which kills fungus. **fungoid** *adj.* like a fungus.

funicular [fə'nɪkjʊlə] *n.* f. (railway) = railway where cars held by cables travel up a slope.

funk 1 [fʌŋk] *in. inf.* fear; to be in a blue f. = to be terrified. **funk 2** *v. inf.* to be afraid to do sth.

funnel 1 ['fʌnl] *n.* (a) tube with a wide mouth and narrow bottom used when pouring liquids from one container into another. (b) chimney on a ship from which the smoke comes. **funnel 2** *v.* (funnelled) to pass through a funnel/through a narrow space.

funny ['fʌni] *adj.* (a) which makes people laugh. (b) odd/unusual; I feel f. = I feel ill. **funnily** *adv.* oddly. **funny bone** *n. inf.* part of the elbow which hurts sharply if it is hit.

fur 1 [fɜː] *n.* (a) soft coat of an animal. (b) deposit in kettles/water pipes, etc. **fur 2** *v.* (furred) to become covered with a deposit. **furry** *adj.* covered with fur.

furbish ['fɜːbɪʃ] *v.* to polish/to clean.

furious ['fjʊərɪəs] *adj.* very angry. **furiously** *adv.* in a furious way.

furl [fɜːl] *v.* to roll up and tie securely.

furlong ['fɜːlɒŋ] *n.* measure of length (= 220 yards).

furlough ['fɜːləʊ] *n.* leave of absence (esp. from the armed forces).

furnace ['fɜːnəs] *n.* (a) large brick or metal oven which can be heated to a very high temperature; blast f. furnace where iron is heated until it melts. (b) heater which warms the water for central heating.

furnish ['fɜːnɪʃ] *v.* (a) to provide with chairs/tables, etc; furnished rooms/flat = rented place where the furniture is provided by the owner. (b) to supply (with). **furnishings** *n. pl.* fittings in a house; soft f. = curtains, cushions, etc. **furniture** ['fɜːnɪtʃə] *n.* (no *pl.*) tables/chairs/cupboards/beds, etc.; a piece of f. = one article of furniture.

furore, *Am.* **furor** [fjuː'rɔːrɪ, fjuː'rɔː] *n.* outburst of anger/excitement.

furrier ['fʌrɪə] *n.* person who sells furcoats, etc.

furrow 1 ['fʌrəʊ] *n.* long groove cut in the earth by a plough. **furrow 2** *v.* to make furrows in (the land, etc.)

further 1 ['fɜːðə] *adv. & adj.* (a) farther/to a greater distance/more distant. (b) additional; College of F. Education = college for people who have left school. **further 2** *v.* to advance (a plan). **furtherance** *n.* advancing (of a plan). **furthermore** [fɜːðə'mɔː] *adv.* also/in addition.

furthermost ['fɜːðəməʊst] *adj.* most distant. **furthest** *adj. & adv.* to the greatest distance/most distant.

furtive ['fɜːtɪv] *adj.* secret; as if hiding something. **furtively** *adv.* in a furtive way. **furtiveness** *n.* being furtive.

fury ['fjʊərɪ] *n.* fierce anger.

furze [fɜːz] *n.* gorse.

fuse 1 [fjuːz] *n.* (a) length of string attached to a bomb which burns slowly when lit. (b) small piece of wire in an electrical circuit which melts and breaks if the circuit is overloaded, and so prevents further damage; to blow a f. = to overload the electric circuit and make the fuse break. **fuse 2** *v.* (a) to break the electrical circuit. (b) to f. together = to join together (wires/companies,etc.).

fusebox *n.* box where the fuses are kept.

fussier *n.* fine wire for putting into fuses.

fuselage ['fjuːzəlɑːʒ] *n.* body of an aircraft.

fusilier [fjuːzə'lɪə] *n.* rifleman in the army.

fusillade [fjuːzɪ'leɪd] *n.* rapid gunfire.

fusion ['fjuːʒn] *n.* (a) melting together of two pieces of metal. (b) joining together of two different things.

fuss 1 [fʌs] *n.* agitated complaints about little things that do not matter; to make a f. about sth = to complain at length about sth unimportant; to make a f. of s.o. = to pay great attention to s.o.

fuss 2 *v.* to be agitated; to show unnecessary care and attention (over little things). **fussily** *adv.* in a fussy way. **fussiness** *n.* being fussy. **fussy** *adj.* (a) unnecessarily careful and

demanding about little things. (b) disliking lots of things.

fusty ['fʌstɪ] *adj.* smelling of dampness. **fustiness** *n.* being fusty.

futile ['fjuːtaɪl, [xx] 'fjuːtl] *adj.* useless. **futility** [fjuː'tɪlɪtɪ] *n.* uselessness.

future 1 ['fjuːtʃə] *n.* time which has not yet happened; in f. = from now on.

future 2 *adj.* coming/not yet happened. **futures** *n.* trade in something, such as foreign currency or commodities, for delivery at a later date.

futuristic [fjuːtʃə'rɪstɪk] *adj.* oddly modern (art).

fuzz [fʌz] *n.* (a) fluffy hair. (b) *Sl.* the f. = the police. **fuzziness** *n.* being fuzzy. **fuzzy** *adj.* (a) fluffy and curly. (b) not clear/blurred.

Gg

g abbrev. for gram.

gab [gæb] *n. inf.* talk/chat; the gift of the g. = talent for speaking.

gabardine [gæbədiːn] *n.* closely woven cotton material, used for making raincoats.

gabble 1 [gæbl] *n.* loud, unintelligible talk. **gabble 2** *v.* to speak very quickly.

gable [geɪbl] *n.* triangular upper part of a wall at the end of a roof. **gabled** *adj.* with gables.

gad [gæd] *v.* (gadded) to g. about = to be constantly out and about. **gadabout** *n.* person who is always out and about. **gadfly** *n.* fly which attacks cows; irritating person.

gadget [gædʒɪt] *n.* useful machine/tool. **gadgetry** *n.* lots of gadgets.

Gaelic ['gædʒɪt, ɪn, g'ælɪk] *n.* language of Scots, Manx and Irish Celts.

gaff 1 [gæf] *n.* stick with iron hook for catching large fish; *inf.* to blow the g. = to let out a secret. **gaff 2** *v.* to catch with a gaff.

gaffe [gæf] *n.* blunder; indiscreet act or remark.

gaffer [gæfə] *n. inf.* (a) old man. (b) boss.

gag 1 [gæg] *n* (a) soft object put into or tied round the mouth to stop s.o. speaking. (b) joke. **gag 2** *v.* (gagged) (a) to bind (s.o.) round the mouth; to g. the press = to impose censorship. (b) to retch/to choke.

gaga ['gɑːgɑː] *adj. inf.* senile/stupid.

gaggle ['gægl] *n.* flock (of geese).

gaiety ['geɪətɪ] *n.* happiness/cheerfulness. **gaily** *adv.* happily.

gain 1 *n.* increase of possessions; profit. **gain 2** *v.* (a) to obtain/to get; to g. the upper hand = to get control. (b) the clock gains five minutes a day = it moves five minutes ahead of the correct time in every twenty four hours. (c) to g. on s.o./sth = to get closer to a person or thing you are chasing. **gainful** *adj.* which earns money; gainful employment. **gainfully** *adv.* g. employed = doing work which earns money. **gainsay** [geɪn'seɪ] *v* (gainsaid) (formal) to deny (sth).

gait [geɪt] *n.* manner of walking. **gaiter** ['geɪtə] *n.* covering of cloth or leather worn over the leg below the knee.

gal *abbrev.* for gallon.

gala ['gɑːlə] *n.* festive occasion; swimming g. = swimming competition.

galaxy ['gæləksɪ] *n.* collection of stars, found singly and in groups and clusters. **galactic** [gə'læktɪk] *adj.* belonging to a galaxy.

gale [geɪl] *n.* very strong wind.

galena [gə'liːnə] *n.* natural form of lead sulphide.

gall 1 [gɔːl] *n.* (a) bile/bitter liquid produced by the liver to digest fat. (b) growth produced by insects on trees, esp. the oak. (c) painful swelling/blister (esp. on horses). (d) *inf.* rudeness/impudence.

gall 2 *v.* to annoy/to humiliate. **galling** *adj.* humiliating; annoying. **gall-bladder** *n.* bag in the body where bile is stored. **gallstone** *n.* small stone like substance which sometimes forms in the gall-bladder.

gallant [gælənt] *adj.* (a) brave/chivalrous. (b) very polite towards women. **gallantly** *adv.* in a gallant way. **gallantry** [gælən] *n.* bravery.

galleon ['gælɪən] *n.* large Spanish warship in the 16th Century.

gallery ['gælərɪ] *n.* (a) room in which pictures are hung. (b) art museum. (c) shop selling pictures/antiques, etc. (d) (in a church/hall, etc) balcony which runs around part of the main hall; (in a theatre/cinema) highest rows of seats; to play to the g. = to appeal to people who have no taste; minstrels' g. = balcony above the end of a castle dining hall from where musicians entertained the diners. (d) shooting g. = long, narrow room at one end of which is a target for shooting.

galley ['gælɪ] *n.* (a) low, flat, single decked ship, rowed by slaves. (b) ship's kitchen. (c) (in printing) rectangular tray which holds type. **galley proof** *n.* proof printed on long sheets of paper.

Gallic ['gælɪk] *adj.* French. **gallicism** ['gælɪsɪzəm] *n.* French word a phrase adopted into another language.

gallivant ['gælɪvænt] *v. inf.* to be always out and about looking for amusement.

gallon ['gælən] *n.* liquid measure equal to 4 quarts or 4.5 litres.

gallop 1 ['gæləp] *n.* (a) fastest pace of a horse running with all feet off the ground in each stride. (b) fast ride on a horse.

gallop 2 *v.* to run/to go fast; he galloped through his speech = spoke it very fast; galloping inflation = rapidly rising inflation.

gallows ['gæləʊz] *n.* structure on which criminals are hanged.

Gallup poll ['gæləp'pəʊl] *n.* test of public opinion on an important topic, esp. how a representative sample of the public will vote, in order to forecast an election result.

galore [gə'lɔː] *adv.* (always after the noun) plenty; apples g.

galoshes [gə'lɒʃɪz] *n. pl.* plastic/rubber shoes worn over other shoes to protect them.

galumph [gə'lʌmf] *v. inf.* to walk about heavily.

galvanize ['gælvənaɪz] *v.* (a) galvanized iron = iron coated with zinc to protect it from rust. (b) to rouse by shock. **galvanization** ['gælvənaɪ'zerʃn] *n.* process of galvanizing.

galvanometer ['gælvə'nɒmɪtə] *n.* instrument for measuring small electric currents.

gambit ['gæmbɪt] *n.* (a) (in chess) opening move whereby a player sacrifices a major piece in order to take a major one later. (b) opening move in some action.

gamble 1 ['gæmbl] *n.* risk taken in the hope of getting good results; It's a bit of a g. = you can't be sure it will succeed.

gamble 2 *v.* to risk (money) on cards or sporting results; to g. on sth happening = to act in the hope that it will happen. **gambler** *n.* person who gambles. **gambling** *n.* risking money; betting on sth.

gambol ['gæmbl] *v.* (gambolled) to frisk about like a lamb.

game 1 *n.* (a) contest played according to rules and decided by skill strength or luck; a g. of tennis/chess; to play the g. = to act honourably; the g.'s up = we have been found out; so that's his little g. = now we know what his plans are. (b) (in tennis/bridge, etc.) single round. (c) wild animals and birds (deer, rabbits, pheasants, etc.) hunted for sport or food; g. soup = soup made from game; big g. = large wild animals (lions/elephants, etc.) shot for sport. **game 2** *adj.* (a) willing/ courageous. (b) lame (leg).

gamekeeper *n.* person employed to breed and look after game. **gamely** *adv.* bravely. **gameness** *n.* being game. **gamesmanship** *n.* (no *pl.*) the art of winning by devious means, such as distracting your opponent. **gaming** *n.* gambling.

gamete ['gæmi:t] *n.* plant or animal cell which can link with another to reproduce.

gamma ['gæmə] *n.* third letter of the Greek alphabet. **gamma globulin** *n.* protein found in blood plasma. **gamma rays** *n. pl.* rays of short wavelength sent out by radioactive substances.

gammon ['gæmən] *n.* smoked or cured ham.

gammy ['gæmɪ] *adj. inf.* lame (leg).

gamut ['gæmət] *n,* (a) whole range of musical notes. (b) whole range or scope; the whole g. of crime = every type of crime imaginable.

gander ['gændə] *n.* male goose.

gang 1 ['gær] *n.* band of people acting or going about together. **gang 2** *v.* to g. up (with) = to team up with; to g. up on (s.o.) = to take sides with one or more people against s.o. **gangland** *n.* all

gangs. **gangplank** *n.* long piece of wood giving access to a boat from the shore. **gangster** *n.* member of a gang of violent criminals. **gangway** *n.* (a) (in a theatre/cinema, etc.) passage between rows of seats. (b) bridge from the shore to a ship. **gangling** ['gæŋglɪŋ] *adj.* tall (person) with long arms and legs.

ganglion ['gæŋglɪən] *n.* (a) nucleus of nerves in the central nervous system. (b) small lump on a tendon.

gangrene ['gæŋgri:n] *n.* rotting of body tissue, caused by a blockage of the blood supply. **gangrenous** ['gæŋgrɪnəs] *adj.* affected by gangrene.

gannet ['gænɪt] *n.* large white sea bird.

gantry ['gæntrɪ] *n.* metal bridge for carrying lights/a crane, etc.

gaol 1 [dʒeɪl] *n.* prison. **gaol 2** *v.* to put (s.o.) in prison. **gaolbird** *n.* person who has been sent to prison often.

gaoler *n.* person in charge of the prisoners in a gaol.

gap [gæp] *n.* (a) space/hole in a hedge/ wall, etc. (b) gorge or pass (between mountains) (c) space/difference; age g.= difference in age; generation g. = difference in years between one generation and another, often resulting in intolerance between them.

gape [geɪp] *v.* to open your mouth wide. **gaping** *adj.* wide open.

garage 1 ['gærɪdʒ, 'gærɑ:ʒ] *n.* (a) building for storing motor vehicles; g. sale = private sale of unwanted household goods (held in the garage of a house). (b) petrol station/place where motor vehicles are repaired. **garage 2** *v.* to put (a vehicle) into a garage.

garb [gɑ:b] *n.* (no *pl.*) (formal) clothing. **garbed** *adj.* dressed (in).

garbage ['gɑ:bɪdʒ] *n.* refuse/rubbish; *Am.* g. can = dustbin.

garble ['gɑ:bl] *v.* to select certain items from speeches in order to give an unfair or malicious representation; to distort/ confuse.

Garda ['gɑ:də] *n.* (*pl.*ai) (in Republic of Ireland) police.

garden ['gɑ:də] *n.* piece of ground used for growing flowers, fruit, or vegetables; g. centre = place where plants, seeds and garden tools are sold; g. of remembrance = garden dedicated to the memory of the dead. **garden 2** v. to look after a garden. **gardener** n. person who looks after a garden.

gardening n. looking after a garden.

gardenia [gɑːˈdiːnɪə] n. shrub with fragrant white or yellow flowers.

gargantuan [gɑːˈgæntuən] adj. huge/ enormous.

gargle 1 [ˈgɑːgl] n. antiseptic liquid used for washing the throat. **gargle 2** v. to wash the throat by holding antiseptic liquid in it and breathing out at the same time.

gargoyle [ˈgɑːgɔɪl] n. water spout on a medieval building, carved like a grotesque head.

garish [ˈgeərɪʃ] adj. bright/showy/ overdecorated. **garishly** adv. very brightly.

garland 1 [ˈgɑːlənd] n. (a) circle of flowers or leaves worn as a decoration. (b) decoration made of linked paper/ ribbon, etc. **garland 2** v. to hang with garlands.

garlic [ˈgɑːlɪk] n. plant whose bulb has a strong smell and taste, used as a flavouring. **garlicky** adj. tasting/ smelling of garlic.

garment [ˈgɑːmənt] n. article of clothing.

garner [ˈgɪnə] v. (formal) to collect and store.

garnet [ˈgɑːnɪt] n. semi-precious dark red stone.

garnish 1 [ˈgɑːnɪʃ] n. thing used to decorate food. **garnish 2** v. to decorate (esp. food).

garret [ˈgærət] n. attic room immediately under the roof of a house.

garrison 1 [ˈgærɪsn] n. (a) troops stationed in a fortress/town, etc. in order to defend it. (b) fortress. **garrison 2** v. to place troops on garrison duty in (a town).

garrotte [gəˈrɒt] v. to strangle (s.o.) with a cord.

garrulous [ˈgærjuəəs] adj. talkative. **garrulously** adv. in a garrulous way. **garrulousness, garrulity** [gæruːlɪtɪ] n. being garrulous.

garter [ˈgɑːtə] n. band worn above or below the knee to keep a stocking or sock up; Order of the Garter = highest order of English knighthood.

gas 1 n. (a) chemical substance like air,

which is completely fluid and has no definite shape or volume. (b) substance, produced from coal or extracted naturally from the ground, which is used for cooking or heating; to cook by g.; g. cooker = which uses gas; natural g. = gas which is extracted from the earth. (c) substance used to make you unconscious while having a tooth removed, etc. (d) Am. petrol; inf. to step on the g. = to accelerate. (e) inf. unimportant talk. **gas 2** v. (gassed) (a) to poison (s.o.) by making them breathe gas. (b) inf. to talk about nothing in particular. **gaseous** [ˈgæsjəs] adj. referring to gas. **gasholder** n. gasometer. **gasmask** n. mask used as protection against poison gases. **gasoline** n. Am. petrol. **gasometer** [gæˈsɒmɪtə] n. large container in which gas is stored. **gas station** n. Am. place where you can buy petrol. **gassy** adj. full of gas/full of bubbles. **gasworks** n. place where gas is manufactured.

gash 1 [gæʃ] n. long deep cut/wound. **gash 2** v. to make a gash.

gasket [ˈgæskɪt] n. piece of thin material used to seal two parts of an engine to prevent air/gas, etc., from escaping.

gasp 1 [gɑːsp] n. sharp intake of breath. **gasp 2** v. to struggle to breathe/to catch your breath in surprise.

gasteropod [ˈgæstərəpɒd] n. type of mollusc, like a snail or limpet.

gastric [ˈgæstrɪk] adj. referring to the stomach; g. flu = infection of the stomach. **gastrectomy** n. operation to remove the stomach. **gastroenteritis** [gæstrəuentəˈraɪtɪs] n. illness of the stomach and intestines. **gastronome** [ˈgæstrənəum] n. expert on food and drink. **gastronomic** [gæstrəˈnɒmɪk] adj. referring to food and drink. **gastronomy** [ˈgæˈtrɒnəmɪ] n. art of cooking.

gate [geɪt] n. (a) barrier, usu. made of wood or iron, closing an opening in a wall/fence, etc. (b) number of people who watch a football match/sports competition; money paid by spectators at a football match, etc. **gatecrash** v. to go uninvited to (a party). **gatecrasher** n. uninvited guest. **gated** adj. (road) with gates. **gate-legged table** n. table

with hinged legs which fold like a gate.
gatepost *n.* post to which a gate is
attached by hinges. **gateway** *n.* gap in
a wall/fence, etc., where a gate can be
fitted.

gateau ['gætəu] *n.* (*pl.*gateaux
['gætəuz]) large decorated cream cake.

gather ['gæðə] *v.* (a) to bring together/
to collect. (b) to gain (speed). (c) to
understand I g. that you are coming. (d)
to pull (material) into folds by means of
tiny stitches. **gathering 1** *n.* (a) group
of people who have come together. (b)
swelling with pus. **gathering 2** *adj.*
imminent a g. storm. **gather up** *v.* to
bring (things) together and pick them up.

gauche [gəuʃ] *adj.* clumsy/tactless.

gaucho ['gauʃəu] *n.* South American
herdsman.

gaudy ['gɔːdɪ] *adj.* (-ier, -iest) too
brightly coloured; showy; lacking in
taste. **gaudily** *adv.* showily.
gaudiness *n.* being gaudy.

gauge 1 [geɪdʒ] *n.* (a) standard
measure of width/thickness, etc. (b)
distance between rails on a railway line.
(c) instrument measuring depth/pressure,
etc. **gauge 2** *v.* (a) to measure exactly.
(b) to estimate/to guess.

gaunt [gɔːnt] *adj.* lean/haggard.
gauntness *n.* being gaunt.

gauntlet ['gɔːntlət] *n.* strong glove with
long wrist cover, for driving, fencing,
etc.; to fling/throw down the g. = to issue
a challenge; to run the g. = to go through
a dangerous area.

gauss [gaus] *n.* unit for measuring the
strength of a magnetic field.

gauze [gɔːz] *n.* thin/transparent
material. **gauzy** *adj.* thin (material).

gave [geɪv] *v.* see give.

gavel ['gævl] *n.* auctioneer's or
chairman's hammer.

gawky ['gɔːkɪ] *adj.* (-ler, -lest)
awkward/ungainly. **gawkiness** *n.*
being gawky.

gawp [gɔːp] *v. inf.* to stare rudely (at).

gay 1 [geɪ] *adj.* (-er, -est) happy; full of
fun. **gay 2** *adj. & n. inf.* homosexual.
gayness *n.* being gay.

gaze 1 [geɪz] *n.* intent look. **gaze 2** *v.*
to look steadily for a long time.

gazebo [gə'ziːbəu] *n.* small
summerhouse.

gazelle [gə'zel] *n.* kind of antelope.

gazette [gə'zet] *n.* official newspaper,
giving details of public appointments,
etc. **gazetteer** [gæzə'tɪə] *n.*
geographical dictionary.

gazump [gə'zʌmp] *v.* to g. s.o. = to
accept a higher price for a house which
s.o. has already agreed to buy.

GBH [dʒiːbiː'ertʃ] Grievous Bodily
Harm.

GDP [dʒiːdiː'piː] gross domestic product.

gear 1 ['gɪə] *n.* (a) equipment; landing
g. = undercarriage of an aircraft. (b) *inf.*
clothing. (c) gears = arrangement of
toothed wheels, levers, etc., connecting
an engine/pedals, etc., with wheels; in g.
= with the gears connected. **gear 2** *v.*
to g. sth to = to fit/to match. **gearbox**
n. casing for gears in cars. **gearing** *n.*
ratio of debt to assets. **gearlever,
gearstick,** *Am.* **gearshift** *n.* handle
by which the gears are changed in a car.
gearwheel *n.* toothed wheel
connecting with another wheel of
different diameter to change the power
ratio of the engine.

gecko ['grkəu] *n.* (*pl.*-os) small tropical
lizard.

gee [dʒiː] *inter.* showing surprise.

gee-gee ['dʒiːdʒiː] *n.* child's name for
a horse.

geese [giːs] *n. pl.* see goose.

gee-up ['dʒiːʌp] *inter* used to tell a
horse to go faster.

geezer ['giːzə] *n. Sl.* (old) man.

Geiger counter ['gaɪg] device for
detecting and recording radioactivity.

geisha ['geɪʃə] *n.* Japanese hostess and
dancing girl.

gel [dʒel] *n.* substance like a jelly.

gelatin(e) ['dʒelətiːn] *n.* substance
obtained after stewing skin, bones, etc.,
and used to make jellies. **gelatinous**
[dʒə'lætɪəs] *adj.* like jelly.

geld [geld] *v.* to castrate. **gelding**
['geldɪŋ] *n.* castrated animal, esp. horse.

gelignite ['dʒelɪgmaɪt] *n.*
nitroglycerine explosive.

gem [dʒem] *n.* precious stone.
gemmology [dʒe'mɒlədʒɪ] *n.* the
science of gems.

Gemini [dʒe'mɪnar] *n.* one of the signs
of the zodiac, shaped like twins.

gen [dʒen] *n. Sl.* information.

gender ['dʒendə] *n.* grammatical
classification of objects roughly

corresponding to the two sexes and absence of sex.

gene [dʒiːn] *n.* part of a chromosome which carries characteristics transmitted by the parent.

genealogical [dʒiːnɪəˈlɒdʒɪkl] *adj.* referring to genealogy. **genealogist** [dʒiːnɪˈælədʒɪst] *n.* person who studies genealogy. **genealogy** *n.* study of family descent through the generations.

genera [ˈdʒeərə] *n.* see genus.

general 1 [ˈdʒenrəl] *adj.* completely or approximately universal; including or affecting all or nearly all parts; g. anaesthetic = anaesthetic which makes the patient lose consciousness; g. election = election in which the whole country is involved; in g. = as a rule.

general 2 *n.* superior officer immediately below a field marshal in the army. **generalissimo** [dʒenrəˈlɪsɪməu] *n.* commander-in-chief of several armed forces. **generality** [dʒenəˈrælɪtɪ] *n.* being general; generalities = general subjects (for a conversation).

generalization [dʒenrəlaɪzerʃn] *n.* general statement. **generalize** [ˈdʒenəraɪz] *v.* to try to express sth as a general notion. **generally** [ˈdʒenrəlɪ] *adv.* as a rule. **general practitioner** *n.* doctor who treats all illnesses/family doctor. **general purpose** *adj.* serving many purposes.

generate [ˈdʒenəreɪt] *v.* to bring into existence; to produce. **generation** [dʒenəˈreɪʃn] *n.* (a) bringing into existence. (b) all people born about the same time; g. gap = age difference between one generation and another, often resulting in intolerance between them (c) period of years separating parents and children. (d) members of a family born about the same time.

generator [ˈdʒenəreɪtə] *n.* apparatus for producing electricity by gas/petrol, etc.

generic [dʒəˈnerɪk] *adj.* referring to a genus/group/type. **generically** *adv.* in a generic way.

generous [ˈdʒenərəs] *adj.* (a) g. with sth = willing to give sth. (b) large; a g. helping. **generosity** [dʒenəˈrɒsɪtɪ] *n.* willingness to give (money, etc.). **generously** *adv.* in a generous way.

genesis [ˈdʒenəsɪs] *n.* origin/beginning.

genetics [dʒəˈnetɪks] *n.* study of heredity. **genetic** *adj.* referring to genes/to genetics. **genetically** *adv.* in a genetic way.

genial [ˈdʒiːnɪəl] *adj.* cheerful/kindly. **genially** *adv.* cheerfully.

genie [ˈdʒiːnɪ] *n.* in the Arabian Nights, a magic slave who appears from a bottle or lamp.

genital 1 [ˈdʒenɪtl] *adj.* referring to the sex organs. **genital 2** *n.* pl.genitals = external sex organs.

genitive [ˈdʒenɪtɪv] *adj. & n.* (in grammar) g. (case) = form of a word showing possession.

genius [ˈdʒiːnɪəs] *n.* a person of great intelligence

genocide [ˈdʒenəsaɪd] *n.* mass killing of a race.

genre [ˈdʒɑːnrə] *n.* particular type (of art, etc.).

gent [dʒent] *n.* inf. gentleman. **gents** *n.* inf. men's toilet. **genteel** [dʒenˈtiːl] *adj.* too refined. **genteelly** *adv.* in a genteel way. **gentility** [dʒenˈtɪlɪtɪ] *n.* refinement (of manners).

gentian [ˈdʒenʃn] *n.* small blue alpine flower.

gentile [ˈdʒentaɪl] *n.* person not of Jewish race.

gentle [ˈdʒentl] *adj.* (-er, -est) mild/tender/soft. **gentlefolk** *n. pl.* (old) people of good breeding. **gentleman** [ˈdʒentlmən] *n.* (*pl.*-men) (a) man of good breeding and manners; g. 's agreement = agreement which is not written down. (b) (polite way of referring to men) Well, gentlemen, shall we begin? **gentlemanly** *adj.* like a gentleman. **gentleness** *n.* softness/carefulness. **gently** [ˈdʒentlɪ] *adv.* softly/carefully; g. does it! = be careful as you do it. **gentry** [ˈdʒentrɪ] *n.* people of high class in society, below the aristocracy.

genuflect [ˈdʒenjʊflekt] *v.* to bend the knee, esp. in worship. **genuflexion** *n.* bending the knee.

genuine [ˈdʒenjʊɪn] *adj.* authentic/true. **genuinely** *adv.* truly. **genuineness** *n.* being genuine.

genus [ˈdʒiːnəs] *n.* (*pl.*genera[ˈdʒiːnəs]) group of animals/plants which have common characteristics, and are distinct from all other groups.

geocentric [dʒi:əʊ'sentrɪk] adj. (astronomy, etc.) using the earth as the starting point when measuring distances.

geodesy [dʒɪ'ɒdɪsɪ] n. science of measurement of the earth. **geodesic** [dʒiəʊ'di:sɪk] adj. referring to geodesy; g. dome = dome made of set of polygons.

geography [dʒɪ'ɒgrəfɪ] n. science of the earth's surface/form/physical features/climate, etc. **geographer** [dʒɪ'ɒgrəfə] n. person who studies geography. **geographic(al)** [dʒɪə'græfɪk(l)] adj. referring to geography. **geographically** adv. in a geographical way.

geology [dʒɪ'ɒlədʒɪ] n. science of the earth's crust, esp. rock formations. **geological** [dʒɪə'lɒdʒɪkl] adj. referring to geology. **geologically** adv. in a geological way. **geologist** [dʒɪ'ɒlədʒɪst] n. person who studies geology.

geometry [dʒɪ'ɒmətrɪ] n. mathematical science of properties and relations of lines/surfaces/solids, etc., in space. **geometric(al)** [dʒɪə'metrɪk(l)] adj. referring to geometry; a g. design = design of lines/curves etc. **geometrically** adv. in a geometrical way.

geophysics [dʒi:əʊ'fɪzɪks] n. study of the physical properties of the earth. **geophysicist** n. person who studies geophysics.

Geordie ['dʒɔːdɪ] adj. & n. (person) from Newcastle.

georgette [dʒɔː'dʒet] n. thin silk cloth.

Georgian ['dʒɔːdʒɪən] adj. referring to the reigns of George I to IV (1714-1830)

geostationary orbit [dʒi:əʊ'steɪʃənrɪ'ɔːbɪt] n. orbit of a satellite which remains over the same point on the earth's surface.

geothermal [dʒi:əʊ'θɜːməl] adj. (energy) derived from the earth's heat.

geranium [dʒə'reɪnɪəm] n. perennial plant with white, pink or red flowers.

gerbil ['dʒɜːbɪl] n. small desert rat which jumps, kept as a pet.

geriatrics [dʒerɪ'ætrɪks] n. branch of medical science dealing with old age and its diseases. **geriatric** adj. for old people. **geriatrician** [dʒerɪə'trɪʃn] n. doctor specializing in geriatrics.

germ [dʒɜːm] n. (a) portion of organism capable of developing into a new one; wheat g. (b) micro-organism, often causing disease. **germicidal** adj. which kills germs. **germicide** n. substance which kills germs. **germ warfare** n. war fought using germs as was a weapon.

German 1 ['dʒɜːmən] adj. referring to Germany; G. measles = mild disease which gives a red rash and which can affect the development of an unborn child if caught by a pregnant woman; Am. G. shepherd = alsation dog.

German 2 n. (a) person from Germany (b) language spoken in Germany, Austria and parts of Switzerland. **Germanic** [dʒɜː'mænɪk] adj. referring to the Germans. Germano, prefix meaning between Germany and another country.

germane [dʒɜː'meɪn] adj. relevant.

germinate ['dʒɜːmɪneɪt] v. (of seeds) to begin to grow/to sprout. **germination** [dʒɜːmɪ'neɪʃn] n. beginning of plant growth from a seed.

gerontology [dʒerɒn'tɒlədʒɪ] n. scientific study of old age and its problems.

gerrymander ['dʒerɪmændə] v. to alter the boundaries of constituencies to improve the chances of a political party in an election.

gerund ['dʒerʌnd] n. noun formed from the -ing form of a verb.

gestation [dʒe'steɪʃn] n. period between conception and birth.

gesticulate [dʒe'stɪkjʊleɪt] v. to make expressive signs with the hands and arms. **gesticulation** [dʒestɪkjʊ'leɪʃn] n. sign with arms or hands.

gesture 1 ['dʒestʃə] n. (a) movement of limb or body, esp. hands, to give an expression of feeling. (b) action which expresses some positive feeling; token g. = small action which symbolizes feelings. **gesture 2** v. to make a movement to express a feeling.

get [get] v. (got; has got; Am. has gotten) (a) to obtain (b) to receive. (c) to have got = possess. (d) inf. to understand; you've got it! = you've found the right answer/you understand correctly. (e) to cause to happen; to make (s.o.) do sth; he got his shoes mended; she got the policeman to show her the way. (f) to have got to = to be obliged to. (g) to g. to

= to arrive at. (h) *inf.* to start; let's get going = let's start now. (i) to catch (a disease). (j) to become; he's getting too old for the job (k) to be doing sth; she's getting dressed. **get about** *v.* (a) to go from place to place (b) to be rumoured. **get across** *v.* (a) to cross (a road). (b) to make (sth) understood. **get along** *v.* (a) to manage. (b) *inf.* get along with you! = I don't believe you. (c) to be on friendly terms (with s.o.). **get at** *v.* (a) to reach. (b) *inf.* to criticize. **get-atable** *adj. inf.* easy to reach. **get away** *v.* to manage to go away; to escape he got away with it = he wasn't found out. **gataway** *n.* escape; g. car = car used to escape in. **get back** *v.* (a) to return. (b) to recover (sth). (c) to get your own back on s.o. = to have your revenge. **get by** *v.* (a) to pass. (b) *inf.* to manage. **get down** *v.* (a) to descend (b) to fetch down (c) to depress; to make (s.o.) gloomy. (d) to make (sth) be written (e) to get down to some hard work = to start to work hard. **get in** *v.* (a) to go inside (a car, etc.). (b) to be elected. **get into** *v.* (a) to go inside (a car, etc.) (b) to get into a temper = to become angry; to get into trouble = to be in a difficult situation. **get off** *v.* (a) to come down from. (b) he got off lightly = he received a light punishment. **get on** *v.* (a) to mount (a bicycle, etc.). (b) to age; he is getting on = he is past middle age. (c) to succeed. (d) to get on with s.o. = to be friendly with s.o.; they don't get on (together) = they don't like each other. **get out** *v.* (a) to bring out/to go out. get out! = leave the room. (b) I've got out of the habit of eating chocolates = I don't eat chocolates any more. (c) to get out of (doing) sth = to avoid doing sth. **get over** *v.* (a) overcome (a difficulty). (b) to recover from (an illness). (c) to climb over. **get round** *v.* (a) to go round (a corner). (b) to flatter (s.o.). (c) to get r. to(doing) sth = to find time to do (sth). **get through** *v.* (a) to pass (a test). (b) to get through to s.o. = to manage to get in contact with s.o. (by telephone). **get-together** *n. inf.* meeting. **get up** *v.* (a) to rise (from sitting or lying position); to get out of bed. (b) to organize (a petition). (c) to get up to = to reach. (d) to get up to mischief = to do sth naughty.

get-up *n.* odd clothes.
geyser ['giːzə] *n.* (a) hot spring of water. (b) gas apparatus for heating water.
ghastly ['gɑːstlɪ] *adj.* (ler, -lest) horrible/frightful. **ghastliness** *n.* being ghastly.
gherkin ['gɜːkɪn] *n.* small vegetable of the cucumber family, used for pickling.
ghetto ['getəʊ] *n.* (*pl.*-os) area in a city where deprived people live.
ghost [gəʊst] *n.* (a) spirit of a dead person; g. story = story about ghosts which aims at frightening the reader. (b) the Holy G. = third person of the Christian Trinity. (c) ghost writer. (d) a g. of a smile = very slight smile. **ghost 2** *v.* to write (book/article/speech, etc.) for s.o. else who then takes the credit.
ghostly *adj.* like a ghost. **ghost writer** *n.* person who writes a book for s.o. else who then takes the credit.
ghoul [guːl] *n.* evil ghost which haunts graves. **ghoulish** ['guːlɪʃ] *adj.* weird/bloodthirsty.
giant 1 ['dʒaɪənt] *n.* (a) (in fairy tales and myths) huge human being. (b) abnormally tall person, animal or plant. (c) very powerful industrial organization. (d) extremely able person. **giant 2** *adj.* very large. **glantess** [dʒaɪən'tes] *n.* (*pl.*-es) female giant.
gibber ['dʒɪbə] *v.* to speak very fast, without any meaning. **gibberish** ['dʒɪbrɪʃ] *n.* (no *pl.*) fast unintelligible speech.
gibbet ['dʒɪbɪt] *n.* gallows/structure on which criminals were hanged.
gibbon ['gɪbən] *n.* long-armed ape.
gibe 1 [dʒaɪb] *n.* sarcastic remark. **gibe 2** *v.* to jeer/to mock.
giblets ['dʒɪbləts] *n. pl.* liver/heart, etc. of poultry, removed before the bird is cooked.
giddy ['gɪdɪ] *adj.* (-ier, -iest) dizzy; feeling as if everything is spinning round. **giddily** *adv.* in a giddy way. **giddiness** *n.* dizzy feeling.
gift [gɪft] *n.* (a) present/thing given; g. token = card given as a present, which allows the person who receives it to buy sth at a shop (b) talent; she has a g. for music. **gifted** *adj.* talented. **gift-wrap** *v.* (gift-wrapped) to wrap (sth) in coloured paper to give as a present.

gig [gɪg] *n.* (a) light carriage on two wheels. (b) *inf.* performance by popular musicians.

giga- ['gɪgə] prefix one thousand million.

gigantic [dʒaɪ'gæntɪk] *adj.* huge/ colossal.

giggle 1 ['gɪgl] *n.* little nervous laugh; to have a fit of the giggles = to be unable to stop giggling. **giggle 2** *v.* to laugh little nervous laughs.

gigolo ['dʒɪgɒləʊ] *n.* (*pl.*-os) man who is paid by a woman to be her lover.

gild [gɪld] *v.* to cover with a thin layer of gold.

gill [dʒɪl] *n.* liquid measure equal to a quarter of a pint (140 ml).

gillie ['gɪlɪ] *n.* (in Scotland) man who helps a huntsman or fisherman.

gills [gɪlz] *n. pl.* (a) breathing organs in fish and other aquatic creatures. (b) thin vertical folds on the underside of mushrooms.

gilt 1 [gɪlt] *adj.* covered with a thin layer of gold. **gilt 2** *n.* (a) young female pig. (b) gilts = safe government bonds. **giltedged** *adj.* (investment) which will not lose its value.

gimbals ['ɪmbəlz] *n. pl.* device (of several rings balanced inside each other) to keep a compass level at sea.

gimcrack ['dʒɪmkræk] *adj.* cheap and badly made.

gimlet ['gɪmlət] *n.* small tool used for boring holes.

gimmick ['gɪmɪk] *n.* device adopted for the purpose of attracting attention or publicity.

gin [dʒɪn] *n.* (a) colourless alcoholic drink flavoured with juniper; glass of this drink. (b) trap for catching wild animals and game. (c) machine for cleaning raw cotton.

ginger 1 ['dʒɪndʒə] *n.* plant with a hot-tasting root used in cooking and medicine. **ginger 2** *adj.* (hair) of reddish colour. **gingerbread** *n.* cake made with treacle and flavoured with ginger. **ginger ale, ginger beer** *n.* fizzy ginger-flavoured drink. **gingerly 1** *adj.* cautious. **gingerly 2** *adv.* delicately/with caution. **ginger up** *v.* to stimulate/to arouse.

gingham ['gɪŋəm] *n.* checked cotton cloth.

gingivitis [dʒɪndʒɪ'vaɪtɪs] *n.* swelling and bleeding of the gums.

ginkgo ['gɪŋgəʊ] *n.* Chinese tree, which is similar to trees which flourished millions of years ago.

gipsy ['dʒɪpsɪ] *n.* member of a wandering race.

giraffe [dʒɪ'rɑːf] *n.* African animal with a very long neck and spotted skin.

gird [gɜːd] *v.* (formal) (girded/girt) to tie a belt round (sth).

girder ['gɜːdə] *n.* iron/steel beam used as a support.

girdle ['gɜːdl] *n.* (a) belt/sash. (b) corset. (c) pelvic g. = bones around the hips supporting the lower limbs. (d) (in N. of England & Scotland) griddle.

girl [gɜːl] *n.* female child; young woman. **girlfriend** *n.* female companion (esp. of a man). **Girl Guides** *n. pl.* social/ training organization for girls. **girlhood** *n.* period when you are a girl (before becoming a woman). **girlie** *adj. inf.* girlie magazine = one with photographs of naked young women. **girlish** *adj.* like a young girl.

giro ['dʒaɪrəʊ] *n.* (a) (also National Girobank) banking system in which money can be transferred directly from one account to another without writing a cheque. (b) payment made through the giro system.

girt [gɜːt] *v.* see gird.

girth [gɜːθ] *n.* (a) circumference/ distance round sth. (b) band of leather or cloth tied round the body of a horse to secure the saddle.

gist [dʒɪst] *n.* real point of matter; basic essentials.

give 1 [gɪv] *v.* (gave; has given) (a) to hand (sth) to s.o.; to transfer (sth) to s.o. (b) to utter (a cry). (c) to collapse; to bend. **give 2** *n.* (a) suppleness; the plank hasn't enough g. (b) g. and take = agreement between two people/parties to make concessions. **give away** *v.* (a) to hand over (sth) without asking for anything in return. (b) to betray/to tell (a secret). (c) to give (a bride) to the bridegroom. **give back** *v.* to return. **give in** *v.* to surrender/to yield. **given** *adj.* (a) she is g. to crying = she cries frequently. (b) particular/which has been identified. (c) g. name = first name/ Christian name. **give off** *v.* to let out.

give out v. (a) to distribute. (b) inf. to fail. (c) to make known. **give over** v. inf. to stop. **giver** n. person who gives. **give up** v. to stop (doing sth); I give up! = I cannot think of the answer; the murderer gave himself up = surrendered to the police. **give way** v. (a) to allow s.o. to go first. (b) to yield; to bend; to collapse.

gizzard ['gɪzəd] n. second stomach of a bird, where its food is ground up into tiny pieces.

glabrous ['glæbrəs] adj. smooth, with no hair.

glacé ['glæseɪ] adj. (cherries) preserved in sugar.

glacier ['glæsɪə] n. mass of ice which moves slowly down from a mountain. **glacial** ['gleɪʃl] adj. (a) referring to ice. (b) very cold; without emotion. **glaciation** [gleɪsɪ'eɪʃn] n. effect of ice on rocks.

glad [glæd] adj. pleased/happy. **gladden** v. to make glad. **gladly** adv. happily. **gladness** n. happiness.

glade [gleɪd] n. (formal) clear open space in the midst of trees.

gladiator ['glædɪeɪtə] n. man who fought in an arena (in ancient Rome). **gladiatorial** [glædɪə'tɔːrɪəl] adj. referring to gladiators.

gladiolus [glædɪ'əʊləs] n. (pl.gladioli[glædɪ'əʊlaɪ]) tall garden plant with sword-shaped leaves and bright flower spikes.

glair [gleːə] n. white of egg. used as a coating.

glamour, Am. **glamor** ['glæmə] n. (a) magic/enchantment. (b) outward charm/ attractiveness (of a woman). **glamorize** v. to make (sth) appear more appealing than it really is. **glamorous** adj. attractive/enchanting.

glance 1 [glɑːns] n. quick look. **glance 2** v. (a) to look briefly. (b) to slide off an object instead of striking it fully. **glancing** adj. sliding off to the side; not straight.

gland [glænd] n. organ of the body which produces a liquid which controls bodily changes, such as growth. **glandular** ['glændjʊlə] adj. referring to glands; g. fever = severe illness which affects the glands.

glare 1 ['gleə] n. (a) strong/fierce light. (b) fierce/fixed look. **glare 2** v. (a) to shine too brightly. (b) to look angrily at s.o. **glaring** adj. g. mistake = very obvious mistake.

glasnost ['glæznɒst] n. openness, freedom of information.

glass [glɑːs] n. (a) (a) substance made from sand and soda or potash, usu. transparent, used for making windows, etc. (b) vessel made of glass used esp. for drinking; contents of such a glass. (c) barometer; looking g. = mirror; stained g. = coloured glass used frequently in the windows of a church. **glass blower** n. person who blows and shapes molten glass into bottles, etc. **glasses** n. pl. spectacles. **glass fibre** n. strong material made of woven fibres of glass; plastic containing fibres of glass. **glasshouse** n. (a) greenhouse, cultivation of plants. (b) Sl. military prison. **glassware** n. (no. pl.) articles made of glass. **glass wool** n. soft substance, made from glass fibre, used as an insulating material in buildings. **glassy** adj. (a) resembling glass. (b) dull/unseeing; a g. stare.

glaucoma [glɔː'kəʊmə] n. disease of the eyes which can cause blindness.

glaze 1 [gleɪz] n. shiny surface (on pottery). **glaze 2** v. (a) to fit with glass; to put glass in (a window). (b) to cover with a shiny coating. **glazier** ['gleɪzɪə] n. person whose trade is to fit glass in windows. **glazing** n. fitting with windows; double g. = windows with two sheets of glass a small distance apart, which help insulation.

gleam 1 [gliːm] n. (a) short-lived weak light. (b) faint/temporary show of some quality. **gleam 2** v. to shine.

glean [gliːn] v. to collect (grain) left after the harvest; to scrape together (news/information, etc.). **gleaner** n. person who gleans. **gleanings** n. pl. odd bits of information.

glee [gliː] n. (a) short song sung by several singers. (b) joy/gaiety. **gleeful** adj. joyful. **gleefully** adv. happily.

glen [glen] n. (in Scotland) narrow valley. **glengarry** n. tartan forage cap with ribbons hanging at the back.

glib [glɪb] adj. fluent but insincere way of speaking. **glibly** adv. smoothly and insincerely.

glide 1 [glaɪd] n. smooth movement.
glide 2 v. to move smoothly. **glider** n.
small aircraft without an engine that
relies on wind currents for propulsion.
gliding n. sport of flying gliders.
glimmer 1 ['glɪmə] n. (a) feeble light.
(b) tiny quantity; faint/temporary show
of (interest, etc.). **glimmer 2** v. to
shine feebly/intermittently.
glimpse 1 [glɪmps] n. quick/passing
sight. **glimpse 2** v. to catch sight of
(sth).
glint 1 [glɪnt] n. flash/glitter/sparkle.
glint 2 v. to flash/to glitter (like metal).
glisten ['glɪsn] v. (of something wet) to
shine/to sparkle.
glitter 1 ['glɪtə] n. bright light/sparkle.
glitter 2 v. to shine brightly/to sparkle.
gloaming ['gləʊmɪŋ] n. twilight.
gloat [gləʊt] v. to g. over = to take
pleasure in (s.o.'s misfortune); to look at
(sth) greedily.
globe [gləʊb] n. (a) the g. = the earth
(b) ball with a map of the world on it. (c)
round object; glass ball which covers an
electric light bulb; g. artichoke = tall
green thistle-like plant of which you eat
parts of the flower head. **global** adj.
world-wide. **globally** adv. all over the
world. **globetrotter** n. tourist who
travels all over the world.
globule ['glɒbjuːl] n. small round
object (such as a drop of water).
globular adj. shaped like a globe.
globulin n. protein found in blood,
which contains antibodies.
glockenspiel ['glɒkənspiːl] n. musical
instrument like a xylophone with metal
bars.
gloom [gluːm] n. (a) darkness/
obscurity. (b) despair/melancholy.
gloomily adv. in a gloomy way.
gloomy adj. (-ier, -iest) melancholy;
pessimistic.
glory 1 ['glɔːrɪ] n. (a) fame/renown. (b)
magnificent sight. **glory 2** v. to g. in =
to get great pleasure from/to pride
oneself on. **glorification** [glɔːrɪfɪ'keɪʃn]
n. transforming into sth more splendid.
glorify v. to make glorious/to transform
into sth more splendid. **glorious**
['glɔːrɪəs] adj. splendid. **gloriously**
adv. in a glorious way. **gloryhole** n.
cupboard/room where you can keep
junk.

gloss 1 [glɒs] n. (a) shine on a surface;
showy appearance; g. paint = paint
which is shiny when dry. (b) comment
about a text. **gloss 2** v. to g. over = to
try to hide (a mistake etc.). **glossiness**
n. being glossy. **glossy** adj. & n. (-ier,
-iest) g. magazines/glossies = colourful,
expensive magazines printed on shiny
paper.
glossary ['glɒsərɪ] n. short explanation
of meanings of words, usu. found at the
end of a book.
glottis ['glɒtɪs] n. space in the vocal
cords, which makes sound when opened
or closed. **glottal** adj. referring to the
glottis; g. stop = type of clicking sound
made by closing the glottis.
glove [glʌv] n. article of clothing worn
on the hand; to handle s.o. with kid
gloves = to deal gently with s.o.; hand in
g. with s.o. = closely associated with
s.o.; g. compartment = small cupboard
on the dashboard of a car, in which you
can put small items.
gloved adj. wearing gloves.
glow 1 [gləʊ] n. (a) brightness/warmth.
(b) blush/bloom. **glow 2** v. to shine; to
show warm colour. **glowing** adj.
shining/warm. **glow-worm** n. female
beetle which gives off a green light in
the dark.
glower ['glaʊə] v. to frown.
gloxinia [glɒk'sɪnɪə] n. type of pot
plant with large trumpet-shaped flowers.
glucose ['gluːkəʊz] n. natural sugar
found in fruit.
glue 1 [gluː] n. substance which will
stick things together. **glue 2** v. to stick
together **gluey** adj. sticky.
glum [glʌm] adj. (glummer, glummest)
sullen; looking dejected/miserable.
glut 1 [glʌt] n. too much of (sth);
supply exceeding demand. **glut 2** v. to
be glutted (with) = to have too much.
gluten ['gluːtən] n. protein left when
starch is removed from flour. **glutinous**
['gluːtɪnəs] adj. sticky.
glutton ['glʌtn] n. (a) person who eats
too much. (b) person with great
enthusiasm for sth. **gluttonous** adj.
referring to overeating. **gluttony** n.
eating too much.
glycerine, Am. **glycerin** ['glɪsərɪn] n.
colourless, sweet liquid (used in
medicines/in explosives, etc.).

gm abbrev. for gram.

GMT [dʒi:em'ti:] abbreviation for Green which Mean Time.

gnarled [nɑ:ld] adj. twisted/rugged; covered with hard lumps.

gnash [næʃ] v. to grind (the teeth).

gnat [næt] n. small, two-winged fly which stings.

gnaw [nɔ:] v. to chew.

gneiss [naɪs] n. type of hard rock.

gnome [nəʊm] n. dwarf/mischievous ugly little man (in fairy stories; inf. the gnomes of Zurich = Swiss international bankers. **gnomic** adj. concise and clever (saying).

GNP [dʒi:en'pi:] gross national product.

gnu [nu:] n. large South African antelope.

go 1 [gəʊ] n. (a) act of moving; inf. he's always on the go = always moving about. (b) inf. energy; she's full of go (c) attempt/try. (d) to try and make a go of it = to try to make the business successful.

go 2 v. (went; has gone) (a) to move from one place to another to travel. (b) to work; my watch won't go.(c) to leave; from the word go = from the start. (d) to be going to do sth = to intend to do sth; to be about to do sth. (e) to fit; It's too big to go into the box (f) to become; she went pale. (g) to make a noise; the guns went bang. (h) to have a certain tune/ certain words; how does the song go? (i) to fail; the brakes went. **go about** v. (a) try to do sth/to plan how do sth. (b) (of sailing boat) to turn to sail in another direction. (c) to move around. **go ahead** v. to start to do sth. **go-ahead 1** n. permission to start. **go-ahead 2** adj. enterprising; active. **go along with** v. to agree with (s.o./sth). **go back** v. to return. **go back on** v. not keep (a promise). **go-between** n. person who carries messages from one person to another **go-cart** n. flat wooden frame with four wheels for children to play with. **go down** v. (a) to descend. (b) to go down well = to be accepted. **go for** v. (a) to apply for. (b) to like. (c) to be sold. (d) to attack. **go getter** n. inf. energetic, ambitious person. **go-go dancer** n. inf. person who performs an energetic (and usu. erotic) dance in a nightclub. **go in** v. to enter; the sun's gone in = is hidden by clouds. **go in for** v. (a) to enter (for a test/examination). (b) to do (sth) as a hobby. **going 1** adj. (a) working. (b) g. rate = usual rate/ current rate. **going 2** n. (a) surface of a race track; do it while the g, is good = while you have the chance. (b) goings-on = unusual things which are happening. **go into** v. (a) to enter. (b) (in maths) to divide. (c) to examine. **go kart** n. flat frame with four wheels and an engine, used as a small racing car. **go-karting** n. racing in go-karts. **go-off** v. (a) to explode. (b) to turn bad. (c) to dislike; I've gone off him = I used to like him, but now I don't. **go on** v. (a) to continue. (b) (showing disbelief) inf. go on! = I don't believe you! (c) to happen; what's going on here? (d) to go on about sth = to talk all the time; to nag. **go out** v. (a) to leave. (b) to be shut off; to die. **go out with** v. to go to parties/the cinema, etc. with (s.o. of the opposite sex). **go round** v. (a) to turn. (b) to be enough for all. (c) to visit. **go slow** n. slowing down of production by workers as a protest. **go under** v. (a) to drown (b) to be ruined. **go up** v. (a) to rise; to go up in flames = to burn. **go with** v. to match/to fit with. **go without** v. not to have.

goad 1 [gəʊd] n. long stick for driving cattle. **goad 2** v. to g. s.o. into doing sth = to urge/to drive s.o. on by annoying him.

goal [gəʊl] n. (a) object of effort/ ambition; aim (b) two posts between which a ball has to be driven to score a point in a game. (c) points won (in football/hockey, etc.) **goalkeepergoalie** n.inf. player who defends the goal. **goalmouth** n. area just in front of the goal. **goalpost** n. one of the two posts between which a ball is driven to score a goal.

goat [gəʊt] n. domestic animal with horns and a beard; to separate the sheep from the goats = to divide the good from the bad; inf. to get s.o.'s g. = to annoy s.o. **goatee** [gəʊ'ti:] n. small beard, like that of a goat.

gob 1 [gɒb] n. Sl. mouth; shut your g.! = stop talking! **gob 2** v. Sl to spit. **gobbet** ['gɒbɪt] n. large lump (of fat).

gobble ["gɒbl] v. (a) to eat quickly and greedily. (b) make a noise like a turkey.
gobbledegook ['gɒbldɪguːk] n. inf. meaningless official/technical language.
goblet ['gɒblət] n. metal or glass drinking cup without handles.
goblin ['gɒblɪn] n. (in fairy stories) mischievous ugly little man.
god [gɒd] n. (a) deity; superhuman power. (b) God = creator and ruler of the Universe, according to Christian/Jewish/Muslim, etc., belief. (c) thing which is worshipped. **godchild** n. (pl.-children) child who was sponsored at baptism. **god-daughter** n. girl who was sponsored at baptism. **goddess** n. female god. **godfather** n. man who sponsors a child at baptism; inf. head of a mafia group. **god-fearing** adj. sincerely religious. **godforsaken** adj. bad/awful. **godlike** adj. like a god. **godliness** n. being godly. **godly** adj. holy. **godmother** n. woman who sponsors a child at baptism. **godparents** n. pl. people who sponsor a child at baptism. **godsend** n. blessing. **godson** n. boy who was sponsored at baptism.
godown ['gaʊdaʊn] n. warehouse (in the Far East).
goggle ['gɒgl] v. to stare (at). **gogglebox** n. inf. television. **goggles** n. pl. protective spectacles against dust and glare.
goitre, Am. **goiter** ['gɔɪtə] n. disease in which the thyroid gland in the neck swells up.
gold 1 [gəʊld] n. (a) element; Au) precious yellow metal. (b) medal made of gold (won in a sports competition).
gold 2 adj. made of gold; g. leaf = thin covering of gold; g. plate = dishes made of gold. **goldcrest** n. very small bird, with an orange crest on its head. **gold-digger** n. (a) person who digs for gold. (b) inf. woman who marries a man for his money. **golden** adj. made of gold; gold-coloured; g. opportunity = wonderful chance; g. rule = very important rule; g. wedding = fiftieth anniversary of marriage; g. handshake = sum of money presented when you leave work; g. disc = award given to a singer whose record has sold one million copies; h. handcuffs = very attractive

salary and benefits, with a penalty if the employee leaves. **goldfield** n. land where gold is mined. **goldfinch** n. brightly coloured song bird. **goldfish** n. (pl.goldfish) small orange fish kept in ponds/bowls. **goldmine** n. mine which produces gold; very profitable business. **goldsmith** n. person who works in gold.
golf [gɒlf] n. game for two people, or two couples, where a small hard ball is struck with long-handled clubs into a series of holes, the object being to use as few strokes as possible. **golfclub** n. (a) wooden-or metal-headed stick for striking the golf ball. (b) group of people who play golf and allow others to join them on payment of a fee; clubhouse where golfers meet. **golf course** n. ground on which golf is played. **golfer** n. person who plays golf.
golliwog ['gɒlɪwɒg] n. doll like a man with a black face and curly black hair.
gonad ['gəʊnæd] n. gland which produces gametes.
gondola ['gɒndələ] n. (a) boat used on the canals in Venice. (b) basket/passenger compartment hanging underneath a balloon. **gondolier** [gɒndə'lɪə] n. man who pushes a gondola, using a pole.
gone [gɒn] v. see go. **goner** ['gɒnə] n. inf. dying person; dead person.
gong [gɒŋ] n. (a) metal disc with a turned rim which gives a resonant sound when struck, used esp. to call people to meals. (b) Sl. medal.
gonna ['gɒnə] v. Sl. = going to.
gonorrh(o)ea [gɒnə'riːə] n. type of venereal disease.
goo [guː] n. inf. (no pl.) sticky stuff. **gooey** adj. inf. sticky.
good 1 adj.. (better, best) (a) having the right qualities/satisfactory; did you have a g. time? = did you enjoy yourself? (b) able; he is g. at French. (c) right/proper; it is a g. idea. (d) morally excellent/virtuous; he is a g. man. (e) well behaved/not troublesome; as g. as gold = exceptionally well behaved. (f) efficient/suitable/competent; he was as g. as his word = he did what he said he would do. (g) g. morning! g. afternoon! g. evening! interjections used when meeting or leaving someone in the

morning, afternoon or evening. (h) valid/ sound/thorough (i) not less than; she waited a g. half-hour (j) a lot of; a g. many people; a g. deal of money. (k) as g. as = practically/almost. **good 2** [gʊd] *n.* (a) the g. = virtuous people. (b) profit/ advantage; what g. will it do him? to do g. = to act kindly; for g. = permanently/ forever; he is up to no g. = he is acting in a suspicious manner. (c) goods = movable property; goods and chattels = personal possessions; goods train = train which carries cargo not passengers. **goodbye** [gʊd'baɪ] *n. & inter.* used when leaving someone. **good-for-nothing** *n.* useless. lazy person. **Good Friday** *n.* Friday before Easter Day. **good-humoured** *adj.* pleasant; in a happy mood. **goodish** *adj.* quite good. **good-looking** *adj.* handsome/pretty. **good-natured** *adj.* kindly/pleasant. **goodness** *n.* virtue/kindness/ generosity; thank g.! = how glad I am! **goodnight** *n. & inter* used when leaving someone late at night. **goodwill** *n.* (a) kindly feeling towards a person. (b) good reputation of a business. **goody** *n. inf.* (a) good person.(b) goodies = good things/money/treasure. **goody-goody** *adj. inf.* (person) who is too good.

goof 1 [guːf] *n. Sl.* stupid person. **goof 2** *v.* to make a stupid mistake. **goofy** *adj. inf.* stupid.

googly ['guːglɪ] *n.* (in cricket) ball which twists sharply in the opposite direction to that expected.

goon [guːn] *n.* silly fool.

goosander [guːsændə] *n.* type of wild duck.

goose [guːs] *n.* (*pl.*geese) (a) web-footed water bird, larger than a duck. (b) *inf.* silly person. **gooseberry** ['guːzbrɪ] *n.* small edible green fruit; bush which bears this fruit. **gooseflesh** *n.* small raised bumps on the skin caused by fear or cold **goose-pimples** *n. pl.* mass of small bumps on the skin caused by fear/ by cold, etc. **goose-step 1** *n.* way of marching without bending the knees. **goose-step 2** *v.* (goosestepped) to march without bending the knees.

gopher ['gəʊfə] *n.* American rodent which lives in burrows.

gore 1 [gɔː] *n.* (a) (formal) blood which

has thickened after coming from a wound. (b) section of a skirt, shaped like a triangle. **gore 2** *v.* to pierce with a horn. **gored** *adj.* (skirt) with a gore.

gorge 1 [gɔːdʒ] *n.* narrow opening between hills. **gorge 2** *v.* to eat greedily; he gorged himself on chocolates.

gorgeous ['gɔːdʒəs] *adj.* magnificent/ splendid; richly coloured. **gorgeously** *adv.* splendidly.

gorgon ['gɔːgən] *n.* fierce woman.

gorilla [gə'rɪlə] *n.* large, powerful African ape.

gormandize ['gɔːməndaɪz] *v.* to eat far too much.

gormless [gɔːmləs] *adj. inf.* foolish/stupid.

gorse [gɔːs] *n.* prickly yellow-flowered shrub.

gory ['gɔːrɪ] *adj.* (-ier, -iest) covered in blood.

gosh [gɒʃ] *inter.* showing surprise.

goshawk ['gɒshɔːk] *n.* type of trained hawk.

gosling ['gɒzlɪŋ] *n.* baby goose.

gospel ['gɒspl] *n.* record of Christ's life in the books of the four evangelists; it's the g. truth = it's absolutely true.

gossamer ['gɒsəmə] *n.* (a) very fine cobweb. (b) very fine material.

gossip 1 ['gɒsɪp] *n.* idle chat, esp. about other people; g. column = section in a paper which gives news about the private lives of famous people. (b) person who spreads rumours. **gossip 2** *v.* to talk idly; to spread rumours. **gossipy** *adj.* full of gossip.

got [gɒt] *v.* (a) see get. (b) to have g. to do sth = to be obliged/to have to do sth.

gothic ['gɒθɪk] *adj.* style of architecture with pointed arches used in Western Europe in 12th-16th centuries.

gotta ['gɒtə] *v. Sl.* = (have) got to.

gotten ['gɒtn] *v. Am.* see get.

gouache [gʊ'ɑːʃ] *n.* kin of thick watercolour paint.

gouge 1 [gaʊdʒ] *n.* kind of chisel used in carpentry. **gouge 2** *v.* to scoop out.

goulash ['guːlæʃ] *n.* Hungarian stew flavoured with paprika.

gourd ['gʊəd] *n.* dried fruit of a climbing plant, used as a bowl.

gourmand ['gʊəmənd] *n.* person who eats too much. **gourmet** ['gʊəmeɪ] *n.* connoisseur of food and wine.

gout [gaʊt] n. painful inflammation of the joints, esp. the big toe. **gouty** adj. afflicted with gout.

govern 1 ['gʌvən] v. (a) to rule with authority. (b) to influence/to determine. **governance** n. (formal) way of governing. **governess** n. female teacher, usu. in a private household. **government** ['gʌvənmənt] n. group of people ruling a country. **governmental** [gʌvən'mentl] adj. referring to a government. **governor** n. person who rules (esp. a prison); Governor-General = person who represents the Queen at the head of a Commonwealth country.

gown [gaʊn] n. (a) (formal) dress. (b) long official robe (worn by a mayor/judge/person with a degree, etc.). (c) dressing-gown = long coat worn over night clothes.

GP ['dʒi:'pi:] abbreviation for general practitioner; family doctor.

GPO [dʒi:pi:'əʊ] abbreviation for General Post Office.

grab 1 [græb] n. sudden seizing with the hands; to make a g. for = to try to seize. **grab 2** v. (grabbed) to seize.

grace 1 [greɪs] n. (a) pleasing quality/attractiveness; with good g. = with a show of willingness. (b) short prayer of thanksgiving before or after a meal. (c) act of mercy; pardon from all sin. (d) favour shown by granting a delay; ten day's g. **grace 2** v. to honour. **graceful** adv. moving with ease. **gracefully** adv. moving with easily. **gracefulness** n. ease of movement. **graceless** adj. with no grace. **grace note** n. note in music which need not be played, but which adds to the attraction of the piece. **gracious** ['greɪʃəs] adj. kind/agreeable; elegant (way of living) good g.! = how surprising! **graciously** adv. kindly. **graciousness** n. being gracious.

grade 1 [greɪd] n. (a) degree/level/rank; to make the g. = to succeed. (b) mark in an exAm. (c) Am. class (in school). **grade 2** v. to arrange in grades/to sort out. **gradation** [grə'deɪʃn] n. series of steps, passing from one level to another. **grade crossing** n. Am. place where a railway line crosses a road. **gradient** ['greɪdɪənt] n. amount of slope in a road, railway, etc.

gradual ['grædjʊəl] adj. slow/progressive. **gradually** adv. little by little.

graduate 1 ['grædjʊət] n. person who has obtained a degree; g. of London University. **graduate 2** ['grædjʊət] v. (a) to obtain a degree (from a university). (b) to regulate. (c) to mark in a scale; graduated measuring glass = one with quantities marked on it. **graduation** [grædjʊ'eɪʃn] n. (a) obtaining a degree. (b) act of marking a scale.

graffiti [grə'fi:ti] n. pl. unofficial drawings or writing on walls.

graft 1 [grɑːft] n. (a) shoot of a plant inserted into another plant from which it receives sap and of which it becomes part. (b) in surgery; piece of transplanted living tissue. (c) Sl. hard work. (d) Sl. bribery; bribe. **graft 2** v. to insert (part of a plant) into another plant so that it can grow; to attach (skin, etc.) to other parts of the body.

Grail [greɪl] n. the Holy G. = precious object (the cup used at the Last Supper) which was sought by medieval knights.

grain [greɪn] n. (a) seed of cereal. (b) small particle of sand/gold, etc. (c) texture of particles (in stone); lines of fibres in wood/material; It goes against the g. = it goes against natural instincts. (d) measurement of weight. **grainy** adj. (wood) with a strongly marked grain.

gram [græm] n. measurement of weight, one thousandth part of a kilogram.

grammar ['græmə] n. (a) art and science of a language; rules of the forms of the words and their relationship in a language. (b) book which explains/teaches the rules of a language. **grammarian** [grə'meərɪən] n. specialist in the study of grammar. **grammar school** n. (old) selective secondary school. **grammatical** [grə'mætɪkl] adj. conforming to the rules of grammar. **grammatically** adv. according to the rules of grammar.

gramophone ['græməfəʊn] n. (old) machine on which records are played and which is wound up with a handle.

grampus ['græmpəs] n. sea animal similar to a dolphin; to puff like a g. = to have difficulty in breathing.

gran [græn] n. inf. grandmother.

granary ['grænərɪ] *n.* storehouse for grain; g. loaf = bread made with whole wheat grain.

grand 1 [grænd] *adj.* (-er, -est) (a) important/imposing. (b) final. (c) conducted with solemnity. (d) very good.

grand 2 *n.* (a) *inf.* grand piano. (b) *Sl.* thousand pounds/dollars. **grandad** *n. inf.* grandfather. **grandchild** *n.* (*pl.*children) child of a son a daughter. **granddaughter** *n.* daughter of a son or daughter. **grandee** [græn'di:] *n.* proud aristocrat (usu. Spanish). **grandeur** ['grændʒə] *n.* splendour/majesty. **grandfather** *n.* father of a mother or father; g. clock = tall clock standing on the floor. **grandiloquence** [græn'dɪləkwəns] *n.* pompous/wordy speech. **grandiloquent** *adj.* speaking in a pompous way. **grandiose** ['grændɪəʊs] *adj.* very splendid. **grandly** *adv.* in a grand way. **grandma** ['grænmɑː] *n. inf.* grandmother. **grandmaster** *n.* chessplayer of international quality. **grandmother** *n.* mother of a mother or father. **grandness** *n.* being grand. **grandpa** ['grænpɑː] *n.* grand father. **grandparents** *n. pl.* parents of a mother or father. **grand piano** *n.* large horizontal piano. **Grand Prix** [grɒŋ'priː] *n.* motor/motorcycle race. **grandson** *n.* son of a son or daughter. **grandstand** *n.* building with a sloping bank of seats for spectators at a racecourse or sportsground.

grange [greɪndʒ] *n.* country house with farm buildings attached to it.

granite ['grænɪt] *n.* hard light-grey stone used for building.

granny ['grænɪ] *n. inf.* grandmother; g. flat = part of a house converted into a separate flat for an old relative; g. knot = insecure type of reef knot.

grant 1 [grɑːnt] *n.* financial aid. **grant 2** *v.* (a) to agree/to give consent; to take sth for granted = not to appreciate it any more. (b) to agree; I g. you it is a difficult job = I admit that it is difficult. **granted** *adj.* admitted/understood. **granulate** ['grænjʊleɪt] *v.* to form into grains. **granular** *adj.* containing grains; like grains. **granule** *n.* very small particle.

grape [greɪp] *n.* small green or purple fruit growing in clusters on a vine, eaten as fruit growing in clusters on a vine, eaten as fruit or made into wine. **grapefruit** *n.* (*pl.*grapefruit) large round yellow citrus fruit. **grapevine** *n.* climbing plant on which grapes grow; I heard it on the g. = I learnt the news the gossip/unofficially.

graph [grɑːf] *n.* mathematical diagram/ curve. **graphic** ['græfɪk] *adj.* (a) referring to graphs/diagrams/signs, etc. (c) vivid (description). **graphical** *adj.* referring to graphs/diagrams/signs, etc. **graphically** *adv.* (a) using graphs/ diagrams/signs, etc. (b) in a graphic way. **graphics** *n.* pictures/charts on a printed document or on a computer screen. **graph paper** *n.* paper with small squares for graphs on. **graphite** ['græfaɪt] *n.* naturally occurring form of carbon; lead (as used in a pencil). **graphology** [græ'fɒlədʒɪ] *n.* science of discovering s.o.'s character from handwriting. **graphologist** *n.* person who practises graphology.

grapnel ['græpnl] *n.* small anchor with several hooks.

grapple ['græpl] *v.* to wrestle/to fight (with). **grappling iron** *n.* grapnel.

grasp [grɑːsp] *n.* (a) tight hold/grip. (b) understanding. **grasp at** *v.* to try to grab. **grasping** *adj.* (person) who is eager to get more things.

grass 1 [grɑːs] *n.* (a) low green plant of which the thin leaves and stalks are eaten by cattle etc.; don't let the g. grow under your feet = waste no time in doing sth. (b) plant of a species related to grass (including bamboo, etc.). (c) lawn/piece of ground covered with grass. (d) *Sl.* police informer. (e) Sl.. marijuana.

grass 2 *v.* (a) to g. over = to cover with grass. (b) *Sl.* to inform the police about a crime. **grasshopper** *n.* green jumping insect with long back legs. **grassland** *n.* prairie pasture. **grassroots** *n. pl.* ordinary members of a political party/a trade union; common people; g. reaction = reaction by the ordinary members (of a party etc.). **grass-snake** *n.* common snake. **grasswidow** *n.* wife whose husband has temporarily gone away. **grasswidower** *n.* husband whose wife has temporarily gone away. **grassy** *adj.* covered with growing grass.

grate 1 [greɪt] n. fireplace. **grate 2** v. (a) to reduce to small bits by rubbing on a rough surface. (b) to make a noise like two rough surfaces rubbing together. (c) to have an irritating effect upon. **grater** n. instrument for grating cheese, etc.

grating 1 n. grille; framework of wooden or metal bars. **grating 2** adj. a g. sound = an irritating sound as of the rubbing together of rough surfaces.

grateful ['greɪtfʊl] adj. thankful. **gratefully** adv. thankfully.

gratify ['grætɪfaɪ] v. (a) to satisfy/to delight (b) to please. **gratification** [grætɪfɪ'keɪʃn] n. satisfaction. **gratifying** adj. pleasing/satisfying.

gratin ['grætæŋ] n. dish cooked with a crust, often of cheese, on top.

gratis ['grɑːtɪs] adv. free/without charge.

gratitude ['grætɪtjuːd] n. appreciation.

gratuity [grə'tjuːɪtɪ] n. (a) present of money. (b) sum of money given to s.o. on retirement. **gratuitous** adj. unasked for; undeserved.

grave 1 [greɪv] n. tomb/hole in the ground to put a dead body in; burial place; to have one foot in the g. = to be very near to death. **grave 2** adj. (-er, -est) serious/solemn. **gravedigger** n. man who digs graves. **gravestone** n. memorial stone placed on a grave.

graveyard n. cemetery/place where people are buried.

gravel ['grævl] n. mixture of sand and small stones.

graven [greɪvn] adj. (old) carved.

gravitate ['grævɪteɪt] v. to move (towards sth). **gravitation** [grævɪ'teɪʃn] n. force of the earth's centre which attracts and causes objects to fall to the ground if dropped. **gravity** ['grævɪtɪ] n. (a) seriousness. (b) weight; specific g. = density of a substance divided by the density of water. (c) force attracting all objects to the earth's centre, causing objects to fall to the ground if dropped.

gravy ['greɪvɪ] n. (no pl.) (a) juices that drip from meat during cooking. (b) brown sauce served with meat.

gravyboat n. small wide jug for serving gravy.

gray [greɪ] adj. & n. (usu. Am.) = grey.

grayling ['greɪlɪŋ] n. (a) type of brown butterfly. (b) grey fish.

graze 1 [greɪz] n. slight surface wound/ scratch. **graze 2** v. (a) to feed on growing grass. (b) to wound slightly in passing. **grazing** n. pasture.

grease 1 [griːs] n. (a) melted animal fat. (b) oily/fatty substance. **grease 2** v. (a) to cover/to coat with oil/fat, etc. (b) inf. to g. s.o.'s palm = to bribe s.o. **greasegun** n. device for putting grease into machines. **greasepaint** n. makeup used by actors. **greaseproof paper** n. paper which will not let oil through. **greasy** adj. smeared with grease; oily.

great [greɪt] adj. (-er, -est) (a) large/big. (b) extreme. (c) distinguished/grand. (d) remarkable. (e) inf. wonderful. **great-aunt** n. aunt of a father or mother. **greatcoat** n. thick army coat. **Great Dane** n. breed of very large dog. **great grandchildren** n. pl. grandchildren of a son or daughter. **great-grand-daughter** n. granddaughter of a son or daughter. **great-grandfather** n. grandfather of a father or mother. **great-grandmother** n. grandmother of a father or mother. **great-grand-parents** n. pl. grandparents of a father or mother. **great-grandson** n. grandson of a son or daughter. **greatly** adv. very much. **greatness** n. remarkable ability. **great-uncle** n. uncle of a father or mother.

grebe [griːb] n. type of diving bird with a long neck.

Grecian ['griːʃn] adj. referring to ancient Greece.

greed [griːd] n. too great appetite; desire for more than is necessary. **greedily** adv. with great appetite. **greediness** n. being greedy. **greedy** adj. (-ier, -iest) wanting to eat too much; g. for = always wanting (power, etc.).

Greek 1 [griːk] adj. referring to Greece. **Greek 2** n. (a) person from Greece (b) language spoken in Greece.

green 1 [griːn] adj. (-ier, -iest) (a) of a colour like grass g. light = light which shows you can go ahead; g. with envy = very envious. (b) immature/gullible. (c) g. bacon = plain bacon which has not been smoked. (d) referring to a concern about the environment; g. issues = problems concerning the environment. **green 2** n. (a) colour like that of grass.

(b) piece of public land covered with grass. (c) piece of land covered with smooth grass on which you can play certain games. **greenback** n. inf. Am. dollar bill. **green belt** n. area of countryside round a town where building is prohibited. **green card** n. (a) insurance certificate to insure a car being taken abroad. (b) work permit for s.o. who is going to live in the USA. **greenery** n. vegetation. **greenfield site** n. site for a factory in fields. **greenfinch** n. bird with yellow and green plumage. **green fingers** n. pl. skill in gardening. **greenfly** n. (pl.greenfly) small green aphis. **greengage** n. kind of green plum. **greengrocer** n. person who sells fruit and vegetables. **greengrocer's, greengrocery** n. shop selling fruits and vegetables. **greenhorn** n. inexperienced person. **greenhouse** n. shelter made of glass and wood or metal for cultivation of delicate plants; g. effect = warming effect on the atmosphere, caused by carbon dioxide in the upper atmosphere. **greenish** adj. rather green. **greenmail** n. buying shares in a company, threatening to take the company over, then selling the shares at a profit. **Green Paper** n. official report by the government on proposals which are being studied. **Green Party** n. political party which is mainly concerned with environmental questions. **green pound** n. value of the pound as used in calculating the Common Market agricultural prices and subsidies relating to the UK. **greenroom** n. room where actors can rest when they are off-stage. **greens** n. pl. inf. cooked green vegetables. **Greens** n. pl. the Green Party. **greenstick fracture** n. fracture of a long bone in a child, where the bone bends, but does not break. **green thumb** n. Am. skill in gardening. **greet** [gri:t] v. to salute/to welcome. **greeting** n. reception/way of welcoming s.o. **greetings** n. pl. good wishes.

gregarious [grɪ'geərɪəs] adj. found of company/sociable.

gremlin ['gremlɪn] n. imaginary imp. supposed to be responsible for faults in machinery.

grenade [grɪ'neɪd] n. small bomb thrown by hand. **grenadier** [grenə'dɪə] n. (a) (old) soldier who threw grenades. (b) member of the Grenadier Guards.

grenadine [grenə'di:n] n. red drink, made from pomegranate juice.

grew [gru:] v. see grow.

grey 1 [greɪ] adj. (-er, -est) of a colour between black and white; g. matter = active part of the brain; inf. intelligence.

grey 2 n. colour between black and white. **grey-haired** adj. with grey hair. **greyhound** n. slender, long logged, swift dog, often used for racing. **greyish** adj. rather grey. **graylag** n. common European wild goose.

grid [grɪd] n. (a) grating/frame of spaced parallel bars. (b) system of numbered squares on a map. (c) national electricity supply system. (d) starting g. = lines drawn on a track to show the start in a car/motorcycle race.

griddle n. iron plate placed over heat for cooking flat cakes.

gridiron n. (a) metal frame for cooking over an open fire. (b) Am. football field.

grief [gri:f] n. deep sorrow; to come to g. = to meet with disaster. **grief-stricken** adj. very sad.

grievance ['gri:vəns] n. real or imagined grounds for complaint; to air one's grievances = to tell everyone about one's complaints. **grieve** [gri:v] v. to feel sad (for); it grieves me = it makes me sad. **grieve over** v. to mourn; to feel sad because of (sth). **grievous** adj. severe; g. bodily harm = severe injury to s.o.

griffin ['grɪfɪn] n. imaginary animal with a lion's head and eagle's wings.

griffon ['grɪfən] n. (a) type of small terrier. (b) type of vulture.

grill 1 [grɪl] n. (a) part of cooker where food is cooked under a direct source of heat; charcoal g. = gridiron over a bed of hot charcoal. (b) (also grillroom) restaurant where most food is cooked under a grill or on a charcoal grill. (c) mixed g. = collection of grilled food. (d) framework of metal/wooden bars. **grill 2** v. (a) to cook under the grill. (b) inf. to interrogate (s.o.) /to ask (s.o.) searching questions.

grille [grɪl] n. grating; frame of spaced parallel bars; radiator g. = parallel/bars in front of a radiator on a car.

grilse [grɪls] *n.* young salmon, returning to the river from the sea for the first time.

grim [grɪm] *adj.* (grimmer, grimmest) (a) sinister/severe. (b) bad/gloomy. **grimly** *adv.* tenaciously; with determination. **grimness** *n.* being grim.

grimace 1 [grɪ'meɪs] *n.* twisted expression on the face. **grimace 2** *v.* to make a grimace.

grime [graɪm] *n.* ingrained dirt. **griminess** *n.* being grimy. **grimy** *adj.* dirty.

grin 1 [grɪn] *n.* wide smile. **grin 2** *v.* (grained) to smile broadly; to g. and bear it = to accept things bravely.

grind 1 [graɪnd] *n.* boring/monotonous work; the daily g. = repetitive work to be done every day. **grind 2** *v.* (ground) (a) to reduce to small pieces by crushing; to g. corn/coffee. (b) *Am.* to mince; ground beef = minced beef (c) to rub surfaces together; to g. your teeth = to rub together the upper and lower teeth, *usu.* in anger; to g. to a halt = to stop. (d) to sharpen (a tool) /to smooth (sth rough); to have an axe to g. = to have a particular interest or point of view which makes your judgement biased. **grinder** *n.* (a) machine for grinding. (b) *Am.* mincer. **grinding** *adj.* terrible (poverty). **grindstone** *n.* stone which turns to sharpen knives; to keep s.o.'s nose to the g. = to keep him working very hard.

gringo ['grɪŋgəʊ] *n. inf.* (esp. in Mexico) foreigner *usu.* American.

grip 1 [grɪp] *n.* (a) firm hold; to come to grips with = to tackle; to keep a g. on = to remain in control of. (b) soft bag/hold all for carrying clothes, etc. (c) pin for holding your hair in place. **grip 2** *v.* (gripped) (a) to seize. (b) to hold (attention). **gripping** *adj.* holding the attention.

gripe [graɪp] *v.* to moan/to complain about sth. **gripe water** *n.* medicine given to babies to stop stomach pains.

grisly ['grɪzlɪ] *adj.* (-ier, -iest) causing horror/dread.

grist [grɪst] *n. inf.* it's all g. to the mill = it's all useful/it all helps. **gristle** ['grɪsl] *n.* tough, whitish, flexible tissue in meat. **gristly** *adj.* full of pieces of gristle.

grit 1 [grɪt] *n.* (a) small particles of stone/sand. (b) *inf.* courage. (c) *Am.* grits = type of porridge made of maize or wheat. **grit 2** *v.* (gritted) (a) to make a surface of grit; to put grit on (an icy road) to prevent cars sliding. (b) to g. your teeth = to clench your teeth together, *usu.* in fear/determination. **grittiness** *n.* being gritty. **gritty** *adj.* full of grit.

grizzle ['grɪzl] *v.* (of children) to whimper/to cry fretfully. **grizzled** ['grɪzld] *adj.* with grey hair. **grizzly 1** ['grɪzlɪ] *adj.* grey; grey-haired. **grizzly 2** *n.* g. (bear) = large, fierce North American bear.

groan 1 [grəʊn] *n.* deep sound expressing pain/grief/disapproval. **groan 2** *v.* (a) to moan deeply. (b) to g. under a weight = to be heavily laden.

groats [grəʊts] *n. pl.* crushed oats.

grocer ['grəʊsə] *n.* dealer in tinned foods, butter, sugar, eggs, etc. and miscellaneous domestic suppliers. **groceries** *n. pl.* items on sale in a grocer's shop. **grocer's, grocery** *n.* grocer's shop.

grog [grɒg] *n.* drink of spirits and water. **groggily** *adv.* unsteadily. **groggy** *adj.* unsteady.

groin [grɔɪn] *n.* (a) hollow where the thigh joins the belly. (b) place where two vaults join. **groined** *adj.* (roof) with joined vaults.

groom 1 [gruːm] *n.* (a) person who looks after horses. (b) bridegroom/new husband. **groom 2** *v.* to look after/to make smart; well-groomed = smart and welldressed.

groove [gruːv] *n.* (a) channel/hollow. (b) routine; to get into a g. = to be stuck in a routine. **groovy** *adj. Sl.* fine/fashionable.

grope [grəʊp] *v.* to feel with your hands as if your were blind.

grosbeak ['grəʊsbiːk] *n.* small bird with a large beak.

gross 1 [grəʊs] *n.* (*pl.*gross) twelve dozen, 144. **gross 2** *adj.* (-er, -est) (a) bloated; horribly fat. (b) great/excessive; g. injustice. (c) total; g. weight = combined weight of container and contents; g. income = total income before tax is deducted. **grossly** *adv.* greatly.

grotesque [grəˈtesk] *adj.* outrageous/fantastic; strange and ugly.

grotto [ˈgrɒtəʊ] *n.* (*pl.*-oes) picturesque cave; room decorated with shells to resemble a cave.

grotty [ˈgrɒti] *adj. inf.* dirty.

grouch 1 [graʊtʃ] *n. inf.* grumble. **grouch 2** *v. inf.* to grumble. **grouchy** *adj. inf.* grumpy.

ground 1 [graʊnd] *n.* (a) soil/earth. (b) surface of the earth to go to g. = to hide away. (c) area of land, to stand one's g. = to maintain one's position/authority; to lose g. = to become less successful; to break new g. = to be the first to start a project; to get (sth) off the g. = to start (sth) successfully/to get (a project) going. (d) large area of land set aside for a particular purpose; football g. (e) grounds = land surrounding a large house. (f) reason; grounds for complaint. (g) coffee grounds = small pieces of ground coffee beans left after the coffee has been made. **ground 2** *v.* (a) to base. (b) to run (a boat) on to the land. (c) to keep (aircraft/pilot) on the ground. (d) see also grind. **grounding** *n.* instruction. **groundless** *adj.* without reason. **groundnut** *n.* peanut. **groundsheet** *n.* rubber/plastic cloth spread on the ground for sitting/sleeping on. **groundsman** *n.* (pl -men) person who looks after sports pitches or gardens. **ground rule** *n.* basic rule of procedure. **groundspeed** *n.* the speed of an aircraft over the ground. **groundswell** *n.* (no *pl.*) large slow-moving waves. **groundwork** *n.* basic work/preliminary work. **groundsel** [ˈgraʊnsl] *n.* common weed with small yellow flowers.

group 1 [gruːp] *n.* (a) number of people or animals gathered close together. (b) classification; blood g.; age g. (c) small number of people playing music together. (d) several different companies linked together in the same organization. **group 2** *v.* to g. (together) = to form into groups. **group captain** *n.* rank in the air force above wing commander. **grouper** *n.* large tropical sea fish, used as food. **groupie** *n. Sl.* girl follower of pop group. **group practice** *n.* several doctors who share patients between them and *usu.* work from the same offices.

grouse 1 [graʊs] *n.* (a) (*pl.*grouse) reddish/black bird shot for sport and food. (b) *inf.* grumble. **grouse 2** *v. inf.* to grumble (about sth). **grouser** *n.* person who grouses.

grout [graʊt] *v.* to fill the spaces between tiles on a floor or wall with cement. **grouting** *n.* cement used to fill spaces between tiles.

grove [grəʊv] *n.* small group of trees.

grovel [ˈgrɒvl] *v..* (grovelled) to humble yourself; to lie with your face on the ground.

grow [grəʊ] *v.* (grew[gruː] has grown) (a) to develop/to exist as a living plant. (b) increase in size/height. (c) to become/to evolve gradually. (d) to cultivate; she grows roses. **grower** *n.* (a) person who cultivates. (b) plant that grows in specified way; a slow g..

growing *adj.* getting bigger. **grown** *adj.* developed to full size. **grow-up** *adj. & n.* adult. **grown on** *v. inf.* to become accepted; this picture grows on you = you gradually come to like it.

grow out of *v.* to become bigger/older (so that clothes no longer fit, etc.).

growth *n.* (a) development; increase in height/size (b) lump of tissue in the body. **growth rate** *n.* speed with which sth grows. **grow up** *v.* to become adult.

growl 1 [graʊl] *n.* sound made in the throat expressing anger. **growl 2** *v.* to murmur angrily.

grown [grəʊn] *v.* see grow.

groyne [grɔɪn] *n.* long breakwater built into the sea.

grub 1 [grʌb] *n.* larva of an insect; short worm which grows into an insect. (b) *Sl.* food. **grub 2** *v.* (grubbed) (also to grub up) to dig. **grubbiness** *n.* dirty appearance. **grubby** *adj.* (-ier, -iest) dirty.

grudge 1 [grʌdʒ] *n.* feeling of resentment/ill with (against s.o.). **grudge 2** *v.* to be unwilling to give (s.o. sth.). **grudging** *adj.* reluctant.

gruel [ˈgrʊəl] *n.* thin porridge.

gruelling [ˈgrʊəlɪŋ] *adj.* exhausting/tiring; very difficult.

gruesome [ˈgruːsəm] *adj.* causing horror/dread.

gruff [grʌf] *adj.* (-er, -est) (a) deep/rough (voice). (b) stern (manner).

gruffly *adv.* in a gruff way. **gruffness** *n.* being gruff.

grumble 1 ['grʌmbl] *n.* moan/complaint. **grumble 2** *v.* to complain (about sth). **grumbler** *n.* person who complains. **grumbling** *adj. inf.* g. appendix = appendix which hurts from time to time.

grumpy ['grʌmpɪ] *adj.* (-ier, -iest) badtempered. **grumpily** *adv.* in a badtempered manner. **grumpiness** *n.* being grumpy.

grunt 1 [grʌnt] *n.* low sound, like that made by pigs. **grunt 2** *v.* to make a low snorting sound.

guano ['gwɑːnəʊ] *n.* (no *pl.*) droppings of sea-birds used as manure.

guarantee 1 [gærən'tiː] *n.* (a) legal document promising that a machine will work for a certain time; the car is still under g. (b) person acting as a security. (c) thing given as security. **guarantee 2** *v.* to give assurance (that sth will happen). **guaranteed** *adj.* assured.

guarantor [gærən'tɔː] *n.* person who promises to pay s.o.'s debts.

guard 1 [gɑːd] *n.* (a) watch/looking out; to be on g./to keep g. = to act as sentry; to be on your g. = to be prepared against attack/surprise etc. to be caught off g. = to be taken unawares. (b) soldier/policeman who protects s.o./a building; g. of honour = group of soldiers acting as a ceremonial escort to an important person. (c) the Guards = special regiments of elite soldiers. (d) person in charge of a train, who gives orders to the driver. (e) device to prevent injury or accident. **guard 2** *v.* (a) to defend/to protect; to watch (prisoners) carefully so that they cannot escape; closely guarded secret = secret which is carefully kept secret. (b) to be careful. **guarded** *adj.* careful/noncommittal (reply). **guardian** *n.* keeper/protector responsible for the upbringing of a child. **guardianship** *n.* protection. **guardroom** *n.* building at the entrance to a military camp, used as a prison. **guardsman** *n.* (*pl.*men) soldier of the Guards.

guava ['gwɑːvə] *n.* orange-coloured tropical fruit.

gudgeon ['gʌdʒn] *n.* (a) small river fish. (b) pin joining a piston rod and connecting rod. (c) pin on which a hinge hangs.

guelder rose ['geldə'rəʊz] *n.* garden shrub with white pompom flowers.

guer(r)illa [gə'rɪlə] *n.* person (nor a regular soldier) -engaged in unofficial fighting; group of these soldiers.

guernsey ['gɜːnzɪ] *n.* (a) breed of cow, which gives rich milk. (b) thick pullover.

guess 1 [ges] *n.* rough estimate; it is anybody's g. = no one really knows. **guess 2** *v.* (a) to estimate. (b) *Am.* think. **guesstimate** *n. inf.* rough calculation. **guesswork** *n.* process of guessing.

guest [gest] *n.* (a) person entertained at another's house; paying g. = lodger/boarder; g. artist/g. conductor = person who is invited to play with/to conduct an orchestra. (b) person staying in a hotel. **guesthouse** *n.* house where people pay for a bed and meals.

guff [gʌf] *n. inf.* words which mean nothing.

guffaw 1 [gə'fɔː] *n.* loud/coarse laugh. **guffaw 2** *v.* to laugh loudly.

guide 1 [gaɪd] *n.* (a) person who shows the way/who describes buildings/works of art, etc., as you see them. (b) indication. (c) book of helpful advice. (d) member of the Girl Guides; the guides = the Girl Guides/social/training organization for girls. **guide 2** *v.* to conduct/to lead; guided tour = tour where the tourists are led by a guide; guided missile = missile which is led to the target by a controlling device. **guidance** *n.* advice. **guide book** *n.* advice/information. **guide dog** *n.* dog which is specially trained to lead a blind person. **guidelines** *n. pl.* advice how to proceed. **guiding** *adj.* directing.

guild [gɪld] *n.* association of merchants of craftsmen. **guildhall** *n.* hall where a guild used to meet, now *usu.* a town hall.

guile [gaɪl] *n.* treachery/cunning/trickery. **guileless** *adj.* honest/straight forward.

guillemot ['gɪlɪmɒt] *n.* black and white sea bird.

guillotine 1 ['gɪlətiːn] *n.* (a) machine with a sharp blade for beheading criminals. (b) machine with a sharp blade for cutting paper. (c) arrangement to limit the length of a debate in Parliament so that a vote can be taken quickly. **guillotine 2** v. (a) to cut the head off (s.o) with a guillotine. (b) to cut (paper) with a guillotine.

guilt [gɪlt] n. having committed a crime; being aware that you have committed a crime. **guiltily** adv. showing that you know you have done wrong. **guiltless** adj. innocent. **guilty** adj. (-ier, -iest) blameworthy/criminal; having done wrong.

guinea ['gɪnɪ] n. (old) coin worth 21 shillings. **guinea fowl** ['gɪnɪfaʊl] n. small black bird with white spots, used for food. **guinea pig** ['gɪnɪpɪg] n. (a) small furry animal with not tail, often kept as a pet. (b) person/animal used in a scientific experiment.

guise [gaɪz] n. (formal) appearance; in the g. of = pretending to be.

guitar [gɪ'tɑː] n. stringed musical instrument played with the fingers; electric g. = guitar which is connected to an amplifier. **guitarist** n. person who plays a guitar.

gulch [gʌltʃ] n. gully.

gulf [gʌlf] n. (a) area of sea partly surrounded by coast. (b) wide difference (between points of view). **Gulf Stream** n. warm current which crosses the Atlantic from West to East.

gull [gʌl] n. long-winged, web-footed sea bird.

gullet ['gʌlɪt] n. food tube from the mouth to the stomach.

gullible ['gʌlɪbl] adj. easily taken in/ready to believe anything. **gullibility** [gʌlɪ'bɪlɪtɪ] n. being gullible.

gully ['gʌlɪ] n. small ravine/water channel.

gulp 1 [gʌlp] n. quick swallow. **gulp 2** v. (also to gulp down) to swallow hastily.

gum 1 [gʌm] n. (a) sticky substance produced by some trees. (b) thin glue. (c) flesh in which the teeth are set. (d) (chewing) g. = sweet sticky substance you chew but do not swallow. **gum 2** v. (gummed) to stick together; gummed label = label with dry glue, which sticks if moistened. **gumboil** n. small abcess on a gum. **gumboot** n. rubber boot. **gumdrop** n. type of hard sweet. **gumshoe** n. Am. Sl. private detective.. **gum tree** n. eucalyptus tree; inf. up a g. t. = in a difficult spot.

gumption ['gʌmpʃn] n. enterprising spirit/resourcefulness.

gun 1 [gʌn] n. weapon which uses an explosive force to send out a bullet; starting g. = weapon used to make a bang to start a race; grease g. = instrument for injecting a small amount of grease into a part of an engine; to stick to one's guns = to maintain one's position; to jump the g. = to start doing sth before you should. **gun 2** v. (gunned) (a) to shoot at. (b) to be gunning for s.o. = to be trying to attack s.o. **gunboat** n. small ship carrying heavy guns. **gun carriage** n. vehicle which carries a heavy gun. **gundog** n. dog trained to accompany hunters shooting birds. **gunfire** n. firing of a gun. **gunman** n. (pl.-men) armed robber. **gunner** n. soldier in the artillery; person who fires a gun. **gunnery** n. management of large guns. **gun metal** n. dark grey metal, made of copper, tin, lead and zinc. **gunpowder** n. explosive substance. **gunroom** n. (a) room where you keep sporting guns. (b) compartment for junior officers in a warship. **gun runner** n. person who brings guns into a country illegally. **gun running** n. illegal importing of guns. **gunshot** n. bullet from a gun; sound made by a gun fired. **gunsmith** n. manufacturer of guns. **gunwale** ['gʌnl] n. upper edge of ship's side.

gunge [gʌndʒ] n. Sl. sticky/dirty stuff.

gung-ho [gʌŋ'həʊ] adj. inf. wildly militaristic.

gunny ['gʌnɪ] n. thick material for making sacks.

guppy ['gʌpɪ] n. small tropical fish often kept as a pet.

gurgle 1 ['gɜːgl] n. bubbling sound. **gurgle 2** v. to make a bubbling sound.

guru ['gʊruː] n. notable thinker who has many disciples.

gush 1 [gʌʃ] n. sudden stream/sudden rush of liquid. **gush 2** v. (a) to flow heavily. (b) to speak effusively; to praise too much. **gusher** n. oil well where the oil comes out so strongly that it does not need to be pumped. **gushing** adj. praising/talking extravagantly.

gusset ['gʌsɪt] n. triangle of cloth inserted in an article of clothing to make it larger. **gusseted** adj. with gussets.

gust 1 [gʌst] *n.* sudden violent rush of wind or rain. **gust 2** *v.* to blow in gusts. **gustily** *adv.* in gusts. **gusty** *adj.* windy. **gusto** ['gʌstəʊ] *n.* (no *pl.*) zest/enthusiasm.

gut 1 [gʌt] *n.* (a) lower part of the intestine; *inf.* g. reaction = natural/instinctive reaction; *inf.* I hate his guts = I dislike him a lot. (b) *inf.* guts = courage. (c) material made from the intestines of animals and used for violin and tennis racket strings. **gut 2** *v.* (gutted) (a) to take out the internal organs of (animal/fish). (b) to remove/to destroy (the contents of sth); the house was gutted by fire. **gutsy** *adj. inf.* brave.

gutta-percha [gʌtə'pɜːʃə] *n.* soft rubbery substance from Malaya.

gutter 1 ['gʌtə] *n.* shallow through below the eaves of a houses or at the side of a street to carry away rainwater; g. press = newspapers which specialize in scandals. **gutter 2** *v.* (of a candle) to flicker so that the molten wax runs down the side. **guttering** *n.* (no *pl.*) curved metal or plastic used to make gutters. **guttersnipe** *n.* dirty child, living in the poor part of a town.

guttural ['gʌtərəl] *adj.* produced in the throat. **gutturally** *adv.* spoken in the throat.

guy 1 [gaɪ] *n.* (a) man/fellow. (b) rope. (c) figure of a man burnt on a bonfire in England on 5th November. **guy 2** *v.* to imitate (s.o.) in a funny way. **guyrope** *n.* rope which holds a tent tight.

guzzle ['gʌzl] *v.* to eat or drink greedily. **guzzler** *n.* person who eats greedily.

gym, gymnasium [dʒɪm], [dʒɪm'neɪzɪəm] *n.* hall for indoor athletics and exercises. **gymnast** ['dʒɪmnæst] *n.* expert in gymnastics. **gymnastic** [dʒɪm'næstɪk] *adj.* referring to gymnastics. **gymnastics** *n.* exercises on wall bars/wooden horse, etc. to help develop muscles and physical coordination. **gymslip** *n.* dark-coloured dress with no sleeves, worn by schoolgirls as part of their uniform. **gymkhana** [dʒɪm'kɑːnə] *n.* competition for horse riding and racing; *Am.* display of car driving.

gynaecology [gaɪnə'kɒlədʒɪ] *n.* study of the diseases of women's reproductive system. **gynaecologist** *n.* doctor specializing in diseases of women's reproductive system. **gynaecological** [gaɪnəkə'lɒdʒɪkl] *adj.* referring to women's diseases.

gypsophila [dʒɪp'sɒfɪlə] *n.* garden plant with masses of small white flowers.

gypsum ['dʒɪpsəm] *n.* sulphate of lime.

gypsy ['dʒɪpsɪ] *n.* see gipsy.

gyrate [dʒaɪ'reɪt] *v.* to turn round; to move rhythmically. **gyration** [dʒaɪ'reɪʃn] *n.* circular movement. **gyratory** [dʒaɪ'reɪtərɪ] *adj.* turning round in a circle.

gyro- ['dʒaɪrəʊ] prefix meaning revolving; gyro-compass = compass which uses a gyroscope to avoid the shock of movement. **gyroscope** ['dʒaɪrəskəʊp] *n.* spinning wheel mounted so that it can rotate on any axis. **gyroscopic** [dʒaɪrə'skɒpɪk] *adj.* rapidly spinning.

Hh

H symbol for hydrogen.

ha [hɑː] (a) inter. showing surprise. (b) abbrev. for hectare.

habeas corpus ['heɪbɪəs 'kɔːpəs] *n.* order to bring a prisoner to answer a charge in court.

haberdashery ['hæbədæʃrɪ] *n.* shop/department selling buttons. ribbons. thread.

habit ['hæbɪt] *n.* (a) custom; regular way of doing sth; from force of h. = because it is sth you ordinarily do. (b) dress. riding h. = special dress for horse riding. **habit-forming** *adj.* (drug) which you can become addicted to. **habitual** [hə'bɪtjʊəl] *adj.* regular/normal. **habitually** *adv.* ordinarily/in the usual way. **habituate** *v.* to accustom (s.o.) to doing sth. **habitué** [hæ'bɪtjʊeɪ] *n.* regular client/visitor. **habitat** ['hæbɪtæt] *n.* place where a certain animal or plant is usually found.

habitation [hæbɪˈteɪʃn] n. place/ building where s.o. lives; not fit for h. = not fit to live in. **habitable** [ˈhæbɪtəbl] adj. fit to live in.

hack 1 [hæk] n. (a) horse which is hired. (b) writer who is paid by the piece (c) Sl. second-rate journalist. **hack 2** v. (a) to chop roughly. (b) to kick. (c) to enter a computer system illegally. using a modem. **hacker** n. person who hacks into a computer system. **hacking** adj. dry and unpleasant (cough). **hackles** [ˈhæklz] n. pl.neck feathers (on a cock); hairs on the neck (of a dog); to puts s.o.' s h. up = to make s.o. annoyed.

hackney [ˈhæknɪ] n. h. carriage = taxi. **hackneyed** [ˈhæknɪd] adj. (phrase) which is often used. **hacksaw** [ˈhæksɔː] n. saw for cutting metal. which has a narrow blade attached to a frame.

had [hæd] v. see have.

haddock [ˈhædək] n. (pl.haddock) common white sea fish.

Hades [ˈheɪdiːz] n. hell.

haematite [ˈhiːmətaɪt] n. iron ore.

haemoglobin [hiːməˈgləʊbɪn] n. substance in red blood cells which contains iron and carries oxygen.

haemophilia [hiːməˈfɪlɪə] n. hereditary disease in males which prevents blood from clotting. **haemophiliac** n. person suffering from haemophilia.

haemorrhage 1 [ˈheməpɪdʒ] n. loss of much blood, usu. internally.

haemorrhage 2 v. to suffer a haemorrhage.

haemorrhoids [ˈheməpɔɪdz] n. pl.small swollen veins at the anus.

haft [hɑːft] n. handle (of a knife, etc).

hag [hæg] n. witch; ugly old woman.

haggard [ˈhægəd] adj. thin/tired (face).

haggis [ˈhægɪs] n. Scottish food. made of sheep's heart, liver, etc., cooked with.

haggle [ˈhægl] v. (over) to discuss a price to try to reduce it.

hagiography [ˈhægɪɒgrəfi] n. writing about saints.

ha-ha 1 [ˈhɑːhɑː] inter. to show that you are amused. **ha-ha 2** n. fence put at the bottom of ditch.

haiku [ˈhaɪkuː] n. very short Japanese poem.

hail 1 [heɪl] n. (a) small piece of ice which fall like frozen rain. (b) small

missiles which fall. (c) call; within h. = near enough to be called. **hail 2** v. (a) to fall as small pieces of ice; to fall in small pieces. (b) to call out to (s.o.); to wave to (a taxi) to stop. (c) to come from. **hailstone** n. small piece of ice falling from the sky. **hailstorm** n. storm when hailstones fall from the sky.

hair [ˈheə] n. (a) single long thread growing on the body of a human or animal. (b) mass of hairs growing on the head; inf. to let your h. down = to relax/ become less formal. **hairbrush** n. special brush for keeping your hair tidy. **haircut** n. making your hair shorter by cutting. **hairdo** n. inf. style of a woman's hair. **hairdresser** n. person who cuts/dyes/styles hair. **hairdresser's** n. shop where people can have their hair cut and styled. **hairdressing** n. cutting/dyeing/styling hair. **hairless** adj. with no hair. **hairline** n. (a) line where the hair meets the forehead. (b) very thin line/ crack. **hairnet** n. light net worn over the hair to keep it in place. **hairpiece** n. small wig; piece of false hair. **hairpin** n. bent piece of wire used to keep hair in place; h. bend = very sharp bend, as on a mountain road. **hair-raising** adj. frightening. **hairspring** n. spiral spring in a watch. **hairstyle** n. way of dressing/cutting, etc., the hair. **hairy** adj. (-ier, iest) (a) covered with hairs. (b) Sl. frighteningly dangerous.

hake [heɪk] n. (pl.hake) common small white sea fish.

halcyon [ˈhælsɪən] adj. calm/beautiful (weather); carefree (days).

hale [heɪl] adj. h. and hearty = very healthy.

half 1 [hɑːf] n. (pl.halves[hɑːvs] (a) one of two equal parts; first h. = first part of a match; to go halves each pays half. (b) midfield player in Rugby. (c) child's ticket which costs half the adult fare. **half 2** adj. being divided into two equal parts; h. an hour = 30 minutes. **half 3** adv. partly/not fully; h. as tall = smaller by half, 50 per cent of the size. **half-and-half** adv. in two equal quantities. **half-back** n. defence player in football/rugby. **half-baked** adj. inf. (plan) which has not been well thought out; (person) who cannot plan. **half-breed** n. person/animal with parents of

different races. **half-brother** *n.*
brother who has one parent the same as
you. **half-caste** *n.* person with
parents of two different races. **half-cock** *n.* to go off at half-cock = have a
bad start. **half-dozen** *n.* six. **half-empty** *adj.* partly empty/not
completely empty. **half-fare** *n.* fare
reduced by half. **half-full** *adj.* partly
full/not completely full. **half-hardy**
adj. (plant) which can stand some cold
but not hard frost. **half-hearted** *adj.*
lacking conviction/enthusiasm. **half-hourly** *adj. adv.* every thirty minutes.
half-life *n.* time taken for a substance
to lose half its radioactivity. **half-mast**
n. the flags are at half-mast = the flags
are flying halfway up the flagpole as a
sign of mourning. **half-nelson** *n.*
hold in wrestling. where the victor
twists the arm of the victim below his
back. **half-open** *adj.* partly open/not
completely open. **halfpenny** ['heɪpnɪ]
n. (*pl.*-pennies = coins, -pence price)
coin worth half a penny. **half-sister** *n.*
sister who has one parent the same as
you. **half-term** *n.* short holiday in the
middle of a term. **half-timbered** *adj.*
(house) whose walls are made of
wooden beams with brick or plaster
walls between. **half-time** *n.* short rest
in the middle of a game. **half-tone** *n.*
photograph reproduced by means of
dots of varying sizes. **half-track** *n.*
vehicle driven by caterpillar tracks
behind and by ordinary wheels in front.
half-volley *n.* (in tennis) hitting the
ball just after it has bounced. **halfway**
adv. in the middle of a distance or
length; to meet s.o. h. = to compromise
with s.o. **halfwit** *n.* idiot. **half-witted**
adj. stupid. **half-year** *n.* six months.
half-yearly *adj. & adv.* (taking place)
every six months.
halibut ['hælɪbət] *n.* (*pl.*halibut) large
white flatfish living in the sea.
halitosis [hælɪ'təʊsɪs] *n.* bad-smelling
breath.
hall [hɔːl] *n.* (a) large room; large
building for public meetings; h. of
residence = large building where
students live in a college. (b) (entrance)
h. = room or passage through which you
enter a house. (c) large house. *usu.* in the
country.

hallelujah [hælɪ'luːjə] *inter.* meaning
praise to God.
hallmark ['hɔːlmɑːk] *n.* mark put on
gold and silver to show that it has the
correct purity. **hallmarked** *adj.* (silver
spoon, etc) with a hallmark stamped on
it.
hallo [hə'ləʊ] *inter.* showing a greeting.
halloo 1 [hə'luː] *n.* call to dogs when
hunting. **halloo 2** *v.* to shout halloo.
hallow ['hæləʊ] *v.* to bless (sth) /to
declare (sth) holy; hallowed ground =
ground (near a church) which has been
blessed. **Hallowe'en** [hæləʊiːn] *n.* 31st
October. the eve of All Saints' Day.
when witches and ghosts are said to
roam about.
hallucination [həluːsɪ'neɪʃn] *n.* seeing
things which are not there; thing seen
when you hallucinate. **hallucinate**
[hə'luːsɪneɪt] *v.* to see things which are
not there. **hallucinatory** [hə'luːsɪnətrɪ]
adj. (drug) which causes hallucinations.
hallucinogen [hə'luːsɪnədʒən] *n.*
substance which gives you
hallucinations. **hallucinogenic** *adj.*
which causes hallucinations.
halo ['heɪləʊ] *n.* (*pl.*-oes) glow of light
(round the moon/round the head of a
saint).
halogen ['hælədʒən] *n.* one of a group
of chemical elements (including
chlorine/fluorine/iodine).
halt 1 [hɔːlt] *n.* (a) complete stop; to
come to a h. = to stop; to call a h. to =
bring to a stop. (b) very small railway
station. **halt 2** *v.* to stop. **halting** *adj.*
hesitant.
halter ['hɔːltə] *n.* rope put round
animal's neck to lead it; h. neck dress =
dress with a piece of material going
round the back of the neck. leaving the
arms and back bare.
halve [hɑːv] *v.* (a) to divide into two
equal parts. (b) to reduce by half.
halves [hɑːv] *pl.*see half.
halyard ['hæljəd] *n.* rope used to pull
up a flag/sail.
ham 1 [hæm] *n.* (a) salted or smoked
meat from a pig's leg *usu.* eaten cold. (b)
inf. bad actor. (c) *inf.* amateur radio
operator working from home. **ham 2** *v.*
(hammed) to act badly. **ham-fisted,
ham-handed** *adj.* clumsy.
hamburger ['hæmbɜːgə] *n.* flat cake of

minced beef, cooked and eaten as a sandwich in a toasted roll.

hamlet ['hæmlət] n. small village.

hammer 1 ['hæmə] n. (a) heavy metal tool for knocking nails into wood/posts into the ground, etc. (b) object which hits sth as part of a machine. (c) metal ball which is thrown in sporting contests. **hammer 2** v. to hit hard. as with a hammer. **hammer out** v. (a) to make (sth) flat with a hammer. (b) to h. out an agreement = to come to an agreement after long difficult discussions. **hammer toe** n. deformed toe which bends downwards.

hammock ['hæmək] n. hanging bed made of a strong cloth or net.

hamper 1 ['hæmpə] n. large basket. **hamper 2** v. to stop/to hinder/to get in the way.

hamster ['hæmstə] n. small rodent. often kept as a pet.

hamstring ['hæmstrɪŋ] n. tendon behind the knee. **hamstrung** adj. incapacitated; unable to do anything.

hand 1 [hænd] n. (a) part of the body at the end of each arm; to have a h. in sth = to help to make sth happen; to give a h./ lend a h. with = to help with; at h. = near; in h. = in reserve; on h. = readily available; put of h. = uncontrollable. (b) workman; sailor; an old h. = very experienced person. (c) cards which have been dealt you in a game. (d) one of pointers on a clock or dial. (e) round of applause. (f) unit of measurement of the height of a horse. **hand 2** v. to pass (sth) to s. o. by hand. **handbag** n. woman's bag for carrying money, handkerchief and other belongings.

handbill n. small poster. **handbook** n. book which gives instructions or information. **handbrake** n. lever in a vehicle which works the brakes.

handclap n. slow h. = regular slow beating of the hands to show impatience/ boredom. **handcuff** v. to attach (s.o.'s. hands) with handcuffs. **handcuffs** n. pl., metal rings linked by a chain for attaching a prisoner's hands together. **handful** n. as much as you can hold in your hand; small number; person who is difficult to control. **handgun** n. small gun which is carried in the hand.

handicap 1 n. (a) physical/metal disability; thing which puts you at a disadvantage. (b) penalty imposed on good sportsmen to make it harder for them to win. **handicap 2** v. (handicapped) to put at a disadvantage; the mentally handicapped = people with a disability of the mind. **handicapper** n. person who calculates a sportsman's handicap. **handicraft** = work done by hand; handicrafts = artistic work done by hand (such as knitting/pottery, etc).

handily adv. in a handy way. **hand in** v. to give in by hand. **handiwork** n. work done by a particular person.

handkerchief ['hæŋkətʃiːf] n. square piece of cloth or paper for wiping your nose. **handmade** adj. made by hand. not by machine. **hand on** v. to pass on by hand. **hand out** v. to distribute. **handout** n. (a) money which is given out. (b) printed information sheet given out to people. **handover** v. to give (sth) to s.o. **handpicked** adj. carefully selected. **handrail** n. bar which you hold on to (next to a staircase, escalator, etc.) **hand round** v. to pass round by hand. **handset** n. the part of a telephone which is held in the hand **handshake** n. greeting when you grasp hands. **handspring** n. gymnastic exercise where you turn a somersault on your hands and land on your feet. **handstand** n. to do a h. = to balance on your hands with your feet in the air. **handwriting** n. writing done by hand. **handwritten** adj. written by hand not typed or printed. **handy** adj. (-ier, -iest) useful; in a convenient place. **handyman** n. (pl.-men) person who can do any sort of work, esp. repairs in the house.

handle 1 ['hændl] n. part of an object which you hold in the hand; inf. to fly off the h. = to lose your temper. **handle 2** v. (a) to move (goods) around (by hand). (b) to deal with (sth); handling charge = charge which has to be paid to s.o. who has delivered or dealt with sth.

handlebar(s) n. (pl.) bar on the front of a bicycle or motorcycle which steers the front wheel.

handsome ['hænsəm] adj. (a) good-looking. (b) fine/large (profit). **handsomely** adv. elegantly; generously.

hang 1 [hæŋ] n. (a) way in which sth hangs/drops/falls; inf. to get the h. of sth = to understand how sth works. (b) inf. he doesn't give/care a h. = he doesn't worry about it at all. **hang 2** v. (hung) (a) to attach/to be attached above the ground to nail or by a string/chain, etc. (b) to stick (wallpaper) on a wall. (c) (hanged) to kill (s.o.) by tying a rope round his neck and suspending him off the ground. **hang about, hang around** v. inf. to wait/to wander aimlessly in a certain place. **hang back** v. to stay behind the others. **hangdog** adj. inf. sheepish (expression). **hang down** v. to hang in a long piece. **hanger** n. object for hanging sth; coat h, = piece of wood/plastic/metal which is placed inside a coat to hang it up. **hanger-on** n. (pl.hangers-on) person who stays near s.o. in the hope of getting money or food. **hang fire** v. to be slow in happening/in taking effect. **hang glider** n. huge kite used in hang gliding. **hang gliding** n. sport of floating through the air by hanging on to a huge kite made of a metal frame covered with plastic. **hanging** n. carpet/tapestry which is hung on a wall as decoration. **hangman** n. (pl.-men) executioner who kills people by hanging them. **hangnail** n. torn skin at the root of a fingernail. **hang on** v. (a) to h. on to sth = to clutch (sth) /to keep (sth). (b) inf. to wait. **hang out** v. inf. to live (in a place). **hangover** n. (a) unpleasant effects of having drunk too much alcohol. **hang up** v. to hang (sth) on a hook; to replace (a telephone receiver). **hang-up** n. (pl.hang-ups) Sl. thing which worries you and prevents you from acting normally. **hangar** ['hæŋə] n. large shed for keeping aircraft in.

hank [hæŋk] n. wool coiled into a loose loop. **hanker** ['hæŋkə] v. to h. after/for = to want (very much). **hankering** n. desire.

hanky ['hæŋkɪ] n. inf. handkerchief. **hankypanky** [hæŋkɪ'pæŋkɪ] n. inf. trouble/bad behaviour; trickery.

Hansard ['hænsɑːd] n. official report of what is said in Parliament.

haphazard [hæp'hæzəd] adj. done at random/unplanned. **haphazardly** adv. at random; without any plan.

hapless ['hæpləs] adj. (formal) unfortunate/unlucky.

happen ['hæpn] v. (a) to take place; what has happened to him? = (i) what is he doing now ? (ii) what harm has come to him? (b) to take place by chance. **happening** n. event/thing which takes place. **happenstance** n. by h. = by a coincidence.

happy ['hæpɪ] adj. (-ier, -iest) glad/full of joy. **happily** adv. joyfully/gladly. **happiness** n. joy/gladness. **happy-go-lucky** adj. easy-going/carefree.

hara-kiri [hærə'kɪrɪ] n. Japanese form of suicide.

harangue 1 [hɪ'ræŋ] n. loud speech. **harangue 2** ['hærəs. [xx] hə'ræs] v. to make a loud speech to (s.o.)

harass v. to bother/to worry (s.o.) **harassment** n. bothering/worrying; many small attacks on an enemy.

harbinger ['hɑːbɪndʒə] n. (formal) thing which shows that sth else is approaching.

harbour, Am. **harbor 1** ['hɑːbə] n. port/safe place where ships can tie up to load or unload. **harbour 2** v. (a) to keep (a grudge) against s.o. (b) to protect (a criminal). (c) to hold (germs) and allow them to spread.

hard 1 [hɑːd] adj. (-er, -est) (a) firm/not soft. (b) h. currency = one which does not lose its value compared to other currencies. (c) difficult; h. lines/h. luck = bad luck; h. labour = punishment involving difficult manual work. (d) strict/severe. (e) (of water) containing calcium. which makes it difficult to form a lather. (f) strong (drink); (drug) which makes you become addicted; h. drinker = person who drinks a lot of alcohol. **hard 2** adv. (a) strongly. (b) with difficulty. **hard-and-fast** adj. strict/absolute (rule). **hardback** n. book with a stiff cover. **hardboard** n. artificial board made of small shreds of wood stuck together. **hard-boiled** adj. (a) (egg) which has been boiled until the white and yolk are set solid. (b) (person) without much feeling/who is not easily shocked. **hard by** adv. nearby. **hardcore 1** n. (a) packed rubble used in making paths. (b) central part (of a group). **hardcore 2** adj. referring to a central group. **hard disk** n. solid disk.

fixed in a computer. **harden** v. to make hard; hardened criminal = regular/permanent criminal. **harden off** v. to bring (tender plants) into the open air. **hard hat** n. protective helmet worn by construction workers, etc. hard-headed, adj. practical/sensible. **hardhearted** adj. cruel. **hardliner** n. person who is very antagonistic/stern towards s.o./an enemy. **hardly** adv. almost not. **hardness** n. being solid/hard/not soft; difficulty; strictness. **hard of hearing** adj. (person) who is quite deaf. **hard sell** n. strenuous efforts to sell sth. **hardship** n. suffering caused by lack of sth. **hard shoulder** n. strip along the edge of a motorway where vehicles can park if they have broken down. **hard up** adj. inf. with no money. **hardware** n. (no pl.) (a) tools. pots and pans; h. shop = shop selling pans/hammers/nails/paint, etc. military h. = guns, tanks and other military equipment. (b) physical parts/machinery of a computer. **hard-wearing** adj. which does not wear out easily. **hardwood** n. wood which comes from deciduous trees. **hardworking** adj. (person) who works hard. **hardy** adj. (-ier, -iest) which can survive in difficult conditions; (plant) which can stay out of doors all the year round.

hare 1 ['heə] n. common field mammal, like a large rabbit. **hare 2** v. to run fast. **hare-brained** adj. mad/senseless (plan). **harebell** n. wild flower shaped like a little blue bell. **harelip** n. split in the upper lip from birth.

harem [ha:'ri:m] n. women in a Muslim household; women's quarters in a Muslim house.

haricot ['hærɪkəʊ] n. h. (bean) = dry white bean eaten cooked.

hark 1 [ha:k] old inter. meaning listen. **hark 2** v. to h. back to = to go back to (a subject talked about earlier).

harlequin ['ha:lɪkwɪn] n. character in old pantomime, wearing a mask and a suit of diamond-patterned cloth.

harlot ['ha:lət] n. (formal) prostitute.

harm 1 [ha:m] n. damage. **harm 2** v. to damage/to hurt. **harmful** adj. which hurts/which causes damage. **harmless** adj. which causes no damage/which does not hurt.

harmony ['ha:mənɪ] n. (a) musical sounds which do not clash, agreeable effect (of music/colour, etc). (b) general agreement. **harmonic 1** [ha:'mɒnɪk] adj. referring to harmony. **harmonic 2** n. higher note which is heard when a note is played. **harmonica** [ha:'mɒnɪkə] n. mouth organ. **harmonious** [ha:'məʊnɪəs] adj. (sounds) which are in agreement/which sound well together. **harmoniously** adv. in a harmonious way. **harmonium** [ha:'məʊnɪəm] n. musical instrument like an organ where the sound comes from air pumped through reeds. **harmonization** [ha:mənaɪ'zeɪʃn] n. act of harmonizing. **harmonize** v. (a) to agree together. (b) to form chords out of the main tune of a piece of music.

harness 1 ['ha:nəs] n. (a) leather straps which attach a horse to a cart; he is still in h. = he is still working. (b) straps for attaching a parachute to s.o.; straps which have a lead attached to control a small child. **harness 2** v. (a) to attach (a horse) to a cart. (b) to use (natural resources/atomic power, etc.) for making energy.

harp 1 [ha:p] n. large upright musical instrument with, many strings which are plucked with the fingers. **harp 2** v. to h. on about = keep talking about.

harpist n. person who plays a harp.

harpoon 1 [ha:'pu:n] n. long barbed spear used to kill whales. **harpoon 2** v. to kill (a whale) with a harpoon.

harpsichord ['ha:psɪkɔ:d] n. old musical instrument. like a piano, but with strings which are plucked.

harpy ['ha:pɪ] n. (a) cruel mythical monster with a woman's body and an eagle's claws. (b) cruel person (esp. woman).

harrier ['hærɪə] n. (a) dog/person who hunts hares. (b) long-distance runner. (c) type of falcon.

harrow 1 ['hærəʊ] n. large rake pulled by a tractor for breaking up heavy soil. **harrow 2** v. to break up soil with a harrow. **harrowing** adj. very sad. causing mental pain.

harry ['hærɪ] v. to bother/to worry (s.o) by continual attacks.

harsh [ha:ʃ] adj. (-er, -est) (a) cruel/sharp (punishment, etc). (b) rough/

hart

238

have

unpleasant (voice, etc). **harshly** *adv.* in a harsh way. **harshness** *n.* cruelty/roughness.

hart [haːt] *n.* male deer.

harum-scarum [heərəmˈskeərəm] *adj. & n.* wild (young person).

harvest 1 [ˈhaːvɪst] *n.* (a) cutting/picking of ripe crops. (b) period of the year when crops are picked. **harvest 2** *v.* to cut/to pick ripe crops. **harvester** *n.* person/machine which cuts crops.

has [hæz] *v.* see have. **has-been** *n.* (*pl.* has-beens) *inf.* person/thing no longer as well known/important as before.

hash 1 [hæʃ] *n.* (a) minced meat; *inf.* he made a h. of it = he did it badly. (b) *inf.* hashish. (c) h. (sign) = printed sign (#) used in computers as an indicator.

hash 2 *v.* to mince (meat, etc); *Am.* hash(ed) brown potatoes = fried grated potatoes.

hashish [ˈhæʃiʃ] *n.* hemp used as a drug.

hasp [haːsp] *n.* metal bar, which closes a door or lid by fitting over a loop which is locked with a padlock.

hassle 1 [ˈhæsl] *n. inf.* bother/struggle to do sth. **hassle 2** *v. inf.* to struggle/to argue.

hassock [ˈhæsək] *n.* cushion for kneeling on in a church.

haste [heɪst] *n.* speed; to make h. = to hurry up. **hasten** [ˈheɪsn] *v.* to make (sth) go faster/come faster; to hurry up. **hastily** *adv.* rapidly. **hastiness** *n.* being hasty. **hasty** *adj.* (-ier, -iest) rapid and with not enough preparation.

hat [hæt] *n.* piece of clothing worn on the head; keep it under your h. = keep it secret; h./trick = three goals, etc. scored by the same person in the same game. **hatband** *n.* piece of ribbon which goes round a hat. **hatless** *adj.* not wearing a hat.

hatch 1 [hætʃ] *n.* opening in a ship's deck; opening in the floor or wall of an aircraft; service h. = small opening in a wall for passing food from a kitchen to a dining room. **hatch 2** *v.* (a) to warm (eggs) until baby birds appear; (of a baby bird) to break out of the egg; to plan (a plot). (b) to indicate shade in a sketch by drawing parallel lines close together. **hatchback** *n.* type of car with a sloping back and a large rear door which

opens upwards. **hatchery** *n.* place where eggs are kept until they develop into young. **hatchway** *n.* opening in a ship's deck.

hatchet [ˈhætʃɪt] *n.* small axe; *inf.* to bury the h. = to make peace; Sl h. man person brought into a firm to sack some of the staff. **hatchet-faced** *adj.* (person) with a grim pointed face.

hate 1 [heɪt] *n.* great dislike. **hate 2** *v.* to dislike intensely. **hateful** *adj.* horrible/unpleasant. **hatred** *n.* great dislike.

hatter [ˈhætə] *n.* person who makes men's hats.

haughty [ˈhɔːti] *adj.* (-ier, -iest) very proud. **haughtily** *adv.* proudly. **haughtiness** *n.* being haughty.

haul 1 [hɔːl] *n.* (a) catch (of fish); the burglars made a good h. = they stole a lot of valuable things. (b) distance travelled. **haul 2** *v.* to pull with difficulty. **haulage** *n.* moving of goods by road; h. contractor person who arranges for goods to be moved by road. **haulier** *n.* haulage contractor.

haulm [hɔːm] *n.* stems of peas/beans/potatoes.

haunch [hɔːnʃ] *n.* thigh and loin (of an animal); the dog was sitting on its haunches = sitting in a squatting position.

haunt 1 [hɔːnt] *n.* place where s.o. goes frequently. **haunt 2** *v.* to go to (a place) frequently; (of ghosts) to appear in (a place). **haunted** *adj.* (house) where a ghost appears.

have [hæv] *v.* (I have, he has; I had, he had) (a) (also have got) to possess. the house has (got) no telephone. (b) to take (a meal/a bath). (c) to play; will you h. a game of tennis? (d) to get (sth) done. (f) (making the past tense of verbs) h. you finished your work? (g) (showing compulsion to do something) you will h. to sing that song again; you had better say nothing. **have got** *v.* to have got to do sth = to be obliged/to have to do sth. **have had** *v. inf.* he's had it = he is finished/he has missed an opportunity. **have on** *v.* (a) to be wearing. (b) to be busy/occupied; have you anything on tonight? (c) *inf.* to trick (s.o.); they're having you on. **have out** *v.* (a) to have a tooth out = to get a tooth removed by a dentist. (b) to have it out with s.o. = to sort out a quarrel with s.o. **have up** v. inf. to call (s.o) to a court, he has been had up for speeding.

haven ['heɪvn] n. safe port; safe place; tax h. = country where taxes are low.

haver ['heɪvə] v. to hesitate.

haversack ['hævəsæk] n. bag carried on the back.

havoc ['hævək] n. damage; to play h. with = do a lot of damage to.

haw 1 [hɔː] n. small red berry on the hawthorn. **haw 2** v. see hum.

hawfinch n. largest European finch.

hawk 1 [hɔːk] n. (a) bird of prey; she has eyes like a h. = she has very good eyesight/notices every detail. (b) person who is in favour of military attacks on an enemy/who is prepared to take a hard line in international relations. **hawk 2** v. (a) to sell goods from door to door. (b) to clear your throat. **hawker** n. person who sells things from place to place.

hawse [hɔːz] n. bow of a ship, with holes for the anchor cable. **hawser** ['hɔːzə] n. thick rope for attaching a boat to the quay.

hawthorn ['hɔːθɔːn] n. common hedge shrub with white flowers and red berries.

hay [heɪ] n. long dried grass used to feed cattle in winter; to make h. while the sun shines = to enjoy yourself/to make money while you can. **hayfever** n. running nose/eyes, etc., caused by an allergy to pollen or dust. **hayfield** n. field of grass which will be cut to make hay. **haymaking** n. cutting of the hay. **hayseed** n. inf. silly country person. **haystack** n. bales of hay stored in a large heap but like a house. **haywire** adj. inf. going h. = he's gone mad.

hazard 1 ['hæzəd] n. (a) risk. (b) rough ground (on a golf course). **hazard 2** v. to risk; he hazarded a guess = he made a rough guess. **hazardous** adj. dangerous/risky.

haze [heɪz] n. light mist. **hazily** adv. vaguely. **haziness** n. being hazy. **hazy** adj. (-ier, -iest) (a) misty. (b) vague.

hazel ['heɪzl] n. tree which bears small nuts. **hazel 2** adj. & n. light brown (colour). **hazel nut** n. nut form a hazel tree.

he [hiː] (a) pronoun referring to a male person or animal; he is my father. (b)

prefix meaning male; he-goat. **he-man** n. (pl.he-men) strong/virile man. **He** symbol for helium.

head 1 [hed] n. (a) part of the body with brain. eyes. ears. mouth, etc., attached to the rest of the body by the neck; the horse won by a h. = by the length of a head; he. over heels = over and over. (b) brain; a good h. for figures; a bad h. for heights. (c) top; leafy part (of a cabbage); foam (on the top of a glass of beer). (d) first one (of a lot/a procession). (e) most important person; h. waiter. (f) top side of a coin; side of a coin with the head of a king on it; to play heads or tails = to spin a coin and try to guess which side will be on top. (g) part of a machine which records/picks up data (as on a tape recorder/computer). (h) (no pl.) number of animals; fifty h. of sheep. **head 2** v. (a) to be first/to lead. (b) to go towards. (c) to hit (a ball) with your head.

headache n. (a) pain in the head. (b) complicated problem. **headboard** n. board/panel at the top of a bed.

headdress n. ornamental covering for the head. **header** n. (a) dive. (b) hitting a ball with the head. **head first** adv. with one's head first. **headgear** n. hat or cap. **headhunt** v. to look for candidates for important jobs.

headhunter n. (a) member of a tribe which cuts off the heads of enemies and collects them. (b) inf. person who tries to find suitably qualified candidates for important jobs. **heading** n. words at the top of a text. **headlamp** n. main light on the front of a car/bicycle, etc.

headland n. (a) promontory. (b) land at the edge of a field, where the tractor turns. **headless** adj. with no head.

headlight n. main light on the front of a car/bicycle, etc. **headline** n. words in large capitals in a newspaper; news headlines short summary of the main items of news on TV/radio. **headlong** adj. & adv. rushing/non-stop; with your head first. **headmaster** n. man in charge of a school. **headmistress** n. woman in charge of a school. **head off** v. to prevent (sth) from taking place. **head-on** adj. & adv. with the front; head first. **headphones** n. pl.apparatus for listening to radio/ records, etc., which fits over your ears.

headquarters *n. pl.*main offices (of an army/of a firm). **headrest** *n.* cushion/part of a seat for leaning your head on. **headroom** *n.* space to pass upright. **headscarf** *n.* (*pl.*-scarves) square piece of cloth worn by women to cover their hair. **headset** *n.* apparatus for listening to radio/records, etc., which fits over your ears with a band across the top of your head. **headship** *n.* position of headmaster/headmistress.
headstone *n.* gravestone.
headstrong *adj.* obstinate/self-willed.
headway *n.* progress/movement forward. **headwind** *n.* wind blowing in your face. headword, n. main word in a dictionary. **heady** *adj.* (-ier, -iest) (drink) which is likely to make you drunk; (news) which is likely to make you excited.
heal [hi:l] *v.* to make (a person/a wound) become healthy; to become healthy. **healing** *n.* making healthy.
health [helθ] *n.* (a) state of the body where there is no sickness; your h.! good h.! = wish said when drinking; h. farm = clinic in the country where people who eat or drink too much go to slim; h. foods = natural foods (such as yoghurt/nuts, etc) which are good for your health; h. service = government run service providing medical treatment for everyone; h. visitor = person who visits sick people in their homes. (b) general state of the body. **healthily** *adv.* in a healthy way. **healthiness** *n.* being healthy. **healthy** *adj.* (a) full of good health/not ill. (b) which gives good health. (c) strong (dislike, etc).
heap 1 [hi:p] *n.* large pile; *inf.* heaps = lots. **heap 2** *v.* to put in a pile.
hear ['hɪə] *v.* (heard[hɜ:'d]) to sense sounds by the ear; to listen to (sth); he's never heard of it = does not know about it; he won't h. of it = he will not allow it. **hearer** *n.* person who hears. **hear hear!** *inter.* used to show agreement.
hearing *n.* (a) ability to hear; h. aid = small device for improving the hearing of s.o who is nearly deaf. (b) listening to s.o. (c) court case. **hearsay** *n.* what people say, rather than what is true.
heard [hɜ:d] *v.* see hear.
hearse [hɜ:s] *n.* vehicle for carrying a coffin.

heart [hɑ:t] *n.* (a) organ in an animal which pumps blood round the body; h. attack = severe illness when the heart stops temporarily; h. failure = dangerous condition when the heart has stopped beating; to learn by h. = learn by memory so that you can repeat it. (b) centre of the emotions; with all my h. = with great emotion; (c) centre (of a town/ forest). (d) courage; to lose h. = to become discouraged; to take h. = to be encouraged. (e) hearts = one of the four suits of playing cards. **heartbeat** *n.* sound of the heart pumping blood.
heart-breaking *adj.* which makes you very sad/upset. **heart-broken** *adj.* extremely sad/disappointed. **heartburn** *n.* burning feeling in the chest and stomach after eating indigestible food.
hearten *v.* to encourage. **heartfelt** *adj.* sincere. **heartily** *adv.* vigorously; warmly. **heartiness** *n.* being hearty.
heartland *n.* central part of a country.
heartless *adj.* cruel. **heartlessly** *adv.* in a heartless way. **heart-rending** *adj.* pitiful. **heartsearching** *n.* deep thought about how to deal with a problem. **heartstrings** *n. pl.*deepest feelings (of pity/love, etc.). **heartthrob** *n.* popular film-star, etc. **heart-to-heart** *adj.* earnest private (conversation). **heartwarming** *adj.* which encourages/pleases. **hearty** *adj.* (-ier, -iest) vigorous/strong; large (meal/ appetite).
hearth [hɑ:θ] *n.* base of a fireplace; a fireplace. **hearthrug** *n.* small rug placed in front of a fireplace.
heat 1 [hi:t] *n.* (a) great warmth. (b) qualifying round in a competition; dead h. = race where two competitors come in a equal first. (c) (of female animal) on h. = sexually excited. **heat 2** *v.* to warm to a higher temperature; heated discussion = discussion where people become quite angry. **heatedly** *adv.* angrily. **heater** *n.* apparatus for warming. **heating** *n.* making sth warm; means of heating; central h. = heating system for a whole building from one source. **heatwave** *n.* period of very hot weather.
heath [hi:θ] *n.* (a) area of wild country covered with low shrubs. (b) heather.

heathland n. wild country covered with low shrubs.

heathen ['hi:ðn] adj. & n. (person) who is not a Christian; (person) who is not a member of any important religious group.

heather ['heðə] n. wild plant with small purple or white bell-shaped flowers, which grows on moors and mountains.

heave 1 [hi:v] n. hard pull. **heave 2** v. (heaved) (a) to pull hard. (b) (hove) to h. to = to stop a ship; to h. in sight = to appear. (c) inf. to throw (d) to breathe noisily.

heaven ['hevn] n. paradise/place where God and the angels live; the heavens = the sky; good heavens! = how surprising! **heavenly** adj. (a) belonging to heaven. (b) inf. beautiful; very fine. **heaven-sent** adj. lucky.

heavy ['hevi] adj. (-ier, -iest) weighing a lot; (meal) which is very filling and indigestible. (a) full (timetable, etc.). (e) h. drinker = person who drinks a lot of alcohol. **heavily** adv. (a) as if weighing a lot. (b) greatly; h. underlined = with thick lines put underneath. (c) (to sleep) soundly. **heaviness** n. being heavy. **heavyduty** adj. (machine, etc.) specially made for rough work. **heavy industry** n. industry which makes large products (like steel/ships/cars, etc.,). **heavy water** n. water containing deuterium in place of hydrogen. **heavyweight** n. heaviest category of boxer.

Hebrew ['hi:bru:] n. (a) member of Jewish people living in ancient Palestine. (b) language of the Jews.

heckle ['hekl] v. to call out; to interrupt a public speaker. **heckler** n. person who interrupts a speaker at a meeting. **heckling** n. interrupting a speaker.

hect-, hecto- ['hekt(əʊ)] prefix meaning one hundred. **hectolitre** n. one hundred litres. **hectare** ['hektɑ:] n. (measure of) area of 10.000 square metres (approx. 2.4 acres).

hectic ['hektɪk] adj. very busy/active. **hectically** adv. in a hectic way.

hector ['hektə] v. to bully/to intimidate. **hectoring** adj. bullying (tone of voice).

hedge 1 [hedʒ] n. (a) screen/fence made of growing shrubs. (b) protection (against). **hedge 2** v. (a) to surround with a hedge. (b) to avoid answering a question. (c) to h. your bets = to arrange things so that you will be protected against losing. **hedgehog** n. small mammal covered with prickles. **hedgerow** n. long hedge, esp. by the side of a country road. **hedge sparrow** n. common sparrow found in the country.

hedonist ['hi:dənɪst] n. person who lives for pleasure. **hedonistic** adj. like a hedonist.

heed 1 [hi:d] n. to take h. of/to pay h. to = to pay attention to. **heed 2** v. to pay attention to. **heedless** adj. careless/imprudent; without paying attention. **heedlessly** adv. in a heedless way.

heel 1 [hi:l] n. (a) back part of the foot; back part of a sock/stocking into which the heel of the foot goes; to take to one's heels = to run away. (b) raised block under the back of a shoe. (c) Sl. unpleasant person. **heel 2** v. (a) (in Rugby) to kick (the ball) backwards. (b) to put a new heel on (a shoe). (c) (of a ship) to h. over = to lean to one side.

hefty ['heftɪ] adj. (-ier, -iest) (large/strong).

hegemony [hɪ'gemənɪ] n. leadership by one country.

heifer ['hefə] n. young cow.

height [haɪt] n. (a) measurement of how tall or high sth is. (b) highest point. **heighten** v. to increase/to make more noticeable.

heinous ['heɪnəs] adj. wicked (crime).

heir, heiress ['eə, eə'res] n. person who is going to inherit money, etc., from s.o. **heirloom** n. valuable object which has belonged to a family for years.

held [held] v. see hold.

helical ['helɪkl] adj. see helix.

helicopter ['helɪkɒptə] n. type of aircraft with revolving blades on top. enabling it to take off vertically. **helipad** n. small marked area where a helicopter may land. **heliport** n. place where helicopters land and take off.

heliograph ['hi:lɪəgrɑ:f] n. apparatus for signalling, using mirrors which flash in the sun.

heliotrope ['hi:lɪətrəʊp] n. & adj. plant

with purple flowers; purple (colour).
helium ['hi:lɪəm] *n.* (element; He) light gas which does not burn.
helix ['hi:lɪks] *n.* spiral shape. **helical** ['helɪkl] *adj.* spiral.
hell [hel] *n.* (a) place where devils live and wicked people are punished after death. (b) *inf.* a h. of a noise = a very loud noise; one h. of a party = a very good party; to give s.o. h. = to make life difficult for s.o.; *Sl.* what the h.? = what on earth? **hell-bent on** *adj. inf.* very determined to do sth. **hellish** *adj.* like hell; *inf.* unbearable.
hellebore ['helɪbɔ:] *n.* winter plant with greenish white flowers.
Hellenic [he'lenɪk] *adj.* referring to Greece.
hello [hə'ləʊ] *inter.* showing a greeting.
helm [helm] *n.* wheel or handle connecting to the rudder of a ship; at the h. = in charge. **helmsman** *n.* (*pl.*-men) person who is steering a ship.
helmet ['helmət] *n.* metal or plastic hat used as a protection; crash h. = helmet worn by motorcyclists.
help 1 [help] *n.* (a) aid/assistance. (b) person who helps. **help 2** *v.* (a) to aid (s.o.) /to come to s.o.'s assistance. (b) to h. yourself = to serve yourself; *inf.* to h. yourself to = to steal. (c) can't h. doing sth = can't stop (doing sth) /can't avoid (sth). **helper** *n.* person who helps.
helpful *adj.* (person) who helps; (thing) which is useful. **helpfully** *adv.* in a helpful way. **helpfulness** *n.* being helpful. **helping 1** *adj.* which helps.
helping 2 *n.* serving/portion (of food).
helpless *adj.* weak/unable to help yourself. **helplessly** *adv.* unable to help. **helplessness** *n.* being helpless. **helpmate** *n.* helper. **help out** *v.* to come to (s.o.'s) assistance in an emergency.
helter-skelter 1 ['heltə'skeltə] *adv.* in a confused rush. **helter-skelter 2** *n.* (in a fairground) tower with a spiral slide round it.
hem 1 [hem] *n.* sewn edge on a piece of cloth/a skirt/table cloth/handkerchief, etc. **hem 2** *v.* (hemmed) (a) to sew a hem. (b) to h. in = to enclose. **hemline** *n.* bottom edge of a dress/skirt, etc.
hemstitch 1 *n.* stitch used in a hem.
hemstitch 2 *v.* to sew a hem using a

hemstitch.
hemi- ['hemɪ] prefix half. **hemiplegia** *n.* paralysis affecting one side of the body. **hemisphere** ['hemɪsfɪə] *n.* half a sphere, esp. half of the earth's globe; northern h./southern h. = parts of the earth north and south of the equator. **hemispherical** [hemɪ'sferɪkl] *adj.* shaped like half a sphere.
hemlock ['hemlɒk] *n.* (a) common poisonous plant. (b) type of American evergreen tree.
hemoglobin [hi:mə'gləʊbɪn] *n.* see haemoglobin.
hemophilia [hi:mə'fɪlɪə] *n.* see haemophilia.
hemorrhage ['hemərɪdʒ] *n.* see haemorrhage.
hemorrhoids ['hemərɔɪdʒ] *n. pl.* see haemorrhoids.
hemp [hemp] *n.* tropical plant, which gives rough fibres for making sacks/ ropes, etc., and which also provides a drug. **hempen** *adj.* (formal) made of hemp.
hen [hen] *n.* (a) female chicken. (b) female bird; *inf.* h. party = party for women only. **henhouse** *n.* wooden hut for keeping chickens in. **henpecked** *adj.* (husband) whose wife nags him continuously and tells him what to do.
hence [hens] *adv.* (a) from this time; five years h. (b) for this reason. **henceforth, henceforward** *adv.* from now on.
henchman ['hentʃmən] *n.* (*pl.*-men) helper/accomplice (of a criminal).
henna ['henə] *n.* red dye used to colour hair. **hennaed** ['henəd] *adj.* (hair) coloured with henna.
hepatitis [hepə'taɪtɪs] *n.* disease of the liver.
heptagon ['heptəgən] *n.* geometrical figure with seven sides. **heptagonal** [hep'tægənl] *adj.* seven-sided.
her 1 [hɜ:] pronoun referring to a female object form of she; have you seen her? **her 2** *adj.* belonging to a female; have you seen her brother?
herald 1 ['herəld] *n.* messenger sent to announce sth; officer nags him with heraldry. **herald 2** *v.* to be a sign that sth is approaching; to announce.
heraldic [he'rældɪk] *adj.* referring to heraldry. **heraldry** ['herəldrɪ] *n.* study

of coats of arms.
herb [hɜːb] *n.* tasty or pungent plant used in cooking or as a medicine. **herbaceous border** [hɜːˈbeɪʃəsˈbɔːdə] *n.* flowerbed planted with flowers which sprout up again every year. **herbage** *n.* grass or other green plants. **herbal** *adj.* containing/using herbs. **herbalist** *n.* person who sells herbs as medicines. **herbarium** *n.* collection of wild plants. **herbicide** *n.* substance which kills weeds. **herbivore** [ˈhɜːbɪvɔː] *n.* animal which eats plants. **herbivorous** [hɜːˈbɪvərəs] *adj.* (animal) which eats plants.

herculean [hɜːkjuːˈliːən] *adj.* showing great strength; (task) which needs great effort.

herd 1 [hɜːd] *n.* group of animals; h. instinct = tendency of people to do what others do. **herd 2** *v.* to form/to make into a group. **herdsman** *n.* (*pl.*-men) man who looks after a herd of cows, etc.

here [ˈhɪə] *adv.* to/in this place. **hereabouts** *adv.* round about here/in this area. **hereafter** *adv.* from this time on. **hereby** *adv.* (formal) in this way. **hereto** *adv.* to this. **herewith** [hɪəˈwɪθ] *adv.* with this.

heredity [hɪˈredɪtɪ] *n.* passing on of characteristics from parent to child. **hereditament** *n.* property which can be inherited. **hereditary** *adj.* which is passed on from parent to child; (title such as Lord, etc.) which is passed from father to son.

heresy [ˈherəsɪ] *n.* heretical belief. **heretic** *n.* person who does not hold generally accepted religious beliefs. **heretical** [həˈretɪkl] *adj.* (belief) which is not generally accepted/which is condemned by the church.

heritage [ˈherɪtɪdʒ] *n.* thing which is passed on from one generation to the next.

hermaphrodite [hɜːˈmæfrədaɪt] *n.* animal/plant which is both male and female.

hermetic [hɜːˈmetɪk] *adj.* sealed; airtight. **hermetically** *adv.* (sealed) tightly so that no air can get in.

hermit [ˈhɜːmɪt] *n.* person who lives alone and refuses to see other people; h. crab = small crab which lives in empty sea shells. **hermitage** *n.* place where a hermit lives.

hernia [ˈhɜːnɪə] *n.* state where part of the bowel has pushed through a weak place in the wall of the abdomen.

hero, heroine [ˈhɪərəʊ, ˈherəʊɪn] *n.* (*pl.*-oes) person who does brave deeds; main character in a book/film, etc. **heroic** [hɪˈrəʊɪk] *adj.* brave/like a hero. **heroically** *adv.* like a hero. **heroism** [ˈherəʊɪzəm] *n.* bravery. **heroin** [ˈherəʊɪn] *n.* drug made from poppies.

heron [ˈherən] *n.* common water bird with long legs and neck.

herpes [ˈhɜːpiːz] *n.* disease which gives blisters on the skin.

herring [ˈherɪŋ] *n.* common sea fish; red h. = distraction/false lead. **herringbone** *adj.* (pattern) in a zigzag. **herring gull** *n.* common large grey and white gull.

hers [hɜːz] *adj.* belonging to her.

herself pronoun referring to a female subject; she was washing h.; all by h.; she wrote to me h.

hertz [hɜːts] *n.* (no *pl.*) standard unit of frequency of radio waves.

hesitate [ˈhezɪteɪt] *v.* to stop for a moment; to be unable to decide. **hesitance, hesitancy** *n.* being hesitant. **hesitant** *adj.* doubtful/ undecided. **hesitantly** *adv.* in a hesitant way. **hesitation** [hezɪˈteɪʃn] *n.* indecision/doubt.

hessian [ˈhesɪən] *n.* rough cloth like sacking.

heterogeneous [hetərəʊˈdʒiːnjəs] *adj.* of varied sorts.

heterosexual [hetərəʊˈseksjʊəl] *adj. & n.* (person) who is attracted to people of the opposite sex.

het up [ˈhet ˈʌp] *adj. inf.* excited; anxious.

heuristic [hjuːˈrɪstɪk] *adj.* which encourages science.

hew [hjuː] *v.* (hewn) to carve/to cut.

hexagon [ˈheksəgən] *n.* geometrical figure with six sides. **hexagonal** [hekˈsægənl] *adj.* six-sided.

hexameter [hekˈsæmɪtə] *n.* line of poetry with six beats.

hey [heɪ] *inter.* showing a greeting/ surprise. **heyday** [ˈheɪdeɪ] *n.* period of greatest glory/success/power.

Hg symbol for mercury.

hi [haɪ] *inter.* esp. *Am.* showing a

greeting.

hiatus ['haɪ'eɪtəs] *n.* (*pl.*-uses) gap/ interruption.

hibernate ['haɪbəneɪt] *v.* (of animals) to sleep during the winter. **hibernation** [haɪbə'neɪʃn] *n.* spending the winter asleep.

hibiscus [hɪ'bɪskəs] *n.* tropical shrub with large trumpet-shaped flowers.

hiccup, hiccough 1 ['hɪkʌp] *n.* repeated spasm in the throat like a small cough. **hiccup, hiccough 2** *v.* (hiccupped) to make a loud noise because of a hiccup.

hick [hɪk] *n. Am.* inf. stupid person from the country.

hickory ['hɪkərɪ] *n.* American tree like a walnut.

hid, hidden [hɪd, 'hɪdn] *v.* see hide.

hide 1 [haɪd] *n.* (a) leather; whole skin of an animal. (b) camouflaged place where you can sit and watch birds, etc.

hide 2 *v.* (hid, has hidden) to be out of sight; to put (a thing) somewhere so that no one can see it. **hide-and-seek** *n.* children's game. where some hide and the others try to find them. **hidebound** *adj.* unwilling to change ideas/narrow-minded. **hide-out** *n.* secret place where you cannot be found. **hiding** *n.* (a) putting yourself/sth out of sight. (b) inf. beating/whipping.

hideous ['hɪdɪəs] *adj.* horribly ugly. **hideously** *adv.* in a hideous way. **hideousness** *n.* being hideous.

hierarchy ['haɪərɑːkɪ] *n.* arrangement in a system of ranks/grades. **hierarchical** [haɪə'rɑːkɪkl] *adj.* arranged in a set system of ranks.

hieroglyphics [haɪərəʊ'glɪfɪks] *n. pl.* system of picture writing used by the Ancient Egyptians. **hieroglyph** *n.* symbol used in hieroglyphics.

hi-fi ['haɪ'faɪ] *adj. & n.* inf. high fidelity radio/stereo (equipment).

higgledy-piggledy [hɪgldɪ'pɪgldɪ] *adv.* in disorder/all over the place.

high 1 [haɪ] *adj.* (-er, -est) (a) going far above; tall. (b) great (rank, price, etc.,) h. fidelity = (radio equipment) which gives excellent reproduction of sound. (c) shrill (note). (d) (of meat) going rotten. (e) main most important. (f) powerful (explosive). (g) inf. influenced by drugs. **high 2** *adv.* (-er, -est) (a) far above. (b)

to a great degree. **high 3** *n.* (a) high-pressure zone in the atmosphere. (b) an all-time h. = the highest point ever reached. (c) inf. state of intoxication produced by a drug, etc. **highball** *n. Am.* whisky and soda. **highbrow** *adj. & n.* intellectual (person). **high chair** *n.* small chair with very long legs for a baby to sit in to eat. **High Church** *adj. & n.* (section of the Anglican Church) which regards ritual as very important. **High Commissioner** *n.* title given to the ambassador of a Commonwealth country. **High Court** *n.* main civil court in England and Wales.

highfalutin *adj. inf.* which sounds/ looks imposing. **high-fidelity** *adj.* which produces sound of a very high quality. **high flyer** *n.* very intelligent/ very ambitious person. **high-handed** *adj.* (action) done without considering other people. **highland** *adj.* coming from the highlands/from a mountain region. **Highlander** *n.* person who lives in the Highlands of Scotland. **Highlands** *n. pl.* mountain region, esp. in northern Scotland. **highlight 1** *n.* most interesting event. **highlight 2** *v.* to accentuate/to draw attention to. **highly** *adv.* very/greatly. **highly-strung** *adj.* very emotional/excitable. **high-minded** *adj.* noble/very serious. **highness** *n.* (a) being high/being above other things. (b) title given to princes, etc. **high-pitched** *adj.* sharp/ shrill (sound); steep (roof). **high-powered** *adj.* very powerful (engine). **high priest** *n.* most important priest. **high-rise** *adj.* (building) with many floors. **highroad** *n.* main road. **high school** *n.* secondary school. **highseas** *n. pl.* the oceans. **high season** *n.* most popular season for holiday travel. **high-speed** *adj.* which goes/works very fast. **high-spirited** *adj.* lively. **high spot** *n.* most enjoyable part of an entertainment. **High Street** *n.* main shopping street. **high tea** *n.* (in North of England and Scotland) large meal of tea, cold meat, cakes, etc., eaten in the early evening. **highwater mark** *n.* highest point (reached by the tide/by sth advancing. **highway** *n.* main road; h. code = official rules for people travelling on public roads. **highwayman** n. (pl.-men) person who attacked travellers and robbed them.

hijack ['haɪdʒæk] v. to take control of (an aircraft/a train, etc.). with passengers on board. by threatening the pilot/driver. **hijacker** n. person who hijacks.

hike 1 [haɪk] n. (a) strenuous walk. (b) Am. increase (in price, etc.). **hike 2** v. (a) to go for a strenuous walk. (b) Am. to increase (prices, etc.). **hiker** n. person who goes for long walks. **hiking** n. walking as a relaxation.

hilarious [hɪˈleərɪəs] adj. very funny/ very happy. **hilariously** adv. in a very funny way. **hilarity** [hɪˈlærɪtɪ] n. great laughter.

hill [hɪl] n. rise in the land. lower than a mountain. **hillbilly** n. Am. person who lives in the country; h. music = country style music. **hillock** n. little hill.

hillside n. side of a hill **hilly** adj. (-ier, -iest) (region) with many hills.

hilt [hɪlt] n. protective shield on the handle of a sword; to the h. = totally.

him [hɪm] pronoun referring to a male; object form of he; have you seen h.?

himself [hɪmˈself] pronoun referring to a male subject; he was washing h.; he is all by h.; he wrote to me h.

hind 1 [haɪnd] n. female deer. **hind 2** adj. h. legs = back legs (of an animal).

hinder ['hɪndə] v. to prevent (s.o.) from doing sth. **hindrance** n. obstacle.

hindmost ['haɪndməʊst] adj. furthest back.

hindsight ['haɪndsaɪt] n. knowing facts about an event in the past which could have been useful if they had been known at the time.

Hindu ['hɪnduː] adj. & n. (person) following the main religion of India. **Hindi** n. language spoken in the central part of India.

hinge 1 [hɪndʒ] n. (a) metal bracket on which a door/a window hangs and opens. (b) stamp h. = small piece of gummed paper for sticking stamps into a stamp album. **hinge 2** v. to centre/to depend (s.o.). **hinged** adj. with hinges.

hint 1 [hɪnt] n. (a) hidden suggestion/ case. (b) sign. (c) hints = helpful advice. **hint 2** v. to suggest/to insinuate.

hinterland ['hɪntəlænd] n. area inland from a sea port/around a large town.

hip [hɪp] n. (a) projecting bone where the legs join the body; wide part of the body where the legs join in it. (b) fruit of a wild rose. (c) h. h. hooray! = words used to give a cheer. **hipped** adj. (roof) which breaks at an angle. **hipsters** n. of trousers which only reach to the hips and not the waist. **hippie** ['hɪpɪ] n. inf. person who lives/dresses in a different way from the majority of people in society.

hippopotamus, hippo [hɪpəpɒtəməs] ['hɪpəʊ] n.inf. (pl.-muses, -mi[-maɪ]; -os) very large African animal living in water and mud.

hire 1 ['haɪə] n. renting (of a car, etc.) usu. for a short time; h. purchase = system where you buy sth by paying instalments. **hire 2** v. to rent (a car, etc.); to engage (staff); he hires out cars = he has cars which people can rent.

hireling n. person who is hired to do a job. **hirer** n. person who hires.

hirsute ['hɜːsjuːt] adj. covered with long hair.

his [hɪz] adj. (a) belonging to a male. (b) belonging to him; a friend of h.

Hispano 1 [hɪsˈpɑːnəʊ] prefix meaning between Spain and another country. **Hispano 2** n. Am. Spanish - speaking immigrant.

hiss 1 [hɪs] n. whistling sound like an 's'. made by snakes/by gas escaping, etc.; similar sound made to show you do not like sth. **hiss 2** v. to make a hissing sound.

histamine ['hɪstəmiːn] n. substance which causes an allergy.

histology [hɪˈstɒlədʒɪ] n. science of body cells. **histologist** n. person who specializes in histology.

history ['hɪstərɪ] n. (a) study of the past; story of what happened in the past. (b) natural h. = study of animals and plants. **historian** [hɪstɔːrɪən] n. person who studies or writes about the past.

historic [hɪˈstɒrɪk] adj. (event) which is so important that it will be remembered. **historical** adj. referring to history; h. novel = novel set in the past. **historically** adv. as in the past.

histrionic [hɪstrɪˈɒnɪk] adj. referring to acting. **histrionics** n. pl. dramatic behaviour.

hit 1 [hɪt] n. (a) blow; he scored three

hits = he hit the target three times. (b) song/play etc. which is very popular. **hit 2** v. (hit; has hit) (a) to knock against; to touch (sth) hard. (b) to affect (badly). **hit and miss** adj. erratic/careless. **hit back** v. to defend yourself against attack. **hit-man** n. (pl.-men) person employed to kill/to hurt s.o. **hit off** v. inf. to hit it off with s.o. = to get on well with s.o. **hit-or-miss** adj. erratic/careless. **hit out** v. (at) to try to attack (s.o.). **hit(up)on** v. to discover.

hitch 1 [hɪtʃ] n. awkward delay/unexpected stoppage. **hitch 2** v. (a) to jerk up/to pull up. (b) to hitch-hike. (c) to attach with a rope; inf. to get hitched = to get married. **hitch-hike** v. to get a free ride in s.o.'s car. stopping the car by pointing your thumb. **hitch-hiker** n. person who hitch-hikes.

hither ['hɪðə] adv. (formal) to this place; h. and thither = all over the place. **hitherto** adv. up till now.

HIV ['eɪtʃaɪ'vi] human immunodeficiency virus.

hive 1 [haɪv] n. (a) box in which bees make their nest. (b) hives = sore red patches on the skin. usu. on the face. **hive 2** v. to h. off = to split off.

HMSO abbrev. for Her Majesty's Stationery Office.

hoard 1 [hɔːd] n. mass/store (of money/food, etc.) which has been collected. **hoard 2** v. to collect and store (money/food, etc.). **hoarder** n. person who buys food when supplies are low. **hoarding** n. (a) buying food, etc., when supplies are low. (b) fence made of rough planks. (c) large advertising board in the street.

hoarfrost ['hɔːfrɒst] n. white frost which covers trees/plants, etc.

hoarse [hɔːs] adj. rough (voice). **hoarsely** adv. in a hoarse voice. **hoarseness** n. roughness/harshness (of voice).

hoary ['hɔːrɪ] adj. (-ier, -iest) (a) (formal) white-haired. (b) inf. very old (joke).

hoax 1 [həʊks] n. trick. **hoax 2** v. to trick/to deceive. **hoaxer** n. person who hoaxes.

hob [hɒb] n. (a) metal stand where a kettle can be put by the side of a fire. (b) flat top to a cooker.

hobble ['hɒbl] v (a) to attach the legs

of (a horse) so that it cannot move easily. (b) to walk with difficulty.

hobby ['hɒbɪ] n. pastime; thing done as a relaxation. **hobbyhorse** n. subject which s.o. always talks about.

hobgoblin [hɒb'gɒblɪn] n. goblin.

hobnail ['hɒbneɪl] n. large nail used to protect the soles of boots. **hobnailed** adj. (boots) with large metal nails. **hobnob** ['hɒbnɒb] v. (hobnobbed) inf. to be on friendly terms (with s.o. important).

hobo ['həʊbəʊ] n. Am. person with no home or money.

hock [hɒk] n. (a) middle joint of an animal's leg; lower part of a leg of an animal used for food. (b) German white wine. (c) Sl. in h. = pawned.

hockey ['hɒkɪ] n. (a) = team game played on grass with long curved sticks and a hard ball. (b) Am. ice hockey.

hocus-pocus ['həʊkəs'pəʊkəs] n. (a) meaningless words (used by conjurers). (b) trickery.

hod [hɒd] n. (a) wooden container on the end of a pole, used by builders for carrying bricks. (b) metal container for coal.

hoe 1 [həʊ] n. garden tool with a blade on the end of a long handle. **hoe 2** v. to take out weeds/to loosen the soil with a hoe.

hog 1 [hɒg] n. castrated male pig; inf. to go the whole h. = to do sth completely. **hog 2** v. (hogged) (a) to eat/to drink like a pig. (b) to monopolize.

hogg [hɒg] n. young female sheep.

Hogmanay [hɒgmə'neɪ] n. Scottish festival on 31st December.

hogshead ['hɒgzhed] n. (a) large barrel. (b) measure of about 50 gallons.

hoick [hɔɪk] v. inf. to pull (out).

hoi polloi [hɔɪpə'lɔɪ] n. the ordinary people.

hoist 1 [hɔɪst] n. apparatus for lifting; goods lift. **hoist 2** v. to lift up.

hoity-toity ['hɔɪtɪ'tɔɪtɪ] adj. inf. snobbish; superior (air).

hold 1 [həʊld] n. (a) grip. (b) influence/power. (c) part of a ship/aircraft where cargo is carried. **hold 2** v. (held) (a) to have in your hand, etc. (b) to contain. (c) to make (sth) take place. (d) to keep in (one's breath, a liquid) (e) to stay. (f) to h. office = to have a post (in a government). **holdall** *n.* large travelling bag. **hold back** *v.* to keep back; not to go forward. **hold down** *v.* to keep (sth) down; to work hard to keep (a job). **holder** *n.* person or thing which holds. **hold forth** *v.* to talk at great length. **holding** *n.* number of shares which you own; h. company = company formed to control shares in other companies. **hold off** *v.* not to act. **hold on** *v.* (a) to cling on to/to take a grip on (sth). (b) to wait. **hold out** *v.* (a) to offer. (b) to last. **hold over** *v.* to postpone (sth). **hold up** *v.* (a) to raise. (b) to support. (c) to hinder/to delay. (d) to attack and rob. **hold-up** *n.* (a) delay; breakdown. (b) armed attack. **hold with** *v. inf.* to accept/to agree with.

hole 1 [həʊl] *n.* opening/space. **hole 2** *v.* (a) to make a hole in. (b) (in golf) to send (the ball) into the hole. **hole up** *v. inf.* to hide away.

holiday 1 ['hɒlɪdeɪ] *n.* period when you do not work. **holiday 2** *v.* to go on holiday. **holidaymaker** *n.* person on holiday away from home.

holiness ['həʊlɪnəs] *n.* see holy.

holistic [hɒ'lɪstɪk] *adj.* (attitude) which considers many sides to a problem; (medical treatment) which deals with the environment of the patient as well as the illness itself.

holler ['hɒlə] *v. inf.* to shout.

hollow 1 ['hɒləʊ] *n.* low-lying land; small depression in a flat surface. **hollow 2** *adj.* empty/with nothing inside; meaningless (success). **hollow 3** *v.* to h. out = to make (sth) hollow.

holly ['hɒlɪ] *n.* very prickly evergreen bush with red berries. **hollyhock** ['hɒlɪhɒk] *n.* common garden flower which produces very tall spikes of blossom.

holm oak ['hɒlməʊk] *n.* evergreen oak found in temperate climates.

holocaust ['hɒləkɔːst] *n.* destruction by fire.

holograph ['hɒləɡrɑːf] *n.* letter, etc., written by s.o. by hand. not typed.

hologram *n.* three-dimensional picture produced by lasers. **holography** *n.* science of making holograms.

holster ['həʊlstə] *n.* leather pouch for carrying a revolver.

holy ['həʊlɪ] *adj.* (-ier, -iest) sacred (place); very pious (person); h. orders = being a priest. **holiness** *n.* being holy; his H. = title given to the Pope. **Holy Week** *n.* the week which ends with Easter Sunday.

homage ['hɒmɪdʒ] *n.* (a) respect; to pay h. to s.o. = to show s.o. signs of respect. (b) (formal) duty/service (to a feudal lord).

home 1 [həʊm] *n.* (a) place where you live/place where you come from originally. (b) (in sports) at h. = playing on a local sports ground. (c) house where people are looked after. (d) top left-hand corner of a computer screen. **home 2** *adv.* to/at the place where you live; to strike h. = to hit the target. **home 3** *adj.* (a) referring to the place where you live. (b) not foreign/internal; h. trade = trade inside the country. (c) (in sports) referring to the local team/the local sports ground; (match) played by the local team on their own ground. **home 4** *v.* to h. in on = to go to a target. **Home Counties** *n. pl.* the counties around London. **home-grown** *adj.* (vegetables) grown in the garden, not bought; (industry) which is developed in a country, and not imported. **home help** *n.* person who helps an invalid with housework in the home. **homeland** *n.* land which is the home of a people. **homeless** *adj.* with nowhere to live. **homeliness** *n.* being homely. **homely** *adj.* (a) simple; not ostentatious. (b) plain/ugly (person). **home-made** *adj.* made at home/not bought. **Home Office** *n.* Government department which deals with internal problems of law and order in England and Wales. **home run** *n.* (in baseball) run made by a batter who touches all the bases. **Home Secretary** *n.* Minister in charge of the Home Office. **homesick** *adj.* unhappy because of wanting to go home. **homesickness** *n.* feeling of being homesick. **homestead** *n.* farmhouse and the fields around it. **homeward** *adj. & adv.* going towards home. **homewards** *adv.* towards home. **homework** *n.* work which children take from school to be done at home in the evening. *adj.* h. pigeon = pigeon trained to return to the place where it usually lives; h. device = device (on

a missile) which guides it to the target.
homicide ['hɒmɪsaɪd] *n.* murder.
homicidal [hɒmɪ'saɪdl] *adj.* likely to
murder.
homily ['hɒmɪlɪ] *n.* sermon/talk to
encourage s.o., to be less wicked.
homoeopathy, *Am.* **homeopathy**
[həʊmɪ'ɒpəθɪ] *n.* method of curing sick
people by accustoming them to very
small quantities of drugs which would
normally make them ill. **homoeopath,**
Am. **homeopath** ['həʊmjəpæθ] *n.*
doctor who practices homeopathy.
homoeopathic, *Am.* **homeopathic**
adj. referring to homeopathy.
homogeneous [hɒməʊ'dʒiːnɪəs] *adj.*
of the same sort/quality (as other things).
homogeneity [hɒməʊdʒə'niːɪtɪ] *n.*
being homogeneous. **homogenize**
[hə'mɒdʒənaɪz] *v.* to mix various parts
until they become a single whole; to mix
the cream into milk. **homogenization**
[həmɒdʒənaɪ'zeɪʃn] *n.* treatment of milk
so that the cream does not separate.
homonym ['hɒmənɪm] *n.* word which
is spelt the same as another word with a
different meaning.
homophone ['hɒməfəʊn] *n.* word
which is pronounced the same as
another, but spelt differently.
homosexual [həʊməʊ'seksjʊəl] *adj. &
n.* (person) who is attracted to persons
of the same sex as himself/herself.
homosexuality [həʊməʊseksjʊ'ælɪtɪ]
n. being homosexual.
hone [həʊn] *v.* to smooth/to sharpen (a
blade).
honest ['ɒnɪst] *adj.* truthful; not
cheating or stealing. **honestly** *adv.*
truthfully. **honesty** *n.* (a) truthfulness.
(b) garden flower with silvery seed
cases, used as a winter decoration.
honey ['hʌnɪ] *n.* sweet substance
produced by bees. **honey-bee** *n.* type
of bee which makes honey.
honeycomb *n.* construction of wax
cells in which bees store honey; pattern
of six-sided shapes like bees cells.
honeycombed *adj.* full of little holes.
honeydew *n.* type of melon which has
green flesh. **honeyed** *adj.* sweet/
flattering (words). **honeymoon 1** *n.*
holiday taken by man and wife
immediately after their wedding.
honeymoon 2 *v.* to go on a

honeymoon. **honeysuckle** *n.* common
climbing plant with scented yellow and
pink flowers.
honk 1 ['hɒŋk] *n.* noise made by a
goose/by a car horn. **honk 2** *v.* to make
a noise like a goose/a car horn.
honorarium [ɒnə'rəerɪəm] *n.* money
paid to s.o. for work which is usually
done free.
honorary ['ɒnərərɪ] *adj.* (a) (person)
who is not paid a salary. (b) given as a
mark of respect.
honour *Am.* **honor 1** ['ɒnə] *n.* (a)
self-respect. (b) mark of respect; title
given as a mark of respect. (c) honours
degree = university degree taken after a
more difficult course of study. (d) title
given to a judge. **honour 2** *v.* (a) to
respect; to give a title/medal to (s.o.) as a
mark of respect. (b) to pay (a bill); (of a
bank) to pay (a cheque). **honourable**
adj. that can be respected. **honourably**
adv. in a way which you can respect.
hooch [huːtʃ] *n. Sl.* alcoholic drink.
hood [hʊd] *n.* (a) loose covering for the
head, attached to a coat. (b) folding roof
on a car or prAm. (c) *Am.* lid covering
the engine of a car. (d) *Sl.* gangster.
hooded *adj.* wearing a hood.
hoodlum ['huːdləm] *n.* thug/violent
hooligan. **hoodwink** ['hʊdwɪŋk] *v.* to
trick.
hoof [huːf] *n.* (*pl.*hooves) hard part of
the foot of a horse, etc. **hoofed** *adj.*
(animal) which has hooves.
hoo-ha ['huːhɑː] *n. inf.* fuss/bother.
hook 1 [hʊk] *n.* (a) bent piece of metal
used for holding or pulling, etc.; to get
s.o. off the h. = to release s.o. from a
difficult situation; by h. or by crook = by
any means available; h. and eye = small
hook and loop for fastening clothing. (b)
very small. bent piece of metal used for
catching fish. (c) (in boxing/cricket)
blow/stroke made with the arm bent.
hook 2 *v.* (a) to hang on a hook; to
attach with a hook. (b) to catch (a fish)
with a hook. **hooked** *adj.* (a) shaped
like a hook. (b) caught with/on a hook.
(c) *inf.* h. on = very interested in (a book,
etc.); addicted to (drugs). **hooker** *n.*
(a) (in Rugby) forward in the centre of
the front line of the scrum, whose job is
to hook the ball backwards to his own
side. (b) *inf.* prostitute. **hook-up** *n.*

radio or T.V. link. **hookworm** *n.* type of parasitic worm.

hookah ['hʊkə] *n.* tobacco pipe where the smoke is cooled by being passed through water.

hookey ['hʊkɪ] *n. Am.* child who avoids going to school; to play h. = to avoid going to school.

hooligan ['huːlɪgən] *n.* rowdy wild person. **hooliganism** *n.* wild behaviour.

hoop [huːp] *n.* large ring of wood or metal. **hoop-la** *n.* game where you throw hoops over little pegs.

hoopoe ['huːpuː] *n.* large cream - coloured bird with a crest.

hooray [hʊ'reɪ] *inter.* showing great pleasure/excitement.

hoot 1 [huːt] *n.* (a) call of an owl; hoots of laughter = sound like an owl call. made when you are laughing. (b) sound made by a car horn. **hoot 2** *v.* (a) (of an owl.) to call; to h. with laughter = laugh hilariously. (b) to sound the horn of a car.

hooter *n.* (a) warning siren. (b) car horn.

Hoover 1 ['huːvə] *n.* trademark for a type of vacuum cleaner. **Hoover 2** *v.* to h. = to clean with a vacuum cleaner.

hop 1 [hɒp] *n.* (a) little jump; *inf.* to catch s.o. on the h. = find s.o. unexpectedly. (b) short flight (in a plane). (c) bitter fruit used in making beer; climbing plant which bears this fruit. **hop 2** *v.* (hopped) to jump on one leg; (of birds) to jump with both feet together; *inf.* hop it! = go away.

hopfield *n.* field where hops are grown. **hop-picker** *n.* person who picks hops.

hope 1 [həʊp] *n.* expectation/wanting sth to happen. **hope 2** *v.* to expect that sth will happen; to want sth to happen. **hopeful** *adj.* full of hope/confident; likely to happen. **hopefully** *adv.* (a) confidently. (b) h. the rain will stop = let's hope/I hope it will stop. **hopeless** *adj.* with no hope; he's h. at chess = he plays very badly. **hopelessly** *adv.* with no hope. **hopelessness** *n.* being hopeless.

hopper ['hɒpə] *n.* very large funnel for channelling loose material (like sand/corn, etc.).

hopsack ['hɒpsæk] *n.* thick rough

material.

hopscotch ['hɒpskɒtʃ] *n.* children's game in which you hop over marked squares on the ground.

horde [hɔːd] *n.* crowd/mass.

horizon [hə'raɪzn] *n.* (a) line where the earth seems to meet the sky. (b) layer of soil. **horizontal** [hɒrɪ'zɒntl] *adj.* lying flat/not upright. **horizontally** *adv.* lying flat.

hormone ['hɔːməʊn] *n.* substance produced by glands in the body, which causes various physical reactions. **hormonal** *adj.* referring to hormones.

horn [hɔːn] *n.* (a) hard bony growth on the head of some animals. (b) feeler on a snail's head. (c) brass musical instrument shaped like an animal's horn. (d) instrument on a car, etc., which makes a loud warning noise. **horned** *adj.* with horns. **horn in(on)** *v. inf.* to join (a meeting) uninvited. **hornpipe** *n.* vigorous dance danced by sailors. **hornrimmed** *adj.* (spectacles) with tortoiseshell frames. **horny** *adj.* hard/rough (hands). **hornbeam** ['hɔːnbiːm] *n.* common hedgerow tree.

hornet ['hɔːnɪt] *n.* large red wasp.

horology [hɒ'rɒlədʒɪ] *n.* study of time and clocks.

horoscope ['hɒrəskəʊp] *n.* description of a person's character/forecasting of what will happen to a person in the future, based on he position of the stars when he or she was born.

horrendous [hɒ'rendəs] *adj.* quite horrible.

horrible ['hɒrəbl] *adj.* terrible/frightening. **horribly** *adv.* frighteningly/badly. **horrid** ['hɒrɪd] *adj.* nasty/unpleasant.

horrific [hə'rɪfɪk] *adj.* frightening/shocking. **horrifically** *adv.* in a horrific way. **horrify** ['hɒrɪfaɪ] *v.* to make (s.o.) very frightened/to shock (s.o.).

horror ['hɒrə] *n.* terror/feeling of being very frightened; h. film = film which aims to frighten the spectators; *inf.* little h. = very naughty child. **horror-stricken, horror-struck** *adj.* very frightened.

hors-d'œuvre [ɔːdɜːv] *n. pl.* cold food served at the beginning of a meal.

horse 1 [hɔːs] *n.* (a) large animal with

hooves, which is used for riding or pulling vehicles; h. racing = racing of horses; dark h. = person you know nothing about and who may win; *inf.* straight from the horse's mouth = from a very reliable source. (b) apparatus made of wood over which you jump in gymnastics. (c) clothes h. = wooden frame used for drying clothes. **horse 2** *v.* to h. around/about = to play roughly. **horseback** *n.* on h. = riding on a horse. **horsebox** *n.* enclosed box on wheels for transporting horses. **horse-chestnut** *n.* type of large tree; shiny inedible nut of this tree. **horsefly** *n.* large fly which bites animals. **horsehair** *n.* hair from the mane or tail of a horse, used for padding furniture. **horse laugh** *n.* loud unpleasant laugh. **horseman** *n.* (*pl.* -men) man riding a horse; man who often rides on horses. **horseplay** *n.* rough fighting/rough games. **horsepower** *n.* unit formerly used when calculating the power of a car engine. **horseradish** *n.* plant with a large root used to make a sharp sauce. **horserider** *n.* person who rides a horse. **horse sense** *n. inf.* commonsense. **horseshoe** *n.* curved metal strip nailed to the hooves of horses. **horsetail** *n.* common leafless weed. **horse trading** *n.* bargaining between parties before coming to an agreement. **horsewoman** *n.* (*pl.* -women) woman riding horse; woman who often rides on horses. **horsy** *adj.* (a) looking like a horse. (b) interested in horses. **horticulture** [ˈhɔːtɪkʌltʃə] *n.* science of gardening. **horticultural** [hɔːtɪˈkʌltʃərəl] *adj.* referring to horticulture. **horticulturist** *n.* person who specializes in gardening. **hose 1** [həʊz] *n.* (a) (also hosepipe) long, flexible tube. (b) stockings/sock; panty h. = tights/stockings and briefs in one piece. **hose 2** *v.* (also hose down) to spray with water, etc. from a hose. **hosiery** [ˈhəʊzjərɪ] *n.* knitted pieces of clothing (esp. socks/gloves). **hospice** [ˈhɒspɪs] *n.* place where poor or terminally ill people can live **hospitable** [hɒˈspɪtəbl] *adj.* welcoming. **hospitably** *adv.* in a welcoming way. **hospitality** [hɒspɪˈtælɪtɪ] *n.* welcome to visitors; giving visitors food, drink,

etc. **hospital** [ˈhɒspɪtl] *n.* place where sick people are treated. **hospitalize** *v.* to put (s.o) in hospital. **host 1** [həʊst] *n.* (a) man who invites guests. (b) hotel keeper. (c) animal/plant on which other animals/plants live. (d) large number. (e) (in church) consecrated bread. **host 2** *v.* to be the host at (a reception/a conference/TV show). **hostess** *n.* (a) woman who invites guests. (b) air h. = woman who looks after passengers on an aircraft. **hosta** [ˈhɒstə] *n.* common garden plant which grows in shade. **hostage** [ˈhɒstɪdʒ] *n.* person kept prisoner until the demands of the captor are met. **hostel** [ˈhɒstl] *n.* (a) building providing rooms for homeless families/students, etc. (b) youth h. = building where young walkers, etc. may stay the night cheaply. **hostile** [ˈhɒstaɪl] *adj.* referring to an enemy; unfriendly. **hostility** [hɒˈstɪlɪtɪ] *n.* (a) dislike (of a plan) /opposition (to a plan). (b) hostilities = warfare. **hot 1** [hɒt] *adj.* (hotter, hottest) (a) very warm; *inf.* to get into. h. water = to get into trouble; to make things h. for s.o. = make life unbearable. (b) highly spiced. (c) very strong; h. line = direct telephone link between heads of state; he's in the h. seat = his job involves him in awkward decisions. (d) *inf.* very recent (news); (goods) which have just been stolen. **hot 2** *v.* (hotted) *inf.* to h. up = to warm up (cold food); things are hotting up = things are getting more dangerous/more exciting. **hot air** *n. inf.* useless excited talk. **hotbed** *n.* place where sth unpleasant breeds rapidly. **hot-blooded** *adj.* (person) with a violent temper. **hot dog** *n.* hot frankfurter eaten in a long roll with pickles or onions. **hotfoot** *adv.* running fast. **hothead** *n.* impetuous person. **hothouse** *n.* heated greenhouse. **hotplate** *n.* piece of metal heated *usu.* by electricity used to heat food. **hotpot** *n.* meat stew with potatoes on top. **hot-tempered** *adj.* (person) with a violent temper. **hotwater bottle** *n.* container filled with hot water which is placed in a bed to warm it. **hotchpotch** [ˈhɒtʃpɒtʃ] *n.* mixture/

jumble.

hotel [həʊˈtel] n. building where you can buy food and drink and rent a room for the night. **hotelier** [həʊˈteliə] n. person who runs a hotel.

hound 1 [haʊnd] n. large hunting dog. **hound 2** v. to chase (s.o.) /to victimize (s.o.).

hour [ˈaʊə] n. (a) period of time lasting sixty minutes; *inf.* they took hours to do it = a very long time. (b) particular point in time; on the h. = at 9.10 etc., o'clock exactly. **hourglass** n. timing device made of two glass containers joined by a narrow tube, through which sand falls. **hourly** adj. & adv. every hour.

house 1 [haʊs, pl. ˈhaʊzɪz] n. (a) building in which people live; *inf.* they get on like a h. on fire = they are very friendly. (b) dynasty/royal family. (c) commercial firm. (d) audience (at a play); members (of a parliament). (e) public h. = inn/building with a licence to sell drinks; drinks are on the h. = drinks offered free by the innkeeper. (f) (in a school) division of the school to which one group of children belongs for competitions or for boarding. (g) the House = one of the two parts of the British Parliament; a debating group. **house 2** v. to provide accommodation for (s.o./sth). **house-agent** n. person who arranges the sale of houses. **house arrest** n. under h. arrest = not allowed to leave one's house which is being guarded by the police. **houseboat** n. large boat which is used for living in. **housebound** adj. not able to leave the house. **housebreaker** n. burglar/person who breaks into a house to steal. **housebreaking** n. breaking into a house to steal. **housecoat** n. light coat/dressing gown worn by women in the house. **housecraft** n. skill at looking after a house. **household** n. family/people who live together in the same house; h. word = saying which everybody uses. **householder** n. head of a family/person who owns/who is in charge of a house. **housekeeper** n. woman employed to look after a house. **housekeeping** n. looking after a house; h. money = money set aside for paying food/heating, etc., in a house. **housemaid** n. girl who looks after the

cleaning of a house. **houseman** n. doctor working and *usu.* living in a hospital. **housemaster, housemistress** n. person in charge of a house in a school. **House of Commons** n. lower house of the British Parliament. **House of Lords** n. upper house of the British Parliament. **House of Representatives** n. lower house of the US Congress. **house physician** n. doctor working and *usu.* living in a hospital. **house plant** n. plant which is kept in the house. **houseproud** adj. taking great pride in the appearance of one's house. **houseroom** n. *inf.* I wouldn't give it h. = I don't like it, and wouldn't have in my house. **Houses of Parliament** n. building in which the two parts of the British Parliament meet. **house surgeon** n. doctor working and *usu.* living in a hospital. **house-trained** adj. (animal) trained not to pass excreta in the house. **housewarming** n. party to celebrate moving into a new house. **housewife.** n. (*pl.*-wives) woman who spends her time looking after a house and *usu.* has no outside work. **housework** n. general cleaning work in a house. **hous(e)y-hous(e)y** n. bingo. **housing** [haʊzɪŋ] n. (a) providing accommodation for people; h. estate = area of houses and flats built at one time. (b) covering for part of a machine.

hove [həʊv] v. see heave.

hovel [ˈhɒvl] n. small dirty house.

hover [ˈhɒvə] v. (a) to fly/to hang in the air without moving forward. (b) to hang (around s.o.) **hovercraft** n. vehicle which moves over water or land on a cushion of air. **hoverfly** n. small insect which hovers.

how [haʊ] adv. (a) in what way/to what extent; h. are you? (b) the means of; tell me h. to do it. (c) (showing surprise) h. green the trees are! how do you do? inter. showing greeting. **however** [haʊˈevə] adv. (a) to whatever extent. (b) in spite of this.

howdah [ˈhaʊdɑː] n. seat on an elephant's back.

howitzer [ˈhaʊɪtsə] n. short gun which fires shells high into the air.

howl 1 [haʊl] n. loud wail. **howl 2** v.

to make a loud wailing noise. **howl down** v. to stop (s.o.) making a speech by shouting at him. **howler** n. inf. bad mistake. **howling** n. loud wailing.

hoyden ['hɔɪdn] n. boisterous girl. **hoydenish** adj. like a hoyden.

HP ['eɪtʃ'piː] hire purchase.

HQ ['eɪtʃ'kjuː] n. headquarters.

hub [hʌb] n. (a) centre of a wheel where it is connected to the axle. (b) centre of activity/business. **hub cap** n. metal plate covering the centre of a car wheel.

hubble-bubble ['hʌblbʌbl] n. inf. hookah.

hubbub ['hʌbʌb] n. confused sound of voices.

huddle 1 ['hʌdl] n. to go into a h. = to meet together to discuss sth in secret. **huddle 2** v. to crowd together.

hue [hjuː] n. (a) colour. (b) h. and cry = loud noise showing anger/alarm.

huff [hʌf] n. in a h. = in a bad temper. **huffy** adj. inf. bad-tempered.

hug 1 [hʌg] n. throwing your arms round s.o. **hug 2** v. (hugged) (a) to throw your arms around (s.o.,). (b) keep close to (sth).

huge [hjuːdʒ] adj. very large/enormous. **hugely** adv. inf. enormously.

hugger-mugger ['hʌgəmʌgə] adv. inf. (a) in secret. (b) in a mess.

hulk [hʌlk] n. (a) rotten old ship which is no longer used for sailing. (b) large and clumsy thing/person. **hulking** adj. big and awkward.

hull 1 [hʌl] n. (a) main body of a ship. (b) pea or bean pod. **hull 2** v. to take (peas) out of their pods.

hullabaloo [hʌləbə'luː] n. loud disorderly noise.

hullo [hə'ləʊ] inter. showing a greeting.

hum 1 [hʌm] n. low buzzing noise. **hum 2** v. (hummed) (a) to make a continual low buzzing noise. (b) to sing the tune of a song without using the words. (c) inf. to give off an unpleasant smell. (d) to h. and haw = not to make up your mind. **hummingbird** n. very small brightly coloured tropical bird which hovers.

human 1 ['hjuːmən] adj. referring to mankind; a h. being = a person; h. immunodeficiency virus = virus which causes AIDS; h. nature = general characteristics of people. **human 2** n.

person. **humane** [hjuː'meɪn] adj. kind/gentle. **humanely** adv. kindly/gently.

humanism ['hjuːənɪzəm] n. concern with human beings rather than with religions. **humanist** n. person who believes in humanism. **humanistic** adj. referring to humanism.

humanitarian [hjuːmænɪ'teərɪən] adj. kind towards other humans. **humanity** [hjuː'mænɪtɪ] n. (a) all people. (b) great kindness. (c) the humanities = arts subjects (not sciences). **humanization** n. act of humanizing. **humanize** v. to make (more) human. **humankind** n. people. seen as a biological group.

humanly adv. we will do everything h. possible = all we can.

humble 1 ['hʌmbl] adj. (-er, -est) modest/not proud; to eat h. pie = to admit you were wrong. **humble 2** v. to make (s.o.) less proud/less important. **humbleness** n. being humble.

humbug ['hʌmbʌg] n. (a) confidence tricks. (b) person who tricks s.o./who pretends to be sth which he is not. (c) kind of hard striped sweet.

humdinger [hʌm'dɪŋə] n. Am. inf. marvellous person/thing.

humdrum ['hʌmdrʌm] adj. dull/ordinary.

humerus ['hjuːmərəs] n. bone in the top part of the arm.

humid ['hjuːmɪd] adj. damp. **humidifier** [hjuː'mɪdɪfaɪə] n. machine which dampens the air (in a house). **humidity** [hjuː'mɪdɪtɪ] n. dampness.

humiliate [hjɜː'mɪlɪeɪt] v. to make (s.o.) feel unimportant/humble/ashamed. **humiliation** [hjuːmɪlɪ'etʃn] n. making s.o. feel unimportant/humble/ashamed. **humility** [hjuː'mɪlɪtɪ] n. humbleness/being humble.

hummock ['hʌmək] n. low hump in the ground.

humour, Am. **humor 1** ['hjuːmə] n. (a) seeing the funny aspects of sth. (b) general feeling/mood. **humour,** Am. **humor 2** v. to do what s.o. wants in order to keep him happy. **humorist** n. person who makes jokes; writer of funny stories or articles. **humorous** adj. funny/amusing. **humorously** adv. in a humorous way.

hump 1 [hʌmp] n. lump on the back small rounded bump in the ground.

hump 2 v. inf. to carry (on your shoulder). **humpbacked** adj. (person) with a hump; (bridge) with a very high arch.

humus ['hjuːməs] n. good soil made rich with decayed animal or vegetable matter.

hunch 1 [hʌntʃ] n. inf. feeling that sth is going to happen. **hunch 2** v. to bend low. **hunchback** n. person with a hunched back.

hundred ['hʌndrəd] n. number 100; hundreds of = very many. **hundredfold** adv. a hundred times. **hundredth, 100th** adj. referring to a hundred. **hundredweight** n. weight of 112 pounds (approx. 50 kilos).

hung [hʌŋ] v. see hang; h. parliament = one where no party has an absolute majority; h. jury = jury which cannot reach a majority decision. **hungover** adj. inf. feeling ill after drinking too much alcohol. **hung up** adj. inf. suffering from an emotional disturbance.

Hungarian 1 [hʌŋ'geərɪən] adj. referring to Hungary. **Hungarian 2** n. (a) person from Hungary. (b) language spoken in Hungary.

hunger ['hʌŋgə] n. wanting/needing to eat. **hunger strike** n. refusing to eat to force s.o. to do sth. **hungrily** adv. in a hungry way. **hungry** adj. feeling hunger.

hunk [hʌŋk] n. large rough piece (of bread/cheese).

hunt 1 [hʌnt] n. (a) chasing of wild animals for sport; group of people who meet regularly to chase wild animals, esp. foxes. (b) search (for s.o.). **hunt 2** v. (a) to look for (s.o./sth). **huntdown** v. to track (a person/an animal) and catch them. **hunter** n. person who chases wild animals; horse used in hunting; bargain h. = person who is looking for bargains in shops. **hunting** n. (a) chasing wild animals. (b) looking for sth. **hunting ground** n. (a) place where wild animals are often found. (b) place where things are often found. **huntsman** n. (pl.-men) man who hunts wild animals; man who looks after a pack of hunting hounds.

hurdle ['hɜːdl] n. (a) moveable fence for keeping sheep in. (b) small fence which has to be jumped over in a race.

(c) obstacle. **hurdler** n. person who takes part in hurdling. **hurdling** n. running a race where you have to jump over fences.

hurdy-gurdy ['hɜːdɪ'gɜːdɪ] n. machine which produces music if a handle is turned.

hurl [hɜːl] v. to throw hard. **hurling** n. game similar to hockey. played in Ireland. **hurly-burly** ['hɜːlɪ'bɜːlɪ] n. rough activity.

hurrah, hurray [hʊ'rɑː, hʊ'reɪ] inter. showing great pleasure/excitement.

hurricane ['hʌrɪkən] n. violent tropical storm, esp. in the West Indies; h. lamp = lamp with a glass shield round the flame.

hurry 1 'hʌrɪ] n. rush. **hurry 2** v. (also hurry up) (a) to go fast. (b) to make (s.o.) go faster. **hurried** adj. quick/rushed. **hurriedly** adv. quickly.

hurt 1 [hɜːt] n. pain. **hurt 2** v. (hurt) to give (s.o.). pain/to make (s.o.) sad. **hurtful** adj. which is painful to the feelings/which makes s.o. sad.

hurtle ['hɜːtl] v. to move quickly/to rush dangerously.

husband 1 ['hʌzbənd] n. man who is married to a certain woman. **husband 2** v. (formal) to look after carefully/not to waste (your resources). **husbandry** n. farming; animal h. = rearing of animals on a farm.

hush 1 [hʌʃ] n. quiet. **hush 2** v. to make quiet. **hush-hush** adj. inf. secret. **hush money** n. money paid to s.o. to stop them revealing a secret. **hush up** v. to suppress (a scandal).

husk 1 [hʌsk] n. hard covering of a seed. **husk 2** v. to take the husk off (a seed). **husky 1** ['hʌskɪ] adj. (-ier, -iest) rough/hoarse (voice). **husky 2** n. dog which pulls sledges in the Arctic. **huskily** adv. in a husky voice. **huskiness** n. hoarseness of the voice.

huss [hʌs] n. (pl.huss) small white sea fish.

hussar ['hʌzaː] n. soldier on horseback.

hussy ['hʌsɪ] n. brazen h. = wicked girl/woman.

hustings ['hʌstɪŋz] n. at the h. = during an election campaign.

hustle 1 ['hʌsl] n. rush/violent activity. **hustle 2** v. to push/to hurry (roughly). **hustler** n. person who gets things going/who hurries business along.

hut [hʌt] *n.* small rough house. *usu.* made of wood.

hutch [hʌtʃ] *n.* wooden box to keep rabbits in.

hyacinth ['haɪəsɪnθ] *n.* strongly-scented spring flower grown from a bulb.

hybrid ['haɪbrɪd] *adj. & n.* (plant/animal etc.) produced from two different species.

hydatid ['haɪdætɪd] *adj.* (cyst) caused by a tapeworm.

hydrangea [haɪ'dreɪndʒə] *n.* garden shrub with large blue or pink flowers.

hydrant ['haɪdrənt] *n.* water pipe in a street to which a hose can be attached; fire h. = one to which firemen can attach fire hoses.

hydrate ['haɪdreɪt] *n.* chemical compound with water.

hydraulic [haɪ'drɔːlɪk] *adj.* worked by fluid. **hydraulically** *adv.* using hydraulic force. **hydraulics** *n.* study of fluids used mechanically.

hydro ['haɪdrəʊ] *n.* (*pl.-os*) *inf.* (a) hotel and clinic which specializes in the use of water to cure people. (b) hydroelectric station.

hydro- ['haɪdrəʊ] prefix meaning water.

hydrocarbon [haɪdrəʊ'kɑːbn] *n.* organic compound of hydrogen and carbon.

hydrochloric [haɪdrəʊ'klɒrɪk] *adj.* (acid) made of hydrogen and chlorine.

hydroelectric [haɪdrəʊɪ'lektrɪk] *adj.* referring to hydroelectricity.
hydroelectricity [haɪdrəʊelek'trɪsɪti] *n.* electricity produced by water power.

hydrofoil ['haɪdrəfɔɪl] *n.* boat which skims over the water on thin legs.

hydrogen ['haɪdrədʒən] *n.* (element H) common gas which combines with oxygen to form water; h. bomb = extremely powerful nuclear bomb.

hydrographer [haɪ'drɒɡrəfə] *n.* person who makes maps of the sea or sea bed.

hydrolysis [haɪ'drɒlɪsɪs] *n.* decomposition of a chemical substance by water.

hydrometer [haɪ'drɒmɪtə] *n.* device for measuring the relative density of water.

hydrophobia [haɪdrə'fəʊbɪə] *n.* rabies;

fear of water (usu. a symptom of rabies).

hydroplane ['haɪdrəpleɪn] *n.* powerful flat-bottomed motorboat which skims over the surface of the water.

hydroponics [haɪdrə'pɒnɪks] *n.* science of growing plants in water without using soil.

hydrostatic [haɪdrəʊ'stætɪk] *adj.* referring to fluids at rest.

hydrotherapy [haɪdrə'θerəpɪ] *n.* treatment of sick people with water.

hyena [haɪ'iːnə] *n.* fierce dog-like African animal.

hygiene ['haɪdʒiːn] *n.* keeping clean and free of germs. **hygienic** [haɪ'dʒiːnɪk] *adj.* (which keeps) clean and free of germs. **hygienically** *adv.* in a hygienic way. **hygienist** person who specializes in (esp. dental) hygiene.

hygrometer [haɪ'grɒmɪtə] *n.* instrument for measuring humidity.

hymen ['haɪmen] *n.* thin tissue which covers the entrance to the vagina of a girl who has never had sexual intercourse.

hymn [hɪm] *n.* religious song. **hymnal, hymn-book** ['haɪml] *n.* book of hymns.

hype 1 [haɪp] *n. inf.* excessive publicity. **hype 2** *v.* to publicize (a product) excessively.

hyper- ['haɪpə] prefix meaning to a great degree; hyperactive = very active.

hyperbola [haɪ'pɜːbələ] *n.* type of curve.

hyperbolic [haɪpə'bɒlɪk] *adj.* referring to a hyperbola. **hyperbole** [haɪ'pɜːbəlɪ] *n.* exaggerated comparison.
hyperbolical [haɪpə'bɒlɪkl] *adj.* referring to hyperbole.

hypercritical [haɪpə'krɪtɪkl] *adj.* extremely critical.

hypermarket ['haɪpəmɑːkɪt] *n.* very large supermarket.

hypersensitve [haɪpə'sensɪtɪv] *adj.* very easily offended.

hypertension [haɪpə'tenʃn] *n.* very high blood pressure.

hyphen ['haɪfn] *n.* short line(-) which joins two words or separates one word into parts. **hyphenate** *v.* to join (words) with a hyphen or separate (one word) into parts with a hyphen.
hyphenation [haɪfə'neɪʃn] *n.* act of hyphenating.

hypnosis [hɪpnəʊsɪs] *n.* putting s.o. into a trance, so that they obey your

orders; under h. = while in a trance.
hypnotic *adj.* referring hypnosis.
hypnotically *adv.* referring to
hypnosis. **hypnotism** ['hɪpnətɪzəm] *n.*
use of hypnosis as a medical process or
for amusement. **hypnotist** *n.* person
who practises hypnosis. **hypnotize** *v.*
to put (s.o.) into a trance.

hypo ['haɪpəʊ] *n.* substance used for
fixing the picture when developing a
photograph.

hypo- ['haɪpəʊ] prefix meaning under/
below.

hypocaust ['haɪpəkɔːst] *n.* Roman
heating system, where hot air flowed
under a raised floor.

hypochondria ['haɪpə'kɒndrɪə] *n.*
being permanently worried about your
health. **hypochondriac** *n.* person who
is always worried about his health.

hypocrisy [hɪ'pɒkrəsɪ] *n.* pretending to
be the opposite of what you really are/to
feel the opposite of what you really feel.
hypocrite ['hɪpəkrɪt] *n.* hypocritical
person. **hypocritical** [hɪpə'krɪtɪkl] *adj.*
referring to hypocrisy.

hypodermic [haɪpə'dɜːmɪk] *adj.* h.
syringe/needle = medical instrument
used for injections just below the surface
of the skin.

hypotension [haɪpəʊ'tenʃn] *n.* very
low blood pressure.

hypotenuse [haɪpɒtənjuːz] *n.* longest
side of a right-angled triangle.

hypothermia [haɪpə'θɜːmɪə] *n.* state
where the temperature of the body is
abnormally low.

hypothesis [haɪ'pɒθəsɪs] *n.* (*pl.*-
theses[-θəsiːz]) suggestion that sth is
true, though without proof.

hypothetical [haɪpə'θetɪkl] *adj.*
suggested as true but necessarily so.
hypothetically *adv.* in a hypothetical
way.

hysterectomy [hɪstə'rektəmɪ] *n.*
surgical operation to remove a woman's
womb.

hysteria [hɪ'stɪərɪə] *n.* nervous
excitement leading to wild fits of
laughing or crying. **hystrical** [hɪ'sterɪkl]
adj. suffering from hysteria; laughing/
crying in a wild manner. **hysterically**
adv. in and uncontrollable way.

hysterics *n.* *pl.*attack of hysteria.

Ii

I, i [aɪ] to dot one's i's and cross one's
t's = to be very careful to settle the final
details.

I [aɪ] pronoun referring to the speaker. **I**
symbol for iodine.

iamb ['aɪæmb] *n.* Greek poetic
measure, formed of a short and a long
syllable. **iambic** *adj.* referring to
iambs.

Iberian [aɪbɪːərɪən] *adj.* referring to
Spain and Portugal.

ibex ['aɪbeks] *n.* (*pl.*ibex(es)) mountain
goat with large curved horns.

ibid, ibidem ['ɪbɪd(em)] *adv.* in the
same way.

ibis ['aɪbɪs] *n.* tropical water bird with
long legs and a curved bill.

i/c ['aɪ'sɪ] *abbrev.* for in charge.

ice 1 [aɪs] *n.* (a) frozen water; to break
the i.= to bring an embarrassing silence
to an end; to keep sth on i. = not do
anything about it for the moment. (b) ice
creAm. (c) dry i. = frozen carbondioxide.
ice 2 *v.* (a) to cool with ice. (b) to
freeze. (c) to cover with sugar icing. **Ice
age** *n.* geological period when parts of
the world were covered with ice. **ice
axe** *n.* axe used by mountaineers to cut
footholds in ice. **iceberg** *n.* large
floating mass of ice at sea; tip of the i. =
small part of sth (usu. unpleasant) which
makes you eventually discover the rest.
icebox *n.* (a) box containing ice to
keep food or drink cool. (b) *Am.*
refrigerator. **ice- breaker** *n.* boat
specially strengthened to break up ice in
shipping lanes. **ice cream** *n.* frozen
sweet made of cream and flavouring.
icefield *n.* large area of ice floating on
the sea. **icefloe** *n.* sheet of ice floating
in the sea. **ice hockey** *n.* form of
hockey played on ice. **icehouse** *n.*
house for storing ice during the summer.
Icelander *n.* person from Iceland.
Icelandic. 1 *adj.* referring to Iceland.
Icelandic. 2 *n.* language spoken in
Iceland. **icicle** *n.* long hanging piece of
ice formed by dripping water in cold
weather. **icily** *adv.* in a cold/unfriendly
way. **iciness** *n.* bitter coldness (of

weather/of greeting). **icing** *n.* sugar topping for a cake; i. sugar = very fine sugar for covering cakes. **icy** *adj.* (-ier, -iest) (a) covered with ice. (b) very cold/unwelcoming.

ichneumon fly [ɪkˈnjuːmən ˈflaɪ] *n.* insect. whose larvae live on other insects.

icon [ˈaɪkən] *n.* (a) picture of Christ or a saint in the Eastern Christian church. (b) little pictorial symbol on a computer screen. **iconoclast** [aɪˈkɒnəklæst] *n.* person who attacks beliefs which are held by many people. **iconoclastic** [aɪkɒnəˈklæstɪk] *adj.* which attacks beliefs which are held by many people. **iconography** *n.* the study of icons; the study of pictures of a particular subject.

id [ɪd] *n.* the basic unconscious drives in a person.

I'd [aɪd] short for I would/I had/I should.

idea [aɪˈdɪə] *n.* thought/plan in the mind; I had no i. = I did not know.

ideal 1 [aɪˈdɪəl] *n.* summit of perfection; man of ideals = person who has standards of perfection. **ideal 2** *adj.* perfect; very suitable. **idealism** *n.* aiming at achieving an ideal. **idealist** *n.* person who aims at achieving an ideal; impractical person. **idealistic** *adj.* aiming at an ideal; too perfect. **idealize** *v.* to make (s.o.) seem perfect. **ideally** *adv.* if everything were perfect.

identify [aɪˈdentɪfaɪ] *v.* (a) to say who s.o. is/what sth is (b) to state that sth belongs to you. (c) to i. with = to feel you have the same characteristics as (s.o.); to have a feeling of sympathy for (s.o./sth). **identical** *adj.* (with/to) exactly the same as. **identically** *adv.* in exactly the same way. **identifiable** *adj.* which can be identified. **identification** [aɪdentɪfɪˈkeɪʃn] *n.* saying who s.o. is/who sth belongs to; i. parade = line of people at a police station from whom a witness is asked to identify the criminal. **identikit** *n.* method of making a portrait of a criminal using pieces of photographs or drawings of different faces to form a composite picture. **identity** *n.* (a) who s.o. is; i. card = card which shows a photograph of the holder, with the name, date of birth and other details; i. parade =

identification parade. (b) being the same/being identical.

ideogram [ˈɪdɪəʊgræm] *n.* picture/character which represents a word.

ideology [aɪdɪˈɒlədʒɪ] *n.* theory of life based on political or economic philosophy rather than religious belief. **ideological** [aɪdɪəˈlɒdʒɪkl] *adj.* referring to ideology.

ides [aɪdz] *npl.* in the Latin calendar, the 15th of some months and the 13th of others.

idiocy [ˈɪdɪəsɪ] *n.* see idiot.

idiom [ˈɪdɪəm] *n.* (a) characteristic way of speaking/of writing. (b) particular expression where the words do not have their literal meaning. **idiomatic** [ɪdɪəˈmætɪk] *adj.* referring to a particular way of speaking.

idiosyncrasy [ɪdɪəʊsɪŋkrəsɪ] *n.* particular way of behaving. **idiosyncratic** [ɪdɪəʊsɪŋˈkrætɪk] *adj.* odd/peculiar; particular to one person.

idiot [ˈɪdɪət] *n.* (a) mentally deficient person. (b) person who is stupid. **idiocy** *n.* stupidity. **idiotic** [ɪdɪˈotɪk] *adj.* stupid. **idiotically** *adv.* in a stupid way.

idle 1 [ˈaɪdl] *adj.* (idler, idlest) (a) lazy. (b) not working, (c) aimless/not worthwhile. **idle 2** *v.* (a) not to work; to spend time doing nothing. (b) (of an engine) to run gently. **idleness** *n.* laziness. **idler** *n.* person who idles. **idly** *adv.* (a) lazily. (b) without being involved.

idol [ˈaɪdl] *n.* (a) statue of a god. (b) favourite person. (c) star performer (who is worshipped by fans). **idolater** *n.* person who worships idols. **idolatry** [aɪˈdɒlətrɪ] *n.* worship of idols. **idolize** *v.* to worship.

idyll [ˈɪdɪl] *n.* pleasant/happy scene. **idyllic** [ɪˈdɪlɪk] *adj.* pleasant/happy (in a romantic way). **idyllically** *adv.* in a idyllic way.

i.e. [ˈaɪˈiː] abbrev. for id est. meaning that is.

if 1 [ɪf] *conj.* (a) (showing what might happen) if it rains the ground gets wet. (b) showing supposition) if only to please him. (c) (exclamation) if only I had known! (d) whether; do you know if the plane is late? (e) although; he is nice, if rather lazy, (f) at any time when. **if 2** *n.* *inf.* undecided question.

igloo ['ɪgluː] n. dome-shaped shelter built by Eskimos out of blocks of snow.

igneous ['ɪgnɪəs] adj. (rock) which was originally formed from solidified lava.

ignite [ɪgnaɪt] v. to set fire to; to catch fire. **ignition** [ɪg'uɪʃn] n. (in a car) electrical device which makes the spark which fires the petrol; i. key = key used to switch on the ignition.

ignoble [ɪg'nəubl] adj. (formal) unworthy.

ignominy ['ɪgnəmɪnɪ] n. shame/ disgrace. **ignominious** [ɪgnə'mɪnɪəs] adj. shameful. **ignominiously** adv. in an ignominious way.

ignore [ɪg'nɔː] v. not to notice (on purpose). **ignoramus** [ɪgnə'reɪməs] n. (pl.-es) person who is stupid/who knows nothing. **ignorance** ['ɪgnərəns] n. not knowing. **ignorant** ['ɪgnərənt] adj. not knowing/stupid. **ignorantly** adv. stupidly.

iguana [ɪgjʊ'ɑːnə] kind of large tropical lizard.

ileum ['ɪlɪəm] n. long part of the small intestine.

ilium ['ɪlɪəm] n. top part of the hip bone.

ilk [ɪlk] n. inf. sort/type.

ill 1 [ɪl] adj. (worse, worst) (a) sick; not well. (b) bad. **ill 2** n. bad thing. **ill 3** adv. badly. **ill-advised** adj. not recommended. **ill-bred** adj. badly brought up; with bad manners. ill-fated, adj. fated to fail. **ill-feeling** n. resentment; dislike. **ill-gotten** adj. illegally acquired. **ill-mannered** adj. badly behaved/with bad manners/rude. **illness** n. sickness. **ill-starred** adj. fated to fail. **ill-treat** v. to treat (animals/children) badly. **ill will** n. to bear s.o. ill will = to want sth bad to happen to s.o..

I'll [aɪl] short for I will/I shall.

illegal [ɪ'liːgl] adj. against the law. **illegality** n. being illegal. **illegally** adv. against the law.

illegible [ɪ'ledʒɪbl] adj. (writing) which cannot be read. **illegibility** n. being illegible. **illegibly** adv. in an illegible way.

illegitimate [ɪlɪ'dʒɪtəmət] adj. (a) (person) born of unmarried parents. (b) against the law. **illegitimately** adv. in

an illegitimate way. **illegitimacy** n. being illegitimate.

illicit [ɪ'lɪsɪt] adj. against the law/illegal. **illicitly** adv. in an illicit way.

illiteracy [ɪ'lɪtərəsɪ] n. inability to read and write. **illiterate** adj. & n. (person) who cannot read or write.

illogical [ɪ'lɒdʒɪkl] adj. not sensible/ not reasonable **illogically** adv. in an illogical way. **illogicality** [ɪlɒdʒɪ'kælɪtɪ] n. being illogical.

illuminate [ɪ'luːmɪneɪt] v. (a) to light up. (b) to draw coloured initials/pictures in a manuscript. **illuminating** adj. which throws light on (a subject). **illumination** [ɪluːmɪ'neɪʃn] n. (a) flood lighting; decoration. (b) coloured initial illustration in a manuscript.

illusion [ɪ'luːʒn] n. impression which is not true; optical i. = thing which appears different from what it really is because the eye is being deceived. **illusionist** n. person who entertains with optical illusions.

illusive adj. false. **illusory** adj. which is an illusion

illustrate ['ɪləstreɪt] v. (a) to add pictures to. (b) to give/to be an example of. **illustration** [ɪlə'streɪʃn] n. (a) picture (in a book). (b) example. **illustrative** ['ɪləstrətɪv] adj. which illustrates/which is an example. **illustrator** ['ɪləstreɪtə] n. person who draws the pictures for a book.

illustrious [ɪ'lʌstrnəs] adj. very famous.

I'm [aɪm] short for I am

image ['ɪmɪdʒ] n. (a) portrait/statue; inf. he's spitting i. of his father = he looks exactly like his father. (b) idea which other people have of a person/a company. (c) picture produced by a lens/ seen in a mirror. (d) comparison/symbols used esp. in poetry. **imagery** n. using comparison/symbols (in writing) as a way of making people imagine things.

imagine [ɪ'mædʒɪn] v. to picture (sth) in your mind. **imaginable** adj. which you can imagine. **imaginary** adj. false/ not real. **imagination** [ɪmædʒɪ'neɪʃn] n. ability to picture things in your mind. **imaginative** [ɪ'mædʒɪnətɪv] adj. (artist) with a strong imagination; (drawing/poem) which shows a lot of imagination. **imaginatively** adv. in an

imaginative way. **imago** [ɪˈmɑːgəʊ] *n.*
final form of an insect (such as a
butterfly) after the larval and pupal
stages.

imam [ˈɪmæm] *n.* Muslim priest.

imbalance [ɪmˈbæləns] *n.* lack of
balance.

imbecile [ˈɪmbəsiːl] *n.* (a) mentally
deficient person. (b) stupid person.

imbecility [ɪmbəˈsɪlɪtɪ] *n.* being
mentally deficient.

imbibe [ɪmˈbaɪb] *v.* (formal) to drink.

imbricated [ˈɪmbrɪkeɪtɪd] *adj.*
overlapping.

imbroglio [ɪmˈbrəʊljəʊ] *n.* (*pl.*-os)
complicated plot.

imbue [ɪmˈbjuː] *v.* (formal) to fill with a
feeling.

IMF [aɪemˈef] abbrev. for International
Monetary Fund.

imitate [ˈɪmɪteɪt] *v.* to copy/to do like
(s.o.). **imitation** [ɪmɪˈteɪʃn] *n.* copy; act
of imitating. **imitative** [ˈɪmɪtətɪv] *adj.*
which copies. **imitator** [ˈɪmɪteɪtə] *n.*
person who copies.

immaculate [ɪˈmækjʊlət] *adj.*
extremely clean/tidy. **immaculacy** *n.*
being immaculate. **immaculately** *adv.*
extremely tidily.

immanent [ˈɪmənənt] *adj.* existing as
an inherent part.

immaterial [ɪməˈtʃʊə] *adj.* not
important.

immature *adj.* not mature/not fully
grown/not fully developed. **immaturity**
n. not being mature.

immeasurable [ɪˈmeʒrəbl] *adj.* which
cannot be measured/very large.
immeasurably *adv.* enormously.

immediate [ɪˈmiːdjət] *adj.* (a) close/
nearest. (b) very soon. **immediacy** *n.*
being immediate. **immediately** *adv.* &
conj. straight away.

immemorial [ɪməˈmɔːrɪəl] *adj.* from
time i. = from very ancient times.

immense [ɪˈmens] *adj.* huge/very
wide/enormous. **immensely** *adv.* very
much. **immensity** *n.* vastness/huge
size.

immerse [ɪˈmɜːs] *v.* to plunge (sth) in a
liquid. **immersion** [ɪˈmɜːʃn] *n.*
plunging (into a liquid); i. heater =
heater inside a water tank.

immigrate [ˈɪmɪgreɪt] *v.* to come to
settle in a country. **immigrant** *n.*

person who comes to a country to settle.

immigration [ɪmɪˈgreɪʃn] *n.* settling in
a new country; i. office = office dealing
with immigrants; i. controls =
restrictions placed by a country on the
numbers of immigrants.

imminent [ˈɪmɪnənt] *adj.* which is
about to happen. **imminence** *n.* being
about to happen.

immobile [ɪˈməʊbaɪl] *adj.* without
moving; unable to move. **immobility**
[ɪməˈbɪlɪtɪ] *n.* state of not moving.
immobilization [ɪməʊbɪlaɪˈzeɪʃn] *n.*
stopping sth moving. **immobilize**
[ɪˈməʊbɪlaɪz] *v.* to stop (sth) moving.

immoderate [ɪˈmɒdərət] *adj.*
extravagant/not moderate.
immoderately *adv.* in an immoderate
way.

immodest [ɪˈmɒdɪst] *adj.* not modest.

immolate [ˈɪməʊleɪt] *v.* (poetic) to
sacrifice.

immoral [ɪˈmɒrəl] *adj.* not concerned
with the principles of good behaviour.
immorality [ɪməˈrælɪtɪ] *n.* lack of
morality. **immorally** *adv.* in an
immoral way.

immortal 1 [ɪˈmɔːtl] *adj.* like a god;
who never dies. **immortal 2** *n.* god.
who never dies. **immortality**
[ɪmɔːˈtælɪtɪ] *n.* being immortal/never
dying. **immortalize** [ɪˈmɔːtəlaɪz] *v.* to
make (s.o) be remembered forever.

immovable [ɪˈmuːvəbl] *adj.* which
cannot be moved. **immovably** *adv.* in
an immovable way.

immune [ɪˈmjuːn] *adj.* (to) (person)
who cannot catch a disease. **immunity**
n. (a) protection (against a disease). (b)
protection against arrest; parliamentary/
diplomatic i. = protection of members of
parliament/diplomats against being
arrested. **immunization**
[ɪmjʊnaɪˈzeɪʃn] *n.* giving protection
against a disease. **immunize**
[ˈɪmjʊnaɪz] *v.* to give protection against
a disease. **immunology** *n.* study of
immunity.

immure [ɪˈmjʊə] *v.* to shut (s.o) in
prison.

immutable [ɪˈmjuːtəbl] *adj.* (formal)
which cannot be changed/which does not
change. **immutability** *n.* being
immutable, **immutably** *adv.* in an
immutable way.

imp [ɪmp] *n.* small devil; wicked child.

impact ['ɪmpækt] *n.* forceful shock/ effect. **impacted** [ɪm'pæktɪd] *adj.* (tooth) which is stuck in the jaw and cannot grow.

impair [ɪm'peə] *v.* to harm. **impairment** *n.* harm

impala [ɪm'pɑːlə] *n.* large African antelope.

impale [ɪm'peɪl] *v.* to jab a sharp object through (s.o.'s body).

impalpable [ɪm'pælpəbl] *adj.* (formal) which cannot be touched.

impart [ɪm'pɑːt] *v.* (formal) to pass on/ to communicate (sth to s.o.).

impartial [ɪm'pɑːʃl] *adj.* not biased. **impartiality** *n.* being impartial. **impartially** *adv.* in an impartial way.

impassable [ɪm'pɑːsəbl] *adj.* which you cannot go through or across. **impasse** ['æmpæs] *n.* deadlock/state where two sides cannot agree.

impassioned [ɪm'pæʃnd] *adj.* very deeply felt/excited (speech).

impassive [ɪm'pæsɪv] *adj.* expressionless. **impassively** *adv.* in an impassive way.

impatient [ɪm'peɪʃnt] *adj.* (a) (with) not patient; unable to wait for sth. (b) in a hurry (to do sth). **impatience** *n.* lack of patience. **impatiently** *adv.* in a hurried way/not patiently.

impeach [ɪm'piːtʃ] *v.* to charge(s.o) with treason or crime against the state. **impeachment** *n.* act of impeaching.

impeccable [ɪm'pekəbl] *adj.* perfect/ perfectly correct. **impeccably** *adv.* perfectly.

impecunious [ɪmpɪ'kjuːnɪəs] *adj.* (formal) with no money.

impede [ɪm'piːd] *v.* to get in the way of (sth) to prevent (sth) happening. **impedance** [ɪm'piːdəns] *n.* resistance to an electric current.

impediment [ɪm'pedɪmənt] *n.* obstacle; speech i. = stammer, etc., which prevents you speaking clearly. **impedimenta** *n. pl.* heavy/awkward baggage or equipment.

impel [ɪm'pel] *v.* (impelled) to push/to force.

impending [ɪm'pendɪŋ] *adj.* imminent/ about to happen.

impenetrable [ɪm'penɪtrəbl] *adj.* which you cannot go through or into.

impenetrability *n.* being impenetrable.

impenitent [ɪm'penɪtənt] *adj.* not penitent/not sorry for having done sth wrong.

imperative [ɪm'perətɪv] *adj.* (a) urgent/obligatory. (b) (in grammar) verb in the i. = verb used as a command.

imperceptible [ɪmpə'septɪbl] *adj.* which you can hardly notice. **imperceptibly** *adv.* scarcely noticeably.

imperfect [ɪm'pɜːfɪkt] *adj.* not perfect/ not complete. **imperfection** [ɪmpə'fekʃn] *n.* flaw.

imperial [ɪm'pɪərɪəl] *adj.* (a) referring to an empire. (b) (weights/measures) used in the UK and the British Commonwealth. **imperialism** *n.* belief in the good of building an empire **imperialist. 1** *n.* person who builds an empire. **imperialist 2** *adj.* (also imperialistic) referring to imperialism.

imperil [ɪm'perɪl] *v.* (imperilled) (formal) to put in danger.

imperious [ɪm'pɪərɪəs] *adj.* arrogant (way of giving orders). **imperiously** *adv.* in an imperious way.

impermanent [ɪm'pɜːmənənt] *adj.* not permanent/not lasting

impermeable [ɪm'pɜːmɪəbl] *adj.* which liquids cannot go through.

impersonal [ɪm'pɜːsnl] *adj.* (a) without a personal touch. (b) (verb) used without a person or thing as the subject. **impersonally** *adv.* in an impersonal way.

impersonate [ɪm'pɜːsəneɪt] *v.* to imitate (s.o.) /to disguise yourself as (s.o) **impersonation** *n.* act of impersonating **impersonator** *n.* person who impersonates.

impertinence [ɪm'pɜːtɪnəns] *n.* rudeness/insolence. **impertinent** *adj.* rude/insolent. **impertinently** *adv.* in an impertinent way.

imperturbable [ɪmpə'tɜːbəbl] *adj.* calm. **imperturbability** *n.* being imperturbable. **imperturbably** *adv.* calmly.

impervious [ɪm'pɜːvɪəs] *adj.* (to) which liquids cannot go through.

impetigo [ɪmp'taɪɡəʊ] *n.* contagious disease of the skin (esp. in children).

impetuous [ɪmˈpetjʊəs] *adj.* thoughtless/hasty (act); (person) who rushes to do sth without thinking. **impetuosity** [ɪmpetjʊˈɒsɪtɪ] *n.* rushing to do sth without thinking. **impetuously** [ɪmˈpetjʊəslɪ] *adv.* without thinking

impetus [ˈɪmpətəs] *n.* (pl -es) movement forward.

impinge [ɪmˈpɪndʒ] *v.* (on) to affect

impious [ˈɪmpɪəs] *adj.* not pious/not religious. **impiety** [ɪmˈpaɪətɪ] *n.* being impious.

impish [ˈɪmpɪʃ] *adj.* like an imp.

implacable [ɪmˈplækəbl] *adj.* who/ which cannot be satisfied. **implacably** *adv.* in an implacable way.

implant 1 [ˈɪmplɑːnt] *n.* tissue which has been implanted. **implant 2** *v.* to fix (sth) in deeply.

implausible [ɪmˈplɔːzəbl] *adj.* not likely to be true.

implement 1 [ˈɪmplɪmənt] *n.* tool/ instrument. **implement 2** [ˈɪmplɪment] *v.* to put into effect. **implementation** [ɪmplɪmənˈtenʃn] *n.* putting into effect.

implicate [ˈɪmplɪkeɪt] *v.* to I.s.o. in sth = to suggest that s.o. was connected with sth. **implication** [ɪmplɪˈkeɪʃn] *n.* (a) suggestion (that s.o. is connected with a crime). (b) thing which is implied

implicit [ɪmˈplɪsɪt] *adj.* which is not definitely said, but is suggested. **implicitly** *adv.* without questioning.

implore [ɪmˈplɔː] *v.* to beg (s.o. to do sth).

imply [ɪmˈplaɪ] *v.* to suggest

impolite [ɪmpəˈlaɪt] *adj.* rude/not polite. **impolitely** *adv.* rudely, **impoliteness** *n.* lack of politeness **impolitic** [ɪmˈpɒlɪtɪk] *adj.* (formal) not wise

imponderables [ɪmˈpɒndrəblz] *n. pl.* things whose importance you cannot easily calculate.

import 1 [ˈɪmpɔːt] *n.* (a) imports = goods which are brought into a country; i. duty = tax paid on goods brought into a country; i. controls = rules limiting goods which can be brought into a country. (b) (formal) meaning (of words). **import 2** [ɪmˈpɔːt] *v.* to bring goods into a country. **importation** [ɪmpɔːˈteɪʃn] *n.* act of importing; goods imported. **importer** [ɪmˈpɔːtə] *n.*

person or country which imports.

importance [ɪmˈpɔːtns] *n.* seriousness/ serious effect/influence. **important** *adj.* (a) serious/with a serious effect/which matters a great deal. (b) with great influence/holding an influential position. **importantly** *adv.* seriously/with a serious effect.

importune [ɪmˈpɔːtjuːn] *v.* (formal) to pester/to bother (s.o.) **importunate** [ɪmˈpɔːtjʊnət] *adj.* pestering/bothering.

impose [ɪmˈpəʊz] *v.* (a) to inflict. (b) to i. on = cause trouble/inconvenience. **imposing** [ɪmˈpəʊzɪn] *adj.* grand/ solemn. **imposition** *n.* (a) making people pay a tax; laying down (of conditions). (b) taking advantage (of s.o.). (c) unfair duty; punishment (in school).

impossible [ɪmˈpɒsɪbl] *adj.* (a) which cannot be done. (b) awkward/difficult (person/situation). **impossibility** *n.* being impossible. **impossibly** *adv.* in an impossible way; *inf.* greatly.

impostor [ɪmˈpɒstə] *n.* person who pretends to be s.o. else. **imposture** [ɪmˈpɒstʃə] *n.* pretending to be s.o. else.

impotence [ˈɪmpətəns] *n.* (a) lack of strength. (b) (of man) inability to have sexual intercourse. **impotent** *adj.* (a) weak. (b) (of man) unable to have sexual intercourse. **impotently** *adv.* without being able to act.

impound [ɪmˈpaʊnd] *v.* to take (sth) away and put it in a safe place.

impoverish [ɪmˈpɒvərɪʃ] *v.* to make poor. **impoverishment** *n.* making poor.

impracticable [ɪmˈpræktɪkəbl] *adj.* (plan) which cannot work; (road) which cannot be used. **impractical** [ɪmˈpræktɪkl] *adj.* (plan) which is not easy to put into practice; (person) who is not good at doing things with his hands.

imprecation [ɪmprɪˈkeɪʃn] *n.* (formal) oath/curse.

imprecise [ɪmprɪˈsaɪs] *adj.* not precise/ not accurate. **imprecision** *n.* lack of precision.

impregnable [ɪmˈpregnəbl] *adj.* (castle) which cannot be captured. **impregnability** *n.* being impregnable

impregnate [ˈɪmpregneɪt] *v.* (a) to soak (with sth) (b) to make pregnant. **impregnation** *n.* act of impregnating.

impresario [ɪmprɪ'sɑːrɪəʊ] *n.* (pl -os) person who organizes concerts and operas.

impress [ɪm'pres] *v.* (a) to make (s.o.) admire/respect s.o./sth. (b) to i. sth on s.o. = to make him understand. (c) to stamp (a pattern on sth). **impression** [ɪm'preʃn] *n.* (a) effect on s.o.'s mind. (b) imitation of how s.o. talks/behaves. (c) mark (of a pattern). (d) printing (of a book). **impressionable** *adj.* (person) who is easily influenced (by others). **impressionism** *n.* art movement where painters tried to convey an impression of reality. In particular of light. **impressionist. 1** *adj.* referring to impressionism. **impressionist 2** *n.* painter in the impressionist movement. **impressionistic** [ɪmpreʃə'nɪstɪk] *adj.* vague/sketchy. **impressive** [ɪm'presɪv] *adj.* which commands respect. **impressively** *adv.* in an impressive way.

imprest ['ɪmprest] *n.* system of purchasing by a government department.

imprimatur [ɪmprɪ'mɑːtə] *n.* official permission to print a book.

imprint 1 ['ɪmprɪnt] *n.* (a) mark made by sth pressed down. (b) name of publishing firm printed in a book.

imprint 2 *v.* to stamp/to mark.

imprison [ɪm'prɪzn] *v.* to put/to keep in prison. **imprisonment** *n.* putting/keeping in prison.

improbable [ɪm'prɒbəbl] *adj.* not probable; unlikely. **improbability** *n.* lack of probability. **improbably** *adv.* not likely.

impromptu [ɪm'prɒmptjuː] *adj. & adv.* without any rehearsal or practice

improper [ɪm'prɒpə] *adj.* (a) rude. (b) (word) used in a wrong way. **improperly** *adv.* (a) not correctly. (b) (word which is used) wrongly.

impropriety [ɪmprə'praɪətɪ] *n.* being improper; improper action.

improve [ɪm'pruːv] *v.* to make/to get better. improvement, n. thing which makes better/is better.

improvident [ɪm'prɒvɪdənt] *adj.* (person) who spends too much money or who does not plan for the future. **improvidence** *n.* being improvident. **improvidently** *adv.* not thinking about saving for the future.

improvise ['ɪmprəvaɪz] *v.* to do/to make (sth) without preparation. **improvisation** [ɪmprəvaɪ'zeɪʃn] *n.* making sth without any preparation.

imprudent [ɪm'pruːdənt] *adj.* careless/ not prudent. **imprudently** *adv.* in an imprudent way.

impudent ['ɪmpjʊdənt] *adj.* rude/ cheeky. **impudence** *n.* rudeness/ cheekiness. **impudently** *adv.* rudely/ cheekily.

impugn [ɪm'pjuːn] *v.* (formal) to attack (s.o's character/the truth of a statement).

impulse ['ɪmpʌls] *n.* (a) shock(which makes sth move/work). (b) sudden feeling/decision; i. buying = buying goods on the basis of a sudden decision. **impulsive** [ɪm'pʌlsɪv] *adj.* acting on a sudden decision/without thinking. **impulsively** *adv.* in an impulsive way. **impulsiveness** *n.* being impulsive.

impunity [ɪm'pjuːnɪtɪ] *n.* with i. = without risk of punishment.

impure [ɪm'pjʊə] *adj.* not pure. **impurities** [ɪm'pjʊərɪtɪz] *n. pl.* substances which make sth impure.

impute [ɪm'pjuːt] *v.* to attribute (sth to s.o.) to say that (sth) is caused by (s.o./ sth) **imputation** *n.* saying that s.o. is at fault.

in 1 [ɪn] *prep & adv.* (a) (showing place) in Russia; in bed. (b) (showing time) in autumn; in January; long skirts are in = fashionable. (c) one in ten = one out of ten. (d) (showing state) dressed in pink; in public; *inf.* all in = tired out; all in price = including everything. **in 2** *n.* the ins and outs = the intricate details. **in 3** *adj inf.* fashionable. **in for** *adv.* to be in for sth = to be about to get sth. **in on** *adv.* to be in on (a secret) = to know a secret. **in tray** *n.* file/basket for incoming letters.

inability [ɪnə'bɪlɪtɪ] *n.* being unable to (to)

inaccessible [ɪnək'sesɪbl] *adj.* impossible to reach.

inaccurate [ɪn'ækjʊrət] *adj.* not exact/ not accurate.

inaccurately *adv.* not accurately. **inaccuracy** *n.* not being exact; lack of accuracy.

inactive [ɪn'æktɪv] *adj.* not active/not doing anything. **inaction, inactivity** [ɪnæk'tɪvɪtɪ] *n.* lack of action/doing nothing.

inadequate [ɪn'ædɪkwət] *adj.* (a) not enough/insufficient. (b) not competent enough. **inadequacy** *n.* being inadequate. **inadequately** *adv.* not enough; insufficiently.

inadmissible [ɪnəd'mɪsəbl] *adj.* (evidence) not allowed to be presented in a court.

inadvertent [ɪnəd'vɜːtbɪt] *adj.* said/done by mistake, not on purpose. **inadvertence** *n.* being inadvertent; thing done invertently. **inadvertently** *adv.* by mistake.

inadvisable [ɪnəd'vaɪzəbl] *adj.* unwise/not recommended.

inalienable [ɪn'eɪljənəbl] *adj.* (formal) which cannot be taken away or refused.

inane [ɪ'neɪn] *adj.* stupid. **inanity** [ɪn'ænɪtɪ] *n.* being stupid.

inanimate [ɪn'ænɪmət] *adj.* not alive.

inapplicable [nə'plɪkəbl] *adj.* unsuitable/which does not apply (to).

inappropriate [ɪnə'prəʊprɪət] *adj.* (to) not appropriate/not suitable/not fitting the circumstances.

inaptitude [ɪn'æptɪtjuːd] *n.* (for) unsuitableness, lack of ability.

inarticulate [ɪnɑː'tɪkjʊlət] *adj.* (a) not speaking clearly. (b) unable to speak.

inartistic [ɪnɑː'tɪstɪk] *adj.* not artistic; not concerned with the arts.

inasmuch as [ɪnəz'mʌtʃæz] *conj.* (formal) seeing that/owing to the fact that.

inattentive [ɪnə'tentɪv] *adj.* not paying attention/not attentive. **inattention** *n.* not paying attention.

inaudible [ɪn'ɔːdɪbl] *adj.* which cannot be heard. **inaudibly** *adv.* so quietly that it cannot be heard.

inaugurate [ɪn'ɔːgjʊreɪt] *v.* to swear in (a new president); to open officially a new building/a festival, etc. **inaugural** *adj.* (speech) given at an opening ceremony; first (use); opening (ceremony). **inauguration** [ɪnɔːgjʊ'reɪʃn] *n.* swearing in (of a new president); official opening.

inauspicious [ɪnɔː'spɪʃəs] *adj.* unlucky/not giving hope for the future.

inboard [ɪn'bɔːd] *adj.* inside a boat.

inborn [ɪn'bɔːn] *adj.* (feelings/ideas) which a person has had since birth.

inbred [ɪn'bred] *adj.* (feelings/ideas) which a person has had since a very

young age. **inbreeding** *n.* breeding between closely related persons/animals, etc.

Inc. [ɪn'kɔːpəreɪtɪd] *Am.* Short for incorporated.

incalculable [ɪn'kælkjʊləbl] *adj.* which cannot be calculated/so large that it cannot be measured.

in camera [ɪn'kæmərə] *adv.* in secret; not in public.

incandescent [ɪnkær'desnt] *adj.* which burns with a very bright light. **incandescence** *n.* very bright light.

incantation [ɪnkæn'teɪʃn] *n.* magic words.

incapable [ɪn'keɪpəbl] *adj.* (a) (of) not able; drunk and i.= so drunk that you cannot stand up. (b) not capable; not competent. **incapability** [ɪnkeɪpə'bɪlɪtɪ] *n.* incompetence/not being capable.

incapacity [ɪn'kə'pæsɪtɪ] *n.* lack of strength/ability to do sth. **incapacitate** *v.* to make (s.o.) unable to do sth.

incarcerate [ɪn'kɑːsəreɪt] *v.* (formal) to put/to keep in prison. **incarceration** [ɪnkɑːsə'reɪʃn] *n.* putting/keeping in prison.

incarnate [ɪn'kɑːnət] *adj.* in human form. **incarnation** [ɪnkɑː'neɪʃn] *n.* appearance in human form.

incautious [ɪn'kɔːʃəs] *adj.* not prudent. **incautiously** *adv.* rashly.

incendiary 1 [ɪn'sendjərɪ] *adj.* which causes fire **incendiary 2** *n.* (a) bomb which causes fire. (b) person who sets fire to buildings.

incense 1 ['ɪnsens] *n.* spice powder which when burnt gives a strong smell. **incense 2** [ɪn'sens] *v.* to make (s.o.) annoyed.

incentive [ɪn'sentɪv] *n.* thing which encourages; i. bonus = extra money paid when production is increased.

inception [ɪn'sepʃn] *n.* beginning

incessant [ɪn'sesnt] *adj.* unceasing/continuous.

incest ['ɪnsest] *n.* sexual intercourse with a close member of a family. **incestuous** [ɪn'sestjʊəs] *adj.* referring to incest

inch 1 [ɪnʃ] *n.* (*pl.*-es) measure of length (2.54 cm.) **inch 2** *v.* to go (slowly)

inchoate [ɪn'kəʊeɪt] *adj.* (formal) not fully developed.

incident ['ɪnsɪdənt] *n.* (a) minor happening. (b) *usu.* violent) action/disturbance. **incidence** *n.* rate.

incidental [ɪnsɪ'dentl] *adj. & n.* (thing) which happens in connection with sth else, but forming an unimportant part; subsidiary; i. music = background music which accompanies a film; i. expenses = secondary expenses. **Incidentally** *adv.* by the way.

incinerate [ɪnsɪnəreɪt] *v.* to destroy by burning. **incineration** [ɪnsɪnə'reɪʃn] *n.* destruction by burning. **incinerator** *n.* furnace for burning rubbish.

incipient [ɪn'sɪpɪənt] *adj.* which is beginning/coming.

incise [ɪn'saɪz] *v.* to make a cut in (esp. a stone). **incision** [ɪn'sɪʒn] *n.* cut. **incisive** [ɪn'saɪsɪv] *adj.* sharp/cutting. **incisively** *adv.* sharply. **incisor** [ɪn'saɪzə] *n.* sharp front tooth for cutting.

incite [ɪn'saɪt] *v.* to encourage (s.o. to do sth) **incitement** *n.* encouragement (to)

incivility [ɪnsɪ'vɪlɪtɪ] *n.* (formal) rudeness.

inclement [ɪn'klemənt] *adj.* (formal) (of weather) bad.

incline 1 ['ɪnklaɪn] *n.* slope. **incline 2** *v.* (a) to slope (b) to encourage (s.o.) to do sth (c) to tend (d) to bend/to bow. **inclination** [ɪnklɪ'neɪʃn] *n.* (a) (angle of) slope. (b) slight bow (of the head). (c) tendency **inclined** *adj.* (a) sloping. (b) likely (to do sth).

include [ɪn'kluːd] *v.* to count (s.o./sth) along with others. **inclusion** [ɪn'kluːʒn] *n.* counting s.o./sth in among others. **inclusive** *adj.* which includes everything from Monday to Friday i.= including both Monday and Friday.

incognito [ɪnkɒg'niːtəʊ] *adv. & n.* to travel i.= under a false name or identity; he kept his i. = people did not find out who he really was.

incoherent [ɪnkəʊ'hɪərənt] *adj.* not coherent; not linked; which does not make sense. **incoherence** *n.* being incoherent **incoherently** *adv.* not in a coherent way; in a way which does not make sense

income ['ɪŋkʌm] *n.* money which you receive; i. tax = tax on income; unearned i. = income from investment/rents.

incoming 1 ['ɪnkʌmɪŋ] *adj.* which is arriving/coming in; i. calls = telephone calls received **incoming 2** *n. pl.* incomings = revenue

incommode [ɪnkɒ'məʊd] *v.* (formal) to inconvenience (s.o.).

incommunicado [ɪnkəmjuːnɪ'kɑːdəʊ] *adv.* not allowed to see or write to any person

incomparable [ɪn'kɒmprəbl] *adj.* which cannot be compared to anything else. **incomparably** *adv.* vastly; so much that it cannot be compared

incompatible [ɪnkəm'pætɪbl] *adj.* (with) which cannot live/work/fit together. **incompatibility** [ɪnkəmpætə'bɪlɪtɪ] *n.* being incompatible (with).

incompetent [ɪn'kɒmpɪtənt] *adj.* not good at doing sth/not competent. **incompetence** *n.* lack of competence. **incompetently** *adv.* in an incompetent way.

incomplete [ɪnkəm'pliːt] *adj.* not complete/not finished. **incompletely** *adv.* not completely.

incomprehensible [ɪnkɒmprɪ'hensɪbl] *adj.* which cannot be understood. **incomprehension** *n.* lack of understanding.

inconceivable [ɪnkən'siːvəbl] *adj.* which cannot be imagined.

inconclusive [ɪnkən'kluːsɪv] *adj.* not final; without a definite result. **inconclusively** *adv.* in an inconclusive way.

incongruous [ɪn'kɒŋgrʊəs] *adj.* which does not fit in with the rest; which seems out of place. **incongruity** *n.* being out of place.

inconsequential [ɪnkɒnsɪ'kwenʃl] *adj.* not of any importance.

inconsiderable [ɪnkən'sɪdərəbl] *adj.* small.

inconsiderate [ɪnkən'sɪdərət] *adj.* not thinking of other people. **inconsiderately** *adv.* not thinking about other people.

inconsistent [ɪnkən'sɪstənt] *adj.* (a) which does not follow/which contradicts. (b) (person) who changes his mind frequently. **inconsistency** *n.* lack of consistency.

inconsolable [ɪnkən'səʊləbl] *adj.* (person) who cannot be comforted.

inconspicuous [ɪnkən'spɔkjʊəs] *adj.*
not very noticeable. **inconspicuously**
adv. without being noticed.

inconstant [ɪn'kɒnstənt] *adj. (formal)*
not constant; unfaithful. **inconstancy**
n. lack of constancy.

incontestable [ɪnkən'tstəbl] *adj.*
which cannot be argued with.

incontinent [ɪn'kɒntɪnənt] *adj.* unable
to control your bladder or bowels.
incontinence *n.* being incontinent.

incontrovertible [ɪnkɒntrə'vɜːtəbl]
adj. (fact) with which you must agree.

inconvenience 1 [ɪnkən'viːnɪəns] *n.*
awkwardness. **inconvenience 2** *v.* to
bother (s.o.). **inconvenient** *adj.*
awkward; not handy. **inconveniently**
adv. awkwardly.

incorporate [ɪn'kɔːpəreɪt] *v.* (a) to
bring into one main part. (b) to form an
official body. (c) *Am.* To form a large
firm. **incorporation** [ɪnkɔːpə'reɪʃn] *n.*
act of incorporating.

incorrect [ɪnkə'rekt] *adj.* not correct/
false. **incorrecly** *adv.* wrongly/falsely.

incorrigible [ɪn'kɒrɪdʒəbl] *adj.*
(person) who cannot be corrected/
improved. **incorrigibly** *adv.* in an
incorrigible way.

incorruptibile [ɪnkə'rʌptəbl] *adj.*
(person) who cannot be corrupted/be
persuaded to behave dishonestly.
incorruptibility [ɪnkərʌptɪ'bɪlnti] *n.*
being incorruptible.

increase 1 ['ɪnkriːs] *n.* growth/
expansion; rise (in salary). **increase 2**
[ɪn'kriːs] *v.* to rise/to grow/to expand.
increasing *adj.* growing.
increasingly *adv.* more and more.

incredible [ɪn'kredɪbl] *adj.* which it is
difficult to believe. **incredibly** *adv.*
unbelievably.

incredulous [ɪn'kredjʊləs] *adj.*
(person) who does not believe.
incredulity [ɪnkrə'djuːlɪtɪ] *n.* lack of
belief. **incredulously** *adv.* as if you do
not believe.

increment ['ɪnkrəmənt] *n.* regular
automatic addition (to salary).
incremental [ɪnkrɪ'mentl] *adj.*
referring to increments.

incriminate [ɪn'krɪmɪneɪt] *v.* to show
that (s.o.) took part in a crime, etc.
incriminating *adj.* which shows that
s.o. took part in a crime. **incriminatory**

[ɪn'krɪmɪnətəri] *adj.* which incriminates.

incrustation [ɪekrʌs'teɪʃn] *n.* layer (of
dirt, etc) encrusted on a surface.

incubate ['ɪnkjʊbeɪt] *v.* to keep (eggs)
war until they hatch; to have (the germs
of a disease) in your body. **incubation**
[ɪnkjʊ'beɪʃn] *n.* keeping eggs warm
until they hatch. i. period = period
during which a disease develops in your
body. **incubator** *n.* war box in which
eggs are kept until they hatch; sterilized
receptacle for keeping very small babies
in until they are strong. **incubus**
['ɪnkjʊbəs] *n.* nightmare; problem which
causes great worry.

inculcate ['ɪnkʌlkeɪt] *v. (formal)* to fix
(ideas, etc.) in the mind of a young
person.

incumbent 1 [ɪn'kʌmbənt] *n.* person
who hold a post, esp. priest in charge of
a parish. **incumbent 2** *adj. (formal)* it
is i. on you = it your responsibility.
incumbency *n.* period when s.o.
holds a post/when a priest is in charge of
a parish.

incur [ɪn'kɜː] *v.* (incurred) to run (a
risk); to be liable to; to bring (sth) on
yourself.

incurable [ɪn'kjʊənəbl] *adj.* which
cannot be made better. **incurably**
adv. in a way which cannot be made
better.

incurious [ɪn'kjʊərɪəs] *adj.* not
curious/not-showing any curiosity.

incursion [ɪn'kɜːʃn] *n.* movement into
sth; attack on sth.

indebted [ɪn'detɪd] *adj.* owing sth to
s.o. **indebtedness** *n.* being indebted.

indecent [ɪn'diːsnt] *adj.* not decent/
rude. **indecency** *n.* being indecent
indecently *adv.* not decently; in a way
which shocks.

indecipherable [ɪndɪ'saɪfnəbl] *adj.*
(writing/message) that cannot be read/
understood.

indecision [ɪndɪ'sɪʒn] *n.* (state of) not
being able to decide; hesitating.
indecisive [ɪndɪ'saɪsɪv] *adj.* without a
positive result; which/who cannot decide
anything.

indecorous [ɪn'dekərəs] *adj. (formal)*
slightly rude.

indeed [ɪn'diːd] *adv.* (a) real/truly. (b)
in fact. (c) inter. meaning really! i. not! =
of course not!

indefatigable [ɪndɪˈfwtɪɡəbl] *adj.*
tireless/who cannot be tries out.
indefatigably *adv.* tirelessly
indefensible [ɪndɪˈfensɪbl] *adj.* which
cannot be defended/excused.
indefinable [ɪndɪˈfaɪnəbl] *adj.* which
cannot be defined/explained
indefinite [ɪnˈdefɪnɪt] *adj.* vague; not
definite; I. article = 'a' (as opposed to
the definite article 'the'). **indefinitely**
adv. for an indefinite period.
indelible [ɪnˈdelɪbl] *adj.* which cannot
be rubbed out **indelibly** *adv.*
permanently (marked).
indelicate [ɪnˈdelɪkət] *adj.* rude/not
polite. **indelicacy** *n.* being indelicate.
indemnify [ɪnˈdemnɪfaɪ] *v.* to pay (s.o.)
for damage, **indemnity** *n.* (a) payment
(for loss/damage). (b) guarantee (of
payment) against loss/damage.
indent [ɪnˈdent] *v.* (a) to start a line
several spaces in from the left-hand
margin. (b) (in commerce) to put in an
order for (sth). **indentation**
[ɪndenˈteɪʃn] *n.* inward cut along an
edge; deep bay/inlet on a coastline.
indented *adj.* with a jagged edge.
indentures [ɪnˈdentʃəz] *n. pl.* contract
by which a person is apprenticed to a
master craftsman.
independent [ɪndɪˈpendənt] *adj.* free/
not ruled by anyone else; not needing/not
relying on anyone else; (candidate) not
belonging to a political party; i. school =
private school, not run by the state,
independence *n.* freedom not
needing/not relying on anyone else.
independently *adv.* freely; separately.
indescribable [ɪndɪˈskraɪbəbl] *adj.*
which cannot be described.
indescribably *adv.* in a way which
cannot be described.
indestructible [ɪndɪˈstrʌktəbl] *adj.*
which cannot be destroyed.
indeterminable [ɪndɪˈtɜːmməbl] *adj.*
which cannot be decided/solved.
indeterminate [ɪndɪˈtɜːmmət] *adj.*
vague/not precise.
index 1 [ˈɪndeks] *n.* (pl -dexes, -dices)
(a) i. (finger) = first finger (next to the
thumb). (b) classified list (showing the
contents/references in a book). (c) cost of
living i. = regular government statistics
which show the rise and falls in the cost
of living. **index 2** *v.* (a) to write and

index for (a book). (b) to relate (pensions
etc.,) to the cost of living index. **indexer**
n. person who compiles indexes.
indexing *n.* (a) (also indexation)
relating sth to the cost of living index,
(b) compiling of an index. **index-linked**
adj. calculated according to the cost of
living index.
Indian 1 [ˈɪndjən] *adj.* referring to
India; referring to the indigenous
people of America; in I. file = in line/
one behind the other; I. ink = black
ink which cannot be removed by
washing; I. summer = period of hot
weather in autumn. **Indian 2** *n.* (a)
person from India, (b) member of one
of the indigenous tribes of America.
indiarubber [ɪndjəˈrʌbə] *n.* rubber
for rubbing out pencil marks.
indicate [ˈɪndɪkeɪt] *v.* to show/to point
out. **indication** [ɪndɪˈkeɪʃn] *n.* sign/
pointer. **indicative** [ɪnˈdɪkətɪv] *adj.* (a)
typical/which indicates (b) (tense of a
verb) which shows that the action
actually took place/is taking place.
indicator *n.* (a) thing which indicates;
flashing light (on a car) which shows
which way you intend to turn. (b) large
board which shows details of train times.
indict [ɪnˈdaɪt] *v.* to cause (s.o.) of a
crime. **indictable** *adj.* (offence) which
you can be charged with. **indictment**
n. detailed accusation.
indifferent [ɪnˈdɪfrənt] *adj.* (a) not
caring; not interested, (b) ordinary/
mediocre; not special. **indifference** *n.*
lack of interest. **indifferently** *adv.* (a)
not bothering. (b) in a mediocre way.
indigenous [ɪnˈdɪdʒənəs] *adj. (formal)*
very poor.
indigence *n.* great poverty.
indigestion [ɪndɪˈdʒestʃn] *n.* not being
able to digest food; pain caused when the
body is unable to digest food.
indigestible *adj.* which cannot be
digested; which causes pain because the
body cannot digest it.
indignant [ɪnˈdɪgnənt] *adj.* feeling
offended/angry **indignantly** *adv.* in an
indignant way. **indignation**
[ɪndɪgˈneɪʃn] *n.* being indignant.
indignity [ɪnˈdɪgnɪti] *n.* rudeness/
offence to dignity.
indigo [ˈɪndɪgəʊ] *n.* blue dye; deep blue
colour.

indirect [ɪndɪˈrekt, ɪndaɪˈrekt] *adj.* (a) not direct/oblique; (tax) added to the price of goods and not paid directly to the government. (b) (speech) reporting what s.o. has said **indirectly** *adv.* not directly.

indiscreet [ɪndɪˈskriːt] *adj.* revealing/not discreet. **indiscretion** [ɪndɪˈskreʃn] *n.* (a) lack of discretion/being careless about what you do or say. (b) doing sth careless.

indiscriminate [ɪndɪˈskrɪmənət] *adj.* widespread/not selective. **indiscriminately** *adv.* (a) in every direction. (b) without selecting/without choosing.

indispensable [ɪndɪˈspensəbl] *adj.* which you cannot do without.

indisposed [ɪndɪˈspəʊzd] *adj.* (a) slightly ill. (b) unwilling. **indisposition** [ɪndɪspəˈzɪʃn] *n.* (a) slight illness. (b) unwillingness.

indisputable [ɪndɪˈspjuːtəbl] *adj.* which cannot be argued over. **indisputably** *adv.* certainly.

indissoluble [ɪndɪˈsɒljʊəl] *adj.* which cannot be destroyed/dissolved.

indistinct [ɪndɪˈstɪŋkt] *adj.* vague/unclear. **indistinctly** *adv.* vaguely/unclearly.

indistinguishable [ɪndɪˈstɪŋgwtʃəbl] *adj.* which cannot be told apart from sth.

individual 1 [ɪndɪˈvɪdjʊəl] *n.* (a) single person. (b) *inf.* person. **individual 2** *adj.* (a) single. (b) belonging to a particular person. (c) for one person. **individualist** *n.* person who emphasizes that he is unique and not a member of a group. **individualistic** *adj.* like an individualist. **individuality** [ɪndɪvɪdjʊˈælɪtɪ] *n.* quality which makes each person different from all others. **individually** *adv.* singly/as a single person.

indivisible [ɪndɪˈvɪzəbl] *adj.* which cannot be divided/separated. **indivisibly** *adv.* in a way which prevents it being divided/separated.

indoctrinate [ɪnˈdɒktrɪneɪt] *v.* to teach (s.o.) esp. political ideas. **indoctrination** [ɪndɒktrɪˈneɪʃn] *n.* teaching s.o., esp. political ideas.

indolence [ˈɪndələns] *n.* laziness. **indolent** *adj.* lazy.

indomitable [ɪnˈdɒmɪtəbl] *adj.* which cannot be overcome.

indoor [ˈɪndɔː] *adj.* done/found inside a building. **indoors** [ɪnˈdɔːz] *adv.* inside a building.

indubitable [ɪnˈdjuːbɪtəbl] *adj.* which cannot be doubted **indubitably** *adv.* certainly/definitely.

induce [ɪnˈdjuːs] *v.* (a) to pursued (s.o.) to do sth. (b) to provoke (sth) /to make (sth) happen; to make (a birth) happen. **inducement** *n.* thing which help persuade you to do sth.

induct [ɪnˈdʌkt] *v.* to place (s.o., esp. a priest) in office. **induction** [ɪnˈdʌkʃn] *n.* (a) entry of a person into a new job; installation of a new priest; i. course = training course for s.o. in a new job. (b) creation of electricity in an object by placing it near a magnet or near sth which is electrically charged. **inductive** *adj.* (reasoning) based on known facts.

indulge [ɪnˈdʌldʒ] *v.* (a) to spoil (s.o.). (b) (in) to give way to (sth enjoyable). **indulgence** *n.* being indulgent; indulgent action. **indulgent** *adj.* kind/soft; too generous. **indulgently** *adv.* kindly; too generously.

industry [ˈɪndəstrɪ] *n.* (a) all manufacturing processes. (b) hard work/steady work. **industrial** [ɪnˈdʌstrɪəl] *adj.* referring to manufacturing work; i. action = strike or protest by workers; i. estate = group of factories built together. **industrialist** *n.* owner/director of a factory. **industrialization** [ɪndʌstrɪəlaɪˈzeɪʃn] *n.* changing of a society from agricultural to industrial. **industrialize** [ɪnˈdʌstrɪəlaɪz] *v.* to create industries (where there were none before). **industrially** *adv.* (made) by industry. **industrious** *adj.* (person) who works steadily and hard. **industriously** *adv.* in an industrious way.

inebriate [niːˈbrɪət] *adj. (formal)* (person) who is often drunk. **inebriated** *adj.* drunk. **inebriation** *n.* drunken state.

inedible [ɪnˈedɪbl] *adj.* which you cannot eat.

ineducable [ɪnˈedjʊkəbl] *adj.* (person) who cannot be educated.

ineffable [ɪnˈefəbl] *adj. (formal)* so wonderful that it cannot be properly described.

ineffective [ɪnɪˈfektɪv] *adj.* which does not have any effect.

ineffectual [ɪnɪˈfektjʊəl] *adj.* (attempt) which is unsuccessful; (person) who is weak/incapable of asserting his authority.

inefficient [ɪnɪˈfɪʃnt] *adj.* not efficient; not competent. **inefficiency** *n.* incompetence/lack of efficiency. **inefficiently** *adv.* in an inefficient way.

inelegant [ɪnˈelɪɡənt] *adj.* not elegant.

ineligible [ɪnˈelɪdʒəbl] *adj.* (person) who is not qualified (for sth. to do sth.)

inept [ɪnˈept] *adj.* stupid (remark); incapable (person). **ineptitude** *n.* stupidity/silliness; being unable to do sth.

inequality [ɪnɪˈkwɒlɪtɪ] *n.* lack of equality. **inequitable** [ɪnˈekwɪtəbl] *adj.* unjust/not fair.

ineradicable [ɪnɪˈrædɪkəbl] *adj.* which cannot be eradicated/removed.

inert [ɪˈnɜːt] *adj.* unmoving; (gas) which does not react with other substances.

inertia [ɪˈnɜːʃə] *n.* (a) lack of motion in a body. (b) continuous movement of a body, unless checked by a force. (c) laziness; i. selling = method of selling goods through the post where it is assumed that they have been bought if they are not returned.

inescapable [ɪnɪˈskeɪpəbl] *adj.* which you cannot avoid.

inessential [ɪnɪˈsenʃl] *adj. & n.* (thing) which is not absolutely necessary.

inestimable [ɪnˈestɪməbl] *adj.* which cannot be estimated/calculated.

inevitable [ɪnˈevɪtəbl] *adj.* which cannot be avoided. **inevitability** [ɪnevɪtəˈbɪlɪtɪ] *n.* being inevitable. **inevitably** *adv.* of course.

inexact [ɪnɪɡˈzækt] *adj.* not exact/not correct. **inexactitude** *n.* error.

inexcusable [ɪnɪkˈskjuːzəbl] *adj.* which cannot be excused/forgiven. **inexcusably** *adv.* in an inexcusable way.

inexhaustible [ɪnɪɡˈzɔːstəbl] *adj.* which cannot be used up.

inexorable [ɪnˈeksərəbl] *adj.* which cannot be changed/influenced.

inexpedient [ɪnɪkˈspiːdɪənt] *adj.* (action) which is not expedient.

inexpensive [ɪnɪkˈspensɪv] *adj.* cheap/not expensive

inexperience [ɪnɪkˈspɪərɪəns] *n.* lack of experience. **inexperienced** *adj.* with no experience/lacking experience

inexpert [ɪnˈekspɜːt] *adj.* (at) not expert/not skilled.

inexplicable [ɪnɪkˈsplɪkəbl] *adj.* which cannot be explained. **inexplicably** *adv.* in a way which cannot be explained.

inexpressible [ɪnɪkˈspresɪbl] *adj.* which cannot be expressed in words.

in extremis [ɪneksˈtriːmɪs] *adv.* at the very end; (of person) when near to death.

inextricable [ɪneksˈtrɪkəbl] *adj.* which you cannot get out of. **inextricably** *adv.* in an inextricable way.

infallible [ɪnˈfæləbl] *adj.* always correct/true; (person) who never makes mistakes. **infallibility** [ɪnfælɪˈbɪlɪtɪ] *n.* being infallible. **infallibly** *adv.* unfailingly/always.

infamous [ˈɪnfəməs] *adj.* very wicked (person/action). **infamy** *n.* (formal) great wickedness.

infant [ˈɪnfənt] *n.* young child; i. prodigy = small child who is exceptionally good at sth, such as music/ chess, etc. **infancy** *n.* young childhood. **infanticide** [ɪnˈfæntɪsaɪd] *n.* killing of a baby. **infantile** [ˈɪnfəntaɪl] *adj.* referring to a small child; childish.

infantry [ˈɪnfəntrɪ] *n.* section of an army which fights on foot.

infatuated [ɪnˈfætjʊleɪtɪd] *adj.* mad (about); wildly in love (with). **infatuation** [ɪnfætjʊˈeɪʃn] *n.* blind love for someone.

infect [ɪnˈfekt] *v.* to make diseased. **infection** *n.* (a) making diseased. (b) disease which spreads. **infectious** *adj.* (disease) which can be passed from one person to another.

infer [ɪnˈfɜː] *v.* (inferred) (a) to deduce (from). (b) to imply/to hint. **inference** [ˈɪnfərəns] *n.* conclusion/deduction.

inferior 1 [ɪnˈfɪərɪə] *adj.* not as good. **inferior 2** *n.* person of a lower rank/ subordinate. **inferiority** [ɪnfɪərɪˈkrɪtɪ] *n.* state of being not as good as s.o. else; i. complex = exaggerated idea that one is not as good as others.

infernal [ɪnˈfɜːnl] *adj. inf.* like hell/ hellish. **infernally** *adv. inf* extremely.

inferno [ɪnˈfɜːnəʊ] *n.* (-os) blaze of fire.

infertile [ɪnˈfɜːtaɪl] *adj.* not fertile/not capable of having young; (land) which is not rich enough to produce crops. **infertility** [ɪmfəˈtɪlɪtɪ] *n.* being unable to have young.

infest [ɪnˈfest] *v.* to cover/to swarm over in large numbers. **infestation** [ɪnfesˈteɪʃn] *n.* being covered with pests.

infidel [ˈɪnfɪdəl] *n.* person who is opposed to Christianity. **infidelity** [ɪnfɪˈdelɪtɪ] *n.* being unfaithful.

infighting [ˈɪnfaɪtɪŋ] *n.* bitter argument between members of a group.

infiltrate [ˈɪnfɪltreɪt] *v.* to enter (a political group) secretly. **infiltration** [ɪnfɪlˈtreɪʃn] *n.* act of infiltrating. **infiltrator** [ˈɪnfɪltreɪtə] *n.* person who infiltrates.

infinite [ˈɪnfɪnət] *adj.* endless/with no end. **infinitely** *adv.* completely; much more. **infinitesimal** [ɪnfɪnɪˈtesɪml] *adj.* tiny/microscopic. **infinitive** [ɪnˈfɪnɪtɪv] *adj. & n.* form of the verb using 'to'. **infinity** *n.* never-ending space.

infirm [ɪnˈfɜːm] *adj.* sick/weak (person). **infirmary** *n.* (a) hospital. (b) sickbay in a factory or school. **infirmity** *n.* physical weakness.

inflame [ɪnˈfleɪm] *v.* (a) (formal) to make violent. (b) to cause inflammation in. **inflammable** [ɪnˈflwməbl] *adj.* which catches fire easily. **inflammation** [ɪnfləˈmeɪʃn] *n.* swelling/redness caused by infection. **inflammatory** [ɪnˈflwmətərɪ] *adj.* (speech) which make people behave violently.

inflate [ɪnˈfleɪt] *v.* to blow up (balloon/tyre); to increase (prices, etc.) artificially. **inflatable** *adj.* which can be blown up. **inflation** [ɪnˈfleɪʃn] *n.* economic state where prices and wages are rising to keep pace with each other. **inflationary** *adj.* (policy) which tends to increase inflation.

inflect [ɪnˈflekt] *v.* to change the ending of (a word, e.g. when used in the plural). **inflection, inflexion** *n.* ending of a word which changes to indicate the plural, the gender, etc.

inflexible [ɪnˈfleksəbl] *adj.* which cannot be bent/altered; (person) who cannot be persuaded to change his mind. **inflexibility** [ɪnfleksɪˈbɪlɪtɪ] *n.* not being able to bend/to adapt. **inflexibly** *adv.* in an unbending way.

inflict [ɪnˈflɪkt] *v.* to i. pain/damage on = to cause pain/damage to; to i. oneself on s.o. = force s.o. to accept one's presence. **infliction** [ɪnˈflɪkʃn] *n.* (act of) inflicting.

inflorescence [ɪnfləˈresəns] *n.* group of flowers arranged on one stem.

inflow [ˈɪnfləʊ] *n.* flowing in.

influence 1 [ˈɪnfluəns] *n.* (on) ability to make s.o./sth change; effect on others. **influence 2** *v.* to make (s.o./sth) change. **influential** [ɪnfluˈenʃl] *adj.* so powerful as to cause change; having an effect on others.

influenza [ɪnfluˈenzə] *n.* virus disease like a bad cold with a high temperature.

influx [ˈɪnflʌks] *n. (pl -es)* entry (of a crowd of people).

inform [ɪnˈfɔːm] *v.* to tell officially; to give details; to i. against s.o. = to tell (the police, etc) about s.o. **informant** *n.* person who passes on information/who gives details. **informatics** *n.* study of information processing. **information** [ɪnfəˈmeɪʃn] *n.* details/knowledge **informative** [ɪnˈfɔːmətɪv] *adj.* which tells you a lot/which conveys much detailed information. **informed** *adj.* up-to-date/reliable. **informer** *n.* person who informs against his accomplices.

informal [ɪnˈfɔːml] *adj.* not formal/relaxed; not following any rules; not official. **informally** *adv.* not formally/unofficially. **informality** [ɪnfɔːˈmwlɪtɪ] *n.* lack of any special ceremony

infra dig [ˈɪnfrəˈdɪg] *adv. inf.* beneath one's dignity. **infra-red** [ɪnfrəˈred] *adj.* (heat rays) which are invisible and have a longer wave-length than visible red heat rays. **infrastructure** [ˈɪnfrəstrʌktʃə] *n.* basic structure; supporting framework.

infrequent [ɪnˈfriːkwənt] *adj.* not frequent; not happening very often **infrequency** *n.* lack of frequency. **infrequently** *adv.* not very often/not frequently.

infringe [ɪnˈfrɪndʒ] *v.* to break (a law). **infringement** *n.* breaking (of a law).

infuriate [ɪnˈfjʊərɪeɪt] *v.* to make furious.

infuse [ɪnˈfjuːz] *v.* to pour hot water (on tea/lime flowers) to make a drink. **infusion** [ɪnˈfjuːʒn] *n.* drink made by pouring hot water on dried leaves.

ingenious [ɪndʒiːnɪəs] *adj.* very clever (device/person). **ingenuity** [ɪndʒəˈnjuːɪtɪ] *n.* cleverness/skill in inventing new techniques.

ingenue [ænʒeɪˈnjuː] *n.* supposedly simple girl. **ingenuous** [ɪnˈdʒenjʊəs] *adj.* naive/innocent; lacking experience. **ingenuousness** *n.* being ingenuous.

ingest [ɪnˈdʒest] *v. (formal)* to take into the body (as food).

inglenook [ˈɪŋɡəlnʊk] *n.* seat at the side of a very large fireplace.

inglorious [ɪnˈɡlɔːrɪəs] *adj. (formal)* dishonourable/not glorious.

ingot [ˈɪŋɡət] *n.* bar (of gold, etc.).

ingrained [ˈɪŋɡreɪnd] *adj.* fixed.

ingratiate [ɪnˈɡreɪʃɪeɪt] *v.* to i. oneself with s.o. = make oneself liked by s.o. **ingratiating** *adj.* which will help you worm your way into s.o.'s favour.

ingratitude [ɪnˈɡrætɪtjuːd] *n.* lack of gratitude; not being grateful.

ingredient [ɪnˈɡriːdɪənt] *n.* substance which goes to make sth.

ingress [ˈɪŋɡres] *n. (formal)* entry.

ingrowing [ˈɪŋɡrəʊɪŋ] *adj.* (toenail) which grows into the flesh.

inhabit [ɪnˈhæbɪt] *v.* to live in. **inhabitable** *adj.* (place) which can be lived in. **inhabitant** *n.* person who lives in a place.

inhale [ɪnˈheɪl] *v.* to draw (sth) into the lungs when breathing. **inhalant, inhalation** *n.* medicine which has to be inhaled. **inhaler** *n.* device which makes a vapour which has to be inhaled.

inherent [ɪnˈhɪərənt] *adj.* natural/inborn. **inherently** *adv.* naturally.

inherit [ɪnˈherɪt] *v.* (a) to take over (money, etc.) from a person who has died; to have (characteristics) passed on from a parent. (b) to take over (a client/a problem) from a predecessor. **inheritance** *n.* money/goods which you receive on the death of s.o. **inheritor** *n.* person who inherits.

inhibit [ɪnˈhɪbɪt] *v.* to restrain (s.o.) from doing sth. **inhibition** [ɪnhɪˈbɪʃn] *n.* thing which prevents you from expressing yourself freely/from letting yourself go. **inhibitory** *adj.* which inhibits.

inhospitable [ɪnhɒˈspɪtəbl] *adj.* not welcoming.

in-house [ˈɪnhaʊs] *adj. & adv.* inside an office or factory.

inhuman [ɪnˈhjuːmən] *adj.* not human; savage/brutal. **inhumane** [ɪnhjuːˈmeɪn] *adj.* not humane; showing barbarity. **inhumanity** [ɪnhjuːˈmænɪtɪ] *n.* cruelty/barbarity. **inhumanly** *adv.* savagely/brutally.

inimical [ɪˈnɪmɪkl] *adj. (formal)* unfriendly. **inimitable** [ɪˈnɪmɪtəbl] *adj.* which cannot be imitated.

iniquitous [ɪˈnɪkwɪtəs] *adj. (formal)* wicked. **iniquity** *n.* wickedness.

initial 1 [ɪˈnɪʃl] *adj.* first. **initial 2** *n.* initials = first letters (of name). **initial 3** *v.* (initialled) to write your initials on (a document) to show you have read and approved it. **initially** *adv.* in the first place/at the beginning.

initiate [ɪˈnɪʃɪeɪt] *v* (a) to start (sth) going. (b) to introduce (s.o.) in to a secret society; to show (s.o.) the basic information about sth. **initiation** [ɪnɪʃɪˈeɪʃn] *n.* introduction to a secret society. **initiative** [ɪˈnɪʃɪətɪv] *n.* decision to get sth going; ability to decide. **initiator** *n.* person who starts (a project).

inject [ɪnˈdʒekt] *v.* to pump a liquid into (sth/s.o.) under pressure; to put (sth new) into. **injection** *n.* act of injecting; liquid which has been injected.

injudicious [ɪndʒuːˈdɪʃəs] *adj. (formal)* unwise.

injunction [ɪnˈdʒʌŋkʃn] *n.* (a) order (by a court) preventing s.o. from doing sth. (b) instruction.

injure [ˈɪndʒə] *v.* to hurt/to wound; the injured party = the party in a court case who has been offended. **injured** *n. (pl)* people who have been wounded. **injurious** [ɪnˈdʒʊərɪəs] *adj.* which can injure. **injury** *n.* hurt/wound

injustice [ɪnˈdʒʌstɪs] *n.* lack of justice; not being fair.

ink 1 [ɪŋk] *n.* liquid for writing with a pen. **ink 2** *v.* to write with a pen and ink; to mark with ink. **ink pad** *n.* pad of cloth soaked in ink for inking date stamps, etc. **inkwell** *n.* pot to put ink in. **inky** *adj.* (black) like ink; covered with ink. **inkling** [ˈɪŋklɪŋ] *n.* suspicion/idea.

inlaid [ɪnˈleɪd] *v.* see inlay.

inland ['ɪnlænd] *adj. & adv.* (to/of) the interior of a country; the I. Revenue = government department dealing with tax.

in-laws ['ɪnlɔːz] *n. pl. inf.* parents related to you by marriage.

inlay 1 [ɪn'leɪ] *n.* thing which is inlaid.

inlay 2 *v.* (inlaid) to insert small pieces of stone/wood/metal in (a surface) to create a pattern.

inlet. ['ɪnlet] *n.* (a) small branch of water off a large stretch of water. (b) i. pipe = pipe for introducing a liquid.

inmate ['ɪnmeɪt] *n.* resident (of a house); person living in a home for old people/in a prison.

inmost ['ɪnməʊst] *adj.* deepest (thoughts, etc.).

inn [ɪn] *n.* small hotel; public house. **innkeeper** *n.* person who runs an inn. **Inns of Court** *n.* four societies of barristers London.

innards ['ɪnədz] *n. pl. inf.* intestines; inside workings (of a machine).

innate [ɪ'neɪt] *adj.* inborn/natural.

inner ['ɪnə] *adj.* inside; i. room = room leading off another room; i. tube = light tube containing air inside a tyre; i. ear = space inside the head, beyond the middle ear, which controls the balance and hearing. **innermost** *adj.* furthest inside.

innings ['ɪnɪŋz] *n.* (*pl.*innings) (in cricket) time when a team/a player bats; he's had a good i. = he 's been a long time at his job/he's lived a long time.

innocent ['ɪnəsnt] *adj.* not guilty; lacking experience/knowledge. **innocence** *n.* lack of guilt. **innocently** *adv.* in a way which shows lack of experience/knowledge.

innocuous [ɪ'nɒkjʊəs] *adj.* inoffensive/harmless.

innovate ['ɪnəveɪt] *v.* to introduce changes/new methods. **innovation** [ɪnə'veɪʃn] *n.* invention which is new; change (in doing sth). **innovative** ['ɪnəveɪtɪv] *adj.* which breaks new ground/which changes everything. **innovator** *n.* person who introduces changes.

innuendo [ɪnjʊ'endəʊ] *n.* (*pl.* -oes) remark which suggests criticism.

innumerable [ɪ'njuːmərəbl] *adj.* countless/which cannot be counted.

inoculate [ɪ'nɒkjʊleɪt] *v.* to i. s.o.

against = to prevent s.o. catching a disease by injecting him with a vaccine. **inoculation** [ɪnɒkjʊ'leɪʃn] *n.* injection to stop you catching a disease.

inoffensive [ɪnə'fensɪv] *adj.* mild/harmless.

inoperable [ɪn'ɒprbl] *adj.* which cannot be operated on.

inoperative [ɪn'ɒprətɪv] *adj.'* which is not in operation/which is not working.

inopportune [ɪn'ɒpətjuːn] *adj.* awkward/badly timed.

inordinate [ɪn'ɔːdɪnət] *adj.* excessive. **inordinately** *adv.* excessively.

inorganic [ɪnɔː'gænɪk] *adj.* not relating to living organisms; i. chemistry = chemistry dealing with substances which are not organic.

in-patient ['ɪn'peɪʃnt] *n.* patient who stays in a hospital.

input ['ɪnpʊt] *n.* (a) electric current put into an apparatus. (b) data/information fed into a computer. (c) inputs = goods or services bought which are subject to VAT.

inquest ['ɪŋkwest] *n.* legal enquiry into a death.

inquire [ɪŋ'kwaɪə] *v.* (a) to ask question (about sth) (b) to conduct an official investigation(into) **inquirer** *n.* person who inquires. **inquiring** *adj.* interested in finding out information. **inquiringly** *adv.* in a questioning way. **inquiry** *n.* (a) formal investigation(into). (b) question.

inquisition [ɪŋkwɪ'zɪʃn] *n.* (a) asking very thorough questions, *usu.* using threats or force. (b) (old) Catholic, tribunal for discovering heretics.

inquisitor [ɪŋkwɪzɪtə] *n.* person who asks very thorough questions.

inquisitive [ɪŋ'kwɪzətɪv] *adj.* curious/asking questions. **inquisitively** *adv.* curiously/inquiringly. **inquisitiveness** *n.* being inquisitive

inquorate [ɪn'kwɔːreɪt] *adj.* without a quorum.

inroads ['ɪnrəʊdz] *n. pl.*to make i. into sth = to use up a large quantity of sth.

inrush ['ɪnrʌʃ] *n.* sudden quick movement inwards.

insalubrious [ɪnsə'luːbrɪəs] *adj.* not healthy.

insane [ɪn'seɪn] *adj.* mad. **insanely** *adv.* madly. **insanity** [ɪn'sænɪtɪ] *n.* madness

insanitary [ɪn'sænɪtərɪ] *adj.* not clean/ not hygienic.

insatiable [ɪn'seɪʃəbl] *adj.* which cannot be satisfied.

inscribe [ɪn'skraɪb] *v.* to write (officially) (in a book/on a stone). **inscription** [ɪn'skrɪpʃn] *n.* writing inscribed on a stone, etc.

inscrutable [ɪn'skruːtəbl] *adj.* mysterious/which you cannot understand

insect ['ɪnsekt] *n.* small six-legged animal with a body in three parts **insecticide** [ɪn'sektɪsaɪd] *n.* liquid/ powder which kills insects **insectivorous** [ɪnsek'tɪvərəs] *adj.* (animal) which eats insects

insecure [ɪnsɪ'kjʊə] *adj.* not safe; wobbly/not firmly fixed. **insecurely** *adv.* not firmly. **insecurity** *n.* feeling of not being safe.

inseminate [ɪn'semɪneɪt] *v.* to introduce male seed into (a female). **insemination** [ɪnsemɪ'neɪʃn] *n.* artificial i. = introduction of sperm from a male into a female by a doctor or veterinary surgeon.

insensate [ɪn'senseɪt] *adj.* without any feeling.

insensible [ɪn'sensəbl] *adj.* (a) not conscious. (b) with not feeling. (c) very small (change). **insensitive** [ɪn'sensɪtɪv] *adj.* not sensitive. **insensitivity** [ɪnsensɪ'tɪvɪtɪ] *n.* lack of sensitivity/lack of awareness of how other people feel.

inseparable [ɪn'seprəbl] *adj.* which cannot be separated. (of people) always together.

insert 1 ['ɪnsɜːt] *n.* thing which is put in. **insert 2** [ɪn'sɜːt] *v.* to put (sth) in. **insertion** [ɪn'sɜːʃn] *n.* act of putting sth in; thing which is put in.

inset 1 ['ɪnset] *n.* small piece which is put into sth larger. **inset 2** *adj.* with sth fixed into it.

inshore [ɪn'ʃɔː] *adj. & adv.* near a coast.

inside 1 [ɪn'saɪd] *n.* (a) inner part; i. out = with the inner part facing outwards; to know i. out = to know very well. (b) (in games) i. left/right = forward player next to the wings. **inside 2** *adj.* (a) indoors; which is in the interior. (b) (information) known only to people working in a certain organization.

inside 3 *adv.* (a) to/in the interior. (b) *inf.* in person. **inside 4** *prep.* (a) to/in the interior of (sth) (b) within; i. three hours = in less than three hours. **insider** *n.* person who works in an organization and therefore knows secret information; i. dealing = illegal buying or selling of shares by people who have secret information about a company.

insidious [ɪn'sɪdɪəs] *adj.* quietly treacherous; working secretly to do harm. **insidiously** *adv.* quietly and dangerously. **insidiousness** *n.* being insidious.

insight ['ɪnsaɪt] *n.* (a) clear thought. (b) deep knowledge; clear understanding.

insignia [ɪn'sɪgnɪə] *n. pl.* badges/ chains/crowns etc. which symbolize an office.

insignificant [ɪnsɪg'nɪfɪkənt] *adj.* unimportant. **insignificance** *n.* being insignificant.

insincere [ɪnsɪn'sɪə] *adj.* not sincere/ false. **insincerity** [ɪnsɪn'serɪtɪ] *n.* lack of sincerity.

insinuate [ɪn'sɪnjʊeɪt] *v.* (a) to suggest (by dropping hints); to i. oneself = work one's way gradually (into a favourable position). **insinuation** [ɪnsɪnjʊ'eɪʃn] *n.* (usu. cruel) hints/suggestion.

insipid [ɪn'sɪpɪd] *adj.* watery/not strong; with no flavour/no excitement. **insipidity** [ɪnsɪ'pɪdɪtɪ] *n.* being insipid.

insist [ɪn'sɪst] *v.* to i. on sth being done = to state firmly that sth should be done. **insistence** *n.* firm demands **insistent** *adj.* demanding firmly. **insistently** *adv.* in a way which demands attention.

in situ [ɪn'sɪtjuː] *adv.* on the site; in its original place.

insole ['ɪnsəʊl] *n.* soft pad which you put inside a shoe to make it more comfortable or fit better.

insolent ['ɪnsələnt] *adj.* rude, **insolence** *n.* rudeness. **insolently** *adv.* rudely.

insoluble [ɪn'sɒljʊbl] *adj.* (a) substance which will not dissolve. *usu.* in water. (b) (problem) which cannot be solved. **insolubility** [ɪnsɒljʊ'bɪlɪtɪ] *n.* inability (of a chemical) to dissolve.

insolvent [ɪn'sɒlvənt] *adj.* bankrupt/ unable to pay one's debts. **insolvency** *n.* being insolvent.

insomnia [ɪnˈsɒmnɪə] n. chronic inability to sleep. **insomniac** n. person who suffers from insomnia

insouciant [ɪnˈsuːsjənt] adj. not caring about anything. **insouciance** n. being insouciant.

inspect [ɪnˈspekt] v. to examine closely. **inspection** [ɪnˈspekʃn] n. examining sth closely. **inspector** n. senior official who examines; school i.= official of the department of education who examines the teaching in schools; police i. = officer in the police force. **inspectorate** n. all inspectors (in a certain area) taken as a group.

inspire [ɪnˈspaɪə] v. to make (s.o.) feel a certain sensation. **inspiration** [ɪnspɪˈreɪʃn] n. (a) sudden urge to write poems/to compose music, etc. (b) sudden good idea.

instability [ɪnstəˈbɪlɪtɪ] n. lack of stability/not being steady.

install [ɪnˈstɔːl] v. to put (a person into a job/machine into a workshop). **installation** [ɪnstəˈleɪʃn] n. (a) putting (a machine in place); (b) group of machines which have been put in place

instalment, Am. **installment** [ɪnˈstɔːlmənt] n. part (of sth which is being delivered in parts); regular payment (of part of a total sum). Am. i. plan = hire purchase.

instance [ˈɪnstəns] n. example/case; for i. = as an example **instance 2** v. to give as an example.

instant 1 [ˈɪnstənt] n. moment/second. **instant 2** adj. immediate; i. coffee = coffee powder to which you add hot water to make coffee rapidly. **instantaneous** [ɪnstənˈteɪnəs] adj. immediate. **instantaneously** adv. immediately. **instantly** adv. straight away/immediately.

instead [ɪnˈsted] adv. in the place of/rather than (sth).

instep [ˈɪnstep] n. arched part of a foot.

instigate [ˈɪnstɪɡeɪt] v. to provoke/to start (sth). **instigation** [ɪnstɪˈɡeɪʃn] n. suggestion. **instigator** n. person who stirs up trouble/who provokes action.

instil [ɪnˈstɪl] v. (instilled) to put (an idea, etc.) into s.o.'s mind gradually.

instinct [ˈɪnstɪŋ̊] n. feeling/ability for doing sth which you have from birth and have not learnt. **instinctive** [ɪnˈstɪŋktɪv] adj. natural/inborn (reaction) **instinctively** adv. because of a natural impulse.

institute 1 [ˈɪnstɪtjuːt] n. (a) organization set up for a purpose. (b) building which houses such an organization. **institute 2** v. to set up/to start. **institution** [ɪnstɪˈtjuːʃn] n. (a) setting up (of an organization). (b) organization/society set up for a purpose (c) permanent feature; long standing custom. **institutional** adj. referring to an institution; i. buying = buying of shares by insurance companies, etc. **institutionalize** v. to make (sth) into an institution; to put (s.o.) into an institution (such as an old people's home, etc.).

instruct [ɪnˈstrʌkt] v. (a) to teach (b) to order. (c) to give orders to (a solicitor) to start legal proceedings. **instruction** [ɪnˈstrʌkʃn] n. (a) teaching (b) instructions = orders; indication of how sth is to be used. **instructive** adj. which teaches. **instructor,** **instructress** n. teacher (esp. of sport).

instrument [ˈɪnstrəmənt] n. (a) piece of equipment. (b) legal document (esp. in international law). (c) musical i. = device which is blown/hit/plucked, etc., to make a musical note. **instrumental** [ɪnstrʊˈmentl] adj. (a) responsible/playing an important role (in getting sth done). (b) referring to a musical instrument. **instrumentalist** n. person who plays a musical instrument.

insubordinate [ɪnsəˈbɔːdɪnət] adj. unruly, not obeying orders. **insubordination** [ɪnsəɔːdɪˈneɪʃn] n. not obeying orders

insubstantial [ɪnsəbˈstænʃl] adj. not substantial/not solid.

insufferable [ɪnˈsʌfrəbl] adj. intolerable/which you cannot bear. **insufferably** adv. intolerably.

insufficient [ɪnsəˈfɪʃnt] adj. not sufficient/not enough. **insufficiency** n. lack. **insufficiently** adv. not enough.

insular [ˈɪnsjʊlə] adj. (a) referring to an island. (b) narrow-minded. **insularity** [ɪnsjʊˈlærɪtn] n. prejudice/narrowness of opinions.

insulate [ˈɪnsjʊleɪt] v. to cover so as to prevent heat/electricity/sound escaping or entering. **insulation** [ɪnsjʊˈleɪʃn] n.

act of insulating; material which insulates. **insulator** ['ɪnsjʊleɪtə] n. material/device which insulates.

insulin ['ɪnsjʊlɪn] n. hormone which regulates the use of sugar by the body and is used to treat diabetes.

insult 1 ['ɪnsʌlt] n. rude word said to or about a person. **insult 2** [ɪn'sʌlf] v. to say rude things about (s.o.). **insulting** adj. rude.

insuperable [ɪn'sjuːpʊrəbl] adj. which cannot be overcome.

insupportable [ɪnsəˈpɔːtəbl] adj. unbearable/which cannot be borne.

insure [ɪn'ʃʊə] v. to agree with a company that if you pay them a regular sum, they will compensate you for loss or damage to property or persons; to i. a jewel for £10,000. **insurance** n. agreement with a company by which you are paid compensation for loss or damage in return for regular payments of money; i. policy = document with the details of an insurance; i. broker = person who arranges an insurance; life i. = insurance paying a sum of money when s.o. dies; National I. = government run insurance which provides for state medical care. unemployment payments etc. **insurer** n. person/company which insures

insurgent [ɪn'sɜːdʒənt] adj. & n. (person) in a state of revolt.

insurmountable [ɪnsəˈmaʊntəbl] adj. which cannot be overcome.

insurrection [ɪnsəˈrekʃn] n. uprising/revolution.

intact [ɪn'tækt] adj. in one piece/not broken

instaglio [ɪn'tɑːlɪəʊ] n. design cut into a surface (as of a precious stone).

intake ['ɪnteɪk] n. thing which is taken in; group of new students/soldiers, etc.

intangible [ɪn'tændʒəbl] adj. which cannot be touched/which cannot be defined.

integral ['ɪntɪgrəl] adj. forming (part of) a whole.

integer ['ɪntɪdʒə] n. whole number (not a fraction).

integrate ['ɪntɪgreɪt] v. to link to form a whole; to make (people) full members of society; integrated circuit = electronic circuit on a microchip **integration** [ɪntɪ'greɪʃn] n. (act of) integrating.

integrity [ɪn'tegrɪtɪ] n. honesty.

integument [ɪn'tegʊmənt] n. (formal) skin.

intellect ['ɪntələkt] n. ability to think or reason; brainpower. **intellectual 1** [ɪntə'lektjʊəl] adj. referring to the intellect; good at using the brain. **intellectual 2** n. person who believes that brainpower is very important/who uses his brain to make a living **intellectually** adv. referring to intelligence. **intelligence** [ɪn'telɪdʒəns] n. (a) quickness of understanding/mental ability; i. quotient = number showing how intelligent you are compared to others. (b) secret information. **intelligent** adj. clever/mentally able. **intelligently** adv. in an intelligent way. **intelligentsia** [ɪntelɪ'dʒensɪə] n. intellectual class of society. **intelligible** [ɪn'telɪdʒəbl] adj. which can be understood. **intelligibility** [ɪntelɪgə'bɪlɪtɪ] n. being intelligible.

intemperate [ɪn'tempərət] adj. wild/not moderate.

intend [ɪn'tend] v. to plan to do (sth) /to mean.

intense [ɪn'tens] adj. (-er, -est) very strong/vigorous (action); extremely serious (person). **intensely** adv. strongly. **intensification** n. becoming stronger. **intensify** v. to grow stronger/to make (sth) stronger. **intensity** n. strength/violence (of pain). **intensive** adj. very concentrated; i. care unit = section of a hospital dealing with seriously ill patients who need a lot of attention. **intensively** adv. very strongly.

intent 1 [ɪn'tent] adj. determined/absorbed. **intent 2** n. with i. to defraud = with the aim of deceiving; to all intents and purposes = virtually/in nearly every way. **intently** adv. fixedly. **intention** [ɪn'tenʃn] n. aim. **intentional** adj. done on purpose. **intentionally** adv. on purpose.

inter [ɪn'tɜː] v. (interred) (formal) to bury.

inter - ['ɪntə-] prefix meaning between.

interact [ɪntə'rækt] v. to have an effect on each other. **interaction** [ɪntər'ækʃn] n. effect of two things on each other. **interactive** adj. (computer program) which allows the user to communicate with the computer.

inter alia [ɪntəˈɑːlɪə] among other things.

interbreed [ɪntəˈbriːd] v. (interbred) to breed (with an adult of another strain).

intercede [ɪntəˈsiːd] v. to plead; to make an appeal. **intercession** [ɪntəˈseʃn] n. pleading (on behalf of s.o.).

intercept [ɪntəˈsept] v. to stop (sth) as it is passing. **interception** [ɪntəˈsepʃn] n. stopping (of sth which is passing). **interceptor** n. person/aircraft which intercepts.

interchange 1 [ˈɪntətʃeɪndʒ] n. (a) exchange (of ideas). (b) large road junction where motorways cross. **interchange 2** v. to exchange one thing for another. **interchangeable** [ɪntəˈtʃeɪndʒəbl] adj. which can be substituted for each other.

intercity [ɪntəˈsɪtɪ] adj. (train/plane) between two cities.

intercom [ˈɪntəkɒm] n. radio for speaking to people over a short distance.

interconnected [ɪntəkəˈnektɪd] adj. which connect with each other.

intercontinental [ɪntəkɒntɪˈnentl] adj. from one continent to another.

intercourse [ˈɪntəkɔːs] n. (a) reproductive act between a male and a female. (b) (formal) communication between people.

interdict [ˈɪntədɪkt] n. (formal) order forbidding sth.

interest 1 [ˈɪntrəst] n. (a) percentage return on investment; percentage payable on a loan. (b) financial share. (c) particular attention. (d) thing which you pay attention to. (e) advantage. **interest 2** v. to attract s.o.'s attention. interested, adj. with a personal (usu.financial) interest in sth. **interesting** adj. which attracts attention.

interface [ˈɪntəfeɪs] n. area where two different systems meet and interact.

interfere [ɪntəˈfɪə] v. (a) to meddle/to get involved (in/with). (b) to affect the reception of radio/TV programmes. **interference** n. (a) involvement/meddling. (b) noise which affects radio/TV programmes.

interferon n. protein which fights a virus.

interim [ˈɪntərɪm] adj. & n. (report) given halfway through an investigation; in the i. = meanwhile.

interior [ɪnˈtɪərɪə] adj. & n. inner part (of a building/car); ministry of the i. = ministry dealing with affairs inside a country.

interject [ɪntəˈdʒekt] v. to make a sudden exclamation. **interjection** [ɪntəˈdʒekʃn] n. exclamation; word used to show surprise.

interlace [ɪntəˈleɪs] v. to weave together.

interlard [ɪntəˈlɑːd] v. to insert comments into (a text).

interleave [ɪntəˈliːv] v. to put (sth) between the pages of a book.

interlock [ɪntəˈlɒk] v. to fit together.

interlocutor [ɪntəˈlɒkjʊtə] n. person who speaks to s.o. else.

interloper [ˈɪntələʊpə] n. person who comes in/who intrudes.

interlude [ˈɪntəluːd] n. quiet time between two lively periods; rest period between parts of a performance.

intermarry [ɪntəˈmærɪ] v. to marry within the same family group. **intermarriage** n. act of intermarrying.

intermediary [ɪntəˈmiːdjərɪ] adj. & n. (person) who goes between two others/who acts as messenger. **intermediate** [ɪntəˈmiːdjət] adj. half way between two extremes.

interment [ɪnˈtɜːmənt] n. (formal) burial.

intermezzo [ɪntəˈmetzəʊ] n. (pl.-os) short piece (of music) linking two other pieces.

interminable [ɪnˈtɜːmɪnəbl] adj. never ending. **interminably** adv. without coming to an end.

intermingle [ɪntəˈmɪŋgl] v. to mix together.

intermission [ɪntəˈmɪʃn] n. (a) interval (in a play/film/concert). (b) without i.= without a break/without stopping.

intermittent [ɪntəˈmɪtənt] adj. which takes place from time to time. **intermittently** adv. (taking place) from time to time/on and off.

intern 1 [ˈɪntɜːn] n. junior doctor who works and lives in a hospital. **intern. 2** v. to put (prisoners) in a prison without trial. **internee** [ɪntɜːˈniː] n. prisoner in a detention camp who has not been tried. **internment** n. putting prisoners in a prison or camp without trial.

internal [ɪnˈtɜːnl] adj. inside; i.

telephone = private telephone inside a building; i. combustion engine = engine in which the fuel is burnt inside a closed space (as in the cylinders in a car engine). **internally** *adv.* inside.

international 1 [ɪntəˈnæʃnl] *adj.* between countries. **international 2** *n.* (a) sportsman who has played for his country's team against another country. (b) game/sporting competition between two countries. **internationally** *adv.* (done) between countries.

internecine [ɪntəˈniːsaɪn] *adj.* (formal) (two things) which destroy each other.

internode [ˈɪntənəʊd] *n.* space between two joints in a plant. **internodal** *adj.* between joints.

interphone [ˈɪntəfəʊn] *n.* short distance internal telephone.

interplanetary [ɪntəˈplænətrɪ] *adj.* between planets.

interplay [ˈɪntəpleə] *n.* reaction between two forces.

interpol [ˈɪntəpɒl] *n.* international police system.

interpolate [ɪnˈtɜːpəleɪt] *v.* to add (words) in between others. **interpolation** [ɪntɜːpəˈleɪʃn] *n.* adding of words between existing words in a text; word(s) thus added.

interpose [ˈɪntəpəʊz] *v.* to place (sth) in between.

interpret [ɪnˈtɜːprɪt] *v.* (a) to explain (sth) to s.o. who does not understand. (b) to translate aloud what is spoken from one language into another. **interpretation** [ɪntɜːprɪˈteɪʃn] *n.* (a) meaning. (b) translating aloud from one language to another. **interpreter** *n.* person who translates aloud from one language to another.

interregnum [ɪntəˈregnəm] *n.* period between the reigns of successive kings; period of inactivity between one management and another.

interrelated [ɪntərɪˈleɪtɪd] *adj.* (several things) which are related.

interrogate [ɪnˈterəgeɪt] *v.* to question severely. **interrogation** [ɪnterəˈgeɪʃn] *n.* severe questioning (of a prisoner). **interrogative** [ɪntəˈrɒgətɪv] *adj. & n.* questioning; i. pronoun = pronoun which asks a question. **interrogator** [ɪnˈterəgeɪtə] *n.* person who questions (a prisoner) closely.

interrupt [ɪntəˈrʌpt] *v.* to break into (a speech); to stop (sth) continuing. **interruption** [ɪntəˈrʌpʃn] *n.* (act of) interrupting; thing which interrupts.

intersect [ɪntəˈsekt] *v.* to cut across; to cut across (each other). **intersection** *n.* place where lines cut across each other; crossroads.

intersperse [ɪntəˈspɜːs] *v.* to scatter.

interstate [ɪntəˈsteɪt] *adj.* (a) between two countries. (b) *Am.* between two states.

interstellar [ɪntəˈstelə] *adj.* between stars.

interstice [ɪnˈtɜːstrs] *n.* small space in between other things.

interwine [ɪntəˈtwaɪn] *v.* to twist (things) together; to be twisted together.

interval [ˈɪntəvl] *n.* period/gap (between two points/between two acts in a play); (in music) difference in pitch.

intervene [ɪntəˈviːn] *v.* to come/to arrive in between. **intervention** [ɪntəˈvenʃn] *n.* coming between; entry into sth.

interview 1 [ˈɪntəvjuː] *n.* (a) discussion (on radio/TV/in the newspaper) between an important or interesting person and a journalist. (b) questioning (by one or more people) of a person applying for a job. **interview 2** *v.* (a) to ask (a famous/interesting person) questions in order to show his answers publicly. (b) to ask questions of (a person applying for a job). **interviewee** [ɪntəvjuːˈiː] *n.* person who is being/who is going to be interviewed. **interviewer** *n.* person who asks the questions at an interview.

interweave [ɪntəˈwiːv] *v.* (interwove; interwoven) to weave/to bind together.

intestate [ɪnˈtesteɪt] *adj.* not having made a will.

intestine [ɪnˈtestɪn] *n.* long tube in the body through which food passes from the stomach to the anus. **intestinal** *adj.* referring to the intestine.

intimate 1 [ˈɪntɪmət] *adj.* (a) very close (friend); detailed (knowledge). (b) sexual (relationship). **intimate 2** [ˈɪntɪmət] *n.* close friend. **intimate 3** [ˈɪntɪmeɪt] *v.* to announce; to suggest. **intimacy** *n.* close relationship (with s.o.). **intimately** *adv.* closely. **intimation** [ɪntɪˈmeɪʃn] *n.* suggestion.

intimidate [ɪn'tɪmɪdeɪt] v. to frighten (s.o.) by threats. **intimidating** adj. frightening. **intimidation** [ɪntɪmɪ'deɪʃn] n. frightening by threats.

into [ɪntʊ] prep. (a) (movement) towards the inside. (b) so as to become; to develop as; the tadpole changed i. a frog; he burst i. tears (c) dividing; four i. three won't go.

intolerable [ɪn'tɒlərəbl] adj. which you cannot bear. **intolerably** adv, unbearably. **intolerant** [ɪn'tɒlərənt] adj. (person) who cannot bear people with different ideas from his own. **intolerance** n. not accepting other people's points of view.

intonation [ɪntə'neɪʃn] n. rise or fall of the voice (in speech or singing). **intone** [ɪn'təʊn] v. to recite (psalms, etc.) in a singing voice.

intoxicate [ɪn'tɒksɪkeɪt] v. to make (s.o.) drunk. **intoxicant** n. substance which intoxicates. **intoxicating** adj. which makes you drunk; exciting. **intoxication** [ɪntɒksɪ'keɪʃn] n. drunkenness.

intra- ['ɪntrə-] prefix meaning within.

intractable [ɪn'træktəbl] adj. very difficult to deal with; (problem) which is impossible to solve.

intransigent [ɪn'trænsɪdʒənt] adj. firm; obstinate/not shifting your position/not changing your mind. **intransigence** n. firmness/being obstinate.

in transit [ɪn'trænzɪt] adv. (goods) which are being transported.

intransitive [ɪn'trænsɪtɪv] adj. (verb) which has no object.

intrauterine [ɪntrə'juːtərɪn] adj. inside the uterus; i. device = contraceptive device which is placed inside a woman's uterus.

intravenous [ɪntrə'viːnəs] adj. (injection) made into a vein.

intrepid [ɪn'trepɪd] adj. fearless/very brave. **intrepidity** [ɪntrə'pɪdɪtɪ] n. being intrepid.

intricate ['ɪntrɪkət] adj. very complicated; made of many different parts. **intricacy** [ɪntrɪkət] n. complexity. **intricately** adv. in an intricate way.

intrigue 1 [ɪn'triːg] n. secret plot. **intrigue 2** v. (a) to plot. (b) to make (s.o.) interested.

intrinsic [ɪn'trɪnzɪk] adj. forming a basic part of sth. **intrinsically** adv. basically.

introduce [ɪntrə'djuːs] v. (a) to present (s.o.) to another person/to people who did not know him previously. (b) to announce (a TV/radio programme, etc.). (c) to make(sth) go in; to bring (sth) in. **introduction** [ɪntrə'dʌkʃn] n. (a) act of presenting sth; thing which presents sth. (b) making s.o. known to another person/ to people who did not know him previously. (c) piece at the beginning of a book which explains the rest of the book. (d) elementary book about a subject. **introductory** adj. (words) which introduce; i. offer = offer of a new range of goods at a specially low price.

introit ['ɪntrɔɪt] n. music sung at the beginning of a church service.

introspective [ɪntrə'spektɪv] adj. inward-looking; thinking a lot about yourself. **introspection** [ɪntrə'spekʃn] n. looking inwards at yourself.

introvert ['ɪntrəvɜːt] n. person who thinks mainly about himself. **introverted** adj. (person) who thinks mainly about himself.

intrude [ɪn'truːd] v. to enter where you are not wanted. **intruder** n. person who has intruded. **intrusion** [ɪn'truːʒn] n. act of intruding. **intrusive** [ɪn'truːsɪv] adj. unwanted.

intuition [ɪntjʊ'ɪʃn] n. thinking of sth/ knowing sth naturally without it being explained. **intuitive** [ɪn'tjɔɪtɪv] adj. based on intuition. **intuitively** adv. in an intuitive way.

Inuit ['ɪnjuːɪt] n. Eskimos.

inundate ['ɪnʌndeɪt] v. to flood. **inundation** [ɪnʌn'deɪʃn] n. flood.

inure [ɪn'jʊə] v. (formal) to accustom to sth unpleasant.

invade [ɪn'veɪd] v. to attack and enter (a country) with an army. **invader** n. person who enters a country with an army.

invalid 1 ['ɪnvəlɪd] adj. & n. sick/ disabled (person); i. carriage = small vehicle for one disabled person. **invalid 2** ['ɪnvəliːd] v. to i. s.o. out = to make s.o. retire because of ill health. **invalid 3** [ɪn'vælɪd] adj. not valid/not legal. **invalidation** [ɪnvælɪdeɪʃn] n. making invalid. **invalidate** [ɪn'vælɪdeɪt] v. to make (sth) invalid. **invalidity** n. being an invalid.

invaluable [ɪn'væljʊəbl] adj. extremely valuable.

invariable [ɪn'veərɪəbl] adj. always the same/not changing. **invariably** adv. always.

invasion [ɪn'veɪʒən] n. (a) entering a country with armed forces. (b) i. of privacy = illegal entering of a person's home in a way which destroys his private life.

invective [ɪn'vektɪv] n. insulting speech/abuse.

inveigh [ɪn'veɪ] v. (formal) to speak violently (against sth).

inveigle [ɪn'veɪgl] v. to trick (s.o.) into doing sth.

invent [ɪn'vent] v. to create (a new process/new machine); to think up (an excuse). **invention** [ɪn'venʃn] n. (a) creation (of new process/new machine). (b) new machine. **inventive** adj. creative. **inventiveness** n. ability to invent. **inventor** n. person who invents new processes/new machines.

inventory ['ɪnvəntrɪ] n. list (of contents of a house, etc.); Am. stock (in a warehouse).

inverse ['ɪnvɜːs] adj. & n. opposite/ contrary. **inversion** [ɪn'vɜːʃn] n. turning sth round in a contrary way.

invert [ɪn'vɜːt] v. to turn (sth) upside down/back to front; inverted commas = printing sign (" ") which indicates speech.

invertebrate [ɪn'vɜːtɪbreɪt] adj. & n. (animal) without a backbone.

invest [ɪn'vest] v. to put (money) into savings/property, etc.. so that it will increase in value. **investment** n. money placed so that it will increase in value. **investor** n. person who puts money into savings or property.

investigate [ɪn'vestɪgeɪt] v. to study/to examine. **investigation** [ɪn'vestɪ'geɪʃn] n. examination. **investigator** n. detective; person who investigates.

investiture [ɪn'vestɪtʃə] n. ceremony where s.o. is given a medal/where s.o. is installed in office.

inveterate [ɪn'vetərət] adj. obstinate/ hardened.

invidious [ɪn'vɪdɪəs] adj. which is likely to offend people unreasonably.

invigilate [ɪn'vɪdʒɪleɪt] v. to supervise an examination. **invigilator** n. supervisor of an examination.

invigorate [ɪn'vɪgəreɪt] v. to make strong/vigorous; to make (s.o.) feel livelier.

invincible [ɪn'vɪnsəbl] adj. which cannot be defeated. **invincibility** [ɪnvɪnsə'bɪlɪtɪ] n. being unbeatable.

inviolable [ɪn'vaɪələbl] adj. which cannot be violated. **inviolability** [ɪnvaɪələ'bɪlɪtɪ] n. being inviolable.

invisible [ɪn'vɪzəbl] adj. which cannot be seen. **invisibility** [ɪnvɪzə'bɪlɪtɪ] n. not being able to be seen.

invite [ɪn'vaɪt] v. (a) to ask (s.o.) to do sth. (b) to ask for (comments, etc.). **invitation** [ɪnvɪ'teɪʃn] n. asking (s.o. to do sth). **inviting** adj. attractive.

in vitro [ɪn'viːtrəʊ] adj (experiment) which is carried out in a laboratory.

invocation [ɪnvə'keɪʃn] n. (formal) calling on s.o. for help/support.

invoice 1 ['ɪnvɔɪs] n. note sent to ask for payment for services or goods. **invoice 2** v. to send a note asking for payment for services or goods. **invoicing** n. sending of an invoice.

invoke [ɪn'vəʊk] v. to call on (s.o./sth) for help/support.

involuntary [ɪn'vɒləntrɪ] adj. not voluntary/not willingly done. **involuntarily** adv. not willingly.

involve [ɪn'vɒlv] v. (a) to bring (s.o./ sth) into (a dispute/a scheme). (b) to make necessary. **involved** adj. intricate/complicated. **involvement** n. contact/collaboration.

invulnerable [ɪn'vʌlnərəbl] adj. which cannot be successfully attacked.

inward ['ɪnwəd] adj. on/to the inside. **inwardly** adv. on the inside. **inwards** adv. towards the inside.

iodine ['aɪədiːn] n. (element:I) substance which is used in solution, e.g. as a disinfectant. **iodize** v. to fill with iodine.

ion ['aɪən] n. atom with an electric charge. **ionize** [aɪ'ɒnəsfɪə] v. to produce ions; to become ions. **ionosphere** [aɪ'ɒnəsfɪə] n. part of the atmosphere surrounding the earth which reflects radio waves back to earth.

iota [aɪ'əʊtə] n. very small piece.

IOU [aɪəʊ'juː] *n.* paper promising that you will pay back money which you have borrowed.

ipecacuanha [ɪpɪkækjuː'ɑːnə] *n.* drug made from the root of a plant, used as an emetic and also as cough medicine.

ipso facto ['ɪpsəʊ'fæktəʊ] *adv.* because of this fact.

IQ ['aɪ'kjuː] abbrev. for intelligence quotient.

IRA ['aɪɑː'eɪ] abbrev. for Irish Republican Army; *Am.* Individual Retirement Account.

Iranian 1 [ɪ'reɪnjən] *adj.* referring to Iran. **Iranian 2** *n.* person from Iran.

Iraqi 1 [ɪ'rɑːkɪ] *adj.* referring to Iraq. **Iraqi 2** *n.* (*pl.*-is) person from Iraq.

irascible [ɪ'ræsɪbl] *adj.* easily becoming angry. **irascibility** [ɪ'ræsɪ'bɪlɪtɪ] *n.* being irascible.

ire ['aɪə] *n.* (formal) anger. **irate** [aɪ'reɪt] *adj.* very angry.

iridescent [ɪrɪ'desnt] *adj.* with changing/shimmering colours. **iridescence** *n.* being iridescent.

iris ['aɪərɪs] *n.* (pl -es) (a) plant with tall flat leaves and *usu.* yellow or purple flowers. (b) part of the eye which is coloured.

Irish 1 ['aɪərɪʃ] *adj.* referring to Ireland. **Irish 2** *n.* (a) Celtic language spoken in parts of Ireland (b) the I. = people from Ireland. **Irishman, Irishwoman** *n.* (*pl.*- men, - women) person from Ireland.

irk ['ɜːk] *v.* to annoy/to bother. **irksome** ['ɜːksəm] *adj.* annoying/bothersome.

iron 1 ['aɪən] *n. & adj.* (element Fe) (a) common grey metal which can be made into a magnet; i. ore = iron in its natural state (b) electric household instrument for smoothing the creases from clothes. (c) in irons = imprisoned with iron chains round one's ankles. (d) metal frame to support a weak leg. (e) gold club with a metal head. **iron 2** *v.* to press (cloth) with an iron; to i. out = to sort out (a problem/difficulty) **Iron Age** *n.* period when man first used iron. **Iron curtain** *n.* border formerly existing between Communist countries in Eastern Europe and non-communist Western Europe. **ironing** *n.* (a) pressing clothes with an electric iron. (b) clothes which need pressing. **ironing board** *n.* high narrow table used for ironing clothes.

iron lung *n.* machine which encloses a patient's body, and in which pressure is increased and reduced to make the patient breathe. **ironmonger** *n.* person who runs a hardware shop, selling tools, paint, pans, etc. **ironmonger's, ironmongery** *n.* hardware shop. **ironwork** *n.* (decorative) locks/ handles/gates.etc. made of iron. **ironworks** *n.* factory which produces iron.

irony ['aɪərənɪ] *n.* (a) way of referring to sth where you say the opposite of what you mean. (b) quality of happening at the wrong moment, as if deliberately planned. **ironic(al)** [aɪ'rɒnɪk(l)] *adj.* mocking/slightly funny. **ironically** *adv.* in a mocking way.

irradiate [ɪ'reɪdɪeɪt] *v.* (of heat/light/ rays) to shine on (sth). **irradiation** [ɪreɪdɪ'eɪʃn] *n.* act of irradiating.

irrational [ɪ'ræʃnl] *adj.* not rational/not sensible/against common sense. **irrationally** *adv.* in an irrational way.

irreconcilable [ɪrekən'saɪləbl] *adj.* which cannot be made to agree.

irrecoverable [ɪrɪ'kʌvərəbl] *adj.* which cannot be recovered.

irredeemable [ɪrɪ'diːməbl] *adj.* (loss) which cannot be made good; (pledge) which cannot be redeemed.

irreducible [ɪrɪ'djuːsəbl] *adj.* which cannot be reduced.

irrefutable [ɪrɪ'fjuːtəbl] *adj.* (argument) which cannot be disproved.

irregular 1 [ɪ'regjʊlə] *adj.* (a) not regular; not level; not happening at the same time. (b) not according to the rules; (verb) which has forms which do not fit the usual patterns of grammar. **irregular 2** *n.* pl irregulars = soldiers who do not form part of the regular army. **irregularity** [ɪregjʊ'lærɪtɪ] *n.* thing which goes against the rules/the law. **irregularly** *adv.* not regularly.

irrelevant [ɪ'reləvənt] *adj.* (to) not relevant/which has no connection to the subject. **irrelevance** *n.* having no connection with the subject.

irreligious [ɪrɪ'lɪdʒəs] *adj.* not religious; not showing respect for religion.

irreparable [ɪ'repərbl] *adj.* which cannot be repaired. **irreparably** *adv.* in a way which cannot be repaired.

irreplaceable [ɪrɪ'pleɪsəbl] *adj.* which cannot be replaced; (thing) for which there is no substitute.

irrepressible [ɪrɪ'presəbl] *adj.* which cannot be held back.

irreproachable [ɪrɪ'prəʊtʃəbl] *adj.* perfect/which cannot be criticized.

irresistible [ɪrɪ'zɪstəbl] *adj.* which cannot be resisted; which you cannot help accepting.

irresolute [ɪ'rezəluːt] *adj.* undecided; (person) who hesitates/cannot decide. **irresolutely** *adv.* not knowing what to do. **irresolution** *n.* being irresolute.

irrespective [ɪrɪ'spektɪv] *prep.* taking no account (of).

irresponsible [ɪrɪ'spɒnsəbl] *adj.* wild/senseless; not responsible. **irresponsibly** *adv.* with no sense of responsibility.

irretrievable [ɪrɪ'triːvəbl] *adj.* which cannot be found again. **irretrievably** *adv.* hopelessly.

irreverent [ɪ'revrənt] *adj.* not serious; disrespectful. **irreverence** *n.* being irreverent. **irreverently** *adv.* not in a serious way; disrespectfully.

irreversible [ɪrɪ'vɜːsəbl] *adj.* (decision) which cannot be changed.

irrevocable [ɪ'revəkəbl] *adj.* (decision) which cannot be changed.

irrigate ['ɪrɪgeɪt] *v.* (a) to water (land) by using canals and pumps. (b) to wash (a wound) with a flow of water.

irrigation [ɪrɪ'geɪʃn] *n.* watering of fields (by using canals and pumps).

irritate ['ɪrɪteɪt] *v.* (a) to annoy. (b) to prickle/to burn. **irritability** [ɪrɪtə'bɪlɪtɪ] *n.* being irritable. **irritable** ['ɪrɪtəbl] *adj.* easily annoyed. **irritably** *adv.* in a bad tempered way. **irritant** *n.* thing which annoys/causes a burning feeling. **irritating** *adj.* which annoys. **irritation** [ɪrɪ'teɪʃn] *n.* annoyance; thing which annoys/which causes a burning feeling.

irrupt [ɪ'rʌpt] *v.* (formal) to appear/to come in suddenly. **irruption** [ɪ'rʌpʃn] *n.* sudden appearance.

is [ɪz] *v.* see be.

isinglass ['aɪzɪŋglɑːs] *n.* type of gelatine.

Islam ['ɪzlæm] *n.* religion of the Muslims. **Islamic** [ɪz'læmɪk] *adj.* referring to Islam.

island ['aɪlənd] *n.* piece of land entirely surrounded by water; traffic i.= small raised piece of pavement in the centre of the road where pedestrians can safely stand. **islander** *n.* person who lives on an island. **isle** [aɪl] *n.* island. **islet** *n.* small island.

isn't ['ɪznt] *v.* short for is not.

isobar ['aɪsəʊbɑː] *n.* line on a weather map showing places of equal barometric pressure.

isolate ['aɪsəleɪt] *v.* (a) to put(sth/s.o.) in a place alone; isolated attack = single attack, not repeated. (b) to separate (a chemical) substance from a compound.

isolation [aɪsə'leɪʃn] *n.* cutting off from communication with other people; i. hospital = hospital for people suffering from dangerous diseases. **isolationism** *n.* policy of not communicating with other countries. **isolationist** *n.* person who advocates isolationism.

isomer ['aɪsəmə] *n.* chemical compound with the same molecular formula as another, but with a different arrangement of atoms. **isometric** [aɪsəʊ'metrɪk] *adj.* (exercises) using muscles acting against each other or a fixed object.

isosceles [aɪ'sɒsɪliːz] *adj.* i. triangle = triangle with two sides of the same length.

isotherm ['aɪsəʊθɜːm] *n.* line on a weather map showing places with equal temperatures.

isotope ['aɪsətəʊp] *n.* one of two or more forms of a chemical element which have atoms which are chemically similar but with different atomic weights.

Israeli 1 [ɪz'reɪlɪ] *adj.* referring to Israel. **Israeli 2** *n.* (*pl.*-is) person from Israel.

issue 1 ['ɪʃuː] *n.* (a) result. (b) problem; to make an i. of = have a big discussion about; the point at i. = the question which is being discussed; to take i. with = disagree with (c) publication (of a book); putting on sale (new stamps); putting into circulation (new coins/notes); giving out (of uniforms/official permits, etc.) (d) one copy of a newspaper or magazine (e) (old) children. **issue 2** *v.* (a) to come out. (b) to put (new stamps) on sale; to publish (books); to put (new banknotes) into circulation; to give out/to hand out (uniforms/official permits, etc.).

isthmus ['ɪsməs] *n.* (*pl.*-es) narrow piece of land connecting two larger pieces of land

it [ɪt] pronoun referring to a thing (a) (standing in the place of thing just mentioned) put it down; it's here. (b) (referring to nothing in particular) it's raining; *inf.* you're for it = you are going to be in trouble.

Italian 1 [ɪ'tæljən] *adj.* referring to Italy. **Italian 2** *n.* (a) person from Italy (b) language spoken in Italy. **italic** [ɪ'tælɪk] *adj. & n.* sloping (letter); this is printed in italics. **italicize** [ɪ'tælɪsaɪz] *v.* to print in italics.

itch 1 [ɪtʃ] *n.* (*pl.*-es) tickling sensation. **itch 2** *v.* to tickle; to be very eager (to do sth) **itching** *n.* tickling sensation

itchy *adj.* tickly; making you feel you want to scratch; i. feet = desire to change jobs/to travel.

item ['aɪtəm] *n.* thing (in a list); news items = separate pieces of news on a news programme. **itemize** *v.* to make a detailed list of (things).

itinerary [ɪ'tɪmərərɪ] *n.* route; list of places to be visited on a tour. **itinerant** *adj.* wandering/travelling.

its [ɪts] *adj.* belonging to a thing/to it. **it's** [ɪts] short of it is/it has.

itself [ɪt'self] pronoun referring to a thing/to it (a) (referring to an object) all by i.; the dog has hurt i. (b) (for emphasis) the television i.

IUD [aɪju:'di:] abbrev. for intrauterine device.

I've [aɪv] short for I have.

ivory ['aɪvərɪ] *adj. & n.* (made of) whitish substance from an elephant's tusk; i. tower = imaginary place where an intellectual can keep away from contact with the everyday world.

ivy ['aɪvɪ] *n.* evergreen plant which climbs up walls and trees.

Jj

jab 1 [dʒæb] *n.* (a) sharp blow (often with a pointed object). (b) *inf.* injection. **jab 2** *v.* (jabbed) to poke firmly (esp. with a pointed object).

jabber 1 ['dʒæbə] *n.* quick, indistinct talk. **jabber 2** *v.* to speak quickly and indistinctly.

jacaranda [dʒækæ'rændə] *n.* tropical tree with scented pale purple flowers.

jack [dʒæk] *n.* (a) instrument for raising a heavy object (esp. a motor vehicle). (b) (in playing cards) the card between the queen and the ten. (c) male of certain mammals. (d) (at bowls) small white ball for players to aim at. (e) flag; the Union J. = flag of the United Kingdom. (f) single-pin electric plug. **jackboot** *n.* high military boot. **jackbooted** *adj.* wearing jackboots. **jackhammer** *n.* power drill held in the hand. **jack-in-the box** *n.* box from which a toy figure springs up when the lid is opened.

jackknife 1 *n.* (*pl.*-knives) type of large folding knife. **jackknife, 2** *v.* (of vehicle pulling a trailer) to fold in half in an accident. **jack-of-all, trades** *n.* person who is reasonably good at a large number of jobs. **jack up** *v.* (a) to raise with a jack. (b) *inf.* to raise (profits or prices).

jackal ['dʒækl] *n.* wild dog, which feeds chiefly on dead flesh.

jackass ['dʒækæs] *n.* laughing j. = kookaburra.

jackdaw ['dʒækdɔ:] *n.* type of small crow.

jacket ['dʒækɪt] *n.* (a) short coat. (b) outer casing or covering; loose paper cover for a book. (c) skin (of a potato). **jacketed** *adj.* with a jacket.

jackpot ['dʒækpɒt] *n.* to win/to hit the j. = to win a high prize in a lottery/to enjoy particular success in sth.

Jacobean [dʒækə'bi:ən] *adj.* referring to the time of James I (1601 - 1625). **Jacobite** ['dʒækəaɪt] *adj. & n.* (person) who supported James II or his descendants in exile.

jade [dʒeɪd] *n.* hard, *usu.* green, precious stone. **jade-green** *adj.* of the bluish green colour of jade.

jaded ['dʒeɪdɪd] *adj.* worn out/tired.

jag [dʒæg] *n. Sl.* drinking session.

jagged [dʒægɪd] *adj.* with an irregular, rough, spiky edge.

jaguar ['dʒægjʊə] *n.* large wild cat of Central and South America.

jail 1 [dʒeɪl] *n.* prison. **jail 2** *v.* to put (s.o.) in prison. **jailbird** *n.* person who

has been sent to prison often. **jailer** *n.* person who guards prisoners in jail.
jalopy [dʒə'lɒpɪ] *n. inf.* dilapidated old car.
jam 1 [dʒæm] *n.* (a) stoppage/blockage caused by too many things in too small a space. (b) *inf.* in a j.= in a difficult situation. (c) sweet food made by boiling together fruit, sugar, etc.; money for j.= money very easily earned. **jam 2** *v.* (jammed) (a) (of machine) to stop/to stick so that it cannot move. (b) to crowd/to force (things) into a small space. (c) to make (a radio broadcast) impossible to understand by broadcasting noise on the same wavelength. **jamming** *n.* marking a radio broadcast impossible to understand. **jammy** *adj.* sticky with jAm. **jam-packed** *adj. inf.* packed full. **jam session** *n.* impromptu jazz concert.
Jamaican 1 [dʒə'meɪkən] *adj.* referring to Jamaica. **Jamaican 2** *n.* person from Jamaica.
jamb [dʒæm] *n.* side post of a door or window.
jamboree [dʒæmbə'riː] *n.* large meeting (esp. of Scouts); big festival/party.
jangle 1 ['dʒæŋgl] *n.* harsh clanging noise. **jangle 2** *v.* (a) to make a harsh changing noise. (b) to disturb/to irritate (the nerves).
janitor ['dʒænɪtə] *n.* caretaker, esp. in a school or college.
January ['dʒænjʊərɪ] *n.* 1st month of the year.
Japanese 1 [dʒæpə'niːz] *adj.* referring to Japan. **Japanese 2** *n.* (a) *pl.*(Japanese) person from Japan. (b) language spoken in Japan.
japonica [dʒə'pɒnɪkə] *n.* flowering quince bush.
jar 1 [dʒɑː] *n.* container for jam, etc., often of glass and *usu.* cylindrical; a j. of jam; jam j. = special jar for putting jam in. **jar 2** *v.* (jarred) (a) to make a nasty/unpleasant sound. (b) to j. on s.o.'s nerves = to annoy. (c) to bump/to give a shock to. (d) to sound/to look unpleasant.
jardinière [ʒɑːdɪnɪ'eə] *n.* ornamental container for plants.
jargon ['dʒɑːgən] *n.* special form of language used by a trade/profession or particular group of people.

jasmine ['dʒæzmɪn] *n.* shrub with sweet smelling white or yellow flowers.
jasper ['dʒæspə] *n.* coloured quartz.
jaundice ['dʒɔːndɪs] *n.* sickness which makes the skin turn yellow, due to a disorder of the liver or bile. **jaundiced** *adj.* (a) suffering from jaundice. (b) miserable/dispirited; envious; resentful.
jaunt [dʒɔːnt] *n.* short excursion.
jaunting car *n.* (in Ireland) light two wheeled carriage. **jaunty** ['dʒɔːntɪ] *adj.* (-ier, -iest) cheerful/lively. **jauntily** *adv.* cheerfully. **jauntiness** *n.* lively manner.
javelin ['dʒævlɪn] *n.* long spear used in battle or in sport.
jaw 1 [dʒɔː] *n.* (a) arrangement of bones which allow the mouth to open and shut. (b) jaws = two parts of a tool which grip. **jaw 2** *v. inf.* to talk (too much). **jawbone** *n.* one of the two bones forming a jaw.
jay [dʒeɪ] *n.* brightly coloured bird of the crow family. **jaywalker** *n.* pedestrian who does not take care when crossing the street. **jaywalking** *n.* crossing a street without taking care.
jazz [dʒæz] *n.* type of music with strong rhythm, originally played by American negroes. **jazz up** *v. inf.* to make bright/attractive. **jazzy** *adj.* bright (colour).
jealous ['dʒeləs] *adj.* (of) feeling sorrow/anger because you want sth which belongs to s.o. else. **jealously** *adv.* in a jealous way. **jealousy** *n.* jealous feeling.
jeans [dʒiːnz] *n. pl.*(often blue) trousers made of a type of strong cotton.
jeep [dʒiːp] *n.* trademark for a strongly built vehicle used for travelling over rough ground.
jeer 1 ['dʒɪə] *n.* mocking/laughing in a nasty way. **jeer 2** *v.* (at) to mock/to laugh at (s.o.) in a nasty way.
Jehovah [dʒɪ'həʊvə] *n.* God of Israel.
jejune [dʒɪ'dʒuːn] *adj.* naive.
jell [dʒel] *v.* (a) (of liquid) to become a jelly. (b) (of plan) to become definite. **jelly** ['dʒelɪ] *n.* (a) semi-solid substance, esp. type of sweet food made of gelatine/water/fruit flavouring, etc. (b) type of jam made of fruit juice boiled with sugar. **jellied** ['dʒelɪd] *adj.* cooked/preserved in a jelly. **jelly bean** *n.* Am. sweet of coloured jelly, shaped like a

bean. **jellyfish** n. sea creature with jelly-like body. **jelly roll** n. Am. swiss roll.

jemmy ['dʒemɪ] n. flat iron bar with a curved end, used by burglars to open doors or widows.

jenny ['dʒenɪ] n. female donkey.

jeopardize ['dʒepədaɪz] v. to put in danger/at risk. **jeopardy** ['dʒepədɪ] n. danger/risk.

jeremiad [dʒerɪ'maɪəd] n. (formal) long complaint about your problems.

jerk 1 [dʒɜːk] n. (a) sudden uneven movement; sharp pull. (b) Am. Sl. stupid person. **jerk 2** v. to make a sudden movement; to pull sharply. **jerkily** adv. with an abrupt/sudden movement. **jerkiness** n. being jerky. **jerky** adj. abrupt/sudden.

jerkin ['dʒɜːkɪn] n. short coat with no sleeves.

jerrican ['dʒerɪkæn] n. large metal container for water/petrol, etc.

jerry-builder ['dʒerɪbɪldə] n. person who builds cheap, poorly constructed, buildings. **jerry-built** adj. (building) which is cheaply built.

jersey ['dʒɜːzɪ] n. (a) close-fitting warm upper garment; special shirt of a football team, etc. (b) j. (cloth) = type of loosely woven, usu. woollen, cloth. (c) type of cow.

jest 1 [dʒest] n. joke; thing done/said for amusement only. **jest 2** v. to make jokes. **jester** n, person who plays jokes, esp. someone employed to do this at a royal court.

jet 1 [dʒet] n. (a) type of black mineral which can be highly polished; j. black = very black. (b) long narrow spray of liquid or gas. (c) opening to allow gas to escape. (d) jet-propelled aircraft; j. lag = tiredness felt by travellers who fly by jet across time zones; j. set = wealthy people who frequently travel by jet. **jet 2** v. (jetted) inf. to travel by jet. **jet engine** n. engine which is propelled by a jet. **jet-propelled** adj. pushed forward by a backward movement of jets of gas. **jet propulsion** n. being jet propelled. **jetstream** n. (a) wind in the upper atmosphere. (b) stream of gases coming from a jet engine.

jetsam ['dʒetsəm] n. (no pl.) things which have been thrown into the water from a boat.

jettison ['dʒetɪzn] v. to throw out (unwanted things) from a ship/balloon, etc.

jetty ['dʒetɪ] n. wall built into water, where boats can tie up.

Jew [dʒuː] n. person descended from the Hebrews of ancient Palestine. **Jewess** n. Jewish woman. **Jewish** adj. referring to Jews. **Jewry** n. the Jews.

jewel ['dʒuːəl] n. (a) precious stone (b) ornament to be worn, made from precious stones and/or precious metals, or of imitation stones. **jewelled** adj. covered with jewels. **jeweller** n. person who makes/sells jewellery. **jewellery** n. ornaments to be worn, made of precious stones/metals.

jib 1 [dʒɪb] n. (a) triangular sail in front of a boat. (b) arm of a crane. **jib 2** v. (jibbed) (of horse) to refuse (a fence, etc) (b) to j. at = to refuse to do sth.

jibe [dʒaɪb] n. & v. see gibe.

jiffy ['dʒɪfɪ] n. inf. very short time.

jig 1 [dʒɪg] n. (a) type of fast lively dance; music for this dance. (b) instrument for guiding a tool and holding the material being worked on. **jig 2** v. (jigged) to jump up and down; to move about jerkily. **jigger** n. (a) small insect which lives in sand. (b) measure for serving alcohol.

jigsaw n. (a) type of saw with very fine blade for cutting out shapes. (b) j. (puzzle) = puzzle of irregularly shaped pieces of wood/cardboard which when fitted together form a picture.

jiggery pockery ['dʒɪgərɪ'pəʊkərɪ] n. inf. tricks.

jiggle ['dʒɪgl] v. inf. to move rapidly/nervously.

jilt [dʒɪlt] v. to (encourage and then) reject (a lover).

jingle 1 ['dʒɪŋgl] n. (a) sound made by small pieces of metal knocking together. (b) verse with a very simple rhyme and/or rhythm; catchy tune advertising a product. **jingle 2** v. to make a tinkling sound (like pieces of metal).

jingoism ['dʒɪŋgəʊɪzəm] n. excessive love for your country and hatred for others. **jingoistic** [dʒɪŋgəʊ'ɪstɪk] adj. full of jingoism.

jinks [dʒɪŋks] n. pl.high jinks = wild amusement.

jinx [dʒɪŋks] n. (pl.-es) inf. bad luck.
jitters ['dʒɪtəz] n. pl.to have the j. = to be (unnecessarily) nervous/flustered.
jittery adj. nervous/flustered.
jive 1 [dʒaɪv] n. type of fast rhythmic dance; music for this dance. **jive 2** v. to dance to jive music.
job [dʒɒb] n. (a) piece of work; to make a good j. of sth = to do it well; inf. it's good j. that = it's lucky that; to give sth up as a bad j. = to stop making useless efforts to do sth; inf. just the j. = exactly what is needed; odd jobs = pieces of work, esp. repairs in the house; odd j. man = person who does odd jobs. (b) difficult task; I had a j. to eat my meal = it was difficult. (c) position in employment; to be out of a j.= to be unemployed; jobs for the boys = giving of employment to your supporters. (d) inf. crime, esp. a theft. **jobber** n. Am. wholesaler. **jobbing** adj. (of a workman) (person) who is paid for each job separately. **jobcentre** n. government office which displays available vacant jobs. **jobless 1** adj. with no job. **jobless 2** n. the j.= people who have no jobs. **job lot** n. group of miscellaneous items sold together.
jockey 1 ['dʒɒkɪ] n. person who rides horses in races. **jockey 2** v. to j. for position = to try to improve your position, esp. by cheating or trickery.
jockstrap ['dʒɒkstræp] n. support for genitals, worn by male sportsmen.
jocose [dʒə'kəʊs] adj. humorous.
jocular [dʒɒkjʊlə] adj. good humoured; treating things as a joke.
jocularity [dʒɒkjʊ'lærɪtɪ] n. good humour. **jocularly** adv. in a joking way. **jocund** ['dʒɒkənd] adj. (formal) cheerful.
jodhpurs ['dʒɒdpəz] n. pl.special trousers for horse riding which are narrow below the knee.
joey ['dʒəʊɪ] n. (in Australia) inf. young kangaroo.
jog 1 [dʒɒg] n. (a) rather slow pace. (b) light blow, esp. from the elbow. **jog 2** v. (jogged) (a) to move at a steady, but rather slow pace. (b) to run at an easy pace, esp. for exercise. (c) to shake/to push lightly; it jogged his memory = it made him remember. **jogger** ['dʒɒgl] n.

person who jogs for exercise. **jogging** n. running at an easy pace for exercise.
jagtrot n. rather slow, easy pace.
joggle v. inf. to move rapidly/ nervously.
john [dʒɒn] n. Sl. toilet.
join 1 [dʒɔɪn] n. place/line where two things come together. **join 2** v. (a) to come together/to be united; to bring together. (b) to (meet and) go along with; to meet and do sth together; to j. forces = to do sth by combined effort. (c) to become a member of (a club). **joiner** n. person who constructs things from wood, esp. furniture and house fittings. **joinery** n. joiner's trade. **join in** v. to take part. **join up** v. to become a member of the armed forces.
joint 1 [dʒɔɪnt] n. (a) (place where) two or more pieces are attached, esp. in building or carpentry. (b) place where bones come together, allowing movement; out of j. = dislocated. (c) large piece of meat, esp. for roasting. (d) inf. low-class night club or gambling den. (e) Sl. cigarette containing marijuana. **joint 2** v. (a) to cut up (a chicken, etc.) into pieces. (b) to provide with joints. **joint 3** adj. together/ combined; shared by two or more; j. account = bank account shared by two people; j. author = author who writes a book with another. **jointed** adj. having joints. **jointly** adv. together; by combined effort.
joist [dʒɔɪst] n. beam which supports a ceiling or floorboards.
joke 1 [dʒəʊk] n. thing said or done for amusement, to cause laughter; practical j. = action which makes s.o. uncomfortable for the amusement of others. **joke 2** v. to tell or make jokes; to say or do sth for amusement; I was only joking = I did not mean it seriously.
joker n. (a) person who jokes. (b) extra card in a pack used as a bonus in certain games. **jokingly** adv. in a joking way.
jolly 1 ['dʒɒlɪ] adj. (-ier, -iest) merry/ happy. **jolly 2** adv. inf. very. **jolly 3** v. inf. to j. s.o. along = to encourage s.o. by keeping him happy. **jollification** [dʒɒlɪfɪ'keɪʃn] n. enjoyment/being jolly. **jollity** n. merriness.
jolt 1 [dʒəʊlt] n. abrupt shake/shock; violent jerk. **jolt 2** v. (a) to move with a

jumping movement. (b) to push/to shake abruptly. (c) to give a sudden shock to.

jonquil ['dʒɒŋkwɪl] *n.* narcissus.

joss stick ['dʒɒsstɪk] *n.* stick with incense painted on it, which burns slowly giving off a pleasant smell.

jostle ['dʒɒsl] *v.* to push/to bump (esp. with the elbows).

jot 1 [dʒɒt] *n.* very small amount. **jot 2** *v.* (jotted) to j. sth down = to make (quick) notes. **jotter** *n.* small pad of paper for making notes. **jottings** *n. pl.*(random) notes.

joule [dʒuːl] *n.* standard unit of work and energy.

journal ['dʒɜːnl] *n.* (a) diary. (b) periodical, esp. on a learned subject. (c) book for recording each day's business. **journalese** [dʒɜːnə'liːz] *n.* style used by bad journalists. **journalism** ['dʒɜːnəlɪzəm] *n.* profession of writing for newspapers or periodicals. **journalist** *n.* person who writes for newspapers or periodicals.

journey 2 ['dʒɜːnɪ] *n.* (a) long trip. (b) long distance travelled; it's two days' j. from here. **journey 2** *v.* (formal) to make a long trip. **journeyman** *n.* (*pl.*-men) craftsman who works for s.o.

joust [dʒaʊst] *v.* to fight with spears on horseback (as an entertainment).

jovial ['dʒəʊvɪəl] *adj.* good-humoured/merry. **joviality** [dʒəʊvɪ'ælɪtɪ] *n.* good humour. **jovially** *adv.* in a jovial way.

jowl [dʒaʊl] *n.* jaw/cheek; cheek by j. = very close together.

joy [dʒɔɪ] *n.* (cause of) very great happiness. **joyful** *adj.* very happy. **joyfully** *adv.* very happily. **joyless** *adj.* very sad. **joyous** *adj.* very happy. **joyride** *n.* excursion for pleasure, esp. in a stolen car. **joystick** *n.* (a) rod which controls the movements of an aircraft. (b) device with a movable arm, which moves a cursor on a computer monitor.

JP ['dʒeɪ'piː] abbreviation for Justice of the Peace.

jubilant ['dʒuːbɪlənt] *adj.* full of happiness/triumph. **jubilantly** *adv.* triumphantly. **jubilation** [dʒuːbɪ'leɪʃn] *n.* great happiness/triumph.

jubilee ['dʒuːbɪliː] *n.* (celebration of the) anniversary of an important event;

silver/golden/diamond j. = celebration 25/50/60 years after an event took place.

Judaism ['dʒuːdeɪɪzəm] *n.* religion of the Jews.

Judas tree ['dʒuːdəstriː] *n.* ornamental tree with pink flowers.

judder 1 ['dʒʌdə] *n.* shaking (of a machine). **judder 2** *v.* (of a machine) to shake.

judge 1 [dʒʌdʒ] *n.* (a) person appointed to make decisions, esp. in a higher court of law. (b) person who decides which is the best entry in a competition. (c) person with good judgement; he's good j. of character. **judge 2** *v.* (a) to make decisions in a court of law/competition, etc. (b) to have as your opinion; to estimate. **judgement** *n.* (a) making a decision. (b) sentence of a court; legal decision. (c) ability to see things clearly/to make good decisions; against my better j. = although I felt it was not the right thing to do. **judicial** [dʒuː'dɪʃl] *adj.* referring to a legal process/to a court of law. **judicature** ['dʒuːdɪkətʃə] *n.* (a) judicial system. (b) judicature. **judicially** *adv.* legally. **judiciary** [dʒuː'dɪʃərɪ] *n.* all the judges in a country. **judicious** *adj.* based on/having good judgement. **judiciously** *adv.* in a well judged way.

judo ['dʒuːdəʊ] *n.* modern form of Japanese wrestling.

jug [dʒʌg] *n.* (a) container with a handle, used for pouring liquids. (b) *Sl.* jail. **jugged hare** *n.* hare soaked in wine and cooked slowly.

juggernaut ['dʒʌgənɔːt] *n.* (a) overpowering force to which people sacrifice themselves. (b) *inf.* very large lorry.

juggle ['dʒʌgl] *v.* (a) to throw and catch several objects so that most of them are in the air at the same time. (b) (with) to change things around very quickly, esp. in order to deceive. **juggler** *n.* person who juggles.

jugular ['dʒʌgjʊlə] *n. & adj.* j. (vein) = main vein in the neck.

juice [dʒuːs] *n.* (a) liquid from fruit/vegetables/meat, etc.; to stew in your own j. = to suffer the consequences of your own mistakes. (b) *inf.* petrol; electricity. **juiciness** *n.* state of being full of juice. **juicy** *adj.* full of juice.

jujitsu [dʒuː'dʒɪtsuː] n. traditional Japanese unarmed combat.

juju ['dʒuːdʒuː] n. African magic charm.

jujube [dʒuːdʒuːb] n. type of soft sweet.

jukebox ['dʒuːkbɒks] n. coin-operated record-playing machine.

julep ['dʒuːləp] n. Am. drink made of alcohol and water, usu. with a mint flavour.

July [dʒʊ'laɪ] n. 7th month of the year.

Julian calendar n. calendar instituted by Julius Caesar, slightly longer than the present-day calendar.

jumble 1 ['dʒʌmbl] n. mixture/ confusion; j. sale = sale of second-hand goods, usu. for charity. **jumble 2** v. (up) to mix; to confuse.

jumbo ['dʒʌmbəʊ] n. (pl.-os) (a) child's name for an elephant. (b) anything very large, esp. a very large aircraft holding several hundred people.

jump 1 [dʒʌmp] n. (a) leap (in the air); (in sports) long j./high j. = competition to see how far/ how high you can leap. (b) sudden movement. (c) (in sports) obstacle to be jumped over. **jump 2** v. (a) to move suddenly, esp. upwards. (b) to move by jumping; to j. over the stream; to j. a page = to miss out a page. (c) to make a sudden movement, esp. from some emotion; to j. to conclusions = to make a decision too quickly; to j. the gun = to begin before your turn/ before the correct time; to j. the queue = to go ahead of your turn. **jump at** v. to seize (an opportunity) eagerly. **jumped-up** adj. (person) who has been promoted faster than his qualities merit. **jumper** n. (a) person who jumps. (b) warm knitted upper garment. **jump jet** n. aircraft which can take off vertically. **jump lead** n. cable which allows two car batteries to be connected to help a car to start. **jump rope** n. Am. skipping rope. **jump suit** n. one-piece suit, with trousers attached to the shirt. **jumpy** adj. (-ier, -iest) inf. nervous; excited.

junction ['dʒʌŋkʃn] n. joining (place), esp. of railway lines/roads; j. box = box where several electric wires join.

juncture ['dʒʌŋktʃə] n. (formal) point in time.

June [dʒuːn] n. 6th month of the year.

jungle ['dʒʌŋgl] n. (a) almost impassable tropical forest. (b) confused mass; place or circumstances where progress is difficult; blackboard j. = schools with uncontrollable pupils; concrete j. = area of tall impersonal buildings.

junior 1 ['dʒuːnɪə] adj. (a) younger; John Smith J. = son of John Smith Senior. (b) for younger children; j. school = school for children from 7 to 11 years old. (c) lower in rank. **junior 2** n. (a) person who is younger/lower in rank. (b) Am. third-year student.

juniper ['dʒuːnɪpə] n. shrub with evergreen leaves and dark berries used as flavouring for gin.

junk [dʒʌŋk] n. (a) large Chinese sailing boat. (b) useless articles/rubbish; j. bonds = bonds giving a high interest, based on the security of a company which is the target of a takeover bid. (c) (inferior) second-hand goods. (d) Sl. drugs, esp. heroin. **junk food** n. bad commercially prepared food with little nutritional value. **junkie** n. Sl. drug addict. **junk shop** n. shop selling junk.

junket 1 ['dʒʌŋkɪt] n. (a) sweet food made of curdled milk. (b) feast/ celebration. (c) pleasure trip made by an official at public expense. **junket 2** v. to have a celebration, esp. by eating and drinking.

junketing n. great celebrations, esp. at public expense.

junta ['dʒʌntə] n. group of soldiers who seize power and rule a country.

jurisdiction [dʒʊərɪs'dɪkʃn] n. (legal) power. **jurisprudence** [dʒʊərɪs'pruːdəns] n. study of the law. **jurist** ['dʒʊərɪst] n. person who specializes in law. **jury** ['dʒʊərɪ] n. (a) group of citizens sworn to decide a verdict on the strength of evidence in a court of law. (b) group of judges in a competition. **juror, juryman** n. (pl.-men) member of a jury. **jurybox** n. place where the jury sits.

just 1 [dʒʌst] adj. showing no favour; true/correct. **just 2** adv. (a) exactly; very nearly/almost; j. by the door; it's j. about ready = almost ready; that's j. it = that is exactly the problem. (b) (used to indicate the immediate past or future) he's j. arrived; I'm j. going. (c) only; we're j. good friends. (d) j. now = (i) at the present moment. (ii) a short time ago (e) j. as = (i) exactly when; (ii) exactly in the manner that. **justly** *adv.* fairly; with justice. **justness** *n.* fairness. **justice** ['dʒʌstɪs] *n.* (a) quality of being fair; to do j. to = to treat (sth) as it deserves; the portrait doesn't do her j. = it is not a good likeness (b) to bring to j. = to bring legal proceedings against. (c) (esp. as title) judge/magistrate. **Justice of the Peace** *n.* local magistrate. **justiciary** *n.* judges/magistrates taken as a group. **justify** ['dʒʌstɪfaɪ] *v.* (a) to show that sth is fair/to prove that sth is right. (b) to space characters so that the right margin is even. **justifiable** *adj.* which can be justified. **justifiably** *adv.* in a way which can be justified. **justification** [dʒʌstɪfɪ'keɪʃn] *n.* (a) reason which shows that sth is fair. (b) making a right margin even.

jut [dʒʌt] *v.* (jutted) to j. (out) = to stick out, *usu.* horizontally.

jute [dʒuːt] *n.* fibre or plants used for making sacks, etc.

juvenile 1 ['dʒuːvənaɪl] *adj.* of/for young people; j. delinquent = young person who is guilty of a crime. **juvenile 2** *n.* young person. **juvenilia** [dʒuːvə'nɪtɪə] *n.* works written by a famous writer when a child.

juxtapose [dʒʌkstə pəʊz] *v.* to place side by side/very close together. **juxtaposition** [dʒʌkstəpə'zɪʃn]çⁿ *n.* being side by side/very close together.

Kk

K. 1 symbol for potassium **K. 2** abbrev. for one thousand.

kaftan ['kæftæn] *n.* long Arab-style gown.

kale [keɪl] *n.* (no *pl.*) type of cabbage with wrinkled leaves.

kaleidoscope [kə'laɪdəskəʊp] *n.* tube with mirrors which reflect small pieces of coloured glass and make patterns which can be seen through a viewer.

kaleidoscopic [kəlaɪdə'skɒpɪk] *adj.* like a kaleidoscope/with bright changing colours; frequently changing.

kamikaze [kæmɪ'kɑːzɪ] *n.* & *adj.* suicidally daring (air attack).

kangaroo [kæŋgə'ruː] *n.* large Australian animal, which carries its young in a pouch; k. court = illegal court set up by terrorists/strikers, etc., to judge one of their members.

kaolin ['keɪəlɪn] *n.* fine white clay used for making porcelain and sometimes in medicine.

kapok ['keɪpɒk] *n.* kind of cotton wool, used for stuffing cushions.

kaput [kə'pʊt] *adj. inf.* finished; broken

karat ['kærət] *n. Am.* measure of purity of gold.

karate [kə'rɑːtɪ] *n.* Japanese style of fighting, where you hit with the side of the hand.

karma ['kɑːmə] *n.* in Buddhism, the way in which a person acts which will affect his future life.

kayak ['kaɪæk] *n.* (a) Eskimo canoe, covered with sealskins. (b) small canoe with a narrow opening for the canoeist.

kebab [kɪ'bæb] *n.* small cubes of meat grilled on a skewer.

kedgeree [kedʒə'riː] *n.* spicy mixture of rice, fish and eggs.

keel 1 [kiːl] *n.* lowest timber in a ship, on which the framework is built; on an even k. = stable/steady. **keel 2** *v.* to k. over = to fall over.

keen 1 [kiːn] *adj.* (-er, -est) (a) (on) eager/willing. (b) sharp. (c) sensitive/acute (sense) (d) *inf.* k. prices = very competitive prices. **keen 2** *v.* to wail/to cry (because s.o. has died). **keenly** *adv.* sharply **keenness** *n.* being keen.

keep 1 [kiːp] *n.* (a) central tower/strongest part of a castle. (b) maintenance; she doesn't earn her k. = she doesn't earn enough money to pay for her food and lodging. (c) *inf.* for keeps = for ever. **keep 2** *v.* (kept[kept]) (a) to continue to have/to possess. (b) to continue; he kept running. (c) to pay regard to (a promise, etc.). (d) to own/to manage (animals). (e) to maintain. (f) to support financially. (g) to have for sale. (h) to detain/to restrain. (i) to conceal. (j) to reserve. (k) to prevent (s.o. from doing sth). (l) to remain; let us k. in touch = we mustn't lose contact with each other; she kept him company = she stayed with him. (m) to k. a diary = to write notes everyday about what you have done. (n) to continue to stay in good condition; raspberries don't k. = go rotten quickly. **keeper** *n.* (a) person in charge of animals in a zoo; person in charge of a museum. (b) fruit which stays in good condition for a long time **keeping** *n.* (a) custody. (b) in k. with = in harmony with. **keep in with** *v.* to stay on friendly terms with (s.o.) **keep on** *v.* to continue (to do sth): he kept on running. **keep on at** *v. inf.* to criticize without stopping: she keeps on at me about painting the kitchen = she tells me all the time that I should paint the kitchen. **keepsake** *n.* memento: thing kept to remind you of the giver. **keep up** *v.* to continue, **keep up with** *v.* (a) to keep yourself informed about (b) to go forward at the same pace: to keep up with the Joneses = to try to maintain the same social level as your neighbours. **keg** [keg] *n.* small barrel; k. beer = beer kept in pressurized metal kegs. **kelp** [kelp] *n.* large seaweed. **kelvin** ['kelvɪn] *n.* standard unit of temperature. **ken 1** *n.* knowledge; beyond our k. = out of our normal range of knowledge. **ken 2** *v.* (kenned) (in Scotland) to know. **kennel 1** ['kenl] *n.* shelter for a dog; kennels = place where dogs can be left when their owners go away/where dogs are bred. **kennel 2** *v.* (kennelled) to keep in a kennel. **kentledge** ['kentlɪdʒ] *n.* iron used as ballast. **Kenyan 1** ['kenjən] *adj.* referring to Kenya. **Kenyan 2** *n.* person from Kenya. **kept** [kept] *v.* see keep. **kerb** [kɜːb] *n.* stone edging to a pavement/path. **kerchief** ['kɜːtʃɪf] *n.* large square scarf worn over your head. **kerfuffle** [kə'fʌfl] *n. inf.* fuss/bother. **kernel** ['kɜːnl] *n.* (a) softer part inside the hard shell of a nut (b) essential part/ centre. **kerosene** ['kerəsiːn] *n.* paraffin. **kestrel** ['kestrəl] *n.* type of small falcon **ketch** [ketʃ] *n.* (*pl.*-es) two-masted sailing boat.

ketchup ['ketʃəp] *n.* sauce made from tomatoes and spices. **kettle** ['ketl] *n.* metal container, with a lid and a spout, used for boiling water; a pretty k. of fish = an awkward state of affairs **kettledrum** *n.* large drum with a round bottom. **key 1** [kiː] *n.* (a) piece of metal for turning locks. (b) solution/explanation. (c) system of musical notes related to each other (d) part of a piano/flute/ typewriter/computer, etc., which you press down to make the instrument work. (e) seed case, shaped like a key. **key 2** *adj.* most important (thing/person). **key 3** *v.* (a) to link to/to make suitable for (b) to type (words/figures) on a keyboard. **keyboard 1** *n.* set of keys on a piano/typewriter/computer etc. **keyboard 2** *v.* to input data into a computer, using a keyboard. **keyed up** *adj.* nervous/tense (before an examination/a battle, etc.). **keyhole** *n.* hole in a lock into which a key is put. **keynote** *n.* (a) dominating musical note (b) main theme in a speech; k. speech = main speech (at a conference). **keypad** *n.* small set of keys on a computer; numeric k. = set of numbered keys on a computer keyboard, used for various functions. **key ring** *n.* ring for carrying several keys together. **keystone** *n.* central supporting block of stone or brick in an arch; important idea on which everything else is based. **kg.** abbrev for kilogram **khaki** ['kɑːkɪ] *adj. & n.* dull yellow brown (colour); the colour of soldiers uniforms. **kibbutz** [kɪ'bʊts] *n.* (*pl.*-tzim[tsiːm]) farming settlement in Israel. **kibosh** ['kaɪbɒʃ] *n. Sl.* to put the k. on sth = to stop sth happening. **kick 1** [kɪk] *n.* (a) blow with the foot (b) *inf.* thrill/excitement; he did it for kicks = to give himself a thrill **kick 2** *v.* to strike with the foot. **kickback** *n.* (a) recoil (of a gun). (b) *Sl.* bribe/ illegal commission paid to s.o. who helps a business deal. **kick off** *v.* to start a game of football. **kick - off** *n.* start (of a football game). **kick start(er)** *n.* pedal to start a motorcycle engine. **kick up** *v. inf.* to make a fuss/a row).

kid 1 [kɪd] n. (a) young goat. (b) inf. child **kid 2** v. (kidded) inf. to make (s.o.) believe sth that is not true; I'm only kidding = I don't mean it: no kidding? = is it really true? **kiddy** n. inf. child. **kidnap** ['kɪdnæp] v. (kidnapped) to steal (a child); to carry (a person) off by force illegally. **kidnapper** n. person who kidnaps. **kidnapping** n. carrying away of a person by force.

kidney ['kɪdnɪ] n. one of a pair of organs in animals that extract impurities from the blood; this organ used as food; k. bean = type of bean with reddish seeds; k. machine = device by which a patient's blood can be purified when his kidneys do not function properly.

kill 1 [kɪl] n. putting an animal to death for sport; to be in at the k. = to be there at the end of the affair. **kill 2** v. to put to death; to make (s.o./an animal/a plant) die; he was killing himself with laughter = he was laughing very heartily; to k. time = to spend time doing very little while waiting for sth: to k. two birds with one stone = to get two successful results from one action; inf. my feet are killing me = my feet hurt. **killer** n. person who kills; k. whale = medium-sized black and white carnivorous whale. **killing 1** adj. inf. very funny. **killing 2** n. (a) putting to death. (b) large profit (on the stock market) **killjoy** n. person who stops others enjoying themselves. **kill off** v. to get rid of (sth) by killing.

kiln [kɪln] n. oven for baking pottery or bricks.

kilo 1 ['kiːləʊ] prefix meaning one thousand. **kilo 2** n. (pl.-os) kilogrAm. **kilobyte** ['kɪləbaɪt] n. storage unit of computer data equal to 1.024 bytes. **kilocycle** ['kɪləʊsaɪkl] n. one thousand cycles as a frequency of radio waves. **kilogram** ['kɪləʊgræm] n. one thousand grams. **kilohertz** ['kɪləʊhɜːʳts] n. one thousand hertz. **kilometre, Am. kilometer** [kɪ'lɒmɪtə] n. one thousand metres. **kilovolt** ['kɪləʊvɒlt] n. one thousand volts. **kilowatt** ['kɪləwɒt] n. one thousand watts.

kilt [kɪlt] n. pleated skirt, usu. of tartan cloth, worn by men in Scotland. and also by women. **kilted** ['kɪltɪd] adj. wearing a kilt.

kimono [kɪ'məʊʊ] n. (pl.-os) long, loose robe worn by Japanese women.

kin [kɪn] n. next of k. = nearest relative(s): see also kith.

kind 1 [kaɪnd] n. type/variety; two of a k. = two the same; it's nothing of the k. = not at all true: payment in k. = payment in goods or natural produce, not in money; inf. k. of sorry = rather sorry. **kind 2** adj. (-er, -est) amiable/thoughtful: friendly/thinking of others. **kindhearted** adj. thoughtful about other people. **kindliness** n. being kindly. **kindly** adj. & adv. thoughtful/pleasant; in a thoughtful/pleasant way; she doesn't take k. to = she doesn't like; k. shut the door = please shut the door. **kindness** n. being kind.

kindergarten ['kɪndəga"tn] n. school for very young children.

kindle ['kɪndl] v. to make a fire; to catch fire.

kindling n. (no pl.) small pieces of wood used to start a fire.

kindred ['kɪndrɪd] adj. similar; k. spirit = person with whom you have sth in common.

kinetic [kɪ'netɪk] adj. produced by moving; (energy) which a body has in motion.

king [kɪŋ] n. (a) male sovereign or hereditary ruler of a country. (b) main piece in chess/draughts; (in cards) card following the queen. **kingcup** n. large buttercup. **kingdom** n. land ruled over by a king. (b) part of the world of nature. (c) until k. come = until the end of the world, **kingfisher** n. small brilliant blue bird that dives for fish. **kingly** adj. like a king. **kingpin** n. central bolt; central person in an organization. **king-size(d)** adj. very large.

kink 1 [kɪŋk] n. (a) knot/twist in a length of cord, wire or rope (b) peculiar mental state. **kink 2** v. to make a kink in (sth). **kinky** adj. Sl. Sexually odd/peculiar.

kinship ['kɪnʃtp] n. family relationship. **kinsfolk** n. pl.relatives. **kinsman, kinswoman** n. (pl.-men, -women) relative.

kiosk ['kiːɒsk] n. small outdoor cabin for the sale of newspapers/sweets etc telephone booth.

kip 1 [kɪp] *n. Sl.* short sleep. **kip 2** *v.* (kipped) *Sl.* to sleep.

kipper ['kɪpə] *n.* split smoked herring. **kippered** *adj.* smoked (fish).

kirk [kɜːk] *n.* (in Scotland) church.

kirsch [kiːəʃ] *n.* cherry brandy.

kiss 1 [kɪs] *n.* (*pl.*-es) touching with the lips; he blew him a k. = signalled to send him a kiss from a distance; k. of life = resuscitation by breathing into a person's mouth: k. of death = act which ruins (a business. etc.). **kiss 2** *v.* to touch with the lips. **kisser** *n. Sl.* mouth.

kit [kɪt] *n.* (a) clothes and personal equipment, *usu.* packed for travelling: first aid k. = supplies for the emergency treatment of injuries. (b) box containing pieces which can be put together to make a model/a piece of furniture, etc. **kitbag** *n.* round bag for carrying a soldier's clothes and equipment. **kit out** *v.* (kitted out) to supply with clothes and equipment.

kitchen ['kɪtʃɪn] *n.* room in which food is cooked. **kitchenette** *n.* very small kitchen. **kitchen garden** *n.* fruit and vegetable plot in a garden.

kite [kaɪt] *n.* (a large bird of prey of the falcon family. (b) toy made of light wood and paper or cloth which is flown in a strong wind on the end of a string; k. mark = mark put on British goods to show that they have met standards: he's just flying a k. = he's putting forward an idea to see how people react to it.

kith [kɪθ] *n.* k. and kin = friends and relatives.

kitsch [kɪtʃ] *n.* lack of artistic taste; tasteless artistic production.

kitten ['kɪtn] *n.* young cat: *inf.* to have kittens = to be afraid/nervous. **kittenish** *adj.* playful/like a kitten.

kittiwake ['kɪtɪweɪk] *n.* type of gull.

kitty ['kɪtɪ] *n.* joint fund.

kiwi ['kiːwiː] *n.* non-flying bird, native of New Zealand. **kiwi fruit** *n.* small tropical fruit, with a hairy skin and green flesh.

Kleenex ['kliːneks] *n.* (*pl.*-es) trademark for a paper handkerchief.

kleptomania [kleptə'meɪnɪə] *n.* irresistible tendency to steal. **kleptomaniac** *n.* person who cannot stop stealing.

km abbrev. for kilometre.

knack [næk] *n.* talent/ability.

knacker ['nækə] *n.* person who buys and kills useless horses. **knackered** *adj. inf.* tired out.

knapsack ['næpsæk] *n.* canvas/leather bag carried on the back.

knave [neɪv] *n.* (a) (old) trickster. (b) (in cards) jack/card between the ten and the queen.

knead [niːd] *v.* to press with the hands.

knee [niː] *n.* joint between your thigh and lower leg; she was sitting on his k.= sitting on his thighs. **kneecap 1** *n.* bone in front of the knee. **kneecap 2** *v.* to punish (s.o.) by shooting him in the kneecap. **knee-deep** *adj.* up to the knees (in) **knees-up** *n. inf.* jolly dance. **kneel** [niːl] *v.* (knelt[nelt]) to go on your knees, **kneel down** *v.* to go down on your knees. **kneeler** *n.* hard cushion for kneeling on.

knell [nel] *n.* (formal) sound of a bell rung at a solemn ceremony such as a funeral.

knelt [nelt] *v.* see kneel.

knew [njuː] *v.* see know

knickerbockers ['nɪkəbɒkəz] *n. pl.*trousers which are gathered at the knees.

knickers ['nɪkəz] *n. pl.*undergarment worn by a woman or girl on the lower part of the body.

knick-knack ['nɪknæk] *n.* small/light article; trinket.

knife 1 [naɪf] *n.* (*pl.*knives[narvz]) cutting blade with a sharpened edge fixed into a handle; to have your k. into s.o. = to try to hurt/to behave nastily towards s.o.; on a k. edge = in a difficult position, where the outcome is not sure. **knife 2** *v.* (knifed) to stab (s.o.) with a knife.

knight 1 [naɪt] *n.* (a) man honoured by a king for personal merit or services to his country (and taking the title Sir). (b) (in medieval times) brave soldier often devoted to the service of a lady. (c) piece in a chess set with a horse's head.

knight 2 *v.* to make (s.o.) a knight. **knighthood** *n.* title of knight.

knit [nɪt] *v.* (a) (knitted) to make (a garment) out of wool, etc, by linking two threads together with the aid of two long needles; to k. one's brows = to frown (b) (knit) (of broken bone) to join together again. **knitter** n. person who knits. **knitting** n. woollen garment which is in the process of being made. **knitting machine** n. machine for knitting. **knitting needle** n. long needle for knitting. **knitwear** n. knitted woollen garments.

knives [naɪvz] n. see knife.

knob [nɒb] n. (a) rounded bump: round lump (b) round handle of door/ drawer. **knobbly, knobby** adj. bumpy; covered with knobs.

knock 1 [nɒk] n. sharp blow; sound of a sharp blow. **knock 2** v. (a) to strike (sth) with a hard blow; he knocked on/at the door = hit the door with the knuckles to call attention. (b) inf. to criticize; knocking copy = publicity material which criticizes a rival's products (c) (of car engine) to make a regular/sharp noise because of misfiring. **knock about** v. (a) to drift aimlessly. (b) to knock (s.o.) about = to beat (s.o.). **knock back** v. inf. (a) to cost (s.o.) a sum. (b) to surprise (s.o.) (c) to swallow quickly. **knock down** v. (a) to hit (s.o./sth) to the ground. (b) to sell (an item) at an auction to a purchaser. **knock-down** adj. very low (price). **knocker** n. knob or ring hinged to a door which can be stuck against it to call attention. **knocking** n. series of sharp blows; noise made by an engine which is misfiring. **knock-kneed** adj. having knees that touch each other when walking. **knock off** v. (a) to hit (sth) so that it falls off. (b) inf. he knocked off work at 4.30 = he stopped working at 4.30. (c) the vendor knocked £110 off the price of the car = he reduced the price of the car by £10. **knock out** v. to hit (s.o.) so hard that he loses consciousness. **knockout** n. (a) hitting s.o. so hard that he loses consciousness (b) k. competition = contest where several teams compete against each other and are eliminated in turn. **knock up** v. (a) to waken (b) to make very tired (c) to score (s.o.) Am. inf. to make pregnant (e) inf. to put (sth) together rapidly. **knock up** n. practice before a tennis match.

knoll [nɒl] n. small hill.

knot 1 [nɒt] n. (a) looping the ends of string/rope etc., and fastening them together; small group (of people): to tie yourself in knots = to get into difficulties. (b) hard round place in a piece of wood where a branch was to join it. (c) measurement by which a ship's/an aircraft's speed is calculated (= one nautical mile per hour). (c) type of small shore bird. **knot 2** v. (knotted) to tie in a knot. **knotty** adj. (-ier, -iest) difficult (problem).

know 1 [nəʊ] n. to be in the k. = to be well informed about sth which is not generally known. **know 2** v. (knew[njuː]; has known) (a) to have in your mind because of learning or experience; do you k. French? = do you speak French? (b) to recognize (s.o.) (c) to be acquainted with: I k. him by sight/by name (d) to k. what it is like to = to have personal experience of;to k. your own mind = to be clear and firm in your views. **know-all** n. person who claims he knows everything. **know-how** n. inf. knowledge about how sth is made/is done. **knowing** adj. understanding; having knowledge. **knowingly** adv. deliberately. **knowledge** n. (a) what s.o. knows (b) what is generally known. **knowledgeable** adj. (person) who knows a lot about sth. **know of** v. to be aware of

knuckle ['nʌkl] n. (a) finger joint: near the k. = verging on the indecent (b) (on an animal) joint on the leg (esp. when used as food) **knuckle down** v. to apply yourself seriously to work. **knuckle duster** n. metal instrument worn on the knuckles, either as a protection or as a weapon. **knuckle under** v. to give in/to submit.

KO abbrev. for knock out.

koala [kəʊ'aːlə] n. k. (bear) = small Australian animal which carries its young in a pouch and lives in trees.

kohl [ləʊl] n. powder used to make eyelids darker.

kohlrabi [ləʊl'raːbiː] n. vegetable with a thick purplish stem which is eaten.

kookaburra ['kʊkəbʌrə] n. large Australian kingfisher.

kop [kɒp] n. (in South Africa) small hill

koran [kɒ'rɔːn] n. holy book of the Muslims.

Korean 1 [kə'rɜən] adj. referring to Korea. **Korean 2** n. (a) person from

Korea (b) language spoken in Korea.

kosher ['kəʊʃə] *adj.* (food) prepared according to Jewish law.

kowtow [kaʊ'taʊ] *v.* to show great respect (to).

kraal [kral] *n.* (in South Africa) village with a fence round it.

Kremlin ['kremlɪn] *n.* the Russian government.

krill [krɪl] *n.* (*pl.*krill) minute shrimps living in the sea

krypton ['krɪptɒn] *n.* (element: Kr) rare gas.

kudos ['kjuːdɒs] *n.* glory/renown.

kudu ['kuːduː] *n.* small African antelope.

kumquat ['kʌmkwɒt] *n.* very small orange.

kung fu [kuːŋ'fuː] *n.* Chinese style of fighting.

Ll

_l [el] L plates = signs with a red L on them. attached to a car etc.. to show that the driver is a learner.

ab [læb] *n.* short for laboratory.

abel 1 ['leɪbl] *n.* (a) piece of paper/ card. etc.. attached to sth to indicate price/contents/name/address. etc. (b) name under which sth is generally known. **label 2** *v.* (labelled) (a) to put a label on. (b) to name/to describe.

abial ['leɪbɪəl] *adj.* referring to the lips.

aboratory ['lə'bɒrətrɪ, *Am.* 'læbrətɔːrɪ] *n.* place where scientific experiments/ research are carried out.

aborious [lə'bɔːrɪəs] *adj.* (a) involving a great deal of work (b) (style) showing signs of effort. **laboriously** *adv.* in a laborious way. **labour,** *Am.* **labor 1** ['leɪbə] *n.* (a) (hard) work; hard l. = prison sentence involving heavy manual work. (b) workers/the workforce. (c) Labour/the Labour Party = socialist political party linked with the trade unions and concerned with the welfare of workers. (d) (pains of) childbirth. **labour** *v.* (a) to work (hard) (b) to l. under a delusion = to have a

(persistently) wrong impression; to l. the point = to argue/to discuss sth too long (c) (of engine, etc.) to work with difficulty. **laboured** *adj.* (a) (of style) heavy/clumsy. (b) (of breathing) heavy/ difficult. **labourer** *n.* person who does heavy manual work. **Labourite** *n. inf.* member of the Labour Party. **labour-saving** *adj.* (of machine/gadget) which lessens work.

labrador ['læbrədɔː] *n.* type of large dog, *usu.* black or yellow.

laburnum [lə'bɜːnəm] *n.* tree with bright yellow flowers and poisonous seeds in pods.

labyrinth ['læbɪrɪnθ] *n.* maze; place where it is difficult to find your way about. **labyrinthine** [læbə'rɪnθaɪn] *adj.* like a labyrinth.

lace1 [leɪs] *n.* (a) thin strip of material for tying a shoe, etc. (b) decorative cloth with open patterns of threads. **lace 2** *v.* (a) to tie with a lace (b) to pour a little alcohol into (sth).

lacerate ['læsəreɪt] *v.* (formal) to wound/to tear (flesh). **laceration** [læsə'reɪʃn] *n.* tearing; place where flesh has been torn.

lachrymose [lækrɪməʊs] *adj.* (formal) (person) who tends to cry. **lachrymal** *adj.* (gland) which produces tears.

lack 1 [læk] *n.* not having sth. **lack 2** *v.* not to have (enough of) sth. **lacking** *adj.* not enough/ without.

lackadaisical [lækə'deɪzɪkl] *adj.* not showing any vigour/any enthusiasm.

lackey ['lækɪ] *n.* servant who obeys without questioning.

lacklustre, *Am.* **lackluster** ['læklʌstə] *adj.* dull/not brilliant.

laconic [lə'kɒnɪk] *adv.* using few words. **laconically** *adv.* in a laconic way.

lacquer 1 ['lækə] *n,* (a) type of hard shiny varnish/paint. often used on metals (b) spray for keeping hair in place. **lacquer 2** *v.* to coat with lacquer.

lacrosse [lə'krɒs] *n.* team game played with a ball and a curved stick with a net at the end.

lactic ['læktɪk] *adj.* referring to milk. **lactation** [læk'teɪʃn] *n.* (of female) production of milk. **lactose** *n.* sugar occurring in milk.

lacuna [lə'kjuːnə] *n.* (*pl.*-ae) gap/space.

lacustrine [ˈlækuːstriːn] *adj.* referring to lakes.

lacy [ˈleɪsɪ] *adj.* (-ier, -iest) like lace; made of a network of fine threads.

lad, laddie [læd, ˈlædɪ] *n. inf.* boy; young man.

ladder 1 [ˈlædə] *n.* (a) object made of horizontal bars between two uprights. used for climbing. (b) long hole in a stocking. **ladder 2** *v.* (of stocking etc.) to get a ladder.

laden [ˈleɪdn] *adj.* (with) carrying a (heavy) load; (of ship) containing a cargo. **lading** *n.* (a) loading of ships, (b) cargo.

ladle 1 [ˈleɪdl] *n.* large deep spoon for serving soup. etc. **ladle 2** *v.* (also ladle out) to serve with a ladle.

lady [ˈleɪdɪ] *n.* (a) woman, esp. of high social standing or with good manners. (b) (as title) Lady = feminine equivalent of Lord; title of wife or sometimes daughter of a peer; title of wife of a knight or baronet. (c) Our Lady = the Virgin Mary. **ladies** *n. inf.* women's toilet. **ladybird**, *Am.* **ladybug** *n.* type of small beetle, *usu.* red with black spots. **Lady Day** *n.* 25th March. **ladykiller** *n. inf.* man who is attractive to women. **ladylike** *adj.* well mannered/polite (as a lady should be). **lady's finger** *n.* okra. **ladyship** *n.* (form of address to a titled lady) Your Ladyship.

lag 1 [læg] *n.* (a) (in time) space/interval. esp. between two parts of an event (b) *Sl.* old l. = person who has been put in prison many times. **lag 2** *v.* (lagged) (a) to go/fall/behind. (b) to cover (a heating appliance, pipes etc.) to prevent heat loss or to prevent freezing. **laggard** [ˈlægəd] *n.* person who is behind the others. **lagging** *n.* material for wrapping round pipes.

lager [ˈlɑːgə] *n.* type of light beer.

lagoon [ləˈguːn] *n.* area of sea water almost completely surrounded by land esp. by a coral island.

laid [leɪd] *v.* see lay. **laid-back** *adj. inf.* unhurried/relaxed.

lain [leɪn] *v.* see lie.

lair [ˈleə] *n.* resting place of a wild animal.

laird [ˈleəd] *n.* (in Scotland) owner of a country estate.

laissez-faire [leseɪˈfɛə] *adj.* (economy) where the government does not interfere on principle.

laity [ˈleɪtɪ] *n.* people who have not been trained as priests.

lake [leɪk] *n.* (a) (large) inland stretch of water. wine l. = large quantity of wine stockpiled because of overproduction. (b) type of reddish dye.

lakh [læk] *n.* (in India) one hundred thousand rupees.

lam [læm] *v. inf.* to hit.

lama [ˈlɑːmə] *n.* Buddhist priest. esp. in Tibet. **lamasery** *n.* monastery for lamas.

lamb [læm] *n.* (a) young sheep (b) flesh of sheep used as food. **lamb 2** *v.* to give birth to lamb. **lambing** [ˈlæmɪŋ] *n.* giving birth to lambs. **lambswool** *n.* (no *pl.*) very soft wool.

lambast [læmˈbeɪst] *v.* to criticize (s.o.) sharply.

lame 1 [leɪm] *adj.* (-er, -est) (a) unable to walk properly. (b) weak/unsatisfactory. **lame 2** *v.* to injure (s.o.) so that he cannot walk properly. **lame duck** *n.* person/company in difficulties and having to rely on outside support. **lamely** *adv.* in a weak way. **lameness** *n.* being lame.

lamé [ˈlɑːmeɪ] *n.* cloth with gold or silver threads.

lamella [læˈmelə] *n.* (*pl.*-ae) thin scale.

lament 1 [ləˈment] *n.* (a) song/music for mourning. (b) expression of grief; complaint. **lament 2** *v.* to be very sad about (the death of s.o.). **lamentable** [ˈlæməntəbl] *adj.* very bad. **lamentably** *adv.* very badly. **lamentation** [læmənˈteɪʃn] *n.* expression of great sorrow.

laminated [ˈlæmɪneɪtɪd] *adj.* (a) formed in thin layers. (b) covered with a thin layer of plastic. **lamination** [læmɪˈneɪʃn] *n.* process of covering a thin plastic film.

Lammas [ˈlæməs] *n.* August 1st.

lamp [læmp] *n.* object which produces light. **lamplight** *n.* light from a lamp. **lamp-post** *n.* large post which holds a street lamp. **lampshade** *n.* (decorative) cover to put over a lamp.

lampoon 1 [læmˈpuːn] *n.* writing which makes s.o. seem ridiculous. **lampoon 2** *v.* to ridicule (s.o.) in writing.

lamprey ['læmprɪ] n. edible fish, like an eel.

lance 1 [lɑːns] n. type of long spear. **lance 2** v. to cut (a wound/an abscess. etc) with a lancet. **lance-corporal** n. non commissioned officer below the rank of corporal. **lancer** n. soldier in a regiment which used to be armed with lances. **lancet** n. (a) pointed two-edged surgical knife (b) tall thin pointed window.

land 1 [lænd] n. (a) solid part of earth's surface. (b) earth/soil to go back to the l. = to go back to being a farmer again (c) country (d) estate owned by s.o. (e) Land = one of the states making up the Federal Republic of Germany. **land 2** v. (a) to come to land; to bring to land; to l. on one's feet = enjoy easy success (b) to bring a fish out of water and on to the land; to obtain (a good job) (c) to give/to deal (a blow). (d) to i. (up) in = to arrive/ to reach. **landed** adj. owning land. **landfall** n. seeing land for the first time from sea or air. **landfill** n. disposing of rubbish in holes in the ground. **landing** n. (a) (esp. of aircraft) touching land: l. gear = wheels on which an aircraft lands. (b) space at the top of a flight of stairs. **landingnet** n. net at the end of a long pole for taking fish out of water. **landing stage** n. (floating) platform where passengers can leave boats. **landlady** n. (a) woman from whom you rent a house/room etc. (b) woman who keeps a hotel or inn. etc. **landlocked** n. (sea/harbour) surrounded by land. **landlord** n. (a) man from whom you rent a house/room etc. (b) man who keeps a hotel or inn, etc. **landlubber** n. inf. person who is not used to going on ships. **landmark** n. (a) object on land which you can see easily, esp. one used by ships to find out their position (b) outstanding/important event etc. **landmine** n. mine hidden in the ground. **landowner** n. person who owns a country estate. **landrace** n. native species. **landscape 1** ['lændskeɪp] n. (a) scenery/appearance of the countryside; l. gardening = making a garden more beautiful by making artificial lakes, hills planting trees etc. (b) painting of a country scene. **landscape 2** v. to improve (a garden) by creating small hills/lakes, planting trees, etc. **landscape gardener** n. person who designs the layout of large gardens/pieces of land. **landslide** n. (a) slipping of large amounts of earth, etc., down a hillside. (b) overwhelming event, esp. an electoral victory in which one party is totally defeated. **landslip** n. landslide. **landward** adj. & adv. towards the land. **landwards** adv. towards the land.

landau ['lændɔː] n. horse-drawn carriage with a folding top.

lane [leɪn] n. (a) narrow road, often in the country. (b) way/road for traffic, usu. in a particular direction; shipping lanes = routes followed by ships; bus l. = part of a road where only buses may drive.

language ['læŋgwɪdʒ] n. (a) way of speaking of a country/a group of people: l. laboratory = room with tape recorders where students can study foreign languages. (b) way of speaking; bad l. = swearing. (c) human speech (d) means of communication esp. signs. letters and other symbols used to instruct a computer.

languid ['læŋgwɪd] adj. slow-moving/ lacking energy. **languidly** adv. lazily. **languish** ['læŋgwɪʃ] v. to become weak/ill. often because of sorrow. **languor** ['læŋgə] n. (a) lack of energy (b) tender emotional mood. **languorous** adj. slow-moving/lazy.

lank [læŋk] adj. (a) (of hair) straight/ dull/lifeless. (b) (of person) thin/ dropping. **lankiness** n. being lanky. **lanky** adj. (-ier, iest) tall/thin/awkward (person).

lanolin ['lænəlɪn] n. fat from sheep's wool used in skin creams.

lantern ['læntən] n. lamp with a covering to protect it, which can be carried in the hand.

lanyard ['lænjəd] n. string worn around your neck or shoulder with a whistle. etc. on it.

lap 1 [læp] n. (a) your body from waist to knees. when you are sitting: in the l. of luxury = in great luxury (b) circuit/ round of a racecourse. (c) part of a long journey. **lap 2** v. (lapped) (a) (of animal) to drink with the tongue. (b) (up) to take in greedily (c) (of waves) to wash against (the shore/the edge of sth). (d) to go so fast that you are a whole lap ahead of (another competitor) (e) to fold (sth) so that it overlaps. **lapdog** *n.* small pet dog. **laptop** *n.* small computer which can be held on the lap.

lapel [lə'pel] *n.* part of collar of coat, etc. which folds back.

lapidary [læpɪdərɪ] *adj.* (a) referring to stones (esp. precious stones) (b) very short and precise(statement).

lapis lazuli [læpɪs'læzjʊlaɪ] *n.* bright blue stone.

lapse 1 [læps] *n.* (a) failure to do sth properly. (b) interval of time. esp. when sth does not take place. **lapse 2** *v.* (a) to fail/ to cease do sth. (b) to cease to be valid (c) to fall into a lower/less active state.

lapwing ['læpwɪŋ] *n.* .bird found in fields and moors.

larboard ['lɑːbəd] *n.* (old) port side (of ship).

larceny ['lɑːsnɪ] *n.* crime of stealing.

larch [lɑːtʃ] *n.* (*pl.*-es) cone-bearing tree which loses its leaves in winter.

lard 1 [lɑːd] *n.* melted down pig fat used in cooking. **lard 2** *v.* to cover (meat) with bacon or lard; to fill (a speech) with quotations, etc. **lardy cake** *n.* type of bread, made with fat and covered with sticky sugar. **larder** ['lɑːdə] *n.* room/ cupboard for storing food.

large [lɑːdʒ] *adj.* (-er, -est) (a) (very) big. (b) at l. = (i) free/not imprisoned; (ii) in general. **largely** *adv.* mostly/for the most part. **large-scale** *adj.* in a large way/involving large number of people or large sums of money.

largesse [lɑː'dʒes] *n.* generous gift of money.

largo ['lɑːgəʊ] *adv. & n.* (piece of music) which is played slowly.

lariat ['lærɪət] *n.* lasso.

lark 1 [lɑːk] *n.* (a) bird which sings and flies high in the sky. (b) *inf.* piece of fun/ joke. **lark 2** *v. inf.* to l. (about) = to fool around/play jokes. **larkspur** *n.* plant with tall spikes of flowers.

larrikin ['lærɪkɪn] *n.* (in Australia) hooligan.

larrup ['lærəp] *v. inf.* to beat (s.o.) up.

larva ['lɑːvə] *n.* (*pl.*-vae) [-vi**X**]) early stage of development of an insect, different in form from the adult.

larynx ['lærɪnks] *n.* (*pl.*-es) upper part

of the windpipe, where sounds are made by the voice. **laryngitis** [lærɪn'dʒaɪtɪs] *n.* inflammation of the larynx causing a sore throat.

lasagne [lə'zænə] *n.* type of pasta which is made of wide flat strips.

lascivious [lə'sɪvɪəs] *adj.* full of sexual desire. **lasciviously** *adv.* in a lascivious way. **lasciviousness** *n.* being lascivious.

laser ['leɪzə] *n.* instrument which produces a highly concentrated beam of light.

lash 1 [læʃ] *n.* (*pl.*-es) (a) stroke with a whip. (b) flexible part of a whip. (c) eyelash. **lash 2** *v.* (a) to beat (sth) with a whip. (b) to make a movement like beating with a whip. (c) to fasten/to tie down tightly with rope/string. **lashing** *n.* (a) whipping. (b) tying/binding with rope, etc. **lashings** *n. pl. inf.* plenty.

lash out *v.* (a) to lash out on = to become (unexpectedly) very extravagant and spend a large sum of money.

lass, lassie [læs, 'læsɪ] *n.* (*pl.*-es) (in N. England & Scotland) *inf.* girl; young woman.

Lassa fever ['læsə'fiːvə] *n.* fatal viral disease which originated in Africa.

lassitude ['læsɪtjuːd] *n.* (*formal*) tiredness.

lasso 1 [lɔː'suː] *n.* (*pl.*-os) rope with looped end for catching horses/cattle, etc. **lasso 2** *v.* to catch (animals) with a lasso.

last 1 [lɑːst] *adj.* (a) placed/coming at the end (of a list/line/period of time); l. thing at night = at the very end of the day; l. but one = the one before the end one; l. but not least = at the end of a list, but not because it is the least important; the l. straw = final piece of trouble which makes everything seem unbearable; the l. word in hats = the very latest fashion; the l. person I would want to go on holiday with = the most unlikely person. (b) most recent l. Monday; l. week. **last 2** *n.* (a) shape on which a shoe is made or repaired. (b) final thing/period/sight; at (long) l. = in the end/after a long time; to the l. = till the very end. **last 3** *adv.* (a) at the end. (b) most recently. **last 4** *v.* to continue (to exist); to remain in good condition. **lasting** *adj.* which continues for a long time. **lastly** *adv.* at the end/finally. **Last Post** *n.* trumpet call sounded at a military funeral. **Last Supper** *n.* last meal take by Christ with his disciples.

latch 1 [lætʃ] *n.* (*pl.*-es) fastening for a door, etc., consisting of a small bar which fits into a catch; the door is on the l. = is held shut by a latch but is not locked. **latch 2** *v.* (a) to close with a latch. (b) *inf.* to on to sth = to seize/to take up. **latchkey** *n.* key for a front door; l. child = child who has a key to the house and lets himself in when he comes home from school because both parents are at work.

late 1 [leɪt] *adj.* (-er, est) (a) at a time after that decided/intended; the train is ten minutes l. (b) at/towards the end of a period of time. (c) at/towards/past the end of a season. (d) latest = last/most recent. (e) (formal) referring to s.o. who has died; my l. father. **late 2** *adv.* (-er, -est) (a) after the appointed time. (b) after a certain time. **latecomer** *n.* person who arrives after others/after the appointed time. **lately** *adv.* during recent days/weeks. **lateness** *n.* being late.

latent ['leɪtənt] *adj.* present but not developed.

lateral ['lætərəl] *adj.* referring to the side;(fin) on the side of a fish's body; l. thinking = solving problems by unusual means. **laterally** *adv.* towards the side.

laterite ['lætəraɪt] *n.* hard clay, like rock.

latex ['leɪteks] *n.* milky juice from a rubber tree.

lath [lɑːθ] *n.* narrow thin strip of wood.

lathe [leɪð] *n.* machine for holding and turning wood/metal, so that it can be shaped.

lather 1 ['lɑːðə] *n.* (a) mass of (soap) bubbles. (b) (esp. on horse) frothy sweat; to get in a l. = to get upset/flustered. **lather 2** *v.* (a) to make (sth) from a lather; to form a lather. (b) to cover with lather.

Latin 1 ['lætɪn] *n.* (a) language formerly spoken by the Romans. (b) person from Italy, Spain, Portugal or South America. **Latin 2** *adj.* (a) referring to the language of ancient Rome. (b) referring to Italy, Spain, Portugal and South America; L. America = countries in

South and Central America where spanish or Portuguese is spoken.

latitude ['lætɪtjuːd] *n.* (a) breadth of view/tolerance/scope. (b) position on the earth's surface measured in degrees north or south of the equator; northern latitudes = in areas north of the equator.

latrine [lə'triːn] *n.* lavatory in a military camp or prison.

latter ['lætə] *adj.* (a) second thing mentioned (of two). (b) recent; of the final part/period. **latterly** *adv.* recently.

lattice ['lætɪs] *n.* pattern (of pieces of wood in a fence, etc.) make of crisscross diagonal lines; l. window = window with small panes and lead frames forming a crisscross pattern.

laud [lɔːd] *v.* (*formal*) to praise. **laudable** *adv.* worthy of praise. **laudably** *adv.* in a laudable way. **laudatory** *adj.* which praises.

laudanum ['lɔːdnəm] *n.* opium in alcohol, used as a sedative.

laugh 1 [lɑːf] *n.* sound made to express amusement/happiness; to do sth for a l. = to do it for amusement only/as a joke.

laugh 2 *v.* (a) to make sounds which express amusement/happiness; to l. up one's sleeve = to laugh secretly. (b) to l. at = to make fun of. **laughable** *adj.* only worth laughing at; ridiculous.

laughing gas *n.* gas which makes you laugh when you breathe it, used esp. by dentists as an anaesthetic. **laughing stock** *n.* person whom everyone makes fun of. **laughter** *n.* (sound/act of) laughing.

launch 1 [lɔːntʃ] *n.* (*pl.*-es) (a) type of small motor boat. (b) act of launching (boat/rocket/new project, etc). **launch 2** *v.* (a) to put (a boat/ship) into the water, esp. for the first time. (b) to send off (a rocket into the air). (c) to give (sth/s.o.) a start. **launching pad** *n.* starting platform for a rocket, etc. **launching out** *v.* to start doing sth expensive or ambitious.

laundry ['lɔːndrɪ] *n.* (a) place where clothes/sheets, etc, are washed. (b) clothes/sheets, etc. for washing or which have been washed. **launder** *v.* (a) to wash clothes. (b) *inf.* to pass (illegal profits, etc.) into the conventional banking system. **laund(e)rette,** *Am.*

laundromat ['lɔːndret, 'lɔːndrəmæt] *n.*
trademark for a shop with coin-operated
washing machines for public use.
laundress *n.* woman who washes
laundry.
laureate ['lɔːrɪet] *n.* person who has
been awarded a prize; Poet L. = leading
poet who is asked to write
commemorative verse for special
occasions. **laurel** ['lɒrəl] *n.* tree with
smooth shiny evergreen leaves; to rest on
your laurels = to enjoy your past success,
without trying to gain more.
lav ['læv] *n. inf.* lavatory.
lava ['lɑːvə] *n.* molten material flowing
from a volcano which becomes solid
when it cools.
lavatory ['lævətrɪ] *n.* (a) small room for
getting rid of waste matter from the body,
usu. with a flushing bowl. (b) bowl with a
seat and a flushing system, for getting rid
of waste matter from the body.
lavender ['lævɪndə] *n.* (a) plant with
sweet-smelling bluish-purple flowers. (b)
bluish-purple colour.
lavish 1 ['lævɪʃ] *adj.* (a) generous/
ample (helping of food etc.). (b)
extravagant/over-generous. **lavish 2** *v.*
(on s.o.) to give (over-) generously.
lavishly *adv.* in a lavish way.
lavishness *n.* being lavish.
law [lɔː] *n.* (a) rules by which a country
is governed and the people controlled.
(b) rule/controlling force; to lay down
the l. = to state sth in a dogmatic way; to
be a l. unto yourself = to do exactly what
you want, regardless of rules or of any
one else. (c) process of upholding the
rules of a country. **law-abiding** *adj.*
obeying the law. **law centre** *n.* local
office whose staff offer legal advice free
of charge. **lawcourt** *n.* court where a
judge/magistrate hears cases. **lawful**
adj. according to law/legal. **lawfully**
adv. in a lawful way. **lawless** *adj.*
wild/uncivilized; paying no attention to
law. **lawlessness** *n.* being lawless.
lawsuit *n.* legal case. **lawyer** *n.*
person who has studied law and can
advise people on legal matters.
lawn. *n.* (a) (area of) short grass in a
garden; l. tennis = tennis played on
grass. (b) very fine cotton material.
lawnmower *n.* machine for cutting
grass.

lax [læks] *adj.* (-er, -est) loose/not rigid.
laxative *adj. & n.* (substance) which
helps to open the bowels. **laxity,**
laxness *n.* being loose/not being rigid.
lay 1 [leɪ] *adj.* (a) (person) who is not
trained as a priest. (b) not belonging to a
profession or specialization. **lay 2** *n.*
(old) short narrative poem. **lay 3** *v.*
(laid) (a) to place/to put, often in a
horizontal position. (b) to place in the
right position; to l. a carpet. (c) to cause
(dust) to settle/to subside. (d) (of bird) to
produce (an egg). (e) to make (a bet). (f)
to set/to place dishes, etc. on (a table); l.
the table for three. (g) to set (a trap/a
scene). (h) see also lie. **layabout** *n. inf.*
person who does no work and wanders
about idly. **lay aside** *v.* to put
(sth) away for future use. **layby** *n.*
place at the side of a road where vehicles
can park. **lay down** *v.* (a) to put (sth)
down/to give (sth) up. (b) to state clearly
in writing. **layer 1** *n.* (a) (horizontal)
thickness of sth. (b) good l. = hen which
produces many eggs. (c) shoot which is
layered. **layer 2** *v.* to make a new plant
by attaching a shoot to the ground so that
it takes root. **lay figure** *n.* large doll
used by artists as a model. **lay in** *v.* to
make a store/to store up. **lay into** *v. inf.*
to attack/to hit (s.o.). **layman** *n.* (*pl.*
men) person who does not belong to a
particular profession or specialization.
lay off *v.* (a) to dismiss (workers)
temporarily. (b) *inf.* to stop doing sth.
lay-off *n.* temporary dismissal from
work. **lay on** *v.* to put on/in; to provide.
lay out *v.* (a) to place in an orderly
way, esp. on a table, etc. (b) to make a
design for (a garden/a book), etc). (c) to
spend (money). (d) to prepare (a corpse)
for burial. **layout** *n.* design, esp. of a
garden/a book. **lay up** *v.* (a) to store
(away). (b) to be laid up = to be ill in
bed. **layette** [leɪ'et] *n.* clothes for a
new-born baby.
lazy ['leɪzɪ] *adj.* (-ier, iest) not wanting
to do any work. **laze** *v.* to do nothing or
very little. **lazily** *adv.* in a lazy way.
laziness *n.* being lazy. **lazybones** *n.*
inf. person who does not like work/who
does nothing.
lb abbrev. for pound (in weight).
LCD abbrev. for liquid crystal display.
lea [liː] *n.* (in poetry) meadow.

leach [li:tʃ] v. to remove a substance from soil, etc., by passing water through it.

lead 1 1 [led] n. (a) (element: Pb) heavy soft bluish-grey metal (b) weight at the end of a rope. used for measuring the depth of water. *inf.* to swing the l. = to avoid doing any work. (c) writing part of a pencil. **leaden** *adj.* of/like lead: l. sky = dull grey sky. **lead 2 1** [li:d] n. (a) front position/first action: to go into the l./to take the l. (b) (in cards) right to play first (c) strap to keep a dog in control (d) electric wire etc.. which joins an appliance to its source of power. (e) (actor who plays a) main role. (f) amount by which one is ahead. **lead 2** v. (led[led]) (a) to go/to be ahead; to show the way: to go towards (b) to be the first/ to have the most important place(c) to make (sth) have; to have; it led me to think he was lying = made me think (d) to be at the head of/to direct (e) (in cards) to play as first card; to play first (f) to go in a particular direction. **leader** n. (a) person who manages/directs others (b) main article in a newspaper which expresses the editor's opinion (c) chief player. esp. of the violin. in an orchestra (d) main barrister in a group of lawyers. **Leader of the House** n. minister who is responsible for the administration of legislation in the House of Commons. **Leader of the Opposition** n. head of the main party which opposes a government. **leadership** n. being the person who manages/directs others. **leading** *adj.* which leads most important: l. article = main article in a newspaper, giving views on topics of current interest: l. aircraftman/seaman = junior rank in the air force/in the navy; l. lady/man = actress/actor taking the main role; l. question = question which is worded in order to get a particular answer. **lead on** v. to go ahead, so that others will follow; to encourage (s.o) to go on. esp. to do sth stupid. **lead time** n. time between placing an order and receiving the goods. **lead up to** v. to prepare the way for sth (in conversation).

leaf 1 [li:f] n. (pl.leaves) (a) flat. *usu.* green part of a plant. growing from a stem or branch; trees in l. = with leaves. (b) sheet of paper forming two pages of a book; to turn over a new l. = to change your ways/to try to improve: to take a l. out of s.o.'s, book = to follow s.o.'s example. (c) flat folding part (of a table). (d) very thin sheet of metal. etc. **leaf 2** v. to l. through the pages of a book = to turn them over rapidly without reading. **leaflet** n. sheet of paper often folded, giving information as an advertisement. **leaf mould** n. compost made of rotted leaves. **leafy** *adj.* covered with leaves.

league 1 [li:g] n. (a) group joined together for some purpose; in l. with s.o. = working with s.o. against s.o. else. (b) association of sports clubs which play against each other (c) (old) measure of distance (about 5 km.). **league 2** v. to join together/to form a group for a particular purpose.

leak 1 [li:k] n. (a) hole through which liquid/gas etc., can escape or enter: the ship sprang a l. = got a hole (b) escape of secret information. **leak 2** v. (a) (of liquid/gas etc.) to flow away/to escape (b) (of container) to allow liquid/gas. etc., to escape or enter(c) to pass on (secret information) **leakage** n. (a) action of leaking (b) amount of liquid. etc., which has escaped. **leaky** *adj.* which leaks.

lean 1 [li:n] *adj.* (-er, -est) (a) thin/with little flesh (b) (of meat) with little fat. (c) poor /unproductive. **lean 2** n. meat with little fat. **lean 3** v. (leaned/ lent[lent]) (a) to support (yourself/sth) (on sth/s.o.) (b) to stand/to be in a position at an angle (c) to have a tendency towards. **leaning** n. tendency towards/interest in. **leanness** n. being thin. **lean over** v. to bend (in a particular direction): to lean over backwards to help = make every effort to help. **lean-to** n. (small) building supported against the wall of a larger building.

leap 1 [li:p] n. (a) jump. (b) upward/ forward movement: to advance by leaps and bounds = to make rapid progress: l. in the dark = action where you are unsure of the consequences. **leap 2** v. (leaped/leapt) (a) to jump (b) to rise suddenly. **leap at** v. to seize/to accept eagerly. **leapfrog 1** n. game in which one person jumps over the bent back to another. **leapfrog 2** v. (leapfrogged) to jump over s.o.'s bent back. **leap year** n. every fourth year, in which February has 29 days.

learn [lɜːn] v. (learned/learnt[lɜːnd/lɜːnt]) (a) to gain knowledge of (sth) /of how to do (sth). (b) to hear (news. etc.). **learned** ['lɜːnɪd] adj. (a) (person) who has much knowledge. (b) (journal) for specialists. **learner** n. person who is learning. **learning** n. (a) gaining knowledge of sth/of how to do sth (b) great study/knowledge.

lease 1 n. letting/renting of a building/ piece of land, etc., for a specified period; it's given him a new l. of life = it's made him want to make a fresh start/to live more fully. **lease 2** [liːs] v. (a) (also lease out) to take/to give on a lease. (b) to hold on a lease. **leasehold. 1** n. (holding of) property on a lease. **leasehold 2** adj. held on a lease. **leaseholder** n. person who holds a property on a lease.

leash [liːʃ] n. (pl.-es) strap/cord to keep a dog in control.

least 1 [liːst] adj. & n. (of the smallest/ most unimportant (amount). **least 2** adv. in the smallest way.

leather ['leðə] n. skin of certain animals. used to make shoes/bags etc. **leather jacket** n. grub of a fly. **leathery** adj. (tough) like leather.

leave 1 [liːv] n. (a) permission to be off; permission to be away. (c) to take l. of = to say goodbye to; to take l. of one's senses = to become quite mad. **leave 2** v. (left[left]) (a) to go away (from) (b) to allow to remain behind/to forget to take; l. me alone = don't pester me; l. it to me = let me deal with it. (c) to abandon (d) to give (sth) to s.o. of your will (e) to have at the time of one's death. **leave behind** v. to forget to take (s.o./sth) with you. **leave off** v. to stop. **leave out** v. to forget/to omit (sth).

leaven 1 ['levn] n. substance which causes a dough to rise; thing which causes a change for the better. **leaven 2** v. to add leaven to (dough); to cause a change.

Lebanese 1 [lebə'niːz] adj. referring to the Lebanon. **Lebanese 2** n. (pl.Lebanese) person from the Lebanon.

lecher ['letʃə] n. man who frequently indulges in sex. **lecherous** adj. indulging in sex. **lechery** n. indulgence in sex.

lectern ['lektən] n. stand with a sloping surface on which you can put a book/ papers, etc., from which you are going to read aloud in public. **lecture 1** ['lektʃə] n. (a) talk. esp. to students or other group of people on a particular subject (b) (long) scolding. **lecture 2** v. to give lecture (on sth). **lecturer** n. (a) person who gives a talk on a particular subject (b) teacher in a university or college. **lectureship** n. position as lecturer.

led [led] v. see lead 2.

ledge [ledʒ] n. flat (narrow) part which sticks out from a cliff or building. **ledger** ['ledʒə] n. book in which accounts are kept. **ledger line** n. ledger line.

lee [liː] n. side of a ship sheltered from the wind l. shore towards which the wind is blowing. **leeward** adj., adv. & n. (side of a ship) sheltered from the wind. **leeway** n. (a) time which has been lost; to make up l. = to make up for lost time/opportunity (b) extra time/extra space.

leech [liːtʃ] n. (pl.-es) (a) type of worm which sucks blood (b) (old inf.) doctor.

leek [liːk] n. vegetable related to the onion. with white stem and long green leaves.

leer 1 ['lɪə] n. nasty sideways look often expressing sexual desire. **leer 2** v. to look with a leer (at s.o.).

lees [liːz] n. pl.sediment left at the bottom of a wine bottle, etc.

left 1 [left] n. (a) side of the body which normally has the weaker hand (b) left hand/fist (c) (in politics) group/policy supporting the rights of the workers. **left 2** adj. (a) of/on the side of the body which normally has the weaker hand; l. bank = bank of a river, etc., on your left when facing down stream (b) of the left (in politics). **left 3** adv. on/to the left. **left 4** see also leave. **left-handed** adj. using the left hand more than the right. **leftist** adj. & n. (person) who is on the left of the socialist party. **left-luggage office** n. place where suitcases,. etc., can be left and collected later for a fee. **leftovers** n. pl.what is not used. esp. food which has not been eaten. **left wing** *adj.* politically on the left. **left winger** *n.* person who is on the left politically.

leg 1 [leg] *n.* (a) part of the body on which a person or animal walks; to be on one's last legs = to be almost exhausted; to give s.o. a l. up = to help him to climb to a higher position; to pull s.o.'s l. = to joke by telling him sth untrue (b) leg of an animal used for food (c) part of a garment which covers the leg (d) part of a piece of furniture which supports. (e) section of a race/journey. **leg 2** *v. inf.* to l. it = to walk. **legged** [legd, 'legɪd] suffix meaning with legs; four legged animal. **leggings** *n. pl.* thick coverings for the lower legs. **leggy** *adj.* with long legs. **legless** *adj.* (a) without any legs. (b) *Sl.* drunk. **leg-pull** *n. inf.* hoax. **legwarmers** *n. pl.* knitted garments for the legs, like long socks with no feet.

legacy ['legəsɪ] *n.* what is left to a person (after s.o.'s death). **legatee** [legə'ti:] *n.* person who receives a legacy.

legal ['li:gl] *adj.* (a) in accordance with/ obeying the law; l. aid = free legal representation given to people without enough money to pay lawyers' fees; l. tender = money which must legally be accepted if you give it in payment. (b) referring to the (processes of the) law. **legalistic** [li:gə'lɪstɪk] *adj.* too concerned with the law. **legality** [lɪ'gælɪtɪ] *n.* being allowed by law. **legalize** *v.* to authorize (sth) by law. **legally** *adv.* in accordance with the law.

legate ['legət] *n.* official envoy (from the Pope). **legation** [lɪ'geɪʃn] *n.* group of officials who represent their government in a foreign country; building where they live and work.

legend ['ledʒənd] *n.* (a) story from the past which may not be based on fact (b) key to symbols used on a map. **legendary** *adj.* referring to a legend. **legerdemain** [ledʒədə'meɪn] *n.* trickery; conjuring.

leger line ['ledʒ'laɪn] *n.* small line on a musical score, written above or below the normal five lines.

legible ['ledʒɪbl] *adj.* clear/able to be (easily) read. **legibility** [ledʒɪ'bɪlɪtɪ] *n.* being easily read. **legibly** *adv.* in a legible way.

legion ['li:dʒən] *n.* (a) division of an army. (b) association/body esp. of soldiers; the Foreign L. = private army, organized by France, which serves overseas (c) very large number. **legionnaire** *n.* member of a legion, such as the Foreign Legion; legionnaires' disease = disease, similar to pneumonia, caused by bacteria in air conditioning systems.

legislate ['ledʒɪsleɪt] *v.* to make laws. **legislation** [ledʒɪ'sleɪʃn] *n.* (making of) laws. **legislative** ['ledʒɪslətɪv] *adj.* referring to laws/law-making. **legislator** *n.* person who makes laws. **legislature** ['ledʒɪsləʃə] *n.* law-making body.

legitimacy [lɪ'dʒɪtɪməsɪ] *n.* being in accordance with the law. **legitimate** *adj.* (a) legal/lawful; (child) born to married parents (b) reasonable/ justifiable. **legitimately** *adv.* in accordance with the law; correctly, **legitimize** *v.* to make legitimate.

legume ['legju:m] *n.* plant (like a pea or bean) which has seeds in pods. **leguminous** [le'gju:mɪnəs] *adj.* (plant) which has seeds in goods.

leisure ['leʒə] *n.* time free to do what you want; at your l. = when there is an opportunity/without hurry; l. pursuits = pastimes. **leisured** *adj.* having plenty of leisure; l. classes = people who do not need to work to earn money. **leisurely** *adj.* without hurry.

leitmotiv ['laɪtməʊti:f] *n.* theme (in music) which reappears and which shows a special feeling/state.

lemming ['lemɪŋ] *n.* small Scandinavian mammal which travels in groups and is said to fall blindly over cliffs into the sea.

lemon ['lemən] *n.* pale yellow sour tasting fruit; tree which bears such fruit l. curd = cream made with eggs and lemons. used to spread on bread. **lemonade** [lemə'neɪd] *n. usu.* fizzy lemon-flavoured drink.

lemur ['li:mə] *n.* monkey-like animal with a long tail

lend [lend] *v.* (lent) (a) to give (sth to s.o.) for a certain period of time: will you l. me your book for a day or two? (b) to give/to contribute (to): to l. a hand = to help; to lend itself to = to be suitable for. **lender** *n.* person who lends (money).

lending library *n.* section of a library from which books may be taken away from a time

length [leŋθ] *n.* (a) measurement of how long sth is from end to end; he won the race by a l. = by the length of a horse/man/boat, etc., throughout the l. and breadth of the country = all over the country (b) piece of sth of a particular length; a l. of rope (c) being long; a stay of some l. = quite a long stay; at l. = (i) at last; (ii) for a long time (d) to go to great lengths = to make great efforts.

lengthen *v.* to make/to become longer.

lengthily *adv.* for a long time/ at length. **lengthiness** *n.* being long.

lengthways, lengthwise *adv.* along the length/along the longest side.

lengthy *adj.* (-ier, -iest) (very) long.

lenience, leniency ['liːnjəns(ɪ)] *n.* being merciful/not being strict. **lenient** *adj.* showing mercy/not strict or severe.

leniently *adv.* in a lenient way.

lens [lenz] *n.* (*pl.*-es) (a) piece of glass/plastic, etc. curved so as to cause light rays to join or spread out, and used in spectacles/telescopes/cameras, etc. (b) part of the eye. (c) contact l. = small lens worn on the eyeball to help you to see.

lent [lent] *v.* see lend.

Lent [lent] *n.* (in the Christian church) period before Easter when many Christians eat less/give up some luxury. **Lenten** *adj.* referring to Lent.

lentil ['lentl] *n.* small round dried seed used as food.

Leo ['liːəʊ] *n.* one of the signs of the Zodiac, shaped like a lion. **leonine** ['liːəʊnaɪn] *adj.* referring to a lion.

leopard ['lepəd] *n.* large spotted animal of the cat family. **leopardess** *n.* female leopard.

leotard ['lɪʊtɑːd] *n.* skintight one-piece costume worn by ballet dancers.

leper ['lepə] *n.* person who has leprosy.

leprosy ['leprəsɪ] *n.* serious infectious skin disease which slowly destroys flesh and nerves. **leprous** *adj.* like leprosy.

lepidoptera [lepɪ'dɒptərə] *n. pl.*group of insects including butterflies and moths.

leprechaun ['leprəkɔːn] *n.* (in Ireland) wicked little elf.

lesbian ['lezbɪən] *adj. & n.* (woman) who is sexually attracted to other

women. **lesbianism** *n.* state of being lesbian.

lesion ['liːʒn] *n.* wound; change in body tissue.

less 1 [les] *adj. & n.* (of a) smaller quantity/size/value. **less 2** *prep.* minus/with a certain amount taken away. **less 3** *adv.* in a smaller amount/to a smaller degree. **lessen** *v.* to make (sth) become less; to reduce. **lesser** *adj.* smaller. **lessee** [le'siː] *n.* person who holds a lease/who pays rent. **lessor** [le'sɔː] *n.* person who gives a lease/who receives rent

lesson ['lesn] *n.* (a) period of time in school, etc. during which you are taught. (b) means by which you learn; he's learnt his l. = he is wiser; to teach s.o. a l. = to make s.o. wiser/to punish s.o. (c) part of the Bible which is read in church.

lest [lest] *conj.* (a) (formal) in order to avoid. (b) for fear that.

let 1 [let] *v.* (let) (a) to permit/to allow. (b) to lend (a house. etc) for a period of time in return for money. **let 2** *v.* (showing command/suggestion) let's hurry; don't let's start yet. **let 3** *n. inf.* period of lease of a property. **letalone** *adv.* even less. **let down** *v.* (a) to take down/to lower. (b) to fail to help/to disappoint. **letdown** *n.* disappointment. **let go** *v.* (a) to lose hold (of sth) (b) to allow (s.o.) to leave. **let in** *v.* (a) to allow to come in (b) to let yourself in for = to allow yourself to get involved in (a difficult situation). **let off** *v.* (a) to make (a gun etc.) fire. (b) to let s.o. off = not to punish s.o. after all. **let on** *v. inf.* to tell a secret. **let out** *v.* (a) to allow to go out/to escape (b) to lend for a period of time in return for money. (c) to make (a garment. etc) wider. **letout** *n.* way of avoiding doing sth which you ought to do. **let up** *v.* to stop/to become less. **let-up** *n.* stopping/slackening.

lethal ['liːθl] *adj.* deadly/causing death.

lethargy ['leθədʒɪ] *n.* (feeling of) unwillingness to do anything; lack of energy. **lethargic** [lə'θɑːdʒɪk] *adj.* feeling/appearing unwilling to do anything; lacking energy.

let's [lets] short for let us.

letter 1 ['letə] *n.* (a) written/printed symbol representing a sound of speech;

to the I. = to the last detail (b) piece of writing sent from one person/ organization to another to pass on information (c) letters = literary learning. **letter 2** v. to mark with letters.
letterbox n. box where letters are posted; hole in a door through which letters are delivered. **letterhead** n. printed heading on writing paper.
lettering n. (a) writing letters (b) letters in an inscription. etc. **letterpress** n. method of printing using metal letters.
lettuce ['letɪs] n. green vegetable whose leaves are often used in salads.
leucocyte ['ljuːkesaɪt] n. white blood cell.
leukaemia, Am. leukemia [luːˈkiːmɪə] n. serious, often fatal, illness, which increases the white cells in the blood.
levee ['levɪ] n. Am. embankment built along the bank of a river which is liable to flood.
level 1 ['levl] n. (a) flat/horizontal position; on the I.= (i) in a flat position; (ii) inf. straight/honest (b) position in relation to height and depth; position on a scale/ in a list (c) instrument for testing whether sth is horizontal or not. **level 2** adj. (a) flat/even/horizontal (b) (with) at the same level as (c) calm/even; inf. to do one's I. best = one's very best. **level 3** v. (levelled) (a) to make/to become level; they levelled the house to he ground = they destroyed it completely (b) to point/to aim (an accusation) at s.o.
level crossing n. place where a road crosses a railway line without a bridge or tunnel. **level-headed** adj. calm/able to act sensibly. **leveller** n. person who believes everyone should be equal in status. **level with** v. inf. to speak frankly.
lever 1 ['liːvə] n. instrument such as a bar which helps to raise a heavy object. or to move part of a machine. etc.: gear I. = handle in a car which changes the gears. **lever 2** v. to move with a lever.
leverage n. (a) force of a lever (b) influence which you can use to reach your aims. **leveraged buyout** n. buying a company, using the company's assets as security for the money borrowed to buy it.
leveret ['levrət] n. young hare.

leviathan [lɪˈvaɪəθən] n. huge powerful monster or machine.
levitate ['levɪteɪt] v. (of person/heavy body) to rise into the air. **levitation** [levɪˈteɪʃn] n. rising into the air.
levity ['levɪtɪ] n. disrespectful way of considering serious things.
levy 1 ['levɪ] n. (a) demand for/ collection of (a tax/a number of soldiers). (b) tax/number of soldiers (which has been collected). **levy 2** v. to demand/to collect (a tax/a number of soldiers).
lewd [luːd] adj. (-er, -est) indecent/rude. **lewdly** adv. in a lewd way. **lewdness** n. lewd action.
lexicon ['leksɪkən] n. dictionary.
lexicography [leksɪˈkɒɡrəfɪ] n. writing of dictionaries. **lexicographer** n. person who writes dictionaries.
ley [leɪ] n. field which is used for pasture.
liable ['laɪəbl] adj. (a) (legally) responsible (for sth) (b) (for) obliged/ bound to do. (c) apt/likely (to do sth).
liability [laɪəˈbɪlɪtɪ] n. (a) (legal) responsibility. (b) obligation; he couldn't meet his liabilities = he couldn't pay his debts (c) tendency to do sth (d) inf. he's a I. = he causes problems.
liaison [lɪˈeɪzən] n. joining/ relationship/connection: I. officer = person responsible for dealings with another group. **liaise** v. to join with others. esp. for discussion (with s.o.).
liar ['laɪə] n. person who tells lies.
lib [lɪb] n. inf. short for liberation.
libation [laɪˈbeɪʃn] n. (formal) drink offered to a god.
libel 1 ['laɪbl] n. untrue statement(s) in writing, damaging to s.o.'s character.
libel 2 v. (libelled) to damage s.o.'s character in writing. **libellous** adj. (writing) which libels s.o.
liberal 1 ['lɪbrəl] adj. (a) wide in views/ meaning. etc. (b) ample/generous. (c) (in politics) Liberal = having views/policies based on freedom of individuals. democratic reform etc. **liberal 2** n. (in politics) Liberal = member or supporter of a Liberal party or policy. **liberalism** n. (in politics) liberal views/policies.
liberality [lɪbəˈrælɪtɪ] n. (a) being open-minded. (b) generosity.
liberalization [lɪbərəlaɪˈzeɪʃn] n. act of liberalizing. **liberalize** ['lɪbərəlaɪz] v. to

make (laws, etc.) more liberal; to become more liberal. **liberally** *adv.* in a liberal way.

liberate ['lɪbəreɪt] *v.* to set/to make (s.o./sth) free (from sth). **liberation** [lɪbə'reɪʃn] *n.* setting free. **liberator** *n.* person who sets s.o. free.

libertarian [lɪbə'teərɪən] *n.* person who believes in freedom of thought and action.

libertine ['lɪbəti:n] *n.* man who is sexually immoral.

liberty ['lɪbətɪ] *n.* freedom; at l. = free/not in captivity; to take liberties = to do sth without permission; to take liberties with sth/s.o. = to treat sth./ s.o. too familiarly.

libido [lɪ'bi:dəʊ] *n.* (*pl.*-os) sexual urge.

Libra ['li:brə] *n.* one of the signs of the zodiac, shaped like a pair of scales.

library ['laɪbrərɪ] *n.* (a) place where books are stored (to be read/borrowed/consulted). (b) collection of records; record l. = collection of records available for borrowing. **librarian** [laɪ'breərɪən] *n.* person who works in a library. **librarianship** *n.* art of being a librarian.

libretto ['lɪbretəʊ] *n.* (*pl.*-os) words of an opera. **librettist** *n.* person who writes a libretto

Libyan 1 ['lɪbjən] *adj.* referring to Libya. **Libyan 2** *n.* person from Libya.

lice [laɪs] *n. pl.* see louse.

licence, *Am.* **license** ['laɪsəns] *n.* (a) (document giving) official permission to have/to do sth (b) freedom; use when used too much or wrongly. (c) poetic l. = use of language in poetry which would not be acceptable in prose. **license 1** ['laɪsəns] *Am.* see licence. **license 2** *v.* to give (s.o.) official permission to do sth; licensed grocer = one allowed by law to sell alcoholic drink. **licensee** [laɪsən'si:] *n.* holder of a licence. esp. landlord of a public house. **licentiate** [laɪ'senʃɪət] *n.* person who has been licensed to practise a profession. **licentious** [laɪ'senʃəs] *adj.* indulging in sex or other pleasures beyond what is normally permitted. **licentiousness** *n.* excessive indulgence in sex.

lichen ['laɪkən] *n.* flat grey/yellow/green plant which grows on stones or on other plants.

licit ['lɪsɪt] *adj.* legal.

lick 1 [lɪk] *n.* (a) stroke with the tongue. (b) thin coating (of paint). (c) *inf.* speed. (d) *inf.* a l. and a promise = a quick wash. **lick 2** *v.* (a) to taste/to stroke with the tongue; to l. s.o.'s boots = to behave very humbly towards him to gain favour; to l. into shape = to train (s.o.) into proper ways. (b) to beat/to hit (c) *inf.* to defeat (in a game). **licking** *n.* (a) stroking with the tongue. (b) beating (c) *inf.* defeat.

licorice ['lɪkərɪs] *n. Am.* see liquorice.

lid [lɪd] *n.* (a).covering for a container. often with a handle: *inf.* that's put the l. on it = that's made it impossible (b) eyelid/covering of the eye.

lido ['li:dəʊ] *n.* (*pl.*-os) swimming pool and terraces round it.

lie 1 [laɪ] *n.* (a) statement which is not true: to give the l. to = to prove (sth) is wrong. (b) position/direction in which sth is situated; the l. of the land = state of affairs. **lie 2** *v.* (a) (lied, lying) to say something which is not true (b) (lay, lying, has lain) to be in a horizontal position: he lay dead on the ground. (c) to be: see how the land lies = see what the condition/position of sth is. **lie down** *v.* to put yourself in a horizontal position (on sth) they won't take that lying down = they won't accept it without protest. **lie-down** *n. inf.* short rest. **lie in** *v.* to stay in bed longer than usual. **lie-in** *n. inf.* to have a lie-in = to stay in bed longer than usual. **lie low** *v.* to hide.

lieder ['li:də] *n.* German romantic song.

liege ['li:dʒ] *n.* (old) lord (to whom people give service).

lien ['lɪən] *n.* legal right to take and hold s.o.'s goods until a debt is paid.

lieu [lju:] *n.* in l. of = instead of.

lieutenant [lef'tenənt, *Am.* lu:'tenənt] *n.* (a) rank in the armed forces (in the army below captain, in the navy below lieutenant-commander); l. -colonel = rank in the army below colonel; l. -commander = rank in the navy below commander; flight l. = rank in the air force below squadron leader. (b) main helper; henchman.

life [laɪf] *n.* (*pl.*lives) (a) state of being alive; run for your lives = as fast as you can: I can't for the l. of me understand =

I can't understand at all; not on your l. = not under any circumstances. (b) liveliness/energy. (c) living things: is there l. on Mars? (d) (length of) time you are alive; in early l.= when he was a child; l. insurance = insurance paid if you die; l. imprisonment = imprisonment for the rest of your life. (e) story of s.o.'s life. **lifebelt** *n.* cork-filled ring to keep s.o. afloat. **lifeboat** *n.* boat used to rescue people at sea. **life cycle** *n.* life of an animal/plant through various stages. **lifeguard** *n.* person who rescues people who get into difficulties while swimming. **life jacket** *n.* cork-filled coat to keep s.o. afloat. **lifeless** *adj.* (a) not alive. (b) not lively. **lifelike** *adj.* (of a picture, etc.) looking like the real person/thing. **lifeline** *n.* rope thrown to a drowning person; help given to s.o. in difficulties. **lifelong** *adj.* lasting your whole life. **life preserver** *n.* (a) short stick, used in self-defence (b) *Am.* lifebelt/life jacket. **lifer** *n.* person who is serving a sentence of life imprisonment **life-saving** *n.* rescuing people from drowning. **life-size(d)** *adj.* (statue/painting. etc) which is the same size as the real thing or person. **life style** *n.* way in which s.o. or a group of people live their daily lives. **lifetime** *n.* time when you are alive: the chance of a l. = the best chance you are ever likely to get.

lift 1 [lɪft] *n.* (a) (act of) raising (b) ride in a car (c) mechanical device for carrying people or goods from one floor of a building to another; ski l. = device to take skiers to the top of a ski slope. **lift 2** *v.* (a) to raise (to a higher position) (b). to pick up (potatoes) out of the ground. (c) to take away/to remove (a ban) (d) *inf.* to steal (e) (of fog/clouds) to rise. **lift-off** *n.* vertical take-off of a space rocket.

ligament ['lɪgəmənt] *n.* tough tissue which holds bones together.

ligature ['lɪgətʃʊə] *n.* thread used for tying in surgical operations; link between two printed letters.

light 1 [laɪt] *n.* (a) brightness which allows you to see; don't stand in my l. = between me and the source of light. (b) bulb/object which gives light (c) in the l. of what he said = in consideration of it;

to throw l. on sth = make it clearer; to come to l. = be discovered (d) appearance/aspect (e) means of making a cigarette, etc., catch fire (f) *pl.*lights = (i) lungs of certain animals used as food; (ii) traffic lights. **light 2** *v.* (lit) (a) to make (sth) start to burn. (b) to give light to. **light 3** *adj.* (-er, - est) (a) having a lot of light, allowing you to see well. (b) pale (colour) (c) not heavy; she's a l. sleeper = wakens easily. (d) not serious; to make l. of = to treat as unimportant. **light 4** *adv.* (to travel) with little luggage. **lighten** *v.* (a) to make lighter/not so dark. (b) to make lighter/not so heavy. **lighter** *n.* (a) small instrument for making cigarettes, etc., burn. (b) boat used for loading other boats.

lighterman *n.* (*pl.*-men) man who works on a lighter. **light-fingered** *adj.* (person) who is likely to steal. **light headed** *adj.* dizzy: feeling excited. **light-hearted** *adj.* cheerful/without a care. **light heavyweight** *n.* weight in boxing between middle weight and heavyweight. **lighthouse** *n.* tall building containing a light to guide ships. **lighting-up time** *n.* time at which street lamps and car lights have to be switched on. **lightly** *adv.* in a light way; l. dressed = wearing thin clothes; to get off l. = with little or no punishment. **lightness** *n.* being light. **light on** *v.* to find. **light pen** *n.* pen with a tip which is sensitive to light and which can ' read' lines or images and transfer them to a computer. **lightship** *n.* ship which carries a large light, acting as a floating lighthouse. **light up** *v.* (a) to give light to (sth) (b) to become bright. (c) to start to smoke (d) to switch car lights on as it gets dark. **lightweight, 1** *n.* (a) weight in boxing between featherweight and welterweight. (b) person without much influence. **lightweight 2** *adj.* (a) light (clothes) (b) not very influential/ important. **light year** *n.* distance travelled by light during one year (about six million million miles.)

lightning 1 ['laɪtnɪŋ] *n.* flash of electricity in the sky; followed by thunder; like l. = very fast; l. conductor = rod for carrying a lightning charge straight to the ground to prevent damage to buildings. **lightning 2** *adj.*

extremely fast. I. strike = strike taking place without warning.

lignite ['lɪgnaɪt] *n.* brown coal.

like 1 [laɪk] *adj.* (nearly) the same/ similar. **like 2** *prep.* in the same way as/ the same as/similar to; I feel I. some chocolate = I would like to eat some chocolate. **like 3** *n.* similar thing(s). **like 4** *adv.* (as) I. as not = probably. **like 5** *conj.* in the same way as. **like 6** *v.* (a) to have pleasant feelings about (b) to desire/to want. **likeable** *adj.* pleasant. **likelihood** *n.* probability. **likely 1** *adj.* (-ier, -iest) (a) probable (b) suitable (for) /apt (to). **likely 2** *adv.* probably: not I.! = certainly not. **like-minded** *adj.* (person) who has the same opinions. **liken** *v.* to I. sth to sth = to compare, by showing how one thing is similar to another. **likeness** *n.* thing which looks like s.o./sth. **likes** *n. pl.*(a) I. and dislikes = things you like and don't like. (b) *inf.* the I. of him = people like him. **likewise** *adv.* (a) in the same way. (b) similarly/the same. **liking** *n.* pleasant feeling towards s.o.; fondness for s.o./sth.

lilac ['laɪlək] *n.* (a) tree with clusters of (pale) purple or white flowers (b) pale purple colour.

lilliputian [lɪlɪ'pju:ʃn] *adj.* very small.

lilt 1 [lɪlt] *n.* song/way of speaking with a light well-marked rhythm. **lilt 2** *v.* to sing/to play a tune with a light well-marked rhythm.

lighting *adj.* (song) which has a lilt.

lily ['lɪlɪ] *n.* type of white flower which grows from a bulb. **lily-of-the-valley** *n.* spring plant with small white flowers growing in clusters.

lima bean ['li:məbi:n] *n.* bean with flat pale seeds.

limb [lɪm] *n.* (a) leg/arm/wing; danger to life and I. = danger that you may be hurt (b) branch of a tree; out on a I.= in a difficult/exposed situation.

limber ['lɪmbə] *v.* to I. up = to do exercises to warm your muscles before taking part in a sporting contest.

limbo ['lɪmbəʊ] *n.* (a) place between heaven and hell. where unbaptized people are said to go when they die. (b) position of not being accepted or rejected; being halfway between two stages. (c) I. dancing = West Indian

dance where the dancer bends his body backwards parallel to the floor to pass under a horizontal bar.

lime [laɪm] *n.* (a) white substance containing calcium, used in making cement. (b) small yellowish-green tropical fruit like a lemon; tree which bears such fruit. (c) northern deciduous tree with smooth leaves and yellowish flowers. **lime green** *adj. & n.* green colour of lime. **limelight** *n.* attention/ publicity. **limestone** *n.* light-coloured stone containing calcium.

limerick ['lɪmərɪk] *n.* type of amusing five-line poem.

limey ['laɪmɪ] *adj. & n. Sl.* English (person).

limit 1 ['lɪmɪt] *n.* furthest point/extent; boundary; end (beyond which you cannot go); *inf.* that's the I. = too much. **limit 2** *v.* to put a limit on/to keep within limits; not to allow (sth) to go beyond a certain point; limited company = private company in which the members only have to pay debts up to the amount of capital they have put in. **limitation** [lɪmɪ'teɪʃn] *n.* (a) act of limiting (b) thing which stops you going further: to know your limitations = to know what you are capable of doing.

limousine [lɪmə'zi:n] *n.* large luxurious car. with a partition between the driver and the passenger.

limp 1 [lɪmp] *n.* way of walking unevenly. **limp 2** *v.* to walk with an uneven step. **limp 3** *adj.* without stiffness/soft; without energy. **limply** *adv.* in a limp way. **limpness** *n.* being limp.

limpet ['lɪmpɪt] *n.* cone-shaped shellfish which clings to rocks.

limpid ['lɪpɪd] *adj.* clear. **limpidity** [lɪm'pɪdɪtɪ] *n.* (formal) being clear.

linchpin ['lɪnʃpɪn] *n.* (a) pin which goes through an axle to hold a wheel on. (b) very important person/piece of machinery.

linctus ['lɪŋktəs] *n.* cough syrup.

lindane ['lɪndeɪn] *n.* powerful insecticide

linden ['lɪndeɪn] *n.* (formal) lime tree.

line 1 [laɪn] *n.* (a) (long) thin mark; to draw the I. at = to stop short of/not to do; to be on the right lines = to be doing things the right way (b) long wire/cord;

hard lines = bad luck (c) telephone l. = cable along which telephone messages are sent; the l. 's bad = it is difficult to make out what s.o. is saying: crossed l. = two telephone conversations which intermingle by error (d) row of people/cars/words. etc.; *inf.* to drop s.o. a l. = to send a short letter; l. printer = computer printer which prints each line separately. (e) *Am.* queue (f) tracks on which trains run (g) shipping/air company (h) sequence of ancestors/descendants (i) lines = shape/outline; general design (j) direction; method; course of action; in l. with = according to/following (a decision); to take a hard l. = to be aggressive/not to weaken in any way. (k) type of work/ goods. **line 2** *v.* (a) to put lines on. (b) to form a line (along the edge of a street). (c) to put a layer of material inside (a piece of clothing); to l. one's pockets = to make money (usu. dishonestly). **lineage** ['lɪnɪɪdʒ] *n.* line of descendants (from an ancestor). **lineal** ['lɪnɪə] *adj.* (descendant) in direct line. **lineaments** *n.* *pl.*outline of the face/features. **linear** ['lɪnɪə] *adj.* referring to lines/to length. **liner** *n.* (a) thing used for lining; bin l. = plastic bag for putting inside a dustbin. (b) large passenger ship. **linesman** *n.* (*pl.*-men) (a) man who looks after electric/telephone/railway lines. (b) person who stays on the sideline in a game to see if the ball goes over the line. **line up.** *v.* to form a line/a queue. **line-up** *n.* row/list of people.

lining *n.* layer of material inside sth.

linen ['lɪnɪn] *n.* (a) cloth made from flax. (b) (household) l. = sheets/pillowcases/tablecloths, etc. (c) underwear; to wash your dirty l. in public = tell shameful personal secrets.

ling [lɪŋ] *n.* (a) type of small edible fish (b) heather.

linger ['lɪŋgə] *v.* (a) to wait/to remain/to say longer than necessary/expected. (b) (of sick person) to remain alive.

lingerie ['lænʃərɪ] *n.* women's underwear.

lingo ['lɪŋgəʊ] *n.* *Sl.* language.

lingua franca [lɪŋgwə'fræŋkə] *n.* language used by speakers of various languages as a common means of communication. **lingual** ['lɪŋgəl] *adj.* referring to the tongue.

linguist ['lɪŋgwɪst] *n.* (a) person who knows foreign languages well. (b) person who studies linguistics. **linguistic** [lɪŋ'geɪstɪk] *adj.* (a) referring to language(s) (b) referring to the science of language. **linguistics** *n.* science of language.

liniment ['lɪnɪmənt] *n.* oily substance which you rub on the skin to lessen pains.

link 1 [lɪŋk] *n.* (a) ring which forms part of a chain (b) thing which connects two parts. **link 2** *v.* to join. **linkage** *n.* act of linking. **linkman** *n.* (*pl.*-men) person who speaks between sections of TV programmes. **links** [lɪŋks] *n.* *pl.*golf course.

linnet ['lɪnɪt] *n.* small singing bird.

lino ['laɪnəʊ] *n.* *inf.* linoleum. **linocut** ['laɪnəʊkʌt] *n.* design printed from a block of linoleum which has been cut into a pattern. **linoleum** [lɪ'nəʊlɪəm] *n.* hard smooth floor covering.

linseed ['lɪnsiːd] *n.* seed of flax.

lint [lɪnt] *n.* soft cloth used for putting on wounds.

lintel ['lɪntl] *n.* piece of wood/stone over a door or window.

lion ['laɪən] *n.* large wild animal of the cat family, the male of which has a long mane: the l. 's share = the biggest part. **lioness** *n.* female lion. **lionize** *v.* to treat (s.o.) as very important.

lip [lɪp] *n.* (a) one of two fleshy parts round the outside of the mouth; to keep a stiff upper l.= not to show emotion in time of trouble; to smack one's lips over = to express great enjoyment of. (b) *Sl.* cheek/rudeness. (c) edge of a bowl/cup etc. **lipped** *adj.* with lips. **lipread** *v.* (lip-read['lɪpred]) (of a deaf person) to follow speech by watching the movements of the lips of the person speaking. **lip salve** *n.* ointment to prevent lips cracking. **lip service** *n.* to pay lip service to sth = to give false impression of respecting/obeying sth. **lipstick** *n.* (stick of) substance for colouring the lips.

lipid ['lɪpɪd] *n.* fatty substance in the tissue in human bodies.

liquefy ['lɪkwɪfaɪ] *v.* to become liquid; to make (sth) become liquid. **liquefaction** [lɪkwɪ'fækʃn] *n.* making/becoming liquid.

liqueur [lɪˈkɜː] n. strong alcoholic drink.

liquid 1 [ˈlɪkwɪd] n. substance which flows easily like water. and which is neither a gas nor a solid. **liquid 2** adj. (a) which is neither gas nor solid. and which flows easily; l. crystal display = display panel, where the figures appear black. (b) (of assets, etc) able to be changed easily into cash. (c) (of sounds) pure/clear. **liquidate** v. (a) to close (a company) which cannot pay its debts. (b) to pay (a debt) (c) inf. to kill. **liquidation** [lɪkwɪˈdeɪʃn] n. closing of a company which cannot pay its debts. **liquidator** n. person named to close a company. **liquidity** [lɪˈkwɪdɪtɪ] n. (in finance) being able to change assets into cash. **liquidize** v. to reduce fruit to liquid. **liquidizer** n. machine which liquidizes. **liquor** [ˈlɪkə] n. (a) alcoholic drink (b) liquid produced in cooking.

liquorice, Am. **licorice** [ˈlɪkərɪs] n. black substance from the root of a plant, used in medicine and in sweets.

lira [ˈlɪrə] n. old unit of money used in Italy.

lisle [laɪl] n. fine cotton (used to make stockings).

lisp 1 [lɪsp] n. speech defect in which 's' is pronounced as 'th'. **lisp 2** v. to speak with a lisp.

lissom [ˈlɪsəm] adj. lithe/supple.

list 1 [lɪst] n. (a) number of items written/spoken one after another; wine l. = list of wines available in a restaurant; to be on the sick l. = to be reported sick; to be on the danger l. = to be dangerously ill; l. price = price of sth as shown in a catalogue. (b) (of ship) leaning to one side. (c) to enter the lists = to be a candidate in an election. **list 2** v. (a) to say/to write (a number of items) one after the other (b) (of ship) to lean over to one side.

listen [ˈlɪsn] v. to pay attention (to s.o./ sth) in order to hear. **listener** n. person who listens.

Listeria [lɪsˈtiːərɪə] n. bacteria found in some foods and in domestic animals, which can cause infections such as meningitis.

listless [ˈlɪstləs] adj. (feeling) dull, without interest or energy. **listlessly** adv. in a way which shows lack of

interest. **listlessness** n. lack of interest/energy.

lit [lɪt] v. see light.

litany [ˈlɪtənɪ] n. form of prayer with repeated responses, used in churches.

litchi [ˈlaɪtʃɪ] n. small Chinese fruit. with a red skin and large stone.

liter [ˈliːtə] n. Am. litre.

literacy [ˈlɪtərɪsɪ] n. ability to read and write.

literal 1 adj. keeping to the exact meaning of the original words. **literal 2** n. typesetting mistake. **literally** adv. in a literal way; (to emphasize) his eyes were l. popping out of his head.

literalness n. being literal. **literary** adj. referring to literature. **literate** [ˈlɪtərət] adj. (a) able to read and write (b) well educated. esp. in literary subjects. **literati** [lɪtəˈrɑːtiː] n. pl. literary people. **literature** [ˈlɪtrɪtʃə] n. (a) book/writing. esp. novels. poetry. drama biography, etc (b) what has been written on a particular subject. (c) written information about sth.

lithe [laɪð] adj. supple/bending easily

lithograph 1 [ˈlɪθəɡrɑːf] n. painting/ drawing, etc., reproduced by lithography. **lithograph 2** v. to print by lithography. **lithographic** [lɪθəˈɡræfɪk] adj. of lithography. **lithography** [lɪˈθɒɡrəfɪ] n. method of printing using oil and ink on a flat surface such as a stone/a sheet of metal etc.

litigate [ˈlɪtɪɡeɪt] v. to go to law; to bring a lawsuit against s.o. **litigant** n. person involved in a lawsuit. **litigation** [lɪtɪˈɡeɪʃn] n. (a) bringing a lawsuit against s.o. (b) lawsuit. **litigious** [lɪˈtɪdʒəs] adj. always ready to go to law.

litmus [ˈlɪtməs] n. blue substance which is turned red by an acid and back to blue by an alkali. **litmus paper** n. paper containing litmus, used to test for acids and alkalis.

litre, Am. **liter** [ˈliːtə] n. measurement for liquids. (almost 2 pints).

litter 1 [ˈlɪtə] n. (a) rubbish left on streets (b) (old) stretcher/bed on which a person is carried (c) bedding of straw etc., for animals (d) (of animals) group of young born at one time. **litter 2** v. (a) to drop rubbish about. (b) (of animals) to produce young.

little 1 ['lɪtl] *adj.* (less, least) (a) small; his l. sister = his younger sister. (b) a l. = small amount of. (c) not much. **little 2** *n.* small amount: l. by l. = gradually. **little 3** *adv.* (by) a small amount: I see him very l. = not very often (b) he l. thought he would win = he had no idea that he would win.

littoral ['lɪtɒrəl] *adj. & n.* (referring to the) coast.

liturgy ['lɪtədʒɪ] *n.* form of public service in church. **liturgical** [lɪ'ɜ:dʒɪkl] *adj.* referring to liturgy.

live 1 [laɪv] *adj.* (a) in a living state. (b) burning (c) (of broadcast) not recorded (d) carrying an electric current: (ammunition) which has not been defused; *inf.* l. wire = very lively and energetic person. **live 2** *v.* (a) to be alive/to have life; l. and let l. = be tolerant (b) to have your (place of) residence (c) to lead a certain type of life; he lives in style; *inf.* to l. it up = lead a life of wild parties, etc. (d) to l. on = to get food/money etc., from. **live down** *v.* to cause (a disgrace) to be forgotten; he'll never l. it down = it will never be forgotten. **live in** *v.* to live in building where you work. **livelihood** ['laɪvlɪhʊd] *n.* (way of getting) your means of living. **liveliness** ['laɪvlɪnəs] *n.* being lively. **livelong** ['lɪvlɒŋ] *adj.* (formal) the l. day = all the day. **lively** ['laɪvlɪ] *adj.* (-ier, -iest) bright/wide-awake (very) active. **liven** *v.* to make lively. **livestock** ['laɪvstɒk] *n.* animals kept on a farm. **liveware** *n. inf.* people who work with computers.

living 1 ['lɪvɪŋ] *adj.* alive. **living 2** *n.* (a) (way of) life. (b) means of subsistence. (c) the l. = people who are alive. (d) position as parish priest. **living room** *n.* room in a house for general use.

liver ['lɪvə] *n.* organ in the lower part of the body which helps the digestion by producing bile; animal's liver used as food. **liverish** *adj.* feeling rather sick and unwell; irritable.

livery ['lɪvrɪ] *n.* (a) special clothing of a group of servants/of an organization. (b) care of horses for payment: l. stable = place where horses may be looked after and may also be hired. **liveried** *adj.* wearing a livery.

livid ['lɪvɪd] *adj.* (a) of the dark grey colour of lead (b) extremely angry.

lizard ['lɪzəd] *n.* type of reptile with four legs and scales.

llama ['lɑ:mə] *n.* thick-haired camel-like animal found in South America.

Lloyd's [lɔɪdz] *n.* central London insurance market.

lo [ləʊ] *inter.* (old) look!

load 1 [ləʊd] *n.* (a) heavy object(s) which have to be carried (b) (on vehicle) what has to be/what is being transported. (c) amount of material transported. (d) amount of power carried by an electric circuit. (e) thing which is difficult to bear; that's a l. off my mind = I feel much less worried. (f) *inf.* loads of = plenty/lots. **load 2** *v.* (a) to put (esp. sth heavy) into/on to. (b) to put ammunition into (a gun) /to put film into (a camera); to put a disk/program into a computer. (c) to l. s.o. with = to give large quantities to. **loaded** *adj.* (a) *inf.* having a lot of money (b) l. question = question which is worded in such a way so as to trap the person who answers (c) (dice) which has a secret weight in it. **loader** *n.* person who loads.

loaf 1 [ləʊf] *n.* (*pl.*loaves (a) (large) piece of bread baked separately. (b) *Sl.* head; use your l. = use your brains. **loaf 2** *v.* to wander about/to waste time doing nothing. **loafer** *n.* person who does nothing all day. (b) *Am.* light casual shoe with no laces.

loam [ləʊm] *n.* fertile soil which crumbles easily.

loamy *adj.* crumbly fertile (soil.).

loan 1 [ləʊn] *n.* (a) lending (b) thing lent (esp. of a sum of money from a bank). **loan 2** *v.* to lend.

loath [ləʊθ] *adj.* very unwilling.

loathe [ləʊð] *v.* to hate very much. **loathing** *n.* feeling of hate/disgust (for). **loathsome** *adj.* disgusting/horrible.

lob 1 [lɒb] *n.* ball which is hit high into the air. **lob 2** *v.* (lobbed) to throw/hit (a ball) slowly in a high curve.

lobby 1 ['lɒbɪ] *n.* (a) entrance hall/corridor. (b) corridor where Members of Parliament go to vote. (c) hall in the House of Commons used esp. for interviews with members of the public; l. correspondent = journalist who reports on parliamentary matters. after confidential briefings from ministers. **lobby 2** *v.* to try to influence (s.o.) (esp. in order to get a bill through Parliament).

lobe [ləʊb] *n.* (a) lower curved part of the ear. (b) division of the lungs/brain/liver etc. **lobar** *adj.* referring to a lobe.

lobotomy [lə'bɒtəmɪ] *n.* operation to remove a lobe.

lobelia [lɒ'biːlɪə] *n.* low plant with blue flowers.

lobster ['lɒbstə] *n.* shellfish with a long body, two large claws, and eight legs, used as food. **lobster pot** *n.* cage left in the sea to catch lobsters.

local 1 ['ləʊkl] *adj.* referring to a place/district; near at hand; l. anaesthetic = which numbs a particular area of the body; l. authority = section of elected government which runs a district. **local 2** *n.* (a) person who lives in a district, esp. the district where you live. (b) *inf.* nearest public house. **locale** [ləʊ'kɑːl] *n.* place where sth takes place. **locality** [ləʊ'kælɪtɪ] *n.* area/district. **localize** ['ləʊkəlaɪz] *v.* to set in a particular place; to be confined to a particular area. **locally** *adv.* in the (same) district. **locate** [ləʊ'keɪt] *v.* (a) to find (the position of). (b) to be located = to be in a particular position. **location** [ləʊ'keɪʃn] *n.* (a) finding the position of sth. (b) place/position (c) on l. = (filming) which takes place in a real setting, not in a studio.

loch [lɒχ] *n.* (in Scotland) lake; arm of the sea.

lock 1 [lɒk] *n.* (a) device for closing a door/container etc.. by means of a key: under l. and key = shut up firmly. (b) part in a gun by which it is fired; l.. stock and barrel = (everything) all together. (c) amount by which the wheels of a car are able to turn. (d) section of a canal/river with barriers which can be opened or closed to control the flow of water thus allowing boats to move up or down to different levels. (e) bundle of hair hanging together. **lock 2** *v.* (a) to close (a door/a box. etc) with a key. (b) to fix/to become fixed in a certain position **lockable** *adj.* which can be locked **locker** *n.* small cupboard for personal belongings which you can close

with a key; l. room = room in a sports stadium where players change and leave their clothes in lockers. **lockjaw** *n.* disease where your jaws become closed tight together. **lock-keeper** *n.* person who looks after a lock in a canal/river. **locknut** *n.* second nut, used to keep the first nut in place. **lock out** *v.* to prevent (s.o.) from going in by locking the door. **lockout** *n.* industrial dispute in which employees are kept out of the factory until they agree to certain terms. **locksmith** *n.* person who makes/repairs locks. **lock up** *v.* (a) to close (a building) by locking doors (b) to keep (a person/thing) inside by locking doors. etc. **lockup** *n.* (a) (old) prison cell. (b) l. garage/shop = garage/shop which can be locked and which is not part of the owner's house. **locket** ['lɒkɪt] *n.* small ornamental case to hold a picture/lock of hair etc., worn round the neck.

locomotive 1 [ləʊkə'məʊtɪv] *adj.* referring to movement. **locomotive 2** *n.* engine of a train. **locomotion** *n.* (power of) movement.

locum (tenena) ['ləʊkəm('tenenz)] *n.* person who does the work of a doctor/clergyman while the latter is away.

locus ['ləʊkəs] *n.* (*pl.*loci['ləʊsaɪ]) point, line, curve etc.. in a technical diagram.

locust ['ləʊkəst] *n.* insect, like a large grasshopper, which destroys crops

lode [ləʊd] *n.* vein of metal ore. **lodestar** *n.* pole star. **lodestone** *n.* magnetic iron ore.

lodge 1 [lɒdʒ] *n.* (a) small house at the gates of a large building (b) house in the country used for shooting parties (c) (meeting place for a) group of freemasons etc. (d) home of beavers. **lodge 2** *v.* (a) to rent a room (in a boarding house). (b) to be/to remain (c) (formal) to make/to place (a complaint). **lodger** *n.* person who rents a room. **lodging** *n.* (a) accommodation. (b) lodgings = rented rooms.

loess ['ləʊəs] *n.* yellow powdery earth found in China, North America etc.

loft [lɒft] *n.* (a) top part of a house immediately under the roof (b) organ l. = gallery for an organ in a church etc (c) hay l. = top part of a barn used for storing hay. **lofty** ['lɒftɪ] *adj.* (-ier, -iest)

(a) very high (b) arrogant/proud. **loftily**
adv. in a proud way.

log 1 [lɒg] *n.* (a) thick piece of a tree
trunk/large branch: to sleep like a I. =
very soundly; as easy as falling off a I. =
very easy (b) device for calculating the
speed of a ship (c) daily detailed record
of speed/position/happenings. esp. on a
ship. (d) short for logarithm. **log 2** *v.*
(logged) (a) to write down details of (sth
which has happened) in a logbook. (b) to
cover a (distance) / to spend (time).
logbook *n.* (a) (on/ship, etc.) book
with record of a journey. (b) official
record book showing details of the
owners of a car. **logging** *n.* Am. cutting
trees for timber.

loganberry ['ləʊgənberɪ] *n.* soft fruit a
cross between a blackberry and a
raspberry.

logarithm ['lɒgərɪðm] *n.* one of a set of
numbers listed in such a way as to help
with calculations by adding and
subtracting instead of multiplying and
dividing. **logarithmic** [lɒgə'rɪθmɪk]
adj. referring to logarithms.

loggerheads ['lɒgəhedz] *n.* to be at I.
= to quarrel constantly.

loggia ['lɒdʒɪə] *n.* (in southern Europe)
covered gallery which is open on one
side.

logic ['lɒdʒɪk] *n.* science of reasoning;
power of reasoning clearly. **logical** *adj.*
(a) clearly reasoned (b) (of person) able
to reason clearly. **logically** *adv.* in a
logical/reasonable way. **logistics**
[lɒ'dʒɪstɪks] *n.* organization of the
movement of supplies/people etc.

logo ['lɒgəʊ] *n.* (pl.-os) symbol/design
used by a company to identify its
products.

loin [lɔɪn] *n.* (a) (meat from the) back of
an animal (b) loins = part of the body
between the hips. **loincloth** *n.* long
cloth wrapped round the hips.

loiter ['lɔɪtə] *v.* to wander about slowly/
aimlessly; to stand about. **loiterer** *n.*
person who wanders/ who is standing
about.

loll [lɒl] *v.* (a) to sit/stand/lie in a lazy
way. (b) (of tongue) to hang out.

lollipop ['lɒlɪpɒp] *n.* sweet on the end
of a stick; *inf.* I. man/woman = person
employed to stop traffic to let
schoolchildren cross a street.

lollop ['lɒləp] *v. inf.* to walk with long
clumsy steps.

lolly ['lɒlɪ] *n.* (a) *inf.* lollipop: ice I. =
lump of flavoured ice on the end of a
stick (b) *Sl.* money.

lone [ləʊn] *adj.* alone; lonely; I. wolf =
person who likes to be alone. **lonely**
adj. (a) with few or no people. (b)
feeling sad because of being alone.
loneliness *n.* being alone; feeling sad
because you are alone. **loner** *n.* person
who prefers to be alone. **lonesome**
adj. lonely/sad because of being alone.

long 1 [lɒŋ] *adj.* (-er, -est) (a) measured
in space from end to end; not short. (b)
measured in time; they stayed for a I.
time. **long 2** *adv.* for a long time; all
night I. = for the whole night (b) as I. as
= while (c) so/as I. as = provided that.
long 3 *n.* long time; before I. = in a
short time; for I. = for a long time. **long
4** *v.* to I. for = to want very much.
long-distance *adj.* (a) (in sport)
(race) run between two places which are
far apart. (b) (telephone call) made over
a long distance. **longhand** *n.* ordinary
writing (not shorthand). **long-haul** *adj.*
(flight) between continents. **longhorn**
n. type of cow with long horns. **longing**
n. great desire (for sth). **long johns** *n.*
pl.inf. long underpants. **long-lived** *adj.*
(person) who lives for a long time. **long-
playing** *adj.* (record) which plays for
about 20 minutes each side. **long-range**
adj. which covers a long distance.
longshoreman *n.* (pl.-men) Am.
person who works at a port. loading or
unloading ships. **long shot** *n.* attempt
which has little chance of being
successful. **long-sighted** *adj.* able to
see things at a distance more clearly than
things which are close. **longstanding**
adj. which has been arranged some time
before. **longsuffering** *adj.* patient/
tolerating much. **long-term** *adj.*
lasting/planned to last for a long time.
long wave *n.* radio wave longer than
1000 metres. **long winded** *adj.*
(person) who talks too much in a boring
way; (talk) which lasts too long.
longevity [lɒn'dʒevɪtɪ] *n.* very long
life. **longitude** ['lɒndʒɪtjuːd] *n.*
position on the earth's surface measured
in degrees east or went of an imaginary
line running through Greenwich,

London. **longitudinal** *adj.* which runs lengthwise. **longitudinally** *adv.* from end to end.

loo [lu:] *n. inf.* lavatory.

loofah ['lu:fə] *n.* type of long sponge made from a dried pod.

look 1 [lʊk] *n.* (a) turning your eyes (often quickly) to see sth. (b) search (for sth). (c) appearance; the way sth appears. (d) good looks = beauty/pleasing personal appearance. **look 2** *v.* (a) (at) to make efforts to see; l. here! = I object. (b) to stare at; he looked me straight in the face. (c) to seem/to have the appearance of; he looks ill; she looks the part = looks right for the job. **look after** *v.* to take care of. **look ahead** *v.* to make plans for the future. **lookalike** *n. inf.* person who looks like s.o. famous. **look at** *v.* to make efforts to see/to examine/to consider. **look back** *v.* (a) to turn round to see what is behind you. (b) after that they never looked back = they were very successful. **look back on** *v.* to think about (sth) in the past. **look down** *v.* to look down on s.o./to look down your nose at s.o. = to think you are better than s.o. **looker-on** *n.* (*pl.*lookers-on) person who is watching (without taking part). **look for** *v.* to try to find. **look forward** *v.* (to) to think about (sth) in the future (usu. with pleasure). **look in (on)** *v. inf.* to visit (s.o.) briefly. **look-in** *n. inf.* chance/opportunity (to share in sth). **looking glass** *n.* mirror. **look into** *v.* to examine/to find out about. **look on** *v.* (a) to watch without taking part. (b) to consider/to think of sth as. **look out** *v.* (a) (on) to have a view towards. (b) (for) to keep looking in order to find. (c) (for) to be careful of. **lookout** *n.* (a) place from which you can see what is happening. (b) careful attention. (c) future hope. (d) affair; that's his l. = he must deal with it himself. (e) person who watches. **look over** *v.* to examine. **look round** *v.* (a) to turn to see behind you. (b) to examine all of a place. **look through** *v.* (a) to examine the whole of (sth) (often quickly). (b) to pretend not to see. **look to** *v.* (a) to expect (help) from. (b) (formal) to take care of. **look up** *v.* (a) to turn your eyes in an upward direction. (b) to get better. (c) to try to

find (sth) in a reference book, etc. (d) to get in contact with. **look up to** *v.* to consider with respect/admiration.

loom 1 [lu:m] *n.* machine on which cloth is woven. **loom 2** *v.* to appear/to come into sight (gradually).

loon [lu:n] *n.* grebe. **loony** ['lu:nɪ] *adj. & n. inf.* mad. (person). **loony bin** *n. inf.* lunatic asylum.

loop 1 [lu:p] *n.* (a) curve formed by a piece of thread/ribbon, etc., which crosses over itself. (b) thing of this shape. **loop 2** *v.* to make a loop/loops; l. back the curtain = to tie it back with a cord; (of aircraft) to l. the loop = to fly in a complete circle vertically, turning upside down at the top. **loophole** *n.* (a) narrow hole in a wall for shooting through. (b) means of escape/of avoiding (a law).

loose 1 [lu:s] *adj.* (-er, -est) (a) not (fully) attached/not fixed; to be at a l. end = to have nothing special to do. (b) not tight. (c) with pieces separated. (d) l. change = money in coins only. (e) translation which is not very exact. (f) of doubtful morals. **loose 2** *v.* to make (sth) become untied/to let (sth) go. **loose 3** *adv.* not tightly. **loose box** *n.* stable where a horse can move about. **loosely** *adv.* (a) not tightly (b) in an inexact way. **looseleaf** *adj.* (book) of which the pages can be removed and replaced. **loosen** *v.* to make (sth) less tight. **looseness** *n.* being loose.

loot 1 [lu:t] *n.* (a) things which have been taken. (b) *Sl.* money. **loot 2** *v.* to steal. **looter** *n.* person who steals (esp. from shops during a riot).

lop [lɒp] *v.* (lopped) to cut off (esp. tree branches). **lope 1** [ləʊp] *n.* running with long strides. **lope 2** *v.* to run with long (slow) strides. **lop-earned** ['lɒprəd] *adj.* (rabbit) with drooping ears. **lopsided** [lɒp'saɪdɪd] *adj.* with one side larger/lower/heavier than the other.

loquacious [lɒ'kweɪʃəs] *adj.* (person) who talks a lot/too much. **loquaciousness, loquacity** [lɒ'kwæsɪtɪ] *n.* talking too much.

lord 1 [lɔ:d] *n.* (a) nobleman/ruler. (b) title for certain peers; House of Lords = upper chamber of the British Parliament. (c) the Lord = Jesus Christ. (d) title for men in certain positions (such as bishops/judges, etc). (e) expression of surprise/shock; Good Lord! **lord 2** *v.* to l. it over s.o. = to behave as if you are superior. **lordliness** *n.* (a) nobility. (b) pride. **lordly** *adj.* (a) referring to the nobility. (b) proud/arrogant. **lordship** *n.* (form of address to a lord) Your Lordship.

lore [lɔː] *n.* (no *pl.*) traditional beliefs and knowledge.

lorgnette [lɔːˈjnet] *n.* glasses which you hold in front of your eyes with a handle.

lorry [ˈlɒrɪ] *n.* large motor vehicle for carrying goods. **lorry driver;** *n.* person who drives a lorry.

lose [luːz] *v.* (lost) (a) to stop having/ owning sth; she lost her gloves = did not know where they were; they lost sight of it = could no longer see it; that joke was lost on him = he did not understand it. (b) to fail to win. (c) to cause the loss of. (d) to get lost/to l. your way = to be/become unable to find the way to where you were going; *Sl.* get lost! = go away! (e) to l. weight = to become lighter. (f) (of clock/ watch) to become/to go slow. **loser** *n.* person who does not win; he's a bad l. = behaves badly, when he loses a game.

lost [lɒst] *adj.* which has been lost; to give sth up for l. = have no hope of ever having it again; he looks l. = looks bewildered. **lost property office** *n.* place where articles which people have left on trains/buses, etc., are stored, and where they can be claimed by the loser.

loss [lɒs] *n.* (*pl.*-es) (a) no longer having sth. (b) thing/amount which you no longer have; they sold it at a l. = for less than they paid for it; *inf.* that's a dead l. = no use at all. (c) to be at a l. what to do = not you know what to do. **loss leader** *n.* article which is sold at a loss to attract customers. **lost** [lɒst] *v.* see lose.

lot [lɒt] *n.* (a) *inf.* a lot (of) /lots (of) = a large amount/number (of); I've seen quite a l. of him lately = seen him many times. (b) the l. = everything. (c) set of things (for selling); thing/group of things together offered at an auction sale. (d) bad l. wicked person. (e) esp. *Am.* piece of land; parking l. = place where cars can be parked. (f) fate/fortune. (g) to draw lots = to decide sth by taking pieces of paper from a box/throwing dice, etc.

loth [ləʊθ] *adj.* very unwilling.

lotion [ˈləʊʃn] *n.* liquid used to soothe/ to soften/to heal the skin.

lottery [ˈlɒtrɪ] *n.* game of chance in which tickets are sold with prizes given for certain numbers.

lotus [ˈləʊtəs] *n.* tropical water plant, with large flowers.

loud 1 [laʊd] *adj.* (-er, -est) (a) having a sound which is (too) easily heard.(b) (of colours, etc.) too striking/showy **loud 2** *adv.* in a way which is easily heard. **loud-hailer** *n.* megaphone operated by electricity. **loudly** *adv.* in a way which is easily heard; she was loudly dressed = in bright/clashing colours. **loud-mouthed** *adj.* talking in a way which is too easily heard. **loudness** *n.* being (too) easily heard. **loudspeaker** *n.* part of a radio, etc., which allows sound to be heard.

lough [lɒk] *n.* (in Ireland) lake.

lounge 1 [laʊndʒ] *n.* (a) room for sitting in. (b) l. (bar) = comfortable/ expensive bar in a hotel; departure l. = room at an airport where passengers wait to board their planes. (c) sitting around doing nothing or very little. **lounge 2** *v.* to sit/to lie doing nothing or very little. **lounger** *n.* person who lounges. **lounge suit** *n.* (man's) informal suit.

louring [ˈlaʊərɪŋ] *adj.* gloomy/ threatening (-looking).

louse [laʊs] *n.* (*pl.*lice small insect which lives on human and animal bodies. **lousy** [ˈlaʊzɪ] *adj.* (a) covered with lice. (b) *inf.* horrible/unfair.

lout [laʊt] *n.* loutish person. **loutish** *adj.* awkward/rude/ill-mannered.

louvre, *Am.* louver [ˈluːvə] *n.* sloping wooden strips in a frame which overlap and only allow some light to enter. **louvered** *adj.* with louvres.

love 1 [lʌv] *n.* (a) great liking/respect for s.o./sth; to do sth for the l. of it = with out looking for profit; it can't be had for l. nor money = not at all/by any means; there's no l. lost between them = they hate each other. (b) great liking/ passion for s.o., esp. strong sexual feeling towards s.o.; to be in l./to fall in l. with s.o.; to make l. (to s.o.) = have sexual intercourse with; l. story = one about sexual love; l. affair = (often short) sexual relationship. (c) person whom you love. (d) *inf.* form of address, esp. to a woman or child. (e) (in tennis, etc) score of zero. **love 2** *v.* (a) to have strong feelings of affection for. (b) to have great liking/passion, esp. strong sexual feelings for (s.o.). (c) to like very much. **loveable** *adj.* pleasant/easy to love. **love bird** *n.* budgerigar. **lovechild** *n.* illegitimate child. **loveless** *adj.* without love. **loveliness** *n.* being very attractive. **lovelorn** *adj.* sad because you love s.o. who does not love you. **lovely** *adj.* (-ier, -iest) (a) beautiful. (b) *inf.* very pleasant. **lover** *n.* (a) person (esp. a man) who is in love. (b) person who loves (sth). **lovesick** *adj.* unhappy because of being in love. **loving** *adj.* affectionate/showing love. **lovingly** *adv.* in a loving way. **low 1** [ləʊ] *adj.* (-er, -est) (a) at/near/ towards the bottom; in a position below (others); l. voice = not easily heard. (b) coarse/mean; inferior. (c) feeling depressed/ill, etc. **low 2** *adv.* in a low direction/way/position; to lie l. = to keep hidden; supplies are running l. = are becoming scarce. **low 3** *n.* (a) low-pressure zone in the atmosphere, bringing bad weather. (b) sales are at an all-time l. = the lowest point ever. **low 4** *v.* to make a sound like a cow. **lowbrow** *adj. & n.* (person) without intellectual interests. **Low Church** *n.* section of Anglican church which stress prayer and preaching, but not ceremony. **lowdown 1** *adj.* mean/bad/to be despised. **lowdown 2** *n. inf.* to give the low down (on sth) = the details (esp. confidential). **lower 1** *adj.* further down; l. deck = deck under another deck; l. case = small (letter), not a capital; Lower House = more important of two parts of a parliament. **lower 2** *v.* (a) to make (sth) reach a position further down; l. your voice = speak more quietly. (b) to l. yourself (so far as to) = to do sth of which you should be ashamed. **low frequency** *n.* radio frequency which is low and can be heard. **low-grade** *adj.* of poor quality. **low-key** *adj.* quite/ without excitement. **lowland** *adj.* coming from a low-lying region. **lowlands** *n. pl.* low-lying region. **lowliness** *n.* being lowly. **lowly** *adj.* (-ier, iest) humble/modest. **low-lying**

adj. (region) which is at a low altitude/ almost at sea level. **low season** *n.* season when there are few tourist. **lowering** ['laʊərɪŋ] *adj.* gloomy/ threatening (-looking). **loyal** ['lɔɪəl] *adj.* (to) faithful/supporting (s.o. sth). **loyalist** *n.* person who is loyal. **loyally** *adv.* in a loyal way. **loyalty** *n.* being faithful. **lozenge** ['lɒzɪndʒ] *n.* (a) diamond shape (esp. as used in heraldry). (b) sweet; medicine tablet. **LP** [el'pi:] abbrev. for long-playing record. **Ltd.** ['lɪmɪtɪd] short for limited. **lubricate** ['lu:brɪkeɪt] *v.* to cover (sth) with oil or grease to make it run smoothly. **lubricant** *adj. & n.* (substance) which makes sth run smoothly. **lubrication** [lu:brɪkeɪʃn] *n.* covering with oil or grease. **lucerne** [lɜ'sɜːn] *n.* plant like clover used as fodder for cattle. **lucid** ['lu:sɪd] *adj.* (a) clear/easily understood. (b) able to think clearly. **lucidity** [lu:sɪdɪtɪ] *n.* being clear. **lucidly** *adv.* in a lucid way. **luck** [lʌk] *n.* (a) chance/fortune; hard l. ! = I am sorry you are unlucky; as l. would have it = as it happened; to be down on your l. = have bad luck. (b) good fortune; to be out of l. = have bad luck. **luckily** *adv.* by good fortune. **luckless** *adj.* with no luck/unlucky. **lucky** *adj.* (-ier, iest) (a) having good fortune/success. (b) having good fortune associated with it; 13's my l. number. **lucre** ['lu:kə] *n. inf.* (filthy) l. money. **lucrative** ['lu:krətɪv] *adj.* bringing in (much) money/profit. **ludicrous** ['lu:dɪkrəs] *adj.* causing laughter; ridiculous. **ludo** ['lu:dəʊ] *n.* game played on a board with dice and counters. **luff** [lʌf] *v.* to sail towards the wind. **lug 1** [lʌg] *n.* small projecting piece on the side of a jar, etc., for carrying it or for attaching sth to it. **lug 2** *v.* (lugged) to pull (sth heavy) along. **lughole** *n. Sl.* ear. **luggage** [lʌgɪdʒ] *n.* (no *pl.*) suitcases/ bags, etc., for carrying your belongings when travelling; l. rack = space for bags, etc., above seats in a train, etc. **lugger** ['lʌgə] *n.* small sailing boat.

lugubrious [lb"gu:brɪəs] *adj.* very miserable/mournful. **lugubriously** *adv.* in a lugubrious way.

lukewarm ['lu:kwɔ:m] *adj.* (a) slightly warm, but not hot. (b) without enthusiasm.

lull 1 [lʌl] *n.* quite(er) /calm(er) interval. **lull 2** *v.* to make calmer/to soothe.

lullaby [lʌləbaɪ] *n.* song/piece of music designed to make a child sleep.

lumbago [lʌm'beɪgəʊ] *n.* pain in the lower part of the back. **lumbar** ['lʌmbə] *adj.* referring to the lower part of the back.

lumber 1 ['lʌmbə] *n.* (a) old articles which are not in use at the moment; junk; l. room = room in which you keep boxes/unwanted articles. (b) *Am.* wood which has been cut. **lumber 2** *v.* (a) *inf.* (with) to give (s.o.) things he doesn't really want. (b) to move with a slow heavy step/pace. **lumberjack** *n.* person who cuts down trees. **lumber jacket** *n.* short thick working coat.

lumen [lu:mɪn] *n.* unit of measurement of light.

luminous ['lu:mɪnəs] *adj.* giving out light (in the dark). **luminary** *n.* learned person. **luminescence** *n.* sending out light without heat. **luminosity** [lu:mɪ'nɒsɪtɪ] *n.* being luminous.

lump 1 [lʌmp] *n.* (a) (often shapeless) mass; sugar l. = solid cube of sugar; l. sum = money (paid) in one amount/not divided up. (b) swelling on the body. (c) *inf.* heavy, clumsy person. **lump 2** *v.* (a) to l. together = to put together in one place/in one group. (b) *inf.* he can l. it = he'll just have to tolerate it. **lumpy** *adj.* (-ier, -iest) having solid parts.

lunacy ['lu:nəsɪ] *n.* madness. **lunatic** *adj. & n.* mad (person). **lunar** [lu:nə] *adj.* referring to the moon; l. month = period from one new moon to the next.

lunch 1 [lʌnʃ] *n.* (*pl.*-es) midday meal. **lunch 2** *v.* (*formal*) to have lunch. **luncheon** ['lʌnʃən] *n.* (*formal*) midday meal; l. meat = tinned meat loaf; l. voucher = ticket given to an employee to buy food with. **lunch hour, lunchtime** *n.* period when the midday meal is usually eaten.

lung [lʌŋ] *n.* one of two organs in the chest, with which you breathe; iron l. = machine which allows a person to breathe if his lungs are not working properly. **lung fish** *n.* type of fish which breaths through lungs.

lunge 1 [lʌndʒ] *n.* sudden forward movement. **lunge 2** *v.* to make a sudden movement forward.

lupin ['lu:pɪn] *n.* garden flower with tall flower spikes.

lupine ['lu:paɪn] *adj.* referring to a wolf.

lurch 1 [lɜ:tʃ] *n.* (*pl.*-es) (a) sudden (unsteady) movement. (b) *inf.* to leave in the l. = to leave/fail in time of trouble or crisis. **lurch 2** *v.* to move with a sudden unsteady movement. **lurcher** *n.* dog used to retrieve game.

lure 1 ['ljʊə] *n.* (a) small object used to attract fish, etc., in order to catch them. (b) thing which traps/attracts. **lure 2** *v.* to attract esp. into sth bad.

lurid ['ljʊərɪd] *adj.* (a) (light, etc.) which glows in an unpleasant sinister way. (b) (of book/film) sensational/ meant to shock. **luridly** *adv.* in a lurid way. **luridness** *n.* being lurid.

lurk [lɜ:k] *v.* to hide/to remain hidden.

luscious ['lʌʃəs] *adj.* good to taste.

lush 1 [lʌʃ] *adj.* (plant) growing thickly/richly. **lush 2** *n. Sl.* drunkard. **lushness** *n.* being lush.

lust 1 [lʌst] *n.* (a) strong sexual desire. (b) great desire for sth. **lust 2** *v.* to l. (after) = to have a great desire for. **lustful** *adj.* full of sexual desire.

lustre, *Am.* **luster** ['lʌstə] *n.* shine/ brilliance. **lustrous** *adj.* brilliant.

lusty ['lʌstɪ] *adj.* (-ier, -iest) strong/ healthy. **lustily** *adv.* strongly. **lustiness** *n.* great strength/health.

lute [lu:t] *n.* old stringed musical instrument played like a guitar.

luv [lʌv] *n. inf.* (form of address) love.

luxuriance [lʌg'ʒu:rɪəns] *n.* great quantity/abundance. **luxuriant** *adj.* growing abundantly. **luxuriantly** *adv.* in a luxuriant way. **luxuriate** *v.* to enjoy freely/to laze happily. **luxury** ['lʌkʃərɪ] *n.* (a) great comfort. (b) thing which is pleasant to have but not necessary. **luxurious** [lʌg'ʒʊrɪəs] *adj.* very comfortable; very expensive. **luxuriously** *adv.* in a luxurious way. **luxuriousness** *n.* being comfortable/ expensive.

lych-gate ['lɪtʃgeɪt] n. gate with roof at the entrance to a churchyard.

lye [laɪ] n. water mixed with ashes, used for washing.

lying ['laɪɪŋ] v. see lie.

lymph [lɪmf] n. liquid found in animal tissues. **lymphatic** [lɪm'fætɪk] adj. referring to lymph.

lynch [lɪnʃ] v. (of a mob) to kill (s.o.) without trial (esp. by hanging).

lynx [lɪŋks] n. (pl.-es) spotted shorttailed animal of the cat family. **lynxeyed** adj. with very good eyesight.

lyre ['laɪə] n. old stringed musical instrument. **lyrebird** n. tropical bird with tail feathers shaped like a lyre.

lyric ['lɪrɪk] adj. & n. (a) (poem, etc) concerned with feeling. (b) (poem etc) intended to be sung. **lyrical** adj. (a) (poem) using suitable language to express feelings. (b) inf. eager/ enthusiastic. **lyrically** adv. in a lyrical way. **lyricism** ['lɪrɪsɪzəm] n. quality of poem which expresses feelings. **lyricist** n. person who writes the words of a song. **lyrics** n. pl. words of a song.

Mm

m abbrev. for metre; mile.

ma [mɑː] n. inf. mother.

ma'am [mɑːm] n. short for madam (now only used to address the Queen).

mac [mæk] n. inf. raincoat.

macabre [mə'kɑːbr] adj. causing horror; gruesome.

macadam [mə'kædəm] n. road surface made of small pieces of broken stone. **macadamized** adj. covered with macadam.

macaroni [mækə'rəʊnɪ] n. Italian food, made of short thick tubes of flour paste.

macaroon [mækə'ruːn] n. small sweet almond biscuit.

macaw [mə'kɔː] n. brightly coloured South American parrot.

mace [meɪs] n. (a) heavy bar of wood/ metal used in ceremonies to symbolize authority. (b) spice made from the outside of a nutmeg.

macerate ['mæsəreɪt] v. to soak in a liquid until soft.

Mach (number) ['mæk('nʌmbə)] n. figure showing the speed of supersonic aircraft in relation to the speed of sound; at M. one = at the speed of sound.

machete [mə'tʃetɪ] n. jungle knife used in South America.

Machiavellian [mækɪə'velɪən] adj. sly/clever (in political plotting).

machination [mækɪ'neɪʃn] n. plot.

machine 1 [mə'ʃiːn] n. (a) device in which power from a motor drives wheels/gears, etc. (b) organization. **machine 2** v. to make/to shape with a machine; to sew with a sewing machine. **machine gun** n. gun which automatically fires many bullets one after the other. **machinery** n. (no pl.) mechanism; (working parts of) machines. (b) organization. **machine tools** n. pl. tools operated by a motor and used to shape metal/wood, etc. **machining** n. working with a machine. **machinist** n. person who works a machine, esp. a sewing machine.

machismo [mə'kɪzməʊ] n. exaggerated sense of male pride. **macho** [mætʃəʊ] adj. (man) who is aggressively male.

mackerel ['mækrəl] n. (pl.mackerel) common sea fish.

mackintosh ['mækɪntɒʃ] n. raincoat.

macramé [mə'krɑːmeɪ] n. (no. pl.) knotted string articles.

macro- ['mækrəʊ] prefix meaning very large/covering a wide area.

macrobiotic [mækrəʊbar'ɒtik] adj. referring to a health-giving diet of cereals/vegetables, etc. **macrocosm** ['mækrəʊkɒzəm] n. large complete system; the universe.

mad ['mæd] adj. (madder, maddest) (a) not sane; wild/silly; inf. like m. = (i) very fast; (ii) very enthusiastically; he's m, with/at you = angry with you; m. cow disease = bovine spongiform encephalopathy. a disease affecting the brains of cattle. (b) very enthusiastic (about s.o./sth),[c] (dog) suffering from rabies. **madcap** adj. & n. wild (person). **madden** v. to make mad; to exasperate/to annoy. **maddening** adj. exasperating. **madhouse** n. place which is full of noise and people rushing

about. **madly** adv. like a madman.
madman n. (pl. -men) lunatic; he
drove like a m. = he drove very fast/
furiously. **madness** n. being mad;
lunacy. **madwoman** n. (pl. -women)
female lunatic.
madam ['mædəm] n. (a) formal way of
addressing a woman. (b) woman who
keeps a brothel.
madder ['mædə] n. plant which gives a
red dye.
made ['meɪd] v. see make.
madeira [mə'dɪərə] n. (a) sweet dessert
wine. (b) m. cake = type of plain cake.
madonna [mə'dɒnə] n. (picture/statue
of) the Virgin Mary.
madrigal ['mædrɪgl] n. group song
popular in the sixteenth and seventeenth
centuries.
maelstrom ['meɪlstrɒm] n. violent
whirlpool in the sea; violent confusion.
maestro ['maɪstrəʊ] n. (pl.-os) inf.
musical genius; conductor.
mafia ['mæfɪə] n. secret (Italian)
organization dealing in crime.
mag [mæg] short for magazine;
magnetic. **magazine** [mægə'ziːn] n. (a)
(illustrated) paper which appears at
regular intervals. (b) radio/TV
programme made up from various items
on the same theme, broadcast
regularly,[c] box containing
ammunition/film/slides which clips on to
a gun/a camera/projector,[d] room/
building used as a store for explosives.
magenta [mə'dʒentə] n. & adj. dark
red-purple (colour).
maggot ['mægət] n. white grub (of a
bluebottle) which lives in rotting meat.
maggoty adj. full of maggots.
Magi ['meɪdʒaɪ] n. pl. wise men who
brought gifts to the infant Christ.
magic 1 ['mædʒɪk] n. spells/conjuring
tricks. etc. which do not appear to follow
normal scientific rules; as if by m. =
suddenly/from nowhere; black m. = evil
spells designed to harm people. **magic
2** adj. enchanted. **magical** adj.
produced by magic; fairy-like.
magically adv. by magic. **magician**
[mə'dʒɪʃn] n. wizard/conjuror.
magisterial ['mædʒɪstɪərɪəl] adj. with
an air of authority. **magisterially** adv.
in a commanding way. **magistrate**
['mædʒɪstreɪt] n. judge in a minor court.

magma ['mægmə] n. (a) molten rock
under the earth's crust. (b) paste.
Magna Carta ['mægnə 'kɑːtə] n.
charter, signed by King John in 1215,
which gave basic rights to some
subjects.
magnanimous ['mæg'nænɪməs] adj.
very generous. **magnanimity**
['mægnənɪmɪtɪ] n. great generosity.
magnanimously adv. in a
magnanimous way.
magnate ['mægneɪt] n. important
businessman.
magnesium [mæg'niːzɪəm] n.
(element: Mg) metal which burns with a
brilliant white light. **magnesia**
['mægnət] n. white powder made from
magnesium used in medicines.
magnet n. thing which attracts, esp. a
metal object which attracts iron and steel
and points roughly north and south when
suspended. **magnetic** ['mæg'nətik] adj.
having a power of attraction; m. pole/m.
north = the point to which the needle of
a compass points; m. field = area around
a magnet which is under its influence;
m. mine = floating bomb which is
attracted to a passing ship; m. tape =
plastic tape for recording music/
information, etc. **magnetically** adv.
by a magnet. **magnetism**
['mægnətɪzəm] n. (a) natural attractive
power of magnets. (b) personal power of
attraction. **magnetize** v. to make (a
piece metal) into a magnet. **magneto**
[mæg'niːtəʊ] n. (pl. -os) device in an
engine which produces electricity used
for ignition.
magnificent [mæg'nɪfɪsnt] adj. very fine/
splendid/very luxurious. **magnificence** n.
splendour/luxury. **magnificently** adv. in a
magnificent way.
magnify ['mægnɪfaɪ] v. to make
(something) appear larger; magnifying
glass = lens which makes small objects
appear larger. **magnification**
[mægnɪfɪkeɪʃn] n. making something
appear larger; degree to which things
appear larger. **magnifier** n. thing
which magnifies. **magnitude**
['mægnɪtjuːd] n. size; (of stars)
brightness.
magnolia [mæg'nəʊlɪə] n. (a) large
tree with huge flowers. (b) very pale pink
colour.

magnum ['mægnəm] *n.* very large bottle (of wine, esp. champagne).

magpie ['mægpaɪ] *n.* common large black and white bird.

maharajah [mɑːhərɑːdʒə] *n.* Indian prince. **maharani** [mɑːhəˈrɑːniː] *n.* Indian princess. **mahatma** [məˈhætmə] *n.* (in India) title given to a holy man.

mahjong *n.* Chinese game played with small counters.

mahogany [məˈhɒɡənt] *n.* dark wood used for making furniture.

maid [meɪd] *n.* female servant; old m. = middle-aged unmarried woman. **maiden 1** *n.* (formal) unmarried girl/woman. **maiden 2** *adj.* (a) unmarried (woman); m. aunt = unmarried aunt; m. name = surname of a woman before she is married. (b) first; m. voyage/flight = first voyage of a new ship/of a new aircraft; m. speech = first speech of a Member of Parliament. **maidenhair** *n.* type of fern. **maidenhood** *n.* (formal) being a maiden. **maidenly** *adj.* (formal) like a maiden. **maiden (over)** *n.* (in cricket) over where no runs are scored.

mail 1 [meɪl] *n.* (a) letters delivered. (b) postal services; m. order = ordering and buying by post; m. merge = computer program which allows the same letter to be written to many different addresses. (c) chain m. = type of armour made of small interlocking metal rings. **mail 2** *v.* to send (sth) by the postal services. **mailbag** *n.* large canvas bag for carrying mail. **mailbox** *n. Am.* letterbox. **mailing list** *n.* list of names and addresses of people to whom information can be sent. **mailman** *n.* (*pl.*-men) *Am.* man who delivers letters.

maim [meɪm] *v.* to wound; to make lame.

main 1 [meɪn] *n.* (a) (formal) with might and m. = with all your strength. (b) in the m. = generally speaking. (c) central pipe for distributing water/gas, etc. (d) the mains = electric power. **main 2** *adj.* most important; to have an eye to the m. chance = to watch out for the best way of making money/of improving your position. **mainland** [meɪnlənd] *n.* large solid mass of land. **mainly** *adv.* mostly/ in a very important way. **mainmast** *n.* most important mast on a ship. **mainsail** [meɪnsl] *n.* most important

sail on a ship. **mainspring** *n.* (a) central spring of a watch. (b) most important force which makes you do sth.

mainstay *n.* principal support.

mainstream *n.* most important trend in a form of art.

maintain [meɪnˈteɪn] *v.* (a) to keep (order); to keep (doing sth). (b) to keep sth in working order. (c) to state/to assert. **maintenance** *n.* (a) keeping. (b) money for upkeep.

maisonette [meɪzəˈnet] *n.* flat on two floors.

maitre d'hôtel, *Am.* **maitre d'** [metrədəʊˈtel, metrəˈdiː] *n.* head waiter.

maize [meɪz] *n.* tall cereal crop.

majesty [mædʒəsɪ] *n.* (a) greatness. (b) form of address to a King or Queen. **majestic** [məˈdʒestɪk] *adj.* grand/ stately. **majestically** *adv.* grandly.

major 1 *n.* (a) army officer above a captain. (b) (formal) legally adult person. **major 2** *adj.* (a) bigger; more important; the m. part of the work = most of the work. (b) musical key where there are semitones between the third and fourth, and between the seventh and eighth notes. **major 3** *v.* to specialize in a subject as an undergraduate.

majordomo *n.* chief servant in a large house. **majorette** [meɪdʒəret] *n.* girl bandleader or marcher. **major-general** *n.* senior army officer below a lieutenant-general. **majority** [məˈdʒɒrɪtɪ] *n.* (a) larger part. (b) larger number of voters; the government has a m. of one = has one vote more than the opposition. (c) legally adult age.

make 1 [meɪk] *n.* (a) brand; country of origin (of an object). (b) *inf.* he's on the m. = all he wants to do is to make money. **make 2** *v.* (made) (a) to prepare; to do; to construct; to m. the beds = to tidy the beds after they have been slept in. (b) to earn; I m. £50 a week. (c) to add up to; to score. (d) to cause (s.o.) to be; he made himself comfortable. (e) to force (s.o.) to do sth. **make away with** *v.* to remove (sth) / to make (sth) disappear. **make believe** *n.* pretending/believing sth is true when it is not. **make do** *v.* (with) to put up with (sth) /to use (sth) even if it is not suitable. **make for** *n.* to aim; to go

towards. **make good** v. (a) to put (sth)
right. (b) to carry out (a promise).[c] to
become successful. **make of** v. to
consider; what do you make of it? = what
do you think of it? **make off with** v. to
run away with (sth) /to steal (sth). **make
out** v. (a) to draw up (a list); to write (a
cheque). (b) to distinguish/to see
properly. (c) to assert/to maintain. (d) inf.
to succeed. **make over** v. to transfer.
maker n. person who makes sth.
makeshift adj. & n. (thing) used
temporarily in place of sth else. **make
up** v. (a) to complete/to fill up; I can't
make up my mind = I can't decide; to
make up for lost time = to act specially
quickly. (b) to put lipstick/powder, etc.,
on your face. (c) to invent. (d) to make it
up = to become friends again. (e) to
make it up to s.o. = to compensate s.o.
for sth lost/damaged, etc. **makeup** n.
(a) composition. (b) character. (c)
lipstick/cream/powder, etc., used to
beautify your face. **makeweight** n.
small quantity added to make up the
weight of sth. **making** n. formation; it
was 3 years in the m. = it took 3 years to
make; it has the making of = it may
develop into.
malacca [məl'ækə] n. tropical cane
used to make walking sticks.
malachite [mæl'əkaɪt] n. green stone.
maladjusted [mælə'dʒʌstɪd] adj.
(person) who does not fit into society.
maladjustment [mælədmɪnɪs'strʃn] n.
being maladjusted.
maladministration [mælə'drɒɪt] n.
incompetent administration.
maladroit [mælə'drɒɪt] adj. (formal)
clumsy.
malady ['mælədɪ] n. (formal) illness.
malaise [mæ'leɪz] n. (formal) awkward
feeling; slight sickness.
malapropism ['mæləprɒpɪzəm] n.
incorrect use of a word which sounds
similar to the correct one.
malaria [mə'leərɪə] n. tropical fever
caused by a parasite carried by
mosquitoes. **malarial** adj. referring to
malaria.
Malaysian 1 [mə'leəʒn] n. referring to
Malaysia. **Malaysian 2** n. person from
Malaysia. **Malay** n. & adj. (person)
from Malaysia; language spoken in
Malaysia.

malcontent ['mælkəntent] n. (formal)
dissatisfied person.
male 1 adj. (a) referring to men/boys.
(b) referring to the sex which fertilizes
eggs produced by females. **male 2** n.
(a) man/boy. (b) animal/insect of the sex
which does not give birth to offspring.
malefactor ['mælɪfæktə] n. (formal)
criminal. **malevolence** [mə'levələns]
n. (formal) ill-will; desire to hurt others.
malevolent adj. wishing (s.o.) ill.
malfeasance [mæl'fɪːzɪns] n. (formal)
an unlawful act.
malformation [mæl'ækə] n. being
wrongly shaped/badly formed.
malformed adj. badly formed/shaped.
malfunction 1 [mæl'fʌŋkʃn] n. bad/
incorrect working (of a machine/of the
heart etc). **malfunction 2** v. to work
badly.
malice ['mælɪs] n. unfriendly
feelings; out of m. = to be spiteful.
malicious [mə'lɪʃəs] adj. wicked/
intentionally spiteful; wanting to hurt
others. **maliciously** adv. in a
malicious way.
malign [mə'laɪn] v. to say bad things
about(s.o.); he has been much maligned
= people have criticized him a lot.
malignancy [mə'lɒgnənsɪ] n. being
malignant. **malignant** [mə'lɪgnənt] adj.
(a) wishing harm to someone. (b) likely
to be fatal. **malignity** n. malignant
feeling.
malinger [mə'lɪŋgə] v. to pretend to be
ill (to avoid work). **malingerer** n.
person who pretends to be ill.
mall [mɔːl] n. Am. shopping precinct or
covered shopping arcade.
mallard ['mæləːd] n. common wild
duck.
malleable ['mælɪəbl] adj. soft/which
can be moulded into shape.
malleability n. being malleable.
mallet ['mælɪt] n. large wooden
hammer.
mallow ['mæləʊ] n. wild flowers
growing in marshy ground.
malnutrition [mælnuː'tnʃn] n. lack of
enough good food.
malodorous [mæl'əʊdərəs] adj.
(formal) which smells bad.
malpractice [mæl'præktɪs] n. illegal
use of your position/authority to gain
money.

malt [mɔːlt] *n.* grain which has been prepared for making beer or whisky by being allowed to sprout and then dried. **malted** *adj.* tasting of malt.

Maltese [mɒlˈtiːz] *adj. & n.* (person) from Malta.

maltreat [mælˈtriːt] *v.* to treat (s.o.) badly. **maltreatment** *n.* rough treatment.

mama [məˈmɑ] *n.* child's name for mother.

mamba [mæmbə] *n.* poisonous African snake.

mambo [mæmbəʊ] *n.* South American dance.

mamma [məˈmɑ] *n.* mama.

mammal [ˈmæm] *n.* type of animal which gives birth to live young and suckles them with milk. **mammalian** [məˈmetlɪən] *adj.* referring to mammals. **mammary** *adj.* referring to the breast.

mammon [mæmən] *n.* evil wealth.

mammoth 1 [mæməθ] *n.* very large prehistoric hairy elephant. **mammoth 2** *adj.* huge.

man 1 *n.* (*pl.*men) (a) human being. (b) person; the m. in the street = the ordinary citizen; no man's land = land between two armies which belongs to neither side. (c) male human adult. (d) husband. (e) servant; ordinary soldier/worker. (f) piece (in chess), etc. **man 2** *v.* (manned) to provide with men; to be the workforce for (a machine/an office, etc.). **maneater** *n.* animal which eats people. **man-eating** *adj.* (animal) which eats people. **manfully** *adv.* like a man; in a strong/forceful way.

manhandle *v.* (a) to move (something large and heavy) by hand. (b) to handle someone roughly. **manhole** *n.* hole in the road or pavement through which you go down into the sewers/into a coal store, etc. **manhood** *n.* (no. *pl.*) state of being an adult male. **man-hour** *n.* work done by one man in one hour.

manhunt *n.* search (for a criminal). **mankind** [mænˈkaɪnd] *n.* (no. *pl.*) the human race. **manliness** *n.* virility/male characteristics. **manly** *adj.* virile/with very strong male features; brave. **man-made** *adj.* artificial (material, etc.). **mannish** *adj.* (woman) who looks/dresses like a man. **manpower** *n.* work force/number of workmen. **man-**

of-war *n.* (a) (old) battleship. (b) Portuguese man-of-war = type of very large jellyfish. **manservant** *n.* male servant. **man-sized** *adj.* of the right size for one man. **manslaughter** *n.* killing s.o. without intending to do so.

manacle 1 [mænəkl] *n.* one of two steel rings connected by a chain. which attach the wrists of a prisoner together. **manacle 2** *v.* to attach (a prisoner's) wrists together.

manage [mænɪdʒ] *v.* (a) to direct. (b) to arrange to do sth; to succeed in doing sth; can she m. all by herself? = can she cope/can she do the work all by herself? **manageable** *adj.* which can be managed/directed. **management** *n.* (a) handling of (a tool); directing (of work). (b) group of people who direct workers; under new m. = with a new owner/manager. **manager** *n.* (a) head of a department in a commercial firm. (b) person who manages/directs; director of a theatre; organizer of a sports team/singer, etc.; person who runs a shop. **manageress** [mænɪdʒəˈres] *n.* (*pl.*-es) woman who runs a shop. **managerial** [mænəˈdʒərɪəl] *adj.* referring to a manager; discussion at m. level = discussion among managers. **managing director** *n.* overall director of a firm.

manatee [mænəˈtiː] *n.* large plant-eating sea mammal.

mandamus [mænˈdeɪməs] *n.* order from a higher court to a lower court.

mandarin [mændərɪn] *n.* (a) small orange with a soft easily-peeled skin. (b) important government official. (c) Mandarin = principal form of the Chinese language.

mandate [ˈmændeɪt] *n.* power given to a person to act on behalf of s.o. else; the government has a m. from the people to cut taxes = people approved of the plan to cut taxes when they voted for the government. **mandated** *adj.* (territory) which is entrusted to a country to administer. **mandatory** [ˈmændətərɪ] *adj.* obligatory/compulsory.

mandible [ˈmændɪbl] *n.* lower jawbone (of birds/insects etc.).

mandolin [ˈmændəlɪn] *n.* stringed instrument like a small guitar.

mandrel [ˈmændrəl] *n.* the turning central shaft of a lathe.

mandrill [ˈmændrɪl] *n.* large baboon.

mane [meɪn] *n.* long hair on neck of a lion or horse; long untidy hair.

maneuver [məˈnuːvə] *n & v.* *Am.* see manœuvre.

manganese [ˈmæŋgəniːz] *n.* (element; Mn) grey metal.

mange [meɪndʒ] *n.* disease of the skin of animals, which makes the hair fall out. **mangy** *adj.* dirty/diseased.

mangel-wurzel [ˈmæŋglwɜːzl] *n.* beet used as food for cattle.

manger [meɪndʒə] *n.* box for food for horses/cows, etc.

mangle 1 [ˈmæŋgl] *n.* device with rollers for squeezing the water out of clothes. **mangle 2** *v.* (a) to squeeze water out of (clothes) by passing them through a mangle. (b) to tear; to chop up; to mess up.

mango [ˈmæŋgəʊ] *n.* (*pl.*-oes) large tropical fruit with a big stone.

mangrove [ˈmæŋgrəʊv] *n.* kind of tropical tree growing in wet areas.

mania [ˈmeɪnɪə] *n.* madness; exaggerated passion (for sth). **maniac** *n.* mad person. **maniacal** [məˈnaɪəkl] *adj.* mad. **manic** [ˈmænɪk] *adj.* referring to mania.

manicure 1 [ˈmænɪkjʊə] *n.* looking after the hands; to have a m. = to have your hands cleaned and nails trimmed. **manicure 2** *v.* to look after the hands. **manicure set** *n.* small box or bag with scissors/nail file, etc. **manicurist** *n.* person who looks after people's hands.

manifest 1 [ˈmænɪfest] *adj.* (formal) obvious/pain to see. **manifest 2** *n.* list of goods in a shipment. **manifest 3** *v.* (formal) to appear/to show. **manifestation** [ˌmænɪfeˈsteɪʃn] *n.* appearance. **manifestly** *adv.* (formal) obviously. **manifesto** [mænɪˈfestəʊ] *n.* (*pl.*-os) programme of action outlined by a political party.

manifold 1 [ˈmænɪfəstʊ] *adj.* (formal) of varying sorts. **manifold 2** *n.* exhaust m. = tubes of an exhaust pipe of a car.

manikin [ˈmænɪkɪn] *n.* very small man.

manilla [məˈnɪlə] *n.* thick brown paper (used for envelopes).

manioc [ˈmænɪɒk] *n.* tropical plant from which a flour is made.

manipulate [məˈnɪpjuleɪt] *v.* to handle; to falsify (accounts) to make them seem more profitable. **manipulation** [məˈnɪpjuˈleɪʃn] *n.* handling (of machinery); falsification (of accounts). **manipulator** *n.* person who manipulates.

manna [ˈmænə] *n.* unexpected help/food.

mannequin [ˈmænɪkin] *n.* person or dummy wearing clothes to show them to possible buyers.

manner [ˈmænə] *n.* (a) way of behaving/acting; (b) manners = way of acting in public. (c) sort; in a m. of speaking = in a sort of way. **mannered** *adj.* full of mannerisms. **mannerism** *n.* affected way of acting/odd way of doing sth. **mannerly** *adj.* well-behaved.

manœuvre, Am. maneuver 1 [məˈnuːvə] *n.* (a) action of moving sth. (b) manœuvres = military exercises. **manœuvre 2** *v.* (a) to move (sth) heavy/awkward. (b) to work to put yourself in a good position. **manœuvrability** [mənuːvrəˈbɪltɪ] *n.* ability to be easily manœuvred. **manœuvrable** *adj.* which can be manœuvred/moved.

manometer [mæˈnɒmɪtə] *n.* instrument for measuring pressure.

manor [ˈmænə] *n.* (land surrounding) a country house. m. house = country house.

mansard [ˈmænsɑːd] *n.* m. (roof) = roof where the top part slopes more gently than the bottom.

manse [mæns] *n.* (in Scotland) church minister's house.

mansion [ˈmænʃən] *n.* very large private house; mansions = large block of flats.

mantelpiece [ˈmæntlpiːs] *n.* shelf above a fireplace.

mantis [ˈmæntɪs] *n.* praying m. = large tropical insect.

mantle [ˈmæntl] *n.* (a) cloak. (b) gauze cover for a gas lamp.

manual 1 [ˈmænjuəl] *adj.* (a) done by hand. (b) (car) where the gears are changed by hand. **manual 2** *n.* (a) book of instructions. (b) keyboard of an organ. **manually** *adv.* (done) by hand.

manufacture 1 ['mænjʊ'fæktʃə] *n.* making of a commercially produced product. **manufacture 2** *v.* to make (products) commercially; manufacturing town = industrial town. **manufacturer** *n.* person/company producing industrial products.

manure 1 [mə'njʊə] *n.* dung of animals used as a fertilizer on land. **manure 2** *v.* to spread manure on (land).

manuscript ['mænjʊskrɪpt] *adj. & n.* (document/novel/poem) written by hand or typed, etc., but not printed.

Manx [mæŋks] *adj. & n.* ((person, etc) from the Isle of Man.

many ['mənɪ] *adj. & n.* (more, most) great number; a good m. prisoners = quite a large number; m. a time = often.

Maori 1 ['maʊrɪ] *adj.* referring to the original natives of New Zealand. **Maori 2** *n.* (a) language spoken by the native race of New Zealand. (b) member of the native race of New Zealand.

map 1 [mæp] *n.* diagram of a town/country as it is seen from above; street m. = diagram showing streets with their names; physical m. = diagram showing mountains/rivers etc.; political m. = diagram showing the borders of countries/administrative districts, etc.

map 2 *v.* (mapped) to draw a diagram of (a town or country); to m. out a route = to plan a journey in advance.

mapping *n.* art of making maps; m. pen = pen with a very fine nib.

maple ['merpl] *n.* northern tree, with sweet sap; m. sugar/m. syrup = sugar/syrup made from the sap of the maple tree.

mar ['mɑː] *v.* (marred) to spoil.

marabou ['mærəbuː] *n.* large stork. with a heavy bill.

maracas [mæ'rækəs] *n. pl.* percussion instrument, formed of a pair of gourds with dried seeds inside them.

maraschino ['mærə'skiːnəʊ] *n.* (*pl.*-os) cherry used to make liqueur or jam.

marathon ['mærəθɒn] *n.* long distance race; (sth) which lasts a long time.

maraud [mə'rɔːd] *v.* to raid; to go about looking for plunder. **marauder** *n.* person who raids. **marauding** *adj.* (person) who raids.

marble ['mɑːbl] *n.* (a) very hard type of limestone which can be brilliantly polished. (b) small glass ball for playing with. **marbled** *adj.* with streaks of different colours.

March [mɑːtʃ] *n.* 3rd month of the year.

march 1 [mɑːtʃ] *n.* (*pl.*-es) (a) military walking in step; route m. = long training march; m. past = ceremonial parade of soldiers; quick m. = rapid walking pace; slow m. = slow walking pace. (b) protest m. = mass of people walking in a line to protest about sth. (c) music for marching. (d) progress/advance of time/events. (e) the marches = border region.

march 2 *v.* (a) to walk in step; quick m.! = order to walk at a rapid pace; the police marched him off to prison = removed him quickly to prison. (b) to walk quickly and purposefully. (c) to walk in a protest march. **marcher** *n.* person who marches.

mare ['meə] *n.* female horse; mare's tails = thin wispy clouds showing a change in the weather; mare's nest = discovery which turns out to be useless.

margarine [mɑːdʒfə'riːn] *n.* mixture of animal or vegetable fat which is used instead of butter. **marge** *n. inf.* margarine.

margin ['mɑːdʒɪn] *n.* (a) edge/border (of a page). (b) extra space/time; leave a m. for error = allow extra space/time in case you have made a mistake in your calculations; safety m. = space/time left to allow for safety. (c) money received which is more than money paid.

marginal *adj.* (a) (note) in a margin. (b) (parliamentary seat) where there is very little difference in the votes of the opposing parties. (c) slight. **marginally** *adv.* slightly.

marguerite [mɑːgə'riːt] *n.* common large white daisy.

marigold ['mærɪgəʊld] *n.* common garden plant with yellow flowers.

marijuana [mærɪ'hwɑːnə] *n.* drug made from hemp.

marina [mə'riːnə] *n.* harbour for yachts/motor boats, etc.

marinade 1 [mærɪ'neːd] *n.* mixture of wine and herbs, etc., in which meat or fish is soaked before cooking.

marinade 2 *v.* (also marinate) to soak (meat or fish) in a mixture of wine and herbs.

marine 1 [mə'ri:n] *adj.* referring to the sea. **marine 2** *n.* (a) the merchant m. = the merchant navy. (b) soldier serving on a ship. **mariner** ['mærɪnə] *n.* sailor.

marionette [mærɪənet] *n.* string puppet.

marital ['mærɪtl] *adj.* referring to marriage.

maritime ['mærɪtaɪm] *adj.* referring to the sea.

marjoram ['mɑːdʒərəm] *n.* common herb used as flavouring.

mark 1 ['mɑːk] *n.* (a) spot/stain; thing which can be seen. (b) target; wide of the m. = far from correct. (c) sign; punctuation m. = printing sign (such as full stop/comma, etc.). (d) number of points given to a student. (e) starting line in a race; on your marks = get ready at your places. (f) line indicating a point reached. (g) unit of money in Germany. **mark 2** *v.* (a) to make a sign on (sth). (b) to correct and give points to. (c) to m. time = (i) to march on one spot; (ii) to stay in one place/not to advance. (d) to follow closely (an opposing player in football/Rugby etc.) **mark down** *v.* to lower the price of (sth). **marked** *adj.* obvious/noticeable; a m. man = man who has been selected by the enemy as a probable target. **markedly** *adv.* obviously. **marker** *n.* thing which marks; person who notes the scores in a competition, etc.; m. buoy = buoy used to indicate a dangerous spot; m. pen = coloured felt pen which makes a wide mark. **marking** *n.* (a) making marks; m. ink = black ink which will not wash off. (b) markings = spots/stripes, etc., on a bird or animal. (c) correcting (exercises/homework, etc). **mark out** *v.* to indicate the boundaries of (a land); to select. **marksman** *n.* (*pl.*-men) person who shoots well. **marksmanship** *n.* ability to shoot well. **mark up** *v.* to increase the price of (sth). **mark-up** *n.* amount added to the cost price to give the selling price.

market 1 ['mɑːkɪt] *n.* (a) selling of produce (from stalls); place where produce is sold (from stalls); m. day = special day when a market is held. (b) sale; on the m. = for sale. (c) place where a product is required/could be sold; need for a product; m. research = examination of the possible sales of a product before it is launched; the Common M. = the European Economic Community; black m. = illegal selling at high prices. **market 2** *v.* to sell (products).

marketable *adj.* which can be sold easily. **market garden** *n.* small farm growing vegetables/fruits for sale in a nearby town. **market gardener** *n.* person who runs a market garden.

marketing *n.* selling techniques (publicity/packing, etc.) for a product. **market place** *n.* place where a market is held/where goods are sold.

marl ['mɑːl] *n.* soil which is a mixture of clay and stone.

marlinespike ['mɑːlɪnspaɪk] *n.* pointed hook, used for unravelling rope.

marmalade ['mɑːməleɪd] *n.* jam made from oranges/lemons or grapefruit.

marmoset ['mɑːməzet] *n.* small American monkey.

marmot ['mɑːmət] *n.* small burrowing animal.

maroon 1 [mə'ruːn] *adj. & n.* deep purple red (colour). **maroon 2** *n.* firework used as a distress signal by ships. **maroon 3** *v.* to abandon in an awkward place.

marquee [mɑːkɪ] *n.* very large tent.

marquetry [mɑːkətrɪ] *n.* (making) patterns on the surface of wood with inlaid pieces of different-coloured wood or ivory.

marram grass [mærəm'grɑːs] *n.* type of grass used to stabilize sand dunes.

marriage [mærɪdʒ] *n.* (a) state of being legally joined as husband and wife. (b) ceremony of being married.

marriageable *adj.* suitable to become married.

marrow ['mærəʊ] *n.* (a) soft interior of bones. (b) large green vegetable growing on a creeping plant. **marrowfat pea** *n.* type of pea with large seeds.

marry ['mærɪ] *v.* (a) to make (two people) husband and wife. (b) to become married to (s.o.) **married** *adj.* joined as husband and wife; m. name = name taken by a woman when she gets married.

marsala [mɑː'sɑlə] *n.* sweet Italian wine.

marsh [mɑːʃ] *n.* (*pl.*-es) wet/swampy land; m. marigold = common yellow flower growing in marshes; m. mallow = common pink flower growing in marshes. **marshmallow** *n.* soft and sticky white or pink sweet. **marshy** *adj.* (-ier, iest) swampy/wet (land).

marshal 1 ['mɑːʃl] *n.* (a) very high ranking military officer; M. of the Royal Air Force = highest rank in the Royal Air Force. (b) organizer (of a race/a show). (c) Am, police chief. **marshal 2** *v.* (marshalled) to set out (facts) in order; to organize (a race/a show). **marshalling yard** *n.* railway yard where wagons are sorted out into trains.

marsupial [mɑːˈsuːpiəl] *adj. & n.* (animal) which carries its young in a pouch.

mart [mɑːt] *n.* market.

martello tower [mɑːˈteləuˈtauəl] *n.* round fort built by the sea in the 19th century.

marten ['mɑːtin] *n.* small wild flesh-eating animal like a weasel.

martial ['mɑːʃl] *adj.* referring to war; m. music = marches played by military bands; m. law = maintenance of law by the army instead of the police; m. arts = oriental fighting techniques using swords/sticks, etc.

Martian ['mɑːʃn] *n.* being which is said to inhabit the planet Mars.

martin ['mɑːtin] *n.* small dark bird similar to a swallow.

martinet ['mɑːtiˈnet] *n.* very strict person.

martingale ['mɑːtiŋgeil] *n.* strap to hold a horse's head down.

martini [mɑːˈtiːni] *n.* drink made of gin/vodka and vermouth.

martyr 1 ['mɑːtə] *n.* person killed because of his religious beliefs; a m. to = suffering a lot from. **martyr 2** *v.* to kill (s.o.) for their religious beliefs. **martyrdom** *n.* death for one's beliefs.

marvel 1 ['mɑːvl] *n.* object of wonder. **marvel 2** *v.* (marvelled) to show wonder/surprise (at s.o./sth). **marvellous** *adj.* wonderful/amazing.

Marxism ['mɑːksizəm] *n.* political theory of the philosopher Marx on which communism is based. **Marxist** *adj. & n.* (person) who follows Marxism.

marzipan ['mɑːzipæn] *n.* paste made from almonds, used for making sweets or covering cakes.

mascara [mæˈskɑːrə] *n.* liquid/paste for making eyelashes dark.

mascot ['mæskət] *n.* object/animal which brings good luck.

masculine ['mæskjolin] *adj.* (a) male/manly. (b) (in grammar) referring to words which have a particular form to indicate the male gender. **masculinity** ['mæskjoˈliniti] *n.* manliness.

maser ['meizə] *n.* device which amplifies microwaves.

mash 1 [mæʃ] *n.* (a) mixture of things crushed together. (b) *inf.* mashed potatoes. (c) food mixture for horses. (d) mixture used as the base for making beer. **mash 2** *v.* to crush (sth) into a paste. **masher** *n.* device for crushing.

mashie *n.* type of heavy metal golf club.

mask 1 [mɑːsk] *n.* covering to disguise/to protect the face. **mask 2** *v.* to cover up/to hide. **masked** *adj.* wearing a mask. **masking tape** *n.* tape used to cover an area which is not being painted.

masochist ['mæsəkist] *n.* person who enjoys being hurt. **masochism** *n.* enjoyment at being hurt. **masochistic** *adj.* referring to masochism.

mason ['meisn] *n.* (a) person who builds with stone. (b) member of a secret society of freemasons. **masonic** [məˈsɒnik] *adj.* referring to freemasons. **masonry** ['meisnri] *n.* art of building with stone; large stones in a building.

masquerade 1 [mɑːskkəˈreid] *n.* (a) dance/party where people wear masks. (b) pretence/hiding of the truth. **masquerade 2** *v.* (as) to pretend to be (s.o.).

mass 1 [mæs] *n. (pl. -es)* (a) Catholic communion service; high m. = mass with full ceremony; low m. = mass without ceremony; Requiem M. = (music for) a mass for the dead. (b) (in physics) solid body. (c) (in physics) amount of matter in a body. (d) large number/large quantity; m. murderer = killer of a large number of people; m. meeting = meeting of a lot of people; m. production = production of a large number of products; m. media = means of communicating (TV/radio/newspapers) which reach a large number of people. (e) the masses = the common people. **mass 2** *v.* group together into a mass. **mass-produce** v. to produce a large number of (products) at the same time.

massacre 1 ['mæwəkə] n. killing of a lot of people/animals. **massacre 2** v. to kill a lot of people/animals.

massage 1 ['mæsɑːʒ] n. rubbing of the body to relieve pain or reduce weight. **massage 2** v. to rub (s.o.'s body) to relieve pain or to reduce weight.

masseur. [mæ'sɜː] n. man who massages. **masseuse** [mæ'sɜːz] n. woman who massages.

massive ['mæsɪv] adj. very large. **massively** adv. very much **massiveness** n. being massive.

mast [mɑːst] n. (a) tall pole on a ship to carry the sails. (b) tall metal construction to carry an aerial. (c) (no pl.) seeds of beech/oak, etc., trees.

mastectomy [mæ'stektəmɪ] n. operation to remove a breast.

master 1 ['mɑːstə] n. (a) person in control; captain (of a ship). (b) male teacher; person with a second degree from a university. (c) head of a college. (d) skilled person; an old m. = painting by a great painter of the past. **master 2** adj. controlling; m. key = main key; m. switch = switch which controls all the other switches; m. tape = main tape from which copies are made; m. bedroom = main bedroom. **master 3** v. to become skilled at (sth.). **master-at-arms** n. (in the navy) petty officer in charge of small arms and discipline. **masterful** adj. commanding/like a commander. **masterfully** adv. in a commanding way. **masterly** adj. clever; like an expert. **mastermind 1** n. very clever person. **mastermind 2** v. to be the brains behind (a plan). **masterpiece** n. very fine painting/book/piece of music, etc. **masterstroke** n. very clever action. **mastery** n. controls over s.o.; complete understanding of a subject; great skill at a game.

mastic ['mæstɪk] n. gum from certain trees.

masticate ['mæstɪkeɪt] v. (formal) to chew. **mastication** [mæstɪ'keɪʃn] n. chewing.

mastiff ['mæstɪf] n. large fierce breed of dog.

mastoid ['mæstɔɪd] n. (a) bone just behind the ear. (b) inf., mastoids = inflammation of the mastoid.

masturbate ['mæstəbeɪt] v. to rub the sex organs to excite them. **masturbation** [mæstə'beɪʃn] v. exciting the sex organs by rubbing.

mat ['mæt] n. (a) small piece of carpet/woven straw etc., used as floor covering; bath m. = small carpet to step on to when getting out of a bath. (b) small piece of cloth/wood/glass put under a plate on a table. **matted** adj. stuck together (like a mat). **matting** n. (material for making) large mats; coconut m. = floor covering made from coconut fibres.

matador ['mætədɔː] n. bullfighter who fights on foot.

match 1 n. (pl.- es) (a) equal (person/thing); they are a good m. = they go well together. (b) game; test m. = international cricket match. (c) small piece of wood/cardboard with a chemical tip which lights when rubbed against a rough surface (d) marriage. **match 2** ['mætʃ] v. (a) to be equal to. (b) to fit/to go with. **match board.** n. tongue-and-groove board. with a projecting tongue along one edge and a corresponding groove along the other. **matchbox** n. small box containing matches. **matchless** adj. with no equal. **matchmaker** n. person who arranges a marriage. **matchstick,** Am. **matchstalk** n. stick of wood forming a match; m. men = sketches of people drawn with single lines for each limb. **matchwood** n. small pieces of wood.

mate 1 ['meɪt] n. (a) one of a pair of animals; husband or wife. (b) inf., friend/companion. (c) workman's helper (d) (in merchant navy) officer. (e) (in chess) position where the king cannot move and the game ends. **mate 2** v. (a) (of animals) to breed. (b) (in chess) to put (your opponent's king) in a position from which he cannot escape. **matey** adj. Inf. friendly.

material 1 ['mətɪərɪəl] n. (a) substance which can be used for making sth. (b) useful implements; writing materials = pen/pencils/ink/paper, etc. (c) cloth. (d) subject matter/notes (for a book, etc.). **material 2** adj. (a) referring to physical things. (b) important.

materialism *n.* interest only in physical things/belief that only physical things are important. **materialist** *n.* person who believes in materialism. **materialistic** *adj.* referring to materialism. **materialize** *v.* to become real/to appear. **materially** *adv.* greatly/noticeably.

maternal [mə'tɜːnl] *adj.* referring to a mother; m. grandfather = father of your mother. **maternally** *adv.* like a mother. **maternity** *n.* becoming a mother; giving birth; m. leave = paid leave from a job while you are having a baby.

mathematics [mæθə'mætɪks] *n.* science of numbers and measurements. **mathematical** *adj.* referring to mathematics. **mathematically** *adv.* by mathematics. **mathematician** [mæθəmə'tɪʃn] *n.* expert at mathematics. **maths**, *Am.* **math** *n. inf.* mathematics.

matinee [mætɪneɪ] *n.* afternoon performance of a play or film.

matins [mætɪnz] *n. pl.* prayers said in the morning.

matriarch [meɪtrɪɑːk] *n.* woman who leads a family/a group. **matriarchal** [meɪtrɪ'ɑːkl] *adj.* referring to a matriarch; (society) where women rule families. **matriarchy** *n.* matriarchal society. **matricide** ['mætrɪsaɪd] *n.* murder of one's mother.

matriculate [mə'trɪkjuleɪt] *v.* to pass an examination which allows you to join a university; to become a member of a University. **matriculation** [mə'trɪkju'leɪʃn] *n.* joining a university after passing an examination; examination which you need to pass in order to join a university.

matrimony ['mætrɪmənɪ] *n.* state of being married. **matrimonial** [mætrɪ'məunɪəl] *adj.* referring to marriage.

matrix ['meɪtrɪks] *n.* (*pl.*-trices) (a) plant/pattern from which copies are made.[ ]b] mathematical arrangement of figures in a series of columns.

matron ['meɪtrən] *n.* (a) (formal) senior nursing officer in charge of a hospital. (b) woman (usu., a nurse) who looks after children in a boarding school. (c) middle-aged married woman. **matronly** *adj.* like a matron.

matt [mæt] *adj.* dull/not shiny.

matter 1 ['mætə] *n.* (a) substance or material. (b) thing/business; that's quite another m. = that's quite different. (c) problem. (d) no m. what = any. **matter 2** *v.* to be important. **matter-of-fact** *adj.* practical.

mattock ['mætək] *n.* type of a pickaxe with a wide blade used for breaking up soil.

mattress [mætrəs] *n.* (*pl.*-es) thick soft part of a bed made of a canvas case with various fillings; sprung m. = mattress with springs inside.

mature 1 [mə'tjuə] *adj.* ripe; older; reasonable/adult (attitude); (student) who is older than normal. **mature 2** *v.* to ripen. **maturation** *n.* becoming mature. **maturity** *n.* ripeness/readiness.

maudlin ['məːdltɪn] *adj.* weeping/silly through drink.

maul [məːl] *v.* to attack/handle roughly. **maulstick** *n.* stick used by a painter to hold his hand steady.

maunder [məːndə] *v.* to mumble disconnected phrases.

Maundy Thursday [məːnɪθɜːzdɪ] *n.* Thursday before Easter Sunday.

mausoleum [məːzə'lɪəm] *n.* important burial building.

mauve [məuv] *adj. & n.* light pinkish purple (colour).

maverick ['mævərɪk] *n.* (a) *Am.* animal which has not been branded and is running loose. (b) person who does not fit into the usual pattern.

maw [məː] *n.* (of animal) large mouth; stomach.

mawkish [məːkɪʃ] *adj.* silly/falsely sentimental.

maxilla [mæk'sɪlə] *n.* upper jaw bone. **maxillary** *adj.* referring to the upper jaw.

maxim ['mæksɪm] *n.* wise saying. **maximum** ['mæksɪməm] *adj. & n.* greatest possible (number or amount); at the m. = at most. **maximize** ['mæksɪmaɪz] *v.* to make as large as possible.

May ['meɪ] *v.* (a) 5th month of the year; M. Day = May 1st. (b) may = hawthorn/wild shrub growing in hedges and flowering in May. **Mayday** *n.* international distress signal. **Mayfly** *n.* small fly which appears in summer.

maypole *n.,* tall pole around which people dance on the 1st of May. **may** [mei] *v.* (might) (a) used with other verbs to mean it is possible; might as well = it would be better if; you might have left it on the train = perhaps you left it on the train; much good m. it do you! = I hope it does you a lot of good (though I doubt if it will). (b) used with other verbs to mean it is allowed.

maybe *adv.* perhaps; may be not = possibly not. **mayhem** ['meihem] *n.* wild confusion.

mayonnaise [meiə'neiz] *n.* cream sauce made with egg yolk and oil.

mayor ['meə] *n.* elected leader of a town. **mayoress** ['meəres] *n.* wife of a mayor; woman mayor.

maze ['meiz] *n.* network of puzzling paths in which you can get lost.

Mb megabyte.

me [mi:] *pron.* referring to the speaker.

mead [mi:d] *n.* alcoholic drink made from honey.

meadow [medəʊ] *n.* large green field. **meadowsweet** *n.* common wild plant with many little white flowers.

meagre, *Am.* **meager** [mi:gə] *adj.* (a) scanty/few. (b) thin. **meagreness** *n.* small amount.

meal [mi:l] *n.* (a) food taken at a sitting. (b) coarse flour. **mealtime** *n.* time when you usually eat. **mealy** *adj.* floury. **mealy-mouthed** *adj.* not straightforward; (person) who tries not to offend and so doesn't say what he thinks.

mean 1 [mi:n] *n.* (a) middle; average; middle point between two extremes. (b) means = way/method of doing sth; by no means = not at all; by all means = certainly. (c) means = money/resources; it's beyond my means = it's too expensive for me; means test = inquiry into the amount of money earned by s.o. in order to calculate how much state benefit he should receive. **mean 2** *adj.* (-er, -est) (a) average/middle. (b) miserable/low; he has no m. opinion of himself = he thinks a lot of himself; m. trick = unkind trick. (c) miserly. (d) *Sl.* very good. **mean 3** *v.* (meant) (a) to intend; he means well = he has good intentions; do you m. Richard? = are you talking about Richard? you are meant to = you are supposed to. (b) to signify/to show.

meaning 1 *n.* signification. **meaning 2** *adj.* significant. **meaningful** *adj.* full of meaning/significant.

meaningfully *adv.* significantly. **meaningless** *adj.* not signifying anything.

meanly *adv.* poorly. **meanness** *n.* miserliness; dislike of sharing things/of spending money. **mean-spirited** *adj.* sly/unpleasant.

meander 1 [mi'ændə] *n.* bend in a river. **meander 2** *v.* to wind/to wander about. **meandering** *adj.* wandering/very winding (path).

meant [ment] *v.* see mean.

meantime 1 ['mi:ntaim] *n.* in the m. = between two events. **meantime 2** *adv.* during this time. **meanwhile.** ['mi:nwail] *adv.* during this time.

measles ['mi:zlz] *n.* children's disease which gives you a red rash; German m. = mild disease which gives a red rash and which can affect an unborn child if caught by a pregnant woman. **measly** *adj. inf.* miserable/small.

measure 1 ['meʒə] *n.* (a) quantity; size; made to m. = made specially to fit. (b) unit for showing the size/quantity of sth. (c) thing for showing the size/quantity of sth; small metal cup; long tape with centimetres/inches marked on it. (d) action; as a precautionary m. = as a precaution (e) seam/layer of coal. (f) plan of a new law/a bill (g) time (in music); rhythm (in poetry). **measure 2** *v.* to be of a certain size/length/quantity, etc., to find out the length/quantity, etc., to find out the length/quantity of (sth).

measurable *adj.* which can be measured. **measured** *adj.* regular; with m. tread = in a slow and stately way. **measureless** *adj.* so large that it cannot be measured. **measurement** *n.* (a) finding out the size/length/quantity of sth. (b) quantity/size etc., found out when you measure. **measure up to** *v.* to be able to do (a difficult job).

measuring *n.* finding out the size/length/quantity of sth; m. tape = long tape with centimetres/inches marked on it. m. glass/jug = glass jar with quantities marked on it by lines.

meat [miːt] *n.* flesh of an animal which is eaten. **meatball** *n.* minced meat rolled into a ball and cooked. **meafy** *adj.* (a) with a lot of meat. (b) with a lot of details/information.

mecca [mekə] *n.* place which attracts a large number of people.

mechanic [mi'kæwwnɪk] *n.* person who works on engines. **mechanical** *adj.* referring to a machine; m. gestures = gestures done automatically as if you were a machine. **mechanically** *adv.* by machine; like a machine; automatically. **mechanics** *n.* (a) the study of force and power. (b) the study of machines. (c) way in which sth works. **mechanism** ['mekənɪəm] *n.* (a) working parts (of a machine). (b) way in which sth works. **mechanization** ['mekənaɪ'zerʃeɪn] *n.* introduction of machines to take the place of manual labour. **mechanize** ['mekənaɪz] *v.* to introduce machines in place of manual labour. **mechanized** *adj.* (soldiers/regiment) with armoured vehicles.

medal ['medl] *n.* metal disc. *usu.* attached to a ribbon. made to commemorate an important occasion or battle; gold/silver/bronze m. = medal for first/second/third place in competitions. **medallion** ['mɪdæljən] *n.* large medal. **medallist** ['medəlɪst] *n.* person who has won a medal in a sports competition etc.

meddle ['medl] *v.* (in/with) to interfere; to get involved with. **meddler** *n.* person who likes to meddle. **meddlesome** *adj.* (person) who interferes. **meddling 1** *n.* interfering. **meddling 2** *adj.* (person) who is always interfering.

media ['miːdɪə] *n.* *pl.*(a) means of communicating information; the (mass) m. = newspapers/TV/radio, etc. m. resources centre = centre for communicating information by television/films/tapes, etc. (b) see also medium.

mediaeval [medɪ'iːvl] *adj.* see medieval.

median ['miːdɪən] *adj. & n.* (point) which is in the middle/(line) which goes through the middle. **medial** *adj.* in the middle.

mediate ['miːdɪeɪt] *v.* to intervene/to try

to bring peace between two opponents. **mediation** [miːdɪ'eɪʃn] *n.* attempt to make two opponents agree. **mediator** *n.* person who tries to make two opponents agree.

medical 1 ['medɪkl] *adj.* referring to the study of disease; the m. profession = all doctors; m. officer to health = person responsible for the health services of a town, etc. **medical 2** *n.* *inf.* examination of the body by a doctor. **medic** *n.* *inf.* doctor. **medically** *adv.* in a medical way. **medicament** *n.* (formal) medicine. **medicate** *v.* to add a medicine to (sth). **medication** *n.* drug. **medicine** ['medsɪn] *n.* (a) study of disease; ill health and their cure. (b) liquid/powder/pill taken to cure an illness; m. ball = large heavy ball used for physical exercises; m. chest = cupboard for keeping medicines in. **medicinal** [me'dɪsnl] *adj.* used to treat an illness. **medicinally** *adv.* (used) as a medicine. **medicine man** *n.* witch doctor.

medieval [medɪ'əʊkə] *adj.* referring to the Middle Ages.

mediocre [miːdɪ'əʊkə] *adj.* ordinary/not good or bad. **mediocrity** [miːdɪ'ʊkrɪtɪ] *n.* (a) not being good or bad/ordinariness. (b) very ordinary person with no special talents.

meditate ['medɪteɪt] *v.* (on/about) to think deeply about (sth). **meditation** [medɪ'teɪʃn] *n.* long deep (often religious) thought. **meditative** *adj.* thoughtful.

medium 1 ['miːdɪəm] *adj.* middle/average. **medium 2** *n.* (*pl.*medium/mediums) (a) middle point; happy m. = compromise. (b) type of paint used by an artist. (c) means of doing sth/of communicating sth. (d) person who thinks the spirits of dead people can talk through him/her.

medlar ['medɪə] *n.* fruit like a brown apple; tree which bears this fruit.

medley ['medlɪ] *n.* mixture.

medulla ['medjuə] *n.* bone marrow; the soft inner part of any organ.

meek [miːk] *adj.* (-er, -est) quiet/humble. **meekly** *adv.* quietly/humbly. **meekness** *n.* quietness/humility.

meerschaum ['mɪəʃəm] *n.* white substance. used to make tobacco pipes.

meet 1 ['mi:t] *n.* gathering of huntsmen. **meet 2** *v.* (met) (a) to come together. (b) to become acquainted with s.o.; we have already met = we know each other already. (c) to satisfy (needs). **meeting** *n.* (a) coming together. (b) group of people who meet for a special purpose; Annual General M. (AGM) = yearly assembly of all the members of a club/society/of all the share holders in a company. **meet with** *v.* (a) to find/to come up against; to have (an accident). (b) *Am.* to meet (s.o.).

mega- ['megə] prefix meaning (a) very large. (b) one million.

megabyte ['megəbait] *n.* unit of storage for a computer, equal to 1048.576 bytes.

megacycle, megahertz ['megəsaikl] ['megəhɜ:ts] *n.* frequency of radio waves of one million cycles per second.

megalith ['megəliθ] *n.* huge stone set up by prehistoric man.

megalomania [megələ'meiniə] *n.* mad belief that you are more important/more powerful than you really are. **megalomaniac** *n.* person suffering from megalomania.

megaphone ['megəfəʊn] *n.* metal trumpet which makes the voice sound louder.

megaton ['megətʌn] *n.* force of an explosion equal to the force produced by exploding one million tons of TNT.

meiosis ['mɪːəsis] *n.* splitting of cells.

melancholy 1 ['melənkəlɪ] *n.* great sadness. **melancholy 2** *adj.* very sad. **melancholia** *n.* (formal) melancholy state. **melancholic** ['melən'kɒlɪk] *adj.* very sad.

melanin ['melənin] *n.* pigment which colours the hair and skin.

melanoma *n.* cancer caused by sunlight.

mêlée ['meleɪ] *n.* crowd of struggling people.

mellifluous ['meləʊ] *adj.* soothing/pleasant (sound).

mellow 1 *adj.* ripe (fruit) (wine) which has matured; soft/rich (voice); calm and relaxed (order person). **mellow 2** *v.* to grow ripe/to mature; to become soft/rich; he has mellowed = he is much less angry/unpleasant than he used to be. **mellowness** *n.* ripeness/maturity.

melodrama ['melədrɑ:mə] *n.* extremely exciting but badly-written play which emphasizes violently alternating passions. **melodramatic** [melədrə'mætɪk] *adj.* arousing violent emotions. **melodramatically** *adv.* in a melodramatic way.

melody ['melədɪ] *n.* tune. **melodic** ['mɪ'lɒdɪk] *adj.* referring to tunes. **melodious** ['mə'ləʊdɪəs] *adj.* tuneful. **melodiously** *adv.* in a tuneful way.

melon ['melən] *n.* large round fruit of a creeping plant; water m. = very large type of melon with red flesh and black seeds.

melt ['melt] *v.* to change from solid to liquid by heating; rioters melted away when the police appeared = they disappeared; to m. down scrap metal = to heat it and make it into blocks so that it can be used again; my heart melted at the sight of puppies = became softened/less angry. **melting point** *n.* temperature at which a solid becomes liquid. **melting pot** *n.* (a) pot in which metals can be melted. (b) place where people of different origins come to live together.

member ['membə] *n.* (a) person who belongs to a group; M. of Parliament = person elected to the lower house of a parliament. (b) limb on a human body. **membership** *n.* (a) belonging to a group; m. card = card which shows you belong to a club/party). (b) all the members of a group.

membrane ['membrein] *n.* thin layer of tissue in the body.

memento [me'mentəʊ] *n.* (*pl.*-oes) thing kept to remind you of sth; souvenir.

memo ['meməʊ] *n.* (*pl.*-os) note/short message between people working in the same organization; m. pad = pad of paper for writing short notes.

memoir ['memwɑ:] *n.* (a) *pl.*memoirs = written account of what you can remember of your life. (b) short official/scientific note.

memorandum ['memə'rændəm] *n.* (*pl.*-da) note/short message.

memory ['meməri] *n.* (a) ability to remember; he recited the poem from m. if my m. serves me right = if I can remember it correctly. (b) what you remember; in m. of = to remind us of. (c) capacity for storing information (in a computer). **memorable** *adj.* which you cannot forget/very striking.

memorial 1 ['mɪ'mɔːrɪəl] *adj.* which reminds you of sth/s.o.; m. service = church service to remember someone who had died. **memorial 2** *n.* monument to remind you of sth/s.o.

memorize *v.* to learn (sth) by heart.

men [men] *n. pl.* see man.

menace 1 ['menəs] *n.* threat; bad thing; that child's a ma. = very naughty. **menace 2** *v.* to threaten; menacing clouds = clouds which threaten to bring rain. **menacingly** *adv.* in a threatening way.

menage [me'nɑːʒ] *n.* household.

menagerie ['mɪnædʒərɪ] *n.* small zoo; collection of more or less wild animals.

mend 1 [mend] *n.* (a) place where a piece of clothing has been repaired. (b) *inf.* on the m. = getting better. **mend 2** *v.* to repair; to be repaired. **mender** *n.* person who mends. **mending** *n.* (a) repairing. (b) clothes which need repairing.

mendacity [men'dæsɪtɪ] *n.* (formal) telling lies. **mendacious** [men'deɪʒəs] *adj.* not truthful.

mendicant ['mendɪkənt] *adj.* (person) who begs.

menfolk ['menfəʊk] *n. pl.* all the men (in a family/group, etc.).

menhir ['menfɪə] *n.* tall standing stone. erected by prehistoric people.

menial ['mɪːnɪəl] *adj.* low; badly paid; m. tasks = dirty jobs which a servant might do.

Ménière's disease ['meɪnɪeəzdɪ'siːz] *n.* disease of the middle ear, causing dizziness.

meningitis [menɪn'dʒaɪtɪs] *n.* inflammation of the membrane covering the brain.

meniscus [me'nɪskəs] *n.* curved surface of a drop of water.

menopause ['menəpɔːz] *n.* period of life (around the age of 50) when women become no longer capable of bearing children; male m. = difficult period in a man's life (around the age of 50).

menstruate ['menstrʊeɪt] *v.* (of women) to lose blood through the vagina at regular periods. **menstrual** *adj.* referring to the regular monthly loss of

blood through the vagina.

menstruation [menstrʊ'eɪʃn] *n.* monthly loss of blood through the vagina.

mensuration [mensjʊə'reɪʃn] *n.* study of measurement.

menswear ['menzweə] *n.* (no *pl.*) clothes for men.

mental ['ment] *adj.* referring to the mind; m. arithmetic = calculations done in the head; m. age = way of showing the development of a person's mind, by expressing it as the age at which such development is normal; m. hospital = hospital for those who suffer from illnesses of the mind. **mentality** [men'tælɪtɪ] *n.* (a) mental power. (b) way of thinking which is typical of s.o./ of a group. **mentally** *adv.* concerning the brain; m. defective = well below normal intelligence.

menthol ['menθɒl] *n.* white substance which tastes strongly of mint. **mentholated** *adj.* treated with menthol; with menthol added.

mention 1 ['menʃn] *n.* reference to sth. **mention 2** *v.* to refer to (sth); not to m. = not forgetting/as well as.

mentor ['mentə] *n.* (formal) person who teaches/helps another (younger) person.

menu ['menjuː] *n.* (a) list of food available in a restaurant. (b) list of options available on a computer program.

meow ['miːaʊ] *Am.* = miaow.

MEP [emiːpiː] *n.* Member of the European Parliament.

mercantile ['mɜːkəntaɪl] *adj.* referring to commerce.

mercenary 1 ['mɜːsənrɪl] *adj.* (person) who is interested in money. **mercenary 2** *n.* person who serves foreigners as a soldier for money.

mercerize ['mɜːsəraɪz] *v.* to make (cotton cloth) shiny.

merchant ['mɜːtʃənt] *n.* businessman; person who buys and sells; m. navy = commercial ships of a country; m. seaman = seaman in the merchant navy; m. bank = bank which lends money to companies, not individuals.

merchandise 1 *n.* goods for sale. **merchandise 2** *v.* to sell (goods) by wide and varied advertising.

merchantman, merchantship n. (pl.-men) commercial ship.

mercury ['mɜːkjərɪ] n. (element: Hg) liquid metal used in thermometers/ barometers, etc. **mercurial** ['mɜːkjuərɪɪəl] adj. (person) whose temper changes frequently.

mercy ['mɜːsɪ] n. (a) compassion/pity; kindness towards unfortunate people; to have m. on = to forgive/not to want to punish/harm s.o.; m. killing = euthanasia, killing of s.o. who is very ill or in pain; (b) gift (of fate); we must be thankful for small mercies = we must be grateful that everything has turned out fairly well so far. **merciful** adj. (person) who forgives/who is kind. **mercifully** adv. thankfully; in a forgiving/kindly way. **merciless** adj. harsh/cruel. **mercilessly** adv. without mercy. **mercilessness** n. lack of pity; hardness (of character).

mere 1 ['mɪə] n. small lake. **mere 2** adj. simply/only; he's a m. boy = only a boy; the m. sight of grass makes me sneeze = simply the sight of grass makes me sneeze. **merely** adv. only/simply.

meretricious ['mer'trɪʃəs] adj. showy and cheap.

merganser [mɜː'gænzə] n. type of large duck with a crest.

merge ['mɜːdʒ] v. to join together (with sth). **merger** n. amalgamation/joining of two companies.

meridian [mə'rɪdɪən] n. imaginary line drawn from the North Pole to the South Pole; the Greenwich m. = line passing through Greenwich (near London) from which longitude is calculated.

meringue [mə'ræŋ] n. sweet baked dessert made of egg whites and sugar.

merino [mə'riːnəʊ] n. (pl.-os) type of long-haired sheep/fine woollen material.

merit 1 ['merɪt] n. value/quality/ excellence; to go into the merits of = to examine the good and bad points of. **merit 2** v. to be worthy of/to deserve (sth). **meritorious** [meri'tɔːrɪəs] adj. (formal) which is valuable/which should be rewarded.

mermaid ['mɜːmeɪd] n. mythical creature, half woman and half fish. **merman** n. mythical creature, half man and half fish.

merry ['merɪ] adj. (-ier, -iest) (a) happy; to make m. = to have a good time; the more the merrier = the more there are the happier everything is. (b) inf. slightly drunk. **merrily** adv. happily. **merriment** n. fun. **merry-go-round** n. roundabout with wooden horse, etc., in a funfair. **merrymaker** n. person who is enjoying himself. **merrymaking** n. festivity/celebration.

mesh 1 [meʃ] n. (pl.-es) space between the threads of a net. **mesh 2** v. (of a cogwheel) to link together with another toothed wheel.

mesmerize ['mezməaɪz] v. to hypnotize.

mess 1 [mes] n. (pl.-es) (a) dirt; disorder/confusion; they made a m. of the repair job = they did the repair job badly. (b) group of soldiers/sailors who eat together; room where officers eat and sleep. **mess 2** v. (with) to eat together. **mess about** v. (a) to spend your spare time doing sth. (b) to waste time. (c) inf. to mess s.o. about = disrupt s.o.'s way of life/to treat s.o. badly. **messily** adv. in a messy way. **mess up** v. inf. (a) to dirty. (b) to run/to spoil. **messy** adj. (-ier, -iest) dirty; disorderly.

message ['mesɪdʒ] n. news/ information sent; inf. he got the m. = he understood. **messenger** n. person who brings a message.

messiah [mɪ'saɪə] n. (a) person whom the Jews expect will come to free them. (b) Jesus Christ. **messianic** [mesɪ'ænɪk] adj. referring to the Messiah.

Messrs ['mesəz] n. used formally as plural of Mr.

met [met] v. see meet. **Met** [met] n. the Met = the Metropolitan Police.

meta- ['metə] prefix meaning change **metabolism** [me'tæbəlɪzəm] n. process by which plants and animals use food to create energy. **metabolic** [metə'bɒlɪk] adj. referring to metabolism.

metacarpus ['metə'kɑːpəs] n. the bones in the hand.

metal ['metl] n. usu. solid mineral substance which can conduct heat and electricity. **metalled** adj. (road) covered with small stones set in tar. **metallic** [mə'tælɪk] adj. referring to metal; m. sheen = shine such as you get

on polished metal. **metallurgist**
[me'tælədʒɪst] *n.* person who studies
metals. **metallurgy** [me'tælədʒɪ] *n.*
study of metals. **metalwork** *n.* making
things with metal; pieces of metal made
into a construction/a work of art.

metamorphosis [metə'mɔːfəsɪs] *n.*
(*pl.*-phoses[-fəsiːz]) change, esp. an
insect's change of form.

metamorphose [metə'mɔːfəʊz] *v.* to
change from one state to another.

metaphor ['metəfə] *n.* way of
describing sth by suggesting it has the
properties of sth else. **metaphorical**
[metə'fɒrɪkl] *adj.* like a metaphor.
metaphorically *adv.* in a
metaphorical way.

metaphysics [metə'fɪzɪks] *n.*
philosophical study of truth/knowledge/
existence etc. **metaphysical** *adj.*
referring to metaphysics.

metatarsus [metə'tɑːsəs] *n.* the bones
in the foot.

metathesis [me'tæθəsɪs] *n.* change of
sounds in a word, where letters are
transposed.

mete out ['miːt'aʊt] *v.* to give
(punishment).

meteor ['miːtɪə] *n.* small object which
flashes through space and shines brightly
as it burns up on entering the earth's
atmosphere. **meteoric** [miːtɪ'ɒrɪk] *adj.*
like a meteor/very rapid. **meteorite**
['miːtɪəraɪt] *n.* lump of rock/iron which
falls to earth from space. **meteorology**
[miːtɪə'rɒlədʒɪ] *n.* study of climate and
weather. **meteorological**
[miːtɪərə'lɒdʒɪkl] *adj.* referring to the
climate and weather; m. station =
research station which notes weather
conditions. **meteorologist**
[miːtɪə'rɒlədʒɪst] *n.* person who studies
climate and weather.

meter 1 ['miːtə] *n.* (a) device for
counting how much time/water/gas, etc.
has been used; parking m. = device into
which you put money to pay for parking.
(b) *Am.* metre. **meter 2** *v.* to count by a
meter.

methane ['miːθeɪn] *n.* colourless gas
which easily catches fire and is found
naturally in the ground. **methanol**
['meθənɒl] *n.* methyl alcohol.

method ['meθəd] *n.* (a) way of doing
sth. (b) well-organized system.

methodical [mɪ'θɒdɪkl] *adj.* ordered/
regulated. **methodically** *adv.* in a well
organized way. **Methodist** *n. & adj.*
(person) following the teaching of
Wesley. **methodology** *n.* methods
used in a certain process or study.

methyl ['meθɪl] *n.* m. alcohol =
poisonous alcohol found in wood.
methylated spirits, inf. meths
['meθɪleɪtɪd'spɪrɪts, meθs] *n.* alcohol
used for lighting or heating.

meticulous [me'tɪkjʊləs] *adj.* attentive
to detail (about doing sth).
meticulously *adv.* carefully/paying
attention to details. **meticulousness**
n. being meticulous.

metier ['metɪeɪ] *n.* profession;
occupation one is good at.

metre, *Am.* **meter** ['miːtə] *n.* (a)
standard measurement of length
(approximately 39.4 inches). (b) regular
rhythm in poetry. **metric** ['metrɪk] *adj.*
(a) referring to metre as a measurement;
the m. system = system of measurement
based on metres litres etc. (b) referring
to metre as rhythm. **metrical** *adj.*
(poem) written in a regular rhythm.
metricate ['metrɪkeɪt] *v.* to express in
metres/centimetres etc. **metrication**
[metrɪ'keɪʃn] *n.* changing of a
measuring system to the metric system.

metronome ['metrənəʊm] *n.* device
which beats time regularly used when
practising/playing music.

metropolis [mə'trɒpəlɪs] *n.* (*pl.*-es)
large capital city. **metropolitan 1**
[metrə'pɒlɪtən] *adj.* referring to a large
capital city; the M. Police = the police
force of Greater London. **metropolitan
2** *n.* chief bishop in the Orthodox
Church.

mettle ['metl] *n.* vigour/strength of
character (of a person); to put s.o. on his
m. = to make s.o. try to do his best.
mettlesome *adj.* (formal) vigorous/
active.

mew 1 [mjuː] *n.* soft cry which a cat
makes. **mew 2** *v.* to make a soft cry
like a cat. **mews** [mjuːz] *n.* (a) row of
former stables or garages converted into
houses. (b) stables.

Mexican 1 ['meksɪkən] *adj.* referring
to Mexico. **Mexican 2** *n.* person from
Mexico.

mezzanine ['metsəniːn] *n.* floor

between the ground floor and the first floor.

mezzo-soprano ['metsəʊsə'prɑːnəʊ] *n.* singer or voice lower in pitch than a soprano.

mezzotint ['mrdzəʊtɪnt] *n.* print made from a plate which has rough and smooth areas.

Mg symbol for magnesium. **mg** abbrev for milligram.

miaow, *Am.* **meow 1** [mi:'aʊ] *n.* call of a cat. **miaow 2** *v* to call like a cat.

miasma [mi:æzmə] *n.* unpleasant/poisonous air.

mica ['maɪkə] *n.* type of mineral which splits into thin glittering layers.

mice maɪs] *n.* *pl.*see mouse.

Michaelmas ['mɪkəlməs] *n.* 29th September; M. daisy = common autumn garden flower.

mickey ['mɪkɪ] *n.* *inf.* to take the m. out of = to make fun of.

micro- 1 ['maɪkrəʊ] prefix meaning. (a) very small. (b) one millionth. **micro-2** *n.* microcomputer.

microbe ['maɪkrəʊb] *n.* germ; tiny living organism.

microchip ['maɪkrəʊtʃɪp] *n.* small piece of silicon used in electronics.

microcomputer [maɪkrəʊkʌm'pjuːtə] *n.* small computer for office or personal use.

microclimate ['maɪkrəʊ'klaɪmət] *n.* climate of a small area.

microcosm ['maɪkrəkɒzəm] *n.* miniature version.

microfiche ['maɪkrəfiːʃ] *n.* index card made of microfilms.

microfilm 1 ['maɪkrəfɪlm] *n.* film on which sth is photographed in very small scale; m. reader = apparatus which an enlarger and a display screen for reading microfilms. **microfilm 2** *v.* to make a very small scale photograph of.

micrometer [maɪ'krɒmɪtə] *n.* instrument for measuring very small distances.

micron ['maɪkrɒn] *n.* one millionth of a metre.

microorganism [maɪkrəʊ'ɔːgənɪzm] *n.* tiny living organism.

microphone ['maɪkrəfəʊn] *n.* apparatus for capturing sound and passing it to a loudspeaker or recording apparatus.

microprocessor [maɪkrəʊ'prəʊsesə] *n.* small central processing unit using microchips.

microscope ['maɪkrəskəʊp] *n.* apparatus which enlarges things which are very small. **microscopic** [maɪkrə'skɒpɪk] *adj.* so small as to be visible only through a microscope.

microwave ['maɪkrəweɪv] *n.* very short electric wave; m. oven = small oven which cooks very rapidly using microwaves.

mid- [mɪd] prefix meaning middle.

midday *n.* twelve o'clock noon.

midland *adj. & n.* (referring to the) central part of a country; the Midlands = the central part of England.

midnight *n.* twelve o'clock at night.

midriff *n.* front part of the body above the waist and below the chest.

midshipman *n.* (*pl.*-men) trainee officer in the Royal Navy.

midst *n.* middle; in our m. = among us.

midstream *n.* middle part of a river.

midsummer *n.* middle of the summer. Midsummer's Day = June 24th.

midway *adv.* half way.

Midwest *n.* central northern part of the United States.

midwinter *n.* middle of the winter.

midden ['mɪdn] *n.* heap of dung.

middle 1 ['mɪdl] *adj.* in the centre; half way between two things; m. sized = neither big nor small, m. class = professional class (between the upper class and the lower/working class); the M. Ages = historical period between the Dark Ages and the Renaissance (about 1000 to 1500 AD). **middle 2** *n.* (a) centre; central point. (b) waistline.

middleaged *adj.* not young and not old (between 40 and 60 years of age). **Middle East** *n.* area between Egypt and Pakistan. **Middle Eastern** *adj.* referring to the Middle East.

middleman *n.* (*pl.*-men) businessman who buys from one source to sell to another. **middle-of-the-road** *adj.* centre/moderate (politics).

middleweight *n.* weight in boxing between welterweight and light heavy weight. **middling** *adj.* neither good nor bad; not very large or small.

midge [mɪdʒ] *n.* small stinging flying insect.

midget ['mɪdʒɪt] *n.* very small person;
m. submarine = submarine which can
only carry one or two people.

midwife ['mɪdwaɪf] *n.* (*pl.*-wives)
person (usu. a woman) trained to help
deliver a baby. **midwifery** ['mɪdwɪfrɪ] *n.*
work of helping deliver babies.

mien [miːn] *n.* way in which a person
behaves or looks.

miff [mɪf] *v. inf.* to offend/to annoy
(s.o.).

might 1 [maɪt] *v.* see may. **might 2** *n.*
force/strength. **mighty 1** *adj.* (-ier, -
iest) (a) strong. (b) great; *inf.* you're in a
m. hurry = you are very impatient.
mighty 2 *adv. inf.* very. **mightily** *adv.*
greatly.

mignonette [mɪnjə'net] *n.* scented
garden plant.

migraine ['miːgreɪn] *n.* recurrent very
bad headache.

migrate [maɪ'greɪt] *v.* to move from one
place to another with the seasons.
migrant ['maɪgrənt] *adj. & n.* (bird)
which moves from one place to another
with the seasons; (workman) who moves
from one job to another or from one
country to another. **migration**
[maɪ'greɪʃn] *n.* movement of birds from
one country to another. **migratory**
['maɪgrətərɪ] *adj.* referring to migration.

mike [maɪk] *n. inf.* microphone.

milch [mɪltʃ] *adj.* m. cow = cow kept
for milk.

mild [maɪld] *adj.* (-er, -est) (a) soft/not
severe (punishment). (b) not harsh
(weather). (c) not strong/powerful.
mildly *adv.* softly/kindly; to put it m. =
not to say anything ruder. **mildness** *n.*
kindness/softness; warmness (of winter
weather).

mildew 1 ['mɪldjuː] *n.* powdery fungus
on plants/paper/leather etc. **mildew 2** *v.*
to become covered with mildew.
mildewed *adj.* covered with mildew.

mile [maɪl] *n.* measure of length (1760
yards/161 kilometres); *inf.* miles of
string = very long piece of string; it's
miles too big = much too big. **mileage**
n. (a) distance travelled in miles; car
with a low m. = car which has not
travelled as much as is normal. (b) *inf.* to
get a lot of m. out of = to gain benefit
from. **mileometer** [maɪ'lɒmɪtə] *n.* dial
showing number of miles travelled.

miler *n.* person who runs in a 1 mile
race. **milestone** *n.* stone showing
distance in miles; important point
(history, etc.).

milieu ['miːljɜː] *n.* surroundings/
environment.

militant ['mɪlɪtənt] *adj. & n.* (person)
who supports a policy of violence;
(person) who is very active in supporting
a cause/a political party. **militancy** *n.*
activity/vigour (in supporting a political
party/a cause). **military 1** ['mɪlɪtrɪ] *adj.*
referring to the army. **military 2** *n.*
the m. = the army. **militarism** *n.* belief in
the use of the army to solve political
problems. **militarist** *n.* person who
believes in militarism. **militaristic** *adj.*
believing that the army should be used to
solve political problems. **militate** *v.* to
work actively (against). **militia** [mɪ'lɪʃə]
n. emergency army; police force
organized like an army.

milk 1 [mɪlk] *n.* white liquid produced
by female mammals for feeding their
young. esp. the milk produced by cows;
m. shake = milk mixed with flavouring
and ice cream; m. chocolate = pale
brown chocolate (flavoured with milk);
m. teeth = first set of teeth produced by a
child. **milk 2** *v.* (a) to take the milk
from (an animal). (b) to get all the
money from (s.o.). **milker** *n.* (a) person
who milks. (b) good m. = cow which
produces a lot of milk. **milk float** *n.*
slow van which delivers milk to houses.
milking *n.* taking milk from a cow; m.
machine = machine which milks cows
automatically. **milkman** *n.* (*pl.*-men)
person who delivers the milk to houses
each morning. **milky** *adj.* (-ier, -iest)
tasting like milk; cloudy like milk;
containing milk; the M. way = luminous
band in the night sky composed of many
stars.

mill 1 [mɪl] *n.* (a) machine for grinding
corn into flour; building which contains
such a machine; *inf.* he's been through
the m. = (i) he has been fully trained; (ii)
he has suffered a great deal. (b) small
instrument for grinding. (c) large factory.
mill 2 *v.* (a) to grind (corn, etc.). (b) to
put vertical lines around the edge of a
coin. **mill about, mill around** *v.* to
move in various directions. **miller** *n.*
man who runs a flour mill. **millpond** *n.*

water dammed to provide power for a watermill; like a m. = perfectly calm.

milestone *n.* (a) large grooved stone used to grind corn. (b) great obstacle which causes trouble.

millennium [mɪˈlenɪəm] *n.* (*pl.*-ia) (a) period of a thousand years. (b) period of great happiness.

millepede [ˈmɪlɪpiːd] *n.* millipede.

millet [ˈmɪlɪt] *n.* grain used for food.

milli- [ˈmɪlɪ] prefix meaning one thousandth.

millibar [ˈmɪlɪbɑː] *n.* unit of atmospheric pressure.

milligram [ˈmɪlɪɡræm] *n.* one thousandth of a gram.

millimetre, *Am.* **millimeter** [ˈmɪlɪmiːtə] *n.* one thousandth of a metre.

milliner [ˈmɪlɪnə] *n.* person who makes/sells women's hats. **millinery** *n.* hats and ribbons.

million [ˈmɪljən] number 1,000.000.

millionaire [mɪljəˈneə] *n.* person who has more than a million pounds; dollar m. = person who has more than a million dollars. millionth, 1,000,000th.

millionth 1 *adj.* referring to a million. **millionth 2** *n.* one of a million parts.

millipede [ˈmɪlɪpiːd] *n.* small creeping animal with a large number of legs.

milometer [maɪˈlɒmɪtə] *n.* mileometer.

milt [mɪlt] *n.* sperm from a male fish.

mime 1 [maɪm] *n.* (a) actor who does not speak, but conveys a story/emotions through gesture. (b) gesture used to convey a story/emotions. (c) story conveyed by gestures. **mime 2** *v.* to convey a story/emotions through gesture.

mimic 1 [ˈmɪmɪk] *n.* person who imitates. **mimic 2** *v.* (mimicked) to imitate. **mimicry** *n.* imitation.

mimosa [mɪˈməʊzə] *n.* semi-tropical tree with yellow, scented flowers.

minaret [mɪnəˈret] *n.* tower attached to a mosque.

mince 1 [mɪns] *n.* meat which has been ground up into very small pieces. **mince 2** *v.* (a) to grind up (meat/vegetables) until they are in very small pieces; he didn't m. his words = he said what he had to say in a straightforward way. (b) to m. along = to walk along in a very affected manner, taking small steps.

mincemeat *n.* mixture of apples,

spices, dried fruit etc.; to make m. out of = to defeat/destroy completely. **mince pie** *n.* small pie filled with mincemeat and eaten at Christmas. **mincer** *n.* machine for grinding up meat, etc.

mincing *adj.* (a) affected (way of walking). (b) m. machine = mincer.

mind 1 [maɪnd] *n.* power of thinking; memory; bear him in m. = remember him; to make up your m. = to decide what to do; I'm in two minds about going = I can't decide whether to go or not; I've good m. to do it myself = I would very much like to do it myself; he's changed his m. twice already = he has changed his decision/his point of view; what do you have in m.? = what are you thinking of? state of m. = general opinion/mood/feeling; he's got sth on his m. = he is worried about sth; try to take her m. off the subject = try to stop her thinking about the subject; not in his right m. = mad. **mind 2** *v.* (a) to be careful about. (b) to bother about/to be busy about; m. your own business = don't interfere in my affairs; never m. = don't bother/don't worry. (c) to object to/to be annoyed by; would you m. shutting the door? = please shut the door; I wouldn't m. a cup of tea = I would rather like a cup of tea. (d) to look after (sth) while the owner is away. **mind-boggling** *adj. inf.* very surprising.

minded *adj.* interested (in doing sth); commercially m. = business like.

minder *n.* (a) person who looks after sth (while the owner is away). (b) bodyguard. **mindful** *adj.* remembering/thinking of sth. **mindless** *adj.* without thinking/stupid. **mind reader** *n.* person who seems to be able to guess what s.o. else is thinking.

mine 1 [maɪn] *n.* (a) deep hole in the ground for digging out minerals; he is a m. of information = he is full of information. (b) explosive device which is planted underground or underwater.

mine 2 *v.* (a) to excavate/to dig for minerals. (b) to plant mines underground or under water. **mine 3** *pron.* belonging to me; he's a friend of m. = one of my friends. **minefield** *n.* area of land/sea full of mines. **minelayer** *n.* ship which specializes in planting mines under water. **miner** *n.* person who

works in a mine; m.'s lamp = special lamp worn by a miner on his helmet.
minesweeper *n.* ship which specializes in removing mines placed under water by the enemy. **mineworker** *n.* worker in a mine. **mining** *n.* (a) action of extracting minerals. (b) placing mines underground or underwater.
mineral ['mɪnrəl] *adj. & n.* (non-living substance) which is extracted from the earth; m. water = (i) water from a spring; (ii) non-alcoholic fizzy drink; m. rights = permission to dig out minerals.
mineralogist [mɪnə'ræIədʒIst] *n.* scientist who studies minerals.
mineralogy *n.* study of minerals.
minestrone [mɪnɪ'strəʊnɪ] *n.* type of Italian vegetable soup.
mingle ['mɪŋgl] *v.* to mix.
mingy ['mɪndʒɪ] *adj. inf.* mean/not generous (with money, etc.).
mini 1 ['mɪnɪ] *n.* (a) trade name for a very small British car. (b) miniskirt.
mini 2 *adj. & prefix.* very small.
minibus *n.* small bus holding about twelve people.
minicomputer *n.* small computer, but larger than a micro.
minimarket *n.* small self-service store.
miniskirt *n.* very short skirt.
miniature 1 ['mɪnɪtʃə] *n.* very small model/portrait/painting. **miniature 2** *adj.* very small. **miniaturize** *v.* to produce a very small version of (sth).
minim ['mɪnɪm] *n.* note in music lasting for two crotchets or half as long as a semibreve.
minimum ['mɪnɪməm] *adj. & n.* (*pl.-* ma) smallest possible (quantity).
minimal *adj.* smallest possible.
minimize *v.* to reduce to the smallest amount; to make (sth) seem very small.
minion ['mɪnjən] *n.* low-grade assistant (who flatters his boss).
minister 1 ['mɪnɪstə] *n.* (a) member of a government in charge of a department; the M. of Defence. (b) Protestant clergyman. **minister 2** *v.* to m. to s.o.'s needs = to look after s.o./to take care of s.o. **ministerial** [mɪnɪ'stɪərɪəl] *adj.* referring to a government minister.
ministering *adj.* (angel) who looks after the needs of people. **ministration** [mɪnɪ'streɪʃn] *n.* care given by a priest.
ministry *n.* (a) government; the

Labour Ministry of 1945. (b) government department; offices of a government department; the Ministry of Defence. (c) work of priest/priesthood.
mink [mɪŋk] *n.* (a) small animal whose fur is very valuable; m. farm = farm where these animals are reared. (b) *inf.* mink coat.
minnow ['mɪnəʊ] *n.* small freshwater fish.
minor 1 ['maɪnə] *adj.* (a) lesser; less important Asia M. = Turkey. (b) (musical key) where there are semitones between the second and third, and between the fifth and sixth notes. **minor 2** *n.* young person under the age of 18.
minority [maɪ'nɒrɪtɪ] *n.* (a) number/ quantity less than half of a total; the men are in the m. = there are more women than men; m. government = with fewer members of parliament than the opposition. (b) period when person is less than 18 years old.
minister ['mɪnɪstə] *n.* (usu. in names) large, important church.
minstrel ['mɪnstrəl] *n.* (old) travelling singer or musician. (b) one of a group of performers made up to look like black people.
mint 1 [mɪnt] *n.* (a) factory where coins are made; in m. condition = perfect/ exactly as when it was made; *inf.* a m. of money = a great deal of money. (b) common herb used as flavouring. (c) small white sweet tasting of peppermint.
mint 2 *v.* to make coins.
minuet [mɪnjʊ'et] *n.* slow stately dance.
minus 1 ['maɪnəs] *prep.* less; *inf.* he came m. his wife = without his wife.
minus 2 *n.* sign (-) meaning less; m. 10 degrees (-10°).
minuscule ['mɪnəskjuːl] *adj.* very small.
minute1 ['mɪnɪt] *n* (a) one sixtieth part of an hour or of a degree in an angle; ten minutes past three = 3.10; five minutes to four = 3.55; m. hand = long hand on watch or clock; m. steak = thin slice of beef which can be cooked quickly. (b) very short space of time; he'll be here any m. now = any time now. (c) minutes = notes of what is said at a meeting.
minutebook *n.* book in which minutes of meetings are kept. **minuted**

adj. put in the minutes of a meeting.
minute 2 [maɪˈnjuːt] *adj.* very small.
minutely [maɪˈnjuːtlɪ] *adv.* in great
detail. **minuteness** [maɪˈnjuːtnəs] *n.*
very small size. **minutiae** [mɪˈnjuːʃiː]
*n. pl.*very small details.
minx [mɪŋks] *n.* naughty girl.
miracle [ˈmɪrəkl] *n.* marvellous thing
which happens apparently by the power
of God; very wonderful happening.
miraculous [mɪˈrækjʊləs] *adj.*
wonderful/inexplicable. **miraculously**
adv. wonderfully/inexplicably.
mirage [ˈmɪrɑːʒ] *n.* imaginary image
caused by heat (such as water and palm
trees seen in a desert).
mire [ˈmaɪə] *n.* (formal) muddy place;
mud.
mirror 1 [ˈmɪrə] *n.* glass backed by
metal which reflects an image; driving
m./rear-view m. = mirror inside a car
which enables the driver to see what is
behind without turning his head; m.
image = exact copy, but reversed as in a
mirror. **mirror 2** *v.* to reflect as in a
mirror.
mirth [mɜːθ] *n.* (formal) gaiety/
happiness.
mis- [mɪs] prefix meaning wrongly.
misadventure [mɪsədˈventʃə] *n.*
unlucky accident.
misanthrope, misanthropist
[ˈmɪzənθrəʊp, mɪˈzænθrəpɪst] *n.* person
who dislikes the human race.
misanthropic [mɪzənˈθrɒpɪk] *adj.*
(person) who dislikes the human race.
misanthropy [mɪˈzænθrəpɪ] *n.* dislike
of the human race.
misapply [mɪsəˈplaɪ] *v.* to use (sth)
wrongly.
misapprehend [mɪsæprɪˈhend] *v.* not
to understand. **misapprehension**
[mɪsæprɪˈhenʃən] *n.* not understanding;
labouring under *Am.* = not understanding
the situation correctly.
misappropriate [mɪsəˈprəʊprɪeɪt] *v.* to
use (public money) for your own
purposes. **misappropriation**
[mɪsəprəʊprɪˈeɪʃn] *n.* using public
money for your own purposes.
misbehave [mɪsbɪˈheɪv] *v.* to act
badly/to behave badly. **misbehaviour**
n. bad behaviour.
miscalculate [mɪsˈkælkjʊleɪt] *v.* to
calculate wrongly. **miscalculation**

[mɪskælkjʊˈleɪʃn] *n.* mistake in
calculating.
miscarry [mɪsˈkærɪ] *v.* (a) (of plan) to
go wrong. (b) to produce a baby which is
not sufficiently developed to live.
miscarriage [ˈmɪskærɪdʒ] *n.* (a)
failure (of a scheme); m. of justice =
wrong decision by a court. (b) loss of a
baby during pregnancy.
miscast [mɪsˈkɑːst] *v.* (miscast) to cast
(an actor/actress) in a part which is
unsuitable.
miscellaneous [mɪsəˈleɪnɪəs] *adj.*
varied/mixed. **miscellany** [mɪˈselənɪ]
n. collection of varied things (usu.
varied pieces of writing).
mischance [ˈmɪsˈtʃɑːns] *n.* (formal)
bad luck.
mischief [ˈmɪstʃɪf] *n.* bad behaviour/
bad action; they mean m. = they are
intending to do damage; to make m. =
to make trouble/to make two people angry
with each other; the boy is always
getting into m.. = he's always doing
something naughty. **mischief-maker**
n. person who tries to start trouble.
mischievous [ˈmɪstʃɪvəs] *adj.*
wicked/naughty. **mischievously** *adv.*
in a mischievous way.
mischievousness *n.* tendency to
cause trouble.
misconception [mɪskənˈsepʃən] *n.*
mistaken idea.
misconduct [mɪsˈkɒndʌkt] *n.* bad
conduct/bad behaviour; professional m.
= behaviour which is not acceptable in a
member of a profession
misconstrue [mɪskənˈstruː] *v.* not to
understand. **misconstruction**
[mɪskənˈstrʌkʃn] *n.* wrong
interpretation of an action.
miscount [mɪsˈkaʊnt] *v.* to count wrongly.
miscreant [ˈmɪskrɪənt] *n.* wicked
person/criminal.
misdeed [mɪsˈdiːd] *n.* wicked action.
misdemeanour, *Am.* **misdemeanor**
[mɪsdɪˈmiːnə] *n.* (not very serious)
unlawful act.
misdirect [mɪsdaɪˈrekt] *v.* to give
wrong directions to.
miser [ˈmaɪzə] *n.* person who hoards
money and refuses to spend it.
miserliness *n.* dislike of spending
money. **miserly** *adj.* not wanting to
spend money.

miserable ['mɪzrəbl] *adj.* sad/
unhappy; awful/bad/unpleasant
(weather); very low (salary). **miserably**
adv. sadly/unhappily.

misericord [mɪ'zerɪkɔːd] *n.* seat in a
medieval church which folds back to
show carrying on its underside.

misery ['mɪzərɪ] *n.* sadness; suffering;
her life was sheer m. = was very
unhappy; to put a dog out of its m. =
kill a dog because it is in pain; to put s.o.
out of his m. = to tell s.o. the result/not
to keep s.o. waiting any longer.

misfire [mɪs'faɪə] *v.* not to fire properly;
the car engine is misfiring = is not
igniting the petrol at the right time; his
plan misfired = went wrong.

misfit ['mɪsfɪt] *n.* person who does not
fit in with a group/fit into society.

misfortune [mɪs'fɔːtjuːn] *n.* bad luck.

misgiving [mɪs'gɪvɪŋ] *n.* doubt/fear.

misguided [mɪs'gaɪdɪd] *adj.* badly
advised; wrongly judged; foolish.

misjudge [mɪs'dʒʌdʒ] *v.* to judge
wrongly; to form a wrong opinion about
(s.o./sth).

mislay [mɪs'leɪ] *v.* (mislaid) to put (sth)
down and not to remember where you
have put it. **mislead** [mɪs'liːd] *v.*
(misled) to give (s.o.) wrong
information/to make (s.o.) make a
mistake. **misleading** *adj.* wrong/
erroneous; likely to cause a mistake.

mismanage [mɪsmænɪdʒ] *v.* to
manage wrongly/badly.
mismanagement *n.* bad
management.

mismatch 1 [mɪsmætʃ] *n.* bad match.
mismatch 2 *v.* to match (two
opponents) badly.

misnomer [mɪs'nəʊmə] *n.* wrong
name/wrong term.

misogynist [mɪ'sɒdʒɪnɪst] *n.* man who
dislikes women. **misogyny** *n.* hatred
of women.

misplace [mɪs'pleɪs] *v.* to put in the
wrong place.

misprint ['mɪsprɪnt] *n.* error in
printing.

mispronounce [mɪsprə'naʊns] *v.* to
pronounce wrongly. **mispronunciation**
[mɪsprənʌnsɪ'eɪʃn] *n.* pronouncing
wrongly.

misquote [mɪs'kwəʊt] *v.* to quote
wrongly/incorrectly. **misquotation**
[mɪskwəʊ'teɪʃn] *n.* incorrect quotation.

misread [mɪs'riːd] *v.* (misread) to read
wrongly; to make a mistake when
reading.

misrepresent [mɪsreprɪ'zent] *v.* to
show (sth) wrongly; to give a wrong idea
of (sth). **misrepresentation**
[mɪsreprɪzen'teɪʃn] *n.* distortion of what
s.o. said or wrote.

misrule 1 [mɪs'ruːl] *n.* bad rule/bad
government. **misrule 2** *v.* to rule badly.

miss 1 [mɪs] *n.* (*pl.*-es) (a) failure to hit;
we'll give it a m. = we will not do it/not
go to see it. (b) title of unmarried
woman; Miss Jones. (c) title given to
schoolmistress/used to call a waitress,
etc. **miss 2** *v.* (a) not to hit/see, etc.;
you didn't m. much = there wasn't much
to see/the performance was not very
good. (b) he just missed being killed =
he was very nearly killed. (c) to regret
the absence of (s.o./sth). **missing** *adj.*
absent/lost; stolen. **miss out** *v.* to
omit/to leave (sth) out. **miss out on** *v.*
inf. not to enjoy (sth) because of being
absent.

missal ['mɪsl] *n.* book containing the text
of the Catholic mass and other prayers.

missel [mɪsl] *n.* m. thrush = type of
woodland thrush.

misshapen [mɪs'ʃeɪpn] *adj.* deformed/
oddly shaped.

missile ['mɪsaɪl, [xx] 'mɪsl] *n.* (a)
weapon which is thrown. (b) explosive
rocket which can be guided to its target

mission ['mɪʃn] *n.* (a) aim/purpose for
which s.o. is sent; her m. in life is to help
orphans = her calling/her chosen task.
(b) house/office of a missionary. (c)
group of people sent somewhere with a
particular aim. (d) embassy or consulate.
missionary ['mɪʃənrɪ] *adj. & n.*
(person) whose duty is to try to convert
people to his religion.

missive ['mɪsɪv] n. (formal) letter.
misspell [mɪs'spel] v. (mispelled/ mispelt) to spell wrongly. **mispelling** n. spelling mistake.
misspent ['mɪsspent] adj. (youth) which has been wasted.
misstatement [mɪs'steɪtmənt] n. wrong statement of facts.
missus ['mɪsɪz] n. inf. wife.
mist 1 [mɪst] n. thin fog/haze. **mist 2** v to get covered with mist; to m. up = to become covered with condensation.
mistiness n. being misty. **misty** adj. (-ier, iest) (a) full of mist. (b) vague (memory).
mistake 1 [mɪs'teɪk] n. error; wrong action. **mistake 2** v. (mistook, mistaken) (a) to understand (sth) wrongly. (b) to m. s.o. for s.o. = to assume (s.o.) is s.o. else. **mistaken** adj. wrong. **mistakenly** adv. by mistake/in error.
mister ['mɪstə] n. inf. form of address to a man.
mistime [mɪs'taɪm] v. to choose the wrong time/an inconvenient time to do something.
mistletoe ['mɪzltəʊ] n. parasitic plant which grows on oaks or apple trees, used as a Christmas decoration.
mistook [mɪs'tʊk] v. see mistake.
mistreatment [mɪs'triːtmənt] n. bad treatment (of prisoners, etc.).
mistress ['mɪstrəs] n. (pl.-es) (a) woman in charge/who employs/teaches; she's her own m. = she is independent. (b) woman who has a sexual relationship with a man without being married to him.
mistrust 1 [mɪs'trʌst] n. wariness/lack of trust. **mistrust 2** v. not to trust (s.o.) /to be doubtful about (s.o.). **mistrustful** adj. not trusting.
misunderstand [mɪsʌndə'stænd] v. (misunderstood) not to understand. **misunderstanding** n. wrong understanding/disagreement.
misuse 1 [mɪs'juːs] n. wrong use.
misuse 2 [mɪs'juːz] v. to use (sth) in a wrong way; to treat (s.o.) badly.
mite [maɪt] n (a) very small child. (b) very small creature like a spider, living in stale food.
miter ['maɪtə] n. Am. = mitre.
mitigate ['mɪtɪgeɪt] v. to make (a

crime) less serious. **mitigation** [mɪtɪ'geɪʃn] n. making less serious.
mitosis [maɪ'təʊsɪs] n. cell division
mitre, Am. **miter** ['maɪtə] n. (a) hat worn by bishops and archbishops. (b) (in woodwork) type of sloping joint/ sloping edge. **mitred** adj. sloping (joint/edge).
mitt, mitten [mɪt, 'mɪtn] n. (a) glove without separate fingers. esp. a glove to wash with or to hold hot dishes with. (b) glove which leaves the fingers bare.
mix 1 [mɪks] n. (pl.-es) blend/mingling of several things. **mix 2** v. to blend/to mingle. **mixed** adj. made up of different things put together; a mixed marriage = marriage between two people of different races; (in tennis) mixed doubles = doubles match where a man and woman play against another man and woman; mixed school = school with both boys and girls; I have very mixed feelings about the project = in some ways I am for it and in others I am against it; it's a mixed blessing = in some ways it a good thing, but in others it is not. **mixer** n. (a) machine for mixing. (b) person who fits in well with other people. **mixture** ['mɪkstʃə] n. blend/mingling together; cough m. = liquid medicine to cure a cough. **mix up** v. (a) to confuse; I always mix him up with his brother = I always think he is his brother. (b) to involve. (c) the speaker got all mixed up = he got confused/lost his notes. **mix-up** n. inf. confusion.
mizzenmast ['mɪzənmɑːst] n. mast nearest the stern of a ship. **mizzen** n. sail on a mizzenmast.
ml abbrev. for millilitre.
mm abbrev. for millimetre.
Mn symbol for manganese.
mnemonic [nɪ'mɒnɪk] adj. & n. (rhyme) which helps you to remember certain facts.
Mo symbol for molybdenum.
moan 1 [məʊn] n. (a) low groan. (b) general complaint. **moan 2** v. (a) to make low groan. (b) to complain (about sth). **moaner** n. inf. person who complains.
moat [məʊt] n. wide ditch with water in it, surrounding a castle/old house. **moated** adj. with a moat.

mob 1 [mɒb] n. (a) crowd of unruly people. (b) inf. criminal gang. **mob 2** v. (mobbed) to surround in a wild crowd. **mobster** n. inf. member of a criminal gang.

mobile 1 ['məʊbaɪl, [xx] 'məʊbl] adj. which can move; he is not very m. = he can't walk easily; m. library = library in a van. which travels around from place to place. **mobile 2** n. artistic creation using pieces of metal/paper, etc., which when hung up can move. **mobility** [məʊ'bɪlɪtɪ] n. ability to move. **mobilization** [məʊbɪlaɪ'zeɪʃn] n. grouping of people together (esp. to join the armed forces). **mobilize** ['məʊbɪlaɪz] v. to group (people) together (esp. to join the armed forces).

moccasins ['mɒkəsɪnz] n. pl. soft leather shoes.

mocha ['mɒkə] n. (a) type of coffee from Arabia. (b) coffee and chocolate flavouring.

mock 1 [mɒk] adj. false/imitation; m. examinations = trial examinations carried out before the real ones. **mock 2** v. to laugh at (s.o./sth). **mockery** n. (a) laughing at (s.o./sth). (b) thing which is only a bad imitation. **mocking** adj. & n. laughing at (s.o./sth). **mocking bird** n. bird from the southern United States which imitates the song of other birds. **mock-up** n. scale model of a new product for testing purposes.

mod [mɒd] adj. inf. short for modern. **mod cons** n. pl. modern conveniences (in a house).

mode [məʊd] n. way (of doing sth).

modal adj. & n. (verb such as can, must, etc.) which is used with other verbs, and not alone.

model 1 ['mɒdl] n. & adj. (a) small scale copy. (b) thing which you can take as a perfect example to be copied; artist's m. = person whose job is to sit while an artist draws pictures of him/her. (c) person whose job is to wear new clothes to show them to customers. (d) style of car, etc., produced in a particular period. **model 2** v. (modelled) (a) to make a model; to make shapes (of clay); modelling clay = special clay for sculpture. (b) be modelled his way of walking on that of his father = he imitated his father's way. (c) to wear

(new clothes) to show to customers.

modem ['məʊdem] n. device for sending data by telephone, linking a computer to the telephone lines.

moderate 1 ['mɒdərət] adj. & n. (a) not excessive; middling. (b) (person) without a violent political bias. **moderate 2** ['mɒdəreɪt] v. to diminish/ to make less strong. **moderately** adv. quite/not excessively. **moderation** [mɒdə'reɪʃn] n. not an excessive use; calming down. **moderator** n. (a) chairman of a learned discussion.

modern ['mɒdən] adj. of the present day; not ancient; m. languages = languages which are spoken today. **modernity** [mə'dɜːnɪtɪ] n. being modern. **modernization** [mɒdənaɪzeɪʃn] n. act of modernizing. **modernize** ['mɒdənaɪz] v. to make modern; to renovate.

modest ['mɒdɪst] adj. (a) not boasting; (b) not demanding/not excessive; a m. flat = one which does not look expensive. **modestly** adv. in a modest way. **modesty** n. (a) not being boastful. (b) not being excessive/ demanding.

modicum ['mɒdɪkəm] n. small quantity.

modify ['mɒdɪfaɪ] v. (a) to change/to alter (sth) to fit a different use. (b) to reduce. **modification** [mɒdɪfɪ'keɪʃn] n. change. **modifier** n. thing which modifies; word which qualifies another word.

modish ['məʊdɪʃ] adj. fashionable.

modulate ['mɒdjʊleɪt] v. to change the pitch of a note/a musical key. **modulation** [mɒdjʊ'leɪʃn] n. change of pitch.

module ['mɒdjuːl] n. section of a larger combination; lunar m. = section of a spacecraft which lands on the moon. **modular** adj. made of various modules.

modus operandi ['məʊdəsɒpə'rændɪ] n. way of working. **modus vivendi** ['məʊdəsvɪ'vendɪ] n. informal way of working together.

moggy ['mɒgɪ] n Sl. cat

mogul ['məʊgəl] n. inf. (a) film m. = boss of a film company. (b) bump on a ski slope.

mohair ['məʊheə] n. very soft wool from a type of goat.

moke [məʊk] n. inf. donkey.

moist [mɔɪst] adj. (-er, -est) slightly wet/damp. **moisten** ['mɔɪsn] v. to make moist. **moistness** n. being moist.

moisture ['mɔɪstʃə] n. slight wetness. **moisturizer** ['mɔɪstʃəraɪzə] n. cream which makes the skin softer. **moisturizing** adj. (cream) which makes the skin softer.

molar ['məʊlə] n. large back tooth used for grinding food.

molasses [mə'læsɪz] n. thick black raw syrup removed from unrefined sugar.

mold [məʊld] Am. = mould.

mole [məʊl] n. (a) small black mammal which lives underground. (b) small dark spot on the skin. (c) inf. member of an organization who is in the pay of the opponent/enemy. (d) stone jetty/pier used as a breakwater. (e) standard measurement of the amount of a substance. **molehill** n. little heap of earth pushed up by a mole; to make a mountain out of a m. = to make a fuss about sth which is really trivial.

moleskin n. skin of a mole used for making clothes.

molecule ['mɒlɪkjuːl] n. smallest unit into which a substance can be divided. **molecular** [mə'lekjʊlə] adj. referring to molecules; m. weight = mass of one molecule of a substance compared to that of one atom of carbon.

molest [mə'lest] v. to attack/to beat (s.o.). **molestation** [mɒlɪs'teɪʃn] n. (formal) act of molesting.

mollify ['mɒlɪfaɪ] v. to make (s.o.) feel less annoyed. **mollification** [mɒlɪfɪ'keɪʃn] n. act of mollifying.

mollusc, Am. **mollusk** ['mɒləsk] n. animal with no backbone, but usu. with a shell (such as snails/oysters etc.).

mollycoddle ['mɒlɪkɒdl] v. to spoil (s.o.) /to treat (s.o.) too softly.

Molotov cocktail ['mɒlətɒf'kɒkteɪl] n. handmade bomb, made of a bottle filled with petrol, with a short wick.

molt [məʊlt] Am. = moult.

molten ['məʊltən] adj. not solid; melted.

molybdenum [mɒ'lɪbdənəm] n. (element; Mo) whitish metal.

moment ['məʊmənt] n. (a) very short space of time; at any m. = very soon; at the m. = just now; for the m. = for the time being. (b) importance. **momentarily** adv. for a short space of time. **momentary** adj. shortlived/passing. **momentous** [mə'mentəs] adj. very important. **momentum** [mə'mentəm] n. impetus; movement forwards; to gain/to lose m. = to progress faster/slower.

monarch ['mɒnək] n. king or queen; ruler. **monarchic(al)** [mə'nɑːkɪk(l)] adj. referring to a monarchy. **monarchist** ['mɒnəkɪst] n. supporter of a monarchy. **monarchy** ['mɒnəkɪ] n. system of government with a hereditary ruler such as a king or queen.

monastery ['mɒnəstrɪ] n. group of buildings where monks live. **monastic** [mɒ'næstɪk] adj. referring to a monastery/to monks.

Monday ['mʌndɪ] n. first day of the week/day between Sunday and Tuesday.

monetary ['mʌnɪtərɪ] adj. referring to money or currency. **monetarism** n. belief that inflation can by checked by reducing the amount of money available in the economy. **monetarist** n. person who believes in monetarism.

money ['mʌnɪ] n. coins or notes which are used for buying and selling; to come into m. = to inherit money; we were offered our m. back = a refund of what we had already paid; we ran out of m. = we had no money left. **moneybox** n. box that can be locked and in which you can keep money. **moneyed** adj. rich. **moneylender** n. person who lends money. **money order** n. order for passing money from one person to another via the post office. **moneyspinner** n. inf. book/record, etc., which sells very well.

mongol ['mɒngəl] adj. & n. (person) born with mongolism. **mongolism.** n. defect in a person from birth of which the symptoms are slanting eyes, flattened skull and low intelligence.

mongoose ['mɒnguːs] n. small tropical mammal which kills snakes.

mongrel ['mʌngrəl] adj. & n. not pure-bred (dog) /(dog) of mixed breeds.

monitor 1 ['mɒnɪtə] *n.* (a) person who watches/surveys the progress of sth. (b) senior pupil (in a school) who has a particular duty to perform. (c) apparatus for checking the progress of sth, esp. the screen of a computer or a small television screen in a television studio.

monitor 2 *v.* to check/to survey (the progress of sth); monitoring station = radio station specially for listening to foreign broadcasts and obtaining information from them.

monk [mʌŋk] *n.* man who is a member of a religious group and lives in a monastery. **monkish** *adj.* like a monk.

monkey 1 ['mʌŋkɪ] *n.* *usu.* a tropical mammal which looks rather like a man. but which normally has a tail; *inf.* naughty child; m. nut = peanut; m. puzzle tree = type of tropical pine tree with spiky branches; m. wrench = large spanner with an adjustable grip.

monkey 2 *inf.* to m. about = to play/ to mess around.

mono 1 ['mɒnəʊ] prefix meaning single. **mono 2** *n. & adj.* not stereophonic; (machine/record) which reproduces sound through a single channel.

monochrome ['mɒnəkrəʊm] *adj. & n.* (in a) single colour, *usu.* black and white.

monocle ['mɒnəkl] *n.* eye glass/single lens worn to correct sight. **monocular** [mɒ'nɒkjuːlə] *adj.* (vision) as with one eye, with no sense of depth.

monogamy [mə'nɒgəmɪ] *n.* system of marriage to one person at a time. **monogamous** *adj.* (marriage) to one husband or wife.

monogram ['mɒnəgræm] *n.* design based on the initials of your name. **monogrammed** *adj.* with your initials on it.

monograph ['mɒnəgrɑːf] *n.* short book about a specialized subject.

monolith ['mɒnəlɪθ] *n.* single standing stone. **monolithic** [mɒnə'lɪθɪk] *adj.* solid/heavy; changeless.

monologue ['mɒnəlɒg] *n.* long speech by one actor alone on the stage.

monomania [mɒnə'meɪnɪə] *n.* mania about a single thing.

mononucleosis [mɒnənjuːklɪ'əʊsɪs] *n. Am.* glandular fever.

monophonic [mɒnə'fɒnɪk] *adj.* not

stereophonic; (record) with sound coming from a single channel.

monoplane ['mɒnəpleɪn] *n.* plane with one pair of wings.

monopoly [mə'nɒpəlɪ] *n.* system where one person or company supplies all needs in one area without any competition. **monopolization** [mənɒpəlaɪ'zeɪʃn] *n.* creating of a monopoly. **monopolize** [mə'nɒpəlaɪz] *v.* to create a monopoly; to use (sth) entirely for yourself; to m. the conversation = to do all the talking and not let anyone else speak.

monorail ['mɒnəreɪl] *n.* train which runs on a single rail.

monosyllable ['mɒnəsɪləbl] *n.* word which only has one syllable. **monosyllabic** [mɒnəsɪ'læbɪk] *adj.* (word) with only one syllable; (conversation) using only monosyllables.

monotheism [mɒnəʊ'θiːɪzəm] *n.* belief that there is only one god.

monotone ['mɒnətəʊn] *n.* flat/level tone of voice. **monotonous** [mə'nɒtənəs] *adj.* not varied/not changing/boring. **monotonously** *adv.* in a monotonous way. **monotony** *n.* lack of variety.

monoxide [mə'nɒksaɪd] *n.* chemical compound containing one atom of oxygen.

monsignor [mɒn'siːnjə] *n.* title given to an important priest in the Roman Catholic church.

monsoon [mɒn'suːn] *n.* (a) season of wind and rain in the tropics. (b) wind blowing in the Indian Ocean.

monster 1 ['mɒnstə] *n.* (a) horrible/ strange creature. (b) very large and terrifying animal/thing. (c) cruel/wicked person. **monster 2** *adj.* very large. **monstrosity** [mɒn'strɒsɪtɪ] *n.* horrible/ strange/ugly thing. **monstrous** ['mɒnstrəs] *adj.* huge/ugly/horrible.

montage [mɒn'tɑːʒ] *n.* picture/piece of music, etc., made of several items brought together; action of putting several items together to make a picture/ piece of music, etc.

month [mʌnθ] *n.* one of the twelve periods which form a year. **monthly 1** *adj. & adv.* occurring every month. **monthly 2** *n.* magazine which appears each month.

monument ['mɒnjʊmənt] n. (a) (to s.o.) stone/building/statue etc., erected in memory of s.o. who is dead. (b) building which is very old. **monumental** [mɒnjʊ'mentl] adj. (a) very large. (b) referring to a monument; m. mason = person who makes gravestones.

moo 1 [muː] n. sound made by a cow.

moo 2 v. to make a sound like a cow.

mooch [muːtʃ] v. (about) to go about aimlessly.

mood [muːd] n. (a) general feeling. (b) bad temper. (c) group of forms of a verb which indicates a fact, a possibility or a condition. **moodily** adv. in a moody way. **moodiness** n. gloomy feeling; quick change from good to bad temper. **moody** adj. (-ier, -iest) often gloomy/ often bad-tempered; changing quickly from good to bad temper.

moon [muːn] n. satellite which travels round a planet, esp. the one which travels round the earth each month and shines with reflected light from the sun; once in a blue m. = very rarely. **moonbeam** n. ray of light from the moon. **moonlight 1** n. light from the moon. **moonlight 2** v to do a second job (for cash). **moonlighter** n. person who does a second job for cash. **moonlighting** n. inf. doing a second job (usu. in the evening) apart from your regular work. **moonlit** adj. lit by light from the moon. **moonshine** n. inf. (a) nonsense. (b) illegal alcohol. **moonstone** n. semi-precious stone with a white shine.

moor 1 ['mʊə,mɔː] n. uncultivated land covered with low shrubs. **moor 2** v. to attach (a boat) to a quayside/to a buoy. **moorhen** n. common water bird. **mooring** n. (a) action of attaching a boat. (b) moorings = place where a boat is moored; ropes; etc., used to moor a boat. **moorland** n. area of uncultivated land covered with low shrubs.

moose [muːs] n. (pl.moose) American elk.

moot 1 [muːt] adj. m. point = question which is open to discussion. **moot 2** v. to raise (a question/a suggestion).

mop 1 [mɒp] n. brush for washing floors with a head made of soft string or foam rubber; m. of hair = long and untidy hair. **mop 2** v (mopped) (a) to wash the floor, using a mop. (b) to wipe.

mop up v. (a) to clear up (liquid) using a mop. (b) to clear up (pockets of resistance).

mope [məʊp] v. to be miserable/ gloomy. **moped** ['məʊped] n. two-wheeled cycle with a low-powered motor.

moquette [mɒ'ket] n. thick cloth for covering chairs, etc.

moraine [mə'reɪn] n. heap of gravel, etc., left by a glacier.

moral 1 ['mɒrəl] adj. (a) referring to right and wrong in human behaviour. (b) referring to good human behaviour; m. support = encouragement without active help. **moral 2** n. lesson to be drawn from a story. **moral 3** morals = personal character and way of behaving. **moralist** n. person who criticizes low moral standards. **morality** [mə'rælɪtɪ] n. correct way of behaving; sense of moral standards. **moralize** ['mɒrəlaɪz] v. to draw a lesson from a story or event. **morally** adv. according to correct human behaviour. **morale** [mə'rɑːl] n. feeling of confidence.

morass [mə'ræs] n. (pl.-es) (a) deep swamp/marsh. (b) mass of things which prevent any progress.

moratorium [mɒrə'tɔːrɪəm] n. (pl.-ia) temporary ban.

moray eel [mɒreɪ'iːl] n. type of large eel.

morbid ['mɔːbɪd] adj. (a) interested in death/unpleasant things. (b) connected with disease. **morbidity** [mɔː'bɪdɪtɪ] n. sickly interest in death/unpleasant things. **morbidly** adv. in a morbid way.

mordant ['mɔːdənt] adj. (formal) cruel (sarcasm).

more 1 [mɔː] adj. extra/additional. **more 2** n. extra/additional amount. **more 3** adv. (a) additionally/to a larger extent. (b) (forming comparative) she is m. intelligent than her brother. (c) not any m. = no longer; m. or less = approximately/practically. **moreover** [mɔː'rəʊvə] adv. besides; in addition.

morganatic [mɔːgə'nætɪk] adj. m. marriage = marriage of a king or queen to s.o. of lower rank who does not take their title.

morgue [mɔːg] n. building where dead bodies are kept before burial.

moribund ['mɒrɪbʌnd] adj. dying; going out of existence.

Mormon ['mɔːmən] adj. & n. (member) of a Christian sect., founded in the USA.

mornay ['mɔːneɪ] adj. cooked with a cheese sauce.

morning ['mɔːnɪŋ] n. early part of the day. before 12 noon; 4 in the m. = 4 a.m. the m. train which leaves every morning.

morocco [mə'rɒkəʊ] n. fine soft leather.

moron ['mɔːrɒn] n. (a) adult with the intelligence of a child. (b) stupid person. **moronic** [mə'rɒnɪk] adj. stupid.

morose [mə'rəʊs] adj. gloomy and bad tempered. **morosely** adv. in a morose way. **moroseness** n. being morose.

morphia, morphine ['mɔːfɪə, 'mɔːfiːn] n. drug which kills pain and makes you go to sleep.

morphology [mɔː'fɒlədʒɪ] n. (a) study of the way in which words change in the plural or according to gender or conjugation. (b) study of the forms of plants or animals. **morphological** [mɔːfə'lɒdʒɪkl] adj. referring to morphology.

morris ['mɒrɪs] n. m. dance = old English dance, danced by men in white clothes with bells on their legs.

morrow ['mɒrəʊ] n. (old) next day.

Morse code [mɔːs'kəʊd] n. system of dots and dashes for sending messages.

morsel ['mɔːsl] n. small piece.

mortal 1 ['mɔːtl] adj. (a) causing death; m. enemy = deadly enemy. (b) referring to the body; m. remains = corpse **mortal 2** n. human being. **mortality** [mɔː'tælɪtɪ] n. (a) human state. (b) m. rate = number of deaths (as a percentage of population). **mortally** adv. so as to cause death.

mortar ['mɔːtə] n. (a) cement mixture for holding together bricks or stones when building. (b) bowl for crushing things with a pestle. (c) short cannon. **mortar-board** n. black cap with a square top worn at ceremonies by people with university degrees.

mortgage 1 ['mɔːgɪdʒ] n. agreement whereby s.o. lends money on the security of a property; money lent on the security of property; second m. = further loan obtained on a property which is already mortgaged. **mortgage 2** v. to give a

property) as security for a loan.

mortgagee [mɔːgɪ'dʒiː] n. person who loans money on mortgage. **mortgagor** [mɔːgɪ'dʒɔː] n. person who borrows money on a mortgage.

mortice ['mɔːtɪs] n. hole cut in the end of a piece of wood into which another piece (a tenon) fits to form a joint; m. lock = lock which is fitted into a door.

mortician [mɔː'tɪʃn] n. Am. undertaker.

mortify ['mɔːtɪfaɪ] v. to humiliate. **mortification** [mɔːtɪfɪ'keɪʃn] n. feeling of shame/humiliation.

mortise ['mɔːtɪs] n. = mortice.

mortuary ['mɔːtjʊərɪ] n. place where dead bodies are kept before burial.

mosaic [mə'zeɪɪk] n. tiny pieces of coloured stone stuck to a wall or floor in patterns.

Moslem ['mɒzləm] adj. & n. = Muslim.

mosque [mɒsk] n. religious building for Muslims.

mosquito [məs'kiːtəʊ] n. (pl.-oes) small flying insect which sucks blood; m. net = thin net spread over a bed to prevent mosquitoes biting at night.

moss [mɒs] n. (pl.-es) primitive green plant growing in compact low clumps on the ground or on stones. **mossy** adj. covered with moss.

most 1 [məʊst] adj. the largest number/ largest quantity (of sth). **most 2** n. the largest number/largest quantity; to make the m. of = get as much profit/value from sth as possible. **most 3** adv. to the largest extent (a) (forming superlative) the m. intelligent child. (b) (intensive) very. **mostly** adv. in most cases/most often.

MOT [eməʊ'tiː] n. MOT (test) = mechanical test for cars over three years old.

motel [məʊ'tel] n. hotel for car drivers where there is parking space for every room.

motet [məʊ'tet] n. music for a small group of unaccompanied singers.

moth [mɒθ] n. flying insect with large wings like a butterfly, but flying mainly at night; clothes m. = type of moth of which the grub eats wool or fur.

mothball v. inf. to store (a ship, etc.) in working order for future use.

mothballs n. pl. balls of a chemical substance put among clothes to keep moths away; in m. = stored for future use. **motheaten** *adj.* full of holes made by moths; old and decrepit.

mother 1 ['mʌðə] *n.* female parent; m. country = country where you or your ancestors were born; m. tongue = first language a child speaks; M. superior = woman head of a religious community. **mother 2** *v.* to look after (s.o.) very attentively. **motherhood** *n.* being a mother. **Mothering Sunday** *n.* festival commemorating mothers. **mother-in-law** *n.* (*pl.* mothers-in-law) mother of your wife or husband; mother in law's tongue = type of house plant with a few tall stiff vertical leaves. **motherless** *adj.* with no mother. **motherly** *adj.* maternal/like a mother. **mother of pearl** *n.* shiny substance found on the inside of oyster shells.

motif [məʊ'ti:f] *n.* distinctive repeating pattern in a design/in a piece of music.

motion 1 ['məʊʃn] *n.* (a) movement/act of moving; in m. = moving. (b) gesture/ movement; to go through the motions = to do sth for the sake of appearances, without believing in it. (c) bowel movement. (d) proposal which is to be put to the vote (at a meeting); to second a.m. = to support the person who proposed the motion. **motion 2** *v.* to make a gesture. **motionless** *adj.* still/ not moving.

motive 1 ['məʊtɪv] *n.* reason for doing sth. **motive 2** *adj.* which makes sth move. **motivate** ['məʊtɪveɪt] *v.* to make (s.o.) do sth; to encourage (s.o.) to do sth; highly motivated = eager. **motivation** [məʊtɪ'veɪʃn] *n.* reason for doing sth/encouragement to do sth.

motley ['mɒtlɪ] *adj.* varied; of varied sorts of colours.

motocross ['məʊtəʊkrɒs] *n.* motorcycle race over rough ground.

motor 1 ['məʊtə] *n.* (a) machine which causes motion; engine. (b) car; m. show = show where new models of cars are shown to the public. **motor 2** *v.* to travel in a car. **motor 3** *adj.* (a) using a motor; motor mower. (b) (nerve) which links the brain to the muscles, so causing motion; m. neurone disease = disease of the nerves which control the muscles. **motorbike** *n. inf.* motorcycle. **motorboat** *n.* small boat with a motor.

motorcade *n. Am.* official procession of cars. **motorcar** *n.* car. **motorcycle** *n.* two-wheeled cycle powered by a motor. **motorcyclist** *n.* person riding a motorcycle. **motoring** *n.* driving of a car; school of m. = driving school. **motorist** *n.* driver of a car. **motorize** *v.* to provide (sth) with an engine; to equip (s.o.) with motor transport. **motorway** *n.* special road for high-speed traffic with very few exist and entry points.

mottled ['mɒtld] *adj.* spotted with different colours.

motto ['mɒtəʊ] *n.* (*pl.*-oes) (a) short phrase which is used to sum up an attitude. (b) amusing phrase on a piece of paper inside a Christmas cracker.

mould, *Am.* **mold 1** [məʊld] *n.* (a) soft earth; leaf m. = soft earth formed from dead leaves. (b) hollow shape into which a liquid is poured, so that when the liquid becomes hard it takes that shape; jelly m. = shape for making jelly. (c) greyish powdery fungus. **mould 2** *v.* to shape (sth). **moulder 1** *n.* person who moulds. **moulder 2** *v.* to rot away. **mouldiness** *n.* being mouldy/rotten. **moulding** *n.* thing which has been moulded. **mouldy** *adj.* rotten/covered with mould.

moult, *Am.* **molt** [məʊlt] *v.* to lose feathers/fur.

mound [maʊnd] *n.* small heap/hill.

mount 1 [maʊnt] *n.* (a) (usu. in names) mountain. (b) cardboard frame for a picture. (c) horse/donkey etc., on which a rider sits. **mount 2** *v.* (a) to climb on to (sth) to rise; mounted police = police on horseback. (b) to m. guard over = to stand on guard to protect sth. (c) to set (sth) in a cardboard frame/in a metal ring/brooch etc. (d) to organize (an expedition). **Mountie** *n. inf.* member of the Royal Canadian Mounted Police. **mount up** *v.* to rise/to increase.

mountain ['maʊntn] *n.* (a) very high land; m. sheep = sheep which are specially bred to live on mountains; m. ash = common northern tree with red berries. (b) large amount; butter m. = large quantity of butter stockpiled by governments because of overproduction. **mountaineer** [maʊntə'nɪə] *n.* person who climbs mountains for pleasure.

mountaineering *n.* climbing of mountains as a sport. **mountainous** *adj.* (area) full of mountains; very high (waves). **mountebank** ['maʊntɪbæŋk] *n.* person who persuades people to pay money by talking cleverly.

mourn [mɔːn] *v.* to regret (sth).

mourner *n.* person who grieves for s.o. who has died; the mourners = people attending a funeral. **mournful** *adj.* very sad. **mournfully** *adv.* in a very sad way. **mourning** *n.* (a) period of time when one grieves over the death of a relative or friend. (b) dark clothes worn as a mark of respect for someone who has died.

mouse [maʊs] *n.* (*pl.* mice[maɪs]) (a) small rodent with long tail, often living in houses. (b) device which is held in the hand and moved across a flat surface, used to control a cursor on a computer monitor. **mousehole** *n.* small hole in which mice live. **mouser** *n.* the cat is a good m. = good at catching mice. **mousetrap** *n.* trap for catching mice; *inf.* m. cheese = strong/old/inferior cheese. **mousy** *adj.* (a) small and insignificant (person). (b) brownish-grey (colour).

moussaka ['muːsækæ] *n.* Greek dish, made of aubergines and minced meat.

mousse [muːs] *n.* light food made of whipped eggs, cream and flavouring.

moustache, *Am.* **mustache** [mə'stɑːʃ, [xx] 'mʌstæʃ] *n.* hair grown on the upper lip.

mouth 1 [maʊθ] *n.* (a) part of the head through which you take in food and drink and through which you speak. (b) wide entrance; m. of a river = place where a river enters the sea. **mouth 2** [maʊð] *v.* to move the mouth as if speaking, without making any sound; to speak without being heard. **mouthful** *n.* (a) quantity contained in the mouth. (b) *inf.* complicated word/phrase. **mouthorgan** *n.* small musical instrument played by blowing with a series of small valves giving different notes. **mouthpiece** *n.* (a) part of a musical instrument which goes into the mouth. (b) person who speaks on behalf of s.o. **mouthwash** *n.* antiseptic solution for clearing the inside of the mouth. **mouthwatering** *adj.* very

delicious.

move 1 [muːv] *n.* (a) action of changing place; movement; get a m. on! = hurry up; *inf.* we must make a m. = we must leave. (b) movement (of a piece in chess); what's the next m.? = what do we have to do next?. (c) changing of place of residence. **move 2** *v.* (a) to change the position (of sth); to change position; don't m.! = stand still! *inf.* we must be moving = we must leave. (b) to leave one place to go to live in another. (c) to change the feelings of (s.o.). (d) to propose (a motion in a debate). **movable, moveable** *adj.* which can be moved. **move about** *v.* (a) to change (sth) from one place to another. (b) to wander about. **move away** *v.* to change to another place further away; to change (sth) to a position further away; we are moving away from London = we are leaving London to live in another town. **move back** *v.* (a) to go backwards; to change (sth) to a place further back. (b) to return to a previous place. **move forward** *v.* to go forward; to make (s.o.) go to a place further forward. **move in** *v.* to settle with furniture in a new house. **movement** *n.* (a) action of changing position/of not being still. (b) mechanism (of a clock). (c) main part of a large piece of music. (d) group of people working towards a certain aim. **move off** *v.* to go away; the train moved off = began to leave. **move on** *v.* to go forward; to make (s.o.) go forward. **mover** *n.* (a) person who moves furniture from one house to another. (b) person who proposes a motion in a debate. **movie** *n. Am.* cinema film. **moving** *adj.* (a) which changes position/which is not still; m. staircase = escalator. (b) which affects your feelings.

mow [maʊ] *v.* (has mown) to cut (grass). **mow down** *v.* to kill/to slaughter. **mower** *n.* (a) person who cuts grass. (b) machine which cuts grass; motor m. = lawnmower powered by a motor.

MP [em'piː] *n.* Member of parliament.
mpg abbrev. for miles per gallon.
mph abbrev. for miles per hour.
Mr ['mɪstə] *n.* title given to a man. **Mrs** ['mɪsɪz] *n.* title given to a married

woman. **Ms** [mʌz, mɪz] *n.* title given to a woman (married or unmarried).
much 1 [mʌtʃ] *adj.* a lot of. **much 2** *adv.* (more/most) to a great extent/very; m. the most expensive = by far the most expensive; *inf.* it's a bit m. ! = it's quite unreasonable! m. to my amazement = to my great surprise. **much 3** *n.* a lot; *inf.* not up to m. = not very good.
muck 1 [mʌk] *n.* dirt; manure. **muck 2** *v.* to m. out of stable = to clean a stable; *inf.* to m. about with = to play about with; *inf.* to m. up = to ruin; *inf.* m. in together = cooperate in the work.
muckraking *n.* discovering and publishing scandalous stories about famous people. **mucky** *adj.* (-ier, -iest) dirty; covered with muck.
mucus [ˈmjuːkəs] *n.* shiny substance which coats the inside of cavities of the body. **mucous** *adj.* referring to mucus; m. membrane = wet membrane which lines inside passages of the body.
mud [mʌd] *n.* very wet earth.
muddiness *n.* being muddy. **muddy 1** *adj.* (-ier, -iest) full of mud; covered with mud. **muddy 2** *v.* to put mud on sth; to m. the waters = to stir up trouble/ confusion. **mudflap** *n.* flap hanging behind the wheel of a car to prevent mud and water being splashed. **mudflats** *n. pl.* flat muddy land covered by the sea at high tide. **mudguard** *n.* strip of metal over the wheel on a bicycle to stop mud and water being splashed. **mudpack** *n.* paste put on the face to improve the texture of the skin. **mudslinging** *n.* insults.
muddle 1 [ˈmʌdl] *n.* confusion/ mixture. **muddle 2** *v.* to confuse/to mix up. **muddleheaded** *adj.* confused. **muddle through** *v.* to get through one's business/to succeed in a muddled way.
muesli [ˈmjuːzlɪ] *n.* breakfast food of flakes of cereal/dried fruit, etc. eaten with milk.
muezzin [muːˈezɪn] *n.* person who calls Muslims to prayer.
muff 1 [mʌf] *n.* warm covering for a particular part of the body, esp. the hands. **muff 2** *v.* to do (sth) badly.
muffin [ˈmʌfɪn] *n.* small round cake eaten warm with butter.
muffle [ˈmʌfl] *v.* (a) to wrap up in

cloths. (b) to deaden (a loud noise).
muffler *n.* (a) long scarf. (b) *Am.* silencer (on car exhaust).
mufti [ˈmʌftɪ] *n. inf.* in m. = in civilian cloths; not in uniform.
mug 1 [mʌg] *n.* (a) large glass/cup with a handle. (b) *inf.* stupid person/person who is easily taken in. (c) *inf.* face. **mug 2** *v.* (mugged) (a) *inf.* to m. up a subject. = to study a subject very hard at the last minute. (b) to attack and rob (in the street). **mugger** *n.* person who attacks and robs s.o. in the street.
mugging *n.* robbery with violence (in the street). **mug shot** *n. inf.* photograph of s.o.'s face. **muggins** [ˈmʌgɪnz] *n. inf.* silly fool. **muggy** [ˈmʌgɪ] *adj. inf.* warm and wet (weather).
mulatto [mjuːˈlætəʊ] *n.* (*pl.*-os) person of mixed Negro and White race.
mulberry [ˈmʌlbərɪ] *n.* soft purple fruit; tree which bears this fruit.
mulch 1 [mʌltʃ] *n.* (*pl.*-es) covering of manure/rotten leaves, etc., spread on the ground to improve the soil. **mulch 2** *v.* to spread mulch on (the ground).
mulct [mʌlkt] *v.* to take money away from (s.o.).
mule [mjuːl] *n.* (a) hybrid between a donkey and a horse; obstinate person. (b) light shoe with an open heel. **muleteer** [mjuːləˈtɪə] *n.* person who drives mules carrying loads. **mulish** *adj.* obstinate/ difficult to deal with.
mull [mʌl] *v.* to heat (wine) with spices/ sugar, etc. **mull over** *v.* to ponder/to think about (sth).
mullah [ˈmʊlə] *n.* Muslim religious thinker.
mullet [ˈmʌlɪt] *n.* small sea fish.
mulligatawny [mʌlɪgəˈtɔːnɪ] *n.* hot soup made with curry.
mullion [ˈmʌljən] *n.* vertical (wooden/ metal) bar between panes of glass in a window.
multi- [ˈmʌltɪ] prefix meaning many.
multicoloured [ˈmʌltɪkʌləd] *adj.* with many colours.
multifarious [mʌltɪˈfeərɪəs] *adj.* very varied/in many different types.
multilateral [mʌltɪˈlætərəl] *adj.* between more than two partners.
multimillionaire [mʌltɪmɪljəˈneə] *n.* person who has several million pounds.

multinational [mʌltɪ'næʃnl] *adj. & n.* (company) which operates in several different countries.

multiple 1 ['mʌltɪpl] *adj.* many/ repeated; m. store = company with many shops in several towns; m. scissors = diseases of the nervous system, which gets progressively worse. **multiple 2** *n.* (a) number which contains another number several times exactly. (b) repeated groups of the same number of sth; sold in multiples of five = you can buy five, ten, fifteen, etc.

multiplication [mʌltɪplɪ'keɪʃn] *n.* action of multiplying; m. sign (X) = sign used to show that numbers are to be multiplied; m. tables = lists of figures to learn by heart how each number is multiplied. **multiplicity** [mʌltɪ'plɪsɪtɪ] *n.* vast and varied mass. **multiply** ['mʌltɪplaɪ] *v.* (a) to calculate the sum of several numbers repeated a stated number of times. (b) to increase in number.

multiracial [mʌltɪ'reɪʃl] *adj.* (society) whose members comes from various races.

multistorey ['mʌltɪstɔːrɪ] *adj.* with many storeys.

multitude ['mʌltɪtjuːd] *n.* great number/crowd. **multitudinous** [mʌltɪ'tjuːdɪnəs] *adj.* in very large numbers.

mum 1 [mʌm] *adj.* silent; he kept m. = he didn't say a word. **mum 2** *n. inf.* mother.

mumble 1 ['mʌmbl] *n.* speech which you can't understand because it is indistinct. **mumble 2** *v.* not to speak distinctly.

mumbo-jumbo [mʌmbəʊ'dʒʌmbəʊ] *n.* nonsense/meaningless talk.

mummer ['mʌmə] *n.* (old) member of a group acting a traditional Christmas play.

mummy ['mʌmɪ] *n.* (a) *inf.* mother. (b) corpse preserved with ointments and bandages as in Ancient Egypt. **mummify** *v.* to preserve (a dead body) in a perfect state.

mumps [mʌmps] *n.* infectious illness with swelling on either side of the neck.

munch [mʌnʃ] *v.* to chew (sth crisp or dry) with large regular movements of the jaws.

mundane [mʌn'deɪn] *adj.* ordinary.

municipal [mjuː'nɪsɪpl] *adj.* referring to a town; m. gardens = park which belongs to a town; m. buildings = town hall. **municipality** [mjuːnɪsɪ'pælɪtɪ] *n.* self-governing town.

munificence [mjuː'nɪfɪsns] *n.* (formal) great generosity. **munificent** *adj.* (formal) extremely generous.

munitions [mjuː'nɪʃnz] *n. pl.* weapons and ammunition.

mural 1 ['mjʊərəl] *adj.* referring to walls. **mural 2** *n.* painting on a wall.

murder 1 ['mɜːdə] *n.* (a) illegal killing of s.o. (b) *inf.* awful or unpleasant thing. **murder 2** *v.* (a) to kill (s.o.) illegally. (b) *inf.* to ruin (a song) by singing it badly. **murderer** *n.* person who has committed a murder. **murderess** ['mɜːdrəs] *n.* woman who has committed a murder. **murderous** ['mɜːdərəs] *adj.* likely to kill.

murk [mɜːk] *n.* (formal) darkness/ gloominess. **murkiness** *n.* being dark/ gloomy. **murky** ['mɜːkɪ] *adj.* (-ier, iest) dark/gloomy (water).

murmur 1 ['mɜːmə] *n.* low whisper of voice/low sound. **murmur 2** *v.* to speak in a low voice; to complain in a low voice. **murmuring** *n.* (a) speaking in a low voice. (b) murmurings = grumblings/complaints.

muscat ['mʌskæt] *n.* type of sweet grape; wine made from this grape.

muscatel [mʌskə'tel] *n.* type of sweet black grape, usually dried.

muscle 1 ['mʌsl] *n.* spring-like parts of the body which allow the limbs to move; he's flexing his muscles = he's preparing to fight/to do sth great. **muscle 2** *v. inf.* to m. in on sth = to push yourself forward to take part in sth which is organized by a s.o. else. **muscular** ['mʌskjʊlə] *adj.* referring to muscles; m. dystrophy = disease causing gradual weakening of the muscles.

muse 1 [mjuːz] *n. (formal)* goddess who inspires poets, musicians, etc. **muse 2** *v.* to think deeply; to day dream.

museum [mjuː'zɪəm] *n.* building in which a collection of valuable or rare objects are put on show permanently.

mush [mʌʃ] *n.* soft half-liquid mess. **mushiness** *n.* being mushy. **mushy**

adj. (a) soft and partly liquid. (b) *inf.* very sentimental.

mushroom 1 ['mʌʃruːm] *n.* edible round white fungus. **mushroom 2** *v.* to spring up rapidly.

music ['mjuːzɪk] *n.* sounds made by playing instruments or singing; to face the m. = to face criticism. **musical 1** *adj.* referring to music; (person) who likes music/plays music a lot; m. chairs = (i) game where people try to sit on chairs when the music stops, with one chair and one person less each time; (ii) *inf.* continual movement from office to office/form job to job. **musical 2** *n.* (also musical comedy) play with songs and popular music. **musicalbox** *n.* small box with a clockwork motor which plays a tune when the box is opened. **musically** *adv.* in a musical way. **music hall** *n.* theatre specializing in verity shows. **musician** [mjuːˈzɪʃn] *n.* person who plays music professionally/skilfully. **musicology** [mjuːzɪˈkɒlədʒɪ] *n.* academic study of music. **musicologist** *n.* specialist in the study of music.

musk [mʌsk] *n.* perfume obtained from glands of deer. **musk ox** *n.* large wild ox, found in North America. **musk-rat** *n.* musquash. **musk-rose** *n.* old fashioned scented rose. **musky** *adj.* with a smell like musk.

muskeg ['mʌskeg] *n.* (in Canada) marsh.

musket ['mʌskɪt] *n.* early portable gun with a long barrel. **musketeer** *n.* soldier who was armed with a musket.

Muslim ['mʊzlɪm] *adj. & n.* (person) following the religion of the prophet Mohammed.

muslin ['mʌzlɪn] *n.* very fine thin cotton cloth.

musquash ['mʌskwɒʃ] *n.* American water rat with fine fur.

muss [mʌs] *v. Am. inf.* to ruffle (hair, etc).

mussel ['mʌsl] *n.* mollusc with a dark blue shell, whose soft parts can be eaten.

must 1 [mʌst] *v.* (a) used with verbs to mean it is necessary. (b) used with verbs to mean it is probable; it m. be the doctor = it cannot be anyone else. **must 2** *n.* (a) *inf.* very necessary thing. (b) grape juice.

mustache ['mʌstæʃ] *n. Am.* = moustache.

mustang ['mʌstæŋ] *n.* wild American horse.

mustard ['mʌstəd] *n.* (a) sharp-tasting yellow powder made from crushed seeds; paste made from this powder; m. gas = poisonous gas which burns the skin; m. yellow = dull yellow colour. (b) plant whose seeds make mustard powder; m. and cress = seedlings of the mustard plant, together with seedlings of cress, eaten as a salad.

muster 1 ['mʌstə] *n.* gathering; parade and inspection of soldiers; to pass m. = to be acceptable. **muster 2** *v.* to gather together.

musty ['mʌstɪ] *adj.* (-ier, -iest) smelling damp/rotten/stale; smelling old. **mustiness** *n.* rotten/stale smell.

mutate [mjuːˈteɪt] *v.* to change genetically. **mutability** [mjuːtəˈbɪlɪtɪ] *n.* being mutable. **mutable** *adj.* which is likely to change/which can be changed. **mutant** ['mjuːtənt] *n.* animal/plant which has changed genetically. **mutation** [mjuːˈteɪʃn] *n.* genetic change.

mute 1 [mjuːt] *adj.* (a) silent/dumb (person). (b) letter which is not pronounced. **mute 2** *n.* (a) person who cannot speak/who is dumb; deaf m. = person who cannot hear or speak. (b) device used to soften the sound of a musical instrument. **mute 3** *v.* to soften the sound of (a musical instrument). **mutely** *adv.* silently.

mutilate ['mjuːtɪleɪt] *v.* to cut off a limb/an ear, etc., from (s.o.); to damage (an object). **mutilation** [mjuːtɪˈleɪʃn] *n.* loss of a limb; great damage.

mutiny 1 ['mjuːtɪnɪ] *n.* uprising, esp. of soldiers/sailors, etc., against the orders of their officers. **mutiny 2** *v.* to refuse to carry out orders/to rise up against officers. **mutineer** [mjuːtɪˈnɪə] *n.* person who mutinies. **mutinous** ['mjuːtɪnəs] *adj.* likely to mutiny/rebellious. **mutinously** *adv.* in a mutinous way.

mutt [mʌt] *n. Sl.* (a) idiot/stupid person. (b) dog.

mutter 1 ['mʌtə] *n.* low indistinct way of speaking. **mutter 2** *v.* to mumble/to speak in a low and indistinct voice.

muttering *n.* speaking indistinctly.
mutton [ˈmʌtn] *n.* meat of a sheep.
mutual [ˈmjuːtjʊəl] *adj.* felt/done by two people to each other; between two people; belonging to two people; our m. friend = the friend of both of us; by m. consent = with the agreement of both parties. **mutually** *adv.* to two people; by two people.
Muzak [ˈmjuːzæk] *n.* trade mark for system of playing recorded music in public places.
muzzle 1 [ˈmʌzl] *n.* (a) nose of an animal. (b) straps placed around the mouth of a dog to prevent it biting. (c) mouth of a gun. **muzzle 2** *v.* to tie up the mouth of (a dog) to prevent it biting; to m. the press = to stop newspapers from printing what they want.
muzzy [ˈmʌzɪ] *adj. inf.* dizzy/in a daze. **muzziness** *n.* feeling muzzy.
my [maɪ] *adj.* belonging to me.
myalgia [maɪˈældʒɪə] *n.* muscle pain.
mycology [maɪˈkɒlədʒɪ] *n.* study of fungi. **mycological** [maɪkəˈlɒdʒɪkl] *adj.* referring to mycology.
myelitis [maɪəˈlaɪtɪs] *n.* inflammation of the spinal cord.
mynah (bird) [ˈmaɪnəˈbɜːd] *n.* black tropical bird which can be taught to talk.
myopia [maɪˈəʊpɪə] *n.* short-sightedness/not being able to see things which are far away. **myopic** [maɪˈɒpɪk] *adj.* shot-sighted.
myriad 1 [ˈmɪrɪəd] *n. (formal)* very large number. **myriad 2** *adj.* very many.
myrrh [mɜː] *n.* sweet-smelling resin used to make incense, etc.
myrtle [ˈmɜːtl] *n.* evergreen plant with scented flower.
myself [maɪˈself] *pronoun.* referring to me. all by m. = on my own.
mystery [ˈmɪstrɪ] *n.* thing which cannot be explained; state of not being able to be explained. **mysterious** [mɪˈstɪərɪəs] *adj.* secret/which cannot be explained. **mysteriously** *adv.* secretly/in a way which cannot be explained.
mystic 1 [ˈmɪstɪk] *n.* person who attempts to make contact with God through prayer/meditation, etc.
mystic 2 *adj.* in contact with God.
mystical *adj.* in contact with God by some process which cannot be

understood. **mysticism** [ˈmɪstɪsɪzəm] *n.* religion based on attempts to contact God by prayer and meditation.
mystify [ˈmɪstɪfaɪ] *v.* to puzzle/to bewilder. **mystification** [mɪstɪfɪˈkeɪʃn] *n.* puzzle/ bewilderment. **mystique** [mɪˈstiːk] *n.* mysterious atmosphere about a person or thing.
myth [mɪθ] *n.* (a) ancient folk story about gods. (b) untrue, but commonly held, notion. **mythical** *adj.* (a) referring to ancient tales of god. (b) untrue/not existing. **mythological** [mɪθəˈlɒdʒɪkl] *adj.* referring to mythology. **mythology** [mɪˈθɒlədʒɪ] *n.* study of myths; ancient folk stories from a particular source.
myxomatosis [mɪksəməˈtəʊsɪs] *n.* fatal disease of rabbits.

Nn

N Symbol for nitrogen.
Na symbol for sodium.
nab [næb] *v.* (nabbed) (a) *inf.* to snatch/ to pull away (sth) suddenly/to steal. (b) *inf.* to catch (s.o.) in the act/to pounce on (s.o.).
nadir [ˈneɪdɪə] *n.* lowest point.
naevus [ˈniːvəs] *n.* birthmark.
naff [næf] *adj. Sl.* worthless.
nag 1 [næg] *n. inf.* horse. **nag 2** *v.* (nagged) to try to persuade (s.o.) by saying the same thing again and again/to criticize without seeming to stop.
nagging *adj.* persistent (pain, etc.).
naiad [ˈnaɪæd] *n.* goddess living in a stream.
nail 1 [neɪl] *n.* (a) hard covering at the ends of fingers and toes; n. scissors = curved scissors for cutting nails. (b) small metal spike with a pointed end, used to hold things together; hard as nails = very tough; *inf.* to hit the n. on the head = to make an accurate judgement/to say the right answer; *inf.* to pay on the n. = to pay immediately/ promptly/on the spot. **nail 2** *v.* to attach with nails.

naive [naɪ'iːv] *adj.* inexperienced and innocent. **naively** *adv.* in a naive way. **naivety** *n.* being naive.

naked ['neɪkɪd] *adj.* with no clothes on; with no covering; n. flame = flame with no protective shield; invisible to the n. eye = which can only be seen using a telescope/microscope. **nakedly** *adv.* with no covering. **nakedness** *n.* being naked.

namby-pamby ['næmbɪpæmbɪ] *adj.* weak and silly.

name 1 [neɪm] *n.* (a) title/word which you use to call people/things; Christian n./first n. = particular name given to someone as a child; he put his n. down to join the club = he applied to join; to call s.o. names = to insult s.o. (b) in n. only = according to the name used, but not really in fact (c) to give a bad n. = a bad reputation; to make a n. for oneself = acquire a high reputation. **name 2** *v.* (a) to call by a name; to give a name to; (b) to specify; to n. the day = to fix the date for a wedding; (c) to appoint s.o. to a post. **nameless** *adj.* with no name; (word/name) not to be used because of disgust or in order to remain anonymous. **namely** *adv.* that is to say. **namesake** *n.* person with the same name as another.

nan, nana [næn, 'nænə] *n.* child's name for grandmother. **nanny** ['nænɪ] *n.* (a) nurse paid to look after children in their own home. (b) n. goat = female goat.

nano- ['nænəʊ] prefix one thousand millionth.

nap 1 [næp] *n.* (a) short sleep, (b) raised surface of cloth, such as velvet. (c) card game. (d) tip for the winner of a horse race. **nap 2** *v.* to sleep for a short time; to catch s.o. napping = to find s.o. off guard.

napalm ['neɪpɑːm] *n.* inflammable substance used in incendiary bombs.

nape [neɪp] *n.* back of the neck.

naphtha ['næfθə] *n.* oil derived from coal/petroleum, used to light fires/clean clothes, etc. **naphthalene** ['næfθəliːn] *n.* strong-smelling white chemical used to make mothballs.

napkin ['næpkɪn] *n.* (a) square piece of cloth or paper used to protect clothes and wipe your mouth at mealtimes. (b) (formal) nappy. **nappy** [næpɪ] *n.* towel used to cover a baby's bottom.

narcissus [nɑːˈsɪsəs] *n.* (*pl.*-issi[-ɪsaɪ]) white flower similar to a daffodil. **narcissism** *n.* great love for your own appearance. **narcissistic** [nɑːsɪˈsɪtɪk] *adj.* loving your own appearance.

narcotic [nɑːˈkɒtɪk] *adj. & n.* (substance) which can make you feel sleepy or become unconscious; *Am.* narcotics squad = police department dealing with drug offences.

nark 1 [nɑːk] *n. Sl.* police spy. **nark 2** *v. Sl.* to annoy.

narrate [nəˈreɪt] *v.* to write/to speak about events; to tell (a story). **narration** [nəˈreɪʃn] *n.* speaking/writing about events. **narrative 1** ['nærətɪv] *n.* what is actually written or told. **narrative 2** *adj.* describing events which took place. **narrator** [nəˈreɪtə] *n.* person who gives an actual account; person who reads a story.

narrow 1 ['nærəʊ] *adj.* (a) not wide; n. squeak/n. escape = escape at the last minute from an awkward or dangerous situation. (b) n. majority = very small margin of votes. (c) restricted (opinions) **narrow 2** *v.* to make/to become less wide; to make/to become smaller. **narrowboat** *n.* long boat used on canals. **narrowly** *adv.* nearly/only just. **narrow-minded** *adj.* not capable of seeing many points of view/not tolerant. **narrowness** *n.* being narrow. **narrows** *n. pl.* narrow stretch of water.

narwhal ['nɑːwəl] *n.* type of whale which lives in the Arctic and has a long tusk.

nary ['neərɪ] *adj.* (old) not one.

nasal ['neɪzl] *adj.* referring to the nose; spoken as if through the nose. **nasally** *adv.* in a nasal way.

nasturtium [nəˈstɜːʃəm] *n.* creeping plant with large orange or yellow flowers.

nasty [nɑːstɪ] *adj.* (-ier, -iest) unpleasant/disagreeable; to turn n. = to become hostile/unfriendly; *inf.* n. piece of work = unpleasant person. **nastily** *adv.* in a nasty way. **nastiness** *n.* being nasty; nasty happening.

natal ['neɪtl] *adj.* referring to birth.

nation ['neɪʃn] *n.* people of a particular country. **national 1** ['næʃnl] *adj.* belonging to the people of a particular country; N. Health Service = British system of free medical care; N. Insurance = system of regular payments by workers and employers to pay for free medical care and other benefits; n. Park = large area of unspoilt land, managed by the state as a public amenity. **national 2** *n.* person of a particular country. **nationalism** ['næʃnəlɪzəm] *n.* feeling of pride in once nation; desire for independence for a country. **nationalist** *n.* person who support nationalism. **nationalistic** *adj.* referring to nationalism **nationality** [næʃə'næliti] *n.* citizenship of a country. **nationalization** [næʃnəlaɪ'zeɪʃn] *n.* conversion of private industries to ownership by the state. **nationalize** ['næʃnəlaɪz] *v.* to put(a private industry) under central government ownership and control. **nationally** *adv.* in a national way (done) all over the land run by the state where building/tourism, etc. are controlled. **national service** *n.* temporary conscription into the armed forces. **nationwide** *adj.* all over the country

native 1 ['neɪtɪv] *n.* (a) person born in a particular country. (b) uncivilized original inhabitant. (c) plant/animal which originally comes from a particular country. **native 2** *adj.* (a) natural; (qualities) with which a person is born. (b) unaltered/undeveloped. (c) belonging to those born in a country. (d) n. to = (plant/animal) which originally comes from a certain country. **nativity** [nə'tɪvɪti] *n.* birth esp. that of Jesus Christ; n. play = play describing the events surrounding the birth of Jesus Christ.

natter 1 *n. inf.* friendly informal conversation/chat. **natter 2** ['nætə] *v. inf.* to have a friendly informal chat.

natty ['næti] *adj.* (-ier, -iest) (a) smart/tidy (personal appearance). (b) cleverly designed (gadget).

natural 1 ['nætʃəl] *adj.* (a) based on inner knowledge or instinct; not learnt. (b) normal not artificial. (c) not surprising/not unexpected. (d) dealing with (the study of) nature; n. gas = gas which is found in the earth. (e) (in music) (note) which is neither sharp nor flat. **natural 2** *n.* person who is

naturally suitable for a job/a part in a play, etc. **natural history** *n.* (also natural science) study of nature. **naturalism** *n.* (in art/literature) showing things as they really are. **naturalist** *n.* person who studies animals or plants. **naturalistic** *adj.* (art etc.) which shows things as they really are. **naturalization** [nætʃərəlaɪ'zeɪʃn] *n.* act of naturalizing; being naturalized. **naturalize** ['nætʃərə laɪz] *v.* (a) to introduce (a plant or animal) into another country. (b) to let cultivated plants become wild. (c) to grant (s.o.) citizenship of a country other than that in which he was born. **naturally** ['nætʃrəli] *adv.* (a) in a natural/unstudied way. (b) as you would expect/of course. **naturalness** *n.* being natural. **nature** ['neɪtʃə] *n.* character (of a person/thing/animal); human n. attitude and behaviour which are typical of human beings. (b) kind/class (of thing). (c) world of plants and animals; the laws of n. = what happens in the world of plants and animals; n. study = the study of plant or animal life in a junior school. **-natured** suffix showing a characteristic; good-natured. **nauturism** *n.* belief in the physical and mental advantages of going about naked. **nauturist** *n.* nudist.

naught [nɔːt] *n.* (formal) nothing. **naughty** ['nɔːti] *adj.* (-ier, -iest) bad/disobedient (child). **naughtily** *adv.* wickedly. **naughtiness** *n.* wickedness/bad behaviour.

nausea ['nɔːzɪə] *n.* feeling of sickness/of extreme dislike. **nauseating** *adj.* horrible/which makes you sick. **nauseous** *adj.* (a) which nauseates. (b) *Am.* feeling unwell.

nautical ['nɔːtɪkl] *adj.* referring to ships, sailing and boating; n. mile = measure of length at sea (2025 yards or 1.85 kilometres). **nautilus** [nɔː'tɪləs] *n.* large type of shell fish.

naval ['neɪvl] *adj.* referring to ships and esp. to a navy; n. engagement = battle at sea; n. base = port for warships; n. college = establishment for training naval officers.

nave [neɪv] *n.* main part of a church. **navel** ['neɪvl] *n.* small hollow in the middle of your stomach where the umbilical cord was attached; n. orange = large seedless orange with a small hollow at the bottom.

navigate ['nævɪgeɪt] v. to guide/to steer (a ship or aircraft); to tell the driver of a car, etc., which way to go. **navigability** [nævɪgə'bɪlɪtɪ] n. being navigable. **navigable** adj. (a) steerable/seaworthy. (b) (river) deep enough for ships to sail in it. **navigation** [nævɪ'geɪʃn] n. guiding/steering a ship/an aircraft along a certain course; inland n. = travel by boat along rivers or canals. **navigator** ['nævɪgeɪtə] n. person who guides/steers a ship or an aircraft; person who tells the driver of a car which way to go. **navvy** ['nævɪ] n. labourer.

navy 1 ['neɪvɪ] n. (a) all a country's warships and crews. (b) Merchant N. = all cargo ships of a country. **navy 2** adj. & n. n. (blue) = dark blue.

nay [neɪ] adv. (old) no.

n.b. [en'biː] short for nota bene, meaning please note.

NCO [ensiːəʊ] n. non-commissioned officer.

neap [niːp] n. n. tide = tide which does not rise or fall very much, midway between the spring tides.

Neapolitan [nɪə'pɒlɪtən] adj. referring to Naples; N. ice cream = ice cream made of layers of different colours and flavours.

near 1 ['nɪə] adv. (-er, -est) close/at only a little distance in space or time. **near 2** prep. close by (an object); not far away in time. **near 3** adj. n. relations = closest relation; n. side = side closest to the kerb (in a car); n. miss = (i) sth which is not quite successful; (ii) narrow escape. **near 4** v. to draw near to/to approach. **nearby** adj. which is situated close by. **near by** adv. close by. **Near East** n. countries at eastern end of the Mediterranean. **nearly** adv. (a) almost. (b) closely; not n. big enough = far too small. **nearness** n. closeness. **near-sighted** adj. short sighted/only able to see clearly things which are near. **neat** [niːt] adj. (-er, -est) (a) tidy/clean, (b) (alcohol) with no water added. (c) apt/precise (words). (d) skilful/well handled. **neatly** adv. in a neat way. **neatness** n. tidy/clean appearance.

nebula ['nebjʊlə] n. (pl.-ae) cloud of dust in space which shines like a star at night. **nebulous** ['nebjʊləs] adj. vague.

necessary 1 ['nesəsərɪ] n. what is essential/what must be done; inf. the n. = the required amount of money.

necessary 2 adj. essential/which cannot be avoided. **necessarily** [nesə'serəlɪ] adv. in an unavoidable way; taking the train isn't n. dearer than the bus = it can be cheaper.

necessitate [nɪ'sesɪteɪt] v. to make essential/to compel. **necessitous** adj. (formal) poor. **necessity** n. (a) need/compulsion (b) absolutely essential thing.

neck 1 [nek] n. (a) part of the body connecting the head to the shoulders; inf. to be up to your n. in work = have a lot of work to do; to breath down s.o.'s n. = to watch s.o. very closely/to follow close behind s.o.; to win by a n. = win a race by a very short distance; to finish n. and n. = to be equal winners; inf. a pain in the n. = a troublesome person/thing; to save you n. = escape hanging/punishment; inf. to get it in the n. = to be severely criticized; inf. to stick your n. out = take a chance/to be asking for trouble. (b) narrow passage leading to a wider area; inf. in this n. of the woods = in this part of the world. (c) part of a garment which goes round your neck. (d) part of an animal eaten as food; best end of n. = joint of lamb consisting of the ribs nearest the neck. **neck 2** v. inf. to fondle/caress. **necklace** n. string of beads/pearls, etc., worn round the neck. **necklet** n. ornament worn tightly round the neck. **neckline** n. edge of a dress, etc., round the neck. **necktie** n. esp. Am. band of material worn round the neck and tied in front with a knot.

necromancy ['nekrəmænsɪ] n. art of black magic/of predicting the future by speaking to the dead. **necromancer** n. person who practises necromancy.

necropolis [ne'krɒpəlɪs] n. large ancient cemetery.

nectar ['nektə] n. (a) sweet substance produced by flowers (b) any extremely pleasant drink. **nectarine** ['nektəriːn] n. fruit like a peach with a smooth skin.

nee [neɪ] adj. with the maiden name of; Mrs Smith, n. Taylor.

need 1 [niːd] *n.* (a) what is necessary. (b) in n. of = requiring. (c) time of difficulty/poverty; a friend in n. is a friend in deed = a person who helps you when you are in difficulties is a real friend. **need 2** *v.* to be necessary/to be required. **needful** *adj.* (old) necessary. **needless** *adj.* unnecessary/not called for. **needs 1** *n. pl.* actual requirements. **needs 2** *adv. inf.* n. must = if it has to be done. **needy** *adj.* (-ier, -iest) in need of/requiring help or food.

needle 1 ['niːdl] *n.* (a) thin metal/plastic/wooden tool with a sharp point at one end; it's like looking for a n. in a haystack = it's a hopeless task. (b) hypodermic n. = needle used for injections. (c) hand/pointer (on a dial); compass n. = the indicator on the dial of a compass. (d) leaf of a pine tree. **needle 2** *v.* to irritate/to provoke (s.o.). **needlestick** *n.* pricking the finger accidentally on a hypodermic needle. **needlewoman** *n.* woman who is good at sewing. **needlework** *n.* sewing done with needle and thread.

ne'er do well ['neəduːwel] *n.* person who is good for nothing.

nefarious [nɪ'feərɪəs] *adj.* very wicked.

negate [nɪgeɪt] *v.* to oppose/to cancel out(sth). **negation** [nɪ'geɪʃn] *n.* what is cancelled out/negated. **negative 1** ['negətɪv] *n.* (a) reply indicating no. (b) reverse image of a photograph. (c) one of the terminals in a battery. **negative 2** *adj.* (a) meaning no; showing opposition/refusal. (b) without good/positive qualities. (c) minus/less than zero. **negative 3** *v.* to contradict/to oppose (sth). **negatively** *adv.* in a way which suggests opposition.

neglect 1 [nɪ'glekt] *n.* disregard/lack of care of attention. **neglect 2** *v.* (a) to fail to look after/to fail to maintain; (b) to omit to do (sth which should be done). **neglected** *adj.* not looked after. **neglectful** *adj.* to be n. of = to forget about.

negligence ['neglɪdʒəns] *adj.* absence of proper care and attention. **negligent** *adj.* not giving proper care and attention. **negligible** *adj.* not significant/not worth regarding. **négligé** ['neglɪʒeɪ] *n.* woman's light dressing gown.

negotiate [nɪ'gəʊsɪeɪt] *v.* a) to discuss so as to make an agreement with s.o.; (b) to make a financial arrangement. (c) to overcome an obstacle/difficulty. **negotiable** [nɪ'gəʊsɪəbl] *adj.* which can be overcome; not n.= not exchangeable for cash. **negotiation** [nɪgəʊsɪ'eɪʃn] *n.* discussing/arranging by discussion. **negotiator** [nɪ'gəʊsɪeɪtə] *n.* person who discusses to try to reach an agreement.

negro, negress ['niːgrəʊ, 'niːgrəs] *adj. & n.* (*pl.*-oes) member of a dark skinned race of people originating in Africa. **negroid** *adj.* having the characteristics of negroes.

neigh 1 [neɪ] *n.* sound made by a horse. **neigh 2** *v.* to make a sound like a horse. **neighbour,** *Am.* **neighbor** ['neɪbə] *n.* (a) person who lives in a nearby house/road/country; (b) person sitting beside. **neighbourhood** *n.* (a) district and its people; n. watch scheme = scheme where people living in an area are encouraged to look out for criminals. (b) in the n. of = around/near to (in space or amount). **neighbouring** *adj.* next to each other. **neighbourly** *adj.* in a friendly/helpful way.

neither 1 ['naɪðə,'niːðə] *adv. & conj.* n...nor = not one.....and not the other. **neither 2** *adj. & pron.* not either of two things or persons.

nelson ['nelsən] *n.* (in wrestling) way of holding the opponent, with the arms under his armpits and the hands on the back of his neck.

nem.con. ['nem'kɒn] *adv.* with no one voting against.

nemesis ['nemɪsɪs] *n.* (no *pl.*) just punishment from which you cannot escape.

neo- ['nɪəʊ] prefix meaning new. **neolithic** [nɪəʊ'lɪθɪk] *adj.* belonging to the late stone Age.

neologism [nɪ'ɒlədʒɪəm] *n.* newly-invented word.

neon ['niːɒn] *n.* (element: Ne) colourless gas often used in tubes to make illuminated signs.

neophyte ['nɪəʊfaɪt] *n.* beginner; person who is learning.

nephew ['nefjuː] *n.* son of your brother or sister.

nephritis [nefraɪtɪs] *n.* kidney disease.
nepotism ['nepətɪzəm] *n.* giving members of your family jobs for which they are not necessarily qualified.
nerve 1 [nɜːv] *n.* (a) one of many thin threads forming part of the body's system for conveying messages to and from the brain; in a state of nerves = in a tense/anxious state; to get on s.o.'s nerves = to irritate/annoy s.o. (b) courage/confidence; *inf.* he's got a n. = he's cheeky/rude; to have the n. to = to be so rude as to. (c) to strain every n. = to make tremendous efforts. **nerve 2** *v.* to n. yourself = to summon up strength/confidence. **nervelessness** *n.* lack of energy/limpness. **nerve-racking** *adj.* disturbing. **nervous** *adj.* (a) the n. system = the pattern of nerve fibres in the body; n. breakdown = physical and mental collapse cause by worry. (b) timid/easily disturbed/easily upset.
nervously *adv.* in worried/frightened way. nervousness, n. being nervous.
nervy *adj. inf.* not relaxed/irritable.
nest 1 [nest] *n.* (a) place built by birds to lay their eggs; to feather you n. = to make a lot of money (usu. fraudulently) (b) hiding place/collecting place for people or animals. (c) n. of tables = tables of different sizes fitting under each other. **nest 2** *v.* (of birds) to build a nest. **nest egg** *n.* investment/money put aside for future use. **nestling** *n.* small bird not yet ready to leave the nest.
nestle ['nesl] *v.* to settle down comfortably. (b) to have close and loving contact.
net 1 [net] *n.* loosely woven material; piece of this material used for fishing/catching/fencing, etc. **net 2** *v.* (netted) (a) to catch in a net (b) to make a true profit; to n. a big profit = to make a lot of money. **net 3** *adj.* (price/weight) left after taking away the weight of the container/the tax paid, etc.; n. profit = actual gain after expenses have been paid; n. weight = true weight without the wrappings. **netball** *n.* team game (usu. played by women) where the ball has to be thrown so that it goes through a ring placed high up at the end of the court.
netting *n.* material made of string/wire loosely woven into a regular pattern of holes. **network** *n.* interconnecting

system (of railways, etc.); radio/TV system; interconnected computer system.
nether ['neðə] *adj.* (formal) lower; **nethermost** *adj.* lowest.
netsuke ['netskɪ] *n.* carved ivory toggle, formerly used in Japan.
nettle 1 ['netl] *n.* (stinging) n. = weed with stinging leaves. **nettle 2** *v.* to anger/to irritate. **nettlerash** *n.* skin rash caused by an allergy.
neural ['njʊrəl] *adj.* referring to nerves.
neuralgia *n.* nerve pains in the face or head. **neuralgic** *adj.* referring to neuralgia. **neuritis** [nju:raɪtɪs] *n.* inflammation of nerves. **neurological** [njʊrə'lɒdʒɪkl] *adj.* referring to neurology. **neurologist** [njʊ:rɒlədʒɪst] *n.* person who studies the nervous system. **neurology** [njʊ:'rɒlədʒɪ] *n.* study of the body's nervous system.
neurone *n.* cell in the nerve system which passes on impulses. **neurosis** [njʊ'rəʊsɪs], *n.* (*pl.*-oses[-əʊsi:z]) mental illness caused by a nervous disorder. **neurotic** [njʊ:rɒtɪk] *adj.* unbalanced (behaviour). **neurotically** *adv.* in an unbalanced way.
neuter 1 ['nju:tə] *adj.* (in grammar) not having a masculine or feminine gender.
neuter 2 *v.* to castrate. **neutral 1** *adj.* (a) not favouring or supporting either side in a dispute. (b) not having a distinctive colour (c) neither acid or alkali. **neutral 2** *n.* (a) citizen of a neutral country. (b) the car is in n. = not in gear. **neutrality** [njʊ'trælɪtɪ] *n.* being uncommitted/neutral; not taking sides.
neutralization [nju:trəlaɪ'zeɪʃn] *n.* act of neutralizing. **neutralize** ['nju:trəlaɪz] *v.* to cancel out by using an opposite.
neutrally *adv.* in a neutral way.
neutron *n.* basic particle with no electric charge; n. bomb = nuclear bomb which kills people but does little damage to buildings.
never ['nevə] *adv.* not ever/not at any time (b) (for emphasis) not at all. (c) (exclamation of surprise) surely not; well I n.! how surprising ! **never-ending** *adj.* which does not stop. **nevermore** *adv.* (formal) not any more. **never-never** *n. inf.* hire purchase system.
nevertheless *adv.* despite all that/all the same. **never-to-be-forgotten** *adj.* memorable.

new [nju:] *adj.* (-er, -est) (a) completely different/not thought of before/not met before. (b) changed/different. (c) fresh/unused; to turn over a n. leaf = become better/start again. (d) most recent; n. moon = moon when it is a thin crescent. (e) just bought/just acquired. **new born** *adj.* just born. **new comer** *n.* person who has just come to an area. **newfangled** *adj.* unpleasant and newly invented. **new-laid** *adj.* (of eggs) freshly laid/just laid. **newly** *adv.* most recently; newly weds = people who have just got married. **newness** *n.* being recent/fresh; not having been used. **news** [nju:z] *n.* spoken or written information about events; it's in the n. = it is of topical interest; to break the n. to s.o. = to tell s.o. bad/unwelcome news; no n. is good n. = the absence of bad news means things may be going well. **newsagent** *n.* person who runs a shop which sells news papers. **newsagent's** *n.* shop selling newspapers. **newscaster** *n.* person who reads the news on television. **newsflash** *n.* short news item. **newsletter** *n.* printed sheet giving news to members of a church/club, etc. **newsman** *n.* (*pl.*-men) journalist. **newspaper** *n.* daily/weekly paper containing information and news. **newsprint** *n.* paper for printing newspapers and magazines. **newsreel** *n.* short film about current events shown in a cinema. **newsvendor** *n.* person who sells news papers in the street. **newsworthy** *adj.* (events) worth recording/mentioning in papers or on television. **newsy** *adj. inf.* full of news. **New World** *n.* North and south America. **new year** *n.* the year which has just started; period just after 1st January. **New Year's Day** *n.* 1st January. **New Year's Eve** *n.* 31st December. **newel** ['nju:əl] *n.* post at the top or bottom stairs to which the banisters are attached. **newt** [nju:t] *n.* small, lizard-like animal which can live either in or out of water. **newton** ['njʊtən] *n.* standard measurement of force. **next 1** [nekst] *adj.* (of time/sequence) coming after (b) (of place) closest to/nearest; she lives n. door = in the house/

flat next to this one. **next 2** *adv.* coming after in place/time; what n. ? = what other amazing or absurd things can we expect ? it costs n. to nothing = it cost very little. **next 3** *n.* person/thing following; the week after n. = not the next week but the following one. **next-door** *adj.* living next door. **next-of-kin** *n.* (no *pl.*) nearest relative(s). **nexus** ['neksəs] *n.* link/connecting point for ideas, organizations, etc. **Ni** symbol for nickel. **nib** [nɪb] *n.* pointed writing end of a pen. **nibble 1** ['nɪbl] *n.* bite/very small amount eaten. **nibble 2** *v.* to take very small, cautious bites. **nibble away** *v.* to remove gradually/in little pieces. **nice** [naɪs] *adj.* (-er, -est) (a) generally pleasant. (b) precise; subtle. **nice-looking** *adj.* pretty/pleasant to look at. **nicely** *adv.* in a satisfactory/good manner. **niceness** *n.* quality of being agreeable. **nicety** *n.* fine/exact detail. **niche** [ni:ʃ] *n.* (a) hollow in a wall or pillar to put a statue/vase/decoration in; to find your n./to find a n. for yourself = to find a completely satisfying or suitable role/job. (b) special place in a market. **nick 1** [nɪk] *n.* (a) small dent/notch (usu. to mark a place); *inf.* in the n. of time = just in time. (b) *Sl.* prison. (c) *Sl* in good n. = in good form. **nick 2** *v.* (a) to make a shall notch/cut. (b) *Sl.* to steal. (c) *Sl.* to catch/arrest. **nickel 1** ['nɪkl] *n.* (a) (element: Ni) silver-coloured metal. (b) *Am.* 5-cent coin. **nickel 2** *v.* (nickelled) to coat with nickel. **nickname 1** ['nɪkneɪm] *n.* abbreviated or pet name. **nickname 2** *v.* to give (s.o.) a nickname. **nicotine** ['nɪkəti:n] *n.* poisonous brown liquid obtained from tobacco. **niece** [ni:s] *n.* daughter of your brother or sister. **nifty** ['nɪftɪ] *adj. inf.* quick and agile; clever (gadget). **Nigerian 1** [naɪ'dʒɪərɪən] *adj.* referring to Nigeria. **Nigerian 2** *n.* person who comes from Nigeria. **niggardly** ['nɪgədlɪ] *adj.* mean; very small (amount). **niggle** ['nɪgl] *v.* to be fussy about relatively unimportant details; to be niggled by s.o. = to be annoyed/upset by s.o's spiteful or petty criticism. **niggling** *adj.* unimportant/insignificant.

nigh [naɪ] *adv.* (formal) near.

night [naɪt] *n.* last part of each day; period of darkness from sunset to sunrise; last n. = yesterday after dark; the first n. = the official opening performance of a play or entertainment; n. out = evening spend outside the home. **nightcap** (a) (old) cap worn in bed (b) bed-time drink. **nightclothes** *n. pl.*clothes worn in bed. **nightclub** *n.* club only open at night. **nightdress** *n.* dress worn by women and girls in bed. **nightfall** *n.* time when night starts. **nightgown** *n.* (old) nightdress. **nightie** *n. inf.* nightdress. **nightingale** *n.* small brown singing bird. **nightjar** *n.* dark-coloured bird which files by night. **night life** *n.* entertainment which takes place in a town at night. **nightlight** *n.* small dim light or candle left burning at night. **nightly** *adv.* every night. **nightmare** *n.* vivid frightening dreAm. (b) horrible event. **nightmarish** *adj.* vividly frightening. **night school** *n.* school which has classes for adults in the evening. **nightshade** *n.* poisonous plant. **nightshirt** *n.* long shirt worn by men in bed. **night soil** *n.* human excreta, used as manure. **night-time** *n.* period of night; night-time flight = flight during the hours of darkness.

nightwatchman *n.* (*pl.*-men) (a) man who guards a building at night. (b) (in cricket) bats man who starts his innings just before the end of the day's play and continues the following morning.

nihilism ['nɪhɪlɪzəm] *n.* belief that nothing which exists is good. **nihilist** *n.* person who believes in nihilism.

nil [nɪl] *n.* nothing/zero.

nimble ['nɪmbl] *adj.* (-er, -est) agile/ fast-moving; physically fit and alert. **nimbly** *adv.* in an expert way.

nimbus ['nɪmbəs] *n.* (a) dark raincloud. (b) shining halo.

nincompoop ['nɪnkəmpuːp] *n.* silly person/fool.

nine [naɪn] *n.* number 9; n. times out of ten = in most cases; *inf.* dressed upto the nines = wearing your most elaborate

clothes; possession in n. tenths of the law = it is easy to claim ownership of something which is already in your possession. **ninepins** *n.* (*pl.*) skittles; they went down like n. = they fell down/ caught the disease very easily. **nineteen** *n.* number 19; the n. hundreds = the years after 1900. **nineteenth, 19th** *adj. n.* referring to nineteen; the n. century = the period from 1800 to 1899. **ninetieth, 90th** *adj. & n.* referring to ninety. **ninety** *n.* number 90; she's in her nineties = she is between 90 and 99 years old. **ninth, 9th** *adj. & n.* referring to nine; the n. century = period from 800 to 899.

ninny ['nɪnɪ] *n.* idiot.

nip 1 [nɪp] *n.* (a) small amount of alcohol (b) short sharp bite/pinch; a n. in the air = a sudden/sharp burst of cold weather. **nip 2** *v.* (nipped) (a) to bite/to pinch sharply or suddenly. (b) *inf.* to go out very quickly. **nipper** *n. inf.* (a) small child. (b) nippers = pincers. **nippy** *adj. inf.* (a) agile/fast-moving. (b) cold.

nipple ['nɪpl] *n.* (a) small projection on the tip of a breast from which, in females the mother's milk comes. (b) projection/ bump on a surface. (c) small hole in a machine for greasing.

nirvana [nɪə'vɑːnə] *n.* (for Buddhists) happy state after death when the dead person's soul joins the divine soul.

nisi ['naɪsaɪ] see decree.

Nissen hut [nɪsən'hʌt] *n.* army shed with a semi-circular roof of corrugated iron.

nit [nɪt] *n.* (a) egg of a louse (b) *Sl.* idiot. **nit-picking** *n. inf.* petty criticism/ finding small faults to criticise. **nitwit** *n. inf.* idiot.

nitrogen ['naɪtrədʒən] *n.* (element: N) gas which makes up four-fifths of the atmosphere. **nitroglycerine** *n.* liquid explosive.

nitrate *n.* salt of nitric acid. **nitric acid** *n.* acid containing nitrogen. **nitrous** *adj.* containing nitrogen.

nitty-gritty [nɪtɪ'grɪtɪ] *n. inf.* basic details (of an argument).

NLQ abbrev. for near letter quality.

no. [nəʊ] abbrev. for number.

no 1 *n. & adv.* showing the negative/ opposite of yes; the noes have it = most people have voted no. **no 2** *adj.* none of/not any of; it's n. distance = not at all far/a very short distance away; it's n. joke = not funny but serious; n. admission = entrance not allowed; *inf.* n. way = certainly not. **no 3** *adv.* not/not at all; n. sooner said than done = it will be done immediately; he's n. more = he is dead. **no claims bonus** *n.* reduction in insurance premiums because no claims have been made. **no-go area** *n.* section of a town where the police/soldiers cannot go.

nob [nɒb] *n. Sl.* (a) head. (b) upper-class person.

nobble ['nɒbl] *n. inf.* to give drug to (a horse) to prevent it running well in a race; to try to influence (s.o.).

noble 1 ['nəʊbl] *n.* person of high rank by title or birth. **noble 2** *adj.* (-er, -est) of high rank/dignified; worthy or praise/splendid. **nobility** [nə'bɪlɪtɪ] *n.* (a) titled members of society/the aristocracy. (b) high-mindedness. **nobleman** *n.* (*pl.*-men) noble. **noble-mindedness** *n.* high-mindedness/worthy thoughts. **nobleness** *n.* being noble. nobility. **noblewoman** *n.* (*pl.*-women) woman of high rank. **nobly** *adv.* in a noble fashion/heroically.

nobody 1 ['nəʊbədɪ] *n.* person of no importance. **nobody 2** *pron.* no one/no person.

nocturnal [nɒk'tɜːnl] *adj.* referring to the night; (animals which are) most active at night. **nocturne** ['nɒktɜːn] *n.* painting/piece of music conveying a feeling of night.

nod 1 [nɒd] *n.* forward movement of the head as a greetings/as a sign of agreement; *inf.* it went through on the n. = it was agreed without any discussion. **nod 2** *v.* (nodded) to show agreement/to give permission/to agree by a forward movement of the head; to n. off = to fall asleep; nodding acquaintance = (i) person you know only slightly. (ii) slight knowledge.

node [nəʊd] *n.* (a) place where leaves grow from a plant's stem. (b) knob on a root/branch/human joint. (c) point where curves cross. **nodal** *adj.* central/at the point where lines meet. **nodule** ['nɒdjuːl] *n.* small node.

Noel [nəʊ'el] *n.* Christmas.

nog [nɒg] *n.* egg n. = drink made of

alcohol and raw eggs. **noggin** *n.* small quantity of alcohol.

noise 1 [nɔɪz] *n.* loud (usu. unpleasant) sound; to make a n. about sth. = to make a fuss/to complain; *inf.* a big n. = an important person. **noise 2** *v.* to n. sth abroad = to make sth public/to spread the news. **noiseless** *adj.* without any sound. **noiselessly** *adv.* in a silent way. **noisily** *adv.* in a noisy/loud way. **noisy** *adj.* (-ier, -iest) making a lot of noise; loud.

nomad ['nəʊmæd] *adj. & n.* (member) of a wandering tribe with no fixed home. **nomadic** [nəʊ'mædɪk] *adj.* not staying in one place/travelling.

no-man's-land ['nəʊmænzlænd] *n.* territory between two armies which belongs to neither side.

nom-de-plume [nɒmdə'pluːm] *n.* name used by an author in place of his own.

nomenclature [nə'menklətʃə] *n.* (formal) system of naming.

nominal ['nɒmɪnl] *adj.* (a) referring to names. (b) in name rather than in fact; n. fee = very small amount of money/token payment. **nominally** *adv.* in name rather than in fact. **nominate** ['nɒmɪneɪt] *v. tr.* to name/to propose. **nomination** [nɒmɪ'neɪʃn] *n.* act of nominating; suggested name. **nominator** *n.* person who nominates. **nominee** [nɒmɪ'niː] *n.* person who is nominated; n. account = bank account held on behalf of s.o. **nominative** ['nɒmɪnətɪv] *n.* form of a noun when it is the subject of a verb.

non- [nɒn] prefix meaning not/the opposite.

nonagenarian [nɒnədʒə'neərɪən] *adj. & n.* (person) who is between 90 and 99 years old.

non-aggression [nɒnə'greʃn] *n.* agreement not to engage in war.

non-alcoholic [nɒnælkə'hɒlɪk] *adj.* not intoxicating/not containing alcohol.

non-aligned [nɒnə'laɪnd] *adj.* (country) which is not linked to a large and powerful bloc of countries. **non-alignment** *n.* policy of being non-aligned.

nonchalant ['nɒnʃələnt] *adj.* casual/unexcited. **nonchalance** *n.* being calm/unmoved. **nonchalantly** *adv.* in a nonchalant way.

non-combatant [nɒn'kɒmbətənt] *adj.* & *n.* (person) who does not flight; doctor/priest, etc., attached to an army.

non-commissioned [nɒnkə'mɪʃnd] *adj.* non-commissioned officer = soldier of a lower rank than a commissioned officer.

non-committal [nɒnkə'mɪtl] *adj.* not favouring a definite course of action/not agreeing with either side in an argument.

non compos mentis [nɒnkɒmpɒs'mentɪs] *adj.* mad.

nonconformist [nɒnkən'fɔ:mɪst] *adj.* & *n.* who does not act in the same way as most people; Nonformist = (person) who does not hold the views of the established church/member of a Protestant church separated from the Church of England. **nonconformity** *n.* being nonconformist.

nondescript ['nɒndɪskrɪpt] *adj.* very ordinary/without individual qualities.

none 1 [nʌn] *pron.* (a) not any (of); n. of your cheek! = don't be rude. (b) no person/no one. **none 2** *adv.* (used with the and comparative or too) not at all; n. too good; n. the worse for the accident.

nonentity [nɒ'nentɪtɪ] *n.* person of no importance.

nonetheless [nʌnθə'les] *adv.* nevertheless.

non-event [nɒnɪ'vent] *n.* happening which was expected to be important but which turns out not to be so.

nonexistent [nɒnɪg'zɪstənt] *adj.* not having any existence in fact/not real.

non -fiction ['nɒnfɪkʃn] *n.* (no *pl.*) books which are not fiction/which are factual.

non-intervention [nɒnɪntə'venʃən] *n.* act of not interfering.

non-iron [nɒn'aɪən] *adj.* not needing ironing.

non-payment [nɒn'peɪmənt] *n.* failing to pay what is due.

non-plussed [nɒn'plʌst] *adj.* puzzled/ confused.

non-profit-making [nɒn'prɒfɪtmeɪkɪŋ] *adj.* (organization such as a charity) which is not allowed to make a profit.

non-refundable [nɒnrɪ'fʌndəbl] *adj.* which will not be refunded.

non-resident [nɒn'rezɪdənt] *adj.* *n.* (person) not living in/not staying very long in a place; a non-residence work

permit = permit which allows s.o. from another country to work.

non-returnable [nɒnrɪ'tɜ:nəbl] *adj.* (bottle) on which there is no deposit and which the manufactures do not want back.

nonsense ['nɒnsəns] *n.* foolish ideas/ ridiculous behaviour. **nonsensical** [nɒn'sensɪkl] *adj.* absurd.

non sequitur [nɒn'sekwɪtə] *n.* phrase which does not follow logically from what has gone before; conclusion drawn incorrectly from the evidence.

non-skid [nɒn'skɪd] *adj.* which prevents skidding.

non-smoker ['nɒnsməʊkə] *n.* (a) person who does not smoke (b) place where smoking is not allowed. **non-smoking** *adj.* where smoking is not allowed.

non-starter [nɒn'stɑ:tə] *n.* (a) horse which is not ready to start at the beginning of a race. (b) *inf.* project/plan which is never going to be accepted.

non-stick ['nɒnstɪk] *adj.* (pan) covered with a substance which prevents food from sticking when cooking.

non-stop 1 ['nɒnstɒp] *adj.* not stopping/travelling directly from point to departure to terminus. **non-stop 2** *adv.* ceaselessly/without stopping.

non-union [nɒn'ju:nɪən] *adj.* not be longing to a union.

non-violence [nɒn'vaɪələns] *n.* absence of physical violence/of aggression.

noodles ['nu:dlz] *n.* *pl.*strips of paste for cooking. **noodle** *n.* *Sl.* fool.

nook [nʊk] *n.* small hiding place; in every n. and cranny = in every little hole and corner.

noon [nu:n] *n.* midday. **noonday** *n.* the n. sun = the sun at noon.

no one ['nəʊwʌn] *pron.* nobody/no person.

noose [nu:s] *n.* rope knotted to form a loop which can be tightened by pulling.

nor [nɔ:] *conj.* (a) (usu. followed by verb then subject) not either/and not. (b) neither...n. = not one...and not the other.

Nordic ['nɔ:dɪk] *adj.* referring to Scandinavia.

norm [nɔ:m] *n.* normal/standard pattern. **normal** ['nɔ:ml] *adj.* usual/regular/ expected. **normality** [nɔ:mælɪtɪ] *n.*

being normal/not/having unusual features. **normally** adv. in the usual way.

Norman ['nɔːmən] adj. & n. (person) from Normandy; (architecture, etc.) developed in England after the conquest by the Noramans in 1066.

Norse 1 [nɔːs] adj. referring to ancient Scandinavia. **Norse 2** n. ancient Scandinavian language. **Norseman** n. (pl.-men) person from ancient Scandinavia.

north 1 [nɔːθ] n. one of the points of the compass, the direction to the right when you are facing the setting sun. **north 2** adv. towards the north. **north 3** adj. referring to the north; n. wind = wind which blows from the north. **northbound** adj. going toward the north. **north-east** n. direction halfway between east and north. **north-easterly** adj. towards/from the north-east. **northeastern** adj. referring to the north-east. **northerly** ['nɔːðəlɪ] adj. & n. in/to/from the north; (wind) from the north. **northern** ['nɔːðn] adj. referring to the north. **northerner** n. person who lives in/comes from the north. **northward** adj. towards the north. **northernmost** adj. furthest north. **northwards** adv. towards the north. **north-west** n. direction halfway between west and north. **north-westerly** adj. towards/from the north west. **north-western** adj. referring to the north-west.

Norwegian 1 [nɔː'wiːdʒən] adj. referring to Norway. **Norwegian 2** n. (a) person from Norway. (b) language spoken in Norway.

nose 1 [nəʊz] n. (a) part of the face used for breathing in air and smelling; as plain as the n. on your face = very obvious; to speak through your n. = speak as if your nose is blocked; inf. I paid through the n. for it = I paid far too much for it; I did it under his very n. = did it right in front of him but he didn't notice; to poke n. into = to interfere unasked; to cut off your n. to spite your face = to do sth when you are angry which in fact harms you; follow your n. = go straight on; to keep s.o's n. to the grind stone = to make s.o. work hard at the time; to look down your n. at s.o. = to

regard s.o. as inferior; to turn up your n. at sth = to reject sth as not good enough. (b) good sense of smell; a good n. for = an instinct for finding sth. (c) front end of a vehicle. **nose 2** v. (a) to discover by smell. (b) to detect/to discover. (c) (of boat) to go in gently. **nose about, nose around** v. to look/to search around. **nose bag** n. bag of food hung around an animal's neck. **nosebleed** n. flow of blood from the nose. **nose cone** n. round pointed part at the top of a rocket. **nosedive 1** n. steep downward dive of an aircraft. **nosedive 2** v to dive down steeply. **nosegay** n. small bunch of flowers. **nosey, nosy** adj. (ier, -iest) inf. curious/interested in the affairs of other people; n. parker = very inquisitive person. **nosily** adv. in a nosey way.

nosh [nɒʃ] n. Sl. food.

nostalgia [nɒ'stældʒɪə] n. longing for/ sentimental recollection of the past. **nostalgic** adj. encouraging nostalgia. **nostalgically** adv. in a nostalgic way.

nostril ['nɒstrl] n. one of the two holes in the nose to admit air and smells.

nostrum ['nɒstrəm] n. quack medicine.

not [nɒt] adv. (a) (used with verbs to make the action negative; short form n't) he will not come/he won't come. (b) (used to make negative words/phrases/ sentences) I think not = I don't think so. (c) (providing emphasis by a form of contrast) not yours but mine (d) (used to show the opposite) not a few = many; not too well = badly; not sorry to leave = glad to leave; not without reason = with good reason. **not half** adv. inf. extremely.

nota bene ['nəʊtə'beneɪ] note well, pay attention to this.

notable 1 ['nəʊtəbl] adj. worth noticing; large. **notable 2** n. important person. **notability** [nəʊtə'bɪlɪtɪ] n. (a) being important. (b) notable/important person. **notably** adv. significantly/ particularly.

notary (public) ['nəʊtərɪˣ'pʌblɪk☐] n. person who has authority to see that legal documents are correctly written and who witness their signing.

notation [nəʊ'teɪʃn] n. system of symbols used to show notes in music/to show mathematical signs.

notch 1 [nɒtʃ] *n.* (*pl.*-es) small cut (usu. V-shaped) used to mark/to record.

notch 2 *v.* to mark with notches; to n. up = to score (a goal/a victory).

note 1 [nəʊt] *n.* (a) music sound (b) written sign which indicates a musical sound. (c) key on a piano, etc.; to strike the right n. = to play the correct note/to provide the appropriate tone/atmosphere/ words in a particular situation. (d) very short letter; very brief written/printed document (e) bank note/piece of paper money. (f) notice/attention/importance; of n. = important; to take n. of = to pay attention to/to be aware of. (g) indication. **note 2** *v.* (a) to write down. (b) to pay attention to. **notebook** *n.* book in which you write notes. **notecase** *n.* wallet or container for banknotes. **noted** *adj.* famous/well-known. **notepad** *n.* pad of paper for notes. **notepaper** *n.* writing paper for letters. **noteworthy** *adj.* deserving attention.

nothing 1 [ˈnʌθɪŋ] *n.* (a) not anything; to say n. about = to keep silent about; there's n. in it = no truth in it; to make sth out of n. = to exaggerate sth; *inf.* n. doing! = I refuse; to get sth for n.= get sth free; there's n. else for it = there's no alternative; to think n. of it = make seem easy; to have n. to do with = not to associate with/not to become involved in; it's n. to do with you = not your concern; to come to n. = be unsuccessful. (b) (used with and adj. following) not any thing. (c) (used as a comparison/to suggest something inferior) that's n. to what I saw. **nothing 2** *adv.* in way/not at all; n. daunted = not intimidated. **nothingness** *n.* void/nothing at all.

notice 1 [ˈnəʊtɪs] *n.* (a) advance information/warning; warning to leave one's job; n. to quit = legal document telling s.o. to leave premises. (b) to take n. of = to pay attention to. (c) written account/ announcement; written information. (d) review in a newspaper. **notice 2** *v.* to pay attention to. **noticeable** *adj.* easily seen. **noticeably** *adv.* in a noticeable way. **noticeboard** *n.* flat piece of wood, etc.. on a wall, on which notices can be pinned. **notify** [ˈnəʊtɪfaɪ] *v.* to announce/to declare/to advise/to inform. **notifiable** *adj.* which has to be notified to the authorities. **notification** [nəʊtɪfɪˈkeɪʃn] *n.* formal information.

notion [ˈnəʊʃn] *n.* (a) vague awareness/ idea/thought. (b) *Am.* notions = shop or department selling buttons/thread/ ribbons etc. **notional** *adj.* vague but assumed to be correct. **notionally** *adv.* in a notional way.

notorious [nəʊˈtɔːrɪəs] *adj.* well known (usu. for doing sth bad). **notoriety** *n.* bad/unfavourable reputation. **notoriously** *adv.* unfavourably significant.

notwithstanding 1 [nɒtwɪθˈstændɪŋ] *prep.* (formal) despite.

notwithstanding 2 *adv.* all the same/ anyway.

nougat [ˈnuːgɑː] *n.* type of white sweet made with nuts honey and egg whites.

nought [nɔːt] *n.* zero/nothing; the sign 0; to come to n. = be unsuccessful; noughts and crosses = same for two players where each puts a cross or a nought in one of nine squares in turn, the object being to be the first to make a line of three noughts or three crosses.

noun [naʊn] *n.* word used as a name of a person or thing.

nourish [ˈnʌrɪʃ] *v.* (a) to provide (sth) with food so that it will grow (b) to keep alive (ideas/feelings). **nourishing** *adj.* providing nourishment. **nourishment** *n.* food which enables plants/animals to grow.

nous [naʊs] *n.* *inf.* common sense/ ordinary intelligent reaction.

nova [ˈnəʊvə] *n.* star which suddenly becomes much brighter and then fades away.

novel1 [ˈnɒvl] *n.* long fictional story in the form of a book. **novel 2** *adj.* new/ original. **novelette** *n.* short novel with no literary merit. **novelist** [ˈnɒvəlɪst] *n.* person who writes novels. **novelty** *n.* (a) new/original thing (b) small/unusual toy or trinket (c) newness.

November [nəˈvembə] *n.* 11th month of the year.

novice [ˈnɒvɪs] *n.* (a) beginner; inexperienced person. (b) person who is intending to join a religious order but who has not yet taken the vows. **noviciate** *n.* state of being a novice in a religious order.

now 1 [naʊ] *adv.* (a) at this moment. (b) immediately/beginning from this time. (c) just n. = in the immediate past. (d) (when relating events) then/next/by that time. **now 2** inter showing criticism n. then! **now 3** *conj.* as a result of since. **now 4** *n.* this time; the present time. **nowadays** ['naʊədeɪz] *adv.* at the present day/in these modern times.

nowhere ['nəʊweə] *adv.* not in/at/to any place; n. near completion = far from being finished; I got n. = I was totally unsuccessful in what I was trying to do.

noxious ['nɒkʃəs] *adj.* unpleasant/harmful.

nozzle ['nɒzl] *n.* special fitting at the end of a pipe or hose for controlling what comes out.

nth [enθ] *adj.* to a very great extent.

nuance ['njuːɑːns] *n.* shade of meaning or colour.

nub [nʌb] *n.* central point.

nubile ['njuːbaɪl] *adj.* (of a young woman) very attractive physically.

nucleus ['njuːklɪəs] *n.* (*pl.*-iei) (a) vital central part around which things collect. (b) central part of an atom. **nuclear** *adj.* concerned with/belonging to a nucleus. esp. of an atom; n. energy = energy produced by nuclear power; n. family = family group consisting of the presents and children; n. reactor = device for producing atomic energy; n. power = power from atomic energy; n. submarine = driven by nuclear power. **nucleonics** [njuːklɪˈɒnɪks] *n.* study of the application of nuclear energy.

nude 1 [njuːd] *n.* (a) naked person. (b) in the n. = naked. **nude 2** *adj.* naked/bare. **nudism** *n.* belief in the physical and mental advantages of going about naked. **nudist** *n.* person who believes in going about naked; n. colony = club/camp for those who wish to go about naked. **nudity** *n.* not wearing any clothes/nakedness.

nudge 1 [nʌdʒ] *n.* slight push/prod with the elbow to attract attention.

nudge 2 *v.* to attract attention, *usu.* by pushing with the elbow.

nugatory ['njuːgətrɪ] *adj.* (formal) worthless; useless.

nugget ['nʌgɪt] *n.* lump of gold in its natural state; n. of information = piece of useful information.

nuisance ['njuːsns] *n.* annoying or disagreeable person/thing; public n. = action which bothers other people in such a way as to be against the law.

null [nʌl] *adj.* without significance/cancelled out; n. and void = no longer valid. **nullify** *v.* to cancel out/to make invalid. **nullity** *n.* nothingness/thing that is null.

numb 1 [nʌm] *adj.* without feeling or sensation/unable to move. **numb 2** *v.* to make incapable of movement or feeling. **numbly** *adv.* not moving because of being numb. **numbness** *n.* having no feeling or sensation/being incapable of action. **numbskull** *n. inf.* stupid person.

number 1 ['nʌmbə] *n.* (a) name of a figure; total of objects or persons; one of their n.= one of them; *inf.* to take care of n. one = to look after yourself/your own interest. (b) numbers = many in quantity. (c) (in grammar) term indicating whether a noun is singular or plural. (d) copy of a periodical/a song/a piece of plain music; back n. = thing which is out of date; *inf.* his number's up = he is dying. **number 2** *v.* to count/to include among/to total; his days are numbered = he hasn't much time to live. (b) to put a number/figure on. **numberless** *adj.* which cannot be counted. **numberplate** *n.* plate on the front and back of a vehicle, showing its registration number.

numeral ['njuːmərəl] *n.* actual sign representing a number. **numeracy** *n.* ability to calculate mathematically/ability to work out sums. **numerate** ['njuːmərət] *adj.* able to calculate mathematically. **numeration** [njuːməˈreɪʃn] *n.* calculation.

numerator *n.* figure above the line in a fraction. **numeric keypad** *n.* set of numbered keys on a computer keyboard. **numerical** [njuːˈmerɪkl] *adj.* referring to numbers; in n. order = in order of numbers. **numerically** *adv.* by/in number. **numerous** ['njuːmərəs] *adj.* many/a lot of.

numismatics [njuːməzˈmætɪks] *n.* study of coins. **numismatist** [njuːˈmɪzmətɪst] *n.* person who collects/studies coins.

nun [nʌn] *n.* woman who is a member of a religious order living in a separate community or convent. **nunlike** adj. very calm/good/restrained. **nunnery** n. convent/community where nuns live.

nuncio ['nʌnsɪəʊ] n. ambassador sent by the Pope to a foreign country.

nuptial ['nʌpʃl] adj. (formal) referring to marriage/wedding ceremonies. **nuptials** n. pl. wedding.

nurse 1 [nɜːs] n. (a) (usu. female) person trained and employed to look after the sick; night n. = nurse who is on duty at night. (b) woman employed to look after children. **nurse 2** v. (a) to look after (a sick person). (b) to look after very carefully to n. a constituency = to look after the needs of electors in the hope that they will vote for you at the next election. (c) to think about/to ponder over. (d) to hold close. **nursemaid** n. young woman who is paid to look after children. **nursery** n. (a) room/building where babies are looked after; day n. = place where babies are looked after during the day time; n. school = school for very young children; n. rhyme = little poem telling a simple story told or sung to young children. (b) place where people are brought up or trained; n. slopes = gentle slopes where you can learn to ski. (c) place where young plants are grown. **nurseryman** n. (pl.-men) man who looks after young plants. **nursing 1** adj. (person) who nurses/looks after; n. mother = who breast-feeds her baby; n. staff = hospital nurses; n. home = small (usu. private) hospital; n. officer = person in charge of the nurses in a hospital. **nursing 2** n. profession of looking after the sick.

nurture ['nɜːtʃə] v. (formal) to protect and bring up carefully.

nut 1 [nʌt] n. (a) fruit with an edible centre inside a hard shell; to crack nuts = to open the shells to get at the edible centres; inf. a tough n. to crack = a hard person/a difficult problem. (b) small metal ring used for tightening a bolt wing n. = nut with two projecting pieces for turning. (c) inf. head; he's off his n. = he's mad. (d) inf. nuts about = very keen on/enthusiastic about. (e) small lump (of butter) **nut 2** v. to go nutting = to gather nuts. **nut case** n. inf. mad person. **nutcrackers** n. pl. pincers for cracking nuts. **nuthatch** n. small grey

and brown bird which climbs up tree trunks. **nutmeg** n. seed of a tropical tree, used as a spice. **nutshell** n. hard outside covering of a nut; in a n. = giving all the important details as briefly as possible. **nutty** adj. (a) tasting of/full of nuts. (b) inf. crazy/very enthusiastic (about s.o./sth).

nutriment ['njuːtrɪmənt] n. thing which nourishes. **nutrient** adj. & n. (food) which feeds/nourishes. **nutrition** n. giving/receiving of nourishment. **nutritious** [njuːˈtrɪʃəs] adj. nourishing/providing food which is necessary for growth. **nutritive 1** n. food which is necessary for growth. **nutritive 2** adj. providing food/nourishment.

nuzzle ['nʌzl] v. to press the nose up to/to snuggle up to.

nylon ['naɪlɒn] n. very tough synthetic material. **nylons** n. pl. women's stockings.

nymph [nɪmf] n. (a) young girl; minor goddess. (b) young insect, esp. young dragonfly. **nymphet** n. sexually desirable young girl. **nymphomania** [nɪmfəˈmeɪnɪə] n. (in woman) uncontrollably strong sexual desire. **nymphomaniac** n. woman who has uncontrollable sexual desires.

Oo

Oo [əʊ] zero/nothing.

O symbol for oxygen.

oaf [əʊf] n. stupid/clumsy/unfeeling person. **oafish** adj. like an oaf.

oak [əʊk] n. type of large deciduous tree; wood of this tree. **oak apple** n. round growth on oak trees caused by an insect. **oaken** adj. (formal) made of oak. **oakum** ['əʊkəm] n. loose pieces of old rope formerly used for stuffing into the seams of wooden ships.

OAP [əʊeɪˈpiː] n. short for old age pensioner.

oar [ɔː] n. long pole with a flat end, used for moving a boat along; inf. to stick your o. in = to interfere. **oarlock** n. Am. row lock. **oarsman** n. person who rows a boat. **oarsmanship** n. being skilled at rowing.

oasis [əʊˈeɪsɪs] n. (pl.-ses[-siːz]) (a) place in the desert with water were plants grow. (b) place which is pleasantly different from its surroundings.

oasthouse [ˈəʊsthaʊs] n. building for drying hops.

oatcake [ˈəʊtkeɪk] n. dry biscuit made of oatmeal.

oath [əʊθ] n. (a) swearing that you are telling the truth. (b) promise. (c) swear word.

oatmeal [ˈəʊtmiːl] n. coarse flour made from oats.

oats [əʊts] n. cereal plant whose grain is used as food; to sow one's wild o. = behave in a very free and unruly way when young.

obbligato [ɒblɪˈgɑːtəʊ] n. (in music) important accompanying part played by a solo instrument.

obdurate [ˈɒbdjʊrət] adj. stubborn/ unyielding/unmoving. **obduracy** n. being obdurate.

obedience [əˈbiːdɪəns] n. being obedient. **obedient** adj. (person) who does what he is told to do. **obediently** adv. in an obedient way.

obeisance [aʊˈbeɪsəns] n. sign of respect, such as a bow or curtsey.

obelisk [ˈɒbəlɪsk] n. four-sided pillar which comes narrower towards the top.

obese [əˈbiːs] adj. very fat. **obesity** [əˈbiːsɪtɪ] n. being obese.

obey [əˈbeɪ] v. to do what you are told to do (s.o.).

obfuscate [ˈɒbfʌskeɪt] v. (formal) to make (sth) difficult to understand.

obituary [əˈbɪtjʊərɪ] n. written report of s.o.'s death, usu. with details of his life; o. column = part of a newspaper which gives obituaries.

object 1 [ˈɒbdʒekt] n. (a) thing; o. lesson = (I) lesson using an object as an object as a teaching aid. (ii) thing which makes a course of action very clear. (b) aim; target/purpose. (C) person/thing to which feeling, etc. is directed. (d) which follows directly from a verb or preposition. (e) money is no o. = is no obstacle/problem. **object 2** [əbˈdʒekt] v. (to) to refuse to agree; to express unwillingness towards disapproval (of).

objection [ɒbˈdʒekʃn] n. act of objecting; reason against.

objectionable adj. (a) causing disapproval. (b) (esp. of person) very unpleasant. **objective 1** [ɒbˈdʒektɪv] adj. (a) (in grammar) referring to the object. (b) referring to the external world. (c) considering matters from a general viewpoint and not just your own. **objective 2** n. (a) aim/object in view. (b) lens in a microscope which is nearest to the object being examined.

objectivity n. being objective.

objector n. person who objects; conscientious o.= person who refuses to join the armed forces to join the armed forces because he feels war is wrong.

objet d'art [ɒbdʒeiˈdɑː] n. ornament.

oblate [ɒbleɪt] n. person who has vowed to do religious work.

oblige [əˈblaɪdʒ] v. (a) to make (s.o) feel it is their duty to do sth. (b) to force (s.o.) to do sth.(c) to do sth useful for/ helpful to (s.o.) (d) to be obliged to s.o. = to owe s.o. gratitude. **obligate** [ˈɒblɪgeɪt] v. to oblige. **obligation** n. (a) duty; legal bond. (b) duty to be grateful; under an o. to s.o. = morally obliged to help s.o. **obligatory** adj. necessary according to rules or laws.

obliging adj. ready to help.

obligingly adv. in an obliging way.

oblique [əˈbliːk] adj. (a) at a slant; o. angle = angle which is not a right angle. (b) from the side; not direct. **obliquely** adv. in an oblique way.

obliterate [əˈblɪtəreɪt] v. to wipe out/to destroy. **obliteration** [əblətəˈreɪʃn] n. act of obliterating; being obliterated.

oblivion [əˈblɪvɪən] n. forgetting totally; being completely forgotten.

oblivious adj. forgetful/unaware.

oblong [ˈɒblɒŋ] n. & adj. (referring to a) rectangular shape with two pairs of equal sides, one pair being longer than the other.

obloquy [ˈɒbləkwɪ] n. (formal) criticism.

obnoxious [ɒbˈnɒkʃəs] adj. very unpleasant/offensive.

oboe [ˈəʊbəʊ] n. high-pitched wood wind instrument. **oboist** n. person who plays the oboe.

obscene [ɒbˈsiːn] adj. offending moral standards/sensitive feelings; indecent.

obscenely adv. in an obscene way.

obscenity [ɒbˈsenɪtɪ] n. (a) being

obscene. (b) obscene word.
obscure 1 [əb'skjʊə] *adj.* (a) (of place) dark/gloomy. (b) not clear. (c) not well known. **obscure 2** *v.* to hide, esp. by covering. **obscurely** *adv.* in an obscure way. **obscurity** *n.* being obscure.

obsequious [əb'si:kwɪəs *adj.* too humble; showing too much respect for/ obedience to (s.o.). **obsequies** ['ɒbsɪkwɪz] *n.* funeral ceremonies. **obsequiously** *adv.* in an obsequious way. **obsequiousness** *n.* being obsequious.

observe [əb'zɜ:v] *v.* (a) to follow/to obey (a law/rule/custom), (b) to watch/to look (at). (c) to notice (d) to remark/to note. **observance** *n.* (act of) observing. **observant** *adj.* noticing (many details). **observation** [ɒbzə'veɪʃn] *n.* (a) (act of) observing; under o. = being carefully watched. (b) calculation of position of a ship. (c) remark. **observatory** *n.* place from which stars and planets can be watched. **observer** *n.* person who attends a meeting and watches (esp. with out taking part).

obsess [ɒb'ses] *v.* to fill s.o.'s thoughts. **obsession** [əb'seʃn] *n.* idea/ subject which fills your mind constantly. **obsessive** *adj.* caused by an obsession. **obsessively** *adv.* in an obsessive way.

obsidian [ɒb'sɪdɪən] *n.* hard glasslike volcanic rock.

obsolete ['ɒbsəli:t] *adj.* (word, custom) no longer in general use. **obsolescence** *n.* being obsolescent. **obsolescent** [ɒbsə'lesənt] *adj.* going out of use/out of fashion.

obstacle ['ɒbstəkl] *n.* thing which is in the way/which prevents progress. **obstacle race** *n.* race in which various obstacles have to be passed.

obstetric (al) [ɒb'stetrɪk(l)] *adj.* referring to obstetrics or childbirth. **obstetrician** [ɒbstə'trɪʃn] *n.* doctor who specializes in obstetrics. **obstetrics** *n.* branch of medicine dealing with childbirth. **obstinate** ['ɒbstɪnət] *adj.* (a) sticking to your opinion/course of action, etc. against all arguments. (b) which will not go away. **obstinacy** *n.* being obstinate.

obstinately *adv.* in an obstinate way.
obstreperous [ɒb'strepərəs] *adj.* behaving in an uncontrolled/wild/loud way.
obstruct [əb'strʌkt] *v.* to get in the way of (sth). **obstruction** [ɒb'strʌkʃn] *n.* (a) act of obstructing. (b) thing which gets in the way. **obstructive** *adj.* which obstructs; which aims to cause an obstruction.
obtain [ɒb'teɪn] *v.* (a) to get. (b) to exist as a rule. **obtainable** *adj.* which can be obtained.
obtrude [əb'tru:d] *v.* (formal) to come/ to put in the way; to form an obstacle. **obtrusion** [əb'tru:ʒn] *n.* (a) (act of) obtruding. (b) thing which is in the way. **obtrusive** [əb'tru:sɪv] *adj.* (thing) which sticks out/which is in the way.
obtuse [əb'tju:s] *adj.* (a) stupid/dull (person). (b) o. angle = angle of between 90° and 180°. **obtusely** *adv.* in an obtuse way. **obtuseness** *n.* being obtuse.
obverse ['ɒbvɜ:s] *n.* side of a coin with the head on it/the main side of a coin.
obviate ['ɒbvɪeɪt] *v.* to avoid/to get round.
obvious ['ɒbvɪəs] *adj.* clear; easily seen/easily noticed. **obviously** *adv.* in an obvious way/clearly. **obviousness** *n.* being obvious.
ocarina [ɒkə'ri:nə] *n.* wind instrument, made of a small pot, with holes to be covered by the fingers.
occasion 1 [ə'keɪʒn] *n.* (a) thing which causes sth else. (b) (time of a) happening; on o. = from time to time. (c) special event. **occasion 2** *v.* to cause (sth) to happen. **occasional** *adj.* happening now and then/not often. **occasionally** *adv.* sometimes/not often.
Occident ['ɒksɪdənt] *n.* (formal) the West; Western countries. **occidental** [ɒksɪ'dentl] *adj.* referring to the occident.
occiput ['ɒksɪpʌt] *n.* back of the head. **occipital** [ɒk'sɪpɪtəl] *adj.* referring to the back of the head.
occlude [ɒ'klu:d] *v.* (formal) to shut up. **occlusion** *n.* (a) movement of warm air upwards, caused by the arrival of colder air. (b) blockage in a blood vessel.

occult ['ɒkʌlt] adj. & n. (referring to the) supernatural; magic.

occupy ['ɒkjʊpaɪ] v. (a) to fill/to take up (space or time). (b) to take/to have possession of. (c) to take possession and remain in control of. (d) to give work/activity to. **occupancy** n. person who occupies a place/who is in a certain seat. **occupation** [ɒkjʊ'peɪʃn] n. (a) (act of) occupying; being occupied. (b) job/position/employment. **occupational** adj. referring to an occupation; c. therapy = treating sick people by encouraging them to do special activities. **occupier** n. person who lives in (a house).

occur [ə'kɜː] v. (occurred) (a) to take place/to happen. (b) (to) come into one's thoughts. (c) to be (found). **occurrence** [ə'kʌrəns] n. happening.

ocean ['əʊʃn] n. large expanse of sea surrounding the land masses of the earth; a part of the sea. **oceanic** [əʊsɪ'ænɪk] adj. referring to the ocean.

oceanography [əʊʃə'nɒgrəfɪ] n. study of the sea.

ocelot ['ɒsɪlɒt] n. leopard-like animal found in Central and South America.

ochre, Am. **ocher** ['əʊkə] n. yellow/red natural material used for colouring; dull yellow colour.

o'clock [ə'klɒk] adv. phrase used with numbers meaning the exact hour; at six o' clock; the six o' clock train.

octagon ['ɒktəgən] n. geometrical figure with eight sides. **octagonal** [ɒk'tægənl] adj. eight-sided. **octane** ['ɒkteɪn] n. o. number/o. rating = number given to types of petrol to indicate their quality. **octave** ['ɒktɪv] n. (in music) space between the first and last notes of an eight note scale. **octavo** [ɒk'teɪvəʊ] n. size of a book. When a sheet of paper is folded to sixteen pages. **octet** [ɒk'tet] n. group of eight people, esp. musicians; piece of music for such a group. **October** [ɒk'təʊbə] n. 10th month of the year. **octogenarian** [ɒktədʒə'neərɪən] adj. & n. (person) who is between 80 and 89 years old; **octopus** ['ɒktəpəs] n. (pl.-es) sea animal with eight arms.

ocular ['ɒkjʊlə] adj. referring to the eyes/to sight. **oculist** n. doctor who specializes in care of the eyes.

odd [ɒd] adj. (-er, -est) (a) (number) which cannot be divided exactly by two. (b) approximately/a little more than, (c) occasional; referring to various individual things/items; (in an auction) o. lots = groups of different items for sale. (d) referring to a member of a set or pair, when separated from the rest.(e) strange/peculiar. **oddball** n. Am. Inf. eccentric person. **oddity** n. (a) being odd, (b) odd thing/person. **oddly** adv. in an odd way; for odd reasons. **oddments** n. pl.bits and pieces; items left over. **oddness** n. being odd. **odds** n. pl. (a) difference between the amount which has been bet and the amount to be won; o. of 10 to 1. (b) more than an equal chance; the o. are against it.(c) it makes no o. = it makes no difference. (d) to be at o. with s.o. = to quarrel constantly.(e) o. and ends = bits and pieces.

ode [əʊd] n. long poem often addressed to a person or thing.

odious ['əʊdɪəs] adj. hateful/horrible. **odiously** adv. in an odious way. **odiousness** n. being odious. **odium** n. great unpopularity/hatred.

odometer [əʊ'dɒmɪtə] n. device for measuring the distance a vehicle travels.

odontology [ɒdɒn'tɒlədʒɪ] n. study of teeth.

odour Am. **odor** ['əʊdə] n. (a) scent/smell. (b) to be in good/bad o. with = to be in/out of favour with. **odorous** adj. with a strong scent. **odourless** adj. with out any smell.

odyssey ['ɒdɪsɪ] n. long voyage of adventure.

oedema [ɪ'diːmə] n. excess liquid gathering in tissues, causing a swelling.

Oedipus complex ['iːdɪpəs'kɒmpleks] n. feeling (in a man) of hatred for his father and love for his mother.

oesophagus Am. **esophagus** [ə'sɒfəgəs] n. part of the throat down which food passes from the mouth to the stomach.

oestrogen ['iːstrədʒən] n. female hormone, controlling bodily changes in the reproductive cycle.

of [ɒv] prep. (a) belonging to/connected with. (b) being a part/a quantity. (c) (who/which) is; a child of ten (d) by/

from; south of the border; made of wool. (e) about/concerning.

off 1 [ɒf] *adv.* (a) away (from); they're o. = they've started running; day o. = day away from work.(b) not on; the deal is o. = has been cancelled; (in restaurant) chicken is o. = not available. (c) no longer fresh., (d) well/badly o. = having plenty/not enough (money). (e) right/ straight o. = immediately; on and o. = from time to time (f) (with verbs) completely; to finish o. **off 2** *prep.* (a) away from. (b) (at sea) a certain distance from. (c) branching from. (d) disliking/ not wanting (food). **off 3** *adj.* away; not on; o. day = one on which you are less successful; o. season = less busy season. **offbeat** *adj. inf.* rather odd/unusual. **offchance** *n.* slight possibility. **off-colour** *adj.* not well. **offhand** *adv. & adj.* (a) without preparation/without thinking carefully. (b) (also offhanded) rude/without courtesy. **offhandedly** *adv.* rudely. **off-licence** *n.* (shop, etc., which has) a licence to sell alcoholic drinks to be taken away. **off-line** *adj.* (computer) which is not connected to a network or to a main system. **offload** *v.* (on to) to pass a load to sth/s.o. else. **off-peak** *adj.* away from the busiest/most used times. **off-putting** *adj. inf.* causing (mild) annoyance. **offseason** *adj. & n.* (period, usually winter) when prices are lower because fewer people travel. **offset 1** ['ɒfset] *n.* method of printing from a plate to a rubber surface and then to paper. **offset 2** [ɒf'set] *v.* to balance (one thing) against another. **offshoot** ['ɒfʃuːt] *n.* small side shoot of a plant; thing which branches from sth else. **offshore** *adj.* (away) from/at a distance from the shore. **off side** *n.* (in a car) side nearest the middle of the road. **offside 1** [ɒf'saɪd] *adv.* (in football) between the ball and the opposing team's goal. **offside 2** *adj.* referring to the side of a car nearest to the middle of the road. **offspring** ['ɒfsprɪŋ] *n.* child; young (of an animal). **offstage** *adv. & adj.* not on the stage/unseen by the audience.

offal ['ɒfl] *n.* internal organs (heart, etc.). of animals, used as food.

offence [ə'fens] *n.* (a) state of offending; being offended; to take o. at =

to be offended by. (b) crime; (act of) offending (esp. against a law). **offend** [ə'fend] *v.* to be/to go against (the law/ opinions/wishes/feelings). **offender** *n.* person who offends (esp. against a law).

offensive 1 *adj.* (a) which is unpleasant. (b) (in army) which is used in an attack. **offensive 2** *n.* (military) attack; to take the o. = to start the attack. **offensively** *adv.* in an offensive way. **offensiveness** *n.* being offensive.

offer 1 ['ɒfə] *n.* (act of) indicating that you will do/give sth; thing which is offered; on o. = offered; special o. = goods which are put on sale at a reduced price. **offer 2** *v.* (a) to say/to indicate that you will do/give (sth). (b) to make/to express (an opinion, etc.). **offering** *n.* thing which is offered. **offertory** *n.* (a) offering of wine and bread in the communion service. (b) collection of money taken while the wine and bread are being offered.

office ['ɒfɪs] *n.* (a) room/building where business or professional activity is carried out; *Am.* doctors o. = room where a doctor sees his patients. (b) position/function. (c) esp. in titles) organization; government dept. (d) help/services. **officer** *n.* (a) person who holds an official position. (b) person who holds one of the commissioned ranks in the armed forces, etc. (c) police o. policeman. **official 1** [ə'fɪʃl] *adj.* referring to an organisation which is recognized by a government, etc. **official 2** *n.* person holding a recognized position. **officialdom** *n.* bureaucracy. **officialese** *n. inf.* clumsy language used by bureaucrats. **officially** *adv.* in an official way. **officiate** [əfɪ'ɪeɪt] *v.* (a) (of clergy man) (at) to perform a religious ceremony. (b) to act as chairman, etc. **officious** *adj.* too ready to interfere or to offer help. **officiously** *adv.* in an officious way. **officiousness** *n.* being officious.

offing ['ɒfɪŋ] *n.* in the o. = coming/ available soon.

often ['ɒfn] *adv.* many times; in many instances. **oftentimes** *adv. Am.* often

ogee ['əʊdʒiː] *n.* S - shaped curve in architecture; an arch with two S - shaped curves, joining at a point.

ogle ['əʊgl] v. to leer/look at (s.o.) with sexual desire.

ogre ['əʊgə] n. cruel giant who eats human beings; cruel terrifying person.

oh [əʊ] inter. expressing surprise/shock.

ohm [əʊm] n. standard measure of electrical resistance.

oil 1 [ɔɪl] n. (a) thick smooth running liquid of various kinds (used in cooking/heating/engineering/painting). (b) liquid found mainly underground and used to produce power. (c) picture painted with oil paints. **oil 2** v. to put oil on/in (esp. to make a machine run more smoothly); to o. the wheels = to help to make things run more smoothly; inf. well-oiled = rather drunk. **oil-bearing** adj. (rocks, etc.) which contain oil. **oilfield** n. area where oil is found. **oiliness** n. being oily. **oilrig** n. structure for drilling for oil. **oilskin (s)** n. (clothing of) material made waterproof with oil. **oilslick** n. thin covering of oil on the surface of the sea. **oil tanker** n. large ship/large lorry for carrying oil. **oily** adj. (-ier, -iest) (a) like oil; covered with oil. (b) (of manner) too smooth and pleasant; insincere.

ointment ['ɔɪntmənt] n. smooth healing or soothing substance spread on the skin.

OK, okay 1 [əʊ'keɪ] inf. inter. & adj. all right **OK, okay 2** n. sign of approval. **OK okay 3** v. to give a sign of approval to.

okapi [ɒ'kɑːpiː] n. African animal, like a large black horse, with white stripes on its rear legs.

okra ['ɒkrə] n. tropical plant with edible green pods.

old [əʊld] adj. (-er, -est) (a) having great age; o. wives' tale belief based on tradition rather than on fact. (b) having been in use for a long time. (c) being of a particular age. (d) having been in a certain state/having been done for a long time. (e) former. (f) term showing vagueness/affection/disrespect, etc.; inf. the o. man = boss/headmaster/father. **Old Bailey** n. central criminal court in London. **old boy network** n. system where men who were at school together help each other get ahead in later life. **olden** adj. (formal) old (times). **old -**

fashioned adj. not in fashion; out of date. **oldie** n. inf. old- fashioned/out of date thing. **oldish** adj. rather old. **old maid** n. older woman who has never married. **old-time** adj. not of the present/done in an old-fashioned way. **old timer** n. former worker/soldier, etc. **Old World** n. Europe, Asia and Africa.

oleaginous [ɒliːæʒɪnəs] adj. (formal) oily.

oleander [ɒlɪ'ændə] n. Tropical shrub with pink flowers.

olfactory [ɒl'fæktərɪ] adj. (formal) referring to the sense of smell.

oligarchy ['ɒlɪgɑːkɪ] n. (country with a) government by a few powerful people.

olive ['ɒlɪv] n. (a) small black or green fruit which produces oil and is used as food; tree which bears this fruit; o. branch = sign of peace. (b) o. (green) = dull green colour of unripe olives; o. skin = yellowish skin.

Olympic [ə'lɪmpɪk] adj. & n. the o. games/the Olympics = international athletic competition held every four years. **Olympiad** n. Major international sporting competition. **Olympian** adj. like a god; rather supercilious.

ombudsman ['ɒmbədzmən] n. (pl.-men) official who investigates complaints by members of the public against a government department.

omega ['əʊmɪgə] n. last letter of the Greek alphabet.

omelette, Am. **omelet** ['ɒmlət] n. cooked egg mixture often with savoury substances added.

omen ['əʊmən] n. thing giving an indication of the future. **ominous** ['ɒmɪnəs] adj. threatening bad results. **ominously** adv. in an ominous way.

omit [ə'mɪt] v. (omitted) (a) to leave out. (b) (to) not to do sth. **omission** [ə'mɪʃn] n. (a) act of omitting. (b) thing omitted.

omnibus 1 ['ɒmnɪbəs] n. (old) bus. **omnibus 2** n. & adj. (book) which includes several books all together.

omnidirectional [ɒmnɪdaɪ'rekʃənəl] adj. (aerial which can capture signals) from any direction.

omnipotence [ɒm'nɪpətəns] n. quality of being all-powerful. **omnipotent** adj. all-powerful.

omnipresent ['ɒmnɪprezənt] *adj.* which is every where.

omniscient [ɒm'nɪsɪənt] *adj.* (person) who knows every thing **omniscience** *n.* knowing every thing.

omnivorous [ɒm'nɪvərəs] *adj.* eating everything; (animal) which eats both plants and other animals.

on 1 [ɒn] *prep.* (a) touching the top/ outer surface of sth.(b) in/at.(c) with; have you any money on you? (d) belonging to/a member of; on the staff. (e) indicating a means of moving; on foot. (f) engaged in; on business. (g) from/by; to live on a small income. (h) (indicating a time) on Sundays; on application = when you apply; on sale = for sale; (i) approximately; just on a year ago. (j) because of; to congratulate s.o. on his success. (k) about/concerning; a book on Wales. (l) towards/against; an attack on s.o. (m) *inf.* paid by; the drinks are on me. (n) (as a bet) to put £10 on a horse = to bet £10 that the horse will win. **on 2** *adv.* (a) in position; put the kettle on; *inf.* it's just not on = cannot be allowed.(b) in action; open; the light is on. (c) happening; what's on at the cinema? (d) being worn, put your shoes on (e) (in a) continuing (way); they worked on. (f) (indicating passing of time) later on. (g) *inf.* on at s.o. = scolding/criticizing. (h) on and off = not continuously/with brakes in between; on and on = without stopping. (i) *inf.* to have s.o. on = to tell s.o. a lie as a joke.

onager ['ɒnədʒə] *n.* wild Asian donkey.

once 1 [wɒns] *adv.* (a) for one time. (b) at all/ever. (c) at a (particular) time in the past. (d) at o. = (i) immediately; (ii) at the same time. **once 2** *conj.* as soon as. **once-over** *n. inf.* quick examination.

oncoming ['ɒnkʌmɪŋ] *adj.* coming towards you.

one 1 [wʌn] *n.* number 1.(a) first number; *inf.* look after number o. = look after yourself first. (b) single unit in quantity or number (c) *inf.* a quick o. = a quick drink; she hit him o. = hit him a blow. **one 2** *adj.* (a) single (example of). (b) the only. (c) the same; it's all o. to me. **one 3** *pron.* (a) thing/person indicated. (b) example of a type. **one 4** *adj.* (on) a certain; o. night. **one 5** *pron.* (a) (*pl.*some/any) an example of sth. (b) (formal) anyone/an indefinite person. **one -armed bandit** *n.* gambling machine worked by a handle. **one-horse town** *n. inf.* small town were very little happens. **one-legged** ['wʌn'legɪd] *adj.* with only one leg. **one-night stand** *n.* performance (of a play/of a show) for one night only. **one-off** *adj.* done/made once only. **oneself** *pron.* referring to a person as an indefinite subject. **one-sided** *adj.* treating or giving justice to one side only. **one-time** *adj.* former. **one-track mind** *n.* mind which concentrates on one thing at a time. **oneupmanship** *n.* art of putting yourself at an advantage over others. **one-way** *adj.* (street) for traffic in one direction only; (ticket) for a single journey only.

onerous ['ɒnərəs] *adj.* causing much (tiring) effort.

onion ['ʌnjən] *n.* strong-smelling vegetable with a round white bulb.

online ['ɒnlaɪn] *adv. & adj.* linked directly to a computer.

onlooker ['ɒnlʊkə] *n.* person who watches.

only 1 ['əʊnlɪ] *adj.* (the) single/(the) one with out any others. **only 2** *adv.* (a) and not anyone/anything else. (b) as recently as. (c) if o. = expressing a strong wish/desire; o. too = very. **only 3** *conj.* but.

onomastics [ɒnə'mæstɪks] *n.* study of names.

onomatopoeia [ɒnəmætə'piːə] *n.* making/using words which imitate a sound. **onomatopoeic** *adj.* using onomatopoeia.

onrush ['ɒnrʌʃ] *n.* rushing in/on.

onset ['ɒnset] *n.* beginning (of an attack, etc.).

onslaught ['ɒnslɔːt] *n.* sudden severe attack.

onto ['ɒntuː] *prep.* on to.

ontology [ɒn'tɒlədʒɪ] *n.* study of reality. **ontological** [ɒntə'lɒdʒikl] *adj.* referring to reality.

onus ['əʊnəs] *n.* responsibility (for a difficult task).

onward 1 ['ɒnwəd] *adj.* forward. **onward 2** *adv.* (also onwards) forward.

onyx ['ɒnɪks] *n.* (*pl.*-es) multicoloured precious stone.

oodles ['uːdlz] *n. pl.*inf. lots (of).

ooh [uː] *inter.* showing surprise/shock.

ooze 1 [uːz] *n.* slimy mud. **ooze2** *v.* to flow slowly and gently.

opacity [ə'pæsɪti] *n.* state of being opaque.

opal ['əʊpl] *n.* semi -precious stone with varied or changing colours. **opalescence** *n.* being opalescent. **opalescent** *adj.* shining like an opal.

opaque [əʊ'peɪk] *adj.* which you cannot see through.

OPEC ['əʊpek] *n.* (Organisation of Petroleum Exporting Countries) group of countries who produce and export oil.

open 1 ['əʊpn] *adj.* (a) not closed. (b) which you can enter. (c) without limits. (d) o. to = with out protection (from sth). (e) ready to accept/to be accepted. (f) with no attempt (being made) to hide sth.(g) with space between the parts. (h) with no fixed idea (s) /conditions. (i) (competition) with out restrictions. **open 2** *v.* (a) to become open. (b) to start (up) /to set going. (c) to have an exit (on to). **open 3** *n.* unlimited area outdoors. **open-air** *adj.* not in a building. **opencaste** *adj.* (mine) dug on the surface of the ground. **open-ended** *adj.* with no definite end. **opener** *n.* device for opening sth. **open handed** *adj.* generous. **openheart** *adj.* (surgery) with the chest cut open to expose the heart. **opening 1** *n.* (a) act of opening. (b) beginning. (c) place where sth opens. (d) opportunity, such as a job vacancy. **opening 2** *adj.* which opens. **open letter** *n.* letter published as an article in a newspaper and not sent to the addressee. **openly** *adv.* in an open way. **open mind** *n.* to have an o.m. = not to have a fixed opinion on sth. **openness** *n.* quality of being open. **open out** *v.* to open (fully); to spread out wildly. **open-plan** *adj.* (offices) with no walls between them, **open prison** *n.* prison with few restrictions **open up** *v.* (a) to open (completely). (b) to bring into use. **open verdict** *n.* verdict by a coroner's jury, which describes the death, but does not state if a crime is involved.

openwork *n.* pattern (on a shoe, etc.) with holes in it.

opera ['ɒprə] *n.* (a) dramatic performance with music, in which the words are partly or wholly sung. (b) company which performs operas. **opera glasses** *n. pl.* small binoculars for looking at performers on the stage. **opera house** *n.* theatre in which opera is performed. **operatic** [ɒpə'rætɪk] *adj.* of/like/for opera. **operatta** [ɒpə'retə] *n.* opera with a light-hearted story in which some of the words are spoken.

operate 1 ['ɒpəreɪt] *v.* (a) to act. (b) to (cause) work. (c) to o. on a patient = to treat a patient by cutting open the body. **operable** ['ɒpərəbl] *adj.* which can be operated on. **operation** [ɒpə'reɪʃn] *n.* (a) (act of) operating; being operated on; to come into o. = begin to be applied. **operational** *adj.* referring to the working of sth. (b) ready for use. **operative 1** ['ɒpərətɪv] *adj.* in operation. **operative 2** *n.* worker, esp. one who operates a machine, etc. **operator** ['ɒpəreɪtə] *n.* (a) person who works instruments, etc. (b) person who carries things out/organizes things; *inf.* smart o.= flower business man.

ophthalmic [ɒp'θælmɪk] *adj.* referring to (the medical treatment of) the eye. **ophthalmologist** [ɒfæl'mɒlədʒɪst] *n.* doctor who specialises in diseases of the eye. **ophthalmology** *n.* study of the eye.

opiate ['əʊpɪət] *n.* drug which sends you to sleep.

opinion [ə'pɪnjən] *n.* (a) (of) what a person thinks/feels about sth; public o. = what people think/feel about sth. (b) view; piece of (usu. expert) advice. **opinionated** *adj.* (person) with rigid opinions/who thinks he is always right.

opium ['əʊpɪəm] *n.* drug which puts you to sleep, made from a type of poppy.

opossum [ə'pɒsəm] *n.* small North American animal which carries its young in a pouch.

opponent [ə'pəʊn/bnt] *n* person/group which is against you.

opportune [ɒpətjuːn] *adj.* coming (by chance) at the right time. **opportunely** *adv.* in an opportune way; at the right time. **opportunism** *n.* being an opportunist. **opportunist** *n.* person who takes advantage of opportunities, esp. at the expense of others.

opportunity [ɒpəˈtjuːnɪtɪ] *n.* chance/ circumstances which allow you to do sth.

oppose [əˈpəʊz] *v.* to act against (s.o./ sth); to try to prevent. **opposed to** *adj.* (a) against. (b) in contrast. **opposite 1** [ˈɒpəzɪt] *adj.* (a) facing. (b) at/in/ towards the other side of sth; o. number = person who is in a similar position in another organizatiion. (c) belonging to a completely different type/position.

opposite 2 *n.* thing which is completely different. **opposite 3** *prep.* in an opposite position to. **opposition** [ɒpəˈzɪʃn] *n.* (a) (act of) opposing. (b) (esp. in politics) the party/group which opposes the government.(c) rivalry.

oppress [əˈpres] *v.* (a) to cause to suffer, esp. by harsh rule. (b) to cause depression/sadness in. **oppression** *n.* (act of) oppressing; being oppressed.

oppressive *adj.* oppressing.

oppressively *adv.* in an oppressive way. **oppressiveness** *n.* being oppressive. **oppressor** *n.* person who oppresses.

opprobrium [əˈprəʊbrɪəm] *n.* (formal) disgrace; (cause of) strong disapproval.

opprobrious *adj.* disgraceful; rude.

opt [ɒpt] *v.* (for) to decide (in favour of). **opt out** *v.* (of) to decide not to(take part).

optical [ˈɒptɪkl] *adj.* referring to the eyes/to the eye sight; referring to optics; o. fibres = fine threads of glass, used for transmitting light signals. **optic** *adj.* referring to the eye/to sight. **optically** *adv.* referring to optics. **optician** [ɒpˈtrʃn] *n.* person who prescribes/ makes/sells spectacles or contact lenses, etc. **optics** *n.* science of light; fibre o. = use of optical fibres to transmit signals.

optimal [ˈptɪməl] *adj.* best. **optimism** *n.* belief that everything is as good as it can be/will work out for the best; confident/cheerful attitude. **optimist** [ˈɒptɪmɪst] *n.* person who believes everything will work out for the best. **optimistic** [ɒptɪˈmɪstɪk] *adj.* feeling that everything will work out for the best; giving cause for optimism.

optimistically *adv.* in an optimistic way.

optimum 1 [ˈɒptɪməm] *n.* best way. **optimum 2** *adj.* best.

option [ˈɒpʃn] *n.* (a) choice/alternative possibility. (b) o. on sth = opportunity to buy/sell sth within a certain time or at a certain price. **optional** *adj.* which may or may not be chosen.

optometrist [ɒpˈtɒmətrɪst] *n. Am.* optician. **optometry** *n,* science of eye sight.

opulence [ˈɒpjʊləns] *n,* being opulent.

opulent *adj.* rich/luxurious/splendid.

opulently *adv.* in an opulent way.

opus [ˈəʊpəs] *n.* (*pl.*-es or opera) (a) piece of music which is given a number. (b) large work of art.

or [ɔː] *conj.* (a) the opposite/the alternative/the other (possibility). (b) approximately. (c) or (else) = if not.

oracle [ˈɒrəkl] *n.* (a) (in Ancient Greece) place were the gods answered questions about the future; person who answered questions about the future. (b) very wise and knowing person.

oracular [ɒˈrækjʊlə] *adj.* referring to an oracle.

oral 1 [ˈɔːrl] *adj.* (a) by speaking. (b) taken by the mouth. **oral 2** *n.* examination where you answer questions by speaking. **orally** *adv.* (a) in/by speech. (b) by the mouth.

orange 1 [ˈɒrɪndʒ] *n. usu.* sweet citrus fruit, reddish yellow when ripe; tree which bears this fruit. **orange 2** *adj. & n.* colour of an orange. **orangeade** [ɒrɪndʒˈeɪd] *n.* fizzy orange-flavoured drink.

orang-utang [ərænjuːtæŋ] *n.* large red ape found in south-east Asia.

oration [əˈreɪʃn] *n.* (formal) speech.

orator [ˈɒrətə] *n.* person who is able to speak forcefully and persuasively to large numbers of people; person making a speech. **oratorical** [ɒrəˈtɒrɪkl] *adj.* full of eloquence. **oratory** [ˈɒrətərɪ] *n.* (a) eloquent/forceful public speaking. (b) private chapel. **oratorio** [ɒrəˈtɔːrɪəʊ] *n.* (*pl.*-os) piece of music for orchestra, choir and soloists often telling a religious story.

orb [ɔːb] *n.* (a) spherical object (such as a planet or an eyeball). (b) ornamental globe with across on top used by a king as a symbol of state power.

orbit 1 ['ɔːbɪt] *n.* (a) curved track (of an object moving through space). (b) extent of influence. **orbit 2** *v.* to move in an orbit round sth.

orchard ['ɔːtʃəd] *n.* field with fruit trees.

orchestra ['ɔːkəstrə] *n.* (a) large group of musicians who play together. (b) part of a theatre, *usu.* next to the stage, where the musicians sit; o. stalls = seats in a theatre very close to where the orchestra sits. **orchestral** [ɔː'kestrəl] *adj.* referring to an orchestra. **orchestrate** [ɔːkɪstreɪt] *v.* (a) to arrange. (a piece of music) for an orchestra. (b) to organize (a demonstration, etc.) **orchestration** [ɔːjɪ'streɪʃn] *n.* (act of) orchestrating; being orchestrated.

orchid, orchis ['ɔːkɪd, 'ɔːkɪs] *n.* flowering plant with showy flowers.

ordain [ɔː'deɪn] *v.* (a) to make (s.o.) a priest/a clergyman in a formal ceremony. (b) (formal) to order/to command (that the sth be done).

ordeal [ɔː'diːl] *n.* painful test of strength/courage; difficult period.

order 1 ['ɔːdə] *n.* (a) command/demand that sth should be done. (b) obeying of rules or laws without unrest or violence. (c) demand/request for goods from a customer; goods supplied to a customer; *inf.* a tall o. = a difficult task. (d) organization of items in succession. (e) good/correct arrangement; in o. = correct/valid; out of o. = not working. (f) arrangement of an army. (g) rules for an assembly/meeting. (h) organization of monks/priests etc.; in holy orders = being a priest. (i) organization of knighthood; group of people to whom a certain honour has been given. (j) type/kind/classification/rank. (k) paper which authorizes the transfer of money. (l) in o. to/that = so that/for the purpose of.

order 2 *v.* (a) to command/to demand/to say (that sth should be done). (b) to demand/to request (goods/services, etc.) (c) to arrange/to put into order.

oderliness ['ɔːdəlɪnəs] *n.* (a) being in good order/tidiness. (b) being quiet/being orderly. **orderly 1** *adj.* (a) in good order; tidy or well-arranged. (b) well behaved. **orderly 2** *n.* person whose duty it is to carry out routine tasks (in a hospital or in armed services).

ordinal ['ɔːdɪnl] *n. & adj.* (referring to a) number indicating the position in a series.

ordinance ['ɔːdɪməns] *n.* laws/rule made by an authority.

ordinary ['ɔːdnrɪ] *adj.* normal/not unusual; typical of its class/not having any special characteristics; out of the o. = extraordinary. **ordinarily** *adv.* in the usual way/usually.

ordination [ɔːdɪ'neɪʃn] *n..* (act/ceremony of) ordaining s.o. as a priest.

ordnance ['ɔːdnəns] *n.* (a) heavy guns. (b) (government department dealing with) military supplies. **ordnance survey** *n.* government departments which produces detailed maps.

ore [ɔː] *n.* material found in the earth from which metals are obtained.

oregano [ɒrɪ'gɑːnəʊ] *n.* spicy herb used in cooking.

organ ['ɔːgən] *n.* (a) part of the body with special function. (b) periodical which gives the views of a group/of an organization. (c) musical instrument with keyboard and many pipes through which air is pumped to make a sound. **organic** [ɔː'gænɪk] *adj.* (a) referring to an organ/to organs. (b) referring to living things; o. chemistry = concerned with carbon compounds; o. farming = using only natural fertilizers. (c) having an organized/structure. **organically** [ɔːgænɪklɪ] *adv.* in an organic way. **organism** ['ɔːgənɪzəm] *n.* living thing. **organist** *n.* person who plays the organ. **organization** [ɔːgənaɪ'zeɪʃn] *n.* (a) (act of) arranging; being arranged. (b) organized group or institution. **organize** ['ɒːgənaɪz] *v.* to arrange/to put into special of order; to put into good order. **organizer** *n.* person who arranges things.

organdie [ɔːgændɪ] *n.* very thin stiff cotton cloth.

orgasm ['ɔːgæzəm] *n.* Climax of sexual excitement.

orgy ['ɔːdʒɪ] *n.* uncontrolled indulgence in drinking/dancing; uncontrolled state or activity.

oriel ['ɔːrɪəl] *n.* o. window = upstairs window which projects from the wall.

orient 1 ['ɔːrɪənt] *n.* the O. = the East/Eastern countries. **orient 2** *v.* to put in a certain direction. **oriental 1** [ɔːrɪ'entl]

adj. referring to the orient. **oriental 2**
n. person from the orient. **orientalist**
n. Person who studies the East.
orientate ['ɒrɪənteɪt] *v.* to put in a
certain direction. **oreintation**
[ɔːrɪən'teɪʃn] *n.* (act of) orientating/
putting in a certain position/direction.
orienteering [ɔːrɪən'tiːərɪŋ] *n.* sport of
finding your way across country by
means of maps and compasses.
orifice ['ɒrɪfɪs] *n.* (formal) hole/
opening.
origami [ɒrɪ'gɑːmɪ] *n. (no pl.)* art of
folding coloured paper to make shapes.
origin [χɒrɪdʒɪn] *n.* beginning/root;
where sth/s.o. comes from. **original 1**
adj. (a) from its beginning(s); form
earliest times. (b) new/different; created
for the first time/not a copy. (c) showing
ideas not based on those of other people.
original 2 *n.* (a) thing from which
other things are copied/translated, etc.
(b) unusual person. **originality**
[ɒrɪdʒɪ'nælɪtɪ] *n.* (a) being original/new/
different. (b) ability to create sth which
has been never done before. **originally**
adv. (a) in an original way. (b) at or from
the beginning. **originate** [ə'rɪdʒɪneɪt] *v.*
(a) to bring into existence for the first
time. (b) to begin/to have its beginning.
origination [ərɪdʒɪ'neɪʃn] *n.* act of
originating. **originator** *n.* person who
originates.
oriole ['ɒrɪəl] *n.* bird with black and
yellow feathers.
ormolu ['ɔːməluː] *n. (no pl.)*
decorations made of bronze covered with
gold leaf.
ornament 1 ['ɔːnəmənt] *n.* thing used
as decoration. **ornament 2** ['ɔːnəment]
v. to decorate/to help to make more
beautiful. **ornamental** [ɔːnə'mentl] *adj.*
acting as an ornament; being pretty
rather than useful. **ornamentation**
[ɔːnəmən'teɪʃn] *n.* act of ornamenting;
group of ornaments. **ornate** [ɔː'neɪt]
adj. having (too) much ornament.
ornery ['ɔːnərɪ] *adj. Am. inf.* bad-
tempered.
ornithology [ɔːnɪ'θɒlədʒɪ] *n.* study of
birds, **ornithological** [ɔːnɪθlɒdʒɪkl]
adj. referring to ornithology.
ornithologist [ɒnɪ'θɒblədʒɪst] *n.*
person who studies birds.
orotund ['ɒrətʌnd] *adj.* pompously calm.

orphan 1 ['ɔːfn] *n.* child who has no
parents. **orphan 2** *v.* to make (s.o,) an
orphan. **orphanage** ['ɔːfenɪdʒ] *n.*
home where orphans are looked after.
orrery ['ɒrərɪ] *n.* mechanical model of
the solar system.
orris root ['ɒrɪs'ruːt] *n.* perfume from
the dried roots of a type of iris,
orthodontics [ɔːθə'dɒntɪks] *n.*
treatment to correct badly formed teeth.
orthodox ['ɔːθədɒks] *adj.* (a) holding
the generally accepted beliefs of a
religion/a philosophy, etc. (b) (Jews)
who observe traditional practices very
strictly; the o. church = the Christian
church of Eastern Europe. **orthodoxy**
n. being orthodox.
orthography [ɔː'θɒgrəfɪ] *n.* (correct)
spelling. **orthographical** [ɔːθə'græfɪkl]
adj. referring to orthography.
orthopaedic [ɔːθə'piːdɪk] *adj.*
referring to diseases and deformities of
bones. **orthopaedics** *n.* branch of
medicine dealing with bones, etc,.
orthopaedist *n.* doctor who
specialises in orthopaedics.
orthoptics [ɔː'θɒptɪks] *n.* correction of
squints.
oryx ['ɒrɪks] *n.* large rare Arabian antelope.
oscillate ['ɒsɪleɪt] *v.* to swing from one
side to the other. **oscillation** [ɒsɪ'leɪʃn]
n. (act of) oscillating. **oscilloscope**
[ɒ'sɪləkəʊp *n.* device which shows
oscillations on a screen.
osier ['əʊzɪə] *n.* type of willow tree
whose branches are used to make
baskets/furniture, etc.
osmosis [ɒz'məʊsɪs] *n.* movement of
liquid into another liquid through the
porous walls of a container.
osprey ['ɒsprɪ] *n.* large bird of prey
which eats fish.
ossicle ['ɒsɪkəl] *n.* small bone in the
middle ear.
ossify ['ɒsɪfaɪ] *v.* to make into bone; to
make rigid. **ossification** [ɒsɪfɪ'keɪʃn]
n. act of ossifying.
ostensible [ɒ'stensɪbl] *adj.* which
shows on the surface; which is meant to
seem real. **ostensibly** *adv.* seemingly.
ostentatious [ɒsten'teɪʃəs] *adj.*
showy/aiming to impress. **ostentation**
n. showing off in luxurious way which
is intended to impress. **ostentatiously**
adv. in an ostentatious way.

osteoarthritis [ɒstɪəʊ:θraɪtɪs] *n.* painful disease of the joints.

osteopath ['ɒstɪəpæθ] *n.* person who treats diseases of the bones and muscles by moving or massaging the patient's limbs. **osteopathic** [ɒstɪə'pæθɪk] *adj.* referring to osteopathy. **osteopathy** [ɒstɪ'ɒpəθɪ] *n.* treatment of diseases of bones and muscles by moving or massaging limbs.

ostracism ['ɒstrəsɪzəm] *n.* being cut off from a group/society. **ostracize** ['ɒstrɪsaɪz] *v.* to force/to keep (s.o.) out of a group.

ostrich ['ɒstrɪtʃ] *n.* (*pl.* -es) large, fast running, flightless bird found in Africa.

other 1 ['ʌðə] *adj.* (a) different/not the one already mentioned/not the same. (b) second of two; every o. week = every second week. (c) (expressing a vague idea) the o. day = a day or two day ago. **other 2** *pron.* (a) different person/ different thing. (b) (used to contrast two things or groups) one after the o. **other 3** *adv.* o. than = apart from. **otherwise** *adv.* (a) in a different way/situation. (b) in other respects. (c) if not/or else.

otherworldly *adj.* (person) who is not interested in material things/who is vague and impractical.

otiose ['əʊtɪəʊs] *adj.* (formal) superfluous/unwanted.

otitis. [əʊ'taɪtɪs] *n.* inflammation of the ear.

otter ['ɒtə] *n.* fish-eating mammal with webbed feet living mainly by rivers.

ottoman ['ɒtəmən] *n.* box for storing goods with a padded seat on top.

ouch [aʊʃ] *inter.* showing reaction to pain.

ought [ɔːt] *v.* (past tense; ought to have) used with other verbs (a) (expressing duty or obligation) you o. to go = it is your duty to go. (b) (expressing something which is vaguely desirable) you o. to hear that concert. (c) (expressing something which is probable) that horse o. to win.

ounce [aʊns] *n.* measure of weight (28 grams).

our ['aʊə] *adj.* belonging to us. **ours** ['aʊəz] *pron.* thing(s) /person/(s) belonging to us. **ourselves** *pron.* referring to the subject we.

oust [aʊst] *v.* to force s.o. to leave a place/position.

out 1 [aʊt] *adv.* (a) not in (a building, etc.); the men are o. = on strike. (b) away from the starting point (of sth). (c) (in a direction) away from the inside/from the starting point. (d) having appeared/ become known; the hawthorn is o. = in flower; her book is just o. = has just been published. (e) o. loud = so that it can be heard. (f) not in the right position/state; o. of practice = not having done enough practice; (in cricket) he is 62 not o. = he has scored 62 and has not been bowled/ caught, etc. (g) mistaken. (h) (of fire/ light) no longer burning; (of hairstyle/ dress) no longer fashionable, (i) finished; having reached the end. **out 2** *n.* to know the ins and outs of = to know the sth in all its details. **out-and out** *adj. adv.* Complete(ly) /total(ly). **outback** *n.* (in Australia) area(s) away from centres of population. **outbid** *v.* (outbid) (at auction) to bid a higher sum than (s.o.). **outboard** *adj.* (engine) which is attached to the outside of a boat. **out break** *n.* sudden occurrence of an illness or unrest. **outbuildings** *n. pl.* buildings standing apart from the main building. **outburst** *n.* sudden display of (violent) emotion. **outcast** *n. & adj.* (person who has been) rejected by/driven away from a society or a group. **outclass** *v.* to be much better than. **outcome** *n.* result. **outcrop** *n.* rock which sticks out of the surface of the ground. **outcry** *n.* loud protest from a number of people. **outdated** *adj.* old-fashioned. **outdo** *v.* (outdid; outdone) to do better than. **outdoor** *adj.* in the open air. **outdoors** *adv. & n.* (in/to) the open air. **outer** *adj.* further out; on the out side; beyond the limits; o. space = space beyond the earth's atmosphere. **outermost** *adj.* furthest out. **outfall** *n.* pipe which takes sewage out to see. **outfit** *n.* (a) set of equipment needed for a purpose (b) set of clothing.(c) *inf.* organisation. **outfitter** *n.* supplier of (esp. men's) clothing. **outflank** *v.* to go by the side of (an enemy). **outflow** *n.* quantity which flows out. **outgoing** *adj.* (a) which is going out. (b) open/lively (personality). **outgoings** *n. pl.* money spent. **outgrow** *v.* (outgrew; outgrown) to grow too big for (clothes); to leave behind as one grows up. **outhouse** *n.* building standing apart from a main building. **outing** *n.* trip, *usu.* for pleasure. **outlandish** *adj.* strange/different from the usual. **outlast** *v.* to live/to last longer than. **outlaw 1** *n.* person who has been outlawed. **outlaw 2** *v.* to declare (s.o.) to be beyond the protection of the law. **outlay** *n.* expenditure. **outlet** *n.* (a) means by which sth can escape. (b) place where sth can be sold or distributed. **outline 1** *n.* line showing the outer edge(s) of sth; broad description without much detail. **outline 2** *v.* to make a broad description of (a plan, etc.). **outlive** *v.* to live longer than. **outlook** *n.* view from a building/of the world/of the future. **outlying** *adj.* away from the centre/from the main part. **outmanœuvre,** *Am.* **outmanœuver** *v.* to beat s.o. by acting/working more cleverly. **outmoded** *adj.* old-fashioned. **outnumber** *v.* to be greater in number than. **out of** *prep.* (a) outside of; away from; o. of your mind = mad. (b) from; one o. of ten. (c) made from. (d) because of. (e) no longer having; o. of print = with no printed copies left; o. of stock = with no stock left. **out of date** *adj.* (a) no longer in fashion. (b) no longer valid. **out of pocket** *adj.* having paid expenses personally. **out of the way** *adj.* (a) very far from the centre. (b) unusual/extraordinary. **outpatient** *n.* person who attends a hospital with out staying overnight. **outpost** *n.* small garrison of soldiers in a distant part of an occupied territory. **outpourings** *n. pl.* flood (of complaints/of emotional speech). **output** *n.* amount which a firm/machine/person produces; information produced by a computer; outputs = goods or services sold. on which VAT is charged. **out rank** *v.* to be of a higher rank than (s.o.). **outreach** *n.* services of a local authority provided out side the offices of the authority. **outrider** ['aʊtraɪdə] *n.* guard on a motorcycle or horse, riding beside a car/carriage in a procession. **outrigger** *n.* long piece with a float at the end, which is attached to the side of a boat to make it more stable. **outright** ['aʊtraɪt] *adv. & adj.*

(a) complete (ly); all at once. (b) straight out/without pretending. **outset** ['aʊtset] *n.* beginning. **outshine** [aʊt'ʃaɪn] *v.* (outshone) to do much better than (s.o.). **outside 1** [aʊt'saɪd] *n.* (a) outer surface (of sth.); what is beyond the outer surface/edge of sth. (b) at the o. = at the most. **outside 2** *adj.* (a) on the outer surface. (b) the most (possible). (c) from the outside/from another group, etc. **outside 3** *adv. & prep.* beyond the outer surface/edge of (sth). **outsider** *n.* (a) person who does not belong to a group, etc. (b) horse which is not expected to win. **outsize** ['aʊtsaɪz] *n. & adj.* (of) size which is larger than the normal or usual range. **outskirts** ['aʊtskɜːts] *n. pl.* outer edges of a town, etc. **outsmart.** [aʊt'smaːt] *v.* to trick (s.o.) by being cleverer. **outspoken.** [aʊt'spəʊkən] *adj.* speaking (too) frankly. **outstanding** [aʊt'stændɪŋ] *adj.* (a) excellent; of unusual quality of very high standard. (b) not yet fulfilled/incomplete. **outstandingly** *adv.* to an outstanding degree. **outstay.** [aʊtsteɪ] *v.* to stay longer than. **outstretched** *adj.* (arm, etc.) which is stretched out. **outstrip** *v.* (outstripped) to run past (s.o.); to do better than (s.o.). **out to** *adj.* trying to/aiming for. **out tray** *n.* basket for correspondence which is to be send out. **outvote** [aʊt'vəʊt] *v.* to defeat by having more votes than. **outward** ['aʊtwəd] *adj. & adv.* (a) towards the outside; away from the centre or starting point.(b) on the outside. **outwardly** *adv.* (appearing) on the outside. **outwards** *adv.* towards the outside. **outweigh** [aʊt'weɪ] *v.* to be more important than (sth). **outwit** [aʊt'wɪt] *v.* (outwitted) to trick (s.o.) by being cleverer. **outwork** *n.* ·work which a company pays s.o. to do at home, **out worker** *n.* person who does outwork. **outworn** *adj.* (formal) worn out (cliché, etc.).

outrage 1 ['aʊtreɪdʒ] *n.* offence; vigorous attack (esp. against moral standards). **outrage 2** *v.* to shock/to be a cause of moral indignation. **outrageous** [aʊt'reɪdʒəs] *adj.* causing (moral) indignation/shock. **outrageously** *adv.* in an outrageous way.

outré ['u:treɪ] *adj.* strange/weird.

ouzel ['u:zl] *n.* type of diving bird.

ova. ['əʊvə] *n. pl.* see ovum.

oval ['əʊvl] *n & adj.* (of) a long rounded shape; egg-shaped (d). .

ovary ['əʊvərɪ] *n.* one of the two organs of a female mammal in which eggs are produced. **ovarian** [əʊ'veərɪən] *adj.* referring to ovaries.

ovation [ə'veɪʃn] *n.* great applause.

oven ['ʌvn] *n.* enclosed box which can be heated for cooking/for baking pottery, etc. **ovenware** *n.* (no *pl.*) dishes which can be put I a hot oven.

over 1 ['əʊvə] *prep.* (a) on the top (surface) of. (b) higher than. (c) across/ to the other side of. (d) from the top of. (e) on the other/on the far side of. (f) everywhere in. (g) during. (h) more than. (i) better than. (j) about. **over 2** *adv.* (a) in all parts of (sth.). (b) repeatedly. (c) above the top of (sth.). (d) downwards from a previous vertical position. (e) into another position; please turn o. = turn the page. (f) to the other side of. (g) more/higher in number. (h) in excess/left behind. (I) past/finished. (j) prefix meaning too (much); overexcited; overtired. **over 3** *n.* one of the sections of a cricket match, during which one bowler bowls six times. **overall 1** *adj.* covering; talking in all aspects. **overall 2** *n.* (a) light coat worn by women at work. (b) overalls = man's one -piece suit worn to protect the other clothes. **overarm** *adv.* (in cricket) (to bowl) with the arm higher than the shoulder. **overawe** [əʊvə'ɔː] *v.* to frighten. **over balance** *v.* to (cause to) lose balance.

overbearing *adj.* trying to dominate others. **overblown** *adj.* (rose) which has almost finished flowering; (claim) which is excessive. **overboard** *adv.* into the water from the edge of a ship, etc.; *inf.* to go o. for = to be enthusiastic about. **overbook** *v.* to book more places than there are rooms/seats. **overcast** *adj.* (of sky) heavy/dull/ cloudy. **overcharge** *v.* to charge too much for sth. **overcoat** *n.* (full - length) coat for outdoor wear. **overcome** *v.* (overcame; has overcome) to gain victory over (an enemy/a problem/an emotion). **over**

crowded *adj.* containing too many people/animals, etc. **overdo** *v.* (overdid, overdone) (a) to do too much; to exaggerate.(b) to cook too much.

overdose *n.* too large a dose (of a drug). **overdraft** *n.* amount by which a bank account is overdrawn; amount which thc bank allows you to borrow.

overdraw *v.* (overdrew, overdrawn) to take out money (from a bank account) when there is no money there.

overdrive *n.* mechanism in a car which gives an extra gear above the top gear. **overdue** *adj.* (debt) which has not been paid at the correct time; (book) which should have been returned to the library; (visit) which should have been made; (plane, etc.) which is late.

overeat *v.* (overate,; overeaten) to eat too much. **overeating** *n.* eating too much. **over estimate** *v.* to estimate too much; to think (sth) is larger than it is. **overexposed** *adj.* (film) which has been exposed too much. **overfed** *adj.* given too much to eat.

overfishing *n.* catching more fish than is allowed. **overflow 1** *v.* (a) to flow over the top. (b) to occupy greater space. **overflow 2** *n.* (a) liquid which has overflowed. (b) pipe to catch overflowing liquid. (c) amount or number which will not fit a given space.

overgrown *adj.* covered (with plants, etc.). **overhanging** *adj.* which juts out over. **overhaul 1** [əʊvə'hɔːl] *v.* (a) to examine carefully, repairing where necessary. (b) to overtake (another ship). **overhaul 2** ['əʊvəhɔːl] *n.* (act of) overhauling **overhead 1** *adv.* above. **overhead 2** *adj.* (a) above; o. projector = projector which projects a picture from a flat surface on to a screen. (b) o. expenses = general expenses incurred by a business as a whole, such as salaries/heating/rent, etc. **overhead 3** *n. Am.* overhead expenses. **overheads** *n. pl.* overhead expenses. **overhear** [əʊvə'hɪə] *v.* (overheard) [əʊvə'hɜːd] to hear accidentally (what you are not meant to hear). **overheat** *v.* to heat too much. **overjoyed** *adj.* very happy. **overkill** *n.* excess of weapons/excessive strength for what is required. **overland** *adv. & adj.* by land. **overlap1** *v.*

(overlapped) to cover a section of (sth). **overlap 2** *n.* amount by which sth overlaps. **overleaf** *adv.* on the other side of a page. **overload** *v.* to put too heavy a load on (sth). **overlook** *v.* (a) not to notice, (b) to pretend not to notice; to pay no attention to.(c) to look out on to. **overlord** *n.* person in supreme command. **overly** *adv.* too much. **overmanning** *n.* having more workers than are needed for the job. **overmuch.** *adv.* too much. **overnight 1** *adv.* until morning. **overnight 2** *adj.* for the night. **overpass** *n.* road which crosses over the top of another road. **overpay** *v.* (overpaid) to pay (s.o.) too much. **overpayment** *n.* paying too much. **overplay** *v.* to o. your hand = to attend (to gain) too much in negotiations. **overpower** *v.* to gain control of (s.o.) by force. **overpowering** *adv.* very strong. **overproduction** *n.* excess production. **overrate** *v.* to estimate/to value (sth) higher than it is. **overreach** *v.* to o. your self = to go too far (and fail in what you are trying to do). **overreact** *v.* to react very violently. **override** *v.* (overrode, overridden) (a) to pay no attention to (an order, etc.). (b) to be more important than other things. **overrider** *n.* rubber pad fixed to the bumper of a car. **overripe** *adj.* too ripe. **over rule** *v.* to rule/to order against. **over run** *v.* (over ran; over run) (a) to go into/to attack all parts of.(b) to continue beyond (a time limit). **overseas** *adv. & adj.* across the sea. **oversee** *v.* (oversaw; overseen) to superintend/supervise. **overseer** *n.* person who supervises other people at a work. **overshadow** *v.* to hide/to make less conspicuous by greater brilliance. **overshoes** *n. pl.* rubber/ plastic shoes worn over ordinary shoes to protect them. **overshoot** *v.* (overshot) to go beyond a natural stopping place. **oversight** *n.* not doing sth because of forgetfulness/not noticing. **oversleep** *v.* (over slept; has overslept) to sleep longer than you meant to. **over spend** *n.* (overspent) to spend more than you should. **overspill** *n.* excess population which

is moved from one area to another. **overstate** *v.* to state too strongly/ with too much detail. **overstatement** *n.* act of overstating; what is overstated. **overstay** *v.* to o. your welcome = to stay for such a long time that you are no longer welcome. **oversteer** *v.* (of vehicle) to turn more sharply than the driver intends. **overstep** *v.* (overstepped) to go further than you ought to. **overstuffed** *adj.* well padded (sofa). **oversubscribed** *adj.* (shares) which more people applied for than there were available. **overtake** *v.* (over took; overtaken) to reach and go past(s.o. ahead of you); to pass (another car) which is going more slowly than you. **overtax** *v.* to demand too much tax from; to o. one's strength = to do more than one is physically capable of. **over-the-counter market** *n.* stop market which deals in shares not listed on a main Stock Exchange. **overthrow 1** *n.* removal (of a government/dictator) from power. **overthrow 2** *v.* (over threw, overthrown) to defeat. **overtime 1** *n.* (a) time worked beyond normal working hours. (b) money paid for working beyond normal hours. **overtime 2** *adv.* beyond normal hours. **overtones** *n. pl.* suggestion of sth which is different from the general content. **overturn** *v.* to (cause to) fall over/to turn upside down. **over view** *n.* general view(of a subject). **overweening** [əʊvə'wiːniŋ] *adj.* excessive/arrogant (pride). **overweight** [əʊvə'welm] *adj.* too heavy. **overwhelm** *v.* (a) to conquer (completely). (b) overwhelmed with work = having more work than you can do. **overwhelming** *adj.* enormous; greater than all others. **overwork 1** [əʊvə'wɜːk] *n.* too much work. **overwork 2** *v.* to (cause to) work too hard. **overwrought** [əʊvə'rɔːt] *adj.* very agitated/under a lot of stress. **overt** [əʊ'vɜːt] *adj.* open/not hidden. **overture** ['əʊvətʃə] *n.* (a) (short) piece of music played at the beginning of an opera/concert., etc. (b) to make overtures to s.o. = to try to begin a conversation/ negotiations with s.o.

oviduct ['ɒvɪdʌkt] n. tube through which ova are passed to the womb. **oviparous** [ɒ'vɪpərəs] adj. which lays eggs.

ovoid ['əʊvɔɪd] adj. shaped like an egg.

ovum ['əʊvəm] n. (pl.ova['əʊvə]) female egg which can develop inside the mother's body when fertilized. **ovulate** ['ɒvjʊleɪt] v. to produce female eggs. **ovulation** n. producing female eggs.

ovule n. part of a plant where the seeds developed.

ow [aʊ] inter. showing pain.

owe [əʊ] v. (a) to be obliged; to be due to pay (s.o.).(b) to o. sth to = to have sth because of (s.o./sth). **owing to** prep. because of.

owl [aʊl] n. bird of prey which is mainly active at night. **owlish** adj. like an owl.

own 1 [əʊn] v. (a) to have/to possess. (b) to recognize as belonging to you. (c) to admit; to say that sth is true.(d) inf. to o. upto sth = to admit/to say that you have done sth wrong. **own 2** adj. belonging to your self (alone). **own 3** n. (a) my o./his o. = mine/his; of your o. = belonging to you; to come into your o. = to have the success which you deserve; inf. to get your o. back = have your revenge; to hold your o. = to remain firm against some threat. (b) on your o. = alone/by yourself. **owner** n. person who owns. **ownership** n. state of owning.

ox [ɒks] n. (pl.oxen) (a) large animal of the cow family. castrate bull. **oxbow** n. curved lake formed in a bent of a river where the current no longer runs. **oxeye** n. daisy with large flowers. **oxtail** n. tail of the ox used as food.

oxalis [ɒk'sælɪs] n. type of flower, which produces a poisonous substance.

oxide ['ɒksaɪd] n. chemical compound of oxygen. **oxidation, oxodization.** [ɒksɪ'deɪʃn, ɒksɪdaɪ'zeɪʃn] n. act of oxidizing. **oxidize** ['ɒksɪdaɪz] v. to (cause to) combine with oxygen.

oxyacetylene [ɒksɪə'setɪliːn] n & adj. (referring to a) mixture of oxygen and acetylene.

oxygen ['ɒksɪdʒən] n. (element: O) gas which forms part of the earth's atmosphere and is essential for plant and animal life.

oyez ['ɒ'jez] int. hear this.

oyster ['ɔɪstə] n. type of double-shelled shellfish highly valued as food; o. bed = part of the sea floor where oysters are found. **oystercatcher** n. common black and white bird which lives on the sea shore.

oz abbrev. for ounce.

ozone ['əʊzəʊn] n. (a) harmful form of oxygen; o. hole = gap which forms in the ozone layer, allowing harmful radiation from the sun to reach the earth; o. layer = layer of ozone in the stratosphere, formed by the action of sunlight on oxygen, which acts as protection against harmful rays from the sun. (b) inf. refreshing sea air.

Pp

P symbol for phosphorous.

pa [pɑː] n. inf. child's name for father.

p.a. abbrev. for per annum.

pace 1 [peɪs] n. (a) stride/step; distance covered by one step. (b) speed; to keep p. with = keep up with; (of a runner) to set the p. = to decide how fast a race should be run. **pace 2** v. (a) to walk; to measure by walking. (b) to set the pace for (a runner, etc.). **pacemaker** n. (a) runner who sets the pace in a race; person who runs alongside a runner to encourage him to run faster. (b) electric device which makes heartbeats regular.

pachyderm ['pækɪdɜːm] n. animal with a thick skin (such as an elephant).

pacify ['pæsɪfaɪ] v. to calm. **pacific** [pə'sɪfɪk] adj. peaceful/calm.

pacifically adv. in a pacific way.

pacification [pæsɪfɪ'keɪʃn] n. calming (of people in revolt). **pacifier** ['pæsɪfaɪə] n. Am. dummy (for babies).

pacifism n. opposition to war.

pacifist n. person who believes in pacifism.

pack 1 [pæk] n. (a) bundle of things. (b) rucksack/bag carried on the back. (c) group of animals/people; the p. = the forwards in a rugby teAm. (d) articles put in a box for selling. (e) face p. = cream which is spread on your face and

left on it for a time to clean the skin. (f) ice p. = bag of ice placed on the forehead to cure a headache, etc. **pack 2** v. (a) to put (things) in order in a case/box. (b) to squeeze (many things) into a small area.
package 1 n. (a) bundle of things/ parcel. (b) p. deal = deal where several items are agreed at the same time; p. tour = tour which is organized and paid for in advance. **package 2** v. to wrap/to present (goods) in an attractive way.
packaging n. wrapping of goods in an attractive way. **packer** n. person who packs goods. **packet** n. (a) small parcel; small box. (b) inf. large amount of money. **pack ice** n. mass of ice covering the sea. **packing** n. (a) putting things into containers; p. case = special wooden box for packing goods (esp. for transport). (b) material used to protect goods which are being packed. (c) to send s.o. p. = to send s.o. away.
pack off v. to send (s.o.) away. **pack up** v. to put things away (before closing a shop/before leaving a place).
pact [pækt] n. agreement/treaty.
pad 1 [pæd] n. (a) soft part under the feet of some animals; soft protective cushion. (b) (in cricket) protective guards for the batsman's leg. (c) set of sheets of paper lightly attached. (d) launching p. = area from which a rocket is launched. (e) Sl. room/flat. **pad 2** v. (padded) (a) to soften (sth hard) by using soft material; to walk about softly; to p. out = to make (a speech/an article) longer by inserting irrelevant material.
padding n. (a) words added to pad out a speech or article. (b) soft material used to make cushions, etc.
paddle 1 ['pædl] n. (a) short oar used to propel canoe. (b) round bat used in table tennis. (c) walk in shallow water. (d) device with a knob. used for moving a cursor on a computer screen. **paddle 2** v. (a) to make (a boat) move forward using a paddle. (b) to walk about in very shallow water. **paddle steamer** n. boat driven by large wheels on either side. **paddle wheel** n. wheel on a paddle steamer. **paddling pool** n. small shallow pool for little children.
paddock ['pædək] n. small field for horses.
paddy ['pædɪ] n. (a) inf. fit of bad

temper. (b) (also paddy field) field where rice is grown.
padlock 1 ['pædlɒk] n. small portable lock with a hook which can be unlocked and twisted to pass through a ring to lock a gate/a box, etc. **padlock 2** v. to lock with a padlock.
padre ['pɑːdrɪ] n. (Army) chaplain.
paean ['piːən] n. (formal) great song praising s.o.
paediatrician [piːdrə'trɪʃn] n. doctor who specializes in paediatrics.
paediatric [piːdɪ'ætrɪk] adj. referring to the medical care of children.
paediatrics n. science of treatment of children's diseases.
pagan ['peɪgən] adj. & n. (person) who does not believe in one of the established religions; (person) who is not a Christian.
page 1 [peɪdʒ] n. (a) one of the sides of a sheet of paper in a book or magazine. (b) messenger boy in a hotel. (c) small boy who accompanies the bride at a wedding **page 2** v. (a) (old) to call (s.o.) over a loudspeaker in a hotel,etc. **pageboy** n. (a) (old) boy attendant on a medieval lord. (b) p. hairstyle = woman's hair cut quite short and straight.
pageant ['pædʒənt] n. grand display of people in costume. **pageantry** n. grand ceremonies where people wear showy costumes.
paginate ['pædʒɪmeɪt] v. to number the pages in a book. **pagination** [pædʒɪ'neɪʃn] n. act of paginating.
pagoda [pə'gəʊdə] n. tall tower made of several storeys. found in the Far East.
paid [peɪd] v. see pay.
pail [peɪl] n. bucket.
pain 1 [peɪn] n. (a) sensation of being hurt. (b) to take pains over sth/to do sth = to take care. (c) on p. of death = at the risk of being sentenced to death. **pain 2** v. to hurt. **pained** adj. sad/sorrowful (expression). **painful** adj. which hurts. **painfully** adv. in a painful way. **painkiller** n. painkilling drug. **painkilling** adj. (drug) which stops part of your body hurting. **painless** adj. which does not hurt. **painlessly** adv. win a painless way. **painstaking** adj. careful/well-done (work).
paint 1 [peɪnt] n. liquid in various colours used to colour. **paint 2** v. (a) to

cover with colour. (b) to make a picture of (s.o./sth). **painter** *n.* (a) person who paints pictures. (b) person who paints houses/cars, etc. (c) rope for typing up a boat. **painting** *n.* (a) making pictures. (b) painted picture. **paintwork** *n.* (no *pl.*) painted surfaces (doors/windows, etc.).

pair 1 ['peə] *n.* (a) two things taken together; two people. (b) two things joined together to make one. (c) agreement between two MPs from opposite parties, by which both can be absent from the House of Commons at the same time. **pair 2** *v.* (a) to join together in twos. (b) to mate.

paisley ['peɪzlɪ] *n.* pattern on textiles of curved shapes.

pajamas [pə'dʒɑːməz] *n. pl.* Am. pyjamas.

Pakistani 1 [pæki'stɑːnɪ] *adj.* referring to Pakistan. **Pakistani 2** *n.* person from Pakistan.

pal [pæl] *n. inf.* friend. **pally** *adj. inf.* friendly.

palace ['pæləs] *n.* large building where a king/queen/president, etc., lives.

palanquin [pælənkwɪn] *n.* seat with a roof, carried by bearers.

palate ['pælət] *n.* top part of the inside of the mouth. **palatable** *adj.* nice to eat/tasting good.

palatial [pə'leɪʃl] *adj.* magnificent/like a palace.

palaver [ə'lɑːvə] *n. inf.* fuss/bother.

pale 1 [peɪl] *adj.* (-er, -est) light coloured. **pale 2** *n.* beyond the p. = doing things which are not acceptable in society. **pale 3** *v.* (a) to lose colour; to become light. (b) to become less important. **paleness** *n.* light colour.

paleography [pælɪ'ɒgrəfɪ] *n.* study of ancient writing. **paleolithic** [pælɪəʊ'lɪθɪk] *adj.* referring to the early part of the Stone Age. **paleontology** [pælɪɒn'tɒlədʒɪ] *n.* study of fossils.

Palestinian [pælɪ'stɪnɪən] *adj. & n.* (person) from Palestine.

palette ['pælət] *n.* (a) flat board on which an artist mixes his colours; p. knife = long flat knife with a rounded end. (b) range of colours available, esp. on a computer graphics program.

palimony ['pælɪmənɪ] *n.* alimony paid to a friend when parting after years of life together.

palindrome ['pælɪndrəʊm] *n.* word or phrase which is spelt the same backwards and forwards.

paling(s) palisade ['peɪlɪŋ(z)] [pælɪ'seɪd] *n.* fence made of pointed pieces of wood.

pall 1 [pɔːl] *n.* (a) (formal) thick layer (of smoke). (b) cloth put over a coffin.

pall 2 *v.* to become less interesting. **pallbearer** *n.* person who walks beside a coffin in a funeral procession.

pallet ['pælɪt] *n.* (a) flat platform on which goods can be stacked and moved from place to place. (b) straw-filled mattress.

palliasse ['pælɪæs] *n.* straw-filled mattress.

palliate ['pælɪeɪt] *v.* to try to reduce (a vice/pain); to cover up (a mistake). **palliative** ['pælɪətɪv] *adj. & n.* (thing) which reduces pain.

pallid ['pælɪd] *adj.* pale (face). **pallor** ['pæləʊ] *n.* paleness (of face).

palm [pɑːm] *n.* (a) soft inside surface of your hand. (b) tall tropical tree with long leaves at the top. **palmist** *n.* person who tells the future by palmistry.

palmistry *n.* telling what will happen to you in the future from the lines in the palm of your hand. **palm off** *v. inf.* (on) to give (sth bad) to s.o. without his knowing. **Palm Sunday** *n.* Sunday before Easter Sunday. **palmy** *adj.* (-ier, -iest) pleasant.

palpable ['pælpəbl] *adj.* which can be felt/which can be easily seen. **palpably** *adv.* in a palpable way. **palpation** [pæl'peɪʃn] *n.* examination of part of the body by feeling it with the hand.

palpitate ['pælpɪteɪt] *v.* to beat very quickly. **palpitations** [pælpɪ'teɪʃnz] *n. pl.* rapid beating of the heart.

palsy ['pɒlzɪ] *n.* (a) Paralysis. (b) trembling (of the hands, etc.). **palsied** *adj.* with trembling limbs.

paltry ['pɔːltrɪ] *adj.* (-ier, -iest) insignificant.

paludism ['pælju:dɪzm] *n.* malaria.

pampas ['pæmpəs] *n. pl.* grass covered plains in South America p. grass = type of tall ornamental grass.

pamper ['pæmpə] *v.* to spoil (a child/a dog) by giving them too much food/by treating them too well.

pamphlet ['pæmflət] *n.* small book with only a few pages which is not bound with a hard cover. **pamphleteer** [pæmflə'trə] n. person who writes political pamphlets.

pan- [pæn] prefix meaning over a wide area; pan-American = covering the whole of America.

pan 1 [pæn] n. (a) metal cooking container with a handle. (b) metal dish; one of the dishes on a pair of scales. (c) bowl of a lavatory **pan 2** (panned) (a) to move a camera sideways to take in a wider view. (b) inf. to criticize. (c) to p. for gold = to sift mud in a stream hoping to find gold in it. **pancake** ['pæŋkeɪk] n. thin soft flat cake made of flour, milk, eggs, etc. **pan out** v. inf. to turn out/to succeed.

panacea [pænə'si:ə] n. thing which cures everything/which solves every problem.

panache [pə'næʃ] n. showy way of doing things.

panama [pænə'mɑ:] n. hat made of fine straw.

panatella [pænə'telə] n. long thin cigar.

panchromatic [pænkrə'mætɪk] adj. (film) which is sensitive to all colours.

pancreas ['pæŋkrɪəs] n. (pl.-es) gland which produces insulin and also a liquid which helps digest food.

panda ['pændə] n. (giant) p. = large black and white Chinese animal; p. car = police car which patrols the streets.

pandemic [pæn'demɪk] adj. (disease) which occurs over the whole world/over a large area.

pandemonium [pændɪ'məʊnɪəm] n. great uproar and confusion.

pander ['pændə] v. to give in (to low tastes).

pane [peɪn] n. sheet of glass (in a window, etc.).

panegyric [pænɪ'dʒɪrɪk] n. (formal) speech in praise of s.o.

panel 1 ['pænl] n. (a) flat surface which is higher/lower/thicker, etc., than the rest of the surface. (b) section of different-coloured material. (c) group of people who answer questions/who judge a competition; group of doctors in the same practice **panel 2** v. (panelled) to cover with sheets of wood. **panel beater** n. person who repairs car bodies. **panel game** n. (on radio/TV)

where a group of people answer questions/guess answers, etc. **panelling** n. sheets of wood used to cover walls, etc. **panellist** n. member of a panel answering questions/judging a competition.

pang [pæŋ] n. sudden sharp pain.

panic 1 ['pænɪk] n. terror/fright. **panic 2** v. (panicked) to become frightened. **panic stricken** adj. wild with fright. **panicky** adj. likely to panic.

panicle ['pænɪkl] n. cluster of flowers which hangs down.

pannier ['pænɪə] n. one of a pair of bags carried on the side of an animal or a bicycle.

panoply ['pænəplɪ] n. fine show/grand display of costume, etc.

panorama [pænə'rɑ:mə] n. wide expanse of landscape. **panoramic** [pænə'ræmɪk] adj. wide.

pansy ['pænzɪ] n. (a) small multicoloured garden flower. (b) inf. effeminate man.

pant [pænt] v. to breathe fast.

pantechnicon [pæn'teknɪkən] n. large lorry for moving furniture.

pantheism ['pænθɪɪzəm] n. belief that God and the universe are one and the same; worship of many gods.

panther ['pænθə] n. large black leopard.

panties ['pæntɪz] n. inf. women's brief undergarment worn on the lower part of the body.

pantile ['pæntaɪl] n. curved tile for a roof.

pantograph ['pæntəgrɑ:f] n. metal frame on the roof of an electric locomotive which rises to touch an overhead electric wire to pick up electricity.

pantomime ['pæntəmaɪm] n. Christmas theatrical entertainment on a traditional fairy-tale subject.

pantry ['pæntrɪ] n. cool cupboard or room for keeping food in.

pants [pænts] n. pl. (a) inf. brief undergarment worn on the lower part of the body. (b) inf. trousers. **panty hose** ['pæntɪ'həʊz] n. pl. women's tights.

pap [pæp] n. soft food for invalids.

papa [pə'pɑ:] n. child's name for father.

papacy ['peɪpəsɪ] n. position of pope. **papal** adj. referring to the pope.

papaw, papaya ['pɔːpɔː, pə'pæjə] *n.* yellow fruit from a tropical tree.
paper 1 ['peɪpə] *n.* (a) thin material made from rags or wood pulp, used for printing/writing, etc. (b) sheet of paper. (c) newspaper. (d) scientific/learned article. **paper 2** *v.* to cover (the walls of a room) with paper. **paperback** *n.* book with a paper cover. **paperboy** *n.* boy who delivers newspapers to houses. **paperchase** *n.* game where people follow a trail of bits of paper. **paperclip** *n.* piece of bent wire for holding pieces of paper together. **paperknife** *n.* (*pl.* knives) long knife for cutting paper (esp. for opening envelopes). **paper round** *n.* group of streets/houses where one paper boy delivers newspapers.
paperweight *n.* heavy block put on papers to prevent them from being blown away. **paperwork** *n.* office work. **papery** *adj.* thin like paper.
papier mâché [pæpɪeɪ'mæʃeɪ] *n.* mixture of wet paper used to make models, etc.
papist ['peɪpɪst] *n.* (rude) Roman Catholic.
papoose [pə'puːs] *n.* Red Indian baby.
paprika ['pæprɪkə] *n.* red spice made from powdered sweet peppers.
papyrus [pə'paɪrəs] *n.* reed growing in the Middle East, used by the ancient Egyptians to make a type of paper.
par [pɑː] *n.* (a) equal level; to be on a p. with = to be equal to. (b) to buy shares at p.= at their face value. (c) (in golf) number of strokes *usu.* needed to hit the ball into the hole; below p. = not very well.
parable ['pærəbl] *n.* *usu.* religious story with a moral.
parabola [pə'ræbələ] *n.* curve like the path of an object which is thrown into the air and comes down again.
parabolic [pærə'bɒlɪk] *adj.* referring to a parabola.
paracetamol [pærə'setəmɒl] *n.* drug used to relieve headaches/colds, etc.
parachute 1 ['pærəʃuːt] *n.* large piece of thin material shaped like an umbrella, with cords and a harness attached, which allows you to flat down safely from an aircraft. **parachute 2** *n.* person who jumps regularly with a parachute.
parachutist *n.* person who jumps regularly with a parachute.

parade 1 [pə'reɪd] *n.* (a) military display/march past; p. ground = square area on a military camp where parades are held. (b) series of bands/decorated cars, etc., passing in a street; fashion p. = display of new clothes by models. (c) wide street (where people like to walk up and down) **parade 2** *v.* to march past in ordered lines.
paradigm ['pærədaɪm] *n.* example to be copied.
paradise ['pærədaɪs] *n.* ideal place where good people are supposed to live after death; any beautiful place.
paradox ['pærədɒks] *n.* thing which appears to contradict itself but may really be true. **paradoxical** [pærə'dɒksɪkl] *adj.* contradictory. **paradoxically** *adv.* in a paradoxical way.
paraffin ['pærəfɪn] *n.* thin oil for lamps/heaters, etc.; liquid p. = refined oil taken as a medicine; p. wax = solid white substance used for making candles.
paragon ['pærəgən] *n.* perfect model (of virtue, etc.).
paragraph ['pærəgrɑːf] *n.* section of several lines of prose. *usu.* starting with a short blank space at the beginning of a new line.
parakeet [pærə'kiːt] *n.* kind of small tropical parrot.
parallax ['pærə'kiːt] *n.* difference in the position of an object when it is seen from different points.
parallel 1 ['pærələl] *adj.* (a) (to/with) (lines) which are side by side and remain the same distance apart without every touching. (b) similar. **parallel 2** *n.* (a) geometrical line which runs parallel to another. (b) line running round the globe from east to west parallel to the equator. (c) closely similar situation; thing which can be compared. **parallel 3** *v.* to be similar to. **parallelogram** [pærə'leləfæm] *n.* four-sided figure where each side is parallel to the one opposite.
paralyse, *Am.* **paralyze** ['pærəlaɪz] *v.* to make unable to move. **paralysis** [pə'ræləsɪs] *n.* being unable to move.
paralytic 1 [pærə'lɪtɪk] *adj.* (a) unable to move. (b) *Sl.* very drunk. **paralytic 2** *n.* paralysed person.

paramedical [pærə'medɪkl] *adj.*
helping in medical treatment.
paramedic *n. inf.* person who is not a
doctor, but who helps give medical
treatment.
parameter [pə'ræmɪtə] *n.* figure which
shows the upper of lower level of some
expected result; data which defines the
limits of sth.
paramilitary [pærə'mɪlɪtrɪ] *adj.*
organized in the same way as the army,
but not a part of it.
paramount ['pærəmaʊnt] *adj.*
extreme/supreme.
paramour ['pærəmuːə] *n.* (old) lover;
mistress.
paranoia [pærə'nɔtə] *n.* type of mental
disease where you feel extremely
important or that everyone is against
you. **paranoiac** *adj. & n.* (person) who
suffers from paranoia. **paranoid** *adj. &*
n. (person) suffering from paranoia.
parapet ['pærəpt] *n.* small wall at the
edge of a ledge/bridge, etc.
paraphernalia [pærəfə'neɪlɪe] *n.* (no
pl.) mass of bits and pieces; equipment.
paraphrase 1 ['pærəfreɪz] *n.* writing
which repeats sth in different words.
paraphrase 2 *v.* to repeat (what s.o.
has said or written) using different
words.
paraplegia [pærə'pliːdʒə] *n.* paralysis
of the legs and lower part of the body.
paraplegic *adj. & n.* (person) who
suffers from paraplegia.
parapsychology [pærəsai'kɒlədʒi] *n.*
study of unexplained psychological
phenomena.
paraquat ['pærəkwæt] *n.* dangerous
weedkiller.
parasite ['pærəsaɪt] *n.* animal/plant
which lives on other animals or plants;
person who does no useful work.
parasitic [pærə'sɪtɪk] *adj.* (insect, etc.)
which lives off others.
parasol ['pærəsɒl] *n.* light umbrella to
keep off the rays of the sun.
parastatal [pærə'stɪtl] *n.* government
run organization in Africa.
paratrooper ['pærətruːpə] *n.* soldier
who is a parachutist. **paratroops** *n.*
pl. paratroopers.
paratyphoid [pærə'taɪfɔɪd] *n.* fever
which is similar to typhoid, but less
dangerous.

parboil ['pɑːbɔɪl] *v.* to half-cook (food)
in boiling water.
parcel 1 ['pɑːsl] *n.* (a) package (to be
sent by post, etc.). (b) small area of land.
parcel 2 *v.* (parcelled) to wrap and tie
(something) up to send. **parcel out** *v.*
to divide up between several people.
parch [pɑːtʃ] *v.* to dry.
parchment ['pɑːtʃmənt] *n.* (a) skins of
animals which have been treated and
which can be used for writing on. (b)
fine quality yellowish paper.
pardon 1 ['pɑːdn] *n.* (a) forgiveness.
(b) freeing s.o. from prison or from
punishment. **pardon 2** *v.* (a) to forgive.
(b) to allow (s.o.) to leave prison; not to
punish (s.o.). **pardonable** *adj.* which
can be excused. **pardonably** *adv.* in a
way which can be excused.
pare ['peə] *v.* to cut the skin/peel (off a
fruit/vegetable, etc.) to cut back
(expenses). **parings** *n. pl.* pieces of
skin cut off a fruit/vegetables, etc.
parent ['peərənt] *n.* father or mother;
(organization) which rules another.
parentage *n.* origin. **parental** *adj.*
referring to parents. **parenthood** *n.*
being a parent.
parenthesis [pə'renθəsɪs] *n.* (*pl.*-ses)
(a) phrase in the middle of a sentence
which is placed in brackets or between
dashes. (b) parentheses = (round)
brackets. **parenthetic(al)**
[pærən'θetɪk(l)] *adj.* which is not part
of a main sentence.
pargetting ['pɑːdʒetɪŋ] *n.* decorated
plaster on the outside of a house.
pariah [pə'raɪə] *n.* person who is
thrown out by civilized society.
parietal [pə'raɪətl] *adj.* referring to the
walls of cavities in the body.
pari passu [pærɪ'pæsuː] *adv.* equally/
with equal shares.
parish [pærɪʃ] *n.* (*pl.*-es) (a)
administrative area round a church and
under the care of a clergyman. (b)
administrative district in a country.
parishioner [pə'rɪʃənə] *n.* person who
lives in or belongs to a parish.
parity ['pærɪtɪ] *n.* equality.
park 1 [pɑːk] *n.* (a) open public place
usu. with grass and trees; business p. =
area with buildings specially built for
businesses; national p. = large area of
countryside kept in a natural state. (b)

car p. = place where cars can be left temporarily. **park 2** v. to leave (one's car) in a particular place; no parking = don't leave your car here; parking meter = device into which you put money to pay for parking; Am. parking lot = car park.

parka ['pɑːlə] n. warm jacket with a hood.

parkin ['pɑːkɪn] n. hard ginger cake.

Parkinson's disease ['pɑːkɪnsənzdɪ'ziːz] n. progressive disease. which affects the parts of the brain which control movement.

parky ['pɑːkɪ] adj. inf. chilly (weather).

parlance ['pɑːləns] n. (formal) way of speaking. **parley 1** ['pɑːlɪ] n. discussion between enemies with a view to agreeing peace terms. **parley 2** v. to discuss peace terms with an enemy.

parliament ['pɑːləmənt] n. group of elected representatives who vote the laws of country; Act of P. = decision which has been passed by parliament and which becomes law.

parliamentarian [pɑːləmən'teərɪən] n. (experienced and knowledgeable) member of a parliament.

parliamentary [pɑːlə'mentərɪ] adj. referring to parliament.

parlour, Am. **parlor** ['pɑːlə] n. (a) sitting room. (b) beauty p. = place where women can have their hair done and their faces made up.

parlous ['pɑːləs] adj. bad/dangerous (state).

parochial [pə'rəʊkɪəl] adj. (a) referring to a parish. (b) restricted (view) narrow-minded (person).

parody 1 ['pærədɪ] n. imitation in order to make fun of s.o./sth. **parody 2** v. to imitate in order to make fun.

parole 1 [pə'rəʊl] n. prisoner on p. = prisoner let out of prison before the end of his sentence on condition that he behaves well. **parole 2** v. to let (a prisoner) out of prison on condition that he behaves well.

paroxysm ['pærəksɪzəm] n. wild fit (of anger, etc.).

parquet ['pɑːleɪ] n. flooring of small wooden blocks.

parricide ['pærɪsaɪd] n. murder of your own father; person who kills his father.

parrot ['pærət] n. colourful tropical bird with a large curved beak. **parrot-**

fashion adv. (repeating words) without really understanding them.

parry ['pærɪ] v. to prevent (a blow) from hitting you.

parse [pɑːz] v. to describe the grammatical function of each word in a sentence.

parsec ['pɑːsek] n. unit of measurement in astronomy (3.26 light years)

parsimony ['pɑːsɪmənt] n. (formal) miserliness. **parsimonious** [pɑːsɪ'məʊnɪəs] adj. miserly. **parsimoniously** adv. in a parsimonious way.

parsley ['pɑːslɪ] n. green herb used in cooking.

parsnip ['pɑːsnɪp] n. vegetable with a long white edible root.

parson ['pɑːsn] n. clergyman in charge of a parish in the Church of England. **parsonage** n. house of a parson.

part 1 [pɑːt] n. (a) piece/bit; in p. = not completely; spare parts = replacement pieces (for a machine) parts of speech = types of words according to usage (noun/verb, etc). (b) role; take p. in = to be active in; to take sth in good p. = without being offended by it. (c) for my p. = as far as I am concerned. **part 2** adv. not entirely; part-cooked. **part 3** v. to separate. **parting** n. (a) separation in the hair. (b) leaving. **partly** adv. not entirely. **part-time** adj. & adv. not for the whole working day. **part with** v. to give away.

partake [pɑːteɪk] v. (partook; partaken) (formal) (of) to eat (food).

parterre [pɑː'teə] n. formal arrangement of flowerbeds.

partial ['pɑːʃl] adj. (a) (to) biased/with a liking for. (b) not complete. **partiality** [pɑːʃɪ'ælɪtɪ] n. strong bias for. **partially** adv. (a) in a biased way. (b) not completely.

participate [pɑː'tɪsɪpeɪt] v. to take part in (sth). **participant** n. person who participates. **participation** [pɑːtɪsɪ'peɪʃn] n. taking part in sth. **participatory** adj. in which you participate.

participle ['pɑːtɪsɪpl] n. part of a verb used either to form compound tenses or as an adjective or noun. **participial** [pɑːtɪ'sɪpɪəl] n. referring to a participle.

particle ['pɑːtɪkl] n. very small piece; minor part of speech.

particoloured Am. **particolored** ['pɑːtɪkʌləd] adj. with one part in one colour, and the other part in another.

particular 1 [pə'tɪkjʊlə] adj. (a) special; referring to one thing or person; in p. = as a special point. (b) fussy.

particular 2 n. detail. **particularity** [pɑːtɪkjuˈlærɪtɪ] n. particular quality.

particularize [pɑːtɪkjʊlə'raɪz] v. to list details. **particularly** adv. specially.

partisan [pɑːtɪ'zæn] adj. & n. (a) (person) who strongly supports a certain point of view. (b) (guerrilla) fighting against an army which has occupied his country. **partisanship** n. being a partisan.

partition 1 [pɑːtɪʃn] n. (a) division into parts. (b) thin wall between two spaces esp. splitting a large room into two.

partition 2 v. to divide (by means of a partition).

partner ['pɑːtnə] n. (a) person who has a part share in a business. (b) person who plays/dances with s.o. **partnership** n. business association between two or more people where the risks and profits are shared.

partridge ['pɑːtrɪdʒ] n, large brown and grey bird, shot for sport and food.

parturition [pɑːtjʊ'rɪʃn] n. giving birth.

party ['pɑːtɪ] n. (a) enjoyable meeting of several people on invitation. (b) group of people. (c) person involved (esp. legal matters); third p. = third person in addition to the two principal people involved; third party insurance = insurance against injuring s.o. not named in the insurance policy. (d) p. line = a shared telephone line; p. wall = wall which forms part of two houses. (e) (political) p. = official group of people with the same political ideas; p. line = official doctrine.

paschal ['pæskəl] adj. referring to pass over to Easter.

pass 1 [pɑːs] n. (pl.-es) (a) lower area between two mountain peaks. (b) (in football, etc.) moving/the ball to another player. (c) acceptance at an examination. (d) bus/train season ticket; permit to go in or out. (e) to make a p. at s.o. = to try to start a sexual relationship with s.o.

pass 2 v. (a) to go past. (b) to move

(sth) to s.o. (c) to get through (an examination/inspection). (d) vote by a majority for (a motion). (e) to p. comments = to make comments. (f) to p. water = to urinate. **passable** adj. fairly good. **passably** adv. fairly well.

passage ['pæsɪdʒ] n. (a) corridor. (b) section of a text. (c) sea p. = journey by sea. **passageway** n. corridor. **pass away** v. to die. **passbook** n. book which records how much money you put in or take out of your savings account in a bank or with a building society.

passenger ['pæsɪndʒə] n. (a) traveller (in a vehicle). (b) weak member of a teAm. **passer-by** [pɑːsə'baɪ] n. (pl.passers-by) person who is walking past. **pass for** v. to be thought to be. **passing** adj. (a) not permanent. (b) which is going past. **pass key** n. main key which opens several doors. **pass off** v. (a) to take place(b) to pass oneself off as = to pretend to be. **pass on** v. to die. **pass out** v. inf. to faint. **pass over** v. (a) to go past above. (b) to pass s.o. over for promotion = to miss s.o. who should have been promoted.

passover ['pɑːsəʊvə] n. Jewish festival which celebrates the freeing of the Jews from captivity in Egypt.

passpost n. official document allowing you to pass from one country to another. **pass up** v. inf. not to take (an opportunity). **password** n. secret word which you say to go past a guard or to access a computer file.

passé ['pæseɪ] adj. old-fashioned.

passim ['pæsɪm] adv. throughout.

passion ['pæʃn] n. violent emotion/ enthusiasm. **passionate** adj. violently, emotional. **passionately** adv. violently. **passionflower** n. climbing plant with green and purple flowers.

passionfruit n. (no pl.) edible tropical fruit.

passive ['pæsɪv] adj. (a) not resisting; which allows things to happen; p. resistance = resisting (the police, etc.) by refusing to obey orders but not using violence. (b) (verb) which shows that the subject is being acted upon. **passively** adv. not offering any resistance/not doing anything positive. **passiveness** n. being passive. **passivity** [pə'sɪvɪtɪ] n. being passive.

past 1 [pɑːst] *adj.* (time) which has gone by. **past 2** *n.* time which has gone by. **past 3** *prep.* after; beyond. **post master** *n.* expert.

pasta ['pæstə] *n.* (*pl.*-pasta) Italian food made of flour and water, such as spaghetti/macaroni, etc.

paste 1 [peɪst] *n.* (a) thin glue, *usu.* made of flour and water. (b) soft substance. (c) imitation jewel. **paste 2** *v.* to glue (paper, etc.). **pasteboard** *n.* cardboard.

pastel ['pæstl] *n.* (a) coloured crayon like chalk; p. colours = soft, light shades. (b) picture done with coloured crayons like chalk.

pastern ['pæstɜːn] *n.* part of a horse's foot above the hoof.

pasteurize ['pɑːstʃəraɪz] *v.* to kill the germs (milk) by heating. **pasteurization** [pɑːstʃəraɪ'zeɪʃn] *n.* action of pasteurizing.

pastiche [pæ'stiːʃ] *n.* poem/piece of music, etc., which is a deliberate imitation of the style of another artist.

pastille ['pæstl] *n.* small sweet made of fruit-flavoured jelly.

pastime ['pɑːstaɪm] *n.* hobby/way of passing your spare time.

pastor ['pɑːstə] *n.* clergyman. **pastoral** *adj.* (a) referring to shepherds. (b) referring to moral guidance.

pastry ['peɪstrɪ] *n.* (a) past made of flour, fat and water which is used to make pies, etc. (b) cooked piecrust. (c) pastries = sweet cakes made of pastry filled with cream/fruit, etc.

pasture 1 ['pɑːstʃəl] *n.* grassy area where cows and sheep can graze. **pasture 2** *v.* to put (cows and sheep) to graze. **pasturage** *n.* (no *pl.*) land used for pasturing.

pasty 1 ['peɪstɪ] *adj.* white (face).

pasty 2 *n.* pastry folded round a filling of meat and vegetables.

pat 1 [pæt] *n.* (a) light hit; a p. on the back = praise. (b) small piece (of butter). **pat 2** *v.* (patted) to give (s.o./sth) a pat. **pat 3** *adj. & adv.* (answer) given promptly.

patch 1 [pætʃ] *n.* (*pl.*-es) (a) small piece of material used for covering up holes; *inf.* not a p. on = not nearly as good as. (b) small area. **patch 2** *v.* to repair by attaching a piece of material

over a hole. **patchily** *adv.* in a patchy way. **patchiness** *n.* being patchy.

patch up *v.* to end (a quarrel).

patchwork *n.* small pieces of material sewn together in patterns. **patchy** *adj.* in small areas; not the same all through.

pate [peɪt] *n.* (old) head.

pâté ['pæteɪ] *n.* paste made of cooked meat or fish finely minced.

patella [pə'telə] *n.* (*formal*) kneecap.

patent 1 ['peɪtənt] *n.* (also[xxxxx]) official confirmation that you have the right to make or sell a new invention.

patent 2 *adj.* (a) covered by an official patent; p. medicine = medicine made under a trade name by one company. (b) p. leather = extremely shiny leather. (c) obvious. **patent 3** *v.* to obtain a patent for. **patentee** [peɪtən'tiː] *n.* person who has obtained a patent. **patently** *adv.* obviously/clearly.

paternity [pə'tɜːnɪtɪ] *n.* being a father. **paternal** *adj.* referring to a father; like a father; my p. grand father = my father's father. **paternalism** *n.* paternalistic way of ruling a country/a company. **paternalistic** [pətɜːnə'lɪstɪk] *adj.* (way of ruling/of managing) which is kindly but does not give enough freedom or responsibility to individuals. **paternally** *adv.* in a paternal way.

path [pɑːθ] *n.* (a) narrow way for walking/cycling, etc. (b) way in which sth moves. **pathway** *n.* track for walking along.

pathetic [pə'θetɪk] *adj.* which makes you feel pity or contempt. **pathetically** *adv.* in a pathetic way.

pathogen ['pæθədʒən] *n.* germ which causes a disease. **pathogenic** *adj.* which causes a disease. **pathology** [pə'θɒlədʒɪ] *n.* study of disease. **pathological** [pæθə'lɒdʒɪkl] *adj.* (a) referring to pathology. (b) caused by mental or physical disease. (c) unhealthy (interest). **pathologist** [pə'θɒlədʒɪst] *n.* doctor specializing in the study of disease; doctor who examines dead bodies to discover the cause of death.

pathos ['peɪθɒs] *n.* quality in sth which makes you feel pity.

patience ['peɪʃns] *n.* (a) being patient. (b) card game for one person. **patient 1** *adj.* (a) person who can wait for a long time/who remains calm/who doesn't lose

his temper. (b) careful/painstaking.
patient 2 *n.* person who is in hospital
or being treated by a doctor/dentist, etc.
patiently *adv.* calmly.
patina ['pætɪnə] *n.* green sheen on old
bronze objects; shine on old wooden
furniture, etc.
patio ['pætɪəʊ] *n.* (*pl.*-os) paved area
outside a house for sitting or eating.
patisserie [pə'tiːsərɪ] *n.* shop selling
continental style cakes and pastries.
patois ['pætwɑː] *n.* dialect spoken in a
small area.
patrial ['peɪtrɪəl] *n.* person who has the
right to live in a country because one of
his parents or grandparents was born
there.
patriarch ['pwɪtrɪɑːk] *n.* (a) bishop/
high dignitary of an Eastern church. (b)
respected old man. **patriarchal** *adj.*
referring to a patriarch.
patrician [pə'trɪʃn] *adj. & n.* (referring
to an) aristocrat.
patricide ['pætrɪsaɪd] *n.* murder of
your own father; person who kills his
father.
patrimony ['pætrɪmənɪ] *n.* inheritance/
property which has been passed from
father to son for generations.
patriot ['peɪtrɪət] *n.* person who fights
for/who is proud of his country.
patriotic [pætrɪ'ɒtɪk] *adj.* proud of
your country; willing to fight for your
country. **patriotically** *adv.* in a
patriotic way. **patriotism**
['peɪtrɪətɪzəm] *n.* pride in your country.
patrol 1 [pə'trəʊl] *n.* (a) keeping guard
by walking or driving up and down. (b)
group of people keeping guard; p. car =
police car which drives up and down the
streets. (c) group of Scouts or Guides.
patrol 2 *v.* (patrolled) to keep guard by
walking or driving up and down.
patrolman *n.* (*pl.*-men) esp. *Am.*
policeman.
patron ['peɪtrən] *n.* (a) person who
protects or supports s.o./sth p. saint =
saint who is believed to protect a special
group of people. (b) regular customer (of
a shop); person who goes regularly to the
theatre. **patronage** ['pætrənɪdʒ] *n.*
giving support/encouragement (to an
artist, etc.). **patroness** *n.* woman
patron. **patronize** ['pætrənaɪz] *v.* (a) to
support/to encourage (an artist, etc.). (b)

to act in a condescending way to (s.o.).
(c) to go regularly to (a shop/public
house/theatre). **patronizing** *adj.*
condescending (tone) which makes s.o.
feel inferior.
patronymic [pætrə'nɪmɪk] *n.* name
which is derived from the name of a
father.
patten ['pætən] *n.* wooden clog with
high sole and heel.
patter 1 ['pætə] *n.* (a) soft repeated
tapping noise. (b) rapid talk by a
conjuror/salesman/trickster to distract
attention from what he is really doing.
patter 2 *v.* to make a soft repeated
tapping noise.
pattern ['pætən] *n.* (a) model/example
which you should copy; paper which
shows how to cut out cloth to make a
piece of clothing; knitting p. =
instructions on how to knit sth. (b)
design of repeated lines/pictures, etc.
patterned *adj.* with a repeated design.
patty ['pætɪ] *n.* small pie.
paucity ['pɔːsɪtɪ] *n.* (formal) small
number/too little (of sth).
paunch [pɔːnʃ] *n.* (*pl.*-es) fat stomach.
pauper ['pɔːpə] *n.* poor person.
pause 1 [pɔːz] *n.* short stop in work,
etc. **pause 2** *v.* to stop doing sth for a
short time.
pave [peɪv] *v.* to cover (a road/path,
etc.) with a hard surface; to p. the way =
to prepare the way. **pavement** *n.* (a)
hard path at the side of a road. (b) *Am.*
hard road surface. **paving stone** *n.*
large flat stone slab used for making
paths/courtyards, etc.
pavilion [pə'vɪljən] *n.* (a) small
building for sportsmen to rest in between
games. (b) building for an exhibition.
paw 1 [pɔː] *n.* (a) hairy foot of an
animal with claws. (b) *inf.* hand. **paw 2**
v. to tap with a paw/hands, etc.; *inf.* to
fondle.
pawky ['pɔːkɪ] *adj.* humorous in a dry
way. **pawkiness** *n.* dry humour.
pawl [pɔːn] *n.* metal piece which
catches in the teeth of a ratchet wheel.
pawn 1 *n.* (a) smallest piece on the
chessboard. (b) person used by s.o. more
powerful. (c) in p. = (object) left in
exchange for money which has been
borrowed. **pawn 2** *v* to leave (an
object) in exchange for borrowing

money (which you claim back when the money is repaid). **pawnbroker** *n.* person who lends money in exchange for valuables left with him. **pawnshop** *n.* shop where goods can be pawned.

pay 1 [peɪ] *n.* wages/salary; in the p. of = paid by. **pay 2** *v.* (paid) (a) to give money for sth; to put paid to = to end. (b) to be worth while. (c) to suffer punishment for. (d) to make (a visit/a call). (e) to make/to show (attention, etc.). **payable** *adj.* which must be paid. **pay-as-you-earn** *n.* system of collecting income tax direct from salaries. **pay back** *v.* (a) to return money to (s.o.). (b) to get your revenge on (s.o.). **pay bed** *n.* bed in a public hospital for which you pay. **paycheck** *n. Am.* salary payment. **payee** *n.* person who receives money. **payer**, *n.* person who pays money. **payload** *n.* load carried by an aircraft or rocket. **paymaster** *n.* officer who pays soldiers. **payment** *n.* giving money for sth. **pay off** *v.* (a) to remove (a debt) by paying the money owed. (b) *inf.* to be successful. **pay-off** *n. inf.* (a) reward. (b) final success. **payola** *n. Am.* bribery. **pay out** *v.* (a) to give money to s.o.. (b) to unroll a rope. **pay roll** *n.* list of people who receive wages. **pay up** *v.* to pay what you owe.

PAYE [piːeːwaɪˈiː] *n.* pay as you earn system.

Pb symbol for lead.

PC [ˈpiːˈsiː] personal computer, police constable.

PCB [piːsiːˈbiː] printed circuit board.

pea [piː] *n.* climbing plant of which the round green seeds are eaten as vegetables; sweet peas = plant of the pea family grown for its scented flowers. **pea-green** *adj.* bright green. **pea-jacket** *n.* double breasted wool jacket worn by sailors. **pea-souper** *n.* thick yellow fog.

peace [piːs] *n.* (a) state of not being at war; p. dividend = money which becomes available for government expenditure as defence spending is reduced following a reduction in international tension. (b) clam/quiet. **peaceable** *adj.* liking peace; not quarrelsome. **peaceably** *adv.* calmly/without quarrelling. **peaceful** *adj.* (a)

calm. (b) liking peace; p. coexistence = living side by side without making war. **peacefully** *adv.* (a) calmly. (b) without making war. **peacefulness** *n.* being peaceful. **peacemaker** *n.* person who tries to bring about peace.

peach 1 [piːtʃ] *n.* (*pl.*-es) (a) sweet fruit, with a large stone and velvety skin; tree which bears peaches. (b) pinkish yellow colour. **peach 2** *v. inf.* to p. on s.o. = to inform (the police) about s.o.

peacock, peahen [ˈpiːkɒk, piːˈhen] *n.* (a) large bird of which the cock has a huge tail with brilliant blue and green feathers. (b) type of brown butterfly with round purple spots.

peak 1 [piːk] *n.* (a) top of a mountain. (b) highest point; p. period = period of the day when most electricity is used/when most traffic is on the roads, etc. (c) front part of a cap which juts out. **peak 2** *v.* to reach a high point. **peaked** *adj.* (cap) with a peak. **peaky** *adj.* looking ill.

peal 1 [piːl] *n.* (a) set of bells of different sizes; sound of bells ringing. (b) loud reverberating noise. **peal 2** *v.* (a) to ring a peal of bells. (b) (of thunder) to roll/to make a loud noise.

peanut [ˈpiːnʌy] *n.* (a) nut which grows in the ground in pods like a pea; p. butter = paste made from crushed peanuts. (b) *inf.* peanuts = very little money.

pear [ˈpeə] *n.* elongated fruit with one end fatter than the other; tree which bears pears. **pear-shaped** *adj.* shaped like a pear.

pearl [pɜːl] *n.* precious round white gem formed inside an oyster; p. barley = barley grains which have been rolled until they are shaped like pearls. **pearldiver** *n.* person who dives to the bottom of the sea to look for oysters with pearls in them. **pearly** *adj.* shiny like a pearl.

peasant [ˈpezənt] *n.* farm labourer or small farmer living in a backward region. **peasantry** *n.* (no *pl.*) peasants (seen as a class in society).

peat [piːt] *n.* decayed vegetable matter cut out of a bog and used as fuel or in gardening.

peaty *adj.* smelling/tasting like peat. **pebble** [ˈpebl] *n.* small round stone. **pebble-dash** *n.* covering for outside walls, where small stones are stuck into wet cement. **pebbly** *adj.* covered with pebbles.

pecan ['pi:kæn] *n.* nut from a tree which grows in the south of the USA.

peccadillo [pekə'dɪləʊ] *n.* (*pl.*-oes) (formal) slight error/fault.

peccary ['pekəri] *n.* wild South American pig.

peck 1 [pek] *n.* (a) bite with a bird's beak. (b) *inf.* little kiss. (c) (old) measurement of quantity of grain. **peck 2** *v.* (a) to bite with a beck; pecking order = unwritten order of importance of people in a firm/office, etc. (b) *inf.* to give (s.o.) a little kiss. **pecker** *n. Sl.* keep your p. up = keep cheerful/optimistic **peckish** *adj. inf.* a bit hungry.

pectin ['pektɪn] *n.* jelly-like substance in fruit which helps jam to set hard.

pectoral 1 ['pektərəl] *adj.* (formal) referring to the chest; p. cross = cross worn by a priest round the neck. **pectoral 2** *n.* muscle in the chest.

peculate ['pekjʊleɪt] *v.* (formal) to embezzle money. **peculation** [pekjʊ'leɪʃn] *n.* embezzlement.

peculiar [pɪ'kju:ljə] *adj.* (a) odd/strange. (b) belonging to one particular place or person. **peculiarity** *n.* being peculiar; strange feature/detail which stands out. **peculiarly** *adv.* oddly/strangely.

pecuniary [pɪ'kju:njəri] *adj.* referring to money.

pedagogical [pedə'gɒdʒɪkl] *adj.* referring to teaching. **pedagogue** ['pedəgɒg] *n.* unpleasant pedantic teacher.

pedal 1 ['pedl] *n.* lever worked by your foot; p. bin = rubbish bin with a lid worked by a pedal. **pedal 2** *v.* (pedalled) to make (a bicycle) go by pushing on the pedals.

pedant ['pedənt] *n.* pedantic person. **pedantic** [pɪ'dæntɪk] *adj.* paying too much attention to detail/showing off knowledge. **pedantically** *adv.* in a pedantic way. **pedantry** ['pedəntri] *n.* being pedantic.

peddle ['pedl] *v.* to go about trying to sell sth. **peddler** *n.* (a) person who sells dangerous drugs. (b) *Am.* pedlar.

pederast ['pedəræst] *n.* person who practises pederasty. **pederasty** *n.* homosexual relations with boys.

pedestal ['pedɪstl] *n.* base (for a statue).

pedestrian 1 [pə'destrɪən] *n.* person who goes about on foot; p. crossing = place where pedestrians can cross a road; p. precinct = street or group of streets closed to traffic so that people can walk about freely. **pedestrian 2** *adj.* (a) referring to pedestrians. (b) heavy/unimaginative.

pediatrician [pi:dɪə'trɪʃn] *n.* doctor who specializes in pediatrics. **pediatrics** [pi:dɪætrɪks] *n.* science of treatment of children's diseases.

pedicure ['pedɪkjʊə] *n.* looking after the feet.

pedigree ['pedɪgri:] *n.* table of ancestors of a person/animal p. bull = bull with a certificate showing it is pure bred.

pediment ['pedɪmənt] *n.* triangular part at the top of the front of a classical building.

pedlar ['pedlə] *n.* person who goes about trying to sell small articles.

pedometer [pe'dɒmɪtə] *n.* instrument which measures how far you have walked.

peduncle [pə'dʌŋkl] *n.* stalk of an inflorescence.

pee 1 [pi:] *n. inf.* (a) waste water from the body. (b) passing waste water from the body. **pee 2** *v. inf.* to pass waste water from the body.

peek 1 [pi:k] *n. inf.* quick look. **peek 2** *v. inf.* to look at sth quickly.

peel 1 [pi:l] *n.* outer skin of a fruit, etc. **peel 2** *v.* (a) to take the outer skin off (a fruit/a vegetable). (b) to come off in layers. **peeler** *n.* special instrument for peeling vegetables. **peelings** *n. pl.* bits of skin from vegetables. **peel off** *v.* (a) (of peel/paint) to come off. (b) *inf.* to take off (clothes).

peep 1 [pi:p] *n.* (a) short/quick look. (b) cheep. **peep 2** *v.* to look quickly and secretly. **peephole** *n.* small hole in a door which you can look through to see who is outside.

peer 1 ['prə] *n.* (a) member of the nobility. (b) person of the same rank/class as another; p. group = group of people of equal (social) status. **peer 2** v. to look at sth hard when you cannot see very well. **peerage** n. (no pl.) all nobles, taken as a group. **peeress** n. woman peer. **peerless** adj. excellent/ which has no equal.

peeved [pi:vd] adj. inf. annoyed/ bothered. **peevish** adj. bad tempered/ complaining. **peevishly** adv. in a peevish way. **peevishness** n. being peevish.

peewit ['pi:wɪt] n. lapwing.

peg 1 [peg] n. small wooden or metal stake/pin; off the p. = ready made. **peg 2** v. (pegged) (a) to attach with a peg. (b) to hold (prices, etc.) stable. **peg away at** v. inf. go on with (piece of work). **peg out** v. Sl. to die.

pejorative [pə'dʒɒrətɪv] adj. disapproving/showing that you feel sth is bad.

pekinese inf. peke [pɪkɪ'ni:z, pi:k] n. breed of low flat faced dogs.

pelagic [pə'lædʒɪk] adj. referring to the top and middle layers of the sea.

pelargonium [pelɑ:'gəʊnɪəm] n. flowering plant, the geranium.

pelican ['pelɪkən] n. large white water bird, with a pouch under its beak in which it keeps the fish it has caught; p. crossing = pedestrian crossing with traffic lights worked by the pedestrians.

pellet ['pelɪt] n. (a) small ball. (b) small lead ball used in shotguns. **palleted** adj. (seeds) made into pellets.

pellicle ['pelɪkl] n. thin layer of skin.

pell mell ['pel'mel] adv. in disorder.

pellucid [pə'lu:sɪd] adj. very transparent.

pelmet ['pelmɪt] n. decorative strip of wood/cloth, etc., over a window which hides the curtain fittings.

pelt 1 [pelt] n. (a) skin of an animal with fur on it. (b) at full p. = going fast.

pelt 2 v. (a) to p. s.o. with = to fling things at s.o. (b) the rain was pelting down = pouring down.

pelvis ['pelvɪs] n. (pl.-es) bones in the lower part of the body forming the hips. **pelvic** adj. referring to the pelvis.

pemmican ['pemɪkən] n. dried meat. used by explorers as rations.

pen 1 [pen] n. (a) small fenced area for sheep. (b) writing instrument using ink; p. name = name used by a writer which

is not his own; p. friend = person whom you have never met but with whom you exchange letters. (c) female swan. **pen 2** v. (penned) (a) to enclose (a) (sheep) in a pen. (b) to write with a pen.

penal ['pi:nl] adj. referring go a legal punishment; p. system = system of punishments relating to various crimes. **penalization** [pi:nəlaɪ'zeɪʃn] n. act of penalizing. **penalize** v. to punish. **penalty** ['penəltɪ] n. (a) punishment. (b) punishment in sport esp. a kick at goal awarded to the opposite side in football. (c) disadvantages.

penance ['penəns] n. punishment which a person accepts to make amends for a sin.

pence [pens] n. see penny.

penchant ['pɑ:nʃɑ:ŋ] n. liking (for sth).

pencil 1 ['pensl] n. instrument for writing made of wood with a graphite centre. **pencil 2** v. (pencilled) to write with a pencil. **pencil sharpener** n. instrument for sharpening pencils.

pendant ['pendənt] n. ornament which hangs from a chain round the neck. **pendent** adj. hanging.

pending ['pendɪŋ] adj. & prep. awaiting; until; p. tray = tray for papers and letters waiting to be dealt with.

pendulum ['pendjʊləm] n. weight on the end of a rod or chain which swings from side to side, such as that which makes a clock work. **pendulous** adj. which hangs down heavily.

penetrate ['penɪtreɪt] v. to go into/ through. **penetrability** [penɪtrə'bɪlɪtɪ] n. ability to be penetrated. **penetrable** adj. which can be penetrated.

penetrating adj. deep/searching (look) very profound (questions).

penetration [penɪ'treɪʃn] n. (a) getting into sth. (b) deep understanding.

penguin ['peŋgwɪn] n. Antarctic bird which swims well but cannot fly.

penicillin [penɪ'sɪlɪn] n. substance made from a mould used to kill bacteria.

peninsula [pə'nɪnsjʊlə] n. large piece of land jutting into the sea. **peninsular** adj. referring to a peninsula.

penis ['pi:nɪs] n. (pl.-es) part of the male body used for urinating and for sexual intercourse.

penitent ['penɪtənt] adj. & n. (person) who is sorry for having done sth wrong.

penitence *n.* being penitent.
penitential [penɪˈtenʃl] *adj.* referring to penance. **penitentiary** [penɪˈtenʃərɪ] *n. Am.* prison.
penknife [ˈpennaɪf] *n.* (*pl.*-knives) small folding pocket knife.
pennant [ˈpemənt] *n.* long thing flag.
pennon [ˈpenən] *n.* small forked flag.
penny [ˈpenɪ] *n.* (*pl.*pennies = coins; pence = price) small coin (the smallest unit in some currencies); (in Britain) one hundredth part of a pound; the penny's dropped = he's understood at last.
penniless *adj.* with no money.
penology [piːˈnɒlədʒɪ] *n.* study of punishment and crime.
pension 1 [ˈenʃn] *n.* money paid regularly to s.o. who has retired from work/to a widow, etc., old age p. = money paid regularly by the state to people over a certain age. **pension 2** *v.* to p. s.o. off = to make s.o. stop working and live on a pension. **pensionable** *adj.* (person) who has the right to have a pension; (job) which gives you the right to have a pension; (age) at which a pension begins to be paid. **pensioner** *n.* person who gets a pension.
pensive [ˈpensɪv] *adj.* thoughtful.
pensively *adv.* thoughtfully.
pensiveness *n.* being pensive.
pent [pent] *adj.* pent up emotions violent emotions which are repressed.
pentagon [ˈpentəgən] *n.* (a) geometrical figure with five sides. (b) the Pentagon = the US ministry of defence. **pentagonal** [penˈtægənl] *adj.* five sided.
pentameter [penˈtæmɪtə] *n.* line of poetry with five beats.
pentathlon [penˈtæθlən] *n.* athletic competition where competitors have to compete in five different sports.
penthouse [ˈpenthaʊs] *n.* flat on the top of a high building.
penultimate [peˈnʌltɪmət] *adj.* next to last.
penumbra [peˈnʌmbrə] *n.* edge of a shadow where only part of the light is cut off.
penury [ˈpenjʊrɪ] *n.* (*formal*) (a) extreme poverty. (b) great lack.
penurious [pɪˈnjʊərɪəs] *adj.* very poor.
peony [ˈpɪənɪ] *n.* perennial summer flower with large scented flowerheads.

people 1 [ˈpiːpl] *n.* (a) (*pl.*) persons; human beings; country p. = persons who live in the country. (b) citizens (of a town or country). **people 2** *v.* to fill with people.
pep 1 [pep] *n. inf.* vigour; p. pill = medicine taken to make you more lively and active; p. talk = talk designed to encourage people to work hard/to win a match, etc. **pep 2** *v. inf.* to p. s.o. up = to make s.o. livelier and more active.
pepper 1 [ˈpepə] *n.* (a) sharp spice used in cooking. (b) green or red fruit used as a vegetable. **pepper 2** *v.* (with) to sprinkle/to throw (things) at.
peppercorn *n.* dried seed of pepper; p. rent = nominal/very low rent.
peppermill *n.* small grinder used for grinding peppercorns. **peppmrint** *n.* (a) common plant with a sharp mint flavour. (b) sweet flavoured with peppermint. **peppery** *adj.* (a) (soup, etc.) with too much pepper in it. (b) very easily angered.
peptic [ˈpeptɪk] *adj.* referring to the digestive system; p. ulcer = ulcer in the stomach.
per [pɜː] *prep.* (a) out of ten p. thousand. (b) in; sixty kilometers p. hour. (c) for; p. annum = in each year; p. capita = for each person.
perambulate [pəˈræmbjʊleɪt] *v.* (*formal*) to walk about slowly. **perumbulation** *n.* slow walk. **perambulator** *n.* (*formal*) pram.
perceive [pəˈsiːv] *v.* to notice through the senses; to become aware of.
perceptible [pəˈseptɪbl] *adj.* which can be seen/heard/smelled, etc. **perceptibly** *adv.* noticeably. **perception** *n.* ability to notice. **perceptive** *adj.* acute; able to notice quickly. **perceptively** *adv.* in a perceptive way **perceptiveness, perceptivity** *n.* being perceptive.
percent [pəˈsent] *adv. & n.* out of each hundred. **percentage** [pəˈsentɪdʒ] *n.* proportion shown as part of a hundred. **percentile** [pəˈsentaɪl] *n.* one of a hundred equal groups into which a large number can be divided.
perch 1 [pɜːtʃ] *n.* (a) (*pl.*-es) branch/ledge on which a bird can sit. (b) (*pl.*perch) type of freshwater fish. **perch 2** *v.* to sit on a perch; to be set in a high place.

perchance [pə'tʃɑːns] *adv.* (old) perhaps.
percipient [pə'sɪpɪənt] *adj.* perceptive/ able to notice quickly. **percipience** *n.* being percipient.
percolate ['pɜːkəleɪt] *v.* to filter (through). **percolation** [pɜːkə'leɪʃn] *n.* filtering. **percolator** *n.* coffee pot where the water boils up and filters through coffee.
percussion [pə'kʌʃn] *n.* (a) action of hitting together; p. instruments = musical instruments which are hit (drums/triangles, etc.); p. cap = piece of paper with a small amount of explosive powder which explodes when hit. (b) the p. = section of an orchestra with percussion instruments.
peregrinations [perɪgrɪ'neɪʃnz] *n. pl.* (formal) travelling/wandering.
peregrine ['perɪgrɪn] *n.* type of falcon.
peremptory [pə'remptəri] *adj.* abrupt (tone/curt refusal). **peremptorily** *adv.* in a peremptory way.
perennial 1 [pə'renɪəl] *adj.* which continues from year to year. **perennial 2** *n.* plant which flowers every year without needing to be sown again. **perennially** *adv.* always.
perestroika [perɪ'strɔɪkə] *n.* reconstruction (of the Soviet economy).
perfect 1 ['pɜːfɪkt] *adj.* (a) without any mistakes/flaws. (b) total (stranger). (c) p. (tense) = past tense of a verb which shows that the action has been completed. **perfect 2** *v.* to make perfect. **perfection** [pə'fekʃn] *n.* state of being perfect; to p. = perfectly.
perfectionist *n.* person who insists that perfection is possible/that everything has to be perfect. **perfectly** ['pɜːfɪktlɪ] *adv.* completely.
perfidy ['pɜːfɪdɪ] *n.* (formal) treachery. **perfidious** [pə'fɪdɪəs] *adj.* (formal) treacherous.
perforate ['pɜːfəreɪt] *v.* to make a hole in/to pierce. **perforation** [pɜːfə'rɪʃn] *n.* (a) action of making a hold. (b) small hole.
perforce [pə'fɔːs] *adv.* (old) because it is necessary.
perform [pə'fɔːm] *v.* (a) to carry out an action(b) to act in public. **performance** *n.* (a) working of a machine; action of a sportsman. (b) public show. **performer** *n.* person who gives public show.

perfume 1 ['pɜːfjuːm] *n.* (a) pleasant smell. (b) liquid scent. **perfume 2** [pə'fjuːm] *v.* (a) to give a pleasant smell to (sth). (b) to pour perfume on.
perfumery *n.* shop which makes and sells perfumes.
perfunctory [pə'fʌŋktərɪ] *adj.* rapid and superficial. **perfunctorily** *adv.* in a perfunctory way.
pergola ['pɜːgələ] *n.* framework of wood over which climbing plants can be trained.
perhaps [pə'hæps] *adv.* possibly/may be.
pericardium [perɪ'kɑːdɪəm] *n.* membrane round the heart. **pericarditis** *n.* inflammation of the pericardium.
perihelion [perɪ'hiːlɪɒn] *n.* point where a planet is nearest to the sun.
peril ['perəl] *n.* great danger. **perilous** *adj.* very dangerous. **perilously** *adv.* in a perilous way.
perimeter [pə'rɪmɪtə] *n.* outside line round an enclosed area.
period ['pɪərɪəd] *n.* (a) length of time; p. furniture = antique furniture from a certain time; p. piece = piece of antique furniture, etc. (b) class time in a school. (c) full stop/dot (.) used in writing to mark the end of a sentence. (d) regular monthly flow of blood from a woman's womb. **periodic** [pɪːrɪ'ɒdɪk] *adj.* repeated at a regular length of time; p. table = list of chemical elements arranged in order of their atomic numbers. **periodical 1** *adj.* periodic; repeated after a regular length of time. **periodical 2** *n.* magazine which appears regularly.. **periodically** *adv.* from time to time.
peripatetic [perɪpə'teɪk] *adj.* (person) who wanders from place to place; p. violin teacher = teacher who goes from school to school teaching children to play the violin.
periphery [pə'rɪfərɪ] *n.* edge. **peripheral 1** *adj.* minor/not very important. **peripheral 2** *n.* peripherals = items of hardware (such as printers) which are attached to a computer
periphrasis [pə'rɪfrəsɪs] *n.* (pl.-ses) way of saying sth which is not straight forward. **periphrastic** [perɪ'fræstɪk] *adj.* not straightforward (expression).
periscope [perɪ'fræstɪk] *n.* long tube with mirrors which allows s.o. in a

submerged submarine to look above the surface of the water.

perish ['perɪʃ] v. (a) (formal) to die. (b) to rot. (c) inf. I'm perished = I'm cold.

perishable adj. (food) which can go bad easily; perishables = perishable food.

peristalsis [perɪ'stælsɪs] n. regular movement of the muscles in the intestine.

peritonitis [perɪtə'naɪtɪs] n. inflammation of the lining of the abdomen.

periwig ['perɪwɪg] n. large wig worn in the 17th and 18th centuries.

periwinkle ['perɪwɪŋkl] n. (a) small creeping plant with blue flowers. (b) edible snail which lives in salt water.

perjure ['pɜːdʒə] v. to p. yourself = to tell lies in a court of law when you have sworn to tell the truth. **perjurer** n. person who has committed perjury. **perjury** n. crime of perjuring yourself.

perk 1 [pɜːk] v. to p. up = to become more alert/more interested. **perk 2** n. inf. valuable extras which you are given by your employer in addition to your salary. **perky** adj. inf. lively/interested

perm 1 [pɜːm] n. inf. (a) curls or a wave put into your hair artificially. (b) combination of football teams on a football pools coupon. **perm 2** v. inf. (a) to put a wave or curl into (s.o.'s hair). (b) to select several football teams in various combinations on a football pools coupon.

permafrost ['pɜːməfrɒst] n. (no. pl.) soil in the Arctic which remains permanently frozen, even in summer.

permanent ['pɜːmənənt] adj. lasting for ever/supposed to last for ever; p. secretary = chief civil servant in a government department. **permanence, permanency** n. state of being permanent. **permanently** adv. always.

permanganate [pə'mæŋgəneɪt] n. salt containing manganese; p. of potash = dark purple crystals used for disinfecting.

permeate ['pɜːmeɪt] v. to filter; to spread right through. **permeability** [pɜːmɪə'bɪlɪtɪ] n. being permeable. **permeable** adj. which lets liquid pass through. **permeation** [pɜːmɪ'eɪʃn] n. act of permeating.

permissible [pə'mɪsəbl] adj. which can be allowed. **permission** [pə'mɪʃn] n. freedom which you are given to do sth. **permissive** [pə'mɪsɪv] adj. free; allowing many things to be done which formerly were not allowed.

permissiveness n. being permissive.

permit 1 ['pɜːmɪt] n. paper which allows you to do sth. **permit 2** v. (permitted) to allow.

permutation [pɜːmjuˈteɪʃn] n. grouping of several items together in varied combinations; combination of various items in a different order.

pernicious [pə'fɪʃəs] adj. harmful/evil.

pernickety [pə'nɪkətɪ] adj. inf. very fussy.

peroration [perəˈreɪʃn] n. (formal) very long speech.

peroxide [pə'rɒksaɪd] n. chemical used for bleaching hair or killing germs.

perpendicular [pɜːpən'dɪkjʊlə] adj. & n. (line) standing vertically/at right angles to a base; style of late medieval English church architecture. **perpendicularly** adv. in a perpendicular way.

perpetrate ['pɜːpɪtreɪt] v. (formal) to commit (a crime). **perpetration** [pɜːpɪ'treɪʃn] n. act of perpetrating. **perpetrator** n. person who commits (a crime).

perpetual [pə'petjʊəl] adj. continuous/without any end. **perpetually** adv. always. **perpetuate** v. to make (sth) continue for ever. **perpetuity** [pɜːpɪ'tjuːɪtɪ] n. (formal) in p. = for ever/without any end.

perplex [pə'pleks] v. to confuse/to puzzle. **perplexity** n. bewilderment/puzzled state.

perquisite ['pɜːkwɪzɪt] n. (formal) valuable extra which is given to you by your employer in addition to your salary.

perry ['perɪ] n. alcoholic drink made from fermented pear juice.

per se [pɜː'seɪ] adv. in itself.

persecute ['pɜːsɪkjuːt] v. to torment/to treat cruelly. **persecution** [pɜːsɪ'kjuːʃn] n. relentless killing (because of religious beliefs); p. mania = mental disease where you feel that everyone is persecuting you. **persecutor** ['pɜːsɪkjuːtə] n. person who persecutes.

persevere [pɜːsɪ'vɪə] v. (with/in) to continue doing sth (in spite of obstacles). **perseverance** n. act of persevering.
Persian 1 ['pɜːʃn] adj. referring o Persia. **Persian 2** n. (a) person from Persia. (b) cat with long silky fur.
persiflage [pɜːsɪ'flɑːʒ] n. (formal) frivolous talk.
persist [pə'sɪst] v. (in) to continue doing sth (in spite of obstacles); to continue to exist. **persistence** n. obtinacy; refusal to stop doing sth. **persistent** adj. continual.
persistently adv. in a persistent way.
person ['pɜːsn] n. (a) human being; he appeared in p. = appeared himself. (b) (in grammar) one of the three forms of verbs or pronouns which indicate who the speaker is first p. = I or we; second p. = you; third p. = he, she, it, they.
persona [pɜː'səʊnə] n. a person's character as seen by others. **personable** adj. attractive/good looking/having a pleasant character. **personage** n. important person. **personal** adj. (a) referring to a person; (letter) addressed so that you an no one else may open it; p. computer = small computer used by a person at home. (b) rude (remarks). (c) (in grammar) p. pronoun = pronoun which refers to s.o. such as 'I', 'he', 'she', etc. **personality** [pɜːsə'nælɪtɪ] n. (a) character(b) famous person; p. cult = publicity given to a political leader making him into a kind of god. (c) legal status. **personalized** adj. with your name or initials printed on it.
personally adv. (a) from your own point of view. (b) in person. (c) don't take it p. = don't think it was meant to criticize you. **persona non grata** [pɜː'səʊnɒnɒn'grɑːtə] n. person (esp. a diplomat) who is not acceptable to a foreign country. **personification** [pəsɒnɪfɪ'keɪʃn] n. good example of an abstract quality in a person. **personify** [pə'sɒnɪfaɪ] v. to be a good example of.
personnel [pɜːsə'nel] n. staff/people employed by a company; p. manager = manager who looks after; pay/sick leave/administration, etc., for all the staff.
perspective [pə'spektɪv] n. (a) (in art) way of drawing objects/scenes. so that they appear to have depth or distance; to

put things in p. = to show things in an objective way. (b) way of looking at sth.
perspex ['pɜːspeks] n. trademark for a type of tough clear plastic.
perspicacious [pɜːspɪ'keɪʃəs] adj. (person) who understands clearly.
perspicacity [pɜːspɪ'kæsɪtɪ] n. clearness of understanding.
perspicuity [pɜːspɪ'kjuːɪtɪ] n. clearness of expression. **perspicuous** [pə'spɪkjʊəs] adj. clearly expressed.
perspire [pə'spaɪə] v. to sweat. **perspiration** [pɜːspə'reɪʃn] n. sweat.
persuade [pə'sweɪd] v. to get s.o. to do what you want by explaining or pleading. **persuasion** [pə'sweɪʒn] n. (a) act of persuading. (b) firm (usu. religious) belief. **persuasive** [pə'sweɪzɪv] adj. which persuades. **persuasively** adv. in a persuasive way. **persuasiveness** n. being persuasive.
pert [pɜːt] adj. cheeky.
pertain [pə'teɪn] v. (formal) to be relevant.
pertinacious [pɜːtɪ'neɪʃəs] adj. obstinate.
pertinacity [pɜːtɪ'næsɪtɪ] n. obstinateness/stubbornness. **pertinent** ['pɜːtɪnənt] adj. relevant; to the point. **pertinence** n. being pertinent. **pertinently** adv. in a pertinent way.
perturb [pɜː'tɜːb] v. to make (s.o.) anxious.
perturbation [pɜːtə'beɪʃn] n. anxiety/bother.
peruse [pə'ruːz] v. (formal) to read carefully. **perusal** n. reading.
Peruvian 1 [pə'ruːvɪən] adj. referring to Peru. **Peruvian 2** n person from Peru.
pervade [pə'veɪd] v. to spread everywhere. **pervasive** [pə'veɪsɪv] adj. penetrating. **pervasiveness** n. penetrating everywhere.
perverse [pə'vɜːs] adj. obstinately awkward; continuing to do sth even if it is wrong. **perversely** adv. in an obstinate way. **perverseness** n. contrariness. **perversion** [pə'vɜːʃn] n. corruption (of s.o. to do sth evil).
perversity n. being perverse. **pervert 1** ['pɜːvɜːt] n. person who commits unnatural sexual acts. **pervert 2** [pə'vɜːt] v. (a) to corrupt (s.o.) to do evil.

(b) to p. the course of justice = to influence a court so that justice is not done.

pervious ['pɜːvɪəs] *adj.* *Am.* (membrane) which allows liquid to pass through.

peseta [pe'seɪtə] *n.* old unit of currency used in Spain.

peso ['peɪzəʊ] *n.* unit of currency used in many S. American countries.

pessary ['pesərɪ] *n.* (a) medicine put in the vagina. (b) contraceptive device placed in the vagina.

pessimism ['pesɪmɪzəm] *n.* belief that only bad things will happen. **pessimist** ['pesɪmɪst] *n.* pessimistic person. **pessimistic** [pesɪ'mɪstɪk] *adj.* gloomy/ believing that only bad things will happen. **pessimistically** *adv.* gloomy.

pest [pest] *n.* (a) troublesome plant. animal or often an insect. (b) *inf.* person who annoys. **pester** *v.* to bother (s.o).

pesticide ['pestɪsaɪd] *n.* poison to kill pests.

pestilence ['pestɪləns] *n.* (*formal*) plague/disease. **pestilential** [pestɪ'lenʃl] *adj.* like a plague/very unpleasant.

pestle ['pesl] *n.* round headed heavy tool for crushing things in a bowl.

pet 1 [pet] *n.* animal kept in the home to give pleasure. **pet 2** *adj.* (a) favourite; p. name = special name given go s.o you are fond of. (b) tame (animal). **pet 3** *v.* (petted) to caress/to fondle.

petal ['petl] *n.* one of several colourful leaf like parts of a flower.

petard [pə'tɑːd] *n.* (*formal*) to be hoist with your own p. = to be caught in a trap which you have set for s.o. else.

peter ['piːtə] *v.* to p. out = to come to an end/to fade away.

petersham ['piːtəʃəm] *n.* thick ribbon used to put inside the waist of skirts/ trousers, etc.

petite [pə'tiːt] *adj.* (of a woman) small and dainty. **petit four** [pətɪ'fʊə] *n.* small fancy cake or biscuit eaten at parties.

petition 1 [pə'tɪʃn] *n.* (a) official request (often signed by many people). (b) legal request. **petition 2** *v.* to ask (s.o.) for sth/to make an official request. **petitioner** *n.* person who makes a petition.

petrel ['petrəl] *n.* sea bird which flies long distances.

petrify ['petrɪfaɪ] *v.* (a) to turn to stone. (b) to strike (s.o.) still with fear. **petrifaction** *n.* act of petrifying.

petrochemical [petrəʊ'kemɪkl] *adj.* & *n.* (chemical) produced from petroleum or natural gas.

petrodollar [petrəʊ'dɒlə] *n.* dollar which is earned by a country selling oil.

petrol ['petrəl] *n.* inflammable liquid produced from petroleum and used as a fuel to drive motor engines, etc.

petroleum [pə'trəʊlɪəm] *n.* raw mineral oil (from the earth); p. products = substances (like petrol/plastics, etc.), which are made from petroleum. **petrology** *n.* study of rocks.

petticoat ['petɪkəʊt] *n.* piece of women's underwear/light skirt worn under another skirt.

pettifogging ['petɪfɒgɪŋ] *adj.* (a) dealing with small useless details. (b) dishonest (lawyer).

petty ['petɪ] *adj.* (a) insignificant/ unimportant; p. cash = small amounts of cash (in an office); p. officer = non-commissioned officer in the Royal Navy; p. sessions = magistrate's court. (b) with a narrow point of view. **pettiness** *n.* (a) unimportance. (b) narrowness of outlook.

petulant ['petjʊlənt] *adj.* irritable/ bad-tempered. **petulance** *n.* irritability. **petulantly** *adv.* in a petulant way.

petunia [pɪ'tjuːnɪə] *n.* common summer garden flower.

pew [pjuː] *n.* long bench seat in a church; *inf.* take a p. = sit down.

pewter ['pjuːtə] *n.* alloy *usu.* a mixture of tin and lead. used for making mugs/ plates, etc.

pH [piː'eɪtʃ] *n.* pH factor = measurement of how much acidity or alkalinity there is (in the soil, etc.).

phalanx ['fælæŋks] *n.* (a) tight mass of people (esp. marching forward). (b) bone in a finger or toe.

phallus ['fæləs] *n.* (*pl.*-es) (formal) penis in erection. **phallic** *adj.* referring to a phallus; p. symbol = thing which resembles a penis. and is taken to symbolize male sex.

phantasm ['fæntæzəm] *n.* seeing sth in the imagination/seeing ghosts. **phantasmagoria** [fæntæzmə'gɒrə] *n.* mass of ghostly shapes. **phantom** ['fæntəm] *n.* ghost.

pharisaic(al) [færɪ'seɪɪk(l)] *adj.* unpleasantly good and religious.

pharmaceutical [faːmə'sjuːtɪkl] *adj.* referring to medicines. **pharmacist** ['faːməsɪst] *n.* person who makes and sells medicines. **pharmacology** [faːmə'kɒlədʒɪ] *n.* study of medicines. **pharmacopoeia** [faːməkə'piːə] *n.* collection of drugs; book which lists drugs. **pharmacy** *n.* study of medicines; shop which makes and sells medicines.

pharynx ['færɪŋks] *n.* (*pl.*-es) passage at the back of the nose leading to the oesophagus. **pharyngitis** [færɪn'dʒaɪtɪs] *n.* inflammation of the pharynx.

phase 1 [feɪz] *n.* period; stage in development of sth. **phase 2** *v.* to p. in/out = to introduce/to remove gradually.

pheasant ['fezənt] *n.* large bright-coloured bird with a long tai. shot for sport and food.

phenobarbitone [fiːnəʊ'baːbɪtəʊn] *n.* drug which makes the patient sleep.

phenol ['fiːnɒl] *n.* carbon derivative used in medicine.

phenomenon [fe'nɒmɪnɒn] *n.* (*pl.*-mena) thing which happens naturally; esp. remarkable thing/happening. **phenomenal** *adj.* remarkable. **phenomenally** *adv.* remarkably.

phial ['faɪl] *n.* (formal) small bottle.

philanderer [fɪ'lændərə] *n.* man who flirts with women.

philanthropy [fɪ'lænθrəpɪ] *n.* love of/caring for human beings. shown esp. by giving money to charity. **philanthropic** [fɪlən'θrɒpɪk] *adj.* kind (towards human beings). **philanthropist** [fɪ'lænθrəpɪst] *n.* person who is philanthropic.

philately [fɪ'lætlɪ] *n.* stamp collecting. **philatelic** [fɪlə'telɪk] *adj.* referring to stamp collecting. **philatelist** *n.* person who studies or collects stamps.

-phile [faɪl] suffix meaning (person) who likes; Francophile = person who likes the French.

philharmonic [fɪlɑː'mɒnɪk] *adj.* liking music (used in names of orchestras/concert halls, etc.).

philistine ['fɪlɪstaɪn] *adj. & n.* (person) who is unsympathetic to the arts.

philodendron [fɪlə'dendrən] *n.* tropical climbing plant. often used as a house plant.

philology [fɪ'lɒlədʒɪ] *n.* study of (the history of) language. **philological** [fɪlə'lɒdʒɪkl] *adj.* referring to philology. **philologist** [fɪ'lɒlədʒɪst] *n.* expert in philology.

philosophy [fɪ'lɒsəfɪ] *n.* study of the meaning of human existence; study of the methods and limits of human knowledge; general way of thinking. **philosopher** *n.* person who studies the meaning of human existence. **philosophical** [fɪlə'sɒfɪkl] *adj.* (a) thoughtful; calm. (b) referring to philosophy. **philosophically** *adv.* thoughtfully; calmly. **philosophize** *v.* to think seriously (like a philosopher).

philtre ['fɪltə] *n.* (old) magic potion to make s.o. fall in love.

phlebitis [flɪ'baɪtɪs] *n.* inflammation of a vein.

phlegm [flem] *n.* (a) slimy substance in the throat, etc., when you have a cold. (b) calmness. **phlegmatic** [fleg'mætɪk] *adj.* calm/not easily annoyed. **phlegmatically** *adv.* in a phlegmatic way.

phlox [flɒks] *n.* (*pl.*phlox) common perennial flower.

-phobe [fəʊb] suffix meaning (person) who does not like; xenophobe = person who dislikes foreigners.

phobia ['fəʊbɪə] *n.* abnormal terror/hatred of something.

phoenix ['fiːnɪks] *n.* mythical bird, said to die by burning and reappear from its ashes.

phone 1 [fəʊn] *n.* telephone. **phone 2** *v.* to call (s.o.) by telephone. **phone book** *n.* book which lists people's names. addresses and phone numbers. **phone box** *n.* small cabin for a public telephone.

phonetic 1 [fə'netɪk] *adj.* referring to spoken sounds. **phonetic 2** *n. pl.* phonetics = (i) study of sounds of a languages; (ii) written signs which indicate sounds. **phonetically** *adv.*

using phonetics; (languages spoken) in a way which closely follows the written letters. **phonetician** [fəʊnə'tɪʃn] n. person who studies phonetics. **phonics** ['fɒnɪks] n. method of teaching reading. using letters as guides to pronunciation. **phonology** [fə'nɒlədʒi] n. study of sounds of speech. **phon(e)y 1** ['fəʊnɪ] adj. (-ier, -iest) inf. false. **phon(e)y 2** n. inf. person who pretends to be richer/more famous, etc., than he really is.

phonograph ['fəʊnəgrɑːf] n. Am. gramophone.

phosphate ['fɒsfeɪt] n. chemical compound containing phosphorus. often used as a fertilizer.

phosphorescence [fɒsfə'resns] n. ability to shine in the dark after being exposed to light. **phosphorescent** adj. which shines in the dark after being exposed to light.

phosphorus ['fɒsfərəs] n. (element: P) poisonous yellow substance which shines in the dark.

photo 1 ['fəʊtəʊ] n. (pl.-os) inf. photograph. **photo 2** photo- prefix meaning (i) light; (ii) photograph.

photochemical adj. (chemical reaction) which is caused by light.

photocopy 1 ['fəʊtəʊkɒpɪ] n. copy (of a document) made by photographing it.

photocopy 2 v. to copy (sth) photographically and make a print of it.

photocopier n. machine which takes photocopies. **photoelectric** [fəʊtəʊ'lektrɪk] adj. referring to electricity controlled by light; p. cell = cell which converts light into electricity or which operates a machine when a beam of light is broken. **photo finish** n. very close end of a raced when a photograph is used to decide who is the winner. **photgenic** [fəʊtəʊ'dʒiːnɪk] adj. (person) who looks well in photographs.

photograph 1 ['fəʊtəgrɑːf] n. picture taken by a camera by means of exposing sensitive film to light. **photograph 2** v. to take a picture with a camera.

photographer [fə'fɒgrəfə] n. person who takes photographs. **photographic** [fəʊtəʊ'græfɪk] adj. referring to photography; p. memory = ability to remember things in exact detail, as if seen. **photography** [fə'tɒgrəfɪ] n. (art of) taking pictures on sensitive film with

a camera. **photogravure**, n. engraving of a photograph. **photo opportunity** n. arranged situation where a famous person can be filmed or photographed by journalists. **photostat 1** ['fəʊtəʊstæt] n. trademark for a type of photographic copy. **photostat 2** v. (photostatted) to make a photographic copy of.

photosynthesis n. process by which plants use sunlight to form carbohydrates.

phrase 1 [freɪz] n. (a) expression; short sentence; group of words taken together; p. book = book of translations of common expressions. (b) group of notes in a piece of music. **phrase 2** v. to express/to word (a sentence, etc.)

phrasal ['freɪzl] adj. referring to a phrase; (verb) making a phrase.

phraseology [freɪzɪ'ɒlədʒɪ] n. way of expressing sth; choice of words and phrases.

phrenology [fre'nɒlədʒɪ] n. study of the outside shape of the skull.

phut [fʌt] adv. inf. to go p. = to stop working.

physical ['fɪzɪkl] adj. (a) referring to matter/energy, etc.; p. geography = study of rocks and earth, etc.; p. chemistry = study of chemical substances. (b) referring to the human body; p. exercise = exercise of the body. **physically** adv. referring to the body or to the laws of nature.

physician [fɪ'zɪʃn] n. doctor

physics ['fɪzɪks] n. study of matter/energy, etc. **physicist** ['fɪzɪsɪst] n. person who studies physics.

physiognomy [fɪzɪ'ɒnəmɪ] n. human face. **physiology** [fɪzɪ'ɒlədʒɪ] n. study of the way in which living things work. **physiological** [fɪzɪʊ'lɒdʒɪkl] adj. referring to physiology. **physiologist** n. person who studies physiology.

physiotherapy [fɪzɪʊ'θerəpɪ] n. treatment of an illness, pain, etc., by exercise or rubbing. **physiotherapist** n. person who practises physiotherapy.

physique [fɪ'ziːk] n. shape of a person's body.

pi [paɪ] n. letter of the Greek alphabet (p). symbolizing the quantity 3. 14159. which is used to calculate the circumference of a circle from a known radius.

piano ['pjænəʊ] *n.* (*pl.*-os) musical instrument with keys which makes notes by striking wires with hammers; grand p. = large piano with horizontal wires.

pianist ['pɪənɪst] *n.* person who plays the piano. **pianoforte** ['pjænəʊfɔːtɪ] *n.* (old) piano. **pianola** [pɪə'məʊlə] *n.* trademark for a piano which plays music mechanically from a reel of perforated paper.

piazza [pɪ'ætsə] *n.* Italian square. often surrounded by arcades.

pibroch ['piːbrɒk] *n.* mournful bagpipe music.

pica ['paɪkə] *n.* measure of type.

picaresque [pɪkə'resk] *adj.* fancifully romantic (story)

piccalilli [pɪkə'lɪlɪ] *n.* pickle made of vegetables, such as cauliflower, onions, etc., in a mustard sauce.

piccolo ['pɪkələʊ] *n.* (*pl.*-os) small wind instrument. like a little flute.

pick 1 [pɪk] *n.* (a) heavy tool (for breaking hard ground/concrete, etc.), with a long handle and a curved metal bar with pointed ends. (b) selected group; to take your p. = choose which one you want. **pick 2** *v.* (a) to break up (hard ground/concrete, etc.) with a pick. (b) to remove things with your fingers/ with a pointed tool; to clean the inside of (your nose) with your fingers. (c) to eat very daintily and without any appetite. (d) to choose. (e) to collect (ripe fruit); to cut (flowers). (f) to open (a lock) with a piece of wire. (g) to steal from (s.o.'s pocket). (h) to p. s.o.'s brains = to ask for ideas/information. **pickaxe** *Am.* **pickax** *n.* pick. **picker** *n.* person who picks. **pickings** *n. pl.* bits and pieces left which people can pick up. **pick-me-up** *n. inf.* tonic. **pick off** *v.* to defeat/kill (an enemy) one by one. **pick on** *v.* to select (s.o.) as a target for criticism/for bullying. **pick out** *v.* to select/to choose. **pickpocket** *n.* person who steals things from people's pockets. **pick up** *v.* (a) to take (sth) which is on the ground. (b) to learn (a language, etc.) unsystematically. (c) to give (s.o.) a lift in a car; (of a bus) to take (passengers) on board; (of police) to arrest/to take to a police station; to start an acquaintanceship with (s.o.) by chance. (d) to get stronger. **pick-up** *n.* (a) *inf.* person who has been picked up. (b) needle and arm of a record player. (c) light van with an open back.

picket 1 ['pɪkɪt] *n.* (a) guard. (b) pointed stake l(c) striking workman/ union official who stands at the entrance to a factory to try to prevent other workmen from going to work; p. line = line of pockets preventing other workmen going to work. **picket 2** *v.* to post strikers at the entrance of a factory to try to prevent workers going to work.

pickle 1 ['pɪkl] *n.* (a) vegetables preserved in vinegar, etc. (b) *inf.* naughty child. **pickle 2** *v.* to preserve (vegetables, etc.) in vinegar. **pickled** *adj. inf.* drunk.

picnic 1 ['pɪknɪk] *n.* (a) (a) excursion with a meal eaten in the open air. **picnic 2** *v.* (picnicked) to eat a picnic. **picknicker** *n* person who goes on a picnic.

pictorial [pɪk'tɔːrɪəl] *adj.* referring to pictures **picture 1** ['pɪktʃəl] *n.* (a) painting/drawing, etc.; *inf.* to put s.o. in the p. = to tell them all the relevant details. (b) image (on a TV screen, etc.). (c) the pictures = cinema. **picture 2** *v.* to imagine. **picturesque** [pɪktʃə'resk] *adj.* which would make a good picture; very artistic.

piddle ['pɪdl] *v. inf.* (child's language) to urinate. **piddling** *adj. inf.* very small.

pidgin ['pɪdʒɪn] *n.* simple language made from several languages used as a lingua franca; p. (English) = simplified form of English used in the Far East.

pie [paɪ] *n.* cooked dish *usu.* of pastry with a filling of meat or fruit; p. in the sky = unattainable ideal. **pie-chart** *n.* diagram shaped like a circle with segments showing how sth is divided up. **pie-eyed** *adj. inf.* drunk. **piebald** ['paɪbɔːld] *adj.* (horse) with black and white patches.

piece 1 [piːs] *n.* (a) small part/bit; he went to pieces = he lost control of himself/had a nervous breakdown. (b) short composition in music. (c) one of the figures used in chess, but not *usu.* a pawn. (d) gun. **piece 2** *v.* to p. together = to join separate parts together. **piecemeal** *adv.* in bits; a bit at a time; separately. **piece rate** *n.* rate of pay for a product produced. **piecework** n. work for which you are paid by the amount of work done and not by the hour.

piéce de résistance [pɪesdəreɪsɪs'tɑ̃s] n. main item.

pied [paɪd] adj. having two colours usu, black and white. **pied-à-terre** [pjeɪdæ'teə] n. small flat/house which you use to live in from time to time when visiting a place.

pier ['pɪə] n. (a) construction going out into the water used as a landing place for ships. (b) pillar (of a bridge).

pierce ['pɪəs] v. to make a hole. **piercing** adj. very loud, shrill (cry); very sharp/severe (cold/wind).

piety ['paɪətɪ] n. being pious; great respect for religion.

piffle [pɪfl] n. inf. nonsense.

pig [pɪg] n. (a) farm animal which gives pork/bacon, etc.; various wild species of this animal. (b) inf. dirty/greedy person. (c) large block of metal; p. iron = iron in rough moulded blocks. (d) Sl. policeman. **piggery** n. place where pigs are kept. **piggy** n. child's name for a pig. **piggyback** n. adj. & adv. carrying s.o. on your back with his arms round your neck. **piggybank** n. child's money box in the shape of a pig. **pigheaded** adj. inf. obstinate. **piglet** n. little pig. **pigmeat** n. meat from a pig. **pigskin** n. leather made from the skin of a pig. **pigsty** n. shed where pigs are kept. **pigtail** n. hair hanging down in a plait at the back of the head.

pigeon ['pɪdʒɪn] n. common greyish bird. **pigeonhole 1** n. small square space used for filing papers/letters, etc. **pigeonhole 2** v. (a) to file letters/ papers, etc. (often as the best way to forget them). (b) to put (s.o./sth) into a particular category. **pigeon-toed** adj. with the feet turned inwards towards each other.

pigment 1 ['pɪgmənt] n. colouring matter. **pigment 2** v. to colour with pigment. **pigmentation** [pɪgmən'teɪʃn] n. colouring of the skin.

pigmy ['pɪgmɪ] n. see pygmy.

pike [paɪk] n. (a) (pl.pike) large ferocious freshwater fish. (b) (old) weapon, like a spear with a broad blade.

pikelet ['paɪklət] n. (in north of England) crumpet. **pikestaff** ['paɪkstɑːf] n. as plain as a p. = very easy to see.

pilaff ['pɪlæf] n. Indian dish of meat with savoury rice.

pilaster [pɪ'læstə] n. rectangular column, usu. attached to a wall.

pilau ['pɪlaʊ] n. see pilaff.

pilchard ['pɪltʃəd] n. small fish similar to a herring.

pile 1 [paɪl] n. (a) heap; inf. he's made his p. = his fortune. (b) large stake/ concrete shaft driven into the earth to provide a foundation. (c) thickness of tufts of wool in a carpet. (d) piles = haemorrhoids. **pile 2** v to p. (up) = to heap up. **piledriver** n. machine for forcing piles into the earth. **pile-up** n. series of cars which have smashed into each other.

pilfer ['pɪlfə] v. to steal small objects or small amounts of money. **pilferer** n. person who pilfers. **pilferage, pilfering** n. stealing small objects or amounts of money.

pilgrim n. person who goes to visit a holy place. **pilgrimage** ['pɪlgrɪm] n. journey to visit a holy place/a famous place.

pill [pɪl] n. small round tablet of medicine; inf. she's on the p. = she takes contraceptive tablets. **pillbox** n. (a) round box for pills. (b) concrete shelter for a small gun.

pillage 1 ['pɪlɪdʒ] n. plundering by soldiers. **pillage 2** v. (of soldiers) to plunder/to steal goods (from a captured town, etc.).

pillar ['pɪlə] n. (a) column. (b) strong supporter. **pillar box** n. round red metal container into which you can post letters; pillar-box red = bright red.

pillion ['pɪljən] n. rear saddle for a passenger on a motorcycle; p. passenger = person riding on the pillion seat; to ride p. = to ride on the pillion seat.

pillory 1 ['pɪlərɪ] n. wooden stand with holes for the head and hands, where criminals were placed so that the public could throw things at them. **pillory 2** v. to make (s.o.) appear ridiculous or foolish in public.

pillow ['pɪləʊ] n. bag full of soft material which you put your head on in bed. **pillowcase, pillowslip** n. cloth bag to cover a pillow with.

pilot 1 ['paɪlət] *n.* (a) person who guides ships into harbour or through dangerous channels; p. scheme = small scheme used as a test before starting a full scale scheme. (b) person who files an aircraft. (c) p. light = small gas light on a cooker/water-heater, etc., from which the main gas jets are lit. **pilot 2** *v.* (a) to guide (a ship). (b) to fly (an aircraft). **pilot officer** *n.* lower rank of officer in the air force.

pimento *Am.* **pimento** [pɪ'mentəʊ, pɪmɪ'entəʊ] *n.* (*pl.*-os) green or red fruit with a hot spicy taste used as a vegetable.

pimp 1 [pɪmp] *n.* man who organizes and makes money from prostitutes. **pimp 2** *v.* to work as a pimp.

pimpernel ['pɪmpənel] *n.* wild plant with small red flowers.

pimple ['pɪmpl] *n.* small bump on the surface of the skin. **pimply** *adj.* covered with pimples.

pin 1 [pɪn] *n.* (a) small sharp metal stick with a round head, used for attaching clothes/papers, etc., together; safety p. = type of bent pin where the sharp point is held by a metal shield. pins and needles = prickling feeling in your hand or foot after it has been numb for a time. (b) blunt wooden or metal bolt used for fastening things together. **pin 2** *v.* (pinned) (a) to attach with a pin; to p. s.o. down = to get him to say what he really thinks/to make his mind up. (b) to hold fast. **pinball** *n.* table game where a ball has to be rolled into holes.

pincushion *n.* round pad in which you can stick pins. **pin money** *n. inf.* money earned by a woman for part-time work. **pinpoint** *v.* to indicate exactly. **pinprick** *n.* slight annoyance. **pinstripe** *n.* dark cloth with a very thin white line in it. **pintable** *n.* table for playing pinball. **pin-up** *n. inf.* photograph of pretty girl which you can pin up on a wall.

pinafore ['pɪnəfɔ:] *n.* apron worn to cover a dress.

pince-nez ['pænsneɪ] *n. pl.* glasses which clip on to your nose.

pincers ['pɪnsəz] *n. pl.* (a) (pair of) p. = scissors-shaped tool for holding sth tight. (b) claws of a crab/lobster.

pinch 1 [pɪnʃ] *n.* (*pl.*-es) (a) squeezing tightly/nipping between finger and thumb; at a p. = if really necessary; to feel the p. = find you have less money than you need. (b) small quantity of sth held between finger and thumb. **pinch 2** *v.* (a) to squeeze tightly, using the finger and thumb. (b) to hold tight and hurt. (c) *inf.* to steal. (d) *Sl.* to arrest.

pine 1 [paɪn] *n.* type of evergreen tree; wood from a pine tree. **pine 2** *v.* (to) waste away (because you want sth).

pineapple ['paɪnæpl] *n.* large tropical fruit, shaped like a pine cone with stiff prickly leaves on top. **pine cone** *n.* fruit of a pine tree. **pine marten** *n.* small carnivorous animal, living in coniferous forests. **pinewood** *n.* a wood of pine trees.

pineal gland *n.* small gland, shaped like a pine cone, found in the brain.

ping 1 [pɪŋ] *n.* noise made when a small bell/a glass, etc., is hit. **ping 2** *v.* to make a ping. **pinger** *n. inf.* bell which makes a ping. **ping pong** ['pɪŋpɒŋ] *n. inf.* table tennis.

pinion 1 ['pɪnjən] *n.* (a) large outer feather on a bird's wing. (b) toothed wheel or cogwheel. **pinion 2** *v.* to tie up (s.o.'s arms) tightly.

pink 1 [pɪŋk] *adj. & n.* (colour) like pale red or flesh colour. **pink 2** *n.* (a) scented garden flower like a small carnation. (b) red jacket worn by a huntsman; in the p. = very well/prosperous. **pink 3** *v.* (of an engine) to make a knocking noise when misfiring. **pinking shears** *n. pl.* large scissors used by dressmakers. which give a zigzag edge to a cut.

pinnacle ['pɪnəkl] *n.* topmost point (of a pointed rock, s.o.'s career); tall, thin stone spire or tower.

pint [paɪnt] *n.* liquid measure (=.568 of a litre or of a gallon). **pinta** *n. inf.* pint of milk.

pioneer 1 [paɪə'nɪə] *n.* (a) person who is among the first to try to do sth/who is the first to explore/settle in a new land. (b) soldier who prepares the way for the main army. **pioneer 2** *v.* to be first to do (sth).

pious ['paɪəs] *adj.* showing great respect for religion. **piously** *adv.* in a pious way.

pip 1 [pɪp] n. (a) small seed. (b) star on the shoulder showing an officer's rank. (c) short high-pitched call used on radio to show a time signal. **pip 2** v. to beat; to p. s.o. at the post = to beat him at the last minute.

pipe 1 [paɪp] n. (a) tube. (b) instrument for smoking tobacco. (c) thin metal flute; the pipes = bagpipes. **pipe 2** v. to send (water/gas, etc.) along a pipe; piped music = recorded music played continuously (in a restaurant, etc.). **pipe down** v. inf. to stop talking. **pipedream** n. plan which is impossible to carry out. **pipeline** n. very large tube for carrying oil/natural gas, etc., over long distances; in the p. = being worked on/on the way. **piper** n. person who plays the bagpipes. **pipe up** v. inf. to start talking (esp. in a high pitched voice) **piping 1** n. (a) collection of tubes; section of metal tube. (b) decoration like white tubes on as cake/on a dress. **piping 2** adv. p. hot = extremely hot.

pipette [pɪˈpet] n. thin glass measuring tube used in laboratories.

pipit [ˈpɪpɪt] n. small signing bird.

pippin [ˈpɪpɪn] n. type of sweet apple.

piquant [ˈpiːkənt] adj. nice sharp (flavour); pleasantly interesting/amusing. **piquancy** n. being piquant. **piquantly** adv. in a piquant way.

pique 1 n. resentment/annoyance. **pique 2** v. (a) to make (s.o.) resentful (b) to arouse s.o.'s curiosity.

piqué [ˈpileɪ] n. cotton material with ribs.

piranha [pɪˈrɑːnə] n. small tropical fish which attacks animals, including man.

pirate 1 [ˈpaɪrət] n. (a) robber (esp. at sea). (b) person who copies a patented invention or a copyright work. (c) person who takes money from s.o. else; p. radio = illegal radio station. **pirate 2** v. to publish books/make recordings which are copied from those of another publisher without having the right to do so. **piracy** n. robbery (at sea); illegal publishing of books/making of records. **piratical** [paɪˈrætɪkl] adj. referring to a pirate.

pirouette 1 [pɪrˈet] n. spinning round on one foot when dancing. **pirouette 2** v. to spin round on one foot.

piscatorial [pɪskəˈtɔːrɪəl] adj. referring to fishing.

Pisces [ˈpaɪsiːz] n. one of the signs of the zodiac, shaped like fish.

pisciculture [pɪsɪˈkʌltʃə] n. raising fish for food.

piss 1 [pɪs] n. inf. & vulgar (a) waste water from the body. (b) passing waste water from the body. **piss 2** v. inf. & vulgar to pass waste water from the body.

pistachio [pɪˈstæʃɪəʊ] n. (pl.-os) small green tropical nut.

piste [piːst] n. track for skiing.

pistil [ˈpstɪl] n. female part of a flower, which produces seeds.

pistol [ˈpɪstl] n. small gun which is held in the hand.

piston [ˈpstn] n. (in an engine) metal disc which moves up and down in a cylinder; p. rod = rod which is attached to a piston and which drives other parts of the engine.

pit 1 [pɪt] n. (a) deep. dark hole in the ground. (b) coalmine. (c) hole in the floor of a garage (for inspecting the underside of a car); (at car races) place where the cars are inspected and repaired. (d) back part of the ground floor of a theatre. (e) depths of your stomach. (f) Am. stone of some fruit. **pit 2** v. (pitted) (a) to try (your strength) against. (b) to mark with a hole. **pithead** n. entrance to a coalmine shaft.

pitch 1 [pɪtʃ] n. (pl.-es) (a) black substance which comes from tar and is used for waterproofing boats/roofs, etc. (b) level of tone in music. (c) ground on which a game is played; place in the street where a trader sells his wares. (d) height (of anger/of excitement). (e) angle of a sloping roof. (f) sales p. = smooth talk, aimed at selling sth. **pitch 2** v. (a) to put up (a tent). (b) to throw (a ball). (c) to set the level of a musical tone. (d) (of boat) to rock with the front and back going up and down. **pitch-black, pitch dark** adj. very black; very dark. **pitchblende** n. mineral which produces radium. **pitched** adj. p. battle = battle fought on a selected piece of ground; fierce argument. **pitcher** [ˈpɪtʃə] n. (a) large earthenware jug. (b) person who pitches a ball. **pitchfork 1** n. large fork for moving bales of hay.

pitchfork 2 v. to put (s.o.) suddenly into an awkward position. **pitch into** v. to attack. **pitchpine** n. type of pine which produces strong resin.

pitfall ['pɪtfɔːl] n. trap/danger.

pith [pɪθ] n. (a) soft part in the centre of a plant stem; soft white stuff under the skin of lemon/an orange, etc. (b) important part (of an argument). **pithily** adv. in a pithy way. **pithy** adj. (-er, -est) (a) (wood) with a soft centre. (b) concise; full of serious meaning.

piton ['piːtɒn] n. metal peg used in rock-climbing.

pittance ['pɪtns] n. low wage.

pitterpatter ['pɪtəpætə] n. series of small sounds

pituitary [pɪ'tjʊɪtrɪ] adj. p. gland = gland in the brain which produces hormones which control the development and function of the body.

pity 1 ['pɪtɪ] n. feeling of sympathy for s.o. unfortunate; to take p. on s.o. = to be sorry for s.o. **pity 2** v. to feel sympathy for (s.o.) **piteous, pitiable** ['pɪtɪəs] adj. which deserves pity. **pitiful** adj. (a) deserving pity; sad. (b) inadequate. **pitifully** adv. in a pitiful way. **pitiless** adj. showing no pity.

pivot 1 ['pɪvət] n. point on which sth turns. **pivot 2** v. to turn on a point; to depend on sth. **pivotal** adj. of great importance.

pixel ['pɪksəl] n. tiny element of colour or light on a TV screen or computer monitor.

pixie ['pɪksɪ] n. small fairy.

pizza ['piːtsə] n. Italian savoury dish, consisting of a flat round piece of dough cooked with tomatoes, onions, etc., on top. **pizzeria** n. shop which sells pizzas.

pizzicato [pɪstɪ'kɑːtəʊ] n. & adv. (music) played by plucking the strings instead of using the bow.

placard 1 ['plækɑːd] n. poster. **placard 2** v. to stick posters up.

placate [plə'keɪt] v. to calm (s.o.); to make (s.o.) less angry. **placatory** adv. which placates.

place 1 [pleɪs] n. (a) location/spot. (b) house/home. (c) open area. (d) name of a smart street in a town. (e) set position; to take p. = to happen/to be held. (f) rank (in a series); in the first p. = first of all.

(g) job. (h) one of the first three positions in a horse race. **place 2** v. (a) to put. (b) to give (an order). (c) to put in a set position. (d) to remember who s.o. is. **placemat** n. mat which a person's plate is put on. **placement** n. placing s.o. in a job. **place setting** n. set of knife/fork/spoon, etc., for one person.

placebo [plə'siːbəʊ] n. (pl.-os) harmless substance given to a patient instead of a drug to make him believe he is receiving treatment.

placenta [plə'sentə] n. tissue in the womb which nourishes the unborn baby.

placid ['plæsɪd] adj. (-er, -est) calm. **placidity** [plə'sɪdɪtɪ] n. calmness. **placidly** adv. calmly.

placket ['plækɪt] n. opening with buttons at the waist of a skirt.

plagiarism ['pleɪdʒərɪzəm] n. copying what s.o. else has written. **plagiarist** n. author who copies the work of s.o. else. **plagiarize** v. to copy the work of (another author).

plague 1 [pleɪg] n. (a) fatal infectious disease transmitted by fleas from rats. (b) great quantity of pests. **plague 2** v. to annoy/to bother (s.o.)

plaice [pleɪs] n. (pl.plaice) common flat sea fish.

plaid [plæd] n. (in Scotland) long piece of (tartan) cloth.

plain 1 adj. (-er, -est) (a) obvious/easy to understand. (b) simple/uncomplicated; p. cover = envelope without any company name on it. (c) not pretty. (d) p. chocolate = dark chocolate, made without milk; p. flour = white flour with no baking powder in it. **plain 2** n. large flat area of country. **plainclothes** n. pl. ordinary/everyday clothes (not uniform). **plainly** adv. (a) obviously. (b) simply. **plainness** n. (a) clearness. (b) simpleness. **plainsong** n. medieval music for church services. **plain-spoken** adj. (person) who speaks in a straightforward way.

plaintiff ['pleɪntɪf] n person who starts a legal action against s.o. else.

plaintive ['pleɪntɪv] adj. sad.

plait 1 [plæt] n. (hair/wool, etc.) with three strands woven into a long rope. **plait 2** v. to weave hair, etc., to form a plait.

plan 1 [plæn] n (a) scheme; according

to p. = as we had intended. (b) drawing of the way sth is to be built or constructed. (c) map of streets. **plan 2** v. (planned) (a) to draw up a scheme to construct sth. (b) to scheme/to propose to do sth. **planner** n. person who draws up schemes; town p. = person who designs how a town should develop.

planning n. making plans; family p. = decision by parents on how many children to have.

plane 1 [pleɪn] n. (a) flat surface. (b) aircraft. (c) tool for smoothing wood. (d) tree often grown in towns, of which bark comes off in large pieces. **plane 2** adj. level/flat. **plane 3** v. to smooth (wood) flat with a plane.

planet ['plænɪt] n. body which revolves round a star esp. round the sun.

planetarium [plænɪ'teərɪəm] n. domed building in which you sit and watch as pictures of the stars are projected against the ceiling. **planetary** ['plænɪtrɪ] adj. referring to the planets.

plangent ['plændʒnt] adj. sad resonant (music).

plank [plæŋk] n. (a) long flat piece of wood used in building. (b) proposal in a political programme. **planking** n. series of planks.

plankton ['plæŋktn] n. tiny organisms living in the sea.

plant 1 [plɑːnt] n (a) thing which grows in the ground, is usu. green. and cannot move from one place to another. (b) factory. (c) machinery. **plant 2** v. (a) to put (a plant) into the ground. (b) to put in a special position. (c) to put (sth) secretly; to put (stolen goods) secretly on s.o., in order to make it look as if they stole them. **plantation** [plɑːm'teɪʃn] n. (a) area of trees specially planted. (b) tropical estate growing a particular crop. **planter** n. (a) person in charge of a plantation. (b) decorative container to hold plants in pots.

plantain ['plæntɪn] n. (a) common weed. (b) tropical fruit.

plaque [plæk] n. (a) decorative plate hung on a wall; stone/metal/earthenware plate with an inscription. (b) deposit which forms on the teeth.

plasma ['plæzmə] n. liquid part of blood.

plaster 1 ['plɑːstə] n. (a) mixture of

fine sand and lime which when mixed with water is used for covering walls of houses. (b) white paste used to make moulds/to make coverings to hold broken arms and legs in place. (c) sticking p. = adhesive cloth/tape used for holding bandages in place/for covering small wounds. **plaster 2** v. (a) to cover with plaster. (b) to cover thickly as if with plaster. **plaster-cast** n. (a) block of plaster put round a broken leg, etc., (b) mould made by covering sth with plaster. (c) copy of a statue made in plaster. **plastered** adj. Sl. drunk. **plasterer** n. person who covers walls with plaster.

plastic 1 ['plæstɪk] n. artificial substance which can be moulded into any shape; p. bomb = explosive material which can be moulded in the hand.

plastic 2 adj. soft/liable; p. surgery = operation to replace damaged skin or to improve s.o.'s appearance. **plasticity** [plæs'tɪsɪtɪ] n. state of being plastic.

plate 1 [pleɪt] n. (a) thin flat sheet of metal/glass etc. (b) flat dish for putting food on. (c) dishes made of gold or silver. (d) thin layer of gold/silver on a less precious metal; objects made of this. (e) book illustration o shiny paper. (f) piece of plastic with false teeth attached with fits into your mouth **plate 2** v to cover with a thin layer of gold or silver. **plateful** n. quantity held by a plate. **plate glass** n. glass in very large sheets. **platelayer** n. railway worker who sets the rails in place/who repairs rails.

plateau ['plætəʊ] n. (pl.-eaux) high flat area of land.

platelet ['pleɪtlət] n. small cell in the blood which helps blood to clot.

platen ['plætən] n. roller round which the paper goes in a typewriter.

platform ['plætfɔːm] n. (a) raised floor space for speakers in a hall. (b) raised pavement by the side of the rails in a railway station so that passengers can get on and off trains easily. (c) proposals put forward by the leaders of a political party before an election.

platinum ['plætɪnəm] n. (element Pt) rare light-coloured precious metal; P. blonde = woman with silvery blonde hair.

platitude ['plætɪtjuːd] n. ordinary saying, esp. one which the speaker thinks is very important.

platonic [plə'tɒnɪk] adj. (love between man and woman) which is not sexual.

platoon [plə'tuːn] n. small group of soldiers/part of a company.

platter ['plætə] n. large serving plate.

platypus ['plætɪpəs] n. (pl.-es) Australian mammal which lays eggs.

plaudits['plɔːdɪts] n. pl.applause.

plausible ['plɔːzɪbl] adj. which sounds as though it is correct when it often is not. **plausibly** adv. in a plausible way. **plausibility** [plɔːzɪ'bɪlɪtɪ] n. being plausible.

play 1 [pleɪ] n. (a) way of amusing yourself; sport. (b) theatrical performance; script of a theatrical performance. (c) freedom to move. **play 2** v. (a) to amuse yourself/to pass the time in a pleasant way. (b) to take part in a game. (c) to perform on a musical instrument. (d) to act a part in a theatrical performance. (e) to aim. (f) to let a fish which has been caught on a hook swim until it is tired and can easily be landed. (g) (of fountain etc.) to work. (h) to make (a record player) work; to make (a beam of light) hit sth. **play at** v. (a) to work in a slack way. (b) (of children) to pretend to be. **play back** v. to listen to (sth) which you have just recorded on tape. **playboy** n. rich man who spends his time amusing himself rather than working. **play down** v. to make (sth) seem less important. **player** n. person who plays. **playfellow** n. child another child plays with. **playful** adj. liking to play. **playfully** adv. in a playful way. **playfulness** n. being playful. **playground** n. area esp. round school buildings, where children can play. **playgroup** n. group of small children who play together under supervision. **playhouse** n. theatre. **playing card** n. one of a set of fifty-two cards, marked in four designs used for playing various games. **playing field** n. area of grass where sports can be played. **playmate** n. playfellow.

play off v. to p. s.o. off against s.o. = to try to benefit by making two people oppose each other. **play on** v. to take advantage by exciting (s.o.'s sympathy).

playpen n. type of cage in which babies can be left to play safely.

plaything n. toy. **playtime** n. time in nursery school when children can play.

play up v. inf. to make trouble.

playwright n. person who writes plays.

plaza ['plɑːzə] n. open area in a town.

Plc [piːel'siː] n. short for public limited company.

plea [pliː] n. (a) answer to a charge in court; p. bargaining = arrangement where an accused person pleads guilty to some charges so as to be let off others. (b) (formal) request. (c) excuse. **plead** [pliːd] v. (a) to answer a charge in a law court. (b) to give an excuse. (c) to p. with s.o. = to try to change s.o.'s mind by asking again and again.

pleasant ['pleznt] adj. (-er. -est) agreeable/which pleases. **pleasantly** adv. in a pleasant way. **pleasantry** n. joke; pleasant remark.

please [pliːz] v. (a) to make (s.o.) happy/satisfied; p. yourself = do as you like. (b) polite expression after an order or request meaning if you would like.

pleased adj. happy; satisfied.

pleasing adj. which pleases.

pleasurable ['pleʒərəbl] adj. pleasant.

pleasure ['pleʒə] n. amusement/happiness.

pleat 1 [pliːt] n. vertical fold (in a skirt, etc.). **pleat 2** v. to iron vertical folds in.

plebiscite ['plebɪsɪt] n. general vote by the inhabitants of a country on an important issue.

plebs [plebz] n. pl. inf. ordinary people. **plebeian** [pliː'biːən] adj. common/ordinary; of the working class.

plectrum ['plektrəm] n. small stick for plucking the strings of a guitar, etc.

pledge 1 [pledʒ] n. (a) object give to the lender when borrowing money, and which will be returned to the borrower when the money is paid back. (b) promise; to take the p. = to swear never to drink alcohol again. **pledge 2** v. (a) to give (sth) as a pledge when borrowing money. (b) to promise. (c) to drink (a toast).

plenary ['pliːnərɪ] adj. complete; p. session = session of a conference where all the delegates meet together.

plenipotentiary [plenɪpə'tenʃərɪ] adj.
& n. (person) who has full powers to act
on behalf of his country.

plenteous ['plentɪəs] adj. (formal)
more than enough. **plenty** ['plentɪ] n.
large quantity. **plentiful** adj. abundant;
in large quantities.

plenum ['pleɪnəm] n. general meeting.

pleonasm ['plɪənæzəm] n. use of more
words than necessary. **pleonastic**
[plɪə'næstɪk] adj. (expression) where
some words are superfluous.

plethora ['pleθərə] n. (formal) too
many (of).

pleura ['pʊərə] n. (formal) membrane
covering the lungs. **pleurisy** n. disease
of the membrane covering the lungs.

plexus ['pleksəs] n. network of nerves.

pliable, pliant ['plaɪəbl] ['plaɪənt] adj.
which can be bent easily (person) who
can be easily persuaded. **pliability,
pliancy** n. being pliable/pliant.

pliers ['plaɪəz] n. pl. (pair of) p. = tool
shaped like scissors for pinching,
twisting or cutting wire.

plight 1 [plaɪt] n. bad state. **plight 2** v.
(formal) to promise.

Plimsoll line ['plɪmsɒlaɪn] n. line
along the side of a ship which shows the
level of the water when the ship is
loaded. **plimsolls** ['plɪmsɒlz] n. pl.
canvas shoes worn when doing
gymnastics.

plinth ['plɪnθ] n. pedestal on which a
statue stands.

plod [plɒd] v. (plodded) (a) to walk
heavily. (b) to work steadily. **plodder** n.
person who works steadily but rather
slowly.

plonk 1 [plɒŋk] n. inf. (a) dull sound.
(b) inferior wine. **plonk 2** v. inf. to put
(sth) down heavily.

plop 1 [plɒp] n. noise made by a stone
falling into water. **plop 2** v. (plopped)
to make a noise like a stone falling into
water.

plot 1 [plɒt] n. (a) small area of land for
building/for growing vegetables, etc. (b)
basic story of a book/play/film. (c)
wicked plan. **plot 2** v. (plotted) (a) to
mark on a map; to draw a graph. (b) to
draw up a wicked plan. **plotter** n.
person who plots.

plough Am. **plow 1** [plaʊ] n. (a) farm
machine for tuning over soil. (b) snow p.

= machine like a tractor with a large
blade in front, used for clearing snow
from streets, railway lines, etc. **plough**
Am. **plow 2** v. (a) to turn over the soil.
(b) to work slowly. **plough back** v. to
invest (profits) back in a business.

ploughman n. (pl.-men) farm worker
who drives a plough; ploughman's lunch
= bread cheese and pickles.

ploughshare n. blade of a plough.

plover ['plʌvə] n. type of wading bird
(found in fields and moors).

plow [plaʊ] n & v. Am. see plough.

ploy [plɔɪ] n. clever trick.

pluck 1 [plʌk] n. courage. **pluck 2** v.
(a) to pull out feathers or eyebrows. (b)
to pick (flowers, etc.). (c) to pull and
release the strings of a guitar to make a
sound; to p. up courage = to get ready to
face a danger. **pluckily** adv. in a
plucky way. **plucky** adj. (-ier, -iest)
brave.

plug 1 [plʌg] n. (a) disc which covers a
hole. esp. the hole for waste water in a
bath/sink, etc. (b) device with pins
which go into the holes in an electric
socket, and allow the current to pass
through; (in a car) sparking p. = device
which passes the electric spark through
the petrol vapour. (c) inf. piece of
publicity. (d) piece of tobacco which you
chew. **plug 2** v. (plugged) (a) to block
up (a hole). (b) inf. to publicize. (c) inf.
to shoot. **plug away** v. inf. to work
hard (at). **plughole** n. hole in a bath/
washbasin through which the dirty water
runs away. **plug in** v. to push an
electric plug into a socket.

plum [plʌm] n. (a) gold. red or purple
fruit with a smooth skin and a large
stone; tree which bears this fruit; p.
pudding = rich boiled fruit pudding. usu.
eaten at Christmas; inf. p. job = very
good job. (b) deep purple colour.

plumage ['pluːmɪdʒ] n. feathers on a
bird.

plumb 1 [plʌm] adj. straight; vertical.
plumb 2 n. lead weight for testing if
sth is straight. **plumb 3** v. (a) to
measure (the depth of water) by using a
plumbline. (b) to reach the bottom (of
feeling of despair). (c) to fix the
plumbing in (a house. **plumb 4** adv.
(a) exactly (in the middle). (b) Am.
completely. **plumber** n. person who

installs water pipes, etc. **plumb in** v. to attach (a washing machine) permanently to the water system. **plumbing** n. system of water pipes in a house.

plumbline ['plʌmlaɪn] n. rope with a weight on the end. dropped over the side from a ship to find how deep the water is or held beside a wall to see if it is vertical.

plume [pluːm] n. tall feather (worn in a hat, etc.); tall column of smoke. **plumed** adj. with a plume.

plummet ['plʌmɪt] v. to fall sharply.

plummy ['plʌmɪ] adj. rich/full (voice).

plump 1 [plʌmp] adj. (-er, -est) fat and tender; round fat (person). **plump 2** v. (a) to p. up = to shake (squashed cushions) until they are fat. (b) inf. to p. for = to decide on. (c) to throw (oneself) down **plumpness** n. fatness.

plunder 1 ['plʌndə] n. booty/goods seized, esp. in war. **plunder 2** v. to seize goods by force.

plunge 1 [plʌndʒ] n. dive; to take the p. = suddenly decide to do sth. **plunge 2** v. to dive deeply; to throw yourself into. **plunger** n. (a) device which goes up and down in a cylinder. (b) handle with a soft rubber head, for clearing blocked pipes by suction.

pluperfect [pluː'pɜːfɪkt] adj. & n. (tense) showing sth which took place before a time in the past.

plural ['pʊərəl] adj. & n. (in grammar) form of a word showing more than one. **pluralism** n. political system where several political parties are allowed to exist **plurality** [plʊə'rælɪtɪ] n. Am. majority.

plus 1 [plʌs] prep. in addition to. **plus 2** adj. & n. (a) sign (+) meaning more than. (b) inf. favourable sign. **plus-fours** n. pl. baggy golfing trousers, attached at the knee.

plush 1 [plʌʃ] n. soft-pile cloth for furnishings. **plush 2** adj. (-er, -est) inf. luxurious.

plutocrat ['pluːtəkræt] n. person who is very rich and powerful **plutocracy** [pluː'tɒkrəsɪ] n. government by the very rich.

plutonium [pluː'təʊnɪəm] n. (element: Pu) radioactive substance, used to produce nuclear power.

ply 1 [plaɪ] n. (a) thickness of wood in plywood. (b) strand of wool. **ply 2** v.

(a) to go backwards and forwards. (b) to p. s.o. with = to force s.o. to eat/drink sth. **plywood** n. sheet made of several thin sheets of wood stick together.

p.m. [piː'em] adv. in the afternoon/after midday.

PM [piː'em] n. 1 = Prime Minister 2 = postmortem.

pneumatic [njuː'mætɪk] adj. driven by compressed air, **pneumatically** adv. using compressed air.

pneumonia [njuː'məʊnɪə] n. illness caused by inflammation of the lungs.

PO ['piː'əʊ] post office.

poach [pəʊtʃ] v. (a) to cook (eggs with out their shells/fish, etc.) in gently boiling water. (b) to catch game illegally. (c) to entice workers to leave their jobs and work for another employer. **poacher** n. person who catches game illegally.

pochard ['pɒtʃəd] n. type of diving duck.

pocket 1 ['pɒkɪt] n. (a) small bag attached to the inside of a coat/trousers, etc., for holding money/keys, etc., a p. dictionary small dictionary which you can keep in your pocket; p. money = money given each week to a child to spend as he pleases. (b) to be in p. = to have made a profit; to be out of p. = to have lost money. (c) hole with a small bag at each corner and side of a billiard table. (d) small patch/small group in a certain place. **pocket 2** v. (a) to put in your pocket. (b) to send (a billiard ball) into a pocket. **pocketbook** n. small wallet. **pocketful** n. amount contained in a pocket.

pockmarked ['pɒkmɑːkt] adj. covered with round scars.

pod [pɒd] n. long case in which peas/ beans, etc., are formed.

podgy ['pɒdʒɪ] adj. inf. (-er, -est) fat.

podium ['pəʊdɪəm] n. raised platform (for winning sportsmen/orchestral conductors, etc., to stand on).

podsol ['pɒdsɒl] n. type of pale acid soil.

poem ['pəʊɪm] n. piece of writing, in a particular rhythm, often with lines of a regular length which rhyme. **poet, poetess** n. person who writes poems. **poetic(al)** ['pəʊ'etɪk(l)] adj. referring to poetry; imaginative/rhythmic (as in a poem). **poetically** adv. in a poetic way. **poetry** ['pəʊətrɪ] n. writing of poems; poems taken as a type of literature.

pogrom ['pɒɡrəm] n. official persecution/massacre (esp. of Jews),

poignant ['pɔɪnjənt] adj. moving/sad (thought). **poignancy** n. sadness.

poignantly adv. sadly/in a way which moves you to sadness.

poinsettia [pɔɪn'setɪə] n. plant with large green leaves. turning red at the top, used as a Christmas decoration.

point 1 [pɔɪnt] n. (a) sharp end (of a pin, etc.). (b) dot; decimal p. = dot used to indicate the division between units and decimals (such as 3.25). (c) place/ spot; p. of no return = place where you can only go on and not go back. (d) reason/purpose. (e) meaning/argument. (f) specific time; on the p. of = just about to. (g) headland; (h) mark in games or competitions; mark on a scale. (i) movable rails which allow trains to cross from one line to another. (j) electric socket; (in an engine) electrical contacts. **point 2** v. (a) to aim (a gun/your finger) at s.o./sth. (b) to sharpen to a point. (c) to fill the spaces in between bricks with mortar. **point-blank** adj. & adv. (a) at very close range. (b) sharply/ directly. **pointduty** n. (of a policeman) to be on pointduty = to direct the traffic. **pointed** adj. (a) with a sharp end. (b) obviously unfriendly (remark). **pointedly** adv. in an unfriendly way. **pointer** n. (a) dog which is trained to point out game with its nose. (b) arrow/ rod which points. **pointless** adj. meaningless. **pointlessly** adv. meaninglessly. **point out** v. to indicate/ to show. **point-to-point** n. type of horse race held over a rough track in the country **point up** v. to make (sth) seem even more obvious.

poise [pɔɪz] n. balance/graceful way of holding your head or of standing upright. **poise 2** v. to balance. **poised** adj. ready (to kill/for action).

poison 1 ['pɔɪzn] n. substance which kills or makes you ill if it is swallowed or if it gets into the bloodstreAm. **poison 2** v. to kill with poison. **poisoner** n. person who poisons. **poisonous** adj. which can kill or harm with poison.

poke [pəʊk] v. (a) to push with your finger/with a stick. (b) to p. about for = to search. **poker** n. (a) long metal rod for stirring up a fire. (b) card game in which the players gamble. **poker face** n. expression which shows no emotion.

pokerfaced adj. showing no emotion.

poky ['pəʊkɪ] adj. (-er, -est) inf. cramped/small (room).

polar ['pəʊlə] adj. referring to the North/Sough Poles. **polar bear** n. white bear which lives in the Arctic.

polarize ['pəʊləraɪz] v. to divide into two opposite groups. **polarization** [pəʊləraɪ'zeɪʃn] n. attraction around two opposite poles; division into main groups.

polder ['pɒldə] n. land which has been reclaimed from the sea.

pole [pəʊl] n. (a) one of the points at each end of the earth's axis. (b) one of the two opposing ends of a magnet; they are poles apart = they are very different/ they will never come to an agreement. (c) long wooden/metal rod; p. vaulting = sport where you have to jump over a high bar with the help of a long pole. (d) Pole = person form Poland. **poleaxe 1** n. (old) large axe used in battle.

poleaxe 2 v. to knock (s.o.) down.

pole star n. star which appears to be near to the North Pole.

polecat ['pəʊlkæt] n. small wild flesh-eating animal, like a weasel.

polemic [pə'lemɪk] n. argument/attack on s.o.'s views. **polemical** adj. controversial/likely to start an argument.

police 1 [pə'liːs] n. group of people who keep law and order in a country; p. constable = ordinary member of the police; p. force = group of police in certain area; p. station = local office of a police force. **police 2** v. to keep law and order in (a town, etc.). **policeman, policewoman** n. (pl.-men, -women) member of the police. **police state** n. country which is terrorized by the police.

policy ['pɒlɪsɪ] n. (a) way of acting. (b) written agreement with an insurance company.

poliomyelitis [pəʊlɪrəʊmarə'laɪtɪs] inf. n polio[pəʊlɪəʊ] disease of the nerve in the spinal cord, sometimes causing paralysis.

polish 1 ['pɒlɪʃ] *n.* (*pl.*-es) (a) shiny surface. (b) rubbing to make sth shiny. (c) substance used to make things shiny. **polish 2** *v.* to rub (sth) to make it shiny. **polished** *adj.* (a) shiny. (b) made perfect by practice. (c) polite (manners). **polisher** *n.* machine which polishes. **polish off** *v.* to finish off (a job) quickly/to eat (a meal) quickly. **polish up** *v. inf.* to improve.

Polish 1 ['pəʊlɪʃ] *adj.* referring to Poland. **Polish 2** *n.* language spoken in Poland.

Politburo [pɒ'lɪtbjuːrəʊ] *n.* central committee of a communist party.

polite [pə'laɪt] *adj.* (-er, -est) not rude; courteous. **politely** *adv.* courteously; in a well-mannered way. **politeness** *n.* good manners.

politics ['pɒlɪtɪks] *n.* study of how to govern a country. **politic** ['pɒlɪtɪk] *adj.* wise/careful. **political** [pə'lɪtɪkl] *adj.* referring to government/party politics. p. party = organized group of people who believe in one method of ruling a country. **politically** *adv.* as far as politics are concerned. **politician** [pɒlɪ'tɪʃn] *n.* person who works in politics. esp. a member of parliament.

polka ['pɒlkə] *n.* type of lively dance; p. dots = small round dots (as a pattern on cloth).

poll 1 [pəʊl] *n.* (a) vote/voting. (b) number of votes. (c) opinion p. = questioning of a sample group of people to guess at the views of the whole population on a question. **poll 2** *v.* (a) to vote. (b) to get a number of votes in an election. (c) to cut the horns off (a cow). **polling.** *n.* voting, elections; p. booth = small cabin in which each voter writes his vote; p. station = place where you vote in an election. **poll tax** *n.* tax which is levied equally on each person.

pollard ['pɒləd] *v.* to cut the branches of (a tree) back to the main trunk.

pollen ['pɒln] *n. usu.* yellow powder in flowers which fertilizes them; p. count = number showing the amount of pollen in the air (which can cause hayfever).

pollinate ['pɒlɪneɪt] *v.* to fertilize with pollen. **pollination** [pɒlɪ'neɪʃn] *n.* fertilizing with pollen.

pollute [pə'luːt] *v.* to make dirty. **pollutant** *n.* substance which pollutes.

polluter *n.* person or company which pollutes; p. pays principle = rule that the person who causes pollution should pay for it to be cleared. **pollution** [pə'luːʃn] *n.* making dirty.

polo ['pəʊləʊ] *n.* (a) ball game in which the two teams ride on ponies; water p. = ball game played by two teams in the water. (b) p. neck pullover = pullover with a high rolled neck.

polony [pə'ləʊnɪ] *n.* red sausage made of cooked pork.

poltergeist ['pɒltəgaɪst] *n.* ghost which knocks things over/makes loud sounds, etc.

poly- ['pɒlɪ] prefix meaning several.

polyanthus [pɒlɪ'ænθəs] *n.* common garden flower, like a primrose with a large flower head.

polychrome ['pɒlɪkrəʊm] *adj.* with several colours.

polyester [pɒlɪ'estə] *n.* type of synthetic fibre used esp. in clothing.

polygamy [pə'lɪgəmɪ] *n.* custom of having several wives at the same time. **polygamist** *n.* man with several wives. **polygamous** *adj.* referring to polygamy.

polyglot ['pɒlɪglɒt] *adj. & n.* (person) who speaks several languages; (dictionary, etc.) written in several languages.

polygon ['pɒlɪgən] *n.* geometrical figure with many sides. **polygonal** [pə'lɪgənl] *adj.* with many sides.

polymer ['pɒlɪmə] *n.* chemical compound whose molecule is made of several single similar molecules. **polymerization** *n.* act of polymerizing. **polymerize** *v.* to make/to become a polymer.

polyp ['pɒlɪp] *n.* (a) small primitive water animal shaped like a tube. (b) growth inside the human body.

polystyrene [pɒlɪ'staɪriːn] *n.* light plastic used as a heat insulator or as packing material.

polysyllable ['pɒlɪsɪləbl] *n.* word with several syllables. **polysyllabic** [pɒlɪsɪ'læbɪk] *adj.* (word) with several syllables.

polytechnic [pɒlɪ'teknɪk] *n.* educational establishment for school-leavers, giving degrees, esp. in technical subjects.

polytheism [pɒlɪˈθiːɪzm] n. belief in the existence of many gods.

polythene [ˈpɒlɪθiːn] n. type of almost transparent plastic used in thin sheets.

polyunsaturated [pɒlɪʌnˈsætjʊreɪtɪd] adj. (fat) which does not form cholesterol in the blood.

polyurethane [pɒlɪˈjʊərɪθeɪn] n. type of plastic used in paints.

pom, pommy [pɒm], [ˈpɒmɪ] adj. & n. inf. (in Australia) (person) from Britain.

pomander [pəˈmændə] n. (box containing) dried scented herbs; p. ball = dried orange with cloves stuck into it.

pomegranate [ˈpɒmɪɡrænɪt] n. tropical fruit with red flesh and many seeds.

pommel [ˈpɒml] n. high front part of a saddle.

pomp [pɒmp] n. splendid ceremony. **pomposity** [pɒmˈpɒsɪtɪ] n. being pompous. **pompous** [ˈpɒmpəs] adj. very solemn/too dignified.

pompom [ˈpɒmpɒm] n. small tufted ball of wool worn as an ornament on a hat, etc.

ponce 1 [pɒns] n. Sl. man who lives off the money earned by prostitutes. **ponce 2** v. Sl. to p. about = to prance about in an effeminate way.

poncho [ˈpɒnʃəʊ] n. (pl.-os) cloak made of a single large piece of material, with a hole in the centre for your head.

pond [pɒnd] n. small lake.

ponder [ˈpɒndə] v. to think deeply. **ponderous** adj. very heavy and slow-moving. **ponderously** adv., in a ponderous way.

pong 1 [pɒŋ] n. Sl. unpleasant smell. **pong 2** v. Sl. to make an unpleasant smell

pontiff [ˈpɒntɪf] n. the Pope. **pontifical** [pɒnˈtɪfɪkl] adj. referring to the Pope. **pontificate** [pɒnˈtɪfɪkeɪt] v. to speak/to write in a pompous way.

pontoon [pɒnˈtuːn] n. (a) boat used to support a floating temporary bridge; p. bridge = one built on pontoons. (b) card game.

pony [ˈpəʊnɪ] n. small horse. **pony tail** n. hairstyle where the hair is tied at the back and falls loosely. **pony-trekking** n. holiday sport riding ponies across country.

poodle [ˈpuːdl] n. type of curly-haired dog, usu. clipped in a curious way.

poof [puːf] n. Sl. homosexual.

pooh-pooh [puːˈpuː] v. inf. to ridicule (an idea).

pool 1 [puːl] n. (a) small lake. (b) area of water or other liquid. (c) swimming p. = enclosed tank of water for swimming. (d) common supply of money/food, etc., for a group of people. (e) group where people share facilities; car p. = arrangement where several people share cars; typing p. = group of typists working for several departments. (f) football pools = system of gambling where you have to forecast the results of football matches. (g) Am. game similar to snooker. **pool 2** v. to group (resources) together. **poolroom** n. Am. public room where you can play pool.

poop [puːp] n. high raised stern of a ship.

poor [ˈpʊə, pɔː] adj. (-er, -est) (a) having little or no money; p. in = with very little (of sth). (b) not very good. **poorly 1** adv. (a) in quite a bad way. (b) without money. **poorly 2** adj. ill **poorness** n. bad quality.

pop 1 [pɒp] n. (a) noise like cork coming out of a bottle. (b) inf. father. (c) inf. popular song. (d) inf. fizzy drink. **pop 2** v. (popped) (a) to make a pop. (b) inf. to go quickly. (c) to put quickly. (d) to ask (a question) quickly. **pop 3** adj. inf. popular. **popcorn** n. sweet corn which has been heated until it bursts. **popgun** n. toy gun which makes a pop.

Pope [pəʊp] n. the head of the Roman Catholic Church.

poplar [ˈpɒplə] n. common tall and slender tree.

poplin [ˈpɒplɪn] n. strong cotton cloth used for making shirts.

poppadom [ˈpɒpədɒm] n. (in Indian food) thin fried cake.

popper [ˈpɒpə] n. inf. snap fastener.

poppet [ˈpɒpɪt] n. inf. nice girl

poppy [ˈpɒpɪ] n. common flower, red when wild.

populace [ˈpɒpjʊləs] n. ordinary people.

popular [ˈpɒpjʊlə] adj. (a) referring to the ordinary people. (b) liked by a lot of people. **popularity** [pɒpjʊˈlærɪtɪ] n.

being popular. **popularization**
[pɒpjʊlərai'zeiʃn] *n.* act of popularizing.
popularize ['pɒpjʊləraiz] *v.* to make
(sth) understood/liked by a lot of people.
popularly *adv.* generally; by most
people.
populate ['pɒpjʊleit] *v.* to put people
to live in (a place). **population**
[pɒpjʊ'leiʃn] *n.* number of people who
live in a place. **populous** ['pɒpjʊləs]
adj. thickly populated.
porbeagle ['pɔːbiːgl] *n.* type of shark.
porcelain ['pɔːslin] *n.* fine china.
porch [pɔːtʃ] *n.* (*pl.*-es) shelter over a
doorway.
porcine ['pɔːsain] *adj.* like a pig.
porcupine ['pɔːkjʊpain] *n.* rodent with
long sharp spikes covering its body.
pore 1 [pɔː] *n.* small hole in the skin
through which water passes. **pore 2** *v.*
to p. over = to look at (a book etc.) very
closely.
pork [pɔːk] *n.* (*no pl.*) meat from a pig.
porker *n. inf.* pig.
pornography [pɔː'nɒgrəfi] *n.*
pornographic films/books/art. **porn**
[pɔːn] *n. inf.* pornography; hard/soft p. =
extremely indecent/less indecent
pornographic material. **pornographic**
[pɔːnə'græfik] *adj.* (book, etc.) which
deals with sex in an indecent way.
porous ['pɔːrəs] *adj.* (solid) which
allows liquid to pass through. **porosity**
[pɔːrɒsiti] *n.* being porous.
porphyry ['pɔːfiri] *n.* type of stone with
crystals in it.
porpoise ['pɔːpəs] *n.* large sea
mammal which tends to swim in groups.
porridge ['pɒridʒ] *n.* (*no pl.*) oatmeal
cooked in water.
port [pɔːt] *n.* (a) harbour. (b) town with
a harbour. (c) left side (when looking
forward on board a ship/aircraft). (d)
strong sweet wine from Portugal. (e)
opening in a ship's side for a gun. (f)
opening in a computer for plugging in an
attachment
portable 1 ['pɔːtəbl] *adj.* which can be
carried. **portable 2** *n.* machine, such
as a small computer, which can be
carried. **portage** [pɔː'tɑːʒ] *n.*
transporting a boat across country.
portal ['pɔːtl] *n.* imposing entrance.
portcullis [pɔːt'kʌlis] *n.* (*pl.*-es) gate
which was dropped to close the entrance

to a medieval castle.
portend [pɔː'tend] *v.* (*formal*) to warn
(that sth unpleasant is going to happen).
portent [pɔː'tənt] *n.* (*formal*) warning
(that sth unpleasant is going to happen).
portentous [pɔː'tentəs] *adj.* important/
significant; warning that sth unpleasant
is going to happen.
porter ['pɔːtə] *n.* (a) person who carries
luggage for travellers. (b) doorkeeper (in
a hotel); (c) person who does general
work in a hospital. (d) (in Ireland) type
of black beer. **porterage** *n.* charge for
carrying sth. **porterhouse (steak)** *n.*
piece of best quality steak.
portfolio [pɔːt'fəʊliəʊ] *n.* (*pl.*-os) (a)
large cardboard case for carrying
paintings, etc. (b) collection of shares.
(c) minister's job in government.
porthole ['pɔːthəʊl] *n.* round window
in the side of a ship.
portico ['pɔːtikəʊ] *n.* (*pl.*-oes) roof
supported by columns forming a
porch in front of the entrance to a
building.
portion 1 ['pɔːʃn] *n.* (a) part. (b)
serving of food. **portion 2** *v.* to p. out
= to share out.
portly ['pɔːtli] *adj.* (-ier, -iest) rather fat.
portmanteau [pɔːt'mæntəʊ] *n.* trunk
for carrying clothes.
portrait ['pɔːtreit] *n.* painting/
photograph of a person. **portraiture**
['pɔːtrətʃə] *n.* art of painting portraits.
portray [pɔː'trei] *v.* to paint/to describe
(a scene or a person). **portrayal** *n.*
painting; description of a scene or
person.
Portuguese 1 [pɔːtjʊ'giːz] *adj.*
referring to Portugal; P. man-of-war =
type of very large jelly fish.
Portuguese 2 *n.* (a) person from
Portugal. (b) language spoken in
Portugal.
pose 1 [pəʊz] *n.* (a) way of standing/
sitting. (b) way of behaving which is just
a pretence. **pose 2** *v.* (a) to p. for s.o. =
to stand/to sit still while s.o. paints/
photographs you. (b) to pretend to be. (c)
to set (a problem) or to put (a question).
poser *n. inf.* difficult question.
poseur [pəʊ'zɜː] *n.* person who
behaves in a false way.
posh [pɒʃ] *adj.* (-er, -est) *inf.* very
smart.

position 1 [pə'zɪʃn] *n.* (a) way of standing/sitting. (b) place. (c) job. **position 2** *v.* to place.

positive 1 ['pɒzɪtɪv] *adj.* (a) meaning yes. (b) certain; sure/convinced. (c) registering the existence of sth. (d) plus/more than zero **positive 2** *n.* (a) photograph printed from a negative, where the light and dark appear as they are in nature. (b) one of the terminals in a battery. **positively** *adv.* absolutely.

positron *n.* positive electron.

posse ['pɒsɪ] *n.* group of armed men/police.

possess [pə'zes] *v.* (a) to own. (b) to occupy s.o.'s mind; what possessed him? = why did he do it? **possession** [pə'zeʃn] *n.* (a) ownership. (b) thing you own. **possessive** *adj.* (a) (in grammar) (word) which indicates possession. (b) (person) who treats another person as if he owns him. **possessively** *adv.* in a possessive way. **possessor** *n.* owner.

possible ['pɒsɪbl] *adj.* (a) which can happen. (b) likely. **possibility** [pɒsɪ'bɪlɪti] *n.* (a) chance; being likely. (b) the plan has possibilities = may well work. **possibly** *adv.* (a) which may happen. (b) perhaps.

possum ['pɒsəm] *n. inf.* to play p. = to pretend to sleep/to be dead so as to trick an opponent.

post 1 [pəʊst] *n.* (a) wooden/concrete stake fixed in the ground. (b) place where a sentry is on duty. (c) job/position. (d) small settlement far from civilization. (e) the last p. = bugle call to commemorate the dead. (f) mail; letters etc., sent by mail **post 2** *v.* (a) to send (s.o.) on duty. (b) to send (a letter, etc.) by mail; to keep s.o. posted = to keep s.o. informed. (c) to stick up (a notice). **postage** *n.* payment for sending a letter by mail; p. stamp = piece of paper which you buy and stick on a letter, etc., to pay for it to be sent to its destination. **postal** *adj.* referring to the post; p. order = order to pay money, which can be bought and cashed at a post office. **postbag** *n.* letters sent to a radio/TV show. **postbox** *n.* box in a wall into which you can put letters, which will then be collected and sent on by the post

office. **postcard** *n.* card (sometimes with a picture) which you send through the post. **postcode** *n.* system of letters or numbers to indicate a town or street in an address to help with the sorting of mail. **poster** *n.* large notice stuck up on a wall, etc.; large picture/advertisement stuck on a wall. **poste restante** [pəʊst 'restɑːnt] *n.* service where letters can be addressed to s.o, at a post office where he can collect them. **post free** *adv.* without paying for postage. **post haste** *adv.* very fast. **postman** *n.* (*pl.*-men) person who delivers letters to houses. **postmark 1** *n.* mark stamped on a letter to show when it was sent off. **postmark 2** *v.* to stamp (a letter) with a postmark. **postmaster, postmistress** *n.* person in charge of a post office. **post office** *n.* (a) building where mail is received/stamps sold etc. (b) organization which runs the postal services. **postpaid** *adj.* (reply) with postage paid by the sender.

post- [pəʊst] prefix meaning later than/after. **postdate** *v.* to put a date on (a cheque) which is later than the day on which you actually write it. **postgraduate** *n.* person who has a first degree at a university and who is studying for further degree. **posthumous** ['pɒstjʊməs] *adj.* after death; p. son = son born after his father's death. **posthumously** *adv.* after death. **post mortem** [pəʊst'mɔːtəm] *adj. & n.* (examination) to find out the cause of death. **postnatal** *adj.* referring to the time just after the birth of a child. **postpone** [pəs'pəʊn] *v.* to put off until later. **postponement** *n.* putting off until later. **postprandial** *adj.* after dinner. **postscript, post scriptum** *n.* additional note at the end of a letter. **postwar** *adj.* referring to the period after the war.

posterior [pɒ'stɪərɪə] *n.* behind/buttocks. **posterity** [pɒ'sterɪti] *n.* generations which will follow.

postern ['pɒstən] *n.* (old) small gate.

postulate 1 ['pɒstjʊleɪt] *n.* basis upon which sth is postulated. **postulate 2** *v.* to suppose (that sth is true). **postulant** *n.* person who is a candidate to join a religious order.

posture 1 ['pɒstʃə] n. way of sitting/standing etc. **posture 2** v. to take up a particular position for effect.

posy ['pəʊzɪ] n. small bunch of flowers.

pot 1 [pɒt] n. (a) container made of glass or clay; inf. pots of money = lots of money. (b) inf. to go to p. = to become ruined/useless. (c) Sl. marijuana. **pot 2** v. (potted) (a) to put in a pot. (b) (in billiards) to send (a ball) into one of the pockets. **potbelly** n. inf. fat stomach. **potboiler** n. worthless novel written rapidly for money. **potbound** adj. (of plant) with roots too large for the pot. **pot-hole** n. (a) hole in rock worn away by water. (b) hole in a road surface. **pot-holler** n. person who climbs down pot-holes as a sport. **potholing** n. sport of climbing inside pot holes. **potluck** n. to take p. = to take whatever comes, with no possibility of choice. **potsherd** n. piece of broken pot. **potshot** n. inf. to take a p. at s.o. = to try to shoot s.o. without aiming properly. **potted** adj. (a) preserved in a pot. (b) condensed. **potting shed** n. shed in a garden where you put plants in pots.

potable ['pɒtəbl] adj. which can be drunk safely.

potash ['pɒtæʃ] n. potassium salts. **potassium** [pə'tæsɪəm] n. (element: K) light white metallic substance.

potato [pə'teɪtəʊ] n. (pl.-oes) common vegetable formed under the soil; sweet p. = yam.

poteen [pɒ'tiːn] n. illegal Irish whiskey.

potency ['pəʊtənsɪ] n. strength. **potent** adj. strong. **potentate** ['pəʊtənteɪt] n. Eastern ruler.

potential 1 [pə'tenʃl] adj. possible. **potential 2** n. (a) possibility of developing into sth valuable. (b) (in physics) electrical property which governs the flow of an electric charge **potentiality** n. being potential. **potentially** adv. possibly.

potentiometer n. instrument for measuring differences in electrical potential.

potion ['pəʊʃn] n. liquid mixture to make you sleep, etc.

potpourri [pəʊpuː'riː] n. (a) dried flowers/herbs kept in a bowl to scent a room. (b) general mixture of bits and pieces.

potter 1 ['pɒtə] n. person who makes pots out of clay. **potter 2** v. to p. about = not to do anything in particular/to do little jobs. **pottery** n. (a) potter's workshop. (b) pots; articles made of clay. earthenware.

potty 1 ['pɒtɪ] n. inf. child's chamberpot. **potty 2** adj. (-ier, -iest) mad.

pouch [paʊtʃ] n. (pl.-es) (a) small bag for carrying coins/ammunition, etc. (b) bag in the skin in front of some marsupials where the young live and grow for some time after birth

pouffe [puːf] n. padded seat shaped like a drum.

poultice 1 ['pəʊltɪs] n. hot wet dressing put on a wound. **poultice 2** v. to dress (a wound) with a poultice.

poultry ['pəʊltrɪ] n. (no pl.) common farm birds such as ducks/hens, reared for eggs or to be eaten. **poulterer** ['pəʊltərə] n. shopkeeper who specializes in selling poultry.

pounce 1 [paʊns] n. act of pouncing. **pounce 2** v. to jump (on sth).

pound 1 [paʊnd] n. (a) measure of weight (= approx. 0.45 kilogram). (b) standard unit of money in Great Britain and several other countries. (c) place where stray animals or illegally-parked cars are put. **pound 2** v. (a) to smash into little pieces; to hit hard. (b) to run heavily. (c) (of heart) to beat fast. **poundage** ['paʊndɪdʒ] n. rate charged for each pound.

pour [pɔː] v. (a) to flow out/down. (b) to transfer liquid from one container to another.

pout 1 [paʊt] n. (a) sulky expression where the lips stick out. (b) type of fish. **pout 2** v. to make a sulky expression with the lips.

poverty ['pɒvətɪ] n. being poor; the p. of = the lack of.

powder 1 ['paʊdə] n. very fine dry grains (like flour); (face) p. = scented flour-like substance for putting on the face; p. compact = small box containing face powder; p. room = women's toilet **powder 2** v. to put powder on. **powdered** adj. covered with powder. **powdery** adj. fine/like powder.

power ['paʊə] n. (a) strength. (b) ability. (c) driving force; p. pack =

portable source of electricity; p. point = wall plug which supplies electricity. (d) (in mathematics) number of times a number is multiplied by itself. (e) (in physics) strength of a lens. (f) (also power base) political/social strength (of a person/a group). (g) political control **powerboat** n. boat which has a powerful engine used for racing. **power drill** n. powerful electric drill. **powered** adj. driven/worked. **powerful** adj. very strong. **powerless** adj. unable to do anything. **powerstation, powerplant** n. works where electricity is produced. **power steering** n. steering (in a car) which is powered by the engine.

powwow ['paʊwaʊ] n. inf. meeting to discuss some problem.

p.p. [piː'piː] adv. on behalf (s.o.) who is absent.

PR [piː'ɑː] n. public relations; proportional representation.

practicable ['præktɪkəbl] adj. which can be done/which can be put into practice. **practicability** [præktɪkə'bɪlɪtɪ] n. ability to be put into practice.

practical 1 ['præktɪkl] adj. interested in practice/action rather than ideas; referring to practice rather than theory; p. joke = trick played on s.o. to make other people laugh. **practical 2** n. inf. examination/test to show how well s.o. can work in practice. **practicality** n. way in which sth works in practice. **practically** adv. (a) in practice (b) almost.

practice 1 ['præktɪs] n. (a) actual application; to put sth into p. = to apply sth/to use sth. (b) habit. (c) repeated exercise; out of p. = capable because of lack of exercise. (d) business of a doctor/dentist/lawyer. (e) practices = ways of doing things **practice 2** v. Am. see practise. **practise, Am. practice** ['præktɪs] v (a) to put sth into practice (b) to do repeated exercises. (c) to carry on a job as a doctor or lawyer. **practised** adj. skilled. **practitioner** [præk'tɪʃənə] n. doctor; general; p. = doctor who treats all patients/all illnesses.

pragmatic [præg'mætɪk] adj. dealing with fact/practical matters, not concerned with theory. **pragmatically** adv. in a pragmatic way. **pragmatism** ['prægmətɪzəm] n. pragmatic approach (to a problem). **pragmatist** n. person who is pragmatic.

prairie ['preərɪ] n. grass-covered plain in North America; p. dog = small American mammal, living in burrows; p. oyster = mixture of raw egg, tomato juice and spices, taken to cure a hangover.

praise 1 [preɪz] n. admiration/expression of approval. **praise 2** v. to express strong approval of (sth). **praiseworthy** adj. which should be praised.

praline ['prɑːliːn] n sweet made of crushed nuts and honey.

pram [præm] n. inf. small carriage in which you push a baby.

prance [prɑːns] v. to jump about/to move lightly.

prank [præŋk] n. trick.

prattle 1 ['prætl] n. children's chatter. **prattle 2** v. to chatter in a childish way.

prawn [prɔːn] n. shellfish like a large shrimp.

praxis ['præksɪs] n. practice.

pray [preɪ] v. to speak to God; to ask God for sth; (formal) p. be seated = please sit down. **prayer** n. act of speaking to God; request

pre- [prɪ] prefix meaning before.

preach [priːtʃ] v. (a) to give a sermon in church. (b) to recommend/to advise; to give moral advice. **preacher** n. person who gives a sermon.

preamble [priː'æmbl] n. introduction/remarks at the beginning (of a speech/treaty, etc.).

prearrange [priːə'reɪndʒ] v. to arrange in advance.

precarious [prɪ'leərɪəs] adj. likely to fall; uncertain. **precariously** adv. unsafely.

precaution [prɪ'kɔːʃn] n. care taken in advance (to avoid sth unpleasant). **precautionary** adj. (measure) taken to avoid sth unpleasant.

precede [prɪ'siːd] v. to take place before (sth). **precedence** ['presɪdəns] n. to take p. over = to go before/to be more important than. **precedent** ['presɪdənt] n. thing which has happened before and which can be a

guide as to what should be done.
preceding [prɪ'siːdɪŋ] *adj.* which
comes before.

precentor [prɪ'sentɔː] *n.* person in
charge of the music in a cathedral.

precept ['priːsept] *n.* (a) command;
guiding rule. (b) order for local taxes to
be paid.

precinct ['priːsɪŋkt] *n.* area surrounded
by a wall; administrative district of a
town; shopping p./pedestrian p. = area of
a town which is closed to traffic

precious ['preʃəs] *adj.* worth a lot of
money; of great value.

precipice ['presɪpɪs] *n.* high cliff (not
usu. near the sea). **precipitous**
[prɪ'sɪpɪtəs] *adj.* very steep.

precipitate 1 [prɪ'sɪpɪtət] *n.* chemical
substance which settles at the bottom of
a liquid. **precipitate 2** [prɪ'sɪpɪteɪt] *v.*
(a) to make sth happen suddenly. (b) to
settle at the bottom of a liquid.

precipitate 3 [prɪ'sɪpɪtət] *adj.* rushed/
hurried. **precipitately** *adv.* in a rushed
way. **precipitation** [prɪsɪpɪ'teɪʃn] *n.* (a)
(formal) great hurry. (b) quantity of rain/
snow etc., which falls on a certain place.

précis 1 ['preɪsiː] *n.* (*pl.*précis)
summary of the main points of a text.
précis 2 *v.* to summarize.

precise [prɪ'saɪs] *adj.* (a) exact. (b)
careful. **precisely** *adv.* (a) exactly. (b)
in a careful way. **precision** [prɪ'sɪʒn] *n.*
accuracy.

preclude [prɪ'kluːd] *v.* to prevent.

precocious [prɪ'kəʊʃəs] *adj.* (child)
who is surprisingly advanced for its age.
precociously *adv.* in a precocious
way. **precociousness, precocity**
[prɪ'kɒsɪtɪ] *n.* being precocious.

preconceive [priːkən'siːv] *v.* to have
an idea or belief from the beginning/
before sth starts. **preconception**
[priːkən'sepʃn] *n.* preconceived idea.

precondition [priːkən'dɪʃn] *n.*
condition which is set in advance.

precursor [prɪ'kɜːsə] *n.* thing which
leads to an invention/person who goes in
advance. **precursory** *adj.* which is in
advance.

predate ['priːdeɪt] *v.* to come before in
date.

predator ['predətə] *n.* animal which
lives by eating other animals.
predatory *adj.* (animal) which eats

other animals; (person) who lives off
other people.

predecease [priːdɪ'siːs] *v.* (formal) to
die before (s.o.). **predecessor**
['priːdɪsesə] *n.* person who has held the
same job, etc., before you.

predestine [priː'destɪn] *v.* to decide the
fate of (s.o.) in advance. **predestination**
[priːdestɪ'neɪʃn] *n.*
being predestined.

predetermine [priːdɪ'tɜːmɪn] *v.* to
decide in advance.

predicament [prɪ'dɪkəmənt] *n.*
troubles/difficult situation.

predicate 1 ['predɪkət] *n.* (in
grammar) statement about the subject.

predicate 2 ['predɪkeɪt] *v.* (formal) to
base a supposition on(sth). **predicative**
[prɪ'dɪkətɪv] *adj.* (adjective, etc.) which
makes a statement about a noun.

predict [prɪ'dɪkt] *v.* to foretell/to tell in
advance what will happen. **predictable**
adj. which could be predicted.
predictably *adv.* in a way which could
have been predicted. **prediction**
[prɪ'dɪkʃn] *n.* foretelling.

predilection [priːdɪ'lekʃn] *n.* liking/
preference.

predispose [priːdɪ'spəʊz] *v* to make
(s.o.) favour sth in advance.
predisposition [priːdɪspə'zɪʃn] *n.*
being predisposed.

predominate [prɪ'dɒmɪneɪt] *v.* to be
bigger/stronger/more numerous.
predominance *n.* being predominant.
predominant [prɪ'dɒmɪnənt] *adj.* most
striking/obvious. **predominantly** *adv.*
in a predominant way.

pre-eminent [priː'emɪnənt] *adj.*
excellent/much better than everything
else. **pre-eminence** *n.* being pre-
eminent.

pre-empt [priː'empt] *v.* to get an
advantage by doing sth before anyone
else. **pre-emption** *n.* act of pre-
empting. **pre-emptive** *adj.* which
gains an advantage by acting before
anyone else.

preen [priːn] *v.* (of bird) to smooth its
feathers; to p. yourself = to smarten
yourself up; to p. yourself on sth = to
congratulate yourself

prefabricated [priː'fæbrɪkeɪtɪd] *adj.*
built in advance; (house) built out of
pieces which are assembled on the site.

prefab ['priːfæb] n. inf. prefabricated house. **prefabrication** [priːfæbrɪ'keɪʃn] n. building in advance.

preface 1 ['prefəs] n. piece written (usu. by the author) to introduce a book. **preface 2** v. to say/to write sth as an introduction. **prefatory** ['prefətrɪ] adj. which acts as a preface.

prefect ['priːfekt] n. (a) school pupil chosen to be in charge of others. (b) high official.

prefer [prɪ'fɜː] v. (preferred) (a) to p. sth to sth = to like (to do) sth better than sth else. (b) (formal) to promote (s.o.). **preferable** ['prefrəbl] adj. which you would prefer. **preferably** adv. if possible. **preference** ['prefrəns] n. liking for one thing more than another. **preferential** ['prefə'renʃl] adj. showing one thing is preferred to another. **preferment** [prɪ'fɜːmənt] n. promotion to a more important post.

prefix 1 ['priːfɪks] n. (pl.-es) part of a word put in front of another. **prefix 2** v. to put some word in front of another/to preface.

pregnancy ['pregnənsɪ] n. state of being pregnant; p. test = test to see if a woman is pregnant. **pregnant** adj. carrying an unborn child; p. pause = pause while everyone waits for sth to happen/for s.o. to speak.

prehensile [priː'hensaɪl] adj. which can grasp/hold on to sth.

prehistory [priː'hɪstərɪ] n. time before written history. **prehistorian** [priːhɪ'stɔːrɪən] n. person who specializes in the study of prehistory. **prehistoric** [priːhɪ'stɒrɪk] adj. belonging to prehistory.

prejudge [priː'dʒʌdʒ] v. to judge (sth) without hearing all the facts.

prejudice 1 ['predʒədɪs] n. (usu. unjust) feeling against s.o. **prejudice 2** v. (a) to make (s.o.) unfriendly towards s.o./sth. (b) to harm. **prejudiced** adj. unfairly biassed (against s.o.). **prejudicial** [predʒʊ'dɪʃl] adj. which might be damaging.

prelate ['prelət] n. person of high rank in a church.

preliminary [prɪ'lɪ'mɪnərɪ] adj. which goes before. **preliminaries** n. pl.things which have to be done before sth can take place. **prelims** ['priːlɪmz] n.

pl. inf. (a) first few pages of a book before the text starts. (b) examinations which decide if you may study at a university.

prelude ['preljuːd] n. thing (esp. piece of music) which introduces sth more important; short piece of music on one theme.

premarital [prɪ'mærɪtəl] adj. before marriage.

premature [premə'tjʊə] adj. which happens before the right time; (baby) born less than nine months after conception. **prematurely** adv. before the right time.

premeditate [priː'medɪteɪt] v. to think over/to plan in advance. **premeditation** [priːmedɪ'teɪʃn] n. planning in advance.

premier 1 ['premɪə] n. Prime Minister. **premier 2** adj. first/most important. **première** ['premɪeə] n. first performance of a film/play etc.

premiership n. being Prime Minister; time when s.o. is Prime Minister.

premise ['premɪs] n. premiss.

premises ['premɪsɪz] n. pl. building and land around it.

premiss ['premɪs] n. (pl.-es) statement which is the basis of reasoning.

premium ['priːmɪəm] n. (a) annual amount paid for an insurance policy. (b) at a p. = scarce and therefore valuable; to put a p. on sth = to show that sth is useful/valuable. (c) bonus; p. offer = specially attractive price. **premium bond** n. British government bond which pays no interest but gives you the chance of winning a monthly prize.

premolar [priː'məʊlə] n. tooth between the canines and the molars.

premonition [premə'nɪʃn] n. feeling that sth is going to happen. **premonitory** [prɪ'mɒnɪtrɪ] adj. warning (sign).

prenatal [priː'neɪtl] adj. referring to the time before the birth of a child.

preoccupation [priːɒkju'peɪʃn] n. only thinking about one thing. **preoccupied** adj. thinking only about one thing; worried. **preoccupy.** v. to make (s.o.) think about only one thing and worry about it.

prep [prep] adj. inf. (a) homework. (b) p. school = preparatory school. (c) preparing a patient for an operation.

prepare [prɪ'peə] v. to get ready.
preparation [prepə'reɪʃn] n. (a)
getting ready. (b) substance which has
been mixed. **preparatory** [prɪ'pærətrɪ]
adj. which prepares; p. school = private
school for children up to the age of 13.
prepared adj. ready (to).
prepay ['priːpeɪ] v. (prepaid) to pay in
advance; prepaid telegram = telegram
where the answer has been paid for in
advance. **prepayment** n. paying in
advance.
preponderate [prɪ'pɒndəreɪt] v.
(formal) to be in a majority.
preponderance [prɪ'pɒndərəns] n.
large number. **preponderant** adj. in a
majority.
preposition [prepə'zɪʃn] n. word
which is used with a noun/pronoun to
show how it is linked to another word.
prepossessing [priːpə'zesɪŋ] adj.
pleasant.
preposterous [priː'pɒstərəs] adj.
silly/absurd.
preprogrammed [priː'prəʊɡræmd]
adj. (chip) which has been programmed
in the factory.
prerequisite [priː'rekwɪzɪt] n. thing
which you must have before you can do
sth.
prerogative [prɪ'rɒɡətɪv] n. privilege
belonging to one person or group.
presbyopia [prezbɪ'əʊpɪə] n. gradual
failing sight (in an old person).
presbytery ['prezbɪterɪ] n. (a) Roman
Catholic priest's house. (b) court of a
church made of ministers and important
laymen. **Prebyterian** [prezbɪ'tiːərɪən]
adj. & n. (member) of a Protestant
church, ruled by a group of laymen.
prescient ['presɪənt] adj. (formal)
(person) who can tell what is likely to
take place in the future. **prescience** n.
being prescient.
prescribe [prɪ'skraɪb] v. to order (sth)
to be done; to tell s.o. to use (sth).
prescription [prɪ'skrɪpʃn] n. paper on
which a doctor has written out
particulars of the medicine to be taken
by the patient. **prescriptive** adj.
which prescribes.
presence ['prezns] n. (a) being
present. (b) p. of mind = sense/calmness;
ability to act quickly. (c) impressive
appearance/way of acting (on the stage).

present 1 ['preznt] adj. (a) being at
the place/at the time. (b) being here now.
(c) (in grammar) (tense) which describes
what is happening now. **present 2**
['preznt] n. (a) at the time we are in
now; at p. = now. (b) gift. **present 3**
['preznt] v. (a) to give. (b) to put on (a
play/show). (c) to introduce (s.o. into
society/an artist to the audience). (d) to
p. oneself = to arrive/to come.
presentable [prɪ'zentəbl] adj. (person)
who is suitable to appear in company.
presentation [prezən'teɪʃn] n. act of
giving. **present-day** adj. modern.
presenter n. person who presents a
TV show. **presently** adv. (a) soon. (b)
Am. & in Scotland now. **presentiment**
[prɪ'zentɪmənt] n. feeling that sth
unpleasant will soon happen.
preserve 1 [prɪ'zɜːv] n. (a) place where
game/fish, etc. are protected so that they
can be killed for sport. (b) preserves =
jam/pickles, etc. **preserve 2** v. (a)
(formal) to keep/to protect. (b) to treat
(food) so that it keeps for a long time.
preservation [prezə'veɪʃn] n.
protecting; p. order = court order to
prevent a building being demolished.
preservative [prɪ'zɜːvətɪv] n.
substance used to make food keep/to
stop food from going bad. **preserver** n.
person/thing that preserves; see also life
preserver. **preserving pan** n. very
large pan for making jam/chutney etc.
preside [prɪ'zaɪd] v. to sit at the head of
the table (at the meeting). **presidency**
['prezɪdnsɪ] n. job of president.
president ['prezɪdənt] n. head of a
republic; chief member of a club (esp.
Am) head of a business firm.
presidential [prezɪ'denʃl] adj.
referring to a president. **presidium**
[prɪ'sɪdɪəm] n. ruling committee (in a
communist country).
press 1 [pres] n. (pl.- es) (a) machine
which squeezes. (b) printing p. =
machine for printing books/newspapers,
etc. (c) newspapers and magazines taken
as a whole. (d) crowd. **press 2** v. (a) to
push down; to push against; to squeeze.
(b) iron the creases from (clothes). (c) to
force (s.o.) to do sth. (d) to p. on/forward
= to continue/to go ahead. **pressed**
adj. I'm p. for time = I haven't much
time; I'd be hard p. to do it = I would

find it difficult. **press conference** *n.* interview given by a famous person to several journalists. **press cutting** *n.* piece cut out from a newspaper with an article which is relevant to s.o./sth.

pressgang 1 *n.* (old) group of people who forced men to join the Royal Navy. **pressgang 2** *v.* to force (s.o.) into doing sth. **pressing 1** *adj.* urgent. **pressing 2** *n.* record/series of records. **press stud** *n.* round fastening where two parts are pressed to clip together. **press-up** *n.* exercise where you lie flat on the floor and push yourself up with your hands.

pressure ['preʃə] *n.* (a) act of squeezing/pushing down; to put p. on s.o. to do sth = to try to force s.o. to do sth. (b) force pushing down/moving/ being heavy etc. blood p. = force with which the blood is driven round the body; p. group = group of people who try to influence the government etc. (c) stress. **pressure cooker** *n.* type of saucepan with a tight-fitting lid, which cooks food rapidly under pressure.

pressurization [preʃəraɪzeɪʃn] *n,.* keeping an aircraft cabin at a constant atmospheric pressure. **pressurize** *v.* to put under pressure to p. s.o., into doing sth = to try to force (s.o.) to do sth.

pressurized *adj.* (aircraft cabin) kept at a constant atmospheric pressure.

prestige [pre'sti:ʒ] *n.* admiration aroused by s.o. because of rank or qualifications or job. **prestigious** [pre'stɪdʒəs] *adj.* which brings prestige.

presto ['prestəʊ] *adv.* (in music) rapidly; hey p.! = words used by magicians when carrying out magic tricks.

prestressed ['pri:'strest] *adj.* which has been stressed in advance.

presume [prɪ'zju:m] *v.* (a) to suppose/ to assume. (b) (to) to take the liberty of doing sth. (c) (formal) to p. (up) on s.o.'s good nature = to take unfair advantage of s.o.'s kindness **presumably** *adv.* probably; as you would expect. **presumption** [prɪ'œʌmpʃn] *n.* (a) thing which is assumed to be true. (b) rudeness. **presumptive** *adj.* which is presumed to be true; heir p. = heir (to a throne) who may be displaced by the birth of s.o. with a better right.

presumptuous [prɪ'zʌm[tjʊəs] *adj.* rude/bold. **presumptuously** *adv.* in a presumptuous way.

presuppose [pri:sə'pəʊz] *v.* to assume in advance (that sth is true/that certain conditions are met). **presupposition** [prɪ:səpə'zɪʃn] *n.* thing which is assumed in advance.

pretax ['pri:tæks] *adj.* before tax is paid.

pretend [prɪ'tend] *v.* (a) to make believe so as to deceive s.o. (b) (to) to be bold enough to claim. **pretence, ** *Am.* **pretense** [prɪ'tens] *n.* making believe. **pretender** *n.* person who has (false) claims to sth, *usu.* person who claims to be king. **pretension** [prɪ'tenʃn] *n.* claim. **pretentious** [prɪ'tenʃəs] *adj.* very showy; claiming to be more important than you are. **pretentiousness** *n.* being pretentious.

preternatural [pri:tə'nætʃrəl] *adj.* supernatural; extraordinary.

pretext ['pri:tekst] *n.* excuse.

pretty 1 ['prɪtɪ] *adj.* (-ier, -iest) pleasant to look at; attractive. **pretty 2** *adv. inf.* quite. **prettily** *adv.* daintily. **prettiness** *n.* attractiveness/ pleasantness.

pretzel ['pretsəl] *n.* hard salty biscuit made in the shape of a knot.

prevail [prə'veɪl] *v. (formal)* (a) to p. upon = to persuade. (b) to be usual/ common. **prevailing** *adj.* usual/ common; p. wind = wind which usually blows from a certain direction.

prevalence ['prevələns] *n.* being wide spread. **prevalent** *adj.* wide spread.

prevaricate [prɪ'værɪkeɪt] *v.* (formal) to try not to tell the truth. **prevarication** [prɪværɪ'keɪʃn] *n.* act of prevaricating; lie. **prevaricator** *n.* person who prevaricates.

prevent [prɪ'vent] *v.* to stop (sth) happening; to p. s.o. from = to stop (s.o.) doing sth. **preventable** *adj.* which could be prevented. **prevention** [prɪ'venʃn] *n.* preventing. **preventative, preventive** [prɪ'vent(ət)ɪv] *adj.* which prevents. **preview** ['pri:vju:] *n.* showing of a film/ exhibition, etc., before it is open to the general public.

previous 1 ['pri:vɪəs] *adj.* former; earlier. **previous 2** *adv.* to p. to = before. **previously** *adv.* before.

pre-war ['pri:wɔ:] *adj. & adv.* existing/ happening before a war.

prey 1 [preɪ] *n.* animal eaten by another; birds of p. = birds which eat other birds/ animals. **prey 2** *v.* to p. (up) on = to attack animals and eat them; sth is preying on his mind = sth is worrying him.

price 1 [praɪs] *n.* quantity of money which has to be paid to buy sth; at a p. = if you are willing to pay a lot. **price 2** *v.* to give (sth) a price. **priceless** *adj.* (a) extremely valuable. (b) very funny (joke). **pricey** *adj. inf.* expensive.

prick 1 [prɪk] *n.* pain caused by sth sharp. **prick 2** *v.* (a) to jab with sth sharp to make small holes in (sth). (b) to p. up your ears = to listen attentively. (c) to p. out seedlings = to plant small seedlings in the open ground after they have been grown in boxes

prickle *n.* thorn/sharp point (on a plant/hedgehog, etc.). **prickliness** *n.* being prickly. **prickly** *adj.* (a) covered with prickles; p. pear = type of cactus; p. heat = skin rash caused by hot climate. (b) (person) who takes offence easily.

pride 1 [praɪd] *n.* (a) pleasure in your own abilities/achievements/ possessions(b) very high opinions of yourself. (c) group of lions. **pride 2** to p. oneself on = to be extremely proud of.

priest [pri:st] *n.* person who has been ordained to serve God/to carry out formal religious duties; parish p. = priest who is in charge of a parish. **priestess** *n.* female priest. **priesthood** *n.* job of being a priest. **priestly** *adj.* referring to priests.

prig [prɪg] *n.* very moral and conceited person. **priggish** *adj.* very moral and conceited. **priggishness** *n.* being priggish.

prim [prɪm] *adj.* (primmer, primmest) very correct/unbending. **primly** *adj.* in a prim way. **primness** *n.* being prim.

prima ballerina [pri:məbælə'ri:nə] *n* leading woman dancer in a ballet company. **prima donna** [pri:mə'dɒnə] *n.* leading woman singer in opera; person who is conceited and liable to outbursts of emotion.

primacy ['praɪməsɪ] *n.* being in first place being most important.

prima facie [praɪmə'feɪʃɪ] *adv. & adj.* based on what seems right at first sight.

primal ['praɪml] *adj.* (formal) primeval.

primary 1 ['praɪmərɪ] *adj.* basic; p. colours = basic colours (red, yellow and blue) which go to make up all the other colours; *Am.* p. election = first election to choose a candidate to represent a political party in a main election; p. school = school for small children (up to the age of eleven). **primary 2** *n. Am.* primary election. **primarily** *adv.* mainly/mostly.

primate ['praɪmət] *n.* (a) leading bishop. (b) ['praɪmeɪt] the primate = members of the highest level of mammals (apes, human beings, etc.).

prime 1 [praɪm] *adj.* (a) most important. (b) of best quality. (c) p. number = number (such as 2, 5,11, etc.) which can only be divided by itself or by 1. **prime 2** *n.* period when your are at your best. **prime 3** *v.* (a) to get (sth) prepared; to give (wood/metal) a first coat of special paint before giving the top coat. (b) to put water into (a water pump) /oil into (a machine) so as to start it working. (c) go give (s.o.) drinks/ information. **Prime Minister** *n.* head of the government in Britain and other countries. **primer** *n.* (a) special paint to cover an unpainted surface. (b) elementary text book.

primeval [praɪ'mi:vl] *adj.* referring to the period at the beginning of the world.

primitive ['prɪmɪtɪv] *adj.* (a) referring to very early/prehistoric times. (b) rough/crude.

primogeniture [praɪməʊ'dʒenɪtʃə] *n.* rule by which the eldest son is the heir.

primordial [praɪ'mɔ:djəl] *adj. (formal)* which existed at the beginning (a long time ago).

primrose ['prɪmrəʊz] *n.* small pale yellow wild spring flower.

primula ['prɪmjʊlə] *n.* garden flower, like a primrose, but with many colours.

prince [prɪns] *n.* son of a king; male ruler of a small state; male member of a royal family. **princely** *adj.* like a prince; large (sum of money/salary).

princess *n.* daughter of a king; female member of a royal family; female ruler of a small state; wife of a prince.

principal 1 ['prɪsɪpl] *adj.* main/most important. **principal 2** *n.* (a) head (of a school/college); main actor (in a play). (b) money on which interest is paid/ capital which has been invested.

principality [prɪnsɪ'pælɪtɪ] *n.* land ruled by a prince. **principally** *adv.* mainly.

principle ['prɪnsɪpl] *n.* (a) law/general rule; in p. = in agreement with the general rule. (b) personal sense of truth; on p. = because of what you believe.

print 1 [prɪnt] *n.* (a) mark made on sth; see also footprint, finger print. (b) letters printed on a page; the small p. = conditions on a contract,. *usu.* written in very small letters. (c) picture which has been printed; photograph which has been reproduced on paper; cloth with a design printed on it. **print 2** *v.* (a) to mark letters on paper by a machine. (b) to write capital letters or letters which are not joined together. (c) to reproduce a photograph/pattern, etc. **printed circuit** *n.* electronic circuit where the connections are printed on a board; p.c. board = flat board on which metal strips are printed to form a circuit. **printer** *n.* (a) person who prints books/newspapers, etc. (b) machine which prints automatically. **printing** *n.* art of printing books/newspapers, etc.; p. press = machine which prints books etc.

printout *n.* printed information from a computer.

prior 1 ['praɪə] *adj. & adv.* before; previous; p. to = before. **prior 2** *n.* male head of a priory. **prioress** *n.* woman head of a priory. **priority** ['prɪ'ɒrɪtɪ] *n.* (a) right to be first. (b) thing which has to be done first. **priory** ['praɪərɪ] *n.* building where monks or nuns live.

prise [praɪz] *v.* to p. up = to lift with the help of a lever; to p. out = to pull out using a lever.

prism ['prɪzəm] *n.* glass block *usu.* with a triangular cross-section, which splits white light up into the colours of the rainbow. **prismatic** [prɪz'mætɪk] *adj.* referring to a prism.

prison ['prɪzn] *n.* place where people are kept by law after they have been found guilty of a crime.

prisoner *n.* person who is in prison; p. of war = soldier/airman, etc. who has been captured by the enemy.

prissy ['prɪsɪ] *adj.* (-ier, -iest) unpleasantly proud of being good.

pristine ['prɪstiːn] *adj.* (formal) fresh/ unspoilt.

private 1 ['praɪvət] *adj.* (a) belonging to one person not to everyone; p. means = personal income from investments; p. parts = sex organs; p. eye = detective employed by an ordinary person. (b) belonging to certain people, but not to the state or the general public; p. view = preview of an exhibition for certain invited guests. **private 2** *n.* (a) in p. = being away from other people. (b) ordinary soldier of the lowest rank. (c) privates = private parts. **privacy** *n.* being away from other people.

privateer *n.* armed ship which belongs to a private individual. **privately** *adv.* (a) in private. (b) (owned) by private individuals. **privatization** ['praɪvətə'zeɪʃn] *n.* act of privatizing. **privatize** ['praɪvətaɪz] *v.* to return (a nationalized industry) to private ownership.

privation [praɪ'veɪʃn] *n.* lack of money/food etc.

privet ['prɪvɪt] *n.* common shrub used for garden hedges.

privilege ['prɪvɪlɪdʒ] *n.* favour/right granted to some people but not to everyone. **privileged** *adj.* having a privilege.

privy 1 ['prɪvɪ] *adj.* (formal) to be p. to a secret = to know the details of a secret. **privy 2** *n. inf.* rough toilet outside a house. **Privy Council** *n.* group of important People who advise a king or queen.

prize 1 [praɪz] *n.* (a) money or object given to a winner. (b) ship captured in war. **prize 2** *v.* (a) to value. (b) *Am.* to prise. **prizefight** *n.* (old) boxing match where the winner wins money. **prizefighter** *n.* boxer.

pro 1 [prəʊ] prefix meaning in favour of. **pro 2** *n.* (a) pros and cons of a case = arguments for and against it. (b) *inf.* professional sportsman/actor etc.

probable ['prɒbəbl] *adj.* likely. **probability** [prɒbə'bɪlɪtɪ] *n.* likelihood. **probably** *adv.* likely.

probate ['prəʊbeɪt] *n.* proving in law that a document (esp. a will) is valid. **probation** [prə'beɪʃn] *n.* (a) period when s.o. is being tested. (b) period when a criminal is supervised instead of being put in prison; p. officer = official who looks after prisoners on probation. **probationary** *adj.* (period) when s.o. is being tested. **probationer** *n.* criminal who is on probation.

probe 1 [prəʊb] *n.* (a) instrument used by doctors to examine wounds, etc. (b) thorough investigation. (c) space p. = spacecraft sent into space for scientific purposes. **probe 2** *v.* to examine (sth) deeply.

probity ['prəʊbɪtɪ] *n.* (formal) total honesty.

problem ['prɒbləm] *n.* thing which is difficult to solve. **problematic(al)** [prɒblə'mætɪk(l)] *adj.* doubtful; likely to cause a problem.

proboscis [prəʊ'bɒsɪs] *n.* (*pl.*-es) long sucking tube coming from the head of an animal (such as the trunk of an elephant/ the sting of a mosquito).

proceed [prə'siːd] *v.* to continue/to go further. **procedural** [prə'siːdʒərəl] *adj.* referring to procedure. **procedure** [prə'siːdʒə] *n.* (a) way in which sth ought to be carried out. (b) medical treatment. **proceed against** *v.* to start a lawsuit against (s.o.). **proceedings** *n. pl.* report of what takes place at a meeting. **proceeds** ['prəʊsiːdz] *n. pl.* money which you receive when you sell sth.

process 1 ['prəʊses] *n.* (*pl.*-es) (a) method of making sth. (b) in the p. (of) = while doing sth. **process 2** *v.* (a) to make manufactured goods using raw materials; processed cheese = cheese which has been treated so that it will keep for a long time. (b) to prepare (figures) for a computer; to sort out (information). (c) *inf.* to walk in a procession **processing** [prə'sefɪn] *n.* treating raw materials; sorting out information. **procession** *n.* group of people marching (with a band, etc.) in line. **processional** *adj.* referring to a procession. **processor** *n.* machine/ person who processes; computer device which processes information.

proclaim [prə'kleɪm] *v.* to state officially and in public. **proclamation** [prɒklə'meɪʃn] *n.* official public statement.

proclivity [prə'klɪvɪtɪ] *n.* (formal) tendency.

procrastinate [prəʊ'kræstɪneɪt] *v.* (formal) to delay/to put sth off until later. **procrastination** [prəkræstɪ'neɪʃn] *n.* delaying/putting off.

procreate ['prəʊkrɪeɪt] *v.* (formal) to produce (young). **procreation** *n.* act of procreating.

proctor ['prɒktə] *n.* university official who keeps law and order.

procure [prə'kjʊə] *v.* (formal) (a) to obtain. (b) to provide (girls) for sex. **procurable** *adj.* which can be obtained. **procurator** ['prɒkjʊreɪtə] *n.* (in Scotland) p. fiscal = public prosecutor. **procurement** *n.* obtaining.

prod 1 [prɒd] *n.* poke; give him a p. = nudge him/try to get him to act. **prod 2** *v.* (prodded) to poke with a finger/stick/ etc.

prodigal ['prɒdɪgl] *adj.* wasteful; (person) who spends a lot. **prodigality** [prɒdɪ'gælɪtɪ] *n.* being prodigal. **prodigally** *adv.* wastefully.

prodigy ['prɒdɪdʒɪ] *n.* remarkable person or thing. **prodigious** [prə'dɪdʒəs] *adj.* remarkable/enormous. **prodigiously** *adv.* remarkably/ enormously.

produce 1 ['prɒdjuːs] *n* things grown on the land. **produce 2** [prə'djuːs] *v.* (a) to bring out. (b) to make/to manufacture. (c) to put on (a play/a film). (d) to yield (crops, etc.) **producer** [prə'djuːsə] *n.* (a) person who puts on a play/a film. (b) person/country which makes/grows sth. **product** ['prɒdʌkt] *n.* (a) thing which is manufactured/ produced. (b) result. (c) (in mathematics) result of multiplying two numbers **production** [prə'dʌkʃn] *n.* (a) manufacturing. (b) putting on a play/ film. **productive** [prə'dʌktɪv] *adj.* which produces. **productivity** [prɒdʌk'tɪvɪtɪ] *n.* rate of output/of production (in a factory); p. bonus = bonus paid for increased output.

profane [prə'feɪn] *adj.* not religious; blasphemous. **profanely** *adv.* in a

profane way. **profanity** [prə'fænɪtɪ] n.
rudeness; swearing/blasphemy.
profess [prə'fes] v. to declare.
professed adj. declared.
professedly [prə'fesɪdlɪ] adv. openly.
profession [prə'feʃn] n. (a) work
which needs special training/skill/
knowledge. (b) declaration (of belief in
sth). **professional 1** adj. (a) referring
to a profession; expert; p. footballer =
footballer who is paid to play.
professional 2 n. (a) expert. (b)
sportsman who is paid to play.
professionalism n. (a) expertise/
skill. (b) being a professional sportsman.
professionally adv. in a professional
way. **professor** n. (a) chief teacher in
a subject at a university. (b) teacher of
music/art, etc. **professorial**
[prɒfə'sɔːrɪəl] adj. referring to a
professor. **professorship** n. position
of professor at a university.
proffer ['prɒfə] v. (formal) to offer.
proficient [prə'fɪʃnt] adj. (at) very
capable of (doing sth). **proficiency** n.
skill in doing sth. **proficiently** adv. in
a capable way.
profile ['prəʊfaɪl] n. (a) view of s.o.'s
head from the side; to maintain a low p.
= to be quiet/unobtrusive. (b) short
biography/description of a famous
person (in a newspaper).
profit 1 ['prɒfɪt] n. money gained; p.
margin = percentage of money gained
against money paid out. **profit 2** v. to
gain. **profitability** [rɒfɪtə'bɪlɪtɪ] n.
ability to produce a profit. **profitable**
['prɒfɪtəbl] adj. likely to produce a
profit. **profitably** adv. at a profit.
profiteer 1 [prɒfɪ'tɪə] n. person who
makes too much profit. **profiteer 2** v.
to make too much profit. **profiteering**
n. making too much profit.
profligate ['prɒflɪgət] adj. & n.
(formal) (person) who is very
extravagant/who leads a wild life.
profligacy ['prɒflɪgəsɪ] n.
extravagance/spending money wildly.
proforma [prəʊ'fɔːmə] adj. & n.
(invoice) sent asking the purchaser to
pay in advance.
profound [prə'faʊnd] adj. very serious/
very deep (understanding/thought).
profoundly adv. extremely.
profundity [prə'fʌndɪtɪ] n. depth (of

thought or understanding).
profuse [prə'fjuːs] adj. abundant/
excessive. **profusely** adv. excessively/
too much. **profuseness** n. being
profuse. **profusion** [prə'fjuːʒn] n. very
large quantity.
progeny ['prɒdʒənɪ] n. (no pl.)
(formal) children/offspring. **progenitor**
[prəʊ'dʒenɪtə] n. ancestor; animal/plant
from which others are descended.
progesterone [prəʊ'dʒestərəʊn] n.
hormone which stops women ovulating
and helps the uterus in the first stages of
pregnancy.
prognathous [prɒg'neɪθəs] adj. with a
lower jaw which is longer than the upper.
prognosticate [prɒg'nɒstɪkeɪt] v.
(formal) to foretell. **prognosis**
[prɒg'nəʊsɪs] n. forecast.
prognostication n. (formal) forecast.
programme, Am. **program 1**
['prəʊgræm, 'prəʊgrəm] n. (a) list of
items in an entertainment. (b) show/item
on TV or radio. **programme 2** v. to
arrange shows on TV/radio. **program 1**
['prəʊgræm] n. instructions given to a
computer. **program 2** v. to give
instructions to (a computer);
programming language = system of signs
and words used to program a computer.
programmable adj. (device) which
can be programmed. **programmer** n.
(a) person who arranges shows on TV/
radio. (b) person who programs a
computer.
progress 1 ['prəʊgres] n. (pl.-es)
movement forwards; work in p. = work
which is being done. **progress 2**
[prə'gres] v. to advance. **progression**
[prə'greʃn] n. advance/movement
forwards. **progressive** adj. (a)
(movement) in stages. (b) advanced
(ideas). **progressively** adv. by stages.
prohibit [prə'hɪbɪt] v. to forbid.
prohibition [prəʊhɪ'bɪʃn] n. forbidding
(esp. the sale of alcohol). **prohibitive**
[prə'hɪbɪtɪv] adj. (price) which is so
high that you cannot pay it.
project 1 ['prɒdʒekt] n. (a) plan. (b)
work planned by students on their own.
project 2 [prə'dʒekt] v. (a) to plan. (b)
to throw (a picture on a screen).
projectile [prə'dʒektaɪl] n. thing which
is thrown/shot. **projecting** adj.
sticking/jutting/standing out.

projection n. (a) thing planned/forecast. (b) (in geography) picture of the shape of the earth on a flat surface. (c) thing which stands/sticks out. (d) action of projecting a picture on a screen

projectionist n. person who operates a projector in a cinema. **projector** n. apparatus for throwing pictures on a screen.

prolapse ['prəʊlæps] n. state where an organ in the body moves out of place.

prolegomena [prəʊle'gɒmɪnə] pl. n. (formal) introduction.

proletariat [prəʊlɪ'teərɪət] n. working class. **proletarian** adj. & n. (member) of the working class.

prolific [prə'lɪfɪk] adj. producing many children; very productive. **prolifically** adv. in a prolific way. **proliferate** [prə'lɪfəreɪt] v. to produce shoots/young, etc., rapidly. **proliferation** [prəlɪfə'reɪʃn] n. rapid spread.

prolix ['prəʊlɪks] adj. (formal) long winded/using too many words. **prolixity** [prəʊ'lɪksɪti] n. being prolix.

prologue ['prəʊlɒg] n. piece spoken as the introduction of a play or poem; preliminary section in a book.

prolong [prə'lɒŋ] v. to lengthen. **prolongation** [prəʊlɒŋ'geɪʃn] n. lengthening. **prolonged** adj. lasting for a long time.

promenade 1 [prɒmə'nɑːd] n. (a) terrace along the seashore where you can walk; (on a ship) p. deck = deck where passengers can stroll about. (b) p. concerts = inexpensive concerts of classical music where part of the audience stands and can walk about.

promenade 2 v. to walk about. **prom** [prɒm] n. inf. promenade; p. concerts/the proms = promenade concerts.

promenader n. (a) person who promenades. (b) person who goes to a promenade concert.

prominence ['prɒmɪnəns] n. (a) standing out; thing which stands out. (b) fame. **prominent** adj. (a) standing out/easily seen. (b) famous. **prominently** adv. so as to be easily seen.

promiscuous [prə'mɪskjʊəs] adj. (person) who does not prefer one thing to another, esp. who has sexual relations with many people. **promiscuity** [prɒmɪ'skjuːɪti] n. having sexual

relations with many people. **promiscuously** adv. in a promiscuous way.

promise 1 ['prɒmɪs] n. (a) act of promising that you will definitely do sth. (b) to show p. = to make people feel that you will do well in the future **promise 2** v. (a) to give your word that you will definitely do sth. (b) to show signs of what may happen in the future.

promising adj. (person) who is likely to succeed. **promissory** ['prɒmɪsəri] adj. (note) in which you promise to pay s.o. money on a certain date.

promontory ['prɒməntəri] n. piece of land jutting out into the sea.

promote [prə'məʊt] v. (a) to give (s.o.) a better job. (b to advertise. (c) to encourage. **promoter** n. person who promotes; person who organizes a boxing match, etc. **promotion** [prə'məʊʃn] n. (a) advancement to a better job. (b) advertising (a new product). **promotional** adj. (material) used in advertising.

prompt 1 [prɒmpt] adj. (-er, -est) done at once; quick/rapid. **prompt 2** v (a) to suggest to (s.o.) that he should do sth. (b) to tell an actor words which he has forgotten. **prompt 3** n. message to a computer user, telling him to do sth.

prompter n. person who prompts an actor. **promptitude** n. being prompt. **promptly** adv. immediately; rapidly. **promptness** n. quickness.

promulgate ['prɒmʌlgeɪt] v. (formal) to make (a law) known to the public. **promulgation** [prɒml'geɪʃn] n. (formal) announcement of a law.

prone [prəʊn] adj. (a) (lying) flat. (b) likely (to).

prong [prɒŋ] n. one of the sharp points of a fork; point of an attack. **pronged** adj. with prongs.

pronoun ['prəʊnaʊn] n. (in grammar) word which stands in place of a noun.

pronounce [prə'naʊns] v. (a) to speak a series of sounds which form a word; to speak clearly. (b) to declare in a formal way **pronounced** adj. noticeable. **pronouncement** n. official/formal statement. **pronunciation** [prənʌnsɪ'eɪʃn] n. way of pronouncing words.

pronto ['prɒntəʊ] adv. inf. immediately.

proof 1 [pru:f] *n.* (a) thing which proves/which shows that sth is true. (b) percentage of alcohol in a drink. (c) test sheet of printing which has to be corrected by the author before the book can be produced; copy of a photograph/lithograph, etc., for the artist to examine to see if it is acceptable. **proof 2** *adj.* (against) safe from/not affected by. **proof 3** *v.* to paint with a protective coat. **proofread** *v.* to read and correct proofs.

-proof [pru:f] *suffix* safe against/protected against.

prop 1 [prɒp] *n.* (a) support; stick which holds sth up. (b) props = articles used in the production of a play/film. (c) (in Rugby) forward in the front row of the scrum. **prop 2** *v.* (propped) to support.

propaganda [prɒpə'gændə] *n.* spreading of (frequently false) political ideas. **propagandist** *n.* person who spreads political ideas.

propagate ['prɒpəgeɪt] *v.* (a) to make (new plants) by sowing seed/taking cuttings. (b) to spread (ideas). **propagation** [prɒpə'geɪʃn] *n.* act of propagating. **propagator** *n.* small glass-covered box for growing new plants.

propane ['prəʊpeɪn] *n.* colourless gas used for heating and cooking.

propel [prə'pel] *v.* (propelled) to send forward. **propellant** *n.* fuel used to propel. **propeller** *n.* mechanism with blades which turns rapidly to drive boats and aircraft.

propensity [prə'pensɪtɪ] *n.* (formal) tendency/leaning.

proper ['prɒpə] *adj.* (a) right. (b) thorough (cleaning, etc.). (c) (in grammar) p. noun = noun which is a name of a person/a country, etc. (d) very correct. (e) (thing) itself exactly. **properly** *adv.* (a) rightly/correctly. (b) thoroughly.

property ['prɒpətɪ] *n.* (a) thing which belongs to s.o. (b) building or buildings. (c) properties = articles used in the production of a play/film; p. man = person responsible for all the articles used in a play/film. (d) quality.

prophecy ['prɒfəsɪ] *n.* act of prophesying; thing prophesied.

prophesy ['prɒfɪsaɪ] *v.* to foretell what will happen in the future. **prophet** ['prɒfɪt] *n.* person who foretells what will happen; religious leader. **prophetess** *n.* woman prophet. **prophetic(al)** [prə'fetɪk(l)] *adj.* which is like a prophecy. **prophetically** *adv.* in a prophetic way.

prophylaxis [prɒfɪ'læksɪs] *n.* prevention of a disease. **prophylactic** [prɒfɪ'læktɪk] *adj. & n.* (substance) which prevents disease.

propinquity [prə'pɪŋkwɪtɪ] *n.* (formal) closeness/nearness.

propitiate [prə'pɪʃɪeɪt] *v.* (formal) to appease/to make (s.o.) less angry. **propitiation** [prəpɪʃɪ'eɪʃn] *n.* act of appeasing. **propitiatory** [prə'pɪʃɪətərɪ] *adj.* which tries to appease/to make less angry. **propitious** [prə'pɪʃəs] *adj.* favourable. **propitiously** *adv.* in a propitious way.

proponent [prə'pəʊnənt] *n.* person who proposes sth.

proportion [prə'pɔ:ʃn] *n.* (a) part (of a total). (b) relationship between a part and a total; in p. = in the right amount. (c) proportions = the relative height/length (of a building/picture, etc.). **proportional** *adj.* which is directly related; p. representation = system of voting where the votes cast for each party are more or less accurately reflected in the number of seats each party has **proportionally** *adv.* in proportion. **proportionate** *adj.* which is in proportion. **proportionately** *adv.* in proportion.

propose [prə'pəʊz] *v.* (a) to suggest/to make a suggestion. (b) to p. to s.o. = to ask s.o. to marry you. **proposal** *n.* (a) suggestion/thing which is suggested. (b) asking s.o. to marry you. **proposer** *n.* person who proposes (a motion).

proposition [prɒpə'zɪʃn] *n.* (a) thing which has been proposed. (b) tough p. = problem which is difficult to solve.

propound [prə'paʊnd] *v.* (formal) to put forward (an idea).

proprietor [prə'praɪətə] *n.* owner. **proprietary** [prə'praɪətrɪ] *adj.* (a) referring to a proprietor. (b) p. medicine = medicine which is sold under a brand name and manufactured by a particular company. (c) (in S. Africa, Australia) p.

company = private limited company.
proprietress *n.* woman proprietor.
proprietorial *adj.* like a proprietor.
propriety [prə'praɪətɪ] *n.* decency;
good behaviour.
propulsion [prə'pʌlʃn] *n.* moving
forward.
pro rata [prəʊ'rɑːtə] *adv. & adj.* in
proportion.
prorogue [prəʊ'rəʊg] *v.* to end a
session of parliament. **prorogation** *n.*
end of a session of parliament.
prosaic [prə'zeɪɪk] *adj.* ordinary; not
poetic; rather dull.
prosaically *adv.* in a prosaic way.
proscenium [prə'siːnɪəm] *n.* part of a
stage in a theatre which sticks out
beyond the curtain; p. arch = arch above
the front part of a stage in a theatre
proscribe [prəʊ'skraɪb] *v.* (formal) to
forbid by law. **proscription**
[prɒs'krɪpʃn] *n.* (formal) act of
proscribing.
prose [prəʊz] *n.* writing which is not in
verse. **prosy** *adj.* wordy/dull in style.
prosecute ['prɒsɪkjuːt] *v.* to bring
(s.o.) to court to answer a charge.
prosecution [prɒsɪkjuːʃn] *n.* (a) court
case against s.o. (b) people who have
accused s.o. of a crime in a court.
prosecutor ['prɒsɪkjuːtə] *n.* person
who prosecutes; public p. = government
lawyer who accuses a criminal in a law
court on behalf of the state
proselyte [prɒsɪlaɪt] *n.* person recently
converted to a religion. **proselytize** *v.*
to try to convert (people) to a religion.
prosody ['prɒsədɪ] *n.* rules of writing .
poetry.
prospect 1 ['prɒspekt] *n.* (a) view. (b)
to have sth in p. = to expect sth to
happen. (c) prospects = future
possibilities. (d) person who may
become a customer. **prospect 2**
[prə'spekt] *v.* to search (a land) for
minerals. **prospective** *adj.* which
may happen in the future. **prospector**
n. person who searches for minerals.
prospectus [prə'spektəs] *n.* paper
giving information about sth in the hope
of attracting clients/customers.
prosper ['prɒspə] *v.* to succeed; to
become rich. **prosperity** [prɒsperɪtɪ] *n.*
being rich. **prosperous** ['prɒspərəs]
adj. wealthy/rich.

prostate ['prɒsteɪt] *n.* gland round the
bladder in men.
prosthesis ['prɒsθəsɪs] *n.* (*pl.*-ses)
(formal) artificial leg/arm, etc.
prostitute 1 ['prɒstɪtjuːt] *n.* person
who receives money for sexual
intercourse. **prostitute 2** *v* to use
(your talents) in a low/unworthy way.
prostitution [prɒstɪ'tjuːʃn] *n.* offering
sexual intercourse for payment.
prostrate 1 ['prɒstreɪt] *adj.* (lying) flat.
prostrate 2 [prə'streɪt] *v.* to p. oneself
before s.o. = to fall down (in front of s.o.
as a mark of respect, fear, etc.); he was
prostrated by malaria = he had to stay
lying down **prostration** [prɒ'streɪʃn] *n.*
lying down/falling down in front of s.o.
protagonist [prə'tægənɪst] *n.* main
character in a play/book, etc.; leader of
one side in a conflict.
protean ['prəʊtɪən] *adj.* which changes
easily.
protect [prə'tekt] *v.* to defend against
attack; to shield against dirt/germs, etc.
protection [prə'tekʃn] *n.* (a) shelter.
(b) defence. **protective** *adj.* which
protects. **protectively** *adv.* in a
protective way. **protector** *n.* person/
thing which protects. **protectorate** *n.*
country which is protected (and *usu.*
controlled) by another country.
protégé ['prɒteʒeɪ] *n.* person (usu.
young) who is supported in work with
money or advice by s.o. else.
protein ['prəʊtiːn] *n.* compound which
is an essential part of living cells; one of
the elements in food which is necessary
to keep the human body working
properly.
pro tempore, pro tem
[prəʊ'tempɒreɪ, 'prəʊ'tem] *adv.*
temporarily.
protest 1 ['prəʊtest] *n.* statement that
you object or disapprove; p. march =
march in procession to show that you
protest against sth. **protest 2** [prə'test]
v (a) to object/to raise a violent
objection (against). (b) to state solemnly.
Protestant ['prɒtɪstənt] *adj. & n.*
(member) of a Western Christian church
which is not part of the Roman Catholic
Church. **Protestantism** *n.* beliefs of
the Protestant church. **protestation**
[prɒtɪ'steɪʃn] *n.* violent statement of
protest.

protocol ['prəʊtəkɒl] n. (a) correct (diplomatic) behaviour. (b) draft agreement.

proton ['prəʊtɒn] n. nucleus of a hydrogen atom, found in all atoms.

protoplasm ['prəʊtəplæzəm] n. basic jelly-like substance in all living matter.

prototype ['prəʊtətaɪp] n. first model of a new machine.

protozoa [prəʊtəʊ'zəʊə] n. pl. simplest types of living creatures.

protracted [prə'træktɪd] adj. very lengthy. **protraction** n. being protracted. **protractor** n. semicircular device used for measuring angles in geometry.

protrude [prə'truːd] v. to stick out. **protrusion** n. thing which protrudes.

protuberance [prə'tjuːbərəns] n. bump/swelling. **protuberant** adj. which swells outwards.

proud [praʊd] adj. (of) full of pride; thinking a lot of yourself/of sth belonging to you; inf. he did himself p. = he gave himself a large meal. **proudly** adv. with pride; with great satisfaction.

prove [pruːv] v. (a) to demonstrate that sth is right. (b) to turn out. **provable** adj. which can be proved. **proven** [prəʊvn] adj. (a) which has been shown to be right. (b) (in Scotland) not p. = decision to release a prisoner because his guilt cannot be proved or disproved

provenance ['prɒvənəns] n. (formal) origin.

provender ['prɒvəndə] n. (no pl.) (formal) food.

proverb ['prɒvɜːb] n. saying which has a moral/which teaches you sth. **proverbial** [prə'vɜːbɪəl] adj. mentioned in a proverb; well-known. **proverbially** adv. in a proverbial way.

provide [prə'vaɪd] v. (a) to supply; to p. for = earn enough to feed and clothe. (b) to take care of. **provider** n. person who provides. **provided that, providing** conj. on condition that.

providence ['prɒvɪdəns] n. (lucky) fate. **provident** adj. careful to think about the future and keep money/stores for use in time of need. **providential** [prɒvɪ'denʃl] adj. lucky. **providentially** adv. luckily.

province ['prɒvɪns] n. (a) large administrative division of a country; the provinces = parts of a country away from the capital. (b) area of knowledge; area of responsibility. **provincial 1** [prə'vɪnʃl] adj. referring to a province/ to the provinces; narrow = minded/not very civilized. **provincial 2** n person from the provinces.

provision 1 [prə'vɪʒn] n. (a) thing that is provided; to make p. for = to see that sth is allowed for in the future. (b) pl.provisions = food. (e) condition in a document **provision 2** v. to stock up with food. **provisional** adj. temporary; conditional. **provisionally** adv. temporarily.

proviso [prə'vaɪzəʊ] n. (pl.-os) condition.

provoke [prə'vəʊk] v. (a) to incite (s.o.) to do sth violent. (b) to make (a reaction) start. **provocation** [prɒvə'keɪʃn] n. action of provoking. **provocative** [prɒ'vɒkətɪv] adj. likely to provoke a violent response. **provocatively** adv. in a provocative way. **provoking** adj. annoying.

provost ['prɒvəst] n. (a) person in charge of a college. (b) (in Scotland) mayor. (c) p. marshal = head of a group of military police

prow [praʊ] n. front end of a ship.

prowess ['praʊes] n. (formal) skill.

prowl 1 [praʊl] n. on the p. = creeping about. **prowl 2** v. to creep about quietly. **prowler** n. person who creeps about, esp. a burglar.

proximate ['prɒksɪmət] adj. (formal) nearest/closest. **proximity** [prɒk'sɪmɪtɪ] n. closeness.

proxy ['prɒksɪ] n. (a) document giving s.o. the power to act/to vote on your behalf. (b) person who acts/votes on your behalf.

prude [pruːd] n. prudish person. **prudery, prudishness** n. state of being prudish. **prudish** adj. with strict principles and easily shocked.

prudence ['pruːdns] n. great care/ caution. **prudent** adj. very careful/very cautious. **prudential** [pruː'denʃl] adj. (formal) showing prudence. **prudently** ad in a prudent way.

prune 1 [pruːn] n. dried plum. **prune 2** v. to cut branches off (a tree); to cut back (a tree/shrub) to keep it in good shape or to encourage it to produce flowers; to cut back (expenditure, etc.); to cut out (parts of a book, etc.).

prurient ['proǝriǝnt] *adj.* which causes indecent thoughts. **prurience** *n.* being prurient.

prussic acid ['prʌsɪk 'æsɪd] *n.* type of poisonous acid.

pry [praɪ] *v.* (a) to look inquisitively into sth. (b) *Am.* to lift open with a lever.

PS [pi:'es] short for post scriptum, additional note at the end of a letter.

psalm [sɑːm] *n.* religious song from the Bible. **psalmist** *n.* person who wrote the psalms. **psalter** ['sɔːltǝ] *n.* book of psalms with music, for use in church.

PSBR short for Public Sector Borrowing Requirement.

psephology [se'fɒlǝdʒɪ] *n.* study of elections/voting patterns and opinion polls of voters. **psephologist** *n.* person who specializes in psephology.

pseud [sjuːd] *n. inf.* person who is not really as he pretends to be.

pseudo- ['sjuːdǝʊ] prefix meaning false.

pseudonym ['sjuːdǝnɪm] *n.* false/invented name. **pseudonymous** [sjuː'dɒnɪmǝs] *adj.* (writer) using a pseudonym.

psittacosis [psɪtǝ'kǝʊsɪs] *n.* serious disease, caught by people from birds.

psoriasis [sɔː'raɪǝsɪs] *n.* itching disease which causes red patches on the skin.

psychedelic [saɪkǝ'delɪk] *adj.* so full of bright moving colours that you become hallucinated.

psychiatry [saɪ'kaɪǝtrɪ] *n.* study of mental disease. **psychiatric** [saɪkɪ'ætrɪk] *adj.* referring to psychiatry. **psychiatrist** [saɪ'kaɪǝtrɪst] *n.* person who studies and treats mental disease.

psychic ['saɪkɪk] *adj. & n.* (person) in contact with supernatural forces. **psychical** *adj.* in contact with supernatural forces.

psychoanalysis [saɪkǝʊǝ'nælǝsɪs] *n.* treatment of mental disorder by discussion. **psychoanalyse** *v.* to treat (s.o.) by psychoanalysis.

psychoanalyst [saɪkǝʊ'ænǝlɪst] *n.* person who treats patients by psychoanalysis.

psychology [saɪ'kɒlǝdʒɪ] *n.* study of the human mind. **psychological** [saɪkǝ'lɒdʒɪkl] *adj.* referring to psychology. **psychologically** *adv.* mentally. **psychologist** [saɪ'kɒlǝdʒɪst] *n.* person who studies the human mind.

psychopath ['saɪkǝpæθ] *n.* psychopathic criminal. **psychopathic** [saɪkǝ'pæθɪk] *adj.* mentally unstable in a dangerous way.

psychosis [saɪkǝʊsɪs] *n. (pl. -oses)* mental illness which changes the patient's personality. **psychotic** [saɪ'kɒtɪk] *adj. & n.* (person) suffering from a psychosis.

psychosomatic [saɪkǝʊsǝ'mætɪk] *adj.* (physical illness) created by a mental state.

psychotherapy [saɪkǝʊ'θerǝpɪ] *n.* treatment of mental disorder by psychological means.

Pt symbol of Platinum.

PTA Parent Teacher Association.

ptarmigan ['tɑːmɪgǝn] *n.* type of mountain bird.

pterodactyl [terǝʊ'dæktɪl] *n.* prehistoric flying dinosaur.

PTO [pi:ti:'ǝʊ] short for please turn over.

Pu symbol for plutonium.

pub [pʌb] *n. inf.* public house/inn; p. crawl = going from inn to inn having a drink in each.

puberty ['pjuːbǝtɪ] *n.* period of adolescence when a person becomes sexually mature.

pubic ['pjuːbɪk] *adj.* referring to the area around the sexual organs.

public 1 ['pʌblɪk] *adj.* (a) referring to the people in general; p. holiday = holiday for everyone; p. house = inn/place where you can buy and drink alcohol. (b) p. school = (in Britain) private fee-paying school which is not part of the state system; (in the USA) a state school. **public 2** *n.* people in general; in p. = in the open; in front of everyone. **publican** *n.* person who runs a public house. **publication** [pʌblɪ'kriʃn] *n.* (a) making public/publishing. (b) book/paper which has been published. **publicist** ['pʌblɪsɪst] *n.* person who attracts people's attention to a product. **publicity** [pʌblɪsɪtɪ] *n.* advertising; attracting people's attention to a product. **publicize** *v.* to attract people's attention to sth/to make publicity for sth. **publicly** adv. in public. **public relations** n. maintaining good relations between an organization and the public. **public service** n. working for the state; all government agencies and their personnel. **Public Sector Borrowing Requirement** n. the amount of money the government needs to borrow, in order to run its services. **public-spirited** adj. (person) who acts energetically for the good of the community.

publish ['pʌblɪʃ] v. to make publicly known; to bring out (a book/newspaper) for sale. **publisher** n. person who produces books/newspapers for sale. **publishing** n. producing books/ newspapers for sale; p. house = firm which publishes books.

puce [pjuːs] adj. dark purplish red.

puck [pʌk] n. small disc which is hit in ice hockey.

pucker 1 [pʌkə] n. wrinkle/fold. **pucker 2** v. to wrinkle (your brow).

puckish ['pʌkɪʃ] adj. mischievous/full of playful tricks.

pudding ['pʊdɪŋ] n. (a) dessert/sweet course at the end of the meat. (b) sweet food which has been cooked or boiled. (c) black p. = dark sausage made of blood.

puddle ['pʌdl] n. small pool of water (e.g. one left after rain).

pudgy ['pʌdʒɪ] adj. soft and fat.

puerile ['pjʊəraɪl] adj. childish/stupid. **puerility** [pjʊə'rɪlɪtɪ] n. being puerile.

puff 1 [pʌf] n. (a) small breath. (b) powder p. = light pad for powdering the skin. (c) p. pastry = light sort of pastry. (d) piece of publicity. **puff 2** v. to blow. **puffball** n. type of round white fungus. **puffed (out)** adj. inf. out of breath. **puffiness** n. being puffy. **puffy** adj. swollen (face).

puffin ['pʌfɪn] n. black and white bird with a large coloured beak, living near the sea.

pug [pʌg] n. type of small dog, with a flat face. **pugnosed** adj. with a flattened nose.

pugilist ['pjuːdʒɪlɪst] n. (formal) fighter/boxer. **pugilism** n. (formal) boxing.

pugnacious [pʌg'neɪʃəs] adj. (formal) (person) who likes fighting; quarrelsome.

pugnaciously adv. in a pugnacious way. **pugnacity** [pʌg'næsɪtɪ] n. being pugnacious.

puisne ['pjuːnɪ] adj. (judge) in the High Court.

puissance ['pwiːsaːns] n. test in show jumping, where a horse has to jump very high fences.

puke [pjuːk] v. inf. to p. (up) = to vomit.

pukka ['pʌkə] adj. inf. real; of good quality.

pulchritude ['pʌlkrɪtjuːd] n. (formal) beauty.

pule [pjuːl] v. (of children) to wait/to whimper.

pull 1 [pʊl] n. (a) act of dragging/ moving sth towards you. (b) inf. influence. (c) handle (which has to be pulled). (d) deep inhaling (of a cigarette). **pull 2** v. (a) to move (sth) by dragging; to move (sth) towards you. (b) to p. a face = make a grimace. (c) to strain (a muscle). **pull down** v. to bring (sth) down by pulling. **pull in** v. to drive close to the side of the road (and stop). **pull-in** n. inf. transport café. **pull off** v. (a) to take off (a piece of clothing/a handle, etc.) by pulling. (b) inf. to succeed in doing (sth). (c) to drive off a road and stop. **pull out** v. (a) to bring (sth) out by pulling. (b) to drive away from the side of the road; to drive towards the middle of the road. **pull round, pull through** v. to recover from an illness. **pull together** v. he pulled himself together = he became calmer/he controlled his emotions. **pull up** v. (a) to stop (in a vehicle). (b) to raise by pulling; inf. to p. one's socks up = to do better/try harder.

pullet ['pʊlɪt] n. young chicken.

pulley ['pʊlɪ] n. apparatus for lifting heavy weights with a grooved wheel round which a rope runs.

pullman ['pʊlmən] n. (a) luxurious railway carriage. (b) Am. sleeping car (on a train).

pullover ['pʊləʊvə] n. piece of clothing made of wool, etc., covering the top part of the body and which you pull on over your head.

pulmonary ['pʌlmənrɪ] adj. referring to the lungs.

pulp 1 [pʌlp] n. squashy mass. **pulp 2** v. to crush to a pulp. **pulpy** adj. in a pulp.

pulpit ['pʊlpɪt] *n.* enclosed platform in a church where the priest preaches.

pulsar ['pʌlsə] *n.* invisible star which sends out radio signals.

pulse 1 [pʌls] *n.* (a) regular beat of the heart. (b) dried seed of peas/beans.

pulse 2 *v.* to pulsate. **pulsate** [pʌl'seɪt] *v.* to throb regularly. **pulsation** [pʌl'seɪʃn] *n.* regular throbbing.

pulverize ['pʌlvəraɪz] *v.* to crush to powder. **pulverization** [pʌlvəraɪ'zeɪʃn] *n.* crushing to powder.

puma ['pjuːmə] *n.* large wild American cat.

pumice (stone) ['pʌmɪs('stəʊn] *n.* block of light grey porous lava used for rubbing stains off your skin.

pummel ['pʌml] *v.* (pummelled) to hit s.o. with many blows.

pump 1 [pʌmp] *n.* (a) machine for forcing liquids or air (b) soft shoe. **pump 2** *v.* (a) to force (liquid/air) with a pump. (b) *inf.* to ask (s.o.) searching questions. **pump priming** *n.* investment by the government in new projects, to stimulate the economy.

pumpkin ['pʌmpkɪn] *n.* large round orange-coloured vegetable.

pun 1 [pʌn] *n.* play with words of different meanings. **pun 2** *v.* (punned) to make puns. **punster** *n.* a person who is always making puns.

punch 1 [pʌntʃ] *n.* (*pl.*-es) (a) blow with the fist; p. line = last sentence of a story/joke which gives the point (b) metal tool for making holes. (c) drink made of wine or spirits and spices.

punch 2 *v.* (a) to hit (s.o.) with your fist.. (b) to make the holes in (sth) with a punch. **Punch and Judy** *n.* form of children's puppet show, with traditional characters. **punch bowl** *n.* (a) bowl for mixing wine and spices to make punch. (b) small valley surrounded by hills. **punch-drunk** *adj.* suffering from brain damage from being punched on the head too often. **punch up** *n. inf.* fight.

punctilious [pʌŋk'tɪlɪəs] *adj.* attentive to detail/extremely fussy. **punctiliously** *adv.* in a punctilious way. **punctiliousness** *n.* being punctilious.

punctual ['pʌŋktjʊəl] *adj.* on time. **punctuality** [pʌŋktjʊ'ælɪtɪ] *n.* being on time/never being late. **punctually** *adv.* on time.

punctuate ['pʌŋktjʊeɪt] *v.* (a) to split a sentence using punctuation marks. (b) to interrupt. **punctuation** [pʌŋktjʊ'eɪʃn] *n.* splitting of a sentence using punctuation marks; p. marks = signs used in writing (such as full stop, comma, dash) to show how a sentence is split up.

puncture 1 ['pʌŋktʃə] *n.* hole in a tyre; very small hole. **puncture 2** *v.* to make a small hole in (sth).

pundit ['pʌndɪt] *n.* expert (esp. in political matters).

pungent ['pʌndʒənt] *adj.* sharp (taste, smell); sarcastic (comment). **pungency** *n.* being pungent. **pungently** *adv.* in a pungent way.

punish ['pʌnɪʃ] *v.* to make (s.o.) suffer because of sth he has done. **punishable** *adj.* (offence) for which you can be punished. **punishment** *n.* treatment given to punish s.o. **punitive** ['pjuːnətɪv] *adj.* which serves to punish.

punk 1 [pʌŋk] *n. inf.* (a) wild hooligan. (b) follower of punk rock. **punk 2** *adj. inf.* bad/inferior. **punk rock** *n.* loud music played by people wearing outrageous costumes.

punnet ['pʌnɪt] *n.* small box made of plastic or thin pieces of wood for holding soft fruit.

punt 1 [pʌnt] *n.* long flat-bottomed boat propelled with a pole. **punt 2** *v.* (a) to push (a punt) with a pole. (b) to kick a ball which is in the air. (c) to bet on a horse race. **punter** *n.* (a) person who gambles, esp. on horseraces. (b) person who pushes a punt along with a pole.

puny ['pjuːnɪ] *adj.* (-ier, -iest) weak/feeble; very small.

pup 1 [pʌp] *n.* young of certain animals. esp. young dog; p. tent = small ridge tent. **pup 2** *n. v..* (pupped) to have pups.

pupa ['pjuːpə] *n.* (*pl.*-pae) resting period in the life of an insect when it is changing from a grub/caterpillar to a butterfly/beetle. **pupal** *adj.* referring to a pupa.

pupate [pju:'peɪt] *v.* (of caterpillar) to turn into a pupa.

pupil ['pju:pl] *n.* (a) child at a school; person learning from a teacher. (b) hole in the central part of the eye, through which the light passes.

puppet ['pʌpɪt] *n.* doll which moves and which is used to give a performance; p. show = performance given using puppets; p. state = country controlled by another country **puppeteer** [pʌpɪ'tɪə] *n.* man who gives a performance using puppets.

puppy ['pʌpɪ] *n.* young dog; p. fat = fatness in young children and adolescents.

purblind ['pɜ:blaɪnd] *adj.* partly blind.

purchase 1 ['pɜ:tʃəs] *n.* (a) thing bought. (b) ability to grip/ability to lift sth by using a lever. **purchase 2** *v.* to buy; purchasing power = quantity that can be bought with a certain amount of money. **purchaser** *n.* person who buys sth.

purdah ['pɜ:də] *n.* seclusion of women (in Eastern countries).

pure ['pjʊə] *adj.* (-er, -est) (a) very clean; not mixed with other things. (b) innocent; with no faults; **purely** *adv.* only/solely.

purée 1 ['pjʊəreɪ] *n.* semi-liquid pulp (of a vegetable/fruit). **purée 2** *v.* to make (sth) into a puree.

purgatory ['pɜ:gətrɪ] *n.* place where you suffer temporarily after death (place of) suffering.

purge 1 [pɜ:dʒ] *n.* (a) medicine which clears the bowels. (b) removal of political opponents. **purge 2** *v.* (a) to clear out (waste matter). (b) to p. one's contempt = to apologize to a court. (c) to remove (political opponents) **purgative** ['pɜ:gətɪv] *adj. & n.* (medicine) which clears the bowels.

purify ['pjʊərɪfaɪ] *v.* to clean/to make pure. **purification** [pjʊərɪfɪ'keɪʃn] *n.* making pure. **purifier** *n.* machine that purifies.

purist ['pjʊərɪst] *n.* person who insists on everything being done in the correct way.

purity *n.* being pure/absolutely clean.

puritan ['pjʊərɪtən] *n.* puritanical person. **puritanical** [pjʊərɪ'tænɪkl] *adj.* very strict concerning morals.

purl [pɜ:l] *v.* to knit putting your needle into the back of the loop.

purlieus ['pɜ:lju:z] *pl. n.* (formal) surroundings.

purloin [pɜ:'lɔɪn] *v.* (formal) to steal.

purple ['pɜ:pl] *adj. & n.* reddish blue (colour). **purplish** *adj.* quite purple.

purport 1 [pɜ:'pɔ:t] *n.* (formal) meaning. **purport 2** *v.* (formal) to mean.

purpose ['pɜ:pəs] *n.* aim/plan; use; on p. = according to what was planned; intentionally. **purpose-built** *adj.* built specially for a purpose. **purposeful** *adj.* intentional; with an aim in view; (person) with set aims. **purposefully** *adv.* in a purposeful way.

purposefulness *n.* being purposeful. **purposely** *adv.* on purpose/intentionally.

purr 1 [pɜ:] *n.* (a) noise made by a cat when pleased. (b) low noise made by a powerful engine. **purr 2** *v.* (a) (of cat) to make a noise to show pleasure. (b) (of engine) to make a low noise.

purse 1 [pɜ:s] *n.* (a) small bag for carrying money. (b) handbag.

purse 2 to p. your lips = to pinch/to press your lips together to show you are displeased. **purser** *n.* officer on a ship who deals with the money, supplies and the passengers' accommodation.

pursue [pə'sju:] *v.* (a) to chase (s.o./sth). (b) to continue to do (sth).

pursuance *n.* (formal) in p. of = while carrying out (duties). **pursuant to** *adv.* relating to. **pursuer** *n.* person who chases s.o. **pursuit** *n.* (a) chase; in p. of = looking for. (b) (formal) career/occupation.

purulent ['pjʊərʊlənt] *adj.* (formal) full of pus.

purvey [pɜ:'veɪ] *v.* (formal) to supply (goods). **purveyor** *n.* person who supplies goods.

purview ['pɜ:vju:] *n.* general scope of a document.

pus [pʌs] *n.* yellowish liquid which gathers in infected wounds/spots.

push 1 [pʊʃ] *n.* (-es) (a) act of pressing sth so that it moves away from you. (b) energy; *inf.* determination to do well. (c) *inf.* at a p. = if necessary. (d) *inf.* to give s.o. the p. = to dismiss s.o. from a job

push 2 *v.* (a) to press; to move (sth) by pressing. (b) *inf.* I am pushed for time = I haven't much time to spare. (c) *Sl.* to

sell (drugs) illegally. **pushbike** *n. inf.*
bicycle. **pushbutton** *n.* switch which
is operated by pushing. **pushchair** *n,.*
light folding carriage for pushing a child
in. **pusher** *n. Sl.* person who sells
drugs illegally. **pushful, pushing** *adj.*
ambitious; eager to get what you want.
push off *v. inf.* to get going/to start a
journey; push off! = go away! **pushover**
n. inf. easy task; person who is easily
influenced. **push-up** *n. Am.* press-up.
pushy *adj. inf.* wanting to succeed/
ambitious.
pusillanimous [pjuːsɪˈlænɪməs] *adj.*
(formal) timid/afraid. **pusillanimity**
[pjuːstləˈnɪmɪtɪ] *n.* being pusillanimous.
puss, pussy, pussycat [pʊs, ˈpʊsɪ,
ˈpʊsɪkæt] *n.* familiar words for a cat.
pussy foot *v. inf.* to p. about = to
dither/to be undecided.
pustule [ˈpʌstjuːl] *n.* blister/spot (on
the skin).
put [pʊt] *v.* (put; putting) (a) to place;
inf. to stay p. = to stay where you are. (b)
to express in words. (c) to estimate at.
(d) to p. a stop to = to stop. (e) (in
sports) to throw (the shot) **put across**
v. to explain (sth) in a convincing way.
put away *v.* to clear (things) away. **put
back** *v.* to place (sth) where it was
before. **put by** *v.* to save. **put down** *v.*
(a) to place at a lower level/on the
ground. (b) to let (passengers) get off. (c)
to note. (d) to kill (a sick animal). (e) to
p. your foot down = (i) to be very strict/
firm; (ii) (in a car) to go faster. **put in** *v.*
(a) to place inside. (b) he p. in three
hour's work = he worked for three hours.
(c) to p. in for a job = to apply. **put off**
v. (a) to delay. (b) to frighten/to
embarrass (s.o.) so that they can't do sth.
put on *v.* (a) to place. (b) to get
dressed in (a piece of clothing).(c) to
switch on (a light, etc.). (d) to add
(weight). **put out** *v.* (a) to place
outside. (b) to stretch out (one's hand,
etc.). (c) to switch off (a light, etc.). (d)
inf. to be p. out = to be annoyed. (e) (of
ships) to p. out to sea = to leave harbour
put up *v.* (a) to fix upright; to build.
(b) to raise. (c) to offer. (d) to find a
place for (s.o.) to sleep. (e) to p. up with
s.o./sth = to accept s.o./sth. even if they
are unpleasant/noisy, etc. (f) to p. s.o. up
to sth = to encourage s.o. to do sth. **put-**

upon *adj.* forced to do sth unpleasant.
putative [ˈpjuːtətɪv] *adj.* (formal) the p.
author = the person who is supposed to
be the author.
putrefy [ˈpjuːtrɪfaɪ] *v.* to rot.
putrefaction [pjɒtrɪˈfækʃn] *n.* rotting.
purtrescent *adj.* which is rotting.
putrid *adj.* rotten; smelling rotten.
putsch [pʊtʃ] *n.* armed overthrow of a
government.
putt 1 [pʌt] *n.* short shot (on a green) in
golf. **putt 2** *v.* to hit a short shot in golf.
putter 1 *n.* golf club for putting.
putter 2 *v. Am.* to p. around = not to
do anything in particular/to do little jobs
here and there.
puttee [ˈpʌtɪ] *n.* long piece of cloth
wound round the leg to act as protection.
putty [ˈpʌtɪ] *n.* soft substance which
hardens after a time, used esp. for
sealing the glass in windows.
puzzle 1 [ˈpʌzl] *n.* (a) problem;
thing which is difficult to solve. (b)
game where you have to solve a
problem. **puzzle 2** *v.* to perplex/to
mystify; to be a problem.
puzzlement *n.* being puzzled.
puzzling *adj.* which does not make
sense/which is a problem.
PVC [piːviːˈsiː] *n.* type of plastic.
pygmy [ˈpɪgmɪ] *adj. & n.* (type of
animal) which is smaller than normal;
very short (person).
pyjamas [prˈdʒɑːməz] *n. pl.* light shirt
and trousers worn in bed.
pylon [ˈpaɪlən] *n.* tall metal tower for
carrying electric cables.
pyorrhea [parəˈrɪə] *n.* infection of the
gums round the teeth.
pyramid [ˈpɪrəmɪd] *n.* shape with a
square base and four sides rising to meet
at a point. **pyramidal** [prˈræmɪdl] *adj.*
shaped like a pyramid.
pyre [ˈpaɪə] *n* ceremonial fire; funeral p.
= pile on which a dead body is cremated.
pyrethrum [parˈruːθrəm] *n.* insecticide
made from a flower.
pyrites [parˈraɪtiːz] *n.* yellowish
chemical substance containing a metal.
pyromaniac [parəʊˈmeɪnɪæk] *n.*
person who sets fire to buildings/who is
mad about fire. **pyrotechnics**
[parəˈtekkns] *n. pl.* science of
fireworks. **pyrotechnic(al)** *adj.*
referring to fireworks.

Pyrrhic victory ['pırık'vıktrı] *n.* victory which costs the victor too much effort/too many losses.

python ['paıθn] *n.* large snake which kills its prey by crushing.

pyx [pıks] *n.* box in church where consecrated bread and wine are kept.

Qq

QC [kju:'si:] *n.* (short for Queen's Counsel) title given to an important lawyer.

qua [kweı] *prep.* taken by itself.

quack 1 [kwæk] *n.* (a) sound made by a duck. (b) *inf.* unqualified doctor. **quack 2** *v.* to make a noise like a duck.

quad [kwɒd] *n. inf.* quadrangle.

quadrangle ['kwɒd'ræŋgl] *n.* open square surrounded by buildings (in a school/college). **quadrant** ['kwɒdrənt] *n.* (a) quarter of a circle. (b) instrument used for measuring angles.

quadraphonic [kwɒdrə'fɒnık] *adj.* (sound) which is reproduced through four loudspeakers.

quadratic [kwɒd'rætık] *adj.* (equation) involving the square of the unknown quantity.

quadrennial [kwɒd'renıəl] *adj.* happening every four years.

quadrilateral [kwɒdrı'lætərəl] *adj. & n.* (shape with four sides).

quadruped ['kwɒdrʊped] *n.* animal with four legs. **quadruple** [kwɒ'drʊpl] *v.* to multiply four times. **quadruplets** ['kwɒdrʊplets] *n. pl.* four babies born at the same birth. **quadruplicate** [kwɒ'dru:plıkət] *n.* in q. = in four copies. **quads** [kwɒdz] *n. pl. inf.* quadruplets.

quaff [kwɒf] *v.* to drink with large gulps.

quagmire ['kwɒgmaıə] *n.* bog/area of dangerous marsh.

quail 1 [kweıl] *n.* small game bird. **quail 2** *v.* to shrink back in fear; to shudder (at sth.).

quaint [kweınt] *adj.* (-er, -est) picturesque/oddly old-fashioned.

quaintly *adv.* in a quaint way.

quaintness *n.* old-fashioned oddness.

quake 1 [kweık] *n. inf.* earthquake.

quake 2 *v.* to shake (with fear/cold).

Quaker *n. inf.* member of a Christian religious society. known as the Society of Friends.

qualify ['kwɒlıfaı] *v.* (a) to q. as = to study for and obtain a diploma which allows you to do a certain type of work. (b) to q. for = to pass a test/a section of a competition and so proceed to the next step. (c) to modify; to attach conditions. **qualification** [kwɒlıfı'keıʃn] *n.* (a) proof that you have studied for and obtained a diploma; what are his qualifications? = what sort of diploma does he have? (b) modification/condition which limits. **qualifier** *n.* (a) person who qualifies. (b) round of a sporting competition which qualifies a team to go to the next round.

quality ['kwɒlıtı] *n.* (a) worth. (b) characteristics. **qualitative** *adj.* referring to quality.

qualm [kwɑ:m] *n.* feeling of guilt/ worry.

quandary ['kwɒndrı] *n.* puzzle/ problem; in a q. = puzzled/not knowing what to do.

quango ['kwæŋgəʊ] *n.* (*pl.*-os) large national body (such as a government commission which investigates a special problem) where the directors are appointed by the government, but without direct government control.

quantify ['kwɒntıfaı] *v.* to calculate in quantities/in amounts. **quantifiable** *adj.* which can be quantified.

quantity ['kwɒntıtı] *n.* amount; a q. of waste paper = a lot; an unknown q. = person/thing you know nothing about; q. surveyor = person who estimates how much material is required for a building. **quantitative** *adj.* referring to quantity.

quantum ['kwɒntəm] *n.* q. theory = theory in physics that energy exists in fixed amounts.

quarantine 1 ['kwɒrənti:n] *n.* period of time when an animal/a person (usu. coming from another country) has to be kept apart to avoid the risk of passing on disease. **quarantine 2** *v.* to put (s.o./an animal) in quarantine:

quark [kwɑːk] *n.* smallest particle.
quarrel 1 ['kwɒrəl] *n.* argument; to pick a q. with s.o. = to start an argument. **quarrel 2** *v.* (quarrelled) to argue (about/over sth). **quarrelling** *n.* arguments. **quarrelsome** *adj.* argumentative/often getting into quarrels.
quarry 1 ['kwɒrɪ] *n.* (a) place where stone. etc. is dug out of the ground. (b) animal which is being hunted; person/ thing which is being looked for. **quarry 2** *v.* to dig (stone) out of the ground.
quart [kwɔːt] *n.* measure of liquid (=2 pints). **quarter 1** ['kwɔːtə] *n.* (a) one of four parts. (b) period of fifteen minutes before or after the hour. (c) period of three months. (d) area. (e) quarters = accommodation for people in the armed forces. (f) *Am.* 25 cent coin.
quarter 2 *v.* (a) to cut into four equal parts. (b) to place (soldiers) in lodgings.
quarterday *n.* day which marks the beginning of a three month period for accounting purposes. **quarterdeck** *n.* top deck of a ship near the stern.
quarter-final *n.* (in sport) one of four matches in a competition, the winners of which go into the semi-finals.
quarterlight *n.* small. *usu.* triangular. window in a car. **quarterly** *adj., adv. & n.* (magazine) which appears every three months. **quartermaster** *n.* (in Army) officer in charge of stores; (in Navy) petty officer in charge of signals.
quartet(te) [kwɔːˈtet] *n.* (a) four people. (b) four musicians playing together. (c) piece of music for four musicians. **quarto** ['kwɔːtəʊ] *adj. & n.* size of paper one quarter of a standard sheet.
quartz [kwɔːts] *n.* hard crystalline mineral. used for making watches because of its very regular vibrations.
quasar ['kweɪsɑː] *n.* distant star which gives off intense radiation.
quash [kwɒʃ] *v.* to annual (a legal sentence).
quasi- ['kweɪzaɪ] prefix meaning almost.
quatrain ['kwɒtreɪn] *n.* stanza of poetry with four lines.
quaver 1 ['kweɪvə] *n.* (a) musical note lasting half as long as a crotchet. (b) tremble (in the voice). **quaver 2** *v.* to tremble (of voice). **quavering** *adj.* trembling (voice).

quay [kiː] *n.* stone jetty/place where ships tie up to load or unload. **quayside** *n.* at the q. = next to the quay.
queasy ['kwiːzɪ] *adj.* feeling sick. **queasiness** *n.* being queasy.
queen [kwiːn] *n.* (a) wife of a king; woman ruler of a country; q. mother = mother of a king or queen who is the widow of a king. (b) (at cards) card between the jack and the king. (c) important piece in chess. (d) q. ant/bee = leading ant/bee in a colony. (e) the best/ the most perfect woman. (f) *Sl.* male homosexual. **queenly** *adj.* like a queen. **Queen Mother** *n.* mother of a king or queen.
queer 1 ['kwɪə] *adj.* (-er, -est) (a) odd/ strange. (b) *Sl.* adj. & n. homosexual. (c) ill. **queer 2** *v.* to make sth go wrong; to q. s.o.'s pitch = to upset s.o.'s plans.
queerness *n.* strangeness/oddness.
quell [kwel] *v.* to claim (a riot): to hold back (your feelings).
quench [kwenʃ] *v.* to q. your thirst = to have a drink.
quern [kwɜːn] *n.* mill for grinding flour by hand.
querulous ['kwerjʊləs] *adj.* bad-tempered/peevish: always complaining.
querulously *adv.* in a querulous way. **querulousness** *n.* being querulous.
query 1 ['kwɪərɪ] *n.* (a) question. (b) question mark. **query 2** *v.* to doubt whether sth is true; to ask a question.
quest ['kwest] *n.* (formal) search.
question 1 ['kwestʃn] *n.* (a) sentence which requires an answer; q. mark = sign (?) which shows that a question is being asked. (b) problem; the human rights q. (c) matter; there is no q. of = it is impossible; the matter in q. = which is being discussed; it's out of the q. = it's unthinkable. **question 2** *v.* (a) to ask (s.o.) questions. (b) to doubt.
questionable *adj.* doubtful. **questioner** *n.* person who asks questions.
questionnaire *n.* printed list of questions given to people to answer.
queue 1 [kjuː] *n.* line of people/cars. etc. waiting one behind the other for sth: to jump the q. = to go in front of people standing in a queue. **queue 2** (also queue up) to form a queue.

quibble 1 ['kwɪbl] *n.* argument about details. **quibble 2** *v.* to argue about details/to argue over the meaning of words. **quibbler** *n.* person who argues about details.

quiche [kiːʃ] *n.* open tart with a filling of eggs/meat/vegetables. etc.

quick 1 [kwɪk] *adj.* (-er, -est) (a) fast/rapid. (b) she has a q. temper = she loses her temper easily. **quick 2** *n.* live flesh (esp. flesh around fingernails/toenails): he was cut to the q. = he was very hurt. **quick-acting** *adj.* (medicine) which takes effect rapidly. **quicken** *v.* (a) to make (sth) go faster. (b) to stimulate (appetite). **quickie** *n. inf.* (a) quick drink/question. etc. (b) quick divorce. **quicklime** *n.* lime. **quickly** *adv.* rapidly. **quickness** *n.* being quick. **quicksand** *n.* dangerous area of soft sand where you can sink in easily. **quicksilver** *n.* mercury. **quickstep** *n.* dance with quick steps. **quick-tempered** *adj.* (person) who loses his temper easily. **quick-writted** *adj.* intelligent (person) /(person) who understands quickly.

quid [kwɪd] *n.* (a) *Sl.* pound (in money). (b) lump of chewing tobacco. **quid pro quo** [kwɪdprəʊ'kwəʊ] *n.* something done in return for something else.

quiescent [kwaɪ'esnt] *adj.* (formal) calm.

quiet 1 ['kaɪət] *n.* (a) absence of noise; calm/tranquillity. (b) to do sth on the q. = in secret. **quiet 2** *adj.* (-er, -est) (a) calm/making no noise. (b) simple; q. wedding = with few guests: q. colour scheme =- where the colours aren't bright. **quiet 3** *v.* to claim; to stop (s.o.) being noisy. **quieten** *v.* to claim; to stop (s.o.) being noisy. **quietly** *adv.* (a) without making any noise. (b) secretly. **quietness** *n.* clam/tranquility. **quietude** *n.* (formal) quietness.

quiff [kwɪf] *n.* hair combed upwards and backwards from a man's forehead.

quill [kwɪl] *n.* long feather (formerly used as a pen).

quilt [kwɪlt] *n.* padded cover for a bed. **quilted** *adj.* made with a pad sewn between two layers of cloth.

quince [kwɪns] *n.* hard fruit used for making jelly; tree producing this fruit.

quinine ['kwɪniːn] *n.* drug made from the bark of a tropical tree. used to treat malaria.

quinquennial [kwɪn'kwenɪəl] *adj.* happening every five years.

quins [kwɪnz] *n. pl. inf.* quintuplets.

quinsy ['kwɪnzɪ] *n.* infection of the tonsils.

quintessence [kwɪn'tesns] *n.* essential part of (sth); perfect example. **quintessential** [kwɪntɪ'senʃl] *adj.* which is a perfect example.

quinte(te) [kwɪn'tet] *n.* (a) group of five musicians playing together. (b) piece of music for five musicians.

quintuple ['kwɪntʊpl] *v.* to multiply five times. **quintuplets** *n. pl.* five babies born at the same birth.

quip 1 ['kwɪp] *n.* joke/clever remark. **quip 2** *v.* (quipped) to make a joke/a clever remark.

quire ['kwaɪə] *n.* 24 sheets of paper.

quirk [kwaːk] *n.* oddity/strange event.

quisling ['kwɪzlɪŋ] *n.* person who betrays his country by helping the enemy who is occupying it.

quit [kwɪt] *v.* (quit/quitted) (a) *inf.* to leave (a job/house. etc.) (b) *Am. inf.* to stop. **quits** *adj.* to be q. = to be equal. **quittance** *n.* (formal) receipt. **quitter** *n. inf.* person who gives up easily.

quite [kwaɪt] *adv.* (a) completely. (b) fairly/relatively; q. a few = several.

quiver 1 ['kwɪvə] *n.* (a) tremor/slight shake. (b) holder for arrows. **quiver 2** *v.* to tremble.

quixotic [kwɪk'sɒtɪk] *adj.* strange/impractical (person). **quixotically** *adv.* in a quixotic way.

quiz 1 [kwɪz] *n.* (*pl.*quizzes) series of questions; TV/radio programme where people are asked questions. **quiz 2** *v.* (quizzed) to ask (s.o.) questions. **quizmaster** *n.* person who asks the questions in a TV/radio quiz. **quizzical** ['kwɪzɪkl] *adj.* amused.

quod [kwɒd] *n. Sl.* prison.

quoin [kɔɪn] *n.* block of stone making a corner of a building.

quoit [kwɔɪt] *n.* large ring used in a game to throw over pegs.

quorum ['kwɔːrəm] *n.* number of people who have to be present to make a vote valid. **quorate** *adj.* with a quorum present.

quota ['kɛəʊtə] n. fixed amount of goods which can be supplied/share; fixed number.

quote 1 [kɛəʊt] n. (a) passage quoted; quotation. (b) estimate. (c) inf. quotes = inverted commas (" "). **quote 2** v. (a) to repeat a number (as a reference): to repeat a text of an author: can I q. you? = can I repeat what you have said? (b) to indicate the beginning of a quotation (when speaking). (c) to give an estimate for work to be done. **quotable** adj. which can be quoted; suitable to be quotable. **quotation** [kwəʊ'teɪʃn] n. (a) passage quoted. (b) estimate. (c) q. marks = inverted commas (" "). **quoth** [kwəʊθ] v. (old) said.

quotient ['kwəʊʃnt] n. result when one number is divided by another.

q.v. [kju:'vi:] abbreviation for quod vide: meaning which see.

qwerty ['kwɜːtɪ] n. normal English keyboard for a typewriter or computer.

Rr

R [ɑː] the three Rs = basic subjects in primary school (reading. writing. arithmetic).

Ra symbol for radium.

rabbi ['ræbaɪ] n. Jewish priest. **rabbinical** [rə'bɪnɪkl] adj. referring to a rabbi.

rabbit 1 ['ræbɪt] n. common wild grey animal with long ears and short white tail which lives in burrows. **rabbit 2** v. inf. (also rabbit on) to talk at great length (about).

rabble ['ræbl] n. crowd/unruly mass of people.

rabid ['ræbɪd] adj. (a) suffering from rabies. (b) wild/fanatic. **rabidity** [rə'bɪdɪtɪ] n. being rabid. **rabies** ['reɪbiːz] n. hydrophobia.

raccoon [rəku:n] n. type of small North American flesh-eating wild animal.

race 1 [reɪs] n. (a) competition to see who is the fastest; to run a r. (b) rush of water in a narrow channel. (c) group of human beings with similar physical characteristics; r. relations = relations between different racial groups in the same country. (d) species/breed of plant/ animal, etc. **race 2** v. (a) to run/to drive, etc., to see who is the fastest. (b) to go very fast. **racecourse** n. grassy track where horse races are run.

racehorse n. horse specially bred and trained to run in races. **racer** n. (a) person who is running in a race. (b) special bicycle/car for racing. **racetrack** n. grassy track where horse races are run. **racial** ['reɪʃl] adj. referring to race; r. discrimination/prejudice = discrimination/prejudice against s.o. because of race. **racialism** n. racism. **racialist** adj. & n. racist. **racially** adv. in a racial way. **racing** n. competitions to see who is fastest.

racism n. prejudice against a group of people because of their race. **racist** adj. & n. (person) who treats s.o. differently because of race. **racy** adj. (-ier, -iest) vigorous (style of writing).

raceme [rə'siːm] n. flowers growing along a stem.

rack 1 [ræk] n. (a) frame to hold things (such as letters/pieces of toast); roof r. = grid attached to the roof or a car for carrying luggage. (b) to go to r. and ruin = to become dilapidated. (c) r. of lamb = joint of roast lamb. formed of a series of chops. **rack 2** v. (a) to r. your brains = to think very hard. (b) to cause pain (to). (c) to draw (wine, beer) off the dregs.

rack and pinion n. toothed wheel which connects with a toothed bar to drive a machine (esp. a mountain railway) forward. **rack railway** n. railway with engines driven by a toothed wheel connecting with a central toothed rail. **rack rent** n. (a) yearly rent. (b) very high rent.

racket ['rækɪt] n. (a) instrument made of a light frame with tight strings across it. used for hitting the ball in tennis. squash and badminton. (b) inf. loud noise. (c) inf. illegal profit-making deal. **racketeer** [rækɪ'tɪə] n. swindler/ gangster. **racketeering** n. crime of running a racket. **rackety** adj. (car) which makes a lot of noise.

raconteur [rækɒn'tɜː] n. person who is good at telling stories.

racquet ['rækɪt] n. (sports) racket.

radar ['reɪdɑː] n. system by which you can detect object and judge their position by sending radio signals to them which are reflected back as dots on a small screen.

radiate ['reɪdɪeɪt] v. to send out/to give off (rays/heat); to spread out (from a central point).

radial adj. which spreads out from central point; (tyre) with grooves which give a better grip of the road surface.

radiance n. brightness. **radiant** adj. bright (smile); (heat) which radiates. **radiantly** adv. in a radiant way. **radiation** [reɪdɪ'eɪʃn] n. sending out/giving off (rays, heat). **radiator** ['reɪdɪeɪtə] n. (a) water-filled metal panel for heating. (b) water-filled metal panel for cooling a car engine.

radical 1 ['rædɪkl] adj. thorough/complete; basic (difference); r. party = a party which believes in the necessity of making great changes in the system of running a country. **radical 2** n. member of a radical party. **radically** adv. in a radical way.

radicle ['rædɪkl] n. small root (on a pea or bean).

radio 1 ['reɪdɪəʊ] n. (pl.-os) system for sending out/receiving messages using atmospheric waves apparatus which sends out/receives messages using atmospheric waves. **radio 2** v. to send (a message) using a radio. **radioactive** [reɪdɪəʊ'æktɪv] adj. (substance) which give off harmful radiation through the breaking up of its atoms. **radioactivity** [reɪdɪəʊæk'tɪvɪtɪ] n. giving off of harmful radiation due to the breaking up of atoms. **radiocarbon** n. radioactive from of carbon; r. dating = calculating the age of sth. by measuring the amount of radiocarbon that has decayed.

radiogram n. (old) piece of furniture containing a radio and a record-player. **radiographer** [reɪd'ɒgrəfə] n. person who takes X-ray photographs. **radiography** n. making X-ray photographs. **radioisotope** n. radioactive isotope. used in radiation treatment. **radiologist** n. person who studies X-rays. **radiology** [reɪdɪ'ɒlədʒɪ] n. science of X-rays and their use in medicine. **radiotelephone** n. long-distance telephone (from a ship) which uses radio. **radiotherapy** n. use of X-rays to treat disease.

radish ['rædɪʃ] n. small red root vegetable, eaten raw.

radium ['reɪdɪəm] n. (element; Ra) radioactive metal used in treating cancer.

radius ['reɪdɪəs] n. (pl.radii['reɪdɪaɪ]) (a) distance from the centre of a circle to the circumference. (b) one of the two bones in the lower part of the arm.

radon ['reɪdɒn] n. (element: Rn) natural radioactive gas occurring in certain types of soil and construction materials.

raffia ['ræfɪə] n. (no pl.) strips from a palm leaf used to make baskets, etc.

raffish ['ræfɪʃ] adj. vulgar and showy; rather disreputable. **raffishness** n. being raffish.

raffle 1 ['ræfl] n. lottery where you buy a numbered ticket in the hope of winning a prize. **raffle 2** v. to offer (a prize) for a lottery.

raft [rɑːft] n. flat boat made of pieces of wood/logs tied together.

rafter ['rɑːftə] n. sloping beam which holds up a roof.

rag 1 [ræg] n. (a) piece of torn cloth; dressed in rags = wearing old, torn clothes; inf. the r. trade = dressmaking trade. (b) inf. newspaper. (c) piece of ragtime music. **rag 2** v. (ragged[rægd]) to play jokes on (s.o.). **ragbag** n. collection of mismatched items. **rag-day** n. day when students dress up to collect money for charity. **ragamuffin** n. dirty boy wearing ragged clothes. **rag doll** n. doll made of bits of cloth. **ragged** ['rægɪd] adj. (a) torn; uneven (edge) (b) (person) wearing rags. **rag rug** n. rug made of strips of torn cloth sewn together. **ragtime** n. music written with a strongly syncopated rhythm.

rage 1 [reɪdʒ] n. violent anger; inf. all the r. = very fashionable. **rage 2** v. to be violently angry; to be violent.

raglan ['ræglən] n. style of coat where the sleeves continue straight to the collar. with no seam on the shoulder.

ragout ['ræguː] n. meat and vegetable stew.

raid 1 [reɪd] n. sudden attack. **raid 2** v. to make a sudden attack on/a sudden visit to. **raider** n. person who takes part in a raid.

rail 1 [reɪl] *n.* (a) bar of wood/metal (in a fence, etc.). (b) rails = metal bars along which trains run; live r. = rail which conducts electricity for electric trains. (c) railway; by r. = on a train (d) small bird which lives near water. **rail 2** *v.* to r. against = to speak violently against. **railhead** *n.* end of a railway line. **railings** *n. pl.*fence made of bars of metal. **raillery** *n.* making fun of s.o. **railroad 1** *n. Am.* railway. **railroad 2** *v. inf.* to force (sth) hurriedly. **railway** *n.* track with two metal rails along which trains run; train system of a country. **railwayman** *n.* (*pl.*-men) man who works on the railways.

raiment ['reɪmənt] *n.* (old) clothing.

rain 1 [reɪn] *n.* water falling from clouds in drops. **rain 2** *v.* to fall like rain. **rainbow** *n.* coloured arch which appears in the sky when the sun's light falls on rain. **rain check** *n. Am.* agreement to have/to do sth later; I'll take a rain check on that = I'll not accept your offer now, but I will take it up again later. **raincoat** *n.* waterproof coat. **raindrop** *n.* drop of rain. **rainfall** *n.* amount of rain which falls in a certain place over a certain period. **rain forest** *n.* thick, lush tropical jungle where it rains frequently. **rainwater** *n.* water which has fallen as rain, and has been collected. **rainy** *adj.* (-ier, -iest) with a lot of rain.

raise 1 [reɪz] *n. Am.* increase in salary. **raise 2** *v.* (a) to lift; to make (sth) higher. (b) to bring up (a subject) for discussion. (c) to rear (animals/a family) (d) to collect.

raisin ['reɪzn] *n.* dried grape.

raison d'être [reɪzɒn'detr] *n.* reason for the existence or sth.

raj [rɑːdʒ] *n* the r. = British rule in India. **rajah** ['rɑːdʒə] *n.* Indian ruler.

rake 1 [reɪk] *n.* (a) tool with a long handle and bent metal teeth. used for smoothing earth/for gathering fallen leaves etc. (b) immoral man. (c) angle of slope. **rake 2** *v.* (a) to smooth/to gather using a rake. (b) to slope. **rake-off** *n. inf.* illegal payment paid as a commission. **rake up** *v.* to start talking again about (sth which had been forgotten). **rakish** *adj.* (that) worn at a slant/tilted sideways.

rally 1 ['rælɪ] *n.* (a) gathering of members of a group/association/political party. (b) car competition where cars have to cross difficult country in a certain time. (c) return to strength (of. s.o. who is ill). (d) long series of shots in tennis. **rally 2** *v.* (a) to gather together. (b) to recover (temporarily) from an illness/a setback.

ram 1 [ræm] *n.* (a) male sheep. (b) heavy machine for pressing down hard. **ram 2** *v.* (rammed) (a) to batter sth down hard. (b) to hit (another ship/car, etc.) hard.

RAM [ræm] *n.* random access memory, memory in a computer which allows access to data.

Ramadan [ræmə'dæn] *n.* 9th month of the year, when Muslims fast.

ramble 1 ['ræmbl] *n.* walk for pleasure in the country. **ramble 2** *v.* (a) to go for a walk. (b) to talk on and on in a confused way. **rambler** *n.* (a) person who goes for walks in the country. (b) type of rose which climbs. **rambling** *adj.* (a) confused (speech). (b) (house) which is full of rooms and corridors.

rambutan [ræmbuː'tæn] *n.* small reddish fruit found in S.E. Asia.

ramekin ['ræməkɪn] *n.* small dish for baking food in an oven; food cooked in this way.

ramification [ræmɪfɪ'keɪʃn] *n.* part of a large complicated system.

ramp [ræmp] *n.* (a) slightly sloping surface joining two different levels; slight hump in a road surface. (b) *inf.* swindle.

rampage 1 [ræm'peɪdʒ] *n.* to go on the r. = to go about breaking things/creating disorder. **rampage 2** *v.* to r. about = to create disorder.

rampant ['ræmpənt] *adj.* (crime) which is widespread and uncontrollable. **rampart** ['ræmpɑːt] *n.* defensive wall.

ramrod ['ræmrɒd] *n.* to stand stiff as a r. = to stand very straight.

ramshackle ['ræmʃækl] *adj.* dilapidated/falling to pieces.

ran [ræn *v.* see run.

ranch [rɑːntʃ] *n.* (in America) farm where horses or cattle are reared. **rancher** *n.* person who owns/runs a ranch.

rancid ['rænsɪd] *adj.* bad/stale (butter). **rancidity** *n.* being rancid.

rancour *Am.* **rancor** ['ræŋkə] *n.* bitterness/dislike. **rancorous** *adj.* bitter/hateful.

rand [rɒnt] *n.* money used in South Africa.

random ['rændəm] *adj. & n.* done aimlessly/without any planning; at r. = aimlessly/with no selection; r. sample = sample for testing taken without any selection. **randomness** *n.* being random.

randy ['rændɪ] *adj.* (-ier, -iest) eager to have sexual intercourse. **randiness** *n.* being randy.

rang [ræŋ] *v.* see ring.

range 1 [reɪndʒ] *n.* (a) series (of buildings/mountains) in line. (b) large open pasture; free-range hens = chickens which are allowed to run about in fields. (c) choices/series (of colours, etc.). (d) distance which a shell/bullet can reach; distance which an aircraft can fly without refuelling; distance for which you can see/hear. (e) old-fashioned kitchen stove which burns wood or coal. **range 2** *v.* to spread/to vary.

rangefinder *n.* device (on a gun/camera) for calculating the distance of an object. **ranger** *n.* person who looks after a forest or park. **rangy** *adj.* with long legs.

rank 1 [ræŋk] *n.* (a) row of soldiers. (b) other ranks = ordinary soldiers; be rose from the ranks = from being an ordinary soldier he became an officer; the r. and file = ordinary people. (c) position in society/in the army. (d) taxi r. = place where taxis wait in line. **rank 2** *v.* to classify/to be classified in order of importance. **rank 3** *adj.* (-er, -est) (a) plants) which grow luxuriantly. (b) complete/total. (c) with an unpleasant smell. **rankness** *n.* being rank.

rankle ['ræŋkl] *v.* to cause bitterness.

ransack ['rænsæk] *v.* to search/to turn over (a room) to find sth.

ransom 1 ['rænsəm] *n.* payment asked for before a hostage is set free; to hold s.o. to r. = to demand payment before s.o. is set free. **ransom 2** *v.* to pay a ransom for (s.o.).

rant [rænt] *v.* to declaim/to shout violently.

rap 1 [ræp] *n.* (a) tap/sharp blow; *inf.* to

take the r. = to accept responsibility. (b) form of West Indian music where the singer improvizes. **rap 2** *v.* (rapped) (a) to tap/to give a sharp blow. (b) sing rap music.

rapacious [rə'peɪʃəs] *adj.* greedy. **rapacity** [rə'pæsɪtɪ] *n.* greed.

rape1 [reɪp] *n.* (a) act of having sexual intercourse with s.o. against their will. (b) vegetable with yellow flowers. whose seeds are used to produce oil. **rape2** *v.* to have sexual intercourse with (s.o.) against their will. **rapist** *n.* person who rapes s.o.

rapid 1 ['ræpɪd] *adj.* fast. **rapid 2** *n. pl.*rapids = place where a river runs fast over boulders and down a steep slope. **rapidity** [rə'pɪdɪtɪ] *n.* speed. **rapidly** *adv.* fast.

rapier ['reɪpɪə] *n.* long. thin sword for thrusting.

rapport [ræ'pɔː] *n.* understanding/close link.

rapprochement [ræ'prɒʃmɒŋ] *n.* becoming closer (of former enemies).

rapt [ræpt] *adj.* with r. attention = very attentively. **raptly** *adv.* attentively.

raptor ['ræptʃə] *n.* bird of prey.

rapture ['ræptʃə] *n.* delight to go into raptures over = to be delighted by. **rapturous** *adj.* excited and delighted (applause, etc.). **rapturously** *adv.* in a rapturous way.

rare [reə] *adj.* (-er, -est) (a) very unusual. (b) (meat) which is very lightly cooked. **rarely** *adv.* hardly ever. **rarefied** ['reəɪfaɪd] *adj.* (air) which is not very dense. **rarity** *n.* (a) (also rareness) uncommonness. (b) rare object. **rarebit** ['reəbɪt] *n.* Welsh r. = cooked cheese on toast.

raring [reərɪŋ] *adj. inf.* r. to go = eager to go.

rascal ['rɑːskəl] *n.* naughty person/child. **rascally** *adj.* wicked.

rash 1 [ræʃ] *n.* red area/red spots on the skin; heat r. = spots caused by hot weather. **rash 2** *adj.* (-er, -est) not cautious/thoughtless; done without thinking. **rashly** *adv.* without thinking. **rashness** *n.* being rash/acting rashly. **rasher** ['ræʃə] *n.* slice (of bacon).

rasp 1 [rɑːsp] *n.* rough metal file used for smoothing surfaces. **rasp 2** *v.* to make a grating noise.

raspberry ['rɑːzbrɪ] *n.* (a) common red soft fruit growing on tall canes; bush which bears this fruit. (b) *inf.* rude noise made with the mouth to show derision.

Rastafarian [ræstə'feərɪən] *adj. & n.* (member) of a West Indian sect.

rat 1 [ræt] *n.* (a) common grey rodent. living in cellars/sewers/on ships. (b) sly unpleasant person. **rat 2** *v.* (ratted) (a) to hunt rats. (b) *inf.* (on) to go back on a promise/to betray (s.o.). **rat race** *n.* competition for success in the business world. **ratty** *adj. inf.* annoyed/ shorttempered.

ratafia [rætə'fiə] *n.* biscuit/drink flavoured with almonds.

ratchet (wheel) ['rætʃət('wiːl)] *n.* wheel with teeth and a catch to prevent it form turning backwards.

rate 1 [reɪt] *n.* (a) number expressed as a proportion of one quantity to another; birth r./death r. = number of births/ deaths per 1000 of population. (b) frequency at which sth is done/level of cost (as compared to a previous level). (c) speed. (d) first r. = very good; second r. = rather bad. (e) at any r. = in any case. (f) business rates = local taxes on business. **rate 2** *v.* to value. **rateable** *adj.* r. value = value of a house as calculated for local taxes. **ratepayer** *n.* company/person who pays local business taxes. **rating** *n.* (a) valuing. (b) TV ratings = comparative estimates of audiences for competing TV shows. (c) naval r. = ordinary seaman.

rather ['rɑːðə] *adv.* (a) relatively/quite. (b) (used with would to show preference) I'd r. stay = I would prefer to stay; I'd r. not = I would prefer not to. (c) r. than = in preference to.

ratify ['rætɪfaɪ] *v.* to approve (a treaty) officially. **ratification** [rætɪfɪ'keɪʃn] *n.* official approval.

ratio ['reɪʃɪəʊ] *n.* (*pl.*-os) proportion.

ratiocinate [rætɪ'ɒsɪneɪt] *v.* to think coherently.

ration 1 ['ræʃn] *n.* amount of food/ supplies allowed. **ration 2** *v.* to allow only a certain amount of food/supplies. **rationing** *n.* allowing only a certain amount of food/supplies.

rational ['ræʃənl] *adj.* reasonable/ based on reason. **rationale** [ræʃə'nɑːl] *n.* set of reasons which are the basis of a system/of a series of actions. **rationality** *n.* being rational. **rationalization** [ræʃnəlaɪ'zeɪʃn] *n.* act of rationalizing. **rationalize** [ræʃnə'laɪz] *v.* (a) to find a reason for *usu.* unreasonable actions. (b) to streamline/to modernize (old-fashioned production methods). **rationally** *adv.* based on reason.

rattan [rə'tæn] *n.* tropical cane. used to make furniture.

rattle 1 ['rætl] *n.* (a) (wooden) instrument which makes a loud repeated noise. (b) repeated clattering noise.

rattle 2 *v.* (a) to make a repeated clattering noise. (b) *inf.* to worry/to upset. **rattle off** *v. inf.* to speak rapidly. **rattlesnake** *n.* American poisonous snake which makes a rattling noise with its tail. **rattling** *adj. inf.* very (good).

raucous ['rɔːkəs] *adj.* rough/hoarse (cough/cry). **raucously** *adv.* in a raucous way. **raucousness** *n.* being raucous.

raunchy ['rɔːntʃɪ] *adj.* (-ier, -iest) *Am.* coarse/openly obscene.

ravage ['rævɪdʒ] *v.* to devastate/to ruin (a town, etc.). **ravages** *n. pl.*damage.

rave [reɪv] *v.* (a) to be wildly mad. (b) *inf.* to be fanatical (about sth). **raving** *adj.* wild (madman). **ravings** *n. pl.*wild mad talk.

ravel ['rævl] *v.* (a) to disentangle (sth which is twisted). (b) to tangle/to make sth knotted and twisted.

raven ['reɪvn] *n.* large black bird of the crow family.

ravenous ['rævənəs] *adj.* very hungry. **ravenously** *adv.* extremely (hungry).

ravine [rə'viːn] *n.* deep narrow valley.

ravioli [rævɪ'əʊlɪ] *n.* Italian dish of small pasta squares filled with a meat stuffing.

ravish ['rævɪʃ] *v.* (a) to steal by force. (b) to enchant. **ravishing** *adj.* very beautiful/very delightful.

raw 1 [rɔː] *adj.* (-er, -est) (a) uncooked. (b) basic/untreated (sewage/skin); untrained (recruits). (c) cold and damp (weather). (d) r. deal = bad/unfair treatment. (e) exposed/sensitive; to touch a r. nerve = to touch a sensitive spot.

raw 2 *n.* (a) sensitive spot. (b) wild natural state. **rawhide** *n.* leather which has not been tanned. **rawness** *n.* being raw.

ray [reɪ] n. (a) beam of light/heat; small quantity (of hope); X-rays = rays which go through the soft tissue, and allow the bones and organs in the body to be photographed. (b) large, flat sea fish..

rayon ['reɪɒn] n. trade name for artificial silk.

raze [reɪz] v. to r. to the ground = to demolish completely.

razor ['reɪzə] n. instrument with a very sharp blade for removing hair. **razorbill** n. type of black and white sea bird. razor-shape, extremely sharp (blade/mind, etc.).

razzle ['ræzl] n. inf. to go on the r. = to have a good time. **razzmatazz** ['ræzmətæz] n. inf. energetic publicizing (in an election campaign).

Rd short for road.

re prep concerning.

re- prefix meaning again.

reach 1 [riːtʃ] n. (pl.-es) (a) distance you can travel easily; distance you can stretch out your hand. (b) straight section of a river. **reach 2** v. (a) to stretch out. (b) to arrive at. (c) to come to (an agreement). **reachable** adj. which can be reached.

react [rɪ'ækt] v. to do/to say sth in reply to words or an action; to r. against = show opposition to; acids r. with metals = change their chemical composition. **reaction** [rɪ'ækʃn] n. act of reacting; thing done/said in reply; what was his r.? = what did he say/do? **reactionary** adj. & n. (person) who is opposed to any political change/to any reforms. **reactivate** v. to make (sth) work again. **reactive** adj. which to active chemically. **reactor** n. device for producing atomic energy.

read 1 [riːd] n. inf. looking at and understanding written or printed words.

read 2 v. (read, has read[red]) (a) to look at and understand written words; to speak aloud words which are written; to r. between the lines = to understand a hidden meaning which is not immediately apparent. (b) to study (a subject) at university. (c) to interpret; to r. s.o.'s palm = to interpret the lines on a hand as indications of what will happen in the future. **readability** n. being readable. **readable** adj. (a) legible/which can be read. (b) (story) which is a pleasure to read. **reader** n. (a) person who reads. (b) senior teacher at a university. (c) school book to help children to read. (d) apparatus for reading microfilms. (e) person who reads manuscripts/proofs to check them.

reading n. (a) act of looking at and understanding printed words. (b) interpretation. (c) one of the stages of the discussion of a Bill in Parliament. **reading room** n. room (in a library) specially for reading.

readdress [riːə'dres] v. to put another address on (an envelope/parcel).

readjust [riːə'dʒʌst] v. to adjust again; to put back to the original position. **readjustment** n. act of readjusting.

ready ['redɪ] adj. (-ier, -iest) (a) prepared (to). (b) fit to be used. (c) quick/rapid. he has a r. reply to anything = he always has an answer. (d) r. cash = cash which is immediately available. **readily** adv. willingly. **readiness** n. willingness to hold sth in r. = to keep sth ready for use. **ready-cooked** adj. (food) which has been cooked in advance. **readymade, ready-to-wear** adj. (clothes) which are made by mass production. to fit any person of a certain size.

reagent [rɪ'eɪdʒnt] n. substance used in a chemical reaction.

real [rɪəl] adj. true/not imitation; (sth) which exists. (b) r. estate = land or buildings which are bought or sold. (c) r. tennis = medieval form of tennis played with a hard ball in a court with high walls. **realism** n. (a) facing facts/accepting life as it is. (b) showing things (in writing/painting) as they really are. **realist** n. (a) artist/writer who shows things as they really are. (b) person who accepts life as it really is and doesn't idealize it. **realistic** ['rɪə'lɪstɪk] adj. (a) which looks as if it is real. (b) accepting life as it really is. **realistically** adv. in a realistic way. **reality** [rɪ'ælɪtɪ] n. what is real/not imaginary. **really** adv. truly.

real time n. action of a computer which takes place at the same time as the problem it is solving.

realign [rɪə'laɪn] v. to set in a new direction; to set in a new group. **realignment** n. change in a series of alliances between countries or political parties.

realize ['rɪəlaɪz] v. (a) to come to understand clearly. (b) to sell property for (money). (c) to make real. to make (sth) come true. **realization** n. (a) gradual understanding. (b) conversion of property into money. (c) carrying out of a plan.

realm [relm] n. (a) kingdom. (b) general area.

Realpolitik [reɪ'ælpɒlɪtɪk] n. politics based on real situations. not on moral principles.

realtor ['rɪəlt] n. Am. estate agent.
realty n. Am. real estate.

ream [ri:m] n. (a) 480 sheets of paper. (b) reams = very large quantity (of paper).

reanimate [rɪ'nɪmeɪt] v. to bring back to life.

reap [ri:p] v. to harvest (corn, etc.). **reaper** n. person/machine which harvests corn.

reappear [rɪə'pɪə] v. to appear again. **reappearance** n. second appearance.

reappraisal [rɪə'preɪzl] n. fresh examination of sth to see if your former opinion was correct.

rear 1 ['rɪə] n. back part; to bring up the r. = march behind. **rear 2** adj. at the back; r. view mirror = mirror in a car so that you can see what is behind you without turning round. **rear 3** v. (a) to breed/to raise (animals). (b) to lift (part of the body). (c) (of horse, etc) to stand up on its back legs. **rear-admiral** n. high-ranking naval officer (beneath vice-admiral). **rearguard** n. soldiers defending the back part of an army.
rearmost adj. furthest at the back.

rearm [rɪ'ɑːm] v. to arm/to stock up with weapons again. **rearmament** n. arming again.

rearrange [rɪə'reɪnʒ] v. to arrange again. **rearrangement** n. new arrangement.

reason 1 ['ri:zn] n. (a) cause/explanation for why sth happens. (b) power of thought; commonsense.
reason 2 v. (a) to think/to plan carefully and logically. (b) to r. with s.o. = to try to calm s.o./to make s.o. change his mind. **reasonable** adj. (a) not extravagant/moderate. (b) sensible.
reasonably adv. in a reasonable way.
reasoning n. putting your mind to

use; I don't follow your r. = I can't see how you reached this conclusion.

reassemble [rɪə'sembl] v. (a) to put back together. (b) to gather together against.

reassure [rɪə'ʃʊə] v. to calm (s.o.) /to make (s.o.) less afraid/less doubtful.
reassurance n. act of reassuring.

rebate ['ri:beɪt] n. (a) reduction in the amount of money which should be paid; money which is returned to the person who paid it. (b) groove cut into a piece of wood to hold the tongue on another piece.

rebel 1 ['rebəl] n. person who fights against the government/against the person in charge. **rebel 2** [rɪ'bel] v. (rebelled) to fight (against s.o./sth).
rebellion [rɪ'beljən] n. revolt/fight against the government/against authority.
rebellious [rɪ'beliəs] adj. fighting against the government/against authority.

rebore 1 ['ri:bɔː] n. cleaning the cylinders on a car. **rebore 2** v. vtr. to clean the cylinders of a car.

rebound 1 ['ri:baʊnd] n. bouncing back; on the r. = (i) as it bounces back; (ii) while still shocked by a disappointment. **rebound 2** [rɪ'baʊnd] v. to bounce back.

rebuff 1 [rɪ'bʌf] n. refusal. **rebuff 2** v. to refuse.

rebuild [ri:bɪld] v. (rebuilt) to build again.

rebuke 1 [rɪ'bju:k] n. (formal) blame/reproof. **rebuke 2** v. to blame/to scold.

rebus ['ri:bu:s] n. trick. where pictures are used to represent words.

rebut [rɪ'bʌt] v. (rebutted) to reject/to disprove (an argument). **rebuttal** n. act of rebutting.

recalcitrant [rɪ'kæsɪtrənt] adj. (formal) difficult/disobedient. **recalcitrance** n. being recalcitrant.

recall 1 [rɪ'kɔːl] n. calling back; gone beyond r. = gone and cannot be called back. **recall 2** v. (a) to call/to summon back (an ambassador/defective cars); to ask Parliament to meet again. (b) to remember.

recant [rɪ'kænt] v. to admit that your former beliefs were wrong. **recantation** [rɪkæn'teɪʃn] n. act of recanting.

recapitulate [ri:kə'pɪtjʊleɪt] v. inf. recap.['ri:kæp] to repeat the main points of an argument. **recapitulation** [ri:kəpɪtjʊ'leɪʃn] n. inf. recap. repeating the main points.

recapture 1 [ri:'kæptʃə] n. act of recapturing. **recapture 2** v. to catch again (an escaped prisoner); to take again (a seat in an election).

recast [ri:'kɑ:st] v. to make again; to write (a statement) again in a different way.

recce ['rekɪ] n. inf. reconnaissance trip.

recd abbrev. for received.

recede [rɪ'si:d] v. to go away/to retreat. **receding** adj. (forehead) which slopes backwards; (hair) which begins to disappear from the front of the forehead.

receipt [rə'si:t] n. (a) receiving; on r. of = when you receive. (b) paper showing that you have paid/that you have received sth. (c) receipts = money taken in a business.

receive [rə'si:v] v. (a) to get sth which has been sent; inf. he was on the receiving end of a lot of criticism = he had to suffer a lot of criticism. (b) to greet/to welcome; to entertain. **receiver** n. (a) person who accepts stolen goods. (b) official put in charge of a bankrupt company. (c) part of a telephone which you can lift and listen to. (d) part of a radio which receives broadcast programmes.

recent ['ri:sənt] adj. which took place not very long ago. **recently** adv. not long ago/only a short time ago.

receptacle [rɪ'septəkl] n. container.

reception [rɪ'sepʃn] n. (a) welcome. (b) (in a hotel) desk where you check in. (c) big party held to welcome special guests. (d) quality of sound of a radio/TV broadcast. **receptionist** n. person in a hotel/doctor's office, etc.. who meets visitors and answers the telephone.

receptive adj. eager to take in new ideas. **receptiveness, receptivity** [risep'tiviti] n. being receptive.

receptor n. cell at the end of a nerve. which receives impulses.

recess [rɪ'ses] n. (pl.-es) (a) alcove/part of the wall of room which is set back. (b) official holiday of the law courts or parliament. (c) Am. recreation period at school. (d) inaccessible part. **recessed** adj. set back. **recessive** adj. (of genes) not likely to predominate.

recession [rɪ'seʃn] n. collapse of world economy/of trade.

recherché [re'ʃeəʃeɪ] adj. chosen with care.

recidivist [rə'sɪdɪvɪst] n. hardened criminal/person who commits a crime repeatedly.

recipe ['resɪpɪ] n. (a) instructions for cooking. (b) effective way to do sth. It's a r. for disaster = it's bound to lead to disaster.

recipient [rɪ'sɪpɪənt] n. person who receives.

reciprocate [rɪ'sɪprəkeɪt] v. to do the same thing in return. **reciprocal 1** adj. mutual; r. trade agreement = agreement on two-way trade between countries.

reciprocal 2 n. (in maths) quantity produced when 1 is divided by a figure. **reciprocally** adv. in a reciprocal way. **reciprocity** n. principle that if one country buys goods from another, the second country will reciprocate.

recite [rɪ'saɪt] v. to speak (verse, etc.) aloud in public. **recital** n. reciting in public sth which has been written. (b) performance of music by one or a few musicians. **recitation** [resɪ'teɪʃn] n. thing recited from memory; recital.

recitative [resɪtə'ti:v] n. (in an opera) speech sung in a rhythmic way.

reckless ['rekləs] adj. foolish/rash/not thinking. **recklessly** adv. in a reckless way. **recklessness** n. foolishness/rashness.

reckon ['rekn] v. (a) calculate/to estimate; (b) to think. (c) to r. on = to count on/to depend on. (d) to r. with = to have to deal with. **reckoner** n. book with tables to help calculations.

reckoning n. calculation; day of r. = time when you have to pay for your mistakes.

reclaim [rɪ'kleɪm] v. to make (useless land) fit for use; to take back (land) from the sea. **reclamation** [reklə'meɪʃn] n. reclaiming (of land).

recline [rɪ'klaɪn] v. to lie back.

recluse [rɪ'klu:s] n. person who lives alone and hidden away.

recognize ['rekəgnaɪz] v. (a) to know (s.o./sth) because you have seen him/it before. (b) to admit (a mistake.) (c) to admit (the value of sth). (d) to r. a government = to accept that a new government is the legal authority

in a country; to r. a union = to agree that a union can officially represent workers in a factory. **recognition** [rekəg'nɪʃn] n. recognizing; he's changed beyond all r. = so much that you can't recognize him.
recognizable [rekəg'naɪzəbl] adj. which can be recognized. **recognizance** [re'kɒgnɪzəns] n. money given as a pledge to a court that s.o. will obey the conditions laid down by the court.
recoil 1 ['riːkɔɪl] n. sudden movement backwards of a gun when it is fired.
recoil 2 [rɪ'kɔɪl] v. to move backwards suddenly; to shrink back from sth unpleasant.
recollect [rekə'lekt] v. to remember.
recollection [rekə'lekʃn] n. remembering.
recommend [rekə'mend] v. (a) to advise s.o. to do sth. (b) to praise (sth/s.o.). **recommendation** [rekəmen'deɪʃn] n. (a) advice. (b) praise; thing which is in your favour.
recompense 1 ['rekəmpens] n. payment for sth done/for the time lost, etc. **recompense 2** v. to pay s.o. for sth done/for time lost, etc.
reconcile ['rekənsaɪl] v. (a) to make two enemies become friendly. (b) to reconcile oneself to = to accept. (c) to make (two accounts/statements) agree.
reconciliation [rekənsɪlɪ'eɪʃn] n. bringing together of two enemies. so that they become friends; making two accounts/statements agree.
recondite [rɪ'kɒndaɪt] adj. (formal) obscure (information). **recondition** [rɪkən'dɪʃn] v. to overhaul thoroughly.
reconnaissance [rɪ'kɒnɪsns] n. survey of land for military information.
reconnoitre, Am. **Reconnoiter** [rekə'nɔɪtə] v. to make a survey to get information/to make a reconnaissance.
reconsider [riːkən'sɪdə] v. to think over again.
reconstitute [rɪ'kɒnstɪtjʊt] v. to form (sth) again as it was before.
reconstruct [riːkən'strʌkt] v. (a) to build again. (b) to work out how (a crime) must have been committed. **reconstruction** n. act of reconstructing; thing reconstructed.
reconvene [riːkən'viːn] v. to meet again.
record 1 ['rekɔːd] n. (a) report of sth which has happened; he is on r. as

saying; she spoke off the r. = in private/ what she said is not to be made public. (b) note/written account. (c) flat plastic disc on which sound is fixed by a recording instrument. (d) description of s.o.'s past career. (e) sporting achievement which is better than any other; at r. speed = very fast. **record 2** v. (a) to report; to make a note; recorded delivery = postal service where you must sign a receipt to show you have received a parcel/a letter, etc. (b) to fix sound on a plastic disc or tape. **record-breaking** adj. which breaks records. **recorder** [rɪ'kɔːdə] n. (a) judge in certain courts. (b) instrument which records. (c) wooden flute held forwards when played.
recording n. (a) act of fixing sounds on tape/on disc. (b) music/speech which has been recorded. **recordist** n. person who records sounds on tape or disc.
record-player n. machine for playing back music/speech, etc. from a record.
recount 1 ['riːkaʊnt] n. counting votes again (when the result is very close).
recount 2 v. (a) to tell (a story). (b) to count again.
recoup [rɪ'kuːp] v. to r. your losses = to get back money which you have lost.
recourse [rɪ'kɔːs] n. to have r. to sth = to use sth in an emergency.
recover [rɪ'kʌvə] v. (a) to get back (sth which has been stolen/lost). (b) (from) to get well again after an illness. (c) (from) to get over (a shock). (d) to put a new cover on (a chair). **recoverable** adj. which can be got back. **recovery** n. (a) getting back (stolen property). (b) getting well again. (c) return to good condition.
recreation [rekrɪ'eɪʃn] n. pleasant occupation for your spare time; r. ground = public sports ground. **recreational** adj. referring to recreation.
recriminate [rɪ'krɪmɪneɪt] v. to accuse (s.o.) who has accused you.
recrimination [rɪkrɪmɪ'nɪʃn] n. accusation made by s.o. who is accused.
recriminatory [rɪ'krɪmɪnətrɪ] adj. (remarks) which accuse s.o.
recrudescence [riːkruː'desns] n. (formal) breaking out again (of a disease).
recruit 1 [rɪ'kruːt] n. new soldier; new member of a club etc. **recruit 2** v. to encourage (s.o.) to join the army/a club

etc. **recruitment** *n.* encouraging people to join the army/a club, etc.

rectal ['rektəl] *adj.* referring to the rectum.

rectangle ['rektæŋgl] *n.* four-sided shape with right angles and two sets of opposite and equal sides. **rectangular** [rek'tæŋjʊlə] *adj.* like a rectangle.

rectify ['rektɪfaɪ] *v.* to correct/to make right. **rectifiable** *adj.* which can be corrected. **rectification** [rektɪfɪ'keɪʃn] *n.* correction.

rectilinear [rektɪ'lɪnɪə] *adj.* with straight lines.

rectitude ['rektɪtjuːd] *n.* (esp. moral) correctness.

recto ['rektəʊ] *n.* right/main side (of a piece of paper page of a book etc).

rector ['rektə] *n.* (a) priest in charge of a parish. (b) official representative of the students at a Scottish university. (c) (in Scotland) head of a school/college/university. **rectory** *n.* house of a rector.

rectum ['rektəm] *n.* lower part of the intestine. leading to the anus.

recumbent [rɪ'kʌmbənt] *adj.* (formal) lying down.

recuperate [rɪ'kjuːpəreɪt] *v.* to recover/to get better after an illness of a loss. **recuperation** [rɪkjuːpə'reɪʃn] *n.* getting better. **recuperative** *adj.* which helps recuperation.

recur [rɪ'kɜː] *v.* (recurred) to happen again. **recurrence** [rɪ'kʌrəns] *n.* reappearance/happening again. **recurrent, recurring** [rɪ'kʌrənt, rɪ'kɜːrɪŋ] *adj.* (a) which happens again. (b) (decimal figure) which is repeated for ever.

recusant ['rekjʊzənt] *adj. & n.* (old) (person) who refused to accept the Anglican Church.

recycle [riː'saɪkl] *v.* to process (waste material) so that it can be used again. **red** [red] *adj. & n.* (redder, reddest) (colour) like blood or fire; *inf.* see r. = get very angry; *inf.* to be in the r. = to be in debt; r. carpet = official welcome; r. tape = official rules which stop you doing sth quickly; r. berring = false track/sth which leads you away from the main problem; *inf.* the Reds = the Communists. **red-blooded** *adj.* strong, vigorous. **redbreast** *n.* robin. **red-brick** *adj.* (British university)

built in the nineteenth century. **Red Crescent** *n.* organization similar to the Red Cross working in Muslim countries. **Red Cross** *n.* international organization which cares for the sick and injured, and also organizes relief work. **red currant** *n.* common red soft fruit growing in small clusters; bush which bears this fruit. **redden** *v.* to turn red/to blush. **reddish** *adj.* rather red. **Red Flag** *n.* flat of the communist party. **red-handed** *adj.* they caught him red-handed = as he was committing a crime. **redhead** *n.* person with red hair. **red-hot** *adj.* (of metal) very hot. **Red Indian** *n.* Indian from North America. **red-letter day** *n.* very special day. **redness** *n.* being red. **redshank** *n.* large sandpiper. **redstart** *n.* small singing bird with red feathers beneath the tail. **redwood** *n.* type of very tall coniferous tree growing on the west coast of North America.

redecorate [riː'dekəreɪt] *v.* to decorate/to paint again.

redeem [rɪ'diːm] *v.* (a) to buy back (sth which you have pledged to borrow money); to pay off (a debt). (b) to compensate. (c) to save from sin. **Redeemer** *n.* Jesus Christ. **redeeming** *adj.* which compensates. **redemption** [rɪ'dempʃn] *n.* (a) payment of a debt. (b) being saved from sin.

redeploy [riːdɪ'plɔɪ] *v.* to move (workers/soldiers) from one place to another. **redeployment** *n.* act of redeploying.

redirect [riːdaɪ'rekt] *v.* to send (a letter) on to another address.

redolent ['redələnt] *adj.* which smells (of sth); which reminds you (of sth). **redolence** *n.* being redolent.

redouble [riː'dʌbl] *v.* to r. your efforts = to try even harder.

redoubt [rɪ'daʊt] *n.* small fort. **redoubtable** [rɪ'daʊtəbl] *adj.* formidable/bold.

redound [rɪ'daʊnd] *v.* (formal) it will r. to your credit = will make you more admired.

redress 1 [rɪ'dres] *n.* compensation done to make up for something wrong. **redress 2** *v.* to correct/to compensate/to repair; to r. the balance = to make things equal again.

reduce [rɪ'djuːs] v. (a) to make smaller/
lower; to r. s.o. to the ranks = to punish
an officer by making him an ordinary
soldier; to r. weight/inf. to r. = get
thinner. (b) to force (s.o.) to do sth
humiliating. **reducible** adj. which can
be reduced. **reduction** [rɪ'dʌkʃn] n.
lowering (of price/speed/standards).

redundant [rɪ'dʌndənt] adj. more than
necessary; to be made r. = to lose your job
because you are not needed any more.
redundancy n. losing a job because
you are no longer needed.

reduplicate [rɪ'djʊplɪkeɪt] v. to repeat
(sth).

re-echo [riːekəʊ] v. to echo again.

reed [riːd] n. (a) marsh plant with tall
stem. (b) part of a wind instrument
which vibrates to make a note.
reediness n. being reedy. **reedy** adj.
(a) high-pitched (voice). (b) (marsh)
which is full of reeds.

reef 1 [riːf] n. (a) ridge of rock in the
sea. (b) r. knot = type of flat knot which
does not come undone easily. **reef 2** v.
to reduce the size of (a sail) by rolling
part of it up. **reefer** n. (a) sailor's short
coat. (b) Sl. marijuana cigarette.

reek 1 [riːk] n. strong smell. **reek 2** v.
to smell strongly (of).

reel 1 [riːl] n. (a) spool for winding
thread/string/film round. (b) vigorous
Scottish dance. **reel 2** v. (a) to wind
round a reel. (b) to r. off = to quote at
length (c) to stagger.

reelect [riːɪ'lekt] v. to elect again.
reelection [riːɪ'lekʃn] n. being
reelected.

reemploy [riːem'plɔɪ] v. to employ
(s.o.) again.

reenter [riː'entə] v. to enter again.
reentry [riː'entrɪ] n. entering again.

ref. [ref] n. inf. (in sports) referee.

refectory [rɪ'fektərɪ] n. eating hall (in a
school, etc.); r. table = long narrow
dining table.

refer to [rɪ'fɜː'tuː] v. (referred) (a) to
mention. (b) to look into sth for
information. (c) to pass (a problem) to
s.o. to decide. (d) to tell (s.o.) to see s.o.
else. **referee 1** n. (a) (in sports) person
who sees that the game is played
according to the rules/who judges
between two sides. (b) person who gives
a report on your character. **referee 2** v.
to act as a referee in a sports match.
reference ['refrəns] n. (a) (to)
mention; with r. to = concerning/about.
(b) direction for further information; r.
book = book (such as dictionary/
encyclopedia) where you can look up
information; r. library = library of
reference books. (c) report on s.o.'s
character, etc. **referral** [rɪ'fɜːrl] n. act of
referring. **referendum** [refə'rendəm] n.
(pl.-da/-dums) vote by all the people of a
country to decide a problem of national
importance.

refill 1 ['riːfɪl] n. container with a fresh
quantity of liquid/ink, etc; another drink.
refill 2 v. to fill again.

refine [rɪ'faɪn] v. to make better/more
pure. **refined** adj. very elegant/polite.
refinement n. (a) elegance. (b)
improvement. **refiner** n. business/
person that refines. **refinery** n. factory
where sth is refined.

refit 1 ['riːfɪt] n. repairs (to a ship). **refit
2** [riː'fɪt] v. to repair (a ship).

reflate [riː'fleɪt] v. to stimulate (an
economy which has previously been
deflated). **reflation** [riː'fleɪʃn] n. action
of stimulating a deflated economy.
reflationary adj. likely to cause
reflation.

reflect [rɪ'flekt] v. (a) to send back
(light/heat/an image). (b) to think back
into the past/to ponder. (c) to r. on = to
be a criticism of. **reflection, reflexion**
[rɪ'flekʃn] n. (a) sending back of light/
heat; reflected image (in a mirror). (b)
thought; on r. = on thinking more about
it. (c) criticism. **reflective** adj.
thoughtful. **reflector** n. apparatus
which reflects.

reflex 1 ['riːfleks] n. (pl.-es) automatic
action/instinctive response. **reflex 2**
adj. (a) which is automatic; r. action =
action done instinctively. (b) which
returns as a reflection; r. camera =
camera where the picture is reflected
from the lens to the viewfinder exactly as
it will appear on the photograph; r. angle
= angle of more than 180°. **reflexive**
[rɪ'fleksɪv] adj. (in grammar) verb or
pronoun which refers back to the
subject.

refloat [riː'fləʊt] v. to float again (a ship
which has gone a ground).

reflux ['riːflʌks] n. flowing back.

reform 1 [rɪ'fɔːm] *n.* improving/ improvement. **reform 2** *v.* (a) to correct/to improve. (b) to become good/ to stop committing crime. **reformation** [refə'meɪʃn] *n.* act of reforming; the Reformation = religious movement in sixteenth century Europe which brought about the creation of the Protestant churches. **reformatory** [rɪ'fɔːmətrɪ] *n.* type of prison school where young criminals are sent in the hope that they will be reformed. **reformer** *n.* person who tries to improve (a system).

refract [rɪ'frækt] *v.* to bend (rays of light, etc.) as they pass through the surface of water. **refraction** [rɪ'frækʃn] *n.* bending of light as it goes from one substance to another (such as into water). **refractive** *adj.* reproducing refraction. **refractor** *n.* object/ substance which refracts. **refractory** [rɪ'fræktərɪ] *adj.* difficult/disobedient.

refrain 1 [rɪ'freɪn] *n.* chorus which is repeated after each section of a song or poem. **refrain 2** *v.* to r. from = not to do sth.

refresh [rɪ'freʃ] *v.* to make fresh again; to make less tired; let me r. your memory = help you to remember sth which you seem to have forgotten. **refresher** *n.* fee paid to a lawyer for appearing again in court a second day; r. course = lessons which bring your knowledge of your job up to date. **refreshing** *adj.* (a) which refreshes. (b) new and invigorating.

refreshment *n.* refreshments = food and drink; r. room = room at a railway station where food and drink are served.

refrigerator [rɪ'frɪdʒəreɪtə] *n.* cooling cupboard for keeping things (esp. food) cold. **refrigerant** *n.* substance used to make other substances very cold. **refrigerated** *adj.* kept cold. **refrigeration** [rɪfrɪdʒə'reɪʃn] *n.* keeping things cold.

refuel [riː'fjʊəl] *v.* (refuelled) to put more fuel into (a ship/plane/car, etc.)

refuge ['refjuːdʒ] *n.* place to hide/to shelter; to take r. = to shelter. **refugee** [refjuː'dʒiː] *n.* person who has been driven out of his own country and needs shelter; political r. = person who has left his country for political reasons.

refund 1 ['riːfʌnd] *n.* repayment of money. **refund 2** [rɪ'fʌnd] *v.* to pay back (money).

refurbish [rɪ'fɜːbɪʃ] *v.* to polish up again.

refuse 1 ['refjuːs] *n.* rubbish. **refuse 2** *v.* (a) to say that you do not accept/that you will not do sth. (b) not to give s.o. (permission). **refusal** [rɪ'fjuːzl] *n.* (a) saying no; to meet with a flat r. = to be refused completely. (b) to give s.o. first r. of sth = to let them have first choice of buying sth.

refute [rɪ'fjuːt] *v.* to prove that (sth) is wrong. **refutation** [refjuː'teɪʃn] *n.* proof that sth is wrong.

regain [riː'geɪn] *v.* to get back. **regal** ['riːgl] *adj.* referring to a king/queen; royal. **regalia** [rɪ'geɪlɪə] *n. pl.* robes/ crown, etc. worn by a king/queen/ mayor. **regally** *adv.* like a king/ queen.

regale [rɪ'geɪl] *v.* to entertain.

regard 1 [rɪ'gɑːd] *n.* (a) concern. (b) esteem. (c) regards = best wishes. **regard 2** *v.* (a) to consider. (b) as regards = concerning. **regarding** *prep.* concerning. **regardless** *adj.* paying no attention to; carry on r. = carry on in spite of everything.

regatta [rɪ'gætə] *n.* series of boat races (for either yachts or rowing boats).

regenerate [rɪ'dʒenəreɪt] *v.* to start up again. **regeneration** [rɪdʒen'reɪʃn] *n.* growing again/starting again.

regent ['riːdʒənt] *n.* person who rules in place of a king or queen. **regency** *n.* period when a regent is ruling.

reggae ['regeɪ] *n.* type of West Indian music.

regicide ['redʒɪsaɪd] *n.* person who kills a king.

régime [reɪ'ʒiːm] *n.* system of government/administration.

regimen ['redʒɪmən] *n.* planned course of action to improve your health.

regiment 1 ['redʒɪmənt] *n.* group of soldiers, usu. commanded by a colonel or lieutenant-colonel. **regiment 2** *v.* to keep (s.o.) under strict discipline. **regimental** [redʒɪ'mentl] *adj.* belonging to a regiment. **regimentals** *n. pl.* military uniform of a certain regiment. **regimentation** [redʒɪmen'teɪʃn] *n.* very strict discipline.

Regina [rɪ'dʒaɪə] *n.* the Queen. i.e. the State in court cases.

region ['riːdʒən] *n.* area; (in Scotland) large administrative area; the London r. = area around London; in the r. of £10,000 = about £10,000. **regional** *adj.* referring to a region.

register 1 ['redʒɪstə] *n.* (a) list (of names). (b) range of notes covered by a voice/a musical instrument. (c) cash r. = device which records sales/money taken in a shop. (d) (in printing) fitting of several printing plates in such a way that various colours correspond exactly on the paper. (e) level of language (such as formal/colloquial, etc.). **register 2** *v.* (a) to write (a name) officially in a list; to r. at a hotel = to write your name and address when you arrive at the hotel. (b) to put into s.o.'s special care. (c) to record (a temperature, etc.). **registered** *adj.* which has been officially recorded.

register office *n.* registry office.

registrar ['redʒɪstrɑː] *n.* (a) person who keeps official records. person who keeps the records of a university. (b) specialist doctor in training.

registration [redʒɪ'streɪʃn] *n.* act of registering; r. plate = number plate of a car; r. number = official number of a car.

registry ['redʒɪstrɪ] *n.* place where official records are kept; r. office = office where records of births, marriages and deaths are kept/place where you can be married in a civil ceremony.

Regius Professor ['riːdʒɪəsprə'fesə] *n.* professor whose post was founded by the king.

regress [rɪ'gres] *v.* to go back to an earlier, and *usu.* worse, condition. **regression** *n.* going back. **regressive** *adj.* which regresses.

regret 1 [rɪ'gret] *n.* sorrow; much to my r. = I am very sorry. **regret 2** *v.* (regretted) to be sorry that sth has happened. **regretful** *adj.* sorry/sad. **regretfully** *adv.* sadly. **regrettable** *adj.* which must be regretted. **regrettably** *adv.* in a regrettable way.

regular 1 ['regjʊlə] *adj.* (a) habitual/ done at the same time each day. (b) usual/ordinary. (c) r. army = permanent, professional army; r. officer = professional officer. (d) (in grammar) r. verb = verb which has no unusual parts. **regular 2** *n.* (a) *inf.* customer who always shops in a particular shop/who always drinks in a certain bar, etc. (b) professional soldier. **regularity** [regjʊ'lærɪtɪ] *n.* being regular.

regularization [regjʊlərɪ'zeɪʃn] *n.* act of regularizing. **regularize** ['regjʊləraɪz] *v.* to make legal.

regularly *adv.* in a regular way.

regulate ['regjʊleɪt] *v.* to adjust (a machine) so that it works regularly. **regulation** [regjʊ'leɪʃn] *n.* act of regulating; rule. **regulator** *n.* person/ instrument which regulates a machine.

regulo ['regjuːləʊ] *n.* system of numbers indicating temperatures on a gas cooker.

regurgitate [rɪ'gɜːdʒɪteɪt] *v.* (formal) to spout out (food which has already been swallowed/information which has already been learnt). **regurgitation** [rigɜːdʒɪ'teɪʃn] *n.* act of regurgitating.

rehabilitate [riːhə'bɪlɪteɪt] *v.* to train (a disabled person/an ex-prisoner, etc.) to lead a normal life and fit into society. **rehabilitation** [riːhəbɪlɪ'teɪʃn] *n.* act of rehabilitating.

rehash 1 ['riːhæʃ] *n.* thing rehashed. **rehash 2** [riː'hæʃ] *v.* to bring out (an old story/book, etc) in more or less the same form as before.

rehearse [rɪ'hɜːs] *v.* to practise (a play/a concert etc.) before a public performance. **rehearsal** [rɪ'hɜːsəl] *n.* practice of play/ concert, etc. before a public performance; dress r. = last rehearsal of a play, etc.. when everyone is in costume.

rehouse [riː'haʊz] *v.* to put (s.o.) into a new house or flat.

reign 1 [reɪn] *n.* period when a king/ queen/emperor rules; r. of terror = period when law and order have broken down. **reign 2** *v.* to rule.

reimburse [riːɪm'bɜːs] *v.* to pay (s.o.) back the money he has spent. **reimbursement** *n.* act of reimbursing; money reimbursed.

rein 1 [reɪn] *n.* strap which controls a horse; to keep on a tight r. = under strict control. **rein 2** *v.* to r. in = to pull on the reins to control (a horse).

reincarnate [riːɪn'kɑːneɪt] *v.* (formal) to make (the should of a dead person) be born again in another body. **reincarnation** [riːɪnkɑː'neɪʃn] *n.* survival of a person's soul born again in another body after death.

reindeer ['reɪndɪə] n. (pl.reindeer) type of deer which lives in the Arctic.

reinforce [riːɪn'fɔːs] v. to strengthen/to consolidate; reinforced concrete = concrete strengthened with metal rods. **reinforcement** n. (a) act of reinforcing. (b) reinforcements = new soldiers to support others already fighting.

reinstate [riːɪn'steɪt] v. to put (s.o.) back into a post which he used to hold. **reinstatement** n. putting s.o. back into a post.

reinsure [riːɪn'ʃuːə] v. to spread the risk of insurance by insuring part of the risk with another insurer.

reinvest [riːɪn'vest] v. to invest again. **reiterate** [riː'ɪtəreɪt] v. to repeat. **reiteration** [riːɪtə'reɪʃn] n. repetition.

reject1 ['riːdʒekt] n. thing which has been thrown away as not satisfactory; rejects = substandard goods sold at a reduced price..

reject2 [rɪ'dʒekt] v. to refuse to accept (sth); to throw (sth) away as not satisfactory. **rejection** [rɪ'dʒekʃn] n. refusal.

rejig [riː'dʒɪg] v. (rejigged) inf. to arrange in a different way.

rejoice [rɪ'dʒɔɪs] v. to be very happy. **rejoicing** n. great happiness; rejoicing = celebrations.

rejoin [rɪ'dʒɔɪn] v. (a) to join again. (b) (formal) to reply. **rejoinder** n. (formal) reply.

rejuvenate [rɪ'dʒuːvəneɪt] v. to make (s.o.) young again; to give (sth) new strength. **rejuvenation** [rɪdʒuːvə'neɪʃn] n. act of rejuvenating.

rekindle [riː'kɪndl] v. to light again.

relapse 1 [riː'læps] n. becoming ill again (after a temporary improvement); getting back into old bad habits. **relapse 2** v. to become ill again; to get back into old bad habits.

relate [rɪ'leɪt] v. (a) to tell (a story). (b) to connect (two things). (c) to have a successful relationship (with s.o.). **related** adj. (a) linked. (b) belonging to the same family. **relation** [rɪ'leɪʃn] n. (a) story. (b) linking/links (between two things); public relations = maintaining good connections with the public, esp. to put across a point of view/to publicize a product. (c) member of a family. **relationship** n. link/connection; being related.

relative 1 ['relətɪv] n. person who is related to s.o.; member of a family. **relative 2** adj. (a) which is compared to sth; their r. poverty = their poverty compared with really wealthy people or with the wealth they used to have. (b) (in grammar) r. pronoun = pronoun (such as 'who' and 'which') which connects two clauses. **relatively** adv. comparatively/ more or less. **relativity** [relə'tɪvɪti] n. (in physics) relationship between objects and time and speed.

relax [rɪ'læks] v. (a) to slacken/to decrease tension; to make less strict. (b) to rest from work. **relaxation** [riːlæk'seɪʃn] n. (a) slackening of a rule, etc. (b) rest. **relaxed** adj. inf. happy/ not upset.

relay 1 ['riːleɪ] n. (a) shift of people working. (b) r. race = running race by teams in which one runner passes a baton to another who then runs on. **relay 2** [rɪ'leɪ] v. to pass on (a message); to pass on (a TV/radio broadcast) through a relay station. **relay station** n. transmitting station which receives signals from a main transmitter and broadcasts them further.

release 1 [rɪ'liːs] n. (a) setting free. (b) new record/piece of information which is made public. **release 2** v. (a) to set free. (b) to make public.

relegate ['relɪgeɪt] v. to put into a worse position; to move (a team) down from one football division to a lower one. **relegation** [relɪ'geɪʃn] n. moving into a worse position.

relent [rɪ'lent] v. to change your mind about a strict decision you have taken/to be less strict. **relentless** adj. pitiless. **relentlessly** adv. with no pity.

relevant ['relɪvənt] adj. which relates/ has to do with sth being spoken of. **relevance** n. being relevant.

reliable [rɪ'laɪəbl] adj. which can be relied on/which can be trusted. **reliably** adv. in a way which can be trusted. **reliability** [rɪlaɪə'bɪlɪti] n. being reliable. **reliance** n. trust/confidence. **reliant** adj. which relies on sth.

relic ['relɪk] n. object which has been left over from the past; holy remains (such as the bones of a saint).

relict n. (formal) widow.

relief [rɪ'li:f] *n.* (a) reducing pain/ tension. (b) help; famine r. fund = money collected to help victims of a famine; r. road = road built to help traffic congestion. (c) person/thing that takes over which another. a. r. nurse. (d) carving in which the details of design stand out; in r. = standing out/prominent; r. map = map where mountains are drawn so that an impression of height is given.

relieve [rɪ'li:v] *v.* (a) to reduce (pain/ tension) to r. oneself = to urinate or defecate. (b) to help. (c) to take over from (s.o.) (d) to remove a weight from (s.o.).

religion [rɪ'lɪdʒən] *n.* belief in gods or in one God; system of worship.

religious *adj.* referring to religion. **religiously** *adv.* regularly/at a fixed time of day.

relinquish [rɪ'lɪŋkwɪʃ] *v.* (formal) to leave/to let go.

reliquary ['relɪkwerɪ] *n.* container for holy relics.

relish 1 ['relɪʃ] *n.* (*pl.*-es) (a) seasoning/flavour; spicy pickles/spicy sauce. (b) enjoyment. **relish 2** *v.* to enjoy.

relocate [ri:lə'keɪt] *v.* to set (offices) in a new location. **relocation** [ri:lə'keɪʃn] *n.* act of relocating.

reluctant [rɪ'lʌktənt] *adj.* not eager/not willing. **reluctantly** *adv.* not willingly. **reluctance** *n.* lack of eagerness.

rely [rɪ'laɪ] *v.* (on) to trust.

remain [rɪ'meɪn] *v.* (a) to stay. (b) it remains to be seen = will see in due course. **remainder 1** *n.* (a) what is left over. (b) remainders = books which are sold off cheaply. **remainder 2** *v.* to sell off (new books) cheaply. **remains** *n. pl.*(a) dead body. (b) things left over/left behind.

remand [rɪ'mɑ:nd] *v.* to order (a prisoner) to appear at a later hearing of a trial when more evidence will be produced; r. home = place where young criminals can be kept while awaiting trial.

remark 1 [rɪ'mɑ:k] *n.* comment/ observation; to pass remarks about = make rude comments. **remark 2** *v.* to notice/to comment. **remarkable** *adj.* unusual/which you might comment on. **remarkably** *adv.* unusually.

remedy 1 ['remədɪ] *n.* thing which may cure. **remedy 2** *v.* to make (sth) better/ to put (sth) right. **remedial** [rɪ'mi:dɪəl] *adj.* which cures/which makes sth better; r. class = class of special instruction for students who are weak in a subject.

remember [rɪ'membə] *v.* (a) to call back into your mind (sth which you have seen/read/heard, etc.. before) (b) to send good wishes to s.o. (c) he remembered me in his will = he left me sth in his will. **remembrance** *n.* memory.

remind [rɪ'maɪnd] *v.* to r. s.o. of sth = to make (s.o.) remember sth. **reminder** *n.* thing which reminds you of sth.

reminiscence [remɪ'nɪsəns] *n.* memory of sth from the past. **reminisce** [remɪ'nɪs] *v.* to talk about memories of the past. **reminiscent** *adj.* which reminds you of the past.

remiss [rɪ'mɪs] *adj.* careless.

remission [rɪ'mɪʃn] *n.* pardon (for your sins); cutting short a prison sentence.

remit 1 ['ri:mɪt] *n.* orders; are of responsibility. **remit 2** [rɪ'mit] *v.* (remitted) (a) to pardon (sins); to cut short (a prison sentence). (b) to send (money). **remittance** *n.* sending money; money which is sent.

remnant ['remnənt] *n.* piece/quantity left over.

remonstrate ['remənstreɪt] *v.* to protest against sth. **remonstrance** [rɪ'mɒnstrəns] *n.* act of remonstrating.

remorse [rɪ'mɔ:s] *n.* regret about sth wicked which you have done. **remorseful** *adj.* full or remorse. **remorseless** *adj.* pitiless/cruel. **remorselessly** *adv.* in a remorseless way.

remote [rɪ'məʊt] *adj.* (-er, -est) (a) distant; r. control = control (of a model plane, etc.) by radio signals. (b) slight (possibility). (c) uncommunicative (person). **remotely** *adv.* distantly. **remoteness** *n.* being remote.

remould 1 ['ri:məʊld] *v.* to mould again. **remould 2** *n.* tyre which has had its tread remoulded.

remount [ri:'maʊnt] *v.* to get back on to (a horse/bicycle, etc.).

remove 1 [rɪ'mu:v] *n.* grade; one r. from = one grade up/down from.

remove 2 v. (a) to take away. (b) to dismiss (s.o.) from a job. **removable** adj. which can be removed. **removal** n. moving of a home; r. van = van in which your furniture is moved from one house to another. **remover** n. (a) person who moves furniture from one house to another. (b) thing which removes; paint r. = liquid which removes old paint.

remunerate [rɪ'mjuːnəreɪt] v. (formal) to pay (s.o.). **remuneration** [rɪmjuːnə'reɪʃn] n. payment. **remunerative** [rɪ'mjuːnərətɪv] adj. well paid.

renaissance [re'neɪsəns] n. rebirth/ starting again; the Renaissance = artistic movement in late medieval Europe based on a renewal of interest in the Greek and Roman civilizations.

renal ['riːnl] adj. referring to the kidneys.

renascent [rɪ'neɪsənt] adj. which is rising again.

rend [rend] v. (rent) (old) to tear.

render ['rendə] v. (a) to give (back) to send in (an account). (b) to translate. (c) to r. (down) = to melt (fat). (d) to cover (a wall) with a coating of cement. (e) to make (s.o.) be (speechless, etc.). **rendering** n. translation; performance (of a song, etc.).

rendezvous 1 ['rɒndeɪvuː] n. meeting place/appointment; meeting.
rendezvous 2 v. rendezvoused ('rKndeNvuːd] to arrange to meet.

rendition [ren'dɪʃn] n. performance (of a song etc.).

renegade ['renɪɡeɪd] adj. & n. (person) who gives up a faith/a belief to adopt another; (person) who leaves one group to join another.

renege [rɪ'neɪɡ] v. to r. on = not to do sth which you had promised to do.

renew [rɪ'njuː] v. to start again; to replace (sth old) with sth new. **renewable** adj. which can be renewed. **renewal** n. act of renewing.

rennet ['renɪt] n. substance which when added to milk makes it curdle and so form cheese.

renounce [rɪ'naʊns] v. to give up officially. **renouncement** n. act of renouncing.

renovate ['renəveɪt] v. to make (sth) like new. **renovation** [renə'veɪʃn] n. making like new. **renovator** n. person/ machine that renovates.

renown [rɪ'naʊn] n. fame. **renowned** adj. famous (for sth).

rent 1 [rent] n. (a) money paid for the hire of a flat/house/office, etc. (b) tear/ slit (in cloth). **rent 2** v. (a) to pay money to hire (a house/flat, etc.) (b) to hire out (a house/flat, etc.) for money. (c) see also rend. **rental** n. rent/money paid to hire a room/flat/office, etc.

renunciation [rɪnʌnsɪ'eɪʃn] n. giving up/renouncing of a claim.

reopen [riː'əʊpən] v. (a) to open again. (b) to start to investigate a case again. (b) to start to investigate a case again.

reorganize [riː'ɔːɡənaɪz] v. to organize in a new way. **reorganization** [riːɔːɡənar'zeɪʃn] n. act of reorganizing.

reorientate [riː'ɔːrɪənteɪt] v. to set (s.o.) in another direction.

rep [rep] n. inf. (a) travelling salesman. (b) repertory theatre. (c) strong corded material used in upholstery.

repaid [riː'peɪd] v. see repay.

repair 1 [rɪ'peə] n. (a) mending. (b) to be in a good state of r./in good r. = to be in good condition. **repair 2** v. (a) to mend. (b) (old) to go. **repairer** n. person who mends. **repairable** adj. which can be mended.

reparation n. thing/money which makes up for a wrong.

repartee [repɑː'tiː] n. series of witty answers in a conversation.

repast [rɪ'pɑːst] n. (formal) meal.

repatriate [riː'pætrɪeɪt] v. to bring/to send (s.o.) back to their home country. **repatriation** [rɪpætrɪ'eɪʃn] n. act of repatriating.

repay [riː'peɪ] v. (repaid) (a) to pay back. (b) to be worth; it repays close examination = it's worth examining carefully. **repayable** adj. which can be repaid. **repayment** n. paying back.

repeal 1 [rɪ'piːl] n. abolition of a law. so that it is no longer valid. **repeal 2** v. to do away with (a law).

repeat 1 [rɪ'piːt] n & adj. performance which is repeated. **repeat 2** v. to say/to do (sth) again. **repeatable** adj. which can be repeated. **repeatedly** [rɪ'piːtɪdlɪ] adv. over and over again. **repeater** n.

old pocket watch which rings the hours; gun which can fire several times without being reloaded.

repel [rɪ'pel] v. (repelled) (a) to drive back (an attack). (b) to disgust/to be so unpleasant that you drive people away. **repelling** adj. disgusting. **repellent** adj. & n. (thing) which drives away/ which repels; insect r. = spray which keeps insects away.

repent [rɪ'pent] v. to be very sorry. **repentance** n. great regret. **repentant** adj. full of repentance.

repercussion [rɪpɜ:'kʌʃn] n. result/ effect.

repertoire ['repətwɑː] n. works which s.o. can play/sing by heart; works which a theatre company has ready for performance. **repertory** ['repətrɪ] n. (a) r. theatre = theatre with a permanent group of actors who play a series of plays. changing them at regular intervals. (b) store (of information/stories, etc).

repetition [repɪ'tɪʃn] n. act of repeating; thing which is repeated. **repetitious, repetitive** [rɪ'petɪtɪv] adj. which repeats sth too frequently.

replace [riː'pleɪs] v. (a) to put (sth) back in place. (b) to put (sth) in place of sth else. **replaceable** adj. which can be. **replacement** n. (a) putting back; replacing sth with sth else. (b) thing which is used to replace; r. parts = spare parts (of an engine) used to replace parts which have worn out.

replay ['riːpleɪ] n. (a) football match which was played again because the first match was a draw. (b) action r. = section of a sporting event which is shown again on TV at a slower speed. so that the action can be appreciated.

replenish [rɪ'plenɪʃ] v. to fill up again. **replenishment** n. act of replenishing; thing which replenishes.

replete [rɪ'pliːt] adj. (formal) full and satisfied.

replica ['replɪkə] n. exact copy.

reply 1 [rɪ'plaɪ] n. answer. **reply 2** v. to answer.

report 1 [rɪ'pɔːt] n. (a) description/story of what has happened. (b) comments by teachers on a child's progress in school; comments by a commission on a problem. (c) explosion. **report 2** v. (a) to write a description of what happened;

you must r. the burglary to the police = given them the details. (b) to make a complaint about (s.o.). (c) to present oneself officially; to r. for work. (d) to r. to = be responsible to. **reportage** [repɔː'tɑːʒ] n. reporting news (esp. for a magazine or TV). **reportedly** adv. according to what has been reported. **reporter** n. journalist who writes articles for a newspaper on events.

repose 1 [rɪ'pəʊz] n. (formal) calm/ resting. **repose 2** v. (formal) (a) to rest. (b) to place (trust) in s.o.

repository [rɪ'pɒzɪtrɪ] n. (a) warehouse where you can store furniture; store (of information, etc.) (b) Am. store for nuclear waste.

repossess [riːpə'zes] v. (of shop) to take back (goods) when the purchaser cannot pay the hire-purchase payments.

repoussé [rə'puːseɪ] adj. & n. (metalwork) which is hammered into relief from the back.

reprehend [rɪprɪ'hend] v. to criticize. **reprehensible** adj. which can be criticized. **reprehensibly** adv. in a reprehensible way.

represent [reprɪ'zent] v. (a) to mean/to show. (b) to speak on behalf of (s.o./a group of people). (c) to sell goods on behalf of (s.o.). **representation** [reprɪzen'teɪʃn] n. (a) being represented. (b) representations = complaints/ protests. **representative 1** [reprɪ'zentətɪv] adj. typical. **representative 2** n. person who represents; travelling salesman; (in the United States) member of the lower house of Congress; the House of Representatives.

repress [rɪ'pres] v. to keep down/to control. **repressed** adj. kept under strict control. **repression** [rɪpreʃn] n. keeping under control. **repressive** adj. severe/sharp.

reprieve 1 [rɪ'priːv] n. pardon given to a prisoner. **reprieve 2** v. to pardon.

reprimand 1 ['reprɪmɑːnd] n. severe rebuke. **reprimand 2** v. to criticize (s.o.) severely.

reprint 1 ['riːprɪnt] n. book which has been printed again. **reprint 2** [riː'prɪnt] v. to print (a book) again.

reprisal [rɪ'praɪzl] n. punishment of people in revenge for sth.

repro ['ri:prəʊ] *n.* proof which is photographed to make a printing film.
reproach 1 [rɪ'prəɪtʃ] *n.* (a) thing which is a disgrace. (b) beyond r. = blameless. (c) rebuke. **reproach 2** *v.* to r. s.o. with sth = to blame s.o. for sth.
reproachful *adj.* which blames.
reproachfully *adv.* in a reproachful way.
reprobate ['reprəbeɪt] *n.* wicked person/scoundrel.
reprocessing [ri:'prəʊsesɪŋ] *n.* treatment of used nuclear fuel. to extract useful substances.
reproduce [ri:prə'dju:s] *v.* (a) to copy. (b) to produce young. **reproduction** [ri:prə'dʌkʃən] *n.* (a) copy (of a painting, etc.); the r. is bad on this record = the quality of the sound is bad. (b) production of young. **reproductive** *adj.* (organs) which produce young.
reprographics [rɪprəʊ'græfɪks] *n. pl.* pictures which are reproduced in a book.
reproof [rɪ'pru:f] *n.* (formal) blame/criticism. **reprove** [rɪ'pru:v] *v.* (formal) to criticize/to blame (someone).
reproving *adj.* criticizing.
reptile ['reptaɪl] *n.* cold-blooded animal which lays eggs and is covered with scales. **reptilian** [rep'tɪlɪən] *adj.* like a reptile.
republic [rɪ'pʌblɪk] *n.* system of government where there may be elected representatives or where the head of state is an elected or nominated president. **republican** *adj. & n.* referring to a republic; (supporter) of a republic. **Republican** *adj. & n. Am.* (member) of one of the two main political parties in the USA.. **republicanism** *n.* belief in the republic as means of government.
repudiate [rɪ'pju:dɪeɪt] *v.* to reject/to refuse to accept. **repudiation** [rɪpjuːdɪ'eɪʃn] *n.* rejection.
repugnant [rɪ'pʌgnənt] *adj.* unpleasant/nasty. **repugnance** *n.* feeling of distaste/dislike.
repulse [rɪ'pʌls] *v.* to push back.
repulsion [rɪ'pʌlʃn] *n.* (a) act of repulsing. (b) feeling of dislike/distaste.
repulsive *adj.* unpleasant/nasty.
repute [rɪ'pju:t] *n.* reputation/general opinion I only know her by r. = I have

never met her. but I know what people think of her. **reputable** ['repjʊtəbl] *adj.* well thought of/with a good reputation.
reputation [repjʊ'teɪʃn] *n.* general opinion (of s.o.). **reputed** [rɪ'pju:tɪd] *adj.* supposed. **reputedly** [rɪpju:tɪdlɪ] *adv.* according to most people.
request 1 [rɪ'kwest] *n.* asking/demand on r. = if asked for; r. stop = bus stop where buses stop only if you signal to them. **request 2** *v.* to ask/to demand politely.
requiem ['rekwɪəm] *v.* mass for the dead; music to be sung at a requiem.
require [rɪ'kwaɪə] *v.* (a) to demand/to request. (b) to need. **requirement** *n.* what is needed.
requisition 1 [rekwɪ'zɪʃn] *n.* official order. **requisition 2** *v.* to demand/to order that sth should be handed over; to demand and take (supplies) for an army; to order (supplies) for a school.
requisite ['rekwɪzɪt] *adj. & n.* (thing) which is necessary, etc.
reredos ['rɪədɒs] *n.* carved screen behind an altar.
rerun ['ri:rʌn] *n.* second showing of a film on TV.
resale [ri:'seɪl] *n.* selling to s.o. goods which you have bought.
rescind [rɪ'sɪnd] *v.* to annual/to cancel (a law).
rescue 1 ['reskju:] *n.* saving; r. squad = group of people who are going to save s.o. **rescue 2** *v.* to save. **rescuer** *n.* person who rescues or tries to rescue.
research 1 [rɪ's3:tʃ] *n.* scientific study/trying to find out facts. **research 2** *v.* to study/to try to find out facts.
researcher *n.* person who researches.
resemble [rɪ'zembl] *v.* to be similar to. **resemblance** *n.* looking like s.o.
resent [rɪ'zent] *v.* to feel annoyed at a real or imaginary injury. **resentful** *adj.* annoyed. **resentfully** *adv.* in a resentful way. **resentment** *n.* annoyance.
reserve 1 [rɪ'z3:v] *n.* (a) quantity kept back for future special use; in r. = waiting to be used. (b) (in sport) extra player; reserves = part-time troops kept to help the regular army if necessary (c) nature r. = area of land where animals and vegetation are protected. (d) shyness; not speaking openly. (e) (at an

auction) price which an item must reach before the owner will allow it to be sold.

reserve 2 v. to keep back for a special use; to book (a seat/a table).

reservation [rezə'veɪʃn] n. (a) booking (of a seat/table). (b) doubt. (c) national park; area where indigenous tribes live.

reserved adj. (a) booked. (b) shy; (person) who does not speak openly.

reservist [rɪ'zɜːvɪst] n. part-time soldier who is a member of the army reserves.

reservoir ['rezəvwɑː] n. (a) large (usu. artificial) lake where water is kept for pumping to a town. (b) container (for pumping to a town. (b) container (for storing liquids); mass (of information/facts) which can be used if necessary.

reshuffle 1 [riː'ʃʌfl] n. reorganization (of ministers in a government).

reshuffle 2 v. (a) to shuffle again. (b) to reorganize the ministers in a government).

reside [rɪ'zaɪd] v. (formal) to live/to have a house. **residence** ['rezɪdəns] n. (a) place where you live. (b) act of living in a place; hall of r. = block of flats where students live. **residency** n. (old) house of a colonial governor.

resident 1 ['rezɪdənt] adj. (a) living permanently in a place. (b) permanently fixed in a computer. **resident 2** n. person who lives in a place. **residential** [rezɪ'denʃl] adj. (part of a town) with houses rather than shops or factories.

residue ['rezɪdjuː] n. what is left over. **residual** [re'zɪdjʊəl] adj. remaining. **residuary** adj. (formal) residual (part of an estate).

resign [rɪ'zaɪn] v. (a) to give up a job. (b) to r. yourself to = to accept. **resignation** [rezɪg'neɪʃn] n. (a) giving up a job; he tendered/handed in his r. = he resigned. (b) acceptance that sth has to happen. **resigned** adj. accepting that sth has to happen. **resignedly** [rɪ'zaɪnɪdlɪ] adv. patiently/calmly/without complaining.

resilient [rɪ'sɪlɪənt] adj. (material) which easily returns to its original shape (after being crushed); (person) who is strong/able to recover easily from a blow. **resilience** n. being resilient.

resin ['rezɪn] n. sticky sap. esp. from pine trees. **resinous** adj. like resin; made of resin.

resist [rɪ'zɪst] v. to oppose/not to give in to (sth). **resistance** n. (a) opposition/fight against sth; r. movement = movement of ordinary people against an invader; he took the line of least r. = he did it the easiest way. (b) (in physics) force which opposes sth; ability not to conduct electricity/heat, etc. **resistant** adj. which results. **resistivity** n. ability to resist the flow of an electric current. **resistor** n. device which increases the resistance to an electric current/which prevents a current from flowing.

resit [riː'sɪt] v. to take (an examination) again after failing.

resolute ['rezəluːt] adj. determined/having made up your mind. **resolutely** adv. in a resolute way. **resolution** [rezə'luːʃn] n. (a) decision reached at a meeting; proposal to be decided at a meeting. (b) (also resoluteness) determination (to do sth/strength of character. (c) solving (of a problem). (d) splitting up into chemical parts. (e) clearness of a computer image (calculated as the number of pixels per unit of area).

resolve 1 [rɪ'zɒlv] n. determination (to do sth). **resolve 2** v. (a) to decide to do sth. (b) to solve (a problem). (c) to split up into chemical parts.

resonant ['rezənənt] adj. which sounds/rings/echoes loudly. **resonance** n. deep loud ringing tone.

resort 1 [rɪ'zɔːt] n. (a) place where people go on holidays. (b) as a last r./in the last r. = when everything else fails. **resort 2** v. to r. to = to use sth in a difficult situation/when everything else has failed.

resound [rɪ'zaʊnd] v. to make a loud echoing, deep noise. **resounding** adj. great/complete.

resource [rɪ'sɔːs] n. source of supply for what is needed/used; natural resources = minerals/oil/trees; r. centre = area in a school which provides books/equipment for school work; left to his own resources = left to look after himself. **resourceful** adj. good at looking after yourself/at dealing with problems. **resourcefully** adv. in a resourceful way. **resourcefulness** n. being resourceful.

respect 1 [rɪ'spekt] *n.* (a) admiration/ regard. (b) concern/detail; with r. to = concerning; in some respects = in some ways. (c) respects = polite good wishes.

respect 2 *v.* (a) to admire/to honour (s.o.) (b) to pay attention to (sth).

respectability [rɪspektə'bɪlɪtɪ] *n.* being respectable. **respectable** [rɪ'spektəbl] *adj.* (a) proper/worthy of respect. (b) quite large/fairly large.

respectably *adv.* properly. **respecter** *n.* person who respects others.

respectful *adj.* full of respect.

respectfully *adv.* showing respect.

respecting *prep.* concerning.

respective *adj.* referring to each one separately. **respectively** *adv.* referring to each one separately.

respire [res'paɪə] *v.* (formal) to breathe.

respiration [respɪ'reɪʃn] *n.* breathing in of air; to give s.o. artificial r. = to force s.o. (who is almost dead from drowning) to breath. **respirator** ['respɪreɪtə] *n.* device which helps you to breathe. esp. a mask worn as protection against gas, smoke, etc.

respiratory *adj.* referring to breathing.

respite ['respaɪt] *n.* rest; without r. = without stopping.

resplendent [rɪ'splendənt] *adj.* very splendid.

respond [rɪ'spɒnd] *v.* to reply/to react (to); he responded to treatment = he began to get better. **respondent** *n.* defendant in a law suit. esp. in a divorce case. **response** *n.* (a) answer. (b) reply made by the congregation to the priest in a church service. **responsibility** [rɪspɒnsɪ'bɪlɪtɪ] *n.* (a) being responsible; he has taken on a lot of r. = he has agreed to be responsible for many things. (b) which you are responsible for.

responsible *adj.* (a) (for) causing. (b) (person) taking decisions for sth/ directing sth. (c) r. to s.o. = being under the authority of s.o. who expects you to carry out the work well. (d) trustworthy (person). (e) r. position = post where decisions have to be taken.

responsibly *adv.* in a responsible way. **responsive** *adj.* (person) who reacts quickly/who shows sympathy.

responsiveness *n.* sensitivity.

rest 1 [rest] *n.* (a) sleep/calm state; to set s.o.'s mind at r. = to calm s.o.'s worries. (b) stop; the car came to r. at the bottom of the hill = stopped moving. (c) (in music) short break between notes. (d) support; arm r. = part of a chair which you put your arms on; head r. = cushion to support your head (usu. attached to a seat in a car). (e) the r. = remains/what is left over/other people. **rest 2** *v.* (a) to sleep/to be calm. (b) to make (sth) be calm. (c) to let the matter r. = not to deal with the problem any more. **restful** *adj.* calm/which makes you feel calm.

restless *adj.* agitated; always on the move. **restlessly** *adv.* in a restless way. **restlessness** *n.* being restless.

restroom *n. Am.* toilet/lavatory.

restaurant ['restrɒnt] *n.* place where you can buy a meal; self-service r. = where you serve yourself; r. car = carriage on a train where you can have a meal. **restaurateur** [restəræ'tɜː] *n.* person who runs a fashionable restaurant.

restitution [restɪ'tjuːʃn] *n.* compensation/paying back.

restive ['restɪv] *adv.* nervous/agitated.

restiveness *n.* agitation.

restore [rɪs'tɔː] *v.* (a) to give back. (b) to repair/to make (sth) new again.

restoration [restə'reɪʃn] *n.* (a) giving back. (b) repairing sth/making sth look like new again. **restorative** [rɪ'stɒrətɪv] *adj. & n.* (medicine) which makes you stronger. **restorer** *n.* person who restores old paintings, etc.; hair r. = liquid which is supposed to make your hair grow again.

restrain [rɪ'streɪn] *v.* to hold back; to prevent/to try and stop. **restrained** *adj.* controlled/calm. **restraint** *n.* control; with great r. = without losing your temper; lack of r. = (excessive) freedom; wage r. = keeping wage increases under control.

restrict [rɪ'strɪkt] *v.* to limit. **restricted** *adj.* limited; r. area = (i) area where cars must obey a speed limit; (ii) area where only certain people are allowed.

restriction [rɪ'strɪkʃn] *n.* limitation.

restrictive *adj.* which restricts/limits.

result 1 [rɪ'zʌlt] *n.* (a) thing which happens because of sth; outcome. (b) score (in a game); marks (in an exam).

result 2 *v.* to r. from = to happen

because of sth which has been done; to r. in = to produce as an effect. **resultant** *adj.* which results.

resume [rɪ'zju:m] *v.* to start again after an interruption. **resumption** [rɪ'zʌmpʃn] *n.* starting again.

résumé ['rezumeɪ] *n.* (a) short summing up of the main points. (b) *Am.* curriculum vitae.

resurface [ri:'sɜːfəs] *v.* (a) to put a new surface (on a road). (b) to reappear on the surface.

resurgent [rɪ'sɜːdʒənt] *adj.* which is rising again/becoming more powerful again. **resurgence** *n.* reappearance/rising again.

resurrect [rezə'rekt] *v.* to bring back to use; to start up again. **resurrection** [rezə'rekʃn] *n.* bringing back to life.

resuscitate [rɪ'sʌsɪteɪt] *v.* to bring (someone who is almost dead) back to life. **resuscitation** [rɪsʌsɪ'teɪʃn] *n.* bringing back to life.

retail 1 ['ri:teɪl] *n.* selling small quantities of goods to an ordinary customer; r. outlet = shop which sells goods direct to the customer. **retail 2** *v.* (a) to sell (goods) direct to customers who will not sell them again; to r. at = to sell for (a certain price). (b) to pass on (gossip). **retailer** *n.* shopkeeper who sells goods to users.

retain [rɪ'teɪn] *v.* to keep; to r. a lawyer to act for you = to agree with a lawyer that he will act for you (and to pay him in advance) retaining wall = wall which holds back a mass of earth/the water in a reservoir, etc. **retainer** *n.* (a) money paid in advance to s.o. for work he will do later. (b) (old) servant.

retaliate [rɪ'tælieɪt] *v.* to hit back/to attack (s.o.) in revenge. **retaliation** [rɪ'tælɪ'eɪʃn] *n.* in r. for = as a reprisal for. **retaliatory** [rɪ'tælɪətrɪ] *adj.* (measures) taken in retaliation.

retard [rɪ'tɑːd] *v.* to make slow/to keep sth late. **retardation** [rɪtɑː'deɪʃn] *n.* act of retarding. **retarded** *adj.* mentally slower than s.o. of the same age. **retardedness** *n.* being retarded.

retch [retʃ] *v.* to have spasms in the throat as if you were about to vomit.

retention [rɪ'tenʃn] *n.* keeping/holding. **retentive** *adj.* (memory) which retains well.

rethink 1 [ri:'θɪŋk] *n. inf.* second thought about a problem. **rethink 2** *v.* (rethought) to think again/to reconsider.

reticent ['retɪsənt] *adj.* uncommunicative/not willing to talk about sth. **reticence** *n.* unwillingness to talk.

retina ['retɪnə] *n.* layer on the inside of the surface of the eye. which is sensitive to light.

retinue ['retɪnjuː] *n.* group of people following an important person.

retire [rɪ'taɪə] *v.* (a) to stop work (and take a pension); to make (s.o.) stop work (and take a pension). (b) to go away into a place by yourself. (c) to r. to bed for the night = to go to bed. **retirement** *n.* (a) act of retiring from work. (b) period of life when you are retired. **retiring** *adj.* quiet and reserved (person).

retort 1 [rɪ'tɔːt] *n.* (a) sharp reply. (b) glass bottle with a long. thin bent neck used for distilling. **retort 2** *v.* to reply sharply.

retouch [ri:'tʌtʃ] *v.* to improve (a picture/a photograph) by adding or removing lines by hand.

retrace [ri:'treɪs] *v.* to go back to the origins (of sth); to r. one's steps = go back over the same path again.

retract [rɪ'trækt] *v.* to pull back; to withdraw (sth said). **retractable** *adj.* (undercarriage of a plane) which folds up into the body of the plane. **retraction** [rɪ'trækʃn] *n.* pulling back; folding up. **retractor** *n.* surgical instrument used to hold back the flesh during an operation.

retread 1 ['ri:tred] *n.* tyre which has had its surface renewed. **retread 2** *v.* to renew the surface of a tyre.

retreat 1 [rɪ'tri:t] *n.* (a) withdrawing of an army from a battle. (b) quiet place. (c) period of calm meditation (in a religious establishment). **retreat 2** *v.* to withdraw from a battle.

retrench [rɪ'trentʃ] *v.* to economize/to cut back on expenditure. **retrenchment** *n.* reduction of expenditure.

retrial [ri:'traɪəl] *n.* second trial.

retribution [retrɪ'bjuːʃn] *n.* well-deserved punishment. **retributive** [rɪ'trɪbjuːtɪv] *adj.* acting as a punishment.

retrieve [rɪ'tri:v] v. to get back (sth) which was lost; to bring back (sth). **retrievable** adj. which can be retrieved. **retrieval** n. getting back; r. system = system (in a catalogue/in a computer program) to allow information to be retrieved. **retriever** n. type of dog trained to fetch birds which have been shot.

retroactive [retrəʊ'æktɪv] adj. which takes effect from a time in the past; r. to last April = which takes effect from last April.

retrograde ['retrəgreɪd] adj. backward; r. step = step which makes things worse than they were before.

retrogress [retrəʊ'gres] v. to move backwards. **retrogression** n. moving backwards.

retrorocket ['retrəʊrɒkɪt] n. rocket which slows down a space vehicle/a plane.

retrospect ['retrəspekt] n. in r. = when you look back. **retrospective** [retrəspektɪv] adj. & n. which looks back on past events; (exhibition) of works of art covering the whole career of an artist.

retroussé [rə'tru:seɪ] adj. turned up (nose).

retsina [re'tsi:nə] n. Greek wine flavoured with resin.

return 1 [rɪ'tɜ:n] n. (a) going back/ coming back; on my r. home = when I got back home; r. ticket = ticket which allows you to go to one place and come back; many happy returns of the day = best wishes for a happy birthday; by r. of post = by the next post service back. (b) profit/income from money invested. (c) sending back; on sale or r. = sale where the wholesaler will take the product back if the retailer cannot sell it. (d) report of results of an election; income-tax r. = statement of income, etc.. to the tax office. (e) (in tennis, etc) sending back of a ball. (f) r. match = match played between two teams who have played each other recently. (g) key on a computer keyboard which shows that data has been completely entered.

return 2 v. (a) to come back/to go back. (b) to give back/to send back. (c) to elect (s.o.) to parliament. **returnable** adj. which can be returned. **returning**

officer n. official who is responsible for an election in a constituency.

reunion [ri:'ju:nɪən] n. meeting of people who have not met for a long time.

reunite [ri:ju:'naɪt] v. to join (two things) together again.

reusable [ri:'ju:zəbl] adj. which can be used again.

rev 1 [rev] n. inf. revolution.

rev 2 v. (revved) inf. (also rev up) to make (a car engine) go quickly while the car is standing still.

Rev ['revrənd] short for Reverend.

revalue [ri:'vlju:] v. to value again (usu. at a higher value). **revaluation** [ri:væljʊ'eɪʃn] n. revaluing/recalculating the value.

revamp [ri:'væmp] v. inf. to improve the appearance of (sth which is slightly old fashioned).

Revd ['revrənd] short for Reverend.

reveal [rɪ'vi:l] v. to show (sth) which was hidden. **revelation** [revə'leɪʃn] n. surprise.

reveille [rɪ'vælɪ] n. (in the army) signal to soldiers to get up in the morning.

revel 1 ['revəl] n. revels = merrymaking/happy celebrations. **revel 2** v. (revelled) to take delight (in); to have a happy time. **reveller** n. person who is celebrating. **revelry** n. celebration.

revenge 1 [rɪ'venʒ] n. action to harm s.o. in return for harm he has caused you. **revenge 2** v. to harm s.o. in return for harm he has caused you. **revengeful** adj. wanting revenge.

revenue ['revənju:] n. money which is received; taxes which a government receives.

reverberate [rɪ'vɜ:bəreɪt] v. to echo/to ring out loudly in an echo. **reverberation** [rɪvɜ:bə'reɪʃn] n. echoing.

revere [rɪ'vɪə] v. to worship/to respect (s.o.) very highly. **reverence** ['revrəns] n. (a) great respect. (b) bow (as a mark of respect). **reverend** adj. (a) worthy of respect. (b) Reverend = title given to priests; Reverend Mother = title given to he head of a convent. **reverent** adj. showing respect. **reverential** adj. extremely respectful. **reverently** adv. in a reverent way.

reverie ['revərɪ] n. daydream.

revers [rɪ'vɪə] n. edge of a coat collar, etc.. which is turned back to form the lapel.

reversal [rɪ'vɜːsəl] n. change to sth opposite/to r. of fortune = bad luck.

reverse 1 [rɪ'vɜːs] adj. opposite; in r. order = backwards. **reverse 2** n. (a) the opposite. (b) gear of a car which makes you go backwards. (c) defeat (in battle). **reverse 3** v. (a) to do the opposite; to make a car go backwards; (on the phone) to r. the charges = to ask the person you are calling to pay for the call. (b) to change a decision to the opposite. **reversible** adj. cloth/coat which can be work with either side out.

reversion [rɪ'vɜːʃn] n. return to an original state/to an original owner.

reversionary adj. (property) which passes to another owner on the death of the existing one.

revert [rɪ'vɜːt] v. to go back/to come back (to); to r. to type = to go back to an original state; to r. to a subject = to start talking about the subject again.

revetment [rɪ'vetmənt] n. stone facing to a wall.

review 1 [rɪ'vjuː] n. (a) written opinion of a book/play/film, etc. (b) magazine which contains articles about new books/films/plays. (c) general examination. (d) general inspection of soldiers/naval vessels, etc. **review 2** v. (a) to write your opinion of (a book/play/film, etc.). (b) to inspect (soldiers/naval vessels). (c) to consider generally. **reviewer** n. person who writes opinions of books/play/films.

revile [rɪ'vaɪl] v. (formal) to insult; to criticize sharply.

revise [rɪ'vaɪz] v. (a) to read/to study a lesson again. (b) to correct/to change. **revision** [rɪ'vɪʒən] n. act of revising; thing revised. **revisionism** n. revising the original pure concept (of a political movement. exp. communism).

revive [rɪ'vaɪv] v. to come back/to bring back to life again. **revival** n. bringing back to life; renewal of interest in sth. **revivalist** n. person who leads a religious revival.

revoke [rɪ'vəʊk] v. to cancel. **revocation** [revə'keɪʃn] n. act of revoking.

revolt 1 [rɪ'vəʊlt] n. uprising against

authority. **revolt 2** v. (a) to rise up against authority. (b) to disgust. **revolting** adj. (a) in revolt. (b) disgusting/which makes you feel ill..

revolution [revə'luːʃn] n. (a) rotation/turning around a central point. (b) uprising against a government. **revolutionary 1** adj. (a) aiming to change things completely/very new. (b) referring to a political revolution. **revolutionary 2** n. person who takes part in an uprising against a government. **revolutionize** v. to change completely.

revolve [rɪ'vɒlv] v. (a) to turn round. (b) to be centred on. **revolver** n. small hand gun with a cartridge chamber which turns after each shot is fired. **revolving** adj. which turns round.

revue [rɪ'vjuː] n. stage show with satirical sketches/songs, etc.

revulsion [rɪ'vʌlʃn] n. (formal) disgust.

reward 1 [rɪ'wɔːd] n. money/present given to s.o. as a prize or for information. **reward 2** v. to give (s.o.) money/a present as a prize or for giving information. **rewarding** adj. which gives moral satisfaction.

rewrite 1 [ˈriːraɪt] n. inf. act of rewriting. **rewrite 2** v. (rewrote, rewritten) to write (sth) again in different words).

Rex [reks] n. the King. i.e. the State. in legal cases.

Rh. abbrev. for rhesus.

rhapsody [ˈræpsədɪ] n. poetry/music/song showing great excitement/passion. **rhapsodical** [ræp'sɒdɪkl] adj. excited/passionate. **rhapsodize** v. (over) to praise (sth) extravagantly.

rheostat [ˈriːəstæt] n. device for making lights fade by cutting down the flow of electric current gradually.

rhesus [ˈriːsəs] adj. r. monkey = small monkey. often used in laboratories for scientific research; r. factor = substance in the blood (or absent from it) which can affect newborn babies and people having blood transfusions; r. positive = having a rhesus factor; r. negative = with no rhesus factor.

rhetoric [ˈretərɪk] n. art of speaking forcefully and eloquently. **rhetorical** [rɪ'tɒrɪkl] adj. referring to rhetoric r. question = question to which you do not expect an answer.

rheumatism ['ru:mətɪzəm] *n.* disease causing pains in the joints or muscles.
rheumatic [ru:mætɪk] *adj.* referring to rheumatism; r. fever = serious disease of children and young people where you joints well. **rheumaticky** *adj. inf.* rheumatic. **rheumatics** *n. pl.inf.* rheumatism. **rheumatoid arthritis** *n.* continuing disease of the joints where they become stiff, swollen and painful.
rhinestone ['raɪnstəʊn] *n.* imitation colourless precious stone.
rhinoceros inf. rhino ['raɪnəʊ] *n.* (*pl.*-es, -os) huge Asiatic or African animal with a thick skin and one or two horns on its head.
rhizome ['raɪzəʊm] *n.* thick stem which lies on the ground like a root and produces shoots.
rhododendron [rəʊdə'dendrən] *n.* large evergreen shrub with clusters of huge colourful flowers.
rhombus ['rɒmbəs] *n.* shape with four equal sides but with no right angles. **rhomboid 1** *adj.* shaped like a rhombus/diamond-shaped. **rhomboid 2** *n.* four-sided shape with opposite sides equal in length and no right angles.
rhubarb ['ru:bɑːb] *n.* garden plant with large poisonous leaves, whose stalks are cooked as a dessert.
rhyme 1 [raɪm] *n.* (a) sameness of sounds between two words (used in poetry). (b) little piece of poetry; nursery r. = (often nonsensical) piece of poetry for children. **rhyme 2** *v.* (with) to have the same sound as; rhyming slang = slang devised in London, where words are replaced by words or phrases which rhyme with them.
rhythm ['rɪðəm] *n.* regular beat in music/poetry, etc. **rhythmic(al)** ['rɪðmɪk(l)] *adj.* with a regular beat. **rhythmically** *adv.* in a rhythmical way.
rib 1 [rɪb] *n.* (a) one of several bones forming a cage across the chest. (b) piece of meat with the rib attached to it; spare ribs = cooked pork ribs in a savoury sauce. (c) curved timber which is part of the structure of a ship; one of the spokes of an umbrella. (d) thicker part in a leaf. (e) thicker line of stitches in knitting. **rib 2** *v. inf.* of tease (s.o.). **ribbed** *adj.* with ribs. **rib-cage** *n.* all the ribs in an animal.

ribald ['rɪbəld] *adj.* rude (song/joke). **ribaldry** *n.* rude jokes.
ribbon ['rɪbn] *n.* long flat thin piece of material for trying or decoration; typewriter r. = flat piece of material covered with ink, which is struck by the letters in a typewriter; r. development = building of lines of houses along the side of a road stretching into the countryside.
riboflavin [raɪbəʊ'fleɪvɪn] *n.* type of vitamin B.
ribonucleic acid [ri:bəʊnju:'kleɪɪk'æsɪd] *n.* substance in cells which takes information from the DNA and converts it to enzymes and proteins.
rice [raɪs] *n.* common tropical cereal, grown in wet ground or water; brown r. = rice which still has its outer covering; wild r. = plant of North America which resembles rice; r. pudding = desert made of rice, milk and sugar; r. paper = very thin paper which you can eat and which is used in cooking.
rich 1 [rɪtʃ] *adj.* (-er, -est) (a) having a great deal of money. (b) (food) with a lot of cream/fat/eggs, etc. in it. (c) deep and resonant (voice); dark (colour). (d) fertile (soil). (e) r. in = with many resources. **rich 2** *n.* the r. = rich people. **riches** ['rɪtʃɪz] *n.* wealth. **richly** *adv.* splendidly; you richly deserve it = you deserve it very much. **richness** *n.* wealth; being rich.
Richter scale ['rɪxtə'skeɪl] *n.* scale for measuring earthquakes.
rick1 [rɪk] *n.* (a) large pile of straw or hay built like a house. (b) sprain. **rick 2** *v.* to twist/sprain (ankle, back). **rickets** ['rɪkɪts] *n.* disease of children (caused by lack of vitamins) where bones become bent. **rickety** *adj.* wobbly (chair).
rickshaw ['rɪkʃɔː] *n.* light wheeled chair pulled by a man.
ricochet ['rɪkəʃeɪ] *v.* (ricocheted ['rɪkəʃeɪd]) to bounce off a surface at an angle.
rid [rɪd] *v.* (rid) to clear away; to get r. of sth = to dispose of sth/to throw sth away. **riddance** *n.* good r. = I am glad to get rid of it.
ridden [rɪdn] suffix meaning filled with/affected by.

riddle1 ['rɪdl] *n.* (a) guessing game where you have to guess the answer to a deliberately puzzling question. (c) large sieve for separating soil from stones. **riddle 2** *v.* (a) to put (soil) through a sieve. (b) to r. with bullets = to shoot many times. **riddled with** *adj.* full of.

ride1 [raɪd] *n.* trip/journey on horseback/on a bicycle/in a car, etc.; *Sl.* he was taken for a r. = (i) they tricked him; (ii) they murdered him. **ride 2** *v.* (rode, has ridden) (a) to go for a trip on horseback/on a bicycle/in a car, etc. (b) (of ships) to r. at anchor = to float; the ships rode out the storm = they remained at anchor during the storm. (c) to r. a blow = to move backwards to make a blow softer. **rider** *n.* (a) person who rides. (b) additional clause to a contract. **riderless** *adj.* (horse) with no rider. **ride up** *v.* (of dress, etc.) to move upwards through movement of the body. **riding** *n.* (a) sport of going on horseback; r. school = school where you learn to ride a horse. (b) (Canada) constituency. **riding lights** *n. pl.* lights on a ship at anchor.

ridge [rɪdʒ] *n.* long narrow raised part; r. tent = tent made of two sloping sides and a horizontal pole. **ridged** *adj.* with ridges.

ridicule 1 ['rɪdɪkjuːl] *n.* mocking/laughing at s.o.; to hold s.o. up to r. = to laugh at s.o. **ridicule 2** *v.* to laugh at (s.o./sth). **ridiculous** *adj.* silly/which can be laughed at. **ridiculously** *adv.* in a silly way. **ridiculousness** *n.* silliness.

rife [raɪf] *adj.* common.

rifflo ['rɪfl] *v.* to flick (through the pages of a book).

riffraff ['rɪfræf] *n.* (no *pl.*) worthless ordinary people.

rifle1 ['raɪfl] *n.* hand gun with a long barrel with spiral grooves inside. **rifle 2** *v.* (a) to search and to steal from. (b) to make spiral grooves inside a gun barrel.

rift [rɪft] *n.* split/crack.

rig 1 [rɪg] *n.* (a) way in which a ship's sails are arranged. (b) metal construction for drilling for minerals. (c) *inf.* set of clothes. **rig 2** *v.* (rigged) (a) to fit out a ship with sails. (b) to arrange a dishonest result. **rigging** *n.* ropes on a ship. **rig our** *n. inf.* bizarre set of clothes. **rig up** *v.* to arrange/to construct (sth) quickly.

rigg [rɪg] *n.* small white sea fish.

right 1 [raɪt] *adj.* (a) good/honest. (b) correct; quite r.! = perfectly correct! (c) to get on the r. side of s.o. = to make s.o. favour you; *inf.* on the r. side of forty = less than forty years old. (d) r. angle = angle of 90*. (e) straight/in order; is he in his r. mind? = is he sane? she's all r. again = she's better. (f) not left; referring to the hand which most people use for writing. **right 2** *n.* (a) what is correct/good; in the r. = not to be criticized. (b) legal title to sth; she has no r. to be here = she should not be here; civil rights = legal entitlements of every citizen; by rights = if things were done properly. (c) the right-hand side/ the right-hand direction; the r. = political parties which are conservative. **right 3** *adj.* (a) r. on = straight on. (b) r. away = immediately. (c) completely. (d) correctly; it serves you r. = you deserved it. (e) to the right hand side. **right 4** *v.* to correct; to make (sth) return to its correct position. **right 5** *inter.* (a) agreed/OK. (b) *inf.* do you understand? **right-angled** *adj.* with a 90° angle. **righteous** ['raɪtʃəs] *adj.* virtuous/very good. **righteously** *adv.* in a righteous way. **righteousness** *n.* virtue/goodness. **rightful** *adj.* legally correct. **rightfully** *adv.* in a rightful way. **right-hand** *adj.* referring to the right hand; right-hand man = most particular helper. **right-handed** *adj.* (person) who uses the right hand for writing/working etc. **rightist** *n.* member of a conservative political group. **rightly** *adv.* correctly; I can't r. say = I am not very sure. **right-minded** *adj.* (person) who has correct ideals/who thinks in the way most people think. **rightness** *n.* correctness. **right of way** *n.* (a) right to walk over s.o. else's property. (b) right (of one vehicle) to go first at a crossroads. **right-wing** *adj.* belonging to the conservative political parties. **right-winger** *n.* person who is on the right politically.

rigid ['rɪdʒɪd] *adj.* stiff/unbending/ inflexible. **rigidly** *adv.* stiffly. **rigidity** [rɪ'dʒɪdɪtɪ] *n.* being rigid.

rigmarole ['rɪgmərəʊl] *n.* long incoherent speech/meaningless jumble of words.

rigour, Am. rigor ['rɪgə] *n.* severity

(of the law, etc.); harshness (of the climate). **rigor mortis** [-'mɔːtɪs] *n.* stiffening of a body after death.
rigorous *adj.* very strict. **rigorously** *adv.* in a rigorous way.
rile [raɪl] *v. inf.* to annoy.
rill [rɪl] *n.* small stream.
rim [rɪm] *n.* edge of a wheel/of a cup; frame of spectacles. **rimless** *adj.* (spectacles) with no frame. **rimmed** *adj.* with a rim.
rime raɪm] *n.* white frost.
rind [raɪnd] *n.* skin on fruit/meat/cheese.
ring 1 [rɪŋ] *n.* (a) circular piece of metal/wood, etc.. with a hole in the centre. (b) anything shaped like a circle; *inf.* to run rings around s.o. = to do things more efficiently than s.o. (c) group of people (usu. criminals). (d) centre of a circus where performances take place; square place where a boxing/wrestling match takes place. (e) sound of a bell. (f) call on the telephone. **ring 2** *v.* (rang, has rung) (a) to make a sound of a bell; *inf.* it rings a bell = it reminds me of sth. (b) my ears are ringing = there is a sound like that of bells in my ears. (c) to telephone; to r. s.o. up = to call s.o. on the telephone; to r. back = to phone in reply to a phone call; to r. off = to stop the telephone call/to put down the receiver. **ring 3** *v.* (ringed) (a) to put a ring on the leg of a wild bird for marking purposes. (b) to mark with a circle.
ringer *n.* (a) person who rings church bells. (b) *inf.* dead r. = person/horse exactly similar to another. **ringleader** *n.* chief of a gang or group/person who organizes a crime. **ringlet** *n.* long curl (of hair). **ringmaster** *n.* master f ceremonies in a circus. **ring road** *n.* bypass/road which goes round a town. **ringside** *adj.* by the side of a ring. **ringworm** *n.* disease of the skin which causes round red patches.
rink [rɪŋk] *n.* place where you can roller-skate or skate on ice; ice for skating.
rinse 1 [rɪns] *n.* (a) putting soapy washing/soapy hair through clean water to remove the soap. (b) coloured liquid for rising hair. **rinse 2** *v.* to put (soapy/dirty things) into clean water to remove the soap/the dirt.
riot 1 ['raɪət] *n.* (a) disorder among

crowds of people; to run r. = to become disordered/to get out of control; to read s.o. the r. act = to warn s.o. to stop being disorderly. (b) mass of (sounds/colours). (c) very amusing film/play, etc. **riot 2** *v.* to take part in a riot/to get out of control.
rioter *n.* person who takes part in a riot. **rioting** *n.* riots/outbreaks of civil disorder. **riotous** *adj.* wild/out of control. **riotously** *adv.* in a riotous way. **riot police** *n.* police specially equipped to deal with rioters.
rip 1 [rɪp] *n.* tear (in cloth). **rip 2** *v.* (ripped) to tear; *inf.* to let r. = to allow sth to go freely **ripcord** *n.* cord you pull to make a parachute open. **rip off** *v.* (a) to tear off. (b) *Sl.* to rip s.o. off = to cheat s.o./to make s.o. pay too much. **rip-off** *n. Sl.* bad deal/thing which costs too much. **rip-roaring** *adj.* wild/noisy (party); great (success). **ripsaw** *n.* saw with large teeth, for rough cutting.
RIP [ɑːrɑː'piː] short for Rest in peace Requiescat in Pace.
riparian [rɪ'peərɪən] *adj.* (formal) referring to the banks of a river.
ripe [raɪp] *adj.* (-er, -est) ready to eat/to be harvested; to a r. old age = until very old; the time is r. for sth = it is the right time to do sth. **ripen** *v.* to become ripe. **ripeness** *n.* readiness; state of being ripe.
riposte 1 [rɪ'pɒst] *n.* quick, sharp reply. **riposte 2** *v.* to make a quick, sharp reply.
ripple 1 ['rɪpl] *n.* little wave. **ripple 2** *v.* to make little waves.
rise 1 [raɪz] *n.* (a) movement upwards; slope upwards. (b) increase in salary. (c) to give r. to sth = to start sth. **rise 2** *v.* (rose, has risen) (a) to move upwards; to get up; to get out of bed. (b) (of court) to stop meeting. (c) (of a river) to start. (d) to r. in revolt/to r. against s.o. = to riot/to rebel. **riser** *n.* (a) early r. = person who gets up early in the morning. (b) vertical board holding up the tread of a staircase. **rising 1** *adj.* which is moving upwards/which is increasing; r. generation = new generation which will follow the present one; r. forty = nearly forty years old. **rising 2** *n.* (a) movement upwards. (b) rebellion/revolt. **risible** ['rɪzɪbl] *adj.* laughable.
risk 1 [rɪsk] *n.* possible harm; dangerous

chance; they run the r. of being caught = they may well be caught. **risk 2** v. to chance/to do sth which may possibly harm. **riskily** adv. in a risky way. **riskiness** n. being risky. **risky** adj. (-ier, -iest) dangerous/which may cause harm.

risotto [rɪ'sɒtəʊ] n. Italian dish of cooked rice with meat/fish/vegetables in it.

risqué ['riːskeɪ] adj. slightly indecent.

rissole ['rɪsəʊl] n. fried ball of meat/fish, etc.

rite [raɪt] n. religious ceremony; last rites = communion for s.o. who is dying. **ritual** ['rɪtjʊəl] adj. & n. (referring to) a religious ceremony. **ritually** adv. in a ritual way.

rival 1 ['raɪvl] n. & adj. (person) who competes. **rival 2** v. (rivalled) to compete with s.o.; to be of similar quality. **rivalry** n. competition.

rive ['rɪvn] adj. (formal) split.

river ['rɪvə] n. large stream of water which goes into another stream or into the sea. **riverside** adj. on the banks of a river.

rivet 1 ['rɪvɪt] n. nail which fastens metal plates together. **rivet 2** v. (a) to fasten metal plates together. (b) to attract s.o.'s attention.

Riviera [rɪvɪ'eərə] n. beautiful south coast.

rivulet ['rɪvjʊlət] n. little stream.

Rn symbol for radon.

RNA [ɑːen'eɪ] abbrev. for ribonucleic acid.

roach [rəʊtʃ] n. (a) (pl.roach) small freshwater fish. (b) (pl.roaches) inf. cockroach.

road [rəʊd] n. (a) path for cars and other vehicles; way of getting somewhere the r. to success = the path which leads to success; on the r. = travelling from place to place (as a salesman/worker). (b) roads = part of the sea near a port where shops can lie at anchor. **roadblock** n. barrier put across a road by the police. **roadhog** n. inf. fast dangerous driver. **roadhouse** n. hotel by a main road. **roadie** n. inf. person who organizes a travelling pop group. **roadmender** n. person who repairs the road surface. **roadside** n. by the side of a road. **roadstead** n. part of the sea near a

port where shops can lie at anchor. **roadway** n. main surface of a road. **roadworks** n. pl.repairs to a road. **roadworthiness** n. being roadworthy. **roadworthy** adj. in a fit state to be driven on a road.

roam [rəʊm] v. to wander.

roan [rəʊn] adj. & n. (brown horse) with grey hairs in its coat

roar 1 [rɔː] n. loud, deep call; loud shouting. **roar 2** v. to make a loud call. **roaring 1** adj. wild (success); to do a r. trade in = to sell sth rapidly. **roaring 2** n. sound of loud, deep calls.

roast 1 [rəʊst] n. meat which has been/which will be cooked in an oven. **roast 2** v. to cook over a fire/in an oven. **roast 3** adj. which has been roasted; r. beef. **roasting** adj. (chicken) which is ready to be roasted.

rob [rɒb] v. (robbed) to steal from s.o. **robber** n. person who steals money from s.o. **robbery** n. stealing.

robe 1 [rəʊb] n. long, loose dress (for men or women); Am. dressing gown. **robe 2** v. to dress in a robe.

robin ['rɒbɪn] n. common small brown bird with a red breast; round r. = letter of complaint signed by many people.

robot ['rəʊbɒt] n. machine which works like a man; (in science fiction) machine which looks a little like a man and which can act like one. **robotics** [rəʊ'bɒtɪks] n. science of electronic robots.

robust [rə'bʌst] adj. strong/vigorous. **robustly** adv. in a robust way. **robustness** n. being robust.

rock 1 [rɒk] n. (a) stone/solid part of the earth's surface. (b) large piece of stone; inf. on the rocks = (i) bankrupt; (ii) (whisky) with ice; r. plant = alpine plant. (c) hard pink sweet shaped like a stick. often with the name of a town printed in it. (d) music with a strong rhythm. **rock 2** v. to sway from side to side; to make (sth) sway from side to side; inf. don't r. the boat = don't disturb what has been arranged. **rock bottom** n. the lowest point. **rock cake** n. small cake with currants in it. **rocker** n. (a) semicircular wooden piece which a rocking chair stands on. (b) Am. rocking chair; inf. off one's r. = mad. (c) type of electric switch which rocks. **rockery** n. garden planted around a collection of rocks. **rocking** adj. swaying rocking-horse = child's wooden horse on rockers; rocking-chair = chair which rocks backwards and forwards on rockers.

rocksalmon n. dogfish. **rocky** adj. (a) full of rocks. (b) inf. wobbly.

rocket 1 ['rɒkɪt] n. (a) type of firework which, when lit, flies up into the sky; spacecraft; type of bomb which is hot through space at an enemy. (b) engine driven by burning gas. which powers a spacecraft or bomb. (c) inf. to give s.o. a r. = to criticize/reprimand s.o. **rocket 2** v. to shoot upwards very fast. **rocketry** n. (no pl.) science of space rockets.

rococo [rə'kəʊkəʊ] adj. & n. ornate flowery (style of architecture of the 18th century).

rod [rɒd] n. (a) long stick. (b) fishing r. = long stick with a line attached used for fishing.

rode [rəʊd] v. see ride.

rodent ['rəʊdənt] n. animal which chews and gnaws (such as mouse/rat, etc.).

rodeo [rəʊ'deɪəʊ] n. (pl.-os) display of skill by cowboys.

roe [rəʊ] n. (a) fish eggs. (b) type of small deer. **roebuck** n. male roe deer.

roentgen ['rʌntjən] adj. referring to X-rays.

roger ['rɒdʒə] inter & signal meaning message received and understood.

rogue [rəʊg] adj. & n. (a) wicked/dishonest person. (b) r. elephant = (i) elephant driven out of the herd by the other elephants; (ii) person who does not behave in the same way as others. **roguery** n. roguish behaviour. **roguish** adj. wicked/dishonest.

roisterer ['rɔɪstərə] n. person who celebrates noisily. **roistering** n. noisy celebrations.

role [rəʊl] n. part played by s.o. (in a play or in real life).

roll 1 [rəʊl] n. (a) thing which has been turned over and over to make a tube; Swiss r./Am jelly r. = cake rolled up with jam or cream in it; sausage r. = small pastry with a sausage inside. (b) very small loaf of bread. (c) list of names; r. of honour = list of prizewinner/list of soldiers who have died during a war. (d) movement from side to side. (e) rumble (of drums). **roll 2** v. (a) to make a tube out of sth flat. (b) to flatten by using a

roller. (c) to make (sth) move forward by turning it over and over; inf. rolling in money = having a great deal of money. (d) to rock from side to side. (e) to r. one's r's = when speaking the letter 'r'. to make the tip of the tongue vibrate. (f) to make a low rumbling noise. (g) Am. inf. to attack and rob (s.o.). **rollcall** n. calling names from a list. **roller** n. (a) round object which rolls; stream r. = machine for flattening new road surfaces. (b) large wave in the sea (c) r. towel = continuous towel hanging on a horizontal bar. (d) plastic tube used for rolling hair into curls. **roller coaster** n. Am. fairground railway which goes up and down steep slopes. **roller-skate 1** n. device with wheels which you strap to your foot so as to glide along fast. **roller-skate 2** v. to glide on roller-skates. **roller-skating** n. sport of going on roller-skates. **rolling** adj. (countryside) which is a mass of small hills; r. pin = wooden roller with handles, for flattening pastry; r. stock = carriages/wagons/engines used on a railway; r. stone = person who never lives long in one place. **rollmop** n. herring fillet, spiced and rolled. **roll on/roll off** n. ferry where cars, lorries and buses can drive straight on and off the ship. **roll-top** adj. r. desk = desk with a cover made of slats of wood which slide upwards to open it.

rollicking ['rɒlɪkɪŋ] adj. noisy and jolly.

roly-poly ['rəʊlɪ'pəʊlɪ] n. (a) cooked pudding made of pastry rolled round jAm. (b) adj. & n. inf. fat (person).

ROM [rɒm] n. read-only memory, computer memory with data programmed into it, which can only be read, but no changed.

Roman ['rəʊmən] adj. referring to Rome; roman = printing type with straight letters; R. candle = type of firework giving a brilliant fountain of light; R. numerals = numbers written in the Roman style (I, II, III, IV, etc.). **Roman Catholic** adj. & n. (person) belonging to the Christian church of which the Pope is the head. **Roman Catholicism** n. beliefs of the Roman Catholic church.

romance 1 [rə'mæns] n. (a) r. language

= language which has derived from Latin. (b) love affair. (c) love story. (d) story remote from daily life. **romance 2** *v.* to invent/to make up a story.

romantic [rə'mæntɪk] *adj.* (a) full of mystery and romance. (b) (literary/ artistic style) which is very imaginative/ based on personal emotions. **romantically** *adv.* in a romantic way. **romanticism** *n.* romantic literary style. **romanticize** *v.* to turn (sth) into a romantic story.

Romanesque [rəʊmə'nesk] *adj. & n.* architectural style with round arches and vaults found in Europe in the early Middle Ages.

Romanian 1 [ru:'meɪnɪən] *adj.* referring to Romania. **Romanian 2** *n.* (a) person from Romania. (b) language spoken in Romania.

Romany ['rəʊmənɪ] *n.* (a) gipsy. (b) language spoken by gipsies.

romp 1 [rɒmp] *n.* energetic children's game. **romp 2** *v.* to play about energetically; to r. home = win easily.

rompers *n.* one-piece suit for a baby.

rondo ['rɒndəʊ] *n.* (*pl.*-os) piece of music where the same theme is repeated several times.

rood [ru:d] *n.* r. screen = screen built across a church, separating the chancel from the nave.

roof 1 [ru:f] *n.* (a) covering over a building. (b) top of the inside of the mouth. (c) top of a car/bus/lorry, etc.; sunshine r. = roof which you can open in fine weather; r. rack = grid fixed to the roof of a car for carrying luggage. **roof 2** *v.* to put a roof on (a building).

rook 1 [rʊk] *n.* (a) large black bird of the crow family. (b) (in chess) piece shaped like a castle. **rook 2** *v. Sl.* to cheat. **rookery** *n.* place where rooks nest; colony of penguins/seals. **rookie** ['rʊkɪ] *n. inf.* new recruit in the armed forces/in the police.

room [ru:m] *n.* (a) one of the divisions inside a house. (b) space; to make r. for = squeeze up to give space for; there's r. for improvement = things could be improved. **room 2** *v.* to live in furnished rooms. **rooming-house** *n. Am.* house with furnished rooms to let. **room-mate** *n.* person with whom you share a room. **roomy** *adj.* (-ier, -iest)

spacious.

roost 1 [ru:st] *n.* perch for a bird; to rule the r. = be in charge/be the boss. **roost 2** *v.* to perch. **rooster** *n.* cockerel.

root 1 [ru:t] *n.* (a) part of plant which goes down into the ground and which takes nourishment from the soil; part of a hair/a tooth which goes down into the skin; to take r. = to start to grow; to put down roots = to begin to feel at home in a place. (b) source. (c) (in language) word which is a base for other words. (d) square r. = number which if multiplied by itself gives the number you have; cube r. = number which if multiplied by itself twice gives the number you have. **root 2** *v.* to put down/to make roots; deeply rooted fear = fear which is very strongly-felt. (b) (for) to dig (sth) up/to look for (sth); *Am.* to r. for team = to cheer a team on. **root bear** *n. Am.* dark fizzy drink. flavoured with roots. **root crop** *n.* crop which is grown for its edible roots (such as carrots turnips, etc.). **rootless** *adj.* with no roots. **rootstock** *n.* plant on which another is grafted. **root up, root out** *v.* to pull up (a plant) by its roots; to remove (sth) completely.

rope 1 [rəʊp] *n.* thick string/thick cord; *inf.* he knows the ropes = he knows all about it/how to go about doing it. **rope 2** *v.* to tie together with a rope; to r. s.o. in = to get s.o. to help/to join; to r. off = to stop people going into a place by putting a rope around it. **ropy** *adj.* (-ier, -iest) *inf.* of bad quality; not healthy.

rosary ['rəʊzərɪ] *n.* string of beads used by Catholics when saying prayers

rose 1 [rəʊz] *n.* (a) scented flower which grows on a prickly bush. (b) pink colour; *inf.* see through r. coloured spectacles = see things as being very good. when they are not. (c) piece of metal/plastic with many holes in it. which is attached to the spout of a watering can. so that water comes out in a spay. **rose 2** *v.* see rise. **roseate** ['rəʊzɪət] *adj.* deep pink. **rosebud** *n.* flower bud of a rose. **rose window** *n.* large round decorated window found *usu.* in the west wall of a church. **rosewood** *n.* fragrant hard red wood. used for making furniture. **rosiness** *n.*

being rosy. **rosy** adj. (-ier, -iest) (a) bright pink. (b) very favourable.

rosé [ˈrəʊˈseɪ] n. pink wine.

rosemary [ˈrəʊzmərɪ] n. common evergreen bush with scented leaves.

rosette [rəˈset] n. ribbon bunched to look like a flower. used as a decoration or as a badge.

rosin [ˈrɒzɪn] n. solid resin used to rub a violin bow..

roster [ˈrɒstə] n. list of duties which have to be done and the people who have to do them.

rostrum [ˈrɒstrəm] n. raised stand for a speaker.

rot 1 [rɒt] n. (a) decay; dry r. = decay in house timbers caused by a fungus; the r. has set in = things are beginning to go badly. (b) nonsense. **rot 2** v. (rotted) to decay; to go bad. **rotten** adj. decayed; inf. to feel r. = (i) to feel ill; (ii) to feel ashamed. **rotter** n. inf. bad person.

rota [ˈrəʊtə] n. list of duties which have to be done in turn and the people who have to do them.

rotate [rəʊˈteɪt] v. to turn round. **rotary** [ˈrəʊtərɪ] adj. which turns/rotates; r. printing press = one where the paper passes round large rollers.. **rotation** [rəʊˈteɪʃn] n. turning/taking turns; r. of crops = growing different crops in turn.. **rotatory** adj. turning (motion). **rotor** n. piece of machinery which rotates; the blades of a helicopter.

rote [rəʊt] n. learning by heart.

rotisserie [rəʊˈtiːsərɪ] n. electric machine for turning meat on a spit in front of heat.

rotund [rəˈtʌnd] adj. round/fat. **rotunda** n. circular building with a dome. **rotundity** n. being rotund.

rouble [ˈruːbl] n. unit of money of the Russian Federation.

rouge [ruːʒ] n. pink cream/powder which you put on your face to give yourself more colour. **rouged** adj. wearing rouge.

rough 1 [rʌf] adj. (-er, -est) (a) not smooth/bumpy/uneven; to give s.o. a r. time = treat s.o. badly; r. house = fight. (b) unfinished; approximate (translation). **rough 2** n. (a) area of long grass on a golf course. (b) unfinished design. (c) hooligan. **rough 3** adv. (a) brutally/harshly. (b) to sleep

r. = without a proper bed. **rough 4** v. to r. out = to make a rough design. to r. it = to live uncomfortably to r. s.o. up = to beat/to attack s.o. **roughage** n. coarse stuff. such as bran. which you eat to help digestion. **rough and ready** adj. approximate not beautifully finished. **rough and tumble** n. violent life; violent game. **roughcast** n. covering for the outside of walls of a house, made of small stones. **rough diamond** n. person who is uncultivated but pleasant. **roughen** v. to make/to become rough. **roughly** adv. in a rough way. **roughneck** n. rowdy hooligan. **roughness** n. being rough. **roughshod** adj. to ride r. over s.o.'s feelings = to pay to attention to s.o.'s feelings.

roulette [ruːˈlet] n. game of chance where bets are made on the number of a box where a small ball will stop in a rotating wheel; Russian r. = game played with a revolver containing a single bullet which is spun round and then fired at the player's head.

round 1 [raʊnd] adj. (-er, -est) (a) circular/shaped like a circle. (b) r. trip = trip to a destination and back. (c) exact (number). **round 2** n. (a) circle. (b) r. of toast = piece(s) of toast from one slice of bread; r. of sandwiches = sandwiches from two slices of bread. (c) regular route; newspaper r. = number of houses where a boy regularly delivers newspapers; r. of golf = going round all the holes in a golf course. (d) part of a contest/of a boxing match. (e) r. of drinks = series of drinks bought by one person; r. of applause = burst of clapping. (f) one bullet; one shell. (g) song for several voices. each starting at a different point. **round 3** adv. (a) in a circle. (b) completely; all year r. = during the whole year. (c) surrounding; he looked r. = (i) he looked around him; (ii) he looked behind him. (d) from one to another; he handed r. the cups of tea = he handed a cup to each person; is there enough cake to go r.? = enough for everybody; come r. for a drink = come to my house. **round 4** prep. in a circle/ around (sth). **round 5** v. (a) (also round off) to make round. (b) to go round (a corner). (c) to r. on s.o. = to attack s.o; to

r. up = to gather together. (d) to make a whole number; to r. a number up = to increase it to the nearest whole number above. **roundabout 1** *n.* (a) place where several roads meet and the traffic moves in a circle. (b) type of children's amusement in a park. a heavy wooden wheel which you push to turn round and then sit on; (in a fair) a revolving machine (with wooden horses) on which you can ride. **roundabout 2** *adj.* not straight. **rounded** *adj.* with smooth/round corners or edges. **rounders** *n.* team game played with a bat and ball. where the batsmen has to run round the pitch to score. **Roundhead** *n.* supporter of Parliament in the English Civil War. **roundhouse** *n.* circular building for repairing railway engines. **roundly** *adv.* sharply/critically; totally. **roundsman** *n.* man who delivers food to houses. **roundup** *n.* gathering together.

rouse [raʊz] *v.* to wake (s.o.) who is sleeping; to get (s.o.) to act. **rousing** *adj.* loud/exciting.

roustabout ['raʊstəbaʊt] *n.* labourer on an oil rig.

rout 1 [raʊt] *n.* complete defeat (of an army). **rout 2** *v.* (a) to defeat completely. (b) to search; to r. s.o. out = to pull s.o. out from where he is hidden.

route 1 [ruːt] *n.* way to be followed to get to a destination; bus r. = normal way which a bus follows; r. march = training march by soldiers. **route 2** *v.* to send (s.o.) along a route.

routine 1 [ruː'tiːn] *n.* (a) normal/regular way of doing things; daily r. = things which you do everyday. (b) instructions which carry out a task as part of a computer progrAm. **routine 2** *adj.* normal/everyday. **routinely** *adv.* (done) as a routine.

roux [ruː] *n.* mixture of fat and flour cooked to make a base for a sauce.

rove [rəʊv] *v.* to wander.

row 1 [rəʊ] *n.* (a) line (of chairs, etc.). (b) short trip in a rowing boat. **row 2** *v.* to make a boat go forwards by using oars. **rowboat** *n. Am.* rowing boat.

rower *n.* person who rows. **rowing** *n.* making a boat move by the use of oars; r. boat = small boat for rowing.

row 1 [raʊ] *n.* (a) loud noise. (b) sharp argument. **row 2** *v.* to make a row.

rowan ['rəʊən] *n.* mountain ash.

rowdy 1 ['raʊdɪ] *adj.* making a great deal of noise. **rowdy 2** *n.* rough person, who makes a lot of noise.

rowdily *adv.* in a rowdy way.

rowdiness *n.* rowdy behaviour.

rowel ['raʊəl] *n.* little wheel with spikes. attached to a spur.

rowlock ['rɒlək] *n.* metal support for oars.

royal 1 ['rɔɪəl] *adj.* referring to a king or queen; R. Assent = signing of a Bill by the Queen, by which it becomes an Act of Parliament; R. Commission = official group appointed by the government to investigate a problem; the R. Family = family of a king or queen; r. blue = bright dark blue; a right r. welcome = a splendid welcome. **royal 2** *n. inf.* the Royals = members of the Royal Family. **royalist** *n.* person who is a political supporter of a king. **royally** *adv.* splendidly/with great pomp.

royalty *n.* (a) state of being royal; members of a king's family. (b) money paid to the author of a book/an actor in a film/the owner of land where oil is found, etc.. as a percentage of the receipts of sale.

RSVP [ɑːesviː'piː] abbreviation for repondez s'il vous plait meaning please reply.

rub [rʌb] *v.* (rubbed) to move sth across the surface of sth else. **rubbing** *n.* action of rubbing; *Am.* r. alcohol = pure alcohol used as an antiseptic. **rub down** *v.* to rub (s.o./a horse) vigorously. **rub in** *v.* to make a (cream) enter the skin by rubbing; *inf.* don't rub it in = don't go on talking about my mistake. **rub out** *v.* to remove (a pencil mark) with a rubber. **rub up** *v. inf.* to rub s.o. up the wrong way = to make s.o. irritable.

rubber ['rʌbə] *n.* (a) elastic material made from the sap of a tree; r. plant = type of indoor plant with thick shiny green leaves. (b) *Am.* rubbers = rubber/plastic shoes worn over ordinary shoes to protect them. (c) number of games of bridge. (d) piece of rubber used for removing pencil marks. **rubberize** *v.* to coat with rubber. **rubberneck 1** *n. inf.* tourist. **rubberneck 2** *v. inf.* to visit a place as a tourist. **rubberstamp**

1 *n.* stamp made of rubber, with words or figures cut on it, which is used for stamping documents. **rubberstamp 2** *v.* to agree to (sth) automatically without examining it. **rubbery** *adj.* flexible and strong like rubber.

rubbish ['rʌbɪʃ] *n.* (no *pl.*) (a) waste/things which are to be thrown away. (b) nonsense. **rubbishy** *adj.* useless; stupid.

rubble ['rʌbl] *n.* small stones/broken bricks, etc. used in constructing paths, etc.

rubella [ruːbelə] *n.* (formal) German measles.

rubicund ['ruːbɪkənd] *adj.* (formal) red (face).

rubric [ruːbrɪk] *n.* written instructions; written heading to a piece of writing.

ruby 1 [ruːbɪ] *n.* red precious stone. **ruby 2** *adj.* dark red (colour).

ruche [ruːʃ] *n.* cloth gathered into folds. **ruched** *adj.* gathered in folds.

ruck 1 [rʌk] *n.* (a) crease in cloth. (b) (in Rugby) group of players who fight for the ball. **ruck 2** *v.* (also ruck up) to form creases. **rucksack** [rʌksæk] *n.* bag carried on the back of a walker.

ruckus ['rʌkəs] *n. inf.* fight.

ructions ['rʌkʃənz] *n. pl.inf.* argument/angry scene.

rudder ['rʌdə] *n.* flat plate at the stern of a boat/on the tail of an aircraft, used for steering.

ruddy ['rʌdɪ] *adj.* (-ier, -iest) (a) red/firecoloured. (b) *Sl.* awful.

rude [ruːd] *adj.* (-ier, -est) (a) impolite; obscene. (b) sudden. (c) rough/primitive. **rudely** *adv.* not politely. **rudeness** *n.* being rude.

rudiments ['ruːdɪmənts] *n.* simple/elementary facts. **rudimentary** [ruːdɪ'mentərɪ] *adj.* basic; not fully developed.

rue 1 [ruː] *n.* bitter herb. **rue 2** *v.* to regret. **rueful** *adj.* sorry/regretful. **ruefully** *adv.* in a rueful way.

ruff [rʌf] *n.* (a) wide collar of ruffed lace. (b) bird with a ring of coloured feathers round its neck.

ruffian ['rʌfɪən] *n.* hooligan/violent person.

ruffle 1 ['rʌfl] *n.* material/lace gathered into a bunch and used as decoration on clothes/curtains, etc. **ruffle 2** *v.* to

disturb (feathers/water/s.o.'s hair); *inf.* ruffled = flustered.

rug [rʌg] *n.* (a) small carpet. (b) thick blanket. esp. one used for travelling.

Rugby ['rʌgbɪ] *n.* type of football played with an oval ball. which can be passed from hand to hand as well as being kicked.

rugged ['rʌgɪd] *adj.* (a) rough/uneven. (b) strict; sturdy. **ruggedly** *adv.* in a rugged way. **ruggedness** *n.* being rugged.

rugger ['rʌgə] *n.. inf.* Rugby.

ruin 1 ['ruːɪn] *n.* (a) wreck; complete loss of all your money. (b) ruins = remains of collapsed buildings. **ruin 2** *v.* (a) to wreck/to spoil completely. (b) to bring to financial collapse. **ruination** [ruɪ'neɪʃn] *n.* act of running. **ruined** *adj.* in ruins. **ruinous** *adj.* so expensive as to cause ruin. **ruinously** *adv.* extremely (expensive).

rule 1 [ruːl] *n.* (a) general way of conduct; as a r. = generally/usually. (b) strict order of the way to behave; (in industry) work to r. = working only according to the rules laid down in the union agreement. (c) government. (d) wood/metal rod with measurements on it. used in carpentry. (e) straight line in printing). **rule 2** *v.* (a) to govern/to control. (b) to give an official/legal decision. (c) to draw a straight line using a ruler; ruled paper = paper with lines on it. **ruler** *n.* (a) person who governs. (b) strip of wood/plastic with measurements marked on it. used for drawing straight lines. **ruling 1** *adj.* (party) which governs; r. party = party which form s the government. **ruling 2** *n.* legal decision. **rule out** *v.* to leave (sth) out/not to consider (sth).

rum 1 [rʌm] *n.* alcoholic drink made from the juice of sugar cane. **rum 2** *adj. inf.* odd/strange.

rumba ['rʌmbə] *n.* Caribbean dance with a strong rhythm.

rumble 1 ['rʌmbl] *n.* (a) low rolling noise. (b) *Am. inf.* street fight. **rumble 2** *v.* (a) to make a low rolling noise. (b) *inf.* to realise that (s.o.) is trying to deceive you.

rumbustious [rʌm'bʌstʃəs] *adj. inf.* wild/rowdy.

ruminate ['ruːmɪneɪt] *v.* (a) to chew

over food which has already been swallowed once (as a cow does). (b) to think over a problem. **ruminant** ['ru:mɪnənt] *adj. & n.* animal (like a cow) which chews its cud. **rumination** [ru:mɪ'neɪʃn] *n.* deep thought. **ruminative** *adj.* thoughtful.

rummage 1 ['rʌmɪdʒ] *n.* (a) searching about for sth. (b) old junk; r sale = sale of unwanted objects for a charity. **rummage 2** *v.* to search about for sth.

rummy ['rʌmɪ] *n.* card game where each player tries to collect sets of similar cards or several cards in sequence.

rumour, *Am.* **rumor** ['ru:mə] *n.* story passed on from one person to another without necessarily being true. **rumoured** *adj.* spread by rumour.

rump [rʌmp] *n.* back part of an animal.

rumple ['rʌmpl] *v.* to crush/to dishevel.

rumpus ['rʌmpəs] *n.* (*pl.*-es) noisy disorder. fuss.

run 1 [rʌn] *n.* (a) act of going quickly on foot; prisoner on the r. = running away from prison; the soldiers broke into a r. = started to run; go far a r. = (i) to take some exercise by running; (ii) to go for short ride in a car. (b) period; for three days on the r. = for three consecutive days; in the long r. = eventually. (c) access to; he has the r. of the house = he can go anywhere in the house. (d) track for running, skiing, etc. (e) caged area where chickens are kept. (f) point made in cricket/baseball. (g) ladder/long hole in a stocking (h) excessive demand; r. on the pound = sudden selling of the pound on foreign exchanges. (i) carrying out of a task by a computer. **run 2** *v.* (ran, has run) (a) to go very quickly on foot; to race. (b) to travel (fast). (c) of motor, transport) to work. (d) to r. to = to amount to. (e) to go in a direction (f) to direct; he runs his own business (g) to own and drive (a car) (h) to r. a bath = to fill a bath with (i) (of liquid) to flow; this colour won't r. = will not come out if put in water, his nose is running = liquid is coming from his nose (because he has a cold). **run across** *v.* (a) to cross quickly on foot. (b) to find/to meet by chance **run along** *v.* to go alongside. **run away** *v.* to escape **runaway 1** *n.* person who has escaped. **run away 2** *adj.* r. success = great success **run**

down *v.* (a) to go down quickly on foot. (b) (of clock machine) to go slower (c) to criticize (s.o.) (d) to reduce the quantity of (e) to knock down (with a vehicle (f) to be r. down = to feel unwell/ tired. **run down 1** *adj.* delapidated/not looked after. **run down 2** *n.* summary **run for** *v. Am.* to be a candidate for (an office) **run in** *v.* (a) to work (a new engine) slowly until it works properly. (b) *inf.* to arrest (s.o.) **run into** *v.* to meet (s.o.) by chance. **runner** *n.* (a) person who is running (in a race) (b) shoot of a plant which makes roots where it touches the soil; r. bean = type of climbing bean (c) sharp blade of a skate/a sledge (d) narrow carpet. **runner up** *n.* (*pl.*runners up) person who comes after the winner in a race.

running 1 *adj.* (a) which runs; r. commentary = commentary on an action while the action is taking place; r. total = total which is carried from one column of figures to the next (b) used in running a race (for three days) = one after another **running 2** *n.* (a) race; in the r. for = a candidate for (b) working **run off** *v.* (a) to escape/to flee. (b) to run off several photocopies = to make several photocopies. **run of the mill** *adj.* ordinary **run on** *v.* (a) to continue (b) to use (sth) as a fuel. **run out** *v.* (of goods) to go short. **run out of** *v.* to be short of **run over** *v.* (a) to look at (sth) quickly. (b) to knock (s.o.) down with a car. **run up** *v.* (a) to go quickly on foot (b) to come closer quickly on foot (c) to run up against sth = (i) to find sth by chance; (ii) to find your way blocked by sth (d) to sew (sth) quickly.

runway *n.* track on which aircraft land.

runes [ru:nz] *pl. n.* ancient form of writing, used by early Germans. **runic** *adj.* referring to runes; magic

rung 1 [rʌŋ] *n.* one of the bars on a ladder. **rung 2** *v.* see ring

runnel ['rʌnl] *n.* gutter

runny ['rʌnɪ] *adj.* liquid; he's got a r. nose = his nose is running (because he has a cold).

runt ['rʌnt] *n.* small person or animal

rupee [ru:'pi:] *n.* money used in India and other countries.

rupture 1 ['rʌptʃə] *n.* (a) break (in

negotiations); burst/break (of part of the body). (b) hernia **rupture 2** *v.* (a) to break off (negotiations.(b) to burst through; he ruptured himself lifting a heavy box = the strain caused a hernia.

rural ['rʊərəl] *adj.* referring to the country side.

ruse ['ruːz] *n.* clever trick

rush 1 [rʌʃ] *n.* (*pl.*-es) (a) type of wild grass growing in water (b) fast movement; r. hour = time of day when traffic is bad/when trains are full (c) rushes = first prints of a film before it has been edited. **rush 2** *v.* (a) to go forward fast; don't r. me = don't keep on hurrying me (b) to attack suddenly.

rusk [rʌsk] *n.* hard biscuit given to babies to suck.

russet 1 ['rʌsɪt] *n.* type of sweet brown apple. **russet 2** *adj. & n.* reddish brown (colour).

Russian 1 ['rʌʃn] *adj.* referring to Russia. **Russian 2** *n.* (a) person from Russia. (b) language spoken in Russia. **Russo-** ['rʌsəʊ] prefix meaning between Russia and another country.

rust 1 [rʌst] *n.* (a) red substance formed on iron or steel which is left in damp air (b) red fungus disease of plants (c) reddish-brown (colour) **rust 2** *v.* to get rusty. **rustiness** *n.* being rusty. **rustless** *adj.* with no rust. **rust proof** *adj.* (metal) which will not rust. **rusty** *adj.* (-ier, -iest) (a) covered with rust (b) not in practice; (person) who lacks practice.

rustic 1 ['rʌstɪk] *adj.* rough/of country style **rustic 2** *n.* rough peasant. **rusticate** *v.* to send (a student) away from university for a period as a punishment.

rustle 1 ['rʌsl] *n.* noise of dry leaves/ silk, etc. rubbing together. **rustle 2** *v.* (a) to make a soft crackling noise. (b) to steal cattle **rustler** *n.* cattle thief. **rustling** *n.* stealing (of cattle).

rut [rʌt] *n.* (a) long deep track made in soft earth by a wheel; to get into a r. = to start to lead a dull life with no excitement or career prospects. (b) period when a male deer is sexually excited. **rutted** *adj.* (path) of ruts. **rutting** *adj.* (deer) in rut.

rutabaga ['uːtəbəɪɡə] *n. Am.* Swede.

ruthless ['ruːθləs] *adj.* pitiless/cruel.

ruthlessly *adv.* cruelly.

ruthlessness *n.* cruelty

rye [raɪ] *n.* (a) type of dark brown cereal. (b) American whisky made from rye.

ryegrass *n.* type of grass grown in pastures.

Ss

S symbol for sulphur.

Sabbath ['sæbəθ] *n.* seventh day of the week; religious day of rest; (for Jews) Saturday; (for Christians) Sunday.

Sabbatical [sə'bætɪkl] *n. & adj.* (leave) granted to teachers, etc., for study and travel after a period of work.

sable ['seɪbl] *n.* small brown-furred arctic animal; fur from this animal.

sabotage 1 ['sæbətɑːʒ] *n.* malicious/ deliberate destruction. **sabotage 2** *v.* to destroy/to render useless deliberately.

saboteur [sæbə'tɜː] *n.* person who commits sabotage.

sabre, *Am.* saber ['seɪbə] *n.* sword with curved blade.

sac [sæk] *n.* bag-like part of an animal/ plant.

saccharin ['sækərɪn] *n.* extremely sweet substance used as a substitute for sugar. **saccharine** *adj.* too sweet/sickly.

sacerdotal [sæsə'dəʊtl] *adj.* referring to priests.

sachet ['sæʃeɪ] *n.* small bag.

sack 1 [sæk] *n.* (a) plundering (of a town). (b) large bag made of strong rough cloth. (c) *inf.* dismissal; to get/to be given the s. = to be dismissed from a job. (d) *inf.* bed. **sack 2** *v.* (a) to plunder. (b) *inf.* to dismiss (s.o.) from a job. **sackcloth** *n.* s. and ashes = (i) clothes worn at times of penitence; (ii) symbol of repentance. **sackful** *n.* amount held in a sack. **sacking** *n.* coarse material from which sacks are made; old sacks.

sacrament ['sækrəmənt] *n.* (a) Christian religious ceremony. (b) the consecrated bread (and wine) taken at Communion. **sacramental** [sækrə'mentl] *adj.* referring to sacrament.

sacred ['seɪkrəd] *adj.* (a) associated

with religion. (b) holy. (c) respected.
sacredcow *n.* belief/idea which is not
to be criticized. **sacredness** *n.* being
sacred.
sacrifice 1 ['sækrɪfaɪs] *n.* (a) killing of
animal/person as an offering to a god. (b)
animal killed as an offering to a god. (c)
thing given up at personal cost in order
to achieve sth else. **sacrifice 2** *v.* (a) to
offer (sth) as a sacrifice. (b) to give up/to
devote. **sacrificial** [sækrɪ'fɪʃl] *adj.* as a
sacrifice.
sacrilege ['sækrɪlɪdʒ] *n.* using sth
sacred in a disrespectful way.
sacrilegious [sækrɪlɪdʒəs] *adj.*
referring to sacrilege.
sacristy ['sækrɪstɪ] *n.* room in a church
where vestments/vessels, etc., are kept.
sacristan *n.* person who looks after a
church, esp. the vestments/holy vessel,
etc.
sacrosanct ['sækrəʊsæŋkt] *adj.* very
sacred/protected by religious respect.
sacrum ['seɪkrəm] *n.* triangular bone at
the base of the spine.
sad [sæd] *adj.* (sadder, saddest)
unhappy/sorrowful. **sadden** *v.* to make
unhappy. **sadly** *adv.* unhappily.
sadness *n.* being sad.
saddle 1 ['sædl] *n.* (a) rider's seat on a
bicycle/on the back of a horse; in the s. =
in control. (b) ridge between two
mountains (c) s. of lamb = joint of meat
from the back of a sheep. **saddle 2** *v.*
(a) to put a saddle on (a horse, etc.). (b)
to burden (s.o.) with a task of
responsibility. **saddlebag** *n.* bag
attached to a bicycle; one of a pair of
bags on a horse. **saddler** *n.* maker of
saddles and other equipment for horses.
saddlery *n.* shop making/selling
saddles.
sadism ['seɪdɪzəm] *n.* pleasure derived
from being cruel or watching cruelty.
sadist ['seɪdɪst] *n.* person who delights
in sadism. **sadistic** [sə'dɪstɪk] *adj.*
referring to sadism. **sadistically** *adv.*
in a sadistic way.
s.a.e. stamped addressed envelope.
safari [sə'fɑːrɪ] *n.* hunting expedition in
Africa; s. park = park where large wild
animals run free, and visitors can look at
them from their cars.
safe 1 [seɪf] *n.* (a) fire-proof and
burglar-proof box for valuables. (b)

ventilated cupboard for food. **safe 2**
adj. (-er, -est) (a) uninjured. (b) secure/
out of danger. (c) certain/to be relied
upon. **safe-conduct** *n.* paper which
allows s.o. to go through enemy territory.
safe deposit box *n.* box (in a bank)
in which you can store valuables.
safeguard 1 ['seɪfgɑːd] *n.* protection.
safeguard 2 *v.* to guard/to protect.
safely *adv.* without any danger;
without being harmed. **safety** ['seɪftɪ] *n.*
freedom from danger or risk; road s. =
care to be taken by pedestrians and
drivers; s. belt = belt worn in a car/in an
aircraft as protection in case of accident;
s. catch = lock which stops a gun being
fired by accident; s. curtain = fireproof
barrier between the stage and the
auditorium in a theatre; s. pin = type of
bent pin whose point is protected by a
guard; s. valve = valve in steam-boiler,
which lets out excess pressure
automatically.
safflower ['sæflaʊə] *n.* plant which
produces on oil used in cooking.
saffron 1 ['sæfrən] *n.* orange-coloured
powder made from crocus flowers, from
which colouring and flavouring are
obtained. **saffron 2** *adj.* orange-
coloured.
sag 1 [sæg] *n.* bending under weight or
pressure. **sag 2** *v.* (sagged) to sink/to
bend (in the middle) under weight or
pressure.
saga ['sɑːgə] *n.* (a) story of heroic
achievement or adventure. (b) series of
books telling the history of a family.
sagacious [sə'geɪʃəs] *adj.* (formal)
wise/shrewd. **sagaciously** *adv.*
wisely. **sagacity** [sə'gæsɪtɪ] *n.*
exceptional intelligence/wisdom. **sage
1** [seɪdʒ] *n.* (a) aromatic herb used in
cookery; s. green = greyish green colour.
(b) very wise man. **sage 2** *adj.* wise/
discreet. **sagely** *adv.* in a wise way.
Sagittarius [sædʒɪ'teərɪəs] *n.* one of
the signs of the zodiac, shaped like an
archer.
sago ['seɪgəʊ] *n.* white powder used as
food; s. palm = palm tree whose pith
yields sago.
said [sed] *v.* see say.
sail 1 [seɪl] *n.* (a) piece of canvas/nylon.
etc., attached to the mast of a boat to
catch the wind. (b) trip in a boat. (c) arm

of a windmill which turns with the wind.
sail 2 v. (a) to travel on water. (b) to
travel in a sailing boat; to s. close to the
wind = (i) to sail nearly against the wind;
(ii) to sail nearly against the wind; (ii) to
come very near to breaking the law. (c)
to control (a sailing boat). (d) to glide in
the air. **sailboat** n. Am. sailing boat.
sailcloth n. canvas for making sails.
sailing 1 adj. (ship) which uses sails.
sailing 2 n. journey by ship; plain s. =
straight forward progress with no
problems. **sailor** ['seɪlə] n. seaman/
person who sails; good/bad s. = person
who is liable/not liable to seasickness.
saint [seɪnt] n. (a) (abbreviated with
names to St.[snt]) person recognised by
the Christian church as having led an
exceptionally holy life, and canonized
after death. (b) very good/devoted
person. **sainthood** n. being a saint.
saintliness n. holiness/piety. **saintly**
adj. holy.
saintpaulia n. African violet.
saithe [seɪð] n. coley.
sake 1 [seɪk] n. for the s. of sth/for sth's
s. = out of consideration for/in the
interest of. **sake 2** ['saːkɪ] n. Japanese
rice wine.
salaam 1 [sə'laːm] n. bow made in
Eastern countries to greet s.o. **salaam 2**
v. to make a salaam.
salacious [sə'leɪʃəs] adj. erotic/
obscene. **salaciously** adv. in a
salacious way. **salaciousness,
salacity** [sə'læsɪtɪ] adj. being
salacious.
salad ['sæləd] n. cold dish of various
cooked or raw vegetables; cold meat
served with a dressing and lettuce; s.
cream = type of sauce made of eggs/oil/
vinegar, etc., used on salad; s. dressing =
mixture of oil/vinegar, etc., used on
salad; fruit s. = mixture of chopped fresh
fruit.
salamander ['sæləmændə] n. small
animal like a lizard.
salami [sə'laːmɪ] n. salty Italian
sausage, eaten cold.
salary ['sælərɪ] n. fixed payment made
to an employee, usu. every month.
salaried adj. (person) who is paid a
salary.
sale [seɪl] n. (a) exchange of sth for
money; on/for s. = ready to be sold. (b)

goods sold at reduced/special prices for a
short period of time. (c) organized
selling of goods; jumble s. = selling of
unwanted household goods; s. of work =
selling of handmade goods. (d) sales =
money received in a business. **saleable**
adj. fit for sale. **saleroom** n. room in
which an auction is carried out. **sales
girl** n. girl in a shop who sells goods to
customers. **sales lady** n. woman who
sells goods to customers. **salesman** n
(pl.-men) (a) person who sells a
producer's goods to a shop. (b) man in a
shop who sells goods to customers.
salesmanship n. the art of selling.
salesperson n. person who sells
goods in a shop. **saleswoman** n. (pl.-
women) woman in a shop who sells
goods to customers.
salient 1 ['seɪlɪənt] n. projecting part of
a fortification/of a line of battle. **salient
2** adj. prominent/conspicuous/most
important.
saline ['seɪlaɪn] adj. containing salt.
salinity [sə'lɪnɪtɪ] n. amount of salt.
saliva [sə'laɪvə] n. liquid formed in the
mouth to help digestion. **salivary** adj.
s. gland = gland which produces saliva.
salivate ['sælɪveɪt] v. to make saliva.
salivation [sælɪ'veɪʃn] n. act of
salivating.
sallow 1 ['sæləʊ] adj. (-er, -est) sickly
yellow (complexion). **sallow 2** n.
willow tree.
sally 1 ['sælɪ] n. (a) sudden rush (of
soldiers) out of a defended position. (b)
witticism. **sally 2** v. (also sally forth) to
go out.
salmon 1 ['sæmən] n. (pl.salmon)
large pink-fleshed fish. **salmon 2** adj.
& n. orange-pink (colour). **salmon
trout** n. large sea trout with pink flesh.
Salmonella [sælmə'nelə] n. type of
bacteria which grows on meat, eggs, and
fish, and causes food poisoning.
salon ['sælɒn] n. hairdresser's/
dressmaker's business; room/building
housing a hairdresser's or dressmaker's.
saloon [sə'luːn] n. (a) large lounge in a
ship. (b) comfortable bar in a public
house. (c) Am. public bar. (d) s.(car) =
covered car.
salsify ['sælsɪfɪ] n. vegetable with a
long white root.
salt 1 [sɔːlt] n. (a) white substance

(sodium chloride) used to season and preserve food; *inf.* to take sth with a pinch of s. = not to believe s.o. completely. (b) (in chemistry) combination of a metal with an acid; (c) *inf.* old s. = experienced sailor. **salt 2** *adj.* containing salt; preserved/seasoned with salt. **salt 3** *v.* to add salt to. **salt away** *v* to put (sth) aside for the future. **salt cellar** *n.* small pot containing salt, *usu.* with a hole in the top so that it can be sprinkled on food. **salt-free** *adj.* without salt. **saltiness, saltness** *n.* being salty. **saltlick** *n.* block of salt put in a field for cattle to lick. **saltpan** *n.* enclosure where salt is formed as sea water evaporates. **saltpetre, *Am.* saltpeter** [sɔːlt'piːtə] *n.* potassium nitrate/powder used to make gunpowder. **salty** *adj.* (-ier, -iest) containing salt.

salubrious [sə'luːbrɪəs] *adj.* (formal) healthy. **salubrity** *n.* healthiness.

saluki [sə'luːkɪ] *n.* breed of hound.

salute 1 [sə'luːt] *n.* gesture expressing respect/homage/recognition. **salute 2** *v.* to give a salute to (s.o.). **salutary** ['sæljʊtərɪ] *adj.* useful/helpful; which has a good effect. **salutation** [sæljʊ'teɪʃn] *n.* words spoken/written in praise of s.o./to greet s.o.

salvage 1 ['sælvɪdʒ] *n.* (a) payment made for saving a ship/its cargo from loss by wreck. (b) objects saved (from a boat/fire, etc.). (c) saving rubbish for use. **salvage 2** *v.* to save (from wreck/fire, etc.).

salvation [sæl'veɪʃn] *n.* saving of the soul from sin; saving of a person from evil. **Salvation Army** *n.* religious organization in missionary and welfare work among poor people.

salve 1 [sælv] *n.* healing ointment; lip s. = ointment which prevents lips cracking in cold weather. **salve 2** *v.* to do sth to s. your conscience = because your conscience tells you to do it.

salver ['sælvə] *n.* large flat plate (usu. made of silver).

salvia ['sælvɪə] *n.* common summer garden plant with red flowers.

salvo ['sælvəʊ] *n.* (*pl.*-oes) (a) simultaneous firing of several guns in a battle at sea or as a salute. (b) round of applause.

sal volatile [sælvə'lætəlɪ] *n.* smelling salts.

Samaritan [sə'mærɪtən] *n.* person who helps s.o. in trouble.

same 1 [seɪm] *adj.* identical; monotonous/unchanging; it's all the s. to me = I don't mind. **same 2** *pron.* the identical thing. **same 3** *adv. inf.* all the s./just the s. = nevertheless. **sameness** *n.* (a) being the same. (b) monotony.

samovar ['sæməʊvɑː] *n.* urn used in Russia for boiling water for tea.

sampan ['sæmpæn] *n.* small Chinese boat.

samphire ['sæmfaɪə] *n.* type of fern which grows near the sea.

sample 1 ['sɑːmpl] *n.* specimen.

sample 2 *v.* (a) to test/to try (by taking a small amount). (b) to ask a group of people questions to find out a general reaction. **sampler** *n.* decorated tapestry panel (usu. with letters, numbers and simple pictures) made to show skill in sewing stitches.

samurai ['sæmʊraɪ] *n.* medieval Japanese warrior.

sanatorium [sænə'tɔːrɪəm] *n.* hospital for the treatment of invalids, esp. people suffering from tuberculosis.

sanctify ['sæŋktɪfaɪ] *v.* to consecrate/to make holy. **sanctification** [sæŋktɪfɪ'keɪʃn] *n.* making holy.

sanctimonious [sæŋktɪ'məʊnɪəs] *adj.* pretending to be holy. **sanctimoniously** *adv.* in a sanctimonious way.

sanctity ['sæŋktɪtɪ] *n.* holiness of life/saintliness.

sanction 1 ['sæŋkʃn] *n.* (a) law/decree. (b) penalty for breaking a rule; economic sanctions = restrictions on trade with a country in order to try to influence its political development. **sanction 2** *v.* (a) to approve. (b) to permit. **sanctuary** ['sæŋktjʊərɪ] *n.* (a) holy place. (b) part of a church where the high altar is placed. (c) place for the protection of wild animals or birds. (d) refuge.

sanctum ['sæŋktəm] *n.* (a) holy place. (b) private room; inner s. = most private/secret office.

sand 1 [sænd] *n.* (a) mass of tiny fragments of worn-down rock, etc., found on seashores/river beds/deserts, etc. **sand 2** *v.* (a) (also sand down) to rub smooth with sandpaper. (b) to spread sand on (icy roads). **sandbag 1** *n.* bag filled with sand and used as a defence/as ballast. **sandbag 2** *v.* (-bagged) (a) to protect (sth) with a wall of sandbags. (b) to knock (s.o.) out by hitting him with a sandbag. **sandbank** *n.* ridge of sand in sea or river. **sand blast** *v.* to clean (the exterior of a building) by directing a powerful jet of sand on to it. **sander** *n.* machine/person who sands. **sandpaper 1** *n.* paper with a coating of sand for smoothing. **sandpaper 2** *v.* to rub (sth) smooth with sandpaper.

sandpiper *n.* small bird with a long bill which lives on beaches. **sandpit** *n.* place with sand where children can play. **sands** *n. pl.*sandy seashore.

sandstone *n.* rock made of compressed sand. **sandstorm** *n.* high wind in a desert blowing clouds of sand. **sandy** *adj.* like sand; made of sand.

sandal ['sændl] *n.* light open shoe worn in the summer. **sandalled** *adj.* wearing sandals. **sandalwood** *n.* (a) tropical tree; fragrant wood from this tree. (b) scent from this tree.

sandwich 1 ['sændwɪtʃ] *n.* (*pl.*-es) two slices of bread with sweet or savoury filling. **sandwich 2** *v.* to insert (sth) between two others. **sandwich board** *n.* pair of boards worn over the shoulders in the street to advertise sth. **sandwich course** *n.* course where students spend time working in a factory between periods of study at a college. **sandwichman** *n.* man who carries a sandwich board.

sane [seɪn] *adj.* (-er, -est) reasonable/ not mad. **sanely** *adv.* in a sane way. **sanity** ['sænɪtɪ] *n.* being sane.

sang [sæŋ] *v.* see sing.

sangfroid [sɑːŋ'frwɑː] *n.* calmness when in danger.

sanguinary ['sæŋgwɪnərɪ] *adj.* delighting in bloodshed or killing. **sanguine** ['sæŋgwɪn] *adj.* confident/ optimistic.

sanitation [sænɪ'teɪʃn] *n.* hygiene/ conditions affecting health. **sanitary** ['sænɪtərɪ] *adj.* referring to sanitation/ hygiene; s. towel = pad of material worn by women to absorb blood lost during menstruation.

sank [sæŋk] *v.* see sink.

Sanskrit ['sænzkrɪt] *n.* classical language of India.

sans serif ['sænz'serɪf] *n.* typeset character with no serifs.

Santa Claus ['sæntə'klɔːz] *n.* Father Christmas.

sap 1 [sæp] *n.* (a) juice circulating in plants and trees. (b) (in warfare) digging a tunnel to get near to the enemy. (c) *inf.* silly person. **sap 2** *v.* (sapped) (a) to weaken/to make insecure by removing foundations. **sapper** *n.* soldier in the Royal Engineers.

sapling ['sæplɪŋ] *n.* young tree.

sapphire 1 ['sæfaɪə] *n.* blue precious stone. **sapphire 2** *adj.* clear blue (colour).

saprophyte ['sæprəʊfaɪt] *n.* fungus which lives on decaying plants. **saprophytic** [sæprəʊ'fɪtɪk] *adj.* living on decaying plants.

saraband ['særəbænd] *n.* slow Spanish dance.

sarcasm ['sɑːkæzəm] *n.* making sharp unpleasant remarks. **sarcastic** [sɑː'kæstɪk] *adj.* scornful, with sarcasm. **sarcastically** *adv.* in a sarcastic way.

sarcoma [sɑː'kəʊmə] *n.* kind of malignant tumour.

sarcophagus [sə'kɒfəgəs] *n.* (*pl.*- gi[gan]) stone coffin often decorated with sculpture.

sardine [sɑː'diːn] *n.* small fish of the herring family; packed like sardines = very tightly.

sardonic [sɑː'dɒnɪk] *adj.* scornful/ cynical. **sardonically** *adv.* in a sardonic way.

sardonyx ['sɑːdɒnɪks] *n.* semi-precious stone, with red layers.

Sargasso Sea [sɑː'gæsəʊ'siː] *n.* area of the Atlantic Ocean, with few currents, covered with drifting weed.

sari ['sɑːrɪ] *n.* long piece of cloth worn by Indian women.

sarong [sə'rɒŋ] *n.* cloth worn wrapped round the lawyer part of the body by S.E. Asian men and women.

sarsaparilla [sɑːspə'rɪlə] *n.* drink made from the roof of an American plant.

sarsen ['sɑːsn] *n.* large block of sandstone.

sartorial [sɔː'tɔːrɪəl] *adj.* (formal)

referring to men's clothes.

sash [sæʃ] *n.* (*pl.*-es) (a) ornamental scarf. (b) wooden frame holding panes of glass. **sash cord** *n.* rope in a sash window which allows the frames to slide up and down smoothly. **sash window** *n.* window made of panes of glass set in two frames which slide up and down.

sashay [səʃeɪ] *v. Am.* to walk confidently.

Sassenach ['sæsənæk] *n.* (in Scotland) Englishman.

sat [sæt] *v.* see sit.

Satan ['seɪtən] *n.* the devil. **satanic** [sə'tænɪk] *adj.* diabolical/like the devil.

satchel ['sætʃəl] *n.* small leather/ canvas bag worn on the shoulders.

sate [seɪt] *v.* (formal) to satisfy (s.o.) by giving him too much.

sateen [sə'tiːn] *n.* type of fine cotton cloth which looks like satin.

satellite ['sætəlaɪt] *n.* (a) heavenly body which goes round a planet. (b) artificial body which was launched from and which goes round the earth; s. broadcast = radio/TV broadcast which is transmitted via a satellite; s. dish = aerial, shaped like a dish, used to capture satellite broadcasts. **satellite state** *n.* country controlled by a more powerful one. **satellite town** *n.* small town dependent on a larger town near by.

satiate ['seɪʃeɪt] *v.* to satisfy totally/to fill to overflowing. **satiation** *n.* act of satiating. **satiety** [sə'taɪətɪ] *n.* being satiated.

satin 1 ['sætɪn] *n.* silk fabric with a glossy surface. **satin 2** *adj.* made of satin. **satinwood** *n.* type of hard tropical wood. **satiny** *adj.* smooth and shiny, like satin.

satire ['sætaɪə] *n.* (a) attacking s.o. in speech/writing by making them seem ridiculous. (b) humorously critical piece of writing. **satiric, satirical** [sə'tɪrɪkl] *adj.* humorously critical. **satirically** *adv.* in a satirical way. **satirist** ['sætɪrɪst] *n.* writer of satires. **satirize** ['sætɪraɪz] *v.* to attack (sth) in a more or less amusing way.

satisfaction [sætɪsfækʃn] *n.* (a) payment of debt; compensation (for damage). (b) good feeling; sense of comfort/happiness. **satisfactory** *adj.* causing satisfaction; quite good.

satisfactorily *adv.* in a satisfactory way. **satisfy 1** ['sætɪsfaɪ] *v.* (a) to comply with/to fulfil. (b) to show adequate proof. (c) to make (s.o.) content/pleased. (d) to be sure/to ascertain. **satisfying** *adj.* which satisfies.

satsuma [sæt'suːmə] *n.* type of small sweet seedless orange.

saturate ['sætʃʊreɪt] *v.* to make very wet. **saturated fat** *n.* fat (such as animal fat) which contains the largest amount of hydrogen possible.

saturation [sætʃʊ'reɪʃn] *n.* complete filling; s. point = point at which a substance cannot absorb any more liquid.

Saturday ['sætədeɪ] *n.* sixth day of the week; day between Friday and Sunday.

saturnalia ['sætə'neɪlɪə] *n.* wild orgy. **saturnine** ['sætənaɪn] *adj.* gloomy character.

satyr ['sætə] *n.* classical god living in woods, with a human body, but with legs and ears like a goat's.

sauce [sɔːs] *n.* (a) liquid poured over food. (b) *inf.* impertinence. **sauceboat** *n.* vessel in which sauce is served.

saucepan *n.* deep metal cooking pot with a long handle. **saucily** *adv. inf.* cheekily. **sauciness** *n. inf.* being saucy. **saucy** *adj.* (-ier, -iest) *inf.* cheeky. **saucer** ['sɔːsə] *n.* shallow dish placed under a cup; flying s. = object shaped like a saucer which people say they have seen in the sky.

Saudi (Arabian) ['saʊdɪ(ə'reɪbɪən)] *adj. & n.* (person) from Saudi Arabia.

sauerkraut ['saʊəkraʊt] *n.* German dish of pickled cabbage.

sauna ['sɔːnə] *n.* (a) very hot steam bath. (b) room where you can have a sauna bath.

saunter 1 ['sɔːntə] *n.* stroll/leisurely walk. **saunter 2** *v.* to walk in a leisurely way/to stroll.

saurian ['sɔːrɪən] *adj. & n.* (animal) like a lizard.

sausage ['sɒsɪdʒ] *n.* tube of edible skin full of minced and seasoned pork or other meat. **sausagemeat** *n.* meat and breadcrumbs minced and seasoned.

sausage roll *n.* small piece of sausage cooked in pastry.

sauté 1 ['saʊteɪ] *adj.* fried in a little fat.

sauté 2 *v.* (sautéed) to fry in a little fat.
savage 1 ['sævɪdʒ] *adj.* (a) uncivilized/primitive. (b) fierce/ferocious. **savage 2** *n.* wild/uncivilized human being. **savage 3** *v.* to attack with teeth. **savagely** *adv.* in a savage way. **savageness, savagery** *n.* being savage.
savanna(h) [sə'vænə] *n.* grassy plain in a tropical country.
savant ['sævɒn] *n.* learned man; idiot s. = person of limited intelligence, but with a highly developed skill in a single faculty (such as memorizing numbers).
save 1 [seɪv] *v.* (a) to rescue from misfortune. (b) to keep for future use/to reserve; (computers) to keep data in storage after it has been keyboarded. (c) to make an economy/not to spend. (d) (in sport) to prevent opponents from scoring. (e) to gain (time). (f) to avoid (trouble). **save 2** *prep. & conj.* except.
Save-As-You-Earn *n.* scheme to encourage people to save by placing money into a savings scheme directly out of one's salary. **saver** *n.* person who saves money. **saving 1** *n.* economy. **saving 2** *adj.* redeeming. **saving 3** *prep.* (old) except. **savings** *n.* money saved. **savings bank** *n.* bank which gives interest on small deposits of money.
saveloy ['sævəlɔɪ] *n.* highly-seasoned dried sausage.
saviour, *Am.* **saviour** ['seɪvjə] *n.* person who saves; our Saviour = Jesus Christ.
savory ['seɪvərɪ] *n.* herb used in cooking.
savour, *Am.* **savor 1** ['seɪvə] *n.* (a) characteristic taste. (b) suspicion/hint.
savour, *Am.* **savor 2** *v.* (a) to appreciate (food and wine). (b) to s. of = to suggest. **savouriness** *n.* appetizing taste or smell. **savoury 1** *adj.* (a) appetizing. (b) salty/not sweet. **savoury 2** *n.* food (which is not sweet) served at the beginning or end of a meal.
savoy [sə'vɔɪ] *n.* curly winter cabbage.
saw 1 [sɔː] *n.* (a) steel tool with a blade with a serrated edge, used for cutting wood/metal etc. (b) old saying. **saw 2** *v.* (sawed; sawn) (a) to cut (wood, etc.) with a saw. (b) see also see. **sawdust** *n.* powder produced from sawing wood.

sawfish *n.* large sea fish with a nose shaped like a saw. **sawmill** *n.* power-driven mill which saws wood mechanically. **sawyer** *n.* person who saws wood.
sax [sæks] *n. inf.* saxophone.
saxe (blue) ['sæks(bluː)] *n.* pale grey blue.
saxifrage ['sæksɪfreɪdʒ] *n.* low alpine plant with pink flowers.
Saxophone ['sæksəfəʊn] *n.* brass musical instrument with keys. **saxophonist** [sæk'sɒfənɪst] *n.* saxophone player.
say 1 [seɪ] *n.* right to decide. **say 2** *v.* (said (sed)) (a) to speak. (b) to speak. (b) to put in writing. (c) to give (an opinion); to put an idea into words. (d) to suggest. **saying** *n.* proverb/phrase which is often used.
SAYE short for save-as-you-earn.
scab [skæb] *n.* (a) dry rough crust formed over a wound when it is healing. (b) *inf.* workman who refuses to take part in a strike. **scabby** *adj.* covered with scabs.
scabbard ['skæbəd] *n.* sheath/holder for a dagger or sword.
scabies ['skeɪbiːz] *n.* (no *pl.*) skin disease which makes you itch.
scabious ['skeɪbɪəs] *n.* perennial plant with pincushion-shaped flowers.
scabrous ['skeɪbrəs] *adj.* (formal) with a rough surface.
scaffold ['skæfəld] *n.* platform on which executions take place.
scaffolding *n.* structure of poles and planks providing workmen with a platform to stand on while working.
scald 1 [skɔːld] *n.* burn caused by boiling liquid. **scald 2** *v.* to injure with hot liquid or steAm. **scalding 1** *n.* being burnt by a hot liquid. **scalding 2** *adj.* very hot.
scale 1 [skeɪl] *n.* (a) thin horny plate protecting the skin of fish and snakes; s. insect = insect which sucks sap from plants and covers itself with a scale. (b) hard deposit struck to a surface. (c) arrangement of musical notes in order. (d) graded system. (e) relative measurements of a small object which are exactly similar to those of a larger object. **scale 2** *v.* (a) to remove scales from. (b) to remove deposit from

(teeth). (c) to s. off = to drop off in thin layers. (d) to climb up/to climb over. (e) to s. up/down = to increase/ to reduce proportionally. **scaleable** *adj.* which can be scaled. **scales** *n. pl.* instrument for weighing; (pair of) s. = weighing machine. **scaly** *adj.* covered in scales.

scallion ['skælɪən] *n.* young onion eaten raw in salad.

scallop ['skɒləp] *n.* (a) type of shellfish with a semi-circular ridged shell. (b) ornamental edging of material in small semicircles. **scalloped** *adj.* with scallops along the edge.

scallywag ['skælɪwæg] *n. inf.* naughty person.

scalp 1 [skælp] *n.* skin and hair on the top of the head. **scalp 2** *v.* (a) to cut off the scalp of (s.o.). (b) *inf.* to sell tickets at a very high price. **scalper** *n. inf.* person who sells tickets at a very high price. **scalpel** ['skælpl] *n.* small surgical knife.

scam [skæm] *n. Am.* fraud.

scamp 1 [skæmp] *n.* rascal. **scamp 2** *v.* to do (sth) in an unsatisfactory way.

scamper 1 ['skæmpə] *n.* run/gallop. **scamper 2** *v.* to run fast.

scampi ['skæmpɪ] *n. pl.* large prawns.

scan 1 [skæn] *v.* (scanned) (a) to test the rhythm of (a line of poetry); (of poetry) to fit a regular rhythm of (a line of poetry); (of poetry) to fit a regular rhythm. (b) to look intently all over. (c) to pass a radar beam over (an area); to pass X-rays through part of the body.

scan 2 *n.* action of passing a radar beam of X-ray over an area; brain s. = examining the inside of the brain by passing X-rays through the head.

scanner *n.* machine for carrying out scanning.

scandal ['skændl] *n.* (a) unkind gossip. (b) thing that produces a general feeling of anger. **scandalize** *v.* to shock. **scandalized** *adj.* shocked. **scandalmonger** *n.* person who spreads gossip. **scandalous** *adj.* shameful. **scandalously** *adv.* terribly.

Scandinavian [skændɪ'neɪvɪən] *n. & adj.* (person) from Scandinavia.

scansion ['skænʃn] *n.* art of scanning poetry.

scant [skænt] *adj.* hardly enough.

scantily *adj.* s. dressed = with very few clothes on. **scantiness** *n.* lack; smallness. **scanty** *adj.* (-ier, -iest) small/not sufficient.

scapegoat ['skeɪpgəʊt] *n.* person who carries the blame for s.o. else.

scapula [skæpjʊlə] *n.* shoulder blade.

scar 1 [skɑː] *n.* mark left after a wound has healed. **scar 2** *v.* (scarred) (a) to wound (s.o.) causing a permanent mark. (b) to leave a mark on the mind of.

scarab ['skærəb] *n.* carved beetle.

scarce [skeəs] *adj.* (-er, -est) insufficient for the demand/hard to find; *inf.* to make oneself s. = to disappear/to keep out of the way. **scarcely** *adv.* hardly/only just. **scarceness, scarcity** *n.* lack/insufficiency.

scare 1 [skeə] *n.* fright/terror. **scare 2** *v.* (a) to frighten. (b) to be alarmed.

scared *adj.* frightened. **scarecrow** *n.* figure looking like a man set up in a field to frighten off birds.

scaremonger *n.* person who likes to alarm others. **scaremongering** *n.* spreading of alarm. **scary** *adj.* (-ier, -est) frightening.

scarf [skɑːf] *n.* (*pl.* scarves) long strip or square of material worn round the neck to keep you warm.

scarify ['skærɪfaɪ] *v.* to make slits in (sth).

scarlet ['skɑːlət] *adj.* brilliant red colour.

scariatina, scariet fever *n.* infectious disease producing a bright red rash.

scarp [skɑːp] *n.* steep hillside. **scarper** ['skɑːpə] *v. inf.* to run.

scathing ['skeɪðɪn] *adj.* very critical.

scatter ['skætə] *v.* (a) to throw here and there. (b) to go/to run in all directions.

scatterbrain *n.* forgetful person.

scatterbrained *adj.* forgetful/ careless. **scattered** *adj.* spread out.

scatty *adj. inf.* silly/slightly mad.

scaup [skɔːp] *n.* type of wild duck.

scavenger ['skævɪndʒə] *n.* (a) animal which feeds on other dead animals. (b) person who looks for useful things among rubbish. **scavenge** *v.* to look for useful things among rubbish.

scenario [sɪ'nɑːrɪəʊ] *n.* (*pl.* -os) written version of a play with details of characters/scenes, etc. **scene** [siːn] *n.*

(a) subdivision of an act in a play; behind the scenes = without being obvious/without many people knowing. (b) place in which events actually occur. (c) view/surroundings. (d) display of temper. (e) *inf.* it's not my s. = it doesn't interest me/it is not the sort of thing I usually do. **scenery** *n.* (a) painted cloth backgrounds and other props used in a theatre to make the stage resemble the supposed scene of action. (b) view of the countryside. **scenic** *adj.* referring to scenery; s. railway = miniature railway running through artificial picturesque scenery at a fair; s. route = road running through beautiful countryside.

scent 1 [sent] *n.* (a) pleasant smell. (b) characteristic smell; on the s. of = following a trail. (c) perfume. (d) sense of smell. **scent 2** *v.* (a) to find out by smelling. (b) to begin to suspect. (c) to make fragrant.

sceptic, *Am.* **skeptic** ['skeptɪk] *n.* person who doubts the truth of religion. (b) person who always doubts the truth of what he is told. **sceptical** *adj.* doubtful/(person) who doubts. **sceptically** *adv.* doubtfully/ distrustfully. **scepticism** *n.* doubt/ uncertainty.

sceptre, *Am.* **scepter** ['septə] *n.* gold stick covered with precious stones carried by a king or queen.

schedule *Am.* **1** ['fedjuːl, [xx] 'skedʒuːl] *n.* (a) timetable. (b) programme/list of events. (c) plan. (d) appendix to a document. **schedule** *Am.* **2** *v.* (a) to list officially. (b) to plan (sth) for a particular time; scheduled service = regular (bus/train, etc.) service.

scheme 1 [skiːm] *n.* (a) plan/ arrangement. (b) plot. **scheme 2** *v.* to plot. **schematic** [skɪ'mætɪk] *adj.* laid out like a diagrAm. **schematically** *adv.* in a schematic way. **schemer** *n.* person who plots. **scheming** *adj.* (person) who plots.

scherzo ['skeətsəʊ] *n.* (*pl.*-os) lively section of a longer piece of music.

schism ['skɪzəm] *n.* division of a religious community into factions. **schismatic** [skɪz'mætɪk] *adj.* tending to break away.

schist [ʃɪst] *n.* rock which splits into thin layers.

schizophrenia [skɪtsəʊ'friːnɪə] *n.* mental illness where thoughts, feelings and actions are all disconnected. **schizoid** ['skɪtsɔɪd] *adj. & n.* (person) suffering from schizophrenia. **schizophrenic** [skɪtsəʊ'frenɪk] *adj.* referring to schizophrenia.

schmaltz [ʃmɒlts] *n.* too much sentimentality (in writing/music, etc.).

schnapps [ʃnæps] *n.* colourless German alcohol.

schnitzel ['ʃnɪtzl] *n.* thin flat piece of veal fried in breadcrumbs.

scholar ['skɒlə] *n.* (a) person who studies. (b) learned person. (c) student at school or university who has a scholarship. **scholarliness** *n.* being scholarly. **scholarly** *adj.* learned/ seeking to learn. **scholarship** *n.* (a) profound learning. (b) money given to a student to help pay for the cost of his study. **scholastic** [skɒ'læstɪk] *adj.* referring to schools or teaching.

school 1 [skuːl] *n.* (a) place for teaching (usu. children); department of a university. (b) followers of a philosopher/artist, etc. (c) large group of fish or sea animals. **school 2** *v.* to teach/to train. **schoolbook** *n.* book used in school. **schoolboy, schoolgirl** *n.* child who goes to school. **schoolchildren** *n. pl.* children who go to school. **schooling** *n.* education at school level. **schoolmaster, schoolmistress** *n.* schoolteacher. **schoolmastering** *n.* profession of teacher. **schoolteacher** *n.* person who teaches in a school.

schooner ['skuːnə] *n.* (a) sailing ship with two or more masts and sails running lengthwise down the ship. (b) tall glass for sherry.

sciatica [saɪ'ætɪkə] *n.* pain in the back and legs. **sciatic nerve** *n.* nerve in the hip.

science ['saɪəns] *n.* (a) knowledge obtained from observation and arranged into a system. (b) study based on observation and experiment (such as chemistry/biology, etc.). **science fiction** *n.* stories on the subject of space travel/life in the future. **scientific** [saɪən'tɪfɪk] *adj.* referring to science. **scientifically** *adv.* according to

scientific experiment. **scientist**
['saɪəntɪst] *n.* person who studies
science.

scilla ['sɪlə] *n.* small blue flower,
coming from a bulb.

scimitar ['sɪmɪtə] *n.* short sword with a
curved blade.

scintillate ['sɪntɪleɪt] *v.* to sparkle.
scintillating *adj.* sparking.
scintillation [sɪntɪ'leɪʃn] *n.* wit/sparkle.

scion ['saɪən] *n.* piece of a plant which
is grafted on to another; young member
of a noble family.

scissors ['sɪzəz] *n. pl.*(a pair of) s. =
instrument for cutting fabric/paper, etc.,
constructed of two blades with handles
for thumb and fingers.

sclerosis [sklə'rəʊsɪs] *n.* hardening of
soft tissue; multiple s. = gradual disease
where hardening of tissue causes general
paralysis.

scoff [skɒf] *v.* (a) to s. at = to make fun
of in a nasty way. (b) *inf.* to eat greedily.
scoffer *n.* person who scoffs.
scoffing *adj.* mocking. **scoffingly**
adv. mockingly.

scold [skəʊld] *v.* to speak to (s.o.)
angrily. **scolding** *n.* rebuke.

sconce ['skɒns] *n.* decorated bracket
which holds a light.

scone [skɒn] *n.* small soft cake *usu.*
eaten with cream and jam.

scoop 1 [skuːp] *n.* (a) short-handled
shovel/spoon; round spoon for serving
ice creAm. (b) portion of ice cream, etc.
(c) piece of news which is published in
one newspaper before any other. **scoop
2** *v.* (a) to lift, using a scoop; to s. out
the inside of sth = to remove the inside
of sth with a spoon, etc. (b) to obtain
against competition. (c) to s. a
newspaper = to print a news item before
another paper does.

scooter ['skuːtə] *n.* (a) child's two
wheeled vehicle with footboard and a
long steering handle, pushed along with
one foot. (b) motor s. = motorized two
wheel bicycle with a curving shield in
front and a platform for the feet. **scoot**
v. inf. to go quite fast. **scooterist** *n.*
person who rides a scooter.

scope [skəʊp] *n.* (a) reach of
observation/action. (b) opportunity.

scorbutus [skɔːˈbuːtəs] *n.* scurvy.

scorch [skɔːtʃ] *v.* to burn slightly/to

brown; scorched-earth policy = tactics in
war where all the resources are destroyed
before retreating and giving up territory
to the enemy. **scorcher** *n. inf.* very hot
day. **scorching** *adj.* very hot/which
scorches.

score 1 [skɔː] *n.* (a) scratch (in paint,
etc.). (b) debt; to settle old scores = to
get your own back on s.o. after a long
delay. (c) number of points made in a
game; *inf.* he knows the s. = he knows all
the facts of the case. (d) piece of music
written out showing the parts for each
instrument or voice. (e) twenty; scores of
= many. (f) question/matter. **score 2** *v.*
(a) to scratch. (b) to make a point in a
game. (c) to write down the score in a
game. (d) to write out (a piece of music)
with parts for each instrument or voice.

scoreboard *n.* large board showing
the score in a tennis match, etc. **scorer**
n. person who makes a point in a game;
person who writes down the scores in a
game. **score off** *v.* to make points
against (s.o.) in a conversation. **score
out** *v.* to cross out.

scorn 1 [skɔːn] *n.* feeling of looking
down/disrespect. **scorn 2** *v.* to look
down on/not to respect. **scornful** *adj.*
disrespectful. **scornfully** *adv.* in a
scornful way.

Scorpio ['skɔːpɪəʊ] *n.* one of the signs
of the Zodiac, shaped like a scorpion.
scorpion ['skɔːpɪən] *n.* poisonous
tropical insect which stings with a long
curved tail.

Scot [skɒt] *n.* person from Scotland.
Scots 1 *adj.* referring to Scotland; S.
pine = common European confer. **Scots
2** *n.* form of English spoken in
Scotland. **Scotsman, Scotswoman**
n. (*pl.*-men, -women) person from
Scotland. **Scottish** *adj.* referring to
Scotland. **Scotch 1** [skɒtʃ] *adj.*
referring to Scotland; (Scottish is
preferred in Scotland, but Scotch is
always used in the following) S. broth =
soup made with mutton, barley, etc.; S.
eggs = hard boiled eggs covered with
sausage meat and fried; S. mist = thick
mist and rain; S. terrier = type of black
or white terrier; S. whisky = whisky
made in Scotland. **Scotch 2** *n.* (a) (*pl.*-
ies) Scotch whisky; a glass of this drink.
(b) trademark for a type of transparent

sticky tape. **Scotch 3** *v.* to s. = to try to stop (a rumour). **scot-free** [skɒt'fri:] *adj.* to get off s. = without being punished.

scoundrel ['skaʊndrəl] *n.* wicked person.

scour ['skaʊə] *v.* (a) to clean by scrubbing with a hard material. (b) to search everywhere. **scourer** *n.* pad of steel wool for cleaning pans.

scourge 1 [skɜːdʒ] *n.* thing which causes suffering. **scourge 2** *v.* to cause suffering.

Scouse ['skaʊs] *adj. & n. inf.* (person) from Liverpool; dialect spoken in Liverpool.

scout 1 [skaʊt] *n.* (a) person sent out to look for information. (b) boy who belongs to the Boy Scouts' Association. **scout 2** *v.* to reconnoitre; to s. around for = to search for. **scoutmaster** *n.* leader of a group of Boy Scouts.

scowl 1 [skaʊl] *n.* angry look made by wrinkling the forehead. **scowl 2** *v.* to make a scowl.

scrabble ['skræbl] *v.* to s. (about) = to scratch wildly with your hands or feet.

scrag [skræg] *n.* s. (end) = sheep's neck used to make soup. **scraggy** ['skrægɪ] *adj.* (-ier, -iest) thin and bony.

scram [skræm] *inter.* meaning go away!

scramble 1 ['skræmbl] *n.* (a) act of scrambling (up sth). (b) rush. (c) cross country motorcycle race. **scramble 2** *v.* (a) to hurry along on hands and knees. (b) to try to get somewhere by pushing. (c) scrambled eggs = eggs mixed together and stirred as they are cooked in butter. (d) to mix up (a radio signal/telephone link) so that it cannot be understood without an apparatus for unmixing it. **scrambler** *n.* machine for scrambling radio signals; s. telephone which scrambles the message.

scrap 1 [skræp] *n.* (a) small piece. (b) waste materials; scraps = bits of waste food/waste material; s. heap = heap of rubbish; s. metal/paper = waste metal/paper. (c) *inf.* fight. **scrap 2** *v.* (scrapped) (a) to throw away as waste. (b) to give up (plans). (c) to fight.

scrapbook *n.* large book with blank pages for sticking photographs/newspaper cuttings, into., etc. **scrappy** *adj.* (-ier, -iest) made of bits and pieces.

scrape 1 [skreɪp] *n.* (a) mark made by

sth hard being pulled across a surface. (b) awkward situation/trouble. (c) very thin layer of butter, etc., spread on bread. **scrape 2** *v.* to scratch with a hard object being pulled across a surface. **scraper** *n.* instrument for scraping. **scrape together** *v.* to collect with difficulty. **scrape through** *v.* to get through (an examination) with difficulty. **scrapie** *n.* disease affecting the brains of sheep, possibly a cause of BSE in cattle. **scrapings** *n. pl.* pieces which have been scraped off.

scratch 1 [skrætʃ] *n.* (*pl.*-es) (a) long slight wound/mark made by a sharp point. (b) sound of a sharp point being pulled across a surface. (c) act of scratching a part of the body which itches. (d) to start from s. = to start at the beginning/with no previous preparation; to come up to s. = to satisfy. **scratch 2** *adj.* (a) s. team = team of players brought together at the least minute. (b) s. player = player who starts with no handicap. **scratch 3** *v.* (a) to make a long wound/mark with a sharp pointed instrument; to s. the surface = to deal with only the first part of the problem and not to get down to he basic details. (b) to make a sound by pulling a sharp point across a surface (c) to rub with your fingernails (a part of the body which itches). (d) (of competitor) to cross one's name off the list of entrants for a race. **scratchy** *adj.* which makes a scratching noise.

scrawl 1 [skrɔːl] *n.* bad/careless handwriting. **scrawl 2** *v.* to write badly/carelessly.

scrawny ['skrɔːnɪ] *adj.* (-ier, -iest) thin and bony.

scream 1 [skriːm] *n.* (a) loud/piercing cry. (b) screams of laughter = loud/piercing laughter. (c) *inf.* very funny thing/person. **scream 2** *v.* (a) to make loud/piercing cries. (b) s. with laughter = laugh uproariously. **screamingly** *adv.* s. funny = extremely funny.

scree [skriː] *n.* loose stones on a mountainside.

screech 1 [skriːtʃ] *n.* (*pl.*-es) piercing cry (of an animal). **screech 2** *v.* to make a piercing cry. **screech owl** *n.* type of owl which screeches.

screed [skriːd] *n.* very long document.

screen 1 [skri:n] *n.* (a) flat surface which protects/divides. (b) thing which acts as protection against draught/fire/noise. etc. (c) flat white surface for projecting films/slides; the small s. = television. (d) device like a large sieve for sifting sand/gravel into varying sizes. **screen 2** *v.* (a) to protect from draught/fire/noise. etc. (b) to show on a film/TV screen. (c) to question/to examine (people) to find out if they have a disease/if they have committed a crime. (d) to sift (sand/gravel) into varying sizes. **screenplay** *n.* scenario of a film. **screenwriter** *n.* person who writes screen plays.

screw 1 [skru:] *n.* (a) metal pin with a groove winding up from the point to the head, so that when twisted it goes into a hard surface. (b) propeller. (c) act of turning a screw with a screwdriver. (d) small piece of twisted paper with sth in it. (e) twisting motion of a ball. (f) *Sl.* pay/wages. (g) *Sl.* prison warder. **screw 2** *v.* (a) to attach with screws. (b) to attach by twisting; *inf.* his head's screwed on the right way = he's very sensible. (c) to twisting. **screwball** *n.* *inf.* odd/crazy person. **screwdriver** *n.* tool with a long handle and small flat end which is used for turning screws.

screw-top jar *n.* jar with a top which screws on and off. **screwy** *adj.* (-ier, -iest) *inf.* mad.

scribble 1 ['skrɪbl] *n.* (a) (child's) meaningless marks. (b) bad writing.

scribble 2 *v.* (a) to make meaningless marks. (b) to write badly/hurriedly.

scribbly *adj.* scribbles (writing).

scribe [skraɪb] *n.* (old) person who writes copies (of letters/books, etc.) by hand.

scrimmage ['skrɪmɪdʒ] *n.* wild struggle.

scrimp [skrɪmp] *v.* to use as little as possible (of sth).

scrimshank ['skrɪmʃæŋk] *v.* to avoid doing work. **scrimshanker** *n.* person who avoids doing work.

scrimshaw ['skrɪmʃɔː] *n.* carvings made by sailors on whalebone or ivory.

scrip [skrɪp] *n.* (no *pl.*) new shares issued by a company instead of paying a dividend.

script [skrɪpt] *n.* (a) style of

handwriting. (b) thing written by hand/manuscript; handwritten answer to an examination. (c) written version of words which are spoken in film/play.

scripture ['skrɪptʃə] *n.* holy writing; the Bible. **scriptural** *adj.* referring to scripture.

scroll 1 [skrəʊl] *n.* (a) roll of paper with writing on it. (b) curved shape. **scroll 2** *v.* to move text up or down on a computer screen.

scrotum ['skrəʊtəm] *n.* bag containing the testicles. **scrotal** *adj.* referring to the scrotum.

scrounge [skraʊndʒ] *v.* to try to get (sth) from s.o. without paying for it. **scrounger** *n.* person who scrounges.

scrub 1 [skrʌb] *n.* (a) (area of land covered by) small bushes. (b) action of cleaning with a stiff brush. **scrub 2** *v.* (scrubbed) (a) to clean by rubbing with a stiff brush. (b) *inf.* to remove what is recorded (on tape); s. that = forget about that. **scrubbing-brush** *n.* stiff brush with no handle, for scrubbing floors, etc. **scrubby** (-ier, -iest) *inf.* dirty, small and unpleasant.

scruff [skrʌf] *n.* skin at the back of the neck. **scruffily** *adv.* in a scruffy way. **scruffiness** *n.* being scruffy. **scruffy** *adj.* (-ier, -iest) untidy/dirty.

scrum, scrummage [skrʌm, 'skrʌmɪdʒ] *n.* (a) (in Rugby football) groups of forwards from both sides pushing against each other to get the ball. (b) struggling crowd.

scrumping ['skrʌmpɪŋ] *n.* *inf.* to go s. = to steal apples from an orchard.

scrumpy *n.* *inf.* strong cider.

scrumptious ['skrʌmʃəs] *adj.* *inf.* very good to eat.

scrunch [skrʌntʃ] *v.* *inf.* to crush.

scruple 1 ['skruːpl] *n.* doubt about whether sth is right which stops you doing it. **scruple 2** *v.* not to s. to do sth = not to have scruples about doing sth. **scrupulous** ['skruːpjʊləs] *adj.* very careful. **scrupulously** *adv.* in a scrupulous way. **scrupulousness** *n.* being scrupulous.

scrutinize ['skruːtɪnaɪz] *v.* to examine very carefully. **scrutineer** [skruːtɪ'nɪə] *n.* official observer of an election. **scrutiny** *n.* careful examination/very close look.

scuba ['skuːbə] *n.* underwater

breathing apparatus.

scud [skʌd] v. (scudded) (of clouds) to rush past.

scuff [skʌf] v. to scrape the outside surface/the soles of (shoes) when walking.

scuffle 1 ['skʌfl] n. small fight. **scuffle 2** v. to fight.

scull 1 [skʌl] n. one of two short oars used by a single rower. **scull 2** v. to row a boat with two oars.

scullery ['skʌlərɪ] n. small room at the back of a kitchen, used for washing up.

sculpt [skʌlpt] n. to carve (figures, etc.) out of wood/metal/stone. **sculptor** ['skʌlptə] n. person who makes figures/artistic constructions out of wood/metal/stone. **sculpture 1** ['skʌlptʃə] n. (a) art of sculpting. (b) figure made by a sculptor. **sculpture 2** v. to sculpt.

scum [skʌm] n. (a) thick dirty foam layer on the surface of a liquid. (b) people of the worst type; worthless person. **scummy** adj. covered with scum.

scupper 1 ['skʌpə] n. hole in the side of the ship to let water run off the deck. **scupper 2** v. to sink (a ship) intentionally by opening holes in the bottom to let water in. (b) inf. to bring to an end/to ruin.

scurf [skɜːf] n. dandruff/bits of dead skin in the hair.

scurrilous ['skʌrɪləs] adj. very insulting/rude. **scurrilously** adv. in a scurrilous way. **scurrilousness, scurrility** [skʌ'rɪlɪtɪ] n. being scurrilous.

scurry 1 ['skʌrɪ] n. fast movement. **scurry 2** v. to run fast, taking short steps.

scurvy ['skɜːvɪ] n. disease caused by lack of Vitamin C which is found in fruit and vegetables.

scut [skʌt] n. little tail (of a rabbit/deer).

scuttle 1 ['skʌtl] n. type of bucket for keeping coal in the house. **scuttle 2** v. (a) to sink (a ship) intentionally by opening holes in the bottom to allow water to come in. (b) to s. off = to run away fast.

scythe 1 [saɪð] n. tool with a wide blade on the end of a long handle, used for cutting grass. **scythe 2** v. to cut

(grass) with a scythe.

sea [siː] n. (a) area of salt water; inf. at s. = not understanding what is happening. (b) salt water. (c) waves; a heavy s. = very large waves. (d) mass (of faces in a crowd). **sea anemone** n. primitive sea animal which looks like a flower. **sea bird** n. bird which lives by the sea. **seaboard** n. land by the edge of the sea. **seaborne** adj. (troops, etc.) brought by sea. **sea breeze** n. light wind blowing inland from the sea. **sea coast** n. land along the edge of the sea. **seafarer** n. person who travels/works on the sea. **seafaring** adj. which works/travels on the sea. **seafood** n. fish and shellfish which can be eaten. **seafront** n. road running along the edge of the sea at a resort town. **seagoing** adj. (boat) which is used on the sea. **seagull** n. white sea bird. **sea horse** n. small black fish which looks like a horse. **sea legs** n. he's got his s. legs = he is used to travelling by sea and isn't seasick. **sea level** n. the level of the sea, taken as a point for measuring altitude. **sealion** n. large type of seal. **seaman** n. (pl.-men) sailor; person who travels/works on the sea. **seamanship** n. art of sailing a ship. **seaplane** n. plane with floats which can land on the sea. **seaport** n. port. **seascape** n. painting of the sea. **seashell** n. shell of a shellfish which lives in the sea. **seasick** adj. ill because of the motion of a ship. **seasickness** n. being seasick. **seaside** n. land by the side of the sea. **sea urchin** n. type of small spiny sea animal. **seaward** adj. towards the sea. seawards, adv. towards the sea. **seaweed** n. plant which grows in the sea. **seaworthy** adj. (boat) which is fit to go to sea.

seal 1 [siːl] n. (a) large animal living mainly in the sea, with flippers for swimming. (b) piece of hard red wax with a design stamped on it, used for showing that a document has been officially approved or for closing an envelope/parcel so that it cannot be opened secretly. (c) metal stamp with a design, used for sealing with wax. (d) tight fit (of a bottle, etc.) **seal 2** v. (a) to attach and stamp a piece of hard wax to show that a document has been officially approved/to prevent an envelope being opened. (b) to close (sth) tightly so that something cannot be opened. (c) to agree on the terms of (an agreement/bargain). **sealant** *n.* substance used for sealing. **sealing-wax** *n.* hard red wax used for making official seals. **seal off** *v.* to close off so as to prevent anyone getting inside. **sealskin** *n.* skin of a seal.

seam [si:m] *n.* (a) line where two pieces of cloth are sewn together/where two pieces of metal are welded together. (b) layer (of coal, etc.). **seamless** *adj.* (stockings, etc.) with no seam. **seamstress** ['semstrəs] *n.* woman who sews.

seamy *adj.* (-ier, -iest) s. side of life = the unpleasant parts of life.

séance ['seɪɑːns] *n.* meeting where people try to get in touch with the spirits of dead people.

sear ['sɪə] *v.* to burn severely/to scorch.

search 1 [sɜːtʃ] *n.* (*pl.*-es) trying to find sth; police s. = inspection by the police looking for stolen goods/bombs. etc.; s. warrant = official permit to carry out a search; s. party = group of people sent to look for s.o. **search 2** *v.* (a) to examine carefully in order to find sth. (b) to s. for = try to find. **searcher** *n.* person who searches. **searching** *adj.* very careful (examination). **searchlight** *n.* powerful light used to try see things. esp. aircraft, at night.

season 1 ['si:zn] *n.* (a) one of four parts into which a year is divided. (b) any period of the year when sth usually takes place; s. ticket = ticket which is valid for unlimited journeys over a long period. **season 2** *v.* (a) to add spices to (food). (b) to dry (wood) until it is ready to be used. **seasonable** *adj.* which fits the season. **seasonably** *adv.* as is usual for the season. **seasonal** *adj.* which only lasts for a season; (work) for the (summer) season only. **seasoned** *adj.* (wood) which has been dried; (traveller) who has much experience of travelling. **seasoning** *n.* spices which are added to food.

seat 1 [si:t] *n.* (a) thing you sit on. (b) place (on a committee/town council, etc.); parliamentary s. = constituency. (c)

part of a chair on which you sit. (d) part of a pair of trousers which covers the buttocks. (e) s. of government = place where the government is carried on; country s. = large house in the country. (f) way of sitting on a horse. **seat 2** *v.* (a) to make (s.o.) sit down. (b) to have room for people to sit down. **seat belt** *n.* belt worn in a car/in an air-craft as protection in case of accident. **seating** *n.* giving seats to people.

sebaceous [sɪ'beɪʃəs] *adj.* which produces fat.

secant ['si:knt] *n.* line which crosses a curve.

secateurs [sekə'tɜːz] *n.* *pl.*(pair of) s. = very strong scissors used in gardening.

secede [sɪ'si:d] *v.* (formal) to break away from a group. **secession** [sɪ'seʃn] *n.* act of seceding.

secluded [sɪ'ljuːdɪd] *adj.* (place) which is quiet/away from crowds. **seclusion** [sɪ'kluːʒn] *n.* quiet/solitude.

second 1 ['sekənd] *n.* (as a number can be written 2nd) (a) sixtieth part of minute; a moment; s. hand = long fast-moving hand on watch. (b) sixtieth part of a degree. (c) person/thing which comes after the first. (d) person who helps a boxer/wrestler. (e) seconds = articles which are not perfect and are sold cheaply. (f) second gear. **second 2** *adj.* (a) coming next after the first; s. class = ordinary railway travel, etc., which is not as luxurious or expensive as first class; s. in command = person directly under the commanding officer/managing director, etc.; the s. century = period from 100 AD to 199. (b) every s. day = every other day/on alternate days. **second 3** *v.* (a) to support (a proposal). (b) to transfer from one job to another for a period of time. **secondary** *adj.* (a) second in importance/in position; s. industry = industry which takes basic raw materials and process them into manufactured goods; s. picketing = picketing of a factory, etc., by people who do not work there. (b) s. education/s. school = education/school for children of about 11 years of age and older. (c) s. colours = colours made by mixing primary colours. **secondarily** *adv.* in second place in importance. **secondbest** *adj. & adv.* in second

place; not as good as the best. **second childhood** *n.* period in old age when old people seem to act like children. **seconder** *n.* person who supports a motion. **second half** *n.* (a) second section (as of a football match). (b) second part of a financial year, from July to December. **secondhand** *adj. & adv.* not new/used; I heard it at s. = not from the original source of the news.
secondly *adv.* in second place. **secondment** [sɪ'kɒndmənt] *n.* being transferred for a period of time to another job. **second nature** *n.* it is s. n. to him = he does it quite naturally. **second-rate** *adj.* not of good quality. **second sight** *n.* being able to tell what will happen in the future. **second thoughts** *n. pl.* to have s. t. about = to change one's mind. **second wind** *n.* he got his s. w. = he could breathe again easily after having lost his breath.
secret 1 ['siːkrət] *adj.* hidden from other people; not known. **secret 2** *n.* thing which is not known/which is kept hidden; in s. = without anyone knowing. **secrecy** ['siːkrəsɪ] *n.* keeping sth secret. **secretive** *adj.* liking to keep things secret. **secretively** *adv.* in a secretive way. **secretiveness** *n.* being secretive. **secretly** *adv.* in secret.
secret service *n.* government department which deals in espionage. **secretaire** [sekrə'teə] *n.* desk with many little drawers. **secretary** ['sekrətərɪ] *n.* (a) person who writes letters/files documents, etc., for s.o. (b) person who deals with correspondence/arranges meetings, etc., in a club/society. (c) minister in a government; S. of State = head of a large government department. (d) official in a government office/in an embassy; first s. = senior official in an embassy; permanent s. = main civil servant in a ministry.
Secretary General *n.* chief administrative officer of an international organization. **secretarial** [sekrə'teərɪəl] *adj.* referring to a secretary.
secretariat *n.* group of officials who administer a large office.
secrete [sɪ'kriːt] *v.* (a) to hide. (b) to produce (a liquid) **secretion** [sɪ'kriːʃn] *n.* liquid produced by an organ/a plant.
sect [sekt] *n.* religious group.

sectarian [sek'teərɪən] *adj.* referring to a religious group.
section ['sekʃn] *n.* (a) cutting; cutting tissue in an operation. (b) part. (c) picture of sth showing what it is like when cut through. (d) part of sth which, when joined to other parts, goes to make up a whole. **sectional** *adj.* (a) (diagram) showing a section through sth. (b) (built) in sections.
sector ['sektə] *n.* (a) section of a circle between two lines drawn from the centre to the circumference; section of the surface of a computer disk. (b) private s. = part of industry which is privately owned; public s. = nationalized industries and the civil service.
secular ['sekjʊlə] *adj.* not religious/not connected with religion. **secularize** *v.* to make secular.
secure 1 [sɪ'kjuːə] *adj.* (a) safe. (b) firmly fixed; s. job = where you can't be sacked. (c) confident. **secure 2** *v.* (a) to make firm/to fasten. **securely** *adv.* in a secure way. **security** *n.* (a) safety. (b) protection against criminals/against hardship; airport s. = measures to protect aircraft against hijackers. (c) thing given to s.o. who has lent you money and which is returned when the loan is repaid. (d) government securities = papers showing that the government will pay back money which people have lent it. **Security Council** *n.* ruling body of the United Nations.
sedan [sɪ'dæn] *n. Am.* covered family car. **sedan-chair** *n.* (old) seat in a box carried on long poles by bearers.
sedate 1 [sɪ'deɪt] *adj.* serious/dignified. **sedate 2** *v.* to give (a patient) sedatives. **sedately** *adv.* in a calm/serious way. **sedateness** *n.* being sedate.
sedative ['sedətɪv] *adj. & n.* (medicine) which makes you calm/which makes you go to sleep. **sedation** [sɪ'deɪʃn] *n.* giving medicine to calm a patient.
sedentary ['sedəntrɪ] *adj.* always sitting down.
sedge [sedʒ] *n.* type of grass which grows in water.
sediment ['sedɪmənt] *n.* solid which forms at the bottom of a liquid. **sedimentary** [sedɪ'mentərɪ] *adj.*

(rocks) which were formed from mud deposited at the bottom of the sea/rivers, etc. **sedimentation** *n.* action of depositing solid particles at the bottom of liquid.

sedition [sə'dɪʃn] *n.* encouraging people to rebel against the government. **seditious** *adj.* which encourages people to rebel.

seduce [sɪ'djuːs] *v.* (a) to persuade (s.o.) to do sth which is perhaps wrong. (b) to persuade (s.o.) to have sexual intercourse. **seducer** *n.* person who seduces. **seduction** [sɪ'dʌkʃn] *n.* act of seducing. **seductive** [sɪ'dʌktɪv] *adj.* attractive.

sedulous ['sedjʊləs] *adj.* very careful and persistent. **sedulously** *adv.* in a sedulous way.

sedum ['siːdəm] *n.* succulent rock plant.

see 1 [siː] *n.* area over which a bishop rules. **see 2** *v.* (saw, seen) (a) to sense with your eyes. (b) to accompany; to s. s.o. home. (c) to understand. (d) to examine. (e) to make sure (that). (f) to visit/to meet. (g) to go to a performance of (a play/film, etc.). **seeing** *n.* action of sensing with the eyes; s. that = since.

see through *v* (a) to understand s.o.'s plans to trick you. (b) to work on (sth) until it is finished. **see-through,** *adj.* transparent. **see to** *v.* to busy yourself about sth; see to it = make sure (that).

seed 1 [siːd] *n.* (a) part of a plant which appears after the flowers and then can produce a new plant; to go/to run to s. = produce flowers and seeds which are not needed; he's gone to s. = he's become lazy/he's got worse. (b) tennis player selected as one of the best players in a tournament (before the tournament starts). **seed 2** *v.* (a) to produce seeds. (b) to select (the best players) in a tennis tournament and arrange them so that they do not play each other until the later rounds. **seedbed** *n.* special area of fine soil where you can sow seeds. **seedless** *adj.* (fruit) with no seeds in it. **seedling** *n.* very young plant. **seedsman** *n.* (*pl.*-men) person who specializes in growing and selling seeds. **seedy** *adj.* (-ier, -iest) worn-out (clothes); sick (person).

seek [siːk] *v.* (sought[sɔːt]) (a) to look

for. (b) to ask for. **seeker** *n.* person who seeks.

seem [siːm] *v.* to appear. **seeming** *adj.* not real, though appearing to be. **seemingly** *adj.* apparently.

seemly *adj.* decent/correct.

seen [siːn] *v.* see see.

seep [siːp] *v.* (of a liquid) to pass through a crack, **seepage** *n.* act of seeping; liquid which has seeped.

seer ['siːə] *n.* (old) person who sees into the future.

seersucker ['sɪəsʌkə] *n.* cotton cloth with a wrinkled surface.

seesaw ['siːsɔː] *n.* children's toy made of a plank with seats at each end, balanced in the middle, so that when one end goes up the other goes down. **seesaws** *v.* to go up and down.

seethe [siːð] *v.* (a) to be very angry. (b) to move about like boiling water. **seething** *adj.* very angry.

segment ['segmənt] *n.* part of sth (which seems to form a natural division); part of a circle or sphere. **segmentation** [segmən'teɪʃn] *n.* being segmented. **segmented** [seg'mentɪd] *adj.* with segments.

segregate ['segrɪgeɪt] *v.* to divide one group from another. **segregation** [segrɪ'geɪʃn] *n.* division of one group from another; racial s. = splitting of a population into groups according to race of colour.

seine [seɪn] *n.* type of fishing net.

seismic ['saɪzmɪk] *adj.* referring to earthquakes. **seismograph** *n.* instrument for recording earthquakes. **seismological** [saɪzmə'lɒdʒɪkl] *adj.* referring to seismology. **seismology** [saɪz'mɒlədʒɪ] *n.* study of earthquakes.

seize [siːz] *v.* (a) to grab/to hold tight. (b) to confiscate/to take by force. **seize up** *v.* (of an engine) to stop working/to become blocked. **seizure** ['siːʒə] *n.* (a) confiscation of goods by the police. (b) stroke/illness caused by lack of blood to the brain.

seldom ['seldəm] *adv.* rarely/not often.

select 1 [sɪ'lekt] *v.* to choose. **select 2** *adj.* (a) of top quality. (b) s. club = club which only lets in certain people; s. area = smart area. **Select Committee** *n.* special committee of the House of Commons, which examines the work of a single ministry. **selection** [sɪ'lekʃn] *n.* (a) choice. (b) things chosen. **selective** *adj.* which chooses (carefully); (weedkiller) which only kills certain plants. **selectively** *adv.* in a selective way. **selectivity** *n.* being able to choose carefully. **selector** *n.* person who chooses players to play in a football team/cricket team, etc.

self [self] *n.* (*pl.*selves) your own person or character; (on cheques) pay s. = pay the person who has signed the cheque. **self-addressed** *adj.* (envelope) on which you have written your own address. **self-assertive** *adj.* (person) who makes others do what he wants. **self assurance** *n.* being self-assured. **self-assured** *adj.* sure you care capable of doing sth. **self-catering** *n.* doing the cooking for yourself; s.-c. holiday = one where you rent accommodation, but cook your own meals. **self-centred** *adj.* (person) who only thinks of himself. **self-confidence** *n.* being self-confident. **self-confident** *adj.* sure you are capable of doing sth. **self-conscious** *adj.* embarrassed because you feel you have certain faults. **self-consciously** *adv.* with embarrassment, **self-consciousness** *n.* being self-conscious. **self-contained** *adj.* (flat) which has its own kitchen/bathroom, etc., and does not share these facilities with others. **self-control** *n.* keeping your feelings under control. **self-defeating** *adj.* (plan) which works in such a way that it defeats its own purpose. **self-defence** *n.* protecting yourself. **self-denial** *n.* refusing to give yourself sth/going without sth which you would like. **self-determination** *n.* choosing your own political future. **self-drive car** *n.* car which you can rent and drive yourself. **self-educated** *adj.* (person) who has taught himself every thing he knows and who has not been to school. **self-effacing** *adj.* (person) who tries to be inconspicuous/who does not want people to notice him. **self-employed** *adj.* (person) who works for himself, and is not paid a salary by s.o. else. **self-esteem** *n.* pride in yourself. **self-evident** *adj.* obvious. **self-explanatory** *adj.* obvious/which

explains itself. **self-governing** *adj.* (country) which governs itself. **self-government** *n.* control of a country by its own people, not by another country. **self-help** *n.* improving one's condition by one's own efforts. **self-important** *adj.* (person) who feels he is very important when he really is not. **self-indulgent** *adj.* (person) who gives himself everything he wants. **self-interest** *n.* working for one's own benefit. **selfish** *adj.* only interested in yourself/doing sth only for yourself. **selfishly** *adv.* (done) only for yourself. **selfishness** *n.* being selfish. **selfless** *adj.* not selfish/thinking only of others. **self-made man** *n.* person who has become rich entirely through his own efforts. **self-pity** *n.* pity for yourself. **self-portrait** *n.* painting which an artist has made of himself. **self-possessed** *adj.* calm/not bothered. **self-raising flour** *n.* flour which contains baking powder to make cakes rise. **self-reliance** *n.* being self-reliant. **self-reliant** *adj.* independent/relying only on yourself. **self-respect** *n.* pride in yourself/concern that you have a good character and work well. **self-righteous** *adj.* feeling sure that you are doing what is right. **self-rule** *n.* self-government. **self-sacrifice** *n.* giving up sth which is right. **self-sacrificing** *adj.* (person) who gives up pleasures. so that others may enjoy them. **selfsame** *adj.* exactly the same. **self-satisfaction** *n.* being self-satisfied. **self-satisfied** *adj.* contented with what you have done. **self-seeking** *adj.* (person) who works to his own advantage, at the expense of others. **self-service** *n & adj.* (shop) where you take things yourself from the counters and pay at a cash desk. **self-styled** *adj.* (person) who has given himself a title. **self-sufficiency** *n.* being self-sufficient. **self-sufficient** *adj.* producing enough food, etc., for all needs. **self-supporting** *adj.* providing for one's own needs, with no help from others. **self-taught** *adj.* (person) who has taught himself a certain skill. **self-willed** *adj.* obstinate/always wanting to have your own way.

sell 1 [sel] *n.* act of selling; hard s. =

forceful selling of a product. **sell 2** *v.*
(sold, has sold) (a) to give goods to s.o.
in exchange for money. (b) *inf.* to betray.
sell-by-date *n.* date on a packet of
food, which is the last date on which the
food is guaranteed to be good. **seller** *n.*
(a) person who sells. (b) good s. = thing
that sells well. **sell off** *v.* (a) to sell
(sth) cheaply to get rid of it. **sell out** *v.*
(a) to sell so many things that you have
none left. (b) *inf.* to abandon your
principles. **sell-out** *n.* (a) show/play,
etc. where all the tickets have been sold
(b) *inf.* abandoning of principles. **sell
up** *v.* to sell a business.
sellotape 1 ['seləteɪpl] *n.* trade mark
for a type of transparent sticky tape.
sellotape 2 *v.* to attack (sth) with
sticky tape.
selvage, selvedge ['selvɪdʒ] *n.* edge
of a piece of cloth which does not fray.
semantics [sɪ'mæntɪks] *n.* study of the
meaning of language. **semantically**
adv. in a way which refers to semantics.
semaphore ['seməfɔː] *n.* way of
signalling using two arms (and flags) in
different positions for each letter.
semblance ['sembləns] *n.* appearance.
semen ['siːmən] *n.* liquid in which
male sperm floats.
semester [sə'mestə] *n. Am.* term in a
school or college year which only has
two terms.
semi 1 ['semɪ] *n. inf.* semi-detached
house. **semi 2** prefix meaning half.
semi-breve *n.* long note in music,
lasting two minims. **semicircle** *n.* half
a circle. **semi-circular** *adj.* like a half
circle in shape. **semi-colon** *n.*
punctuation mark (;) showing a pause.
semiconductor *n.* material (such as
silicon) which is partly able to conduct
electricity. **semi-conscious** *adj.* half
conscious. **semi-detached** *adj.*
(house) which is joined to another
similar house on one side, but is not
joined on the other. **semi-final** *n.* one
of two matches in a competition, the
winners of which go into the final game.
semi-finalist *n.* team/player in a semi-
final. **semi-official** *adj.* not quite
official. **semi-precious** *n.* (stone)
which is quite valuable, but not in the
same class as diamonds/rubies/
sapphires, etc. **semi-quaver** *n.* note in

music lasting half as long as a quaver.
semi-skilled *adj.* (worker) who has
been trained to a certain level.
semitone *n.* (in music) half a tone on
the scale.
seminal [semɪnl] *adj.* which acts as the
starting point for sth new.
seminar ['semɪnɑː] *n.* class given to a
small group of students who meet to
discuss a problem with a teacher.
seminary ['semɪnərɪ] *n.* college for
priests.
Semitic [sə'mɪtɪk] *adj.* referring to a
group of races including Jews and Arabs.
semolina [semə'liːnə] *n.* hard crushed
wheat, used to make spaghetti and milk
puddings.
senate ['senət] *n.* (a) upper house of
parliament in some countries. (b) main
committee which governs a university.
senator *n.* member of the upper house
of parliament.
send [send] *v.* (sent) (a) to tell (s.o.) to
go somewhere; to make (sth) go from
one place to another. (b) to give (s.o.) a
sensation; it sent him crazy. (c) to put
out (roots, etc.). (d) *inf.* to make (s.o.)
excited. **send away** *v.* (a) to make
(s.o./sth) go away, (b) to send away for =
to write asking s.o. to send sth to you.
send back *v.* to return (sth). **send
down** *v.* to dismiss (a student) from a
university. **sender** *n.* person who
sends. **send for** *v.* to pass a message to
(s.o.) asking them to come. **send off** *v.*
(a) to make (s.o./sth) go off. (b) to post;
to send off for = send away for. (c) to tell
(a player) to leave the football field
because of bad conduct. **send-off** *n.*
party to say goodbye to s.o. leaving on
along journey. **send out** *v.* to
make(s.o./sth) go out. **send up**, *v.* (a) to
make (s.o./sth) go up. (b) *inf.* to make
fun of (s.o.)
senile ['siːnaɪl] *adj.* old and mentally
weak. **senility** [sə'nɪlɪtɪ] *n.* being
senile.
senior 1 ['siːnjə] *adj.* (a) order; J.
Smith S. = father of J. Smith Junior; s.
school = school for older children; s.
citizen = old person living on pension.
(b) more important (rank, etc.); the
Senior Service = the Royal Navy. **senior
2** *n.* (a) older person; the seniors = the
older children in a school. (b) *Am.* fourth

year student. **seniority** [siːnɪ'ɒrɪtɪ] *n.* being senior.

senna ['senə] *n.* s. pods = dried pods used as a laxative.

sensation [sen'seɪʃn] *n.* (a) feeling. (b) (thing/person that causes) great excitement. **sensational** *adj.* very exciting. **sensationally** *adv.* in a sensational way.

sense 1 [sens] *n.* (a) one of the five ways in which you notice sth; sixth s. = ability to feel that sth has taken place/will take place, without using any of the five senses. (b) feeling. (c) senses = power of reasoning; to come to one's senses = become reasonable. (d) meaning; to make s. = to have a meaning; to make s. of = understand. (e) reasonableness/good judgement. **sense 2** *v.* to feel. **senseless** *adj.* (a) stupid. (b) unconscious. **senselessness** *n.* stupidity.

sensible ['sensɪbl] *adj.* (a) reasonable/well judged. (b) (person) who has commonsense. (c) s. walking shoes = strong, but not fashionable, walking shoes. (d) (formal) s. of = aware of. **sensibility** [sensɪ'bɪlɪtɪ] *n.* being capable of delicate feeling. **sensibly** *adv.* in a sensible way.

sensitive ['sensɪtɪv] *adj.* (a) able to feel keenly/sharply. (b) (instrument) which measures very accurately. (c) (substance) which reacts to light, etc. **sensitivity, sensitiveness** [sensɪ'tɪvɪtɪ] *n.* being sensitive. **sensitively** *adv.* in a sensitive way. **sensitize** ['sensɪtaɪz] *v.* to make sensitive (to light, etc.).

sensor ['sensə] *n.* apparatus which detects sth by sense of heat/light/smell of smoke, etc. **sensory** *adj.* referring to the senses.

sensual ['sensjʊəl] *adj.* referring to pleasures of the body, not of the mind. **sensuality** *n.* experience of sensual pleasure. **sensually** *adv.* in a sensual way.

sensuous *adj.* which gives pleasure to the senses. **sensuously** *adv.* in a sensuous way.

sent [sent] *v.* see send.

sentence 1 ['sentəns] *n.* (a) words put together to form a complete separate statement, *usu.* ending with a full stop.

(b) decision of a judge which gives the details of punishment. **sentence 2** *v.* to condemn (s.o.) to a certain punishment. **sententious** ['sen'tenʃəs] *adj.* too full of moral sense.

sententiously *adv.* in a sententious way.

sentient ['senʃnt] *adj.* able to feel.

sentiment ['sentɪmənt] *n.* (a) show of feeling. (b) sentiments = opinions. **sentimental** [sentɪ'mentəl] *adj.* full of emotion/full of feeling. **sentimentality** [sentɪmən'tælɪtɪ] *n.* playing on the emotions (in literature/music). **sentimentally** *adv.* by feeling.

sentinel ['sentɪnl] *n.* sentry.

sentry ['sentrɪ] *n.* soldier on duty at a gate, etc. **sentry-box** *n.* wooden shelter for a sentry.

sepal ['sepəl] *n.* green leaf under the petals of a flower.

separate 1 ['seprət] *adj.* detached/not together. **separate 2** ['sepəreɪt] *v.* to detach/to divide. **separate 3** *n.* separates = pieces of women's clothing (skirts/blouse/jumper, etc.) which can be worn in different combinations. **separable** ['seprəbl] *adj.* which can be separated. **separately** *adv.* in a separate way. **separation** [sepə'reɪʃn] *n.* dividing/living apart. **separatism** ['sepərətɪzəm] *n.* political ideal of separating from a large country. **separatist** *adj. & n.* (person) who wants his region to separate from a large country. **separator** *n.* person/machine that separates.

sepia ['siːpɪə] *n.* brown colour.

sepsis ['sepsɪs] *n.* being septic.

September [sep'tembə] *n.* 9th month of the year.

septennial [sep'tenɪəl] *adj.* for seven years.

septet [sep'tet] *n.* group of seven musicians; piece of music for seven instruments.

septic ['septɪk] *adj.* (wound) which has gone bad/become poisoned; s. tank = underground tank near a house for collecting sewage. **septicaemia** [septɪ'siːmɪə] *n.* poisoning of the blood.

septuagenarian [septjʊədʒə'neərɪən] *n.* person who is between seventy and seventy-nine years old.

septum ['septəm] *n.* (*pl.*-ta) wall

between two sections of the body/a plant.
sepulchre, *Am.* **sepulchar** ['sepəlkə]
n. tomb. **sepulchral** [se'pʌlkrəl] *adj.*
referring to a sepulchre; very deep
gloomy (voice).
sequel [si:kwəl] *n.* (a) continuation of a
story, play, etc. (b) result. **sequence**
['si:kwəns] *n.* (a) series of things
happening; series of numbers which
follow each other. (b) sense in a film.
sequential *adj.* in sequence.
sequentially *adv.* in sequence.
sequester [sɪ'kwestə] *v.* (formal) to
seclude. **sequestrate** ['sekwɪstreɪt] *v.*
(formal) to confiscate (property).
sequestrator *n.* person who seizes
property on the orders of a court.
sequin [si:kwɪn] *n.* small round shiny
metal ornament. **sequinned** *adj.*
covered with sequins.
sequoia [sɪ'kwɔɪə] *n.* redwood.
seraglio [se'ræljəʊ] *n.* harem.
seraph ['serəf] *n.* (*pl.*seraphim) highest
angel. **seraphic** *adj.* like a seraph.
serenade 1 [serə'neɪd] *n.* love song.
serenade 2 *v.* to sing a love song to
(s.o.).
serendipity [serən'dɪpɪtɪ] *n.* pleasure
which you get from finding things by
accident.
serene [sə'ri:n] *adj.* calm/not worried.
serenely *adv.* in a serene way.
serenity [sə'renɪtɪ] *n.* being serene.
serf [sɜ:f] *n.* peasant/slave working on a
farm. **serfdom** *n.* state of being a serf.
serge [sɜ:dʒ] *n.* type of thick cloth.
sergeant ['sɑ:dʒənt] *n.* senior non-
commissioned officer in the army/the
police. **sergeant-major** *n.* rank in the
army above sergeant.
serial 1 ['sɪərɪəl] *adj.* (number) of a
series. **serial 2** *n.* story/TV play which
is told in several instalments. **serialize**
v. to make (a novel, etc.) into a serial.
seriatim [sɪərɪ'ɑ:tɪm] *adv.* in order.
series ['sɪəri:z] *n.* (*pl.*series) (a) group
of things which come one after the other
in a set order. (b) group of things.
serif ['serɪf] *n.* little line added to the
end of a stroke in a typeset character.
serious ['sɪərɪəs] *adj.* (a) not
humorous. (b) important/bad. **seriously**
adv. in a serious way. **seriousness** *n.*
being serious.
serjeant ['sɑ:dʒənt] *n.* s.-at-arms =

office of a court/of parliament.
sermon ['sɜ:mən] *n.* serious speech
made in church. **sermonize** *v.* to
preach to (s.o.).
serpent ['sɜ:pənt] *n.* snake.
serpentine *adj.* like a snake; winding.
serrated [sɜ:reɪtɪd] *adj.* toothed (blade);
with a zigzag edge. **serration** *n.* being
serrated; serrated edge.
serried ['serɪd] *adj.* in s. ranks = in
ranks close together.
serum ['sɪərəm] *n.* yellow liquid in the
blood, which can be injected into s.o.'s
body to fight disease.
serve 1 [sɜ:v] *n.* act of serving the ball
at tennis. **serve 2** *v.* (a) to provide/to
give (food); to help at table; (of a recipe)
to make enough food for. (b) to work for.
(c) to be useful (as). (d) to deal with (a
customer). (e) to undergo punishment.
(f) to start a game of tennis by hitting the
ball first. (g) it serves you right = you
deserve the punishment you have got. (h)
to assist a priest (at mass). **servant** *n.*
(a) person who is paid to work in the
house. (b) civil s. = government
employee. **server** *n.* (a) person who
serves at table. (b) large flat knife for
serving food; spoon/fork for serving fish
or salad. (c) person who helps a priest (
at mass).
service 1 ['sɜ:vɪs] *n.* (a) working for
s.o.; military s. = period which you
spend in the army/navy/air force; s. flat =
flat where cleaning, etc., is provided; s.
charge = charge added to a bill for the
work carried out; s. road = road which
leads to a house, etc., but nowhere else.
(b) group of people working together;
civil s. = all the government employees;
the foreign s. = people who represent
their country abroad; the services = the
army, navy and air force. (c) providing
basic essentials which people require;
bus s. = regularly passing bus. (d)
regular religious ceremony. (e) act of
starting a game of tennis by hitting the
ball first. (f) set of china for use at tea/
dinner. (g) repairs to a machine, done on
a regular basis; the car needs a s. =
examination by the garage; s. area =
place by a motorway where you can stop
and buy petrol/get food, etc. **service 2**
v. to do any repairs which need doing to
(a car, etc.). **serviceable** *adj.*

practical; which will be useful.
serviceman *n.* (*pl.*-men) member of
the army/navy/air force. **service-
station** *n.* garage which sells petrol/
oil, etc. **servicewoman** *n.* (*pl.*-
women) woman member of the army/
navy/airforce.
serviette [sɜːvɪ'et] *n.* square of cloth or
soft paper used to protect your clothes
and wipe your mouth at table.
servile ['sɜːvaɪl] *adj.* like a slave.
servilely *adv.* in a servile way.
servility [sɜː'vɪlɪtɪ] *n.* acting like a
slave.
servitude ['sɜːvɪtjuːd] *n.* slavery.
servo ['sɜːvəʊ] prefix meaning power
assisted.
sesame ['sesəmiː] *n.* tropical plant
whose seeds produce oil or are eaten.
session ['seʃn] *n.* (a) meeting of a
committee/parliament, etc.; in s. = in the
process of meeting. (b) meeting to study/
to practise.
set 1 [set] *n.* (a) group of things which
go together; (in mathematics) group of
numbers, etc., which are linked. (b)
apparatus. (c) one of the main parts of a
tennis match. (d) group of people. (e)
scenery on a stage. (f) position/direction.
(g) arranging of hair. (h) onion s. = very
small onion which is planted and then
grows into a large one. (i) burrow of a
badger. **set 2** *v.* (set) (a) to put/to place;
to s. the table = put the knives and forks.
etc. on the table. (b) to arrange/to fix (a
machine, etc.). (c) to arrange in place.
(d) to give work to. (e) to make (free,
etc.). (f) to become solid. (g) (of sun/
stars) to go down. (h) to write music to
go with (a poem, etc.). (i) to place
scenery on a stage; to put (the action of a
story) in a certain period. (j) to arrange
letters in rows for printing. **set 3** *adj.*
(a) fixed/which cannot be changed. (b)
ready. **set about** *v.* to start doing (sth).
set aside *v.* (a) to put to one side/to
reject. (b) to keep to one side (for future
use). **set-aside** *n.* system of using land
previously used for farming. for another
purpose. **set back** *v.* (a) to make late.
(b)inf. it s. me back £10 = it cost me
£10. **setback** *n.* holding back
progress. **set down** *v.* (a) to write
down on paper. (b) to let passengers get
off. **set forth** *v.* (old) (a) to start a
journey. (b) to write out (a list, etc.). **set
in** *v.* to start; to become fixed. **set off**
v. (a) to start a journey (b) to light
(fireworks); to make (a bomb) explode;
to start (a reaction). (c) to show up. **set
out** *v.* (a) to put out, (b) to start a
journey. **set-square** *n.* instrument to
help you draw lines, shaped like a right
angled triangle. **setting** *n.* (a) action of
setting. (b) background for a story; frame
in which a diamond is fixed. (c) place s.
= set of knives/forks/spoons. etc., for one
person. **set to** *v.* to get to work. **set-to**
n. inf. argument/fight. **set up** *v.* to
build/to establish. **set-up** *n. inf.*
arrangement/organization **set upon** *v.*
to attack.
sett [set] *n.* burrow of a badger.
settee ['setiː] *n.* sofa.
setter ['setə] *n.* hunting dog trained to
point out game by standing still.
settle 1 ['setl] *n.* long wooden bench
with a back. **settle 2** *v.* (a) to arrange/
to agree; to end (a dispute); to s. up =
pay the bill; to s. on/for = to decide on/to
choose. (b) (also settle down) to place
yourself in a comfortable position/to rest.
(c) to go to live in a new country. (d) (of
sediment) to fall to the bottom of a
liquid; (of building) to sink into the
ground. (e) to s. money on s.o. = to pass
money to s.o. by a legal process. **settled**
adj. fixed/unchanging. **settlement** *n.*
(a) payment (of a bill); agreement in a
dispute. (b) place where a group of
people has settled. (c) settling money,
etc., on s.o. (d) (of building) act of
sinking into the ground. **settler** *n.*
person who goes to settle in a new
country.
seven ['sevn] *n.* number7. **seventeen**
n. number 17. **seventeenth, 17th**
adj. & n. referring to seventeen; the s.
century = period from 1600 to 1699.
seventh, 7th *adj. & n.* referring to
seven. **seventieth, 70th** *adj. & n.*
referring to seventy. **seventy** *n.*
number 70.
sever ['sevə] *v.* to cut off. **severance**
n. cutting off; s. pay = money paid as
compensation to s.o. who is losing a job.
several ['sevrəl] *adj. & pron.* more
than a few, but not very many.
severally *adv.* separately.
severe [se'vɪə] *adj.* (-er, -est) (a) very

strict. (b) very bad (illness, weather, etc.). **severely** *adv.* (a) strictly. (b) badly. **severity** [sə'verɪtɪ] *n.* being severe.

sew [səʊ] *v.* (sewn) to attach/to mend by using a needle and thread; to make (with a needle and thread). **sewing** *n.* (a) action of attaching/mending with needle and thread. (b) work which s.o. is in the process of sewing. **sewing machine** *n.* machine which sews. **sew up** *v.* (a) to close (a hole) by sewing. (b) *inf.* to settle (a deal).

sewer ['sʊə] *n.* large tube in the ground used for taking away waste and dirty water from houses. **sewage** ['suːɪdʒ] *n.* waste and dirty water; s. work/s. farm = place where waste is collected and treated to kill germs. **sewerage** *n.* system of sewers for removing waste and dirty water.

sex 1 [seks] *n.* (*pl.*-es) (a) one of two groups (male and female) into which animals and plants can be divided. s. appeal = attractiveness to members of the other sex. (b) to have s. with s.o. = to have sexual intercourse. **sex 2** *v.* to s. chickens = to tell whether chickens are male or female. **sexism** *n.* bias against one sex. **sexist** *adj. & n.* (person) who is biased against one of the sexes. **sexless** *adj.* without sex; not involving sexual feeling. **sexological** *adj.* referring to sexology. **sexologist** *n.* person who studies human sex. **sexology** [sek'sɒlədʒi] *n.* study of human sex. **sexual** ['seksjʊəl] *adj.* referring to sex; s. intercourse = reproductive act between a male and female. **sexuality** *n.* interest in sexual way. **sexually** *adv.* in a sexual way. **sexy** *adj.* sexually attractive.

sexagenarian [seksədʒə'neərɪən] *adj. & n.* (person) who is between sixty years and sixty-nine years old.

sextant ['sekstənt] *n.* instrument for calculating the position of a ship by referring to the stars.

sextet [seks'tet] *n.* (a) group of six musicians playing together. (b) piece of music for six musicians.

sexton ['sekstən] *n.* man who works in a church/rings the bells/digs graves, etc.

sh [ʃ] *inter.* used to make silence.

shabby ['ʃæbɪ] *adj.* (-ier, -iest) poor/

worn out (clothes); mean (trick). **shabbily** *adv.* in a shabby way. **shabbiness** *n.* being shabby.

shack 1 [ʃæk] *n.* rough wooden but.

shack 2 *v. Sl.* to s. up with s.o. = to go to live with s.o.

shackle 1 ['ʃækl] *n.* thing which hampers movement; shackles = chains (for attaching a prisoner). **shackle 2** *v.* to attach (s.o.) with a chain.

shade 1 [ʃeɪd] *n.* (a) dark place which is not in the sunlight; to put s.o. in the s. = to make s.o. seem less important/ hardworking, etc. (b) dark part of a picture. (c) cover put on lamp; *Am.* blind on a window. (d) type of colour; slight difference. (e) little bit. (f) *Am. inf.* shades = sunglasses. (g) (formal) ghost. **shade 2** *v.* (a) to protect (sth) from sunlight. (b) to make (a picture) darker. (c) (also shade off) to change from one colour to another gradually. **shadiness** *n.* being shady. **shading** *n.* action of making shade; making part of a picture darker. **shady** *adj.* (-ier, -iest) (a) full of shade. (b) dishonest/disreputable.

shadow 1 ['ʃædəʊ] *n.* (a) shade made by an object in light; five o'clock s. = dark tint on a man's chin as his beard begins to grow. (b) small amount. (c) person who follows s.o. (d) opposition in parliament which parallels the government; s. cabinet = senior members of the opposition who parallel the government. **shadow 2** *v.* to follow (s.o.). **shadowy** *adj.* vague/indistinct.

shaft [ʃɑːft] *n.* (a) long stick which is the main part of an arrow/a javelin, etc.; long pole in front of a cart to which a horse is attracted. (b) ray of light. (c) rod which turns in an engine. (d) pillar. (e) deep hole in the ground; lift s. = hole down the centre of a building in which a lift moves up and down.

shag [ʃæg] *n.* (a) thick tobacco. (b) type of black sea bird. **shaggy** ['ʃægɪ] *adj.* (-ier, -iest) with long hair; s. dog story = very long story with an unexpectedly silly ending. **shag-pile carpet** *n.* carpet with thick wool fibres.

shake 1 [ʃeɪk] *n.* (a) act of moving from side to side or up and down. (b) drink made by mixing milk and flavouring. **shake 2** *v.* (shook[ʃuːk]; shaken) to move from side to side or up and down; to s. one's head = to move one's head from side to side to indicate 'no'. **shake down** v. to settle down (after a period of uncertainty). **shakedown** n. rough bed. **shaken** adj. very upset/disturbed. **shake off** v. to get rid of (sth unpleasant). **shaker** n. person/machine which shakes; container for mixing cocktails. **shake-up** n. inf. total change. **shakily** adv. in a shaky way. **shakiness** n. being shaky.

shaky adj. (-ier, -iest) (a) wobbly; trembling. (b) not very reliable.

shale [ʃeil] n. type of rock which splits into soft thin slices.

shall [ʃæl] v. used with I and we to form future (negative; shan't; past should) (a) (suggestion/request) s. we sit down? (b) (emphasis in the future) yes I s.! (c) (negative future) I shan't say anything. (note: except for (a) shall is gradually being replaced by will; see also should.

shallot [ʃə'lɒt] n. type of small onion which grows in clusters.

shallow 1 [ʃæləʊ] adj. (er, -est) (a) not deep. (b) superficial (mind). **shallow 2** n. shallows = water which is not deep. **shallowness** n. being shallow.

sham 1 [ʃæm] adj. false. **sham 2** n. thing which is false. **sham 3** v. (shammed) to pretend.

shamble [ʃæmbl] v. to s. along = to wander along dragging your feet. **shambles** [ʃæmblz] n. disorder/mess.

shame 1 [ʃeim] n. (a) feeling caused by being guilty/being ashamed. (b) what a s. = what a pity/how sad. **shame 2** v. to s. s.o. into = to make s.o. ashamed so that he does sth. **shamefaced** adj. embarrassed/ashamed. **shamefacedly** adv. in embarrassment. **shameful** adj. scandalous/disgraceful. **shamefully** adv. in a shameful way. **shameless** adj. without shame. **shamelessly** adv. in a shameless way.

shampoo 1 [ʃæm'puː] n. liquid soap for washing your hair/a carpet, etc. **shampoo 2** v. to wash (your hair/the carpet, etc.) with a shampoo.

shamrock [ʃæmrɒk] n. small clover like plant with leaves which are split into three parts.

shandy [ʃændɪ] n. mixture of beer and lemonade.

shanghai 1 [ʃæŋ'hai] n. (in Australia)

catapult. **shanghai 2** v. (shanghaied) to capture (s.o.) and force them to obey your orders.

shank [ʃæŋk] n. (a) straight shaft. (b) leg.

shan't [ʃɑːnt] v. see shall.

shanty [ʃæntɪ] n. (a) rough wooden hut; s. town = group of huts belonging to poor people. (b) sea s. = song sung by sailors.

shape 1 [ʃeip] n. (a) form; the picture is taking s. = is beginning to look like sth. (b) mould for making a jelly. (c) condition. **shape 2** v. (a) to form/to make into a shape. (b) to s. well = turn out well. **shapeless** adj. with no definite shape. **shapelessness** n. being shapeless. **shapeliness** n. being shapely. **shapely** adj. with an attractive shape.

shard [ʃɑːd] n. piece of broken pottery.

share 1 [ʃeə] n. (a) part which belongs to someone. (b) contribution which each person makes. (c) one of the parts into which a company's capital is divided. (d) ploughshare, the metal blade of a plough. **share 2** v. (a) (also share out) to divide up among several people. (b) to s. sth s.o. = to allow s.o. to use sth which you also use. (c) to have/to use (sth) in common. **shareholder** n. person who owns shares in a company. **shareholding** n. group of shares in a company owned by one person. **share-out** n. division of sth among several people.

shark [ʃɑːk] n. (a) large dangerous fish which can kill a man. (b) inf. crook/ swindler.

sharp 1 [ʃɑːp] adj. (-er, -est) (a) with a fine cutting edge. (b) very cutting/harsh. (c) with a very acute angle. (d) bitter. (e) clever/intelligent. (f) with a highly-developed sense. (g) high pitched (sound). (h) (in music) (note) which is slightly higher than the correct pitch. (i) clear (image). **sharp 2** n. note in music which is a semitone higher. **sharp 3** adv. (a) acutely. (b) exactly. (c) (in music) higher than the correct pitch. **sharpen** v. to make sharp. **sharpener** n. pencil s. = instrument for sharpening pencils. **sharper** n. person who cheats at cards. **sharply** adv. (a) acutely. (b) completely. (c) harshly. **sharpness** n.

being sharp. **sharp practice** n. dishonest activity. **sharpshooter** n. soldier who is trained to shoot very accurately. **sharp-witted** adj. clever.

shatter ['ʃætə] v. to break into little pieces; to upset (s.o.) very badly.

shave 1 [ʃeɪv] n. act of cutting off the hair on your face with a razor; close s. = near miss. **shave 2** v. (a) to cut off the hair on your face. (b) to slice very thin pieces off (sth). **shaven** adj. (old) shaved. **shaver** n. razor/machine for shaving. **shaving** n. (a) act of cutting off hair; s. cream = cream which you put on your face before shaving. (b) shavings = small thin slices of wood cut off by a plane.

shawl [ʃɔːl] n. large square of warm material for wrapping round your shoulders/your head.

she [ʃiː] (a) pron. referring to a female person. (b) prefix meaning female; she wolf.

sheaf [ʃiːf] n. (pl. sheaves [ʃiːvz]) bundle of corn of papers.

shear ['ʃɪə] v. (sheared/shorn [ʃɔːn]) to cut the wool off (sheep, etc.); to cut (through sth). **shearer** n. person who cuts the wool off sheep. **shears** n. cutting tool like large scissors. **shearwater** n. type of small dark sea bird.

sheath [ʃiːθ] n. (a) holder (for a knife, etc.). (b) rubber contraceptive. **sheathe** [ʃiːð] v. to put a knife back into its sheath. **sheath-knife** n. (pl.-knives) knife kept in a sheath.

sheaves [ʃiːvz] n. see sheaf.

shed 1 [ʃed] n. wooden building. **shed 2** v. (shed) (a) to lose (leaves); to lose/to take off (clothes). (b) to let flow (blood, tears, light); to s. light on = to make clearer.

sheen [ʃiːn] n. brilliant shining surface.

sheep [ʃiːp] n. (pl. sheep) farm animal, reared for wool or for meat; s. station = large sheep farm in Australia. **sheep dip** n. bath of disinfectant into which sheep are put to kill parasites. **sheepdog** n. type of dog specially trained for herding sheep. **sheepish** adj. ashamed/embarrassed. **sheepishly** adv. with a sheepish air.

sheepishness n. know tied to make a rope shorter. sheepmeat, n. meat from a sheep/lamb. sheepshank, n. knot tied to

make a rope shorter. **sheepskin** n. skin of a sheep with the wool attached.

sheer 1 ['ʃɪə] adj. (a) complete/total. (b) very steep. (c) very fine (stockings, etc.). **sheer 2** adv. straight up or down. **sheer 3** v. to swerve to avoid sth.

sheet [ʃiːt] n. (a) large piece of thin cloth which is put on a bed. (b) large flat piece (of paper/cardboard/plywood, etc.); s. feed = device which allows separate sheets of paper to be fed into a printer. s. lightning = lightning which appears as a sheet and not as a single flash. (c) rope for attaching a sail. **sheetanchor** n. large anchor used if a ship is in difficulties.

sheikh [ʃeɪk] n. Arab leader.

sheikhdom ['ʃeɪkdəm] n. country ruled by a sheikh.

sheila ['ʃiːlə] n. (in Australia) inf. girl.

sheldrake, shelduck ['ʃeldreɪk, 'ʃeldʌk] n. type of wild duck.

shelf [ʃelf] n. (pl. shelves [ʃelvz]) (a) plank attached to a wall/in a cupboard on which things can be put; inf. on the s. = (i) left behind/forgotten about; (ii) not married (when all your friends are married); s. life = length of time food can be kept in a shop before it goes bad. (b) narrow edge of rock.

shell 1 [ʃel] n. hard outside of some animals. (b) hard outside of an egg/a nut. (c) exterior of a car/building. (d) metal tube full of explosive fired from a gun.

shell 2 v. (a) to take (peas) out of their pods/(a hardboiled egg) out of its shell. (b) to bombard with shells. **shellfish** n. (no. pl.) sea animal with a shell (such as a crab/mussel, etc.). **shell out** v. inf. to pay money. **shellshock** n. illness in soldiers caused by being in battle.

shellac ['ʃelæk] n. resin used to make varnish.

shelter 1 ['ʃeltə] n. place where you can go for protection. **shelter 2** v. to give (s.o.) protection; to take shelter. **sheltered** adj. protected from wind/cold/unpleasant happenings; s. housing = small flats provided for elderly people, often with a resident warden.

shelve 1 [ʃelv] v. (a) to put off discussing a problem. (b) to slope down (c) to put (sth) on a shelf. **shelve 2** n. pl. see shelf. **shelving** n. set of shelves.

shemozzle [ʃɪ'mɒzl] n. inf. fight/row.

shenanigans [ʃɪ'nænɪgənz] n. pl.inf. (a) wild behaviour. (b) dishonest trick.

shepherd 1 ['ʃepəd] n. man who looks after sheep; s.'s pie = mashed potatoes on top. **shepherd 2** v. to guide.

shepherdess n. woman who looks after sheep.

sherbet ['ʃɜːvət] n. (a) fizzy powder/ fizzy drink. (b) Am. water ice.

sheriff ['ʃerɪf] n. (a) Am. country police officer. (b) (in England) ceremonial chief official in a country. (c) (in Scotland) chief judge of an area.

sherry ['ʃerɪ] n. type of strong wine, originally from Spain.

shibboleth ['ʃɪbələθ] n. slogan/policy formerly considered important.

shield 1 [ʃiːld] n. (a) large protective plate carried by riot police/knights in armour, etc. (b) protection against sth dangerous. **shield 2** v. to protect.

shift 1 [ʃɪft] n. (a) change of place/of direction; s. key = key on a typewriter/ computer which makes capital letters. (b) group of workers who work for a period and whose place is then taken by another group. (c) loose dress. **shift 2** v. (a) to change position/direction; to move. (b) inf. to s. for yourself = to look after yourself. **shiftiness** n. dishonest look. **shiftless** adj. lazy. **shifty** adj. (-ier, - iest) looking dishonest.

shillelagh [ʃɪ'leɪlɪ] n. (in Ireland) thick stick.

shilling ['ʃɪlɪŋ] n. currency used in Kenya and some other countries; old British coin worth 12 pence.

shilly-shally ['ʃɪlɪ'ʃælɪ] v. to hesitate.

shimmer 1 ['ʃɪmə] n. soft quivering light. **shimmer 2** v. to quiver with light.

shin 1 [ʃɪn] n. (a) front of the bottom part of your leg. (b) s. of beef = meat from the bottom part of the legs of cattle. **shin 2** v. (shinned) to s. up a tree = to climb up.

shindig, shindy ['ʃɪndɪg, ʃɪndɪ] n. inf. row/noisy party.

shine 1 [ʃaɪn] n. (a) brightness. (b) act of polishing. **shine 2** v. (shone[ʃɒn]) (a) to glint brightly. (b) to be brilliant. (c) to polish. **shining** adj. brilliant. **shiny** adj. (-ier, -iest) bright/polished.

shingle [ʃɪŋgl] n. (a) mass of small stones. (b) flat piece of wood/asbestos

nailed on a wall or roof as a covering (c) shingles = infectious disease related to chickenpox causing a painful rash.

shingly adj. covered with small stones.

ship 1 [ʃɪp] n. large boat for carrying goods/passengers. **ship 2** v. (shipped) (a) to put/to take on board a ship. (b) to send (goods), not necessarily on a ship.

shipbuilder n. person who builds ships. **shipbuilding** n. building of ships. **shipmate** n. sailor on the same ship as you. **shipment** n. (a) sending of goods; s. company = which specializes in the sending of goods. (b) quantity of goods shipped. **shipowner** n. person who owns a ship. **shipper**, n. person who sends goods. **shipping** n. (a) sending of goods; s. company = which specializes in the sending of goods. (b) (group of) ships. **shipshape** adj. neat/tidy. **shipwreck** n. wrecking of a ship. **shipwrecked** adj. (person) involved in a shipwreck. **shipyard** n. works where ships are built.

shire ['ʃaɪə] n. country; s. horse = large powerful horse used for farm work.

shirk [ʃɜːk] v. to try not to do sth/not to work. **shirker** n. person who shirks.

shirr [ʃɜː] v. (a) to gather (cloth) by running threads through it. (b) Am. to bake (beaten eggs).

shirt [ʃɜːt] n. piece of light clothing worn on the top part of the body; inf. keep your s. on! = keep calm/don't lose your temper. **shirtsleeves** n. in one's s. = not wearing a jacket. **shirtwaister** n. woman's dress where the top part looks like a shirt. **shirty** adj. inf. angry.

shishkebab ['ʃɪʃkbæb] n. small pieces of meat and vegetables cooked on a skewer.

shit 1 [ʃɪt] n. (vulgar) (a) excreta/solid waste matter from the body. (b) dirt. (c) nonsense. **shit 2** v. (vulgar) to pass solid waste matter from the body.

shiver 1 ['ʃɪvə] n. tremble (with cold/ fear). **shiver 2** v. (a) to tremble (with cold/fear/fever). (b) to break into tiny pieces. **shivery** adj. trembling (esp. with fever).

shoal [ʃəʊl] n. (a) (also shoals) bank of sand under the water. (b) group of fish swimming about.

shock 1 [ʃɒk] n. (a) untidy mass (of

hair). (b) sudden (unpleasant) surprise.
(c) mental/physical collapse (after a
blow/a sudden surprise). (d) electric s. =
sudden painful passing of electric
current through the body; electric s.
treatment = medical treatment of mental
illness using electric shocks. (e) great
blow; s. absorbers = part of a car/aircraft
which reduces the effect of bumps.
shock 2 v. to give (s.o.) a sudden
(unpleasant) surprise. **shocker** n. inf.
shocking person/thing. **shock-headed**
adj. with a mass of stiff hair. **shocking**
adj. in a shocking way. **shockingly**
adv. in a shocking way. **shock-proof**
adj. (watch, etc) which is not affected
by shocks. **shock troops** n. soldiers
specially trained to attack violently.
shod [ʃɒd] adj. wearing shoes.
shoddy 1 ['ʃɒdɪ] n. poor quality cloth.
shoddy 2 adj. (-ier, -iest) (a) badly
made. (b) low/nasty (trick). **shoddily**
adv. in a shoddy way. **shoddiness** n.
bad quality.
shoe [ʃuː] n. (a) article of clothing
which you wear on your feet both inside
and outside the house, not covering your
ankles; in his shoes = in his place/in the
situation he is in. (b) ring of metal nailed
under a horse's hoof. (c) brake shoes =
curved metal blocks which tighten round
a wheel. **shoe 2** v. (shod/shoed) to
attach metal horseshoes to the hooves of
(a horse). **shoehorn** n. curved piece of
plastic/metal which you put into the heel
of a shoe to make it easier to put on.
shoelace n. lace for tying up shoes.
shoemaker n. person who makes and
mends shoes. **shoeshine** n. polishing
of shoes. **shoestring** n. shoelace; on a
s. = with only a little money. **shoetree**
n. device which is put in a shoe to help
keep its shape.
shone [ʃɒn] v. see shine.
shoo 1 [ʃuː] inter. meaning go away.
shoo 2 v. to s. away = to frighten away
(birds/small children. etc.).
shook [ʃʊk] v. see shake.
shoot 1 [ʃuːt] n. (a) new growth on a
plant. (b) slide for goods/rubbish, etc. (c)
expedition to kill wild animals with
guns. (d) land where game can be shot.
(c) inf. the whole s. = everything. **shoot
2** v. (shot[ʃɒt]) (a) to fire a bullet from
a gun/an arrow from a bow; to kill (s.o./

an animal) with a bullet from a gun/an
arrow from a bow; to kill (s.o./an animal)
with a bullet or an arrow. (b) to hunt
with a gun. (c) to rush/to go fast; to s. the
rapids = to race through rapids in a light
boat. (d) to send out new growths. (e) to
kick a ball hard; to score (a goal). (f) to
make (a film). **shoot down** v. (to
make (an aircraft) crash by hitting it with
a shell. **shooting 1** n. action of
shooting with a gun; s. stick = walking
stick with a handle which unfolds to
make a seat. **shooting 2** adj. which
goes very fast; s. star = meteor. **shoot
up** v to go up fast.
shop 1 [ʃɒp] n. (a) place where you can
buy goods; s. assistant = person who
serves in a shop; inf. all over the s. =
scattered everywhere. (b) workshop/
place where goods are made; closed s. =
works where all the workers have to
belong to single union; to talk s. = to talk
about your job/about your office. **shop
2** v. (shopped) (a) to buy things in a
shop; to s. around = to go to various
shops and compare prices before buying
what you want. (b) Sl to report (s.o.) to
the police. **shopfloor** n. working area
in a factory. **shopkeeper** n. person
who runs a shop. **shoplifter** n. person
who steals things from a shop.
shoplifting n. stealing from a shop.
shopper n. person who buys goods
from a shop. **shopping** n. (a) goods
which you have bought in a shop. **shop-
soiled** adj. made dirty by being on
display in shop. **shop steward** n.
elected union representative in a factory.
shopwalker n. person who supervises
a department in a shop.
shore 1 [ʃɔː] n. (a) land at the edge of
the sea or a lake; beach. (b) prop. **shore
2** v. to hold up (sth) which might fall
down.
shorn [ʃɔːn] adj. cut off; s. of sth =
lacking sth; see also shear.
short 1 [ʃɔːt] adj. (a) not long (b) not
long in time; in s. = briefly. (c) not tall
(d) rude. (e) not enough/not as much as
in needed (of); s. weight as supposed (f)
light/crumbly (pastry). **short 2** n. (a)
short film. (b) short circuit. (drink of
spirits (d) pl.shorts = trousers not going
below the knee. **short 3** adv. (a)
abruptly: to stop s. (b) not far enough: to

fall s. **short 4** v. to short-circuit.
shortage n. lack. **shortbread** n.
thick sweet crumbly biscuit. **shortcake**
n. (a) shortbread (b) Am. cake with fruit
and creAm. **shortchange** v. to cheat
(s.o.). **short-circuit 1** n. jump of
electric current between two points.
missing out part of the normal circuit.
short-circuit 2 n. (a) to make a short
circuit(b)to get through difficulties by
taking a short cut. **shortcoming** n.
fault/defect. **short cut** n. way which is
shorter than usual quicker way of
reaching your destination. **shorten** v.
to/make/to become shorter. **shortening**
n. lard/cooking fat. **shortfall** n.
amount which is missing to make up an
expected total. **shorthand** n. way of
writing fast by using a system of signs. s.
typist who can take shorthand. **short-
handed** adj. with not enough workers.
shorthold n. tenancy of a property
guaranteed for less than five years.
shorthorn n. type of cattle with short
horns. **short list** n. list of some of the
people who have applied for a job, and
who have been chosen to come for an
interview. **short-list** v. to make a short
list of (candidates) for a job to put (s.o.'s
name)on a short list. **shortlived** adj.
which does not last long. **shortly** adv.
(a) soon (b) abruptly/rudely. **shortness**
n. (a) state of being short (b)rudeness.
short order n. Am. order given for sth
to be cooked on the spot (such as ham
and eggs). **short-sighted** adj. (a)
(person) who can only see near
objects(b) not paying attention to what
may happen in the future. short-
sightedness, n. being short-sighted.
short sleeved adj. (shirt etc.) with
short sleeves. **short-staffed** adj. with
not enough workers. **short-tempered**
adj. (person) who easily gets angry.
short term adj. not lasting long.
short time n. shorter working hours
than usual. **short wave** n. radio wave
about 50 metres long.
shot 1 [ʃɒt] adj. (silk) which changes
colour according to the light. **shot 2** n.
(a) small pellets/bullets fired from a gun.
(b) large heavy ball thrown in a
competition; to put the s. = throw the
weight in a competition. (c) act of
shooting; the sound of shooting; like a s.

= very rapidly. (d) person who shoots. (e)
inf. attempt. (f) Sl. injection. (g) Sl. small
drink of alcohol. (h) inf. photograph. see
also shoot. **shotgun** n. gun which fires
small pellets.
should [ʃʊd] v. used to show certain
moods. (a) ought; they s. have arrived by
now = they ought to have arrived. (b)
must; why s. I be the one to go? = why
must I be the one? (c) who s. we meet
but my aunt = what a surprise we had
when we met my aunt. (d) tentative
suggestion) s. I try again? (e) future after
that it is strange that he s. want to go.
shoulder 1 [ˈʃəʊldə] n. (a) part of the
body at the top of the arm/between the
top of the arm and the neck. (b) part of a
piece of clothing between the top of the
arm and the neck. (c) top part of the front
leg of a sheep. (d) hard s. = reinforced
side part of a road. **shoulder 2** v. (a) to
put on your shoulder. (c) to take on (a
burden). **shoulder bag** n. bag which
can be carried over the shoulder.
shoulderblade n. large flat bone in
the shoulder.
shout 1 [ʃaʊt] n. loud cry. **shout 2** v.
to make a loud cry; to s. s.o. down = to
shout so loudly that s.o. cannot speak.
shove 1 [ʃʌv] n. sharp push. **shove 2**
v. inf. to give a push to. **shove off** v.
inf. to go away.
shovel 1 [ˈʃʌvl] n. wide spade. **shovel
2** v. (shovelled) to lift up with a shovel.
shovelful n. contents of a shovel.
shoveller n. wild duck with a wide
flat beak.
show 1 [ʃəʊ] n. (a) exhibition/display;
s. house = house which is built to show
what similar houses can look like. (b)
performance: s. business = actors/
actresses/producers. etc. (considered as a
group); the entertainment world. (c)
pretence. (d) inf. affair/business. **show
2** v. (shown) (a) to make (sth) seen; to
allow s.o. to see (sth); to be seen. (b) to
indicate. (c) to point out/to direct. (d) to
prove/to demonstrate. **showcase** n.
cupboard with a glass front/box with a
glass top for putting things on show in a
shop or museum. **showdown** n. final
argument which will solve a crisis.
showily adv. in a showy way.
showiness n. being showy.
showjumper n. horse specially

trained for show-jumping. **show-jumping** n. riding competition where horses have to jump over different obstacles in a short time. **showman** n. person who puts on shows (such as circuses, etc.); person who is good at publicising. **showmanship** n.. art of putting on attractive shows. **show off** v. (a) to display (sth) to great effect. (b) to try to make people look at you by doing sth which will attract their attention. **show-off** n. inf. person who shows off. **showpiece** n. important item in an exhibition. **showroom** n. room where goods are shown to customers. **show up** v. (a) to reveal/to show (b) to stand out. (c) inf. to arrive. **showy** adj. too bright (colours); too ostentatious.

shower 1 ['ʃaʊə] n. (a) light fall of rain/small stones, etc. (b) spray device in a bathroom for washing your whole body. (c) bath taken in a spray of water from above. (d) Am. party where presents are given to a girl about to get married. **shower 2** v. (a) (also shower down) to pour/to fall in a quantity. (b) to wash under a spray. **shower bath** n. (a) spray device in a bathroom for washing your whole body. (b) bath taken in a spray of water. **showerproof** adj. (coat) which can protect against light rain. **shower room** n. room with a shower bath in it. **showery** adj. with many showers.

shrank [ʃræŋk] v. see shrink.

shrapnel ['ʃræpnl] n. pieces of metal from an exploded shell or bomb. etc.

shred 1 [ʃred] n. (a) long strip torn off sth. (b) small piece. **shred 2** v. (shredded) to tear into long strips; to cut into very thin strips. **shredder** n. machine for tearing waste paper into long strips; device for cutting vegetables into long thin strips.

shrew [ʃruː] n. (a) animal like a mouse with a long nose. (b) unpleasant bad-tempered woman who is always criticizing. **shrewish** adj. bad-tempered (woman).

shrewd [ʃruːd] adj. clever/wise. **shrewdly** adv. in a shrewd way. **shrewdness** n. being shrewd.

shriek 1 [ʃriːk] n. loud high-pitched cry. **shriek 2** v. to make a shriek.

shrift [ʃrɪft] n. to get short s. = to be treated curtly.

shrike [ʃraɪk] n. bird which pins insects to spines before eating them.

shrill [ʃrɪl] adj. high-pitched. **shrilly** adv. in a shrill way. **shrillness** n. being shrill.

shrimp [ʃrɪmp] n. (a) small shellfish with a long tail. (b) inf. small person. **shrimping** n. fishing for shrimps.

shrine [ʃraɪn] n. tomb/chapel where a saint is buried.

shrink 1 [ʃrɪŋk] n. Sl. psychiatrist. **shrink 2** v. (shrank; shrunk) (a) to make smaller; to get smaller. (b) to move back (from). **shrinkage** n. action of shrinking; amount by which sth shrinks,

shrivel ['ʃrɪvl] v. (shrivelled) to make/ to become dry and wrinkled.

shroud 1 [ʃraʊd] n. (a) long cloth covering a dead body. (b) shrouds = ropes from a mast to the sides of a ship. **shroud 2** v. to cover up. **Shrove Tuesday** ['ʃrəʊ'tjuːzdeɪ] n. the Tuesday before Lent.

shrub [ʃrʌb] n. small bush. **shrubbery** n. part of garden planted with shrubs.

shrug 1 [ʃrʌg] n. raising the shoulders to show you are not interested. **shrug 2** v. (shrugged) to s. your shoulders = to raise your shoulders to show you are not interested. **shrug off** v. to treat (sth) as if its not a cause of worry.

shrunk [ʃrʌŋk] v. see shrink.

shrunken ['ʃrʌŋkən] adj. wrinkled; dried up.

shuck 1 [ʃʌk] n. Am. shell/outer covering. **shuck 2** v. to take the shell off (sth).

shudder 1 ['ʃʌdə] n. tremble of horror. **shudder 2** v. to tremble violently with horror.

shuffle ['ʃʌfl] v. (a) to walk dragging your feet. (b) to mix (playing cards).

shun [ʃʌn] v. (shunned) to avoid.

shunt 1 [ʃʌnt] n. accident where one car bumps into the back of the car in front of it. **shunt 2** v. to move (a train) into a siding; to move (s.o.) backwards and forwards. **shunting yard** n. area of railway lines where wagons are kept/ sorted into trains.

shush [ʃʊʃ] inf. inter. meaning be quiet.

shut [ʃʌt] v. (shut) (a) to close. (b) to

lock up (sth) so that it cannot escape. (c) to close for business. **shut down** v. to make (a factory) stop working.
shutdown n. closure of a factory.
shuteye n. inf. sleep. **shut in** v. to look inside; to surround. **shut off**, v. to switch off (an engine/the water supply. etc.). **shut out** v. (a) to block. (b) to lock (s.o.) outside. **shutter** n. (a) folding wooden/metal cover which covers a window. (b) (in camera) part which opens and closes very rapidly to allow the light to go on to the film.
shuttered adj. with shutters. **shut up** v. (a) to close. (b) inf. to be quiet; to make (s.o.) be quiet.
shuttle 1 [ʃʌtl] n. part of a loom which carries the thread from side to side; s. service = bus/plane which goes backwards and forwards between two places; s. diplomacy = action of a diplomat going backwards and forwards between two countries to try to make them reach agreement. **shuttle 2** v. to go backwards and forwards; to send (s.o.) backwards and forwards.
shuttlecock n. light ball with feathers stuck in it, which is hit in badminton.
shy 1 [ʃaɪ] adj. timid/afraid to do sth; to fight s. of doing sth = to prefer not to.
shy 2 n. throwing (of a ball); coconut s. = game at fairs where you try to knock down a coconut with a hard ball. **shy 3** v. (a) to throw. (b) (of horse) to jump with fear. **shyly** adv. timidly. **shyness** n. being shy. **shyster** n. Sl. dishonest businessman.
SI abbrev. for Système International. the international system of units for measuring physical properties. such as weight, speed, heat, etc.
Siamese [saɪəˈmiːz] adj. referring to Siam: S. twins = twins born with parts of their bodies joined together; S. cat = type of cat with pale fawn fur, dark brown face and blue eyes.
sibilant [ˈsɪbɪlənt] adj. & n. (sound) like a hiss.
sibling [ˈsɪblɪŋ] n. brother or sister.
sic [sɪk] adv. thus (used to indicate a mistake).
sick [sɪk] adj. (a) ill/not well; s. leave = time off work because of illness. (b) vomiting; feeling ready to vomit. (c) (of) showing disgust/dislike. **sickbay** n. (a)

hospital ward (on a ship). (b) small hospital attached to a factory/school. etc.
sickbed n. bed where a sick person is lying. **sicken** v. to become ill.
sickening adj. which makes you sick; s. for = beginning to show signs of (a disease). **sickly** adj. not well; weak.
sickness n. (a) illness; s. benefit = payment made by the government to s.o. who is ill and cannot work. (b) feeling of being about to vomit. **sick pay** n. wages paid to s.o. who is ill and cannot work. **sickroom** n. room where a sick person is in bed. **sickle** [ˈsɪkl] n. tool with a semi-circular blade. used for cutting corn.
side 1 [saɪd] n. (a) edge; area near the edge; on the s. = (i) apart from one's usual job; (ii) dishonestly. (b) one of four parts which (with the top and bottom) make a box. etc. wall (of a house). (c) part of the body between the hips and the shoulder; s. by s. = close together (in a row). (d) surface (e) slope (of a mountain); surface/part. (f) teAm. (g) group holding a particular point of view; to take sides = to support one party or another in a quarrel. (h) family connection. (i) inf. conceited attitude.
side 2 adj. (a) secondary/less important (road, etc.). at the side (not the front or back). **side 3** v. to s. with s.o. = to support s.o. in an argument.
sideboard n. (a) piece of dining room furniture for holding plates, a type of table with a cupboard beneath. (b) sideboards = sidewhiskers. **sideburns** n. Am. sidewhiskers. **sidecar** n. small compartment for one passenger attached to the side of a motorcycle. **side effects** n. secondary and unexpected effects (of a drug). **side issue** n. secondary problem. **sidekick** n. inf. companion/helper. **sidelight** n. (a) unusual information. (b) small light on the front of a car. **sideline** n. (a) business which is extra to your normal work. (b) pl.sidelines = lines at the edge of a football pitch, etc. **sidelong** adj. from one side. **sidesaddle** adv. (of woman) (to ride) with both legs on the same side of the horse. **sideshow** n. small show/stall with a game of skill (at a fair, etc.). **sideman** n. assistant in a church. **sidestep** v. (sidestepped) to

avoid. **sideswipe** v. inf. (of car) to hit another vehicle in passing. **sidetrack** v. to attract s.o.'s attention away from the main problem. **sidewalk** n. Am. pavement. **sidewards** adv. to the side. **sideways** adv. to the side; with the side in front. **sidewhiskers** n. pl. whiskers down the side of your face. **siding** n. minor railway line where trains are kept until needed.

sidereal [saɪ'dɪərɪəl] adj. referring to the stars.

sidle ['saɪdl] v. to walk sideways, not directly forwards.

siege [si:dʒ] n. act of surrounding an enemy town with an army to make it surrender.

sienna [sɪ'enə] n. burnt s. = reddishbrown colour; raw s. = yellowish brown colour.

siesta [sɪ'estə] n. afternoon rest.

sieve 1 [sɪv] n. kitchen utensil with very small holes for passing liquid through to hold back lumps/for sorting out large pieces in a powder. **sieve 2** v. to pass (a liquid/a powder) through a sieve to sort out large lumps.

sift [sɪft] v. (a) to sieve. (b) to examine carefully. **sifter** n. container with small holes in the lid for sprinkling sugar or flour.

sigh 1 [saɪ] n. deep breath. showing sadness/relief, etc. **sigh 2** v. to breathe deeply showing sadness, relief, etc.

sight 1 [saɪt] n. (a) one of the five senses, the ability to see. (b) glimpse; act of seeing. (c) range of vision. (d) spectacle; thing which you ought to see. (e) funny/odd thing. (f) part of a gun through which you look to take aim. (g) inf. a s.. more = a lot more. **sight 2** v. (a) to see for the first time. (b) to aim a gun. **sightless** adj. blind. **sightread** v. to play written music without having practises it. **sightscreen** n. large white screen placed behind the bowler in cricket. **sightseeing** n. visiting the sights of a town. **sightseer** n. tourist/ person seeing the sights.

sign 1 [saɪn] n. (a) movement (of hand/ head, etc.) which means sth; s language = signs of the hands used by deaf and dumb people to communicate. (b) mark. (c) indication/thing which suggests that sth may happen. (d) trace. (e) advertising

board; panel showing directions on a road. **sign 2** v. (a) to write your signature at the end of (a letter or on a document, etc.). (b) to make a movement which has a meaning. **sign away** v. to lose possession of (sth) by signing a document. **signboard** n. panel with a sign. **sign off** v. to end a letter/a radio broadcast. **sign on** v. to join the armed services for a period; to start work.

signpost 1 n. post with a sign showing directions to a place. **signpost 2** v. to indicate a direction with signs.

signup v. (a) to join the armed services for a period. (b) to sign a contract to play only for a particular football club, etc.; make (a player) sign a contract.

signal 1 ['sɪgnl] n. (a) movement of the hand/head, etc., which tells s.o to do sth. (b) lights/mechanical flags, etc., used to tell s.o. to do sth. (c) sound heard on a radio receiver. **signal 2** adj. (formal) remarkable. **signal 3** v. (signalled) to make signs to tell s.o. to do sth. **signal box** n. building by the side of the railway where the signalman controls the signals. **signaller** n. person who signals. **signally** adv. (formal) remarkably. **signalman** n. person who controls railway signals.

signatory ['sɪgnətrɪ] n. person who signs (a treaty, etc.). **signature** ['sɪgnətʃə] n. (a) name which has been signed. (b) group of pages of a book (usually 32 or 64) which are folded out of one sheet of paper. (c) s. tune = tune which is used regularly at the beginning or end of a broadcast to identify the broadcast.

signet ['sɪgnɪt] n. seal (for sealing with wax); s. ring = ring worn on the little finger with a design carved on to it to use as a seal.

signify ['sɪgnɪfaɪ] v. (a) to mean. (b) to show; that signifies = that makes sense. (c) to be of importance. **significance** n. (a) meaning. (b) importance. **significant** adj. which is important/ which has a lot of meaning. **significantly** adv. in a significant way. **signification** n. meaning.

silage ['saɪlɪdʒ] n. green crops fermented in a silo and used to feed animals.

silence 1 ['saɪləns] n. (a) lack of noise.

(b) not saying anything. **silence 2** v. (a) to make (s.o.) stop talking. (b) to stop (sth) making a noise. **silencer** n. (a) apparatus to stop the noise of the exhaust of a car. (b) apparatus attached to a gun to stop the noise of it being fired. **silent** adj. quiet. **silently** adv. in a silent way.

silhouette 1 [sɪluːet] n. black outline of s.o.'s head in profile. **silhouette 2** v. to stand out in profile.

silica [ˈsɪlɪkə] n. mineral compound of silicon. **silica gel** n. hard crystals used to keep things dry in humid conditions.

silicate n. common silicon compound. **silicon** [ˈsɪlɪkən] n. (element: Si) common element which is not a metal, and which is usu. found in compounds; s. chip = small piece of silicon used in transistors and very small electronic devices. **silicone** [ˈsɪlɪkəʊn] n. chemical substance used in making oils. **silicosis** [sɪlɪˈkəʊsɪs] n. disease of the lungs caused by breathing in dust.

silk [sɪlk] n. (a) thread which is produced by a caterpillar; cloth woven from this thread. (b) to take s. = to be accepted as a leading barrister. **silken** adj. soft and shiny. **silkscreen printing** n. printing by forcing colours through a taut piece of cloth. **silkworm** n. caterpillar which of cloth. **silky** adj. soft and shiny.

sill [sɪl] n. ledge beneath a window/a door.

silly [ˈsɪlɪ] adj. stupid/idiotic. **silliness** n. being silly.

silo [ˈsaɪləʊ] n. large tower for storing grain for storing green crops (as food for animals). (b) deep hole in the ground in which rockets are kept.

silt 1 [sɪlt] n. fine mud washed down by a river. **silt 2** v. to s. up = to fill with silt.

silver [ˈsɪlvə] n. (a) (element: Ag) precious white metal; s. jubilee = 25th anniversary of an important event; s. wedding = anniversary of 25 years of marriage. (b) s. foil/paper = sheet of thin shiny metal which looks like silver, used for wrapping food in. (c) coins made of white metal. (d) light shining colour like silver. **silver birch** n. common northern tree with white bark.

silverfish n. small silvery insect found

in kitchens, etc. **silverside** n. good quality beef, cut from the back part of the animal. **silversmith** n. craftsman who makes things in silver. **silverware** n. articles made of silver. **silvery** adj. (a) shiny like silver. (b) light ringing (sound).

simian [ˈsɪmɪən] adj. like a monkey.

similar [ˈsɪmɪlə] adj. very alike but not quite the same. similarly, adv. in a similar way. **similarity** n. sameness/likeness.

simile [ˈsɪmɪlɪ] n. comparison using 'like' or 'as'.

simmer [ˈsɪmə] v. to boil gently; to s. down = to become calmer.

simnel [ˈsɪmnl] n. s. cake = fruit cake covered with marzipan.

simper 1 [ˈsɪmpə] n. silly affected smile. **simper 2** v. to make a simper.

simple [ˈsɪmpl] adj. (a) not complicated; not difficult. (b) inf. not very intelligent. (c) s. interest = interest calculated as a percentage per annum on the original sum without adding each year's interest to the capital. (d) plain/ordinary. **simple-minded** adj. not very intelligent. **simpleton** n. person who is not very intelligent. **simplicity** [sɪmˈplɪsɪtɪ] n. being simple. **simplification** [sɪmplɪfɪˈkeɪʃn] n. making simple. simplify[ˈsɪmplɪfaɪ] v. to make (sth) simple. **simply** [ˈsɪmplɪfaɪ] adv. (a) without complication. (b) absolutely. (c) purely/only.

simulate [ˈsɪmjʊleɪt] v. to pretend. **simulation** [sɪmjʊˈleɪʃn] n. pretence. **simulator** [ˈsɪmjʊleɪtə] n. machine which allows a learner to experience simulated conditions (as in a car/aircraft, etc.)

simultaneous [sɪməlˈteɪnɪəs] adj. happening at the same time. **simultaneously** adv. at the same time.

sin 1 [sɪn] n. wicked deed; action which goes against the rules of religion; to live in s. = to live together without being married. **sin 2** v. (sinned) to do sth wicked/wrong. **sinful** adj. wicked (person/action). **sinner** n. person who has sinned.

since 1 [sɪns] adv. from then onwards. **since 2** prep. from a certain time. **since 3** conj. (a) from a certain time.

(b) because.

sincere [sɪn'sɪə] *adj.* very honest/open. **sincerely** *adv.* really/truly; yours s. = greeting written at the end of a letter. **sincerity** [sɪn'serɪtɪ] *n.* honesty.

sine [saɪn] *n.* (in mathematics) ratio between the length of one of the shorter sides opposite and acute angle to that of the hypotenuse in a right-angled triangle.

sinecure ['saɪnɪkjʊə] *n.* job for which you get paid but which does not involve much work.

sine die ['sɪneɪdɪeɪ] *adv.* to a later date, which is unspecified. **sine qua non** ['sɪneɪkwaː'nɒn] *n.* condition without which something cannot function.

sinew ['sɪnjuː] *n.* strong cord which joins a muscle to a bone. **sinewy** *adj.* very strong.

sing [sɪŋ] *v.* (a) to make music with your mouth. (b) to make a buzzing noise. **singer** *n.* person who sings. **singsong 1** *adj.* (voice) with a rising and falling tone. **singsong 2** *n.* singing party.

singe ['sɪndʒ] *v.* to burn slightly.

single 1 ['sɪŋgl] *adj.* (a) alone/one by itself; s. figures = numbers from 1 to 9. (b) for one person. (c) unmarried. (d) s. ticket = ticket for one journey. (e) s. cream = light creAm. **single 2** *n.* (a) singles = tennis game played between two people. (b) ticket for one journey. (c) (in cricket) one run. (d) small record of pop music with only one piece of music on each side. **single 3** *v.* to s. out = to select. **singlebreasted** *adj.* (coat) which does not fold over widely in the front to button. **singledecker** *n.* bus with only one deck. **singlehanded** *adj.* all by yourself. **singleminded** *adj.* thinking only of one aim. **singlemindedness** *n.* being singleminded. **singleness** *n.* (a) being single. (b) s. of purpose = having only one aim. **singly** *adv.* one by one.

singlet ['sɪŋglət] *n.* man's (sleeveless) undergarment for the top part of the body.

singular 1 ['sɪŋgjʊlə] *adj. & n.* referring to one person/thing. **singular 2** *adj.* (a) odd/peculiar. (b) remarkable. **singularity** [sɪŋgjʊ'lærɪtɪ] *n.* oddness/peculiarity. **singularly** *adv.* (a) strangely. (b) particularly.

sinister ['sɪnɪstə] *adj.* looking evil;

which promises evil.

sink 1 [sɪŋk] *n.* (a) basin for washing in a kitchen. (b) place where substances pass to be absorbed out of the atmosphere. **sink 2** *v.* (sank; sunk) (a) to (cause to) go to the bottom of water/mud. etc. (b) to go down. (c) to make (a well). (d) to s. your teeth into = to bite. (e) to invest. **sinker** *n.* lead weight used to pull down a fishing-line into the water. **sink in** *v.* to become fixed in the mind.

Sino- ['saɪnəʊ] prefix meaning Chinese/between China and another country.

sinuous ['sɪnjʊəs] *adj.* winding. **sinuosity** *n.* (a) being sinuous. (b) bend (in a pipe or road).

sinus ['saɪnəs] *n.* hole in the bones of the head connected with the nose and air passages. **sinusitis** [saɪnə'saɪtɪs] *n.* infection of the sinuses.

sip 1 [sɪp] *n.* small quantity of liquid. **sip 2** *v.* (sipped) to drink taking only a small quantity at a time.

siphon 1 ['saɪfn] *n.* (a) device for making fizzy water. (b) bent tube to allow you to take liquid from one container to another placed at a lower level. **siphon 2** *v.* (a) to remove (liquid) by using a siphon. (b) to remove (money) from a source illegally.

sir [sɜː] *n.* respectful way of addressing a man (usu. and older or more important man). (b) title given to a knight or baronet. (c) way of addressing a man in a formal letter.

sire 1 ['saɪə] *n.* (a) male horse which is a father. (b) (old) Sire = way of addressing a king. **sire 2** *v.* (of a horse) to be father of.

siren ['saɪrən] *n.* loud warning signal which wails.

sirloin ['sɜːlɔɪn] *n.* best cut of beef from the back of the animal.

sisal ['saɪsl] *n.* rope made from fibres from a tropical plant.

siskin ['sɪskɪn] *n.* small finch.

sissy ['sɪsɪ] *n.* weak girlish man/boy.

sister 1 ['sɪstə] *n.* (a) female child whose parents are the same as yours. (b) senior nurse. (c) nun; title given to nuns. **sister 2** *adj.* similar/identical; s. ship = ship of the same design. **sisterhood** *n.* group of nuns/nurses, etc. **sister-in-**

law *n.* wife of your brother; sister of your husband or wife. **sisterly** *adj.* like a sister.

sit [sɪt] *v.* (sat) (a) to be seated; to make (s.o.) be seated; to rest in a seated position with your behind on a chair/on the ground, etc.; to s. for your portrait = to pose (not necessarily in a seated position). (b) to be in session/to meet. (c) to be a member of. (d) (of bird) to sit on her eggs. (e) to take (an examination). **sit back** *v.* to be seated and lean backwards. **sit down** *v.* to take a seat. sit-down, *adj.* (a) sit-down meal = meal where you sit at a table. (b) sit-down strike = strike where workers do not move from their place of work. **sit-in** *n.* occupation of the place of work by workers/students. etc. **sit on** *v.* (a) to be a member of (a committee). (b) *inf.* to delay (a request). **sitter** *n.* person who sits/poses for a painter; baby-sitter = person who looks after a child when its parents are out. **sit tight** *v.* to stay where you are/to refuse to move. **sitting** *n.* act of sitting; session. **sitting room** *n.* room where you can relax in comfortable chairs. **sit up** *v.* (a) to straighten yourself up on your chair. (b) to stay up/not to go to bed.

site 1 [saɪt] *n.* (a) place where a building/town is situated. (b) place where an event took place. **site 2** *v.* to place (a building/town) on a particular piece of land.

situate ['sɪtjʊeɪt] *v.* to place. **situation** [sɪtjʊ'eɪʃn] *n.* (a) place where a building is. (b) state of affairs. (c) job; situations vacant = list of vacancies in jobs.

sitz bath ['sɪtsbɑːθ] *n.* small low bath in which a person can sit, but not lie down.

six [sɪks] *n.* number 6; *inf.* they're all at sixes and sevens = they're very disorganized/they can't agree. **sixteen** *n.* number 16. **sixteenth, 16th** *adj. & n.* referring to sixteen. **sixth, 6th** *adj. & n.* referring to six; s. form = top class in a secondary school. **sixtieth, 60th** *adj. & n.* referring to sixty. **sixty** *n.* number 60; she's in her sixties = she is ages between 60 and 69.

size 1 [saɪz] *n.* (a) largeness of sth. (b) measurements. (c) type of pastelike glue. **size 2** *v.* (a) to s. s.o. up = to judge

s.o.'s capabilities. (b) to cover with glue. **sizeable** *adj.* quite large.

sizzle ['sɪzl] *v.* to make a hissing sound when frying; *inf.* to be very hot.

skate 1 [skeɪt] *n.* (a) large flat fish with white flesh. (b) sharp blade worn under boots for sliding on ice. **skate 2** *v.* (a) to slide on ice wearing skates. (b) to s. over/round sth = not to mention sth which could be embarrassing.

skateboard *n.* board with two pairs of wheels which you stand on to glide about. **skater** *n.* person who goes skating.

skedaddle [skɪ'dædl] *v.* *inf.* to go quickly.

skein [skeɪn] *n.* length of wool loosely wound round and round into a loop.

skeleton ['skelɪtn] *n.* (a) bones inside a body; s. in the cupboard = secret that a family or person is trying to keep hidden. (b) s. staff = few staff left to carry on essential work while the others are away. (c) s. key = key which will fit any lock in a building. (d) rough outline. **skeletal** *adj.* like a skeleton.

skep [skep] *n.* straw beehive.

skeptic ['skeptɪk] *n.* *Am.* see sceptic.

skerry ['skerɪ] *n.* low rocky outcrop in the sea.

sketch 1 [sketʃ] *n.* rough drawing. (b) short amusing play. **sketch 2** *v.* to make a rough drawing/a rough plan of. **sketch-book** *n.* book of drawing paper for sketching. **sketchily** *adv.* in a sketchy way. **sketchiness** *n.* being sketchy. **sketch-map** *n.* roughly drawn map. **sketchpad** *n.* pad of paper for sketching. **sketchy** *adj.* rough/incomplete.

skew [skjuː] *adj.* not straight on the s. = askew/not straight. **skewbald** ['skjuːbɔːld] *adj.* (horse)with patches of white with another colour, but not black.

skewer 1 ['skjʊə] *n.* long thin metal rod for putting through pieces of meat when cooking. **skewer 2** *v.* to stick a long metal rod through (sth).

ski 1 [skiː] *n.* long flat narrow piece of wood etc. which you attach under your boot for moving over snow; water skis = similar pieces of wood for gliding over water. **ski 2** *v.* to travel on skis to go skiing = to travel on skis as a sport. **skiboots** *n. pl.* special boots for skiing. **skier** n. person travelling on skis. **ski jump** n. slope with a sudden drop at the bottom to allow a skier to jump high in the air. **ski lift** n. device to take skiers to the top of a slope.

skid 1 [skɪd] n. sliding sideways (b) plank for sliding heavy objects along. **skid 2** v. (skidded) to slide sideways in a vehicle with the wheels not gripping the surface.

skidoo [skɪ'duː] n. Am. & Canada small powered sledge for travelling over snow.

skiff [skɪf] n. light rowing boat.

skill [skɪl] n. cleverness/ability to do something **skilful** adj. clever/very able. **skilfully** adv. in a skilful way. **skilled** adj. having/requiring a particular skill

skillet ['skɪlɪt] n. Am. frying pan.

skim [skɪm] v. (skimmed) (a) to remove things floating on the surface of (a liquid). (b) to dash over the surface of sth: to s. through a book = to read a book quickly.

skimp [skɪmp] v. (a) to do a job badly. (b) not to give enough of: they s. on food = they don't spend much money of food. **skimpy** adj. (-ier, -iest) insufficient (meal); tight/short (clothes).

skin 1 [skɪn] n. (a) outer surface of an animal's body; by the s. of their teeth = only just. (b) outer surface **skin 2** v. (skinned) to remove the skin of. **skin-deep** adj. on the surface/superficial. **skindiver** n. person who goes skindiving. **skindiving** n. sport of swimming underwater with breathing apparatus but without special clothing. **skinflint** n. miser. **skinny** adj. (-ier, -iest) inf. thin. **skintight** adj. (clothes) which are close-fitting.

skint [skɪnt] adj. Sl. having no money.

skip 1 [skɪp] n. (a) act of skipping (b) large metal container for builder's rubbish. **skip 2** v. (skipped) (a) to jump over a rope; to run along half hopping and half jumping (b) to miss out (part of a book). **skipping rope** n. child's rope which you jump over as it turns.

skipper 1 ['skɪpə] n. captain (of a ship/ team). **skipper 2** v. robe the captain of (a team).

skirl [skɜːl] n. wailing sound made by bagpipes.

skirmish ['skɜːmɪʃ] n. (pl.-es) slight

battle between opposite sides.

skirt 1 [skɜːt] n. piece of woman's clothing covering the lower part of the body from the waist to the knees or ankles. **skirt 2** v. to go round/to avoid going through. **skirting board** n. decorative board running along the bottom edge of a wall in a room.

skit [skɪt] n. play/story which makes fun of s.o./sth. **skittish** ['skɪtɪʃ] adj. (of horse, girl, etc.) liable to jump about unexpectedly.

skittle ['skɪtl] n. bottle-shaped wooden object which is to be knocked down with a ball in a game.

skive [skaɪv] v. inf. to avoid working. **skiver** n. inf. person who skives. **skivvy** ['skɪvɪ] n. inf. girl who does the dirty work in a house.

skua ['skjuːə] n. type of large sea bird.

skulduggery [skʌl'dʌgərɪ] n. inf. some vague unspecified crime.

skulk [skʌlk] v. (a) to hide away (because you are planning sth wicked) (b) to creep about mysteriously

skull [skʌl] n. bony part of the head. **skullcap** n. small round hat which fits tight on the head.

skunk [skʌŋk] n. American mammal with black and white fur which produces a bad smell.

sky [skaɪ] n. area above the earth which is blue during the day, and where the moon and stars appear at night. **sky-blue** adj. & n. bright light blue(colour). **sky-diver** n. person who jumps from an aircraft, and falls freely for some time before opening his parachute. **sky-high** adv. as high as the sky; to blow sth sky-high = to blow sth up with a powerful explosive. **skylark 1** n. small singing bird which sings as it flies upwards. **skylark 2** v. to play wild games. **skylight** n. window in a roof or ceiling. **skyline** n. horizon; shape of buildings silhouetted against the sky. **skyscraper** n. very tall building.

slab [slæb] n. thick flat rectangular block.

slack 1 [slæk] adj. (-er, -est) (a) not taut/not tight(b) not busy (c) lazy/not working well. **slack 2** n. (a) looseness; loose part of a rope (b) very small pieces of coal (c) slacks = trousers **slack 3** v. to s.(off) = to be lazy/to do less work.

slacken *v.* (a) to loosen (b) to s. off = to work less. **slacker** *n.* person who doesn't work hard. **slackly** *adv.* (a) loosely (b) lazily. **slackness** *n.* being slack.

slag [slæg] *n.* waste material left after metal has been extracted from ore; s. heap = mountain of slag left near a metal works or coalmine.

slain [sleɪn] *v.* see slay.

slake [sleɪk] *v.* (a) to s. your thirst = to drink to remove your thirst (b) to mix lime with water.

slalom ['slɑːləm] *n.* test in skiing where you have to ski fast between a series of posts.

slam 1 [slæm] *n.* (a) banging of door (b) grand s. = winning all the card games in a competition. **slam 2** *v.* (slammed) (a) to bang (b) *inf.* to criticize very unfavourably.

slander 1 ['slɑːndə] *n.* untrue thing said about a person which hurts his reputation; crime of saying such things **slander 2** *v.* to say untrue things about a person. **slanderous** *adj.* (statement) which is slander.

slang [slæŋ] *n.* words or phrases used by certain groups of people in popular speech which are not used in correct or written language. **slanging match** *n.* bitter argument where two people call each other rude names. **slangy** *adj. inf.* using slang.

slant 1 [slɑːnt] *n.* (a) slope; on the s. = sloping (b) point of view **slant 2** *v.* (a) to slope (b) to show (news or information) in a biased way. **slanting** *adj.* sloping. **slantwise** *adv.* at an angle; on a slope.

slap 1 [slæp] *n.* smack with your hand flat. **slap 2** *v.* (slapped) (a) to hit with your hand flat (b) to bring (sth) down flat on to a surface; to s. down = tell off sharply. **slap 3** *adv.* to run s. into the wall = right into the wall. **slapdash** *adj.* careless. slaphappy, adj. & *inf.* happily careless. **slapstick** *adj. & n.* rough (comedy) which depends on physical jokes. **slap-up** *adj. inf.* good expensive(meal).

slash 1 [slæʃ] *n.* (*pl.*-es)long cut. **slash 2** *v.* (a) to make a long cut (b) to shorten; to reduce (a price) drastically.

slat [slæt] *n.* thin flat piece of wood.

slatted *adj.* made of slats.

slate 1 [sleɪt] *n.* dark-grey stone which splits into thin sheets; piece of this stone used as a roof covering or for writing on; to start a clean s. = to start again (without any faults held against you) (b) group of candidates in an election. **slate 2** *v. inf.* to criticize (a play/a book. etc.). **slate grey** *adj. & n.* very dark blue-grey (colour).

slattern ['slætən] *n.* dirty woman. **slatternly** *adj.* (of a woman) dirty.

slaughter 1 ['slɔːtə] *n.* (a) killing of animals for meat (b) killing of people (in war). **slaughter 2** *v.* (a)to kill (animals) for meat (b) to kill (many People) in war. **slaughterhouse** *n.* place where animals are slaughtered.

slave 1 [sleɪv] *n.* person who belongs to and works for s.o. **slave 2** *v.* (also slave away) to work hard. **slave driver** *n. inf.* employer who makes his workers work very hard. **slavery** *n.* being a slave; buying and selling slaves. **slavish** *adj.* exact (imitation) without any imagination. **slavishly** *adv.* (to obey rules) exactly without exercising any imagination. **slaver 1** ['sleɪvə] *n.* liquid which dribbles out of your mouth.

slaver 2 *v.* to dribble/to let liquid trickle out of your mouth.

slay [sleɪ] *v.* (formal)('slew[sluː].slain) to kill.

sleazy ['sliːzɪ] *adj.* (-ier, -est) *inf.* dirty/ disreputable.

sled [sled] *n.* sledge.

sledge 1 [sledʒ] *n.* small vehicle with runners for sliding over the snow.

sledge 2 *v.* to go sledging = to play at sliding on the snow on a sledge. **sledge-hammer** *n.* very large heavy hammer.

sleek 1 [sliːk] *adj.* (-er, -est) smooth/ shiny; well-kept. **sleek 2** *v.* to smooth down (hair) with oil. **sleekly** *adv.* in a sleek way. **sleekness** *n.* being sleek.

sleep 1 [sliːp] *n.* state of resting naturally and unconsciously; to go/to get to s. = to start sleeping; to send s.o to s. = to make s.o. go to sleep (from boredom/by hypnosis); to put to s. = to kill; my foot has gone to s. = has become numb. **sleep 2** *v.* (slept) (a) to be in a state of natural rest and unconsciousness; I'll s on it = I will make a decision on the problem in the morning; to s. sth off = to get rid of the effects of sth by sleeping; to s. with s.o. = to have enough beds for. **sleeper** n. (a) person who is asleep(b) wooden bar which rails are attached to (c) sleeping car (d) overnight train with sleeping cars. **sleepily** adv. in a sleepy away. **sleepiness** n. being sleepy. **sleeping 1** adj. asleep; s. partner = partner who does not take an active interest in the business. **sleeping 2** n. being asleep; s. pill = medicine which makes you go to sleep; s. car = carriage on a train with beds where passengers can sleep; s. bag = quilted bag for sleeping in a tent. etc.; s. sickness = carriage on a train with beds where passengers can sleep; s. bag = quilted bag for sleeping in a tent.etc.; s. sickness = tropical disease which affects the nervous system. sleepless, adj. with no sleep. **sleeplessness** n. having no sleep not able to get to sleep. **sleepwalk** v. to walk about when you are asleep. **sleepwalker** n. person who sleepwalks. **sleepy** adj. (-ier, -iest) half asleep; ready to go to sleep. **sleet 1** [sli:t] n. mixture of snow and rain. **sleet 2** v. it is sleeting = snow and rain are falling together.

sleeve [sli:v] n. (a) part of clothing which covers the arm; to keep sth up your s. = to have a plan which you are keeping secret (b) cover for a piece of machinery (c) square cardboard cover for a gramophone record. **sleeveless** adj. with no sleeves.

sleigh [sleɪ] n. large sledge pulled by horses or reindeer etc.

sleight [slaɪt] n. s. of hand = quickness of a conjurer's movements when performing a card trick.

slender ['slendə] adj. (a) very thin/slim (b) not strong; not large. **slenderness** n. being slender.

slept [slept] v. see sleep.

sleuth [slu:θ] n. inf. detective.

slew [slu:] v. (a) to turn/to twist (b) see slay.

slice 1 [slaɪs] n. (a) thin piece cut off sth (b) fish s. = flat broad knife for serving fish (c) (in games) strike which makes the ball spin towards the right.

slice 2 v. (a)to cut into slices (b) to cut sharply (c) to hit a ball so that it spins towards the right **slicer** n. machine for slicing meat/bread etc.

slick 1 [slɪk] adj. (-er, -est) clever (in a way which tricks people). **slick 2** n. oil s. = layer of oil which has spilled on the sea from a tanker or oil rig. **slick 3** v. to s. down = to make (hair) sleek.

slid [slɪd] v. see slide.

slide 1 [slaɪd] n. (a) action of slipping on a smooth surface (b) slippery surface (on ice); slippery metal slope for children to slide down (c) thin glass plate to put under a microscope (d) plastic transparent photograph which can be projected on a screen (d) clip which slips into the hair to hold it in place

slide 2 v. (slid[slɪd]) (a) to move smoothly (b) to let things s. = to allow things to become worse/not to care if things get worse. **slide-rule** n. device for calculating made of a ruler marked with numbers and a central part which slides sideways. **sliding scale** n. system of marks/points/taxes etc., which vary according to a scale.

slight 1 [slaɪt] adj. (-er, -est) (a) thin/slender (person) (b) not very large; not very important. **slight 2** n. insult. **slight 3** v. to insult/to be rude to (s.o.). **slightingly** adv. rudely/insultingly. **slightly** adv. not very much

slim 1 [slɪm] adj. (slimmer, slimmest) (a) thin/slender/not fat. (b) small. **slim 2** v. (slimmed) to diet in order to become thin. **slimmer** n. person who is trying to lose weight. **slimness** n. being slim.

slime [slaɪm] n. thin mud; dirty sticky liquid. **sliminess** n. being slimy. **slimy** adj. (ier, -iest) unpleasantly muddy/slippery/sticky.

sling 1 [slɪŋ] n. a device for throwing a stone (b) carrying strap; bandage tied round your neck to hold steady your wounded arm (c) apparatus made of ropes and pulleys for hoisting and carrying goods. **sling 2** v. (slung) (a) to throw (b) to hold up/to hang by a sling. **slingshot** n. Am. catapults/strong elastic band on a forked stick used for throwing stones.

slink [slɪŋk] v. (slunk) to creep about furtively. **slinky** adj. (-ier, -iest) smooth (shape); tight smooth (clothes).

slip 1 [slɪp] n. (a) action of sliding by mistake (b) mistake; s. of the tongue =

mistake in speaking(c) to give s.o. the s. = to escape from s.o. (d) pillow s, = cloth bag to cover a pillow (e) small piece of paper (f) petticoat (g) slips = long smooth slope on which ships are built (h) mixture of clay and water which is used in pottery. **slip 2** v. (slipped) (a) to slide by mistake (b) to go quietly (c) (of machinery) to miss/not to connect; slipped disc = painful state where one of the cushioning discs in the spine has become displaced. **slipper** n. light comfortable shoe worn indoors.

slippery adj. (a) so smooth that one can easily slip on it (b) inf. (who) cannot be trusted. **slippy** adj. inf. slippery. **slip road** n. road which leads on to a motorway. **slipshod** adj. badly carried out (work); point just behind a fast moving vehicle. **slipstream** n. air blown backwards by an aircraft engine; point just behind a fast-moving vehicle. **slip up** v. in to make a mistake. **slip-up** n. in mistake. **slipway** n. smooth slope on which ships are built or repaired.

slit 1 [slɪt] n. long cut; narrow opening. **slit 2** v. (slit) to make a slit.

slither ['slɪðə] v. to slide about in various directions.

sliver ['slɪvə]ɪ n. thin piece of wood or meat.

slob [slɒb] n. inf. sloppy/untidy fat person. **slobber** ['slɒbə] v. to dribble saliva from your mouth. **slobbery** adj. covered with saliva.

sloe [sləʊ] n. bitter wild fruit like a plum; tree which bears this fruit.

slog 1 [slɒg] n. difficult work; difficult walk. **slog 2** v. (slogged) to work hard at sth difficult. slogger, n. person who works hard.

slogan ['sləʊgn] n. phrase used in publicity for a product/for a political party, etc.

sloop [sluːp] n. type of small ship.

slop [slɒp] v. (slopped) to spill. **sloppily** adv. in a sloppy way. **sloppiness** n. being sloppy. **sloppy** adj. (-ier, -iest) (a) untidy; badly done (work). (b) stupidly sentimental. **slops** n. pl. (a) liquid food given to people who are too ill to eat. (b) waste food given to pigs. (c) liquid refuse.

slope 1 [sləʊp] n. slanting surface; angle of a slanting surface; slanting piece of ground. **slope 2** v. to slant upwards or downwards. **slope off** v. inf. to creep away quietly. **sloping** adj. (roof. etc) which slopes.

slosh [slɒʃ] v. (a) to splash (b) inf. to hit. **sloshed** adj. inf. drunk.

slot 1 [slɒt] n. narrow opening(for putting a coin into); s. machine = machine which (which (when you put a coin into the slot) will give chocolate/ cigarettes, etc., automatically. **slot 2** v. (slotted) to s. into = to fit into (a slot).

sloth [sləʊθ] n. (a) (formal) laziness (b) slow-moving South American Mammal, like a bear. **slothful** adj. (formal).

slouch [slaʊtʃ] v. to stand/to sit in a bad position/with bent shoulders; to s. along = to walk along bending forwards. **slouch hat** n. hat with a wide a brim which can be turned down.

slough 1 [slʌf] n. (a) old skin of a snake. (b) marshy place. **slough 2** v. (of a snake) to lose (its skin).

slovenly ['slʌvənlɪ] adj. untidy; careless (work). **slovenliness** n. being slovenly.

slow 1 [sləʊ] adj. (-er, -est) (a) not fast; s. train = train which stops at each station. (b) (of clock, etc.) to be s. = to show a time which is earlier than the correct time. (c) not quick to learn; inf. to be s. on the uptake = not to understand quickly. **slow 2** adv. not fast; to go s. = (i) to advance less quickly; (ii) to protest by working slowly. **slow 3** v. to s. down = to make (sth) go slowly; to go more slowly. **slowcoach** n. inf. person who goes slower than others. **slowdown** n. slowing down (of business activity). **slowly** adv. in a slow way. **slow motion** n. (in firms) action which appears to take place very slowly because the film speed has been slowed down. **slowness** n. being slow. **slow-worm** n. snake-like lizard.

sludge [slʌdʒ] n. wet mud; wet refuse.

slug 1 [slʌg] n. (a) common garden animal like a snail with no shell. (b) small metal pellet. **slug 2** v. (slugged) inf. to hit (s.o.) a heavy blow.

sluggard n. lazy/person. **sluggish** adj. lazy/slow-moving. **sluggishly**

adv. in a slow way.
sluice 1 [sluːs] *n.* (a) channel for taking water round a dam; gate which allows water to enter this channel. (b) washing with buckets of water. **sluice 2** *v.* to wash (sth) with lots of water. **sluice gate** *n.* gate which allows water to enter the sluice channel.
slum [slʌm] *n.* poor, rundown area of a town. **slumming** *n.* visiting slums; visiting people who you think are of a lower class or less rich than yourself.
slumber 1 ['slʌmbə] *n.* gentle sleep. **slumber 2** *v.* to sleep gently. **slumberer** *n.* person who slumbers. **slumberwear** *n.* (no *pl.*) clothes worn to go to bed.
slump 1 [slʌmp] *n.* collapse (of prices); economic collapse (of a country). **slump 2** *v.* (a) to fall suddenly. (b) to sit/to lie clumsily/heavily.
slung [slʌŋ] *v.* see sling.
slunk [slʌŋk] *v.* see slink.
slur 1 [slɜː] *n.* (a) insult. (b) slurring of several notes; mark on a musical score to show that notes should be slurred. **slur 2** *v.* (slurred) to a speak words indistinctly. (b) (in music) to play several notes without a break between them.
slurp [slɜːp] *v. inf.* to drink noisily.
slurry ['slʌrɪ] *n.* (no *pl.*) watery mud/cement; liquid waste from farm animals.
slush [slʌʃ] *n.* (a) half-melted snow. (b) sentimentality. **slush fund** *n. inf.* money kept for the purposes of bribery. **slushy** *adj.* (a) covered with half-melted snow. (b) very sentimental.
slut [slʌt] *n. inf.* dirty, untidy woman. **sluttish** *adj.* like a slut.
sly [slaɪ] *adj.* (-er, -est) cunning (person); on the s. = without any knowing. **slyly** *adv.* in a sly way. **slyness** *n.* being sly.
smack 1 [smæk] *n.* (a) blow with the flat of the hand. (b) fishing s. = small fishing boat. (c) loud kiss. (d) particular taste. **smack 2** *v.* (a) to hit (s.o.). (b) to s. one's lips = make a loud noise (as if hungry). (c) to smell/to taste; that smacks of bribery = it sounds as though bribery is involved. **smack 3** *adv. inf.* straight/directly. **smacker** *n.* (a) *inf.* loud kiss. (b) *inf.* pound note.
small 1 [smɔːl] *adj.* (-er, -est) (a) not large; little. (b) delicate/soft/(voice). (c)

not imposing. (d) petty/thinking only of trivial things. **small 2** *n.* (a) the s. of the back = the lower part of the back. (b) *inf.* smalls = underwear. **small 3** *adv.* into little bits. **smallholder** *n.* person who owns a smallholding.
smallholding *n.* very small farm.
small hours *n.* period just after midnight. **small-minded** *adj.* thinking only of yourself/of trivial things.
smallness *n.* being small. **smallpox** *n.* dangerous infectious disease causing a rash which leaves marks on the skin.
small talk *n.* general conversation about sth unimportant. **smalltime** *n.* unimportant (criminal).
smarmy ['smɑːmɪ] *adj.* (-ier, iest) (person) who is unpleasantly smooth. **smarminess** *n.* being smarmy.
smart 1 [smɑːt] *n.* sharp pain (from a wound). **smart 2** *v.* to hurt/to feel as if burning. **smart 3** *adj.* (-er, -est) (a) sharp (blow). (b) rapid/efficient. (c) clever; s. card = plastic card with a microprocessor embedded in it. (d) well-dressed/elegant. **smarten** *v.* to s. yourself up = to make yourself look smart. **smartly** *adv.* in a smart way. **smartness** *n.* being smart.
smash 1 [smæʃ] *n.* (*pl.*-es) (a) crash (of a car). (b) financial collapse. (c) powerful shot (in tennis). **smash 2** *v.* (a) to break (sth) to pieces. (b) to hit sth hard. (c) to hit (a ball) hard. **smash-and-grab raid** *n.* burglary done by breaking a shop window and stealing as much as you can get hold of. **smash hit** *n. inf.* play/film, etc., which is very successful. **smashing** *adj. inf.* very good/fantastic.
smattering ['smætrɪŋ] *n.* small knowledge (of a language).
smear 1 ['smɪə] *n.* (a) dirty mark; thing which is smeared (esp. a small amount of sth for examining under a microscope); s. test = test for cancer esp. of the cervix. (b) insult; s. campaign = campaign to discredit s.o. by spreading gossip about his private life. **smear 2** *v.* (a) to make dirty marks. (b) to spread (sth greasy).
smell 1 [smel] *n.* (a) one of the five senses, fell through the nose. (b) thing which you can sense through the nose. (c) unpleasant thing which you can sense

through the nose. **smell 2** v. (smelled/ smelt) (a) to notice (sth) by the nose. (b) to sniff in order to sense the smell. (c) to give off a smell. **smelling salts** n. pl.crystals of a compound of ammonia, which are smelled to cure faintness. **smelly** adj. (-ier, -iest) which gives off an unpleasant smell.

smelt 1 [smelt] n. (pl.smelt) small edible fish. **smelt 2** v. (a) to produce metal by melting ore. (b) see also smell. **smelter** n. works where metal is extracted from ore. **smelting** n. production of metal by heating ore with coke and limestone.

smidgen ['smɪdʒn] n. inf. very small amount.

smile 1 [smaɪl] n. expression of pleasure with the mouth turned up at the corners. **smile 2** v. to make an expression of happiness by turning up the corners of the mouth.

smirk 1 [smɜːk] n. unpleasant superior smile. **smirk 2** v. to give a smirk.

smite [smaɪt] v. (smote, has smitten) (formal) to hit; smitten with = liking.

smith [smɪθ] n. person who works in metal. **smithy** [smɪðɪ] n. workshop where a blacksmith works.

smithereens [smɪðə'riːnz] n. very small bits.

smitten ['smɪtn] v. see smite.

smock [smɒk] n. long loose overall worn over clothes to protect them. **smocking** n. embroidery on gathered material.

smog [smɒg] n. mixture of fog and exhaust fumes of cars.

smoke 1 [sməʊk] n. (a) vapour and gas given off when sth burns. (b) action of smoking a cigarette. **smoke 2** v. (a) to send out clouds of vapour and gas. (b) to cure (bacon/fish, etc.) by hanging in wood smoke. (c) to suck in smoke from a burning cigarette/pipe, etc. **smokeless** adj. which makes no smoke; s. zone = area where you are not allowed to make any smoke. **smoker** n. (a) person who smokes cigarettes, etc. (b) railway carriage where you can smoke. **smokescreen** n. thick smoke made so that the enemy cannot see; anything which is deliberately used to hide what is going on. **smoky** adj. (-ier, -iest) full of cigarette smoke.

smooth 1 [smuːð] adj. (-er, -est) (a) (surface) with no bumps/no roughness. (b) with no bumps/jolts. (c) with no hair. (d) too pleasant (person). **smooth 2** v. to make smooth; to s. the way for sth = to make it easy; to s. the way for sth = to make it easy; to s. things over = settle an argument. **smoothly** adv. in a smooth way. **smoothness** n. being smooth.

smorgasbord ['smɔːgəsbɔːd] n. Swedish buffet of many cold dishes.

smote [sməʊt] v. see smite.

smother ['smʌðə] v. (a) to stifle and kill (s.o.) (b) to cover.

smoulder, Am. smolder ['sməʊldə] v. to burn slowly.

smudge 1 [smʌdʒ] n. dirty (ink) stain. **smudge 2** v. to make a mark, such as by rubbing ink which is not dry. **smudgy** adj. (paper) with a dirty mark on it.

smug [smʌg] adj. (smugger, smuggest) self-satisfied. **smugly** adv. in a way which shows you are pleased with yourself. **smugness** n. being smug.

smuggle ['smʌgl] v. to take (goods) past the customs without declaring them for duty; to take (sth) into or out of a prison without the warders seeing. **smuggler** n. person who smuggles goods.

smut [smʌt] n. (a) small black mark. (b) indecent stories. **smutty** adj. (-ier, -iest) indecent.

Sn symbol for tin.

snack [snæk] n. light meal. **snackbar** n. restaurant where you can have light meal, usu. sitting at a counter.

snaffle 1 ['snæfl] n. horse's bit. **snaffle 2** v. inf. to take/to steal.

snag 1 [snæg] n. (a) obstacle; thing which prevents you from doing sth. (b) sharp point; place where a piece of clothing has been caught on a sharp point. **snag 2** v. (snagged) to catch and tear (your clothes) on a sharp point.

snail [sneɪl] n. common slimy animal with a shell; at a s.'s pace = extremely slowly.

snake 1 [sneɪk] n. long, sometimes poisonous, reptile which wriggles along the ground. **snake 2** v. to wriggle like a snake.

snap 1 [snæp] n. (a) sudden dry noise. (b) cold s. = sudden spell of cold weather. (c) type of brittle biscuit. (d) photograph. (e) card game where you say 'snap' if you play the same card as your opponent. **snap 2** *adj.* (decision) taken hurriedly. **snap 3** *v.* (snapped) (a) to try to bite. (b) to speak sharply. (c) to break sharply; to make a dry noise (in breaking). (d) to take a photograph of (s.o.) (e) to s. up = to buy quickly. (f) *inf.* to s. out of it = to get out of a state of depression. **snapdragon** *n.* antirrhinum. **snap fastener** *n.* fastening for clothes, make of two small metal studs which fit into each other. **snapper** *n.* type of American fish. **snappily** *adv.* in a snappy way. **snappy** *adj.* (-ier, iest) (a) irritable/ short-tempered. (b) *inf.* make it s.! = do it quickly. **snapshot** *n.* informal photograph taken quickly. **snare 1** ['sneə] *n.* trap for catching animals made with a noose which is pulled tight. **snare 2** *v.* to catch with a snare. **snarl 1** [snɑːl] *n.* (a) angry growl. (b) tangle. **snarl 2** *v.* (a) to growl angrily. (b) to make a tangled. **snarl-up** *n. inf.* traffic jam. **snatch 1** [snætʃ] *n.* (a) (*pl.*-es) (a) grabbing sth; wages s. = grabbing a company's wages from the pay office. (b) short piece (of a song, etc.). **snatch 2** *v.* to grab (sth) rapidly. **snazzy** ['snæzɪ] *adj.* (-ier, -iest) *inf.* smart/in fashion. **sneak 1** [sniːk] *n. inf.* person who tells tales about s.o. **sneak 2** *v.* (a) to creep without being seen. (b) *inf.* to s. on s.o. = to report that s. o. has done sth wrong. **sneakers** *n. pl.*Am. soft sports shoes with rubber sales. **sneaking** *adj.* secret. **sneaky** *adj. inf.* deceitful/not open. **sneer 1** ['snɪə] *n.* sarcastic smile; unpleasant smile. **sneer 2** *v.* to give s.o. a sarcastic smile to show contempt; to speak in a contemptuous way. **sneeze 1** [sniːz] *n.* sudden blowing out of air through your mouth and nose because of irritation in your nose. **sneeze 2** *v.* make a sneeze; *inf.* it's not to be sneezed at = you should not refuse it/despise it. **snick 1** [snɪk] *n.* (a) small cut (with a knife). (b) (in cricket) sharp stroke.

snick 2 *v.* to hit (a ball) a sharp glancing blow. **snicker** *n* & *v.* snigger. **snide** [snaɪd] *adj. inf.* unpleasant/ envious (remark). **sniff 1** [snɪf] *n.* short intake of air through the nose. **sniff 2** *v.* to take in air rapidly through the nose; *inf.* it's not to be sniffed at = you should not refuse it/despise it. **sniffer** *n.* person who sniffs. **sniffle 1** *n.* slight cold in the head. **sniffle 2** *v.* to keep on sniffing because of a cold. **snigger 1** ['snɪgə] *n.* quiet unpleasant laugh. **snigger 2** *v.* to laugh quietly in an unpleasant way. **sniggering** *n.* hidden laughter. **snip 1** [snɪp] *n.* (a) piece which has been cut off. (b) *inf.* bargain. **snip 2** *v.* (snipped) to cut with scissors. **snippet** *n.* little bit (of cloth, etc.). **snipe 1** [snaɪp] *n.* large marsh bird with a long beak. **snipe 2** *v.* to s. at s. o. = to shoot at s. o. from a hiding place/to make continuous criticism of s.o **sniper** *n.* hidden soldier who shoots at the enemy. **snitch** [snɪtʃ] *v. inf.* to steal. **snivel** ['snɪvl] *v.* (snivelled) (a) to have a runny nose. (b) to cry and complain. **snob** [snɒb] *n.* person who likes people who are of a higher social class than himself; intellectual s. = person who looks down on those who are not as well-educated as he feels he is himself. **snobbery, snobbishness** *n.* being a snob. **snobbish** *adj.* referring to a snob. **snood** [snuːd] *n.* (old) ornamental bag shaped net for holding a woman's hair at the back of the head. **snook** [snuːk] *n.* to cock a s. at = to make a rude gesture at (s. o.)/to disregard (a rule). **snooker** [snuːkə] *n.* game like billiards played on a table with twenty-two balls of various colours. **snoop** [snuːp] *v.* to creep about investigating sth secretly. **snooper** *n.* person who spies on s.o. secretly. **snooty** ['snuːtɪ] *adj.* (-ier, -iest) *inf.* superior (air/expression). **snootily** *adv.* in a snooty way. **snootiness** *n.* being snooty. **snooze 1** [snuːz] *n.* short sleep. **snooze 2** *v.* to sleep lightly for a short time.

snore 1 [snɔː] *n.* loud noise in the throat made by breathing air when you are asleep. **snore 2** *v.* to make a snore. **snorer** *n.* person who snores.

snorkel ['snɔːkl] *n.* tube which goes from the mouth or mask of an underwater swimmer to the surface to allow him to breathe in air. **snorkelling** *n.* to go s. = go swimming with a snorkel.

snort 1 [snɔːt] *n.* (a) snorting nose. (b) *inf.* small drink. **snort 2** *v.* to make a loud noise blowing air out through the nose.

snot [snɒt] *n.* *inf.* mucus in the nose.

snout [snaʊt] *n.* nose of an animal (esp. a pig).

snow 1 [snəʊ] *n.* water vapour which freezes and falls in light white flakes. **snow 2** *v.* to fall in flakes of snow; snowed under = overwhelmed.

snowball 1 *n.* ball of snow. **snowball 2** *v.* (a) to throw snowballs. (b) to get bigger and bigger. **snowblindness** *n* painful lack of sight caused by the brightness of snow. **snowdrift** *n.* heap of snow which has been piled up by the wind. **snowdrop,** *n.* small spring bulb with little white flowers. **snowfall** *n.* amount of snow which has fallen.

snowflake *n.* flake of snow.

snowline *n.* point on a high mountain above which there is always snow.

snowman *n.* figure of a man made out of snow. **snowmobile** ['snəʊməbiːl] *n.* vehicle with caterpillar tracks specially designed for driving on snow. **snow plough,** *Am.* **snowplow** heavy vehicle with a plough on the front for clearing snow off road/railways, etc.

snowshoes *n. pl.* frames shaped like tennis rackets, with a light web, which are tied under the feet for walking on snow. **snowstorm** *n.* storm which brings snow. **snow white** *adj.* pure white. **snowy** *adj.* covered with snow; white like snow.

snub 1 [snʌb] *n.* insult; insulting refusal to speak to s.o. **snub 2** *v.* (snubbed) to insult (s.o.) by refusing to speak to them/by not paying any attention to them. **snub 3** *adj.* s. nose = small nose which is turned up at the end.

snuff 1 [snʌf] *n.* powdered tobacco which is sniffed into the nose. **snuff 2** *v.* (a) to put out (a candle). (b) *Sl.* to. s. it = to die.

snuffle 1 ['snʌfl] *n.* loud sniff. **snuffle 2** *v.* to sniff noisily.

snug [snʌg] *adj.* (snugger, snuggest) warm and comfortable. **snuggle** *v.* to curl yourself up to warm; to curl up close to s.o. for warmth. **snugly** *adv.* in a snug way.

so 1 [səʊ] *adv.* (a) to such an extent. (b) in this way. (c) true/correct; I think s. = I think it is true. (d) in the same way. (e) or s. = approximately. (f) and s. on = and in a similar way; etcetera. **so 2** *conj.* (a) therefore. (b) s. that/s as to = for the purpose of. so-and-so, n. (a) somebody (whom you do not want to name). (b) *inf.* naughty person. **so called** *adj.* wrongly called. **so-so** *adj. & adv. inf.* not very well.

soak 1 [səʊk] *n.* being very wet. **soak 2** *v.* to put (sth) to lie in a liquid; to get/ to make very wet. **soakaway** *n.* hole in the ground into which rainwater drains. **soaking 1** *n.* (action of) being soaked. **soaking 2** *adj. & adv.* wet through. **soak up** *v.* to absorb (a liquid).

soap 1 [səʊp] *n.* material made of oil and fat used for washing. **soap 2** *v.* to wash with soap. **soapbox** *n.* box on which a speaker stands to talk at a meeting outdoors. **soap opera** *n.* trite serial story on television. **soapstone** *n.* type of soft grey stone which can be easily carved. **soapsuds** *n.pl.* foam made from soap. **soapy** *adj.* full of soap; covered with soap.

soar [sɔː] *v.* (a) to fly high into the air; (of bird) to glide without beating its wings. (b) to rise rapidly.

sob 1 [sɒb] *n.* short breath like a hiccup when crying. **sob 2** *v.* (sobbed) to weep, taking short breaths like hiccups.

sober 1 ['səʊbə] *adj.* (a) not drunk. (b) serious. (c) dark (colour). **sober 2** *v.* to s. up = to recover from drunkenness. **soberly** *adv.* seriously. **soberness, sobriety** [sə'braɪtɪ] *n.* being sober.

sobriquet ['səʊbrɪkeɪ] *n.* nickname.

soccer ['sɒkə] *n.* football/game played between two sides of eleven players who can only kick or head the ball.

sociable ['səʊʃebl] *adj.* friendly/liking the company of other people. **sociability** [səʊʃə'bɪlɪtɪ] *n.* being sociable.

social 1 ['səʊʃl] *adj.* (a) referring to society; s. science = study of the problems of society; s. security = money/ help provided by the government to people who need it; s. services = state services to help people's problems; s. worker = person who works to help families in need; the s. system = the way society is organized. (b) living in groups. (c) s. evening = evening party for a group of people. **social 2** *n.* party.

socialism *n.* political system where the state owns and runs the wealth of the country; belief that all property should belong to the state and that every citizen is equal. **socialist** *adj. & n.* (person) who believes in socialism; (policies) which follow the principles of socialism. **socialite** *n.* person who moves in high society. **socialize** *v.* (a) to be friendly with other people (at a party). (b) to organize (a country) along the principles of socialism. **socially** *adv.* in a social way. **society** [sə'saɪtɪ] *n.* (a) way in which people are organized; group of people who live in the same way. (b) group/club/association of people with the same interests. (c) (also high society) top class of people. **sociology** [səʊsɪ'ɒlədʒɪ] *n.* study of society and how people live in society. **sociological** [səʊsɪə'lɒdʒɪkl] *adj.* referring to society and the way in which society changes. **sociologist** [səʊsɪ'ɒlədʒɪst] *n.* person who studies society and how people live in it.

sock 1 [sɒk] *n.* woollen covering for the foot and lower part of the leg; *inf.* you'll have to pull your socks up = try to do better. **sock 2** *v. inf.* to hit.

socket ['sɒkɪt] *n.* hole(s) into which sth is fitted; electric s. = one which a plug/ bulb can be fitted into.

sod [sɒd] *n.* (a) piece of soil with grass growing on it. (b) *Sl.* unpleasant/nasty man.

soda ['səʊdə] *n.* compound of sodium; s. (water) = water made fizzy by putting gas into it; ice cream s. = sweet fizzy drink mixed with ice creAm. **soda**

fountain *n.* bar where sweet drinks and ice cream are served.

sodden ['sɒdn] *adj.* very wet.

sodium ['səʊdɪəm] *n.* (element: Na) white soft metal, which can catch fire, and is use, found in combination with other substances.

sodomy ['sɒdəmɪ] *n.* anal sexual intercourse between men.

sofa ['səʊfə] *n.* long seat with a soft back for several people.

soffit ['sɒfɪt] *n.* underside of an arch.

soft [sɒft] *adj.* (a) not hard; (pencil) which makes wide blurred marks. (b) quiet (voice). (c) not strict. (d) *inf.* stupid. (e) (water) with little calcium in it; (drink) which is not alcoholic; (drugs) which are not addictive. **soft-boiled** *adj.* (egg) which has not been boiled very much. **soften** ['sɒfn] *v.* to make/to become soft; to s. up = to make weak before attacking or before asking for a favour. **softener** *n.* water s. = apparatus for making hard water soft. **soft fruit** *n. pl.* small fruit (like raspberries/strawberries, etc.). **soft-hearted** *adj.* not strict/too kind. **softly** *adv.* in a soft way. **softness** *n.* being soft. **soft soap** *n. inf.* flattery. **software** *n.* computer programs (as opposed to the machines). **softwood** *n.* wood from pine and fir trees.

soggy ['sɒgɪ] *adj.* wet and soft. **sogginess** *n.* being soggy.

soil 1 [sɔɪl] *n.* earth. **soil 2** *v.* to make dirty.

sojourn 1 ['sʌdʒən] *n.* (formal) stay. **sojourn 2** *v.* (formal) to stay.

solace ['sɒləs] *n.* (formal) comfort.

solar ['səʊlə] *adj.* referring to the sun; s. energy/s. power = electricity produced from the radiation of the sun; s. heating = heating system run by light from the sun; s. system = series of planets orbiting the sun; s. plexus = (i) group of nerves behind the bottom of the lungs and the stomach; (ii) *inf.* the lower part of the body where the stomach is. part of the body where the stomach is. **solarium** [sə'leərɪəm] *n.* room where you can enjoy real or artificial sunlight.

sold [səʊld] *v.* see sell.

solder 1 ['səʊldə] *n.* soft metal used to join metal surfaces together when it is melted. **solder 2** *v.* to join (metal surfaces together) with solder.

soldering iron *n.* tool which is heated to apply solder.

soldier 1 ['səʊldʒə] *n.* member of the army. **soldier 2** *v.* (a) to be on military service. (b) to s. on = to continue doing a hard job. **soldiery** *n.* soldiers.

sole 1 [səʊl] *n.* (a) underside of the foot; bottom part of a shoe. (b) flat sea fish. **sole 2** *v.* to put a new sole on (a shoe). **sole 3** *adj.* (a) only. (b) belonging to one person; he has the s. right to = he is the only person allowed to. **solely** *adv.* only.

solecism ['sɒlɪsɪzəm] *n.* embarrassing mistake made in speaking.

solemn ['sɒləm] *adj.* (a) special and religious (ceremony). (b) very serious. **solemnity** [sə'lemnɪtɪ] *n.* being solemn. **solemnization** [sɒlemnaɪ'zeɪʃn] *n.* celebration (of a marriage/of a religious ceremony). **solemnize** ['sɒlemnaɪz] *v.* to celebrate/ to perform (a marriage/a religious ceremony). **solemnly** *adv.* in a solemn way.

solenoid ['sɒlənɔɪd] *n.* coiled wire which produces a magnetic field when an electric current passes through it.

solfa [sɒl'fɑː] *n.* system of indicating tones in music by syllables (doh-ray-me, etc.).

solicit [sə'lɪsɪt] *v.* to ask for. **solicitation** [səlɪsɪ'teɪʃn] *n.* soliciting. **solicitor** *n.* lawyer who gives advice to people on legal problems. **solicitous** *adj.* worried/anxious about sth. **solicitously** *adv.* in a solicitous way. **solicitude** *n.* anxiety/worry about sth.

solid 1 ['sɒlɪd] *adj.* (a) not liquid. (b) not hollow. (c) made all of one material; for eight hours s. = without stopping. (d) trustworthy. **solid 2** *n.* (a) solid sustance. (b) three-dimensional shape. **solidarity** [sɒlɪ'dærɪtɪ] *n.* common interest with s.o. **solidification** [sɒlɪdɪfɪ'keɪʃn] *n.* act of solidifying. **solidify** [sə'lɪdɪfaɪ] *v.* to (math sth) become solid. **solidity** [sə'lɪdɪtɪ] *n.* being solid. **solidly** *adv.* completely. **solid-state** *adj.* (TV set, etc.) which uses, transistors and not valves.

soliloquy [sə'lɪləkwɪ] *n.* speech spoken by a character alone on the stage.

soliloquize *v.* to speak all alone.

solitaire [sɒlɪ'teə] *n.* (a) game for one person, made of balls which have to be jumped from hole to hole removing the intervening balls one at a time. (b) single diamond (in a ring, etc.).

solitary ['sɒlɪtrɪ] *adj.* (a) single/sole. (b) lonely; s. confinement = imprisonment alone in a cell. **solitude** *n.* being alone.

solo 1 ['səʊləʊ] *n.* piece of music for one person. **solo 2** *adj. & adv.* carried out by one person. **soloist** *n.* musician who plays a solo.

solstice ['sɒlstɪs] *n.* summer s. = period of the longest day (June 21st); winter s. = period of the longest night (December 21st).

soluble ['sɒljʊbl] *adj.* (a) which can be dissolved. (b) (problem) which can be solved. **solubility** [sɒljʊ'bɪlɪtɪ] *n.* ability to be dissolve/solved. **solution** [sə'luːʃn] *n.* (a) liquid in which sth has been dissolved. (b) act of solving a problem; answer to a problem.

solve [sɒlv] *v.* to find the answer to (a problem). **solvable** *adj.* which can be solved. **solver** *n.* person who solves a problem.

solvency ['sɒlvənsɪ] *n.* state of being solvent. **solvent 1** having enough money to pay your debts. **solvent 2** *n.* liquid which dissolves another substance.

somatotrophin [səmə'təʊ'trɒfɪn] *n.* growth hormone.

sombre, *Am.* **somber** ['sɒmbə] *adj.* dark and gloomy. **sombrely** *adv.* in a sombre way.

sombrero [sɒm'breərəʊ] *n.* hat with a wide brim worn in South America.

some 1 [sʌm] *adj.* (a) not a particular one. (b) certain; (c) several/a few; a little. (d) *inf.* wonderful; that was s. party! **some 2** *pron..* several out of a group; part of a whole. **some 3** *adv.* approximately. **somebody** ['sʌmbədɪ] *pron..* (a) a particular unknown person. (b) *inf.* important person. **somehow** ['sʌmhaʊ] *adv.* (a) in one way or another. (b) for no particular reason. **someone** ['sʌmwɒn] *pron..* somebody. **someplace** ['sʌmpleɪs] *adv. Am.* somewhere. **something** ['sʌmθɪŋ] *pron..* (a) particular·unknown thing. (b) thing which is possibly important. (c) (replacing a forgotten detail) the 4 s. train = the train which leaves at some time after 4 o'clock. **sometime** ['sʌmtaɪm] adv. (a) at a particular unknown time. (b) (old) formerly. **sometimes** ['sʌmtaɪmz] adv. from time to time/at times. **somewhat** ['sʌmwɒt] adv. rather. **somewhere** ['sʌmweə] adv. at some particular unknown place.

somersault 1 ['sʌməsɔːlt] n. rolling over, with your head underneath and feet over your head. **somersault 2** v. to do a somersault/to roll over.

somnambulism [sɒm'næmbjʊlɪzəm] n. walking in your sleep.
somnambulist [sɒm'næmbjʊlɪst] n. person who walks when asleep.

somnolence ['sɒmnələns] n. (formal) being sleepy/sleepiness. **somnolent** adj. sleepy.

son [sʌn] n. male child of a parent.
son-in-law n. husband of a daughter.

sonar ['səʊnɑː] n. device for finding underwater objects by using sound waves.

sonata [sə'nɑːtə] n. piece of music in three or four movements for one or two instruments.

sonde [sʌnd] n. device attached to a balloon, used for taking samples of the atmosphere.

son et lumière [sɒneɪluː'mɪ'ɜː] n. entertainment consisting of sound and lighting effects, shown in the open air at night.

song [sɒŋ] n. (a) singing. (b) words and music to be sung; for a s. = for very little money; inf. he made a great s. and dance about it = a great fuss. **songbird** n. bird which sings particularly well.
songster n. person or bird that sings.

sonic ['sɒnɪk] adj. referring to sound waves; s. boom = bang made by an aircraft travelling faster than the speed of sound.

sonnet ['sɒnɪt] n. poem with fourteen lines.

sonny ['sʌnɪ] n. inf. way of addressing a boy.

sonorous ['sɒnərəs] adj. which makes a loud ringing noise.

soon [suːn] adv. (a) in a very short time; sooner or later = at some to come. (b) I

would as s./sooner stay than go away - I would rather stay.

soot [sʊt] n. black carbon dust which collects in chimneys. **sooty** adj. (-ier, -iest) black; covered with soot.

soothe [suːð] v. to calm. **soothing** adj. which calms. **soothingly** adv. in a soothing way.

soothsayer ['suːθseɪə] n. person who foretells the future.

sop 1 [sɒp] n. (a) piece of bread dipped in liquid (b) sth given as a bribe to make s.o. keep quiet. **sop 2** v. (sopped) to soak in liquid; to soak up (a liquid). **sopping** adj. s. wet. = soaked. **soppy** adj. inf. silly and sentimental.

sophistication [səfɪstɪkeɪʃn] n. (a) cultured way of life. (b) advanced idea behind the construction of the machine.
sophisticated adj. (a) cultured (b) complicated/advanced (machine).

sophistry ['sɒfɪstrɪ] n. clever argument which is probably wrong.

sophomore ['sɒfəmɔː] n. Am. second year student.

soporific [sɒpə'rɪfɪk] adj. &n. (medicine) which makes you go to sleep.

soprano [sə'prɑːnəʊ] n. (pl.-os) high pitched singing voice; woman or boy with such a voice.

sorbet ['sɔːbeɪ] n. water ice.

sorcery ['sɔːsərɪ] n. witchcraft/magic.
sorcerer, sorceress n. person who makes magic.

sordid ['sɔːdɪd] adj. unpleasant/dirty.
sordidly adv. in a sordid way.
sordidness n. being sordid.

sore 1 [sɔː] adj. (-er, -est) (a) painful/which hurts (b) inf. upset/annoyed. **sore 2** n. painful spot on the skin. **sorely** adv. very much. **soreness** n. being sore.

sorghum ['sɔːgəm] n. type of grass, used as a cereal.

sorority. [sə'rɒrɪtɪ] n. Am. students society for women.

sorrel ['sɒrəl] n. (a) common sour - tasting. edible plant (b) (horse which is) a reddish brown colour.

sorrow ['sɒrəʊ] n. sadness. **sorrowful** adj. very sad. **sorrowfully** adv. in a sorrowful way. **sorry** adj. (-ier, -iest) (a) regretting sth. (b) feeling pity/ sympathy for s.o. (c) pitiful.

sort 1 [sɔːt] n. type/variety; good s. = pleasant type of person; inf. s. of tired =

rather tired; a meal of sorts = not a very good meal; out of sorts slightly unwell. **sort 2** *v.* to arrange in different groups. **sorter** *n.* person who sorts. esp. letters in a post office; sorting office = department in a post office where letters are sorted according to their addresses. **sortie** ['sɔːtiː] *n.* (a) sudden attack; bombing raid (by aircraft) (b) sudden excursion into an unpleasant area **SOS** [esəʊ'es] *n.* international code for showing that you are in distress. **soufflé** ['suːfleɪ] *n.* light cooked dish, made from beaten up eggs. **sought** [sɔːt] *v.* see seek. **sought after** *adj.* which people want. **soul** [səʊl] *n.* (a) the spirit in a person (as opposed to the body) (b) he was a life and s. of the party = made the party go well. (c) she is the s. of owner = a fine example of owner. (d) person **soul-destroying** *adj.* (work) which is very dull or does not allow you to use your mind. **soulful** *adj.* with a lot of feeling. **soulfully** *adv.* in a soulful way. **soulless** *adj.* very dull/inhuman. **soul music** *n.* popular music played by black musicians, which conveys deep feelings. **soul-searching** *n.* examination of your own motives/conscience. **sound 1** [saʊnd] *n.* (a) noise; s. wave = wave in the air which carries sound; s. barrier = the speed of sound; s. bite = short sentence spoken by a famous person when being interviewed, which is of suitable length for showing on a TV news broadcast. (b) stretch of sea water. **sound 2** *v.* (a) to make a noise (b) to s. like = to be similar to sound to (sth) (c) s.o. out = to tack to someone to test his opinion. (d) to measure the depth of water. **sound 3** *adj.* (-er, -est) (a) healthy/not rotten (b) reasonable/trustworthy (c) deep (sleep). **sound effects** *n. pl.* noises made in a plane/film, etc., which imitate the real sounds (such as thunder/gunfire, etc). **sounding** *n.* (a) making of noise; s. board = (i) board (as above a pulpit) which reflects sound; (ii) way of spreading ideas. (b) investigation (c) measuring the depth of water. **soundless** *adj.* which does not make any noise. **soundlessly** *adv.* not

making any noise. **soundly** *adv.* thoroughly/deeply. **soundness** *n.* being sound. **sound off** *v. inf.* to start talking loudly about sth. **soundproof 1** *adj.* made so that sound cannot get through. **soundproof 2** *v.* to make (a building) soundproof **soundtrack** *n.* part of a film where the sound is recorded. **soup** [suːp] *n.* liquid dish *usu.* eaten at the beginning of a meal; *inf.* in the s. the real trouble. **soup-kitchen** *n.* place where soup and other food is given to the poor/to victims of a disaster. **soup up** *v. inf.* to increase the power of (an engine). **soupcon** ['suːpsɒn] *n.* slight taste; very small amount. **sour 1** ['saʊə] *adj.* (-er, -est) (a) not sweet; sharp-tasting; *inf.* s. grapes = saying unpleasant things because of envy. (b) (milk) which has gone bad. (c) bird-tempered/unpleasant person. **sour 2** *v.* to make bad. **sourly** *adv.* in a bad/tempered way. **sourness** *n.* being sour. **sourpuss** *n. inf.* unpleasant-bad tempered person. **source** [sɔːs] *n.* place of origin/place where something starts or comes from. **souse** [saʊs] *v.* (a) to soak in water (b) to pickle (herrings) in salt water. **south 1** [saʊθ] *n.* one of the points of the compass; (in areas north of the equator) the directions of the sun at midday. **south 2** *adj.* of the south. **south 3** *adv.* towards the south. **southbound** *adj.* going towards the south. **south-east** *adj. adv. & n.* directions between south and east. **south-easterly, south-eastern** *adj.* referring to the south-east. **southerl** ['sʌðəlɪ] *adj.* (a) (wind) from the south (b) in a s. direction = towards the south. **southern** ['sʌðən] *adj.* referring to the south. **southerner** ['sʌðənə] *n.* person who lives in the south. **southern most** *adj.* furthest south. **southpaw** *n. inf.* boxer who is left-handed. **southward** *adj.* towards the south. **southwards** *adv.* towards the south. **south-west** *adj. adv. & n.* direction between the south and west. **south-westerly, south-western** *adj.* referring to the south-west. **souvenir** [suːvə'nɪə] *n.* thing which reminds you of a place/an event.

sou'wester [sau'westə] *n.* waterproof sailor's hat

sovereign 1 ['sɒvrɪn] *n.* (a) ruler/king or queen (b) British gold coin worth £ 1. **sovereign 2** *adj.* (a) powerful (remedy) (b) self-governing.

sovereignty *n.* total power; self - government.

soviet ['səʊvɪət] *adj. & n.* council/ committees in the former Soviet Union. **Soviet Union.** former Union of Soviet Socialist Republics.

sow 1 [saʊ] *n.* Female pig. **sow 2** [səʊ] *v.* (sowed, sown) to put seed into earth so that it grows. **sower** ['səʊə] *n.* person who sows seed.

soy, soya [sɔɪ, 'sɔjə] *n.* kind of very nutritious tropical bean; s. sauce = salty Chinese sauce made from soya beans.

sozzled ['sɒzld] *adj. inf.* drunk.

spa [spɑ:] *n.* place where mineral water comes out of the ground naturally and where people go to drink or bathe in the water because of its medicinal properties.

space 1 [speɪs] *n.* (a) place; empty area between two objectives a sheet of paper, etc. (b) short of paper, etc. (b) short period of time: s, bar = key on a typewriter/computer which makes a space between letters. (c) (also outer space) area beyond the earth's atmosphere. **space 2** *v.* to s. out = to time (things) at intervals, to place (things) with gaps between them.

spacecraft *n.* rocket in which astronauts travel in space. **spaceman** *n.* person who travels in space.

spacesaving *adj.* (piece of furniture, etc) which is compact or which folds, and so saves space. **spaceship** *n.* rocket in which astronauts travel in space. **spacesuit** *n.* special clothes worn by spacemen.

spacious ['speɪʃəs] *adj.* very large/ with lots of space. **spaciousness** ['speɪʃəsnəs] *n.* state of being spacious.

spade [speɪd] *n.* (a) long handled tool for digging holes in the ground; s. work = the preliminary work, to call a s, a s = to say what you think without trying to hide your opinions (b) spades = one of the four suits in a pack of cards.

spaghetti [spə'getɪ] *n.* Italian food formed of long strips of pasta.

span 1 [spæn] *n.* (a) width (of wings/an arch, etc.) (b) arch of a bridge, (c) length of time. **span 2** *v.* (spanned) to stretch across.

spandrel ['spændrəl] *n.* wall between adjoining arches.

spangle ['spæŋgl] *n.* small piece of bright metal which is sewn on a dress as an ornament. **spangled** *adj.* covered with spangles.

Spaniard ['spæbjəd] *n.* person from Spain.

spaniel ['spænjəl] *n.* type of dog with large hanging cars.

Spanish 1 ['spænɪʃ] *adj.* referring to Spain. **Spanish 2** *n.* language spoken in Spain and Latin America.

spank [spæŋk] *v.* to smack on the behind. **spanking 1** *adj. inf.* (a) fast (pace) (b) bright new **spanking 2** *n.* series of smacks on the behind.

spanner ['spænə] *n.* metal tool with an opening which fits round a out so that it can be twisted to loosen or tighten; to throw a s., in the works = to bring things to a state of confusion.

spar 1 [spɑ:] *n.* (a) ship's mast or a wooden beam for holding the sails. (b) type of mineral crystal **spar 2** *v.* (sparred) to practise boxing. **sparring partner** *n.* person a boxer spars with.

spare 1 ['speə] *adj.* (a) not used/extra; s. parts = replacement parts for a machine; a. wheel carried to replace one that has a puncture. *inf.* s. type = fold of fat found the waist of a plump person. (b) thin (person/body). **spare 2** *n.* extra thing/replacement. **spare 3** *v.* (a) to do without. (b) to give up; not to need. (c) to s. s.o's life = not to kill s.o. whom you have defeated, to have mercy on s.o. (d) he was spared the embarrassment = it saved him from being embarrassed.

spare ribs *n. pl.* cooked pork ribs in a savoury sauce. **sparing** *adj.* to be s. with = to economize. **sparingly** *adv.* using little.

spark 1 [spɑ:k] *n.* little flash of fire/of electricity of life. **spark 2** *v.* to send out sparks/to make electric sparks. **sparking plug am, spark plug** *n.* (in a car engine) desire which produces a spark which ignites petrol vapour. **sparkle 1** ['spɑ:kl] *n.* bright shiny light; small spark. **sparkle 2** *v.* to glitter/to shine brightly; sparkling wine = wine which bubbles. **sparkler** *n.* type of firework which sends out sparks. **spark off** *v. inf.* to start.

sparrow ['spærəʊ] *n.* common small brown and grey bird. **sparrowhawk** *n.* common small hawk.

sparse ['spɑːs] *adj.* not thick thinly spread. **sparsely** *adv.* with few (things); thinly. **sparseness, sparsity** *n.* being sparse.

spartan ['spɑːtən] *adj.* harsh/hard (discipline) uncomfortable (conditions).

spasm ['spæzəm] *n.* sudden uncontrollable pulling of muscles. (b) sudden fit (of work). **spasmodic** ['spæz'mɒdɪk] *adj.* coming in spasms/ from time to time. **spasmodically** *adv.* from time to time.

spastic ['spæstɪk] *adj. & n.* (person who has suffered from brain damage which causes partial paralysis.

spat 1 [spæt] *n.* (a) small gaiter which just covers the shoe. (b) minor argument. **spat 2** *v.* see spit.

spate [speɪt] *n.* river in s. = in flood (b) sudden rush (of orders, etc).

spathe [speɪθ] *n.* leaf which encloses a flower.

spatial ['speɪʃəl] *adj.* referring to space. **spatially** *adv.* in a spatial way.

spatter ['spætə] *v.* to splash with little sports of liquid.

spatula ['spætjʊlə] *n.* (a) wide flat blunt flexible knife, (b) doctor's instrument used to hold down your tongue while examining your throat.

spawn 1 [spɔːn] *n.* eggs (of a fish/frog, etc.); Mushroom s. = material like seeds from which mushrooms grow **spawn 2** *v.* to produces eggs.

spay [speɪ] *v.* to make (a female animal) sterile by removing her ovaries.

speak [spiːk] *v.* (spoke, spoken) (a) to say words and phrases; I know him to s. to = I know him enough to get into conversation with him, (b) to talk in public (c) to be able to say things in a foreign language). **speaker** *n.* (a) person who speaks, (b) (in parliament) the S, of the Houses of Commons = the chairman. (c) loudspeaker. **speak for** *v.* to plead on s.o, 's behalf. **speaking** *n.* action of talking; we've not on s; terms = we have quarrelled and don't speak to

each other, **speak up** *v.* (a) to speak more loudly, (b) to s. up for = to support.

spear 1 ['spɪə] *n.* long pointed throwing weapon. **spear 2** *v.* to jab (s.o./sth) with a spear. **spearhead 1** *n.* front part of a force of attackers.

spearhead 2 *v* to be in the front of an attacking force. **spearmint** *n.* common type of mint, often used in chewing gum.

spec [spek] *n. inf.* to buy on s, = without being sure of the value/ condition.

special 1 ['speʃəl] *adj.* (a) particular/ referring to one particular thing. (b) extraordinary/rare/unusual. **special 2** *n.* (a) particular edition of a newspaper, (b) particular dish on a menu, (c) article reduced in price. **specialist** *n.* person who has studied sth very deeply.

speciality [speʃɪ'ælɪtɪ] *n.* particular interest; subject which you have studied/ thing you are known for.

specialization [speʃəlaɪ'zeɪʃn] *n.* act of specializing; thing you specialize in. **specialize** ['speʃəlaɪz] *v.* to s. to sub = to study/to produce sth in particular. **specially** *adv.* particularly; unusually.

species ['spiːʃɪz] *n.* (pl.species) (a) group of animals/plants which are closely similar, and which can breed together, (b) *inf.* sort.

specie *n. pl.*(formal) coins.

specify *v.* to state clearly what is required. **specific** ['spesɪfɪk] *adj.* particular/precise (details). **specifically** *adv.* particularly. **specification** [spesɪfɪ'keɪʃn] *n.* detailed plan/ information. **specific gravity** *n.* density of a substance divided by the density of water.

specimen ['spesɪmən] *n.* (a) sample which is selected for study or exhibition (b) sample/example.

specious ['spiːʃəs] *adj.* not really true as it seems. **speciously** *adv.* in a specious way. **speciousness** *n.* being specious.

speck [spek] *n.* tiny spot. **speckle** *n.* small (usu. brown) spot. **speckled** *adj.* covered with speckles.

specs [speks] *n. pl.*inf. glasses.

spectacle ['spektəkl] *n.* (a) show, (b) spectacles = glasses worn in front of your eyes to correct defects in your sight. **spectacular** [spek'tækjʊlə] *adj.*

impressive (show/display).
spectacularly *adv.* in a spectacular
way. **spectator** *n.* person who watches
a show/ football match, etc.
spectre, *Am.* **specter** ['spektə] *n.* (a)
ghost, (b) feat.
spectral *adj.* like a ghost.
spectrum ['spektrəm] *n.* hands of
colours varying from red to blue (as seen
in a rainbow); range (of ideas etc.).
spectrography *n.* recording of a
spectrum, used to analyse the chemical
composition of a substance.
speculate ['spekjʊleɪt] *v.* (a) to s.
about = to make guesses about, (b) to
gamble by buying things whose value
you hope will rise. **speculation**
[spekjʊ'leɪʃn] *n.* (a) guesses made about
sth. (b) gambling by buying things whose
value you hope will rise. **speculative**
['spekjʊlətɪv] *adj.* (a) made by guessing,
(b) gambling; s. share = one whose
future price is quite uncertain.
speculator ['spekjʊleɪtə] *n.* person
who buys goods in the hope or reselling
them again at a profit.
speculum ['spekjʊləm] *n.* (a) reflector
in a telescope, (b) tube for inspecting the
interior of the body.
sped [sped] *v.* see speed.
speech [spiːtʃ] *n.* (a) ability to talk. (b)
spoken language; the parts of s. =
different groups of words (nouns/verbs,
etc.) which are used in a similar way in
language. (c) talk given in public; s. day
= day when children are given prizes at
school for good work, etc. **speechify** *v.*
to make long speeches. **speechless**
adj. incapable of saying anything.
speed 1 [spiːd] *n.* (a) quickness of
movement (b) rate of movement. **speed
2** *v.* (a) (sped) to go fast. (b) (speeded)
to drive a car faster than the legal speed
to make (progress) go faster. **speedboat**
n. racing motor boat. **speedily** *adj.*
vary fast. **speediness** *n.* being
speedy. **speedometer** [spiː'dɒmɪtə] *n.*
dial which shows you how fast you are
travelling. **speed up** *v.* to go faster; to
make go faster. **speedway** *n.* racing
track for motor cycles. **speedwell** *n.*
small wild plant with blue flowers.
speedy *adj.* (ier, -iest) very fast.
speleology [spiːlɪ'ɒlədʒi] *n.* potholing; climbing down into caves or

holes in the ground. **speleological**
adj. referring to speleology.
speleologist *n.* person who climbs in
or explores caves and holes in the
ground.
spell 1 [spel] *n.* (a) magic curse: words
which may have a magic effect (b) period
of time. **spell 2** *v.* (spelt) (a) to say
aloud/to write correctly the letters which
form a word; to s. out = (i) to read with
difficulty; (ii) to explain very clearly. (b)
to mean. **spellbinder** *n.* thing which
enchants/attracts and keeps the attention.
spellbound *adj.* bewitched/
enchanted. **spell check** *v.* to check the
spelling of text using a computer
progrAm. **speller** *n.* person who
spells. **spelling** *n.* way in which a
word is spelt; writing words correctly.
spelling checker *n.* computer
program which checks spelling.
spencer ['spensə] *n.* type of sleeved
vest worn by women.
spend [spend] *v.* (spent) (a) to pay
(money) in exchange for sth., (b) to pass
(time), (c) to s. oneself = to tire oneself
out. **spender** *n.* person who spends.
spending *n.* action of using money to
buy sth. **spendthrift** *adj.* (Person) who
spends money fast. **spent** [spent] *adj.*
used; s. fuel = fuel which has been used
in a nuclear reactor; see also spend.
sperm [spɜːm] *n.* (a) male fluid which
fertilizes the eggs of a female, (b) s.
whale = large whale which provides oil.
spermaceti [spɜːmə'setɪ] *n.* white
substance taken from a sperm whale. and
used as a base for perfumes.
spermatozoa [spɜːmətə'zəʊə] *n.*
sperms. **spermicidal** *adj.* which kills
sperm.
spew [spjuː] *v.* to s. (out) = to vomit; to
pour out.
sphagnum ['sfægnəm] *n.* type of
moss.
sphere ['sfɪə] *n.* (a) object which is
perfectly round, (b) area (of influence);
society. **spherical** ['sferɪkl] *adj.*
shaped like a sphere/perfectly round.
sphincter ['sfɪŋktə] *n.* circular muscle
which controls an opening.
sphinx [sfɪŋks] *n.* legendary animal in
Egypt with the head of a women and the
body of a lion; large stone monument of
this animal.

spice 1 [spaɪs] n. (a)flavouring made from seeds/leaves of plants etc. (b) thing which excites interest. **spice 2** v. to add spices to (a dish). **spiciness** n. being spicy. **spicy** adj. (a)with a lot of spices, (b) rather rude(story).

spick and span ['spɪkən'spæn] adj. very clean/tidy

spider ['spaɪdə] n. eight legged animal, which makes a web and eats flies; s. plant = common house plant, with long yellow and green leaves. **spider's-web** n. web made by a spider. **spidery** adj. thin and scrawling(handwriting).

spiel [spi:l] n. long flow of talk (aimed at persuading).

spigot ['spɪgət] n. tap(in a barrel).

spike 1 [spaɪk] n. (a)long sharp point, (b)spikes = sharp points in the soles of running shoes. **spike 2** v. (a) to attach spikes to (b) to jam (a gun), (c) to cut (another runner) with your spikes, **spiked** adj. covered with spikes. **spiky** adj. standing up in sharp points.

spill 1 [spɪl] (a)fall (b)long thin piece of of wood for lighting cigarettes/candles. etc. **spill 2** v. (spilled/split) to pour (liquid) out of a container by mistake. **spillage** n. action of spilling; amount of liquid spilt.

spin 1 [spɪn] n. (a) action of turning round and round flat s. = state of confusion (b)short fast trip. **spin 2** v. (spun) (a) to turn round and round very fast: to throw (a coin) up into the air and catch it. so as to decide which side plays first, etc: to form a thread. **spin drier** n. machine for drying washing by turning it round very fast. **spindry** v. to dry (washing) in a spin-drier. **spinner** n. person who spins thread. **spinneret** [spɪnə'ret] n. part of the spider which spins the threads to make a web.

spinning wheel n. apparatus for twisting and winding wool. **spin-off** n. secondary result: useful by product. **spin out** v. to make (sth) last a long time.

spina bifida [spaɪnə'bɪfɪdə] n. condition from birth where the spine is badly formed allowing the membrane covering the spinal cord to protrude.

spinach ['spɪnɪtʃ] n. common greenleaved vegetable

spindle ['spɪndl] n. (a) pin used for twisting thread in a spinning machine.

(b) central pin round which sth turns. **spindly** ['spɪndlɪ] adj. long, thin and weak.

spindrift ['spɪndrɪft] n. spray which is blown from breaking waves.

spine [spaɪn] n. (a) backbone. (b) back of a book. (c) prickle (on a cactus/hedgehog, etc.). **spinal** n. referring to the spine; s. column = backbone; s. cord = group of nerves running down the inside of the spine. **spineless** adj. (person) who is weak and indecisive. **spiny** adj. covered with prickles.

spinet [spɪ'net] n. old musical instrument, like a small rectangular harpsichord.

spinnaker ['spɪnəkə] n. large balloon like sail on the front of a racing yacht.

spinney ['spɪnɪ] n. small wood.

spinster ['spɪnstə] n. unmarried woman (usu. middle-aged).

spiral 1 ['spaɪərəl] n. (a) thing which is twisted round. **spiral 2** adj. twisted round and round like a spring. **spiral 3** v. (spiralled) to go round and round and rise at the same time. **spirally** adv. in a spiral shape.

spire ['spaɪə] n. pointed construction on top of a church tower.

spirit 1 ['spɪrɪt] n. (a) soul. (b) ghost; Holy S. = the third person of the Christian Trinity. (c) energetic way of doing sth. (d) real meaning (not always expressed in words). (e) alcohol; surgical s, = pure alcohol used for rubbing on the skin, etc. (f) spirits = strong alcoholic drink (whisky/gin. etc.) **spirit 2** v. to a away = to remove as if by magic.

spirited adj. very vigorous.

spiritedly adv. in a spirited way.

spirit lamp n. lamp which burns spirit. **spirit level** n. tool for testing if a surface is level using a glass tube containing an airbubble. **spiritual 1** adj. referring to the spirit; dealing with the soul. **spiritual 2** n. religious song sung by black people in the southern United States. **spiritualism** n. belief that you can communicate with the spirits of dead people. **spiritualist** n. person who tries to communicate with the spirits of dead people. **spirituality** n. love of religion. **spiritually** adv. in a spiritual way. **spirituous** adj. alcoholic.

spit 1 [spɪt] n. (a) long metal rod passed through meat which turns so that the meat is evenly cooked. (b) long thin stretch of land going out into the sea. (c) depth of earth dug by a spade. (d) liquid formed in the mouth; s. and polish = excessive cleaning; inf. he is the dead s. and image of his father = he looks exactly like his father. **spit 2** v. (a) (spitted) to put (meat) on a spit to roast. (b) (spat) to send liquid out of the mouth; inf. he is the splitting image of his father = he looks exactly like his father. (c) to send sparks out; to rain slightly. **spittle** ['spɪtl] n. saliva. **spittoon** [spɪ'tu:n] n. dish for spitting into.

spite 1 [spaɪt] n. (a) bad feeling against s.o./desire to hurt s.o. (b) in s. of sth = without bothering about. **spite 2** v. to try to annoy. **spiteful** adj. full of bad feeling/wishing to hurt s.o. **spitefully** adv. in a spiteful way. **spitefulness** n. being spiteful.

splash 1 [splæʃ] n. (a) noisy throwing of liquid; sound of liquid being thrown noisily. (b) mark made by dirty liquid being scattered. (c) bright patch of colour. (d) short spurt (of soda water, etc,). (e) sudden show; sudden spending of money. **splash 2** v. (a) (of liquid) to make a noise while hitting (a solid). (b) to send dirty liquid on to. (c) to display. **splash down** v. (of space capsule) to land in the sea. splashdown, n. landing (of a spacecraft) in the sea. **splash out** v. inf. to spend a lot of money. **splashy** adj. which splashes.

splatter ['splætə] v. to splash.

splay 1 [spleɪ] adj. turned outwards. **splay 2** v. to slant outwards.

spleen [spli:n] n. organ near the stomach which keeps the blood in good condition.

splendid ['splendɪd] adj. magnificent/wonderful. **splendidly** adv. wonderfully/extremely well. **splendour,** Am. **splendor** n. magnificence.

splenetic [splə'netɪk] adj. violently angry.

splice 1 [splaɪs] n. joint which links two pieces of rope. **splice 2** v. to join (two pieces of rope) by twisting the threads together; to join (two pieces of

film) together; inf. to get spliced = to get married. **splicer** n. device for joining pieces of film together.

splint [splɪnt] n. stiff bar tied to a broken leg,.etc,. to keep it straight.

splinter 1 ['splɪntə] n. small pointed piece (of wood/metal); s. group = group of people who have separated from a main group. **splinter 2** v. to split into thin pointed pieces.

split 1 [splɪt] n. (a) thin crack; sharp break. (b) the splits = gymnastic exercise where you sit on the floor with one leg stretched out in front, and the other behind you. (c) banana s. = dessert of bananas, cream, ice cream and nuts. **split 2** v. (a) to divide (sth) into parts; to make (sth) divide/crack; inf. my head is splitting = I have a bad headache. (b) inf. to s. on s.o. = to report s.o. **split 3** adj. which has been cracked; s. pass = dried peas broken in half; in a s. second = very fast; to have a s. personality = to have two ways of behaving which are quite different in varying circumstances. **splitlevel** adj. (room, etc.) with part of the floor higher than the rest. **split up** v. to divide.

splodge, splotch [splɒdʒ], [splɒtʃ] n. dirty mark; oddly-shaped spot of colour.

splurge 1 [splɜ:dʒ] n. inf. spending spree. **splurge 2** v. inf. to spend money extravagantly.

splutter ['splʌtə] v. (a) to spit when speaking; to speak rapidly. (b) (of kettle) to hiss (when boiling).

spoil 1 [spɔɪl] v. (a) to ruin/to make bad. (b) to treat (a child) so leniently that it ruins their character. **spoil 2** n. pl. spoils (a) booty, goods taken by soldiers from a defeated enemy. (b) rubbish from a mine. **spoiler** n. decorative panel at the intended to slow the vehicle down. **spoil for** v. to be eager for (a fight). **spoilsport** n. person who spoils other people's enjoyment. **spoilt** adj. badly brought up (child).

spoke 1 [spəʊk] n. one of the rods running from the axle of a wheel to the rim. **spoke 2** v. see also speak. **speak, spokeshave** n. tool with a curved blade for smoothing sth round. **spoken** ['spəʊkn] v. see speak. **spokesman, spokeswoman, spokesperson** [spəʊksmən, -wʊ:mən, -pɜ:sən] n. (pl.-

men, -women) person who speaks on behalf of s.o.

spoliation [spəʊlɪ'eɪʃn] *n.* (formal) act of destroying.

spondee ['spɒndeɪ] *n.* measure (two long syllables) used in Latin poetry.

sponge 1 [spʌnʒ] *n.* (a) soft skeleton of a sea animal/block of plastic full of small holes. which soaks up water and is used for washing; s. bath = washing a patient in bed. using a sponge. *inf.* to throw up/in the s. = to give in/to admit you are beaten. (b) act of washing with a sponge. (c) s. cake/pudding = light soft cake/pudding. **sponge 2** *v.* (a) to wash with a sponge. (b) *inf.* to s. on s.o. = to live by begging for money from s.o. **spongebag** *n.* small plastic bag for carrying washing things. **sponger** *n.* person who doesn't work but gets money by begging for it from friends. **spongy** *adj.* soft and full of holes.

sponsor 1 ['spɒnsə] *n.* (a) person who helps s.o./sth by taking responsibility. (b) person or firm who pays for a television show/cricket match, etc., as a form of advertisement. (c) person who pays money to a charity if s.o, else walks, swims, runs, a certain distance, etc. **sponsor 2** *v.* to be a sponsor; to be responsible for (a bill in parliament) to pay for (a television show/a cricket match, etc.); (of god-parent) to s. a child at baptism = to promise to help the child to lead a Christian life. **sponsorship** *n.* action of sponsoring.

spontaneous [spɒn'teɪnɪəs] *adj.* which happens freely/which is not forced. **spontaneously** *adv.* in a spontaneous/natural way. **spontaneity** [spɒntə'nɪətɪ] *n.* acting in a natural way.

spoof [spu:f] *n.* *inf.* hoax/amusing imitation.

spook [spu:k] *n.* ghost. **spooky** *adj.* *inf.* frightening; (place) which is likely to be haunted.

spool *n.* cylinder round which sth is wound.

spoon 1 [spu:l] *n.* eating utensil with a small bowl and a long handle; wooden s. = (i) spoon made of wood; (ii) silly prize given to s.o. who is last in a competition. **spoon 2** *v.* to s. sth up/into = to lift sth up/to put sth in with a spoon. **spoonbill** *n.* large white bird with a spoon-shaped

end to its bill. **spoonfeed** *v.* to give (a baby) food with a spoon; to teach (people) by giving them answers to questions and not allowing them to work by themselves; to provide everything for (s.o.) so that they need to nothing to help themselves. **spoonful** *n.* amount contained in a spoon. **spoonerism** ['spu:nərɪzəm] *n.* exchanging letters of words by mistake (queer old dean for dear old queen).

spoor ['spʊə] *n.* tracks left by an animal.

sporadic [spə'rædɪk] *adj.* which happens at irregular intervals. **sporadically** *adv.* in a sporadic way.

spore [spɔ:] *n.* plant cell which reproduces without requiring to be fertilized.

sporran ['spɒrən] *n.* leather bag worn by Scotsmen in front of the kilt.

sport 1 [spɔ:t] *n.* (a) game (such as football/hockey/tennis. etc.); blood sports = hunting animals as a sport; sports car = light fast open car; sports jacket/sports coat - man's tweed jacket. (b) *inf.* good s. = pleasant person always willing to help. (c) animal/plant which is very different from its parents. **sport 2** *v.* to wear. **sporting** *adj.* (person) who plays according to the rules/who is pleasant and willing to help; s. chance = quite a good chance. **sportive** *adj.* playful. **sportsman** *n.* (a) person who takes part in a sport. (b) person who plays properly. **sportsmanlike** *adj.* (playing a game) in a proper way/ according to the rules; not cheating. **sportsmanship** *n.* quality of being a good sportsman/of not cheating. **sportswear** *n.* clothes worn to play sports. **sportswoman** *n.* woman who takes part in a sport. **sporty** *adj.* interested in sport (and in nothing else).

spot 1 [spɒt] *n.* (a) place; on the s. = on duty/at your post; in a s. = in a difficult position; to put s.o. on the s. = in a position where he has to act. (b) pimple. (c) *usu.* round coloured mark; *inf.* to knock spots off = to defeat easily. (d) *inf.* small amount. (e) spotlight/bright light which only shines on one spot. **spot 2** *v.* (a) to mark with a spot. (b) it's spotting with rain = drops are falling here and there. (c) to notice. spot check,

n. surprise check (on items at random).
spotless *adj.* very clean. **spotlessly**
adj. s. clean = extremely clean.
spotlight 1 *n.* bright light which
shines on one small area. **spot 2** *v.* to
highlight/to draw attention to (sth).
spot-on *adj. inf.* absolutely correct.
spotter *n.* person who notes things.
spotty *adj.* covered with pimples.
spouse ['spaʊz] *n.* husband or wife.
spout 1 [spaʊt] *n.* tube for pouring
liquid out of a kettle, etc.; tube for
sending waste water/rainwater away
from the wall of a building. *inf.* up the s.
= lost/ruined/wasted. **spout 2** *v.* (a) to
come out in a jet. (b) *inf.* to speak
continuously.
sprain 1 [spreɪn] *n.* twist of a joint.
sprain 2 *v.* to twist (a joint).
sprang [spræŋ] *v.* see spring.
sprat [spræt] *n.* very small herring like
fish.
sprawl 1 [sprɔːl] *n.* irregular spread;
urban s. = unregulated spread of houses
built over what formerly was
countryside. **sprawl 2** *v.* (a) to lie with
arms and legs spread out. (b) to spread
out in an irregular way.
spray 1 [spreɪ] *n.* (a) branch with
flowers on it. (b) liquid in the form of
tiny drops/in a mist. (c) sprayer. **spray 2**
v. to send out liquid in a fine mist.
sprayer *n.* machine for spraying.
spray gun *n.* tool shaped like a pistol
with a small container attached (used for
spraying paint/insecticide, etc.).
spread 1 [spred] *n.* (a) wide expanse;
width. (b) act of sending out over a wide
area. (c) *inf.* feast. (d) soft paste of meat/
cheese. (e) double-page s. = text which
runs over two facing pages in a book or
newspaper. **spread 2** *v.* (spread) (a) to
send out/to go out over a wide area. (b)
to space out over a period of time. (c) to
cover with a layer of sth. **spreadeagled**
adj. lying flat of sth. **spreadsheet** *n.*
computer printout of tables of figures.
spree [spriː] *n.* happy time; to go on a
spending s. = to have a happy time
spending money.
sprig [sprɪg] *n.* (a) small branch. (b)
design of small branches. (c) small
headless nail.
sprightly ['spraɪtlɪ] *adj.* light and
vigorous. **sprightliness** *n.* being

sprightly.
spring 1 [sprɪŋ] *n.* (a) small stream of
water coming out of the ground. (b)
season of the year following winter when
plants begin to grow and put out leaves;
s. onion = thin white onion plant eaten
raw in salads. (c) leap in the air. (d)
coiled wire which returns to its original
shape after being stretched or
compressed; strong bent metal plates
which allow a vehicle to ride over
bumps; s. clip = clip which closes with a
spring; s. balance = device for weighing
made of a large spring which stretches
when a weight is attached to it. (e)
bounciness. **spring 2** *v.* (sprang, has
sprung) (a) to leap/to bounce. (b) to set
(sth) off/to make (sth) happen suddenly.
(c) to come from. (d) to s. a leak = to
start taking in water through a crack.
springboard *n.* long flexible board
used to give an impetus to a diver or
jumper. **springbok** ['sprɪŋbok] *n.* type
of African deer. **spring-clean** *v.* to
clean thoroughly after the winter. **spring
fever** *n. Am.* feeling of excitement at
the coming of spring. **springiness** *n.*
being springy. **springlike** *adj.*
(weather) which is mild like in spring.
spring tide *n.* tide which rises and
falls very sharply, and occurs at the new
and full moon. **springtime** *n.* spring/
the season after winter. **springy** *adj.*
which bends; (carpet/grass) which is
very soft.
sprinkle ['sprɪŋkl] *v.* to scatter water/sand.
etc. **sprinkler** *n.* device for sprinkling; s.
system = system of automatic fire control
which sprinkles water on a fire and is set off
by rising heat. **sprinkling** *n.* (a) action of
scattering water/sand, etc. (b) small
quantities.
sprint 1 [sprɪnt] *n.* short fast running
race. **sprint 2** *v.* to run very fast over a
short distance. **sprinter** *n.* number
who specializes in sprint races.
sprit [sprɪt] *n.* small spar which goes
diagonally across a sail. **spritsail** *n.*
sail held by a sprit.
sprite [spraɪt] *n.* fairy.
sprocket ['sprɒkɪt] *n.* small tooth on a
wheel. **sprocket-wheel** *n.* toothed
wheel which connects with a chain.
sprout 1 [spraʊt] *n.* young shoot of a
plant; Brussels sprouts = edible shoots

from a type of cabbage. **sprout 2** *v.* to send out (shoots/horns).

spruce 1 [spru:s] *n.* type of fir tree.
spruce 2 *adj.* smart. **spruce 3** *v.* to s. yourself up = to make yourself neat.
sprucely *adv.* in a spruce way.
spruceness *n.* being spruce.
sprung [sprʌŋ] *v.* see spring.
spry [sprai] *adj.* (old person) who is vigorous and active. **spryly** *adv.* in a spry way. **spryness** *n.* being spry.
spud [spʌd] *n.* *inf.* potato.
spume [spju:m] *n.* foam (on the sea).
spun [spʌn] *v.* see spin.
spunk [spʌŋk] *n.* *inf.* courage.
spur 1 [sp3:] *n.* (a) metal point attached to the heels of a rider's boots which pricks a horse to make it go faster; to win your spurs = to show for the first time how good you are. (b) low hill running from a higher range of mountains; minor road/railway line leading off a main one. (c) impetus/stumulus; on the s. of the moment = without planning in advance.
spur 2 *v.* (spurred) to urge (s.o.) on.
spurge [sp3:dʒ] *n.* common weed with bitter white sap.
spurious ['spjuəriəs] *adj.* false.
spuriously *adv.* in a spurious way.
spuriousness *n.* being spurious.
spurn [sp3:n] *v.* to reject (an offer) scornfully.
spurt 1 [sp3:t] *n.* (a) jet of liquid. (b) sudden effort. **spurt 2** *v.* (a) to s. out = to come out in a jet. (b) to run fast suddenly.
sputter ['spʌtə] *v.* to spit/to send out sparks or fat.
sputum ['spju:təm] *n.* mucus which is spat out of the mouth.
spy 1 [spai] *n.* person who is paid to try to find out what the enemy/a criminal gang/a rival firm is planning to do. **spy 2** *v.* to see; to s. on s.o. = to try, in secret, to find out what s.o. is doing.
spying *n.* trying to find out information about the enemy. **spy out** *v.* to examine (the land) secretly.
squab [skwɒb] *n.* small pigeon.
squabble 1 ['skwɒbl] *n.* quarrel/argument. **squabble 2** *v.* to argue.
squad [skwɒd] *n.* (a) small group of soldiers; firing s. = group of soldiers who shoot s.o. who has been condemned to death. (b) small group of workmen/

police; s. car = police car on patrol. (c) (sports) team.
squadron ['skwɒdrən] *n.* group of soldiers on horseback; group of aircraft, group of naval ships; s. leader = rank in the air force above flight lieutenant.
squalid ['skwɒlɪd] *adj.* sordid/unpleasant/dirty. **squalidly** *adv.* in a squalid way. **squalor** *n.* dirt; dirty state.
squall 1 [skwɔ:l] *n.* sudden gust of wind. **squall 2** *v.* to cry loudly.
squally *adj.* accompanied by gusts of wind.
squander ['skwɒndə] *v.* to waste (money/energy).
square 1 ['skweə] *n.* (a) shape with four equal sides and four right angles; *inf.* we're back to s. one = we'll have to start planning again from the beginning. (b) open area in a town, surrounded by buildings. (c) instrument for drawing right angles. (d) a number multiplied by itself. **square 2** *adj.* (a) shaped like a square. (b) s. corner = corner with a right angle. (c) fair/straightforward; s. deal = honest treatment; s. meal = a good filling meal. (d) straight. (e) multiplied by itself; s. metre = area of one metre multiplied by one metre; s. root = number which when multiplied by itself produces the number you have. **square 3** *adv.* (a) in a level/straight way. (b) directly. **square 4** *v.* (a) to make (a round stone, etc.) square; squared paper = paper with squares drawn on it (for making graphs, etc.) (b) to balance (accounts); to pay (s.o.) what is owed; to pay (s.o.) a bribe. (c) to multiply (sth) by itself. (d) to straighten (your shoulders); to s. up to s.o. = to prepare to fight.
squarely *adv.* in a straightforward way.
squash 1 [skwɒʃ] *n.* (a) crowded mass of people. (b) concentrated juice of a fruit to which water is added. (c) fast game played with rackets in a court with high walls. (d) vegetable like a marrow/pumpkin, etc. **squash 2** *v.* (a) to crush (b) to stop (a revolt) by force; to sop (s.o.) speaking by being rude to them.
squash court *n.* court for playing squash. **squashy** *adv.* soft and wet.
squat 1 [skwɒt] *n.* (a) action of occupying an empty house without the

permission of the owner. (b) empty house which is suitable for squatting in. **squat 2** v. (squatted) (a) to crouch down. sitting on your heels. (b) to crouch down sitting on your heels. (b) to occupy an empty house without the permission of the owner. **squat 3** adj. (squatter, squattest) short and thick. **squatter** n. person who occupies and empty house without the permission of the owner.

squaw [skwɔː] n. American Indian woman.

squawk 1 [skwɔːk] n. short harsh cry. **squawk 2** v. to make short harsh cries.

squeak 1 [skwiːk] n. little high-pitched cry (like that of a mouse); high-pitched sound (like a rusty hinge); inf. narrow s. = near miss/narrow escape. **squeak 2** v. to make a squeak. **squeaky** adj. (gate) which squeaks.

squeal 1 [skwiːl] n. long loud high pitched cry. **squeal 2** v. to make long loud high-pitched cries.

squeamish ['skwiːmɪʃ] adj. easily made sick/easily shocked.

squeamishness n. being squeamish.

squeegee ['skwiːdʒi] n. implement for cleaning floors, made of a wad of sponge attached to a hinged plate.

squeeze 1 [skwiːz] n. (a) pressure; crushing; tight w. = crowd of people crushed together. (b) credit s. = restriction on credit. (c) s. of lemon = few drops of lemon juice. **squeeze 2** v. (a) to crush/to force/to press. (b) to push together; to push to get into/through a small space. **squeezer** n. device for pressing citrus fruit to get the juice out.

squeeze up v. to crush together to make room for s.o. else.

squelch 1 [skweltʃ] n. noise made by a wet sticky substance. **squelch 2** v. to make a wet sucking noise.

squib [skwɪb] n. small firework which bangs. damp s. = exciting/new thing which doesn't work properly.

squid [skwɪd] n. sea animal like a small octopus.

squiggle 1 ['skwɪgl] n. illegible curly marks/handwriting. **squiggle 2** v. to make squiggles.

squint 1 [skwɪnt] n. (a) state where your two eyes look in different directions. (b) inf. look/glance. **squint 2** v. (a) to have eyes which look in

different directions. (b) to half-close your eyes to look at a bright light.

squire ['skwaɪə] n. (a) gentleman living in the country, often the owner of a large house. (b) inf. way of addressing a man.

squirm [skwɜːm] v. to wriggle about; it makes me s. = it makes me very embarrassed.

squirrel ['skwɪrəl] n. common small mammal with a large bushy tail, living in trees.

squirt 1 [skwɜːt] n. (a) sharp jet of liquid. (b) inf. little s. = small insignificant person. **squirt 2** v. to send out a sharp jet of liquid.

squishy ['skwɪʃɪ] adj. soft and squashy.

Sr symbol for strontium.

St [snt, striːt] short form of Saint or Street.

stab 1 [stæb] n. would made with a sharp knife; s. in the back = attack by s.o. who is thought to be loyal; inf. to have a s. at = to try to do. **stab 2** v. (stabbed) to wound with a sharp knife; to s. s.o. in the back = to attack s.o. who thinks you are his friend.

stable 1 ['steɪbl] n. (a) building for keeping a horse. (b) stables = place where horses are kept for breeding/racing. etc. **stable 2** v. to keep (a horse) in a stable. **stable 3** adj. solid; steady/not wobbly. (b) (in chemistry) (compound) which does not change or decompose easily. **stability** [stə'bɪlɪtɪ] n. steadiness. **stabilization** [steɪbɪlaɪ'zeɪʃn] n. making stable.

stabilize ['steɪbɪlaɪz] v. to make steady.

stabilizer n. (a) fin attached to the hull of a ship to prevent rolling; small wheels attached to the back wheel of a child's bicycle to allow the child to learn to ride without falling off. (b) substance added to processed food to keep it in a stable condition. **stableboy, stablelad** n. man who looks after horses in a stable.

stably adv. in a stable way.

staccato [stə'kɑːtəʊ] adj. & n. sharp (noise).

stack 1 [stæk] n. (a) heap; inf. lots (of). (b) brick pillar housing a chimney. (c) inner part of a library where books are kept without being open to the public.

stack 2 v. (a) to pile up. (b) of aircraft to circle round waiting in turn for permission to land at a busy airport.

stadium ['steɪdɪəm] *n.* large building for sport.

staff 1 [stɑːf] *n.* (a) long thick stick. (b) people working in a school/college/firm; s. room = room for teachers in a school. (c) officers who help the commander organize a military force; general s. = officers who work at headquarters. (d) set of five lines on which musical notes are written. **staff 2** *v.* to provide employees for (a firm. etc.). **staffer** *n. Am.* member of staff.

stag 1 [stæg] *n.* (a) make deer; s. party = party for men only. (b) person who buys new issues of shares and sells them at a profit. **stag 2** *v.* to buy shares at a new issue and sell them at a profit. **stag-beetle** *n.* large black beetle with horns.

stage 1 [steɪdʒ] *n.* (a) platform (on which a play is acted, etc); s. directions = notes in the script of a play showing what the actors have to do; s. fright = nervousness before appearing before an audience; s. whisper = loud whisper which everyone can hear; to go on the s. = to become an actor. (b) period/phase. (c) each of the parts of a rocket. (d) landing s. = wooden platform for boats to tie up to. (e) part of a journey. **stage 2** *v.* (a) to put on/to arrange (a performance of a play, etc.). (b) to make/to organize. **stagecoach** *n.* (old) horsedrawn passenger coach which ran regularly along certain routes.

stagecraft. *n.* art of the theatre.

stagehand *n.* person who moves scenery/prepares the stage (in a theatre).

stage-manage *v.* to arrange/to organize (a performance): to plan (a trick/a coup). **stage manager** *n.* person who organizes a performance of a play/opera, etc. **stager** *n. inf.* old s. = old experienced person. **staging** *n.* (a) putting on (of a play). (b) racks for storing. (c) s. post = place where planes/travellers regularly stop on a long journey. **stagy** *adj.* unreal: looking too much as if being acted on a stage.

stagflation [stæg'fleɪʃn] *n.* inflation and stagnation combined.

stagger ['stægə] *v.* (a) to walk unsteadily. (b) to astonish. (c) to arrange things so that they do not coincide exactly. **staggering.** *adj.* astonishing.

staggeringly *adv.* astonishingly.

stagnant ['stægnənt] *adj.* (a) (water) which does not flow/which is not pure enough to drink. (b) (business) which does not make increased sales.

stagflation [stæg'fleɪʃn] *n.* period when the economy stagnates but inflation increases. **stagnate** [stæg'neɪt] *v.* to stay static; not to advance.

stagnation [stæg'neɪʃn] *n.* being stagnant.

staid [steɪd] *adj.* serious/not adventurous.

stain 1 [steɪn] *n.* (a) dirty mark which is difficult to remove. (b) liquid used to change the colour of wood. **stain 2** *v.* (a) to make a dirty mark on (sth). (b) to change the colour of (wood, etc.); stained glass = coloured glass for windows (esp. in church). **stainless** *adj.* without any stain; s. steel = steel which contains nickel and chromium so that it does not rust in contact with air or water.

stair ['steə] *n.* (a) step (on a staircase) (b) (flight of) stairs = series of steps leading from one floor of a building to the next. **staircarpet** *n.* long narrow piece of carpet for covering stairs.

staircase *n.* flight of stairs (usu. with a handrail). **stair rod** *n.* metal rod which keeps a staircarpet in place.

stairway *n.* staircase.

stake 1 [steɪk] *n.* (a) strong pointed stick. (b) money which is gambled; he has a s. in the company = he has invested some money in the company. hoping to make a profit; at s. = which may be lost. **stake 2** *v.* (a) to put a stick in the ground; to s. your claim to = to suggest that you hold the right to own sth. (b) to bet (money, etc.).

stalactite ['stæləktaɪt] *n.* long point of limestone hanging from the ceiling of a cave, formed by mineral deposits from dripping water.

stalagmite ['stæləgmaɪt] *n.* long point of limestone rising from the floor of a cave formed by mineral deposits from dripping water.

stale [steɪl] *adj.* (-er, -est) (a) no longer fresh; (joke) that has been repeated many times. (b) to go s. = to become bored/tired so that you cannot work well.

stalemate *n.* (a) (in chess) position

where a player cannot move with out being checkmated. (b) situation where neither side will compromise. **staleness** *n.* being stale. **stalk 1** [stɔːk] *n.* (a) thin stem of a plant. (b) small part of the stem which attaches a fruit to the plant. **stalk 2** *v.* (a) to try to get close enough to an animal to shoot it. (b) to march along proudly. **stalker** *n.* person who stalks animals. **stalking horse** *n.* thing or person used to hide your real plans.

stall 1 [stɔːl] *n.* (a) compartment for one animal in a stable, etc. (b) stalls = seats in church for the choir and priests; seats on the ground floor (in a theatre/ cinema). (c) table with goods laid out for sale; small moveable shop. **stall 2** *v.* (a) (of a car engine) to stop unintentionally. (b) (of an aircraft) to go so slowly that it falls suddenly. (c) to put off making a decision. **stallholder** *n.* person who runs a stall in a market.

stallion ['stæljən] *n.* male horse, esp. one kept for breeding.

stalwart 1 ['stɒlwət] *adj.* strong/ vigorous/brave. **stalwart 2** *n.* strong/ vigorous/brave person.

stamen ['stemən] *n.* one of the thin spikes in the centre of a flower which carry the pollen.

stamina ['stæmɪnə] *n.* ability to do sth for a long time.

stammer 1 ['stæmə] *n.* unintentional repetition of sounds when speaking. **stammer 2** *v.* to repeat sounds when speaking. **stammerer** *n.* person who stammers.

stamp 1 [stæmp] *n.* (a) banging your foot on the ground. (b) object for making a mark on sth. (c) device for cutting out a design. (d) small piece of gummed paper for sticking on an envelope/parcel, etc., to pay for it to be sent by mail; s. machine = machine which sells stamps automatically. (e) any small piece of gummed paper used to show you have made a payment. (f) mark made by a rubber stamp. **stamp 2** *v.* (a) to bang your foot hard on the ground. (b) to make a mark on sth; stamped addressed envelope = envelope with your own name, address and a stamp, which you enclose in a letter so that the person you are writing to can reply. **stamp out** *v.*

to stop/to eradicate.
stampede 1 [stæm'piːd] *n.* mad rush (of animals/people). **stampede 2** *v.* to rush madly.
stance [stɑːns] *n.* (a) way of standing. (b) attitude/position.
stanch [stɑːnʃ] *v.* to stop blood flowing.
stanchion ['stænʃn] *n.* vertical post/ bar which holds sth up.
stand 1 [stænd] *n.* (a) position; to make a s. against = to resist. (b) support; thing which holds sth up; flat base. (c) an exhibition. (d) stands = series of seats for spectators at a football match. (e) *Am.* witness s. = witness box. (f) taxi s. = place where taxis wait. (g) one-night s. = stop for a single performance (of a play/ by a pop group) before moving to another location the following night.
stand 2 *v.* (stood) to be/to place in an upright position. (b) to be on your feet/ not to be sitting down. (c) to stay/to remain. (d) to bear/to accept. (e) to put your name forward in an election. (f) to pay for. **stand aside** *v.* to step to one side. **stand back** *v.* to step backwards; to be behind. **stand by** *v.* (a) to be ready. (b) to stand at one side without taking part in the action. (c) to support/to be faithful. **standby** *n.* (a) thing which is ready to go into action if necessary; good s. = thing which is good to have at hand in case of need. (b) waiting; he is on s. = he is waiting to see if he is needed; (at an airport) s. ticket = cheap ticket which allows you to wait to see if there are any empty places. **stand down** *v.* withdraw from an election, etc. **stand for** *v.* (a) to mean. (b) to accept/to allow. (c) to be candidate for (an elected position). **stand in for** *v.* to take s.o.'s place. **stand-in** *n.* person who takes s.o.'s place. **standing 1** *n.* (a) being on your feet; s. room only = room for people to stand, not to sit. (b) social position. **standing 2** *adj.* (a) upright/not lying or sitting. (b) permanent; s. order = permanent order to send sth or pay sth regularly; it is a s. joke = it is sth we always laugh about. **standoffish** *adj.* (person) who is cold/ who does not make friends. **standoffishness** *n.* unfriendliness. **stand out** *v.* to be obvious. **stand over** *v.* to be just behind (s.o.) and supervise what

he is doing. **standpipe** *n.* upright pipe connected to the water main in the street, with a tap which allows water to be taken off when the supply to houses has been cut. **standpoint** *n.* point of view/ position from which you look at a problem. **standstill** *n.* state of being stopped. **stand to** *v.* (in army, etc.) to be ready to go into action. **stand up** *v.* (a) to get to your feet. (b) s. up straight! = hold yourself straight. (c) to s. up for sth = to fight s. o. bravely; to s. s. o. up = not to meet s.o. at a rendezvous. **stand-up** *adj.* stand-up buffet = buffet where you eat standing up; stand-up fight = real fight where people come to blows.

standard 1 ['stændəd] *n.* (a) model with which sth is compared. (b) excellent quality which is set as a target. (c) large flag. (d) lamp s. = tall pole with a light on top for lighting a street. (e) tree/bush grown with a tall trunk.

standard 2 *adj.* (a) normal/usual; s. authors = the classical authors/authors everyone usually reads; s. pronunciation = pronunciation which is generally used by educated speakers. (b) on a tall pole; s. lamp = lamp in a room on a tall pole; s. rose = rose grown with a tall trunk. (c) which is taken as a measure.

standardization [stændədar'zeɪʃn] *n.* setting of a standard; making sure that everything conforms to a standard.

standardize ['stændədaɪz] *v.* to make everything conform to a standard.

stank [stæŋk] *v.* see stink.

stanza ['stænzə] *n.* section of a poem made up of a series of lines.

stapes ['steɪpɪz] *n.* one of the ossicles in the ear.

staphylococcus [stæfɪlə'kɒkəs] *n.* (*pl.*-cocci) type of bacterium which causes food poisoning and infection in the blood.

staple 1 ['steɪpl] *n.* piece of strong bent wire used to hold things in place; small wire clip for attaching papers together by being passed through them and then bent over. **staple 2** *adj.* (a) main product of a country/town. etc. (b) s. diet = main part of what you eat. **staple 3** *v.* to attach with a staple. **stapler** *n.* small instrument for stapling.

star 1 [stɑː] *n.* (a) body in the sky like a very instant sun which shines at night.

(b) the sign of the zodiac which marks your birth; *inf.* thank your lucky stars = consider yourself very lucky. (c) shape with several regular points. (d) asterisk (e) actor/actress who is very well known to the public. **star 3** *v.* (starred) (a) to play an important part (in a film). (b) to have (a famous actor) playing. (c) to mark with a star. **stardom** *n.* being a film star. **starfish** *n.* sea animal shaped like a star. **starless** *adj.* (night) when no stars are visible. **starlet** *n.* young film actress. **starlight** *n.* light from the stars. **starlit** *adj.* (night) lit by the light of the stars. **starry** *adj.* covered with stars. **starry-eyed** *adj.* wildly hopeful. **stars and stripes** *n.* the flag of the USA.

starboard ['stɑːbəd] *n & adj.* right side of a ship when facing forwards.

starch 1 [stɑːtʃ] *n.* (a) white energy giving carbohydrate in bread/potatoes/ rice, etc. (b) white powder mixed with water to make cloth stiff. **starch 2** *v.* to make (cloth) stiff with starch. **starchy** *adj.* (a) full of starch. (b) very formal (manner)

stare 1 ['steə] *v.* fixed look from the eyes. **stare 2** *v.* to look at s.o./sth with a fixed gaze; *inf.* it's staring you in the face = it is very obvious. **staring** *adj.* adv. with a fixed look.

stark 1 [stɑːk] *adj.* (-er, -est) (a) total/ pure (nonsense). (b) bare (landscape/ details). **stark 2** *adv.* completely (naked); s. staring mad = completely mad. **starkly** *adv.* in a stark way. **starkness** *n.* being stark.

starling ['stɑːlɪŋ] *n.* common dark bird with a green sheen to its feathers.

start 1 [stɑːt] *n.* (a) beginning; for a s. = in the first place. (b) to give s. o. two metre's s. = to place them at the beginning of a race two metres in front of you. (c) sudden jump/sudden movement; by fits and starts = at odd moments. **start 2** *v.* (a) to begin. (b) to (cause to) begin to work. (c) to set (sth) going. (d) to jump (in surprise). **starter** *n.* (a) person or animal who starts. (b) person who gives the signal for the start of a race. (c) *inf.* first course in a meal. (d) machine which starts a car engine. **starting** *n.* beginning (of a race, etc.); starting point = point from which everything begins. **start off, start out** *v.* to begin to do/to go. **start up** *v.* to make (an engine, etc.) begin to work.

startle ['stɑːtl] *v.* to make (s.o.) jump in surprise. **startling** *adj.* remarkable/ surprising.

starve [stɑːv] *v.* not to give enough food to (s.o.); to die from lack of food; *inf.* I'm starving = I am very hungry; starved of = not having enough of. **starvation** [stɑːˈveɪʃn] *n.* lack of food.

stash [stæʃ] *v. inf.* to s. away = to store in a safe place.

state 1 [steɪt] *n.* (a) condition; *inf.* in a s. = very angry. (b) government of a nation; state-owned = owned by the country/government (not privately owned). (c) independent country. (d) one of the semi-independent parts of a federal country; great show. **state 2** *adj.* belonging to/run by/given by the government. **state 3** *v.* to say clearly/to claim. **stated** *adj.* fixed/regulated. **State Department** *n. Am.* section of the US government dealing with foreign affairs. **stateless** *adj.* (person) who is not a citizen of any state. **stateliness** *n.* being stately. **stately** *adj.* noble/ dignified; s. home = palace/castle belonging to a lord, etc. **statement** *n.* declaration clearly written or spoken. **state-of-the-art** *adj.* very advanced technically. **stateroom** *n.* large cabin on a ship. **States** *n. pl.inf.* the United States of America. **stateside** *adj. & adv. Am.* in/to the United States of America. **statesman** *n.* (*pl.*-men) person who is or was a member of a government. **statesmanlike** *adj.* like a statesman. **statesmanship** *n.* skill in government of a country.

static 1 ['stætɪk] *adj.* not moving; s. electricity = electricity which stays in one place (in a car/cloth). **static 2** *n.* electrical interference in the air which disturbs a radio signal. **statics** *n. pl.*study of physical forces in equilibrium or of motionless bodies.

station 1 ['steɪʃn] *n.* (a) place where trains stop to pick up and put down passengers; place where coaches/buses begin or end their journeys. (b) central building for some sort of service. (c) radio s./TV s. = broadcasting headquarters with its own frequency. (d) position in society. (e) sheep s. = large sheep farm in Australia. **station 2** *v.* to place (s.o.) at a spot. **stationary** *adj.* not moving. **stationmaster** *n.* man in charge of a railway station. **station wagon** *n.* long car with a part at the back for carrying goods. **stationer** ['steɪʃənə] *n.* person who sells stationery. **stationery** *n.* materials for writing, such as paper/pens/ink.

statistic [stəˈtɪstɪk] *n.* fact given in the form of a figure; statistics = study of facts given in the form of figures, **statistical** *adj.* referring to statistics. **statistically** *adv.* in a statistical way. **statistician** [stætɪsˈtɪʃn] *n.* person who studies/analysis statistics.

statue ['stætjuː] *n.* figure of a person carved in stone/made of metal, etc. **statuary** *n.* collection of statues. **statuesque** [stætjʊˈesk] *adj.* (woman) who is beautiful but large and dignified. **statuette** [stætjʊˈet] *n.* small statue. **stature** ['stætʃə] *n.* (a) height. (b) importance.

status ['steɪtəs] *n.* (no. *pl.*) (a) legal position. (b) importance/position in the eyes of other people; s. symbol = object which may make other people think more highly of you. **status quo** ['steɪtəsˈkwəʊ] *n.* state of things as they are at the moment.

statute ['stætjuːt] *n.* law. **statutory** ['stætjʊtrɪ] *adj.* officially imposed.

staunch 1 [stɔːnʃ] *adj.* (-er, -est) firm (friend). **staunch 2** *v.* (a) to stop (a flow of blood). **staunchly** *adv.* firmly.

stave 1 [steɪv] *n.* (a) curved piece of wood which forms part of a barrel. (b) set of five lines on which music is written. **stave 2** *v.* (a) (stove) to s. in = to batter a hole in a boat/a barrel. (b) to s. off = to hold off/to prevent.

stay 1 [steɪ] *n.* (a) time which you spend in a place. (b) s. of execution = delay ordered by a judge in carrying out a sentence. (c) strong rope which supports. e.g. a mast on a ship. (d) (old) stays = corset. **stay 2** *v.* to stop in a place. **stay-at-home** *n.* person who does not go out much. **stay away** *v.* to keep away/not to come. **stayer** *n.* person who can work hard/horse which can run long distances without tiring. **stay in** *v.* to stay at home. **stay out** *v.*

not to come home. **stay up** v. not to go to bed.

STD short for Subscriber Trunk Dialling.

stead [sted] n. (a) it stood him in good s. = it was very useful to him. (b) in your s. = in place of you. **steadfast** ['stedfɑːst] adj. firm/constant.

steadfastly adv. firmly/constantly.

steady 1 ['stedɪ] adj. (-ier, -iest) (a) firm/not wobbling. (b) continuing regularly. (c) (person) who is not easily upset. **steady 2** n. inf. boyfriend/girl friend with whom you go out regularly. **steady 3** inter. s. on! = be careful. **steady 4** v. to make/to keep firm. **steadily** adv. (a) firmly. (b) regularly/continuously. **steadiness** n. being steady.

steak [steɪk] n. (a) thick slice of beef cut from best part of the animal. (b) thick slice of fish. **steakhouse** n. restaurant serving steak and other grilled food.

steal [stiːl] v. (stole; stolen) (a) to take (sth which does not belong to you). (b) to s. glance at = to look at quickly and secretly. (c) to s. a march on s.o. = to do sth stealthily before s.o. can do it. (d) to creep very quietly (into).

stealth [stelθ] n. by s. = in a secret way/without anyone knowing.

stealthily adv. in a stealthy way. **stealthiness** n. being stealthy. **stealthy** adj. (-ier, -iest) without anyone knowing or seeing.

steam 1 [stiːm] n. (a) vapour which comes off hot water/from warm breath; s. engine = engine which runs on steam pressure; inf. s. radio = old-fashioned radio (as opposed to television). (b) in the days of s. = when railways used steam locomotives. (c) inf. to let off s. = (i) to use up your excess energy; (ii) to explode with anger. **steam 2** v. (a) to cook by steAm. (b) to send out steAm. (c) to move by steam power. (d) (of window) to s. up = to be covered by a mist; inf. to get steamed up about = to get very annoyed. **steamboat** n. boat powered by steAm. **steamer** n. (a) large passenger ship (powered by steam). (b) type of pan with holes in the bottom which is placed over boiling water for steaming vegetables/puddings.

steamroller n. vehicle with a very heavy roller for flattering newly laid road surfaces. **steamship** n. large passenger ship (powered by steam). **steamy** adj. full of steam.

steatite ['stɪətaɪt] n. soft grey stone which can be carved.

steed [stiːd] n. (in literature) horse.

steel 1 [stiːl] n. (a) hard flexible metal made from iron and carbon; s. band = West Indian band which plays music on steel drums of varying sizes. (b) bar of rough steel for sharpening knives. **steel 2** v. to s. yourself to do sth = to get up enough courage to do sth. **steeliness** n. being steely. **steel wool** n. very fine steel wire used in wads for cleaning metal. **steelworks** n. factory which produces steel. **steely** adj. sharp/hard like steel.

steep 1 [stiːp] adj. (-er, -est) (a) which rises or falls sharply. (b) inf. excessive. **steep 2** v. to soak in a liquid for a long time. **steepen** v. to become steeper. **steeply** adv. (rising) sharply. **steepness** n. being steep.

steeple ['stiːpl] n. church tower with the top rising to a point. **steeplechase** n. race run across open country, over fences, hedges, etc.; race on a track over hurdles. **steeplechaser** n. person/horse that runs in a steeplechase. **steeplejack** n. person who climbs towers/factory chimneys, etc., to do repairs.

steer 1 ['stɪə] n. young bull raised for meat. **steer 2** n. to guide/to make (a vehicle) go in a certain direction; to s. clear of = to avoid. **steerage** n. (a) act of steering. (b) cheapest berths in a passenger ship. **steering** n. mechanism in a car which steers it; s. wheel = wheel which is turned by the driver to alter the direction of a car; s. column = metal tube to which the steering wheel is attached; s. committee = small committee which does detailed work on the agenda for a large committee meeting. **steersman** n. (pl.-men) who steers a ship.

stele [stiːl] n. carved slab of stone, placed upright.

stellar ['stelə] adj. referring to stars.

stem 1 [stem] n. (a) long stalk on which flowers and leaves grow. (b) thin part of a wine glass/of a tobacco pipe. (c) basic part of a word to which endings or prefixes are added. (d) from s. to stern = from the bows to the stern of a boat.

stem 2 v. (stemmed) (a) to result from. (b) to stop/to prevent (a flow, etc.).

stench [stentʃ] n. (a) strong unpleasant smell.

stencil 1 ['stensl] n. (a) sheet of cardboard or metal with a pattern cut out of it, so that if it is placed on a surface and colour is passed over it, the pattern will appear on the surface; pattern/ letters/numbers, etc., which are painted in this way. (b) sheet of waxed paper used for making large numbers of copies.

stencil 2 v. (stencilled) (a) to mark with a stencil. (b) to make a copy of (a document) using a stencil.

stengun ['stengʌn] n. small machine gun.

stenographer [stə'nɒgrəfə] n. person who can write down fast in shorthand.

stenography [stə'nɒgrəfɪ] n. shorthand.

stenosis [sten'əʊsɪs] n. condition where an artery becomes narrow.

stentorian [sten'tɔːrɪən] adj. (formal) very loud (voice).

step 1 [step] n. (a) single movement of the foot when walking/running; distance covered by this movement; s. by s. = little by little. (b) sound made by moving a foot forward. (c) regular movement of the feet; keep in s. = move at the same pace as everyone else; out of s. = not moving at the same pace as everyone else; out of s. = not moving at the same pace as everyone else. (d) action. (e) stair (on a staircase); flat rung (on a ladder); (a pair of) steps = ladder with two parts hinged at the top, which can stand solidly without learning against anything. **step 2** v. (stepped) to make a movement with a foot; to s. on the brakes = to push the brake pedal hard. **step in** v. to involve yourself/to interfere.

stepladder n. pair of steps.

stepping-stone n. one of a series of stones in a stream which allow you to cross it, **step up** v. to increase.

step- [step] prefix showing a family relationship which is through a parent who has remarried. **stepbrother** n. male child of your stepfather or step

mother. **stepdaughter** n. daughter of your wife/husband by another marriage. **stepfather** n. husband of your mother who is not your father. stepmother, n. wife of your father, who is not your mother. **stepsister** n. female child of your stepfather or stepmother. **stepson** n. son of your wife/husband by another marriage.

steppe [step] n. wide grass-covered plain in Russia and Asia.

stereo- ['sterɪəʊ] prefix referring to sth which has two dimensions. **stereo** ['sterɪəʊ] n. & adj. (machine) which reproduces sound through two different channels and loudspeakers.

stereophonic [sterɪə'fɒnɪk] adj. referring to sound which comes from two places at once.

stereoscope ['sterɪʊskəʊp] n. apparatus which shows a picture which appears to have depth and be three dimensional.

stereoscopic [sterɪə'skɒpɪk] adj. referring to seeing in three dimensions; s. vision = ability to see the same object with both eyes, and so judge distance.

stereotype ['sterɪətaɪp] n. pattern for certain types of person. **stereotyped** adj. fitting certain patterns.

sterile ['steraɪl] adj. (a) not capable of bearing fruit/children. (b) so clean that no germs/bacteria can grow. **sterility** [ste'rɪlɪtɪ] n. inability to grow fruit/to produce children or ideas. **sterilization** [sterɪlaɪzeɪʃn] n. action of sterilizing. **sterilize** ['sterɪlaɪz] v. (a) to make (s.o.) incapable of producing children. (b) to make so clean that bacteria/ germs cannot grow. **sterilizer** n. apparatus for sterilizing.

sterling 1 ['stɜːlɪŋ] adj. of a certain standard/of good quality; s. sliver = sliver of a certain high purity. **sterling 2** n. standard measure of British currency.

stern 1 [stɜːn] adj. (-er, -est) harsh/ strict. **stern 2** n. rear part of a ship. **sternly** adv. in a stern way. **sternness** n. being stern. **sternwheeler** n. large pleasure ship (on American rivers) with a paddle wheel at the stern.

sternum ['stɜːnəm] n. central bone on the chest. **sternal** adj. referring to the sternum. **steroid** ['stɪərɔɪd] n. one of a group of natural substances in plants and animals, including hormones.

stertorous ['stɜːtərəs] *adj.* making a snoring sound.

stet [stet] *v.* word showing that a correction should not be made.

stethoscope ['steθəskəʊp] *n.* doctor's instrument for listening to a patient's chest.

stetson ['stetsən] *n.* tall cowboy hat with a wide brim.

stevedore ['stiːvədɔː] *n.* person who works at a port, unloading or loading ships.

stew 1 [stjuː] *n.* dish of meat and vegetables cooked together for a long time; *inf.* in as = in an awkward situation. **stew 2** *v.* to cook for a long time in liquid. **stewed** *adj. Sl.* drunk

steward ['stjʊəd] *n.* (a) man who serves meals or drinks on a ship/aircraft in a club. (b) person who organizes a meeting, person who looks after a farm or estate for the owner. (c) shop. s = elected union representative.

stewardess *n.* woman who looks after passengers on a ship or aircraft.

stick 1 [stɪk] *n.* Piece of wood; strong piece of wood with a handle used as a support when walking; hockey = stick with a curved end, used in playing hockey (b) long piece. **stick 2** *v.* (stuck) (a) to jab or push (sth sharp) into sth (b) to glue or attach (c) to stay close/ to keep (to) (d) to be fixed not be able to move (e) *inf.* to bear/to accept. **stick at** *v.* (a) to stick at nothing = to be ruthless. (b) to stay at. **sticker** *n.* small piece of paper or plastic which you can stick on a surface as a decoration or advertisement. **stickily** *adv.* in a sticky way. **stickiness** *n.* state of being sticky. **sticking plaster** *n.* strip of cloth which can be stuck to the skin to cover a wound. **stick-in-the-mud** *n. inf.* person who will not accept new ideas. **stick-on** *adj.* (label)which sticks on to a surface. **stick out** *v.* (a) to push out to be further out than usual(b) to be easily seen. **stick up** *v.* (a)to put your hands up(a notice etc.) s. them up = put your hands up (to show you surrender)(b) *inf.* to s. up for s.o = to defend s.o. **sticky** *adj.* (-ier, -iest)(a) covered with glue which sticks easily (b)

inf. difficult/awkward; he came to a s. end = he died/was put in prison/was ruined etc. s. wicket = difficult situation.

stickleback ['stɪklbæk] *n.* common small freshwater fish with spines along its back.

stickler ['stɪklə] *n.* (for) person who attaches great importance to sth.

stiff [stɪf] *adj.* (a) which cannot be bent or moved easily; (brush) with hard bristles; starched (collar); bored s. = very bored. (b) solid/thick (paste). (c) strong (breeze). (d) difficult/hard (examination, penalty). (e) (whisky, etc.) with not much water added. (f) high (price). (g) unfriendly/unsociable. **stiffen** *v.* (a) to become/make stiff. (b) to become cautious/unfriendly. (c) (of wind) become stronger. (d) to make (resistance) stronger. **stiffener** *n.* thing which stiffens. **stiffly** *adv.* in a stiff way. **stiff-necked** *adj.* obstinate. **stiffness** *n.* being stiff.

stifle ['staɪfl] *v.* (a) to prevent (s.o.) from breathing. (b) to hold back (a yawn, etc.). **stifling** *adj.* suffocating; extremely hot.

stigma ['stɪgmə] *n.* (a) disgrace; feeling of shame. (b) top of the centre of a flower which receives pollen to make seeds. **stigmatize** ['stɪgmətaɪz] *v.* to give a bad name to (sth).

stile [staɪl] *n.* steps which allow people, but not animals, to get over a wall or fence.

stiletto [stɪ'letəʊ] *n.* (a) long thin dagger. (b) s. heels = high thin heels on women's shoes.

still 1 [stɪl] *n.* (a) apparatus for producing alcohol. (b) one picture from a moving film. **still 2** *adj.* calm/ motionless; (lemonade, etc.) which is not fizzy; s. life = picture of flowers or objects, not people or animals. **still 3** *adv.* (a) up until this/that moment. (b) even. (c) however. **stillbirth** *n.* birth of a dead child. **stillborn** *adj.* (child) which is born dead; (idea) which is never put into practice. **stillness** *n.* calm. **stillroom** *n.* pantry/store in a large house.

stilts [stɪlts] *n. pl.* poles to raise (sth) above the ground; pair of stilts = two poles with foot rests to enable you to walk high in the air. **stilted** *adj.* (style of writing) which is very formal/not natural.

stimulate ['stɪmjʊleɪt] v. to excite/to encourage; to make more active.

stimulant n. drug which makes you more active. **stimulation** [stɪmjʊ'leɪʃn] n. being stimulated. **stimulus** n. (pl.[-laɪ]) thing that encourages further activity.

sting 1 [stɪŋ] n. (a) tiny needle in the tail of an insect/leaf of a plant which injects poison. (b) wound made by an insect or plant. (c) burning feeling. **sting 2** v. (stung[stʌŋ]) (a) to wound with a sting. (b) to have a burning feeling. (c) to hurt (s.o.) so that he reacts. (d) inf. to ask (s.o.) for money. **stinging nettle** n. common wild plant which causes a rash. **stingray** n. large flat fish with a sting in its tail.

stingy ['stɪndʒɪ] inf. mean; not free with money. **stinginess** n. meanness.

stink 1 [stɪŋk] n. unpleasant smell; inf. to create a s. = to object vigorously. **stink 2** v. (stank; stunk) to make an unpleasant smell.

stint 1 [stɪnt] n. (a) amount of work. (b) without s. = in large quantities/with no restriction. **stint 2** v. to give (s.o.) a very small amount.

stipend ['staɪpend] n. salary of a priest or a magistrate. **stipendiary** [staɪ'pendjərɪ] adj. (magistrate) who is paid.

stipple ['stɪpl] v. to colour with small dots.

stipulate ['stɪpjʊleɪt] v. to insist; to make a condition. **stipulation** [stɪpjʊ'leɪʃn] n. condition (in a contract).

stir 1 [stɜː] n. (a) mixing up a liquid. (b) fuss/agitation. **stir 2** v. (stirred) (a) to mix up (a liquid). (b) to cause fuss/agitation. (c) to move. **stirring** adj. exciting. **stir up** v. to cause (trouble).

stirrup ['stɪrəp] n. metal loop hanging from the saddle into which the rider puts his foot; s. cup = drink taken on horseback before setting off on a ride.

stitch 1 [stɪtʃ] n. (pl.-es) (a) small loop of cotton or wool made with a needle in sewing or knitting; inf. I haven't got a s. to wear = I have no suitable clothes. (b) small loop of thread used by a surgeon to attach a wound together. (c) sharp pain

in the side of the body which comes after you have been running; inf. in stitches = laughing uproariously. **stitch 2** v. to attach with a needle and thread.

stoat [stəʊt] n. small brown flesh-eating animal whose fur turns white in winter.

stock 1 [stɒk] n. (a) plant on which other plants are grafted. (b) race/family. (c) handle of a rifle. (d) stocks = yard where ships are built; on the stocks = being worked on. (e) stocks = wooden frame with holes for the feet, in which criminals were placed. (f) quantity of things for use; quantities of goods for sale; to take s. = (i) to count what you have in stock; (ii) to assess a situation. (g) farm animals; fat s. = animals reared for meat. (h) liquid made from building bones, etc,. in water, used as a base for soups and sauces. (i) common scented garden flower. (j) capital invested in a business; government stocks = loans made to the state; s. market = buying and selling of shares; s. exchange = building in which shares are bought and sold. (k) reputation (of s.o.). **stock 2** v. (a) to keep (goods) for sale. (b) to provide with goods/animals/plants, etc. **stock 3** adj. usual; s. size = normal size; s. argument = one which is frequently used.

stockbreeder n. farmer who specializes in breeding animals.

stockbreeding n. breeding animals.

stockbroker n. agent who buys shares on the stock exchange. **stockcar** n. car adapted for brutal racing. **stockholder** n. owner of government stocks.

stockiness n. being stocky. **stock-in-trade** n. things needed to carry on a business; habitual way of acting.

stockist n. person/shop which stocks a certain brand of goods. **stockjobber** n. dealer in shares on the stock exchange. **stockman** n. man who looks after farm animals. **stockpile 1** n. supplies kept in reserve (in case of an emergency). **stockpile 2** v. to collect supplies in case of emergency. **stockpot** n. large pot for making soup.

stockroom n. room where stocks are kept. **stock-still** adv. without moving. **stocktaking** n. counting of goods in stock at the end of a period. **stock up with** v. to buy supplies for use in the future. **stocky** adj. short and strong.

stockyard n. place where animals are kept before they are slaughtered or shipped.

stockade [stɒ'keɪd] n. strong fence made of thick upright poles.

stockinet [stɒki'net] n. elastic material.

stocking ['stɒkɪŋ] n. long close-fitting piece of clothing to cover your leg and foot; in his s. (also stockinged) feet = without his shoes on.

stodge [stɒdʒ] n. heavy filling food (such as puddings). **stodgy** adj. heavy (food); dull (book).

stoep [stuːp] n. (in South Africa) verandah.

stoic ['stəʊɪk] n. person who accepts problems or pain without complaining. **stoical** adj. accepting problems or pain without complaining. **stoically** adv. in a stoical way. **stoicism** ['stəʊɪsɪzəm] n. being stoical.

stoke [stəʊk] v. to put fuel in (a furnace). **stoker** n. person who stokes a furnace; seaman who looks after the engines.

stole 1 [stəʊl] n. wide light scarf worn around the shoulders. **stole 2** v. see steal. **stolen** ['stəʊlən] v. see steal.

stolid ['stɒlɪd] adj. slow and heavy; not excitable. **stolidity** [stɒ'lɪdɪtɪ] n. being stolid. **stolidly** adv. in a stolid way.

stoma ['stəʊmə] n. pore in a plant.

stomach 1 ['stʌmək] n. (a) bag inside the body in which food is digested; s. ache = pain in the stomach. (b) part of the body lower than the chest. (c) desire/courage. **stomach 2** v. to put up with/to tolerate.

stomp [stɒmp] v. to stamp/to walk with a heavy tread.

stone 1 [stəʊn] n. (a) small piece of rock. (b) piece of rock which has been cut for building, etc.; Stone Age = prehistoric period when men made tools out of stone; precious s. = rate mineral which is very valuable. (c) hard seed piece of mineral which forms inside the body (in the kidneys, etc.) and causes pain. (e) measure of weight (= 14 pounds or 6.35 kilograms). **stone 2** adv. completely (deaf); Am. s. broke = stony broke. **stone 3** v. (a) to s. (s.o.) to death = to throw stones at (s.o.) and kill him. (b) to take the stones out of

(fruit). **stonechat** n. small dark bird with a red breast. **stonecrop** n. type of plant which grows among stones. **stoned** adj. Sl.(a) drunk. (b) drugged. **stonemason** n. person who cuts and builds with stone. **stonewall** v. to speak for a long time without answering the question. **stoneware** n. pottery made of rough clay and fired at high temperatures. **stonework** n. walls, etc., made of stone. **stonily** adv. with no feeling. **stony** adj. (a) covered with stones. (b) hard; with no feeling. (c) inf. s. broke = with no money.

stood [stʊd] v. see stand.

stooge 1 [stuːdʒ] n. inf. (a) person who does what he is told to do. (b) the stupid one of a pair of comedians. **stooge 2** v. inf. to s. about = to wander about waiting to be told what to do.

stook [stuːk] n. group of sheaves of corn. leaning together.

stool [stuːl] n. (a) seat with no back; to fall between two stools = (i) to miss each of two targets; (ii) not to take up either of two opportunities. (b) lump of waste matter passed from the bowels.

stoolpigeon n. criminal who helps the police to trap another criminal.

stoop 1 [stuːp] n. bending forward. **stoop 2** v. (a) to bend forward. (b) he stoops = he has a permanently bent back. (c) to s. to do sth = to allow yourself to do sth which you feel is beneath you.

stop 1 [stɒp] n. (a) act of not moving/not doing sth. (b) place where buses. etc., usually stops to pick up or put down passengers. (c) full s. = round dot (.) showing the end of a sentence. (d) block which prevents a door, etc., closing. (e) knob on an organ which switches on a different set of pipes; set of pipes on an organ which produce a particular sound; to pull out all the stops = to do everything possible. **stop 2** v. (stopped) (a) to make (sth which is moving) come to a halt; to come to a halt. (b) to make (sth) cease working; to cease working/doing sth. (c) to stay in a place. (d) to block; to fill (a gap). (e) to cut off (supply); to prevent (money) being paid; to s. a cheque = to tell the bank not to pay a cheque which you have written: to s. s.o.'s wages = not to pay s.o. **stop by** v. inf. to visit s.o. for a short time. **stopcock** *n.* tap which stops the supply of water. **stop down** *v.* to make the aperture of a lens smaller. **stopgap** *n. & adj.* thing which is used temporarily while waiting for sth more suitable to turn up. **stop off** *v.* to make a stop on a long journey. **stop over** *v.* to make an overnight stop on a long journey. **stopover** *n.* overnight stop on a long journey. **stoppage** *n.* action of stopping/blocking. **stopper** *n.* piece of glass/cork, etc., which fits the mouth of a jar to close it. **stop press** *n. & adj.* last piece of new added to a newspaper before it is printed. **stop watch** *n.* watch which can be started and stopped by pressing a button, used for timing races.

store 1 [stɔː] *n.* (a) supply of food, etc., kept for later use; to set great s. by sth = think that sth is very important. **store 2** *v.* (a) to keep (sth) for future use. (b) to put (sth) in a warehouse. **storage** *n.* (a) act of keeping/putting in store; night s. heater = electric heater where the electricity warms bricks which then store the heat and release it gradually. (b) memory, the part of a computer where data is stored. **storehouse** *n.* place where things are stored. **storekeeper, storeman** *n.* shopkeeper. **storeroom** *n.* room where things are stored.

storey, *Am.* **story** ['stɔːrɪ] *n.* whole floor in a building. **storeyed** *adj.* with several storeys.

stork [stɔːk] *n.* large, *usu.* white, bird with long legs and long beak.

storm 1 [stɔːm] *n.* (a) period of bad weather with wind; s. in a teacup = lot of fuss for no good reason. (b) s. of applause = loud burst of clapping and cheering. (c) to take a town by s. = (i) to attack a town suddenly and capture it; (ii) to become suddenly very popular in a town; s. troops = soldiers who are specially trained to attack and capture. **storm 2** *v.* (a) to be violently angry. (b) to attack and capture. stormy, adj. referring to a storm; like a storm.

story ['stɔːrɪ] *n.* (a) tale of what has happened. (b) piece of fiction. (c) *inf.* lie. (d) *Am.* storey. **storyline** *n.* plot of a novel/film, etc. **storyteller** *n.* (a) person who tells a story. (b) *inf.* person who tells lies.

stoup [stuːp] *n.* bowl for holy water in a church.

stout 1 [staʊt] *adj.* (a) fat. (b) strong/thick (material). (c) brave. **stout 2** *n.* strong dark beer. **stout-hearted** *adj.* brave. **stoutly** *adv.* (a) vigorously. (b) solidly/strongly. **stoutness** *n.* being stout.

stove [stəʊv] *n.* machine for heating or cooking. **stovepipe** *n.* metal chimney which carries the smoke from a stove.

stow [stəʊ] *v.* to put away; to pack. **stow away** *v.* (a) to pack. (b) to travel secretly on a ship/aircraft without paying the fare. **stowaway** *n.* person who stows away.

strabismus [strə'bɪzməs] *n.* squint.

straddle ['strædl] *v.* to stand with legs apart and your feet on either side of (sth).

strafe [strɑːf] *v.* to attack (sth) by shooting at it from a low-flying plane.

straggle ['strægl] *v.* to hang/to walk in an untidy way. **straggler** *n.* person who walks well behind the main group of people. **straggling, straggly** *adj.* which grows untidily.

straight 1 [streɪt] *adj.* (a) not curved; s. hair = not curly. (b) honest/frank. (c) simple/not complicated; (whisky, etc.) with nothing added; s. fight = election where there are only two candidates. (d) tidy; not crooked. (e) serious (actor/play); to keep a s. face = to stop yourself smiling. (f) *Sl.* not homosexual. **straight 2** *n.* the s. = part of a racecourse (usu. near the finish) which is not curved.

straight 3 *adv.* (a) in a straight line. (b) immediately. (c) directly. (d) honestly; *inf.* to go s. = to lead an honest life after having been a criminal. **straight away** *adv.* immediately/at once. **straighten** *v.* to make/to become straight. **straightforward** *adj.* frank/honest. **straightforwardly** *adv.* in an honest way. **straightness** *n.* being straight. **straight off** *adv.* at once. **straight out** *adv.* directly.

strain 1 [streɪn] *n.* (a) act of pulling tight; tension. (b) hurt caused by pulling a muscle too hard. (c) stress; mental/physical tension. (d) way of speaking. (e) breed. (f) quality or defect which is inherited. (g) tune. **strain 2** *v.* (a) to pull/to work too hard. (b) to make a great effort (to). (c) to put too much stress on (credulity/patience). (d) to pass (a liquid) through a sieve to separate it from solids. **strained** *adj.* (a) which has been pulled/worked too hard. (b) tense/ unfriendly. **strainer** *n.* sieve for separating liquids from solids.

straits [streɪts] *n. pl.* (a) narrow piece of sea water between two masses of land. (b) money difficulties. **straitened** *adj.* in s. circumstances = not having enough money to live on. **straitjacket** *n.* (a) strong coat whose sleeves are tied behind the back to prevent a mad person from attacking people. (b) thing which prevents you from acting freely.

straitlaced *adj.* with very strict ideas about correct moral behaviour.

strake [streɪk] *n.* plank which runs along a ship lengthwise.

strand 1 [strænd] *n.* (a) long piece of hair/thread, etc. (b) (formal) shore.

strand 2 *v.* to leave (your ship) on the shore. **stranded** *adj.* alone and helpless.

strange [streɪnʒ] *adj.* (a) odd/bizarre. (b) which you have never seen/heard before. **strangely** *adv.* oddly/curiously. **strangeness** *n.* being strange.

stranger *n.* person whom you do not know; you're quite a s. = I haven't seen you for a long time; he is a s. to the town = he does not know it well.

strangle ['stæŋgl] *v.* to kill (s.o.) by pressing on his throat so that he cannot breath; to crush (initiative/a plan). **stranglehold** *n.* control which prevents you doing what you want to do. **strangler** *n.* person who strangles. **strangulation** [stræŋgjʊ'leɪʃn] *n.* being strangled.

strap 1 [stræp] *n.* long flat piece of leather or material for attaching sth.

strap 2 *v.* (strapped) (a) to attach with a strap. (b) to wrap a bandage tightly round a wound. (c) to hit (s.o.) with a strap. **strap-hanging** *n.* travelling standing in a crowded bus/train, holding on to a strap attached to the roof.

strapless *adj.* with no straps.

strapping *adj.* big/strong (young man/ girl).

strata ['strɑːtə] *n.* see stratum.

stratagem ['strætədʒəm] *n.* clever plan to trick an enemy.

strategic, strategical [strə'tiːdʒɪk(l)] *adj.* referring to strategy (position) which gives an advantage over the enemy. **strategically** *adv.* according to strategy. **strategist** ['strætədʒɪst] *n.* officer who plans military attacks.

strategy ['strætədʒɪ] *n.* planning of war/of an action.

stratify ['strætɪfaɪ] *v.* to form layers; to be arranged in layers. **stratification** [strætɪfɪ'keɪʃn] *n.* forming layers; arranging in layers.

stratosphere ['strætəsfɪə] *n.* upper layer of the earth's atmosphere.

stratum ['strɑːtəm] *n.* layer (esp. rock); social strata = levels of society.

stratus ['stɑːtəs] *n.* s. clouds = low flat clouds.

straw [strɔː] *n.* (a) dry stalks of plants like corn. (b) one single dry stalk of a plant; thin plastic tube for sucking liquid; *inf.* that's the last s. = that is all I can stand/as much as I can take; s. poll = random questioning to test the general opinion of the public/of a group.

strawberry *n.* common red summer fruit growing on low plants; s. mark = red mark on the skin, which is present from birth.

stray 1 [streɪ] *adj. & n.* (animal, etc.) which is wandering away from home.

stray 2 *adj.* (bullet, etc.) wandering off course. **stray 3** *v.* to wander.

streak 1 [striːk] *n.* (a) band/line (of colour); flash (of light). (b) quality of character. **streak 2** *v.* (a) to rush. (b) *inf.* to run about naked in public.

streaker *n. inf.* person who runs about naked in public. **streaky** *adj.* (a) with smudges of colour of dirt. (b) (bacon) with fat and lean streaks.

stream 1 [striːm] *n.* (a) small flow of water; small river. (b) continuous flow. (c) current. (d) to come on s. = to start to be produced/to function. (e) (in school) group of children selected for a certain class. **stream 2** *v.* (a) to flow (b) (in school) to put (children) into a streAm.

streamer *n.* long thin flag; long paper or ribbon used as a decoration.

streaming *adj.* dripping (wet).

streamline *v.* (a) to design (a car/ plane/boat, etc.) so that it can move easily through water or air. (b) to make more efficient; to modernize.

street [stri:t] *n.* road in a town, with houses or shops on each side; the man in the s. = the ordinary citizen; at s. level = on the same level as the street; *inf.* streets ahead = much more advanced *inf.* right up my s. = I am very interested in/ sth I know a lot about. **streetcar** *n.* *Am.* tram.

strength [strenθ] *n.* (a) being strong. (b) numbers; in full s. = all together. (c) number of people employed. (d) on the s. of = because of. **strengthen** *v.* to make stronger.

strenuous ['strenjʊəs] *adj.* energetic. **strenuously** *adv.* vigorously. **strenuousness** *n.* being strenuous.

streptococcus [streptə'kɒkəs] *n.* (*pl.*- cocci[-kɒkaɪ]) bacterium which causes infections, such as a sore throat.

streptomycin [streptə'maɪsɪn] *n.* type of antibiotic.

stress 1 [stres] *n.* (a) force; pressure. (b) nervous strain. (c) emphasis. **stress 2** *v.* to emphasize; to put stress on (sth).

stretch 1 [stretʃ] *n.* (a) act of being pulled out. (b) act of putting out your arms and legs as far as they will go. (c) long piece (of road); long period (of time); *Sl.* time spent in prison. **stretch 2** *v.* (a) to pull out (sth elastic)/(b) to pull (sth) out too far. (c) to be able to be pulled out. (d) to put out your arms or legs as far as they will go. (e) to s. to = to be enough for. (f) to lie for a great distance. (g) to relax (a rule). **stretcher** *n.* (a) portable bed with handles at each end for carrying sick people; s. bearer = person who lifts one end of a stretcher. (b) thing which stretches.

strew [stru:] *v.* (strewn) to scatter.

striated [straɪ'eɪtɪd] *adj.* marked with parallel furrows. **striation** *n.* furrow/ ridge parallel to several others.

stricken ['strɪkn] *adj.* hit/struck by disease/emotion, etc.

strict [strɪkt] *adj.* (a) exact (meaning). (b) (orders) which must be obeyed. (c) severe/harsh; (person) who insists that rules are obeyed. **strictly** *adv.* in a strict way. **strictness** *n.* being strict. **stricture** ['strɪktʃə] *n.* criticism/words of blame.

stride 1 [straɪd] *n.* long step with your legs. **stride 2** *v.* (strode[strolled]) to take long steps. **strident** ['straɪdənt]

adj. unpleasantly loud harsh high (sound). **stridency** *n.* being strident. **stridently** *adv.* in a strident way.

strife [straɪf] *n.* fighting; trouble between people.

strike 1 [straɪk] *n.* (a) stopping of work by workers (because of disagreement with management). (b) air s. = rapid attack from the air. (c) oil s. = discovery of oil. **strike 2** *v.* (struck[strʌk]) (a) to hit. (b) to light (a match) to make (a coin/a medal); to make/to agree (a bargain). (c) to be struck down with flu = to have a sudden attack of flu. (d) to make and impression on (s.o.) (e) to discover (oil, etc.). (f) to lower (a flag); to pack up (a tent). (g) to make (a note) sound in music; (of clock) to ring (the hour). (h) to go in a certain direction. (i) to stop working because of disagreement or in protest. **strikebound** *adj.* not able to move because of a strike.

strikebreaker *n.* worker who continues to work when his colleagues are on strike. **strike off** *v.* to cross off (a list). **strike out** *v.* (a) (for) to swim hard towards. (b) to cross off (a list). **strike pay** *n.* wages paid to striking workers by their union. **striker** *n.* (a) person who goes on strike. (b) football player whose job is to score goals. **strike up** *v.* (a) to start playing a piece of music, (b) to s. up an acquaintance with s.o. = to start getting to know s.o. **striking** *adj.* remarkable. **strikingly** *adv.* remarkably.

string 1 [strɪŋ] *n.* (a) thin rope for tying things together; *inf.* strings = hidden conditions; *inf.* to pull strings = to try to obtain sth through influential friends. (b) series of things tied together. (c) thin wire in a musical instrument; the strings = part of an orchestra playing stringed instruments. (d) tough thread (in meat/ vegetables). **string 2** *v.* (strung[ ]strHE]) (a) to tie together in a series. (b) to put a string in (a musical instrument). (c) highly strung = excitable; very nervous. **string along** *v.* (a) to go along in a line behind s.o. (b) to make (s.o.) promises to get him to co-operate. **string bag** *n.* shopping bag made of a net of knotted string. **string bean** *n.* *Am.* runner bean. **string course** *n.* horizontal line of projecting bricks.

stringed adj. (musical instrument) with strings. **string out** v. to put (things) in a long line. **string up** v. to hang up with a string; inf. to hang (s.o.). **string vest** n. vest made of cotton woven like a net. **stringy** adj. (meat/vegetables) with tough threads.

stringent ['strɪndʒənt] adj. strict/severe. **stringency** n. being stringent. **stringently** adv. in a stringent way.

strip 1 [strɪp] n. long narrow piece; s. cartoon/comic s. = cartoon story made of a series of small drawings side by side.

strip 2 v. (stripped) (a) to make naked; to take off your clothes. (b) to remove (sth). **strip down** v. to take (an engine) to pieces. **strip lighting** n. lighting using long round tubes. **stripper** n. (a) liquid for removing old paint; sharp tool for stripping off old paint or old wallpaper. (b) woman who performs a striptease. **striptease** n. entertainment where s.o. takes their clothes off piece by piece.

stripe [straɪp] n. (a) long strip of colour. (b) strip of coloured cloth sewn to a uniform to show a certain rank in the army. **striped** adj. with stripes. **stripy** adj. covered with many stripes.

stripling ['strɪplɪŋ] n. very young man.

strive [straɪv] v. (strove[strəʊv]) has striven) to try very hard (to).

strobe [strəʊb] n. light which flashes on and off very rapidly. **stroboscope** n. illuminated figures on a turntable. which enable you to tell if it is turning at the correct speed; device which makes lights flash on and off (on a dance floor).

strode [strəʊd] v. see stride.

stroke 1 [strəʊk] n. (a) gentle touch. (b) line made by a pen/brush, etc.; oblique s. = printing sign (/) used to show an alternative. (c) blow. (d) illness/paralysis caused by damage to part of the brain. (e) one movement; s. of luck = piece of luck. (f) particular style of swimming. (g) one ring of a bell. (h) rower seated in the stern who gives the time for all the others in a boat. **stroke 2** v. (a) to run your hands gently over. (b) to set the time for the other rowers in a boat.

stroll 1 [strəʊl] n. short leisurely walk. **stroll 2** v. to walk slowly along. **stroller** n. (a) person who strolls. (b) light pram for babies.

strong 1 [strɒŋ] adj. (a) powerful. (b) large (in numbers). (c) with a powerful smell/noise, etc.; s. drink = alcohol.

strong 2 adv. inf. still going s. = still working well after a long time.

strongbox n. small safe for keeping jewels. **stronghold** n. fortress; place which is difficult to capture. **strongly** adv. powerfully. **strong man** n. powerful man. **strong-minded** adj. with clear fixed ideas. **strong point** n. quality/good characteristic.

strongroom n. room with thick walls and door where a bank keeps money/jewels, etc. **strongwilled** adj. with a strong character.

strontium ['strɒntɪəm] n. (element: Sr) white radioactive metal.

strop 1 [strɒp] n. leather strap for sharpening razors. **strop 2** v. (stropped) to sharpen (a razor) on a strop.

stroppy adj. inf. angry/obstinate.

strove [strəʊv] v. see strive.

struck [strʌk] v. see strike.

structure 1 ['strʌktʃə] n. (a) way in which things are put together. (b) building. **structure 2** v. to arrange in a certain way. **structural** adj. referring to a structure. **structurally** adv. referring to a structure.

struggle 1 ['strʌgl] n. bitter/violent fight. **struggle 2** v. to fight violently.

strum [strʌm] v. (strummed) to play (a piano/guitar) in an informal way.

strung [strʌŋ] v. see string.

strut 1 [strʌt] n. (a) bar of wood, metal, etc., which supports sth. (b) strutting way of walking. **strut 2** v. (strutted) to walk in a proud and important manner.

strychnine ['strɪkniːn] n. bitter poison.

stub 1 [stʌb] n. (a) small piece left after sth has been used. (b) piece of paper left after a cheque or a ticket has been torn out of a book. **stub 2** v. (stubbed) (a) to hurt (your toe) by hitting it against a rock. (b) to put out (a cigarette) by pressing the stub against sth. **stubby** adj. short and fat (fingers).

stubble ['stʌbl] n. (a) short stems left after corn has been cut. (b) short hairs which grow if a man does not shave for several days. **stubbly** adj. covered with short bristles.

stubborn ['stʌbən] adj. obstinate;

(person) who will only do what he wants to do; (thing) which will not do what you want it to do. **stubbornly** *adv.* obstinately. **stubbornness** *n.* being stubborn.

stucco ['stʌkəʊ] *n.* plaster put on walls and painted; plaster used to make moulded decorations in buildings. **stuccoed** *adj.* covered with stucco.

stuck [stʌk] *v.* see stick. **stuck-up** *adj. inf.* supercilious/proud.

stud 1 [stʌd] *n.* (a) nail with a large head; metal marker on a road to show a pedestrian crossing, etc. (b) type of button with two heads for passing through two holes to fasten a shirt. (c) horses which are kept for breeding; (also stud farm) farm where horses are kept for breeding; s. book = register of pedigree horses, etc. **stud 2** *v.* (studded) to cover with nails. **studded** *adj.* covered (with nails/stars, etc.)

student ['stjuːdənt] *n.* person who is studying at college/university; *Am.* person studying at high school.

studio ['stjuːdɪəʊ] *n.* (a) place where artists paint/where photographers take photographs. (b) place where films/broadcasts/recordings are made. (c) very small flat.

studious ['stjuːdɪəs] *adj.* (a) showing careful study. (b) careful. **studiously** *adv.* carefully. **studiousness** *n.* being studious.

study 1 ['stʌdɪ] *n.* (a) act of examining sth carefully to learn more about it; course at university, etc. (b) room in which s.o. works/studies. (c) piece of music which aims to improve the players technique; work of art in which new ideas are practised; her face was a s. = it was instructive/amusing to watch her expression. **study 2** *v.* (a) to examine (sth) in detail to learn more about it. (b) to follow a course at college or university. **studied** *adj.* done very carefully; done on purpose.

stuff 1 [stʌf] *n.* (a) material of which sth is made. (b) *inf.* equipment/belongings; do your s. = do what you have to do; that's the s. = that's it's and nonsense! = rubbish! (c) cloth. **stuff 2** *v.* (a) to fill (sth) very full. (b) to block (a hole). (c) to fill the skin of (a dead animal) with material to make it look

lifelike. (d) to put stuffing into (a chicken, etc.); *Sl.* you can s. it = I don't want to have anything to do with your plan; *Sl.* get stuffed! stop bothering me!

stuffing *n.* (a) savoury mixture put inside a chicken, etc., before cooking. (b) material used to fill cushions/chair seats, etc. **stuffy** ['stʌfɪ] *adj.* (a) (room) full of bad air from lack of ventilation. (b) prudish; old-fashioned. **stuffily** *adv.* in a stuffy way. **stuffiness** *n.* being stuffy.

stultify ['stʌltɪfaɪ] *v.* (formal) to make (s.o.) stupid. **stultification** [stʌltɪfɪ'keɪʃn] *n.* act of stultifying.

stumble 1 ['stʌmbl] *n.* tripping over; awkward step. **stumble 2** *v.* (a) to trip over sth; to walk awkwardly. (b) to s. across = to find by chance. **stumbling block** *n.* thing which prevents you doing sth.

stump 1 [stʌmp] *n.* (a) short piece left after sth has been finished or cut down. (b) one of the three sticks placed in the ground as a target in cricket; stumps were drawn = the game of cricket came to an end (temporarily). **stump 2** *v.* (a) to s. along = to walk along heavily. (b) *inf.* to puzzle. (c) (in cricket) to put (a batsman) out by touching the stumps with the ball when he is not in the hitting area. **stump up** *v. inf.* to pay up. **stumpy** *adj. inf.* short and squat.

stun [stʌn] *v.* to knock out; to shock completely. **stunning** *adj.* extraordinary/marvellous.

stung [stʌŋ] *v.* see sting.

stunk [stʌŋk] *v.* see stink.

stunt 1 [stʌnt] *n.* trick; dangerous action done to attract attention. **stunt 2** *v.* to shorten/to prevent (sth) from growing. **stunt man** *n.* person who carries out dangerous actions in films in place of a film star.

stupefy ['stjuːpɪfaɪ] *v.* (a) to make stupid. (b) to astonish. **stupefaction** [stjuːpɪ'fækʃn] *n.* astonishment.

stupendous [stjuː'pendəs] *adj.* extraordinary/management.

stupid ['stjuːpɪd] *adj.* (a) not very intelligent; with no sense. (b) dull; with a dull mind. **stupidity** [stjuː'pɪdɪtɪ] *n.* being stupid. **stupidly** *adv.* in a stupid way.

stupor ['stjuːpə] *n.* being in a daze;

being half senseless.

sturdy ['stɜːdɪ] *adj.* strong and vigorous. **sturdily** *adv.* in a sturdy way. **sturdiness** *n.* being sturdy.

sturgeon ['stɜːdʒən] *n.* large edible fish whose eggs are caviare.

stutter 1 ['stʌtə] *n.* speech defect where you stutter. **stutter 2** *v.* to repeat the same sounds when speaking.

sty [staɪ] *n.* shed in which a pig lives; see also stye.

stye, sty [staɪ] *n.* infected pimple near the eye.

style 1 [staɪl] *n.* (a) way/manner of doing sth; in s. = very grandly. (b) fashion. (c) elegance. **style 2** *v.* (a) to name. (b) to give a certain style to (hair, etc.). **stylish** *adj.* elegant/fashionable. **stylishness** *n.* fashion/elegance. **stylist** *n.* person who gives (a) style to sth; hair s. = hairdresser. **stylistic** [staɪ'lɪstɪk] *adj.* referring to style in art. **stylistically** *adv.* referring to style in art. **stylistics** *n.* study of style of writing. **stylization** [staɪlaɪ'zeɪʃn] *n.* showing sth in a stylized way. **stylize** *v.* to show (sth) according to a fixed pattern/not in a natural way.

stylus ['staɪləs] *n.* needle of a record player.

stymie ['staɪmɪ] *v.* to block (a plan).

styptic ['stɪptɪk] *adj.* which stops bleeding; s. pencil = small stick of white substance (alum) which stops bleeding from cuts.

suave [swɑːv] *adj.* extremely polite with very smooth manners (but often with an unpleasant character). **suavely** *adv.* in a suave way. **suavity** *n.* being suave.

sub 1 [sʌb] *n. inf.* (a) subsidy; money lent to s.o. until he gets his wages. (b) subscription. (c) subeditor. (d) submarine. **sub 2** *v. inf.* (a) to subedit. (b) to act as a substitute. **sub 3** prefix sub. = below/under.

subaltern [sʌbəltən] *n.* junior army officer.

subaqua [sʌb'ækwə] *adj.* referring to underwater sports.

subcommittee ['sʌbkəmɪtɪ] *n.* small committee which is part of a large committee.

subconscious 1 [sʌb'kɒnʃəs] *adj.* which you have in your mind without being aware of it. **subconscious 2** *n.*

part of your mind which has subconscious ideas or feelings. **subconsciously** *adv.* in a subconscious way.

subcontinent [sʌb'kɒntɪnənt] *n.* mass of land which is part of a continent.

subcontract 1 [sʌb'kɒntrækt] *n.* agreement between a main contractor and another firm who will do part of the work which the contractor has agreed to do. **subcontract 2** *v.* to agree with a firm that they will do part of the work which you have agreed to do. **subcontractor** *n.* person/company who does work for a contractor.

subcutaneous [sʌbkjʊ'teɪnɪəs] *adj.* (formal) under the skin.

subdivide [sʌbdɪ'vaɪd] *v.* to divide (sth) which has already been divided. **subdivision** *n.* (a) division of sth into smaller units. (b) *Am.* land which has been divided up into plots for houses.

subdue [sʌb'djuː] *v.* (a) to overcome/to conquer. (b) to make quiet/to make less bright. **subdued** *adj.* (a) over come/beaten. (b) low (light); s. colours = (i) dull colours; (ii) pastel shades.

subedit [sʌb'edɪt] *v.* to correct (what s.o. has written) before it is printed. **subeditor** *n.* person who subedits.

subheading ['sʌbhedɪŋ] *n.* secondary heading.

subhuman [sʌb'hjuːmən] *adj.* less advanced than a human.

subject 1 ['sʌbdʒɪkt] *n.* (a) person who belongs to a country. (b) word which shows the person or thing which does an action. (c) thing which is being discussed. (d) thing which is being studied. **subject 2** ['sʌbdʒɪkt] *adj.* (a) belonging to; under the power of (a king). (b) s. to = (i) likely to be ruled by/to suffer from; (ii) depending on. **subject 3** [sʌb'dʒekt] *v.* to make (sth/s.o.) undergo sth unpleasant. **subjection** [sʌb'dʒekʃn] *n.* being subjected. **subjective** [sʌb'dʒektɪv] *adj.* seen from your own point of view. **subjectively** *adv.* in a subjective way. **subjectivity** *n.* being subjective. **subject-matter** *n.* subject dealt with in a book/TV programme.

subjoin [sʌb'dʒɔɪn] *v.* to add (sth) at the end.

sub judice [sʌb'dʒuːdɪsɪ] *adv.* being

considered in a court of law (and therefore not to be mentioned in the press).

subjugate ['sʌbdʒʊgeɪt] v. (formal) to bring (a country) under your control. **subjugation** [sʌbdʒʊ'geɪʃn] n. act of subjugating.

subjunctive [sʌb'dʒʌŋktɪv] adj. & n. (referring to) a form of a verb used to show doubt/desire, etc.

sublease 1 [sʌb'liːs] n. lease of a building which is already leased. **sublease 2** v. to sublet.

sublet [sʌb'let] v. (sublet) to lease (a building/room) which you yourself rent.

sublieutenant [sʌbleftenənt] n. junior officer in the navy below the rank of lieutenant.

sublimate 1 ['sʌblɪmət] n. substance formed when a substance is changed from solid to vapour. **sublimate 2** ['sʌblɪmeɪt] v. (a) to change a substance from solid to vapour. (b) (formal) to channel (crude energy/emotion) into an activity which is accepted in society. **sublimation** n. act of sublimating.

sublime [sə'blaɪm] adj. grand/wonderful; noble; very great. **sublimely** adv. wonderfully.

subliminal [sʌb'lɪmɪnl] adj. below the consciousness of the senses.

submachine gun [sʌbmə'ʃiːngʌn] n. light machine gun.

submarine 1 [sʌbmə'riːn] adj. which lives/takes place under the water. **submarine 2** n. ship which can travel under the water. **submariner** [sʌb'mærɪnə] n. member of the crew of a submarine.

submerge [sʌb'mɜːdʒ] v. (a) to (make sth) go under the surface of the water. **submergence, submersion** [sʌb'mɜːʃn] n. being submerged.

submission [sʌb'mɪʃn] n. (a) state of giving in/giving way. (b) evidence/document/opinion submitted to s.o. **submissive** [sʌb'mɪsɪv] adj. meek (person) who gives in easily. **submissively** adv. in a submissive way. **submissiveness** n. meekness. **submit** v. (a) to give way; to yield. (b) to give (evidence/documents/opinion) for s.o. to examine.

subnormal [sʌb'nɔːml] adj. less than normal; below normal standard.

subordinate 1 [sə'bɔːdnət] adj. & n. (person) who is under the control of s.o. else; s. clause = phrase in a sentence which cannot stand alone, and which is dependent on another clause.

subordinate 2 [sə'bɔːdɪneɪt] v. to put (sth) in a less important position; to consider (sth) is less important. **subordination** [sʌbɔːneɪʃn] n. act of subordinating.

suborn [sə'bɔːn] v. (formal) to bribe (s.o) to commit perjury.

subpoena 1 [sʌb'piːnə] n. order to come to a court. **subpoena 2** v. to order (s.o) to come to a court.

subscribe [sʌb'skraɪb] v. (a) to give money (to a charity). (b) to pay for a series of issues of magazine/for a series of tickets to concerts, etc. (c) to s. to an opinion = agree with it. **subscriber** n. person who subscribes to a charity/to a magazine; person who has a telephone; s. trunk dialling = telephone system where you can dial long distance or international numbers without asking the operator to do so for you. **subscription** [sʌb'skrɪpʃn] n. (a) money paid to a charity. (b) money paid to a magazine/to a club for a series of a issues/a year's membership.

subsection ['sʌbsekʃn] n. part of a section.

subsequent ['sʌbsɪkwənt] adj. which follows later. **subsequently** adv. later.

subservient adj. weak/always giving in to s.o. **subserviently** adv. in a subservient way. **subservience** n. being subservient.

subside [sʌb'saɪd] v. (a) to sink down. (b) to become less violent. **subsidence** [sʌb'saɪdəns] n. sinking down (of ground).

subsidiary [sʌb'sɪdjərɪ] adj. & n. (thing) which is less important; s. (company) = company which is controlled by another.

subsidy ['sʌbsɪdɪ] n. money given to help pay for sth unprofitable. **subsidize** ['sʌbsɪdaɪz] v. to help by giving money.

subsist [sʌb'sɪst] v. to exist (with difficulty). **subsistence** [sʌb'sɪstəns] n. existence; survival with very little

money or food; s. level = having only
just enough to live on.
subsoil ['sʌbsɔɪl] *n.* layer of soil under
the topsoil.
subsonic ['sʌbsɒnɪk] *adj.* (plane)
which files at a speed less than the speed
of sound.
substance ['sʌbstəns] *n.* (a) matter/
material of which things can be made.
(b) basis (of an argument/report). (c) a
man of s. = a wealthy man. **substantial**
[sʌb'stænʃl] *adj.* (a) large/important. (b)
large/solid. **substantially** *adv.* mostly/
mainly. **substantiate** [sʌb'stænʃɪeɪt] *v.*
to justify; to prove that (sth) is true.
substantiation [sʌbstænʃɪ'eɪʃn] *n.* act
of substantiating.
substandard [sʌb'stændəd] *adj.*
second-rate; below the normal standard.
substantive 1 ['sʌbstəntɪv] *adj.* (a)
real; existing. (b)[sʌb'stæntɪvl]
permanent (military rank). **substantive
2** *n.* noun.
substation ['sʌbsteɪʃn] *n.* small local
electricity station.
substitute 1 ['sʌbstɪtjuːt] *n.* person/
thing taking the place of s.o./sth else.
substitute 2 *v.* to put (sth/s.o.) in the
place of (s.o./sth). **substitution**
[sʌbstɪ'tjuːʃn] *n.* act of substituting.
substratum [sʌb'strɑːtəm] *n.* lower
layer of rock/soil.
subsume [səb'sjuːm] *v.* (formal) to
include in a certain category.
subtenant [sʌb'tenənt] *n.* person to
whom a flat/house has been sublet.
subtenancy *n.* act of subletting.
subterfuge ['sʌbtə'fjuːdʒ] *n.* trick;
clever plot.
subterranean [sʌbtə'remɪən] *adj.*
under the ground.
subtitle 1 ['sʌbtaɪtl] *n.* (a) secondary
title on a book. (b) subtitles = translation
of the dialogue of a foreign film which is
shown on the bottom of the screen.
subtitle 2 *v.* to give a subtitle or
subtitles to (sth).
subtle ['sʌtl] *adj.* (a) difficult to
explain; very delicate (scent). (b)
cunning. **subtlety** ['sʌtltɪ] *n.* thing
which is difficult to explain/to describe.
subtly *adv.* in a subtle way.
subtopia [sʌb'təupɪə] *n. inf.*
supposedly ideal suburbs.
subtotal ['sʌbtəʊtl] *n.* total of one

section of a set of figures.
subtract [sʌb'trækt] *v.* to take away
(sth from a group). **subtraction**
[sʌb'trækʃn] *n.* act of subtracting.
subtropical [sʌb'trɒpɪkl] *adj.* referring
to the subtropics **subtropics** *n.* areas
of the world between the tropics and the
temperate zones.
suburb ['sʌbɜːb] *n.* residential area on
the outskirts of a town; the suburbs =
area all round a town where most people
live. **suburban** [sə'bɜːbən] *adj.*
referring to the suburbs; s. trains = trains
which go from the town centre to the
suburbs. **suburbia** *n. inf.* the suburbs.
subvention [sʌb'venʃn] *n.* subsidy.
subversion [shb'vɜːʃn] *n.* act of
subverting. **subversive** [sʌb'vɜːsɪv]
adj. which tries to subvert. **subvert**
[sʌb'vɜːt] *v.* to try to destroy the
authority of (the government).
subway ['sʌbweɪ] *n.* underground
passage (b) *Am.* underground railway
system.
subzero [sʌb'zɪərəʊ] *adj.*
(temperature) below zero degrees.
succeed [sək'siːd] *v.* (a) to follow on;
too take the place of (b) to do well; to do
what you have been trying to do
success [sək'ses] *n.* (*pl.*-es) (a) doing
what you have been trying to do (b)
thing/person who does well.
successful *adj.* which succeeds.
successfully, adv. in a successful way.
succession [sək'seʃn] *n.* (a)series (b)
right to take s.o.'s place; act of taking
s.o.'s place. **successive** [sək'sesɪv]
adj. one after the other. **successively**
adv. one after the other. **successor** *n.*
person who takes someone's place.
succinct [sək'sɪŋkt] *adj.* concise/not
using many words. **succinctly** *adv.* in
a succinct way.
succour, *Am.* succor 1 ['sʌkə] *n.*
(formal) help. **succour, *Am.* succor 2**
v. (formal) to help.
succulent 1 ['sʌkjʊlənt] *adj.* juicy/
full of juice. **succulent 2** *n.* type of
plant with thick fleshy leaves and stems
(like a cactus).
succumb [sə'kʌm] *v.* (to) to give in/to
yield; to die (from).
such 1 [sʌtʃ] *adj.* (a) like/similar (b) so
large/so great (c) of this type. **such 2**
pron. thing/person of a certain kind; s.

as it is = although it is not very good.
such and-such *pron.* a particular/a certain. **suchlike** *adj. pron.* similar (people/things).

suck 1 [sʌk] *n.* action of drawing in liquid through the mouth. **suck 2** *v.* (a) to pull (liquid) into your mouth (b) to pull in (sth) by suction. **sucker** *n.* (a)shoot which sprouts from a stock, not from the grafted plant. (b) thing which sticks on to a surface by suction (c) *inf.* person who is easily tricked. **suckle** *v.* to give (a child) milk from the breast. **suckling** *n.* young animal/child still taking milk from its mother. **suck up to** *v. inf.* to try to make (s.o) like you (by giving presents/making compliments. etc).

suction ['sʌkʃən] *n.* action of sucking in air/liquid so that sth will be pulled in/will stick to a surface because of the vacuum created; s. pad = small concave pad which will stick to a surface if pressed hard; s. pump = pump which sucks up liquid when air is pulled out of it.

sucrose ['su:krəʊz] *n.* sugar found in plants.

sudden ['sʌdn] *adj.* which happens rapidly/unexpectedly; all of a s. = suddenly. **suddenly** *adv.* rapidly/unexpectdly **suddenness** *n.* being rapid/unexpected.

suds [sʌdz] *n. pl.* foam made with soap.

sue [su:] *v.* to take(s.o) to court/to start a lawsuit against (s.o).

suede [sweɪd] *n.* soft leather with a rough/furry surface.

suet ['sɔɪt] *n.* hard fat from an animal used in cooking. **suety** *adj.* made of suet; like suet.

suffer ['sʌfə] *v.* (a) to feel pain; to be in a difficult situation (b) to put up with. (c) to undergo. **sufferance** *n.* he is only here on s. = we allow him to be here but we don't really want him. **sufferer** *n.* person who suffers. **suffering** *n.* feeling pain.

suffice [sə'faɪs] *v.* (formal) to be enough. **sufficiency** [sə'fɪʃənsɪ] *n.* enough supplies. **sufficient** [sə'fɪʃənt] *adj.* enough. **sufficiently** *adv.* enough.

suffix ['sʌfɪks] *n.* (*pl.*-es) part added after a word to make another word.

suffocate ['sʌfəkeɪt] *v.* not to be able

to breathe; to kill/to die by stopping breathing. **suffocation** [sʌfə'keɪʃn] *n.* not being able to breathe.

suffragan ['sʌfrəgən] *n.* bishop who helps another bishop run a large diocese. **suffrage** ['sʌfrɪdʒ] *n.* right to vote in elections. **suffragette** *n.* (old) women who campaigned for the right to vote.

suffuse [sə'fju:z] *v.* to cover with (colour). **suffusion** *n.* act of suffusing.

sugar 1 ['ʃʊgə] *n.* sweet substance made from the juice of a sugar cane or from sugar beet. **sugar 2** *v.* to put sugar into; to s. the pill = - to make some unpleasant news more acceptable.

sugar beet *n.* plant with a large root which when crushed give sugar and rum. **sugar cane** *n.* tropical plant whose stalks when crushed gives sugar and rum. **sugarcoated** *adj.* covered with a coating of hard sugar. **sugar daddy** *n.* old man who entertains young girls and gives then presents. **sugar soap** *n.* soft material for cleaning paintwork. **sugary** *adj.* with too much sugar.

suggest [sə'dʒest] *v.* (a) to propose (an idea). (b) to hint/to insinuate.. **suggestible** *adj.* (person) who can easily be influenced. **suggestion** *n.* proposal. **suggestive** *adj.* (a) which suggests (b) which gives an impression of indecency. **suggestively** *adv.* in a suggestive way.

suicide ['sʊɪsaɪd] *n.* (a) killing yourself; to commit s. = to kill yourself (b) person who has killed himself. **suicidal** [sʊɪ'saɪdl] *adj.* referring to suicide.

suit 1 [su:t] *n.* (a) two or three piece of clothing made of the same cloth (jacket/waistcoat and trousers or skirt). (b) lawsuit/court case. (c) one of the four groups with the same symbol in a pack of cards; to follow s. = to do what s.o. else has done. **suit 2** *v.* (a) to fit together. (b) to be completely acceptable/convenient; s. yourself = do what you want. (c) to fit s.o.'s appearance.

suitability [su:tə'bɪlɪtɪ] *n.* being suitable. **suitable** ['su:təbl] *adj.* convenient; (thing) which fits. **suitably** *adv.* in a convenient/fitting way.

suitcase *n.* box with a handle for carrying clothes in when you are travelling. **suitor** *n.* person who wants to marry a certain girl.

suite [swiːt] n. (a) series of rooms/ pieces of furniture which make a set. (b) group of people accompanying a king, queen or other important person. (c) several short pieces of music which are played together as a group. (d) ens.['ɒn'swiːt] = attached.

sulfa ['sʌlfə] n. Am. see sulpha.

sulfur ['sʌlfə] n. Am. see sulphur.

sulk 1 [sʌlk] n. sulks = being grumpy/ annoyed in silence. **sulk 2** v. to show you are annoyed by not saying anything. **sulkily** adv. in a sulky way. sulkiness, n. being sulky. **sulky** adj. bad-tempered/grumpy.

sullen ['sʌln] adj. silently angry; unpleasant. **sullenly** adv. in a sullen way.

sully ['sʌlɪ] v. (formal) to dirty (a reputation).

sulpha, Am. sulfa ['sʌlfə] n. s. drug = sulphonamide. **sulphur, Am. Sulfur** ['sʌlfə] n. (element; s.) solid substance, usu. found as a yellow powder.

sulphate n. salt formed from sulphuric acid. **sulphide** n. combination of sulphur with another substance.

sulphonamide n. drug used against bacteria. **sulphuric acid** [sʌl'fjʊərɪk'æsɪd] n. very strong acid containing sulphur. **sulphurous** ['sʌlfərəs] adj. like sulphur.

sultan ['sʌltən] n. Muslim prince. **sultana** [sʌl'tɑːnə] n. (a) wife of a sultan. (b) type of seedless raisin. **sultanate** n. country ruled by a sultan.

sultry ['sʌltrɪ] adj. (-ier, -iest) (a) hot/heavy (weather). (b) attractive in a dark way; passionate. sultriness, n. being sultry.

sum 1 [sʌm] n. (a) total of numbers added together(b) quantity of money. (c) arithmetic problem. **sum 2** v. (summed) to s. up = to make a summary/ to tell briefly what has happened.

summarize ['sʌməraɪz] v. to make a brief account of(sth). **summary. 1** n. short account of what has happened; short version of sth longer. **summary. 2** adj. (a) brief. (b) done quickly with out wasting too much time. **summarily** adv. quickly. **summing- up** n. summary of evidence made by a judge at the end of a trial.

summer ['sʌmə] n. season of the year following spring, when plants begin to make fruit; the warmest season; s. holidays = main/longest holidays during a school year; s. school = classes held at a school/university during the summer holiday. **summerhouse** n. small house in a garden where you can sit in the summer. **summertime** n. summer season. **summer time** n. system of altering the clocks during the summer to take advantage of the longer period of daylight. **summery** adj. like the summer.

summit ['sʌmɪt] n. (a) top of a mountain). (b) s. (meeting) = meeting of heads of government to discuss international problems. **summitry** n. inf. diplomacy carried on at summit meetings.

summon ['sʌmən] v. (a) to call (b) to s. up courage = to get together courage to do sth. **summons 1** n. (a) official legal order to appear in court. **summons 2** v. to order (s.o)to appear in court.

sump [sʌmp] n. (a) part of a car engine containing the oil (b) pit in which water collects.

sumptuous ['sʌmtʃʊəs] adj. very luxurious/splendid. **sumptuously** adv. in a sumptuous way.

sun 1 [sʌn] n. (a) very hot body around which the earth revolves and which provides heat and daylight (b) light from the sun. **sun 2** v. (sunned) to s. yourself = to sit in the sun. **sunbathe** v. to lie in the sun to get your body brown. **sunbeam** n. ray of sunlight. **sunburn** n. painful inflammation of the skin caused by being in the sun for too long. **sunburnt** adj. made brown or red by the sun. **sundeck** n. top deck of a passenger ship where people can sit in the sun. **sundial** n. round clock face with a central pointer whose shadow with a central pointer whose shadow points to the time when the sun shines on it. **sundown** n. moment when the sun goes down. **sundrenched** adj. (always) very sunny. **sunflower** n. very large yellow flower on a tall stem; s. oil = oil made from its seeds. **sunglasses** n. dark glasses to protect your eyes from the sun. **sunlamp** n. lamp which gives off ultraviolet rays like

the sun, used to give a suntan indoors.
sunless *adj.* with no sun. **sunlight**
n. light from the sun. **sunlit** *adj.* lit by
the sun. **sunnily** *adv.* in a happy way.
sunny *adj.* (-ier, -iest) full of sunlight,
happy (character) *Am. inf.* a side up =
(egg) fried without being turned over.
sunrise *n.* time at which the sun ruses.
sunroof *n.* part of a roof of a car
which slides open. **sunset** *n.* time
when the sun goes down behind the
horizon; colourful sky as the sun goes
down. **sunshade** *n.* light bright
coloured umbrella to protect from the
sun. **sunshine** *n.* light from the sun.
sunshine roof *n.* sunroof. **sunspot**
n. dark spot which appears on the
surface of the sun. **sunstroke** *n.*
illness caused by being too much in the
sunlight. **suntan** *n.* brown colour of
the skin caused by the sun. **suntanned**
adj. with a skin made brown by the sun.
suntrap *n.* very sunny place. **sun-up**
n. sunrise. **sundae** ['sʌndɪ] *n.* dessert
of ice cream, cream and fruit. **Sunday**
['sʌndɪ] *n.* last day of the week; day
between Saturday and Monday; S. best =
best clothes; S. school = school for
teaching religion to children, *usu.* held
on a Sunday.
sunder ['sʌndə] *v.* (formal) to split into
parts.
sundew ['sʌndjuː] *n.* wild plant which
catches insects for food.
sundry 1 ['sʌndrɪ] *adj.* various.
sundry 2 *n.* (a) all and s. = everyone.
(b) sundries = various small articles/
small items on a bill.
sung [sʌŋ] *v.* see sing.
sunk [sʌŋk] *adj.* ruined/lost; see also
sink. **sunken** *adj.* (a) which is beneath
the surface. (b) lower than the
surrounding area.
sup 1 [sʌp] *n.* mouthful of liquid. **sup
2** *v.* (supped) to drink in small
mouthfuls.
super 1 ['suːpə] *adj. inf.* wonderful. **super
2** *n. inf.* (a) police superintendent. (b) extra
actor. 3. super - prefix meaning more/
greater/of better quality.
superabundance [suːpərə'bʌndəns]
n. great abundance; very large quantity.
superabundant *adj.* very abundant/in
very large quantities.
superannuated [suːpə'rænjʊeɪtɪd] *adj.*

too old to work properly; old-fashioned.
superannuation [suːpərænjʊ'eɪʃn] *n.*
(a) retirement of workers when they
reach a certain age. (b) pension paid to
s.o. who has retired.
superb [suː'pɜːb] *adj.* marvellous/
wonderful. **superbly** *adv.* wonderfully.
supercharged ['suːpətʃɑːdʒd] *adj.*
(motor/person) with much increased
energy. **supercharger** *n.* apparatus
on a car engine for increasing the
power.
supercilious [suːpə'sɪlɪəs] *adj.*
looking down on others; considering
others as inferior. **superciliously** *adv.*
in a supercilious way.
superciliousness *n.* being
supercilious.
superficial [suːpə'fɪʃl] *adj.* touching
only the top surface; not going deeply
beneath the surface. **superficiality**
[suːpəfɪ'ælɪtɪ] *n.* being superficial.
superficially *adv.* in a superficial way.
superfine [suːpə'faɪn] *adj.* very fine.
superfluous [suː'pɜːfluːəs] *adj.* which
is more than is needed. **superfluity**
[suːpə'fluːɪtɪ] *n.* being superfluous/more
than is needed; excess. **superfluously**
adv. in a superfluous way.
superhighway [suːpə'haɪweɪ] *n. Am.*
important motorway.
superhuman [suːpə'hjuːmən] *adj.*
more than is normal in human beings.
superimpose [suːpərɪm'pəʊz] *v.* to
place on top of sth.
superintend [suːpərɪn'tend] *v.* to be in
charge. **superintendent** *n.* (a) person
in charge. (b) senior police officer.
superior 1 [suː'pɪərɪə] *adj.* (a) of better
quality; of a larger quality. (b) higher in
rank. (c) thinking yourself to be better
than others. **superior 2** *n.* (a) person
of higher rank. (b) leader of a religious
community. **superiority** [suːpɪərɪ'ɒrɪtɪ]
n. being superior.
superlative 1 [suː'pɜːlətɪv] *adj.* of the
best quality. **superlative 2** *n.* form of
an adjective or adverb showing the
highest level of comparison.
superlatively *adv.* extremely well.
superman ['suːpəmæn] *n.* man who
has superhuman strength/power/ability.
supermarket ['suːpəmɑːkɪt] *n.* large
store selling mainly food, where you
serve yourself.

supernatural [su:pə'nætʃərəl] *adj.* & *n.* (things) which happen not in accordance with the laws of nature. **supernaturally** *adv.* in a supernatural way.

supernova [su:pənəʊvə] *n.* large star which explodes and suddenly appears in the sky.

supernumerary ['su:pə'nju:mərərɪ] *adj.* & *n.* (person) who is in addition to the usual number of people.

superphosphate [su:pə'fɒsfeɪt] *n.* fertilizer based on phosphates.

superpower ['su:pəpaʊə] *n.* extremely powerful country.

superscription [su:pə'skrɪpʃn] *n.* words written above sth.

supersede [su:pə'si:d] *v.* to take the place of (sth which is older or less efficient).

supersonic [su:pə'sɒnɪk] *adj.* faster than the speed of sound.

superstition [su:pə'stɪʃn] *n.* belief in magic and the supernatural.

superstitious [su:pə'stɪʃəs] *adj.* believing an magic and the supernatural.

superstore ['su:pəstɔ:] *n.* large supermarket.

superstructure ['su:pəstrʌktʃə] *n.* top structure of a ship; structure built on top of sth else.

supertanker ['su:pətæŋkə] *n.* very large oil tanker.

supertax ['su:pətæks] *n.* tax on very high incomes.

supervene [su:pə'vi:n] *v.* to happen so that things are changed.

supervise ['su:pəvaɪz] *v.* to watch over work, etc., to see that it is well done. **supervision** [su:pə'vɪʒn] *n.* act of supervising. **supervisor** ['su:pəvaɪzə] *n.* person who supervises. **supervisory** [su:pə'vaɪzərɪ] *adj.* as a supervisor.

superwoman ['su:pəwʊmən] *n.* woman who has superhuman strength/power/ability.

supine ['su:paɪn] *adj.* (formal) (a) lying flat on your back. (b) uninterested/lazy.

supper ['sʌpə] *n.* evening meal.

supplant [sə'plɑ:nt] *v.* to take (s.o.'s) place by cunning manœuvres.

supple ['sʌpl] *adj.* flexible/which bends easily. **suppleness** *n.* being supple. **supplely, supply** ['sʌplɪ] *adv.*

in a supple way.

supplement 1 ['sʌplɪmənt] *n.* (a) thing which is in addition. (b) addition to a book; magazine which is part of a newspaper. **supplement 2** ['sʌplɪment] *v.* to add to. **supplementary** [sʌplɪ'mentrɪ] *adj.* in addition; s. benefits = payments from the Government to people who have very low incomes.

suppliant ['sʌplɪənt] *n.* person who begs for help.

supplicate ['sʌplɪkeɪt] *v.* (formal) to beg for sth. **supplicant** *n.* person who begs for help. **supplication** [sʌplɪ'keɪʃn] *n.* (formal) begging for help.

supply 1 [sə'plaɪ] *n.* (a) providing sth which is needed; Supply Bill = bill which provides money which the government needs. (b) stock of sth which has been provided. (c) supplies = food, etc., which has been stocked/which is going to be provided. **supply 2** *adj.* s. teacher = teacher who replaces a permanent teacher who is away. **supply 3** *v.* (a) to provide (sth which is necessary). (b) to s. s.o. with sth = to provide sth to s.o. (c) to satisfy. **supply 4** ['sʌplɪ] *adv.* see supple. **supplier** [sə'plaɪə] *n.* person/shop/country which supplies.

support 1 [sə'pɔ:t] *n.* (a) thing which supports. (b) moral/financial encouragement. **support 2** *v.* (a) to hold up. (b) to provide/to earn money so that s.o. can live. (c) to encourage/to agree with. **supporter** *n.* person who encourages a plan/a football team, etc. **supporting cast** *n.* group of actors who play the minor parts in a play.

suppose [sə'pəʊz] *v.* (a) to assume sth to be correct (even if it is not). (b) to think. (c) what happens if? **supposedly** [sə'pəʊzɪdlɪ] *adv.* as it is assumed. **supposing** *conj.* what happens if? **supposition** [sʌpə'zɪʃn] *n.* thing which is assumed; guess.

suppository [sə'pɒzɪtərɪ] *n.* tablet of medicinal material which is put into the rectum or vagina where it melts.

suppress [sə'pres] *v.* (a) to crush; to stop (a revolution). (b) to forbid the publication of (sth). (c) to hide (feelings). **suppression** [sə'preʃn] n. act of suppressing. **suppressor** n. machine which prevents an electric appliance from interfering with radio/TV signals.

suppurate ['sʌpjʊreɪt] v. (formal) to produce pus.

supra- ['suːprə] prefix. beyond.

supranational [suːprə'næʃnl] adj. over/beyond the interests of a single nation or several nations.

supreme [su'priːm] adj. highest; total (indifference). **supremely** adv. totally/completely. **supremacy** [sʊ'preməsɪ] n. highest power.

supremo [sʊ'priːməʊ] n. inf. person in charge of many organizations; officer in charge of several armies.

surcharge 1 ['sɜːtʃɑːdʒ] n. extra charge. **surcharge 2** [sɜː'tʃɑːdʒ] v. to charge an extra amount.

surd [sɜːd] n. (in mathematics) quantity (like a root) which cannot be expressed as a whole number.

sure 1 [ʃɔː, 'ʃʊə] adj. (a) without any doubt; certain; for s. = for certain. (b) reliable. (c) s. of yourself = confident. **sure 2** adv. certainly. **sure-fire.** adj. Am. inf. absolutely certain. **surefooted** adj. able to walk on slippery rocks/narrow ledges without slipping. **surely** adv. (a) carefully. (b) naturally/of course. **sureness** n. being sure.

surety n. (a) person who takes the responsibility that s.o. will do sth. (b) money paid as a guarantee that s.o. will appear in court.

surf 1 [sɜːf] n. line of breaking waves along a shore; foam from breaking waves. **surf 2** v. to ride on breaking waves on a board. **surfboard** n. board which you stand on to ride on breaking waves. **surfboat** n. light boat for riding on surf. **surfer** n. person who surfs. **surfing, surf-riding** n. riding on breaking waves as a sport.

surface 1 ['sɜːfəs] n. top layer; outside of sth. **surface 2** v. (a) to come up from under/to appear on the top of water, etc. (b) to cover (a road, etc.) with a hard substance. **surface mail** n. post which travels by van/train/ship, etc., and not by air.

surfeit 1 ['sɜːfɪt] n. (formal) too much. **surfeit 2** v. to feed (s.o.) too much.

surge [sɜːdʒ] n. (a) rising up of water

into waves. (b) sudden increase. **surge 2** v. (a) to rise up. (b) move (forward) in a mass.

surgeon ['sɜːdʒən] n. doctor who carries out operations; house s. = young surgeon in a hospital; dental s. = dentist.

surgery n. (a) treatment of disease or wounds by cutting open part of the body. (b) doctor's/dentist's consulting room. (c) consultation given by a member of parliament to any of his constituents.

surgical ['sɜːdʒɪkl] adj. referring to surgery; s. gloves = gloves worn by a surgeon; s. spirit = pure alcohol used to rub on the skin. **surgically** adv. in a surgical way.

surly ['sɜːlɪ] adj. grumpy/sullen. **surliness** n. being surly.

surmise 1 [sə'maɪz] n. guess/supposition. **surmise 2** v. to guess.

surmount [sɜː'maʊnt] v. (a) to overcome (an obstacle). (b) to be on top of (sth). **surmountable** adj. which can be surmounted.

surname ['sɜːneɪm] n. family name.

surpass [sə'pɑːs] v. to do better than.

surplice ['sɜːpləs] n. long white robe worn by priests/choirboys.

surplus ['sɜːpləs] adj. & n. (pl.-es) extra (stock); (material) left over.

surprise 1 [sə'praɪz] n. shock caused by sth unexpected. **surprise 2** v. (a) to give (s.o.) a surprise/an unexpected shock. (b) to catch (s.o.) unexpectedly. **surprising** adj. astonishing/unusual. **surprisingly** adv. in an unusual way.

surrealism [sə'rɪəlɪzəm] n. 20th century art movement in which an artist depicts realistic objects in an unreal environment, emphasizing the meaning he sees beyond reality. **surrealist** adj. & n. (artist) following the principles of surrealism. **surrealistic** adj. very strange/totally unreal.

surrender 1 [sə'rendə] n. (a) giving in (to an enemy). (b) giving up (of goods); giving up (of an insurance policy); s. value = amount of money you will receive if you end an insurance before the normal completion date. **surrender 2** v. (a) to give in (to an enemy). (b) to give up (a ticket/insurance policy, etc.).

surreptitious [sʌrəp'tɪʃəs] adj. done in secret. **surreptitiously** adv. in secret.

surrogate ['sʌrəgɪt] n. deputy/person who acts in place of s.o.

surround 1 [sə'raʊnd] n. border; edge; bare floor space round a carpet.

surround 2 v. to be/to come all round (sth). **surrounding** adj. which surrounds. **surroundings** n. pl. area around a place/person.

surtax. ['sɜːtæks] n. extra tax on high incomes.

surveillance [sɜː'veɪləns] n. strict watch.

survey 1 ['sɜːveɪ] n. (a) general account. (b) careful examination of a building to see if it is in good condition. (c) way measurements of land heights/distances/roads/buildings, etc., to produce accurate plans or maps. **survey 2** [sə'veɪ] v. (a) to look at/to talk about (sth) in a general way. (b) to make a survey of (a building). (c) to measure (land) in order to produce an accurate plan or map. **surveyor** n. person who surveys buildings or measures land.

survive [sə'vaɪv] v. (a) to continue to live (after an accident, etc.). (b) to live longer than (s.o.). **survival** n. continuing to live. **survivor** n. person who survives.

susceptible [sə'septɪbl] adj. (a) s. of proof = which can be proved; s. to = likely to catch (a disease). (b) easily upset. **susceptibility** [səseptə'bɪlɪtɪ] n. being susceptible.

suspect 1 ['sʌspekt] adj. & n. (person) who is thought to have committed a crime; (food) which might be poisonous. **suspect 2** [sə'spekt] v. (a) to s. s.o. of = to think that (s.o.) may have committed a crime. (b) to guess/to think.

suspend [sə'spend] v. (a) to hang; to make (sth) hang in a liquid. (b) to stop (sth) for a time. (c) to take (sth) away as a punishment; to stop (s.o.) from doing sth. **suspenders** n. pl. elastic straps to hold up stockings or socks. (b) Am. braces. **suspense** n. impatient wait for sth to happen or for a decision to be reached. **suspension** n. (a) act of suspending; being suspended; s. bridge = one which hangs by ropes/chains, etc., from tall towers. (b) system of springs, etc., in a car which attaches the chassis to the axles.

suspicion [sə'spɪʃn] n. (a) feeling that

sth is wrong or that s.o. has committed a crime. (b) guess; general feeling. (c) slight hint. **suspicious** adj. which can be suspected. **suspiciously** adv. (a) in a suspicious way. (b) as if suspecting sth.

suss 1 [sʌs] n. Sl. suspicion. **suss 2** v. Sl. to suspect; to s. s.o. out = to find out.

sustain [sə'steɪn] v. (a) to keep (sth) going. (b) to suffer. (c) to support. **sustained** adj. which continues for a long time. **sustaining** adj. which will support or nourish.

sustenance ['sʌstənəns] n. (a) food. (b) means of s. = way of keeping alive/of keeping strong.

suture ['suːtʃə] n. thread used for stitching wounds together; stitching (of a wound); stitch made to hold a wound together.

suzerain ['suːzəreɪn] n. (formal) overlord. **suzerainty** n. rule over (a state).

svelte [svelt] adj. slim and graceful.

swab 1 [swɒb] n. (a) cloth for wiping floors clear of water. (b) piece of material (like cottonwool) used for cleaning a wound or for taking samples of infection for analysis. (c) sample of infection taken for analysis. **swab 2** v. (swabbed) to clean (a floor) with a swab.

swaddle ['swɒdl] v. (old) to wrap (a baby) in pieces of cloth.

swag [swæg] n. inf. (a) stolen goods (esp. jewellery/silver, etc.). (b) (in Australia) bundle of belongings. **swagman** n. (in Australia) tramp.

swagger 1 ['swægə] n. proud way of walking. **swagger 2** v. to walk in a proud way, swinging your body.

swallow 1 ['swɒləʊ] n. (a) mouthful of liquid which you drink in one movement; act of swallowing. (b) common fast-flying bird with long wings and tail. **swallow 2** v. (a) to make (food/liquid) pass down your throat from your mouth to the stomach. (b) to accept (a story) as true. **swallow dive** n. dive where the arms are stretched out sideways at the start. **swallow hole** n. cave formed in limestone rock. **swallow up** v. to make (sth) disappear inside.

swam [swæm] v. see swim.

swamp 1 [swɒmp] n. area of wet soft land. **swamp 2** v. to fill (a boat) with water; swamped with = having so much (work, etc.) that it is impossible to deal with. **swampy** *adj.* wet (land) like a marsh.

swan 1 [swɒn] *n.* large white water bird with a long curved neck. **swan 2** *v.* (swanned) *inf.* to travel about in a leisurely way. **swan song** *n.* last performance by an artist (esp. a singer); last work by a writer.

swank 1 [swæŋk] *n. inf.* (a) showing off. (b) person who shows off. **swank 2** *v. inf.* to show off; to show that you think a lot of yourself. **swanky** *adj. inf.* pretentious; (acting) in a swanking way.

swap, swop 1 [swɒp] *n. inf.* (a) exchange. (b) swaps = stamps/coins, etc., which a collector has ready to exchange for others. **swap, swop 2** *v.* (swapped/swopped) *inf.* to exchange (sth for sth).

sward [swɔːd] *n.* soft grassy surface.

swarm 1 [swɔːm] *n.* large group of insects, etc., flying about together.

swarm 2 *v.* (a) to move about in a large group. (b) (up) to climb using your hands and feet like a monkey.

swarthy ['swɔːðɪ] *adj.* with a dark complexion.

swashbuckling ['swɒʃbʌklɪŋ] *adj.* daring; living dangerously.

swastika ['swɒstɪkə] *n.* ancient sign, shaped like a cross with each arm bent at right angles.

swat 1 [swɒt] *n.* flat disc on a handle for killing flies etc. **swat 2** *v.* (swatted) to hit and kill (a fly, etc). **swatter** *n.* swat.

swatch [swɒtʃ] *n.* (*pl.*-es) small sample of fabric.

swath [swɒθ] *n.* strip cut by a scythe/ harvester/mower.

swathe [sweɪð] *v.* to wrap up.

sway 1 [sweɪ] *n.* (a) power. (b) act of swaying. **sway 2** *v.* (a) to (cause to) move from side to side. (b) to influence.

swear ['sweə] *v.* (swore[swɔː]; sworn[swɔːn]) (a) to promise solemnly. (b) to (make s.o.) take an oath. (c) to curse. (d) to s. by = to believe completely or enthusiastically in. **swear word** *n.* word used as a curse or to show annoyance.

sweat 1 [swet] *n.* drops of liquid which come through your skin when you are hot. **sweat 2** *v.* to produce sweat; we'll have to s. it out = keep on with it, even if it is unpleasant/difficult. **sweat band** *n.* band of towelling worn round your head or wrist to stop seat trickling down. **sweated** *adj.* s. labour = (i) people who work hard for little money; (ii) hard work which is very badly paid. **sweater** *n.* pullover. **sweatshirt** *n.* light long-sleeved cotton shirt with no collar or buttons. **sweat shop** *n.* factory using sweated labour. **sweaty** *adj.* damp with sweat.

Swede [swiːd] *n.* (a) person from Sweden. (b) swede = type of root vegetable like a yellow turnip. **Swedish. 1** *adj.* referring to Sweden. **Swedish 2** *n.* language spoken in Sweden.

sweep 1 [swiːp] *n.* (a) act of sweeping (with a brush); act of swinging (a sword or your hand); to make a clean s. = to clear sth away completely/to win completely. (b) wide stretch (of water, etc.). (c) person who cleans chimneys. (d) sweepstake. **sweep 2** *v.* (swept[swept]) (a) to clean with a brush; to. s. the board = to win completely. (b) to clear up (dust/snow, etc.) with a brush. (c) to make a wide movement. (d) to move rapidly; to carry (sth) along rapidly. **sweeper** *n.* person/machine that sweeps. **sweeping** *adj.* wide-ranging/far-reaching; s. statement = statement which is partly true but too general. **sweepstake** *n.* form of gambling on a horserace where the holders of the winning tickets take all the money which has been bet.

sweet 1 [swiːt] *adj.* (-er, -est) (a) tasting like sugar; not sour; s. tooth = liking for sweet things. (b) pleasant; s. pea = pea with scented flowers. (c) fresh (air).

sweet 2 *n.* (a) small piece of sweet food, made with sugar or chocolate. (b) sweet course at the end of a meal. **sweetbread** *n.* pancreas of an animal eaten as food. **sweet corn** *v.* maize, eaten as food. **sweeten** *v.* (a) to make sweet. (b) *inf.* to give (s.o.) a bribe to make sure he is favourable to you. **sweetener** *n.* (a) thing/material which sweetens. (b) *inf.* bribe. **sweetening** *n.* act of making sweet; substance which makes sweet. **sweetheart** *n.* darling; boy/girl friend. **sweetie** *n.* *inf.* (a) sweet (b) darling. **sweetly** *adv.* in a sweet way. sweetmeat, n. (old) sweet.

sweetness *n.* being sweet. **sweet potato** *n.* yAm. **sweetshop** *n.* shop which sell sweets and chocolates. **sweet william** *n.* type of common scented garden flower.

swell 1 [swel] *n.* (a) rising movement of the sea. (b) increasing loudness. **swell 2** *adj.* *Am.* fine. **swell 3** *v.* (swollen/swelled) (a) to increase. (b) to s. (up) = to be come larger/to increase in size. (c) to s. (out) = to become/to make (sails) fully rounded. **swelling** *n.* part of the body which has swollen up.

swelter ['sweltə] *v.* to be very hot. **sweltering** *adj.* very hot.

swept *v.* see sweep.

swerve 1 [swɜːv] *n.* movement to the side. **swerve 2** *v.* to move to one side.

swidden ['swɪdən] *n.* type of farming. where forest is cut down to create space for growing crops.

swift 1 [swɪft] *adj.* (-er, -est) fast. **swift 2** *n.* fast-flying bird like a swallow but with shorter wings and tail. **swiftly** *adv.* fast. **swiftness** *n.* rapidity.

swig 1 [swɪg] *n.* *inf.* large mouthful of liquid. **swig 2** *v.* (swigged) *inf.* to drink in large mouthfuls.

swill 1 [swɪl] *n.* (a) washing a floor with a lot of water (b) food for pigs. **swill 2** *v.* (a) to wash a floor with a lot of water. (b) *inf.* to drink a lot of alcohol.

swim 1 [swɪm] *n.* act of moving in the water using arms/flippers, etc.; in the s. = up to date/knowing what's going on. **swim 2** *v.* (swam; swum) (a) to move in water using arms legs, flippers etc (b) to cross (a river, etc) by swimming (c) to be covered with liquid. (d) (of head, room) to seem to turn. **swimmer** *n.* person who swims. **swimming** *n.* action of swimming; s. trunks = shorts worn for swimming. **swimming bath** *n.* large public pool for swimming. **swimmingly** *adv.* *inf.* very well. **swimming pool** *n.* pool for swimming. **swimsuit** *n.* bathing costume.

swindle 1 ['swɪndl] *n.* trick to get money from s.o. **swindle 2** *v.* to get money from (s.o.) by a trick. **swindler** *n.* person who swindles s.o.

swine [swaɪn] *n.* (no *pl.*) (a) pig. (b) *inf.* unpleasant person. **swine fever** *n.* infectious disease of pigs. **swineherd** *n.* (old) person who looks after pigs.

swing 1 [swɪŋ] *n.* (a) movement from side to side or forwards and backwards; movement of voters to vote for a certain party. (b) to go with a s. = (i) to have a regular beat; (ii) to go very well; in full s. = going very well. (c) seat on the end of two ropes which you can sit on and swing backwards and forwards. **swing 2** *v.* (swung[swʌŋ]) (a) to move from side to side or forwards and backwards. (b) to make (sth) turn round; to turn round. (c) to move in a rhythmic way with a regular motion. **swing bridge** *n.* bridge which can be made to turn to allow ships to pass underneath. **swing door** *n.* door which is not attached with a catch, and which opens when you push it. **swinger** *n.* person who is fashionably modern. **swinging 1** *n.* action of moving backwards and forwards. **swinging 2** *adj.* (a) moving backwards and forwards. (b) *inf.* lively; fashionably modern. **swing-wing** *adj.* (aircraft) with adjustable wings.

swingeing ['swɪndʒɪŋ] *adj.* harsh (tax); severe (blow, measure).

swipe 1 [swaɪp] *n.* *inf.* sweeping hit/blow. **swipe 2** *v.* (a) *inf.* to hit (s.o.) with a sweeping blow. (b) *Sl.* to steal.

swirl 1 [swɜːl] *n.* whirling/twisting movement. **swirl 2** *v.* (a) to move with a whirling/twisting motion.

swish 1 [swɪʃ] *adj.* *inf.* smart. **swish 2** *n.* soft rustle (of a dress/of dead leaves); whistle (of a stick). **swish 3** *v.* to make a whistling noise with a whip/stick.

Swiss 1 [swɪs] *adj.* (a) referring to Switzerland. (b) swiss roll = type of thin sponge cake rolled up with cream or jam as a filling. **Swiss 2** *n.* (*pl.*Swiss) person from Switzerland.

switch 1 [swɪtʃ] *n.* (*pl.*-es) (a) apparatus for starting or stopping an electric current. (b) sudden change. (c) whip made of a thin stick. (d) lock of hair tied at one end. **switch 2** *v.* (a) to send (a train. etc.) in a different direction; to do sth quite different. (b) to hit with a switch. **switchback** *n.* (a) fairground railway which goes up and down steep slopes. (b) road or railway which goes up and down hills.

switchboard *n.* central telephone panel where calls can be transferred to different rooms. **switch off** *v.* to stop an electric current; *inf.* to stop listening to what s.o. is saying. **switch on** *v.* to start an electric current flowing; *inf.* switched on = up to date/knowing all that is happening. **switch over to** *v.* to change to sth quite different.

swivel 1 ['swɪvl] *n.* joint between two parts which enables either part to turn without the other. **swivel 2** *v.* (swivelled) to turn around; to pivot.

swivel chair *n.* chair which pivots, so that the seat can turn while the legs stay stationary.

swizzle ['swɪzl] *n. inf.* swindle/trick. **swizzlestick** *n.* small stick put into a glass of fizzy drink to make it less fizzy.

swollen ['swəʊlən] *adj.* blown up; increased in size; swollen-headed = (person) who has a high opinion of himself; see also swell.

swoon [swu:n] *v.* to faint.

swoop 1 [swu:p] *n.* coming rapidly down from a height to attack; sudden attack; at one fell s. = in sudden move/all at once. **swoop 2** *v.* to come down rapidly to attack; to attack suddenly.

swop [swɒp] *n. & v.* see swap.

sword [sɔːd] *n.* weapon with a long sharp blade held by a handle; to cross swords with = to get into an argument with. **swordfish** *n.* fish with a long pointed upper jaw like a sword.

swordsman *n.* (*pl.*-men) person who fights well with a sword. **swordstick** *n.* hollow walking stick containing a long sharp blade.

swore [swɔː] *v.* see swear.

sworn [swɔːn] *adj.* s. enemies = total enemies; see also swear.

swot 1 [swɒt] *n. Sl.* (a) hard school work; (b) person who studies hard. **swot 2** *v.* (swotted) *Sl.* to study hard.

swum [swʌm] *v.* see swim.

swung [swʌŋ] *v.* see swing.

sybarite ['sɪbəraɪt] *n.* person who enjoys luxury. **sybaritic** [sɪbə'rɪtɪk] *adj.* very comfortable and luxurious.

sycamore ['sɪkəmɔː] *n.* common deciduous tree with very large leaves.

sycophant ['sɪkəfænt] *n.* person who

flatters s.o. in power. **sycophantic** [sɪkə'fæntɪk] *adj.* which flatters excessively.

syllable ['sɪləbl] *n.* unit of sound which forms a whole word or part of a word. **syllabic** [sɪ'læbɪk] *adj.* referring to a syllable.

syllabub ['sɪləbʌb] *n.* sweet food made of cream whipped with wine.

syllabus ['sɪləbəs] *n.* (*pl.*-es) list of subjects to be studied.

syllogism ['sɪlədʒɪzəm] *n.* logical reasoning where a conclusion is reached from two statements.

sylph [sɪlf] *n.* thin girl. **sylphlike** *adj.* very slim.

sylvan ['sɪlvən] *adj.* (*formal*) referring to woods.

symbiosis [sɛmbɪ'əʊsɪs] *n.* state where two living organisms live close together and depend on each other to a certain extent. **symbiotic** [sɪmbaɪ'ptɪk] *adj.* referring to symbiosis.

symbol ['sɪmbl] *n.* sign/letter/picture/object which represents sth/which is a short way of indicating sth.

symbolic(al) [sɪm'bɒlɪk(l)] *adj.* which acts as a symbol. **symbolically** *adv.* used as a symbol. **symbolism** *n.* (a) movement in literature and art which used symbols to express emotion. etc. (b) using symbols to express emotion etc. **symbolist** *adj. & n.* (follower) of symbolism. **symbolize** ['sɪmbəlaɪz] *v.* to represent (sth) by a symbol; to be a symbol for sth.

symmetry ['sɪmətri] *n.* state where two sides of sth are exactly similar.

symmetrical [sɪ'metrɪkl] *adj.* referring to symmetry.

sympathy ['sɪmpəθɪ] *n.* (a) feeling of pity or sorrow because s.o. else has problems. (b) common feeling; sharing ideas. **sympathetic** [sɪmpə'θetɪk] *adj.* showing sympathy. **sympathetically** *adv.* in a sympathetic way. **sympathize** *v.* (with) (a) to show sympathy to (s.o in trouble.) (b) to approve; to agree.

sympathizer *n.* person who sympathizes with s.o.'s political views.

symphony ['sɪmfənɪ] *n.* piece of music in several parts for a full orchestra.

symphonic [sɪm'fɒnɪk] *adj.* referring to a symphony.

symposium [sɪm'pəʊzɪəm] *n.* (*pl.*- ia)

organized meeting to discuss a specific subject; collection of articles written on a specific subject.

symptom ['sɪmptəm] *n.* thing which shows visibly that feelings exist/that changes are taking place. **symptomatic** [sɪmptə'mætɪk] *adj.* (of) which shows visibly that changes are taking place or that feelings exist.

synagogue ['sɪnəgɒg] *n.* building where Jews worship.

synapse ['sɪnæps] *n.* point in the nervous system where neurones join.

sync [sɪŋk] *n. inf.* synchronization; out of s. = not synchronized.

synchromesh ['sɪŋkrəmeʃ] *n.* type of gear system where the gears revolve at the same speeds before being engaged.

synchronize ['sɪŋkrənaɪz] *v.* to adjust (watches) to the same time; to arrange (things) so that they happen at the same time. **synchronization** [sɪŋkrənaɪ'zeɪʃn] *n.* act of synchronizing.

syncopate ['sɪŋkəpeɪt] *v.* (in music) to stress (a beat) which would not normally be stressed and so change the rhythm. **syncopation** [sɪŋkə'peɪʃn] *n.* act of syncopating.

syncope ['sɪŋkəpɪ] *n.* fainting attack.

syndicalism ['sɪndɪkəlɪzm] *n.* form of socialism, where control is in the hands of the trade unions. **syndicate 1** ['sɪndɪkət] *n.* group of people or companies working together to make money. **syndicate 2** ['sɪndɪkeɪt] *v.* to produce (an article/a cartoon) which is then sold to a series of newspapers. **syndication** [sɪndɪ'keɪʃn] *n.* act of syndicating.

syndrome ['sɪndrəʊm] *n.* (a) series of symptoms which show an illness. (b) symptoms which show a general feeling/ way of approaching a problem etc.

synergy ['sɪnədʒɪ] *n.* (of two organizations) working together to be better than working separately.

synod ['sɪnəd] *n.* meeting of religious leaders.

synonym ['sɪnənɪm] *n.* word which means the same thing as another word. **synonymous** [sɪ'nɒnɪməs] *adj.* which has the same meaning.

synopsis [sɪ'nɒpsɪs] *n.* (*pl.*-ses) summary (of main points made in a book or article).

synovitis ['saɪnəʊ'vaɪtɪs] *n.* inflammation of the membrane covering a joint.

syntax ['sɪntæks] *n.* grammatical rules for putting words together into sentences. **syntactic** [sɪn'tæktɪk] *adj.* referring to syntax.

synthesis ['sɪnθəsɪs] *n.* (*pl.*-ses) bringing several parts together to form a whole. **synthesize** ['sɪnθəsaɪz] *v.* to combine (several things) together to make a whole. **synthesizer** *n.* electronic device which can make musical sounds similar to those of different instruments.

synthetic 1 [sɪn'θetɪk] *n.* artificial/man made material. **synthetic 2** *adj.* artificial; made in such a way that it looks natural. **synthetically** *adv.* in a synthetic way.

syphilis ['sɪfɪlɪs] *n.* serious disease transmitted by sexual intercourse or inherited. **syphilitic** *adj. & n.* (person) suffering from syphilis.

Syrian ['sɪrɪən] *adj. & n.* (person) from Syria.

syringa [sɪ'rɪŋgə] *n.* tall shrub with scented white flowers.

syringe 1 [sɪ'rɪdʒ] *n.* tube with a piston or rubber bulb so that liquids can be sucked into it then squeezed out, as in giving injections; garden s. = instrument for spraying trees with insecticide. etc. **syringe 2** *v.* to clean by blowing liquid with a syringe.

syrup ['sɪrəp] *n.* thick sweet liquid; thick golden juice from sugar. **syrupy** *adj.* like syrup; very sweet.

system ['sɪstəm] *n.* (a) arrangement of things which work together (b) way of organizing things to work together. (c) method (d) body. **systematic** [sɪstə'mætɪk] *adj.* orderly/methodical. **systematically** *adv.* in a methodical way. **systematize** ['sɪstəmətaɪz] *v.* to organize into a system. **systemic** [sɪs'temɪk] *adj.* which affects the whole system. **systems analysis** *n.* use of a computer to forecast needs etc., by analysing the way in which a system is actually operating. **systems analyst** *n.* person who specializes in systems analysis.

systole [sɪs'təʊlɪ] *n.* phase in the heart beat, when the heart contracts and pumps blood out.

Tt

T, t [tiː] *inf.* it suits him to a T = it suits him perfectly; to dot one's i's and cross one's t's = to settle the final details (of an agreement)/to be very careful about sth; T-bone steak = type of beef steak with a bone shaped like a T in it; T-junction = junction where one road joins another at right angles; T shirt = light short-sleeved shirt with no buttons or collar; T square = device shaped like a T for drawing right angles.

ta [tɑː] *inter. inf.* thank you.

tab [tæb] *n.* (a) small loop of cloth for hanging up a coat/for pulling open a box. (b) little coloured marker attached to cards in an index so that they can be found easily; *inf.* to pick up the t. = to pay the bill; to keep tabs on s.o. = to keep watch on s.o.

tabard ['tæbɑːd] *n.* short sleeveless coat worn by heralds.

tabasco [təˈbæskəʊ] *n.* trademark for a hot red sauce.

tabby (cat) ['tæbi(kæt)] *n.* striped black, brown, and grey cat.

tabernacle ['tæbənækl] *n.* (a) place of worship. (b) ornamental box for consecrated bread and wine.

table 1 ['teɪbl] *n.* (a) piece of furniture with a flat top and legs, used for eating at/for working at, etc.; to set the t. = to get the table ready for a meal; to clear the t. = to remove dirty plates/knives, etc. after a meal; to turn the tables on s.o. = to put yourself in a superior position, where before you were in an inferior one. (b) printed list of figures/facts; multiplication tables = lists of figures to learn by heart how each number is multiplied. t. of contents = list of contents of a book. **table 2** *v.* to suggest (items for discussion); to put (additional information) on the table at a committee meeting. **tablecloth** *n.* cloth for covering a table during a meal. **tableland** *n.* high flat land. **table linen** *n.* tablecloth/serviettes, etc. **table manners** *n. pl.* polite way of eating according to the rules of society. **table mat** *n.* mat for protecting the surface of a table. **tablespoon** *n.* large spoon for serving food at table. **tablespoonful** *n.* quantity held in a tablespoon. **table tennis** *n.* game played on a large table with a net across the centre, using small round bats and a very light white ball. **tableware** *n.* knives, forks, spoons, plates, etc.

tableau ['tæbləʊ] *n.* (*pl.*-eaux[-əʊz]) scene where actors represent a historic occasion, etc., without moving.

table d'hôte ['tɑːblədəʊt] *n.* menu which has a restricted number of dishes at a reduced price.

tablet ['tæblət] *n.* (a) small round pill of medicine. (b) flat stone with an inscription on it. (c) bar (of soap/chocolate)

tabloid ['tæblɔɪd] *n.* popular newspaper with a small page size. *usu.* with a large number of pictures.

taboo 1 [təˈbuː] *adj.* forbidden (by religion/by custom). **taboo 2** *n.* (religious) custom which forbids sth.

tabor ['teɪbɔː] *n.* small drum beaten with the hand.

tabular ['tæbjʊlə] *adj.* arranged in a table. **tabulate** ['tæbjʊleɪt] *v.* to arrange (figures) in a table. **tabulation** [tæbjʊˈleɪʃn] *n.* arrangement (of figures) in a table. **tabulator** *n.* device on a typewriter/in a computer program which allows the typist to make columns automatically.

tachograph ['tækəɡrɑːf] *n.* machine placed in the cab of a lorry which records details of the mileage and time spent on a journey. **tachycardia** [tækɪˈkɑːdɪə] *n.* rapid heartbeat.

tacit ['tæsɪt] *adj.* (agreement, etc.) which is understood, but not actually given. **tacitly** *adv.* (agreement given) without speaking, but nevertheless understood.

taciturn *adj.* (person) who does not say much. **taciturnity** [tæsɪˈtɜːnɪtɪ] *n.* silence/not saying much.

tack 1 [tæk] *n.* (a) small nail (with a large head); *inf.* to get down to brass tacks = to talk real business/to start discussing the real problem. (b) (in sewing) light stitch to hold cloth in place and which can be taken out later. (c) diagonal movement of a ship so that it is sailing against the wind on the right t. = doing the right thing. n. (d) saddle and equipment for horse-riding. (e) (Scotland) lease. **tack 2** v. (a) to nail (sth) using tacks; (b) to make a light temporary stitch. (c) to change direction so that you are sailing into the wind. they were tacking up the river = they sailed in a zigzag way up the river against the wind. **tack on** v. to add (sth) at the end.

tackle 1 ['tækl] n. (a) equipment. (b) block and t. = arrangement of ropes. pulleys and hooks for lifting heavy weights. (c) (in football, etc.) trying to get possession of the ball from an opposing player; (in Rugby) grabbing an opposing player so that he falls to the ground and releases the ball. **tackle 2** v. (a) to grab (s.o./sth); to try to deal with (a problem). (b) (in football, etc.) to try to get possession of the ball from an opposing player; (in Rugby) to grab (an opposing player) so that he falls to the ground. **tackler** n. person who tackles.

tacky ['tækɪ] adj. (-ier, -iest) sticky. **tackiness** n. being tacky.

tact [tækt] n. care in your relationships with people so that you do not offend them. **tactful** adj. using tact. **tactfully** adv. in a tactful way. **tactless** adj. lacking tact/unintentionally offensive. **tactlessly** adv. in a tactless way. **tactlessness** n. lack of tact.

tactic ['tæktɪk] n. (often pl.) way of doing sth so as to be at an advantage; way of placing troops/guns, etc., so as to be in a better position than the enemy. **tactical** adj. (a) referring to tactics; tactical error = mistake in planning. (b) (nuclear weapon) which is used in a limited area. **tactically** adv. in a tactical way. **tactician** [tæk'tɪʃn] n. person who is expert at tactics.

tactile ['tæktaɪl] adj. sensitive to touch; referring to the sense of touch.

tadpole ['tædpəʊl] n. baby frog/toad in its first stage after hatching.

taffeta ['tæfɪtə] n. thin shiny stiff cloth.

taffrail ['tæfreɪl] n. guard rail round the stern of a ship.

tag 1 [tæg] n. (a) small loop of cloth; metal piece at the end of a shoelace. (b) label. (c) common old saying. (d) children's game where you have to try to touch another child who chases the others in his turn. **tag 2** inf. to t. on to

s.o. = to stay close to s.o.; to t. along behind = to follow closely.

taiga ['taɪgə] n. forest in north Siberia.

tail 1 [teɪl] n. (a) part of an animal at the rear of its body, usu. sticking out at the back to turn t. = run away. (b) back part of a long coat/of a shirt, etc.; wearing tails = wearing evening-dress. (c) back part (of a line); back (of a car). (d) tails = reverse side of a coin/the side of a coin without the head of a king, etc., on it. (e) inf. detective who is following s.o. closely. **tail 2** v. (a) to take the stems off (gooseberries, etc.). (b) to follow (s.o) closely. **tail away** v. to die away/to fade away. **tailback** n. long line of cars held up by an accident, etc. **tailboard, tailgate** n. hinged board at the back of a lorry which can be let down to load or unload the contents. **tail coat** n. man's black evening jacket with a long tail at the back. **tail end** n. back part (of a queue); last part (of a film, etc). tailless, adj. (animal) with no tail. taillight, n. rear light (of a car, etc.). **tail off** v. to die away/to fade away. **tailpipe** n. Am. exhaust pipe. **tailplane** n. flat wings on the tail of an aircraft. **tailspin** n. dive by an aircraft, where the machine turns round and round. **tail wind** n. wind blowing behind an aircraft, making it go faster.

tailor 1 ['teɪlə] n. person who makes outer clothes (suits/coats, etc.) usu. for men. **tailor 2** v. (a) to make clothes which fit. (b) to make (sth) fit particular circumstances. **tailor-made** adj. made to fit.

taint 1 [teɪnt] n. slight trace of evil/of corruption. **taint 2** v. to infect/to corrupt; tainted food = food which has become rotten (by touching other rotten food).

take 1 [teɪk] n. (a) one scene of a film which has been filmed. (b) money taken in a shop/in a business. **take 2** v. (took; has taken) (a) to hold/to grasp/to carry. (b) to remove/to steal. (c) to buy/to rent/ to occupy; to have a (newspaper) delivered to your house regularly; to t. a seat = sit down; to t. the chair = to act as chairman (at a meeting). (d) to win (a prize). (e) to be a candidate for (an examination). (f) to eat/to drink (usually); do you t. sugar in your tea? (g) to make (a photograph) (h) to accept; t. it from me = believe what I say; she's taking legal advice = she is consulting a lawyer; t. my advice = do as I suggest. (i) to need; it took three men to lift the piano; we took two days/it took us two days to get to London. (j) to lead; to go (in a direction); can you t. me to the station? = can you drive me to the station? (k) to hold; (of machine) to accept/to be able to work with. (l) to do (a certain action); to t. a walk/a bath/a holiday; to t. a decision = to decide. (m) to stand/to put up with. (n) to be successful/to have effect; the kidney transplant has taken = has been successful; the cuttings have taken = have sprouted roots. **take after** v. to be like (a parent). **take away** v. (a) to remove. (b) to subtract. **takeaway** n. & adj. inf. (shop where you can buy) hot food to eat elsewhere. **take back** v. (a) to return. (b) I take it all back = I withdraw what I said and apologise for having said it. **take down** v. (a) to lower (sth which is hanging). (b) to write down (what s.o. says). (c) to demolish. **take-home pay** n. amount of money you actually receive out of your wages, after tax, etc., has been deducted. **take in** v. (a) to accept/to bring inside. (b) to include. (c) to trick (s.o.). (d) to understand. (e) to make (a skirt, etc.) smaller, **taken with** adj. inf. attracted by. **take off** v. (a) to remove (clothes). (b) to fly into the air. (c) inf. to imitate. **takeoff** n. (a) departure (of an aircraft). (b) inf. imitation. **take on** v. (a) to agree to do (some work). (b) to agree to employ (s.o.). (c) to fight; to play against. (d) to make a scene. **take out** v. (a) to pull (sth) out. (b) to invite (s.o) to go out. (c) to take out an insurance policy on = to start to insure. (d) to take it out on s.o. = to make s.o suffer to help relieve your own feelings. (c) the heat takes it out of me = makes me very tired. **takeout** n. Am. takeaway. **take over** v. (a) to buy (a business), (b) to take over from s.o. = to start to do sth in place of s.o. else. **takeover** n. buying of a business; t. bid = offer to buy a business. t. bid = offer to buy a business. **taker** n. person who wants to buy. **take to** v. (a) to start to do sth to help you out of a bad

situation; he took to the woods = went into the woods to hide; she took to drink = started to drink alcohol regularly. (b) to start to like (s.o.). **take up** v. (a) to pick up; they've taken up the road = removed the road surface. (b) to occupy (space). (c) to start to do (a sport/a craft). (d) to start to work on (an idea); to start to discuss (a case). (e) to make (a skirt, etc.) shorter. (f) inf. to take s.o, up on sth = to accept a suggestion which s.o. has made. **take up with** v. to become friendly with (s.o.), **takings** n. pl. money received in a shop/in a business.

talaq ['tælæk] n. Islamic form of divorce.

talc [tælk] n. smooth soft mineral used to make powder to put on the body; powder made from this mineral. **talcum powder** n. powder made from talc.

tale [teɪl] n. story; old wives' t. = superstitious belief.

talent ['tælənt] n. (a) natural gift/ability. (b) people with natural ability. t. contest = contest to find new singers/comedians, etc. **talented** adj. very gifted.

talisman ['tælɪzmən] n. object kept because it supposedly brings good luck.

talk 1 [tɔːk] n. (a) spoken words; idle t. = gossip; double t. = saying one thing and thinking the opposite. (b) conversation. (c) lecture/informal speech. **talk 2** v. (a) to speak (a language). inf. now you're talking = that's a good idea. (b) to gossip. (c) to give information (usu. unwillingly). **talkative** adj. (person) who likes to chat/to gossip. **talk down** v. (a) to speak in a condescending way/in an exaggeratedly simple way (to s.o.). (b) to give instructions over the radio to a pilot for landing his aircraft when visibility is bad. **talker** n. person who talks. **talking** n. speech, conversation; he did all the t. = the others said nothing. **talking-point** n. thing people argue about. **talking-shop** n. place where things are discussed but no action is ever taken. **talking-to** n. inf. scolding. **talk into** v. to talk s.o. into doing sth = to persuade. **talk over** v. I talked him over = I persuaded him to change his mind; come and talk it over = come and discuss it. **talk round** v. I talked him round = I persuaded him to change his mind; we just talked round the subject = we never discussed the main problem.

tall [tɔːl] *adj.* (-er, -est) (a) high. (b) *inf.* unbelievable (story); t. order = command which is extremely difficult to carry out.

tallboy *n.* type of tall chest of drawers.

tallow ['tæləʊ] *n.* fat from animals, used to make candles.

tally 1 ['tælɪ] *n.* note/account. **tally 2** *v.* to agree (with).

talon ['tælən] *n.* claw (of a bird).

tamarisk ['tæmərɪsk] *n.* shrub with feathery evergreen leaves. which is often grown near the sea.

tambourine [tæmbə'riːn] *n.* small drum with metal pieces loosely attached to the rim, so that they jangle when it is beaten.

tame 1 [teɪm] *adj.* (-er, -est) (a) (animal) which is not wild/which can be approached by human beings; *inf.* our t. tax expert = the tax expert whom we call on regularly for advice. (b) not very exciting. **tame 2** *v.* to make (an animal) tame; to make safe. **tamely** *adv.* humbly. **tameness** *n.* being tame. **tamer** *n.* person who tames wild animals.

tam-o'-shanter [tæmə'ʃæntə] *n.* flat Scottish cap, like a beret.

tamp [tæmp] *v.* to press down.

tamper ['tæmpə] *v.* to t. with = to meddle with.

tampon ['tæmpɒn] *n.* pad of cotton wool used to soak up blood.

tan 1 [tæn] *n. & adj.* brownish yellow (colour). **tan 2** *n.* brown colour of the skin after being in the sun. **tan 3** *v.* (tanned) to treat (animal skin) to make leather. (b) to get brown by sitting in the sun. **tanner** *n.* person who makes animal skins into leather. **tannery** *n.* factory where skins are made into leather.

tandem ['tændəm] *n.* bicycle for two people; in t. = in pairs/together.

tang [tæŋ] *n.* sharp smell/taste. **tangy** *adj.* with a sharp taste/smell.

tangent ['tændʒənt] *n.* line which touches a curve without cutting through it; to go off at a t. = to change direction/ to follow another line of thought. **tangential** [tæn'dʒənʃl] *adj.* referring to a tangent.

tangerine ['tændʒə'riːn] *n.* small

orange with soft skin which peels easily.

tangible ['tændʒəbl] *adj.* which can be touched; real. **tangibility** [tændʒɪ'bɪlɪtɪ] *n.* being tangible. **tangibly** *adv.* in a real/definite way.

tangle 1 ['tæŋgl] *n.* mix of threads/ string/hair; in a t. = all mixed up. **tangle 2** *v.* to mix (things) together in knots; to t. with s.o. = to get into an argument.

tango ['tæŋgəʊ] *n.* (*pl.*- os) dance where you glide sideways.

tank [tæŋk] *n.* (a) large (metal) container for liquids. (b) t. wagon = railway wagon for carrying liquids. (c) armoured vehicle with caterpillar tracks and a powerful gun. **tanker** *n.* (a) special ship for carrying liquids (esp. oil). (b) special lorry for carrying liquids.

tank up *v. inf.* to drink a lot. **tankard** ['tæŋkəd] *n.* large metal mug for drinking beer.

tannin ['tænɪn] *n.* red-brown liquid (found in the bark of trees/in tea) which is used to make leather. **tannic** *adj.* t. acid = tannin.

tannoy ['tænɔɪ] *n.* trademark for a public loudspeaker system.

tansy ['tænzɪ] *n.* herb with yellow flowers.

tantalize ['tæntəlaɪz] *v.* to tease (s.o.) by offering him sth which he can't have. **tantalizing** *adj.* which tantalizes. **tantalizingly** *adv.* in a tantalizing way.

tantamount ['tæntəmaʊnt] *adj.* equivalent/equal (to).

tantrum ['tæntrəm] *n.* attack of uncontrollable bad temper.

Taoiseach ['tiːʃək] *n.* (in Republic of Ireland) Prime Minister.

tap 1 [tæp] *n.* (a) apparatus with a twisting knob and a valve which, when you turn it, allows liquid to come out of a pipe/container; t. water = water which comes from the mains and not from a well; on t. = readily available. (b) slight blow; light knock. **tap 2** *v.* (tapped) (a) to run liquid out of (a barrel) by fixing a tap; to cut a ring round the stem of (a rubber tree) so that the sap flows down and drips from a small spout. (b) to attach a secret listening device to (a telephone). (c) to start to exploit (sth new). (d) to hit lightly. **tap dance** *n.* dance done by beating time to the music with metalsoled shoes. **tap dancer** *n.* dancer who specializes in tap dancing.

tap dancing *n.* dancing with special shoes with metal soles, so that the dancer beats time to the music. **tap root** *n.* main root (of a tree) which goes straight down into the soil.

tape 1 [teɪp] *n.* (a) long thin flat strip (of cloth/plastic, etc.); sticky t. = glued plastic strip for sticking things together, etc., insulating t. = sticky tape for wrapping round electrical connections; measuring tape = long strip marked in centimetres/inches, etc., for measuring; magnetic t. = sensitive plastic tape for recording. (b) long string held across the finishing line of a race. **tape 2** *v.* (a) to attach to a tape. (b) to record (5th) on magnetic tape. (c) *inf.* I've got him taped = I know exactly what he's like/I understand him completely; we've got it all taped = everything is under control/ we know how to do it perfectly. **tape deck** *n.* apparatus which plays tape and records on tape, but does not have its own amplifier or loudspeakers. **tape measure** *n.* long strip of cloth/metal marked in centimetres/inches, etc., used for measuring. **tape-record** *v.* to record (sth) on tape. **tape-recorder** *n.* apparatus which records on tape and plays back these tapes. **tape-recording** *n.* recording done on tape. **tapeworm** *n.* long flatworm which lives in the intestines of man and other animals.

taper 1 [ˈteɪpə] *n.* long slender candle, made of wick covered with a thin layer of wax. **taper 2** *v.* to make (sth) become thinner at the end; (also taper off) to become thinner at the end.

tapestry [ˈtæpɪstrɪ] *n.* thick woven cloth with a picture or design, *usu.* hung on walls or used to cover chairs.

tapioca [tæpɪˈəʊkə] *n.* white starchy powder which comes from a tropical plant and is used to make puddings.

tapir [ˈteɪpə] *n.* South American animal like a pig with a short trunk.

tappet [ˈtæpɪt] *n.* small projecting piece which opens or closes a valve by tapping on it.

tar 1 [tɑː] *n.* (a) black oily substance which comes from coal and is used for covering roads. (b) *inf.* sailor. **tar 2** *v.* (tarred) to cover with tar; tarred paper = thick brown waterproof paper with, an inner layer of tar; to t. and feather s.o. = to cover s.o. with hot tar and feathers as a punishment; to be tarred with the same brush = to have the same weaknesses/to make the same mistakes (as s.o.).

tarantula [tæˈræntjʊlə] *n.* large mildly poisonous tropical spider.

tardy [ˈtɑːdɪ] *adj.* (-ier, -iest) (formal) late. **tardily** *adv.* late. **tardiness** *n.* being tardy.

tare [teə] *n.* (a) allowance made for the weight of the lorry, etc., in calculating transport costs. (b) (old) weed.

target [ˈtɑːgɪt] *n.* thing which you aim at; t. practice = practising at shooting at a target; t. language = language which you are learning/into which you are translating.

tariff [ˈtærɪf] *n.* (a) tax to be paid for importing goods; to lift t. barriers = to reduce import/hotel taxes. (b) list of prices (in a restaurant/hotel/bar, etc.).

tarmac [ˈtɑːmæk] *n.* (a) trademark for a hard surface of a road made of tar mixed with small stones. (b) runway of an airport, **tarmacked** *adj.* covered with tarmac.

tarn [tɑːn] *n.* small mountain lake in the Lake District.

tarnish [ˈtɑːnɪʃ] *v.* (of metal) to become discoloured; to ruin (a reputation).

tarot [ˈtærəʊ] *n.* set of cards designed for use in telling fortunes.

tarpaulin [tɑːˈpɔːlin] *n.* large waterproof cloth.

tarragon [ˈtærəgən] *n.* common herb used in cooking.

tarry [ˈtærɪ] *v.* (old) to stay behind.

tarsus [ˈtɑːsəs] *n.* set of bones in the ankle.

tart 1 [tɑːt] *n.* (a) small pastry dish filled with sweet food. (b) *Sl.* prostitute. **tart 2** *adj.* (-er, -est) (a) bitter (taste) (b) sharp (answer). **tart 3** *v.* *inf.* to t. yourself up = to make yourself look smart. **tartly** *adv.* sharply. **tartness** *n.* sourness (of taste).

tartan [ˈtɑːtən] *n. & adj.* (cloth) woven into a special pattern for one of the Scottish clans; distinctive pattern in such a cloth.

tartar [ˈtɑːtə] *n.* (a) hard substance which forms on teeth. (b) cream of t. = white powder used in cooking and in medicine. (c) *inf.* fierce person. **tartaric** [tɑːˈtærɪk] *adj.* t. acid = acid used in cooking. **tartare sauce** [tɑːtɑːˈsɔːs] *n.*

mayonnaise containing finely chopped pieces of vegetables.

task [tɑːsk] *n.* (a) work which has to be done. (b) to take s.o. to t. for = to criticize.

task force *n.* special group (esp. of soldiers) chosen to carry out a hard task. **taskmaster** *n.* person who sets a hard task.

tassel ['tæsl] *n.* group of threads tied together at one end to form a ball, with the other ends hanging free. **tasselled** *adj.* with tassels.

taste 1 [teɪst] *n.* (a) sense by which you can tell differences of flavour between things you eat; t. buds = cells on the tongue which enable you to tell differences in flavour. (b) flavour of food or drink. (c) very small quantity (of food/drink); he's had a t. of prison = he has been in prison once. (d) liking (for sth); expensive tastes = liking for expensive things. (c) good/bad t. = ability/inability to judge what is fine/ beautiful/refined. **taste 2** *v.* (a) to sense the flavour of (sth). (b) to have a flavour (of). (c) to try (sth); to experience (freedom). **tasteful** *adj.* showing good taste. **tastefully** *adv.* in good taste. **tastelessly** *adv.* in a tasteless way. **taster** *n.* person whose job is to taste food to test its quality.

tasty *adj.* (-er, -iest) with a particular pleasant flavour.

tat [tæt] *n.* (no *pl.*) *inf.* shabby/cheap things; see also tit.

ta-ta [tə'tɑː] *int. inf.* goodbye.

tatters ['tætəz] *n.* in t. = (i) torn (clothes); (ii) (person) wearing old torn clothes.

tattered ['tætəd] *adj.* torn and old.

tatting ['tætɪŋ] *n.* type of lace made by hand.

tattle ['tætl] *v.* (formal) to gossip.

tattoo 1 [tə'tuː] *n.* (a) military parade in the evening. (b) rapid beating (of drums). (c) decoration on skin made by pricking with a needle and putting colour into the wound. **tattoo 2** *v.* to make decorations on s.o.'s skin by pricking it and putting colour into the wound.

tatty ['tætɪ] *adj.* (-ier, -iest) untidy/ shabby.

taught [tɔːt] *v.* see teach.

taunt 1 [tɔːnt] *n.* sarcastic jeering.

taunt 2 *v.* to jeer at (s.o.) sarcastically.

Taurus ['tɔːrəs] *n.* one of the signs of the zodiac, shaped like a bull.

taut [tɔːt] *adj.* stretched tight. **tauten** *v.* to make tight; to become tight. **tautly** *adv.* tightly. **tautness** *n.* being taut.

tautology [tɔːtɒlədʒɪ] *n.* unnecessary use in a phrase of different words which mean the same thing. **tautological** *adj.* using tautology.

tavern ['tævən] *n.* inn/public house.

taw [tɔː] *n.* big marble.

tawdry ['tɔːdrɪ] *adj.* (-ier, -iest) cheap and bad taste.

tawny ['tɔːnɪ] *adj.* (-ier, -iest) orange brown.

tawse [tɔːz] *n.* (in Scotland) strap for beating school children.

tax 1 [tæks] *n.* (*pl.*-es) (a) money taken by the state from incomes/sales, etc., which pays for government services; t. free = without having to pay any tax. (b) burden; it's a severe t. on our resources = it strains our resources. **tax 2** *v.* (a) to put a tax on (sth/s.o.). (b) to strain. (c) (formal) to t. s.o. with = to accuse s.o. of.

taxable *adj.* which can be taxed.

taxation [tæk'seɪʃn] *n.* (a) (system of) imposing taxes. (b) money raised from taxes. **taxman** *n.* (*pl.*-men) *inf.* civil servant who deals with tax (usu. income tax). **taxpayer** *n.* person who pays taxes. **tax point** *n.* date on which goods are supplied and VAT becomes chargeable. **tax return** *n.* form to be filled in to report your earnings and allowances to the tax office.

taxi 1 ['tæksɪ] *n.* car which can be hired; t. rank = place in the street where taxis can wait. **taxi 2** *v.* (of an aircraft) to go along the ground before take-off or after landing. **taxicab** *n.* taxi. **taximeter** *n.* machine fitted inside a taxi which shows the price for the journey.

taxidermy ['tæksɪdɜːmɪ] *n.* art of stuffing the skins of dead animals so that they look lifelike. **taxidermist** *n.* person who stuffs the skins of dead animals so that they look lifelike.

taxonomy [tæk'sɒnəmɪ] *n.* scientific classification (esp. of plants and animals). **taxonomist** *n.* person who specializes in taxonomy.

TB ['tiːbiː] abbreviation for tuberculosis.

TD [ti:di:] abbrev. for Teachta Dala, a Member of the Irish Parliament.

tea [ti:] n. (a) dried leaves of a tropical plant which are used to make a common drink. (b) drink made by pouring boiling water on to dried leaves of the tea plant. (c) any hot drink made in a similar way; lime t. = tea made with the dried flowers of the lime tree. (d) afternoon meal; t. service/t. set = plates/cups/saucers, etc., used at tea; high tea = large meal eaten in the early evening in the North of England and Scotland. **teabag** n. small paper bag full of tea which is put into the pot instead of loose tea. **tea break** n. rest period at work, when you can drink tea. **teacake** n. type of bun with raisins in it, usu. eaten hot with butter. **teachest** n. light wooden packing case in which tea is shipped. **teacloth** n. cloth for drying dishes. **tea cosy** n. cover for putting over a teapot to keep it warm. **teacup** n. large cup for tea. **tealeaf** n. (pl.-leaves) small piece of tea left in the cup after you have drunk the tea. **tea party** n. party (held in the afternoon or early evening) when you drink tea, eat cakes, etc. **teapot** n. special pot with a handle and spout for making tea in. **tearoom, teashop** n. small restaurant which serves mainly tea and light meals. **teaspoon** n. small spoon for stirring tea. **teaspoonful** n. quantity contained in a teaspoon. **teatime** n. time when you have tea (about 4 o'clock in the afternoon). **tea towel** n. cloth for drying dishes. **tea trolley** n. small table on wheels from which you can serve foods.

teach [ti:tʃ] v. (taught[tɔ**x**t]) to give (s.o.) information; to give lessons (in a school); to show (s.o.) how to do sth; inf. that'll t. him to be so rude = will punish him for being rude. **teachable** adj. which can be taught. **teacher** n. person who teaches. **teach-in** n. inf. informal discussion on a topic. **teaching** n. (a) action of giving knowledge/giving lessons; the t. profession = teachers as a group. (b) political or moral ideas/philosophy.

teak [ti:k] n. large tropical tree; hard wood of this tree, which does not warp, and is used for making furniture, etc.

teal [ti:l] n. (pl.teal) small type of wild

duck.

team 1 [ti:m] n. (a) group of people playing together/working together; t. spirit = good feeling of those who play or work well together as a teAm. (b) group of animals working together. **team 2** v. to t. up with s.o. = to join s.o. to work together. **teamster** n. Am. lorry driver. **teamwork** n. ability to work together as a group; working together as a group.

tear 1 [tɪə] n. drop of water formed in the eyes when you cry; he burst into tears = suddenly started to cry; in tears = crying. **teardrop** n. one tear. **tearful** adj. sad/crying. **tearfully** adv. in a tearful way. **tear-gas** n. gas which makes you cry, used to control crowds of rioters. **tear-jerker** n. inf. film/novel which makes you cry. **tear-stained** adj. (face) with the marks of tears.

tear2 1 [teə] n. (a) hole torn in a piece of cloth; (b) wear and t. = normal usage (of a house/car, etc.) which wears sth away. **tear2 2** v. (tore[tɔ**x**], has torn[tɔ**x**nl]) (a) to make a hole in (sth) by pulling; torn between = unable to decide between; inf. that's torn it = that has ruined what we were planning/that has spoilt everything. (b) to pull to pieces; to t. into s.o. = to attack s.o.; they tore up the road = dug up the road surface; to t. oneself away from = to leave reluctantly. (c) inf. to go fast; in a tearing hurry = very fast. **tearaway** n. inf. wild young hooligan.

tease 1 [ti:z] n. person who annoys/irritates people on purpose. **tease 2** v. (a) to annoy (s.o.)/to irritate (s.o.) on purpose. (b) to disentangle threads (with a comb); to brush (cloth) to make it soft. **teaser** n. inf. problem which is difficult to solve/question which is difficult to answer.

teasel ['ti:zl] n. tall plant with prickly flower heads.

teat [ti:t] n. (a) projection on a cow's udder through which milk passes. (b) rubber cap put on a baby's feeding bottle through which the baby sucks milk.

technical ['teknɪkl] adj. (a) referring to a particular industry/practical work, etc.; t. term = term used by specialists; t. college = college where technical skills are taught; t. subjects = subjects which teach practical skills (such as woodwork, engineering, etc.); t. training = training in a practical skill. (b) referring to a fixed interpretation of the rules; t. knockout = where the referee stops the fight because a boxer is too hurt to continue. **tech** [tek] *n. inf.* technical college. **technically** *adv.* (a) in a technical way; (b) strictly speaking. **technicality** [teknɪ'kælɪtɪ] *n.* (a) technical detail. (b) strict interpretation of rules/of laws. **technician** [tek'nɪʃn] *n.* person who is specialized in industrial or scientific work. **technique** [tek'niːk] *n.* skilled way of doing sth. **technocrat** [teknəkræt] *n.* person with particular technical/organizational skills, brought in to run a country/an organization. **technological** [teknə'lɒdʒɪkl] *adj.* referring to technology. **technologically** *adv.* in a technological way. **technologist** *n.* specialist in technology. **technology** [tek'nɒlədʒɪ] *n.* knowledge/study of new industrial or scientific skills. **tectonics** [tek'tɒnɪks] *n.* study of the earth's crust and its movements.

teddy (bear) ['tedɪ ('beə)] *n.* child's toy bear.

tedious ['tiːdɪəs] *adj.* boring. **tediously** *adv.* in a boring way. **tediousness, tedium** ['tiːdɪəm] *n.* boredom/being boring.

tee 1 [tiː] *n.* (a) spot on a golf course where the ball is placed before you hit it. (b) little peg, on which the golf ball is placed. **tee 2** *v.* to t. off = to hit the ball from a tee.

teem [tiːm] *v.* (a) to be full of/covered with sth; (b) *inf.* it's teeming = it's pouring (with rain).

teens [tiːnz] *n. pl.* age between 13 and 19. **teenage** ['tiːneɪdʒ] *adj.* adolescent; referring to s.o. aged between 13 and 19. **teenager** *n.* person aged between 13 and 19.

teeny(-weeny) ['tiːnɪ'(wiːnɪ)] *adj. inf.* very small.

tee-shirt ['tiːʃɜːt] *n.* light short-sleeved shirt with no buttons or collar.

teeter ['tiːtə] *v.* to wobble. **teeter-totter** *n. Am.* seesaw.

teeth [tiːθ] *n.* see tooth. **teethe** [tiːð] *v.* to grow your first teeth. **teething troubles** *n.* problems which develop when a baby grows its first teeth/when

anything is in its first stages.

teetotal [tiː'təʊtl] *adj.* (person) who never drinks any alcohol. **teetotaller** *n.* person who never drinks any alcohol.

Teflon ['teflɒn] *n.* trademark for a nonstick surface, used on frying pans, etc.

tele- ['telɪ] prefix meaning over a distance.

telecast ['telɪkɑːst] *n.* TV broadcast.

telecommunications [telɪkəmjuːnɪ'keɪʃnz] *n. pl.* system of passing messages over a great distance (such as telephone/radio, etc.).

telegram ['telɪgræm] *n.* message sent by telegraph.

telegraph 1 ['telɪgrɑːf] *n.* system of sending messages along wires; t. line = wire along which telegraph messages are sent; t. pole = pole which holds up a telegraph line; *inf.* bush t. = passing information by gossip. **telegraph 2** *v.* to send (a message) along wires. **telegrapher** [tə'legrəfə] *n.* person who sends messages by telegraph. **telegraphese** *n.* abbreviated language used when writing telegrams. **telegraphic** [telɪ'græfɪk] *adj.* referring to telegraph; t. address = short form of an address used on telegrams. **telegraphist** [tə'legrəfɪst] *n.* person who sends messages by telegraph. **telegraphy** [tə'legrəfɪ] *n.* sending messages by telegraph.

telepathy [tə'lepəθɪ] *n.* sending feelings/sympathy/mental images from one person to another without the use of the senses. **telepathic** [telɪ'pæθɪk] *adj.* referring to telepathy.

telephone 1 ['telɪfəʊn] *n.* device/system for speaking to s.o. over a distance using electric current running along wires, or by radio; on the t. = (i) speaking into the telephone; (ii) (house) with a telephone; t. box = outdoor booth with a public telephone in it.

telephone 2 to speak to (s.o.) by telephone. **telephonic** [telɪ'fɒnɪk] *adj.* referring to the telephone. **telephonist** [tə'lefənɪst] *n.* person who connects telephone calls in a central exchange. **telephony** *n.* science of telephones.

telephoto lens [telɪ'fəʊtəʊ'lenz] *n.* lens for a camera which gives a large picture of sth which is at a distance.

teleprinter ['telɪprɪntə] *n.* apparatus like a typewriter which sends out and receives messages by telegraph, and which prints them when they are received.

telesales [telɪ'seɪlz] *n.* sales made by telephone.

telescope 1 ['telɪskəʊp] *n.* tube with a series of lenses for looking at very distant objects; radio t. = apparatus which detects radio signals from stars and follows their movements.

telescope 2 *v.* to push together, so that one piece slides into another; to crush together. **telescopic** [telɪ'skɒpɪk] *adj.* (a) referring to a telescope. (b) (parts) which slide together like a telescope.

teletypewriter [telɪ'taɪpraɪtə] *n. Am.* teleprinter.

television [telɪ'vɪʒn] *n.* system for sending pictures by radio waves; t. (set) = apparatus for showing pictures sent by radio waves. **televise** ['telɪvaɪz] *v.* to broadcast (sth) by television. televised live = shown direct/not recorded and broadcast later.

telex 1 ['teleks] *n.* (*pl.*-es) system of sending messages by teleprinter; message sent by teleprinter. **telex 2** *v.* to send a message to (s.o.), using the teleprinter.

tell [tel] *v.* (told) (a) to say. (b) to pass on information. (c) to give instructions (how to do sth). (d) to make out (the difference) between two things); to notice a quality. (e) to have an effect; his age told in the end = finally he lost because he was older than the other competitors. (g) to count (money/votes); all told = altogether. **teller** *n.* person who counts votes, clerk in a bank who counts money and pays it out to customers. **telling** *adj.* which has an effect. **tellingly** *adv.* in a telling way. **tell off** *v. inf.* to reprimand/to criticize (s.o.). **tell on** *v. inf.* to tell on s.o. = to let out a secret about someone. **telltale 1** *n.* person who gives away a secret. **telltale 2** *adj.* (thing) which gives away a secret.

telly ['telɪ] *n. inf.* television.

temerity [tə'merɪtɪ] *n.* audacity; daring to do sth.

temp 1 [temp] *n. inf.* short for

temporary secretary. **temp 2** *v. inf.* to work as a temp.

temper 1 ['tempə] *n.* (a) usually calm state of mind; he lost his t. = he became very angry; she kept her t. = she stayed calm and did not get angry. (b) (good/bad) state of mind. (c) fit of anger. (d) hardness of a metal due to beating.

temper 2 *v.* (a) to harden (steel). (b) to moderate/to make less strong.

tempera ['tempərə] *n.* type of thick paint which can be diluted with water.

temperament ['tempərəmənt] *n.* state of mind; nature of a person.

temperamental [temprə'mentl] *adj.* (person) likely to change his state of mind frequently; likely to get easily excited or depressed.

temperamentally *adv.* according to a state of mind.

temperance ['tempərəns] *n.* (a) being moderate/controlled. (b) not drinking alcohol; t. movement = group of people who try to persuade others not to drink alcohol. **temperate** ['tempərət] *adj.* (a) moderate/sober (language/habits). (b) (climate) which is neither extremely hot nor cold.

temperature ['tempərətʃə] *n.* (a) amount of heat measured in degrees. (b) state where the temperature of the body is higher than it should be.

tempest ['tempɪst] *n.* storm.

tempestuous [tem'pestjʊəs] *adj.* violently stormy/very wild; very enthusiastic (applause).

template ['templeɪt] *n.* thin sheet used as a pattern for cutting pieces of wood/metal, etc., to an exact shape.

temple ['templ] *n.* (a) flat part of the front of the head on each side of the forehead. (b) building for worship (not *usu.* Christian or Muslim).

tempo ['tempəʊ] *n.* (*pl.*-os/ tempi['tempiX]) rhythm; beat (of music, etc.).

temporal ['tempərəl] *adj.* (a) referring to the temple/the flat part of the side of the head near the forehead. (b) referring to this world/not eternal/not spiritual. (c) referring to time.

temporary ['tempərɪ] *adj.* which only lasts a short time/which is meant to last a short time. **temporarily** ['tempərəlɪ] *adv.* for a short time.

temporize v. to try to gain time.
tempt [temt] v. (a) to attract (s.o.); to try to persuade (s.o.) to do sth. (b) I am tempted to accept = I think I will accept. (c) to t. providence = to take a great risk.
temptation [tem'teɪʃn] n. state of being tempted; thing which attracts you.
tempter, temptress n. person who tempts. **tempting** adj. attractive.
ten [ten] n. number 10; inf. t. to one be finds out = he's very likely to find out.
tenable ['tenəbl] adj. (theory) which can be held/supported.
tenacious [tɪ'neɪʃəs] adj. which holds on to sth tightly; obstinate; determined. **tenaciously** adv. in a tenacious way. **tenacity** [tə'næsɪtɪ] n. holding to sth too tightly.
tenant ['tenənt] n. person who rents a room/flat/house/land; to buy a house with a sitting t. = with s.o. living in it and paying rent. **tenancy** n. period during which a tenant rents a property.
tench [tentʃ] n. (pl.tench) type of small fish.
tend [tend] v. to look after. (b) to be likely (to do sth). (c) to lean (in a certain direction). **tendency** n. being likely to do sth.
tendentious [ten'denʃəs] adj. (book/ article/speech) which puts over a strong point of view which is not generally approved.
tender 1 ['tendə] n. (a) boat which brings supplies to a large ship; wagon carrying coal behind a coal burning locomotive. (b) offer to do work at a certain price. (c) legal t. coins/notes which are legally acceptable when offered in payment. **tender 2** adj. (a) soft/delicate; t. meat = which can be chewed/cut easily. (b) t. plants = which cannot stand frost; child of t. years = very young child. (c) with a t. heart = very affectionate/very loving. (d) painful; inf. you've touched him on a t. spot = you mentioned sth which he is very touchy about. **tender 3** n. (a) (formal) in offer. (b) (for) to offer to do work at a certain price. **tenderfoot** n. inexperienced person. **tenderhearted** adj. kind. **tenderize** v. to make (meat) tender. **tenderloin** ['tendələɪn] n. piece of tender beef or pork from the side of the backbone **tenderly** adv.

gently with kindness. **tenderness** n. being tender.
tendon ['tendən] n. strong cord of tissue attaching a muscle to a bone.
tendril ['tendrəl] n. thin curling part with which a plant clings to a support.
tenement ['tenəmənt] n. (a) large (often dilapidated) building which is divided into flats. (b) (in Scotland) building which is rented as flats.
tenet ['tenet] n. basic principle/belief.
tenfold ['tenfəʊld] adv. ten times as much.
tenner ['tenə] n. inf. ten pound note.
tennis ['tenɪs] n. game for tow players or two pairs of players who use rackets to hit a ball backwards and forwards over a net; t. court = specially marked ground for playing tennis; t. elbow = painful condition of the elbow joint caused by strain.
tenon ['tenən] n. small projection from the end of a piece of wood which fits into a corresponding mortise in another piece to form a joint.
tenor ['tenə] n. (a) man who sings with the highest male voice. (b) highest male voice; musical instrument with a high pitch. (c) (formal) general meaning. (d) (formal) general way (of living).
tense 1 [tens] n. form of a verb which shows when the action takes place.
tense 2 adj. (-er, -est) (a) stretched right. (b) nervous and anxious. (c) warlike (state between countries). **tense 3** v. to make/to become tense. **tensely** adv. in a tense way. **tenseness** n. being tense.
tensile ['tensail] adj. referring to tension; t. strength = force needed to stretch sth until it breaks.
tension ['tenʃn] n. (a) tightness; being stretched; (in knitting) tightness of the stitches calculated as the number of stitches or rows per centimetre. (b) nervous anxiety. (c) state of aggravation (between countries). (d) electric power; high-tension cables.
tent [tent] n. small canvas shelter held up by poles and attached to the ground with pegs and ropes; to pitch a t. = to put up a tent; oxygen t. = cover put up over a sick person's bed to allow oxygen to be pumped in.

tentacle ['tentəkl] *n.* long arm with suckers (such as that of an octopus).

tentative ['tentətɪv] *adj.* uncertain; done as a trial; t. proposal = made to find out what the response is. **tentatively** *adv.* in a tentative way.

tenterhooks ['tentəhuːks] *n. pl.* on t. = impatiently waiting/anxious and uncertain.

tenth, 10th [tenθ] *adj. & n.* referring to ten; the t. century = period from 900 to 999

tenuous ['tenjʊəs] *adj.* thin; not strong. **tenuously** *adv.* in a tenuous way. **tenuousness** *n.* being tenuous.

tenure ['tenjə] *n.* (a) right to hold property/to have employment; holding of a property or employment. (b) right to hold a job permanently.

tepee ['tiːpiː] *n.* cone-shaped tent of North American Indians.

tepid ['tepɪd] *adj.* slightly warm.

tequila [te'kiːlə] *n.* Mexican alcoholic drink.

tercentenary [tɜːsen'tiːnərɪ] *n.* anniversary of 300 years.

term 1 [tɜːm] *n.* (a) length of time; in the long t./in the short t. = for a long period from now/for a short period from now. (b) end of a period of time; she was approaching her t. = nearly at the end of her pregnancy. (c) part of a school/ university year. (d) conditions; terms of reference = areas which a committee/an inspector has to examine or discuss; to come to terms with = to accept as inevitable; they came to terms = they reached agreement; terms of payment = way in which a payment shall be made 'our terms are ninety days = we allow 90 days' credit. (e) relationship; on good/ bad terms = having a friendly/unfriendly relationship. (f) particular word. (g) expressing; in terms of health/in health terms = regarding health; I'm thinking in terms of weekly payments = my idea is that the payments should be made each week. **term 2** *v.* to call.

termagant ['tɜːməgənt] *n.* noisy woman who bullies people.

terminal 1 ['tɜːmɪnl] *adj.* (a) at the end; t. shoot = shoot at the end of a branch. (b) referring to a school term. (c) in the last period of life; t. case = patient who is soon going to die.

terminal 2 *n.* (a) building at an airport where passengers arrive or leave. (b) terminus; air t. = building in the centre of a town where coaches arrive from an airport. (c) electric t. = one of the connecting points in an electric circuit. (d) apparatus which can be used for putting information into and getting information from a distant computer (to which it is linked by cable). **terminable** *adj.* which can be terminated. **terminally** *adv.* in a terminal way; t. ill = in the last stages of an illness before death. **terminate** ['tɜːmɪneɪt] *v.* to finish/to bring (sth) to an end. **termination** [tɜːmɪ'neɪʃn] *n.* bringing to an end. **terminology** [tɜːmɪ'nɒlədʒɪ] *n.* special words or phrases used in a particular science. **terminological** [tɜːmɪnə'lɒdʒɪkl] *adj.* referring to terminology.

terminus ['tɜːmɪnəs] *n.* (*pl.*-ni[-naɪ]) station at the end of a railway line; station at the end of a journey for a bus or a coach.

termite ['tɜːmaɪt] *n.* destructive white insect, rather like an ant, which lives in tropical countries.

tern [tɜːn] *n.* white sea bird similar to a gull.

terrace 1 ['terəs] *n.* (a) flat area which is raised above another area. (b) row of houses connected together and built in a similar style. (c) terraces = rows of wide steps on which the spectators stand (at a football stadium). **terrace 2** *v.* (a) to make a flat raised area. (b) terraced houses = connected houses built all in a similar style.

terracotta [terə'kɒtə] *n.* red clay used to make small statues; statue made of red clay

terra firma ['terə'fɜːmə] *n.* dry land.

terrain [tə'reɪn] *n.* area of country.

terrapin ['terəpɪn] *n.* type of small American turtle.

terrarium [te'reərɪəm] *n.* glass box in which flowers are grown.

terrazzo [te'rætsəʊ] *n.* polished surface, made of little chips of stone embedded in mortar.

terrestrial [tə'restrɪəl] *adj.* referring to the earth.

terrible ['terɪbl] *adj.* (a) awful/which

makes you very frightened. (b) *inf.* very bad. **terribly** *adv.* (a) frighteningly. (b) *inf.* very.

terrier ['terɪə] *n.* small dog (originally used in hunting).

terrific [tə'rɪfɪk] *adj. inf.* awful/ wonderfully/awfully. **terrifically** *adv. inf.* wonderfully/awfully. **terrify** ['terɪfaɪ] *v.* to frighten completely. **terrifying** *adj.* frightening

terrine [tə'riːn] *n.* type of pate

territory ['terɪtrɪ] *n.* (a) land which belongs to a country; large stretch of land. (b) area which an animal/bird, etc. considers as its own. (c) area visited by a travelling salesman. **territorial** [terɪ'tɔːrɪəl] *adj.* referring to territory; t. water = area of sea round a country which that country controls. **Territorial Army** *n.* volunteer reserve army. **Territorials** *n. pl.inf.* the Territorial Army.

terror ['terə] *n.* (a) extreme fear. (b) thing which causes fear. (c) *inf.* naughty/ uncontrollable person. **terrorism** *n.* policy of using violence in a political cause. **terrorist** *adj. & n.* (person) who practises terrorism. **terrorize** *v.* frighten (s.o.) very much. **terror-stricken, terror-struck** *adj.* extremely frightened.

terry ['terɪ] *n.* type of cloth where uncut loops stand above the surface.

terse [tɜːs] *adj.* concise/short; using few words. **tersely** *adv.* briefly/concisely. **terseness** *n.* being terse.

tertiary ['tɜːʃərɪ] *adj.* referring to third stage, esp. to the level of education after the secondary; t. sector/t. industry = industries which provide services.

Terylene ['terɪliːn] *n.* trademark for a type of man-made thread; cloth made of this thread.

tessellated ['tesəleɪtɪd] *adj.* covered with mosaic.

test 1 [test] *n.* (a) examination to see if sth works well/is reliable/if s.o. is healthy. t. pilot = pilot who flies a new aircraft to see if it work well. (b) short written or practical examination to see if s.o. knows information/knows how to do sth; intelligence t./aptitude t. = test to show how intelligent/how capable you are; driving t. = to see if you can drive a car. (c) to put sth/s.o. to the t. = to try sth/s.o. out to see if they can stand up to

certain conditions. (d) international cricket match. **test 2** *v.* (a) well; to examine (s.o) to see if he healthy. (b) to give (s.o.) a short examination. **test case** *n.* court case where the decision sets a precedent for other similar cases to follow. **test-drive** *v.* to drive (a new car) before you buy it to see if it works well. **test match** *n.* international cricket match. **test tube** *n.* small round-bottomed glass tube used in a laboratory for making chemical tests; t.-t. baby = baby born through artificial insemination.

testament ['testəmənt] *n.* (a) last will and t. = document written by a person before death, to indicate what should happen to his property after he dies. (b) Old T./New T. = the two main sections of the Bible. **testamentary** [testə'mentərɪ] *adj.* referring to a will

testate ['testeɪt] *adj.* (person who has died) leaving a will **testator, testatrix** [tes'teɪtə, -teɪtrɪks] *n.* (*pl.-trices*[-trɪsiːz]) man/woman who makes a will

testicle ['testɪkl] *n.* one of two male glands which produce sperm

testify ['testɪfaɪ] *v.* to give evidence that sth is true.

testimonial [testɪ'məʊnɪəl] *n.* (a) statement showing what you know of a person's qualities. (b) thing done for a person/given to a person to show appreciation; t. dinner = dinner organized to give a present to s.o.

testimony ['testɪmənɪ] *n.* evidence that sth true.

testis ['testɪs] *n.* (*pl.*testes['testiːz]) (formal) testicle.

testosterone [tes'tɒstərəʊn] *n.* male sex hormone.

testy ['testɪ] *adj.* irritable; easily made angry.

testily *adj.* irritably/angrily.

tetanus *n.* serious disease caused by infection in a wound, which can make esp. the jaw muscles stiffen.

tetchy ['tetʃɪ] *adj.* (-ier, -iest) bad tempered **tetchily** *adv.* in a tetchy way.

tête-à-tête [teɪtɑːteɪt] *n.* private conversation between two people.

tether 1 ['teðə] *n.* rope which attaches an animal to a post; he's at the end of his t. = he can't stand any more/he has lost all patience. **tether 2** *v.* to attach (an animal) to a post with a rope.

tetrahedron [tetrə'hi:drən] *n.* solid shape with four sides, each of which is a triangle.

Teutonic [tju:'tɒnɪk] *adj.* German

text [tekst] *n.* (a) main written part of a book (not the notes or pictures, etc.). (b) original words of a speech. (c) quotation from the Bible used as a moral guide. **textbook** *n.* book which students read for information about the subject they are studying **textual** *adj.* referring to a text.

textile ['tekstaɪl] *adj. &n.* (referring to) cloth.

texture ['tekstʃə] *n.* quality which can be felt; degree of fineness. **textured** *adj.* with certain feel.

than [ðæn, ðən] *conj.. & prep.* used to introduce the second part of comparisons and clauses; I have less t. you; there are more t. twenty people in the room; no sooner had we arrived t. the music started.

thank [θæŋk] *v.* to t. s.o. for = to show gratitude to (s.o.) **thankful** *adj.* showing gratitude; glad because an anxiety has gone **thankfully** *adv.* showing relief that an anxiety has gone. **thankfulness** *n.* being thankful **thankless** *adj.* (work) for which no one will thank you; difficult/hopeless (task) **thanklessly** *adv.* in a thankless way. **thanklessness** *n.* being thankless **thanks** *n. pl.* (a) word which shows you are grateful; to pass a vote of t. to s.o. = to thank s.o. officially in the minutes of a meeting. (b) thank you; no t. = no, thank you. (c) thank to = as a result of. **thanksgiving** *n.* (religious) festival where thanks are shown to God; Thanksgiving = American and Canadian festival when thanks are given for safe harvest. **thank you** *inter.* showing gratitude (for); thank you letter = in which you thank s.o. for sth.

that 1 [ðæt] *adj. & pron.* (*pl.*those [ðɒʊz]) used to indicate something further away (as opposed to this). **that 2** *pron.* linking a subject or object to a verb where is the letter t. he sent you? **that 3** *adv. inf.* to such an extent; so much; I knew they were going to be early, but not t. early. **that 4** *conj..* introducing a clause he knew t. we were

late.

thatch 1 [θætʃ] *n.* reeds/straw, etc., used to make a roof. **thatch 2** *v.* to cover (a house) with a roof of reeds/ straw, etc. **thatcher** *n.* a person who thatches houses.

thaw 1 [θɔ:] *n.* warm weather (which results in the melting of snow/ice). **thaw 2** *v.* (a) to melt; to unfreeze (sth which is frozen). (b) to get less unfriendly/less shy.

the 1 [ðə] (before a vowel or when stressed[ðiːX] 1. definite article (a) referring to a particular person or thing) the man with the red nose. (b) (referring to something in general) the Russians are lively people. (c) (stressed) it is the shop for furniture. **the 2** *adv.* (in comparisons) it will be all easier = that much easier; the sooner the better

theatre, *Am.* **theater** ['θɪətə] *n.* (a) building in which plays are performed. (b) *Am.* cinema. (c) art of acting/of producing plays. (d) collection of plays. (e) place where important events happen. (f) operating t. = room in a hospital where operations take place.

theatregoer *n.* person who goes to the theatre **theatrical** [θɪ'ætrɪkl] *adj.* (a) referring to the theatre. (b) very dramatic/not acting naturally.

theatrically *adv.* in a theatrical way.

theatricals *n. pl.* amateur t. = performances of play by amateurs.

thee [ðiː] *pron.* (old) you.

theft [θeft] *n.* stealing.

their ['ðeə] *adj.* belonging to them.

theirs ['ðeəz] *pron.* belonging to them; she's a friend to t.

theism ['θiːɪzəm] *n.* belief that a god exists. **theist** *n.* person who believes that a god exists.

them [ðem] *pron.* referring to persons/ things which are objects of a verb.

themselves [ðem'selvz] *pron.* referring to a plural subject; all by t. = without any help from anyone else.

theme [θiːm] *n.* (a) subject (of book/ article). (b) main tune in a piece of music; t. tune/t. song = catchy tune/song played several times in a film or TV serial which makes the audience recognize it. **thematic** [θɪ'mætɪk] *adj.* referring to a theme.

then 1 [ðen] *adv.* (a) at that time; t. and

there = immediately; now and t. = from time to time (b) afterwards. (c) also/in any case. (d) therefore; the result is. **then 2** *n.* that time. **then 3** *adj.* existing at that time; the t. Prime Minister.

thence [ðens] *adv.* (formal) (a) from that place; from there. (b) so/therefore. **thenceforth** *adv.* (formal) from that time onwards.

theodolite [θɪˈɒdəlaɪt] *n.* device for measuring angles when surveying land.

theology [θɪˈɒlədʒɪ] *n.* study of belief in God; study of God and God's relations with man. **theologian** [θɪəˈləʊdʒɪən] *n.* person who specializes in the study of God/in the interpretation of religion. **theological** [θɪəˈlɒdʒɪkl] *adj.* referring to theology; t. college = college where people study to become priests. **theologically** *adv.* in a theological way.

theorem [ˈθɪːərəm] *n.* thing which has to be proved in mathematics.

theory [ˈθɪərɪ] *n.* (a) explanation of sth which has not been proved but which you believe to be true. (b) statement of general principles (which may not apply in practice); in t. it should work = if you follow general principles. **theoretical** [θɪəˈretɪkl] *adj.* referring to a theory; not proved in practice. **theoretically** *adv.* in theory, but not in practice. **theoretician, theorist** [θɪərəˈtɪʃn, ˈθɪərɪst] *n.* person who forms (political) theories. **theorize** [ˈθɪəraɪz] *v.* to make up a theory about sth.

theosophy [θɪˈɒsəfɪ] *n.* religion which states that certain people can understand the working of God.

therapy [ˈθerəpɪ] *n.* treatment of illness (esp. without using medicine); speech t. = treatment of difficulty in speaking; occupational t. = treatment by getting patients to do things; group t. = treatment by getting patients together in groups to discuss their problems. **therapeutic** [θerəˈpjuːtɪk] *adj.* which may cure. **therapeutically** *adv.* in a therapeutic way. **therapeutics** *n. pl.* study of curing diseases. **therapist** *n.* person who applies therapy.

there 1 [ˈðeə] *adv.* in that place/to that place. *inf.* t. she goes again = that is her doing it again. **there 2** *inter.* showing

various feelings t., t., don't cry. **there 3** *pron.* used as subject of a clause usually with the verb to be, when the real subject follows the verb there's a big car coming up the hill; t. weren't very many people at the meeting; t. appears to be a mistake. **thereabouts** [ðeərəˈbaʊts] *adv.* approximately. **thereafter** [ðeərˈɑːftə] *adv.* (formal) after that. **thereby** [ðeəˈbaɪ] *adv.* (formal) by doing this. **therefore** [ˈðeəfɔː] *adv.* consequently; for this reason. **thereupon** [ðeərəˈpɒn] *adv.* (formal) immediately after that.

therm [θɜːm] *n.* measure of heat, used for measuring gas in Britain. **thermal 1** *adj.* referring to heat; t. baths = baths of natural hot water; t. underwear = which keeps you warm; t. current = current of warm air/water. **thermal 2** *n.* current of warm air. **thermionic** [θɜːmɪˈɒnɪk] *adj.* (radio valve) made of a vacuum tube containing heated electrodes. **thermo-** [ˈθɜːməʊ] *adj.* referring to heat.

thermodynamics [θɜːməʊdaɪˈnæmɪks] *n.* study of heat and its relationship to power. **thermometer** [θɜːˈmɒmɪtə] *n.* instrument for measuring the temperature. **thermonuclear** [θɜːməʊˈnjuːklɪə] *adj.* referring to the high temperature caused by atomic fusion. **thermoplastic** [θɜːməˈplæstɪk] *adj. & n.* (material) which becomes soft when heated and hard when cold. **Thermos (flask)** [ˈθɜːməsˈflɑːsk] *n.* trademark for a type of vacuum flask. **thermostat** [ˈθɜːməstæt] *n.* instrument which controls the temperature by setting off heating or cooling devices. **thermostatic** [ˈθɜːməstætɪk] *adj.* referring to a thermostat. **thermostatically** *adv.* (controlled) by a thermostat.

thesaurus [θəˈsɔːrəs] *n.* book with words collected according to their similar meanings, and not in alphabetical order.

these [ðiːz] *adj. & pron.* see this.

thesis [ˈθiːsɪs] *n.* (*pl.*-ses[-siːz]) (a) long piece of written research done for a higher university degree. (b) particular point of view.

Thespian ['θespɪən] n. actor, actress.

thews [θjuːz] n. pl. strength

they [ðeɪ] pron. subject (a) referring to several persons or things. (b) (referring to people in general) t. say it's going to rain.

thiamine ['θaɪəmiːn] n. Vitamin B. found in cereals, liver and pork.

thick 1 [θɪk] adj. (-er, -est) (a) fat/not thin/with a large distance between the two surfaces. (b) with a large diameter. (c) dense/packed close together. (d) (liquid) which does not flow easily. (e) (voice) which is not clear. (f) inf. that's a bit t = that's very unreasonable. (g) inf. stupid; she's a bit t. (h) inf. very friendly. **thick 2** n. (a) centre of a battle). (b) through t. and thin = through times of difficulty as well as through easy times. **thick 3** adv. in a thick layer; inf. to lay it on t. = to praise s.o. excessively; t. and fast = rapidly and heavily. **thicken** v. to make thick/to become thick. **thicket** ['θɪkɪt] n. small wood of trees and bushes growing close together. **thickly** adv. in a thick way. **thickness** n. being thick; distance between sides. **thickset** adj. (a) (hedge) planted with bushes close together. (b) short stocky (person). **thick-skinned** adj. (a) (fruit) with a thick skin. (b) (of person) insensitive/not easily hurt.

thief [θiːf] n. person who steals. **thieve** v. to steal. **thievery** n. stealing. **thieving** n. act of stealing. **thievish** adj. like a thief.

thigh [θaɪ] n. thick top part of the leg between the knee and the hip.

thimble ['θɪmbl] n. small cover worn to protect the end of your finger when sewing. **thimbleful** n. inf. very small quantity (of liquid).

thin 1 [θɪn] adj. (thinner, thinnest) not thick/with only a distance between the two surfaces. (b) not fat. (c) with a small diameter. (d) not very dense/not close together. (e) very watery (liquid). **thin 2** adv. in a thin way. **thin 3** v. (thinned) (a) to become thin. (b) to make liquid thin. (c) to make less dense; to become less dense. **thin down** v. to reduce; to make (sth) thinner. **thinly** adv. in a thin way. **thinner** n. substance used to thin paint. **thinness** n. being thin.

thinnings n. small plants which are removed to allow others more space.

thin out v. to remove (seedlings) to give more room to those which are left.

thin-skinned adj. (a) (fruit) with a thin skin. (b) (of person) sensitive/easily hurt.

thine [ðaɪn] pron. (old) your.

thing [θɪŋ] n. (a) object. (b) inf. person/ animal. (c) things = clothes/equipment. (d) item; unspecified subject; object referred to; It's a just one t. after another = one problem after another; It's a good t. you came with us = it's lucky. (e) first t. in the morning/last t. at night = as soon as you get up-just before you go to bed. (f) inf. to have a t. about sth = to like/ dislike sth irrationally. (g) inf. he wants to do his own t. = to do what he really feels like doing. **thingamajig, thingummy** ['θɪŋəmədʒɪg, 'θɪŋəmɪ] n. inf. some object/person whose name you have forgotten.

think 1 [θɪŋk] n. time when you have thoughts/when you consider plans in your mind; inf. you've got another t. coming = you'll have to change your ideas, as this idea won't work. **think 2** v. (thought[θɔːt]) (a) to use your mind; to t. aloud = to speak your thoughts as they come into your mind. (b) to believe; to have as your opinion. (c) to expect. (d) to plan; to t. again = to change your mind; inf. t. big = consider only large-scale projects. **thinkable** adj. which can be thought. **think about** v. (a) to consider (sth) in your mind. (b) to plan (sth). (c) to have an opinion. **think back** v. to remember. **thinker** n. person who thinks; great t. = philosopher. **thinking** n. reasoning; to my way of t. = my opinion is. **think of** v. (a) to consider (sth) in your mind. (b) to plan (sth). (c) to remember. (d) to have an opinion; I told him what I thought of him = I criticized him; he thinks highly of his teacher = has a high opinion of him; she thinks nothing of working 12 hours a day = she finds it easy; think nothing of it = don't bother to thank me for it; he thought better of it = changed his mind. **think out** v. to consider carefully all the details. **think over** v. to consider (sth) seriously. **think tank** n. group of experts who advise the government on matters of general policy. **think through** v. to consider carefully all the details. **think up** v. to invent. **third, 3rd** [θɜːd] n. & adj. referring to three; t. person = pronoun or part of a verb referring to a person or thing who is being referred to the car went up the hill in t. = in third gear; the Third World = countries with no strong connections to the superpowers. **third degree** n. hard questioning (by the police). **third party** n. any person who is not one of the two parties involved in a contract; person (usu. s.o. injured in an accident) who is not the driver of the car or the insurance company which insured it. t. party insurance = insurance which covers s.o. not named in it; **third-rate** adj. very bad.

thirst 1 [θɜːst] n. (a) wanting to drink. (b) desire (for). **thirst 2** v. (formal) to desire (after/for sth). **thirsty** adj. (-ier, -iest) wanting to drink; t. work = hard/ hot work which makes you thirsty.

thirstily adv. in a thirsty way.

thirteen [θɜːˈtiːn] n. number 13; the t. hundreds = years between 1300 and 1399. **thirteenth, 13th** adj. & n. referring to thirteen; the t. century = period from 1200 to 1299.

thirty [ˈθɜːtɪ] n. number 30; she's in her thirties = she is more than thirty years old but less than forty. **thirtieth, 30th** adj. & n. referring to thirty.

this 1 [ðɪs] adj. & pron. (pl.these[ðiːz]) used to indicate something near (as opposed to that). (a). t. is the book I meant, not that one. (b) t. morning/t. evening = today in the morning/evening. **this 2** adv. inf. to such an extent; I didn't expect you to be t. late = so late.

thistle [ˈθɪsl] n. large prickly weed with purple flowers. **thistledown** n. soft white feathery substance attached to thistle seeds.

thither [ˈðɪðə] adv. (formal) to that place.

thole [θəʊl] n. peg used as a rowlock.

thong [θɒŋ] n. (a) thin leather strap used for tying. (b) light sandal, held by a strap between the toes.

thorax [ˈθɔːræks] n. part of the body between the neck and the abdomen; chest (of an animal/a person); part of an insect's body to which the wings and legs are attached. **thoracic** [θɔːˈræsɪk] adj. referring to a thorax.

thorn [θɔːn] n. spike (of a prickly plant); a t. in the flesh = a constant annoyance. **thorny** adj. (-ier, -est) covered with thorns; (problems) which is difficult to solve.

thorough [ˈθʌrə] adj. (a) very careful/ detailed. (b) complete. **thoroughbred** adj. & n. pure-bred (horse). **thoroughfare** n. way through which the public can go. **thoroughgoing** adj. complete. **thoroughly** adv. completely/totally. **thoroughness** n. completeness.

those [ðəʊz] adj. & pron. see that.

thou [ðaʊ] pron. (old) you.

though 1 [ðəʊ] conj.. although; in spite of the fact that; strange t. it may seem = although it may seem strange; as t. = as if. **though 2** adv. in spite of this.

thought 1 [θɔːt] n. (a) action of thinking; he was lost in t. = thinking so hard that you could not attract his attention. (b) considering in your mind; after much t. = after considering (the plan) for a long time; on second thoughts = having considered everything a second time. (c) plan. (d) regard. **thought 2** v. see think. **thoughtful** adj. (a) thinking hard. (b) considerate to other people. (c) showing deep thought. **thoughtfully** adv. in a thoughtful way. **thoughtfulness** n. being thoughtful. **thoughtless** adj. without thinking; not thinking about. **thoughtlessly** adv. in a thoughtless way. **thoughtlessness** n. being thoughtless. **thought reader** n. person who claims to be able to say what s.o. else is thinking.

thousand [ˈθaʊzənd] n. number 1000. **thousandth, 1000th 1** adj. referring to thousand. **thousandth, 1000th 2** n. one of a thousand parts.

thrall [θrɔːl] n. (formal) in t. = in slavery.

thrash [θræʃ] v. (a) to beat (with a stick) (b) to beat (another team) decisively. **thrash about** v. to move/to wave your arms and legs violently. **thrashing** n. beating. **thrash out** v. to discuss in detail.

thread 1 [θred] n. (a) long thin piece of cotton/silk, etc.; his life hangs by a t. = he is very likely to die (b) to lose the t. of conversation = to miss what the conversation is about. (c) spiral ridge going round a screw/a bolt or inside a nut; a screw with a left - handed t. = which you have to turn to the left to tighten. **thread 2** v. (a) to put a piece of cotton etc, through the eye of a needle; to pass (a magnetic tape) through a slit. (b) to put (beads, etc.) on a string (c) to t. your way through a crowd = to squeeze through a crowd carefully. **threadbare** adj. worn out (clothes). **threadlike** adj. long a thin like a thread. **threadworm** n. long thin worm which lives in human intestines.

threat [θret] n. (a) warning that sth unpleasant will happen or will be done. (b) person/thing which may harm. **threaten** v. to warn that sth unpleasant will be done/that some action will be taken. **threateningly** adv. menacingly.

three [θriː] n. number 3. **three-act** adj. (play) with three acts. **three-cornered** adj. with three corners; (election) where there are three candidates. **three-dimensional** adj. (picture) which has depth as well as length and breadth. **threefold** adv. three times as much. **three-piece** adj. with three parts; (suit) with jacket. trousers and waistcoat; (suite of living room furniture) consisting of a sofa and two armchairs. **three-ply** adj. (wool) with three threads twisted together; (plywood) made of three layers stuck together **three-point turn** n. turning a car in a narrow street in three movements. **three-quarter 1** adj. referring to three fourths of a whole. **three-quarter 2** n. (a) three-quarters = three fourths of a whole; three-quarters of an hour = 45 minutes. (b) (in Rugby) one of the fast attacking players behind the forwards. **three-quarter 3** adv. three-quarters = three fourths. **threescore** n. (old) sixty. **threesome** n. group of three people, esp. three players playing a game.

threnody ['θrenədɪ] n. (formal) funeral song.

thresh [θreʃ] v. to beat (corn) so that the grain falls out; threshing machine = machine which threshes corn automatically. **thresher** n. person/

machine that threshes. **threshold** ['θreʃəʊld] n. (a) bar across the floor of a doorway. (b) edge/beginning; tax t. = point at which a higher level of tax is charged. (c) limit; t. of pain = point at which pain becomes felt.

threw [θruː] v. see throw.

thrice [θraɪs] adv. three times.

thrift [θrɪft] n. (a) saving (money) by wise use and restricting spending. (b) type of seashore plant with small tufts of pink flowers. **thriftily** adv. in a thrifty way. **thriftiness** n. being thrifty. **thrifty** adj. (-ier, -iest) careful with money.

thrill 1 [θrɪl] n. (shudder of) excitement. **thrill 2** v. to give (s.o.) a shudder of excitement; to be excited. **thriller** n. exciting novel/film etc. (usu. about crime). **thrilling** adj. very exciting.

thrips [θrɪps] n. pl. small insects which live on plants.

thrive [θraɪv] v. (thrived/throve[θrəʊv]) to grow well/to be strong.

throat [θrəʊt] n. (a) front part of your neck below the chin. (b) pipe running from the back of your mouth down the inside of your neck; to clear your t. = to give a short cough; inf. he's always ramming figures down my t. = telling me figures. **throatily** adv. in a throaty voice. **throaty** adj. t. voice = low. rough-sounding voice.

throb 1 [θrɒb] n. beating (of heart/ machine). **throb 2** v. (throbbed) to beat regularly; to have a regular pain.

throes [θrəʊz] n. pl.death = great suffering just before death; in the t. of = in the middle.

thrombosis [θrɒm'bəʊsɪs] n. clot in a blood vessel, esp. in the heart.

throne [θrəʊn] n. ceremonial chair for a king/queen, etc.; the t. = the position of king.

throng 1 [θrɒŋ] n. great crowd of people. **throng 2** v. to crowd together.

throttle 1 ['θrɒtl] n. valve on a pipe which allows variable quantities of steam/petrol, etc.. to pass into an engine; to open up the t. = to make the engine go faster. **throttle 2** v. to strangle (s.o.) by squeezing the neck and preventing them breathing. **throttle back, throttle down** v. to reduce the supply of petrol

to an engine. making it go more slowly.
through 1 [θruː] *prep.* (a) crossing sth
on the inside/going in at one side and
coming out at the other. (b) during. (c)
Am. up to and including; Monday t.
Friday = from Monday to Friday
inclusively. (d) be means of. (e) because
of. **through 2** *adv.* (a) from one side to
another. (b) completely/to the finish; we
must see the plan t. = see that it is
completed. (c) in contact by telephone.
through 3 *adj.* (a) which goes from
one side to the other without stopping; t.
ticket = ticket for a whole journey, with
possibly changes of transport; t. traffic =
traffic going through a town without
stopping. (b) finished/completed; *inf.*
I'm t. with her = I've broken off our
friendship. **through and through** *adv.*
completely. **throughout 1** [θruː'aʊt]
prep. in every part; at all times. from
beginning to end. **throughout 2** *adv.*
everywhere; at all times. **throughput**
['θruːpʊt] *n.* amount of work done/of
goods produced in a certain time.
throughway *n. Am.* motorway.
throve [θrəʊv] *v.* see thrive.
throw 1 [θrəʊ] *n.* (a) sending sth
through the air. (b) distance sth is sent
through the air; they live a stone's t.
away = quite close. **throw 2** *v.* (threw;
has thrown) (a) to send (sth) through the
air. (b) to shine (a light) on; can you t.
any light on the problem? = make the
problem clearer. (c) to make (a pot) with
clay on a wheel. (d) *inf.* to hold (a party).
(e) *inf.* to surprise/to confuse (s.o.).
throw away *v.* (a) to get rid of (sth)
which you no longer need. (b) to waste.
throwaway *adj.* which can be got rid
of. **throwback** *n.* person/animal
showing characteristics of distant
ancestors; thing which shows a
connection with the past. **thrower** *n.*
person who throws. **throw in** *v.* (a) to
add. (b) (in football) to throw the ball
back into play. **throw-in** *n.* (in
football) throwing the ball back into play
from the touch line. **throw off** *v.* to get
rid of (sth). **throw out** *v.* (a) to put
(sth/s.o.) outside using force. (b) to send
out (heat). (c) to reject. **throw over** *v.*
to reject (a lover). **throw up** *v.* (a) to
send up into the air. (b) to vomit. (c) to
give up/to abandon.

thru [θruː] *prep., adv. & adj. Am.* inf. =
through. **thruway** *n. Am.* =
throughway.
thrum [θrʌm] *v.* (thrummed) to make a
continuous low-pitched sound.
thrush [θrʌʃ] *n.* (a) (*pl.*-es) common
brown bird with a speckled breast. (b)
infectious throat disease caused by the
bacterium Candida.
thrust 1 [θrʌst] *n.* (a) push; force which
pushes. (b) stab with a sword or dagger.
thrust 2 *v.* (thrust) (a) to push
energetically. (b) to t. yourself on s.o. =
to forces s.o. to accept you as a guest/
companion, etc.
thud 1 [θʌd] *n.* dull heavy noise. **thud
2** *v.* (thudded) to make a dull noise.
thug [θʌg] *n.* ruffian/violent person.
thumb 1 [θʌm] *n.* (a) short thick finger
which is placed apart from the other four
fingers on each hand; his fingers are all
thumbs = he is awkward with his hands.
it's a useful rule of t. = (i) a useful way
of calculating approximately; (ii) a
practical way of approaching a problem;
to be under s.o.'s t. = to be dominated by
s.o.; *inf.* thumbs up (sign) = gesture to
show that everything is all right; *inf.*
thumbs down (sign) = gesture to show
disapproval. (b) part of a glove into
which the thumb goes. **thumb 2** *v.* (a)
to t. through = to flick through (a book)
using your thumb; well-thumbed book =
one which has been used often. (b) to t. a
lift = to get a lift from a passing car by
making a sign with your thumb.
thumbnail *n.* nail on a thumb; t.
sketch = rapid. very small sketch/
description. **thumbindex 1** *n.* series
of notches cut in the edges of the pages
of a book so that you can easily see
where a new letter starts. **thumbindex
2** *v.* to give a book a thumb index.
thumbscrew *n.* machine for torturing.
which squeezes the victim's thumb.
thumbtack *n. Am.* drawing pin.
thump 1 [θʌmp] *n.* (a) dull noise. (b)
punch; heavy blow with the fist. **thump
2** *v.* (a) to hit with the fist. (b) to make a
dull noise. **thumping** *adj. inf.* very
large.
thunder 1 ['θʌndə] *n.* (a) rumbling
noise in the air caused by lightning; to
steal s.o.'s t. = to take the credit for sth
done by s.o. else/to do sth remarkable so

that no one notices what another person has done. (b) loud rumbling noise.
thunder 2 v. (a) to make a rumbling noise. (b) to speak loudly. **thunderbolt** n. (a) flash of lightning and thunder. (b) sudden (unpleasant) surprise.
thunderclap n. sudden noise of thunder. **thundercloud** n. large black cloud which will bring thunder and lightning. **thundering** adj. inf. very big/terrible. **thunderous** adj. very loud (applause). **thunderstorm** n. rainstorm with thunder and lightning. **thunderstruck** adj. astonished.
thundery adj. (weather) when thunder is likely.
Thursday ['θɜːzdeɪ] n. fourth day of the week/day between Wednesday and Friday
thus [ðʌs] adv. (formal) (a) in this way. (b) and so.
thwack 1 [θwæk] n. sound made when hitting sth hard. **thwack 2** v. to hit (sth) hard.
thwart 1 [θwɔːt] n. seat for a rower in a boat. **thwart 2** v. to prevent (s.o.) doing sth.
thy [ðaɪ] adj. (old) your. **thyself** pron. (old) yourself.
thyme [taɪm] n. common herb used as flavouring.
thymus ['θaɪməs] n. lymph gland at the base of the neck.
thyroid (gland) ['θaɪrɔɪd (glænd)] n. gland in the neck which influences the growth, etc. of the body.
thyroidectomy n. operation to remove the thyroid.
Ti symbol for titanium.
tiara [tɪ'ɑːrə] n. headpiece with jewels. like a small crown.
tibia ['tɪbɪə] n. one of the two large bones between the knee and the ankle.
tic [tɪk] n. twitch of the muscles which cannot be controlled.
tick 1 [tɪk] n. (a) inf. very short moment. (b) mark on paper to indicate that sth is correct. (c) small insect or similar creature which lives on the skin of birds and animals. (d) inf. on t. = on credit. (e) small click made by a clock/watch, etc.
tick 2 v. (a) to mark with a tick. (b) to make a small clicking noise; inf. what makes s.o. t. = what is the reason for his behaviour. **tick away** v. (of time) to

pass. **ticker** n. inf. (a) watch. (b) heart.
tickertape n. long paper tape which carries information printed automatically by telegraph. **tick off** v. (a) mark with a tick. (b) inf. to reprimand (s.o.). **tick over** v. (of car engine) to run gently while the car is stationary. **tick-tack** n. system of hand signals used by bookmakers to pass information at racecourses.
ticket 1 ['tɪkɪt] n. (a) piece of paper/card allowing you to travel. to go into a theatre/cinema, etc.; piece of paper showing a price/information; receipt for a coat in a cloakroom; parking t. = piece of paper showing that you have parked illegally and must pay a fine. (b) master's t. = licence held by the captain of a ship which shows he is qualified. (c) Am. list of candidates sponsored by a political party. **ticket 2** v. to stick a ticket on (sth for sale).
ticking ['tɪkɪŋ] n. thick cloth for covering mattresses, etc.
tickle 1 ['tɪkl] n. irritation which makes you laugh/cough. **tickle 2** v. (a) to irritate mildly (a part of s.o.'s body) in order to make him laugh; inf. tickled pink = very pleased and amused. (b) to itch/to be irritated. **ticklish** adj. (a) (person) who is easily made to laugh by tickling. (b) inf. difficult (problem).
tickly adj. irritated so as to make you want to scratch.
tic-tac-toe [tɪktæk'təʊ] n. Am. noughts and crosses.
tidbit ['tɪdbɪt] n. Am. see titbit.
tiddler ['tɪdlə] n. inf. very small fish.
tiddly ['tɪdlɪ] adj. (-ier, -iest) inf. rather drunk. **tiddly-winks** n. game where small discs have to be flicked into a little cup.
tide 1 [taɪd] n. (a) regular rising and falling movement of the sea. (b) movement (of public opinion, ect); to swim against the t. = to go against what most people think. **tide 2** v. to t. s.o. over = to help him get past a difficult period. **tidal** adj. referring to the tide; t. wave = huge wave in the sea; t. stretch of the river = part of the river near its mouth where the movement of the tides is noticeable. **tidemark** n. (a) mark showing the top limit of a tide. (b) inf. dirty line round a bath showing where the water reached to; line(as on your

neck) showing which part of the body has been washed and which has not.

tideway *n.* current caused by the tide running in a tidal stretch of a river.

tidings ['taɪdɪŋz] *n. pl.*(formal) news.

tidy 1 ['taɪdɪ] *adj.* (-ier, -iest) (a) neat/in good order. (b) *inf.* quite large (sum). **tidy 2** *n.* small container for putting things to keep them tidy. **tidy 3** *v.* to make (sth) neat. **tidily** *adv.* in a tidy way. **tidiness** *n.* being tidy. **tidy up** *v.* to make (sth) completely tidy; to remove (a mess).

tie 1 [taɪ] *n.* (a) thing which attaches/ which restricts; the ties of friendship. (b) band of cloth which is worn knotted round the neck under the shirt collar old school t. = particular tie which shows which school you went to. (c) linking mark in music to show that several notes are to be played as one long note. (d) equal score in a competition/election; there was a t. for second place = two people were equal second. (e) cup t. = football match as a result of which one team is eliminated from a championship. **tie 2** *v.* (a) to attach/to fasten; she's tied to her work = can never get away from it. (b) to make (a knot). (c) to come equal in a competition. **tie-breaker** *n.* (in tennis) game to decide the winner of a set. played when the score is 6-6. **tied** *adj.* attached; t. house = public house which belongs to a brewery; t. cottage = cottage belonging to a farmer who rents it to his farmworkers. **tie down** *v.* to attach (to the floor/ground); to tie s.o. down = to make s.o. accept certain conditions. **tie-dyed** *adj.* (shirt, etc) which has been tied and then dyed to give a mottled effect. **tie-on** *adj.* tie-on label = label which is attached so that it can be tied. **tiepin** *n.* pin for attaching a tie. **tie up** *v.* (a) to attach/to fasten. (b) to keep motionless; *inf.* rather tied up = rather busy. (c) to use (money) to purchase sth. so that it is not available for other purposes. **tie-up** *n.* link/ connection.

tier ['tɪə] *n.* one of a series of steps. *usu.* a row of seats in a theatre; wedding cake with four tiers = made of four separate cakes balanced one on top of the other. **tiered** *adj.* with tiers.

tiff [tɪf] *n.* small argument/quarrel.

tiffin ['tɪfɪn] *n.* (in. India, etc.) lunch.

tiger ['taɪgə] *n.* large striped cat-like-wild animal; t. lily = lily with spotted orange flowers; paper t. = thing which seems fierce but is really harmless.

tigress *n.* female tiger.

tight 1 [taɪt] *adj.* (-er, -est) (a) which fits (too) closely; (b) closely packed together; (schedule) which allows no spare time. (c) stretched taut. (d) *inf.* (money) which is difficult to get. (e) *inf.* drunk. **tight 2** *adv.* (a) closely/firmly (shut). (b) closely packed. (c) *inf.* to sit t. = to stay where you are. **tighten** *v.* to make/to become tight; we must t. our belts = be prepared to eat less/to spend less. **tightfisted** *adj.* & *n.* mean/not generous. **tightfitting** *adj.* which fits tightly. **tightlipped** *adj.* with the mouth firmly closed; (person) who refuses to speak. **tightly** *adv.* in a tight way. **tightness** *n.* being tight.

tightrope *n.* rope stretched between two poles on which s.o. can walk/can perform tricks. **tights** *n. pl.*closefitting piece of clothing worn by girls, women, dancers, etc., on the legs and lower part of the body.

tile 1 [taɪl] *n.* flat piece of baked clay used to cover floors/wall/roofs; carpet tiles = square piece of carpet which can be laid on a floor like tiles. **tile 2** *v.* to cover (a roof/a floor/a wall) with tiles. **tiler** *n.* person who tiles (a roof, etc.).

till 1 [tɪl] *n.* drawer for keeping cash in a shop. **till 2** *v.* to cultivate (land). **till 3** *prep.* until/up to (a time). **till 4** *conj.*. up to/until. **tiller** ['tɪlə] *n.* handle which is attached to a rudder and so steers a boat.

tilt 1 [tɪlt] *n.* (a) slope/slant. (b) at full t. = at full speed. **tilt 2** *v.* to slope; to place at a slope.

tilth [tɪlθ] *n.* good crumbly soil.

timber ['tɪmbə] *n.* (a) cut wood ready for building t. merchant = person who sells timber. (b) growing trees which could be cut down and used for building. (c) large beam/plank used in building. **timbered** *adj.* (house) made of wooden beams. **timberyard** *n.* place where cut wood is sold.

timbre ['tæmbə] *n.* quality of sound (of voice/musical instrument).

time 1 [taɪm] *n.* (a) existence for a

period (such as years/centuries, etc.); t. alone will tell = the result will only become apparent later; to have t. one your hands = to have a period with nothing to do; there's no t. to be lost = we must hurry; to make up for lost t. = to do things rapidly because time has been wasted. (b) period between two happenings; in three weeks' t. = three weeks from now; all the t. = continuously. (c) particular period; *inf.* to do t. = to serve a prison sentence. (d) times = age/period; behind the times = out of date. (e) particular point at which sth took place; I was away at the t. = when it happened; at the present t. = now; by the t. I got there = when I got there; from t. to t./at times = occasionally; for the t. being = temporarily. (f) point expressed in hours and minutes; Greenwich Mean Time = internationally accepted correct time system. (g) hour at which sth usually happens; the train arrived on t. = at the right time; we were in t. = we were early enough. (h) (pleasant/bad) period. (i) one of several occasions. (j) times = multiplied by. (k) rhythm. **time 2** *v.* (a) to choose the right moment. (b) to calculate the time sth takes. **time bomb** *n.* bomb with a clock attached, which sets off the bomb at a particular moment. **time-honoured** *adj.* (custom) observed for a long time and therefore respected. **timekeeper** *n.* (a) person who times a race. (b) good t. = (i) person who is always on time; (ii) watch which always shows the correct time. **timekeeping** *n.* being on time. **timelag** *n.* delay. **timeless** *adj.* permanent; untouched by time. **timelessness** *n.* being timeless. **time limit** *n.* period during which sth should be done. **timeliness** *n.* being timely. **timely** *adj.* which happens at the right moment. **timepiece** *n.* old-fashioned watch or clock. **timer** *n.* (a) person/device which times; egg t. device which times how long an egg boils. (b) time switch. **timesaving** *adj.* (device) which saves time. **timeserver** *n.* person who changes his opinions to match those of people in power. **timesharing** *n.* system where several people buy shares in a property, each one

being allowed to use it for a limited period each year. **time-signal** *n.* accurate radio signal showing the exact time. **timeswitch** *n.* switch which can be set to start a machine/to stop a light, etc. at a particular time. **timetable 1** *n.* list which shows the times of trains/aircraft/classes in school/appointments. **timetable 2** *v.* to draw up a list of times; to appear on a list of times. **time-work** *n.* work which is paid for at a rate of money for a particular time. **time zone** *n.* zone on the earth in which a uniform time is kept. **timing** *n.* (a) action of recording the time (of a race). (b) controlling the time at which sth happens. (c) (in a car engine) rate at which the spark coincides with the flow of petrol.
timid ['tımıd] *adj.* afraid/frightened. **timidity** [tı'mıdıtı] *n.* being timid. **timidly** ['tımıdlı] *adv.* in a timid way.
timorous ['tımərəs] *adj.* very frightened.
timpani ['tımpənı] *n. pl.* group of kettledrums in an orchestra. **timpanist** *n.* person who plays the timpani.
tin 1 [tın] *n.* (a) (element; Sn) silvery metal. (b) metal covered with a thin layer of tin. (c) (usu. round) metal box for keeping food in; cake t. = tin for baking or keeping cakes in. **tin 2** *v.* (tinned) to preserve (food) by packing it in a tin. **tinfoil** *n.* thin metal sheet used esp. to wrap food up. **tinny** ['tını] *adj.* (-ier, -iest) weak metallic (sound); (car) which rattles. **tin opener** *n.* device for opening tins. **tin pan alley** *n. inf.* area where publishers of popular music have offices. **tin plate** ['tınpleıt] *n.* thin sheet of iron covered with tin. **tinpot** *adj. inf.* not of good quality. **tin tack** *n.* nail with a large head used to fasten down carpets etc.
tincture ['tıŋktʃə] *n.* medicine dissolved in alcohol.
tinder ['tındə] *n.* very dry material for starting a fire.
tine [taın] *n.* prong of a fork.
tinge 1 [tınʒ] *n.* slight colour/taste, etc.. of sth. **tinge 2** *v.* to give a slight colour/taste of (sth).
tingle 1 ['tıŋgl] *n.* sharp prickling feeling. **tingle 2** *v.* to have a sharp prickling feeling; tingling with

excitement = very excited.

tinker 1 ['tɪŋkə] n. mender of saucepans who travels from place to place. **tinker 2** v. to t. with sth = to try (often in a clumsy way) to make sth work better.

tinkle 1 ['tɪŋkl] n. ringing (like a little bell). **tinkle 2** v. to make a little ringing noise.

tinnitus [tɪ'naɪtəs] n. ringing noise in the ears.

tinsel ['tɪnsl] n. thin strips of glittering metal for decorating Christmas trees, etc.

tint 1 [tɪnt] n. slight shade of colour. **tint 2** v. to give a slight shade of colour; tinted glass = glass which has a slight shade of brown/ blue, etc.

tiny ['taɪnɪ] adj. (-ier, -iest) very small.

tip 1 [tɪp] n. (a) pointed end; the t. of the iceberg = small part of sth (usu. unpleasant) which makes you eventually discover the rest. (b) money given to a waiter, etc., to show thanks for his services. (c) piece of helpful information; racing tips = suggestions as to which horses are likely to win; take my t. = take my advice. (d) rubbish t. = public place where rubbish can be dumped. **tip 2** v. (tipped) (a) to put a tip on (sth); (b) to make (sth) slope/lean. (c) to pour out/to empty (sth). (d) to throw away (rubbish). (e) to give (a waiter, etc.) a small gift of money. (f) to give (s.o.) a piece of helpful information; to t. s.o. off/inf. to t. s.o. the wink = to warn s.o. (g) to forecast confidently that s.o. with do sth. **tip-off** n. inf. piece of useful information; warning. **tip over** v. to lean and fall over; to make (sth) lean and fall over. **tipper** n. truck, etc. which tips. **tipster** n. person who gives advice on which horse is likely to win a race. **tiptoe 1** n. on t. = quietly on the tips of your toes. **tiptoe 2** v. to walk quietly on the tips of your toes. **tiptop** adj. inf. excellent. **tip up** v. (a) to turn (sth) over so that the contents fall out. (b) to swing on a hinge. **tip-up** adj. (chair/lorry) which tips up.

tipple 1 ['tɪpl] n. inf. drink. **tipple 2** v. inf. to drink alcohol regularly.

tipstaff ['tɪpstɑːf] n. official of a law court.

tipsy [tɪpsɪ] adj. (-ier, -iest) inf. rather drunk; t. cake = cake soaked in sherry, etc. **tipsily** adv. in a tipsy way. **tipsiness** n. being tipsy.

tirade [taɪ'reɪd] n. long angry speech.

tire 1 [taɪə] n. Am. see tyre. **tire 2** v. (a) to become/to make weary; to need a rest after physical exercise. (b) (of) to lose interest in doing sth. **tired** adj. (a) feeling sleepy/in need of rest. (b) t. of sth = bored with sth/having no patience with sth. **tiredness** n. feeling in need of rest. **tireless** adj. full of energy/never needing to rest. **tirelessly** adv. in a tireless way. **tiresome** adj. annoying/ bothering. **tiring** adj. which makes you tired.

tiro ['taɪrəʊ] n. (pl.-os) complete beginner/person with no experience.

tissue ['tɪʃuː] n. (a) group of cells which make up a part of an animal or plant. (b) thin cloth. (c) soft paper handkerchief. (d) t. of lies = mass of lies. **tissue paper** n. thin soft paper used for wrapping delicate objects.

tit [tɪt] n. (a) type of common small bird. (b) Sl. teat; breast. (c) t. for tat = paying back a blow with another blow.

titan ['taɪtn] n. very large/strong person. **titanic** [taɪ'tænɪk] adj. very large.

titanium [tɪ'teɪnɪəm] n. (element; Ti) light grey metal.

titbit Am. **tidbit** ['tɪtbɪt] n. special little piece (of food/of information).

tithe [taɪð] n. (old) produce paid to the church. **tithebarn** n. barn in which tithes were kept.

titillate ['tɪtɪleɪt] v. to excite. **titillation** n. act of titillating.

titivate ['tɪtɪveɪt] v. inf. to t. (yourself) = to make yourself look smart.

title ['taɪtl] n. (a) name of a book/play/ film, etc.; t. page = page at the beginning of a book. where the title is written in large letters; t. role = part in a play/film which gives the name to the play/film; credit titles = words at the beginning of a film showing who is the director, etc. (b) word (usu. put in front of a name) to indicate an honour/a qualification. (c) (in sport) position of champion. (d) right to own (property); t. deed = paper showing that you are the owner of a property. **titled** adj. with a title (such as Lord, Sir, etc.) to show that you are a nobleman.

titmouse ['tɪtmaʊs] *n.* (*pl.*-mice) type of small bird.

titrate [taɪ'treɪt] *v.* to analyse the concentration of a chemical solution.

titration [taɪ'treɪʃn] *n.* act of titrating.

titter 1 ['tɪtə] *n.* little laugh. **titter 2** *v.* to give a little laugh. **tittle-tattle** ['tɪtl'tætl] *n. inf.* gossip.

titular ['tɪtjʊlə] *adj.* holding a title but without direct power.

tiz, tizwaz, tizzy [tɪz, 'tɪzwɒz, 'tɪzɪ] *n. inf.* bother/nervous state.

TNT ['ti:en'ti:] abbreviation for trinitrotoluene, common high explosive.

to1 [tu:] *prep.* (a) (showing direction or position) he went to France; move to the right. (b) (showing time) from day to day; it's ten to six = ten minutes before six o'clock. (c) (showing person who receives something) give it to me. (d) (showing relationship) is this the key to the box? secretary to the managing director. (e) concerning; there's nothing to it = there's no difficulty in doing it. (f) (showing ratio) they lost by six goals to four; the rate is two dollars to the pound. (g) (showing comparison) I prefer butter to margarine. **to 2** *adv.* (a) he came to = he regained consciousness. (b) pull the door to = pull it until it is almost shut. **to 3** (forming infinitive) (a) after verbs they came to help us. (b) after adjectives good to eat. (c) after nouns he made no attempt to run away. (d) when the verb is a subject to refuse the invitation would have been rude. **to and fro** *adv.* backwards and forwards. **to-be** suffix showing something in the near future a mother-to-be.

toad [təʊd] *n.* amphibian like a large frog, which lives mostly on land; t. in the hole = sausages cooked in a dish of batter. **toadstool** *n.* fungus shaped like a mushroom but *usu.* not edible, and sometimes poisonous. **toady 1** *n.* person who flatters s.o. (in the hope of getting sth in return). **toady 2** *v.* to flatter (s.o.).

toast 1 [təʊst] *n.* (a) slices of bread which have been grilled brown. (b) taking a drink and wishing s.o. success. **toast 2** *v.* (a) to grill (bread, etc.) until it is brown; to warm. (b) to drink and wish s.o. success. **toaster** *n.* electric device for toasting bread. **toastmaster**

n. person (at a banquet) who calls on people to speak and announces the toasts. **toastrack** *n.* device for holding slices of toast.

tobacco [tə'bækəʊ] *n.* (dried leaves of a) plant used for smoking in cigarettes/ cigars and in pipes. **tobacconist** *n.* person who sells tobacco/cigarettes, etc.

toboggan 1 [tə'bɒgən] *n.* long sledge curved upwards at the front. **toboggan 2** *v.* to slide on a toboggan.

tobogganing *n.* sport of sliding on a toboggan.

toby jug ['təʊbɪ 'dʒʌg] *n.* small mug made in the shape of a head.

toccata [tɒ'kɑːtə] *n.* piece of music for the organ or piano.

tocsin ['tɒksɪn] *n.* warning bell.

today [tə'deɪ] *adv. & n.* (a) this present day; t/week/a week t. = in exactly seven day's time. (b) this present time.

toddle ['tɒdl] *v.* to walk unsteadily.

toddler *n.* child who is just learning to walk.

toddy ['tɒdɪ] *n.* alcohol and hot water and sugar.

to-do [tə'duː] *n. inf.* excitement/ confusion/bother.

toe 1 [təʊ] *n.* (a) one of the five parts like fingers at the end of your foot; big t./ little t. = the largest/smallest of the five toes; to be on your toes = to be ready/ prepared. (b) end part of a shoe/a sock; t. cap = hard end to a shoe. **toe 2** *v.* to touch with the toe; to t. the line = to do what you are told to do. **toehold** *n.* grip with the toes; small foothold.

toenail *n.* nail at the end of a toe.

toff [tɒf] *n. inf.* aristocrat.

toffee ['tɒfɪ] *n.* sticky sweet made with sugar and butter; t. apple = apple covered with toffee; *inf.* he can't do it for t. = he can't do it at all. **toffeenosed** *adj. inf.* supercilious.

toga ['təʊgə] *n.* robe worn by men in Ancient Rome.

together [tə'geðə] *adv.* (a) in a group/ all at the same time; get t. = meet. (b) into contact one with another; stick the pieces t. **togetherness** *n.* being together with other people.

togged [tɒgd] *adj. inf.* t. out/up in = wearing.

togs [tɒgz] *n. pl.inf.* clothes.

toggle ['tɒgl] *n.* short piece of wood

attached to a coat with string. used in place of a button; small clasp used for attaching a scarf.

toil 1 [tɔɪl] *n.* hard work. **toil 2** *v.* to work hard.

toilet ['tɔɪlət] *n.* (a) washing and dressing. (b) bowl with a seat on which you sit to pass waste matter from the body; room with this bowl in it; t. paper = soft paper for wiping your anus after getting rid of waste matter. t. roll = roll of toilet paper; t. water = scented water. **toiletries** *n. pl.* facecloths/soap/ perfume, etc., uses in washing.

token ['təʊkən] *n.* (a) visible thing which is a mark/sign (of respect, etc.); by the same t. = in a similar way; t. strike = short strike which stands as a symbol of grievances; t. payment = a small symbolic payment; t. woman/black person appointed to a position (on a committee, etc.) to placate rights movements. (b) piece of paper/card/ plastic which is used to replace money; book/flower/record t. = card which can only be exchanged for books/flowers/ records.

told [təʊld] *v.* see tell.

tolerate ['tɒləreɪt] *v.* (a) to suffer (noise, etc.) without complaining. (b) to allow (sth which you do not agree with) to exist. **tolerable** ['tɒlərəbl] *adj.* (a) bearable. (b) fairly good. **tolerably** *adv.* in a fairly good way; a t. good film = quite a good film. **tolerance** *n.* (a) putting up with (unpleasantness etc); allowing (sth which you do not agree with) to exist. (b) amount by which a measurement can vary from what is specified on a plan. (c) ability to stand the effect of a drug/a poison. **tolerant** *adj.* (person) who tolerates. **tolerantly** *adv.* in a tolerant way. **toleration** [tɒlə'reɪʃn] *n.* allowing (sth which you do not agree with) to exist.

toll 1 [təʊl] *n.* (a) payment for using a road/a bridge/a ferry; t. bridge = one where a toll is paid. (b) loss/damage; death t. = number of deaths. (c) solemn ringing of a bell. **toll 2** *v.* to ring (a bell) solemnly as for a funeral. **toll call** *n. Am.* long-distance telephone call. **toll free** *adv. Am.* without having to pay the charge for a long-distance call. **tollgate**

n. gate across a road where a toll has to be paid. **tollhouse** *n.* house where the tollkeeper lives. **tollkeeper** *n.* person who takes the toll on a road/bridge, etc.

tom(cat) ['tɒm(kæt)] *n.* male cat.

tomahawk ['tɒməhɔːk] *n.* light North American Indian axe.

tomato [tə'mɑːtəʊ, *Am.* tə'meɪtəʊ] *n.* (*pl.*-oes) red fruit growing on annual plants and used in salads; plant which bears tomatoes; t. sauce = sauce made with tomatoes.

tomb [tuːm] *n.* large grave (usu. with an underground vault in which to put a dead person). **tombstone** *n.* large stone placed on a grave with the name of the dead person written on it.

tombola [tɒm'bəʊlə] *n.* game where people buy numbered tickets and one or more tickets win prizes.

tomboy ['tɒmbɔɪ] *n.* girl who plays rough games like a boy.

tome [təʊm] *n.* (formal) large book.

tomfool ['tɒmfuːl] *adj. inf.* idiotic. **tomfoolery** *n.* stupid behaviour.

tommy gun ['tɒmɪgʌn] *n.* small machine gun.

tomorrow [tə'mɒrəʊ] *adv. & n.* (a) the day which follows today. (b) the future.

tomtom ['tɒmtɒm] *n.* small drum beaten with your hands.

ton [tʌn] *n.* (a) weight equal to 2240 pounds; metric t. = 1000 kilograms. (b) space in a ship equivalent to 100 cubic feet. (c) *inf.* tons of = lots. (d) *Sl.* to do a t. = to go at 100 miles per hour.

tonnage *n.* (a) space in a ship measured in tons. (b) total number of ships in a navy/belonging to a company calculated by adding together their individual sizes. **tonne** [tʌn] *n.* metric ton.

tone 1 [təʊn] *n.* (a) quality of sound of music/voice. (b) (in music) difference between to notes which have one note between them on the piano. (c) way of speaking/writing which shows a particular emotion. (d) shade of colour. (e) strength of the body and muscles. (f) general quality or appearance. **tone 2** *v.* to t. in with = to fit in well/to harmonize. **tonal** ['təʊnl] *adj.* referring to tone. **tonality** [tə'nælɪtɪ] *n.* quality of tone (in colours of a painting/in a piece of music). **tone-deaf** *adj.* not able to recognize differences in musical pitch. **tone down** v. to reduce (sth) excessive. **toneless** adj. with no variation in tone. **tone up** v. to make fitter.

tongs [tɒŋz] n. pl.(pair of) t. = instrument for picking things up. with small claws on the end of two arms; sugar t. = tongs for picking up lumps of sugar.

tongue [tʌŋ] n. (a) long, movable piece of muscular flesh in the mouth, which is used for tasting and speaking; to say sth. with one's t. in one's cheek = not really to mean it seriously; to hold one's t. = not to speak; it's on the tip of my t. = I will remember it in a moment. (b) peace of moveable flesh in an animal's mouth, used as food. (c) language; mother t. = first language. (d) loose piece of leather under the laces in a shoe. (e) long, thin flame/piece of land. **tongue-and-groove** n. type of interlocking board, with a projecting tongue along one edge which fits into a corresponding groove along the edge of the next board. **tongue-tied** adj. so shy as to be unable to say anything. **tonguetwister** n. phrase (like red lorry, yellow lorry) which is difficult to say quickly.

tonic 1 ['tɒnɪk] adj. (a) referring to a musical tone; t. solfa = system of writing the tones in music using syllables (doh-ray-me, etc). (b) referring to physical strength/wellbeing. **tonic 2** n. (a) note which sets the key to a scale of music. (b) anything (such as medicine) which strengthens the body; to act as a t. on s.o. = make s.o. more energetic. (c) t. (water) = fizzy drink containing quinine.

tonight [tə'naɪt] adv. & n. the night of the present day.

tonnage ['tʌnɪdʒ] n. see ton.

tonne [tʌn] n. see ton.

tonsil ['tɒnsl] n. one of two soft lumps of flesh at the back of your throat. **tonsillectomy** n. operation to remove the tonsils. **tonsillitis** [tɒnsɪ'laɪtɪs] n. painful infection of the tonsils.

tonsure ['tɒnʃə] n. shaving off all or part of the hair of people becoming monks; part of the head which has been shaved. **tonsured** adj. with a tonsure.

tontine ['tɒntiːn] n. type of investment where the survivors each receive more as investors die.

too [tuː] adv. (a) more than necessary. (b) as well/also. (c) inf. very; t. bad! = it's a shame!

took [tʊk] v. see take.

tool 1 [tuːl] n. hard instrument for doing work (such as hammer/spade, etc.); person used by s.o. else. **tool 2** v. to decorate using a tool. **tool up** v. to equip (a factory) with machinery.

toot 1 [tuːt] n. short sound made by a horn. **toot 2** v. to blow a horn sharply.

tooth [tuːθ] n. (pl.teeth[tiːθ]) (a) one of a set of bony structures in the mouth, used by animals for chewing and biting; milk teeth = first set of teeth grown by a baby, and replaced by permanent teeth as a child; false teeth = set of plastic teeth of replace teeth which have been taken out; in the teeth of = running against/into; long in the t. = old; armed to the teeth = fully armed. (b) part of a saw/of a comb/of a cogwheel shaped like a tooth. **toothache** ['tuːθeɪk] n. pain in a tooth. **toothbrush** n. small brush with a long handle used for cleaning your teeth. **toothcomb** n. comb with teeth set close together; to go through sth with a (fine) t. = to inspect sth very carefully. **toothed** adj. with teeth; t. wheel = cogwheel. **toothless** adj. with no teeth. **toothpaste** n. paste used with a toothbrush for cleaning your teeth. **toothpick** n. small pointed piece of wood/metal etc. for pushing between the teeth to remove pieces of food. **toothsome** adj. good to eat. **toothy** adj. showing a lot of teeth.

tootle 1 ['tuːtl] n. inf. little toot. **tootle 2** v. inf. (a) to make a tootle. (b) to go (along/off).

top 1 [tɒp] n. (a) highest point; on t. of everything else = in addition to everything else. (b) flat upper surface; lid. (c) Am. roof (of a car). (d) highest/most important place. (e) big t. = large circus tent. (f) at the t. of his voice = as loud as possible. (g) (in vehicle) highest gear. (h) child's toy which spins when twisted sharply. (i) piece of clothing covering the upper part of the body. **top 2** adj. (a) highest. (b) most important. **top 3** v. (topped) (a) to cut the top off. (b) to put sth on top. (c) to go higher than; inf. to t. it all = in addition to everything else. (d) *Sl.* to execute (s.o.). **topcoat** *n.* overcoat. **top dog** *n. Sl.* winner. **top dressing** *n.* scattering fertilizer on the surface of the soil; fertilizer to be scattered in this way. **top flight** *adj. inf.* excellent/of very high quality. **top hat** *n.* man's tall black hat. **top-heavy** *adj.* unstable because the top part is heavier than the bottom. **topknot** *n.* small bunch of hair tied on the top of the head. **topless** *adj.* (of woman) wearing nothing on the top part of the body. **top-level** *adj.* (talks) involving important people. **topmost** *adj.* highest. **top notch** *adj.* top flight. **topper** *n. inf.* top hat. **topping 1** *n.* cream etc. put on the top of a cake. **topping 2** *adj. inf.* very good. **topping out** *n.* ceremony to mark the completion of the main work on a new building. **top secret** *adj.* very secret. **topside** *n.* best quality beef for roasting. **topsoil** *n.* layer of good light soil on the surface (of a field, etc.). **top up** *v.* to fill completely (sth which is half empty).

topaz ['təʊpæz] *n.* yellow semi-precious stone.

topee, topi ['təʊpɪ] *n.* helmet worn in hot countries to protect your head from the sun.

topiary ['təʊpjərɪ] *n.* art of cutting bushes into odd shapes for ornament.

topic ['tɒpɪk] *n.* subject (for discussion/ of a conversation). **topical** *adj.* which is of interest at the present time. **topicality** *n.* being topical. **topically** *adv.* in a topical way.

topography [tə'pɒgrəfɪ] *n.* description of land mentioning rivers, mountains, roads, buildings, etc. **topographer** *n.* person who studies topography. **topographical** [tɒpə'græfɪkl] *adj.* which describes land. **topology** [tə'pɒlədʒɪ] *n.* study of the properties of geometrical shapes which remain the same even when the shapes change.

topple [tɒpl] *v.* to make a government/ dictator lose power. **topple over** ['tɒpl'əʊvə] *v.* to make (sth) fall down; to fall down.

topsy-turvy ['tɒpsɪ'tɜːvɪ] *adj. & adv.* upside down/in confusion.

toque [təʊk] *n.* round hat (for a woman) with no brim.

tor [tɔː] *n.* rocky hill.

torch [tɔːtʃ] *n.* (*pl.*-es) (a) portable electric light which you can hold in your hand. (b) flaming piece of wood. **torchlight** *n.* light from a flaming torch; t. procession = procession of people carrying flaming torches.

tore [tɔː] *v.* see tear.

toreador ['tɒrɪədɔː] *n.* Spanish bullfighter.

torment 1 ['tɔːmənt] *n.* extreme pain; in t. = in great pain. **torment 2** *v.* to make (s.o.) suffer. **tormentor** *n.* person who torments.

torn [tɔːn] *v.* see tear.

tornado [tɔː'neɪdəʊ] *n.* (*pl.*-oes) violent whirlwind.

torpedo 1 [tɔː'piːdəʊ] *n.* (*pl.*-oes) self propelled missile which travels through the water. **torpedo 2** *v.* to sink (a ship) using a torpedo; to ruin (s.o.'s plans). **torpedo boat** *n.* small fast naval ship which carries torpedoes.

torpid ['tɔːpɪd] *adj.* half asleep with heat; dull; sluggish.

torpor *n.* being half asleep/sluggish.

torque [tɔːk] *n.* (a) mechanical force to make sth rotate. (b) prehistoric necklace made of twisted gold or silver.

torrent ['tɒrənt] *n.* (a) fast rushing streAm. (b) fast flow. **torrential** [tə'renʃəl] *adj.* like a torrent

torrid ['tɒrɪd] *adj.* (a) very hot. (b) intense (passion)

torsion ['tɔːʃn] *n.* being twisted; strain caused by twisting.

torso ['tɔːsəʊ] *n.* (*pl.*-os) body (excluding the head. arms and legs)

tort [tɔːt] *n.* act which is the subject of a civil action in court

tortilla [tɔː'tiːjə] *n.* type of Spanish omelette, with vegetables.

tortoise ['tɔːtəs] *n.* reptile covered with a hard domed shell, which moves very slowly and can live to a great age. **tortoiseshell** *adj. & n.* speckled brown material (from the shell of a tortoise) used for making combs/frames for glasses, etc.; t. cat = brown. yellow and black cat; t. butterfly = common brown and red butterfly.

tortuous ['tɔːtjʊəs] *adj.* which twists and turns. **tortuously** *adv.* in a tortuous way.

torture 1 ['tɔːtʃə] *n.* pain inflicted on s.o. as a punishment or to make them reveal a secret. **torture 2** *v.* to inflict torture on s.o. **torturer** *n.* person who tortures.

Tory ['tɔːrɪ] *adj. & n.* (member) of the Conservative party.

toss 1 [tɒs] *n.* (*pl.*-es) (a) action of throwing sth into the air; t. of a coin = throwing a coin up to see which side is on top when it comes down; to argue the t. = to argue about s.o.'s final decision; (in sport) to win the t. = guess correctly which side of the coin comes down on top and so play first. (b) sharp disdainful movement of the head. **toss 2** *v.* (a) to throw (sth) into the air; to t. a coin = to throw a coin to see which side is on top when it comes down; let's t. for it = the person who guesses right. starts to play first/has first choice. (b) to move (sth) about; to mix (a salad); she tossed her head = made a sharp disdainful movement of her head. **toss up** *v.* to toss a coin. **toss-up** *n. inf.* it's a toss-up which one will win = you can't tell which one will win.

tot 1 [tɒt] *n.* (a) little child. (b) *inf.* small glass of alcohol. **tot 2** *v.* (totalled) t. up = to add up.

total 1 ['təʊtl] *adj. & n.* complete/whole (amount). **total 2** *v.* (totalled) to add up (to). **totality** [təʊˈtælɪtɪ] *n.* whole amount. **totalize** *v.* to add up (figures). **totally** *adv.* completely.

totalitarian [təʊtælɪˈteərɪən] *adj.* (state) governed by a single party/group which refuses to allow the existence of any opposition.

totalizator ['təʊtəlaɪzeɪtə] *n.* machine which calculates the amount to be paid to people who bet on a winning horse.

tote 1 [təʊt] *n. inf.* the t. = totalizator. **tote 2** *v. Am.* to carry. **tote-bag** *n.* large carrying bag.

totem pole ['təʊtəmpəʊl] *n.* tall carved pole on which North American Indians carve figures of gods.

totter ['tɒtə] *n.* to walk unsteadily/to wobble. **tottery** *adj.* wobbly/likely to fall.

toucan ['tuːkæn] *n.* American tropical bird with huge coloured beak.

touch 1 [tʌtʃ] *n.* (*pl.*-es) (a) sense by which you feel sth. (b) way of bringing your fingers into contact with sth; she's lost her t. = she isn't as successful as she was. (c) slight tap. (d) slight stroke (of a paintbrush); to put the finishing touches to sth = to finish sth off. (e) contact; to get into t. with/to lose t. with = to contact/to lose contact with. (f) slight taste/trace. (g) (in football) part of the field outside the playing area. **touch 2** *v.* (a) to feel (with the fingers); to come into contact; I wouldn't t. it = I wouldn't have anything to do with it; don't t. my things = don't interfere with them/don't move them. (b) to t. one = to refer to (a subject). (c) to eat or drink. (d) to affect the emotions of (s.o.). (e) to reach the same level as (s.o.). (f) *inf.* to ask (s.o.) for a loan. **touch and go** *n.* it was touch and go = it was doubtful. **touch down** *v.* (a) (of plane) to land. (b) (in Rugby) to score a try. **touchdown** *n.* (a) landing (of a plane). (b) (in Rugby) scoring a try. **touché** ['tuːʃeɪ] *inter.* meaning you have scored a point against me. **touched** *adj.* (a) grateful/pleased with (b) slightly mad. **touchiness,** *n.* being susceptible/easily offended. **touching 1** *adj.* which affects the emotions. **touching 2** *prep.* concerning/about. **touch line** *n.* white line along one side of a football pitch. **touch off** *v.* to set off (an explosion, etc.). **touch on** *v.* to refer to (a question) briefly. **touchpaper** *n.* chemically treated paper used as a fuse to light a firework. **touch screen** *n.* computer screen which is sensitive to touch, and where a cursor can be positioned by touching the screen. **touchstone** *n.* thing used as a standard to test other things against. **touch type** *v.* to type without looking at the keys on the typewriter. **touch up** *v.* to add little strokes of paint to improve the appearance of sth. **touchy** *adj. inf.* highly susceptible/easily offended.

tough 1 [tʌf] *adj.* (-ier, -est) (a) hard; difficult to chew/to cut/to break; *inf.* it's as t. as old boots = extremely tough. (b) strong/hardy. (c) difficult; to get it with s.o. = to deal roughly/harshly with s.o. (d) *inf.* t. luck! = hard luck! **tough 2** *n.*

inf. rough criminal. **toughen** *v.* to make tough; toughened glass = specially strengthened glass. **toughness** *n.* being tough.

toupee ['tuːpeɪ] *n.* small wig.

tour 1 ['tʊə] *n.* journey which goes round various places and returns to its starting point; package t. = one which has been totally organized in advance.

tour 2 *v.* to visit; to go on a tour; touring company = theatre company which goes from one town to another in the provinces. **tourism** *n.* business of providing lodging and entertainment for tourists. **tourist** *adj. & n.* person who goes on holiday to visit places; t. class = type of seating in an aircraft which is cheaper than first class; t. trap = place which overcharges tourists. **tour de force** [tuːdə'fɔːs] *n.* act showing remarkable skill.

tourmaline ['tʊəməliːn] *n.* type of semiprecious stone.

tournament ['tʊənəmənt] *n.* (a) (old) contest between groups of knights. (b) sporting competition with many games which eliminate competitors.

tournedos ['tʊənədəʊ] *n.* piece of fillet steak.

tourniquet ['tʊənɪkeɪ] *n.* tight bandage put round an arm or leg to stop bleeding from a wound.

tousle ['taʊzl] *v.* to make (hair) untidy.

tout 1 [taʊt] *n.* (a) person who tries to sell something to people he meets; ticket t. = person who sells tickets at high prices to people in the street. (b) person who touts. **tout 2** *v.* (also tout for) to try to persuade people to vote/to buy things/to stay in a hotel.

tow 1 [təʊ] *n.* (a) pulling a car/a ship behind you; he had his family in t. = coming behind him. (b) short, coarse pieces of flax. **tow 2** *v.* to a pull (a car/a ship) which cannot move itself.

towbar *n.* bar fitted to a car, to attach a caravan/trailer. **tow-headed** *adj.* with yellow hair. **tow-line, tow-rope** *n.* rope which attaches a car/a ship to sth being towed. **towpath** *n.* path along the bank of a river/canal (along which horses used to walk to tow barges)

towards [tə'wɔːdz] *prep.* (also toward) (a) in the direction of. (b) to (a person/a

country, etc.) (c) as part payment for. (d) near (a time).

towel 1 ['taʊəl] *n.* piece of soft absorbent cloth for drying; to throw in the t. = to give up/not to continue a contest. **towel 2** *v.* (towelled) to rub dry with a towel. **towelling** *n.* rough soft cloth used for making towels.

tower 1 ['taʊə] *n.* tall building; control t. = tall airport building containing the control room; t. of strength = very strong and sympathetic person. **tower 2** *v.* to rise very high (above). **towering** *adj.* (a) very tall. (b) very great (rage).

town [taʊn] *n.* place where people live and work, with houses, shops, offices and factories (as opposed to the country); t. clerk = formerly, senior administrative and legal officer in a town (now called Chief Executive) t. council = elected committee which runs a town; t. hall = offices of the town council; public building used for meetings; t. planning = science of planning the development of a town; *inf.* to go to t. over sth = to spend a lot of money/time on sth; *inf.* to paint the t. red = to have a wild party in the town.

townee *n. inf.* person who lives in a town. **town house** *n.* (a) house in a town. (b) expensive modern terraced house. **townsfolk** *n. pl.* people who live in a town. **township** *n.* (a) (in US and Canada) small town and the administrative area round it. (b) (in South Africa) area where black people live near a large town. **townsman, townswoman** *n.* (*pl.*-men, -women) person who lives in a town.

townspeople *n. pl.* people who live in a town.

toxaemia, *Am.* **toxemia** [tɒk'siːmɪə] blood poisoning.

toxic ['tɒksɪk] *adj.* poisonous. **toxcity** *n.* being toxic. **toxicologist** [tɒksɪ'kɒlədʒɪst] *n.* scientist who studies poisons. **toxicology** *n.* scientific study of poisons. **toxin** *n.* poisonous substance.

toxophily [tɒk'sɒfɪlɪ] *n.* (formal) archery.

toy 1 [tɔɪ] *adj. & n.* thing which children play with. **toy 2** *v.* to t. with = (i) to eat (food) reluctantly; (ii) to turn over (an idea) in your mind. **toyshop** *n.* shop which sells toys.

trace 1 [treɪs] *n.* (a) traces = set of tracks/footprints left by an animal. (b) small amount; he's vanished without a t. = leaving nothing behind to show where he has gone. (c) traces = straps by which a horse is attached to a carriage; to kick over the traces = to rebel (against authority). **trace 2** *v.* (a) to follow the tracks left by (sth); to try to find where (s.o./sth) is. (b) to copy (a picture/a map) by placing a piece of thin transparent paper over it and drawing on it. **traceable** *adj.* which can be traced. **trace element** *n.* chemical element of which a tiny amount is needed by a plant or animal to grow properly. **tracer** *n.* type of bullet/shell which leaves a visible stream of sparks/smoke as it flies. **tracery** *n.* delicate stone patterns holding the glass in a church window. **tracing** *n.* drawing done by tracing; t. paper = thin transparent paper for tracing drawings. **trachea** [træ'kiːə] *n.* windpipe. **tracheotomy** [trækɪ'ɒtəmɪ] *n.* operation to make a hole in the windpipe from the outside of the neck. **trachoma** [trə'kəʊmə] *n.* eye disease caused by a virus. **track 1** ['træk] *n.* (a) footprints of animal/marks of wheels, etc.; the police are on his t. = they are following him; to keep t. of = to keep an account/to keep oneself informed of; lose t. of sth = not to know where it is any longer; to make tracks for home = to set off for home. (b) path; on the wrong t. = working wrongly/ making a wrong assumption. (c) course for racing; t. events = running competitions in an athletics tournament; t. suit = type of warm two-piece suit worn by sportsmen when practising; t. shoes = running shoes with spikes in the soles; he has a good t. record = he has been very successful in the past. (d) line of rails; single-track railway = on which trains go up and down the same rails with passing places at intervals; *inf.* to have a one-track mind = to think on only one thing/have only one interest. (e) endless belt on which a caterpillar tractor/tank, etc., runs. (f) part of a magnetic tape on which sth can be recorded. (g) one song on a record containing several popular songs. **track**

2 *v.* to follow (an animal); to follow (a moving subject) with a camera. **track down** *v.* to follow and catch (an animal/a criminal). **tracker** *n.* animal/ person who follows tracks. **trackless** *adj.* with no paths.
tract [trækt] *n.* (a) wide stretch of countryside. (b) short (religious) pamphlet. (c) system of organs in the body which are linked together. **tractable** ['træktəbl] *adj.* which can be tamed/made to do what is necessary. **tractability** [træktə'bɪlɪtɪ] *n.* being tractable.
traction ['trækʃn] *n.* (a) pulling force; t. engine = large steam-driven engine which used to be used for pulling heavy loads. (b) pulling (a broken leg, etc.) up with pulleys. **tractor** ['træktə] *n.* farm vehicle with large back wheels for pulling a plough, etc.; t. feed = paper feed in a printer. where the paper is pulled by sprocket wheels.
trad [træd] *adj. inf.* traditional.
trade 1 [treɪd] *n.* (a) business; buying and selling. (b) people who buy and sell a particular type of goods/who work in a particular industry; t. price = special price to another dealer in the same business. (c) job. **trade 2** *v.* (a) to carry on a business. (b) to exchange (sth for sth). **trade in** *v.* to exchange of an old car, etc., as part payment for a new one. **trade-in** *n.* exchange of an old car, etc., for a newer one. **trademark, trade name** *n.* particular name, sign, etc., which has been registered by a producer and which cannot be copied by other manufacturers. **trade on** *v.* to exploit/ to profit from. **trader** *n.* person who does business. **tradesman** *n.* (*pl.- men*) person who runs a shop. **tradespeople** *n. pl.*shopkeepers. **trade union, trades union,** *n.* organization which groups together workers from similar industries to represent them in wage bargaining with employers. **trade unionist** *n.* member of a trade union. **tradewind** *n.* tropical wind blowing towards the equator. **trading** *n.* business. **trading estate** *n.* group of factories built together. **tradition** [træ'dɪʃn] *n.* customs/habits/ stories which are passed from generation

to generation. **traditional** adj.
referring to tradition. **traditionalist** n.
person who does things in a traditional
way. **traditionally** adv. according to
tradition.

traduce [trə'djuːs] v. (formal) to slander
(s.o.).

traffic 1 ['træfɪk] n. (a) movement of
vehicles, esp. cars/lorries/buses, etc., on
the roads; t. jam = blockage of traffic on
a road; Am. t. circle = roundabout; air t.
= aircraft flying. (b) illegal international
business. **traffic 2** v. (trafficked) to
deal in (drugs) illegally. **trafficator** n.
light on a car which flashes to show that
the car is about to turn. **traffic lights** n.
red, green and amber lights which
regulate the movement of traffic. **traffic
warden** n. person who controls traffic,
esp. the parking of cars. **trafficker** n.
person who traffics (in drugs).

tragedy ['trædʒədɪ] n. play/film/story
with a sad story; unhappy event.
tragedian [trə'dʒiːdɪən] n. person who
acts in tragedies.

tragic adj. referring to tragedy; very
sad. **tragically** adv. very sadly.

trail 1 [treɪl] n. (a) tracks left by an
animal. (b) path. (c) thing which
stretches a long way behind. **trail 2** v.
(a) to let (sth) drag behind you. (b) to
follow the tracks of (an animal/a person).
(c) trailing plant = one which hangs or
creeps along the ground. **trailer** n. (a)
goods vehicle pulled behind a car. (b)
caravan. (c) short film showing parts of a
full-length film as an advertisement.

train 1 [treɪn] n. (a) series of coaches or
wagons pulled by a railway engine; t.
ferry = boat which carries a train across
water. (b) series of events; line of animal
carrying goods; retinue (of an important
person); t. of thought = series of
thoughts following one another. (c) long
fuse (to light an explosive). (d) part of a
dress which hangs down on to the
ground at the back. **train 2** v. (a) to
teach (s.o./an animal) to do sth; to learn
how to do sth; to t. a plant up a stick = to
attach a plant so that it will clim
upwards. (b) to practise (for a sport). (c)
to point (a rifle/a telescope) at sth.

trainable adj. which can be trained.
trainee [treɪ'niː] n. person who is being
taught. **trainer** n. (a) person who trains

animals/sportsmen. (b) small aircraft in
which you learn to fly. **training** n.
action of being taught/of practising; in t.
= (i) practising (for a sport); (ii) fit/in
good physical condition; t. college =
college where teachers are trained.

traipse [treɪps] v. inf. to walk about in a
heavy/tired way.

trait [treɪ(t)] n. particular point of s.o.'s
character.

traitor ['treɪtə] n. person who sides with
the enemy/who gives away secrets to the
enemy. **traitorous** adj. like a traitor.

trajectory [trə'dʒektrɪ] n. curved
course taken by sth which has been
thrown through the air.

tram [træm] n. form of public transport.
consisting of carriages running on rails
laid in the street. **tramcar** n. single
carriage of a trAm. **tramlines** n. pl.(a)
rails along which a tram runs. (b) two
parallel side lines on a tennis court.
tramway n. rails, etc., on which trams
run.

trammel 1 ['træml] n. (a) type of fishing
net. (b) thing which prevents you from
doing sth. **trammel 2** v. (trammelled)
(formal) to stop (s.o.) doing sth.

tramp 1 [træmp] n. (a) noise of feet
hitting the ground heavily. (b) long
energetic walk. (c) person who has
nowhere to live and walks from place to
place begging for food or money. **tramp
2** v. (a) to walk heavily. (b) to trample
on (sth); to crush (grapes) by stepping on
them to extract the juice. **tramp
steamer** n. cargo boat which goes
from port to port but not on a regular
route.

trample ['træmpl] v. (on) to crush (by
walking).

trampoline ['træmpəliːn] n. frame with
a large sheet of elastic material on which
you can bounce/perform exercises, etc.

trance [trɑːns] n. state when you are not
fully conscious, and do not notice what
is going on.

tranny ['trænɪ] n. inf. transistor radio.

tranquil ['træŋkwɪl] adj. calm/peaceful.
tranquillity [træŋ'kwɪlɪtɪ] adj. calm.
tranquillize ['træŋkwɪlaɪz] v. to make
(s.o.) calm (by giving drugs).
tranquillizer n. drug which makes a
person calm. **tranquilly** adv. in a
tranquil way.

trans- [trænz] prefix meaning through/across.

transact [træn'zækt] v. to carry out (a piece of business). **transaction** n. piece of business; cash t. = piece of business paid for in cash; transactions = report of what takes place at a meeting of a learned/scientific society.

transatlantic [trænzət'læntɪk] adj. across the Atlantic; from the other side of the Atlantic; involving countries on both sides of the Atlantic.

transceiver ['trænzsi:və] n. transmitter and receiver.

transcend [træn'send] v. to go better/further than sth. **transcendent** adj. which transcends. **transcendental** [trænsən'dentəl] adj. which rises above the level of ordinary thought or reasoning.

transcontinental [trænzkɒntɪ'nentl] adj. across a continent.

transcribe [træn'skraɪb] v. to write out the text (of sth which is heard); to write out in full (what has been written down in shorthand); to rewrite (a piece of music) for another instrument than the one for which it was originally written.

transcript ['trænskrɪpt] n. written text of what was said (on the radio/at a trial, etc.). **transcription** n. act of transcribing.

transept ['trænsept] n. one of the two branches at right angles to the nave and choir in a cross-shaped church.

transfer 1 ['trænsfə] n. (a) movement of sth/s.o. to a new place; t. list = list of footballers whom a club would agree to see move to another teAm. (b) design which can be stuck on to a surface.

transfer 2 [træns'fɜ:] v. (transferred) to move (sth/s.o.) to another place.

transferable [trænz'fɜ:rəbl] adj. which can be transferred; not t. = (ticket) which can only be used by the person to whom it was issued. **transference** n. act of transferring.

transfigure [trænz'fɪgə] v. to change for the better (appearance of sth/s.o.). **transfiguration** n. act of transfiguring.

transfix [trænz'fɪks] v. to prevent (s.o.) from moving (by giving a shock).

transform [trænz'fɔ:m] v. to change completely. **transformation** [trænzfə'meɪʃn] n. complete change of appearance. **transformer** [træn'fɔ:mə] n. apparatus for changing the voltage of an alternating electric current.

transfuse [trænz'fju:z] v. to move liquid from one container to another. **transfusion** [trænz'fju:ʒn] n. moving of liquid from one container to another; blood t. = giving blood to a sick patient.

transgress [trænz'gres] v. (formal) to go against (a rule). **transgression** n. act of transgressing. **transgressor** n. person who transgresses.

tranship [trænz'ʃɪp] v. (transhipped) to move (goods) from one ship or lorry to another.

transience ['trænzɪəns] n. state of not being permanent. **transient** ['trænzɪənt] adj. & n. which will not last; Am. transients = people who stay in a hotel for a short time.

transistor [træn'zɪstə] n. (a) device made of semi-conductors which can increase an electric current. (b) t. (radio) = small pocket radio which uses transistors. **transistorize** v. to put transistors into (sth).

transit 1 ['trænzɪt] n. (a) movement of passengers/goods (on the way to another destination); t. lounge = waiting room in an airport where you wait for a connecting flight. (b) moving of a planet across the face of the sun or other planet. **transit 2** v. (formal) to go across.

transition [træn'zɪʃn] n. movement between one state and another. **transitional** adj. referring to transition; t. government = temporary government between two different constitutions.

transitive ['trænzɪtɪv] adj. (verb) which has an object.

transitory ['trænzɪtrɪ] adj. which does not last for long.

translate [trænz'leɪt] v. (a) to put (words) into another language. (b) to move (a bishop) to another see. **translatable** adj. which can be translated. **translation** [trænz'leɪʃn] n. text which has been translated; action of translating; simultaneous t. = translating directly into another language what a speaker is saying. **translator** n. person who translates.

transliterate [trænz'lɪtəreɪt] v. to put (words) into the letters of a different alphabet. **transliteration** n. act of transliterating.

translucent [trænz'luːsnt] adj. which light can pass through. but which you cannot see through. **translucence** n. being translucent.

transmigration [trænzmaɪ'greɪʃn] n. moving of a soul from a dead body to a living one.

transmit [træz'mɪt] v. (transmitted) (a) to pass (from one person to another). (b) to send out by radio/T.V. **transmission** [trænz'mɪʃn] n. (a) passing (of disease) from one person to another. (b) sending out by radio/TV; a radio/TV broadcast. (c) (in a car) series of moving parts which pass the power from the engine to the wheels. **transmitter** n. apparatus for sending out radio/TV signals.

transmogrify [trænz'mɒgrɪfaɪ] v. to change (sth) totally.

transmute [trænz'mjuːt] v. to make (sth) change its shape or substance. **transmutation** n. act of transmuting.

transom ['trænsəm] n. (a) cross beam in a window; beam across the top of a door. (b) stern piece of a boat.

transparency [træns'pærənsɪ] n. (a) being transparent. (b) photograph which is printed on transparent film so that it can be projected on to a screen.

transparent adj. (a) which you can see through. (b) obvious (lie). **transparently** adv. obviously.

transpire [træn'spaɪə] v. (a) to happen. (b) to pass moisture through the surface of the skin/of a leaf, etc. **transpiration** [trænspɪ'reɪʃn] n. act of transpiring.

transplant 1 ['trɑːnsplɑːnt] n. (a) act of taking an organ from one person and grafting it into another's body. (b) small plant which is moved to another place to grow. **transplant 2** [træns'plɑːnt] v. (a) to graft (an organ) into s.o.'s body. (b) to plant (small plants) in another place where they will grow permanently.

transport 1 ['trænspɔːt] n. (a) movement of goods/people; means of moving goods/people; public t. system = system of buses/trams/underground trains for moving the public.; t. café = restaurant where lorry-drivers eat. (b) ship/aircraft which carries goods or soldiers. (c) great emotion. **transport 2** [træn'spɔːt] v. (a) to move (goods/people) from one place to another. (b) transported with joy = very happy. (c) (old) to send (a criminal) to a prison in a colony. **transportable** adj. which can be transported. **transportation** [trænspɔː'teɪʃn] n. (a) movement of goods/people; means of moving goods/people. (b) (old) sending of a criminal to a prison in a colony. **transporter** [træn'spɔːtə] n. large lorry for carrying several cars; t. bridge = platform which is suspended from a bridge and moves across a river on cables, carrying cars, etc.

transpose [træn'spəʊz] v. to make (two things) change places. **transposition** [trænspə'zɪʃn] n. act of transposing.

tranship [træns'ʃɪp] v. (transshipped) to move (goods) from one ship or lorry to another.

transubstantiation [trænsʌbstænʃɪ'eɪʃn] n. belief that the wine and bread become the blood and body of Christ at the Communion service.

transuranic [trænzjʊ'rænɪk] adj. (element) which has atoms heavier than those of uranium.

transverse ['trænzvɜːs] adj. which lies across.

transvestite [trænz'vestaɪt] n. person who wants to wear the clothes of the opposite sex. **transvestism** [trænz'vestɪzəm] n. desire to wear the clothes of the opposite sex.

trap 1 [træp] n. (a) device to catch an animal; plan to catch (s.o.)/to take (s.o.) by surprise; police radar t. = device to catch a motorist who is driving too fast. (b) gate which allows a greyhound to start to run in a race. (c) t. door = door in a floor/in a ceiling. (d) bend in a waste pipe which is filled with water and so stops unpleasant smells coming back up the pipe from a sewer. (e) Sl. mouth. (f) small light horse-drawn carriage. **trap 2** v. (trapped) to catch. **trapper** n. person who catches wild animals for their fur.

trapeze [træ'piːz] n. bar which hangs from ropes, and which acrobats use in a circus.

trapezium [træ'piːzɪəm] n. (a) foursided shape, where two of the sides are parallel. (b) Am. trapezoid. (c) little bone in the wrist.

trapezoid ['træpɪzɔɪd] n. (a) four-sided shape. where none of the sides is parallel. (b) A. trapezium.

trappings ['træpɪŋz] n. pl. ornaments/ clothes/decorations which are suitable for a particular occasion.

trash [træʃ] n. rubbish. **trash-can** n. Am. dustbin. **trashy** adj. (-ier, -iest) very bad/completely worthless.

trauma ['trɔːmə] n. (a) sharp shock/ unpleasant experience which affects your mental outlook. (b) injury. **traumatic** [trɔː'mætɪk] adj. which gives a sharp and unpleasant shock. **traumatically** adv. in a traumatic way.

travel 1 ['trævl] n. moving from one country to another/from one place to another. **travel 2** v. (travelled) (a) to move from one country to another/from one place to another. (b) to be a sales representative (in an area). **travel agency** n. office which arranges tickets/hotel reservations etc., for you when you are making a journey. **travel agent** n. person who runs a travel agency. **travelator** n. moving belt which you stand on to move from one point to another (such as in an airport) **traveller** n. (a) person who is travelling from one place to another; traveller's cheques = cheques which you can buy at your bank and which can then be cashed in a foreign country. (b) (commercial) t. = sales representative. **travelogue** n. film describing travel.

traverse 1 ['trævɜːs] n. (a) crossing. (b) thing which crosses another. (c) (in mountaineering) crossing of a dangerous flat rock face. **traverse 2** [trə'vɜːs] v. to cross.

travesty 1 ['trævəstɪ] n. parody; ridiculous copy/poor imitation. **travesty 2** v. to imitate (sth) in a ridiculous way.

trawl 1 [trɔːl] n. long net shaped like a bag, pulled at sea by a trawler. **trawl 2** v. to fish with a trawl. **trawler** n. fishing boat which uses a trawl.

tray [treɪ] n. (a) flat board for carrying glasses/cups and saucers, etc. (b) flat open box/basket for papers.

treachery ['tretʃərɪ] n. act of betraying/ being a traitor to your friends, etc. **treacherous** adv. (a) likely to betray. (b) dangerous. **treacherously** adv. in a treacherous way.

treacle ['triːkl] n. thick dark-brown syrup produced when sugar is refined. **treacly** adj. thick and sticky like treacle.

tread 1 [tred] n. (a) way of walking. (b) sound of a footstep. (c) part of a step (on stairs/an escalator) on which you put your foot. (d) surface of tyre marked with a pattern of lines. **tread 2** v. (trod[trɒd]; has trodden) (a) to walk. (b) to trample on/to crush with your feet; to t. water = to keep afloat in water by moving your legs up and down.

treadle 1 ['tredl] n. foot pedal which makes a machine turn. **treadle 2** v. to push a treadle with the foot. **treadmill** n. (a) device turned by people/animals as they walk around a circular path or inside a large wheel. (b) dull routine work.

treason ['triːzn] n. betraying your country/giving your country's secrets to the enemy. **treasonable** adj. which can be considered as treason.

treasure 1 ['treʒə] n. (a) store of money/jewels/gold, etc.; t. trove = buried treasure found by accident which then becomes the property of the state; t. hunt = game where you follow clues from place to place until you find a prize. (b) thing which is highly valued. **treasure 2** v. to value (sth) very highly **treasurer** n. person who looks after the finances of a club, etc. **treasury** n. (a) place where treasure is kept. (b) government department which deals with the nation's money.

treat 1 [triːt] n. special meal/outing etc., which should give pleasure; a t. in store = a special future surprise; this is my t. = I am paying the bill **treat 2** v. (a) to deal with; to write about (a subject). (b) to t. s.o. to = to give (s.o.) a special meal/ outing as a surprise gift. (c) to look after (a sick person). (d) to pass (a substance) through a certain process. (e) (formal) to negotiate (with an enemy). **treatment** n. (a) way of dealing with sth. (b) way of looking after a sick person.

treatise ['tri:tɪz] *n.* long learned piece of writing on a subject.

treaty ['tri:tɪ] *n.* (a) agreement between two or more countries. (b) agreement between private people; to sell a house by private t. = in private, after having offered it for auction.

treble 1 ['trebl] *n.* (a) voice which sings high-pitched notes; high-pitched musical instrument. (b) thing which is three times as large; three points. **treble 2** *adj.* (a) three times as large; t. chance = possible way of winning the football pools, where you try to forecast the matches which will be drawn. (b) high (voice/note); t. cief = sign in music showing that the notes are in a high pitch. **treble 3** *adv.* three times as much. **treble 4** *v.* to increase by three times. **trebly** *adv.* three times as much.

tree [tri:] *n.* (a) large plant with a wooden stem and branches. (b) family t. = diagram showing the development of a family over a long period of time. **treecreeper** *n.* small bird which creeps up the trunk of trees, looking for insects. **treeless** *adj.* with no trees. **treeline** *n.* line at a certain altitude above which trees do not grow. **treen** *n.* (no *pl.*) small spoons/rings, etc. made of wood. **treetop** *n.* top of a tree.

trefoil ['tri:fɔɪl] *n.* design/leaf shaped in three equal parts like that of a clover.

trek 1 [trek] *n.* long and difficult journey. **trek 2** *v.* (trekked) to make a long and difficult journey.

trellis ['trelɪs] *n.* (*pl.*-es) openwork fence made of thin pieces of wood in a crisscross pattern

tremble 1 ['trembl] *n.* shaking/ shuddering. **tremble 2** *v.* (a) to shake/ to quiver. (b) to be very worried. **trembly** *adj.* shaky/doddery.

tremendous [trɪ'mendəs] *adj.* (a) enormous/very large. (b) wonderful **tremendously** *adv.* greatly.

tremolo ['tremələʊ] *n.* (*pl.*-os) trembling note in music.

tremor ['tremə] *n.* shaking; earth t. = slight earthquake.

tremulous ['tremjʊləs] *adj.* shaking/ quivering.

trench 1 [trentʃ] *n.* (*pl.*-es) long narrow ditch in the ground **trench 2** *v.* to dig a long narrow ditch. **trench coat** *n.* belted waterproof coat.

trenchant ['trentʃənt] *adj.* sharp/biting (remark) vigorous (style).

trencher ['trentʃə] *n.* (old) wooden plate for food. **trencherman** *n.* good t. = person who eats a lot.

trend [trend] *n.* general tendency. **trendiness** *n.* being trendy. **trendsetter** *n.* person who sets the fashion. **trendy 1** *adj.* (-ier, -iest) *inf.* following fashion; fashionable. **trendy 2** *n. inf.* person who follows fashion.

trepan, trephine 1 [trɪ'pæm, trɪ'fi:n] *n.* saw for cutting out round pieces of bone. **trepan, trephine 2** *v.* (trepanned) to cut a round piece of bone out of (esp. the skull).

trepidation [trepɪ'deɪʃn] *n.* anxiety

trespass ['trespəs] *v.* (on) to go into s.o.'s property without permission. **trespasser** *n.* person who trespasses.

tresses ['tresɪz] *n. pl.* long hair.

trestle ['tresl] *n.* pair of folding legs which can be used to hold up a table; t. table = table made of planks resting on folding legs.

trews [tru:z] *n. pl.* close-fitting trousers made of tartan cloth.

tri- [traɪ] prefix meaning three.

triad ['traɪæd] *n.* Chinese secret society.

trial ['traɪəl] *n.* (a) court case to judge a criminal; to stand t. = to appear in court. (b) test; sheepdog trials = competition to select the best sheepdogs; on t. = being tested to see if it is acceptable; t. and error = testing and rejecting various things until you find the one which works. (c) game played to test the skills of players before they are selected for a teAm. (d) motorcycle competition held on rough ground.

triangle ['traɪæŋgl] *n.* (a) geometrical shape with three sides and three angles; eternal t. = situation where s.o. is in love with s.o. who is in love with a third person. (b) musical instrument made of a piece of metal bent into the shape of a triangle. **triangular** [traɪ'æŋgjʊlə] *adj.* shaped like a triangle. **triangulation** [traɪæŋgjʊ'leɪʃn] *n.* method of measuring land to produce maps.

tribe [traɪb] *n.* (a) group of people ruled by a chief. (b) *inf.* large family/group.
tribal *adj.* referring to a tribe.
tribalism *n.* organization of tribes.
tribesman *n.* (*pl.*-men) member of a tribe.
tribulation [trɪbjʊ'leɪʃn] *n.* (formal) great misery.
tribunal [traɪ'bjuːnl] *n.* court/official committee which judges special problems or writes a report on a special problem; industrial t. = court which decides in disputes between employers and workers; rent t. = court which decides if a rent is fair or excessive.
tribune ['trɪbjuːn] *n.* leader who upholds the rights of the people.
tribute ['trɪbjuːt] *n.* (a) money paid to a conqueror by people who have been conquered. (b) words/gifts, etc., to show thanks/praise; to pay t. to = to praise; floral tributes = flowers sent to a funeral.
tributary 1 *adj.* (person) who pays tribute. **tributary 2** *n.* river which flows into a larger river.
trice [traɪs] *n.* in a t. = very rapidly.
trichology [trɪk'ɒlədʒɪ] *n.* study of the diseases of the hair. **trichologist** *n.* person who studies the diseases of the hair.
trick 1 [trɪk] *n.* (a) clever action which can deceive/confuse s.o.; to play a t. on s.o. = to deceive/confuse s.o.; *inf.* tricks of the trade = clever dealings which are associated with a certain trade; card tricks/conjuring tricks = clever games with cards/with hats, handkerchiefs, etc., to amuse an audience; *inf.* that should do the t. = should do what is wanted/should make it work; *inf.* he doesn't miss a t. = he is very alert. (b) (in card games) points won at the end of a round (c) odd way of doing sth. **trick 2** *adj.* which deceives; t. question = one which is intended to catch people out **trick 3** *v.* to deceive/to confuse; to t. s.o. into doing sth = to deceive s.o. so that he does sth which he did not intend to do. **trickery** *n.* act of deceiving. **trickiness** *n.* being tricky **trickster** *n.* person who tricks; confidence t. = person who cheats s.o. out of his money by some fraudulent scheme which seems to be honest. **tricky** *adj.* (-ier, -iest) (a) difficult/awkward. (b) *inf.* sly/deceitful/untrustworthy.

trickle 1 [trɪkl] *n.* small flow of water; t. charger = device which charges a car battery slowly. **trickle 2** *v.* to flow/move in a small quantity.
tricolour ['trɪkələ] *n.* flag with three bands of colour, esp. the national flag of France.
tricycle ['traɪsɪkl] *n.* three-wheeled pedal vehicle like a bicycle with two back wheels.
trident [traɪdənt] *n.* spear with three prongs.
tried [traɪd] *v.* see try.
triennial [traɪ'enɪəl] *adj.* happening every three years.
trier ['traɪə] *n.* person who tries.
trifle 1 ['traɪfl] *n.* (a) small insignificant thing. (b) small amount. (c) pudding made of cake/biscuits/jelly/jam/sherry and creAm. **trifle 2** *v.* (with) to play with/not to treat (sth) seriously. **trifler** *n.* person who trifles with s.o./sth.
trifling *adj.* slight/very small.
trigger 1 ['trɪgə] *n.* small metal lever on a gun which you pull to fire it.
trigger 2 *v.* to t. off = to start (a series of things) happening. **trigger-happy** *adj.* ready to shoot/ready to act quickly without thinking.
trigonometry [trɪgə'nɒmɪtrɪ] *n.* science which deals with the relationships between the sides and angles of triangles.
trike [traɪk] *n. inf.* tricycle.
trilateral [traɪ'lætrəl] *adj.* with three people/groups taking part.
trilby ['trɪlbɪ] *n.* type of man's hat.
trilingual [traɪ'lɪŋwəl] *adj.* (person) who can speak three languages.
trill 1 [trɪl] *n.* (a) warbling song (like a bird). (b) (in music) two notes rapidly repeated **trill 2** *v.* to warble/to sing like a bird.
trillion ['trɪljən] *n.* (a) one million million millions. (b) esp. *Am.* one million millions
trilobite ['traɪləbaɪt] *n.* ancient shellfish found in fossils.
trilogy ['trɪlədʒɪ] *n.* novel/play in three separate related parts.
trim 1 [trɪm] *n.* (a) neatness. (b) cutting (of hair/bush, etc.). (c) decoration (on a car.) **trim 2** *adj.* (trimmer, trimmest) neat. **trim 3** *v.* (trimmed) (a) to cut (sth) so hat it is tidy. (b) to cut back; to

reduce. (c) to ornament/to decorate. (d) (on a sailing boat) to put sails into the best position. (e) to change your political opinions to fit the current popular trend. **trimly** *adv.* in a trim way. **trimmer** *n.* person/device which trims; hedge t. = electric cutter for hedges. **trimming** *n.* (a) ornament added to decorate sth; roast pork with all the trimmings = with the usual sauces and vegetables. (c) trimmings = pieces cut off (a hedge, etc.) when it is being trimmed. **trimness** *n.* being trim.

trimaran ['traɪməræn] *n.* yacht with three parallel hulls.

trinitrotoluene [traɪnaɪtræʊ'tɒljʊiːn] *n.* high explosive/TNT.

trinity ['trɪnɪtɪ] *n.* (a) group of three. (b) the T. = the three persons in the Christian God - the Father, Son and Holy Ghost. **Trinity House** *n.* body which runs lighthouses and pilots.

trinket ['trɪŋkɪt] *n.* cheap ornament

trio ['triːəʊ] *n.* (*pl.*-os) (a) piece of music for three instruments. (b) three musicians; group of three people.

trip 1 [trɪp] *n.* (a) journey; day t. = journey lasting one day. (b) switch which activates a motor/light, etc. (c) *Sl.* trance caused by drugs. **trip 2** *v.* (tripped) (a) to t. along = to go along with light footsteps. (b) to catch your foot so that you stagger and fall. (c) to set off (a switch). (d) *Sl.* to go into a trance induced by drugs. **tripmeter** *n.* dial on a car dashboard which shows how far you go on particular journey. **tripper** *n.* person on a short (usu. one day) trip.

trip up *v.* to t. s.o. up = (i) to make s.o. fall down; (ii) to force s.o. to make a mistake **trip wire** *n.* wire stretched low above the ground, which when you touch it. sets off a gun/camera, etc.

tripartite [traɪ'pɑːtaɪt] *adj.* with three parts; (agreement) between three countries.

tripe [traɪp] *n.* (a) part of cow's/sheep's stomach used as food. (b) *inf.* rubbish/nonsense.

triple 1 ['trɪpl] *adj.* made of three parts; three times as big. **triple 2** *v.* to become three times as large; to make (sth) three times as large. **triplet** *n.* (a) (in music) three notes played quickly together. (b) one of three children born at

the same birth. **triplex** *adj.* with three layers. **triplicate** *n.* in t. = in three copies.

tripod ['traɪpɒd] *n.* stand with three legs.

tripos ['traɪpɒs] *n.* final examination at Cambridge University.

triptych ['trɪptɪk] *n.* religious picture formed of three parts, often placed on or above an altar.

trite [traɪt] *adj.* very ordinary/unexciting (remark). **tritely** *adv.* in a trite way. **triteness** *n.* being trite.

triumph 1 ['traɪəmf] *n.* (a) great victory. (b) celebration of a victory, **triumph 2** *v.* to t. over s.o. = to win a victory over s.o.; to show that you are very glad that you won a victory. **triumphal** [traɪ'ʌmfl] *adj.* referring to triumph; t. arch = archway set up to celebrate a victory. **triumphant** *adj.* victorious. **triumphantly** *adv.* in victory.

triumvirate [traɪ'ʌmvɪrət] *n.* group of three people who rule/manage.

trivet ['trɪvət] *n.* (a) small three-legged stand for a kettle, etc. (b) metal stand for putting inside a pan to stop food sticking to the bottom.

trivial ['trɪvəl] *adj.* not important; ordinary. **trivia** *n. pl.* unimportant details. **triviality** [trɪvɪ'ælɪtɪ] *n.* being unimportant; unimportant detail. **trivialize** *v.* to make (sth) trivial. **trivially** *adv.* in a trivial way.

trochee ['trəʊkiː] *n.* poetic measure made of one beat followed by a weak one **trochaic** [trəʊ'keɪɪk] *adj.* referring to trochee.

trod, trodden [trɒd, 'trɒdn] *v.* see tread.

troglodyte ['trɒglədaɪt] *n.* person who lives in a cave

troika ['trɔɪkə] *n.* (a) Russian carriage pulled by three horse. (b) three people holding power together (usu.) in Communist countries.

Trojan ['trəʊdʒn] *adj. & n.* to work like a T. = to work very hard; T. horse = trick carried out to infiltrate an enemy and ruin his plans.

troll [trəʊl] *n.* (in Scandinavia) bad tempered dwarf

trolley ['trɒlɪ] *n.* (a) wheeled cart for carrying luggage (such as at an airport);

wheeled cart for pushing round a supermarket; small wheeled table for putting food on; sweet t. = trolley with a selection of desserts in a restaurant. (b) *Am.* trAm. **trolley-bus** *n.* bus which works on electricity taken from overhead wires by contact poles

trollop ['trɒləp] *n.* dirty woman.

trombone [trɒm'bəʊn] *n.* brass wind instrument with a sliding tube **trombonist** *n.* person who plays the trombone

troop 1 [tru:p] *n.* (a) group of people. (b) group of boy scouts. (c) troops = soldiers; t. ship/t. train = ship/train which carries soldiers. **troop 2** *v.* to move in a large group. **trooper** *n.* (a) cavalry soldier. (b) *Am.* policeman from a state police force. **trooping** *n.* t. the colour = military parade with the regimental flag.

trophy ['trəʊfɪ] *n.* (a) prize given for winning a competition. (b) thing taken from the enemy and kept as a prize.

tropic ['trɒpɪk] *n.* (a) T. of Cancer/of Capricorn = two imaginary lines running round the earth, parallel to the equator, and about 23O north/south of it. (b) the tropics = the hot areas of the world lying between these two imaginary lines **tropical** *adj.* very hot; (plant, etc.) growing in the tropics.

tropism ['trɒpɪzəm] *n.* growth of a plant towards or away from sth.

troposphere ['trɒpəsfɪə] *n.* layer of atmosphere between the surface of he earth and the stratosphere

trot 1 ['trɒt] *n.* running with short regular steps; they broke into a t. = started to run; *inf.* to keep s.o. on the t. = to make s.o. work continuously, *inf.* four games on the t. = one after the other. **trot 2** *v.* (trotted) to run with short regular steps; *inf.* to t. out = to produce (the same excuse, etc.) again. **trotter** *n.* pig's foot cooked for food.

troth [trəʊθ] *n.* (old) promise.

Trotskyite ['trɒtskɪaɪt] *n.* person opposed to the central authority of a communist party, but who advocates continual revolution giving power to small groups of activists.

troubadour ['tru:bədu:ə] *n.* wandering medieval singer.

trouble 1 ['trʌbl] *n.* (a) misfortune. (b)

problem/difficult situation; it's just asking for t. = that type of behaviour will simply cause problems for you; he's in t. with the police = has been accuses by the police of a crime; to get s.o. into t. = (i) to make s.o. be accused of doing sth wrong; (ii) to make s.o. pregnant. (c) care which is put into an action. (d) illness; mechanical defect. (e) troubles = riots/disturbances. **trouble 2** *v.* (a) to worry (s.o.). (b) to create problems for (s.o.); to bother (s.o.). (c) to bother (to do sth) **troublemaker** *n.* person who creates problems/who stirs up unrest. **trouble-shooter** *n.* person whose job is to sort out problems. **troublesome** *adj.* causing trouble. **troublespot** *n.* area where trouble is likely to occur.

trough [trɒf] *n.* (a) large container for animal food or drink; horse t./water t. = container for water for horses to drink. (b) low place; low point between two peaks (on a graph); low-pressure area in the atmosphere; low -pressure area in the atmosphere; low part of the sea between two waves.

trounce [traʊns] *v.* to beat (s.o.) soundly.

troupe [tru:p] *n.* company (of actors/ circus clowns, etc.). **trouper** *n.* member of a troupe.

trousers ['traʊzəz] *n.* *pl.*(pair of) t. = outer clothes which cover the legs and the lower part of the body.

trousseau ['tru:səʊ] *n.* clothes and linen collected by the bride before her wedding.

trout [traʊt] *n.* (*pl.*trout) type of edible freshwater fish; salmon t. = large sea trout with pink flesh like that of a salmon.

trove [trəʊv] *adj.* see treasure.

trowel ['traʊəl] *n.* (a) small hand spade used in gardening. (b) tool with a flat blade used for spreading mortar between bricks.

troy [trɔɪ] *n.* t. weight = system for weighing gold/silver.

truant ['tru:ənt] *adj. & n.* (child) who is absent from school without permission; to play t. = not to go to school. **truancy** ['tru:ənsɪ] *n.* being away from school without permission.

truce [tru:s] *n.* period when two armies/ enemies, etc., agree to stop fighting temporarily.

truck [trʌk] n. (a) open railway wagon for carrying goods. (b) heavy lorry. (c) small hand cart. (d) to have no t. with = not to have anything to do with. (e) Am. fruit and vegetables grown for sale in a town market. **truck driver, trucker** n. lorry driver. **trucking** n. Am. transport of goods by lorry. **truckload** n. amount carried in a truck. **truckle** ['trʌkl] v. to give in (to s.o.) weakly. **truckle bed** n. low bed which can be pushed under another bed in daytime.

truculence ['trʌkjʊləns] n. being truculent. **truculent** adj. threatening/ fierce; eager to quarrel. **truculently** adv. in a truculent way.

trudge 1 [trʌdʒ] n. tiring walk. **trudge 2** v. to walk heavily.

true 1 [truː] adj. (-er, -est) (a) correct. (b) real. (c) correctly adjusted. t. north = north towards the north pole, and not the magnetic north. (d) faithful. **true 2** adv. correctly; to come t. = to happen as forecast; the wheel wasn't running t. = wasn't turning straight. **true 3** n. out of t. = not quite straight/not correctly adjusted. **true-blue** adj. completely typical; totally loyal. **trueness** n. being true. **truly** adv. really; yours t. = ending of a slightly formal letter.

truffle ['trʌfl] n. (a) type of round black edible fungus found under the earth. (b) soft chocolate-covered sweet (usu. flavoured with rum).

trug [trʌg] n. long shallow basket for picking flowers.

truism ['truːɪzəm] n. saying which is quite obviously true and therefore need not be said.

trump 1 [trʌmp] n. (in card games) suit which is chosen as being of higher value than the other suits; inf. to turn up trumps = very generous/helpful; t. card = advantage which is kept ready for use to win an argument. **trump 2** v. (a) to t. a card = to play a card of the suit which is trumps, and so win. (b) t. up = to invent; trumped-up charge = false charge.

trumpery ['trʌmpəri] adj. (formal) useless and showy.

trumpet 1 ['trʌmpɪt] n. brass musical instrument with three keys; inf. to blow your own t. = to praise what you yourself have done. **trumpet 2** v. (a) to play the trumpet. (b) to make a loud noise. (c) (of elephant) to call. **trumpeter** n. person who plays the trumpet.

truncated [trʌn'keɪtɪd] adj. cut off; shortened.

truncheon ['trʌnʃn] n. short. heavy stick used by policemen.

trundle ['trʌdl] v. to roll/to push along (sth heavy).

trunk [trʌŋk] n. (a) main stem (of a tree); body (of a person). (b) long nose of an elephant. (c) large box for sending clothes, etc., in. (d) Am. boot of a car. (e) trunks = men's shorts for swimming **trunk call** n. long-distance telephone call. **trunk road** n. main road.

truss 1 [trʌs] n. (pl.-es) (a) bundle of straw. (b) beam holding up a bridge/a roof. (c) belt to support a hernia **truss 2** v. (a) to tie up (straw) into bundles. (b) to tie up (a chicken) ready for the oven; to tie up

trust 1 [trʌst] n. (a) confidence that sth is correct/is good/will work well, etc.; to take on t. = without examining to see if it is all right. (b) hope. (c) responsibility. (d) passing of goods/money to s.o. who will look after it; family t. = family money put in the hands of a group of people who will administer it. (e) group of business companies which combine to avoid competing with each other. **trust 2** v. (a) to be sure of (s.o.); to have confidence in (s.o.); inf. t. him to be late = as usual, he is late. (b) to hope.

trustee [trʌs'tiː] n. person who has charge of money on trust for s.o.; person who administers a family trust/who directs a charity, etc. **trusteeship** n. position of trustee. **trustful, trusting** adj. full of confidence (in s.o.). **trustfully, trustingly** adv. in a trustful/trusting way. **trustworthiness** n. being trustworthy. **trustworthy** adj. which can be depended upon. **trusty 1** ['trʌstɪ] n. prisoner who is given certain responsibilities because he can be trusted. **trusty 2** adj. (-ier, -iest) which can be depended upon.

truth [truːθ] n. thing which is true; true story; to tell s.o. a few home truths = to tell s.o. what you think of them/to criticize s.o.'s behaviour/character.

truthful adj. (person) who always tells the truth. **truthfully** adv. in a truthful way. **truthfulness** n. being truthful.

try 1 [traɪ] *n.* (a) attempt (to do sth). (b) goal scored in Rugby by touching the ball down behind the opposing goal line. **try 2** *v.* (a) to test. (b) to attempt. (c) to make (sth) suffer. (d) to judge (a case/a person) in court **trying** *adj.* difficult to put up with **try on** *v.* to put (clothes) on to see if they fit; *inf.* to try it on with s.o. = to act boldly to see if s.o. with accept your behaviour. **try out** *v.* to test (sth).

trypanosome [trɪ'pænəsəʊm] *n.* parasite. carried by the tsetse fly. causing sleeping sickness.

tryst [trɪst] *n.* (old) lovers meeting.

tsar [zɑː] *n.* former title of the emperor of Russia.

tsetse ['tsetsɪ] *n.* type of African fly which transmits disease by biting.

tub [tʌb] *n.* (a) round (wooden) container; small. round cardboard box for ice creAm. (b) bath. (c) *inf.* old ship. **tubbiness** *n.* being tubby. **tubby** *adj.* (-ier, iest) *inf.* fat.

tuba ['tjuːbə] *n.* large bass brass instrument.

tube [tjuːb] *n.* (a) long pipe for carrying liquids or gas; inner t. = rubber pipe for air inside a tyre. (b) long pipe (in the body); bronchial tubes = tubes leading to the lungs. (c) soft pipe with a screw top which contains paste, etc. (d) (esp. in London) the underground railway system. (e) glass bulb in a television set which projects the picture on the screen. **tubeless** *adj.* (tyre) with no inner tube. **tubing** *n.* tubes made of metal/plastic etc. **tubular** ['tjuːbjʊlə] *adj.* like a tube; t. bells = pieces of metal tubing of varying lengths which when hung up and hit with a hammer give different notes.

tuber ['tjuːbə] *n.* thick piece of root which can be planted to make a new plant grow **tuberous** *adj.* (root) which produces tubers.

tubercle ['tjuːbəkl] *n.* rounded bump on the skin; scar caused by tuberculosis. **tuberculosis** [tjʊbɜːkjʊ'ləʊsɪs] *n.* disease of the lungs. **tubercular** [tjuː'bɜːkjʊlə] *adj.* suffering from tuberculosis. **tuberculin-tested** *adj.* (milk/cow) which has been tested to show that it is free from tuberculosis.

TUC [tiːjuː'siː] *abbrev.* for Trades Union Congress.

tuck 1 [tʌk] *n.* (a) little fold/pleat in a piece of cloth. (b) *inf.* cakes/sweets, etc., eaten by school children; t. shop = shop in a school selling sweets/cakes, etc.

tuck 2 *v.* (a) to fold (a blanket) around s.o. and push the ends underneath. (b) to fold cloth into little pleats. **tucker** *n.* (in Australia) *inf.* food. **tuck in** *v.* (a) to push the edge of a piece of cloth underneath s.o. to keep them warm. (b) *inf.* to eat a large quantity of food. **tuck-in** *n.* *Sl.* big meal. **tuck up** *v.* to tuck s.o. up (in bed) = push the edge of the bed clothes around (s.o.) to keep them warm

Tuesday ['tjuːzdeɪ] *n.* second day of the week/day between Monday and Wednesday.

tufa ['tjuːfə] *n.* type of porous volcanic rock.

tuft [tʌft] *n.* small bunch of grass/hair, etc. **tufted** *adj.* with tufts.

tug 1 [tʌg] *n.* (a) sudden pull. (b) tugboat. **tug 2** *v.* (tugged) to pull hard. **tugboat** *n.* powerful boat used for towing barges/ships. **tug-of-war** *n.* (a) competition where two teams pull against each other on a strong rope. (b) bitter struggle where two sides win alternately.

tuition [tjʊ'ɪʃn] *n.* teaching (esp. of one student)

tulip ['tjuːlɪp] *n.* common spring bulb with brilliant flowers shaped like cups. **tulip tree** *n.* large evergreen tree, with big shiny leaves and large white flowers. **tulle** [tjuːl] *n.* thin silk/artificial material like a veil.

tumble 1 ['tʌmbl] *n.* fall. **tumble 2** *v.* (a) to fall (down) (b) to come down in confusion. **tumbledown** *adj.* (house) which is falling down/coming to pieces. **tumbler** *n.* round. straight glass for drinking **tumbler dryer** *n.* machine which dries washing. **tumble to** *v.* *inf.* to understand.

tumescent [tjuː'mesənt] *adj.* swollen.

tummy ['tʌmɪ] *n.* *inf.* stomach. **tumyache** *n.* *inf.* pain in the stomach.

tumour *Am.* **tumor** ['tjuːmə] *n.* abnormal growth in or on the body.

tumult ['tjuːmʌlt] *n.* loud, excited noise (of a crowd). **tumultuous** [tjʊ'mʌltjʊəs] *adj.* noisy/excited.

tumulus ['tjuːmjʊləs] *n.* (*pl.*-li) mound of earth covering an ancient tomb.

tun [tʌn] *n.* large barrel (for wine/beer).
tuna ['tjuːnə] *n.* (*pl.*tuna) large sea fish (used for food).
tundra ['tʌndrə] *n.* Arctic plain with no trees.
tune 1 [tjuːn] *n.* (a) series of musical notes which make a recognizable melody; he's changed his t. = he has changed his way of thinking; *inf.* to the t. of £100 = at least £100. (b) in t. = with the correct musical tone; in t. with = harmonizing with/similar to. **tune 2** *v.* (a) to adjust (a musical instrument) so that it has the correct tone. (b) to adjust (an engine) so that it works more efficiently. **tuneful** *adj.* full of catchy tunes. **tune in** *v.* to adjust a radio to a particular station. **tuner** *n.* piano t. = person who tunes pianos. **tune up** *v.* (a) to adjust instruments before playing. (b) to adjust (an engine) so that it works more efficiently. **tuning fork** *n.* metal fork which gives a correct note when it is hit.
tungsten ['tʌŋstən] *n.* (element; W) hard grey metal used to make steel and electric light filaments.
tunic ['tjuːnɪk] *n.* (a) loose top garment. (b) short jacket worn by soldiers/policemen, etc.
tunnel 1 ['tʌnl] *n.* long hole in the ground. **tunnel 2** *v.* (tunnelled) to make a long passage under the ground.
tunny ['tʌnɪ] *n.* (*pl.*tunny) tuna.
tup [tʌp] *n.* male sheep.
turban ['tɜːbən] *n.* long piece of cloth wrapped round the head to cover the hair.
turbid ['tɜːbɪd] *adj.* muddy (water). **turbidity** [tɜː'bɪdɪtɪ] *n.* being turbid.
turbine ['tɜːbaɪn] *n.* engine driven by the force of water/steam which turns a wheel with blades. **turbo-jet** ['tɜːbəʊ'dʒet] *n.* jet engine driven by a turbine; aircraft powered by this engine.
turbo-prop ['tɜːbəʊ'prɒp] *n.* jet and propeller engine driven by a turbine; aircraft powered by this engine.
turbot ['tɜːbət] *n.* (*pl.*turbot) large flat edible sea fish.
turbulent ['tɜːbjʊlənt] *adj.* (a) disturbed/violently moving (water/air). (b) likely to riot. **turbulence** *n.* disturbance in the air causing an aircraft to rock suddenly; disturbance in water.

turd [tɜːd] *n.* lump of human excreta
tureen [tjʊ'riːm] *n.* large bowl for serving soup
turf 1 [tɜːf] *n.* (a) stretch of grassy lawn. (b) (*pl.*turves) piece of grass and soil which can be planted to form a lawn; (in Ireland) block of peat for burning. (c) the t. = the world of horse racing; t. accountant = bookmaker. **turf 2** *v.* (a) to make a lawn by putting turves on the ground. (b) *inf.* to t. s.o. out = the to throw s.o. out.
turgid ['tɜːdʒɪd] *adj.* swollen; grand sounding; meaningless (words). **turgidly** *adv.* in a turgid way.
Turk [tɜːk] *n.* person from Turkey.
turkey ['tɜːkɪ] *n.* large domestic bird. often eaten at Christmas.
Turkish 1 ['tɜːkɪʃ] *adj.* referring to Turkey; T. bath = steam bath after which you plunge into cold water; T. delight = scented sweet jelly eaten in lumps.
Turkish 2 *n.* language spoken in Turkey.
turmeric ['tɜːmərɪk] *n.* yellow spice. used esp. in curries.
turmoil ['tɜːmɔɪl] *n.* wild disorder.
turn 1 [tɜːn] *n.* (a) circular movement (of a wheel, etc.); the meat is done to a t. = properly cooked all through. (b) change of direction; to take a t. for the better/for the worse = suddenly to start to get better/worse; the tide is on the t. = is about to start rising/falling; at the t. of the century = about 1900. (c) sudden attack (of illness). (d) chance to do sth in order; (of several people) to take (it in) turns to do sth = to do sth. each person doing it in order. (e) way of speaking/thinking/acting. (f) to do s.o. a good t. = to do sth to help them. (g) performance (in a variety show). **turn 2** *v.* (a) to go round; to make (sth) go round in a circle. (b) to change direction; (of tide) to start to rise/fall; his luck turned = changed. (c) to change (into sth else); (of milk) to go sour. (d) to aim (a gun) (e) to t. s.o.'s head = to make s.o. very proud/vain; t. s.o.'s stomach = to make s.o. feel sick. (f) to shape (a round piece of wood) by carving it on a lathe. (g) to pass a particular point in time; It's turned seven = it is past seven O'clock; he's turned fifty = he's more than fifty years old.

turnabout *n.* act of turning to face in another direction. **turn aside** *v.* to move to one side. **turn away** *v.* (a) to move away. (b) to send (s.o.) away. **turn back** *v.* (a) to turn and go back in the opposite direction. (b) send (s.o.) back. **turncoat** *n.* person who switches from one opinion to another. **turncock** *n.* stopcock. **turndown** *v.* (a) to refuse. (b) to reduce. (c) to fold back (a sheet on a bed). so that the pillow is uncovered. **turner** *n.* person who makes chair legs, etc., on a lathe. **turnery** *n.* (a) trade of a turner. (b) articles which are turned on a lathe. **turn in** *v.* (a) to hand back (equipment) to s.o. in authority. (b) *inf.* to go to bed. (c) to t. oneself in = to give oneself up to the police. **turning** *n.* (a) action of moving in a circle/of changing direction. (b) point where a road leaves another road. **turning point** *n.* important/decisive moment. **turn off** *v.* (a) to switch off. (b) to change direction away from a straight line **turn on** *v.* to switch on. (b) to attack. **turn out** *v.* (a) to throw (s.o.) out. (b) to clear out. (c) to produce. (d) to switch off. (e) to happen. (f) to come out in a crowd. (g) well turned out = well dressed. **turnout** *n.* crowd of people who turn out. **turn over** *v.* (a) to move (the page of a book) so that you can read the next one; to turn over a new leaf = to be better behaved. (b) to think about. (c) to roll over. (d) (of engine) to run gently. (e) to have sales of (a certain amount). (f) to hand (a criminal) to the police **turnover** *n.* (a) type of pie made with pastry turned over a filling. (b) change (in staff). (c) amount of sales. **turnpike** *n. Am.* motorway with tolls. **turnstile** *n.* gate which turns round on a pivot, allowing only one person to go through at a time. **turntable** *n.* (a) flat part of a record player which turns with the record on it. (b) flat turning platform with rails on it, to enable railway locomotives to go off in a different direction. **turn up** *v.* (a) to arrive; to be found. (b) to increase. (c) to roll up. (d) to unfold/unroll (a collar). **turnup** *n.* folded part at the bottom of each leg of a pair of trousers. **turnip** [ˈtɜːnɪp] *n.* common vegetable with a round white root.

turpentine [ˈtɜːpəntaɪn] *n.* oil which comes from fir trees, used for removing or thinning paint. **turps** [tɜːps] *n. inf.* turpentine.
turpitude [ˈtɜːpɪtjuːd] *n.* (formal) wickedness.
turquoise 1 [ˈtɜːkwɔɪz] *n.* green-blue precious tone. **turqoise 2** *adj.* green-blue (colour).
turret [ˈtʌrɪt] *n.* small tower; small armoured construction housing a gun (on a ship/tank, etc.). **turreted** *n.* with turrets.
turtle [ˈtɜːtl] *n.* sea reptile with a hard shell like a tortoise; to turn t. = to capsize. **turtledove** *n.* type of wild pigeon with a soft, cooing call. **turtleneck pullover** *n.* pullover with a high rolled neck.
turves [tɜːvz] *n.* see turf.
tusk [tʌsk] *n.* long tooth coming far out from the mouth of some animals (such as elephants/walruses, etc.). **tusker** *n. inf.* elephant.
tussle 1 [ˈtʌsl] *n.* fight/argument. **tussle 2** *v.* to fight/to struggle.
tussock [ˈtʌsək] *n.* large tuft of grass.
tussore [ˈtʌsə] *n.* type of coarse silk.
tutelage [ˈtjuːtəlɪdʒ] *n.* being responsible for s.o.; training given to pupil.
tutor 1 [ˈtjuːtə] *n.* teacher (esp. one who teaches one student or small group of students). **tutor 2** *v.* to teach (a small group of students).
tutorial [tjʊˈtɔːrɪəl] *n.* discussion meeting between a tutor and students.
tutti frutti [ˈtʊtɪˈfruːtɪ] *n.* icecream with pieces of preserved fruit in it.
tut-tut 1 [tʌtˈtʌt] *n.* sound made to show you disapprove. **tut-tut 2** *v.* (tut-tutted) to make disapproving sounds.
tutu [ˈtuːtuː] *n.* girl ballet dancer's short stiff skirt.
tuxedo [tʌkˈsiːdəʊ] *n.* (*pl.*-os) *Am.* dinner jacket.
TV [tiːˈviː] *n.* (a) television. (b) television set.
twaddle [ˈtwɒdl] *n. inf.* rubbish/nonsense.
twain [tweɪn] *n.* (formal) two things.
twang 1 [twæŋ] *n.* (a) sound made, such as when a guitar string is pulled and released. (b) nasal t. = accent made by speaking through the nose. **twang 2** *v.* to make a twang.

tweak 1 [twiːk] *n.* sharp pull. **tweak 2** *v.* to pull suddenly.

twee [twiː] *adj. inf.* small delicate and sentimental.

tweed [twiːd] *n.* rough woollen cloth made of strands of different colours. **tweeds** *n. pl.* suit made of tweed.

tweet 1 [twiːt] *n.* little sound made by a small bird. **tweet 2** *v.* to make a little sound like a bird. **tweeter** *n.* loudspeaker which reproduces high sounds.

tweezers ['twiːzəz] *n. pl.* (pair of) t. = small pincers.

twelve [twelv] *n.* number 12. **twelfth, 12th** [twelfθ] *adj. & n.* referring to twelve; the t. century = period from 1100 to 1199.

twenty ['twentɪ] *n.* number 20; she's in her twenties = she is over twenty but under thirty years old. **twentieth, 20th** *adj. & n.* referring to twenty; the t. century = period from 1900 to 1999.

twerp [twɜːp] *n. Sl.* stupid person.

twice [twaɪs] *adv.* two times; double; he's t. my age = two times; as old as I am.

twiddle ['twɪdl] *v.* to turn/to twist with no particular aim; to t. your thumbs = holding your hands together, to turn your thumbs round and round as a sign of not having anything to do. **twiddly** *adj. inf.* awkward and curly.

twig 1 [twɪg] *n.* little branch. **twig 2** *v.* (twigged) *inf.* to understand.

twilight ['twaɪlaɪt] *n.* (period of) weak light between night and sunrise or between sunset and night.

twill [twɪl] *n.* thick cloth woven in diagonal lines.

twin 1 [twɪn] *adj. & n.* (child) born at the same birth as another; identical twins = two children born at the same time who look very similar. **twin 2** *adj. & prefix* made of two similar parts. **twin 3** *v.* (twinned) (with) to join (a town) to a similar town in another country for exchange visits and to encourage international understanding. **twinset** *n.* matching jumper and cardigan.

twine 1 [twaɪn] *n.* thick, rough string. **twine 2** *v.* to twist round and round.

twinge [twɪnʒ] *n.* short sharp pain; short worry.

twinkle 1 ['twɪŋkl] *n.* little flicker of light; with a t. in his eye = with his eyes shining with amusement. **twinkle 2** *v.* (a) to glitter. (b) (of eyes) to shine (with amusement/wickedness, etc.). **twinkling** *n.* little flicker; in the t. of an eye = very fast.

twirl 1 [twɜːl] *n.* (a) spinning movement. (b) spiral shape. **twirl 2** *v.* (a) to spine round. (b) to twist in your fingers. **twirly** *adj. inf.* twisting.

twirp [twəːp] *n.* twerp.

twist 1 [twɜːst] *n.* (a) thing which has been twisted; t. of paper = small container made of a piece of paper with its end twisted. (b) thing which twists. (c) act of twisting; a new to the story = an unexpected change. **twist 2** *v.* (a) to turn round and round. (b) to wind (sth) round sth. (c) to bend in the wrong way; to sprain (an ankle); *inf.* to t. s.o.'s arm = to persuade s.o. to do what you want. (d) to change the meaning of (words).

twister *n. Sl.* (a) dishonest person. (b) *Am.* whirlwind. **twisty** *adj.* which twists.

twit 1 [twɪt] *n. Sl.* silly idiot. **twit 2** *v.* (twitted) to make fun of (s.o.).

twitch 1 [twɪtʃ] *n.* (pl.-es) sudden jerk/ sudden movement. **twitch 2** *v.* to jerk suddenly/to make a sudden movement. **twitcher** *n. inf.* birdwatcher who travels long distances to see a rare bird.

twitter 1 ['twɪtə] *n.* little calls made by birds; she was all of a t. = very excited. **twitter 2** *v.* to make little sounds (like birds).

twixt [twɪkst] *prep.* (old) between.

two [tuː] *n.* number 2. (a) one or t. = a few; to put t. and t. together = to come to a conclusion by comparing various facts; to be in t. minds about sth = not to be able to decide. **two-bit** *adj. Am. inf.* cheap/second-rate. **two-edged** *adj.* (a) (knife) with two sharp edges. (b) (remark/action) which has two results (one good, one bad). **two faced** *adj.* deceitful. **twofold** *adv.* twice as much. **two-legged** [tuːˈlegɪd] *adj.* with two legs. **twopenny** ['tʌpnɪ] *adj.* costing two pence. **two-piece** *adj.* made of two pieces; to-piece suit = suit made of a jacket and skirt/trousers. **two-ply** *adj.* made of two threads/two pieces. **two-seater** *n.* car/aircraft with only two

seats. **twosome** *n.* two people (playing) a game; game for two people.
twostep *n.* dance with smooth steps.
two-stroke *adj.* (engine) with two pistons; two-stroke fuel = fuel for small engines. **two-time** *v. inf.* to be unfaithful (to a girlfriend/boyfriend).
two-timer *n. inf.* unfaithful person.
two-tone *adj.* coloured with two tones of the same colour. **two-way** *adj.* going in two directions.
tycoon [taɪˈkuːn] *n.* wealthy businessman.
tying [ˈtaɪɪŋ] *v.* see tie.
tyke [taɪk] *n.* (in N. of England) naughty child; small dog.
tympanum [tɪmˈpɑːnəm] *n.* (formal) eardrum.
type 1 [taɪp] *n.* (a) sort/kind. (b) example; a real northern t. = a good example of a northerner. (c) small pieces of metal with letters moulded on them, used for printing; collection of pieces of metal for printing. **type 2** *v.* to write with a typewriter. **typecast** *v.* (typecast) to give (an actor) the same type of part all the time. **typescript** *n.* document typed on a typewriter.
typesetter *n.* person who sets manuscripts in type ready for printing.
typesetting *n.* action of setting type; type which has been set. **typewriter** *n.* machine which prints letters on a piece of paper when you press the keys.
typewritten *adj.* (document) which has been written with a typewriter.
typing *n.* (a) action of writing letters with a typewriter; t. pool = group of typists who work for several departments in a company; t. paper = special paper for typewriters. (b) action of classifying into types; blood t. = classification of blood into a certain group. **typist** *n.* person whose job is to type letters on a typewriter. **typographer** *n.* specialist in typography.
typographic(al) [taɪpəˈɡræfɪk(l)] *adj.* referring to typography. **typography** [taɪˈpɒɡrəfɪ] *n.* (a) art of arranging material for printing/of designing a printed page. (b) study of the appearance of printed characters.
typhoid [ˈtaɪfɔɪd] *adj. & n.* t. (fever) = serious disease caused by infected food or drink.

typhoon [taɪˈfuːn] *n.* tropical storm (in the Far East). **typhus** [ˈtaɪfəs] *n.* serious fever, where the virus is carried by lice.
typical [ˈtɪpɪkl] *adj.* obviously belonging to particular group; characteristic; that's t. of him = that's exactly what he always does. **typically** *adv.* in a typical way.
typify *v.* to be an excellent example of.
typo [ˈtaɪpəʊ] *n. Am.* typesetting mistake.
tyranny [ˈtɪrənɪ] *n.* cruel rule by undemocratic government/ruler.
tyrannical, tyrannous [tɪˈrænɪkl, ˈtɪrənəs] *adj.* cruel. **tyrannize** *v.* to rule (s.o.) in a cruel way. **tyrant** [ˈtaɪrənt] *n.* cruel. undemocratic ruler.
tyre *Am.* **tire** [ˈtaɪə] *n.* thick rubber cover round a wheel; flat t. = the tyre has a hole in it so that the air has come out.
tyro [ˈtaɪrəʊ] *n.* (*pl.*-os) complete beginner/person with no experience.

Uu

U, u [juː] U-turn = turn made by a car in a road so that it faces in the opposite direction; to do a U-turn = change policy completely; *inf.* non U = not polite in upper class style. **U-boat** *n.* German submarine. **U** symbol for uranium.
ubiquitous [juːˈbɪkwɪtəs] *adj.* (thing) which is/which seems to be everywhere. **ubiquity** *n.* being everywhere.
udder [ˈʌdə] *n.* bag producing milk which hangs under the body of cow or goat.
UDI [juːdiːˈaɪ] abbrev. for unilateral declaration of independence.
UFO [juːefˈəʊ] *n.* abbrev. for unidentified flying object.
ugh *inter.* showing a feeling that something is unpleasant.
ugly [ˈʌɡlɪ] *adj.* (-ier, -iest) (a) not pleasant to look at. (b) dangerous (mood). **ugliness** *n.* being ugly.
UHF [juːeɪtʃˈef] abbrev. for ultra high frequency.
UHT [juːeɪtʃˈtiː] *adj.* abbrev. for ultra heat treated.

UK [juːˈkeɪ] abbrev. for United Kingdom.

ukulele [juːkəˈleɪlt] n. very small guitar.

ulcer [ˈʌlsə] n. sore on the body. **ulcerate** v. to cover with ulcers; to become covered with ulcers. **ulceration** n. being covered with ulcers; place where an ulcer is. **ulcerous** adj. covered with ulcers.

ullage [ˈʌlɪdʒ] n. amount of missing liquid which would make a container full.

ulna [ˈʌlnə] n. one of the two bones of the lower arm.

ulterior [ʌlˈtɪərɪə] adj. hidden/secret; u. motive = reason for doing sth. which anticipates the result of the action.

ultimate [ˈʌltɪmət] adj. final. **ultimately** adv. finally. **ultimatum** [ʌltɪˈmeɪtəm] n. message sent to an opponent stating that unless demands are met by a certain time. violent action (usu. war or a strike) will start.

ultra [ˈʌltrə] prefix meaning extremely/ very.

ultramarine [ʌltrəməˈriːn] adj. & n. (colour) of deep sea blue.

ultramodern adj. extremely modern.

ultrasonic adj. (sound waves) which cannot be heard by humans. **ultrasound** n. very high frequency sound wave. used to detect objects in the body or under water.

ultraviolet [ʌltrəˈvaɪələt] adj. (light rays) which are beyond the violet of the spectrum and which tan the skin.

ultra vires adv. (acting) beyond one's powers.

umbel [ˈʌmbl] n. flower head made of many single flowers on long stalks. **umbelliferous** [ʌmbəˈlɪfərəs] adj. (plant) with umbels.

umber [ˈʌmbə] adj. & n. brown (colour) like earth; burnt u. = reddish-brown (colour).

umbilical [ʌmˈbɪlɪkl] adj. u. cord = tube joining the mother to her baby before birth. and through which nourishment passes.

umbra [ˈʌmbrə] n. (formal) shadow.

umbrage [ˈʌmbrɪdʒ] n. to take u. at = to feel insulted by.

umbrella [ʌmˈbrelə] n. round shade of folded cloth which opens on a frame and is held over your head to keep off the rain; u. organization = large organization which includes small ones.

umpire 1 [ˈʌmpaɪə] n. person who acts as a judge in cricket/tennis/baseball. etc.. to see if the game is played according to the rules. **umpire 2** v. to act as umpire.

umpteen [ʌmˈtiːn] adj. & n. inf. very large number. **umpteenth** adj. inf. referring to umpteen.

un- [ʌn] prefix meaning not; the opposite.

'un [ʌn] pron. inf. one.

UN [ˈjuːˈen] abbrev. for United Nations..

unabashed [ʌnəˈbæʃt] adj. not ashamed/not timid.

unabated [ʌnəˈbeɪtɪd] adj. with no loss of vigour.

unable [ʌnˈeɪbl] adj. not able.

unabridged [ʌnəˈbrɪdʒd] adj. (text) which has not been shortened.

unacceptable [ʌnekˈseptəbl] adj. which cannot be accepted.

unaccompanied [ʌnəˈkʌmpɪnd] adj. alone; (singer/instrument) without any accompaniment.

unaccountable [ʌnəˈkaʊntəbl] adj. which cannot be explained **unaccountably** adv. without explanation. **unaccounted for** adj. lost. with no explanation for the loss.

unaccustomed [ʌnəˈkʌstəmd] adj. not accustomed.

unacquainted [ʌnəˈkweɪntɪd] adj. to be u. with = not to know.

unadopted [ʌnəˈdɒptɪd] adj. (road) which it is not the duty of the local council to keep in good repair.

unadulterated [ʌnəˈdʌltəreɪtɪd] adj. pure; with nothing added.

unaffected [ʌnəˈfektɪd] adj. sincere/ natural.

unaided [ʌnəˈɪdɪd] adj. without help.

unalloyed [ʌnəˈlɔɪd] adj. pure.

unalterable [ʌnˈɒltrəbl] adj. which cannot be altered. **unaltered** adj. which has not been changed.

unambiguous [ʌnæmˈbɪgjʊəs] adj. clear/not ambiguous.

unanimous jʊˈnænɪməs] adj. where every agrees. **unanimously** adv. all agreeing together. **unanimity** [jʊnənɪmɪtɪ] n. being unanimous.

unannounced [ʌnəˈnaʊnst] adj. which has not been announced.

unappetizing [ʌnˈæpɪtaɪzɪŋ] *adj.* which does not make you want to eat/ which takes away your appetite.

unapproachable [ʌnəˈprəʊtʃəbl] *adj.* (person) who is very formal; (place) which cannot be approached easily.

unarmed [ʌnˈaːmd] *adj.* with no weapons.

unashamed [ʌnəˈʃeɪmd] *adj.* not ashamed.

unasked [ʌnˈaːskt] *adj.* without being asked.

unassuming [ʌnəˈsjuːmɪŋ] *adj.* quiet/ modest.

unattached [ʌnəˈtætʃt] *adj.* not attached; not married.

unattainable [ʌnəˈteɪnəbl] *adj.* which cannot be reached.

unattended [ʌnəˈtendɪd] *adj.* alone; not looked after.

unattractive [ʌnəˈtræktɪv] *adj.* not attractive.

unauthorised [ʌnˈɔːθəraɪzd] *adj.* which is not permitted.

unavoidable [ʌnəˈvɔɪdəbl] *adj.* which cannot be avoided. **unavoidably** [ʌnɪˈweə] *adv.* in an unavoidable way.

unaware *adj.* (of) not knowing/not aware. **unawares** *adv.* without noticing; to catch s.o. u. = by suprise.

unbalanced [ʌnˈbælənst] *adj.* erratic/ slightly mad.

unbearable [ʌnˈbeərəbl] *adj.* which cannot be borne. **unbearably** *adv.* so much that you cannot bear it.

unbeatable [ʌnˈbiːtəbl] *adj.* which cannot be beaten. **unbeaten** *adj.* which has not been beaten.

unbecoming [ʌnbɪˈkʌmɪŋ] *adj.* which is not decent.

unbeknown [ʌnbɪˈnəʊn] *adj. inf.* u. to anyone = without anyone knowing.

unbelievable [ʌnbɪˈliːvəbl] *adj.* incredible/which you cannot believe. **unbelievably** *adv.* incredibly/ amazingly. **unbeliever** *n.* person who does not believe in god.

unbend [ʌnˈbend] *v.* (unbent) to stop being stiff and start behaving naturally. **unbending** *adj.* inflexible/harsh (rule).

unbiased [ʌnˈbɪdn] *adj.* impartial/not biased.

unbidden [ʌnˈbɪdn] *adj.* (formal) without having been asked.

unbleached [ʌnbliːtʃt] *adj.* (cloth. etc.) which has not been bleached.

unblock [ʌnˈblɒk] *v.* to take a blockage away from (sth).

unblushing [ʌnˈblʌʃɪŋ] *adj.* showing no shame.

unbolt [ʌnˈbəʊlt] *v.* to pull back the bolt on (a door).

unborn [ʌnˈbɔːn] *adj.* not yet born.

unbosom [ʌnˈbʊzəm] *v.* to u. oneself to s.o. = tell all one's private thoughts and troubles.

unbounded [ʌnˈbaʊndɪd] *adj.* with no limits.

unbreakable [ʌnˈbreɪkəbl] *adj.* which cannot be broken.

unbridled [ʌnˈbraɪdld] *adj.* (passion) which is not controlled.

unbroken [ʌnˈbrəʊkn] *adj.* which has not been broken; (case of wine) which has not been opened.

unburden [ʌnˈbɜːdn] *v.* to u. yourself to s.o. = to tell (s.o.) all your troubles/ secrets.

unbutton [ʌnˈbʌtn] *v.* to undo the buttons on.

uncalled for [ʌnˈkɔːldfɔː] *adj.* not necessary; not deserved.

uncanny [ʌnˈkænɪ] *adj.* mysterious/ which seems unnatural.

uncared for [ʌnˈkeədfɔː] *adj.* not looked after.

unceasing [ʌnˈsiːsɪŋ] *adj.* ceaseless; without any stopping.

unceremonious [ʌnserɪˈməʊnɪəs] *adj.* not dignified; not polite.

unceremoniously *adv.* in an undignified way.

uncertain [ʌnˈsɜːtən] *adj.* (a) not certain/not sure. (b) which cannot be forecast. **uncertainty** *n.* being uncertain; lack of certainty.

unchallenged [ʌnˈtʃælənʒd] *adj.* without a challenge; to let sth pass u. = to let sth be said or written without questioning it.

uncharacteristic [ʌnkærəkteˈrɪstɪk] *adj.* not in character.

uncharitable [ʌnˈtʃærɪtəbl] *adj.* unkind. **uncharitably** *adv.* in an uncharitable way.

unchecked [ʌnˈtʃekt] *adj.* with no check.

unchristian [ʌnˈkrɪstʃn] *adj.* not kind/ generous. etc.

uncial ['ʌn'siəl] *adj. & n.* (rounded) letters used in early medieval manuscripts.

uncivilized [ʌn'sɪvɪlaɪzd] *adj.* not civilized; barbarous.

unclaimed [ʌn'kleɪmd] *adj.* which has not been claimed; u. baggage = cases. etc.. which have been left in a left-luggage office and not been taken back by their owners.

unclassified [ʌn'klæsɪfaɪd] *adj.* not classified/not secret.

uncle ['ʌŋkl] *n.* brother of your father or mother; husband of your aunt. **Uncle Sam** *n. inf.* person symbolizing the USA.

unclean [ʌn'kliːn] *adj.* dirty.

unclouded [ʌn'klaʊdɪd] *adj.* not troubled/clear (liquid).

uncluttered [ʌn'klʌtəd] *adj.* tidy.

uncoil [ʌn'kɔɪl] *v.* to unwind.

uncomfortable [ʌn'lʌmftəbl] *adj.* (a) not comfortable. (b) embarrassed; ill at ease. **uncomfortably** *adv.* in an uncomfortable way.

uncommitted [ʌnkə'mɪtɪd] *adj.* with no strong beliefs; (country) which has not decided which group to support; (voter) who has not decided which way to vote.

uncommon [ʌn'kɒmən] *adj.* (-er, -est) strange/odd; rare. **uncommonly** *adv.* in an uncommon way; *inf.* very.

uncommunicative [ʌnkə'mjuːnɪkətɪv] *adj.* silent/not talkative.

uncomplimentary [ʌnkɒmplɪ'mentərɪ] *adj.* rude/not complimentary.

uncompromising [ʌn'kɒmprəmaɪzɪŋ] *adj.* unwilling to give in or to change ideas.

unconcealed [ʌnkən'siːld] *adj.* open; not hidden.

unconcerned [ʌnkən'sɜːnd]. not worried/not bothered.

unconditional [ʌnkən'dɪʃnl] *adj.* without any conditions. **unconditionally** *adv.* without insisting on conditions.

unconnected [ʌnkə'nektɪd] *adj.* with no connection.

unconscious 1 [ʌn'kɒnʃəs] *adj.* (a) not conscious. (b) not aware.

unconscious 2 *n.* the u = deep level of the mind, with thoughts or feelings of which you are not conscious.

unconscionable [ʌn'kɒnʃnəbl] *adj. inf.* unreasonable/excessive.

unconsciously *adv.* in an unconscious way. **unconsciousness** *n.* being unconscious.

unconstitutional [ʌnkɒnstɪ'tjuːʃənl] *adj.* going against the constitution.

uncontested [ʌnkən'testɪd] *adj.* (divorce) which is not disputed.

uncontrollable [ʌnkən'trəʊləbl] *adj.* which cannot be controlled.

unconventional [ʌnkən'venʃnl] *adj.* not usual.

uncooked [ʌn'kʊkt] *adj.* not cooked.

uncooperative [ʌnkəʊ'ɒpərətɪv] *adj.* unhelpful/not cooperative.

uncork [ʌn'kɔːk] *v.* to take the cork out of (a bottle).

uncorroborated [ʌnkə'rɒbəreɪtɪd] *adj.* (evidence) which has not been confirmed.

uncouple [ʌn'kʌpl] *v.* to detach (things) which are coupled.

uncouth [ʌn'kuːθ] *adj.* rude/badly brought up.

uncover [ʌn'kʌvə] *v.* (a) to take the cover off. (b) to find (sth hidden).

uncritical [ʌn'krɪtɪkl] *adj.* (person) who does not think critically.

uncrossed [ʌn'krɒst] *adj.* (check) which has not been crossed.

uncrowned [ʌn'kraʊnɪ] *adj.* (king) who has not been crowned; (leader) who is like a king.

uncrushable [ʌn'krʌʃəbl] *adj.* (material) which does not make creases if it is crushed.

unction ['ʌŋkʃn] *n.* putting oil on a person in a religious ceremony.

unctuous ['ʌŋkʃʊəs] *adj.* extremely and unpleasantly polite. **unctuously** *adv.* in an unctuous way.

uncultivated [ʌn'kʌltɪveɪtɪd] *adj.* (land) which has not been cultivated.

uncut [ʌn'kʌt] *adj.* which has not been cut; (film) which has not been censored; (book) with pages still joined together at the edges.

undaunted [ʌn'dɔːntɪd] *adj.* bold/with no fear.

undecided [ʌndɪ'saɪdɪd] *adj.* (person) who has not made up his mind.

undeclared [ʌndɪ'kleəd] *adj.* which has not been declared.

undefended [ʌndɪˈfendɪd] *adj.* not defended; (divorce case) which the defended does not defend.

undemanding [ʌndɪˈmaːndɪŋ] *adj.* not difficult.

undemocratic [ʌndemoˈkrætik] *adj.* not democratic.

undeniable [ʌndɪˈnaɪəbl] *adj.* which cannot be denied/which is quite clearly true.

under 1 [ˈʌndə] *prep.* prep. (a) in a place which is directly below; u. water = below the surface of the water. (b) less than; u. age = younger than the legal age. (c) being ruled/managed/commanded by s.o. (d) because of/according to (terms). (e) in a state of; u. repair = being repaired; u. lock and key = locked up; u. treatment = being treated; u. control = controlled. **under 2** *adv.* in a lower place; to go u. = to fail/to go bankrupt; *inf.* down u. = in Australia and New Zealand. **under 3** *adj.* lower/bottom.

under 4 under- prefix meaning less important; not enough.

underachieve [ʌndərəˈtʃiːv] *v.* to do less well than expected.

underachiever *n.* student who does not do as well as expected.

underarm [ˈʌndəraːm] *adv. & adj.* (thrown) with the hand kept lower than the shoulder.

undercarriage [ˈʌndəkærɪdʒ] *n.* aircraft's wheels and supports.

undercharge [ʌndəˈtʃaːdʒ] *v.* to charge less than you should.

underclothes [ˈʌndəkləʊðz] *n. pl.* clothes worn next to the skin, under other clothes.

undercoat [ˈʌndəkəʊt] *n.* first coat of paint.

undercover [ˈʌndəkʌvə] *adj.* secret; u. agent = spy.

undercurrent [ˈʌndəkʌrənt] *n.* (a) current of water under the surface. (b) hidden feelings.

undercut [ˈʌndəkʌt] *v.* (undercut) to sell more cheaply than (s.o.).

underdeveloped [ʌndədɪˈveləpt] *adj.* not, developed; not industrially advanced.

underdog [ˈʌndədog] *n.* person who is weaker/who always loses.

underdone [ˈʌndədʌn] *adj.* not cooked enough; not too cooked.

underestimate 1 [ʌndərˈestɪmət] *n.*

estimate which is less than the real quantity. **underestimate 2** [ʌndərˈestɪmeɪt] *v.* to estimate at less than the real quantity.

underexposes [ʌndərɪkˈspəʊzd] *adj.* (film) which has not been exposed sufficiently.

underfed [ʌndəˈfed] *adj.* with not enough to eat.

underfelt [ˈʌndəfelt] *n.* soft material put beneath a carpet.

underfloor [ʌndəˈflɔː] *adj.* (heating system) which is under the floor.

underfoot [ʌndəˈfʊt] *adv.* under the feet.

undergarment [ˈʌndəgaːmənt] *n.* piece of clothing worn next to the skin. under other clothes.

undergo [ʌndəˈgəʊ] *v.* (underwent, undergone) to suffer/to experience.

undergraduate [ʌndəˈgrædjʊət] *n.* student at university who has not yet passed the final examination.

underground 1 [ʌndəˈgraʊnd] *adv.* (a) under the ground. (b) in hiding.

underground 2 [ˈʌndəgraʊnd] *adj.* (a) under the ground. (b) secret; against the ruling authorities. **underground 3** [ˈʌndəgraʊnd] *n.* (a) city railway which runs beneath the ground. (b) secret organization.

undergrowth [ˈʌndəgrəʊθ] *n.* bushes which grow thickly together under trees.

underhand(ed) [ʌndəˈhænd(ɪd)] *adj.* cunning; deceitful.

underlay [ˈʌndəleɪ] *n.* material for putting under a carpet; see also underlie.

underlie [ʌndəˈlaɪ] *v.* (underlay, underlain) to be underneath; to be the basic cause (of sth). **underlying** *adj.* basic (cause).

underline [ˈʌndəlaɪn] *v.* to write a line under (a word); to emphasize.

underling [ˈʌndəlɪŋ] *n.* person who works for s.o. else.

undermanned [ʌndəˈmænd] *adj.* with not enough staff.

undermentioned [ʌndəˈmenʃənd] *adj.* mentioned lower down on the page.

undermine [ʌndəˈmaɪn] *v.* to weaken.

underneath 1 [ʌndəˈniːθ] *prep.* under/ beneath. **underneath 2** *adv.* under. **underneath 3** *n.* the bottom part.

undernourished [ʌndəˈnʌrɪʃt] *adj.* not having enough to eat.

underpaid [ʌndə'peɪd] *adj.* not paid enough.

underpants ['ʌndəpænts] *n. pl.* men's undergarment for the lower part of the body.

underpass ['ʌndəpɑːs] *n.* (*pl.*-es) place where one road goes under another.

underpin [ʌndə'pɪn] *v.* (underpinned) to support. **underpinning** *n.* support.

underprivileged [ʌndə'prɪvɪlɪdʒd] *adj.* not having the same opportunities as other people.

underrate [ʌndə'reɪt] *v.* to value (sth) less than you ought.

underscore [ʌndə'skɔː] *v.* to underline.

undersea ['ʌndəsiː] *adj. & adv.* under the sea.

underseal 1 ['ʌndəsiːl] *n.* protective paint to stop the underneath of a car rusting. **underseal 2** *v.* to paint the underneath of (a car) with underseal.

undersecretary [ʌndə'sekrətrɪ] *n.* person in charge of a government department under a minister.

undersell [ʌndə'sel] *v.* (undersold) to sell more cheaply than (s.o.).

undershirt ['ʌndəʃɜːt] *n. Am.* vest.

underside ["ʌndəsaɪd] *n.* side which is underneath.

undersigned ['ʌndəsaɪnd] *n.* person who has signed a letter.

undersize(d) ['ʌndəsaɪz(d)] *adj.* smaller than normal.

underslung ['ʌndəslʌŋ] *adj.* (car chassis) which hangs below the axles.

understaffed [ʌndə'stɑːft] *adj.* with not enough staff.

understand [ʌndə'stænd] *v.* (understood) (a) to know; to see the meaning of (sth). (b) to be an expert in (sth). (c) to think/to have an impression. (d) to take sth for granted. even if it is not written or spoken. (e) to know why (sth is done) and accept it.

understandable *adj.* which can be understood. **understandably** *adv.* in a way which can be understood.

understanding 1 *n.* (a) ability to understand. (b) sympathy for another person's problems. (c) private agreement. **understanding 2** *adj.* sympathetic.

understate [ʌndə'steɪt] *v.* to make (sth) seem less important than it really is.

understatement *n.* statement which does not tell the facts forcefully enough.

understeer [ʌndə'stɪə] *v.* (of car) to turn a corner less sharply than it should.

understood [ʌndə'stʊd] *v.* see understand.

understudy 1 ['ʌndəstʌdɪ] *n.* actor who learns a part in the play so as to be able to act it if the main actor is ill.

understudy 2 *v.* to be the understudy of (an actor).

undertake [ʌndə'teɪk] *v.* (undertook, has undertaken) to promise to do (sth); to accept do (sth). **undertaker** *n.* person who organizes funerals. **undertaking** *n.* (a) business. (b) promise. (c) job; quite an u. = very difficult job.

undertone ['ʌndətəʊn] *n.* (a) quiet voice. (b) hidden feeling.

undertow ['ʌndətəʊ] *n.* strong current under the surface of water. which flows in a different direction to that on the surface.

undervalue [ʌndə'væljuː] *v.* to value at less than the true value.

underwater [ʌndə'wɔːtə] *adj.* below the surface of the water.

underwear ['ʌndəweə] *n.* (no *pl.*) clothes worn next to your skin under other clothes.

underweight [ʌndə'weɪt] *adj.* which weighs less than usual.

underwent [ʌndə'went] *v.* see undergo.

underworld ['ʌndəwɜːld] *n.* (a) (in mythology) place inhabited by the dead. (b) criminal world; u. killing = murder of a criminal by other criminals.

underwrite [ʌndə'raɪt] *v.* (underwrote, has underwritten) to insure (esp. ships); to accept responsibility for (sth). **underwriter** *n.* person who insures (esp. ships).

undeserved [ʌndərɪztə] *adj.* not deserved. **undeservedly** [ʌndɪ'zɜːvd] *adv.* in an undeserved way.

undesirable 1 [ʌndɪ'zaɪərəbl] *adj.* not wanted; not pleasant. **undesirable 2** *n.* person who is not wanted/who is considered a bad influence.

undesirability [ʌndɪzaɪərə'bɪlɪtɪ] *n.* being undesirable.

undetected [ʌndɪ'tektɪd] *adj.* not noticed. **undetectable** *adj.* which cannot be detected.

undeterred [ˌʌndɪˈtɜːd] *adj.* not put off.

undeveloped [ˌʌndɪˈveləpt] *adj.* which has not been developed.

undid [ʌnˈdɪd] *v.* see undo.

undies [ˈʌndiz] *n. pl.inf.* (women's) underwear.

undignified [ʌnˈdɪgnɪfaɪd] *adj.* not dignified.

undiluted [ˌʌndaɪˈljuːtɪd] *adj.* without any water added.

undischarged [ˌʌndɪsˈtʃɑːʒd] *adj.* (debt) which has not been paid; u. bankrupt = person who is still legally a bankrupt.

undistinguished [ˌʌndɪsˈtɪŋgwɪʃt] *adj.* ordinary.

undivided [ˌʌndɪˈvaɪdɪd] *adj.* complete/not split.

undo [ʌnˈduː] *v.* (undid, has undone) (a) to untie (a knot); to unbutton. (b) to ruin. **undoing** *n.* ruin. **undone** *adj.* (a) unfastened. (b) not complete.

undoubted [ʌnˈdaʊtɪd] *adj.* certain. **undoubtedly** *adv.* certainly.

undreamt of [ʌnˈdremtɒv] *adj.* which no one can imagine.

undress [ʌnˈdres] *v* to take off (usu. all your) clothes. **undressed** *adj.* not wearing clothes.

undrinkable [ʌnˈdrɪŋkəbl] *adj.* (liquid) which is so unpleasant/so polluted that you cannot drink it.

undue [ˈʌndjuː] *adj.* excessive/too much. **unduly** [ʌnˈdjuːlɪ] *adv.* excessively/too much.

undulant [ˈʌndjʊlənt] *adj.* u. fever = brucellosis. **undulate** [ˈʌndjʊleɪt] *v.* to rise and fall like waves. **undulation** [ˌʌndjʊˈleɪʃn] *n.* rise and fall (of land. etc.).

undying [ʌnˈdaɪɪŋ] *adj.* (emotion) which lasts for ever.

unearned [ˈʌnɜːnd] *adj.* (income) from investments/rents. etc.

unearth [ʌnˈɜːθ] *v.* to dig up; to discover. **unearthly** *adj.* supernatural; *inf.* very early/late (hour).

uneasy [ʌnˈiːzɪ] *adj.* (-ier, -iest) worried. **uneasily** *adv.* in an uneasy way. **uneasiness** *n.* worry/anxiety.

uneatable [ʌnˈiːtəbl] *adj.* (food) which is so unpleasant that you cannot eat it.

uneconomic(al) [ˌʌniːkəˈnɒmɪk] *adj.* which is not economic/which does not make a profit.

uneducated [ʌnˈedjʊkeɪtɪd] *adj.* not educated; (person) who has not been well brought up; (way of speaking) which is not refined.

unemployed [ˌʌnɪmˈplɔɪd] *adj.* without any permanent work; the u. = people with no jobs. **unemployment** [ˌʌnɪmˈplɔɪmənt] *n.* lack of jobs; mass u. = situation where large numbers of people are out of work.

unending [ʌnˈendɪŋ] *adj.* ceaseless/with no end.

unenlightened [ˌʌnɪnˈlaɪtənd] *adj.* lacking knowledge.

unenviable [ʌnˈenvɪəbl] *adj.* which no one would envy.

unequal [ʌnˈiːkwəl] *adj.* (a) not equal. (b) u. to = not good/strong enough for. **unequalled** *adj.* which has no equal.

unequivocal [ˌʌnɪˈkwɪvəkl] *adj.* clear; easily understood; which cannot be misunderstood.

unerring [ʌnˈɜːrɪŋ] *adj.* faultless/making no mistake.

unethical [ʌnˈeθɪkl] *adj.* (conduct) which does not follow the usual rules of a profession.

uneven [ʌnˈiːvn] *adj.* (a) bumpy/not flat. (b) not always very good. **unevenness** *n.* being uneven.

uneventful [ˌʌnɪˈventfəl] *adj.* without any particularly exciting incidents.

unexampled [ˌʌnɪgˈzɑːmpld] *adj.* extraordinary; of which there is no other example.

unexceptionable [ˌʌnɪkˈspʃənəbl] *adj.* very satisfactory. **unexceptional** [ˌʌnɪkˈsepʃnəl] *adj.* ordinary.

unexpected [ˌʌnɪkˈspektɪd] *adj.* which was not expected. **unexpectedly** *adv.* in an unexpected way.

unexplored [ˌʌnɪkˈsplɔːd] *adj.* which has never been explored.

unexposed [ˌʌnɪkˈspeʊzd] *adj.* (film) which has not been used.

unexpurgated [ʌnˈekspɜːgeɪtɪd] *adj.* (book, etc.) which has not had offensive parts removed.

unfailing [ʌnˈfeɪlɪŋ] *adj.* which never fails. **unfailingly** *adv.* without fail.

unfair [ʌnˈfeə] *adj.* not fair; u. dismissal = removing of a person from his job for reasons which are not fair.

unfaithful [ʌnˈfeɪθfəl] *adj.* not faithful (to your husband or wife).

unfamiliar [ʌnfə'mɪlɪə] *adj.* not familiar.

unfasten [ʌn'fɑːsn] *v.* to undo (sth which is fastened).

unfathomable [ʌn'fæðəməbl] *adj.* (mystery) which cannot be solved.

unfavourable [ʌn'feɪvrəbl] *adj.* not favourable.

unfeeling [ʌn'fiːlɪŋ] *adj.* insensitive; not sympathetic to s.o.

unfettered [ʌn'fetəd] *adj.* free.

unfit [ʌn'fɪt] *adj.* (a) (person) who is not fit/not in good physical condition. (b) not suitable.

unflagging [ʌn'flægɪŋ] *adj.* tireless.

unflappable [ʌn'flæpəbl] *adj.* (person) who is always calm.

unflinching [ʌnflɪntʃɪŋ] *adj.* brave. **unflinchingly** *adv.* bravely.

unfold [ʌn'fəʊld] *v.* (a) to spread out (a newspaper). (b) (of story) to become clear/be told.

unforeseen [ʌnfɔː'siːn] *adj.* not foreseen/not anticipated.

unforgettable [ʌnfə'getəbl] *adj.* which cannot be forgotten.

unfortunate [ʌn'fɔːtʃənət] *adj.* (a) unlucky. (b) sad; to be regretted. **unfortunately** *adv.* sadly.

unfounded [ʌn'faʊndət] *adj.* without any basis in truth.

unfreeze [ʌn'friːz] *v.* (unfroze, unfrozen) to warm (sth) so that it stops being frozen.

unfrequented [ʌnfrɪ'kwentɪd] *adj.* (place) where few people go.

unfriendly [ʌn'frendlɪ] *adj.* (-ier, -iest) not like a friend.

unfrock [ʌn'frɒk] *v.* to remove (a priest) from holy orders.

unfurl [ʌn'fɜːl] *v.* to unroll (like a flag).

unfurnished [ʌn'fɜːnɪʃt] *adj.* (house) with no furniture in it.

ungainly [ʌn'geɪnlɪ] *adj.* awkward/ clumsy (way of walking).

ungentlemanly [ʌn'dʒentəlmənlɪ] *adj.* (behaviour) not like that of a true gentleman.

ungetatable [ʌnget'ætəbl] *adj.* which you cannot reach easily.

ungodly [ʌn'gɒdlɪ] *adj.* wicked unpleasant/inconvenient; *inf.* very early/ late (hour).

ungracious [ʌn'greɪʃəs] *adj.* not gracious/not polite.

ungrammatical [ʌngrə'mætɪkl] *adj.* which goes against the rules of grammar.

ungrateful [ʌn'greɪtfəl] *adj.* not grateful.

unguarded [ʌn'gɒːdɪd] *adj.* careless; in an u. moment = without thinking about the consequences.

unguent ['ʌngʊənt] *n.* (formal) ointment.

ungulate ['ʌngjʊleɪt] *n.* animal with hooves.

unhappy [ʌn'hæpɪ] *adj.* (-er, -iest) sad. **unhappily** *adv.*. sadly/unfortunately. **unhappiness** *n.* being unhappy.

unharmed [ʌn'hɑːmd] *adj.* safe.

unhealthy [ʌn'helθɪ] *adj.* (-ier, -iest) (a) not healthy. (b) unnatural.

unheard of [ʌn'hɜːdɒv] *adj.* strange/ odd.

unheated [ʌn'hiːtɪd] *adj.* which has no heating.

unhelpful [ʌn'helpfəl] *adj.* not helpful.

unheralded [ʌn'herəldɪd] *adj.* not announced/publicized beforehand.

unhinged [ʌn'hɪndʒd] *adj.* mad.

unholy [ʌn'həʊlɪ] *adj. inf.* unpleasant.

unhook [ʌn'hʊk] *v.* to take (sth) off a hook; to unfasten (sth) which is attached with hooks.

unhoped for [ʌn'həʊptfɔː] *adj.* unexpected.

unhorse [ʌn'hɔːs] *v.* to make (s.o.) fall off his horse.

unhurt [ʌn'hɜːt] *adj.* not hurt; safe and sound.

unhygienic [ʌnhaɪ'dʒiːnɪk] *adj.* dirty/ not hygienic.

unicameral [jʊnɪ'kæmərəl] *adj.* system of government where the parliament has only one chamber.

unicorn ['juːnɪkɔːn] *n.* mythical animal like a horse, with one long, straight horn.

unidentified [ʌnaɪ'dentɪfaɪd] *adj.* which has not been identified; u. flying object = mysterious object in the sky which cannot be identified.

unification [jʊnɪfɪ'keɪʃn] *n.* act of unifying; joining together into one.

uniform 1 ['juːnɪfɔːm] *n.* specially designed clothing worn by all members of a group. **uniform 2** *adj.* all the same; never changing. **uniformity** [jʊnɪ'fɔːmɪtɪ] *n.* being uniform. **uniformly** *adv.* in a uniform way.

unify ['juːnɪfaɪ] *v.* to join together into one.

unilateral [ju:nɪ'lætərəl] adj. on one side only; done by one side only.
unilaterally adv. (done) by one side only.

unimaginative [ʌnɪ'mædʒɪnətɪv] adj. lacking flair.

unimpaired [ʌnɪm'peəd] adj. not damaged. **unimpeachable** [ʌnɪm'pi:tʃəbl] adj. which can be trusted completely.

unimportant [ʌnɪm'pɔːtənt] adj. not important.

uninformed [ʌnɪn'fɔːmd] adj. without full knowledge.

uninhabitable [ʌnɪn'hæbɪtəbl] adj. which cannot be lived in. **uninhabited** adj. not lived in.. **uninhibited** [ʌnɪn'hɪbɪtɪd] adj. free; not bound by the customs of society.

uninitiated [ʌnɪ'nɪʃɪeɪtɪd] n. the u. = people who are not experts.

unintelligible [ʌnɪn'telɪdʒəbl] adj. which cannot be understood.

uninterrupted [ʌnɪntə'rʌptɪd] adj. with no breaks; continuous.

uninvited [ʌnɪn'vaɪtɪd] adj. without an invitation. **uninviting** adj. not very attractive.

union ['ju:nɪən] n. (a) being joined together; countries or states which are joined together. (b) (formal) marriage. (c) group of people working in the same type of industry joined together for mutual protection. **unionist** n. member of a trade union. **unionize** v. to form a trade union in (a factory/a group of workers). **Union Jack** n. national flag of the United Kingdom.

unique [ju'niːk] adj. so special that there is nothing similar to it. **uniquely** adv. in a special or unique way.

unisex ['ju:nɪseks] adj. which can be used by both men and women.

unison ['ju:nɪsn] n. in u. = (i) singing the same note all together; (ii) in total agreement.

unit ['ju:nɪt] n. (a) one part (of a larger whole); one cupboard/one set of shelves. etc.. which can be matched with others to form a whole kitchen. (b) one part (of an army). (c) standard measurement by which sth is counted. (d) one single part of a group investment; u. trust = company which invests its members' money in a varied range of investments.

each member buying one or more units. (e) number one; single number. **unitary** adj. referring to a unit. **unite** [ju:'aɪt] v. to join together as a whole. **unity** ['ju:nɪtɪ] n. being one whole

univalve ['ju:nɪvælv] n. animal (such as a snail) with a single shell.

universe ['ju:nɪvɜːs] n. all that exists. including the earth. the planets and the stars. **universal** [ju:nɪ'vɜːsəl] adj. which is everywhere; which affects everyone; u. joint = mechanical joint made so that each of two connected rods can move in any direction; u. suffrage = situation where all adults have the right to vote. **universally** adv. everywhere; by everyone.

university [ju:nɪ'vɜːsɪtɪ] n. place of high learning. where degrees are given to successful students, and a wide range of specialized subjects are taught.

unjust [ʌn'dʒʌst] adj. not fair. **unjustly** adv. in an unjust way. **unjustified** [ʌn'dʒʌstɪfaɪd] adj. which is not justified.

unkempt [ʌn'kemt] adj. dishevelled/ untidy.

unkind [ʌn'kaɪnd] adj. (-er, -est) harsh/ cruel. **unkindly** adv. in a cruel way.

unknown [ʌn'nəʊn] adj. not known.

unladen [ʌn'leɪdn] adj. without a load.

unladylike [ʌn'leɪdɪlaɪk] adj. (behaviour) which is not like that of a lady.

unlawful [ʌn'lɔːfəl] adj. against the law.

unleaded [ʌn'ledɪd] adj. (petrol) with out lead additives.

unleash [ʌn'liːʃ] v. to unfasten the leash (of a dog); to set free/to set loose.

unleavened [ʌn'lend] adj. (bread) made without yeast.

unless [ʌn'les] conj. (a) if. not. (b) except if.

unlike ['ʌnlaɪk] adj. & prep. not similar to; different from; it is u. him to be rude = he is not usually like that. **unlikely** [ʌn'laɪklɪ] adj. improbable; (story) which is probably not true.

unlimited [ʌn'lɪmɪtɪd] adj. with no limits.

unlined [ʌn'laɪnd] adj. (a) without lines. (b) without a lining.

unlisted [ʌn'lɪstɪd] adj. not included in a list; (shares) which are not dealt with on the Stock Exchange.

unload [ʌn'ləʊd] v. to remove a load from (a vehicle). **unloaded** adj. (gun) with no bullets in it.

unlock [ʌn'lɒk] v. to open (sth) which was locked.

unlooked for [ʌn'lʊktfɔː] adj. not expected.

unlucky [ʌn'lʌkɪ] adj. (-ier, -iest) not lucky; bringing bad luck. **unluckily** adv. unfortunately.

unmanageable [ʌn'mænɪdʒəbl] adj. difficult to control.

unmanned [ʌn'mænd] adj. without a crew/without any staff. **unmannerly** [ʌn'mænəlɪ] adj. with no manners.

unmarried ['ʌnmærɪd] adj. not married; u. mother = woman who has a child but is not married.

unmask [ʌn'mɒːsk] v. to remove a mask; to show (s.o.) as they really are.

unmatched [ʌn'mætʃt] adj. which has no equal.

unmentionable [ʌn'menʃnəbl] adj. which you must not talk about because it is so indecent/unpleasant. etc.

unmistakable [ʌnmɪs'teɪkəbl] adj. which is easily recongnized/which cannot be mistaken.

unmitigated [ʌn'mɪtɪgeɪtɪd] adj. total/ complete.

unmoved [ʌn'muːvd] adj. not touched/ not affected.

unmusical [ʌn'mjuːzɪkl] adj. not interested in music; not able to play a musical instrument.

unnamed [ʌn'neɪmd] adj. (person) who has not been named.

unnatural [ʌn'nætʃərəl] adj. which is not natural; which does not follow the usual pattern.

unnecessary [ʌn'nesəsərɪ] adj. which is not necessary. **unnecessarily** adv. uselessly; for no good reason.

unnerve [ʌn'nɜːv] v. to make (s.o.) lose his nerve/his courage.

unnoticed [ʌn'nəʊtɪst] adj. not noticed; without anyone noticing.

unnumbered [ʌn'nʌmbəd] adj. with no numbers; which cannot be counted.

unobservant [ʌnəb'strʌktɪd] adj. not observant; (person) who does not notice things.

unobstructed [ʌnəb'strʌktɪd] adj. with nothing in the way.

unobtainable [ʌnəb'teɪbəbl] adj. which cannot be obtained. **unobtrusive** [ʌnəb'truːsɪv] adj. not obvious; not easily noticed.

unoccupied [ʌn'ɒkjʊpaɪd] adj. not occupied; empty.

unofficial [ʌnə'fɪʃl] adj. not official; (strike) which has not been officially approved by a union. **unofficially** adv. in an unofficial way.

unopposed [ʌnə'pəʊzd] adj. with no opposition; (elected) because there is no other candidate.

unorthodox [ʌn'ɔːθədɒks] adj. not usual.

unpack [ʌn'pæk] v. to take (things) out of containers in which they were transported.

unpaid [ʌn'peɪd] adj. (person) who is not paid a salary; (bill) which has not been settled.

unpalatable [ʌn'pælətəbl] adj. not pleasant to the taste; unpleasant (fact).

unparalleled [ʌn'pærəleld] adj. with no parallel or no equal.

unpardonable [ʌn'pɑːdnəbl] adj. which cannot be excused.

unparliamentary [ʌnpɑːlɪ'mentərɪ] adj. (in Parliament) offensive (language/ behaviour).

unpatriotic [ʌnpætrɪ'ɒtɪk] adj. not patriotic.

unperson ['ʌnpɜːsən] n. person who is treated as if he did not exist (because of opposition to the government).

unpick [ʌn'pɪk] v. to remove (stitches).

unplaced [ʌn'pleɪst] adj. (horse) which is not one of the first three in a race.

unpleasant [ʌn'plezənt] adj. not pleasing. **unpleasantness** n. argument/disagreement.

unpopular [ʌn'pɒpjʊlə] adj. not popular. **unpopularity** [ʌnpɒpjʊ'lærɪtɪ] n. being unpopular.

unprecedented [ʌn'presɪdentɪd] adj. which has never happened before.

unprejudiced [ʌn'predʒʊdɪst] adj. fair; not prejudiced.

unpremeditated [ʌnprɪ'medɪteɪtɪd] adj. which has not been planned.

unprepared [ʌnprɪ'peəd] adj. not ready.

unprepossessing [ʌnprɪpə'zesɪŋ] adj. not very attractive.

unpretentious [ʌnprɪˈtenʃəs] *adj.* modest/not showing off.

unprincipled [ʌnˈprɪnsɪpld] *adj.* without any moral standards.

unprintable [ʌnˈprɪntəbl] *adj.* (words) so rude that you cannot print them.

unproductive [ʌnprəˈdʌktɪv] *adj.* (discussion) which does not produce any result; (land) which does not produce any crops.

unprofessional [ʌnprəˈfeʃnəl] *adj.* (conduct) which is not of the sort you would expect from a member of the profession.

unprofitable [ʌnˈprɒfɪtəbl] *adj.* which does not make a profit; which is useless.

unprompted [ʌnˈprɒmptɪd] *adj.* without anyone suggesting it.

unpronounceable [ʌnprəˈnaʊnsəbl] *adj.* (name) which is difficult to say.

unprovoked [ʌnprəˈvəʊkt] *adj.* (action) which was not provoked.

unqualified [ʌnˈkæ̈lɪfaɪd] *adj.* (a) (person) who has not passed the examinations to qualify for a profession. (b) total/complete (success).

unquestionable [ʌnˈkweʃʃənəbl] *adj.* which is certain/not doubtful. **unquestionably** *adv.* certainly. **unquestioning** *adj.* without doubting.

unquote [ˈʌnkwəʊt] *v.* to indicate the end of a quotation (when speaking).

unravel [ʌnˈrævl] *v.* (unravelled) to disentangle (sth knotted); to solve (a mystery).

unreadable [ʌnˈriːdəbl] *adj.* (book) which is so boring that you cannot read it.

unreal [ʌnˈriːl] *adj.* not like the real world. **unrealistic** [ʌnrɪəˈlɪstɪk] *adj.* impractical/not facing facts.

unreasonable [ʌnˈriːznəbl] *adj.* not reasonable/too large.

unrecognizable [ʌnrekəgˈnaɪzəbl] *adj.* which cannot be recognized.

unreel [ʌnˈriːl] *v.* to undo (sth wound round a reel).

unrefined [ʌnrɪˈfaɪnd] *adj.* (sugar/oil) which has not been refined.

unrelated [ʌnrɪˈleɪtɪd] *adj.* not related/ with no connection.

unrelenting [ʌnrɪˈlentɪŋ] *adj.* which never stops/weakens.

unreliable [ʌnrɪˈlaɪəbl] *adj.* which cannot be relied on.

unrelieved [ʌnrɪˈliːvd] *adj.* not lessened.

unremitting [ʌnrɪˈmɪtɪŋ] *adj.* never ceasing.

unrequited [ʌnrɪˈlwaɪtɪd] *adj.* (love) which is not returned.

unreserved [ʌnrɪˈzɜːvd] *adj.* not reserved. **unreservedly** [ʌnrɪˈzɜːvɪdlɪ] *adv.* definitely.

unrest [ʌnˈrest] *n.* being restless/ dissatisfied; agitation to get political/ industrial change.

unrivalled [ʌnˈraɪvəld] *adj.* with no equal.

unroll [ʌnˈrəʊl] *v.* to undo (sth which is rolled up).

unruffled [ʌnˈrʌfld] *adj.* calm/not anxious.

unruly [ʌnˈruːlɪ] *adj.* wild/with no discipline. **unruliness** *n.* rowdy behaviour.

unsafe [ʌnˈseɪf] *adj.* (-ier, -est) dangerous).

unsaid [ʌnˈsed] *adj.* better leave it u. = better not to say it.

unsalted [ʌnˈsɒltɪd] *adj.* (butter. etc.) with no salt.

unsatisfactory [ʌnsʌtɪsˈfæktrɪ] *adj.* not satisfactory.

unsatisfied [ʌnˈsætɪsfaɪd] *adj.* not satisfied.

unsaturated [ʌnˈsʌtjuːreɪtɪd] *adj.* (fat) which contains little hydrogen, and so can be broken down easily in the body.

unsavoury, *Am.* **unsavory** [ʌnˈseɪvərɪ] *adj.* unpleasant/disgusting.

unscathed [ʌnˈskeɪðd] *adj.* not harmed.

unscheduled [ʌnˈʃedjuːld] *adj.* not on a schedule.

unschooled [ʌnˈskuːld] *adj.* not taught; without any experience (in).

unscientific [ʌnsaɪənˈtɪfɪk] *adj.* not scientific.

unscramble [ʌnˈskræmbl] *v.* to put back in order; to put (a coded message) back into plain language.

unscrew [ʌnˈskruː] *v.* to open by twisting a screw or a screw lid anticlockwise.

unscripted [ʌnˈskrɪptɪd] *adj.* (broadcast) made without a script.

unscrupulous [ʌnˈskruːpjʊləs] *adj.* not worrying too much about honesty.

unsealed [ʌnˈsiːld] *adj.* (envelope. etc.) which has not been sealed.

unseasonable [ʌnˈsiːzənəbl] *adj.* not usual for the season.

unseat [ʌnˈsiːt] *v.* to make (s.o.) fall off a horse; to remove (a Member of Parliament) at an election.

unseemly [ʌnˈsiːmlɪ] *adj.* offensive/ rude (behaviour).

unseen [ʌnˈsiːn] *adj. & n.* not seen/ invisible; (piece of writing) which you have not seen before. and which you have to translate in an examination.

unselfish [ʌnˈselfɪʃ] *adj.* not selfish/ thinking of others before yourself.

unserviceable [ʌnˈsɜːvɪsəbl] *adj.* not in a good enough state to be used.

unsettle [ʌnˈsetl] *v.* to upset. **unsettled** *adj.* (weather) which changes often..

unshakeable [ʌnˈʃeɪkəbl] *adj.* solid/ firm (belief/faith).

unsightly [ʌnˈsaɪtlɪ] *adj.* ugly.

unsigned [ʌnˈsaɪnd] *adj.* not signed.

unskilled [ˈʌnskɪld] *adj.* (worker) who has no particular skill.

unsociable [ʌnˈsəʊʃəbl] *adj.* not friendly; now wishing to make friends.

unsocial [ʌnˈsəʊʃəl] *adj.* (hours of work) where the worker is rarely free at the same time as his family.

unsolicited [ʌnsəˈlɪsɪtɪd] *adj.* which has not been asked for.

unsolved [ˈʌnsɒlvd] *adj.* (problem) which has not been solved.

unsophisticated [ʌnsəˈfɪstɪkɪtɪd] *adj.* simple; not sophisticated.

unsound [ˈʌnsaʊnd] *adj.* (a) of u. mind = mad. (b) (reasoning) not based on fact or logic.

unsparing [ʌnˈspeərɪŋ] *adj.* generous; not reluctant.

unspeakable [ʌnˈspiːkəbl] *adj.* extremely unpleasant.

unspoilt [ˈʌnspɔɪlt] *adj.* (countryside) which has not been spoilt.

unstable [ʌnˈsteɪbl] *adj.* (a) not stable; changeable; (government) which is likely to fall at any moment. (b) dangerously mad.

unsteady [ʌnˈstedɪ] *adj.* not steady; wobbly.

unstick [ʌnˈstɪk] *v.* (unstuck) to remove sth which is stuck on; to come unstuck = to go badly wrong.

unstoppable [ʌnsˈstɒpəbl] *adj.* which cannot be stopped.

unsuccessful [ʌnsəkˈsesfəl] *adj.* not successful.

unsuitable [ʌnˈsuːtəbl] *adj.* not suitable.

unsullied [ʌnˈsʌlɪd] *adj.* pure.

unsung [ʌnˈsʌŋ] *adj.* (hero) who is not famous.

unsure [ʌnˈʃʊə] *adj.* not sure; u. of oneself = lacking self-confidence.

unsuspected [ʌnsəsˈpektɪd] *adj.* which is not suspected to exist.

unsuspecting *adj.* (person) who does not realize sth/that a danger is imminent.

unsweetened [ʌnˈswiːtənd] *adj.* (food) with no sugar added.

unswerving [ʌnˈswɜːvɪŋ] *adj.* (loyalty) which does not change.

unsympathetic [ʌnsɪmpəˈθetɪk] *adj.* not sympathetic.

untangle [ʌnˈtæŋgl] *v.* to disentangle.

untapped [ʌnˈtæpt] *adj.* not previously used.

untenable [ʌnˈtenəbl] *adj.* (position/ theory) which cannot be defended.

unthinkable [ʌnˈθɪŋkəbl] *adj.* which cannot be considered or thought of. **unthinking** [ʌnˈθɪŋkɪŋ] *adj.* done without thinking. **unthought-of** *adj.* which no one has thought possible.

untidy [ʌnˈtaɪdɪ] *adj.* (-ier, -iest) not tidy/in disorder. **untidily** *adv.* in an untidy way. **untidiness** *n.* being untidy.

untie [ʌnˈtaɪ] *v.* to unfasten (sth which is tied with a knot).

until [ʌnˈtɪl] *prep. & conj.* (a) up to (a certain time). (b) up to (a certain place).

untimely [ʌnˈtaɪmlɪ] *adj.* (a) happening too soon. (b) not suitable.

unto [ˈʌntʊ] *prep.* (old) to.

untold [ʌnˈtəʊld] *adj.* very large; so large that it cannot be counted.

untouchable 1 [ʌnˈtʌtʃəbl] *adj.* which cannot be touched. **untouchable 2** *n.* person from the lowest caste in India.

untoward [ʌntəˈwɔːd] *adj.* unlucky/ inconvenient; nothing u. took place = everything went off well.

untrained [ʌnˈtreɪnd] *adj.* (person) who has had no training.

untried [ʌnˈtraɪd] *adj.* which has not been tested.

untrue [ʌnˈtruː] *adj.* wrong/not true.

untrustworthy [ʌn'trʌstwɜːði] *adj.* (person) who cannot be trusted.

untruth [ʌn'truːθ] *n.* lie. **untruthful** *adj.* (person) who does not tell the truth; (statement) which is wrong.

unusable [ʌn'juːzəbl] *adj.* which cannot be used. **unused** [ʌn'juːzd] *adj.* (a) new/clean; which has not been used. (b) not accustomed (to).

unusual [ʌn'juːʒʊəl] *adj.* strange/ extraordinarily. **unusually** *adv.* strangely/extraordinarily

unutterable [ʌnʌ'tərəbl] *adj.* so terrible that it cannot be expressed.

unvarnished [ʌn'vɑːnɪʃt] *adj.* with no varnish; plains/simple (truth)

unveil [ʌn'veɪl] *v.* to uncover (a new statue/a new plan. etc.).

unversed [ʌn'vɜːst] *adj.* with no experience (in).

unwanted [ʌn'wɒntɪd] *adj.* which is not wanted.

unwarranted [ʌn'wɒrəntɪd] *adj.* which is not justified.

unwary [ʌn'weərɪ] *adj.* (person) who does not take care.

unwell [ʌn'wel] *adj.* sick/ill.

unwholesome [ʌn'həʊlsəm] *adj.* not healthy/which might harm.

unwieldy [ʌn'wiːldɪ] *adj.* large and awkward.

unwilling [ʌn'wɪlɪŋ] *adj.* reluctant; not willing.

unwind [ʌn'waɪnd] *v.* (unwound) (a) to undo (sth which has been wound). (b) *inf.* to relax.

unwise [ʌn'waɪz] *adj.* rash/imprudent; not wise.

unwitting [ʌn'wɪtɪŋ] *adj.* not knowing/ intending. **unwittingly** *adv.* without intending to; not intentionally.

unwonted [ʌn'wɒntɪd] *adj.* not usual.

unworkable [ʌn'wɜːkəbl] *adj.* (plan) which will not work in practice.

unworthy [ʌn'wɜːði] *adj.* (of) (a) which does not deserve (sth). (b) not as good as one might expect from (a person).

unwound [ʌn'waʊnd] *v.* see unwind.

unwrap [ʌn'ræp] *v.* (unwrapped) to take the wrapping off (sth).

unwritten [ʌn'rɪtən] *adj.* u. law = custom which has grown up over a period f time but which is not written down..

unzip [ʌnzɪp] *v.* (unzipped) to undo a zip fastener.

up 1 [ʌp] *adv.* (a) towards a higher place; hands u.! = lift your hands into the air to show you surrender. (b) in a higher place; this side u. = this side must be on top. (c) to an important town; towards the north. (d) to a higher level. (e) to the end; completely. (f) not in bed. (g) close to. **up 2** *prep.* (a) towards a higher part of (sth). (b) along; towards the source of (a river); to walk up and down = backwards and forwards. **up 3** *adj.* (a) which is going up. (b) which is in a higher position; completely built; the road is all up = being dug up for repairs. (c) not in bed. (d) finished; your time is up = you have to stop now; his leave is up = he has to go back to the army. (e) *inf.* what's up = what is the matter. **up 4** *n.* the ups and downs of business = the good and bad periods. **up 5** *v.* (upped) (a) to raise (prices. etc.). (b) *inf.* to get up suddenly. **up-and-coming** *adj.* (person) who looks as though he might succeed. **up-and-up** *n.* to be on the up-and-up = to be doing well.

upcoming· *adj.* imminent/likely to happen soon.. **up for** *prep.* ready for; up for sale = on sale. **up-market** *adj.* aiming at the expensive end of the market. **up to** *prep* (a) as many as. (b) capable enough to do (sth). (c) it's up to you = it is your responsibility. (d) doing (sth bad). **up to date** *adj. & adv.* modern/using the most recent information etc.

upbraid [ʌp'breɪd] *v.* (formal) to scold.

upbringing ['ʌpbrɪŋɪŋ] *n.* education; training of a child.

update [ʌpdeɪt] *v.* to revise (sth) so that is more up to date.

upend [ʌp'end] *v.* to stand (sth) on its end.

upgrade [ʌp'greɪd] *v.* to put (s.o.) into a more important job; to improve the quality of (sth).

upheaval [ʌp'hiːvəl] *n.* great change/ disturbance.

uphill 1 [ʌp'hɪl] *adj.* going upwards; difficult. **uphill 2** *adv.* upwards.

uphold [ʌp'həʊld] *v.* (upheld) to support; to say that (a decision) is right.

upholster [ʌp'həʊlstə] *v.* to cover (chairs, etc.) with padded seats and covers. **upholsterer** *n.* person who upholsters. **upholstery** *n.* (a) covering chairs. etc. with padded seats and covers. (b) covers for chairs; padded seats and cushions.

upkeep [ʌpˈkiːp] *n.* (cost of) keeping a house/a car. etc. in good order.

upland [ʌplənd] *n.* mountainous area (of a country).

uplift 1 [ˈʌplɪft] *n.* (a) thing which gives a feeling of happiness or goodness. (b) increase/raising. **uplift 2** [ʌpˈlɪft] *v.* to lift up/to raise.

upon [ʌˈpɒn] *prep.* (formal) on; battle u. battle = one battle after another.

upper 1 [ˈʌpə] *adj.* (a) higher. (b) further up. (c) more important; of higher rank; the u. classes = the nobility; (in a school) the u. forms = forms with older pupils; u. case = capital (letters); u. chamber/house = (in UK) House of Lords; (in other countries) senate; to get the u. hand = begin to win. **upper 2** *n.* top part of a shoe. **uppercut** *n.* blow with the first upwards on the chin.

uppermost 1 *adj.* (a) highest (b) furthest up. (c) most important. **uppermost 2** *adv.* what is u. in their minds = the subject they think about most.

uppish, uppity *adj. inf.* feeling superior to other people.

upright 1 [ˈʌpraɪt] *adj.* (a) vertical. (b) very honest. **upright 2** *n.* (a) vertical post. (b) piano with the strings and body vertical. **uprising** [ˈʌpraɪzɪŋ] *n.* revolt (against authority).

uproar [ˈʌprɔː] *n.* loud noise/ disturbance. **uproarious** [ʌpˈrɔːrɪəs] *adj.* noisy.

uproot [ʌpˈruːt] *v.* (a) to dig up (a plant) with its roots. (b) to make (a family) move to a totally new area.

upset 1 [ˈʌpset] *n.* (a) complete change for the worse. (b) great worry/clause of unhappiness. (c) slight illness. (d) (at an auction) u. price = price which an item has to reach before the owner allows it to be sold. **upset 2** [ʌpˈset] *v.* (upset) (a) to knock over; to fall over. (b) to change completely (for the worse). (c) to make (s.o) worried/unhappy. (d) to make (s.o.) slightly ill. **upset 3** [ʌpˈset] *adj.* (a) very worried/unhappy/anxious. (b) made ill.

upshot [ˈʌpʃɒt] *n.* result.

upside down [ˈʌpsaɪdˈdaʊn] *adv.* with the top turned to the bottom.

upstage 1 [ʌpˈsteɪdʒ] *adv.* at the back of the stage. **upsage 2** *v.* (a) to move nearer the front of the stage than (s.o.) (b) to take attention away from (s.o. who feels he ought to have it.).

upstairs 1 [ʌpˈsteəz] *adv.* towards the upper part of a house. **upstairs 2** *adj.* on the upper floors of a house. **upstairs 3** *n.* the upper floors of a house.

upstanding [ʌpˈstændɪŋ] *adj.* strong/ honest.

upstart [ʌpˈstaːt] *n.* inexperienced person who has become unexpectedly important.

upstream [ʌpˈstriːm] *adv. & adj.* (moving) towards the source or a river against the flow of the current.

upsurge [ˈʌpsəːdʒ] *n.* sudden increase (of emotion).

uptake [ˈʌpteɪk] *n.* slow/quick on the u. = slow/quick to understand.

uptight [ˈʌpteɪt] *adj. inf.* nervous and annoyed.

upturn [ˈʌptəːn] *n.* movement upwards (in sales. etc). **upturned** *adj.* (boat, etc.) turned upside down.

upward [ˈʌpwəd] *adj.* moving towards a higher level. **upwards** *adv.* (a) on towards a higher level. (b) on the top. (c) more. **upwards of** *prep.* more than.

uranium [jʊˈreɪnɪəm] *n.* (element: U) radioactive metal used in producing atomic energy.

urban [ˈəːbən] *adj.* (a) referring to towns (b) living in towns. (b) living in towns. **urbanization** *n.* act of urbanizing. **urbanize** *v.* to make (an area) into a town; to make (sth/s.o. from the country) become accustomed to the town. **urbane** [əːˈbeɪn] *adj.* very polite. **urabanity** [əːˈbænɪtɪ] *n.* being urbane.

urchin [ˈəːtʃɪn] *n.* dirty little boy; sea u. = small sea creature with a round shell covered with spikes.

urea [juːˈriːə] *n.* substance produced by the liver and excreted into the urine.

ureter [juːˈriːtə] *n.* tube taking urine from the kidneys to the bladder. **urethra** [juːˈriːθrə] *n.* tube taking urine from the bladder out of the body.

urge 1 [əːdʒ] *n.* strong desire. **urge 2** *v.* (a) to encourage; to push (s.o.) to do sth. (b) to suggest strongly **urgency** ['əːdʒənsɪ] *n.* being urgent; need for sth to be done quickly; what's the u.? = why are you all hurrying? **urgent** *adj.* which needs to be done quickly.

urgently *adv.* quickly/immediately.

urine ['jʊərɪn] *n.* liquid waste matter from the body. **urinal** [jʊəˈraɪnəl] *n.* place where men can pass waste liquid from the body; bowl to catch waste liquid passed from the body **urinary** ['jʊərɪnərɪ] *adj.* referring to urine; (tube) one uses to pass urine; u. system = organs which create and excrete urine.

urinate *v.* to pass waste liquid from the body.

urn [ɜːn] *n.* very large vase; tea u. = large metal container with a tap, in which large quantities of tea can be made.

us [ʌs] *pron.* (a) referring to we. (b) *inf.* referring to I; let us/let's have a go = let me have a go.

US, USA ['juːˈes, ˌjuːesˈeɪ] abbreviations for United States (of America).

use 1 [juːs] *n.* (a) being used; way in which sth is used. (b) ability to be used. (c) usefulness. **use 2** [juːz] *v.* (a) to put to a purpose. (b) to take advantage f (s.o.). (c) *inf.* I could use a beer = I would like a beer. (d) to do sth regularly in the past; she used not to smoke/she did not u. to smoke. **usable** ['juːzəbl] *adj.* which can be used. **usage** ['juːsɪdʒ] *n.* (a) custom; way of dairy things. (b) way of using a word. **used** [juːzd] *adj.* (a) not new; which has been put to a purpose. (b) accustomed (to).

useful ['juːsfəl] *adj.* which helps; to make oneself u. = to do helpful things.

usefully *adv.* in a helpful way.

usefulness *n.* being useful. **useless** ['juːsləs] *adj.* which does not help; *inf.* she is quite u. = of no help at all.

uselessness *n.* being useless. **user** ['juːzə] *n.* person who uses; road u. = person who drives on the road.

userfriendly *adj.* (program/machine) which a user finds easy to use. **use up** *v.* to finish.

usher 1 ['ʌʃə] *n.* person who shows people to their seats (in a theatre/in a church). **usher 2** *v.* to u. in = (i) to bring (s.o.) in; (ii) to be the beginning of.

usherette [ʌʃəˈret] *n.* girl who shows people to their seats in a cinema.

USSR [ˌjuːesesˈɑ] abbreviation for former Union of Soviet Socialist Republics.

usual ['juːʒʊəl] *adj.* ordinary; which happens often. **usually** *adv.* mostly/ ordinarily.

usurer ['juːʒʊrə] *n.* person who lends money for high interest. **usurious** [juːˈʒʊərɪəs] *adj.* excessively high (interest rate). **usury** *n.* lending money for high interest.

usurp [juːˈzɜːp] *v.* to take the place of (s.o.). **usurpation** [juːzɜːˈpeɪʃn] *n.* act of usurping. **usurper** *n.* person who usurps (a throne).

utensil [juːˈtens] *n.* tool/pan/knife, etc., used for work in kitchen.

uterus ['juːtərəs] *n.* part of a female body where an unborn baby is carried. **uterine** ['juːtəraɪn] *adj.* referring to the uterus.

utility [juːˈtɪlɪtɪ] *n.* (a) usefulness; u. van = small van for carrying goods; u. room = room in a house where you put the washing machine/freezer, etc. (b) utilities = essential public services (such as electricity/gas/water. etc.). **utilitarian** [juːtɪlɪˈteərɪən] *adj.* used for a practical purpose, not decoration. **utilizable** [juːtɪlaɪzəbl] *adj.* which can be used. **utilization** [juːtɪlaɪzeɪʃn] *n.* making use of sth. **utilize** ['juːtɪlaɪz] *v.* to use; to make use of (sth) for profit.

utmost ['ʌtməʊst] *adj.* (a) greatest that can be. (b) furthest.

utopia [juːˈtəʊpɪə] *n.* imaginary perfect would. **utopian** *adj.* very perfect (ideas).

utter 1 ['ʌtə] *adj.* complete/total. **utter 2** *v.* to speak; to make (a sound). **utterance** *n.* thing spoken.

utterly *adv.* completely. **uttermost** *adj.* (a) greatest that can be. (b) furthest.

UV ['juːˈviː] abbrev. for ultraviolet.

uvula ['juːvjʊlə] *n.* small lump of flesh hanging down at the back of the mouth.

uxorious [ʌkˈsɔːrɪəs] *adj.* (man) who is very fond of his wife.

Vv

V v [viː] V-neck pullover = one with a neckline shaped like a V; V sign = sign made with two fingers raised in the air (either meaning victory or showing extreme rudeness).

V. ['vɜːsəs] *prep.* against; see versus.

vac [væk] *n. inf.* vacation.

vacancy ['veɪkənsɪ] *n.* (a) being vacant. (b) empty place/room/job.

vacant *adj.* (a) empty/not occupied; to sell a house with v. possession = with no one living in it; situations v. = jobs **vacantly** *adv.* with a vacant expression.

vacate [və'keɪt] *v.* to leave/to make (sth) empty. **vacation 1** [və'keɪʃn] *n.* (a) holiday (esp. in universities and low courts). (b) act of vacating (an office, etc.). **vacation 2** *v. Am.* to go on holiday.

vaccinate ['væksɪneɪt] *v.* to v. s.o. against a disease = to put a vaccine into s.o., that his body will react against it and thus protect him from catching the disease. **vaccination** [væksɪ'neɪʃn] *n.* act of vaccinating. **vaccine** ['væksɪːn] *n.* substance which contains the virus of a disease which when injected, gives protection against the disease.

vacillate ['væsɪleɪt] *v.* to waver/to hesitate. **vacillation** ['væsɪ'leɪʃn] *n.* hesitation/wavering.

vacuous ['vækjʊəs] *adj.* with no meaning/sense; silly/vacant (expression). **vacuity, vacuousness** [və'kjuːɪtɪ] *n.* emptiness of meaning/silliness.

vacuum 1 ['vækjʊəm] *n.* space from which all matter, including air, has been removed; vacuum-packed = (food) packed in vacuum, so that no air can enter the package. **vacuum 2** *v. inf.* to clean with vacuum cleaner. **vacuum cleaner** *n.* cleaning machine which sucks up dust. **vacuum flask** *n.* bottle with double walls to keep liquids warm or cold.

vagabond ['vægəbɒnd] *adj. & n.* (person) who wanders about/who has no home.

vagary ['veɪgərɪ] *n.* oddity/strange behaviour.

vagina ['və'dʒaɪnə] *n.* tube in a female mammal connecting the uterus to the vulva and through which a baby is born. **vaginal** *adj.* referring to the vagina.

vagrant ['veɪgrənt] *adj. & n.* (tramp/person) who wanders from place to place with no home or work. **vagrancy** *n.* being a vagrant.

vague [veɪg] *adj.* (-er, -est) not clear/not precise; I haven't the vaguest idea = I have no idea at all. **vaguely** *adv.* more or less; in a vague way. **vagueness** *n.* being vague.

vain [veɪn] *adj.* (-er, -est) (a) useless; meaningless; (b) very proud of one's appearance; (c) in v.= without any success/result. **vainly** *adv.* with no success/with no result.

valance ['væləns] *n.* short frilled curtain.

vale [veɪl] *n.* (used in names of places) valley.

valediction [vælɪ'dɪkʃn] *n.* (formal) farewell. **valedictory** *adj.* which says farewell

valence, valency ['veɪləns, 'veɪlənsɪ] *n.* (in chemistry) power of an atom to combine.

valentine ['væləntaɪn] *n.* (a) person chosen as a loved one on February 14th (St Valentine's Day).(b) (usu. unsigned) card sent to someone you love on February 14th.

valerian [və'lɪərɪən] *n.* type of wild plant with pink flowers.

valet ['vælet, 'vælɪt] *n.* male servant who looks after his master's clothes; v. service = cleaning service in a hotel.

valetudinarian [vælɪtjuːdɪ'neərɪən] *n.* person who likes to feel he is an invalid.

valiant ['vælɪənt] *adj.* brave. **valiantly** *adv.* bravely.

valid ['vælɪd] *adj.* (a) which is acceptable because it is true. (b) which can be lawfully used for a time. **validate** *v.* to make valid. **validation** [vælɪ'deɪʃn] *n.* act of validating. **validity** [və'lɪdɪtɪ] *n.* (a) legal force. (b) truth.

valley ['vælɪ] *n.* long stretch of low land through which a river runs.

valour, *Am.* **valor** ['vælə] *n.* bravery.

value 1 ['væljuː] *n.* (a) worth (in money or esteem); to get v. for money = to get a good bargain. (b) usefulness. (c) values =

principles/important things in life. **value 2** v. (a) to put a price in money on (an object). (b) to set a high value on (sth). **valuable 1** adj. worth a lot of money; very useful. **valuable 2** n. valuables = objects of great value. **valuation** [væljʊ'eɪʃn] n. estimate of the worth of sth; act of estimating the worth of sth. **value added tax** n. tax imposed on the value of goods or services. **valueless** adj. worthless/with no value which is more than their cost. **valuer** n. person who estimates the value of property. **valve** [vælv] n. (a) mechanical device which allows air/liquid to pass through in one direction only; safety v. = valve which allows gas/steam, etc., to escape if the pressure is too great. (b) flap in a tube in the body which allows air/blood etc., to circulate in one direction only. (c) part of radio/TV set which controls the flow of electricity. (d) part of a brass musical instrument which lengthens the tube. (e) single shell (of a shellfish). **valvular** ['vælvjʊlə] adj. referring to a valve in the heart.

vamp [væmp] n. (a) front part of the upper of a shoe or boot. (b) (old) flirtatious woman. **vampire** [væmpaɪə] n. person who supposedly sucks blood from his victims. **vampire bat** n. type of small bat which sucks blood from animals.

van [væn] n. (a) small vehicle for carrying goods by road or rail; guard's v.= wagon at the end of a train where the guard rides. (b) in the v. = in the front (of a movement/of an attack).

vandal ['vændl] n. person who destroys property for the pleasure of destruction. **vandalism** n. meaningless destruction of property. **vandalize** to smash (sth) for no reason at all.

vane [veɪn] n. one of the blades on a water wheel/pump, etc.

vanguard ['væŋgɑːd] n. front part of an army; in the v.= in the front (of a movement).

vanilla [və'nɪlə] n. flavouring made from the seed pods of a tropical plant.

vanish ['vænɪʃ] v. to disappear/to go out of sight; to v. into thin air = disappear completely. **vanishing cream** n. scented cream rubbed into the skin to make it soft. **vanishing point** n. point in a drawing where the horizontal lines seem to meet at eye level.

vanity ['vænɪtɪ] n. (a) pride/feeling that you are more handsome that you really are. (b) uselessness. **vanity case** n. small bag for carrying makeup/powder, etc.

vanquish ['væŋkwɪʃ] v. to defeat. **vantage point** ['vɑːntɪdʒpɔɪnt] n. place from which you can see well.

vapid ['væpɪd] adj. dull (conversation). **vapidity** [və'pɪdɪtɪ] n. dullness.

vaporize ['veɪpəraɪz] v. to turn into vapour. **vaporization** [veɪpəraɪ'zeɪʃn] n. changing into vapour. vaporizer, n. machine which turns liquids (esp. in water) into vapour. **vapour**, Am. **vapor** n. gas form of a liquid, usu. caused by heating; v. trail = line of white vapour left in the sky by an aircraft.

variability [veərə'bɪlɪtɪ] n. being variable. **variable 1** ['veərɪəbl] adj. which varies/changes all the time. **variable 2** n. thing which varies. **variance** ['veərɪəns] n. to be at v. with = to disagree. **variant** adj. & n. (version/spelling, etc.) which is slightly different. **variation** [veərɪ'eɪʃn] n. (a) act of varying. (b) amount by which sth varies. (c) variations = pieces of music which repeat the same theme but written in a different fashion.

varicella [værɪ'selə] n. chicken pox. **varicoloured** ['vɜːrɪkʌləd] adj. variegated.

varicose vein ['værɪkəʊs'veɪn] n. swollen vein, esp. in the leg.

variegated ['veərɪgeɪtɪd] adj. (plant which is) striped/marked in contrasting colours. **variegation** [veərɪ'geɪʃn] n. irregular marking in contrasting colours.

variety [və'raɪətɪ] n. (a) being of different sorts; for a v. of reasons = for several different reasons. (b) different type (of plant). (c) v. show = entertainment which includes several different types of performer (such as singers/conjurors/ventriloquists, etc).

varietal adj. referring to a variety of plant.

various ['veərɪəs] adj. different/several. **variously** adv. in different ways.

varnish 1 ['vɑːnɪʃ] n. (a) liquid which when painted on sth gives it a shiny surface. (b) shiny surface made by painting with varnish. **varnish 2** v. (a) to paint with a liquid varnish; to give a shiny surface to sth. (b) to cover up (a mistake/disagreement).

vary ['veərɪ] v. (a) to make different; to become different; you ought to v. your diet = eat different sorts of food. (b) to have different views. **varied** adj. of various kinds/different.

vas [væs] n. tube in the body. **vascular** ['væskjələ] adj. referring to veins, etc.,which carry blood or sap.

vase [vɑːs] n. container for cut flowers.

vasectomy [və'sektəmɪ] n. operation on a man to cut the tubes through which sperm flows and so to make him sterile.

vassal ['væsl] n. (a) servant. (b) v. state = country which is under the rule of another.

vast [vɑːst] adj. very large. **vastly** adv. very much. **vastness** n. large size.

vat [væt] n. large container for liquids (esp. wine). **VAT** [væt, viːeɪ'tiː] abbrev. for value Added Tax, government tax on goods or services. **vatman** n. (pl.-men) inf. government inspector dealing with VAT.

vaudeville ['vɔːdəvɪl] n. variety show.

vault 1 [vɔːlt] n. (a) arched stone ceiling. (b) underground room (for keeping things safe). (c) underground room for burying people. (d) high jump; pole v. = leap over a high bar, using a pole to swing you up. **vault 2** v. to jump over (sth) by putting one hand on it to steady yourself. **vaulted** adj. with a stone arch.

vaunt [vɔːnt] v. to boast about (sth).

VD ['viː'diː] abbrev. for venereal disease. **VDU** [viːdiː'juː] abbrev. for visual display unit.

veal [viːl] n. meat from a calf.

vector ['vektə] n. (in mathematics) (a) thing which has both direction and size. (b) insect, etc., which carries disease.

veer ['vɪə] v. to turn.

veg [vedʒ] n. (no pl.) inf. (cooked) vegetable(s).

vegan ['viːgən] adj. & n. (person) who only eats vegetables and fruit.

vegetable ['vedʒɪtəbl] adj. & n. (a) (referring to) plants; the v. kingdom = all

plant life. (b) plant grown for food, not usu. sweet. (c) person who is more less incapable of movement or thought.

vegetarian [vedʒɪ'teərɪən] adj. & n. (person) who does not eat meat; (restaurant) which does not serve meat.

vegetarianism n. belief that not eating meat is good for you. **vegetate** v. to live like a vegetable, not moving or doing anything. **vegetation** [vedʒɪ'teɪʃn] n. (a) act of vegetating. (b) plants.

vehemence ['vɪəməns] n. forceful way (of saying what you think). **vehement** ['vɪəmənt] adj. forceful. **vehemently** adv. in a forceful way.

vehicle ['vɪəkl] n. (a) machine on wheels which travels along the road; rocket which travels in space; commercial v. = one which carries goods. (b) v. for = means of expressing (sth). **vehicular** [vɪ'ɪkjələ] adj. referring to vehicles.

veil 1 [veɪl] n. light cloth which can cover a woman's head or face; to draw a v. over sth = not to mention sth which is wrong/unpleasant; to take the v. = to become a nun. **veil 2** v. to cover with a veil; veiled = half-hidden.

vein [veɪn] n. (a) small tube in the body along which blood runs to the heart. (b) thin line on the leaf of a plant. (c) thin layer of mineral in a rock. (d) mood; in poetic v, = feeling poetic. **veined** adj. covered with veins.

veldt [velt] n. grass-covered plain in South Africa.

vellum ['veləm] n. (a) good quality writing paper. (b) skin of an animal made very thin and used for binding books or writing on.

velocity [və'lɒsɪtɪ] n. speed.

velour [və'lʊə] n. thick, soft cloth with a soft surface like velvet.

velum ['viːləm] n. soft membrane.

velar adj. referring to a soft membrane.

velvet [velvət] adj. & n. (a) cloth (made from silk, etc.) with a soft surface of cut threads; v. lawn = soft and smoothly cut like velvet. (b) soft skin covering a deer's antlers. **velveteen** n. velvet made of cotton. **velvety** adj. with soft surface like velvet.

venal ['viːnəl] adj. (person) who will take a bribe; (act) which is dishonest/

which is done for a bribe. **venality** [vɪ'nælɪtɪ] n. being venal.

vendetta [ven'detə] n. private quarrel between families/persons.

vending ['vendɪŋ] n. selling; v. machine = machine which provides cigarettes/chocolate, etc., when money is put into a slot. **vendor** ['vendə] n. person who sells.

veneer1 [və'nɪə] n. (a) thin layer of expensive wood glued to the surface of ordinary wood. (b) thin layer of politeness/knowledge which covers a person's bad qualities. **veneer 2** v. to cover (wood) with a veneer.

venerate ['venəreɪt] v. to respect greatly. **venerable** adj. very old and likely to be respected. **veneration** [venə'reɪʃn] n. respect; to hold s.o. in v. = to respect s.o. greatly.

venereal [və'nɪərɪəl] adj. (disease) transmitted during sexual intercourse.

venetian blind [və'niːʃn'blaɪnd] n. blind to shut out light, made of horizontal strips of plastic/wood, etc., which can be opened or shut and raised and lowered by pulling a string.

vengeance ['vendʒəns] n. harm caused to s.o. in return for harm they have caused you; inf. with a v. = very strongly.

venial ['viːnɪəl] adj. slight (mistake); (sin) which can be excused. **veniality** [viːnɪ'ælɪtɪ] n. being venial

venison ['venɪzn] n. meat from a deer.

venom ['venəm] n. (a) poison (from a snake, etc.). (b) bitter hatred.

venomous adj. (a) poisonous. (b) bitterly spiteful.

venous ['viːnəs] adj. referring to veins (in the body).

vent 1 [vent] n. (a) hole through which air/gas can escape. (b) slit in the back of a coat. (c) to give v. to = to let (an emotion) come out. **vent 2** v. he vented his anger on her = he made her the target of his anger. **ventilate** ['ventɪleɪt] v. (a) to allow fresh air to come into. (b) to discuss (a question) in the open.

ventilation [ventɪ'leɪʃn] n. (a) bringing in fresh air; v. shaft = tube which allows fresh air to go down into a coal mine. (b) public discussion (of sth). **ventilator** ['ventɪleɪtə] n. opening which allows fresh air to come in; machine which pumps in fresh air.

ventral ['ventrəl] adj. (formal) referring to the abdomen.

ventricle ['ventrɪkl] n. space in the heart which fills up with blood and then pumps it out into the arteries.

ventriloquist [ven'trɪləkwɪst] n. person who can make his voice appear to come from a puppet. **ventriloquism** n. act of being a ventriloquist.

venture 1 ['ventʃə] n. commercial deal which involves risk. **venture 2** v. to dare/to be bold enough to do sth dangerous.

venturesome adj. (person) who dares to take a risk.

venue ['venjuː] n. agreed place where sth will take place.

veracious [və'reɪʃəs] adj. truthful. **veracity** [və'ræsɪtɪ] n. truth.

veranda(h) [və'rændə] n. covered terrace along the side of a house with no outside wall.

verb [vɜːb] n. part of speech which shows how s.o./sth acts or feels. **verbal** adj. (a) referring to a verb. (b) spoken; not written down. **verbalize** v. to express in words. **verbally** adv. in spoken words. **verbatim** [vɜː'beɪtɪm] adj. & adv. word for word; in exactly the same words. **verbena** [vɜː'biːnə] n. type of scented herb, used to make soap or in hot drinks. **verbiage** ['vɜːbɪɪdʒ] n. lot of useless words. **verbose** [vəː'bəʊs] adj. using more words than necessary. **verbosity** [və'bɒsɪtɪ] n. being verbose.

verdant ['vɜːdənt] adj. (formal) green (grass).

verdict ['vɜːdɪkt] n. (a) judgement/ decision by a judge or jury. (b) opinion.

verdigris ['vɜːdɪgrɪs] n. green discolouring of copper, etc. through contact with damp.

verdure ['vɜːdjʊə] n. (formal) green vegetation.

verge1 [vɜːdʒ] n. edge; grass strip along the side of a road; on the v. of = near to. **verge2** v. to v. on = to be near to. **verger** ['vɜːdʒə] n. man who looks after a church.

verify ['verɪfaɪ] v. to check/to see if (a statement) is correct. **verifiable** [verɪ'faɪəbl] adj. which can be verified. **verification** [verɪfɪ'keɪʃn] n. checking that sth is correct.

verily ['verɪlɪ] adv. (old) truly.

verisimilitude [verɪsɪ'mɪlɪtjuːd] *n.* appearance of being true.

veritable ['verɪtəbl] *adj.* true/real.

vermicelli [vɜːmɪ'selɪ] *n.* type of very thin spaghetti.

vermiculite [vɜː'mɪkjuːlaɪt] *n.* grains of silica, used as a growing medium for some types of pot plants.

vermiform [və'mɪfɔːm] *adj.* shaped like a worm.

vermilion [və'mɪlɪən] *adj. n.* bright red (colour).

vermin ['vɜːmɪn] *n.* (a) insects which live on other animals. (b) unwanted animals or birds which are pests. **verminous** *adj.* covered with fleas.

vermouth ['vɜːməθ] *n.* type of strong wine flavoured with herbs.

vernacular [və'nækjʊlə] *adj. & n.* (referring to) the ordinary spoken language of a country or region.

vernal ['vɜːnl] *adj.* (formal) referring to the spring.

veronica [və'rɒnɪkə] *n.* low creeping plant with blue flowers.

verruca [və'ruːkə] *n.* wart.

versatile ['vɜːsətaɪl] *adj.* (person/machine) able to do various things equally well; (musician) who can play many different instruments. **versatility** [vɜːsə'tɪlɪtɪ] *n.* ability to do various things with equal skill.

verse [vɜːs] *n.* (a) group of lines of poetry which form a part of a poem. (b) poetry; lines of writing with a rhythm and sometimes rhyme. (c) one line of a poem. (d) short (numbered) sentence from the Bible; to give chapter and v. for sth = to quote exactly the origin of a statement. **versed** *adj.* well v. in = knowing a lot about/being well skilled in. **versification** [vɜːsɪfɪ'keɪʃn] *n.* making of poetry; way in which a poem is written. **versify** ['vɜːsɪfaɪ] *v.* to write (usu. bad) poetry.

version ['vɜːʃn] *n.* (a) story of what happened as seen from a particular point of view. (b) translation. (c) model (of car, etc.).

verso ['vɜːsəʊ] *n.* left side/back (of a piece of paper/a page of a book, etc.).

versus ['vɜːsəs] *prep.* (usu. written v.) (in a civil court case/in sport) against.

vertebra ['vɜːtɪbrə] *n.* (*pl.*-brae[-briː]) one of the bones which form the spine.

vertebrate ['vɜːtɪbrət] *adj. & n.* (animal) which has a backbone.

vertex ['vɜːteks] *n.* (*pl.*-tices[-tɪsiːz]) top; angle at the top of a triangle.

vertical 1 ['vɜːtɪkl] *adj.* upright.

vertical 2 *n.* upright line (in geometry); out of the v. = leaning at an angle. **vertically** *adv.* straight up/down.

vertigo [vɜː'tɪgəʊ] *n.* dizziness caused by heights. **vertiginous** [vɜː'tɪdʒɪnəs] *adj.* which makes one dizzy.

verve [vɜːv] *n.* enthusiasm/feeling of liveliness.

very 1 ['verɪ] *adv.* (a) to a high degree, v. much the same = almost the same. (b) exactly; the same = exactly the same.

very 2 *adj.* (-ier, -iest) exactly the same/exactly the right (person); at the v. beginning = right at the beginning.

vesicle ['vesɪkl] *n.* small hollow in the body (usu. filled with liquid). **vesicular** [ve'sɪkjʊlə] *adj.* referring to a vesicle.

vespers ['vespəz] *n.* church service in the evening.

vessel ['vesl] *n.* (a) container (for liquid); blood v. = tube which carries blood round the body. (b) ship.

vest [vest] *n.* (a) light undergarment for the top half of the body. (b) *Am.* waistcoat. **vested** *adj.* v. interest = sth which is to s.o.'s advantage, and makes him want to avoid changes, because it is in his interest to keep the present system.

vestibule ['vestɪbjuːl] *n.* entrance hall.

vestige ['vestɪdʒ] *n.* trace/remains.

vestigial [ves'tɪdʒəl] *adj.* which exists as a vestige; v. tail = very small tail.

vestments ['vestmənts] *n. pl.* clergyman's robes.

vestry ['vestrɪ] *n.* clergyman's room in a church.

vet 1 [vet] *n. inf.* veterinary surgeon.

vet 2 *v.* (vetted) to examine carefully.

vetch [vetʃ] *n.* (*pl.*-es) type of wild pea.

veteran 1 ['vetrən] *n.* (a) person who has given long service. (b) old/retired soldier. (c) *Am.* person (not necessarily old) who has served in the armed services. **veteran 2** *adj.* old; experienced; v. car = car made before 1916. **veterinary** ['vetrɪnrɪ] *adj.* referring to the treatment of sick animals; v. surgeon = doctor who specializes in treating sick animals.

veterinarian [vetərɪ'neərɪən] *Am.* veterinary surgeon.

veto 1 ['viːtəʊ] *n.* (*pl.*-os) power to forbid sth. **veto 2** *v.* to forbid.

vex [veks] *v.* to annoy. **vexation** [vek'seɪʃn] *n.* annoyance. **vexatious** [vek'seɪʃəs] *adj.* annoying; v. litigant = person who starts legal actions very often, for no solid reason. **vexed** *adj.* (a) annoyed. (b) (question) which is often discussed but which has not been solved.

VHF [viːeɪtʃ'ef] abbreviation for very high frequency.

via ['vaɪə] *prep.* (travelling) through.

viable ['vaɪəbl] *adj.* (a) able to work in practice. (b) (of new born young) sufficiently developed to survive. **viability** [vaɪə'bɪlɪtɪ] *n.* being viable

viaduct ['vaɪədʌkt] *n.* long bridge carrying a road/railway over a wide valley.

vial ['vaɪəl] *n.* small glass bottle.

viands ['vaɪəndz] *n. pl.* (formal) food.

vibes [vaɪbz] *n. pl. inf.* (a) vibraphone. (b) sensations. **vibrate** [vaɪ'breɪt] *v.* to shudder/to shake. **vibrancy** *n.* being vibrant. **vibrant** ['vaɪbrənt] *adj.* full of (energy). **vibraphone** *n.* instrument like a xylophone with an amplifier. **vibration** [vaɪ'breɪʃn] *n.* act of vibrating; rapid movement. **vibrato** [vɪ'brɑːtəʊ] *n.* (in music) trembling effect. **vibrator** *n.* machine which vibrates. **vibratory** *adj.* which vibrates.

viburnum [vaɪ'bɜːnəm] *n.* common shrub with pink or white flowers.

vicar ['vɪkə] *n.* clergyman in charge of a parish. **vicarage** ['vɪkrɪdʒ] *n.* vicar house.

vicarious [vɪ'keərɪəs] *adj.* felt through imagining what another person feels; (pleasure) felt because you imagine how s.o. is enjoying sth. **vicariously** *adv.* in a vicarious way.

vice [vaɪs] *n.* (a) sexual wickedness/ immorality; v. squad = police department dealing with prostitution, etc. (b) great wickedness. (c) bad habit. (d) tool with jaws that screw tight to hold sth. **vice-like** *adj.* tight like a vice.

vice- [vaɪs] prefix meaning deputy; second in rank. **vice-chancellor** [vaɪs'tʃɑːnsələ] *n.* executive head of a university. **vice-president** [vaɪs'prezɪdənt] *n.* deputy to a president.

viceroy ['vaɪsrɔɪ] *n.* person who represents a king or queen.

viceregal [vaɪs'riːgl] *adj.* referring to viceroy.

vice versa [vaɪsə'vɜːsə] *adv.* the other way round.

vicinity [vɪ'sɪnɪtɪ] *n.* area around sth; in the v. (of) = near (by).

vicious ['vɪʃəs] *adj.* (a) wicked. (b) v. circle = interlocking chain of bad circumstances from which it is impossible to escape. **viciously** *adv.* in a wicked/spiteful way.

vicissitude [vɪ'sɪsɪtjuːd] *n.* (formal) variation in luck.

victim ['vɪktɪm] *n.* person who suffers an attack/an accident. **victimization** [vɪktɪmaɪ'zeɪʃn] *n.* act of victimizing. **victimize** ['vɪktɪmaɪz] *v.* to choose (s.o.) as a victim; to treat s.o. more harshly than others.

victor ['vɪktə] *n.* person who wins (a game/a battle). **Victorian** [vɪk'tɔːrɪən] *adj.* referring to the reign of Queen Victoria (1837 - 1901). **victorious** [vɪk'tɔːrɪəs] *adj.* (person/general) who has won a game/a battle. **victory** ['vɪktrɪ] *n.* win; winning of a battle.

victual 1 ['vɪtl] *n.* victuals = food. **victual 2** *v.* to supply (a ship/an army) with food. **victualler** ['vɪtlə] *n.* licensed v. = innkeeper.

vicuna [vɪ'kjuːnə] *n.* soft wool from a South American animal.

vide ['vɪdeɪ] Latin word meaning see.

video ['vɪdɪəʊ] *adj. & n.* (system) which shows pictures on a television screen. **videocassette** *n.* small cassette containing a videotape.

videodisc *n.* disc which contains recorded sound and pictures. **video-recorder** *n.* machine which records television pictures on tape, so that they can be played back later. **videotape 1** *n.* magnetic tape which can record pictures and sound for playing back through a television set. **videotape 2** *v.* to record (picture/film, etc.) on magnetic tape.

vie [vaɪ] *v.* to v. with s.o. = to rival/to try to beat s.o.

view 1 [vjuː] *n.* (a) scene (which you can see from a certain place). (b) sight/

action of looking at sth; on v.= on show for people to look at. (c) opinion; I share your v. = I agree with your opinion; to take a dim v. of = to disapprove of. (d) in v. of = when you consider. (e) intention/ what you hope to do; with a v. to = planning to. **view 2** *v.* (a) to look at (sth)/to consider (a problem). (b) to watch television; the viewing public = people who watch television. **viewer** *n.* (a) person who watches television. (b) small device for looking at colour slides. **viewfinder** *n.* small window in a camera which you look through when taking a picture, and which shows the exact picture you are about to take. **viewpoint** *n.* way of looking at things/ of considering things.

vigil ['vɪdʒɪl] *n.* keeping awake/on guard all night. **vigilance** *n.* being watchful/on guard. **vigilant** *adj.* watchful/on guard. **vigilante** [vɪdʒɪ'læntɪ] *n.* person who tries to enforce law and order, esp. when the police find it impossible to do so.

vignette [vɪ'njet] *n.* small sketch.

vigour, *Am.* **vigor** ['vɪgə] *n.* energy. **vigorous** *adj.* energetic/very active; strong. **vigorously** *adv.* in a vigorous way.

vile [vaɪl] *adj.* extremely unpleasant/ bad. **vilely** *adv.* in a vile way. **vileness** *n.* being vile. **vilify** ['vɪlɪfaɪ] *v.* to say extremely bad things about (s.o.). **vilification** [vɪlɪfɪ'keɪʃn] *n.* act of vilifying.

villa ['vɪlə] *n.* (a) large country (or seaside) house (usu. in a warm country). (b) suburban house.

village ['vɪlɪdʒ] *n.* small group of houses (usu. with a church) in the country. **villager** *n.* person who lives in a village.

villain ['vɪlən] *n.* wicked person. **villainous** *adj.* wicked. **villainy** *n.* wickedness. **villein** ['vɪleɪn] *n.* medieval agricultural labourer.

vim [vɪm] *n.* energy.

vinaigrette [vɪneɪ'gret] *n.* (a) small bottle of smelling salts. (b) sauce made of oil and vinegar.

vindicate ['vɪndɪkeɪt] *v.* to justify; to show that (s.o.) was right. **vindication** [vɪndɪ'keɪʃn] *n.* (of) proving that sth was right.

vindictive [vɪn'dɪktɪv] *adj.* wanting to take revenge; spiteful. **vindictively** *adv.* spitefully. **vindictiveness** *n.* spite; desire to take revenge.

vine [vaɪn] *n.* (a) climbing plant which bears grapes. (b) climbing plant. **vinegar** ['vɪnɪgə] *n.* liquid made from sour wine/cider, used in cooking and for preserving food. **vinegary** *adj.* (wine, etc.) tasting like vinegar; bad-tempered (person). **vineyard** ['vɪnjəd] *n.* field of vines for producing wine. **vino** ['vi:nəʊ] *n.* Si. cheap wine. **vinous** ['vaɪnəs] *adj.* referring to wine. **vintage** ['vɪntɪdʒ] *n.* (a) collecting of grapes to make wine; grapes which are collected. (b) fine wine made in a particular year; v. wine/v. port = fine/expensive old wine/port. (c) year of make; v. car = one made between 1917 and 1930. (d) of typical high quality. **vintner** ['vɪntnə] *n.* person who sells wine.

vinyl ['vaɪnl] *n.* type of plastic sheet which looks like leather/tiles, etc.

viol [vaɪəl] *n.* early stringed instrument. **viola** [vaɪ'əʊlə] *n.* (a) small pansy-like garden flower. (b) stringed instrument slightly larger than a violin.

violate ['vaɪəleɪt] *v.* (a) to break/to go against (the law/a treaty). (b) (formal) to rape. **violation** [vaɪə'leɪʃn] *n.* act of violating; in v. of an agreement = against the terms of the agreement. **violator** *n.* person who violates

violence ['vaɪələns] *n.* (a) force/ strength. (b) rough action. **violent** *adj.* (a) strong. (b) rough. **violently** *adv.* strongly; roughly.

violet ['vaɪələt] *n. & adj.* (a) small wild plant with bluish purple flowers. (b) bluish purple (colour).

violin [vaɪə'lɪn] *n.* stringed musical instrument played with a bow. **violinist** *n.* person who plays the violin.

violoncello [vaɪələn'tʃeləʊ] *n.* (*pl.*-os) (formal) cello.

VIP [vi:aɪ'pi:] abbreviation for very important person; VIP treatment = being treatment like a very important person.

viper ['vaɪpə] *n.* adder/poisonous snake.

virago [vɪ'rɑ:gəʊ] *n.* (*pl.*-os) fierce loudmouthed woman.

viral ['vaɪrəl] *adj.* referring to a virus.

virement ['vaɪəmənt] *n.* moving money from one area of a budget to another.

virgin 1 ['vɜːdʒɪn] n. (a) person who has never had sexual intercourse. (b) the V. (Mary) = the mother of Jesus Christ. **virgin 2** adj. pure/untouched. **virginal** adj. pure like a virgin. **virginals** n. pl.type of 16th century harpsichord. **virginity** [vəˈdʒɪnɪtɪ] n. being a virgin; to lose your v. = to have sexual intercourse for the first time. **virginia creeper** [vɜːˈdʒɪnɪəˈkriːpə] n. common climbing plant which grows on walls, with leaves which turn bright red in autumn.

Virgo ['vɜːgəʊ] n. one of the signs of the zodiac, shaped like a girl.

virile ['vɪraɪl] adj. manly; masculine. **virility** [vɪˈrɪlɪtɪ] n. being virile; strength; manliness.

virology [vaɪˈrɒlədʒɪ] n. study of viruses. **virologist** n. scientist who studies viruses.

virtual ['vɜːtjʊəl] adj. almost, if not in fact. **virtually** adv. almost.

virtue ['vɜːtjuː] n. (a) particular goodness (of character); good quality. (b) special quality. (c) by v. of = because of. **virtuous** adj. very good/very honest. **virtuously** adv. in a virtuous way. **virtuoso** [vɜːtjʊˈəʊzəʊ] n. (pl.-os/-si[ ]-si]) person who is skilled in an art, esp. who can play a musical instument extremely well. **virtuosity** [vɜːtjʊˈɒsɪtɪ] n. ability to play a musical instrument/sing, etc., extremely well.

virulence ['vɪrjʊləns] n. (of a disease) great strength. **virulent** adj. very bad (attack of disease); very harsh (attack). **virulently** adv. in a virulent way. **virus** ['vaɪrəs] n. (pl.-es) (a) germ which is smaller than bacteria and which causes colds/pneumonia, etc. (b) hidden routine placed in a computer program, which corrupts or destroys files.

visa ['viːzə] n. special mark on a passport/special paper allowing you to enter a country; 30-day v. = visa which allows you to stay in a country for 30 days.

vis-à-vis [viːzəˈviː] prep. (a) in relation to. (b) compared with.

viscera ['vɪsərə] n. organs inside the body, esp. the intestines. **visceral** adj. referring to the viscera.

viscosity [vɪsˈkɒsɪtɪ] n. state of being viscous. **viscose** ['vɪskəʊz] n. man-made silk material, made from viscous cellulose. **viscid, viscous** ['vɪsɪd, 'vɪskəs] adj. thick/sticky (liquid).

viscount ['vaɪkaʊnt] n. title of a nobleman below an earl. **viscountess** n. (pl.-es) wife of a viscount.

vise [vaɪs] n. Am. tool with jaws that screw tight to hold sth. **viselike** adj. Am. tight, as in a vise.

visible ['vɪzɪbl] adj. which can be seen. **visibility** [vɪzɪˈbɪlɪtɪ] n. ability to seen clearly; good v. = ability for things to be seen at long distances because the air is clear. **visibly** adv. obviously; in a way which can be seen.

vision ['vɪʒn] n. (a) ability to see; field of v. = range from one side to another over which you can see clearly; tunnel v. = seeing only the area immediately in front of the eye. (b) ability to look and plan ahead. (c) thing which you imagine; he has visions of himself as Prime Minister = he imagines he will be Prime Minister one day. (d) ghost; strange sight. **visionary 1** adj. idealistic/impracticable (plan). **visionary 2** n. person whose plans are idealistic and impracticable.

visit 1 ['vɪzɪt] n. short stay; to pay a v. to = to go to see (s.o.)/to stay a short time in (a place). **visit 2** v. to stay a short time (in a place/with s.o.); visiting hours = times when you can visit patients in hospital; visiting team = opposing team who has come to play on the home ground. **visitant** n. ghost. **visitation** [vɪzɪˈteɪʃn] n. (a) trouble which is thought to be sent as a divine punishment. (b) official visit. **visitor** ['vɪzɪtə] n. person who visits; summer v. = person/bird which only comes to this country in the summer; prison v. = private person who regularly spends time visiting prisoners and talking to them.

visor ['vaɪzə] n. moveable part of a helmet, which drops down to protect the face; folding shield above the windscreen which protects the driver of a car from bright sunshine.

vista ['vɪstə] n. wide view.

visual ['vɪzjʊəl] adj. referring to what can be seen; v. arts = painting/sculpture, etc. (as opposed to music); v. aids =

slides/films used for teaching purposes.
visualize ['vɪzjʊəlaɪz] v. to picture/to
see (sth) in your mind. **visually** adv. in
a visual way.
vital ['vaɪtl] adj. (a) very important. (b)
vigorous/energetic (person). (c) (organs
in the body) which are essential to life.
vitally adv. in a very important way.
vitality [vaɪ'tælɪtɪ] n. great energy.
vitalize v. to make (sth) more
energetic. **vitals** n. pl.important organs
in a body. **vital statistics** n. (a)
official statistics concerning populations,
births, deaths, etc. (b) inf. measurements
of bust, waist and hips of a woman.
vitamin ['vɪtəmɪn] n. chemical
substance occurring in food which is
important for the development or health
of the human body. **vitaminized**
['vɪtəmɪnaɪzd] adj. with vitamins added.
vitiate ['vɪʃɪeɪt] v. to make bad/to make
weak. **vitiation** [vɪʃɪ'eɪʃn] n. act of
vitiating.
vitreous ['vɪtrɪəs] adj. like glass.
vitrification [vɪtrɪ'keɪʃn] n. act of
vitrifying. **vitrify** ['vɪtrɪfaɪ] v. to make
into glass; to become like glass.
vitriol ['vɪtrɪəl] n. sulphuric acid.
vitriolic [vɪtrɪ'ɒlɪk] adj. very violent/
very rude (attack).
vituperation [vɪtjʊpə'reɪʃn] n.
(formal) abuse; insulting words.
vituperative adj. (formal) insulting/
abusive.
viva (voce) ['varvə ('vəʊsɪ)] n. oral
examination.
vivacious [vɪ'veɪʃɪs] adj. full of life/
full of excitement. **vivaciously** adv. in
a vivacious way. **vivaciousness**,
vivacity [vɪ'væsɪtɪ] n. being vivacious.
vivid ['vɪvɪd] adj. (a) very bright (light/
colour). (b) very lifelike (description);
very lively (imagination). **vividly** adv. in
a vivid way **vividness** n. being vivid.
viviparous [vɪ'vɪpərəs] adj. (animal)
which produces live young (that is,
which does not lay eggs).
vivisection [vɪvɪ'sekʃən] n. operating
on a live animal for the purpose of
scientific research.
vixen ['vɪksn] n. female fox.
viz. [vɪz or 'neɪmlɪ] adv. namely.
vocabulary [və'kæbjʊlərɪ] n. (a) words
used by a person or group of persons. (b)
printed list of words.

vocal 1 ['vəʊkl] adj. referring to the
voice; v. cords = muscles in the throat
which produce sounds. (b) very loud/
insistent (opposition). **vocal 2** n.
pl.vocals = popular songs performed
with a group. **vocalic** [vəʊ'kælɪk] adj.
referring to vowels. **vocalist** n. singer.
vocalize v. to make a sound with your
voice. **vocally** adv. in a loud way.
vocation [və'keɪʃn] n. job which you
feel you have been called to do/for which
you have a special talent; she missed her
v. = she should be in another job for
which she is better suited. **vocational**
adj. referring to a vocation; v. training =
training for a particular job.
vociferate [və'sɪfəreɪt] v. (formal) to
shout protests against sth. **vociferous**
adj. loud/shouting. **vociferously** adv.
loudly.
vodka ['vɒdkə] n. colourless alcohol
made originally in Russia or Poland.
vogue [vəʊg] n. fashion; popularity; in
v. = fashionable.
voice 1 [vɔɪs] n. (a) sounds made by a
person speaking or singing; she's lost her
v. = she can't speak (because of a cold);
in a low v. = quietly; don't raise your v. =
don't talk so loudly. (b) right to express
an opinion. (c) active v./passive v. =
forms of a verb which show whether the
subject is doing sth or having sth done to
it. **voice 2** v. to express (an opinion).
voiceless adj. silent; with no voice.
void 1 [vɔɪd] adj. (a) empty. (b) null
and v. = not valid. **void 2** n. emptiness.
void 3 v. to empty.
voile [vɔɪl] n. very thin cotton or silk
material.
volatile ['vɒlətaɪl] adj. (a) (liquid)
which can easily change into vapour. (b)
(person) who changes his mind/his mood
frequently. **volatility** [vɒlə'tɪlɪtɪ] n.
being volatile. **volatize** v. to make sth
evaporate.
vol-au-vent [vɒlə'vɒn] n. small
pastry case with savoury mixture inside.
volcano [vɒl'keɪnəʊ] n. (pl.-oes)
mountain with a hole on the top through
which lava, ash and gas can come.
volcanic [vɒl'kænɪk] adj. referring to
volcanoes. **volcanology**
[vɒlkə'nɒlədʒɪ] n. volcanology.
vole [vəʊl] n. small animal. resembling
a mouse.

volition [və'lɪʃn] n. (formal) wish/will of one's own v. = because one wants to and not because of one is told to.

volley 1 ['vɒlɪ] n. (a) series of shots/ missiles which are fired/thrown at the same time. (b) (in sport) hitting the ball before it touches the ground. **volley 2** v. (a) to fire several shots/throw several missiles at the same time. (b) (in sport) to hit the ball before it touches the ground. **volleyball** n. team game in which a large ball is thrown across a high net and must not touch the ground.

volt [vɒlt] n. standard unit of electric potential. **voltage** n. amount of electric force. **voltmeter** n. instrument for measuring voltage. **volt face** ['vɒlt'fæs] n. sudden unexpected change of opinion.

voluble ['vɒljʊbl] n. (person) who speaks easily with a lot of words. **volubility** [vɒljʊ'bɪlɪtɪ] n. use of a lot of words. **volubly** adj. with a lot of words.

volume ['vɒlju:m] n. (a) book (esp. one book of a series). (b) space taken up by sth. (c) amount. (d) loudness; **voluminous** [və'lju:mɪnəs] adj. large; taking up a lot of space.

volunteer 1 [vɒlən'tɪə] n. (a) person who offers to do sth without being told to do it. (b) soldier who has joined the army of his own free will. **volunteer 2** v. (a) to offer to do sth; to join the armed services of your own free will. (b) to give (information) without being forced to do so. **voluntarily** adv. freely. **voluntary 1** ['vɒləntrɪ] adj. (a) done of your own free will. (b) done for no payment; v. organization = charity/organization which is organized by voluntary help and not subsidized by the government.

voluntary 2 n. organ v. = solo piece of music played on the organ during or at the beginning or end of a church service

voluptuous [və'lʌptjʊəs] adj. absorbed in/evoking sensual pleasure. **voluptuary** n. person who enjoys sensual pleasure. **voluptuously** adv. in a voluptuous way.

vomit 1 [vɒmɪt] n. food vomited. **vomit 2** v. to bring up food through your mouth when you are sick.

voodoo ['vu:du:] n. witchcraft practised in the West Indies.

voodooism n. belief in voodoo.

voracious [və'reɪʃəs] adj. greedy; wanting to eat a lot; v. reader = person who reads a lot. **voraciously** adv. greedily. **voraciousness, voracity** [vɒ'ræsɪtɪ] n. being voracious.

vortex ['vɔːteks] n. (pl. -tices[ ]-tɪsi:z]) matter which is turning round and round very fast.

votary ['vəʊtrɪ] n. (formal) person who worships/who admires sth fervently.

vote 1 [vəʊt] n. (a) expressing your opinion by marking a paper/by holding up your hand/by speaking. (b) action of voting; to put sth to the v. = to ask people to vote on sth; v. censure = vote criticizing (the government, etc). (c) to v. = the right to vote in an election/to vote on a proposal. **vote 2** v. (a) to express an opinion by making a paper/ by holding up your hand/by speaking. (b) he was voted on to/off the committee = he was elected/was not re-elected a member of the committee.

voter n. person who votes/who has the right to vote; floating v. = person who has not decided which party to vote for in an election.

votive ['vəʊtɪv] adj. (offering) given to fulfil a promise made to a god or to a saint.

vouch [vaʊtʃ] v. to v. for sth = to guarantee sth. **voucher** n. paper which guarantees payment; gift v. = ticket bought from a shop, which you give as a present, and which can be used to buy articles in the shop; luncheon v. = ticket (given by an employer) which can be exchanged for food in a restaurant.

vouchsafe [vaʊtʃseɪf] v. (formal) to ensure/to guarantee (that s.o. has the right to do sth).

vow 1 [vaʊ] n. solemn promise (esp. one sworn to God). **vow 2** v. to make a solemn promise.

vowel ['vaʊəl] n. sound made without using the teeth, tongue or lips; one of the five letters (a, e, i, o, u) which represent these sounds.

voyage 1 ['vɔɪdʒ] n. long journey (esp. by sea). **voyage 2** v. to make a long journey (by sea). **voyager** n. person who voyages.

voyeur [vwɑː'jɜː] n. person who watches people making love.

vulcanize ['vʌlkənaɪz] *v.* to treat rubber with sulphur so that it is made stronger, harder and more elastic. **vulcanite** *n.* vulcanized rubber. **vulcanization** *n.* process of vulcanizing. **vulcanology** [vʌkə'nɒlədʒɪ] *n.* study of volcanoes.

vulgar ['vʌlgə] *adj.* (a) rude/indecent. (b) not in good taste. (c) v. fraction = fraction written as one number above and another below a line. **vulgarian** [vʌl'geərɪən] *n.* vulgar person. **vulgarism** *n.* rude expression. **vulgarity** [vʌl'gærɪtɪ] *n.* rudeness; lack of good taste. **vulgarization** *n.* making common/popular. **vulgarly** *adv.* in a rude/indecent way.

vulnerable ['vʌlnərəbl] *adj.* which can be easily attacked/easily hurt. **vulnerability** [vʌlnərə'bɪlɪtɪ] *n.* being vulnerable.

vulpine ['vʌlpaɪn] *adj.* referring to foxes.

vulture ['vʌltʃə] *n.* large tropical bird that eats mainly dead flesh.

vulva ['vʌlvə] *n.* part of female body around the opening of the vagina.

Ww

wacky ['wækɪ] *adj.* (-ier, -iest) *inf.* crazy/silly.

wad 1 [wɒd] *n.* (a) thick piece of soft material. (b) thick pile of banknotes/papers.(c) inf.thick sandwich. **wad 2** *v.* (wadded) to stuff/to press into a wad. **wadding** *n.* thick, soft material used for lining a coat/quilting/stuffing.

waddle1 ['wɒdl] *n.* walk swaying from side to side like a duck. **waddle 2** *v.* to walk with a waddle.

wade [weɪd] *v.* to walk through deep water or mud; to w. through = to find (a book) difficult to read; to w. into a pile of work = to start dealing with a pile of work vigorously. **wader** *n.* (a) bird which spends most of its time in shallow water or mud. (b) waders = long waterproof boots worn by fishermen.

wafer ['weɪfə] *n.* (a) thin sweet, biscuit eaten with ice creAm. (b) thin disc of bread eaten at communion or mass.

waffle 1 *n.* (a) type of crisp cake cooked in an iron mould and eaten with syrup. (b) unnecessary or muddled speaking/writing. **waffle 2** *v.* to talk too much without saying anything clearly. **waffleiron** *n.* iron mould used for making waffles.

waft 1 [wɒft] *n.* gentle smell. **waft 2** *v.* to carry (sth) gently through the air.

wag 1 [wæg] *n.* (a) movement from side to side or up and down. (b) *inf.* person who likes making jokes/facetious remarks. **wag 2** *v.* (wagged) to move from side to side or up and down. **waggish** *adj.* joking (remark).

wage 1 [weɪdʒ] *n.* (also wages) weekly payment given for work done; w. freeze = period of standstill in wages. **wage 2** *v.* to fight (a war); to w. war (on sth) = to fight against sth. **wage-earner** *n.* person who works for wages.

wager 1 ['weɪdʒə] *n.* bet/money which you promise to pay if sth you expect to happen does not take place. **wager 2** *v.* to bet.

waggle ['wægl] *v.* to move from side to side.

wagon, waggon ['wægn] *n.* (a) fourwheeled vehicle pulled by horses and used for carrying heavy loads. (b) railway truck. (c) *inf.* to be on the w. = to drink only non-alcoholic drinks. **wag(g)oner** *n.* person who drives a wagon.

wagtail ['wægteɪl] *n.* small bird which wags its tail up and down as it walks.

waif [weɪf] *n.* homeless child or animal; waifs and strays = homeless abandoned children or animals.

wail 1 [weɪl] *n.* high-pitched sad cry. **wail 2** *v.* to make a high-pitched mournful cry.

wainscot(ing) ['weɪnzkət(ɪŋ)] *n* wood panelling covering the lower part of a wall in a house. **wainscoted** *adj.* with a wainscot.

waist [weɪst] *n.* (a) narrow part of the body between the chest and the hips. (b) narrow part (of a bottle, etc.).

waistband *n,* band of cloth round the waist of a pair of trousers/skirt.

waistcoat ['weɪskəʊt] *n.* short close-fitting sleeveless garment which goes over a shirt and under a jacket. **waistlline** *n.* measurement around the waist.

wait 1 [weɪt] *n.* act of staying until sth happens or s.o. arrives; to lie in w. for s.o. = to hide waiting for s.o. to pass by in order to attack him. **wait 2** *v.* (a) (for) to stay somewhere until sth happens or s.o./sth arrives. (b) to w. on s.o. = to serve food to s.o. at table. **waiter** *n.* man who serves food to people in a restaurant; head w. = person in charge of other waiters; dumb w. = (i) small table (usu. with wheels) for keeping food on; (ii) lift for carrying food from one floor to another. **waiting-room** *n.* room where travellers wait for their trains/buses, etc./where patients wait to see a doctor, etc. **waiting list** *n.* list of people waiting to see s.o. or do sth. **waitress** *n.* (*pl.*-es) woman who serves food to people in a restaurant. **waits** *n pl.*(old) carol singers. **wait up** *v.* to stay up/not to go to bed.

waive [weɪv] *v.* to give up (a right/a claim). **waiver** *n.* giving up (of a right/ claim).

wake 1 [weɪk] *n.* (a) waves left by a boat, etc., moving through water; in the w. of = immediately behind. (b) staying up all night with a dead body before a funeral. **wake 2** *v.* (woke[wəʊk]; has woken) to stop (s.o) sleeping; to stop sleeping. **wakeful** *adj.* not at all sleepy/not able to go to sleep. **waken** *v.* to stop (s.o.) sleeping. **wakes** *n. pl.*holiday for industrial workers in the North of England. **wake up** *v.* (a) to stop sleeping. (b) to wake up to = to realize. **wakey-wakey** *inter.* used to wake s.o. **waking** *adj.* not asleep.

walk 1 [wɔːk] *n.* (a) journey on foot. (b) way of walking. (c) wide path in a park or garden. (d) w. of life = social position or occupation. **walk 2** *v.* (a) to move along the feet at a normal speed. (b) to accompany (s.o./an animal) on foot. **walk about** *v.* walk among a crowd by an important person. **walker** *n.* person who walks, or who is fond of walking. **walkie-talkie** *n.* portable two-way radio-telephone. **walk in** *v.* to enter. **walk-in** *adj.* (cupboard) which you can walk into. **walking stick** *n.* stick used

to rest on when walking. **walk into** *v.* (a) to entry. (b) to hit by accident. **walk off** *v.* (a) to go away; to walk off with = (i) to win (a prize) easily; (ii) to steal. (b) to walk off your dinner = to go for a walk after a big dinner to help you digest it. **walk on** *v.* (a) to continue walking. (b) to have a non-speaking part in a play. **walk-on** *adj.* (part) in a play where the actor doesn't have to speak. **walk out** *v.* (a) to go out. (b) to leave angrily. (c) to go on strike. (d) to walk out on s.o. = to leave s.o. suddenly. **walkout** *n.* strike of workers. **walk over** *v.* to walk across; to cross (a room) to see s.o./to go up to s.o. **walkover** *n. inf.* easy victory. **walk up** *v.* (a) to climb (on foot). (b) to walk up (to s.o.) = to approach/to go to speak (to s.o.). **walkway** *n.* passage/path where you can walk.

wall [wɔːl] *n.* structure of bricks/stone, etc., forming the side of a room/building, or the boundary of a piece of land; w. painting = mural; to go to the w. = to be defeated; *inf.* he sends me up the w. = he makes me furious. **walled** *adj.* with walls. **wall-eyed** *adj.* (person) who squints badly. **wallflower** *n.* (a) garden flower with a sweet scent. (b) (at a dance) *inf.* woman who is not asked to dance and is left sitting alone. **wall in** *v.* to surround with walls. **wallpaper 1** *n.* decorative paper stuck on the walls of a room. **wallpaper 2** *v.* to stick paper on the walls of (a room). **Wall Street** *n.* American finance centre. **wall-to-wall** *adj.* (carpet) which covers all the floor space of a room. **wall up** *v.* to close/to block with a wall.

wallaby ['wɒləbɪ] *n.* Australian animal like a small kangaroo.

wallet ['wɒlɪt] *n.* small leather case used for holding banknotes in a pocket.

wallop1 ['wɒləp] *n. inf.* (a) hard blow. (b) beer. **wallop2** *v. inf.* to hit hard. **walloping** *adj. inf.* huge.

wallow 1 ['wɒləʊ] *n.* mud hollow where animals can roll. **wallow 2** *v.* (a) (of animals) to roll delightedly around in mud. (b) (of person) to take too much pleasure in.

walnut ['wɒlnʌt] *n.* (a) hard round nut with a wrinkled shell. (b) tree on which walnuts grow. (c) wood from a walnut tree.

walrus ['wɒlrʌs] *n.* (*pl.*-es) Artic animal like a large seal with two long tusks pointing downwards; w. moustache = moustache whose long ends point downwards.

waltz 1 [wɒls] *n.* (*pl.*-es) (a) dance in which a man and woman turn around together as they move forwards. (b) music suitable for such a dance. **waltz 2** *v.* (a) to dance together. (b) *inf.* to walk smoothly/happily.

wan [wɒn] *adj.* pale/looking ill. **wanly** *adv.* in a wan way. **wanness** *n.* being wan.

wand [wɒnd] *n.* slim magic stick.

wander ['wɒndə] *v.* (a) to walk about with no special purpose or direction. (b) to w. off = to walk away from the correct path. (c) to go away from the subject when talking. (d) to be confused because of illness or old age. **wanderer** *n.* person who wanders. **wanderings** *n.* long random journeys. **wanderlust** *n.* passion for going off on journeys and adventures.

wane 1 [weɪn] *n.* the moon is on the w. = appears to be getting smaller; his influence is on the w. = is diminishing. **wane 2** *v.* to appear smaller; to decrease.

wangle 1 ['wæŋgl] *n. inf.* trick/thing dishonestly obtained. **wangle 2** *v. inf.* to get (sth) by a trick. **wangler** *n. inf.* person who gets things by a trick.

want 1 [wɒnt] *n.* (a) state of being without; for w. of sth better = as sth better is not available. (b) desire/wish. (c) wants = things needed. **want 2** *v.* (a) to wish/to desire/to long for. (b) to need/to require.(c) to look for (s.o) to ask him questions. **wanted** *adj.* (a) desired/needed. (b) searched for by the police, *usu.* because of a crime.

wanting *adj.* (a) needing. (b) having very little of sth.

wanton ['wɒntn] *adj.* wild undisciplined.

war [wɔː] *n.* (a) fighting carried on between two or more nations; civil w. = war between two parties in one country; *inf.* he's been in the wars = he looks as though he has had a fight. (b) fight/battle; w. of words = bitter argument.

warcry *n.* loud shout given when going into battle; slogan used in a

political campaign. **war-dance** *n.* dance before the start of a battle.

warfare *n.* fighting a war; type of war.

warhead *n.* explosive top of a missile.

warhorse *n.* (a) heavy, strong horse formerly used for carrying soldiers into battle. (b) old soldier/politician who has seen many battles. **warlike** *adj.* for war; like war. **warlord** *n.* militarty leader who rules part of country.

warmonger *n.* person who wants to start a war. **warpaint** *n.* bright colour put on the face and body before battle to make the enemy afraid. **warpath** *n. inf.* to be on the w. = to be angry and looking for a fight. **warring** *adj.* at war.

warship *n.* armed fighting ship.

wartime *n.* time of war.

warble 1 ['wɔːbl] *n.* trembling song (of a bird). **warble 2** *v.* to sing with a trembling note. **warbler** *n.* type of bird which sings with a trembling note.

ward 1 [wɔːd] *n.* (a) young person in the care of s.o. other than his parents; w. of court = child who is under the protection of the court. (b) large room in a hospital; section of a hospital.(c) part of a town for election purposes. **ward 2** *v.* to w. (sth) off = to keep away.

warden *n.* (a) person in charge of an institution/old people's home/students' hostel, etc. (b) person who looks after a park or forest; traffic w. = person who controls the parking of cars, etc., in town. **warder, wardress** *n.* prison officer/person who guards prisoners.

wardrobe ['wɔːdrəʊb] *n.* (a) large cupboard in which clothes may be hung. (b) a person's clothes. (c) costumes in a theatre; w. mistress = women in charge of the costumes in theatre. **wardroom** [wɔːdrʊm] *n.* general living room of officers on a warship.

ware ['weə] *n.* (a) suffix meaning goods made of a certain material/for a special purpose. (b) *pl.* wares = things that have been made and are for sale.

warehouse 1 ['weəhaʊs] *n.* large building for storing goods. **warehouse 2** *v.* to store (goods) in a large building. **warehouseman** *n.* (*pl.*-men) person who works in a warehouse.

warm 1 [wɔːm] *adj.* (-er, -est) (a) quite hot/pleasantly hot; (in a game) you're getting w. = you're near the right answer.

(b) kind and friendly (welcome). **warm 2** *n.* (a) being/keeping warm; warm place. (b) British w. = man's military style beige overcoat. **warm 3** *v.* to make hot or hotter; to w. to s.o. = to feel more and more friendly towards s.o. **warm-blooded** *adj.* having warm blood. **warm-hearted** *adj.* friendly and welcoming. **warming pan** *n.* metal container in which hot coals were put and which was used to warm beds. **warmly** *adv.* in a warm way. **warmth** *n.* (a) heat/state of being warm. (b) enthusiasm. **warm up** *v.* (a) to heat/to make warm again; to become warm again. (b) to exercise before a game/a contest.

warn [wɔːn] *v.* to tell of possible danger; to inform (s.o.) in advance; to w. s.o. off sth = to advise s.o. not to eat/drink/touch sth. **warning 1** *n.* (a) notice of danger. (b) without w. = suddenly. **warning 2** *adj.* which tells of danger.

warp 1 [wɔːp] *n.* (a) twisting out of shape of a piece of wood. (b) threads running lengthwise in a piece of material.(c) heavy rope used for moving boats along. **warp 2** *v.* (a) to twist out of shape. (b) to make (mind/character) evil.(c) (of boats) to move by pulling on a rope. **warped** *adj.* twisted (wood/character).

warrant 1 ['wɒrənt] *n.* (a) written official paper permitting s.o. to sth. (b) w. officer = highest non-commissioned officer in the army. **warrant 2** *v.* (a) to guarantee/to promise. (b) to justify/to deserve. **warranty** *n.* guarantee/legal document promising that a machine will work, etc.

warren [wɒt] *n.* land with rabbit burrows

warrior ['wɒrɪə] *n.* person who fights in a war.

wart [wɔːt] *n.* small, hard, dark lump on the skin; warts and all = with all faults shown. **warthog** *n.* type of wild African pig.

wary ['weərɪ] *adj.* (-ier, -iest) careful/cautious. **warily** *adv.* cautiously/looking around all the time. **wariness** ['weərɪnəs] *n.* being wary.

was [wɒz] *v.* see be.

wash 1 [wɒʃ] *n.* (pl.-es) (a) act of cleaning with water or another liquid;

inf. it will all come out in the w. = it will all be made clear in due course. (b) clothes which are being washed. (c) movement of the sea or water.(d) waves left behind a boat. (e) thin mixture of liquid; colour w. = thin pale mixture of paint and water. **wash 2** *v.* (a) to clean with water or another liquid. (b) to be able to be washed; inf.to be believable. (c) (of water) to flow past/to touch.(d) to be washed overboard = to be swept off the deck of a ship by a wave. **wash away** *v.* to remove by water. **washable** *adj.* able to be washed. **washbasin** *n.* fixed container, with taps, for holding water for washing the hands and face. **washbowl** *n.* bowl for holding water, but not fixed and with no taps. **wash cloth** *n. Am.* flannel. **washday** *n.* day when the clothes are washed. **wash down** *v.* (a) to clean with a lot of water. (b) to w. down the medicine with a drink of water = to drink water to help swallow the medicine. **washdown** *n.* quick wash all over. **washer** *n.* (a) person who washes. (b) steel or rubber ring inside a tap which prevents water escaping when the tap is turned off. (c) machine for washing.(d) windscreen w. = attachment on a car which squirts water on to the windscreen to clean the glass. **washerwoman** *n.* (pl.-women) woman who washes clothes. **washing** *n.* (a) act of cleaning with water. (b) clothes which are to be washed/which have just been washed. **washing day** *n* day when clothes are washed. **washing machine** *n.* machine for washing clothes. **washing up** *n.* washing of cups/plates/knives and forks, etc., after a meal. **washing up bowl** *n.* bowl or container in which the plates/cups/knives and forks, etc., are washed after a meal. **washleather** *n.* piece of soft leather used for cleaning windows. **wash off** *v.* to clean away with water. **wash out** *v.* (a) to clean/to be cleaned with water. (b) washed out = tired and without energy. (c) the game was washed out = could not be played because of rain. **washout** *n. inf.* (a) useless person. (b) thing that has failed.(c) removal of pollutants by the rain. **washroom** *n.* room where you can wash your hands and use the toilet.

wash stand *n.* (a) (old) table on which a washbowl and jug of water stood in a bedroom. (b) *Am.* fixed bowl, with taps, for holding water for washing the hands and face. **wash up** *v.* (a) to clean with water the cups/plates/knives and forks, etc., used during a meal. (b) *Am.* to wash yourself. (c) (of the sea) to throw (wreckage) on to the shore.

wasp [wɒsp] *n.* striped insect, like a bee. which can sting but which does not make honey; w. waist = (woman's) very slim waist. **WASP** *n. Am.* White Anglo-Saxon Protestant. **waspish** *adj.* irritable/quick-tempered. **waspishly** *adv.* in a waspish way.

wassailing ['wɒseɪlɪŋ] *n.* (old) going from house to house singing Christmas carols.

waste 1 [weɪst] *n.* (a) wild/uncultivated land. (b) unnecessary use (of time/money). (c) rubbish; w. pipe = pipe which takes dirty water from a sink to the drains; w. disposal unit = machine attached to a kitchen sink which grinds up and washes away kitchen rubbish. **waste 2** *v.* (a) to use more than necessary/to use badly. w. not, want not = don't throw anything away. you may need it later. (b) to. w. away = to become thin/to lose weight. **waste 3** *adj.* (a) (of land) uncultivated/not used for any particular purpose; to lay w. = to destroy the crops and houses in an area. esp. in time of war. (b) old and useless; w. paper basket = small container where useless papers can be put. **wastage** *n.* (a) loss; natural w. = reducing numbers of workers by not replacing those who leave. (b) amount lost by waste. **wasteful** *adj.* extravagant/which wastes a lot. **wastefully** *adv.* in an extravagant way. **waster** *n.* (a) person/thing which wastes a lot. (b) wastrel. **wastrel** *n.* person who is useless and idle.

watch 1 [wɒtʃ] *n.* (*pl.*-es) (a) act of looking at s.o./sth; observation. (b) (old) group of people who patrolled a town or village at night. (c) period of duty for sailors on a ship. (d) small clock worn on the arm or carried in a pocket; digital w. = watch which shows the time in numbers (10.27) rather than on a circular dial. **watch 2** *v.* (a) to look at/to observe. (b) to be careful. **watch committee neighbourhood watch** *n.* group of people in a town or village who make sure that people and houses are safe at night. **watchdog** *n.* (a) dog which guards a house or other buildings. (b) person/committee which examines public spending/public morals, etc. **watcher** *n.* person who watches/observes. **watchful** *adj.* very careful. **watchfully** *adv.* very carefully. **watching** *n.* act of looking/observing. **watchmaker** *n.* person who makes and mends clocks and watches. **watchman** *n.* (*pl.*-men) person who guards a building, *usu.* when it is empty. **watchout** *v.* to be careful; to watch out for = to careful to avoid. **watch tower** *n.* tower from the top of which you can see if the enemy is coming. **watchword** *n.* slogan/password.

water 1 ['wɔːtə] *n.* (a) compound of hydrogen and oxygen; liquid that is in rain/rivers/lakes and the sea; drinking w. = water that is safe to drink; hot w. bottle = rubber or stone bottle filled with hot water and used to warm a bed; by w. = on a boat; to be under w. = to be covered by water; to have pipes put from the main water supply to the house; high w. / low w. = high/low tide; to keep your head above w. = (i) to swim with your head out of the water; (ii) to be able to keep out of difficulties; to pass w. = to urinate. (b) waters = large amount of water in a lake/sea; to take the waters = to drink mineral water at a spa. (c) *inf.* w. on the brain = illness where liquid forms on the brain, causing mental deficiency.(d) mixture of water with other substances.(e) (of diamonds/precious stones) brilliance; of the first w. = of the finest quality. **water 2** *v.* (a) to give water to. (b) (down) to add water to (wine or spirits); to make (a statement) less forceful.(c) (of eyes/mouth) to fill with water. (d) (of boats) to take in supplies of drinking water. **water bed** *n.* mattress made of a plastic bag filled with water. **water biscuit** *n.* thin hard biscuit eaten with cheese. **water-boatman** *n.* insect which skims across the surface of lakes/rivers, etc. **waterborne** *adj.* (troops) carried in boats; (disease) carried in water.

waterbrash *n.* bitter liquid which comes up from the stomach into the mouth. **water buffalo** *n.* large Asian animal, with a hump, which is used for farm work. **waterbutt** *n.* barrel for collecting rain water. **water cannon** *n.* machine for sending strong jets of water (for dispersing rioters, etc.). **water closet** *n.* (formal) lavatory. **water colour** *n.* (a) paint used by artists which is mixed with water, not oil. (b) picture painted in watercolours. **watercourse** *n.* path of a stream/ river. **watercress** *n.* creeping plant grown in water and eaten in salads. **watered** *adj.* (silk) with wavy marking in it. **waterfall** *n.* fall of a river, etc., from a high level over the edge of a cliff. **waterfowl** *n. pl.* birds which like to live around ponds and lakes (such as duck/geese, etc.). **waterfront** *n.* bank of river/shore of the sea and the buildings along it. **waterhole** *n.* pond in the desert, where wild animals come to drink. **water ice** *n.* type of light ice cream made of water and flavouring. **watering** *n.* (a) act of giving water. (b) w. down = dilution (of wine or spirits) by adding water. (c) filling of the eyes with water. **watering-can** *n.* container with a long spout used for giving water to plants, etc. **watering hole** *n. inf.* bar where a group of people often get together. **waterless** *adj.* without water. **waterlevel** *n.* level of water. **waterlily** *n.* plant with round leaves and big flowers, growing in water. **waterline** *n.* line where the water reaches on the hull of a ship. **waterlogged** *adj.* very wet/full of water. **Waterloo** *n.inf* to meet one's w. = to have a disaster. **water-main** *n.* principal pipe carrying water underground along a road, and into buildings. **waterman** *n.* (*pl.*-men) man who ferries people in a rowing boat. **watermark** *n.* (a) faint design put in paper to show who made it. (b) mark showing where the tide reaches. **watermeadow** *n.* meadow often flooded by a river. **water-melon** *n.* large juicy fruit with red flesh. **water-mill** *n.* mill driven by the power of water running over a large wheel. **water pistol** *n.* toy gun which squirts water

when the trigger is pressed. **water-polo** *n.* ball game played in water between two teams. **water-power** *n.* power/ energy of running water, used to drive machines. **waterproof 1** *adj.* which will not let water through. **waterproof 2** *n.* coat which will not let water through. **waterproof 3** *v.* to make (sth) waterproof. **water rat** *n.* small mammal living in holes in a river bank. **watershed** *n.* (a) high ground separating different rivers and the streams that run in to them. (b) point where the situation changes permanently. **waterside** *n.* bank of a river/lake/sea; houses which front a river/lake/sea. **waterskier** *n.* person who goes in for waterskiing. **water-skiing** *n.* sport of gliding along the surface of water standing on a pair of skis pulled by a fast boat. **water softener** *n.* chemical/ device for removing the hardness in water. **watersplash** *n.* place where a shallow stream flows over a road. **waterspout** *n.* (a) pipe carrying rainwater away from a roof. (b) tornado at sea when the water rises in a high column. **water supply** *n.* system of pipes/tanks, etc., bringing water to people's homes; amount of water in the system. **water table** *n.* natural level of water below ground. **watertight** *adj.* (a) fitting so tightly that water cannot get in or out. (b) (argument) so strong that it cannot be disproved. **water tower** *n.* tower holding a large tank of water. **water way** *n.* canal or deep river along which boats can safely travel. **waterweed** *n.* weed which grows in water. **waterwheel** *n.* wheel which is turned by water and so makes a machine work. **waterwings** *n.* inflatable rings attached to the arms of children learning to swim. **waterworks** *n.* (a) buildings from which water is piped to houses and factories. (b) *inf.* urinary system; to turn on the w. = to cry. **watery** *adj.* which has a lot of water.

watt [wɒt] *n.* standard unit of electrical power. **wattage** ['wɒtɪdʒ] *n.* amount of electricity in watts.

wattle ['wɒtl] *n.* (a) woven twigs/laths used to make light walls; w. and daub = type of medieval construction consisting of woven strips of wood covered with mud. (b) type of Australian tree. (c) fold of red skin hanging under the throat of some birds (such as turkeys).

wave 1 [weɪv] n. (a) ridge on the surface of the sea. (b) up-and-down movement; she gave me a w. = she waved to me. (c) ridge on the surface; permanent w. = treatment which makes hair wave and curl. (d) sudden feeling (usu. affecting many people); sudden spell (of hot/cold weather). **wave 2** v. (a) to move up and down; to w. to s.o. = to signal to s.o. with the hand; to w. s.o. aside = to dismiss s.o. with a movement of the hand; to w. s.o. on = to tell s.o. to go on by a movement of the hand. (b) to have/to make ridges on the surface. **waveband** n. group of wavelengths which are close together. **waved** adj. (of hair) treated to look wavy. **wavelength** n. distance between similar points on radio waves; inf. they're not on the same w. = they do not understand each other at all. **wavy** adj. (-ier, -iest) which goes up and down. **waver** ['weɪvə] v. (a) to tremble/to move from side to side. (b) to hesitate. **waverer** n. s.o. who hesitates. **wavering** adj. trembling/hesitant.

wax 1 [wæks] n. (a) solid substance made by bees to build the cells of their honeycomb. (b) solid substance similar to this. **wax 2** v. (a) to put polish on (furniture, etc.). (b)(of the moon) to grow bigger. **waxen** adj. pale (like wax). **waxwing** n. small bird with bright marks on its wings. **waxworks** n. exhibition of wax models of famous people. **waxy** adj. (a) like wax. (b) yellowish (potatoes).

way 1 [weɪ] n. (a) road/path; to make your w. through a crowd = to push through a crowd; w. in = entrance; w. out = exit; by the w. = incidentally in passing; by w. of = (i)via; (ii) as a sort of. (b) right direction/right road; to go out of your w. to help s.o. = to make a special effort to help s.o. (c) particular direction; one-way street = street where the traffic can only move in one direction. (d) method/means/manner; she always gets her own w. = she gets what she wants; to have a w. with = know how to amuse and please; I know all his little ways = I know all the odd little things he does; w.

out of a difficulty = solution to a problem. (e) distance (from one place to another); he'll go a long w. he will be very successful. (f) space in which s.o. wants to move. (g) state/condition; in the ordinary w. = usually; out of the w. = unusual; in many ways = in lots of aspects/points; (in) no w. = not at all. (h) progress/movement forwards; under w. = moving forwards; to make your w. in the world = to be successful; to pay your w. = to pay for yourself. **way 2** adv. inf. away/far. **waybill** n. list of goods/passengers carried. **wayfarer** n. (formal) traveller. **waylay** [weɪ'leɪ] v. (waylaid) to wait for (s.o.) in order to attack/to ambush. **waymark** v. to show a public path, using special signs. **way-out** adj. Sl. strange/unusual. **wayside** adj.& n. (referring to the) side of the road. **wayward** adj. (child) who wants to do what he wants. **waywardness** n. being difficult/uncontrollable.

WC ['sʌbljʊ'siː] n. short for water closet.

we [wiː] pron. (a) referring to people who are speaking/to the person speaking and others. (b) inf. you.

weak [wiːk] adj. (-er,-est) (a) not strong in body or in character. (b) (of a liquid) watery/not strong. (c) not good at (a subject). (d) (in grammar) (verb) which forms its past tense using a suffix. **weaken** v. to make/to become weak. **weak-kneed** adj. soft/timid/cowardly. **weakling** n. weak person. **weakly 1** adj. not strong. **weakly 2** adv. not strongly/feebly. **weak-minded** adj. not strong in character. **weakness** n. (a) being weak. (b) inf. liking (for).

weal [wiːl] n. raised mark left on the skin by a blow from a whip or a stick.

wealth [welθ] n. (a) riches. (b) large amount. **wealthy** adj. & n. (-ier, -iest) very rich (person).

wean [wiːn] v. to make (a baby) start to eat solid food after only drinking milk; to w. s.o. off/away from sth = to gets s.o. to drop a (bad) habit.

weapon ['wepən] n. object with which you fight. **weaponry** n. (no pl.) weapons.

wear 1 ['weə] n. (a) act of carrying on your body as a piece of clothing; normal w. and tear = normal use. (b) clothes. (c) damage through much use. (d) ability to stand much use. **wear 2** v. (a) to carry on your body as a piece of clothing. (b) to become damaged through much use. (c) to stand up to much use/to last a long time. (d) to have (an expression) or your face. (f) inf. to accept/to put up with (sth); the boss won't wear it = will never accept this suggestion. **wearable** adj. able to be worn. **wear away, wear down** v. to disappear/to make (sth) disappear by rubbing or much use. **wearer** n. person who wears clothes. **wearing** adj. tiring. **wear off** v. to disappear gradually; to make (sth) disappear. **wear on** v. (of time) to pass **wear out** v. (a) to become useless through much use; to make sth become useless through much use. (b) to wear yourself out/to be worn out = to become tired through doing a lot.

weary 1 ['wɪərɪ] adj. (-ier,-iest) very tired/tiring. **weary 2** v. to become tired/to make tired. **wearily** adv. in a tired way. **weariness** n. tiredness. **wearisome** adj. tiring/boring.

weasel ['wi:zl] n. small animal with a long thin body and short legs, which kills and eats rabbits, etc.

weather 1 ['weðə] n. state of the air and atmosphere at a certain time; in all weathers = in every sort of weather; to make heavy w. of a job = to have unnecessary difficulty in doing the job; under the w. = miserable/unwell. **weather 2** v. (a) (of sea/frost/wind, etc.) to wear down (rocks, etc.). (b) to season (planks of wood); to make (wood) suitable for use by leaving it outside for several years. (c) to survive (a storm/crisis). **weather-beaten** adj. (a) marked by the weather. (b) (of face) tanned/made brown by the wind, rain and sun. **weather boarding** n. overlapping boards of wood used for covering the sides of a building to protect them against bad weather. **weather bureau, weather centre** n. office where the weather is forecast. **weathercock** n. weather vane in the shape of a cock. **weather forecast, weather report** n. description of the weather about to come in the next few hours or days. **weatherman** n. (pl.-men) inf. expert who describes the coming weather, usu. on TV or radio. **weatherproof** adj. able to keep out the wind and the rain. **weather station** n. place where weather conditions are recorded. **weather strip(ping)** n. strip of plastic foam/of metal which is attached to the inside of a window frame to prevent draughts. **weather vane** n. metal pointer on a high building which turns round to show the direction of the wind.

weave 1 [wi:v] n. pattern of cloth; way in which cloth has been woven. **weave 2** v. (wove[wəʊv], has woven) (a) to make cloth by winding threads in and out. (b) to make (sth) by a similar method, using straw, etc. (c) to twist and turn **weaver** n. person who weaves. **weaving** n. action of making cloth by winding threads in and out; inf. to get weaving = to start work.

web [web] n. (a) thing that is woven. (b) net spun by spiders. (c) skin between the toes of a water bird, etc. **webbed** adj. with skin between the toes. **webbing** n. strong tape used in upholstery. **webfooted** adj. with webbed feet.

wed [wed] v. (wedded) (a) (formal) to marry (s.o.); to become husband and wife. (b) to be wedded to an idea = to be firmly attached to an idea. **wedding** n. marriage ceremony; silver/golden w. = anniversary of 25/50 years of marriage; w. breakfast = meal eaten after the wedding ceremony; w. ring = ring which is put on the finger during the wedding ceremony. **wedlock** n. being married.

wedge 1 [wedʒ] n. (a) V-shaped piece of wood/metal, used for splitting wood, thin end of the w. = small beginning which will bring greater changes later. (b) V-shaped piece. **wedge 2** v. (a) to split with a wedge. (b) to fix firmly with a wedge. (c) to become tightly fixed.

Wednesday ['wenzdɪ, 'wedənzdeɪ] n. third day of the week/day between Tuesday and Thursday.

wee 1 [wi:] adj. (in Scotland) very small. **wee 2** v. (child's word) (also wee-wee) urine. **wee 3** v. (child's word) (also wee-wee) to urinate.

weed 1 [wi:d] n. (a) plant that you do not want in garden. (b) (old) weeds = black clothes worn by a widow. (c) inf.

weak person. (d) *inf.* tobacco; *Sl.* marijuana. **weed 2** *v.* (a) to pull out unwanted plants from. (b) to w. out = to remove. **weedkiller** *n.* chemical which kills unwanted plants. **weedy** *adj.* (- ier,-iest) (a) covered with weeds. (b) thin and weak (person).

week [wi:k] *n.* (a) period of seven days. a w. from now/a w. today = this day next week; yesterday w. = a week ago yesterday. (b) part of a seven day period; he works a 35 hour w. = he works 35 hours every week. **weekday** *n.* any day of the week except Sunday (and sometimes Saturday). **weekend** *n.* period from Friday evening or Saturday morning until Sunday evening. **weekly 1** *adv. & adj.* once a week. **weekly 2** *n.* magazine published once a week.

weeny ['wi:nɪ] *adj. inf.* very small.

weep [wi:p] *v.* (wept[wept]) to cry. **weeping** *adj.* (a) crying. (b) (of tree) with branches hanging down.

weevil ['wi:vl] *n.* type of beetle which eats plants, grain, etc.

weft [weft] *n.* threads going across a length of material.

weigh [weɪ] *v.* (a) to measure how heavy sth is. (b) to have a certain heaviness; time weighs heavily on his hands = he has nothing to do. (c) to w. anchor = to lift the anchor of a ship in order to sail away. **weighbridge** *n.* large machine for weighing heavy lorries and their goods. **weigh down** *v.* (a) to press down. (b) to make (s.o.) gloomy. **weigh in** *v.* (of boxers/jockeys) to be weighed before a fight or race. **weighing machine** *n.* device for weighing. **weigh up** *v. inf.* to guess rightly what s.o./sth is like; to weigh up the pross and cons = to examine all the arguments for and against.

weight 1 [weɪt] *n.* (a) heaviness (of sth); to lose/put on w. = to get thinner/ fatter; to pull your w. = to do your best. (b) piece of metal used to measure the exact heaviness of sth else. (c) heavy object; that's a w. off my mind! = I no longer need to worry about that. (d) importance; *inf.* to throw your w. about = to use your authority in an arrogant way. **weight 2** *v.* (a) to attach a weight to (sth). (b) to add (a quantity) to a sum to produce a certain result. **weighting** *n.*

additional salary paid to compensate for living in an expensive area. **weightless** *adj.* with no weight. **weightlessness** *n.* having no weight. **weightlifter** *n.* person who lifts heavy weights as a sport. **weightlifting** *n.* sport of lifting heavy weights. **weighty** *adj.* (-ier, - iest) (a) heavy. (b) important (problem, etc.).

weir ['wɪə] *n.* (a) small dam built across a river to control the flow of water. (b) fence across a lake or river to trap fish.

weird ['wɪəd] *adj.* (-er,-est) strange/odd. **weirdly** *adv.* in a strange way. **weirdness** *n.* being weird. **weirdo** ['wɪədəʊ] *n.* (*pl.*-os) *inf.* strange/odd person; person who behaves in a strange way.

welcome 1 ['welkəm] *n.* greeting/ reception. **welcome 2** *v.* (a) to greet (s.o.) as he arrives. (b) to hear (news) with pleasure. **welcome 3** *adj.* (a) pleasing/received with pleasure. (b) (to) willingly permitted. (c) *Am. inf.* (as a reply to thank you) you're w. = it was pleasure to do it.

weld 1 [weld] *n.* joint made by joining two pieces of metal together by first heating. then pressing. **weld 2** *v.* to join (two pieces of metal) together by first heating, then pressing. **welder** *n.* person/machine that welds metal. **welding** *n.* process of joining two pieces of metal together; place where two pieces are welded.

welfare ['welfeə] *n.* happiness/comfort/ freedom from want; welfare state = state which looks after the health and wellbeing of its citizens; child w. = health and wellbeing of children.

welkin ['welkɪn] *n.* (old) sky.

well 1 [wel] *n.* (a) deep hole at the bottom of which is water or oil. (b) deep holes; space in the centre of a building where the staircase or lift is. (c) low part of a courtroom where clerks. etc., sit.

well 2 *v.* to w. up = to start to flow.

well 3 *adv.* (better, best) (a) in a good way/properly; to do w. = to prosper; to go w. = (i) to be successful/to have good results. (ii) to fit/to suit; to speak w. of = to praise/to say nice things about. (b) to large degree; w. after 7 o'clock = a long time after 7 o'clock; pretty w. all the family = almost all the family to be w. up

in = to know a lot about (a subject). (c) lucky/desirable; you may w. be right = you probably are right; all's w. that ends w. = if the result is fine then every thing is fine; to wish s.o. w. = to wish them good luck. (d) as w. = also/too. **well 4** *adj.* healthy and in good condition. **well 5** *inter.* starting a sentence and meaning nothing in particular or showing surprise. **well-advised** *adj.* wise. **well-appointed** *adj.* luxuriously furnished. **well-balanced** *adj.* steady/ sensible. **well-behaved** *adj.* good/ having good manners. **wellbeing** *n.* health and happiness. **well-born** *adj.* of an aristocratic family. **well-bred** *adj.* polite/well educated. **well-connected** *adj.* with influential friends or family. **well-disposed** *adj.* kindly. **well done** *adj.* (meet) which has been cooked a long time. **well-earned** *adj.* which has been deserved. **wellfounded** *adj.* (fears) which are justified. **well-groomed** *adj.* clean and tidy (person). **well-grounded** *adj.* (fears) which are justified. **well-heeled** *adj. inf.* rich. **well-informed** *adj.* knowing a lot about a subject. **well-intentioned** *adj.* (person) with good intentions. **well-knit** *adj.* strong (body). **well-known** *adj.* famous/known by many people. **well-mannered** *adj.* polite/with good manners. **well-meaning** *adj,* (person) who does sth with good intentions. **well-meant** *adj.* (action) done with good intentions. **wellnigh** *adv.* (formal) almost. **well-off** *adj. inf.* rich. **well-oiled** *adj. Sl.* drunk. **well-read** *adj.* having read many books and therefore knowing a lot. **well-spoken** *adj.* (person) who speaks politely and correctly. **well-timed** *adj.* which happens at the right time. **well-to-do** *adj. inf.* wealthy. **well-wisher** *n.* person who is friendly towards another. **well-worn** *adj.* used a lot.
wellington boots, wellingtons, *inf* wellies ['welɪŋtən'buːts, 'welɪŋtənz, 'welɪz] *n. pl.* rubber waterproof boots.
Welsh 1 [welʃ] *adj.* referring to Wales; W. rarebit = toasted cheese on bread.
Welsh 2 *n.* (a) *pl.*the W. = the people of Wales. (b) language spoken in Wales.
Welsh 3 *v.* to w. = to leave without paying your debts; to w. on s.o.

Welshman, Welshwoman *n.* person from Wales.
welt [welt] *n.* (a) leather edging for attaching the upper part of a shoe to the sole. (b) strong edge to a piece of knitting. (c) weal. **welter** ['weltə] *n.* confused mass. **welterweight** *n.* medium weight in boxing between middle weight and lightweight.
wen [wen] *n* tumour.
wench [wenʃ] *n.* (*pl.*-es) (old) young woman.
wend [wend] *v.* to w. one's way = to go.
went [went] *v.* see go.
wept [wept] *v.* see weep.
were [wɜː] *v.* see be.
werewolf ['wɪəwʊlf] *n* (*pl.*-wolves) person who changes into a wolf.
west 1 [west] *n* (a) one of the points of the compass, the direction in which the sunsets; w. wind = wind coming from the west. (b) the w. = the non-communist world. **west 2** *adv.* towards the west; *inf.* gone w. = broken; disappeared.
westbound *adj.* going towards the west. **West End** *n.* the fashionable part of London, where the main shopping area is found. **westerly** *adj.* (a) (wind) from the west. (b) towards the west. **western 1** *adj.* of the west.
western 2 *n.* novel/film about cowboys and Indians in the USA.
westerner *n.* person who lives in the west. **westernization** *n.* act of westernizing. **westernize** *v.* to make more European or American.
westernmost *adj.* furthest west.
West Indian *n.& adj.* (person) from the West Indies. **Westminister** *n,* borough in London where the Houses of Parliament are situated; Parliament itself. **westward** *adj.* towards the west.
westwards *adv.* towards the west.
wet 1 [wet] *adj.* (wetter,wettest) (a) covered or soaked with water or other liquid; I'm w. through/soaking w. = all my clothes are very wet; *inf.* w. blanket = person who spoils any fun. (b) rainy. (c) *inf.* dull/uninteresting/weak (person).
wet 2 *n.* (a) rain. (b) *inf.* weak/ moderate person. **wet 3** *v.* (wetted) to dampen with water. **wetlands** *n.* marshy areas which are often covered by water. **wetness** *n.* being wet. **wetsuit** *n.* suit worn by divers which keeps the

body warm with a layer of warm water.
wetting *n.* soaking/getting wet.
wether [weðə] *n.* castrated ram.
whack1 [wæk] *n.* (a) hard. noisy blow.
(b) *inf.* let's have a w. at it ! = let's try to
do it. **whack 2** *v.* (a) to hit hard,
making a loud noise. (b) to defeat (in a
match). **whacked** *adj.* (a) beaten. (b)
inf. worn out/tired. **whacker,** *n. inf.*
huge thing. **whacking 1** *adj. inf.* huge.
whacking 2 *n.* beating.
whale [weɪl] *n.* (a) huge sea mammal.
(b) *inf.* we had a w. of a time = we
enjoyed ourselves very much.
whaleboat *n.* boat used when hunting
whales. **whalebone** *n.* thin bone taken
from the jaws of whales and formerly
used in corsets. **whaler** *n.* (a) boat
used when hunting whales. (b) person
who hunts whales. **whaling** *n.* hunting
of whales.
wharf [wɔːf] *n.* (*pl.*wharfs/
wharves)[wɔːvz] place in a dock where a
ship can tie up and load or unload.
wharfinger *n.* person who is in charge
of wharf.
what 1 [wɒt] *adj.* (a) that which. (b)
(asking a question) which? w. good is
this to us? = what is the use of this? (c)
(showing surprise) how much/how great/
how strange. **what 2** *pron.* (a) that
which; come w. may = whatever
happens. (b) (asking a question) which
thing or things; w. is the German for
table? = which is the German word
meaning table? What's is the use of
learning Latin? = why learn Latin? w.
about stopping for lunch now? = do you
think we should stop for lunch now? w.
did you say?/(not polite) w. ? = I didn't
hear what you said, please say it again;
w. if ? = what will happen if; he knows
what's w. = he knows what the situation
is and what to do. **what 3** *inter.*
showing surprise. **what's-it, what-
d'you-call-it** *n. inf.* thing of which you
have forgotten the name for the moment.
whatever 1 [wɒ'evə] *pron.* anything at
all. **whatever 2** *adj.* (a) (strong form
of what). (b) none w. = none at all. **what
for** *pron* (a)why. (b) what is the
purpose of. (c) inf.to give s.o. what for =
to be angry with s.o. **what not** *n.* (a)
vague object/idea. (b) wooden stand with
shelves for small books and ornaments.

whatsoever [wɒtsəʊ'evə] *adj.& pron.*
(strong form of whatever) none w. =
none at all.
wheat [wiːt] *n.* cereal plant. **wheatear**
n. brown bird living in fields. **wheaten**
adj. made of wheat. **wheatgerm** *n.*
central part of a grain of wheat.
wheatmeal *n.* brown flour containing
most of the grain. **wheatsheaf** *n.* large
bundle of stalks of wheat bound together.
wheedle [wiːdl] *v.* to ask s.o. for sth in
a flattering way.
wheel 1 [wiːl] *n.* (a) circular frame
which turns around a central axis (as a
support for cars/trains/bicycles, etc.). (b)
any similar circular object; steering w. =
wheel which the driver of a car holds and
turns to follow the road; to take the w. =
to drive; potter's w. = horizontal disc on
which a potter throws the clay to make
pottery. **wheel 2** *v.* (a) to push along
(sth) that has wheels. (b) to w. round = to
turn around suddenly. (c) (in army) to
change direction; left w. ! = turn left ! (d)
to fly in circles. gulls wheeling above the
boats. (e) to w. and deal = to negotiate to
obtain concessions in business.
wheelbarrow *n.* small handcart used
by builders and gardeners, which has
one wheel in front, and two handles
behind. **wheelbase** *n.* distance
between the front and rear axles of a car/
lorry, etc. **wheelchair** *n.* chair on
wheels used by people who cannot walk.
wheeler-dealer *n.* businessman who
lives by making deals. **wheelwright** *n.*
man who makes wheels.
wheeze 1 [wiːz] *n.* (a) noisy breathing.
(b) *inf.* clever trick. **wheeze 2** *v.* to
breathe noisily and with difficulty.
wheezily *adv.* in a wheezy way.
wheeziness *n.* being wheezy.
wheezy *adj.* (person) who wheezes.
whelk [welk] *n.* type of edible sea snail.
whelp 1 [welp] *n.* young of a dog.
whelp 2 *v.* to give birth to a young
dog.
when 1 [wen] *adv.* (asking a question)
at what time. **when 2** *conj.* (a) at the
time that. (b) if. **whenever** [we'nevə]
adv. at any time that.
whence [wens] *adv* (formal) from
where.
where 1 ['weə] *adv.* (asking a question)
in/at/to what place? **where 2** *adv.* in

the place. **whereabouts 1** ['weərbaʊts] *n. pl.*place where s.o./sth is.
whereabouts 2 [weərə'baʊts] *adv.* in what place? **whereas** [weər'æz] *conj.* on the other hand/while/in contrast with the fact that. **whereby** [wɜə'baɪ] *adv.* (formal) by which; according to which. **wherefore** *conj.& adv.* (old) why. **wherein** [wɜər'ɪn] *adv.* (formal) in which. **whereupon** [weərə'pɒn] *conj.* at that point/after that. **wherever** [weər'evə] *adv.* in every place. **wherewithal** *n.* (formal) necessary money.
wherry ['werɪ] *n.* small rowing boat.
whet [wet] *v.* (whetted) (a) to sharpen (a knife). (b) to w. your appetite = to make you more interested in sth by giving you a little taste of it. **whetstone** *n.* stone used to sharpen knives, etc.
whether ['weðə] *conj.* (a) if. (b) either.
whey [weɪ] *n.* liquid left when milk is made into cheese.
which 1 [wɪtʃ] *adj.* what (person/thing). **which 2** *pron.* (a) asking a question what person/what thing. (b) (only used with things not person) that/the thing that. **whichever** *pron.& adj.* (a) anything that. (b) no matter which.
whiff [wɪf] *n.* slight smell.
while 1 [waɪl] *n.* length of time; quite a w./a good w. = a fairly long time; once in a w. = from time to time. (b) to be worth w. = to be worth doing. **while 2** *v.* to w. away the time = to make the time pass while you are waiting for something.
while 3 *conj.* (a) during/as long as. (b) although.(c) where as/in contrast with.
whilst [waɪlst] *conj.* while.
whim [wɪm] *n.* sudden wish or desire.
whimsical ['wɪmzɪkl] *adj.* odd/fanciful. **whimsicality** *n.* being whimsical. **whimsy** *n.* strange/fanciful idea.
whimper 1 ['wɪmpə] *n.* sad/weak cry.
whimper 2 *v.* (of small dogs) to cry weakly.
whine 1 [waɪn] *n.* complaint/moan.
whine 2 *v.* to moan/to complain in a long high voice.
whinge [wɪndʒ] *v. inf.* to complain in a whining voice.
whinny 1 ['wɪnɪ] *n.* sound which a horse makes when pleased. **whinny 2** *v.* (of a horse) to make a happy neigh.

whip 1 [wɪp] *n.* (a) long, thin piece of leather fixed to a handle and used for hitting animals. (b) party w. = member of parliament whose job it is to keep order among members of his party. (c) instructions given by a party whip; three line w. = the strictest instructions. (d) instant w. = sweet milk pudding made quickly by adding milk to a packet of powder. **whip 2** *v.* (whipped) (a) to hit with a whip. (b) to beat sharply. (c) to beat (cream) until it is firm.(d) to wind string round (the end of a piece of rope). (e) inf.to move quickly; to w. out a gum = to pull a gun out quickly. **whipcord** *n.* type of corduroy. **whiphand** *n.* advantage. **whiplash** *n.* (a) piece of thin leather which is part of a whip. (b) neck injury, caused by the head moving back suddenly. **whip off** *v.* to move quickly; to remove quickly.
whippersnapper *n.* boy/young man who is too sure of himself. **whipping** *n.* beating **whip round** *v.* to turn round quickly. **whipround** *n. inf.* to have a whip-round = to ask everyone to give some money. **whip up** *v.* to encourage/to make (sth) increase. **whippet** ['wɪpɪt] *n.* breed of small thin do trained for racing.
whirl1 [wɜːl] *n.* (a) rapid turning movement. (b) giddy/dizzy feeling.
whirl 2 *v.* (a) to turn round quickly/to spin. (b) to move quickly. **whirligig** *n.* something which turns round rapidly (like a top). **whirlpool** *n.* water which turns rapidly round and round.
whirlwind *n.* (a) wind blowing round and round in a circle. (b) confused rush; w. engagement = very rapid engagement before marriage.
whirr, Am. whir 1 [wɜː] *n.* noise of sth spinning round quickly. **whirr, Am. whir 2** *v.* to make a spinning noise.
whisk 1 [wɪsk] *n.* (a) swift movement. (b) light brush for removing dust. (c) kitchen utensil used for beating eggs/cream, etc. **whisk 2** *v.* (a) to move quickly. (b) to beat (eggs/cream) very quickly.
whisker ['wɪskə] *n.* (a) long stiff hair at the side of an animal's mouth. (b) whiskers = moustache and beard on the side of a man's face. **whiskery** *adj.* covered with whiskers.

whisky ['wɪskɪ] n. alcoholic drink (usu.made in Scotland), distilled from grain; glass of this drink. **whiskey** ['wɪskɪ] n. whisky (made in Ireland and North America).

whisper 1 ['wɪspə] n. (a) quiet sound/ words quietly spoken. (b) rumour.

whisper 2 v. (a) to speak very quietly. (b) to make a very quiet sound.

whist [wɪst] n. card game for four people; w. drive = competition of several games of whist played at the same time in a large room.

whistle1 ['wɪsl] n. (a) simple instrument played by blowing; penny w. /tin w. = cheap metal flute. (b) small pipe which gives a loud shrill noise when blown.(c) musical sound made by almost closing the lips and blowing air through the small hole; to wet one's w. = to have a drink. **whistle 2** v. (a) to blow through the lips and make a musical or shrill sound; inf. you can w. for it = you will never get it. (b) to make a shrill sound. **whistlestop tour** n. Am. election tour where a candidate stops for a brief period in many different towns. **whistle up** v. to create (sth) out of nothing.

whit [wɪt] n. very small amount; not a w. more = nothing more. **Whit** [wɪt] adj. referring to Whitsun.

white 1 [waɪt] adj. (-er, -est) colour of snow; w. coffee = coffee with milk; white Christmas = Christmas with snow on the ground. **white 2** n. (a) colour of snow. (b) person whose skin is not black, brown, yellow or red. (c) light-coloured meat (on a chicken); w. of an egg = part of the egg which is not yellow. **white ant** n. termite **whitebait** n. (pl.whitebait) small young fish eaten fried. **whitecollar worker** n. office worker. **white elephant** n. thing which is big and expensive but useless to its owner. **white ensign** n. flag of the Royal Navy. **white flag** n. symbol of surrender. **white goods** n. households linen (sheets, pillowcases, etc.); household machines, such as refrigerators and washing machines, which are usually white. **white-haired** adj. with white hair. **Whitehall** n. inf. British Civil Service; W. mandarins = top civil servants. **white heat** n. very

high temperature, when white light is produced by heated metal. **white hot** adj. extremely hot. **White House** n. house of the President of the USA; inf. the US government. **white knight** n. person/company which rescues another threatened with a takeover. **white lie** n. innocent lie. **whiten** v. to make white. **whitener, whitening** n. white liquid for making shoes, etc., white. **whiteness** n. being white. **white out** n. blinding conditions caused by wind and snow. **White Paper** n. government report on a problem. **white sale** n. sale of sheets/pillowcases, etc. **white slave** n. white girl captured and sent abroad as a prostitute. **white slavery** n. trade in white slaves. **white spirit** n. turpentine substitute used for cleaning paint-brushes, etc. **whitewash 1** n (a) mixture of water and lime used for painting the walls of houses. (b) attempt to cover up (mistakes). **whitewash 2** v. (a) to paint with a mixture of water and lime. (b) to attempt to cover up (mistakes). **whitewood** n. unpainted soft wood, such as pine. **whitish** adj. quite white.

whither ['wɪðə] adv. (formal) to which place.

whiting ['waɪtɪŋ] n. (pl.whiting) type of small sea fish.

whitlow ['wɪtləʊ] n. infected spot near a nail.

Whitsun ['wɪtsən] n. Christian festival on the seventh Sunday after Easter.

whittle ['wɪtl] v. (a) to shape (a piece of wood) by cutting off small pieces with a knife. (b) to w. sth away/down = to make sth gradually smaller.

whiz [wɪz] v. (whizzed) to move very fast. **whiz-kid** n. inf. brilliant young businessman.

who [hu:] pron. (asking a question) which person/which people? (b) the person/people that. **whodunit** [hu:dʌnɪt] n. inf. detective story. **whoever** pron. (a) anyone who/no matter who. **WHO** abbrev. for World Health Organization.

whoa [wəʊ] inter. used to tell a horse to stand still.

whole 1 [həʊl] adj. complete; not broken/not damaged; he ate the w. cake = he ate all the cake; he ate the cake w. =

he put it all in his mouth at once and ate it, without cutting it up. **whole 2** *n.* all; as a w. = altogether; on the w. = for the most part. **wholefood** *n.* food, grown naturally, which has not been given artificial fertilizers, and has not been processed. **wholehearted** *adj.* complete/total. **wholeheartedly** *adv.* completely/totally. **whole life insurance** *n.* insurance where a sum of money is paid when the insured person dies. **wholemeal** *n.* brown flour containing all parts of the grain. **whole number** *n.* number which is not a fraction. **wholesale 1** *n. & adj.* sale of goods in large quantities to shops which then sell them to people in small quantities. **wholesale 2** *adj.* in a large quantities/on a large scale. **wholesaler** *n.* person who buys and sells goods in large quantities. **wholesome** ['həʊsəm] *adj.* healthy/good; w. food = food that is good for your health. **wholesomeness** *n.* being wholesome. **wholewheat** *n.* brown flour containing all the grain.

wholly *adv.* completely/altogether.

whom [huːm] *pron.* (a) (formal) (object in questions) which person/which persons. (b) (object in statements) the person/persons that.

whoop [wuːp] *n.* loud cry. **whoopee** [wʊˈpiː] *inter.* showing excitement; to make w. = to enjoy yourself noisily.

whooping cough ['huːpɪŋkɒf] *n.* children's illness which causes coughing and loud noises when the child tries to breathe. **whoops** *inter.* showing surprise.

whoosh [wuːʃ] *n.* sound of air blowing past.

whopper ['wɒpə] *n. inf.* (a) very large thing. (b) very big lie. **whoopping,** *adj. inf.* very large.

whore ['hɔː] *n.* (formal) prostitute.

whorl [wɜːl] *n.* coiled/spiral shape.

whose [huːz] *pron.* (a) (asking a question) of who. (b) belonging to who.

whosoever [huːsəʊˈevə] *pron.* whoever.

why 1 [waɪ] *adv.* (asking a question) for what reason. **why 2** *n.* the reason. **why 3** *inter.* showing surprise.

wick [wɪk] *n.* length of string in the middle of a candle/piece of material in an oil lamp which is lit and burns slowly.

wicked ['wɪkɪd] *adj.* very bad/very nasty. **wickedly** *adv.* in a wicked way. **wickedness** *n.* evil; being wicked.

wicker ['wɪkə] *n.* thin twigs used to make chairs or baskets. **wickerwork** *n.* (no *pl.*) objects made of thin twigs woven together.

wicket ['wɪkɪt] *n.* (a) small door set in or next to a larger one (as in a castle gate or city wall). (b) *Am.* position on the counter in a post office/bank, etc. (c) (in cricket) set of three sticks put in the ground and used as the target; main playing area between two sets of these sticks; slow/fast w. = where the ball moves slowly/fast off the ground; *inf.* a sticky w. = an awkward/difficult situation. **wicket-keeper** *n.* (in cricket) player standing behind the wicket to stop the balls that the batsman does not hit.

wide 1 [waɪd] *adj.* (-er, -est) (a) stretching far from side to side. (b) measurement from side to side. (c) enormous (range). **wide 2** *adv.* (a) greatly/a long way apart/fast. (b) to fall w. of the target = miss the target. **wide 3** *n.* (in cricket) ball which passes too far to the side of the wicket. **wide-angle** *adj.* (lens) which takes in a wider area than an ordinary lens. **wide awake** *adj.* very much awake/not at all sleepy.

widely *adv.* (a) greatly; w. read = (i) (book) which many people have read; (ii) (person) who has read many books. **widen** *v.* to make larger/to become wide. **wide-ranging** *adj.* (discussion) which covers a wide field to subjects. **wide-spread** *adj.* far/over a large area.

widgeon ['wɪdʒn] *n.* (*pl.* widgeon) type of small wild duck.

widow ['wɪdəʊ] *n.* woman whose husband has died; grass w. = woman whose husband is away from home on business. **widowed** *adj* (woman) who has become a widow; (man) who has become a widower. **widower** *n.* man whose wife has died; grass w. = man whose wife is away from home on business. **widowhood** *n.* being a widow.

width [wɪdθ] *n.* (a) measurement from side to side. (b) piece of material (cut right across a roll).

wield ['wi:ld] v. (a) to hold (sth) *usu.* by the handle, and use it. (b) to use/to control (power)

wiener ['wi:nə] n. *Am.* frankfurter. **wiener schnitzel** n veal escalope, fried in breadcrumbs.

wife [waɪf] n. (*pl.*wives) woman to whom a man is married. **wifely** adj. like a wife.

wig [wɪg] n. false hair worn on the head. **wigging** n. (old) *inf.* sharp rebuke.

wiggle ['wɪgl] v. *inf.* to move slightly up and down or from side to side. **wiggly** adj. *inf.* wavy; (line) which goes up and down

wigwam ['wɪgwæm] n. cone-shaped tent of the North American Indians.

wild 1 [waɪld] adj. (-er, -est) (a) not tame/free to live naturally. (b) (plant) which is not a garden plant. (c) stormy/ rough (sea/wind). (d) savage/angry/fierce (animal); *inf.* to be w. with s.o. = to be angry with s.o.; to be w. with excitement = to be over-excited; *inf.* w. about = very enthusiastic about. (e) rough/uncivilized (country). (f) rash/reckless (plan); badly aimed (shot). **wild 2** n. in the w. = in country which is uninhabited and where animals can live freely. **wildcat 1** n. small wild animal of the cat family. **wildcat 2** adj. risky/reckless; w. strike = unofficial strike/strike of workers without the union's permission. **wilderness** ['wɪldənəs] n. uncultivated/uninhabited country; desert. **wildfire** n. like w. = very quickly. **wildfowl** n. *pl.*wild birds shot for sport (such as ducks and geese). **wildfowler** n. person who shoots wildfowl. **wild goose chase** n. hopeless search. **wildlife** n. (no *pl.*) birds/plants/animals living free, untouched by man; w. park = park where wild animals are allowed to run wild. **wildly** adv. in a wild way; w. inaccurate = completely wrong. **wildness** n. being wild. **wildebeest** ['wɪldɪbri:st] n. large African antelope.

wiles [waɪlz] n. *pl.*clever tricks.

wilful ['wɪlfəl] adj. (a) (person) determined to do what he wants. (b) done on purpose; w. murder = murder which was planned. **wilfully** adv. intentionally/on purpose.

will 1 [wɪl] n. (a) strength of mind and character; to work with a w. = to work very hard and earnestly. (b) wish; of one's own free w. = not forced; at w. = as you wish. (c) written instructions made by s.o. as to what should happen to his belongings when he dies. **will 2** v. (a) to w. s.o. to do sth = to suggest strongly to s.o. else by power of mind. (b) to leave (your belongings) after death to others by writing down your wishes. **will 3** v. (used with an infinitive) (a) to wish; I won't have it! = I will not allow it. (b) (polite form of asking someone to do something) would you please sit down?/ won't you sit down? (c) (stressed) to be certain to happen. **will 4** used with verbs forming future tense. **willing 1** adj. wanting (to do sth); eager (to help). **willing 2** n. eagerness to help; to show w. = to show you are ready to help. **willingly** adv. eagerly. **willingness** n. eagerness. **willpower** n. strength of will.

willies ['wɪlɪz] n. *pl.inf.* it gives me the w. = it makes me scared.

will-o'-the-wisp ['wɪləðəwɪsp] n. bluish light caused in marshes by burning methane gas.

willow ['wɪləʊ] n. tree with thin supple branches often found along river banks. **willowherb** n. common weed with tall spikes of pink flowers. **willow pattern** n. china with a blue and white Chinese design on it. **willowy** adj. tall and slender.

willy-nilly [wɪlɪ'nɪlɪ] adv. whether you want to or not.

wilt 1 [wɪlt] n. disease of plants which makes them droop **wilt 2** v. to become weak and droop.

wily [waɪlɪ] adj. (-ier, -iest) crafty/full of tricks. **wiliness** n. being wily.

wimp [wɪmp] n. weak individual.

wimple ['wɪmpl] n. linen covering worn by nuns over their heads.

win 1 [wɪn] n. action of beating s.o. in a competition/game. **win 2** v. (won[wʌn]) (a) to defeat s.o. in a contest/race, etc; to be first in a race/competition. (b) to gain/to get (a prize). **win back** v. to get back/to regain. **winner** n. (a) person who has won a race/prize, etc. (b) *inf.* thing which is (certain to be) successful. **winning 1** adj. (a) which wins. (b) attractive (smile). **winning 2** n. (a) victory; w. post = post which marks the end of the race. (b) winnings = money etc., which has been won at a game of chance. **win over** v. to persuade. **win through** v. to succeed in the end after many difficulties.

wince1 [wɪns] n. movement which shows you feel pain. **wince 2** v. to show signs of pain, esp. by moving the face.

winceyette [wɪnsɪ'et] n. soft cotton material, often used for night clothes.

winch 1 [wɪnʃ] n. (pl.-es) device which pull things up by winding a rope around a drum. **winch 2** v. to pull up/to lift by using a winch.

wind 1 1 [wɪnd] n. (a) moving air; in high winds = in very strong winds; head w. = wind blowing straight towards the face; in the teeth of the w. = against the wind; inf. to go like the w. = to run quickly; inf. to get/to have the w. up = to be frightened; inf. to put the w. up s.o. = to frighten s.o.; to sail close to the w. = (i) to sail a boat almost directly into the wind; (ii) to be very near to being dishonest or rude; to take the w. out of s.o.'s sails = to spoil s.o.'s plans, usually by doing what he was going to do. (b) breath; to get your second w. = to get enough breath again after being tired; to be able to make a second effort. (c) smell/scent, when hunting; to get w. of = to hear a rumour about. (d) gas in the stomach. (e) (also wind instruments, wind section) woodwind instruments in an orchestra. **wind 1 2** v. (a) make (s.o.) breathless, esp. by hitting him in the chest. (b) to smell/scent when hunting. **windbag** n. inf. person who talks too much. **windbreak** n. fence/hedge which protects sth against the wind. **windburn** n. inflammation of the skin caused by cold wind.

windcheater, Am. **windbreaker** n. short jacket, often with a hood, to keep out the wind. **windchill factor** n. air temperature including the effect of the wind. **windfall** n. (a) fruit which has been blown to the ground from a fruit tree. (b) unexpected good fortune.

windgauge n. instrument for measuring the force of the wind.

windjammer n. (old) large sailing ship. **windless** adj. with no wind.

windmill n. mill driven by sails

pushed around by the wind. **windpipe** n. pipe leading from the nose and mouth to the lungs. **windscreen** n. glass window in the front of a car/lorry, etc.

windshield n. (a) screen on a motorcycle. (b) Am. windscreen.

windsock n. tube of material at the end of a tall pole, which shows the direction of the wind at an airfield.

windsurfer n. person who does windsurfing. **windsurfing** n. sport of riding on the sea on a surfboard with a sail attached. **windswept** adj. blown by strong winds. **windward** adj. adv. & n. (side of a ship) from which the wind blows. **windy** adj. (-ier, -iest) (a) having much wind. (b) inf. cowardly.

wind 2 1 [waɪnd] n. bend/twist/turn. **wind 2 2** v. (wound[waʊnd] (a) to turn. (b) to roll up/to roll round. (c) to turn a key of (a watch/clock) until the spring is tight. **winding 1** adj. turning/twisting. **winding 2** n. action of turning/rolling. **wind up** v. (a) to roll up. (b) to tighten a spring on a watch/clock work toy, etc. (c) to finish to put (a company) into liquidation. (d) inf. to be would up = to be nervous/tense. **windlass** ['wɪndləs] n. (pl.-es) hand winch for pulling sth up by winding a rope round a drum.

window ['wɪndəʊ] n. (a) opening in a wall/door, etc. filled with glass; stained-glass w. = window made of esp. in churches; w. of opportunity = short moment when the conditions for something are especially favourable. (b) section of a computer screen reserved for a special purpose. **window box** n. long box for plants kept on an outside windowledge. **window dressing** n. (a) displaying goods in an artistic way in a shop window. (b) putting on a display to hide the real state of affairs.

windowledge, windowsill n. ledge/flat piece of wood, etc., inside and outside a window. **window-pane** n. single piece of glass, used as part of a whole window. **window shopping,** n. looking at goods in shop windows with out buying them.

wine 1 [waɪn] n. (a) alcoholic drink made from the juice of grapes; w. list = list of wines which are available at restaurant. (b) alcoholic drink made from the juice of fruit or flowers. **wine 2** v.

to w. and dine s.o. = to take s.o. out for an expensive dinner and drinks. **wine cellar** n. cool room underground where wine is kept. **wineglass** n. glass used for drinking wine. **wine-growing** adj. (district) where vines are grown to produce wine. **wine merchant** n. person who sells wines and spirits in a shop. **wine waiter** n. person in charge of serving the wines in a restaurant.

wing 1 [wɪŋ] n. (a) one of the two limbs which a bird/butterfly, etc., used to fly; to take s.o. under your w. = to protect/to look after. (b) one of the two flat projecting parts on an aircraft. (c) side part of a large building which leads off the main part. (d) part of a car body which covers the wheel. (e) part of an army which stretches to one side; part of a political party which has a certain tendency. (f) group of squadrons in the air force; w. commander = rank in the air force below group captain. (g) wings = side of the stage in a theatre where actors wait before going on stage. (h) wings = pilot's badge. (i) side of a football/hockey pitch. (f) (in football/hockey) forward player on the side of pitch. **wing 2** v. (a) to fly. (b) to shoot (in the wing/arm). **winged** adj. with wings. **winger** n. (a) toward player on the side of the pitch in football/hockey. (b) suffix showing person on the right/left of a political party. **wingless** adj. having no wings. **wing nut** n. nut with two projecting parts for screwing easily. **wingspan** n. distance from the tip of one wing to the tip of another (of a bird/aircraft, etc.).

wink 1 [wɪŋk] n. act of quickly shutting and opening one eye; inf. to have party winks = to have short sleep; inf. to tip s.o. the w. = to warn s.o of sth. **wink 2** v. (a) to shut one eye and then quickly open it again. (b) (of light/stars) to shine on and off. **winker** n. flashing light (on a car).

winkle 1 ['wɪŋkl] n. edible snail which lives in salt water. **winkle 2** v. to w. sth out = to get sth out with difficulty.

winnow ['wɪnəʊ] v. to separate the grain from chaff, by allowing the wind to blow the chaff away.

winsome ['wɪnsəm] adj. pleasant/charming.

winter 1 ['wɪntə] n. coldest season of the year; w. sports = sports which are played on snow or ice. **winter 2** v. to spend the cold months of the year. **wintry** adj. like winter; unfriendly/cold (smile).

wipe 1 [waɪp] n. act of cleaning or drying with a cloth. **wipe 2** v. to clean/to dry with a cloth. **wipe away** v. to clean away. **wipe out** v. (a) to clean and dry the inside of (sth). (b) to kill/to destroy. **wiper** n. thing that wipes; device on a car which wipes rain away from the windscreen; rear w. = device for wiping the rain from the rear window of a car.

wire 1 ['waɪə] n. (a) thin metal line or thread; w. netting = pieces of wire twisted together to make a net, used as a fence; barbed w. = wire with sharp pieces of metal twisted in at intervals, used to stop animals or people from getting in or out; live w. = (i) wire which carries an electrical current; (ii) person who is full of energy; telegraph/telephone w. = wire along which telegraph/telephone messages are sent; inf. we must have got our wires crossed = we must has misunderstood each other; w. service = news agency sending news to subscribers by teleprinter; w. tapping = listening to other people's telephone conversations with special equipment. (b) inf. telegrAm. **wire 2** v. (a) to fasten with wires. (b) to put in wires to carry electricity to (a house). (c) to send a telegrAm. **wireless 1** n. radio. **wireless 2** adj. without wires. **wireworm** n. type of small insect which attacks plants. **wiring** n. system of wires used to carry electricity. **wiry** adj. (-ier, -iest) (a) (of person) thin but strong. (b) (of hair) stiff and strong, not easily combed.

wisdom ['wɪzdəm] n. intelligence/knowledge/common sense; w. tooth = one of four back teeth which grow when you are an adult. **wise** [waɪz] adj. (-er, -est) having intelligence and common sense/knowing a great deal/prudent; no one will be any the wiser = no one will know anything about it; I'm none the wiser = I know not more than I did before. **wisecrack 1** n. clever remark. **wisecrack 2** v. to make a joke/a wisecrack **wise guy** *n.* person who pretends to know more than anyone else. **wisely** *adv.* (a) in a wise way. (b) prudently. **wish 1** [wɪʃ] *n.* (*pl.*-es) want/desire. (b) good wishes = kind feelings/greetings. **wish 2** *v.* (a) to want/to desire sth which is unlikely to happen. (b) to express a desire or a hope. **wishbone** *n.* V-shaped bone in a chicken's breast, which you are supposed to pull with your partner, the person who holds the larger piece being in luck. **wishful** *adj.* w. thinking = believing sth because you would like it to happen.

wishy-washy [ˈwɪʃɪwɒʃɪ] *adj.* watery; not strong (colour/character, etc.).

wisp [wɪsp] *n.* small strand; little piece. **wispy** *adj.* thin/slight.

wistaria, wisteria [wɪˈsteərɪə, wɪˈstɪərɪə] *n.* climbing plant with sweetsmelling blue flowers.

wistful [ˈwɪstfəl] *adj.* longing for sth, but sad as there is not hope of getting it. **wistfully** *adv.* in a wistful way. **wistfulness** *n.* being wistful.

wit 1 [wɪt] *n.* (a) (usu. wits) intelligence; at your wit's ends = not knowing what to do next; to keep your wits about you = to keep calm in a difficult situation and think hard what to do next. (b) ability to say clever/funny things. (c) person who says clever and funny things. **wit 2** *v.* (old) to w. = namely/that is.

witch [wɪtʃ] *n.* (*pl.*-es) woman believed to have evil magic powers. **witchcraft** *n.* art of magic. **witch doctor** *n.* man in a primitive tribe who appears to cure illnesses by magic. **witchery** *n.* witchcraft. **witch hazel** *n.* shrub with tiny yellow flowers blooming in early spring. **witch hunt** *n.* cruel investigation of people who are supposed to be politically unreliable.

with [wɪð, wɪθ] *prep* (a) accompanied by/together/beside. (b) having/possessing. (c) in spite of (faults). (d) using; pouring w. rain = raining hard. (e) from/because of (f) showing (an emotion). (g) (used after many verbs to show a connection) to part w. sth = to give sth away; to meet w. = to have/to experience unexpectedly; I can do nothing w. him = I can't change him; to have nothing to do w. = to have no

connection with; I'm w. you there! = (i) I agree with you! (ii) I understand you; *inf.* to be w. it = to be fashionable/ modern. **withdraw** [wɪθˈdrɔː] *v.* (withdrew; withdrawn) to move back/to take back/to pull back; to take (money) out of a back account; to retract (sth which has been said). **withdrawal** *n.* taking back; removing of money (from a bank account); w. symptoms = symptoms shown by s.o. who is trying to stop taking a drug/smoking, etc. **withdrawn** *adj.* shy; (person) who does not like meeting other people.

wither [ˈwɪðə] *v.* (a) (of plants) to grow weaker and dry up (b) to make (sth) grow weaker and dry up; to make (s.o.) feel embarrassed by looking disapprovingly. **withering** *adj.* scornful/disapproving (look). **withers** [ˈwɪðəz] *n.* *pl.*part of a horse's back just below the neck. **withhold** [wɪθˈhəʊld] *v.* (withheld) to keep back/to refuse to give. **within** [wɪˈðɪn] *prep.* inside.

without [wɪˈðaʊt] *prep.* not having/not with; to go w. = not to have (sth); it goes w. saying that = it hardly needs to be said that. **withstand** [wɪθˈstænd] *v.* (withstood) to resist/to endure.

withy [ˈwɪðɪ] *n.* thin willow twig used to tie things together.

witness 1 [ˈwɪtnəs] *n.* (*pl.*-es) (a) person who sees sth happening. (b) to bear w. to = to be evidence of. (c) person who witnesses s.o.'s signature. **witness 2** *v.* (a) to see (sth) happen. (b) to sign your name on a legal paper to say that s.o.'s signature is genuine. (c) to give evidence in court. **witness-box,** *Am.* **witness stand** *n.* place where a witness stands in a law court.

wittingly [ˈwɪtɪŋlɪ] *adv.* on purpose/ intentionally.

witty [ˈwɪtɪ] *adj.* (-ier, -iest) clever and funny. **witticism** [ˈwɪtɪsɪzəm] *n.* clever/ funny remark.

wives [waɪvz] *n.* see wife.

wizard [ˈwɪzəd] *n.* (a) man who is believed to have magic powers. (b) clever person/expert. **wizardry** *n.* being a wizard; cleverness.

wizened [ˈwɪzənd] *adj.* dried up and wrinkled (face).

woad [wəʊd] *n.* wild plant with blue flowers. used to make a blue dye.

wobble 1 ['wɒbl] n. shaking movement. **wobble 2** v. to shake/to move unsteadily. **wobbly** adj. unsteady/shaking.

wodge [wɒdʒ] n. inf. thick piece.

woe [wəʊ] n. sadness/trouble. **woebegone** adj. very sad (look). **woeful** adj. full of sadness. **woefully** adv. sadly; inf. totally.

wog [wɒg] n. Sl. foreigner.

woke, woken [wəʊk, wəʊkn] v. see wake.

wold [wəʊld] n. (used in place names) area of gently rounded hills.

wolf 1 [wʊlf] n. (pl.wolves) (a) wild animal like a dog, usu. living in a large group in cold northern regions; pack of wolves = group of wolves living together; lone w. = person who prefers to be alone/who does not associate with other people; she-wolf = female wolf; w. cub = young wolf; w. in sheep's clothing = person who seems inoffensive but really is wicked; to keep the w. from the door = to have enough food to live on; to cry w. = to raise a false alarm. (b) inf. man who chases women; w. whistle = whistle of admiration given by men as a pretty woman passes. **wolf 2** v. to eat quickly. **wolfhound** n. large hunting dog. **wolfish** adj. like a wolf.

wolverine ['wʊlvəriːn] n. dark-furred North American carnivorous mammal.

woman ['wʊmən] n. (pl.women['wɪmɪn]) (a) female adult human being; inf. fussy old man; Women's Lib = movement to free women so that they can have equal status in society. (b) female. **womanhood** n. state of being a woman. **womanish** adj. (man) who behaves like a woman. **womanize** v. to try to seduce women often. **womanizer** n. man who womanizes. **womankind** n. all women. **womanliness** n. being womanly, **womanly** adj. feminine like a woman. **womenfolk** n. pl.all women (in a family, etc.).

womb [wuːm] n. uterus.

wombat ['wɒmbæt] n. small Australian animal.

won [wʌn] v. see win.

wonder 1 ['wʌndə] n. (a) amazing thing; no w. = it isn't surprising. (b) astonishment/surprise. **wonder 2** v. (a)

to be surprised/to marvel (at). (b) to want to know/to ask yourself (why). (c) (used when asking someone politely to do something) I w. if you could open the door. **wonderful** adj. marvellous/very good/exciting. **wonderfully** adv. in a wonderful way. **wonderland** adv. in a marvellous place **wonderment** n. astonishment/wonder. **wondrous** adj. (old) wonderful.

wonky ['wɒŋkɪ] adj. (-ier, -iest) inf. unsteady/wobbly.

wont [wəʊnt] n. (formal) habit; as is his w. = as he usually does. **wonted** adj. (formal) habitual.

won't [wəʊnt] v. see will.

woo [wuː] v. to try to attract (a woman) to marry you; to try to get (s.o.) to support you/to vote for you, etc. **wooer** n. person who woos.

wood [wʊd] n. (a) large group of trees/small forest; not to see the w. for the trees = concentrate on the details and not appreciate the main problem; we're not out of the w. yet = our problems are not over. (b) material that a tree is made of **woodbine** n. wild climbing plant **woodburning stove** n. stove which is designed to use wood as a fuel. **woodcarving** n. (i) art of sculpture in wood; (ii) wooden sculpture. **woodchuck** n. North American rodent. **woodcock** n. small brown bird shot for sport or food. **woodcraft** n. skill at finding your way about woods and forests and living in them. **woodcut** n. print made from a carved wooden plate. **wooded** adj. covered in trees. **wooden** adj. (a) made of wood. (b) stiff/showing no feeling. **woodenly** adv. stiffly. **woodland** n. country covered in woods. **woodlouse** n. (pl.-lice) very small animal with a hard shell, which curls up when attacked, and lives in rotten wood, etc. **woodpacker** n. bird with a long sharp beak which finds insects under the bark of trees.

woodpigeon n. common wild pigeon. **wood pulp** n. fragments of wood made into a pulp, used for making paper. **woodshed** n. small shed/hut used for storing wood. **wood(s) man** n. (pl.-men) man who works in woods and forests. **woodwind** n. wind instruments in an orchestra which are *usu.* made of wood. **woodwork** *n.* (a) carpentry. (b) wooden parts of a building. **woodworn** *n.* small grub which bores holes in wood. **woody** *adj.* (-ier, -iest) like wood; made of wood.

woof 1 [wʊf] *n.* (a) weft. (b) sound of a dog's bark. **woof 2** *v* (of dog) to bark. **woofer** *n.* loudspeaker which reproduces low sounds.

wool [wʊl] *n.* (a) short, thick hair of a sheep/goat, etc. (b) long threads of twisted hair, used to make clothes/carpets, etc; cloth woven from hair; to pull the w. over s.o.'s eyes = to deceive s.o. (c) material which looks like sheep's wool; cotton w; steel w. **wool-gathering** *n.* daydreaming/not thinking of what you are doing. **woollen** *adj.* made of wool. **woollens** *n. pl.* clothing made of knitted wool. **wooliness** *n* being woolly. **woolly 1** *adj.* (-ier, -iest) (a) made of wool/like wool. (b) vague/not clear. **woolly 2** *n. inf.* cardigan/jumper. **woolsack** *n.* large cushion on which the Lord Chancellor sits.

woozy ['wuːzɪ] *adj. inf.* dizzy/in a daze.

word 1 [wɜːd] *n.* (a) unit of speech either spoken or written; to have words with s.o. = to quarrel with s.o.; to have a w. with s.o. = to have a short talk with s.o.; in other words = explaining sth in a different way; you've taken the words out of my mouth = you've said what I was going to say; without a w. = without speaking; w. for w. = exactly as I said or written. (b) message/news; by w. of mouth = by spoken message. (c) promise; to give one's w. = to promise; he kept his w. = he did what he promised to do; I'll take your w. for it = I'll believe what you say. (d) my w. ! *inter.* expressing surprise (e) w. of command = order. **word 2** *v.* to put in words, either written or spoken. **wordily** *adv.* in a wordy way. **wordiness** *n.* being wordy. **wording** *n.* choice of words. **word-perfect** *adj.* able to repeat exactly what has been learnt. **word processor** *n.* typewriter with a computer memory and a screen on which the text can be displayed. **wordy** *adj.* (-ier, -iest) using too many words.

wore ['wɔː] *n.* see wear

work 1 [wɜːk] *n.* (a) mental or physical activity; to have one's w. cut out = find it difficult (to do sth). (b) job; out of w. = with no job. (c) thing that has been made by s.o. (d) works = factory. (e) road works = repairs to a road. (f) works = moving parts of a machine; *inf.* to give s.o. the works = to give s.o. everything/the full treatment. **work 2** *v.* (a) to use energy/to make s.o. use energy in carrying out an activity. (b) (of machine) to operate/to move. (c) to make (a machine) function. (d) to have a job. (e) to be successful. (f) to embroider/to sew. (g) to w. one's way = to move gradually; he was working himself into a rage = he was becoming more and more angry. (h) to take coal/copper, etc., from (a mine); worked out = (mine) where all the ore has been extracted. **workable** *adj.* able to be worked. **workaday** *adj.* plain/ordinary. **workaholic** *n. inf.* person who cannot stop working. **workbook** *n.* book of exercises to help teach a subject. **worked up** *adj.* excited/annoyed (about). **worker** *n.* (a) person who works. (b) member of the working class. (c) type of female bee which works to provide the queen with honey, but which is sterile. **workforce** *n.* all the workers (in a factory). **workhorse** *n.* person who can work hard. **workhouse** *n.* (old) place where poor people were made to live and work. **working 1** *adj.* which works; referring to work; w. party = group of experts who investigate a certain problem and report on it; w. class = people who work with their hands/who earn wages not salaries. **working 2** *n.* (usu. *pl.* workings) (a) place where mineral has been dug. (b) way sth works. **workman** *n.* (*pl.*-men) man who works with his hands. **workmanlike** *adj.* skilful/expert. **workmanship** *n.* skill of a good workman. **work off** *v.* to get rid of (sth) by working. **work on** *v.* (a) to continue to work. (b) to be busy doing sth. (c) to try to influence/to persuade. **work out** *v.* (a) to succeed/to do well. (b) to plan (sth) in detail/to find an answer to (sth). (c) (at) to amount to (a price). **workout** *n.* exercise/practice before a sports contest. **workroom** *n.* room where work is done. **work-sharing** *n.* arrangement where two

people work part-time to do one job.
workshop *n.* place where things are made in a small factory or house.
workshy *adj.* reluctant to work.
workspace *n.* memory available on a computer for current use. **workstation** *n.* desk with terminal, monitor, keyboard, etc., where a computer operator works. **work to rule** *v.* to protest by working strictly according to the rules laid down, in such a way that the work is done excessively slowly.
worktop *n.* top of a kitchen cupboard, etc., for working on. **work up** *v.* to develop/to reach slowly.
world [wɜːld] *n.* (a) the earth; particular part of the earth; the old W. = Europe, Asia and Africa; the New W. = North and South America; the Third W. = countries with no strong connections to the superpowers; W. War = war in which many countries all over the world take part. (b) people on Earth; everything; to come into the w. = to be born; to be all alone in the w. = to have no family; out of this w. = magnificent; to think the w. of s.o. = to think very highly of s.o.; it will do you the w. of good = it will help you greatly. (c) people with a particular interest/things which form a particular group. **world-famous** *adj.* know everywhere. **worldliness** *n.* being worldly/not being idealistic. **worldly** *adj.* (a) of the material world. (b) not idealistic. **worldly-wise** *adj.* wise about worldly things. **worldwide** *adj.* & *adv.* throughout the whole world.
worm 1 [wɜːm] *n.* (a) small spineless burrowing creature which looks like a very small snake and lives in earth. (b) similar animal which lives in the intestines of animals. (c) woodworm. (d) spiral thread of a screw. **worm 2** *v.* to move slowly like a worm; to w. yourself into s.o.'s favour = to make s.o. like you by being especially nice to them; to w. information out of s.o. = to get information by asking many persistent questions. **wormcast** *n.* small pile of earth thrown up by a worm.
wormeaten *adj.* which has been eaten by woodworms. **wormwood** *n.* bitter plant.
worn [wɔːn] *adj.* much used; see also wear. **worn out** *adj.* (a) used so much

that t is now useless. (b) tired.
worry 1 ['wʌrɪ] *n.* (a) thing which makes you anxious. (b) being anxious.
worry 2 *v.* (a) to be upset/anxious; to make (s.o.) upset/anxious. (b) (of dogs) to shake and tear with the teeth; to w. sheep = to chase and attack sheep.
worried *adj.* anxious/troubled.
worrier *n.* person who worries.
worrisome *adj.* which makes you worried/anxious.
worse 1 [wɜːs] *adj.* (a) more bad. (b) more ill. **worse 2** *n.* more awful thing.
worse 3 *adv.* more badly. **worsen** *v.* to become or make worse. **worse off** *adj.* with less money.
worship 1 ['wɜːʃɪp] *n.* (a) praise and honour shown to God. (b) praise and honour shown to s.o./sth. (c) Your W. = title of respect used when speaking to a mayor or a magistrate in a law court.
worship 2 *v.* (worshipped) (a) to praise and love (God). (b) to take part in a church service. (c) to praise and love (s.o./sth). **worshipper** *n.* person who worships; sun w. = person who loves sunbathing.
worst 1 [wɜːst] *adj.* very bad/worse than anyone/anything else. **worst 2** *n.* most awful thing. **worst 3** *adv.* very badly/worse than anyone/anything else.
worsted ['wʊstɪd] *n.* fine woollen cloth.
worth 1 [wɜːθ] *adj.* (a) having a value/ price (b) useful; giving satisfaction; it is w. (your) while = it is worth the effort. (c) having riches/money, etc.; for all you are w. = as much as possible. **worth 2** *n.* value. **worthily** *adv.* in a worthy way. **worthiness** *n.* being worthy.
worthless *adj.* having no worth/no use. **worthwhile** [wɜːθ'waɪl] *adj.* which is worth doing. **worthy 1** ['wɜːðɪ] *adj.* (-ier,-iest) deserving. **worthy 2** *n.* notable person (in a town).
would [wʊd] *v.* see will.
wound 1 [wuːnd] *n.* (a) cut/damage to the skin, *usu.* received in a fight. (b) hurt to the feelings. **wound 2** *v.* (as) to hurt. (b) to hurt the feelings of (s.o.). (c)[waʊnd] see also wind2.
wove, woven [wəʊv, 'wəʊvn] *v.* see weave.
wow 1 [waʊ] *n.* *inf.* (a) great success. (b) fluctuation of sound in a record-

player. **wow 2** *v. inf.* (of a singer, etc.) to excite (the audience).

WPC ['dʌblju:pi:'si:] *n* woman police constable.

wrack [ræk] *n.* seaweed.

wraith [raɪθ] *n.* ghost.

wrangle 1 ['ræŋgl] *n.* argument/dispute. **wrangle 2** *v.* to argue.

wrap 1 [ræp] *n* shawl; *inf.* to keep sth under wraps = to keep sth a secret. **wrap 2** *v.* (wrapped) to cover (sth) all round with paper/cloth, etc. **wrap up** *v.* (a) to cover up completely. (b) to wear warm clothes. (c) to be wrapped up in your work = to think only of the work and take no notice of other things. **wrapper** *n.* piece of paper used to cover sth.

wrapping *n.* paper/cardboard/plastic, etc., used to wrap things w. paper = paper used to wrap presents.

wrasse [ræs] *n.* type of sea fish.

wrath [rɒθ] *n.* great anger. **wrathful** *adj.* angry.

wreak [ri:k] *v.* to carry out/to do (sth violent).

wreath [ri:θ] *n.* (a) circle of flowers or leaves esp. given at funeral in memory of the dead person. (b) winding clouds (of smoke/mist). **wreathe** [ri:ð] *v.* (a) to put a circle of flowers on (s.o./sth). (b) to cover with twisting clouds of smoke/mist.

wreck 1 [rek] *n.* (a) ship which has been sunk/badly damaged on rocks, etc. (b) action of being wrecked. (c) anything which has been damaged and is useless. (d) person who, because of illness, can do very little. **wreck 2** *v.* to cause severe damage to (sth); to ruin (sth).

wreckage *n.* broken remains of a building/ship, etc., after a disaster.

wrecker *n.* (a) person who destroys a building/plan. etc., on purpose or tries to make a ship crash on to rocks. (b) person who is employed to destroy old buildings/break up old cards, etc. (c) *Am.* truck which goes to help cars which have broken down on the road; engine which goes to help a train which has broken down on the track.

wren [ren] *n.* (a) very small brown songbird. (b) Wren = woman member of the Royal Navy.

wrench 1 [renʃ] *n.* (*pl.*-es) (a) violent twisting movement. (b) large spanner for turning nuts. (c) sadness at leaving. **wrench 2** *v.* to turn and pull (sth) violently.

wrest [rest] *v.* (formal) to twist/to wrench away. **wrestle** ['resl] *v.* (a) to fight with s.o. in a contest by trying to throw him to the ground. (b) to fight/struggle which (a problem). **wrestler** *n.* person who wrestles in contests.

wrestling *n.* w. match = contest of wrestlers watched by crowds of people.

wretch [retʃ] *n.* (*pl.*-es) (a) person who looks poor and miserable. (b) naughty/annoying person. **wretched** ['retʃɪd] *adj.* (a) miserable and poor; to feel w. = to feel ill. (b) terrible/annoying.

wretchedly *adv.* miserably.

wretchedness *n.* being wretched.

wriggle ['rɪgl] *v.* to twist and turn; to w. out of = to get out of (a difficult situation) by trickery.

wring [rɪŋ] *v.* (wrung) to twist (sth), esp. to get water out of it; to w. information from = to manage to get information with difficulty; to w. one's hands = to twist and turn one's hands, showing sadness and emotion. **wringer** *n.* machine for squeezing the water out of wet washing. **wringing** *adj.* very (wet).

wrinkle 1 ['rɪŋkl] *n.* (a) line/fold of the skin. (b) line or crease in cloth. **wrinkle 2** *v.* to make lines/creases in.

wrist [rɪst] *n.* joint between the arm and the hand; w. watch small watch worn on a strap around the wrist. **wristlet** *n.* band worn round the wrist.

writ [rɪt] *n.* legal paper ordering s.o. to do/not to do with. **Holy Writ** *n.* the Bible.

write [raɪt] *v.* (wrote[rəʊt], has written) (a) to put down words on paper. (b) to be the author of books/music, etc. (c) to put a letter in writing and send it to s.o. *inf.* that's nothing to w. home about = it's nothing special. **write in** *v.* (a) to write to (a radio station, etc.). (b) *Am.* to vote for a candidate whose name does not appear on the ballot paper by writing the name there. **write off** *v.* to remove (sth) from a written list; to cancel (a debt); to see that (sth) is a failure; the car was written off = the insurance company considered it a total loss. **write-off** *n. inf.* total loss. **writer** *n.* person who writes, esp. to earn money. **write up** v. to describe fully in writing. **write-up** n. inf. article in a newspaper. **writing** n. (a) thing that is written; w. paper = paper used for writing letters. (b) handwriting. **writings** n. pl.books, etc., written by an author.

writhe [raɪð] v. to twist and turn (in agony).

wrong 1 [rɒŋ] adj. (a) bad/not right. (b) not right/incorrect. (c) what's w. ? = what is the matter? I hope nothing's w. = I hope nothing bad has happened.

wrong 2 n. bad/incorrect thing; to be in he w. = to have made a mistake.

wrong 3 adv. badly/incorrectly; to go w. = to break down/not to work properly.

wrong 4 v. to treat (s.o.) unfairly.

wrongdoer n. person who has committed a crime. **wrongdoing** n. crime/unlawful act. **wrongful** adj. unjust/unlawful. **wrongfully** adv. in a wrongful way. **wrongheaded** adj. mistaken but refusing to admit it.

wrongly adv. incorrectly/badly.

wrote [rəʊt] v. see write.

wrought [rɔːt] adj. w. iron = hammered, twisted and bent iron used for making decorative gates/balconies, etc.

wrung [rʌŋ] v. see wring.

wry [raɪ] adj. showing dislike by twisting the mouth.

wych elm ['wɪtʃelm] n. elm with wide spreading branches.

WYSIWYG ['wɪzɪwɪg] what-you-see-is-what-you-get (when the text on a computer screen is exactly the same as the printed output).

Xx

X x [eks] (a) a twenty-fourth letter of the alphabet. (b) symbol for an unknown quantity

X-ray 1 n. (a) ray which will pass through solids and is used esp. in hospitals for photographing the inside of the body. (b) photograph taken with X-rays. **X-ray 2** v. to take an X-ray photograph of.

xenophobe ['zenəfəʊb] n. person who dislikes foreigners.

xenophobia [zenə'fəʊbɪə] n. hatred of foreigners. **xenophobic** adj. hating foreigners.

xerox 1 ['zɪərɒks] n. (pl.-es) trademark for a type of photocopier. (b) photocopy made with this machine. **xerox 2** v. to make a photocopy with a Xerox machine.

Xmas ['krɪsməs, 'eksməs] n. short for Christmas.

xylophone ['zaɪləfəʊn] n. musical instrument consisting of wooden bars of different lengths which make different notes when they are tapped with a hammer.

Yy

yacht [jɒt] n. sailing boat; boat used for pleasure and sport; y. club = sailing club.

yachting n. art of sailing a boat.

yachtsman n. (pl.-men) person who sails a yacht.

yahoo ['jɑːhuː] n. inf. crude boorish person.

yak 1 [jæk] n. long-haired ox from Asia.

yak 2 v. inf. to talk incessantly.

yam [jæm] n. tropical plant with an edible root.

yank 1 [jæŋk] n. inf. short sharp pull.

yank 2 v. inf. to pull hard and sharply.

Yank, Yankee n. inf. American (esp. from the northern states).

yap 1 [jæp] n. short sharp bark of a dog.

yap 2 v. (yapped) to make short sharp barks.

yard [jɑːd] n. (a) measure of length (= 0.91 metre). (b) piece of wood attached to the mast holding a sail. (c) enclosed space (often paved) behind a house of other building. (d) Am. small garden round a house. (e) enclosed space used for a certain purpose; builder's y. = place where a builder keeps stocks of wood/bricks, etc.; goods' y. = space where trains are loaded with goods; Scotland Y./inf. the Y. = headquarters of the London Metropolitan Police. **yardage**

n. length in yards or area in square yards. **yardarm** *n.* end of the yard holding a sail. **yardstick** *n.* standard for measurement.

yarn 1 [jɑːn] *n.* (a) long thread of wool/ fibre used in knitting or weaving. (b) *inf.* long story. **yarn 2** *v. inf.* to tell stories.

yarrow ['jærəʊ] *n.* wild plant with clusters of small white flowers.

yashmak ['jæʃmæk] *n.* veil worn by Muslim women.

yaw [jɔː] *v.* (of ship/aircraft) to go away from the course).

yawl [jɔːl] *n.* type of two-masted fishing boat.

yawn 1 [jɔːn] *n.* movement of opening the mouth when tired; to stifle a y. = to try to stop yawning. **yawn 2** to open the mouth wide when feeling sleepy, and to breath in and out; to y. your head off = to yawn again and a again. **yawning** *adj.* open wide; y. hole = deep wide hole.

yaws [jɔːz] *n. pl.* tropical skin disease.

yd short for yard.

ye 1 [jiː] *pron.* (old) you. **ye 2** article used in false old names the.

yea [jeɪ] *adv.* (old) yes.

year ['jɜː] *n.* (a) period of twelve months starting on Ist January and ending on 31st December; the New Y. = the first few days of the year; to see the New Y. in = to stay up until midnight on 31st December and celebrate with a party the beginning of the next year; calendar y. = year beginning on Ist January and ending on 31st December; leap y. = year with 366 days in it. one more than the normal year. (b) any period of twelve months; school y. = year starting in September and ending in July of the following year; financial y. = (i) twelve month period for a firm's accounts; (ii) (in UK) period beginning on April 6th and ending on the following April 5th considered for tax purposes; all (the) y. round = through the whole year. y. in, y. out = happening regularly over a long period of time. (c) his early years = his childhood; getting on in years = quite old; I haven't seen him for (donkey's) years = I haven't seen him for a long time. **yearbook** *n.* reference book which comes out each year with up to date information.

yearling *n.* one year old animal.

yearly *adj. & adv.* every year; once a year.

yearn [jɜːn] *v.* to long for sth/to wants sth. **yearning** *n.* desire/longing.

yeast [jiːst] *n.* living fungus used to make bread and beer. **yeastly** *adj.* like yeast; referring to yeast.

yell 1 [jel] *n.* loud shout. **yell 2** *v.* to shout loudly.

yellow 1 ['jeləʊ] *n. & adj.* (a) colour of the sun/of gold; y. fever = type of tropical fever; y. pages = section of a telephone directory giving a classified list of businesses. (b) cowardly. **yellow 2** *v.* to turn yellow. **yellowhammer** *n.* small bird with a yellow breast.

yellowish *adj.* rather yellow.

yelp 1 [jelp] *n* cry of pain. **yelp 2** *v.* (usu. of animals) to cry out in pain.

yen [jen] *n.* (a) currency of Japan. (b) *inf.* strong desire.

yeoman ['jəʊmən] *n.* (*pl.*-men) (old) farmer with his own land; to y. service = work long and hard. **yeomanry** *n.* (old) all yeomen.

yes [jes] *adv. & inter.* expression of agreement. **yes man** *n.* person who always agrees with a person in authority.

yesterday ['jestədeɪ] *adv. & n.* (a) the day before today; the day before y. = two days before today. (b) recent times.

yesteryear *adv. & n.* (formal) times past.

yet 1 [jet] *adv.* (a) up till now/up till this time. (b) in spite of everything. (c) even.

yet 2 *conj.* still/but.

yeti ['jetɪ] *n* large animal, like an ape or bear, which is said to exist in the snows of the Himalayas.

yew [juː] *n.* evergreen tree with small cones and poisonous red berries.

Yiddish ['jɪdɪʃ] *n.* language spoken by European Jews.

yield 1 [jiːld] *n.* crop/product; return on your investment. **yield 2** *v.* (a) to give/ to produce. (b) to produce money. (c) (to) to give up/to surrender. (d) to give way when pressed. (e) (t0) (of traffic) to allow other vehicles to pass first.

yob(bo) ['jɒb(əʊ)] *n. Sl.* (*pl.*-os) rude/ violent young man.

yodel ['jəʊdl] *v.* to sing with quick changes from low to high notes. **yodeller** *n.* person who yodels.

yoga ['jəʊgə] *n.* system of exercises and meditation practised by Hindu thinkers, and now popular in western countries.

youghurt, yogurt ['jɒgət] *n.* fermented milk *usu.* eaten as a dessert.

yogi ['jəʊgɪ] *n.* Hindu thinker who practises yoga.

yoke 1 [jəʊk] *n.* (a) piece of wood placed over the neck of a pair of animals when they are used for ploughing, etc.; y. of oxen = two oxen attached together. (b) part of a dress which covers the shoulders and upper chest. **yoke 2** *v.* to join together (with a yoke).

yokel ['jəʊkl] *n.* stupid man from the country.

yolk [jəʊk] *n.* yellow part of an egg.

yon, yonder [jɒn, 'jɒndə] *adj. & adv.* (which is) over there.

yore [jɔː] *n.* (formal) in days of y. = in the past.

yorker ['jɔːkə] *n.* (in cricket) ball which pitches just under the bat. **york** *v.* to bowl (s.o.) out with a yorker. **Yorkshire pudding** ['jɔːkʃə'pʊdɪŋ] *n.* batter pudding eaten with roast beef.

you [juː] *pron.* (a) (referring to the personal/persons to whom we are speaking) (b) (referring to anybody/people in general).

young 1 [jʌŋ] *adj.* (-er, -est) not old/recently born. **young 2** *n.* (a) young animals or birds. (b) young people.

yongster *n.* young person.

your ['jɔː] *adj.* belonging to you. **yours** ['jɔːz] *pron.* belonging to you.

yourself, yourselves [jɔː'self, jɔː'selvz] *pron.* referring to the subject you.

youth [juːθ] *n.* (a) time when you are young. (b) young man. (c) young people; y. club = club where young people meet; y. hostel = building where young walkers, etc., can stay the night cheaply. **youthful** *adj.* young. **youthfulness** *n.* being youthful.

yowl [jaʊl] *v.* (esp. of animals) to howl/to cry out loudly.

yo-yo ['jəʊjəʊ] *n.* toy made of a circular piece of wood/metal with a groove round the edge, which can be made to run up and down a string.

yucca ['jʌkə] *n.* type of large succulent plant.

Yugoslav ['juːgəʊslɑːv] *adj. & n.* (person) from Yugoslavia.

yukky ['jʌkɪ] *adj. inf.* which has a nasty taste.

yule [juːl] *n.* Christmas; y. log = log burnt at Christmas. **Yuletide** *n.* the Christmas period.

yumyum ['jʌmjʌm] *inter.* showing liking for food. **yummy** *adj. inf.* nice to eat.

Zz

zany ['zeɪnɪ] *adj.* (-ier, -iest) *inf.* wildly mad.

zap [zæp] *v.* (zapped) *inf.* to hit/kill.

zeal ['ziːl] *n.* keenness/eagerness.

zealous ['zeləs] *adj.* eager. **zealot** ['zelət] *n.* person who is too enthusiastic about religion or politics.

zebra ['zebrə] *n.* African animal similar to a horse, but with a striped coat; z. crossing = pedestrian crossing painted with white stripes.

zenith ['zenɪθ] *n.* (a) point of the sky directly overhead. (b) highest point.

zephyr ['zefə] *n.* (formal) gentle (often westerly) breeze.

zero ['zɪərəʊ] *n.* (a) number 0/nothing/nil. (b) freezing point of water when measured on a Celsius thermometer. **zero hour** *n.* time fixed to start sth important. **zero in on** *v.* to aim at (sth)/to go straight to (sth). **zero-rated** *adj.* (item) which has a 0% VAT applied to it.

zest [zest] *n.* (a) enthusiasm/enjoyment. (b) added pleasure/spice. (c) thin piece of orange or lemon peel. **zestful** *adj.* enthusiastic.

zigzag 1 ['zɪgzæg] *adj. & n.* (line) which turns sharply one way, then the opposite way. **zigzag 2** *v.* (zigzagged) to move in a zigzag.

zilch [zɪltʃ] *n. Am. Sl.* nothing/zero.

zinc [zɪŋk] *n.* (element: Zn) hard bright light-coloured metal.

zinnia ['zɪnjə] *n.* annual garden plant with bright flowers.

zip 1 [zɪp] *n.* (a) whistling sound made by a bullet as it goes through the air. (b) *inf.* energy. (c) (also zip fastener) device for closing openings on trousers/dresses, etc., consisting of two rows of teeth which lock together. (d) *Am.* z. code = post code. **zip 2** *v.* (zipped) (a) to go fast; to whistle by. (b) to z. up = to close a zip (fastener). **zipper** *n. inf.* zip (fastener). **zippy** *adj. inf.* quick and lively.

zirconium [zɜ:'kəʊnɪəm] *n.* (element: Zr) rare metal used in alloys.

zither ['zɪðə] *n.* flat musical instrument played by plucking strings.

Zn symbol for zinc.

zodiac ['zəʊdɪæk] *n.* part of the sky (divided into twelve imaginary sections) through which the sun and planets are supposed to travel during the year; signs of the z. = twelve signs named after groups of stars. **zodiacal** [zəʊ'daɪəkəl] *adj.* referring to the zodiac.

zombie ['zɒmbɪ] *n.* (a) (West Indian) dead body which is revived and controlled by witchcraft. (b) *inf.* person who is half-asleep/moving slowly.

zone 1 [zəʊn] *n.* (a) region/area/part (of a country/town). (b) region of the Earth showing a particular type of climate.

zone 2 *v.* to divide (a town) into parts of planning purposes. **zonal** *adj.* of a zone. **zoning** *n.* the splitting up (of a town or area) into zones.

zoo [zu:] *n.* place where wild animals are kept in enclosures and which the public can visit. **zoology** [zu:'ɒlədʒɪ] *n.* study of animals. **zoological** [zu:ə'lɒdʒɪkl] *adj.* referring to the study of animals; z. gardens = zoo. **zoologist** [zu:'ɒlədʒɪst] *n.* person who studies animals.

zoom 1 [zu:m] *n.* deep buzzing noise made by sth travelling fast. **zoom 2** *v.* (a) to make a deep buzzing noise when moving fast. (b) (of prices, etc.) to rise suddenly and steeply. (c) to z. in on sth = to focus a camera lens so that it makes a distant object appear to come closer.

zoom lens *n.* camera lens which allows you to change quickly from distant to close-up shots while still keeping in focus.

zoonosis [zəʊə'nəʊsɪs] *n.* disease which can be caught from animals.

zucchini [zʊ'ki:nɪ] *n.* courgette.

zwieback ['zwi:bæk] *n. Am.* type of hard crumbly biscuit.

Information Section

Currencies of the World

Afghanistan	afghani	Af
Albania	lek	L
Algeria	dinar	DA
American Samoa	*see* United States of America	
Andorra	euro	
Angola	"kwanza (new kwanza, 2001-)"	Kz
Anguilla	dollar	EC$
Antarctica	each Antarctic base uses the currency of its home country	
Antigua and Barbuda	dollar	EC$
Argentina	peso	$
Armenia	dram	
Aruba	guilder (a.k.a. florin or gulden)	Af.
Australia	dollar	A$
Austria	*see* European Union	
Azerbaijan	manat	
Bahamas	dollar	B$
Bahrain	dinar	BD
Bangladesh	taka	Tk
Barbados	dollar	Bds$
Belarus	ruble	BR
Belgium	*see* European Union	
Belize	dollar	BZ$
Benin	franc	CFAF
Bermuda	dollar	Bd$
Bhutan	ngultrum	Nu
Bolivia	boliviano	Bs
Bosnia-Herzegovina	convertible mark	KM
Botswana	pula	P
Bouvet Island	*see* Norway	
Brazil	real (1994-)	R$
British Indian Ocean Territory	"legal currency is GBP, but mostly USD is used"	
British Virgin Islands	*see* United States	
Brunei	ringgit (a.k.a. Bruneian dollar)	B$
Bulgaria	leva	Lv
Burkina Faso	franc	CFAF
Burma	now Myanmar.	
Burundi	franc	FBu
Cambodia	new riel	CR
Cameroon	franc	CFAF
Canada	dollar	Can$
Canton and Enderbury Islands	see Kiribati	
Cape Verde Island	escudo	C.V.Esc.
Cayman Islands	dollar	CI$
Central African Republic	franc	CFAF
Chad	franc	CFAF

Chile	peso	Ch$
China	yuan renminbi	Y
Christmas Island	*see* Australia	
Cocos (Keeling) Islands	*see* Australia	
Colombia	peso	Col$
Comoros	franc	CF
Congo	franc	CFAF
"Congo, Dem. Rep. "	franc	
Cook Islands	*see* New Zealand	
Costa Rica	colon	slashed C
Côte d'Ivoire	franc	CFAF
Croatia	kuna	HRK
Cuba	peso	Cu$
Cyprus	pound	£C
Cyprus (Northern)	*see* Turkey	
Czech Republic	koruna	Kc (with hacek
on c)		
Denmark	krone (pl. kroner)	Dkr
Djibouti	franc	DF
Dominica	dollar	EC$
Dominican Rep.	peso	RD$
Dronning Maud Land	*see* Norway	
East Timor	*see* Indonesia	
Ecuador	country has adopted the US Dollar	
Egypt	pound	£E
El Salvador	colon	¢
Equatorial Guinea	franc	CFAF
Eritrea	nakfa	Nfa
Estonia	kroon (pl. krooni)	KR
Ethiopia	birr	Br
European Union	Euro	•
Faeroe Islands (Føroyar)	*see* Denmark	
Falkland Islands	pound	£F
Fiji	dollar	F$
Finland	*see* European Union	
France	*see* European Union	
French Guiana	*see* France	
French Polynesia	franc	CFPF
Gabon	franc	CFAF
Gambia	dalasi	D
Gaza	*see* Israel and Jordan	
Georgia	lari	
Germany	*see* European Union	
Ghana	new cedi	¢
Gibraltar	pound	£G
Great Britain	*see* United Kingdom	
Greece	*see* European Union	
Greenland	*see* Denmark	
Grenada	dollar	EC$

Guadeloupe	*see* France	
Guam	*see* United States	
Guatemala	quetzal	Q
Guernsey	*see* United Kingdom	
Guinea-Bissau	franc	CFAF
Guinea	syli	FG
Guinea	franc	
Guyana	dollar	G$
Haiti	gourde	G
Heard and McDonald Islands	*see* Australia	
Honduras	lempira	L
Hong Kong	dollar	HK$
Hungary	forint	Ft
Iceland	króna	IKr
India	rupee	Rs
Indonesia	rupiah	Rp
Iran	rial	Rls
Iraq	dinar	ID
Ireland	*see* European Union	
Israel	new shekel	NIS
Italy	*see* European Union	
Ivory Coast	*see* Côte d'Ivoire	
Jamaica	dollar	J$
Japan	yen	¥
Jersey	*see* United Kingdom	
Johnston Island	*see* United States	
Jordan	dinar	JD
Kampuchea	*see* Cambodia	
Kazakhstan	tenge	
Kenya	shilling	K Sh
Kiribati	*see* Australia.	
"Korea, North"	won	Wn
"Korea, South"	won	W
Kuwait	dinar	KD
Kyrgyzstan	som	
Laos	new kip	KN
Latvia	lat	Ls
Lebanon	pound (livre)	L.L.
Lesotho	"loti, pl., maloti"	"L, pl., M"
Liberia	dollar	$
Libya	dinar	LD
Liechtenstein	*see* Switzerland	
Lithuania	"litas, pl., litai"	
Luxembourg	*see* European Union	
Macao (Macau)	pataca	P
Macedonia (Former Yug. Rep.)	denar	MKD
Madagascar	ariayry = 5 francs	FMG
Malawi	kwacha	MK
Malaysia	ringgit	RM

Maldives	rufiyaa	Rf
Mali	franc	CFAF
Malta	"lira, pl., liri"	Lm
Martinique	*see* France	
Mauritania	ouguiya	UM
Mauritius	rupee	Mau Rs
Micronesia	*see* United States	
Midway Islands	*see* United States	
Mexico	peso	Mex$
Moldova	"leu, pl., lei"	
Monaco	*see* France	
Mongolia	tugrik (tughrik?)	Tug
Montserrat	dollar	EC$
Morocco	dirham	DH
Mozambique	metical	Mt
Myanmar	kyat	K
Nauru	*see* Australia	
Namibia	dollar	N$
Nepal	rupee	NRs
Netherlands Antilles	guilder (a.k.a. florin or gulden)	Ant.f. or NAf.
Netherlands	*see* European Union	
New Caledonia	franc	CFPF
New Zealand	dollar	NZ$
Nicaragua	gold cordoba	C$
Niger	franc	CFAF
Nigeria	naira	double-dashed N
Niue	*see* New Zealand	
Norfolk Island	*see* Australia	
Norway	krone (pl. kroner)	NKr
Oman	rial	RO
Pakistan	rupee	Rs
Palau	*see* United States	
Panama	balboa	B
Panama Canal Zone	*see* United States	
Papua New Guinea	kina	K
Paraguay	guarani	slashed G
Peru	inti	
Peru	new sol	S/.
Philippines	peso	dashed P
Pitcairn Island	*see* New Zealand	
Poland	zloty	z dashed l
Portugal	*see* European Union	
Puerto Rico	*see* United States	
Qatar	riyal	QR
Reunion	*see* France	
Romania	leu (pl. lei)	L
Russia	ruble	R
Rwanda	franc	RF

Samoa (America)	*see* United States	
San Marino	*see* Italy	
Sao Tome & Principe	dobra	Db
Saudi Arabia	riyal	SRls
Senegal	franc	CFAF
Serbia	*see* Yugoslavia	
Seychelles	rupee	SR
Sierra Leone	leone	Le
Singapore	dollar	S$
Slovakia	koruna	Sk
Slovenia	tolar	SIT
Solomon Island	dollar	SI$
Somalia	shilling	So. Sh.
South Africa	rand	R
Spain	*see* European Union	
Sri Lanka	rupee	SLRs
St. Helena	pound	£S
St. Kitts and Nevis	dollar	EC$
St. Lucia	dollar	EC$
St. Vincent and the Grenadines	dollar	EC$
Sudan	dinar	
Suriname	guilder (a.k.a. florin or gulden)	Sur.f. or Sf.
Svalbard and Jan Mayen Islands	*see* Norway	
Swaziland	"lilangeni, pl., emalangeni"	"L, pl., E"
Sweden	krona (pl. kronor)	Sk
Switzerland	franc	SwF
Syria	pound	£S
Tahiti	*see* French Polynesia	
Taiwan	new dollar	NT$
Tajikistan	somoni	100 dirams
Tanzania	shilling	TSh
Thailand	baht	Bht or Bt
Togo	franc	CFAF
Tokelau	*see* New Zealand	
Tonga	pa'anga	PT or T$
Trinidad and Tobago	dollar	TT$
Tunisia	dinar	TD
Turkey	lira	TL
Turkmenistan	manat	
Turks and Caicos Islands	*see* United States	
Tuvalu	*see* Australia.	
Uganda	shilling	USh
Ukraine	Hryvnia	
United Arab Emirates	dirham	Dh
United Kingdom	pound	£

United States of America	dollar	$
Uruguay	peso uruguayo	$U
Uzbekistan	som	
Vanuatu	vatu	VT
Venezuela	bolivar	Bs
Vietnam	(new) dong "dashed d, or D"	
Virgin Islands	*see* United States	
Wake Island	*see* United States	
Wallis and Futuna Islands	franc	CFPF
Western Samoa	tala	WS$
Yemen	rial	YRls
Yugoslavia	dinar	Din
Zambia	kwacha	ZK
Zimbabwe	dollar	Z$

The Solar System

	distance from Sun (millions of km)	diameter diameter	rotation period on its axis (days hours minutes)	revolution round the sun
Sun	0	"1,392,000"	25 09 00	
Mercury	58	"4,880"	59 00 00	87.97 days
Venus	108	"12,100"	243 00 00	224.70 days
Earth	150	"12,756"	00 23 56	365.25 days
Mars	228	"6,790"	00 24 37	1.88 years
Jupiter	778	"142,800"	00 09 50	11.86 years
Saturn	"1,427"	"120,000"	00 10 14	29.45 years
Uranus	"2,870"	"52,000"	00 16 00	84.00 years
Neptune	"4,497"	"48,000"	00 10 00	164.79 years
Pluto	"5,950"	"?3,000"	06 09 14	247.7 years

The World's Largest Cities

The following list is of those urban areas in the world which have a population of more than six million. City limits often fall short of, or exceed, the built-up or urban area.

Mexico City	"18,748,000"	LosAngeles	"8,505,000"
Cairo	"14,000,000"	São Paulo	"8,490,763"
Shanghai	"12,620,000"	Bombay	"8,202,000"
Tokyo	"11,680,282"	London	"6,696,000"
Seoul	"9,991,089"	Manila	"6,720,050"
Buenos Aires	"9,968,000"	Jakarta	"6,503,449"
Beijing	"9,957,000"	Karachi	"6,500,000"
Calcutta	"9,166,000"	Delhi	"6,220,000"

Moscow	"8,815,000"	Chicago	"6,199,000"
Paris	"8,706,963"	Tehran	"6,000,000"
New York	"8,529,000"		

The Highest Mountain in each of the Continents

Continent		Height (m)	Country
Asia	Everest	"8,848"	Nepal/China
South America	Aconcagua	"6,960"	Argentina
North America	McKinley	"6,194"	Alaska
Africa	Kilimanjaro	"5,895"	Tanzania
Europe	El'brus	"5,642"	Russia/Georgia
Australia	Kosciusko	"2,228"	N.S.W.

The World's Ten Longest Rivers

	Length	Outflow
Nile	"6,690km"	Mediterranean
Amazon	"6,280km"	Atlantic Ocean
Mississippi-Missouri	"6,270 km"	Gulf of Mexico
Ob-Irtysh	"5,570km"	Gulf of Ob
Zaire (Congo)	"4,670km"	Atlantic Ocean
Amur	"4,410km"	Tatar Strait
Huang Ho (Yellow River)	"4,350km"	Yellow Sea
Lena	"4,260km"	LaptevSea
Yangtze	"4,090km"	EastChinaSea
Mackenzie	"4,040km"	Arctic Ocean

The Largest Lakes in the World

	Continent	Area in 1,000km²
Caspian Sea	Asia	424
Lake Superior	N. America	82
Lake Victoria	Africa	69
Aral Sea	Asia	63
Lake Huron	N. America	59
Lake Michigan	N. America	58
Lake Tanganyika	Africa	32
Lake Baikal	Asia	31
Great Bear Lake	N. America	31
Great Slave Lake	N. America	28

The Largest Oceans and Seas

	Area in 1,000km²
Pacific Ocean	"165,721"
Atlantic Ocean	"81,660"
Indian Ocean	."73,442"
Arctic Ocean	"14,351"
Mediterranean Sea	"2,966"
Bering Sea	"2,274"
Caribbean Sea	"1,942"

Time Zones

Standard time is reckoned from Greenwich, England, which is recognised as being on the Prime Meridian of Longitude. The world is divided into twenty-four zones, each fifteen degrees of arc, or one hour in time apart. Greenwich meridian (0) extends through the centre of the first zone. The zones to the east are numbered from minus one to minus twelve, the minus indicating the number of hours which must be subtracted to obtain Greenwich Time. The zones to the west are numbered plus one to plus twelve, the plus indicating the number of hours which must be added to obtain Greenwich Time. These zones are generally used in sea areas, but in many countries Standard Time does not coincide with zone time.

The International Date Line is a zig-zag line that approximately follows the 180° meridian. The time must be advanced by twenty-four hours when it is crossed in a westerly direction and must be set back by twenty-four hours when it is crossed in an easterly direction.

The following list gives the Standard Time in various cities of the world when it is 12.00 (midday) in Greenwich, England.

City	Time	City	Time
Adelaide	2100	Dubai	1600
Algiers	1300	Dublin	1200
Amsterdam	1300	Gibraltar	1300
Ankara	1500	Helsinki	- 1400
Athens	1400	Hobart	2200
Beijing	2000	Hong Kong	2000
Beirut	1400	Istanbul	1500
Belgrade	1400	Jerusalem	1400
Berlin	1300	Kuwait City	1500
Berne	1300	Lagos	1300
Bonn	1300	Leningrad	1500
Bombay	1730	Lima	0700
Brasilia	0900	Lisbon	1300
Brisbane	2200	London	1200
Brussels	1300	Luxemburg	1300
Bucharest	1400	Madeira	1200
Budapest	1300	Madrid	1300
Buenos Aires	0900	Malta	1300

Cairo	1400	Mexico City	0600
Calcutta	1730	Montevideo	0830
Cape Town	1400	Montreal	0700
Caracas	0800	Moscow	1500
Chicago	0600	Nairobi	1500
Colombo	1730	New Orleans	0600
Copenhagen	1300	New York	0700
Delhi	1730	Oslo	1300
Ottawa	0700	Singapore	2000
Panama	0700	Stockholm	1300
Paris	1300	Suez	1400
Perth (Austr)	2000	Sydney	2200
Prague	1300	Tehran	1500
Pretoria	1400	Tokyo	2100
Quebec	0700	Toronto	0700
Rangoon	1830	Tunis	1300
Rio de Janeiro	0900	Valetta	1300
Riyadh	1500	Vancouver	0400
St Louis (USA)	0600	Vienna	1300
San Francisco	0400	Warsaw	1300
Santiago	0800	Wellington (NZ)	2400

The United States of America: the states

	Zip code	*Capital*
Alabama	(AL)	Montgomery
Alaska	(AK)	Juneau
Arizona	(AZ)	Phoenix
Arkansas	(AR)	Little Rock
California	(CA)	Sacramento
Colorado	(GO)	Denver
Connecticut	(CI)	Hartford
Delaware	(DE)	Dover
Florida	(FL)	Tallahassee
Georgia	(GA)	Atlanta
Hawaii	(HI)	Honolulu
Idaho	(ID)	Boise
Illinois	(IL)	Springfield
Indiana	(IN)	Indianapolis
Iowa	(IA)	Des Moines
Kansas	(KS)	Topeka
Kentucky	(KY)	Frankfort
Louisiana	(LA)	Baton Rouge
Maine	(ME)	Augusta
Maryland	(MD)	Annapolis
Massachusetts	(MA)	Boston
Michigan	(MI)	Lansing

Minnesota	(MN)	St Paul
Mississippi	(MS)	Jackson
Missouri	(MO)	Jefferson City
Montana	(MT)	Helena
Nebraska	(NE)	Lincoln
Nevada	(NV)	Carson City
New Hampshire	(NH)	Concord
New Jersey	(NJ)	Trenton
New Mexico	(NM)	Santa Fe
New York	(NY)	Albany
North Carolina	(NC)	Raleigh
North Dakota	(ND)	Bismarck
Ohio	(OH)	Columbus
Oklahoma	(OK)	Oklahoma City
Oregon	(OR)	Salem
Pennsylvania	(PA)	Harrisburg
Rhode Island	(RI)	Providence
South Carolina	(SC)	Columbia
South Dakota	(SD)	Pierre
Tennessee	(TN)	Nashville
Texas	(TX)	Austin
Utah	(UT)	Salt Lake City
Vermont	(VT)	Montpelier
Virginia	(VA)	Richmond
Washington	(WA)	Olympia
West Virginia	(WV)	Charleston
Wisconsin	(WI)	Madison
Wyoming	(WY)	Cheyenne
District of Columbia	(DC)	Washington

Australia: the states

	Abbreviation	*Capital*
New South Wales	(N.S.W.)	Sydney
Queensland	(Qld.)	Brisbane
South Australia	(SA.)	Adelaide
Tasmania	(Tas.)	Hobart
Victoria	(Vic.)	Melbourne
Western Australia	(W.A.)	Perth

The Territories

Northern Territory	(N.T.)	Darwin
Australian Capital Territory	(A.C.T.)	Canberra

Canada: the provinces

	Abbreviation	*Capital*
Alberta	(Alta.)	Edmonton
British Columbia	(B.C.)	Victoria
Manitoba	(Man.)	Winnipeg
New Brunswick	(N.B.)	Fredericton
Newfoundland	(Nfld.)	St John's
Nova Scotia	(N.S.)	Halifax
Nunavut	(N.U.)	Iqaluit
Ontario	(Ont.)	Toronto
Prince Edward Island	(PEl.)	Charlottetown
Quebec	(Que.)	Quebec
Saskatchewan	(Sask.)	Regina

The Territories

Yukon Territory	(Y.T.)	Whitehorse
Northwest Territories	(N.W.T.)	Yellowknife

Kings and Queens of England from 1066

The House of Normandy
William I	1066-1087
William II	1087-1100
Henry I	1100-1135
Stephen	1135-1154

The House of Anjou or Plantagenet
Henry II	1154-1189
Richard I	1189-1199
John	1199-1216
Henry III	1216-1272
Edward I	1272-1307
Edward II	1307-1327
Edward III	1327-1377
Richard II	1377-1399

The House of Lancaster (sub-division of Plantagenet)
Henry IV	1399-1413
Henry V	1413-1422
Henry VI	1422-1461

The House of York (sub-division of Plantagenet)
Edward IV	1461-1483
Edward V	1483
Richard III	1483-1485

The House of Tudor

Henry VII	1485-1509
Henry VIII	1509-1547
Edward VI	1547-1553
Mary I	1553-1558
Elizabeth I	1558-1603

The House of Stuart

James I	1603-1625
Charles I	1625-1649
The Commonwealth	1649-1659
Charles II	1660-1685
James II	1685-1688
Mary II & William III	1689-1694
William III	1689-1702
Anne	1702-1714

The House of Hanover

George I	1714-1727
George II	1727-1760
George III	1760-1820
George IV	1820-1830
William IV	1830-1837
Victoria	1837-1901

The House of Saxe-Coburg

Edward VII	1901-1910

The House of Windsor

George V	1910-1936
Edward VIII	1936
George VI	1936-1952
Elizabeth II	1952-

The Prime Ministers of Great Britain

(with their political party and dates in office)

Sir R Walpole	(Whig)	1721-1742
Earl of Wilmington	(Whig)	1742-1743
H Pelham	(Whig)	1743-1754
Duke of Newcastle	(Whig)	1754-1756
Duke of Devonshire	(Whig)	1756-1757
Duke of Newcastle	(Whig)	1757-1762
Earl of Bute	(Tory)	1762-1763
G Grenville	(Whig)	1763-1765
Marquis of Rockingham	(Whig)	1765-1766
Earl of Chatham	(Whig)	1766-1768
Duke of Grafton	(Whig)	1768-1770
Lord North	(Tory)	1770-1782

Marquis of Rockingham	(Whig)	1782
Earl of Shelburne	(Whig)	1782-1783
Duke of Portland	(Coalition)	1783
W Pitt	(Tory)	1783-1801
H Addington	(Tory)	1801-1804
W Pitt (the younger)	(Tory)	1804-1806
Lord Grenville	(Whig)	1806-1807
Duke of Portland	(Tory)	1807-1809
S Perceval	(Tory)	1809-1812
Earl of Liverpool	(Tory)	1812-1827
G Canning	(Tory)	1827
Viscount Goderich	(Tory)	1827-1828
Duke of Wellington	(Tory)	1828-1830
Earl Grey	(Whig)	1830-1834
Viscount Melbourne	(Whig)	1834
Sir Robert Peel	(Tory)	1834-1835
Viscount Melbourne	(Whig)	1835-1841
Sir Robert Peel	(Tory)	1841-1846
Lord Russell	(Whig)	1846-1852
Earl of Derby	(Tory)	1852
Earl of Aberdeen	(Peelite)	1852-1855
Viscount Palmerston	(Liberal)	1855-1858
Earl of Derby	(Conservative)	1858-1859
Viscount Palmerston	(Liberal)	1859-1865
Earl Russell	(Liberal)	1865-1866
Earl of Derby	(Conservative)	1866-1868
Benjamin Disraeli	(Conservative)	1868
W E Gladstone	(Liberal)	1868-1874
Benjamin Disraeli	(Conservative)	1874-1880
W E Gladstone	(Liberal)	1880-1885
Marquis of Salisbury	(Conservative)	1885-1886
WE Gladstone	(Liberal)	1886
Marquis of Salisbury	(Conservative)	1886-1892
WE Gladstone	(Liberal)	1892-1894
Earl of Rosebery	(Liberal)	1894-1895
Marquis of Salisbury	(Conservative)	1895-1902
A Balfour	(Conservative)	1902-1905
Sir H Campbell-Bannerman	(Liberal)	1905-1908
H H Asquith	(Liberal)	1908-1915
H H Asquith	(Coalition)	1915-1916
D Lloyd George	(Coalition)	1916-1922
A Bonar Law	(Conservative)	1922-1923
S Baldwin	(Conservative)	1923-1924
J R MacDonald	(Labour)	1924
S Baldwin	(Conservative)	1924-1929
J R MacDonald	(Labour)	1929-1931
J R MacDonald	(Coalition)	1931-1935
S Baldwin	(Conservative)	1935-1937
N Chamberlain	(Conservative)	1937-1940

WS Churchill	(Coalition)	1940-1945
WS Churchill	(Conservative)	1945
C R Attlee	(Labour)	1945-1951
Sir W S Churchill	(Conservative)	1951-1955
Sir A Eden	(Conservative)	1955-1957
H Macmillan	(Conservative)	1957-1963
Sir A Douglas-Home	(Conservative)	1963-1964
J H Wilson	(Labour)	1964-1970
E R G Heath	(Conservative)	1970-1974
J H Wilson	(Labour)	1974-1976
J Callaghan	(Labour)	1976-1979
Mrs Margaret Thatcher	(Conservative)	1979-1990
J Major	(Conservative)	1990-1997
Tony Blair	(Labour)	1997-

The Presidents of the United States

(and their political affiliation)

George Washington	(Federalist)	1789-1797
John Adams	(Federalist)	1797-1801
Thomas Jefferson	(Republican)	1801-1809
James Madison	(Republican)	1809-1817
James Monroe	(Republican)	1817-1825
John Quincy Adams	(Republican)	1825-1829
Andrew Jackson	(Democrat)	1829-1837
Martin Van Buren	(Democrat)	1837-1841
William Harrison	(Whig)	1841
John Tyler	(Whig)	1841-1845
James Polk	(Democrat)	1845-1849
Zachary Taylor	(Whig)	1849-1850
Millard Fillmore	(Whig)	1850-1853
Franklin Pierce	(Democrat)	1853-1857
James Buchanan	(Democrat)	1857-1861
Abraham Lincoln	(Republican)	1861-1865
Andrew Johnson	(Republican)	1865-1869
Ulysses Grant	(Republican)	1869-1877
Rutherford Hayes	(Republican)	1877-1881
James Garfield	(Republican)	1881
Chester Arthur	(Republican)	1881-1885
Grover Cleveland	(Democrat)	1885-1889
Benjamin Harrison	(Republican)	1889-1893
Grover Cleveland	(Democrat)	1893-1897
William McKinley	(Republican)	1897-1901
Theodore Roosevelt	(Republican)	1901-1909
William Taft	(Republican)	1909-1913
Woodrow Wilson	(Democrat)	1913-1921
Warren Harding	(Republican)	1921-1923

Calvin Coolidge	(Republican)	1923-1929
Herbert Hoover	(Republican)	1929-1933
Franklin Roosevelt	(Democrat)	1933-1945
Harry Truman	(Democrat)	1945-1953
Dwight Eisenhower	(Republican)	1953-1961
John Kennedy	(Democrat)	1961-1963
Lyndon Johnson	(Democrat)	1963-1969
Richard Nixon	(Republican)	1969-1974
Gerald Ford	(Republican)	1974-1977
Jimmy Carter	(Democrat)	1977-1981
Ronald Reagan	(Republican)	1981-1989
George Bush	(Republican)	1989-1993
Bill Clinton	(Democrat)	1993-2001
George W Bush	(Republican)	2001-